P9-DVQ-527

SECOND EDITION

LIFE-SPAN HUMAN DEVELOPMENT

Carol K. Sigelman is a professor of psychology at The George Washington University. She has also taught at Texas Tech University, Eastern Kentucky University (where she won her college's Outstanding Teacher Award), and the University of Arizona. She has taught courses in child, adolescent, adult, and life-span development for 20 years. She has published extensively on such topics as the communication skills of individuals with developmental disabilities, peer acceptance of children and adolescents who are different, and children's developing understanding of diseases and disorders. Recently, through a grant from the National Institute of Child Health and Human Development, she has been studying children's theories of AIDS and evaluating an experimental curriculum to teach them the basic facts of HIV infection.

David R. Shaffer is a professor of psychology, chair of the Social Psychology program, and past chair of the Life-Span Developmental Psychology program at the University of Georgia, where he has taught courses in human development to graduate and undergraduate students for the past 20 years. His many research articles have concerned such topics as altruism, attitudes and persuasion, moral development, sex roles and social behavior, self-disclosure, and social psychology and the law. He has also served as associate editor for the *Journal of Personality and Social Psychology, Personality and Social Psychology Bulletin,* and *Journal of Personality.* In 1990 Dr. Shaffer received the Josiah Meigs Award for Excellence in Instruction, the University of Georgia's highest instructional honor.

SECOND EDITION

LIFE-SPAN HUMAN DEVELOPMENT

Carol K. Sigelman
THE GEORGE WASHINGTON UNIVERSITY

David R. Shaffer
UNIVERSITY OF GEORGIA

Brooks/Cole Publishing Company
Pacific Grove, California

Brooks/Cole Publishing Company
A Division of Wadsworth, Inc.

Printed in the United States of America
10 9 8 7 6 5 4 3 2 1

Library of Congress Cataloging-in-Publication Data
Sigelman, Carol K.
Life-span human development / Carol K. Sigelman and David R. Shaffer. — 2nd ed.
p. cm.
Includes bibliographical references and index.
ISBN 0-534-19578-4
1. Developmental psychology. I. Shaffer, David R. (David Reed), [date] . II. Title.
BF713.S53 1994 94-6251
155—dc20 CIP

Sponsoring Editor: *Jim Brace-Thompson*
Marketing Representative: *Mark Francisco*
Editorial Associate: *Cathleen S. Collins*
Production Coordinator: *Fiorella Ljunggren*
Production: *Cecile Joyner, The Cooper Company*
Manuscript Editor: *Micky Lawler*
Permissions Editor: *May Clark*
Interior Design: *Katherine Minerva*
Cover Design: *Susan Haberkorn*
Cover Illustration: *Katherine Minerva*
Interior Illustration and Electronic Art: *John and Judy Waller, Scientific Illustrators*
Other Interior Illustration: *Cyndie C. H. Wooley and Wayne Clark*
Photo Researcher: *Terri Wright*
Typesetting: *ColorType, Inc.*
Cover Printing: *Phoenix Color Corporation, Inc.*
Printing and Binding: *Arcata Graphics/Hawkins*

(Credits continue on p.647.)

BRIEF CONTENTS

CONTENTS

3

THE GENETICS OF LIFE-SPAN DEVELOPMENT 55

4

ENVIRONMENTAL INFLUENCES ON LIFE-SPAN DEVELOPMENT 85

5

THE PHYSICAL SELF 115

6

PERCEPTION 145

7

COGNITION AND LANGUAGE 173

8

LEARNING AND INFORMATION PROCESSING 209

9

INTELLIGENCE, CREATIVITY, AND WISDOM 239

10

SELF-CONCEPTIONS, PERSONALITY, AND EMOTIONAL EXPRESSION 267

11

GENDER ROLES AND SEXUALITY 299

12

CHOICES: THE DEVELOPMENT OF MORALITY AND MOTIVATION 329

13

PARTICIPATION IN THE SOCIAL WORLD 359

14

THE FAMILY 389

15

LIFESTYLES: PLAY, SCHOOL, AND WORK 419

16

PSYCHOLOGICAL DISORDERS THROUGHOUT THE LIFE SPAN 449

PREFACE

Our purpose in writing this overview of life-span human development has been to create the book that we would most want our students to read—one that arouses their curiosity about how and why human beings change (and remain the same) from their beginnings as fertilized eggs to their last years of life, and one that shares with them the best theories, research, and practical advice that developmentalists have to offer. We want our students to understand that human development is an incredibly complex process that grows out of the interactions between a changing person and a changing world and that continues throughout the entire life span. We want them to appreciate how major theories of human development guide researchers but can also help anyone analyze the "real-life" issues that developing persons face. And we want them to appreciate that the best advice about such matters as raising children, working with troubled adolescents, or smoothing the adjustment of new nursing-home residents is based on research reports rather than on armchair speculation.

Guided by these goals, we have written a text that delves into important theoretical issues and incorporates the best of both classic and contemporary research from the several disciplines concerned with understanding developmental processes. But we also recognize that solid scholarship is of little good to students unless they want to read it and can understand it. Fortunately, our own excitement about human development has made it easy for us to bring our subject to life. Moreover, we are convinced that even the most complex issues in human development can be made simple through clear and straightforward writing, apt use of concrete examples and analogies, and attempts to highlight the relevance of course concepts to students' lives and to the work of parents, teachers, psychologists, nurses, day-care workers, and other human service professionals. In short, we have aimed for a book that is both rigorous and readable, both research oriented and "real."

Our Integrated Topical/Chronological Approach

The large majority of life-span development textbooks adopt a chronological or "age/stage" approach, carving the life span into age ranges and describing the prominent characteristics of individuals within each age range. By contrast, we use a topical approach blended with a chronological approach within topics. We focus on domains of development such as physical growth, cognition, and personality, and trace developmental trends in each domain from infancy to old age.

Why have we bucked the tide? Like many other instructors, we have typically favored topically organized textbooks when teaching child, adolescent, or adult development courses. As a result, it seemed only natural to use that same topical approach in introducing students to the whole life span. Besides, chronologically organized texts seem to have to repeat themselves as they remind readers of where development left off in an earlier age period.

More important, a topical organization allows us to convey more effectively the flow of development—the systematic, and often truly dramatic, transformations that take place in the course of human life, as well as the developmental continuities that make each individual a reflection of his or her past self. The topical approach also lends itself to a strong emphasis on developmental *processes*; it helps us clarify the ways in which nature and nurture interact over the life span to bring about normal developmental changes, as well as differences among individuals.

Finally, a predominantly topical approach facilitates a *life-span perspective* on human development. Events within any one period of the life span can be viewed from the vantage point of what comes before and what is yet to come. In chronologically organized textbooks, many topics are discussed only in connection with the age group to which they seem most relevant—for example, attachment in relation to infancy, play in relation to the preschool years, or sexuality in relation to adolescence and adulthood. As we have gone about creating a topical life-span text, we have repeatedly found ourselves grappling with intriguing questions that we might otherwise not even have asked. Consider the topic of attachment: Could the approaches used to assess the quality of infants' attachments to their parents also be used to analyze attachments between childhood chums or adult romantic partners? Do securely attached infants later have a greater capacity to form and sustain friendships or romantic partnerships than infants whose early social experiences are less favorable? What are the consequences at different points in the life span of lacking someone to whom one is closely attached? Attachments are important throughout the life span, and we try to make that clear. Similarly, we have found it fascinating and instructive to ask whether the learning and memory difficulties faced by some elderly adults bear any resemblance to those faced by young children, and to think about how the sexual curiosity evident even during infancy evolves into mature sexuality.

In short, we have adopted a topical approach because we consider it the best way to introduce the how and why of human development. However, we also appreciate the strengths of the chronological approach, particularly its ability to portray "the whole person" in each period of the life span. For this reason, we have integrated the age/stage approach within our topical organization, hoping to have the best of both worlds.

Each topical chapter contains major sections on infancy, childhood, adolescence, and adulthood. The very existence of these sections is proof that we have indeed traced development in each of the domains we cover across the *whole* life span, although we do, of course, vary our emphasis on each period of the life span depending on its significance for the domain of development under consideration. These age/stage sections help students appreciate the distinctive qualities of each phase of life and make it easier for them to find material on an age period of particular interest to them. Moreover, they allow instructors who wish to move further in the direction of an age/stage approach to cover infancy, childhood, and adolescence in the first portion of the course and save all the material on adulthood for the end of the course.

We have also attempted to highlight, throughout the text, the intimate interrelationships among physical, cognitive, personal, and social development at any age. And, to focus even more attention on the "whole person," we have written a concluding chapter that summarizes (1) major developments in each of seven periods of the life span and (2) broad themes in life-span development emphasized throughout the book. This integrative chapter serves as a handy reference for students who want the "big picture." Indeed, some instructors like to assign Chapter 18 at both the beginning and the end of the course.

Organization of the Text

The book begins by orienting students to the scientific study of life-span development (Chapter 1) and to the central issues and theoretical perspectives that have dominated the field (Chapter 2). It then explores developmental processes in some depth, examining genetic influences (Chapter 3) and environmental influences (Chapter 4) on development. These chapters show how genes contribute to maturational changes and individual differences throughout the life span and how people are also the products of a prenatal environment and of postnatal experiences that vary as a function of age, culture, and historical period. If students gain nothing else from their study of human development, we hope they gain an appreciation of the many forces acting on the developing person.

Chapters on the growth and aging of the body and nervous system (Chapter 5) and on the development of sensory and perceptual capacities (Chapter 6) launch our examination of the development of basic human capacities. Chapter 7 introduces the Piagetian perspective on cognitive development and describes the development of language in relation to the development of thought; Chapter 8 views learning, memory, and problem solving from an information-processing perspective; and Chapter 9 highlights the psychometric approach to cognition, exploring individual differences in intelligence and creativity.

The next three chapters concern the development of the self—changes in self-conceptions and personality (Chapter 10), in gender roles and sexuality (Chapter 11), and in personal priorities as they are reflected in morality and achievement motivation (Chapter 12). The self is set more squarely in a social context as we trace life-span changes in relationships and social competencies (Chapter 13), in roles and relationships within the family (Chapter 14), and in lifestyles as expressed in play, school, and work activities (Chapter 15). Finally, we offer a life-span perspective on developmental problems and disorders (Chapter 16), examine why people die and how they cope with death (Chapter 17), and summarize key trends and issues in life-span development (Chapter 18). Even though links between chapters are noted throughout the book, instructors who are teaching short courses or who are otherwise pressed for time can omit a chapter here or there without fear of rendering other chapters incomprehensible.

New to This Edition

The basic structure of this edition is the same as that of the first one. One goal we set in rewriting the book was to perfect the integration of topical and chronological coverage through judicious reorganization of some chapters. The age/stage organization is no longer used in Chapters 3 and 4 so that these chapters can more efficiently lay out the terms of the nature/nurture debate and prepare students for upcoming chapters. In some chapters, topics that had been interwoven throughout (for example, cognitive development and language development in Chapter 7) are now covered separately so that students will have an easier time understanding the flow of development in each area.

A second goal was to place even more emphasis on interactions between nature and nurture, giving serious attention to genes, hormones, and other biological forces in development while also raising more questions about the extent to which development can be pushed one way or another depending on the cultural and subcultural context in which the individual develops. Third, the book has been updated from start to finish, incorporating hundreds of new research reports, so that it conveys the most recent discoveries and insights developmentalists have to offer.

In pursuing these goals, we have added some exciting new topics and greatly expanded and updated coverage of other topics. A sampling:

- Historical changes and cross-cultural differences in the treatment of aging adults (Chapter 1)
- The "world views" behind major theories of human development and their implications for raising children (Chapter 2)
- Breakthroughs in the understanding of genetic diseases and disorders such as cystic fibrosis (Chapter 3)
- Biological and social contributors to postpartum depression in new mothers (Chapter 4)
- Lifestyle choices that contribute to a long, healthy old age (Chapter 5)
- Biological and experiential influences on perceptual development and the role of perception in learning to read (Chapter 6)
- Lev Vygotsky's influential thinking about social influences on cognitive development and the relationship between thought and language (Chapter 7)
- Our amnesia regarding our earliest years of life and the challenges of ensuring that elders with failing memories remember to take their medicines (Chapter 8)
- The possibilities for gaining wisdom in later life (Chapter 9)
- Issues facing minority youth as they attempt to forge a positive ethnic identity (Chapter 10)
- Childhood sexual abuse and its many implications for later development (Chapter 11)
- Cultural influences on morality and the origins of violent, antisocial behavior among teenagers (Chapter 12)
- Applications of attachment theory to understanding not only the infant's emotional development but the college student's anxiety upon leaving home for college and the lover's jealousy (Chapter 13)
- Influences of poverty and economic stress on family functioning and child rearing (Chapter 14)
- Ethnic differences in school achievement and a cross-national analysis of why Asian students outperform American students (Chapter 15)
- Cultural influences on the diagnosis of childhood problems (Chapter 16)
- Cross-cultural and racial/ethnic differences in responses to death (Chapter 17)

Chapter Organization

Although not all of the following features will be found in the first four chapters or in the last, most chapters follow a standard format and contain, in this order:

- A *chapter outline* that orients students to what lies ahead.
- *Introductory material* that stimulates interest, lays out the plan for the chapter, and introduces key concepts, theories, and issues relevant to the area of development to be explored.
- *Developmental sections* that describe key changes and continuities, as well as the mechanisms underlying them, during four developmental periods: infancy, childhood, adolescence, and adulthood.
- *Applications*, an examination of how knowledge has been applied to optimize development in the domain at issue. "Applications" sections deal with such topics as genetic counseling; recent innovations in care for premature babies; and programs designed to improve intellectual functioning, self-esteem, moral reasoning, social skills, and family functioning at different ages.
- *Reflections*, a section in which we make some concluding observations and challenge students to step back from the material, appreciate its broader significance, or think about a chapter's themes in new ways.
- *Summary points* that succinctly overview the chapter's main themes to aid students in reviewing the material.
- *Key terms*, a list of the new terms introduced in the chapter. The terms are printed in boldface, defined when they are first presented in a chapter, and included in the Glossary at the end of the book.

In addition, each chapter is sprinkled with photographs, tables, and figures. Although some of these are intended to stimulate interest or to entertain, they have a serious educational purpose as well: summarizing stage theories, presenting revealing research data, or illustrating concepts discussed in the chapter.

Similarly, the "boxes" in each chapter are integral parts of the text. They offer a closer look at selected topics, such as ways of combatting an infant's fear of strangers in the doctor's office, misconceptions about hyperactivity, the implications of growing up bilingual, the advantages and disadvantages of working part time during adolescence, cultural differences in the experience of menopause, problems facing middle-aged people who must care for their ailing parents, and interventions to increase the well-being of nursing-home residents.

Finally, a word on referencing: Each chapter cites the authors and dates of publication for a large number of books and articles, which are fully referenced in the chapter-by-chapter bibliographies at the end of the book. Although some students may find these citations distracting, they are included for good reasons: because we are committed to the value of systematic research, because we believe in giving proper credit where credit is due, and because we want students to have the resources they need to pursue their interests in human development.

Supplementary Aids

For the instructor, there is an instructor's manual that contains chapter outlines, learning objectives, graphics that can be converted to transparencies for use in class, and suggestions for class discussion, projects, films, videos, and additional readings. The test bank (available in print and in computerized format) offers a variety of multiple-choice, true/false, and essay questions for each chapter. Also available are acetate transparencies, as well as videotape options. The student study guide is designed to promote active learning through a guided review of the important principles and concepts in the text. The study materials for each chapter also include a comprehensive multiple-choice self-test and a number of "applications" exercises that challenge students to think about and apply what they have learned.

Acknowledgments

A project of this magnitude cannot be carried out without the efforts of many people, all of whom deserve our deepest thanks. We are very grateful to the reviewers of the manuscript for their constructive criticism and useful suggestions. Reviewers of the first edition included Freda Blanchard-Fields of Louisiana State University, Janet Fritz of Colorado State University, John Klein of Castleton State College, Rosanne Lorden of Eastern Kentucky University, Robin Paikovitz of the University of Delaware, Suzanne Pasch of the University of Wisconsin–Milwaukee, and Katherine Van Giffen of California State University–Long Beach. Reviewers of this revised edition were David Beach of the University of Wisconsin–Parkside, Charles Harris of James Madison University, Malia Huchendorf of Normandale Community College, Vivian Jenkins of the University of Southern Indiana, Nancy Macdonald of the University of South Carolina –Sumter, Jim O'Neill of Wayne State University, Marjorie Reed of Oregon State University, and Ruth Wilson of Idaho State University. We would also like to thank the many reviewers of the first, second, and third editions of David Shaffer's *Developmental Psychology: Childhood and Adolescence*. Their contributions to that book are reflected in the coverage of child development here.

For her dedicated performance of numerous library-search, proofreading, and referencing tasks, Kathleen Dwyer deserves many thanks; she was just the obsessive/compulsive personality for the job. Corinne Alfeld, Jennifer Johnson, and Janette Smidt were a great help too. Credit for excellent supplementary materials goes to Elizabeth Rider of Elizabethtown College, who prepared the study guide and material for the instructor's manual, and to Richard Pisacreta of Ferris State University, who prepared the test bank.

Producing this book required the joint efforts of Brooks/Cole and The Cooper Company. We want to express our gratitude to Fiorella Ljunggren of Brooks/Cole for overseeing the process, to Cecile Joyner for her contributions to the book's production, and to Micky Lawler for all the care she invested in copy editing. These pros were a joy to work with, and the book is much better because of them.

We are also deeply indebted to a line of sponsoring editors that has run from C. Deborah Laughton through Vicki Knight to Jim Brace-Thompson. It was C. Deborah who saw the need for a life-span text like this one, pestered us unmercifully until we agreed to write it, and nurtured us as we began. We have not forgotten our debt to her. We are equally grateful to Vicki, who skillfully shepherded the first edition through its final stages and oversaw the second edition until placing the project in the capable hands of Jim. All three have been invaluable sources of advice and moral support. Finally, Lee Sigelman cannot be thanked enough for putting up with this process not once but twice, and Andrew and Gooseberry Sigelman can rest assured that they will have more of their mother's attention in the coming months.

Carol K. Sigelman
David R. Shaffer

SECOND
EDITION

LIFE-SPAN HUMAN DEVELOPMENT

1

UNDERSTANDING LIFE-SPAN HUMAN DEVELOPMENT

The boy's father, a traveling salesman for an auto parts dealer, died in a car accident before he was born. His grandparents raised him from the age of 2 to the age of 7 while his mother concentrated on earning some money to support him. Then his mother remarried, but her new husband turned out to be an abusive alcoholic. The boy and his mother and stepbrother never knew when the stepfather's violent side might show itself. It was critical to try to keep the peace, to avoid conflicts at all cost. Through it all, he talked to no one: ". . . you didn't reveal your pain and agony. Those were not things you shared with people" ("You Didn't Reveal," 1992).

Do you want to try your hand at predicting the course of this boy's development? What lasting impacts might growing up in a single-parent home and then with an alcoholic, abusive parent have on a child? How well adjusted is this boy likely to be as an adult? Is he likely to abuse alcohol or abuse his children, as his stepfather did? His stepbrother, it turns out, got into serious trouble with drugs and served time in prison as a result. But he—yes, the boy is Bill Clinton—became President of the United States, and we can only wonder what it was about him and his life experiences that allowed him to overcome his early disadvantages.

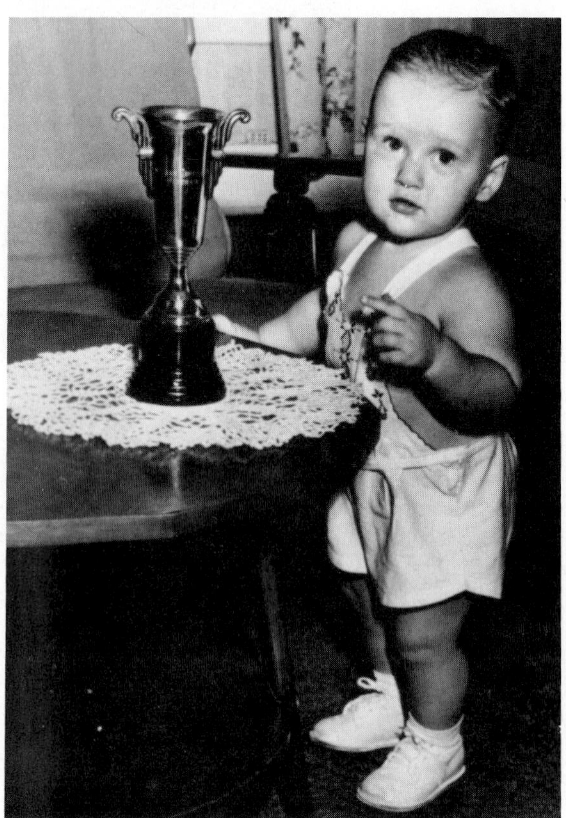

The young Bill Clinton.

Predicting the course of human lives is risky business, but it is the business of those of us who study the process of human development. This book is about development from conception to death. Among the many, many questions it addresses are these: What does the world actually look like to newborn infants? Does experiencing the divorce of one's parents as a child have any lasting effects on one's personality or later relationships with the other sex? What leads some teenagers to attempt suicide? Why do some college students seem to have so much trouble deciding on a major or committing themselves to a serious relationship? How do adults' lives change when they become parents? Do most adults really experience a midlife crisis that leads them to question what they have done with their lives? How well can people expect to remember things when they are 70 or 80, and how do aging adults feel about the prospect of death? How in the world does a fertilized egg evolve into a thinking, feeling, ever-changing adult?

Do any of these questions intrigue you? Probably so, for we are all developing persons who interact daily with other developing persons. What *are* we interested in if not in ourselves and the people close to us? Most college students genuinely want to understand how they personally have been affected by experiences in their lives, how they have changed over the years, and where they may be heading. They are also curious about the behavior of people they know. Many students also have very practical motivations for learning about human development—for example, a desire to be a better parent or to work more effectively as a psychologist, nurse, teacher, or other human service professional.

This introductory chapter lays the groundwork for the remainder of the book by addressing some questions about what the nature of life-span human development is and how knowledge of it is gained. What does it mean to say that people "develop" over the life span? How should the life span and its phases be viewed? How is our experience of the life span different from that of developing individuals in past eras or in other cultures? When were scientific studies of human development first conducted, why are they needed, and how do today's researchers investigate development over the life span?

WHAT IS DEVELOPMENT?

Let us define **development** as systematic changes and continuities in the individual that occur between conception and death, or from "womb to tomb." By describing changes as "systematic," we imply that they are orderly, patterned, and relatively enduring; temporary and unpredictable changes such as mood swings are therefore excluded. We are also interested in "continuities" in development, or ways in which we remain the same or continue to reflect our past.

For decades the study of human development focused primarily on changes during childhood, and the term *development* typically referred to changes of a positive sort, changes that make humans more competent or more complex. Most developmental scholars today, though, argue that developmental change can take many forms: It may indeed be positive (as when a 2-year-old's vocabulary expands), it may be negative (as when a girl progressing through school loses some of the curiosity and love of learning she had as a 4-year-old), or it may simply represent a difference between earlier behavior and later behavior (as when a boy who once feared loud noises comes to fear hairy monsters under the bed instead).

The systematic changes of interest to students of human development fall into three broad realms: physical, cognitive, and psychosocial. **Physical development** includes the growth of the body and its organs during childhood, the appearance of physical signs of aging during adulthood, and the gains and losses in motor abilities that occur over the years. **Cognitive development** involves changes in the mental processes involved in perception, language use, learning, and thought. And **psychosocial development** refers to changes in personal and interpersonal phenomena such as motives and emotions, personality traits, interpersonal skills and relationships, and roles played within the family and in the larger society. Even though developmentalists sometimes specialize in studying one or another of these three aspects of development, they have come to appreciate that humans are *whole* beings and that changes in these three areas of functioning are intimately intertwined. The baby who develops the ability to crawl, for example, now has new opportunities to develop her mind by exploring the contents of bookshelves and kitchen cabinets and to hone her social skills by accompanying her parents wherever they go.

When in life are changes in the physical, cognitive, and psychosocial domains most likely to occur? Many people picture the life span this way: First there are tremendous gains in capacity and positive changes from infancy to young adulthood; then there is little change at all from young adulthood through middle age; and finally there is nothing but a loss of capacities — a process of deterioration — in the later years.

This vision of the life span, though grim, has some truth to it, particularly if we focus on biological change. Biologists typically define **growth** as the physical changes that occur from conception to maturity. We do indeed become more biologically mature and physically competent during the early part of the life span. *Aging*, to the biologist, is the deterioration of organisms (including human beings) that leads inevitably to their death. So, from a biological perspective, development really is growth in early life and aging in later life.

However, most developmentalists today have rejected this biological perspective. They prefer to use the term **aging** to refer to a wide range of changes, both positive and negative, in the *mature* organism (Birren & Zarit, 1985). They also maintain that both positive and negative changes — gains and losses — occur in every phase of the life span (Baltes, Smith, & Staudinger, 1992). Consider this: From early childhood to young adulthood, although we certainly do gain many new abilities, suicide rates rise steeply (Kagan, 1986). From our teenage years to our 40s, when we are supposedly not changing much, we are typically gaining self-confidence and other psychological strengths (Haan, 1981), and we are aging as well. And, although many elderly adults do find themselves becoming somewhat forgetful or hard of hearing, many are also still acquiring knowledge or even gaining a kind of wisdom about life that young people lack (Baltes et al., 1992; Clayton & Birren, 1980). In short, *development involves gains, losses, and just plain changes in each phase of the life span.* Above all, we should abandon the idea that aging involves only deterioration and loss.

To grasp the meaning of life-span development more fully, we should also understand two important processes that underlie developmental change: maturation and learning. **Maturation** is the biological unfolding of the individual according to a plan contained in the *genes*, or the hereditary material passed from parents to child at conception. Just as seeds systematically unfold to become mature plants (assuming that they receive the necessary nourishment from their environment), human beings "unfold" within the womb. Their genetic "program" then calls for them to walk and utter their first words at about 1 year of age, to achieve sexual maturity at about age 12 to 14, and even to undergo the aging process and die on a roughly similar schedule. Since the brain undergoes maturational changes, maturation also contributes to

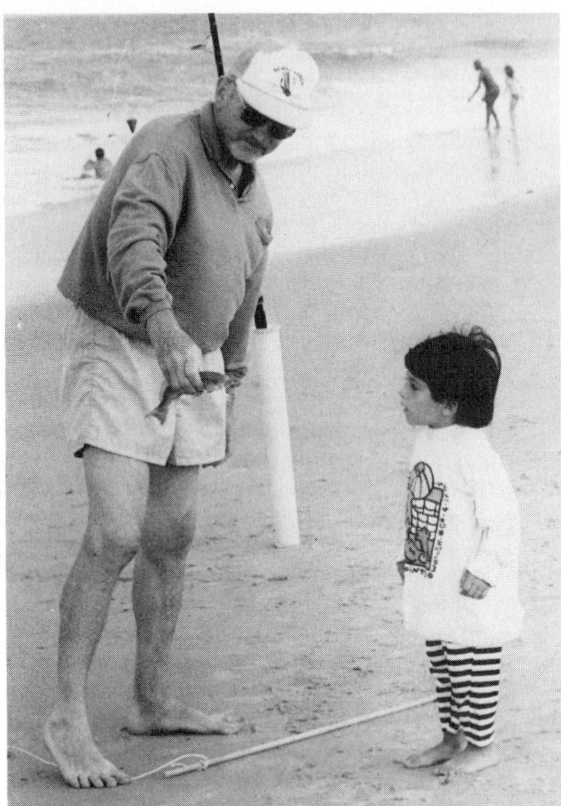

The child is not the only developing person in this photo. Younger members of the family can contribute to the ongoing development of their aging relatives.

psychological changes such as increased abilities during the school years to remember material for tests and to understand what other people are feeling. Thus, one reason human beings are so similar in many important respects is that genetically programmed maturational processes guide all of us through many of the same developmental changes at about the same points in our lives.

The second critical developmental process is **learning,** or the process through which *experience* brings about relatively permanent changes in thoughts, feelings, or behavior. A certain degree of physical maturation is clearly necessary before a child can run, much less run while dribbling a basketball. However, careful instruction and long, hard hours of practice are just as clearly required if this child is ever to approximate the basketball feats of a Michael Jordan. Many of our abilities and habits do not just "mature" as part of nature's grand plan; parents, teachers, and other important people show us how to behave in new ways, and we are changed by the events we experience during our lives. That is, we change in response to the *environment* in which we develop—particularly in response to the actions and reactions of the people around us. As it turns out, developmental changes are generally the products of both "nature" (genetic endowment and maturation) and "nurture" (environmental influences and learning).

In summary, development is a multifaceted and complex process, involving gains and losses, growth and aging, and more, brought about by both maturation and learning. As we shall now see, development also takes place in a historical and cultural context that influences how the life span and its phases are viewed.

HOW DO PEOPLE VIEW THE LIFE SPAN?

Most of us do not see the life span as a single, long period between conception and death. Rather, we divide it into periods or phases, each of which is believed to be distinct in some way from the others. Table 1.1 lists the periods of the life span that many of today's developmentalists regard as distinct. You will want to keep these age ranges in mind as you read this book, for we will constantly be speaking of infants, preschoolers, school-aged children, adolescents, and young, middle-aged, and older adults. Remember that these ages are only approximate, and a person's age is merely a rough indicator of his or her level of development: There are many differences among individuals of the same age.

It is generally more useful to focus on the individual's functioning than to consider only his or her age. For example, those 10-year-olds who have already experienced puberty might more appropriately be classified as adolescents than as children, and those teenagers who are fully self-supporting with children of their own might have more in common with young adults than with other adolescents. Similarly, some older adults are physically and psychologically much "older" than others. This observation led Bernice

TABLE 1.1 An overview of periods of the life span.

Period of Life	*Approximate Age Range*
Prenatal period	Conception to birth
Infancy	First 2 years of life
Preschool period	2 to 5 or 6 years (some prefer to describe as "toddlers" children who have begun to walk and are age 1 to 3)
Middle childhood	6 to 12 or so (until the onset of puberty)
Adolescence	12 or so to 20 or so (when the individual is relatively independent of parents and assumes adult roles)
Early adulthood	20 to 40 years
Middle adulthood	40 to 65 years
Late adulthood	65 years and older

Neugarten (1975) to distinguish between two distinct subgroups within the aging population. The **young-old,** who are usually somewhere between 55 and 75 but can be older, are relatively healthy, active, and socially involved. They are the ones you see on the tennis courts and in the halls of Congress. The **old-old,** most of whom are 75 or older, have chronic diseases and impairments, have suffered declines in their abilities, and often depend on others for care. According to Neugarten, these two groups have very different needs: The young-old need meaningful roles in society, whereas the old-old need long-term medical care.

The life span has not always been carved up into the age periods contained in Table 1.1. In fact, even today different cultures view the life span quite differently. Age, like gender and other significant human characteristics, means what a society chooses to have it mean. All societies appear to view age as a significant attribute, but each society has its own ways of dividing the life span and of treating the individuals who fall into different age groups. Each socially defined age group in a society — called an **age grade,** or age stratum — is assigned a different status and different roles, privileges, and responsibilities. We, for example, grant "adults" (18-year-olds, by law) a voting privilege that we do not grant to children, and we give senior-citizen discounts to older adults but not to young or middle-aged adults. Just as high schools have their "elite" seniors and their "lowly" freshmen, whole societies are "layered" into age grades.

Once it has defined age grades, each society also establishes expectations about what people should and should not be doing at different points in the life span — expectations called **age norms.** Age norms are a society's way of telling people how to act their age; in our culture, for example, 10-year-olds are told that they are "too young" to date, 25-year-olds get the message that it is a good time to marry, and 65-year-olds are expected to think about retiring if they have not already done so. With that as background, let us briefly examine how concepts of the life span, in the form of age grades and age norms, have evolved through history and how they vary from culture to culture in the world today.

Historical Changes in Phases of the Life Span

Every human develops in a historical context: Being a developing person today is quite different from being a developing person in past eras. Moreover, the quick historical tour that we are about to take should convince you that the phases of the life span that we recognize today were not always perceived as distinct.

Childhood in Premodern and Modern Times

Imagine that you are a newborn baby boy in the ninth century B.C. in the city-state of Sparta. The Spartan elders soon inspect you and decide that you are strong and healthy enough to live (lucky for you, because otherwise you would have been taken into the wilderness and left to die) (Despert, 1965). Having passed the test, you will now be exposed to a strict regimen designed to train you for the grim task of serving a military state. As an infant you will be given cold-water baths to "toughen" you (Despert, 1965). At 7 years of age, when children in our society are entering the second grade, you will be taken from your home and raised in a barracks. You will be beaten often and may go for days at a time without food — all to instill in you the discipline you will need to become an able warrior and a credit to Sparta (deMause, 1974; Despert, 1965).

Not all ancient societies treated their children as harshly as the Spartans did. And yet deplorable treatment of children has been the rule rather than the exception through much of recorded history (deMause, 1974). Children have generally been viewed as family "possessions," pieces of property to be used as seen fit; they have had no rights (Hart, 1991). It was not until the 12th century A.D. in Christian Europe that the law finally defined infanticide — the killing of children — as murder (deMause, 1974)! Yet the beatings continued. One mother in early America described a struggle with her 4-month-old infant: "I whipped him til he was actually black and blue, and until I *could not* whip him any more, and he never gave up one single inch" (deMause, 1974, p. 41).

Not only were children of past eras subjected to discipline that we would brand as child abuse, but they were expected to grow up fast. In medieval Europe (500–1500 A.D.), as soon as children turned 6 they were dressed in miniature versions of adult clothing and expected to work alongside adults (often parents or other relatives) at home, at a shop, or in the fields (Ariès, 1962; deMause, 1974). Children participated in many of the same social and sexual activities that adults favored, and they were treated as adults by the law. A 10-year-old convicted of stealing stood to be hanged for it (Kean, 1937).

Historian Phillippe Ariès (1962) concluded that European societies had no concept of "childhood" as we know it before 1600, or the start of the 17th century. Children, he claimed, were simply viewed as miniature adults. It is now clear that this is an overstatement (see Borstelmann, 1983). Parents in the Middle Ages seem to have recognized that children were different from adults. However, before about 1600 parents *did* view children as potentially evil beings and pressured them to overcome their deficiencies, adopt adult roles, and contribute economically to the family's survival as soon in life as possible (Borstelmann, 1983).

During the 17th century, our modern concept of childhood came into being. Children were now seen as more distinctly childlike — as innocent souls who

Although medieval children were pressured to abandon their childish ways as soon as possible and were dressed like miniature adults, it is doubtful that they were viewed as nothing but miniature adults.

should be protected, given a proper moral and religious education, and taught skills such as reading and writing so they would eventually become good workers (Ariès, 1962). Although children were still considered economic possessions, parents were discouraged from beating them and were urged to treat them with warmth and affection (Ariès, 1962; Despert, 1965). By the end of the 19th century, at least in highly industrialized countries, the modern concept of childhood became even more firmly rooted. As child laborers were replaced by adult immigrants in the factories of the United States, children came to be regarded as "economically worthless but emotionally priceless" (Zelizer, cited in Remley, 1988).

And what is it like to be a child in our society today? We do not have to look far to find ample evidence that the historical tradition of child abuse and neglect continues to this day. And yet the lives of most children are infinitely better than they were a few centuries ago. Modern industrial societies regard children as a special class of human beings who need guidance and protection in order to develop well. Such societies have devised schools and other institutions to serve children's special needs and have finally enacted laws granting rights to children (Hart, 1991).

Some observers claim that our society has been shifting toward still another conception of childhood, one in which children are no longer treated as innocents to be protected but as sophisticates who can learn to protect themselves from a wide range of threats (see Elkind, 1992; Postman, 1982; Winn, 1983). Modern parents, not unlike medieval ones, seem to be asking today's children to grow up very quickly, and children, with a good deal of help from television, are learning more and more about topics once considered to be "for adults only." Think of it: Many of today's elementary school children have learned to converse intelligently about AIDS and condoms, "good" touches and "bad" touches, "crack" and "smack." They are expected to learn to protect themselves from drug dealers in their schoolyards and to let themselves into empty houses after school. Concerned about this trend, child psychologist David Elkind (1992) believes that adults will once again step forward to protect children and relieve them of some of this pressure to grow up so quickly.

The Invention of Adolescence

Because the modern concept of childhood arose only in the 17th century, it is not surprising that adolescence did not come to be viewed as a distinct period of the life span in Western societies until the end of the 19th century (Kett, 1977). The spread of industry had a great deal to do with the emergence of adolescence. At first, developing industries in the United States and elsewhere needed cheap child labor, and children left farms to work in factories. But, as immigrants began to fill the labor shortage in the late 19th century and as industry advanced, what was needed was an *educated* labor force. So laws were passed restricting child labor and making schooling compulsory. Now adolescents spent their days in school, separated from the adult world. They came to be regarded as distinct from adults, and they began to develop their own "peer culture" as they spent more time with their friends.

The adolescent experience has continued to change during the 20th century (Elder, 1980). It has been argued that a new stage of the life span, called "youth," came into being after World War II as adolescents began to attend college and graduate school in large numbers (Keniston, 1970). The age of entry into the adult world became postponed even longer than it had been with the introduction of compulsory secondary education. Youth—those individuals who pursued an advanced education instead of going to work after high school—found themselves in an ambiguous territory between adolescence and adulthood, struggling to establish their own identity as a group. This distinct identity became particularly clear in the late 1960s and early 1970s: the days of student protests against civil rights violations and the war in Vietnam, the days of hippies, flower children, and "acid-heads."

Today's youth may not be hippies, but they continue to take quite some time to strike out on their own as adults. People in their 20s in the 1990s have been taking even longer than those of the 1960s and

1970s did to achieve some of the milestones of adulthood: to settle on careers, to leave home, to marry, and to have children (Hartung & Sweeney, 1991; Vobejda, 1991). It seems, then, that today's children, under the guidance of this society's current age norms, are expected to cease being helpless children very quickly but to assume adult roles very slowly.

A Changing Adulthood

And how is adulthood today different from adulthood in past eras? For one thing, more people are living longer now. In ancient Rome the average age of death was about 20 to 30; in the late 17th century it was 35 to 40 years (Dublin & Lotka, 1936). These figures, which are *averages*, are low mainly because so many individuals died in infancy. In medieval times, for example, one, and sometimes two, out of three babies did not survive their first year (Borstelmann, 1983). However, those fortunate enough to make it through early childhood then had relatively low odds, by modern standards, of living to be 65 or older.

The average life expectancy has continued to increase dramatically during this century. In about 1900 a newborn in the United States could expect to live 49 years; in 1989 the life expectancy for a newborn was 79 for a white female, 74 for a black female, nearly 73 for a white male, and 65 for a black male (National Center for Health Statistics, 1992).

The makeup of the U.S. population has also changed significantly in this century. In 1900 about 4% of the population was 65 and older; today the figure is 12.5% (U.S. Bureau of the Census, 1992). Meanwhile, the percentage of the population under age 16 fell from 35% in 1900 to 23% in 1990 (Pifer & Bronte, 1986; U.S. Bureau of the Census, 1992). And we have not seen anything yet. Census takers are now watching the **baby boom generation**—the huge generation of people born between the close of World War II (in 1945) and 1964—move into middle age. The election of Bill Clinton and Al Gore as President and Vice-President of the United States in 1992 was widely regarded as a marker of this generation's assumption of power from the previous generation. By 2035, when most "baby boomers" will have retired from work, 20% of the U.S. population—1 of 5 Americans—is expected to be 65 or older (Pifer & Bronte, 1986). No wonder the news media are discussing the "graying of America" and the strains on society that an ever-aging population will exert.

With changes in longevity over the course of history have come changes in the experience of adulthood and aging (Cole, 1992; Minois, 1987/1989). Yet there does not seem to have been any simple historical trend toward a better and better (or worse and worse) experience of aging over the centuries. Although older adults have received more favorable treatment in some eras than in others, historian Georges Minois (1987/1989) concludes that most societies from ancient times onward have held ambivalent attitudes toward aging and old people. On the one hand, the old have been devalued and mocked; on the other hand, they have often been idealized as sources of wisdom and have been placed in positions of great power. As Minois (1987/1989) puts it, old people have been "... respected or despised, honoured or put to death according to circumstance" (p. 11).

In most periods of history, negative views of aging have outweighed positive ones, and the lives of older adults have been accorded less worth than those of younger adults. In the early Middle Ages, for example, the murder of a man 20 to 50 years of age warranted a fine of 300 gold solidi, but the life of a man over 65 was valued at only 100 solidi, the same as that of a child under 10 (Minois, 1987/1989). This devaluing of the old was even more pronounced where women were concerned: The life of a woman of child-bearing age was worth 250 solidi, the life of a woman over 60 almost nothing. According to Minois, the status of the elderly has been especially low in societies that have placed high value on youth and beauty; ancient Greece is a good example, and perhaps our society is as well. The status of the elderly has been especially high in societies that have lacked writing and have therefore depended on old people to serve as the "collective memory" of the culture—to be experts on matters of cultural tradition.

For most of history, the adult portion of the life span has been conceptualized as one long stretch extending from the beginning of productive activity, usually in childhood, to death (Minois 1987/1989). Because adults did not retire unless they became infirm, and because harsh life conditions tended to make everyone age rapidly, there were not many meaningful differences in lifestyle or status between older and younger adults. In the 20th century, however, Western societies began to recognize a distinct period of life called *middle age,* marked in part by the emptying of the nest as children venture out on their own (Neugarten & Neugarten, 1986). In the 19th century, when fewer people lived to a ripe old age and when people had larger families, many adults never experienced this phase of family life (Hareven, 1986). Now family sizes are smaller, and adults today spend whole decades of their lives without children in the house.

Concepts of old age have also changed in the 20th century due to the introduction of Social Security and other programs that serve an ever-larger aging population (Cole, 1992). In the 1800s, as in previous centuries, people who survived to old age literally worked until they dropped. Now old age has come to mean the retirement phase of the life span—the time when adults over 65, like adolescents, are given few meaningful roles in the labor force, even though many of them are healthy, active, and capable (Rosenmayr, 1985). Old age has become a problem to be solved with modern technology rather than a phase of life to be accepted (Cole, 1992).

In sum, one's age—whether it is 7, 17, or 70—has meant something quite different in each historical era. Quite possibly, the experience of being 7, 17, or 70 may be quite different in the 21st century than it is now. Our modern way of "carving up" the life span into age grades is not the only way in which it can be done.

Cultural Differences in Phases of the Life Span

Just as the life span has been viewed differently in different historical eras, each culture has its own way of regarding the life span and dividing it into socially meaningful periods or age grades. In Western industrialized societies, the life span is often visualized as a straight line extending from birth to death. In certain other cultures, however, the recognized phases of the life span include a period before birth as well as an afterlife (Fry, 1985). In still other cultures, the life span is pictured as a circle, with those who die being "recycled" and born again (Fry, 1985). The Hindu concept of reincarnation illustrates this concept of the life span. So does the Inuit Eskimo belief that the indestructible names of the dead wait in the underworld until they can reenter the world as newborns bearing the same names (Guemple, 1983).

Different societies also have established different age grades. Anthropologist Jennie Keith (1985) reports that the St. Lawrence Eskimo simply distinguish between boys and men (or girls and women). By contrast, the Arusha people of East Africa have *six* socially meaningful age strata of males: youths, junior warriors, senior warriors, junior elders, senior elders, and retired elders. On top of that, all of the adolescent boys who are circumcised in coming-of-age ceremonies during a given five-year period are recognized as a distinct social group.

Each January 15 in Japan, 20-year-olds are officially pronounced adults in a national celebration. Young women receive kimonos, young men receive suits, and all are reminded of their responsibilities to society. Young adults also gain the right to drink, smoke, and vote. The modern ceremony grew out of an ancient one in which young samurai became recognized as warriors (Reid, 1993). The age-grading system in Japanese culture clearly marks the beginning of adulthood.

Consider, too, how societies define who is old and who is not. In our society age 65 is widely viewed as the beginning of old age and the retirement period, although many adults resist viewing themselves as "old" until they are a good deal past 65. Most other cultures define old age in terms of *functional,* rather than chronological, age (Keith, 1985). Thus, among the !Kung hunter/gatherers of central Africa, one becomes old when one is no longer bearing or raising children (Biesele & Howell, 1981)—a good deal earlier than in our society.

If there is anything universal in all of this, it is perhaps the tendency of all societies, past and present, to use age in *some* manner as a basis for categorizing people and assigning them privileges and responsibilities. Otherwise, we have no choice but to view human development within its particular historical and social context. Age simply does not have the same meaning across times and places; each society settles on its own definitions of the nature of the life span, the phases within it, and the lot of those individuals who fall into each phase. Most significantly, human development in one historical and cultural context differs from human development in other eras and settings. This fact must continually be borne in mind by those who study development.

WHAT IS THE SCIENCE OF LIFE-SPAN HUMAN DEVELOPMENT?

If development consists of systematic changes from conception to death, the science of development consists of the study of those changes. In this section we consider the goals of the science of life-span development and the ways this science has "developed" over time.

Goals of Study

Three broad goals guide the study of life-span development: the description, explanation, and optimization of human development (Baltes, Reese, & Lipsitt, 1980). To achieve the goal of *description,* developmentalists characterize the behavior of human beings of different ages and trace how it changes with age. Developmentalists attempt to describe both *normal development* and variations, or *individual differences,* in development. Although "average" trends in human development across the life span can be described, it is clear that no two of us (even identical twins) develop along precisely the same pathways. Some babies are considerably more alert and active than others; some 80-year-olds are out on the dance floor, whereas others are bedridden.

Description is the starting point in any science, but ultimately scientists want to achieve the goal of *explanation,* or understanding *why* humans develop as they typically do and *why* some individuals turn out different from others. Again, developmentalists are interested in explaining both typical changes *within* individuals and differences in development *between* individuals. For instance, descriptive studies tell us that late adolescence is a time when many individuals are deciding what career to pursue. Is this mainly because social pressures are placed on adolescents to become self-supporting, or does it have more to do with changes in cognitive abilities that allow adolescents to imagine and think productively about alternative careers? And why is it that some young people meet this challenge relatively easily while others struggle for years before they have any clue what to do with their lives? Both maturational processes and learning experiences must be considered. Obviously it is easier to describe development than to explain it.

Finally, the *optimization* of human development is the most practical goal of the science of life-span development. How can human beings be helped to develop in positive directions? How can their capacities be enhanced, and how can any developmental problems they suffer be overcome? Among the many important practical discoveries made by developmentalists are these:

- Ways to stimulate the normal growth of fragile, premature babies who must be kept in intensive-care units after birth
- Ways to help children with learning problems achieve more success in school
- Ways to help adults cope with life crises such as the death of a spouse

The goal of optimizing development often cannot be achieved, however, until researchers are able to describe development and explain how it comes about.

In summary, the scope of this book, like the scope of the science of human development, is large. We want to show you what developmentalists have learned about human development from conception to death—about typical physical, cognitive, and psychosocial changes and about individual differences in these interrelated aspects of development. Moreover, we will not be content with describing development; we also want to explain it and to identify ways to optimize it or channel it in positive directions.

Historical Beginnings

Just as human development itself has changed through the ages, attempts to understand development have evolved over time. Philosophers have long expressed their views on the nature of human beings and the proper methods of raising children, but it was not until the 19th century that scientific investigations of the developmental process were undertaken. Most notably, a number of people began to carefully observe the growth and development of their own children and to publish their findings in the form of **baby biographies.** Perhaps the most influential of these baby biographers was Charles Darwin (1809–1882), who made daily records of his own son's development (Darwin, 1877; see also Charlesworth, 1992). Darwin's curiosity about child development stemmed from his theory of evolution. Quite simply, he believed that young, untrained infants share many characteristics with their nonhuman ancestors and that the evolution of the individual child parallels that of the entire species. He inspired others as well to study child development in the interest of gaining insights into our evolutionary history.

Baby biographies left much to be desired as works of science. Because different baby biographers emphasized very different aspects of their children's behavior, baby biographies were difficult to compare. Then, too, parents are not always entirely objective about their own children, and baby biographers like Charles Darwin may also have let their assumptions about the nature of development bias their observations so that they "found" what they were looking for. Finally, each baby biography was based on a single child—and often the child of a distinguished individual, at that. Conclusions based on a single case may not hold true for other children.

We can give Charles Darwin and other eminent baby biographers much credit for making human development a legitimate topic of study. Still, the man who is most often cited as the founder of developmental psychology is G. Stanley Hall (1846–1924). Well aware of the shortcomings of baby biographies, Hall set out in the late 19th century to collect more objective data on large samples of individuals. He developed a now-all-too-familiar research tool, the questionnaire, to explore "the contents of children's minds" (Hall, 1891). By asking children questions about every conceivable topic, he discovered that children's understanding of the world grows rapidly during childhood and that the "logic" of young children is often not very logical at all.

Hall went on to write an influential book entitled *Adolescence* (1904), which was the first to call attention to adolescence as a unique phase of the life span. Influenced by evolutionary theory, Hall drew parallels between adolescence and the turbulent period in history during which barbarism gave way to modern civilization. Adolescence, then, was a tempestuous period of the life span, a time of emotional ups and downs and rapid changes—a time of what Hall called **storm and stress.** Thus it is Hall we have to thank

G. Stanley Hall is widely recognized as the founder of the scientific study of human development.

for the notion — a largely inaccurate notion, as it turns out — that most teenagers are just short of emotionally disturbed. Later, this remarkable pioneer turned his attention to the end of the life span in his book *Senescence* (1922).

Today's Life-Span Perspective on Development

G. Stanley Hall viewed all phases of the life span as worthy of study. Unfortunately, however, the science of human development began to break up into age-group specialty areas during the 20th century. Some researchers focused on infant or child development, others specialized in adolescence, and still others formed the specialization called **gerontology,** the study of aging and old age. (Almost no one specialized in development during early and middle adulthood; after all, people supposedly do not change during those years!) Students of infancy, adolescence, and old age each went about their own work and rarely communicated with one another.

Only since the 1960s and 1970s has a true **life-span perspective** on human development emerged. Paul Baltes (1987; see also Baltes et al., 1980) has laid out seven assumptions that are part of this newly emerging life-span perspective. You will see these themes echoed again and again throughout this book:

1. *Development is a lifelong process.* Today's life-span developmentalists have moved beyond the traditional (and incorrect) notions that development occurs only from conception to adolescence and that all we do in adulthood is lose everything we gained early in life. One is never too old to be a developing person. Thus it is useful to place development in any one period of life in the context of the whole life span. If you were interested in the question of how adolescents go about deciding what they want to be in life, wouldn't it be helpful to know how children form ideas about their strengths and weaknesses and how they learn about different adult careers or society's expectations about "proper" vocations for men and women? After all, it seems likely that the choices adolescents make are related to their earlier experiences. And shouldn't we also know something about vocational development during adulthood? Do adults actually carry through with the vocational plans that they made as adolescents, or do they reformulate their life goals later on? Our understanding of adolescent development is bound to be richer if we concern ourselves with what led up to it and where it is leading.

2. *Development is multidirectional.* Traditionally, developmental changes were regarded as universal ones that build toward some "mature" form of functioning, as when young children all over the world progress from speaking one-word to two-word to multiword sentences in a predictable sequence leading to adultlike speech. Today's developmentalists recognize that humans of any age can be experiencing growth in one set of capacities, decline in another set, and no change at all in still another. Moreover, some individuals can be gaining capacities while others of the same age are losing those same capacities, as when one older person seems to be becoming more knowledgeable every day while another is becoming more and more forgetful. Indeed, the differences among us seem to become wider and wider as we progress through the life span, because we travel along different developmental paths (Morse, 1993). You are likely to find more diversity in a group of 70-year-olds than in a group of 7-year-olds.

3. *Development always involves both gain and loss.* As we noted earlier, development at every age involves both growth and decline. Indeed, for every gain there may be a corresponding loss (Baltes, 1987). Gaining a capacity for logical thought as a school-aged child means losing some of the capacity for fanciful, imaginative thinking one had as a preschooler; specializing in one field of study means losing some of one's command of other fields of study.

4. *There is much plasticity in human development.* **Plasticity** refers to a capacity to change in response to positive or negative experiences. Developmentalists have known for a long time that child development can be damaged by deprivational experiences such as poverty and malnutrition and optimized by enriching experiences such as participation

in a stimulating preschool education program. Increasingly, they have come to appreciate that this plasticity continues into later life—that the aging process can be altered considerably depending on the individual's experiences. For example, elderly adults who have been losing intellectual abilities can, with the help of special training and practice, regain some of those abilities (Baltes et al., 1992).

5. *Development is shaped by its historical/cultural context.* We have already encountered ample justification for this assumption about human development. Not only is our development different from that of people in past eras, but we are affected by societal changes in our own time: by historical events such as wars, technological breakthroughs such as the development of the home computer, and social movements such as the women's movement. Each generation develops in its own way, and each generation changes the world for generations that follow. Glen Elder (1974; Elder & Caspi, 1988; Elder, Liker, & Cross, 1984) vividly demonstrates this point in his fascinating studies of the effects of the Great Depression of the 1930s on development. This economic crisis had lasting negative effects on some (though by no means all) children, especially those whose out-of-work fathers became less affectionate and less consistent in disciplining them. Such children displayed many behavior problems (especially boys), had low aspirations and poor records in school as adolescents, and often as men had erratic careers and unstable marriages or as women were seen by their own children many years later as ill tempered. Clearly we can be affected by the times in which we grow up.

6. *Development is multiply influenced.* Some early developmental scholars believed that development is almost entirely due to biologically programmed maturational processes—that our human genes dictate exactly how we will unfold from conception on. Other scholars believed just as strongly that how we develop is almost entirely the result of the unique learning experiences we have in life. Today's life-span developmentalists maintain that human development is the product of ongoing interactions between a changing person and his or her changing world; *a wide range of factors,* both inside and outside the person, affect development.

7. *Understanding development requires multiple disciplines.* Because human development is influenced by everything from biochemical changes in the cells to historical changes in society, it is simply impossible for any one discipline to have all the answers. A full understanding of human development will come only when many disciplines, each with its own perspectives and tools of study, join forces. Table 1.2 lists some of the most important of these disciplines and the kinds of questions that they commonly raise about development. Some universities have established human development programs that explicitly attempt to bring members of different disciplines together in order to forge new, truly interdisciplinary, perspectives.

In summary, by adopting a life-span perspective on human development in this book, we will be assuming that development (1) occurs throughout the life span rather than just in childhood, (2) can take many different directions, positive or negative, depending on the aspect of functioning being considered and on the individual, (3) involves gains *and* losses at every age, (4) is characterized by plasticity at every age, (5) is very much affected by the historical and cultural context in which it occurs, (6) is influenced by multiple causal factors interacting with one another, and (7) can best be understood if scholars from multiple disciplines join forces to understand it.

TABLE 1.2 Some disciplines that are part of the multidisciplinary effort to study human development.

Discipline	*Major Focus Sample Questions of Interest*
Anthropology	The effects of culture on development: How much do such cultural practices as methods of rearing children or of caring for the frail elderly differ across societies, and what are the implications? Are there aspects of development that are universal, or evident in all known cultures?
Biology	The growth and aging of cells and organs: How does one fertilized egg become a fully developed human being? How does the functioning of human organs change as we age?
History	Changes in human development over the centuries: What has it been like to be a child or an elderly person in different historical periods? How is the family of today different from the family of the 19th century? How do major historical events affect people's lives?
Home economics or human ecology	Development within its family and societal context: What is the nature of the family as an institution, and how do family relationships contribute to the individual's development and adjustment?
Psychology	The functioning of the individual: How do mental abilities, personality traits, and social skills typically change with age? How stable or how changeable are each individual's qualities, and why?
Sociology	The nature of society and the individual's relationship to society: What does society expect of us at different ages? What roles do we play in the larger social system as we progress through life? How are we affected by social institutions and changes in these institutions?

HOW IS DEVELOPMENTAL RESEARCH CONDUCTED?

How can we gain understanding of this complex phenomenon called life-span development? Through the same scientific method applied in any physical or social science. Let us review for you, briefly, some basic concepts of scientific research and then turn to certain research strategies devised specifically for describing, explaining, and optimizing development.

The Scientific Method

There is nothing mysterious about the **scientific method.** It is really more of an *attitude* than a method: a belief that investigators should allow their systematic observations (or *data*) to determine the merits of their thinking. For example, for every "expert" who believes that psychological differences between males and females are largely biological in origin, there is likely to be another expert who just as firmly insists that boys and girls differ because they are raised differently. Whom shall we believe? It is in the spirit of the scientific method to believe the data — for example, research findings regarding the effects of sexist and nonsexist learning experiences on the interests, activities, and personality traits of girls and boys. The scientist values conclusions that are based on factual evidence. Above all, the scientist is willing to abandon a pet theory if the data contradict it. Ultimately, then, the scientific method can protect the scientific community and society at large from flawed or erroneous ideas, even when those ideas are generated by great minds or "authorities."

The scientific method involves a process of generating ideas and testing them by making research observations. Often, casual observations provide the starting point for a scientist. Sigmund Freud, for instance, carefully observed the psychologically disturbed adults whom he treated, began to believe that many of their problems stemmed from experiences in early childhood, and ultimately formulated his *psychoanalytic theory* of development. A **theory** is simply a set of concepts and propositions intended to describe and explain some aspect of experience.

Theories generate specific predictions, or **hypotheses,** about what will hold true if we observe a phenomenon that interests us. Consider, for example, a theory stating that psychological differences between the sexes are largely due to the fact that parents and other adults treat boys and girls differently. Based on this theory, a researcher might hypothesize that, if parents grant boys and girls the same freedoms, the two sexes will be similarly independent, whereas, if parents allow boys to do many things that girls are prohibited from doing, boys will be more independent than girls. Suppose, though, that the study designed to test this hypothesis indicates that boys are more independent than girls no matter how their parents treat them. Then the hypothesis would be disconfirmed by the research data, and the researcher would want to rethink this theory of sex-linked differences. If other hypotheses based on this theory were also inconsistent with the facts, the theory would have to be significantly revised or abandoned entirely in favor of a better theory.

This, then, is the heart of the scientific method — a persistent effort to put ideas to the test, to retain ideas that carefully gathered facts support, and to abandon those that carefully gathered facts contradict. Theories generate hypotheses that are tested through observation of behavior, and new observations indicate which theories are worth keeping (see Figure 1.1). Now let's look at the more specific ways in which researchers study human development — at the types of data they collect, the techniques they use to describe how human beings change with age, and the methods they use to explain developmental changes.

Data Collection Techniques

No matter what aspect of human development we are interested in — whether it is the formation of bonds between infants and their parents, adolescent drug use, or the changes in communication that occur over time in a marriage — we must find a way to measure what interests us. Scientists insist that any measure should have two important qualities: **reliability** and **validity.** A measure is *reliable* if it yields consistent

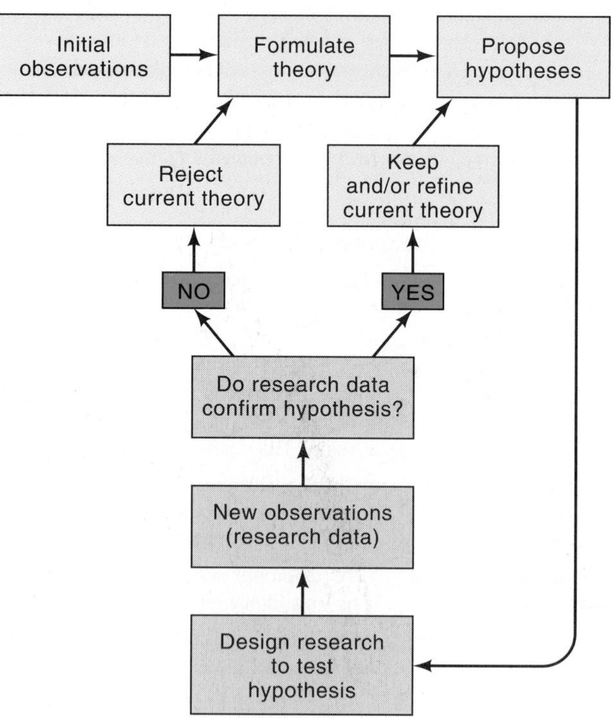

FIGURE 1.1 The scientific method in action.

information from occasion to occasion. For example, if a personality test is supposed to measure the extent to which adults are assertive, the test score an individual receives one week should be similar to the score he or she receives the next week, not wildly different. Similarly, if two observers watch adults in a situation in which they have the opportunity to act assertively, the two observers' assessments of each adult's degree of assertiveness should be consistent (that is, in agreement).

A measure is *valid* if it measures what it is supposed to measure. A personality scale intended to measure assertiveness could be highly reliable but not valid. For example, it could actually measure the extent to which a person wants to create a favorable impression on the tester rather than that person's true tendency to act assertively in everyday life. Researchers must demonstrate that they are actually assessing the trait they believe they are assessing rather than some other trait—for instance, by establishing that high scorers on the assertiveness scale are more likely than low scorers to assert themselves in a range of situations.

Keeping in mind the importance of establishing the reliability and validity of measures, let's look briefly at some of the pros and cons of the major methods of data collection used by developmental researchers.

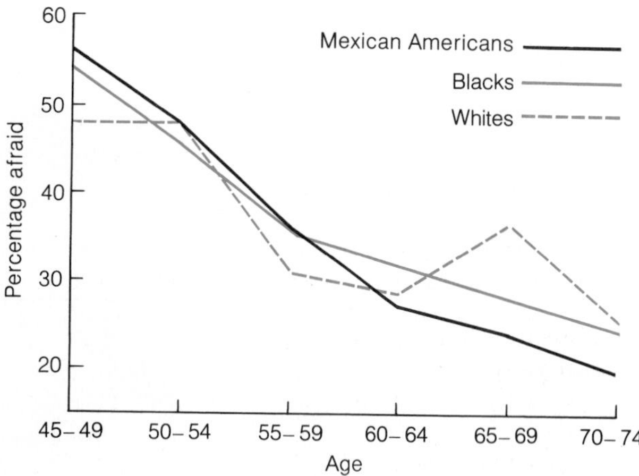

FIGURE 1.2 *How afraid are you of death? Would you say you are: not at all afraid?/somewhat afraid?/or very afraid?* Vern Bengtson, Jose Cuellar, and Pauline Ragan (1977) asked this question in interviews with adults in Los Angeles. The graph shows the percentage of adults of each age who said they were "very afraid" or "somewhat afraid" of death. But how many people who claimed they were "not at all afraid" simply did not want a strange interviewer to know that they were fearful? Could older adults in particular have been trying to present themselves as bravely accepting the inevitability of death? Responses to interviews and questionnaires are not always valid indicators of what they are attempting to measure. (From Bengtson, Cuellar, & Ragan, 1977.)

Self-Report Measures: Interviews, Questionnaires, and Tests

Collecting information through an *interview* involves orally asking people questions about some aspect of their lives, attitudes, or behaviors, whereas collecting data via a *questionnaire* involves putting one's questions on paper and asking people to write responses to them. A *psychological test* poses questions or presents tasks designed to measure a person's abilities, aptitudes, or personality traits. Such self-report measures are *standardized* if they ask the same questions in precisely the same order of all research participants. This technique allows researchers to compare the responses of different individuals.

Interviews, questionnaires, and tests such as intelligence (IQ) tests are widely used to study human development. Yet these "self-report" methods have their shortcomings. First, they typically cannot be used with infants, very young children, or other individuals who cannot read or understand speech very well. Second, because individuals of different ages may not interpret questions in the same way, the trends in responses may reflect age differences in comprehension rather than differences in the quality of interest to the researcher. Developmental researchers always face the challenge of ensuring that their data-gathering tools measure the same thing at all ages they intend to study. Third, answers to interviews and questionnaires may be misleading if respondents try to present themselves in a positive or socially desirable light. The interview findings in Figure 1.2, for example, suggest that older adults fear death less than younger adults do. But could it be that elderly adults were more reluctant to admit to a stranger that they were afraid? Might some other method of data collection have revealed a higher level of death anxiety among older adults than this single, direct question did? Very possibly.

Behavioral Observations

Naturalistic observation involves observing people in their common, everyday (that is, natural) surroundings. Ongoing behavior is observed in homes, schools, playgrounds, workplaces, nursing homes, or wherever people are going about their lives. Box 1.1 describes a study that used naturalistic observation of the social behavior of physically abused children in day-care settings.

Naturalistic observation has been used more often to study child development than adult development, largely because infants and young children often cannot be studied through techniques that demand verbal skills. The greatest advantage of naturalistic observation is that it is the only technique that

BOX 1.1 The Legacy of Child Abuse: Naturalistic Observations of Peer Interactions in Day-Care Settings

Many developmental researchers have attempted to assess the effects of physical abuse on a child's development, and several have found that abused children have difficulty relating to other children. Aware of this research, Mary Haskett and Janet Kistner (1991) set out to determine whether physically abused children would continue to show disturbed patterns of social behavior after spending at least a year in day-care centers where they had opportunities to interact with nonpunitive adults and to learn new social skills. Their study illustrates the research method of naturalistic observation.

The investigation centered on 14 girls and boys, ranging in age from 3 to 6, who had been physically abused by their mothers (11 of them) or fathers and had incurred injuries ranging from bruises to bone fractures. None had been abused for at least six months, so any maladaptive social behavior on their part would most likely be attributable to past rather than current abuse. A control group of 14 nonabused children was formed by matching them with abused children on the basis of age, gender, race, IQ, and family background characteristics. All children were from lower-income families.

Observations were made of one abused or one nonabused child playing with six randomly chosen peers in an enclosed area of the day-care classroom. The researchers equipped the area with a standard set of play materials such as blocks and dress-up clothes. Because the size of the group and the toys available for play were standardized, the observations were not strictly naturalistic. Still, they were naturalistic in the sense that children were observed interacting with familiar playmates in their natural setting.

Children were observed during three 10-minute play sessions on three different days. Observers stood outside the play area and recorded the occurrence, during each 10-second interval that passed, of these behaviors: appropriate initiation of conversation or play, appropriate response to a peer who attempts to initiate interaction, instrumental aggression (biting, kicking, hitting aimed at gaining possessions or territory during struggles), hostile aggression (similar acts that are not related to achieving instrumental goals such as possessing a toy), negative verbalizations, and rough play (negative or threatening acts that do not qualify as aggressive behavior). Importantly, observers were "blind" to which children had abuse histories and therefore could not be biased one way or the other toward abused children.

The findings were disturbing. Compared to nonabused children, abused children initiated fewer interactions with peers overall, suggesting that they tended to be socially withdrawn. When they *did* interact, they engaged in more negative behavior than nonabused children did, particularly more instrumental aggression aimed at getting things from other children. Overall, the average percentage of social acts that were negative rather than positive was over 25% among abused children and about 13% among nonabused children. In addition, peers less often responded when abused children attempted to start interactions with them, as if they did not want to get involved. Teachers' ratings of the children's usual social behavior and peers' ratings of how much they liked to play with the other children in their day-care class generally confirmed the observational findings: Despite the fact that abused children had not been abused for at least six months and had spent a year in day care, they were judged by their teachers to have more behavior problems and were less liked by their peers than control children.

As in other studies relying on naturalistic observation as a method of data gathering, it is difficult to know which of many influences operating in the natural environment is actually causing behavior. We cannot be certain, for example, whether the aggressive behavior of abused children causes peers to back off from them or whether peer rejection causes abused children to behave more aggressively. Meanwhile, Haskett and Kistner note that the only real therapeutic "treatment" many abused children in this country receive is placement in day care. They conclude that day care alone may not be enough to help children who have acquired maladaptive patterns of relating to peers learn more appropriate social skills, and they fear that many abused children will continue to be rejected by other children unless something is done.

can tell us what children or adults actually do in everyday life (Willems & Alexander, 1982). Yet naturalistic observation also has its limitations. First, some behaviors (for example, heroic efforts to help other people) occur too infrequently and unexpectedly to be observed in this manner. Second, many events are usually happening at the same time in a natural setting, and any of them may be affecting people's behavior. This makes it difficult to pinpoint the causes of the behavior or of any developmental trends in the behavior. Finally, the mere presence of an observer can sometimes make people behave differently than they otherwise would. Children may "ham it up" when they have an audience; parents may be on their best behavior. For this reason, researchers sometimes videotape the proceedings from a hidden location or spend time in the setting before they collect their "real" data so that the individuals they are observing become used to their presence and behave more naturally.

Sometimes, to achieve greater control over the conditions under which they gather behavioral data, researchers make **contrived observations**; that is, they create special conditions designed to elicit the behavior of interest. Thus a researcher might bring children individually to a laboratory room and stage an emergency in which a loud crash and scream are heard from the adjoining room. The researcher might then observe whether each child intervenes and, if so, in what way and how quickly. Contrived observations permit the study of behaviors that are rarely observable in natural settings. By exposing all subjects to the same stimuli, this approach also increases the investigator's ability to compare the behavior of different individuals. Concerns about this method center on whether conclusions based on behavior in contrived settings will generalize to behavior in natural settings.

Case Studies

Any or all of the data collection methods we have described—interviews, questionnaires, tests, and behavioral observations (naturalistic or contrived)—can be used to compile a detailed picture of a single individual's development through the **case study** method. The early baby biographies were a form of case study, and Sigmund Freud wrote many fascinating case studies of his patients. Using the case study approach, a clinical psychologist might, for example, attempt to reconstruct the developmental history of a suicidal teenager by interviewing the teenager and his or her parents to gather information about family background, recent stresses, and the quality of the parent/child relationship. The psychologist might also give the youth a battery of personality tests and observe parent/child interaction. The case study approach has much to contribute to our understanding of the development of specific individuals, especially those with psychological disorders. However, case studies have some of the same limitations that the early baby biographies had. In particular, we cannot always be confident that what we learn about a specific individual will apply to people in general.

These, then, are the most commonly used techniques of collecting data about human development. Since each method has its limitations, our knowledge is advanced the most when *multiple* methods are used to study the same aspect of human development and these different methods lead to similar conclusions.

Describing Development: Cross-Sectional, Longitudinal, and Sequential Research Designs

Once developmental researchers have figured out what they want to measure and how they want to measure it, they can turn their attention to the goal of describing developmental changes. Two developmental research designs have been relied on extensively to achieve this descriptive goal: the cross-sectional design and the longitudinal design. A third design, the sequential study, has come into use in an attempt to overcome the limitations of the other two techniques. Let's first define the original two approaches and then explore their strengths and weaknesses.

The Cross-Sectional and Longitudinal Designs in Brief

In a **cross-sectional design,** the performances of people of different age groups are compared. A researcher interested in the development of vocabulary might gather samples of speech from a number of 2-, 3-, and 4-year-olds; calculate the mean (or average) number of distinct words used per child for each age group; and compare these means to describe how the vocabulary sizes of children of ages 2, 3, and 4 differ. A cross-sectional study of memory abilities in adulthood might use a memory test to compare the performance of adults in their 20s with that of adults in their 60s. In each case, what we learn about are *age differences*; by seeing how age groups differ, we can attempt to draw conclusions about how performance changes with age.

In a **longitudinal design,** the performance of one group of individuals is assessed repeatedly over time. The language development study just described would be longitudinal rather than cross-sectional if we identified a group of 2-year-olds, measured their vocabulary sizes, waited a year until they were age 3 and measured their vocabularies again, and did the same thing a year later when they were age 4. In any longitudinal study, whether it covers only 2 years or 20 or 50 years, the same individuals are studied *as they develop*. Thus the longitudinal design provides information about *age changes* rather than age differences.

Now, what difference does it make whether we choose the cross-sectional or the longitudinal design to describe development in some domain? Suppose we were interested in this question: How do attitudes about the roles of men and women in society typically change over the adult years? We have a gender-role attitudes questionnaire that allows us to characterize any adult as having traditional attitudes about gender roles or liberated attitudes that emphasize equality of the two sexes. In 1995 we conduct a cross-sectional study comparing the gender-role attitudes of adults 20, 40, and 60 years old. We were also clever enough to have started a longitudinal study way back in 1955 with a group of 20-year-old men and women. We administered the gender-role questionnaire at that time and again in 1975, when they were 40. We give it a third time in 1995, when they are 60. Figure 1.3 outlines these two alternative designs, and Figure 1.4 portrays hypothetical age trends that they might generate.

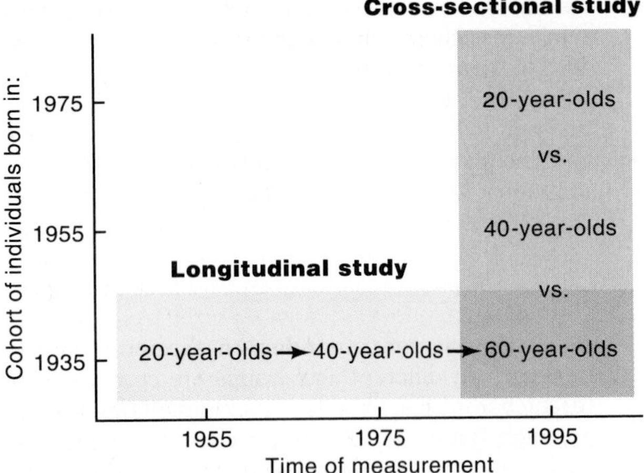

FIGURE 1.3 Cross-sectional and longitudinal studies of development from age 20 to age 60.

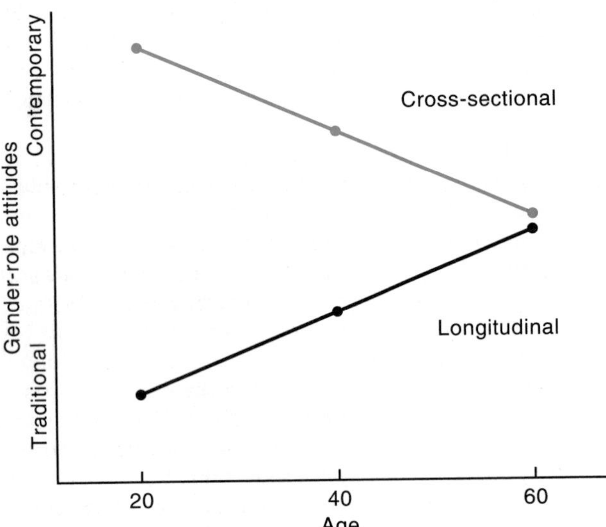

FIGURE 1.4 Conflicting findings of hypothetical cross-sectional and longitudinal studies of gender-role attitudes.

What is going on here? The cross-sectional study seems to be indicating that, as people get older, their attitudes about gender roles become more traditional. The longitudinal study suggests precisely the opposite: As people get older, their attitudes about gender roles seem to become more liberated. How could the two studies lead to totally different conclusions?

Age, Cohort, and Time of Measurement Effects

To unravel the mystery we have posed, we must realize that the findings of developmental studies can be influenced by three factors: *age effects*, *cohort effects*, and *time of measurement effects*. **Age effects** are simply the effects of getting older; note that the whole purpose of our developmental study is to describe how attitudes about gender roles change as a function of *age* during adulthood. **Cohort effects** are the effects of being born at a particular time and growing up in a particular historical context. Any *cohort* is a group of people born at the same time, either in the same year or within a specified, limited span of years. People who are in their 40s today not only are older than people in their 20s, but they belong to a different cohort or generation. Finally, **time of measurement effects** in developmental research are the effects on findings of historical events occurring at the time when the data are being collected. Once one is aware that age, cohort, and time of measurement can all influence developmental research findings, one can appreciate that both the cross-sectional and the longitudinal designs have their problems.

Strengths and Weaknesses of the Cross-Sectional Design

In our cross-sectional study, the three age groups studied represent three different cohorts of people. The 60-year-olds were born in 1935, the 40-year-olds in 1955, and the 20-year-olds in 1975. Certainly these three groups had different formative experiences. The oldest group grew up in an era when traditional attitudes about the roles of the sexes were strongly held: Women were to stay at home and raise families, and men were to head the household and bring home the bacon. Perhaps, then, older adults' unliberated responses to the questionnaire in 1995 reflect traditional views they learned early in life rather than some shift toward more traditional attitudes that occurred as they developed. The 20-year-olds are a different cohort entirely; they grew up when the women's movement was going strong and may have formed relatively liberated gender-role attitudes as a result. The cross-sectional study *does* tell us how people of different ages or cohorts differ, and this can be useful information. But the cross-sectional technique does not necessarily tell us how people develop *as a function of age*. Do 60-year-olds have more conservative gender-role attitudes than 20-year-olds because they are older, or because of cohort effects—because they are members of a different cohort raised in a more traditional historical period? We cannot tell. *Age effects and cohort effects are hopelessly tangled.*

This, then, is the central problem in cross-sectional research, and it is a very real problem in studies designed to describe how adults develop over the years. As we shall see in Chapter 9, cross-sectional studies of performance on intelligence tests once appeared to indicate that we lose our intellectual facul-

Children growing up earlier in this century (for example, these boys working the night shift at a glassworks in 1908) had different experiences than today's youth have. Each cohort or generation develops somewhat differently as a result.

ties starting in middle age and perform quite poorly indeed in old age. Yet the older people who were being compared with younger adults in these studies were part of a cohort that grew up in a time when many people ended their education before completing high school. Did these older people lose intellectual abilities in old age? Perhaps not; longitudinal studies of the same people tested repeatedly over the years have revealed far less decline in intellectual performance. What cross-sectional studies often detect is a cohort effect, not a true developmental trend or age effect.

Despite this central problem, the cross-sectional design is still the one most often used by developmentalists. Why? Because it has the great advantage of being quick and easy; we can go out this year, sample individuals of different ages, and be done with it. Moreover, this design should yield valid conclusions if it is unlikely that the cohorts studied have had widely different growing-up experiences—as when 3- and 4-year-olds rather than 30- and 40-year-olds are compared. It is when researchers attempt to make inferences about development over the span of many years that cohort effects are a serious problem.

The second major limitation of the cross-sectional design is this: It tells us nothing about the development of *individuals,* because each person is observed at only one point in time. We can compare the average performances of the different age groups studied, but we do not watch a single person actually develop. We cannot, for example, see whether different people show divergent patterns of change in their gender-role attitudes over time, or whether individuals who are especially liberated in their attitudes as 20-year-olds are later among the most liberated of the 60-year-olds. To address issues like these, we need longitudinal research.

Strengths and Weaknesses of the Longitudinal Design

Because the longitudinal design actually traces changes in individuals as they develop, it can tell us whether most people change in the same direction or whether different individuals travel different developmental paths. It can indicate whether traits remain consistent over time so that the bright or aggressive or dependent young person retains those same traits in later life. And it can tell us whether experiences early in life predict traits and behaviors later in life. The cross-sectional design can do none of this.

What, then, are the limitations of the longitudinal design? In our longitudinal study of gender-role attitudes, adults were first assessed at age 20 and then reassessed at age 40 and age 60. This study centers on *one cohort* of individuals: people who were 20 years old in 1955, when they were first surveyed (and therefore were members of the 1935 birth cohort). These people were raised in a particular historical context and then experienced changes in their social environment as they aged. Thus we must focus attention on *time of measurement effects* on the gender-role attitudes they expressed.

In 1955 these adults' responses were undoubtedly influenced by the prevailing traditional views of that time. By the time they are interviewed in 1995, as 60-year-olds, the times had changed immensely because of the women's movement and other social changes. Why, then, are their responses in 1995 more liberal than their responses in 1955? Perhaps it is not because people's gender-role attitudes *generally* become more liberal as they get older but only because society changed in a particular way from one time of measurement to the next during the time frame of our study. Perhaps we would obtain entirely different "developmental" trends if we did this longitudinal study in an era in which sexism suddenly became the rage again!

In the longitudinal study, then, *age effects and time of measurement effects are tangled.* We cannot tell for sure whether the age-related changes observed are true developmental trends or whether they reflect historical events occurring during the study. Since it is clear that people are affected by the historical context in which they develop, we may not be able to generalize what we find in a longitudinal study to people developing in a different era.

There are still other disadvantages of the longitudinal design. One is fairly obvious: This approach is not at all easy; it is costly and time-consuming, particularly if it is used to trace development over a long span of time and at many points in time. Second, because knowledge of human development is constantly changing, questions that seemed very exciting when a study was launched may seem rather trivial by the time the project ends, or researchers might wish that they had measured something that they did not originally anticipate would be important. Third, participants drop out of long-term studies; they may move, lose interest, or, in studies of aging, die during the course of the study. The result is a smaller and often less representative sample on which to base conclusions. Finally, researchers must be on guard for the effects of repeated testing; sometimes simply taking a test improves performance on that test the next time around.

Are both the cross-sectional and longitudinal designs hopelessly flawed, then? That would be overstating their weaknesses. As we have noted, the cross-sectional design is still very efficient and useful, especially when the cohorts studied are not widely different in age or formative experiences. Moreover, longitudinal studies are extremely valuable for what they can reveal about the actual changes in performance that occur as individuals get older—even though it must be recognized that the cohort studied may not develop in precisely the same way that an earlier or later cohort does. However, in an attempt to overcome the limitations of both cross-sectional and longitudinal designs, developmentalists have devised a new and more powerful method of describing developmental change: the sequential design.

Sequential Designs: The Best of Both Worlds

Sequential designs combine the cross-sectional approach and the longitudinal approach in a single study (Schaie, 1965, 1986). How might we conduct such a study to measure changes in attitudes about gender roles that occur as adults grow older? We might begin in 1955 with a sample of 20-year-olds (the 1935 birth cohort) and reassess these people's attitudes when they are 40 and 60. In 1975 we might also launch a second longitudinal study with a sample of 20-year-olds (the 1955 birth cohort) and then reassess them every 20 years. Notice that there are actually *two* longitudinal studies here, each involving a different cohort of people. Notice too that cross-sectional comparisons can also be made; for instance, in 1975 we can compare the responses of 20-year-olds with those of 40-year-olds from the 1955 birth cohort.

TABLE 1.3 Summary of the cross-sectional, longitudinal, and sequential development designs.

	Cross-Sectional Method	*Longitudinal Method*	*Sequential Method*
Procedure	Observe people of different ages (or cohorts) at one point in time	Observe people of one age group repeatedly over time	Combine cross-sectional and longitudinal approaches; observe different cohorts on multiple occasions
Information Gained	Describes age differences	Describes age changes	Describes age differences *and* age changes
Advantages	Demonstrates age differences in behavior; hints at developmental trends Takes little time to conduct; is inexpensive	Actually indicates how individuals are alike and different in the way they change over time Can reveal links between early behavior or experiences and later behavior	Helps separate the effects of age, cohort, and time of measurement Indicates whether developmental changes experienced by one generation or cohort are similar to those experienced by other cohorts
Disadvantages	Age trends may reflect cohort effects (differences between cohorts) rather than true developmental change Provides no information about change over time in individuals	Age trends may reflect historical (time of measurement) effects during the study rather than true developmental change Relatively time-consuming and expensive Measures devised may later prove inadequate Participants drop out Participants can be affected by repeated testing	Often complex and time-consuming Despite being the strongest method, may still leave questions about whether a developmental change is generalizable

Sequential designs, by combining the cross-sectional and longitudinal approaches, improve on both. (See Table 1.3 for a summary of these three basic designs.) They can tell us: (1) which age-related trends are truly developmental in nature and reflect how most people can be expected to change over time regardless of their cohort (age effects); (2) which age trends suggest that each generation is affected by its distinct growing-up experiences (cohort effects); and (3) which trends imply that historical events during a specific time period change most people who experience them, regardless of which cohort they belong to (time of measurement effects). In short, sequential designs can at least begin to untangle the effects of age, cohort, and time of measurement and to indicate which age trends are truly developmental in nature.

Explaining Development: Experimental and Correlational Methods

Researchers are not content to describe development through the use of cross-sectional, longitudinal, and sequential studies; they also want to achieve their goal of *explaining* it. We change with age but do not change *because* we get older. Instead, we change because we are affected by maturational processes and learning experiences that occur as we get older. So how can researchers identify the factors responsible for developmental change?

The most powerful method for explaining behavior and identifying the causes of developmental changes in behavior is the experiment. When experiments cannot be conducted, correlational research techniques may suggest answers to important "why" questions.

The Experimental Method

An **experiment** is a research technique in which the investigator manipulates or alters some aspect of people's environment in order to see what effect this has on their behavior. Let's examine an experiment conducted by Lynette Friedrich and Aletha Stein (1973) to study the effects of different kinds of television programs on the behavior of preschool children. These researchers divided children in a nursery school into three groups: One group was exposed to violent cartoons like *Superman* and *Batman* (aggressive treatment condition), another group watched episodes of *Mister Rogers' Neighborhood* portraying many helpful and cooperative acts (prosocial treatment condition), and a third group saw programs featuring circuses and farm scenes with neither aggressive nor altruistic themes (neutral treatment condition).

The whole idea of an experiment is to see whether the different treatments that form the **independent variable** — the variable being manipulated so that its causal effects can be assessed — have differing effects on the behavior being studied: the **dependent variable** in the experiment. The independent variable in Friedrich and Stein's experiment was the type of treatment condition children experienced — specifically, the type of television they watched (aggressive, prosocial, or neutral). The dependent variables that Friedrich and Stein chose to study, using a complicated observation system, were the number of aggressive behaviors and the number of helpful, cooperative, or affectionate behaviors children displayed toward other children in the nursery school. These behaviors were observed before each child spent a month watching daily episodes of one of the three kinds of television programs and were recorded again during the two weeks after the month-long treatment period to see if they had changed.

And what were the findings? The children who watched violent programs became more aggressive — although only if they were already relatively aggressive. By contrast, many of the children who watched altruistic programs, especially those from lower-income families, became friendlier and more helpful than children in the other experimental treatment groups. Thus this experiment demonstrated clear cause-and-effect relationships between the kind of behavior children watched on television and their own subsequent behavior, although not all children were affected equally by their viewing experiences.

This study has the three critical features shared by any true experiment. First, an experiment involves *manipulation of an independent variable*; the investigator must arrange for different groups to have different experiences so that the effects of those experiences can be assessed. If children had been allowed to choose for themselves what kind of television programs they would watch, this study would not be an experiment.

Second, an experiment involves **random assignment** of individuals to treatment conditions, as by drawing their names from a hat in an unbiased manner so that each child has an equal chance of being in each treatment condition. Randomly assigning participants to experimental conditions is a way of ensuring that the treatment groups are similar (in, for example, previous tendencies to be aggressive or helpful, socioeconomic status, ethnic background, and numerous other individual characteristics that could be related to positive or negative social behavior). Only if experimental groups are similar in all respects initially can we be confident that any differences among groups at the end of the experiment were caused by differences in the experimental treatments they received.

Finally, an experiment is characterized by **experimental control**; that is, all other factors besides the independent variable must be controlled or held constant. Random assignment of children to experimental conditions helped to control for unwanted differences among the groups before they were exposed to any television. In addition, Friedrich and Stein did all they could to ensure that children in the three treatment conditions were treated similarly *except for* the type of television they watched. It would have ruined the experiment, for example, if the children exposed to violent programs had to watch them in a small, hot, crowded room, whereas children in the other two groups watched in larger, more comfortable rooms. To establish that the independent variable, and not some uncontrolled other factor, caused any change in the dependent variable, it is essential to control extraneous aspects of the situation.

The greatest strength of the experimental method is its ability to establish unambiguously that one thing *causes* another—that manipulating the independent variable causes a change in the dependent variable (or, here, that watching a particular kind of television program causes a change in children's behavior). When experiments are properly conducted, they do indeed contribute to our ability to *explain* human development. They also contribute to the goal of *optimizing* development when they establish that some experiences have more beneficial effects on human development than others.

Does the experimental method have any limitations? Absolutely! First, the findings of laboratory experiments may not invariably hold true in the real world, because the situations created in laboratory experiments can be quite contrived and artificial—very unlike the situations that people encounter in everyday life. Urie Bronfenbrenner (1979) has been critical of the fact that so many developmental studies are contrived experiments. Indeed, he once charged that developmental psychology had become "the science of the strange behavior of children in strange situations with strange adults" (p. 19). Similarly, Robert McCall (1977) notes that experiments indicate what *can* cause a developmental change but not necessarily what actually *does* most strongly influence developmental change in natural settings.

A second limitation of the experimental method is that it simply cannot be used to address many significant questions about human development. Suppose we were interested in how older women are affected by their husbands' deaths? How could we study this question experimentally? Simple: We would identify a sample of women aged 65 and older, randomly assign them to either the experimental group or the control group, and then manipulate the independent variable by shooting the husbands of all those women in the experimental group! Only textbook writers trying to make a point would propose such an outrageously immoral study. Ethical principles demand that developmentalists use correlational methods rather than experimental ones to study many, many important questions about development.

The Correlational Method

The **correlational method** involves determining whether two or more variables are related. In an experiment the researcher manipulates the independent variable, randomly assigns participants to treatment conditions, and controls extraneous factors. In a correlational study none of these steps is followed. Instead, the researchers take people as they find them—already "manipulated" by their life experiences—and attempt to determine whether differences in people's experiences or characteristics are associated with differences in their behavior.

How would a *correlational* study of the effects of television programs on preschool children differ from Friedrich and Stein's experiment on this issue? Consider a project by Jerome and Dorothy Singer (1981). Parents completed detailed logs describing the TV viewing habits of their preschool children: how much they watched and what they watched during a year's time. On four occasions, observers rated how aggressive the children were in interactions with other children in their nursery schools. In this manner the researchers gathered data on the two variables of interest to them: amount of exposure to TV and level of aggression.

The Singers were then able to determine the strength of the relationship between these two variables by calculating a **correlation coefficient**—a measure of the extent to which individuals' scores on one variable are systematically associated with their scores on another variable in either a positive or negative way. A correlation coefficient (symbolized *r*) can range in value from +1.00 to −1.00. A large positive correlation of +.80 or +.90 between TV viewing and aggression would indicate that, as the number of hours of TV a child watches increases, so does the number of aggressive acts he or she commits (see Figure 1.5). A large negative correlation of −.80 or −.90 would result if the heaviest TV viewers were quite consistently the *least* aggressive children and the lightest viewers were the *most* aggressive children. A correlation of .00 would be obtained if the dots in Figure 1.5 were scattered randomly about rather than falling neatly along a line. This would mean that there is no relationship between the two variables—that one cannot predict how aggressive a child is based on knowing his or her TV viewing habits.

Like most other researchers, Singer and Singer found a moderately strong positive correlation between TV watching and aggression (see also Huston et al., 1992). Specifically, children who frequently watched action and adventure programs were more

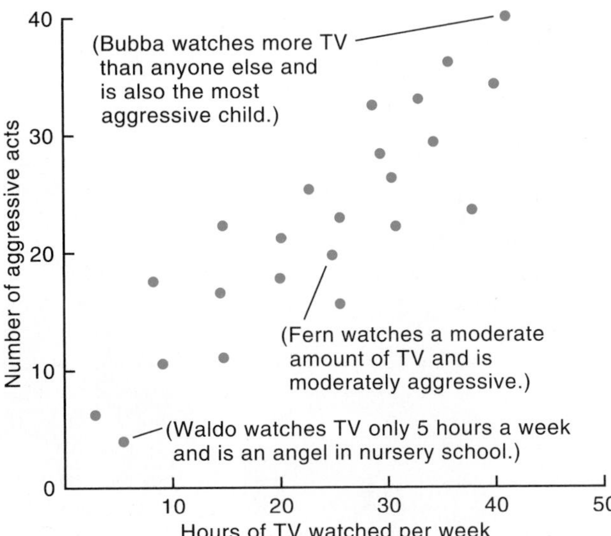

FIGURE 1.5 Plot of a hypothetical correlation between the amount of TV children watch and the number of aggressive acts they display. Each dot represents a specific child who watches a particular amount of TV and commits a particular number of aggressive acts. Here the correlation is large and positive: The more TV a child watches, the more aggressive he or she is.

aggressive in the nursery school than children who rarely watched such programs; the correlation was +.33.

Does this correlational study firmly establish that watching action-packed programs *causes* children to become more aggressive? No, because there are alternative explanations for the correlation between TV watching and aggression. One possibility is that aggression causes violent TV watching—that children who are already highly aggressive seek out violence wherever they can get it, whereas nonviolent children shy away from guns and gore. Television viewing habits could then be the *effect* rather than the cause of aggression in children.

A second possibility is that the association between TV watching and aggression is actually due to some third variable. For example, some children might have parents who are harsh and rejecting and might watch a lot of TV simply because there is nothing better to do in their homes (see Tangney, 1988). These harshly treated children may be aggressive because they have watched their parents being aggressive or are acting out in the nursery school the negative feelings that have resulted from their being rejected by their parents. If any of these possibilities were true, TV watching did not cause these children to become more aggressive than their peers; the treatment they received from their parents was the real cause.

Now that we have compared an experiment and a correlational study of the same topic, you can see that the correlational method has one major limitation: *It cannot unambiguously indicate that one thing caused another.* Correlational studies can *suggest* that a causal relationship exists. Indeed, Singer and Singer (1981) used complex statistical techniques to show that watching violent television probably did contribute to aggression in children and that several alternative explanations for the relationship between TV viewing and aggression could probably be ruled out. Nonetheless, they could not establish a definite cause/effect link.

Despite this important limitation, the correlational method is extremely valuable. First, as already noted, many problems can be addressed only through the correlational method because it would be unethical to conduct experiments. We can compare the adjustment of widows and nonwidows in a correlational study, but we simply cannot conduct an experiment on the effects of widowhood. Second, correlational studies often have a "real world" quality that experiments lack. The Singer and Singer (1981) study, for example, says something about relationships between children's actual, everyday TV viewing

TABLE 1.4 Comparison of the experimental method and the correlational method.

Experimental Method	*Correlational Method*
Manipulation of an independent variable (investigator exposes participants to different experiences)	Studies people who have already had different experiences
Random assignment to treatment groups to ensure similarity of groups	Assignment by "nature" to groups (groups may not be similar in all respects)
Experimental control of extraneous variables	Lack of control over extraneous variables
Can establish a cause/effect relationship between independent variable and dependent variable	Can suggest but not firmly establish that one variable causes another
May not be possible for ethical reasons	Can be used to study issues that cannot be studied experimentally
May be artificial (findings from contrived experimental settings may not generalize well to the "real world")	Can be applied to data collected in natural settings (findings may generalize better to the "real world")

habits and their behavior. Experiments sometimes expose children to only a short dose of violent TV in an artificial situation, making it difficult to be sure whether their behavior in such situations has any implications for their conduct in the natural environment. Overall, our ability to understand why humans develop as they do is advanced the most when the results of different kinds of studies *converge*—when experiments demonstrate a clear cause-and-effect relationship under controlled conditions *and* when correlational studies reveal that this very same relationship seems to be operating in everyday life (Miller, 1987).

WHAT PROBLEMS ARISE IN STUDYING DEVELOPMENT?

Designing good developmental research is not easy. Researchers must first draw on theories and previous research to form a clear notion of what questions they want to answer and what hypotheses they want to test. They must then define the variables that interest them, decide how to measure those variables, and demonstrate that their measures are good ones (that is, that they are reliable and valid). And of course they must decide on a research design, choosing a cross-sectional, longitudinal, or sequential design if they are trying to describe age-related changes, and weighing the pros and cons of experimental or correlational methods if they wish to uncover possible influences on development. But there are many additional issues that researchers must grapple with. Here we will highlight just two: choosing the individuals to be studied and protecting their rights.

Choosing Samples to Study

A research **sample** is simply a group of individuals chosen for study. Researchers study a sample and hope to generalize their findings to a larger **population**—a well-defined group such as American high school students or Canadian nursing-home residents. In many kinds of research, the ideal sample is a **random sample**—that is, a sample formed by identifying all members of the larger population of interest and then, by a random means (such as drawing names blindly), selecting a portion of that population to participate in the study. Random sampling increases confidence that the sample studied is representative or typical of the larger population of interest and therefore that conclusions based on studying the sample will hold true of the whole population.

In actual practice, developmentalists often draw their samples—sometimes random, sometimes not—from their local communities. Thus a researcher might survey a random sample of students at a local high school about their drug use but then be unable to make statements about American teenagers in general if, for example, the school is in a high-income suburb where drug-use patterns are different than they might be in a low-income inner-city area. As a result, researchers must be careful to describe the characteristics of the sample they studied and to avoid overgeneralizing their findings to populations that might be socioeconomically or culturally different from their research sample.

Developmental findings established through the study of a sample of white children do not always hold true in a sample of African-American or Hispanic children. It is important to study development in a wide range of subcultural settings.

When developmentalists conduct cross-sectional studies, one of their main challenges is to make sure that the age groups they study are similar to one another in all characteristics except age—that is, similar in average family income, intelligence, ethnic or racial background, and so on. But suppose we want to compare the memory abilities of 20-year-olds and 60-year-olds. If we randomly sample people in these age groups, we encounter a major problem: Older adults today typically have had less education than young adults today have had. We would have no trouble at all showing that elders do worse than young people on our memory tests, but we would not be justified in blaming that poor performance on the aging process. This age difference would most likely be due to cohort differences in education.

What is the solution? Many researchers cope with this problem by selecting younger and older adults with equivalent years of education—for example, college graduates only. Then any performance differences between the age groups would not be the result of differences in the amount of education they have received. But notice that the samples chosen are no longer representative of their age groups. Conclusions about college-educated older people might not hold true of the large number of older adults who did *not* graduate from college. Again, researchers need to describe their samples carefully to make it clear that their findings might not generalize to other kinds of individuals.

Finally, cross-cultural studies show that human development differs from society to society, as we will see in Chapter 4 and throughout this book. Unfortunately, the vast majority of our knowledge of human development is based on studies of children and adults in Western societies in the 20th century—and often white, middle-class ones at that. So bear in mind that we cannot just assume that findings based on children or adults in Peoria will also hold true of children or adults in Paris or Peking. Nor can we assume that what holds for one subcultural group in our own society holds for others; developmental experiences can differ widely across racial, ethnic, and socioeconomic groups. The message is clear: What we learn about human development often depends on whom we sample.

Protecting the Rights of Research Participants

Developmental researchers sometimes also face thorny issues centering on **research ethics,** the standards of conduct that investigators are ethically bound to honor in order to protect their research participants from physical or psychological harm. Some ethical issues are easily resolved: One simply does *not* conduct experiments that will cause physical or psychological damage—experiments in which children are physically abused or the husbands of elderly women are shot. But most ethical issues are far more subtle. For example, is it ethical to deceive people by telling them that they performed poorly on a test in order to create in them a temporary sense of failure? Is it an invasion of a family's privacy to ask children questions about the ways in which their parents punish them?

The American Psychological Association (1982), the Society for Research in Child Development (1990), the federal government, and many other agencies have established guidelines for ethical research with human beings (see also Hartmann, 1992; Miller, 1987; Thompson, 1990). In addition, universities, research foundations, and government agencies that fund research have set up "human-subjects review committees" to determine whether proposed research projects conform to ethical standards. However, the ultimate responsibility for research ethics rests with the investigator. Deciding whether a proposed study is on safe ethical ground involves weighing the possible *benefits* of the research (gains in knowledge and potential benefits to humanity or to the participants themselves) against the potential *risks* to participants. If the potential benefits greatly outweigh the potential risks, and if there are no other, less risky, procedures that could produce these same benefits, the investigation will generally be approved and will be carried out. Box 1.2 describes some of the ethical issues that arise in developmental research and some of the ethical guidelines that researchers are urged to follow.

REFLECTIONS

Each upcoming chapter will close with a "Reflections" section that encourages you to think about larger themes and issues. Here we'll simply mention what you have no doubt noticed already: Understanding life-span human development is an incredibly complex undertaking. Developmentalists must somehow make sense of continuities and changes in all facets of human functioning over entire lifetimes in response to numerous influences. Is this an impossible task? It would indeed be impossible if researchers merely conducted study after study without any guiding ideas. To understand human development, we need *theories* of human development. Theories provide the "big picture," calling our attention to regularities in development and to critical processes underlying development and guiding new research. This is why we devote Chapter 2 to theories.

SUMMARY POINTS

1. Life-span human development consists of systematic changes and continuities in the individual occurring between conception and death. Developmental changes involve gains and losses, growth and aging, and more neutral changes; they occur through genetically programmed maturation as well as through environmental influence or learning.

2. Concepts of the life span and its distinctive periods (or age grades and corresponding age norms) have changed greatly over history and vary greatly from culture to culture today. Until the 17th century, children were expected to assume adult roles very early and were treated quite harshly. In Western cultures, adolescence apparently did not come to be viewed as a distinct phase of the life span until the late 19th century; also, a lengthening of the average life

BOX 1.2 Guidelines for Conducting Ethical Research

Drawing primarily on the principles of research ethics set forth by the American Psychological Association (1982) and the Society for Research in Child Development (1990), we can highlight some of the main ethical responsibilities that an investigator has. These responsibilities boil down to respecting the rights of research participants: allowing them to make informed and uncoerced decisions about taking part in research, protecting them from harm, and treating any information they provide as confidential (Miller, 1987).

Informed consent

Researchers generally should inform potential participants of all aspects of the research that might affect their decision to participate. The idea is to ensure that each person who chooses to participate in research has made a voluntary decision based on knowledge of what the research involves. But are young children or mentally impaired older adults capable of understanding what they are being asked to do and of giving their *informed* consent? Probably not (see Miller, 1987; Ratzan, 1986). Therefore researchers who study such individuals should obtain informed consent both from the individual (if possible) and from someone who can act on the individual's behalf: the parent or guardian of a child, school officials, superintendents, directors of institutions, or legal representatives. Children 7 years of age and older generally should provide their own informed consent after receiving a clear and simple explanation of the study; younger children may not be able to provide truly informed consent but still should be told what will happen and given a chance to decide for themselves whether they want to do it (Society for Research in Child Development, 1990). Investigators also must not pressure anyone to participate and must respect any participant's right to refuse to participate in the first place, to drop out at any point during the study, and to refuse to have his or her data used by the investigator. Again, treating children ethically is tricky: Even if they understand that they can stop participating in a study at any time, they may not really grasp how to go about doing so or may not really believe that there will be no penalties if they do (Abramovitch, Freedman, Thoden, & Nikolich, 1991).

Protection from harm

Researchers are bound not to harm research participants either physically or psychologically. It may be difficult to predict whether any psychological harm is possible, but researchers must try to do so and should consult with others if they are in doubt. If harm to the participants seems likely, another way of obtaining the information should be considered—or the research should be abandoned.

Debriefing about any deception or concealment of information

Ideally, researchers are able to tell participants about the true purposes of the study in advance. However, in some cases doing so would make the study worthless. Suppose, for example, that we are interested in the moral development of children and adolescents and want to know if they would cheat if they thought they could get away with it. If we told all the participants that the study was about cheating, do you think a single person would cheat? Instead, we might propose setting up a situation in which children have an opportunity to cheat and believe that they are alone but are actually being observed from behind a one-way mirror. Our ethical responsibility now is to *debrief* the participants—that is, to explain to them afterward what the true purpose of the study was and why they were misled about it. In this example we would also have an obligation to make sure that children do not leave feeling upset about the fact that they cheated. Indeed, in research with young children who may not be able to understand a debriefing, the most important thing may be to leave them feeling good (Society for Research in Child Development, 1990). A research ethics committee looks very closely at any study that involves deception to make sure that the deception is really necessary and is justified by the benefits of the research.

Confidentiality

Researchers also have an ethical responsibility to keep in confidence the information they collect. It would be unacceptable, for example, to tell a child's teacher that the child performed poorly on an intelligence test or to tell an adult's employer that he or she revealed a drinking problem in an interview. Only if participants give explicit permission to have information about them shared with someone else would that information be passed on. However, there are a few circumstances in which researchers must violate confidentiality. For example, many states now have laws that prohibit an investigator from withholding the names of children who are believed to be the victims of abuse.

---

span and a decline in birth rates have led to a middle-aged "empty nest" phase and a period of old age in which people are retired.

3. The science of life-span development has three goals—the description, explanation, and optimization of development—and got its start at the end of the 19th century with the first baby biographies. Although many developmentalists have specialized in studying one age group or another, today's developmentalists are increasingly adopting a life-span perspective and viewing development as a lifelong, multidirectional process that involves gain and loss, is characterized by considerable plasticity, is shaped by its historical/cultural context, has many causes, and is best viewed from a multidisciplinary perspective.

4. Through the scientific method, data, or systematic observations, are used to decide which ideas are best. It involves formulating theories based on observations, testing specific hypotheses (predictions based on theory) by collecting new observations in research investigations, and using the data to evaluate the worth of theories.

5. To study human development, researchers must devise measures of human attributes and behaviors and ensure that these measures are reliable (consistent) and valid (accurate). The most widely used data collection techniques are self-report measures (interviews, questionnaires, tests) and behavioral observations (either naturalistic or contrived). These techniques can be combined to study one individual in depth through the case study method.

6. Developmental researchers rely principally on the cross-sectional and longitudinal research designs to describe development. The cross-sectional design, which compares different age groups (cohorts) at a single time of measurement, is easy to conduct but may be misleading if an age trend is actually due to differences in life experiences (cohort effects) rather than to true developmental change (age effects). In the longitudinal design, one group (cohort) is assessed repeatedly as its members develop. However, participants in a longitudinal study may change over the years, not as a function of age itself but in response to historical events (time of measurement effects). To counteract the limitations of cross-sectional and longitudinal designs, researchers devised sequential designs that combine the two approaches.

7. To achieve the goal of explaining (and often of optimizing) development, researchers rely primarily on experiments. In an experiment an independent variable is manipulated to see what effects this has on a dependent variable, participants are randomly assigned to treatment groups, and extraneous factors are experimentally controlled. Properly conducted, an experiment can firmly establish that a cause-and-effect relationship exists. The alternative correlational method cannot yield firm conclusions about cause and effect but can suggest causal relationships between variables and may be mandatory in many situations for ethical or practical reasons.

8. Developmentalists who want to conduct good research must decide which samples to study and must ensure that the different age groups studied are similar in everything but age; they must also adhere to standards of ethical research practice, with attention to informed consent, protection from harm, debriefing, and confidentiality.

KEY TERMS

age effects
age grades
age norms
aging
baby biographies
baby boom generation
case study
cognitive development
cohort effects
contrived observation
correlational method
correlation coefficient
cross-sectional design
dependent variable
development
experiment
experimental control
gerontology
growth
hypothesis
independent variable
learning
life-span perspective
longitudinal design
maturation
naturalistic observation
old-old
physical development
plasticity
population
psychosocial development
random assignment
random sample
reliability
research ethics
sample
scientific method
sequential design
storm and stress
theory
time of measurement effects
validity
young-old

THEORIES OF HUMAN DEVELOPMENT

Sheila is an attractive 15-year-old whose relationship with James has become the center of her life. She gets by in school, but most of what goes on in the classroom bores her. Her relationship with her parents has been a bit strained lately, partly because her mother does not want her to spend so much time with James and nags her about doing her homework and chores. James, age 16, is also struggling at school as he tries to juggle his part-time job, family responsibilities, and time with Sheila. And these two teenagers have a far more serious problem: Sheila is pregnant. The sex "just happened" one night after a party about five months ago and continued thereafter. Neither Sheila nor James wanted a baby.

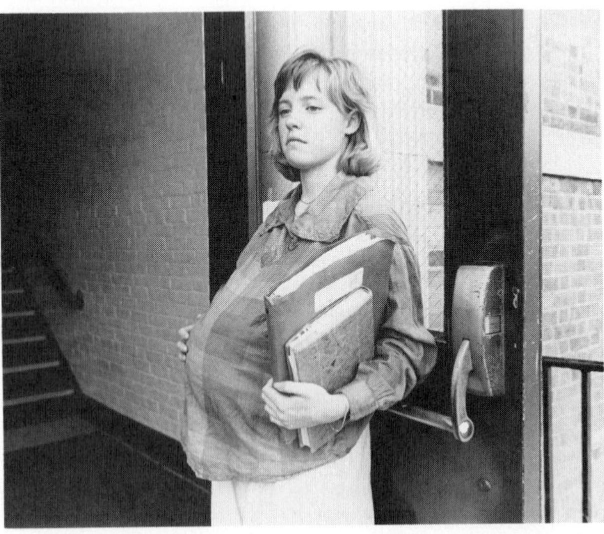

Teenage pregnancy is one of the many facts about human development waiting to be explained by theories.

Here is a specific event in the lives of two developing individuals. How can we explain this unwanted teenage pregnancy? What is your theory? What explanations do the leading theories of human development offer? More practically, what can be done to reduce the high rate of teenage pregnancy in our society? Over 1 in 10 females aged 15 to 19 become pregnant each year, and about half of pregnant teenagers give birth (Henshaw, Koonin, & Smith, 1991). The consequences sometimes include an interrupted education, low income, and a difficult start for both new parent and new child (Brooks-Gunn & Furstenberg, 1989; Furstenberg, Lincoln, & Menken, 1981). Meanwhile, sexually transmitted diseases are epidemic among adolescents, more and more teenagers are becoming infected with the HIV virus that causes AIDS, and all too many continue to engage in risky sex (Hingson & Strunin, 1992). What practical solutions to the problems of unwanted teenage pregnancy and sexually transmitted disease might different theorists offer? We will attempt to answer those questions in this chapter to illustrate the fact that different theories of human development often differ radically in their positions on the very same issue.

THE NATURE OF THEORIES

As we noted in Chapter 1, a *theory* is a set of ideas proposed to describe and explain certain phenomena. Basically, then, a theory is no more than a perspective on something (Kaplan, 1983). Theories of human development should give us insights into many developmental phenomena, including teenage pregnancy. Indeed, the beauty of theories is that they can organize our thinking about a wide range of specific facts or events.

In science it simply is not enough to catalog fact after fact without somehow organizing this information around some set of concepts and propositions. We would soon be swamped by unrelated facts, becoming trivia experts who lack a big picture. A theory of human development provides needed organization; it offers a lens through which we can interpret any number of specific facts or observations. A theory also guides the collection of new facts or observations. Each theory tells researchers what is particularly important to study, what can be hypothesized or predicted about it, and how it should be studied. Because different theories often have radically different views on these critical matters, the progress of any science depends a good deal on which theoretical perspectives become dominant.

What qualities should a good theory have? Everyone has at least half-baked theories about human development. Indeed, we hope that reading this chapter makes you more aware of your own assumptions about human development and how they compare to those of the major theorists. Scientific theories are expected to be more rigorous than our everyday theories, though. First, a good developmental theory should be capable of explaining a wide range of phenomena but should at the same time be *parsimonious*—as simple and concise as possible. A theory that can account for a large number of empirical observations or findings using only a few assumptions, concepts, and principles is generally more valuable than a theory that must introduce all kinds of assumptions and terms in order to explain the same phenomena. Second, a good theory should be *falsifiable*—that is, capable of generating hypotheses or predictions that are precise, that can be tested through research, and that can then be either confirmed or disconfirmed. If a theory is vague or generates contradictory hypotheses about development, it cannot guide research, cannot be adequately evaluated, and therefore will not be very useful in advancing our knowledge. Third—and perhaps most obviously and importantly—a good theory should be *valid*; its predictions should be supported by the facts gathered through research. That is, a good theory should indeed help us better describe, predict, and explain human development (and even help us optimize development by solving practical problems such as teenage pregnancy). Theories that fail to meet these evaluation criteria—theories that are not parsimonious, falsifiable, or valid—need to be revised or, ultimately, discarded altogether.

In this chapter we examine four major theoretical viewpoints:

- The *psychoanalytic* viewpoint, as developed by Sigmund Freud and revised by his heirs
- The *learning* perspective developed by B. F. Skinner, Albert Bandura, and others
- The *cognitive-developmental* viewpoint associated with Jean Piaget
- The newly emerging *contextual-dialectical* approach to human development across the life span

Each theory makes particular assumptions or statements about the nature of human development. To aid us in comparing theories, we'll first examine some of the basic developmental issues on which theorists—and people in general, we should add—often disagree.

BASIC ISSUES IN HUMAN DEVELOPMENT

What are developing humans like? How does development come about? What courses does it follow? Let's look at five major issues on which developmental theories often disagree.

Assumptions about Human Nature

Are people inherently good, inherently bad, or neither? Well before modern theories of human development were proposed, philosophers of the 17th and 18th centuries were taking stands on the nature of human beings. Thomas Hobbes (1588–1679), for one, portrayed children as inherently selfish and bad; it was society's task to control their selfish and aggressive impulses and teach them to behave in positive ways. Jean Jacques Rousseau (1712–1778) took exactly the opposite stand: He believed that children were innately good, that they were born with an intuitive understanding of right and wrong, and that they would develop in positive directions as long as society did not interfere with their natural tendencies. In the middle was the English philosopher John Locke (1632–1704), who maintained that an infant is a ***tabula rasa,*** or "blank slate" waiting to be written on by his or her experiences. Locke believed that children were neither innately good nor innately bad; they could develop in any number of directions depending on their experiences, and so it was up to adults to help them develop good habits.

These different visions of human nature are all represented in one or more modern theories of development and have radically different implications for how one might best raise children. In teaching children to share and help others, for example, should one assume that the child's innate selfish tendencies must be combatted every step of the way, or that children are predisposed to care about their fellow humans and will naturally develop prosocial behaviors such as helping if they are simply allowed to grow in their own way, or that children have the potential to become either selfish beasts or selfless wonders depending on how they are brought up? Many developmentalists today have settled on the assumption that human nature is inherently neither good nor bad. But there is still controversy about what behaviors we are predisposed to display by virtue of having a human genetic makeup.

The Nature/Nurture Issue

Is development primarily the result of nature (biological forces) or nurture (environmental forces)? Perhaps no controversy in the study of human development has been more heated than the **nature/nurture issue.** On the nature side of the debate have been those who emphasize the influence of heredity, universal maturational processes guided by the genes, and biologically based predispositions. A strong believer in nature would claim that all normal children achieve the same developmental milestones at similar times because of maturational forces and that differences among children or adults are largely due to differences in their genetic makeups. On the nurture side of the debate have been those who emphasize *environment*—forces outside the person, including life experiences, changes achieved through learning, and the influence of methods of child rearing, societal changes, and culture on development. A strong believer in nurture would argue, as John Locke did, that human development can take many different forms depending on which specific events the individual experiences over a lifetime. Most developmentalists today take a middle ground, holding that human attributes such as intelligence and personality are the products of an involved interplay between both biological and environmental forces (see Plomin, 1990). They believe that it is high time to stop asking about the influences of nature *versus* nurture and to start trying to understand how these two sets of influences combine and interact to produce developmental change.

The Activity/Passivity Issue

Are people active in their own development, or are they more passively shaped by forces outside themselves? With respect to this **activity/passivity issue,** some theorists believe that children are curious, active creatures who in a very real sense orchestrate their own development by exploring the world around them or by shaping their own environments. For example, a 4-year-old girl who asks her mother for clothes to play "dress-up" and studiously watches how her teenage sister acts around boys would be viewed as actively contributing to her own sex-role development. Similarly, adults who choose marriage partners and influence their partners every day may actively produce many of the developmental changes they experience. According to this view, developmental problems might also be partially attributable to the individual. Highly aggressive children may not just be the victims of poor parenting; they may have helped create the climate in which they were raised by angering their parents and provoking punishment.

Other theorists view humans as passive beings who are largely the products of forces beyond their control—usually environmental influences (but possibly strong biological forces). From this vantage point, children's academic failings might be blamed on the failure of their parents and teachers to provide them with the proper learning experiences rather than on their own failure to benefit from instruction. Or, the problems of socially isolated older adults might be traced to the effects of a society that devalues its elderly rather than to the lifestyle decisions of older adults themselves. Theorists do disagree about how active individuals are in creating their own environments and, in the process, producing their own development.

The Continuity/Discontinuity Issue

Do you believe that humans change gradually, in ways that leave them not so different than they were before, or do you believe that human development takes dramatic turns that make people become very different than they were earlier in life? One aspect of the **continuity/discontinuity issue** concerns whether the changes we undergo over the life span are gradual or abrupt. *Continuity* theorists view human development as a process that occurs in small steps, without sudden changes. In contrast, *discontinuity* theorists picture the course of development as more like a series of stairsteps, each of which elevates the individual to a new (and presumably more advanced) level of functioning. When a child rather rapidly gains six inches in height and achieves sexual maturity, the change may seem quite discontinuous.

A second aspect of the continuity/discontinuity issue concerns whether changes are *quantitative* or *qualitative* in nature. Quantitative changes are changes in *degree*: A person becomes taller, or knows more vocabulary words, or interacts with friends more or less frequently. By contrast, qualitative changes are changes in *kind*—changes that make the individual fundamentally different in some way than he or she was before. The transformations of a caterpillar into a butterfly, of a tadpole into a frog, and of a nonverbal infant into a speaking toddler are examples of qualitative changes.

Different societies sometimes take different positions on the continuity/discontinuity issue. In some cultures of the Pacific and Far East, for example, terms for infant qualities are never used to describe adults, and infants are never described with adult trait terms such as *intelligent* or *angry* (Kagan, 1991). In such cultures, personality development is viewed as discontinuous, and infants are regarded as so fundamentally different from adults that they cannot be judged on the same personality dimensions. North Americans seem more willing to assume continuity in personality development and to search for the seeds of adult personality in babies (Kagan, 1991).

So, continuity theorists typically hold that developmental changes are gradual and quantitative, whereas discontinuity theorists hold that they are rather abrupt and qualitative. Discontinuity theorists are the ones who often propose that we progress through **developmental stages,** each of which is a distinct phase of the life cycle characterized by a particular set of abilities, motives, emotions, or behaviors that form a coherent pattern. Each stage is perceived as qualitatively different from the stage before or the stage after. Thus the child may be said to solve problems in an entirely different manner than the infant, adolescent, or adult.

The Universality/Particularity Issue

Do we all follow the same developmental path, or do we follow different paths? Developmental theorists often disagree on the **universality/particularity issue**—on the extent to which developmental changes are common to everyone (*universal*) or different from person to person (*particularistic*). Stage theorists typically believe that the stages they propose are universal. For example, a stage theorist might claim that virtually all children enter a new stage in their intellectual development at about the time they start school, or that most adults, sometime around the age of 40, experience a "midlife crisis" in which they raise major questions about their lives. From this perspective, development proceeds in certain universal directions.

But other theorists believe that human development is far more varied than this. Paths of development followed in one culture may be very different from paths followed in another culture; even within a single culture, sequences of developmental change may differ from subcultural group to subcultural group, from family to family, from individual to individual. As we saw in Chapter 1, the belief that development may proceed in many directions is part of the emerging life-span perspective on development.

These, then, are some of the major controversies about human development that different theories resolve in different ways. We invite you to clarify your own stands on these issues by completing the brief questionnaire in Box 2.1. At the end of the chapter, Box 2.6 indicates how the major developmental theorists might answer these same questions, so you can compare your own assumptions to theirs. For now, let's begin our survey of the theories, starting with Freud's psychoanalytic perspective.

PSYCHOANALYTIC THEORY

It is difficult to think of a theorist who has had a greater impact on Western thought than Sigmund Freud, the Viennese physician who lived from 1856 to 1939. This revolutionary thinker challenged prevailing notions of human nature and human development by proposing that we are driven by motives and emotions of which we are largely unaware and that we are shaped by our earliest experiences in life (see Hall, 1954). His name is a household word, and his **psychoanalytic theory** continues to influence thinking about human development.

Human Nature: Instincts and Unconscious Motives

Central to Freudian psychoanalytic theory is the notion that human beings have basic biological urges or drives that must be satisfied. What kinds of urges? Undesirable ones! Freud viewed the newborn as a "seething cauldron," an inherently selfish creature "driven" by two kinds of **instincts,** or inborn biological forces that motivate behavior. The *life instincts* aim for survival: They direct life-sustaining activities such as breathing, eating, copulation, and the fulfillment of other bodily needs. The *death instincts* are destructive forces said to be present in all human beings and expressed through such behavior as aggression, sadism, murder, and even masochism (harm

BOX 2.1 How Do You Stand on Major Developmental Issues?

Choose one answer for each question, and write down the corresponding letter or fill it in at the end of the box. Compare your results with those in Box 2.6 at the end of this chapter.

1. Children are:
   a. creatures whose basically negative or selfish impulses must be controlled.
   b. neither inherently good nor inherently bad.
   c. creatures who are born with many positive and few negative tendencies.
2. Biological influences (heredity, maturational forces) and environmental influences (culture, parenting styles, learning experiences) are thought to contribute to development. Overall,
   a. biological factors contribute far more than environmental factors.
   b. biological factors contribute somewhat more than environmental factors.
   c. biological and environmental factors are equally important.
   d. environmental factors contribute somewhat more than biological factors.
   e. environmental factors contribute far more than biological factors.
3. People are basically
   a. active beings who are the prime determiners of their own abilities and traits.
   b. passive beings whose characteristics are molded either by social influences (parents and other significant people, outside events) or by biological changes beyond their control.
4. Development proceeds
   a. through stages, so that the individual changes rather abruptly into a quite different kind of person than he or she was in an earlier stage.
   b. in a variety of ways, some stage-like, some gradual or continuous.
   c. continuously—in small increments without abrupt changes or distinct stages.
5. Traits such as aggressiveness or dependency
   a. emerge in childhood and remain largely consistent over the years.
   b. first appear in childhood but often disappear or give way to quite different traits at some later time.
6. When we compare the development of different individuals, we see
   a. many similarities; children and adults develop along universal paths and experience similar changes at similar ages.
   b. many differences; different people often undergo different sequences of change and have widely different timetables of development.

	Question					
	1	2	3	4	5	6
Your pattern of answers:	___	___	___	___	___	___

Sigmund Freud's psychoanalytic theory was one of the first, and certainly one of the most influential, theories of how the personality develops from childhood to adulthood.

directed against the self). According to Freud, these biological instincts are the source of the psychic (or mental) energy that fuels human behavior and is channeled in new directions over the course of human development.

Freud strongly believed that human beings are often unaware of the instincts and other inner forces that motivate their behavior. A teenage boy, for example, may not realize that his devotion to body building could be a way of channeling his sexual or aggressive urges. Freud's concept of **unconscious motivation** refers to underlying forces and inner conflicts that influence thinking and behavior, even though they are not conscious or cannot be recalled. As Freud developed his psychoanalytic therapy, he came to rely on such therapy methods as hypnosis, free association (a quick spilling out of ideas), and dream analysis because he believed that only these techniques would uncover underlying unconscious motives. Our teenage boy's dreams, for instance, might reveal deep desires for sex or power that he is unaware of or could not express in the light of day. So, we immediately see that Freud's theory is highly biological in nature: Biological instincts—forces that often provide an unconscious motivation for our actions—are said to guide human development.

Three Components of Personality: Id, Ego, and Superego

According to Freud (1933), each individual has a fixed amount of psychic energy that can be used to satisfy basic urges or instincts and to grow psychologically. As the child develops, this psychic energy is divided among three components of the personality: the id, the ego, and the superego.

At birth all psychic energy resides in the **id.** The id's entire mission is to satisfy the instincts. It obeys the "pleasure principle," seeking immediate gratification, even when biological needs cannot be realistically or appropriately met. If you think about it, young infants do seem to be "all id" in many ways. When they are hungry or wet, they simply fuss and cry until their needs are met; they are not known for their patience. The id is the impulsive, irrational, and selfish part of the personality, and it is with us throughout the life span.

The second component of the personality is the **ego,** the rational side of the individual that operates according to the "reality principle" and tries to find realistic ways of gratifying the instincts. According to Freud (1933), the ego begins to emerge during infancy when psychic energy is diverted from the id to energize important cognitive processes such as perception, learning, and problem solving. The hungry toddler may be able to do more than merely cry when she is hungry; she may be able to draw on the resources of the ego to hunt down Dad, lead him to the kitchen, and say "cake." However, toddlers' egos are still relatively immature; they want what they want NOW. As the ego matures further, children become more and more able to postpone their pleasures until a more appropriate time or to devise logical and realistic plans for meeting their needs. In order to find realistic ways to meet the id's basic needs, Freud said, the ego must use some of its energy to block the id's irrational and impulsive thinking. Thus the ego is both servant and master to the id. It masters the id by delaying gratification until needs can be realistically met, but it also serves the id by weighing courses of action and selecting a plan that is most likely to satisfy the id's needs.

The third part of the Freudian personality is the **superego,** the individual's internalized moral standards. The superego develops from the ego and strives for *perfection* rather than for pleasure or realism (Freud, 1933). It begins to develop as 3- to 6-year-old children *internalize* (take on as their own) the moral standards and values of their parents. Typically, it grows stronger as children continue to absorb the values of adults. Once the superego emerges, children have a parental voice in their heads that tells them that it would be wrong to satisfy their ids by grabbing or stealing other children's snacks, and that voice makes them feel guilty or ashamed when they do violate society's rules and standards. The superego insists that we find socially acceptable or ethical outlets for the id's undesirable impulses.

Obviously the three parts of the personality do not see eye to eye. Conflict among the id, ego, and superego is inevitable, Freud claimed. In the mature, healthy personality, a dynamic balance operates: The

The three parts of the personality proposed by Freud are inevitably in conflict.

id communicates its basic needs, the ego restrains the impulsive id long enough to find realistic ways to satisfy these needs, and the superego decides whether the ego's problem-solving strategies are morally acceptable. The ego is clearly "in the middle"; it must somehow strike a balance between the opposing demands of the id and the superego, all the while accommodating to the realities of the external world.

According to Freud (1940/1964), psychological problems often arise when psychic energy is unevenly distributed among the id, the ego, and the superego. Because there is a fixed amount of psychic energy to be spent, too much energy devoted to one part of the personality inevitably means less to be channeled into the other parts. For example, the sociopath who routinely lies and cheats to get his way may have a very strong id and a normal ego but a very weak superego, never having learned to respect the rights of other people. In contrast, the woman who is crippled by anxiety over the thought of having sex with her boyfriend may be controlled by an overly strong superego, perhaps because she was made to feel deeply ashamed about any interest she took in her body as a young girl. Analysis of the dynamics operating among the three parts of the personality provided Freud and his followers with an important means of understanding individual differences in personality and the origins of psychological disorders.

The Stages of Psychosexual Development

Freud viewed the sex instinct as the most important of the life instincts because the psychological disturbances of his patients often revolved around childhood sexual conflicts. Certainly the notion of childhood sexuality was one of the most controversial of Freud's ideas. Yet he used the term *sex* to refer to much more than what you are probably thinking of, regarding many simple bodily actions such as sucking, biting, and urinating as "erotic" activities.

Although the sex instinct is presumably inborn, Freud (1940/1964) felt that its character changes over time as dictated by biological maturation. Freud's view was that the sex instinct's psychic energy, which he called **libido,** shifts from one part of the body to another over the years, seeking to gratify different biological needs. In the process the child moves through five stages of *psychosexual development*: oral, anal, phallic, latency, and genital.

The Oral Stage (Birth to 1 Year)

Young infants suck, bite, or chew just about anything they can get their mouths on, even when they are not particularly hungry or thirsty. So, not surprisingly, Freud concluded that the libido seeks pleasure through the mouth during the **oral stage.** Freud went on to argue that later psychological development would be very much affected by how adequately the infant's oral needs were met and thus how closely attached the infant became to its mother. For example, the infant boy who was weaned too early or was fed only on a rigid schedule would be deprived of "oral gratification" and might later become a man who still craves "mother love" and becomes overdependent on his wife. In this way, Freud argued, *early experiences may have long-term effects on personality development.*

The Anal Stage (1 to 3 Years)

As the sphincter muscles mature in the second year of life, infants acquire the ability to withhold or expel fecal material at will. Voluntary defecation becomes the primary method of gratifying the sex instinct during the **anal stage.** Infants now face their first major conflict between biological urges and social demands, for parents insist that they control their bowels and become toilet trained. According to Freud, the way in which parents handle toilet training can leave lasting imprints on the personality. For example, the child who is harshly punished for mistakes or forced to sit for hours on the potty seat may become an inhibited or stingy adult.

The Phallic Stage (3 to 6 Years)

Starting at about age 3, Freud proposed, psychic energy is redirected from the anus to the genitals, and preschool children find pleasure in stroking and fondling their genitals. And—as if that were not controversial enough—Freud believed that preschool children develop a strong incestuous desire for the parent of the other sex. He called this period the **phallic stage** because he believed that the phallus (penis) assumes a critically important role in the psychosexual development of both boys and girls.

Consider the events of the phallic stage for boys. According to Freud, a 3- to 5-year-old boy, already strongly attached to his mother, develops an intense longing for her and begins to view his father as a rival for Mom's affection. Freud called this state of affairs the **Oedipus complex** after Oedipus, the legendary King of Thebes who unwittingly killed his father and married his mother. The problem is that young boys, unlike Oedipus, are no match for their fathers. In fact, Freud claimed, they come to fear that their fathers might castrate them as punishment for their rivalrous conduct.

When this *castration anxiety* becomes sufficiently intense, the boy will resolve his Oedipus complex. How? First, said Freud, through **repression** of his incestuous and rivalrous desires (that is, through a defensive process of forcing these anxiety-provoking thoughts out of conscious awareness) and, second, through **identification** with his father (that is, by emulating his father and taking on as his own the father's attitudes, attributes, and behaviors; this, too, is defensive, for presumably a father would not retaliate against someone so much like himself). There are two important outcomes of the boy's identification with his father: He will learn his masculine sex role, and he will develop a superego by internalizing his father's moral standards.

What about preschool girls? Freud admitted that he was unsure about them. Once a 4-year-old girl discovers that she lacks a penis, she is believed to blame her mother for this "castrated" condition. She transfers her affection from her mother to her father, envies her father for possessing a penis, and hopes that he will share with her the valued organ that she lacks. (Freud assumed that her real underlying motive is to bear her father's child, especially a male child, to compensate for her lack of a penis.) This is the heart of the girl's **Electra complex.**

But how is the girl's conflict resolved? Boys fear castration, and that fear motivates them to identify with their fathers. But what do girls fear? After all, they supposedly believe that they have already been castrated. Freud (1924/1961) assumed that the Electra complex may simply fade away as the girl faces reality and recognizes the impossibility of possessing her father. The next best thing for her may be to identify with her mother, who *does* possess her father.

Although the inner conflicts of the phallic period may be more emotionally intense for a boy than for a girl, the similarities between the sexes are also clear. Children of each gender value the male phallus: Girls hope to gain one, and boys hope to keep theirs. Moreover, both boys and girls perceive the parent of the same sex as their major rival for the affection of the other parent. And, finally, if development proceeds normally, both boys and girls resolve their conflicts by identifying with the parent of the same sex, thereby taking on a "masculine" or "feminine" role and developing a superego.

The Latency Period (6 to 12 Years)

During the **latency period,** or the elementary school years, the sexual conflicts of the phallic stage have been repressed, and libidinal energy is channeled into socially acceptable activities such as schoolwork and play with friends of the same sex. The ego and the superego continue to grow stronger, Freud claimed, as the child gains new problem-solving abilities and internalizes additional societal values. But this lull period in childhood sexuality will end abruptly with the coming of puberty.

The Genital Stage (12 Years Onward)

With the onset of puberty comes the **genital stage,** which is characterized by maturation of the reproductive system, a flooding of the body with sex hormones, and a reactivation of the genital zone as an area of sensual pleasure. The underlying goal of the sex instinct now becomes biological reproduction through sexual intercourse. But adolescents face conflicts in learning how to manage their new sexual urges in socially appropriate ways and how to form genuinely loving relationships. They may have difficulty accepting their new sexuality, they may reexperience some of the conflicting feelings toward their parents that they felt during their preschool years (as part of the Oedipus and Electra complexes), and they may even distance themselves from their parents to defend against these anxiety-producing feelings. Out of the intense psychic conflicts of this period comes a more fully formed personality.

Freud's theory of psychosexual development stopped with adolescence. Presumably teenagers and young adults invest libido in activities such as forming friendships, preparing for a career, dating, and marrying. They develop a greater capacity to love and eventually satisfy the fully mature sex instinct by having children. Freud imagined that the individual remains in this genital stage throughout adulthood.

Early Experience, Defense Mechanisms, and Adult Personality

Freud's psychoanalytic theory tended to emphasize nature more than nurture. He believed that inborn biological instincts drive behavior and that biological maturation determines the child's progress through the five psychosexual stages. Much as he emphasized the role of biology in development, however, Freud also viewed nurture—especially early experiences within the family—as an important cause of individual differences in adult personality.

At each psychosexual stage the id's impulses and social demands inevitably come into conflict. And parents' child-rearing methods can heighten this conflict and the child's anxiety. To defend itself against such anxiety, the ego, without being aware of it, adopts **defense mechanisms** (Freud, 1940/1964). We all use these mechanisms, but some people become overdependent on them because of unfavorable experiences early in life. We mentioned repression and identification a moment ago, but now we'll consider two other defense mechanisms, fixation and regression, that have major developmental implications and illustrate how early experience can leave lasting imprints on the personality.

Fixation is a kind of arrested development in which part of the libido remains tied to an early stage. Why might a child become fixated at the oral stage? Perhaps he or she was rarely allowed to linger at the breast, was screamed at for mouthing and chewing paychecks and other fascinating objects around the house, or was otherwise deprived of oral gratification. This infant might become fixated at the oral stage to satisfy unmet oral needs and to avoid the potentially even greater conflicts of the anal stage. He or she might display this oral fixation by becoming a chronic thumbsucker and, later in life, by chain-smoking, talking incessantly (as college professors are prone to do), or being overdependent on other people.

Another important defense mechanism, **regression,** involves retreating to an earlier, less traumatic stage of development. The child who is temporarily made insecure by the arrival of a new baby in the house may revert to infantile behavior—throwing temper tantrums, gooing like a baby, and demanding juice from a baby bottle. Similarly, the man who has had a terrible day at work may want his wife to act like his mother and "baby" him.

In short, Freud insisted that the past lives on. Early childhood experiences may haunt us in later life and influence our adult personalities, interests, and behaviors. Parents significantly impact a child's success in passing through the biologically programmed psychosexual stages. They can err by overindulging the child's urges, but more commonly they create lasting and severe inner conflicts and anxieties by denying an infant oral gratification, using harsh toilet-training practices with a toddler, or punishing the preschooler who is fascinated by naked bodies. Heavy reliance on fixation, regression, and other defense mechanisms may then become necessary just to keep the ego intact and functioning.

Now, what might Freud have said about the causes of teenage pregnancy and about the case of Sheila and James described at the start of the chapter? In Box 2.2 we speak for Freud. In this box and in Boxes 2.3 through 2.5, describing how other theorists would view teenage pregnancy, we have taken the liberty of commenting for the theorists, whether they are dead or alive. You might want to anticipate what each theorist will say before you read each such box to see if you can successfully apply the theories to a specific problem. It is our hope that, as you grasp the major theories, you will be in a position to draw on their concepts and propositions to make sense of your own and other people's development.

Strengths and Weaknesses of Freud's Psychoanalytic Theory

Are we really driven by sexual and aggressive instincts? Could we really have experienced an Oedipus or Electra complex and simply repressed these traumatic events? Or did Freud get carried away with sex? Could the sexual conflicts he thought so important merely have been reflections of the sexually repressive Victorian culture in which he and his patients lived? And could the lessons Freud learned from psychoanalyzing disturbed adults have little bearing on the development of normal children?

Many developmentalists fault Freud for proposing a theory that is difficult to test and therefore not very falsifiable. Testing hypotheses that require studying unconscious motivations and the workings of the unseen id, ego, and superego has been challenging indeed. In addition, even when the theory has been tested, many of its specific ideas have not been supported (Fisher & Greenberg, 1977). For example, there is not much evidence that oral and anal experiences in childhood predict one's later personality. It also turns out that many preschool children are quite ignorant of male and female anatomy; it is therefore hard to imagine that they could experience castration anxiety or penis envy in the phallic stage (Bem, 1989; Katcher, 1955). In fact, the whole idea that children experience Oedipus and Electra complexes has come under fresh attack. It seems that Freud initially uncovered evidence that many of his patients had been sexually or physically abused in childhood; however, unable to believe that such abuse was as widespread as it appeared to be, he claimed instead that children wished for and fantasized about, but did not actually experience, seduction by their parents (Emde, 1992). Now, of course, we know that child sexual abuse not only is widespread but can contribute to lasting psychological difficulties (see Chapter 11).

Despite the fact that some of Freud's specific ideas have been difficult to test or have not been supported by research, many of his broad insights have stood up well and have profoundly influenced later theories of human development (Emde, 1992). Perhaps Freud's greatest contribution was his concept of unconscious motivation—his notion that much of our behavior is caused by forces and conflicts of which we are not consciously aware. Freud also deserves considerable credit for focusing attention on the potential importance of early experience in the family for later development. Debates continue about exactly how

BOX 2.2 Psychoanalytic Theory Applied: Freud on Teenage Pregnancy

I welcome this opportunity to return to life to comment on the problem of teenage pregnancy. As you know, I was always fascinated by sex. This matter of teenage pregnancy is right up my alley! We must realize that teenagers experience intense conflicts during the genital stage of psychosexual development. Their new sexual urges are anxiety provoking and must somehow be managed. Moreover, the sexual conflicts of earlier psychosexual stages often reemerge during adolescence. Of course, I would need to find out more about the early childhood experiences and psychic conflicts of Sheila and James to pinpoint the specific causes of their behavior, but I can offer a few suggestions.

Since I've been back, I have uncovered some revealing psychoanalytic studies of pregnant teenagers. In one study of 30 teenage girls,[1] many of them were found to be very dependent individuals who had weak egos and superegos. Perhaps Sheila and James did not have strong enough egos and superegos to keep their selfish ids in check; perhaps they sought immediate gratification of their sexual urges with no thought for future consequences or morality.

But it is also quite possible that these teenagers were motivated by inner conflicts that had their roots in infancy or the preschool years. For instance, many pregnant girls come from homes without fathers.[1] Perhaps Sheila never fully resolved the Electra complex of the phallic stage and was unconsciously seeking to possess her father by possessing James and having a baby. James, of course, might have been seeking to gratify his unconscious desire for his mother through Sheila. Teenagers often distance themselves from their parents as a defense against reawakened Oedipal feelings of love for the other-sex parent.

All these possibilities suggest that Sheila and James may have had an especially difficult time dealing with their newfound sexuality. I'll bet my reputation that one or both of them has personality problems rooted in early childhood experiences. Without being consciously aware of what is motivating them, they may well be seeking to gratify needs that were never adequately met in their early years.

[1]For further information about the works "Dr. Freud" refers to, see Babikian and Goldman (1971), Hatcher (1973), and Schaffer and Pine (1972).

critical early experience is, but few developmentalists today doubt that early experiences *can* have lasting impacts. We might also thank Freud for exploring the emotional side of human development: the loves, fears, anxieties, and other powerful emotions that play such an important role in our lives. Emotional development has often been slighted by developmentalists who focus intently on observable behavior or on rational thought processes. Finally, Freud reminds us that people are individuals and find different meanings in their life experiences (Emde, 1992).

The Neo-Freudians

Still another sign of Freud's immense influence is the fact that he inspired so many disciples and descendants to contribute in their own right to our understanding of human development (see Tyson & Tyson, 1990). Among these well-known *neo-Freudians* were Alfred Adler, who suggested that siblings (and rivalries between siblings) are significant in development; Karen Horney, who challenged Freud's ideas about sex differences; Harry Stack Sullivan, who wrote extensively about how close friendships in childhood set the stage for intimate relationships later in life (see Chapter 13); and Freud's daughter Anna, who developed methods of psychoanalysis appropriate for children. These and other neo-Freudians typically placed more emphasis than Freud did on *social* influences on personality development—and less emphasis on the role of sexual instincts.

Another theme developed by some neo-Freudian theorists was the idea that development continues beyond adolescence. Carl Jung (1933), for example, claimed that adults experience a midlife transition, after which, if all goes well, they stop clinging to youth, set new goals for themselves, and become freer to express both the "masculine" and "feminine" sides of their personalities. Jung was one of the first theorists, then, to write about something akin to a "midlife crisis" (see Chapter 15) and to suggest that gender roles change during the adult years (see Chapter 11).

Finally, influential theorist Erik Erikson (1963, 1968, 1982), like Jung, saw possibilities for continued growth beyond adolescence. Like other neo-Freudians, he also believed that Freud put too much emphasis on biological and sexual forces and not enough on social and cultural influences on development. Erikson described eight stages of psycho*social* (as contrasted with psycho*sexual*) development extending from infancy to old age. Although his theory is considered in some detail in Chapter 10, its stages are outlined briefly in Table 2.1, alongside the corresponding Freudian stages.

Both biological maturation and the demands of the social environment influence the individual's progress through Erikson's stage sequence. For development to proceed normally, Erikson believed, a healthy balance must be struck between the terms of the critical conflict characterizing each developmental period. Thus, infants whose parents are loving and responsive to their needs would resolve the crisis of *trust versus mistrust* by gaining a solid sense of trust balanced by a dose of skepticism. They would become neither gullible "suckers" nor suspicious standoffs.

TABLE 2.1 The stage theories of Freud and Erikson compared.

Freud (Psychosexual Theory)		*Erikson (Psychosocial Theory)*	
Stage/age range	*Description*	*Stage/age range*	*Description*
Oral stage (birth to 1 year)	Libido is focused on the mouth as a source of pleasure. Obtaining oral gratification from a mother figure is critical to later development.	*Trust versus mistrust* (birth to 1 year)	Infants must learn to trust their caregivers to meet their needs. Responsive parenting is critical.
Anal stage (1 to 3 years)	Libido is focused on the anus, and toilet training creates conflicts between the child's biological urges and society's demands.	*Autonomy versus shame and doubt* (1 to 3 years)	Children must learn to be autonomous—to assert their wills and do things for themselves—or they will doubt their abilities.
Phallic stage (3 to 6 years)	Libido centers on the genitals. Resolution of the Oedipus or Electra complex results in identification with the same-sex parent and development of the superego.	*Initiative versus guilt* (3 to 6 years)	Preschoolers develop initiative by devising and carrying out bold plans, but they must learn not to impinge on the rights of others.
Latency period (6 to 12 years)	Libido is quiet; psychic energy is invested in schoolwork and play with same-sex friends.	*Industry versus inferiority* (6 to 12 years)	Children must master important social and academic skills and keep up with their peers or they will feel inferior.
Genital stage (12 years and older)	Puberty reawakens the sexual instincts as youths seek to establish mature sexual relationships and pursue the biological goal of reproduction.	*Identity versus role confusion* (12 to 20 years)	Adolescents ask who they are and must establish social and vocational identities or else remain confused about the roles they should play as adults.
		Intimacy versus isolation (20 to 40 years)	Young adults seek to form a shared identity with another person but may fear intimacy and experience loneliness and isolation.
		Generativity versus stagnation (40 to 65 years)	Middle-aged adults must feel that they are producing something that will outlive them, either as parents or as workers, or they will become stagnant and self-centered.
		Integrity versus despair (65 and older)	Older adults must come to view their lives as meaningful in order to face death without worries and regrets.

Important neo-Freudians such as Erikson continue to shape our understanding of human development. However, many developmentalists have rejected the whole psychoanalytic perspective in favor of theories that are more precise and testable.

LEARNING THEORIES

Give me a dozen healthy infants, well formed, and my own specified world to bring them up in and I'll guarantee to take any one at random and train him to become any type of specialist I might select—doctor, lawyer, artist, merchant, chief, and yes, even beggar-man and thief, regardless of his talents, penchants, tendencies, abilities, vocations, and race of his ancestors [Watson, 1925, p. 82].

There is a bold statement! It reflects a belief that nurture is everything and nature, or hereditary endowment, counts for nothing. It was made by John B. Watson, a strong believer in the importance of learning in human development and the father of the school of thought in psychology called behaviorism (see Horowitz, 1992).

A basic premise of Watson's (1913) **behaviorism** is that conclusions about human development and functioning should be based on observations of overt behavior rather than on speculations about unconscious motives or cognitive processes that remain unobservable. Moreover, said Watson, *learned* associations between external stimuli and observable responses are the building blocks of human development. Like John Locke, Watson believed that the infant is a *tabula rasa* to be written on by experience. Children have no inborn tendencies; how they turn out will depend entirely on the environment in which they grow up and the ways in which their parents and other significant people in their lives treat them. According to a behavioral perspective, then, it is a mistake to assume that children advance through a series of distinct stages partly programmed by biological maturation, as Freud, Piaget, and others have argued. Instead, development is viewed as a continuous process of behavior change that is particularistic and can differ enormously from person to person. Watson's basic view of development as learning was advanced by the influential work of B. F. Skinner.

John B. Watson was the father of behaviorism.

Skinner's Operant-Conditioning Theory

B. F. Skinner (1905–1990), whose name is as well known as that of any psychologist, had a long, distinguished career at Harvard University. Through his research with animals, Skinner (1953) gained understanding of one very important form of learning. He would put a rat in a special cage called a "Skinner box." On one side of the box was a bar; pressing the bar caused a food pellet to be delivered. Upon entering the Skinner box, a rat does what rats normally do in a new environment: some moving around, sniffing, scratching, and so forth. The rat happens to press the lever and then happens to find a food pellet in the food receptacle. The rat goes on sniffing and exploring, hits the bar again in its meanderings, and again receives food. Through a series of such experiences, an association forms between the behavior of pressing the bar and its consequence, the delivery of a food pellet. Before long the rat is no longer behaving as it was initially; it has formed a new habit and is pressing the bar as fast as its paws will let it!

In such **operant** (or instrumental) **conditioning,** a learner's existing behaviors become either more or less probable depending on the consequences they produce. **Reinforcers** (such as the food pellets delivered to the rat) are consequences that increase the probability that a response (such as bar pressing) will occur in the future. A boy may form a long-term habit of sharing toys with playmates if his parents reinforce his sharing with praise, or a computer saleswoman may work harder at making sales if she receives a commission for each sale. **Punishers,** on the other hand, are consequences that suppress a response and decrease the likelihood that it will occur in the future. If the rat that had been reinforced with a food pellet for pressing the bar were suddenly given a painful shock each time it pressed the bar, the "bar pressing" habit would begin to disappear. Similarly, a teenage girl whose car keys are confiscated every time she stays out beyond her curfew and a man who is criticized for interrupting people during meetings are likely to cut down on the responses that resulted in punishment. Very simply, we learn to keep doing the things that have positive consequences and to stop doing the things that have negative consequences.

Like Watson, then, Skinner believed that human development results from the individual's learning experiences. One boy's aggressive behavior may be reinforced over time because he gets his way with other children and his parents encourage his "macho" behavior. Another boy may quickly learn that aggression is prohibited and punished. The two may develop in entirely different directions based on their different histories of reinforcement and punishment.

B. F. Skinner's operant-learning theory emphasized the role of the environment in controlling behavior.

In this view, there is no cause for speaking of an "aggressive stage" in child development or an "aggressive drive" within human beings. Skinner did acknowledge that evolution has provided us with a brain that allows us to learn from experience and that even influences what we can learn most easily and what we find most reinforcing. However, he believed that the essence of human development is the continual acquisition of new habits of behavior and that these learned behaviors are controlled by *external* stimuli (reinforcers and punishers).

From a learning theory perspective, even development that seems stagelike need not be caused by biological maturation. Instead, age-related changes in the environment could produce age-related changes in behavior (Bijou & Baer, 1961). Six-year-olds starting school might change in response to a new system of reinforcements and punishments imposed by their teachers, or older adults might change when they are forced to retire and lose access to the reinforcers that employment brought them.

Most developmentalists appreciate that Skinner's operant-conditioning principles can explain many aspects of human development (Gewirtz & Pelaez-Nogueras, 1992; Schlinger, 1992). They also appreciate that human development can take varied forms and that habits can emerge and disappear over a lifetime depending on whether they have positive or negative consequences. Yet some theorists believe that Skinner placed too much emphasis on a single type of learning and too little emphasis on the role of cognitive processes such as attention, memory, and reflection in learning. For this reason, today's developmental scholars are more attracted to Albert Bandura's cognitive social learning theory.

Bandura's Cognitive Social Learning Theory

Albert Bandura's (1977, 1986, 1989) **social learning theory** (or "social cognitive theory," as he has come to call it) claims that humans are cognitive beings whose active processing of information from the environment plays a major role in learning and human development. To Skinner the mind was a "black box" between external stimuli and responses. Because Skinner believed that the mind could not be studied objectively and felt that the true causes of behavior lay in the environment rather than within the person, he paid little attention to cognitive processes. The same learning principles that shape the behavior of rats were also believed to shape the behavior of human beings.

But Bandura would argue that human learning *is* different from rat learning because humans have far more sophisticated cognitive capabilities. Bandura agrees with Skinner that operant conditioning is an important type of learning, but he notes that humans *think* about the connections between their behavior and its consequences, anticipate what consequences are likely to follow from their future behavior, and often are more affected by what they *believe* will happen than by the consequences they actually encounter. For example, a woman may continue to pursue a medical degree despite many punishments and few immediate rewards because she *anticipates* a greater reward when she completes her studies. We are not just passively shaped by the external consequences of our behavior; we actively think about past and present experiences and anticipate the future. We also reinforce or punish ourselves with mental "pats on the back" and self-criticism.

Nowhere is Bandura's cognitive emphasis clearer than in his highlighting of **observational learning** as the most important mechanism through which human behavior changes. Observational learning is simply learning that results from observing the behavior of other people (called *models*). A 5-year-old boy may learn how to make sandwiches, build model cars, or swear a blue streak by watching every move his older brother makes. A teenager may pick up the latest dress styles, dances, and slang by watching and listening to other teenagers. A middle-aged executive may learn how to use a computer program by observing a colleague.

Albert Bandura highlighted the role of cognition in human learning. He is on the faculty at Stanford University.

Such observational learning could not occur unless cognitive processes were at work. We must, for example, pay attention to the model, actively digest what we observe, and store this information in memory if we are to imitate at a later date what we have observed. Over the years we are exposed to hundreds of social models and have the opportunity to learn thousands of behavior patterns (some good, some bad) simply by observing others perform them. We need not be reinforced in order to learn this way. We do, however, take note of whether the model's behavior has positive or negative consequences and use that information to decide whether to imitate what we have observed.

Watson and Skinner may have believed that humans are passively shaped by the environment to become whatever those around them groom them to be, but Bandura does not. Because he views humans as active, cognitive beings, he holds that human development occurs through a continuous reciprocal interaction among the person, the person's behavior, and the environment—a perspective he called **reciprocal determinism.** Our personal characteristics and behaviors affect the people in our social environment, just as these individuals influence our personal characteristics and future behaviors.

What does Bandura think about the idea of universal stages of human development? He is skeptical, believing that development can proceed along many different paths depending on the kinds of social learning experiences the individual receives and helps to create. As in other learning theories, there are no "stages" of development; changes occur gradually through a lifetime of learning. Bandura does acknowledge that children's cognitive learning capacities mature over childhood. As children get older, for example, they can remember more about what they have seen and can imitate a greater variety of novel behaviors. Yet Bandura also believes that much development, especially the acquisition of complex knowledge, depends on experiences that are not universal—for example, on encountering specific material in school.

Obviously there is a fundamental disagreement between stage theorists like Freud and learning theorists like Bandura. Learning theorists do not give us a general description of the normal course of human development, because they insist that there is no such description to give. Instead, they offer a rich account of the *mechanisms* through which behavior can change over time. They ask us to apply basic principles of learning to understand how specific individuals change with age. So, can you apply learning principles to the matter of teenage pregnancy? Skinner's and Bandura's points of view appear in Box 2.3.

Strengths and Weaknesses of Learning Theory

Behavioral learning theories and Bandura's cognitive social learning theory have contributed immensely to our understanding of development (see Gewirtz & Pelaez-Nogueras, 1992; Grusec, 1992; Horowitz,

One is never too old to learn by observing others.

BOX 2.3 Learning Theory Applied: Skinner and Bandura on Teenage Pregnancy

I ("B. F. Skinner") will get right to the point: Teenage pregnancy occurs because teenagers have learned to engage in sexual behavior! By the same token, they also have not learned to practice contraception. My point has been made well by one team of researchers: "It is quite likely that if teenagers had to take a pill to become pregnant, early childbearing would quickly vanish as a social problem."[1] Let me expand. Sexual stimulation, like food, is naturally reinforcing; we tend to keep doing things that result in sexual pleasure. But other stimuli—for example, attention and positive comments from other people—become reinforcers through learning processes. Suppose that, during their early dating history, James was especially attentive and complimentary to Sheila each time she returned his kisses or responded positively to his attempts to fondle her but became quite withdrawn and took her home early when she said "no." Reinforced for engaging in sexual activities and punished for refusing, Sheila's behavior would gradually be "shaped" in the direction of sexual intercourse. (If that sounds sexist, let me note that it could just as easily work the other way, with attentive behavior on Sheila's part reinforcing James's sexual behavior.) Meanwhile, the use of contraception is an unlikely behavior because it detracts from the spontaneity of sex (it's a "punisher" in that respect) and has no immediate reinforcement value to speak of. Surely we need not assume, as Dr. Freud did, that young people are riddled by inner conflicts. It's much simpler to assume that the consequences of their past sexual behavior influenced their present sexual behavior.

* * *

I ("Albert Bandura") appreciate Professor Skinner's account of teenage pregnancy, but I believe that my cognitive social learning theory yields additional insights. Sheila and James have been learning a great deal about sexual behavior through observation. Today's adolescents live in a social world filled with messages about sex from their peers, the media, and, to a lesser extent, their parents. They actively process this information for future use. They learn that their friends are "doing it" and are enjoying themselves. They view sex on TV all the time—often exploitive sex, with never a mention of birth control and rarely a mention of such consequences as HIV infection or the stresses of teenage parenthood.

In a recent study, adolescents were asked which people they regarded as models of "responsible sexual behavior" or of "irresponsible sexual behavior."[2] These teenagers had a hard time even thinking of positive sexual role models. Almost half of them named their parents as adults whom they *generally* respected as role models, but only about a quarter of them cited their parents as positive sexual role models. Media personalities and friends readily came to mind as models of *irresponsible* sexual behavior. These findings suggest that adolescents today have more opportunities to learn sexually irresponsible behavior than to learn sexually responsible behavior through observation.

Finally, let me emphasize, though Dr. Skinner did not, the importance of cognition in all of this. As I have argued for years, people's *expectations* about the consequences of their actions are often more important than the actual reinforcers and punishers operating in a situation. If James, for example, *believes* that using a condom will decrease his sexual enjoyment, or if Sheila *believes* that James will resent it if she asks him to use a condom, those beliefs will surely decrease the chances that they will use protection.

"B. F. Skinner" is referring to Furstenberg et al. (1981),[1] and "Albert Bandura" is citing Fabes and Strouse (1984).[2] See also Balassone (1991) for a social learning theory model of adolescent contraceptive use.

1992). Learning theories are very precise and testable, and carefully controlled experiments have established that the learning processes these theories propose do in fact operate. Learning theorists have been able to demonstrate how we might learn everything from altruism to alcoholism. We will see the fruits of research on human learning throughout this text (especially in Chapter 8).

Moreover, the learning principles involved in operant conditioning, observational learning, and other forms of learning operate *across the entire life span*; learning theorists can go about trying to understand middle-aged or older adults in the same way that they attempt to understand infants. Finally, learning theories have very practical applications; they have been the basis for many highly effective techniques for optimizing development and treating developmental problems. Parents and teachers can certainly be more effective when they systematically reinforce the behavior they hope to instill in children and when they serve as role models of desirable behavior. And many psychotherapists today apply behavioral and cognitive learning techniques to treat psychological problems.

At the same time, learning theories leave something to be desired as models of human development. Consider the following demonstration. Paul Weisberg (1963) reinforced 3-month-old infants with smiles and gentle rubs on the chin whenever they happened to babble. He found that these infants babbled more often than did infants who received the same social stimulation randomly rather than only after each babbling sound they made. But does this demonstration of the power of social reinforcement mean that infants normally begin to babble *because* babbling is reinforced by their caregivers? Not necessarily. All normal infants, even deaf ones, babble at about 4 months of age. Moreover, no matter what experiences we provide to a newborn, he or she will not be maturationally ready to begin babbling. We must suspect, then, that the maturation of the neural and muscular control required for babbling has more than a little to do with the onset of babbling during infancy.

This example really highlights two criticisms of learning theories as theories of human development. First, learning theorists rarely demonstrate that learning is actually responsible for commonly observed developmental changes; they show only that learning *might have* resulted in developmental change. Some critics wish that learning theorists would provide a fuller account of normal changes across the life span. Second, learning theorists may have oversimplified their account of development by downplaying biological influences. Children simply cannot achieve certain developmental milestones or benefit from certain learning experiences until they are maturationally ready. And, although individuals differ from one another partly because they have different experiences in life, they also differ because they have different genetic endowments. After a number of years in which learning theories dominated the study of development, many scientists began to look for a theory that was more clearly "developmental," that showed how human beings change systematically as they get older—and they found what they wanted in the remarkable work of Jean Piaget.

COGNITIVE-DEVELOPMENTAL THEORY

No theorist has contributed more to our understanding of children's minds than Jean Piaget (1896–1980), a Swiss scholar who began to study children's intellectual development during the 1920s. This remarkable man developed quickly himself, publishing his first scientific article, about a rare albino sparrow, at the tender age of 10. His interest in zoology and the adaptation of animals to their environments was accompanied by an interest in philosophy. He finally put the two areas together by devoting his career to the study of how humans acquire knowledge and use it to adapt to their environments.

Piaget's lifelong interest in cognitive development (the development of intellectual processes) emerged when he accepted a position in Paris at the Alfred Binet laboratories to work on the first standardized intelligence test. In this testing approach to the study of mental ability, an estimate of a person's intelligence is based on the number and types of questions that he or she answers correctly. Piaget soon found that he was more interested in children's *incorrect* answers than in their correct ones. He first noticed that children of about the same age were producing the same kinds of wrong answers. Then, by questioning children to find out how they were thinking about the problems presented to them, he began to realize that young children do not simply know less than older children do; their thought *processes* are completely different. Eventually Piaget developed a full-blown theory to account for changes in thinking from infancy to adolescence.

Piaget's Basic Perspective on Intellectual Development

Influenced by his background in biology, Piaget (1950) viewed intelligence as a process that helps an organism adapt to its environment. The infant who can grasp a cookie and bring it to the mouth is behaving adaptively, as is the adolescent who can solve algebra problems or fix a broken fan belt. As children mature, they acquire ever more complex "cognitive structures," or organized patterns of thought or action, that aid them in adapting to their environments.

How do children develop more complex cognitive structures and increase their understanding of the world? Piaget insisted that children are not born with innate ideas about reality, as some philosophers have claimed. Nor are they simply filled with information by adults, as others have claimed. Instead, Piaget took a position called **constructivism,** claiming that children actively construct new understandings of the world based on their experiences. How? By being the curious and active explorers that they are: by watching what is going on around them, by seeing what happens when they experiment on the objects they encounter, and by recognizing when their current understandings are faulty. What children seek out and what they can absorb from their experiences change as their brains develop, so biological maturation plays a role in development too. Ultimately, it is the *interaction* of a biologically maturing child and his or her environment that is responsible for cognitive development.

Consider 4-year-old Cheri. Like a fair number of children her age, she believes that the sun is alive. At least in our culture, this idea was probably not learned from adults; it was apparently constructed by the child based on her experience. After all, many moving things *are* alive, so why not the sun? As long as Cheri clings to this understanding, she will tend to regard any new object that moves as alive; that is, new experiences will be interpreted in terms of current cognitive structures, a process Piaget called **assimilation.** But suppose Cheri continues to encounter animate and inanimate objects in daily life and begins to notice that a wind-up toy and a paper airplane move but are not alive and that trees do not move from one part of the yard to another but are alive. Now a contradiction or "disequilibrium" exists between the child's understanding and the facts to be understood. It becomes clear to her that the objects-that-move-are-alive concept needs to be revised. A new and more adequate understanding of the distinction between living and

Swiss psychologist Jean Piaget revolutionized the field of human development with his theory of cognitive growth.

nonliving things will be constructed through the process of **accommodation,** an alteration of existing cognitive structures so that they better fit new experiences.

So it goes throughout life. Piaget believed that we bring the complementary processes of assimilation and accommodation to bear on our experiences. We naturally attempt to understand our experiences and solve problems using our current cognitive structures (through assimilation), but we sometimes find that our current understandings are flawed. This gives us reason to *revise* our understandings (through accommodation) so that our cognitive structures "fit" reality better (Piaget, 1952). Gradually, children whose brains are maturing and who are exploring the world, developing new understandings, and reorganizing their knowledge of reality progress far enough to be thinking about old issues in entirely new ways; that is, they pass from one stage of cognitive development to a new, qualitatively different, stage.

Four Stages of Cognitive Development

Piaget proposed four major periods of cognitive development: the *sensorimotor stage* (birth to age 2), the *preoperational stage* (ages 2 to 7), the *concrete operations stage* (ages 7 to 11), and the *formal operations stage* (ages 11 to 12 or later). These stages form what Piaget called an *invariant sequence*; that is, all children progress through them in exactly the order in which they are listed. There is no skipping of stages, because each successive stage builds on the previous one and represents a more complex way of thinking. There is no regression to earlier stages, either.

The key features of each stage are summarized in Table 2.2. The big message is that humans of different ages think in very different ways. We will be exploring Piaget's theory in depth in Chapter 7, but for now let's look at one example of how children who are at different stages of cognitive development might approach the same problem. The problem is to figure out, given a number of objects and a bucket of water, why some objects float and others do not. This is one scientific problem used by Barbel Inhelder and Jean Piaget (1958) to explore the child's developing understanding of the physical world. They asked children to classify objects such as a wooden plank, a pebble, and a candle according to whether they would float or not and to explain their classifications. Then they allowed children to experiment with the objects and try to formulate a general law to explain why some objects float and others do not.

What might the infant in the **sensorimotor stage** do in this problem-solving situation? Inhelder and Piaget were not foolish enough to try to find out. The problem is obviously far beyond the grasp of infants, who can deal with the world directly through their perceptions and actions but are unable to use symbols (gestures, images, or words representing real objects and events) to help them *mentally* devise solutions to problems. Infants *will* use their eyes, ears, and hands to actively explore the fascinating materials placed before them. A 6-month-old infant might merely bang a block of wood repeatedly against the bucket and listen to the clanking sound that results. A 1-year-old might experiment with the materials, perhaps throwing and dropping objects into the water, carefully watching the splashes that are produced, and shrieking with delight. From the start, human beings are curious about the world; moreover, Piaget maintained, they learn about the world and acquire tools for solving problems through their sensory experiences and their actions (hence the label *sensorimotor* stage).

The preschooler who has entered the **preoperational stage** of cognitive development now has command of symbolic thought. The 4- or 5-year-old can use words to talk about the task and can imagine doing something before actually doing it. Preoperational children will take great interest in placing objects in the water to see what will happen. However, lacking the tools of logical thought, they must rely on their perceptions and as a result are easily fooled by appearances. Preoperational children's "experiments" are likely to be unsystematic, and they are unlikely to form any general rule about floating objects. Being easily fooled by appearances, they tend to think that a large object will sink, even if it is light. And being egocentric thinkers who have some difficulty adopting perspectives other than their own, they may cling to incorrect ideas because they *want* them to be true:

> Mic (5 years) predicts that a plank will sink. The experiment which follows does not induce him to change his mind: [He leans on the plank with all his strength to keep it under the water.] *"You want to stay down, silly!"*—"Will it always

TABLE 2.2 Jean Piaget's four stages of cognitive development.

Stage	*Age Range*	*Features*
Sensorimotor	Birth to 2	Infants use their senses and motor actions to explore and understand the world. At the start they have only innate reflexes, but they develop ever more "intelligent" actions and, by the end, are capable of symbolic thought using images or words and can therefore plan solutions to problems mentally.
Preoperational	2 to 7	Preschoolers use their capacity for symbolic thought in developing language, engaging in pretend play, and solving problems. But their thinking is not yet logical; they are egocentric (unable to take others' perspectives) and easily fooled by perceptions.
Concrete Operations	7 to 11 or later	School-aged children acquire logical operations that allow them to mentally classify and otherwise act on concrete objects in their heads. They can solve practical, real-world problems through a trial-and-error approach.
Formal Operations	11 or later	Adolescents can think about abstract concepts and purely hypothetical possibilities and can trace the long-range consequences of possible actions. With age and experience they can form hypotheses and systematically test them through the scientific method.

stay on the water?"—"*Don't know.*"—"Can it stay at the bottom another time?"—"*Yes*" [Inhelder & Piaget, 1958, p. 22].

School-aged children who have advanced to the **concrete operations stage** will seem much more logical in problem-solving situations. These children can perform a number of important actions, or *operations,* in their heads. For example, they can mentally form categorization schemes, which help them realize that either small or large objects can be heavy or light. They now begin to try to resolve contradictions such as the fact that a small object (a key) may sink while a large one (a plank) may float. They can also draw sound general conclusions based on what they observe. But they have difficulty formulating an abstract, general rule to explain why some large objects float and some small objects sink; they must depend instead on a trial-and-error approach to problem solving using the concrete materials before them.

Adolescents who have reached the **formal operations stage** are able to formulate hypotheses or predictions in their heads, plan in advance how to systematically test their ideas, and imagine the consequences of their tests. Consider one 11-year-old:

> Ala (11 years, 9 months): "Why do you say that this key will sink?"—"*Because it is heavier than the water.*"—"This little key is heavier than that water?" [The bucket is pointed out.]—"*I mean the same capacity of water would be less heavy than the key.*"—"What do you mean?"—"*You would put them [metal or water] in containers which contain the same amount and weigh them*" [Inhelder & Piaget, 1958, p. 38].

This ability to imagine *possible* solutions to a problem and to test them out through systematic experiments is a key feature of formal-operational thought. It often takes some years beyond age 11 or 12 before adolescents can adopt a thoroughly systematic and scientific method of solving problems and can think through the implications of hypothetical ideas. However, once this kind of systematic hypothesis-testing strategy has developed, a teenager might

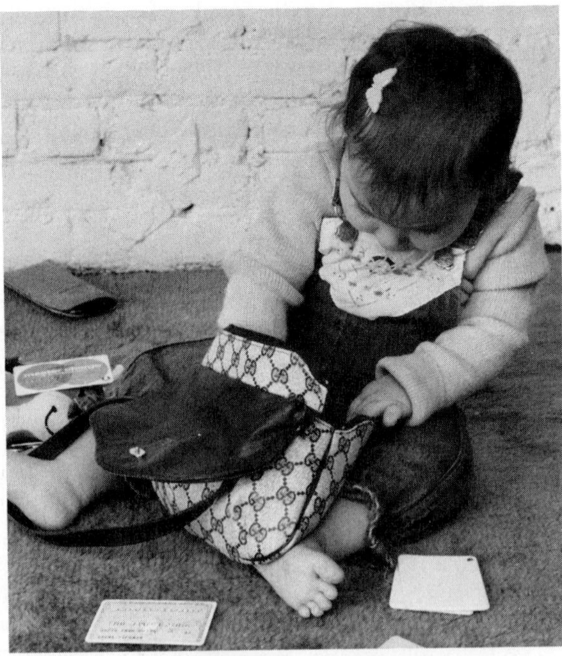

Piaget believed that children are naturally curious explorers who try to make sense of their surroundings.

be able to formulate the general law of floating objects: An object will float if its *density* is less than that of water. This same adolescent might also be able to devise grand theories about what's wrong with the older generation or the school system or the federal government.

Obviously children's cognitive capacities change dramatically between infancy and adolescence as they progress through Piaget's four stages of cognitive development. Young children simply do not think as we do. But what might "Piaget" have to say about the issue of teenage pregnancy? See Box 2.4 for an answer.

Strengths and Weaknesses of Cognitive-Developmental Theory

Like Freud, Piaget was a true pioneer whose work has left a deep and lasting imprint on thinking about human development (see Beilin, 1992). Indeed, his cognitive-developmental perspective dominated the study of child development for two or three decades until the *information-processing approach* to studying cognitive development took command in the 1980s (see Chapter 8). You will see his influence throughout this text, for the same mind that "constructs" understanding of the physical world also comes, with age, to understand sex differences, moral values, emotions, death, and a range of other important aspects of the human experience. To cite just one example, Lawrence Kohlberg's well-known theory of moral development is based on a Piagetian cognitive-developmental perspective and claims that all humans progress through an invariant sequence of stages of moral reasoning (see Chapter 12).

The majority of developmentalists today accept Piaget's basic beliefs that thinking changes in qualitative ways during childhood, that children are active in their own development, and that development occurs through the interaction of person and environment. Piaget's description of intellectual development has been put to the test and has been largely supported (with some important qualifications that we discuss in detail in Chapter 7). And, finally, Piaget's ideas have influenced education and child rearing by encouraging teachers and parents to aim their educational efforts at the child's level of understanding and to stimulate children to discover concepts through their firsthand experiences.

In spite of these many contributions, Piaget has come in for his share of criticism. Some theorists would fault Piaget for saying too little about the influences of motivation and emotion on thought processes and for underestimating the significance of social interactions with adults as a source of cognitive growth. In addition, there is some question about whether Piaget's stages really "hang together" as the coherent modes of thinking that he believed they were. Children do not always act as if they are at only one particular stage, and they often acquire different cognitive skills at different rates. Other critics feel that Piaget may have been wrong to choose formal operations as the most "mature" mode of thinking—that

BOX 2.4 **Cognitive-Developmental Theory Applied: Piaget on Teenage Pregnancy**

You may be wondering what in the world I might have to say about teenage sexual behavior. After all, my main interest has been the development of the mind. Yet, don't you see, teenagers must *decide* whether or not to have sex and whether or not to use birth control. These decisions demand cognitive abilities.

Now, you might think that an adolescent who has reached my stage of formal operations would be ready to consider all the possible consequences of his or her actions and make sound decisions. This is true. But different children achieve formal-operational thinking at different rates. I noticed that Sheila and James were not doing particularly well in school. Perhaps they are slow developers still functioning in the stage of concrete operations and do not yet have the cognitive skills required to consider all the implications of a decision to have sex without protection.

I also find that many adolescents who show the beginning signs of formal-operational thought have not yet developed the full capacity to plan solutions to problems in advance or to consider all possible alternatives. This sometimes takes a few years. Moreover, adolescents just entering the stage of formal operations often get carried away with their new cognitive powers. They sometimes begin to feel that they are unique and not subject to the laws of nature that affect others: "Other teenagers may get pregnant, but it won't happen to me" (see Chapter 7). Studies show that many teenagers act impulsively, fail to anticipate that they will need contraception, misunderstand the risks of becoming pregnant, do not think about the future consequences of their behavior, and are seriously misinformed about sex and birth control.[1]

I conclude, then, that the cognitive limitations and knowledge gaps of many teenagers have quite a bit to do with today's high rate of teenage pregnancy. These adolescents are not necessarily in the throes of personality conflicts, as Dr. Freud would have you believe, or deprived of the proper learning experience, as Drs. Skinner and Bandura argue. They may simply be cognitively immature and uninformed.

[1]For further information about the studies "Dr. Piaget" cites, see Balassone (1991), Cobliner (1974), Finkel and Finkel (1978), and Morrison (1985).

he should have allowed for the possibility of continued cognitive growth during adulthood. And many have felt that Piaget described cognitive development well enough but did not fully explain *how* children progress from one stage of intellect to the next.

The more developmentalists tested Piaget's ideas, the more they began to question his assumption that all humans everywhere develop through the same stages, toward the same end points. They began to seek theoretical perspectives that allowed for more diversity in the paths that human development could take while still retaining Piaget's emphasis on the interaction of nature and nurture in development.

Klaus F. Riegel.

CONTEXTUAL-DIALECTICAL PERSPECTIVES ON DEVELOPMENT

Contextual-dialectical theories of development hold that changes over the life span arise from the ongoing interrelationships between a changing organism and a changing world (see, for example, Lerner & Kauffman, 1985; Riegel, 1976, 1979; Sameroff, 1975, 1983). Changes in the person produce changes in his or her environment; changes in the environment produce changes in the person; and this interchange goes on continuously. This perspective arose in part because scholars who began to study human development during the adult years soon realized that adult development was too complex and varied to be captured by a set of universal stages. Instead, adult development seemed to take a variety of forms depending on the individual and the historical, cultural, and social context in which he or she was developing.

Riegel's Dialectical Theory

To illustrate the flavor of the contextual-dialectical perspective, let's consider the **dialectical theory** of development put forth by Klaus Riegel (1976, 1979), who, until he died in 1977, taught at the University of Michigan. The term *dialectic* means a kind of dialogue or argument; dialectical theory holds that development results from continuous dialogues between a changing person and a changing world. Riegel questioned stage theories such as Piaget's because they seem to assume that we function at one stable and coherent stage or another for long periods of our lives. In this view, we experience disequilibrium or conflict between our understandings and the reality of things only during transition periods between stages. By contrast, Riegel argues that, although we seek equilibrium or harmony with our environments, we rarely achieve it. When person and world are in continual flux and conflict, there are no stable periods that can be described as stages. And the course of development is not quite as predictable as a stage theory implies.

Riegel focused attention on four major dimensions of development, two of them lying within the person and two of them lying outside the person:

1. An *inner-biological* dimension that involves such changes as the maturation of the nervous system, pubertal changes, menopause, wrinkling, and the onset of illnesses
2. An *individual-psychological* dimension that includes changing thoughts, emotions, and personality processes
3. An *outer-physical* dimension, or the physical world of changing weather conditions, physical settings, and so on
4. A *cultural-sociological* dimension that includes a changing social environment, historical events, and cultural values

Each of these four dimensions is like a river, constantly changing, and each is interacting with the other dimensions and with other elements within the same dimension. So intimately intertwined are these dimensions that we really cannot easily separate person and environment.

Using Riegel's four dimensions, we can analyze the dialectics of growth and change—that is, the interaction among dimensions of development. According to Riegel, changes in one dimension of development inevitably lead to changes in other dimensions. Usually the adjustment process resembles a quiet conversation. For example, we easily adjust our steps as we confront curbs and stairs in the physical environment or respond to requests from people in our social environment. Sometimes, however, we experience crises in which a major change in one dimension puts two or more of the dimensions "out of sync." Out of our efforts to resolve the conflict can come major developmental growth.

Let's look at the dynamic interplay of dimensions of development in the lives of Tom and Marcia, a middle-aged married couple who live in Los Angeles. Marcia began working as a personnel manager five years ago and has just been offered a promotion—one that would require her to move to New Jersey. Tom is quite comfortable with his current job as a teacher. Picture these two people at the kitchen table carrying on a dialogue about the possibility of moving. Consider first the short-term development that may take place during their conversation. We immediately notice that what Tom says influences what Marcia says next, and that what Marcia says influences what Tom says. Marcia and Tom affect and are affected by each other so much that we have to view them as a couple or unit rather than as two independent people. Moreover, there is a structure to their conversation: They take turns speaking (except when someone interrupts in the heat of debate), and their statements are related to what came before. Finally, unless one or the other stomps off in disgust, the whole dialogue may lead somewhere—perhaps to some meeting of the minds or to a new insight into their relationship. A dialogue like this, Riegel (1979) believes, is an excellent model of the developmental process.

To understand the longer-term development of Tom and Marcia, we must place them in the context of changes that have been taking place in the cultural-sociological dimension of development. When this couple married, traditional gender-role beliefs prevailed in society; women were to be housewives, or at least were to subordinate their careers to those of their husbands. But Tom and Marcia have been developing as individuals in a historical period of rapidly changing beliefs regarding the roles of men and women. This cultural-sociological change has helped create the present conflict in their lives; there would have been none if traditional ideas about gender roles had remained strong and Marcia had been content as a homemaker. Tom, who is satisfied with his current lifestyle, now experiences an *asynchrony*, or a lack of meshing, between the individual-psychological dimension of development (his own vocational goals and his traditional gender-role attitudes) and the cultural-sociological dimension (a wife and a larger social world now asking him to view women as equals). Moreover, his individual-psychological development now clashes with Marcia's individual-psychological development. She is psychologically ready for new challenges in her career, but he wants to follow the career path he is already on. Marriage partners are constantly changing, and, when changes in one partner do not mesh with changes in the other partner, the relationship can be thrown off balance.

Riegel argues that such conflicts between individuals and among the four dimensions of development affecting individuals produce developmental change. We cannot always predict in advance what the outcomes will be; that is, we cannot assume that development will inevitably move through a series of universal stages. Instead, we must analyze the ongoing transactions between people and their changing world. Perhaps Marcia and Tom will simply decide to divorce. Or perhaps they will be able to forge a new agreement out of their disagreement—maybe a plan to postpone the move until Tom has more time to locate a new teaching job for himself. Whatever resolution is achieved, harmony or balance will not last long. Once resolutions to this conflict are achieved, new conflicts will inevitably arise in the lives of these two people. Riegel summarizes it this way:

> Specifically, development is brought about by crises in these progressions [the four dimensions of development] which create discordance and conflicts. Through the actions of individuals in society, synchronization is reestablished and thereby progress achieved. But as such a coordination is attained, new discrepancies emerge producing a continuous flux of contradictions and changes [1979, p. 2].

In short, contextual-dialectical theorists believe that person and environment form a unit, that both are in continual flux, and that changes in one produce

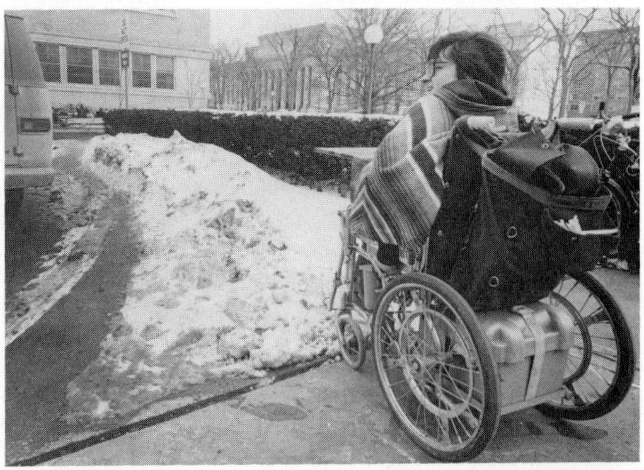

The inner-biological, individual-psychological, and outer-physical dimensions of development proposed by Riegel can become "out of sync" when a person who loves hiking becomes disabled. This disequilibrium may stimulate growth and change.

changes in the other (Lerner & Kauffman, 1985). We cannot ignore the fact that people develop in a changing historical context—something that Piaget and other stage theorists tend to do. Nor can we focus all of our attention on external events and ignore the effects of human beings on their environments—something that Skinner and other behavioral theorists tend to do. We must view development as consisting of changes in the *relationship* between person and environment. A contextual-dialectical perspective on teenage pregnancy is presented in Box 2.5.

Strengths and Weaknesses of Contextual-Dialectical Theory

Contextual-dialectical perspectives on development began to emerge in response to some of the deficiencies of earlier stage theories and learning theories of development. Contextual-dialectical perspectives are complex, but that is because life-span human development appears to be far more complex than it once appeared to be. We can applaud Riegel and like-minded theorists for emphasizing some very important truths about human development. Development *does* occur in a context. People *do* change their environments and actively contribute to their own development, just as they are influenced by other people and by events in the world around them. And not all developmental changes lead inevitably to some "mature" end point such as the achievement of formal-operational thought. Instead, development takes many different directions, and we cannot always predict where lives will turn unless we look more closely at the ongoing transactions between the person and the environment.

The life-span developmental perspective introduced in Chapter 1 is contextual in its orientation. It emphasizes historical influences on development and interactions between person and environment. Life-span researchers have come to see that, although the development of infants and young children appears to be influenced in part by universal maturational processes, the developmental paths of children, and especially adults, differ widely from one another because of the operation of social and historical forces.

BOX 2.5 Contextual-Dialectical Theory Applied: Riegel on Teenage Pregnancy

To understand why Sheila and James are faced with an unintended pregnancy, we can start by analyzing their ongoing relationship. People select and shape their environments and therefore help to produce their own development. James and Sheila each influenced the other, just as each was influenced by the other. Their sexual behavior evolved over time through their ongoing "dialogue." Indeed, the most important influence on an adolescent's sexual behavior and use of contraceptives is his or her partner.[1]

Of course, I would also want to emphasize the relevant relationships between these young people and the changing world in which they are developing. Our society has undergone a number of important historical, or cultural-sociological, changes that have had an impact on developing adolescents. Think of it: increased sexual permissiveness, more working mothers and therefore less supervision of teenagers, the introduction of the Pill, the legalization of abortion, and more.[2] Sheila and James have undoubtedly been influenced by these social changes (though perhaps not enough by the spread of the AIDS epidemic).

Moreover, the different dimensions of development are out of synchrony for today's youth. Adolescents are reaching sexual maturity earlier today than in past eras because of improved nutrition and health care (see Chapter 5); that is, their inner-biological development is proceeding rapidly. So today's young teenagers are biologically ready for sex, and society gives them plenty of messages that sex is desirable. And, yet, in terms of the individual-psychological dimension of development, these young people may still be socially immature, overdependent on others, and psychologically unready for committed relationships.[3] In short, a conflict among the different dimensions of development exists for many teenagers like James and Sheila. They will take some action to reduce the conflict—perhaps in this case by convincing themselves that they are really psychologically mature enough for a sexual relationship.

My dialectical approach is also illustrated well by Beatrix Hamburg's[4] intriguing analysis of teenage pregnancy in high-poverty areas. Many advantaged youth will postpone sexual pleasure for a time—or use birth control—because they are working toward long-term career goals. But what hope does the disadvantaged teen have when inner-city unemployment is rampant and educational systems are poor? Use of contraception becomes less likely in lower-socioeconomic environments where employment opportunities are scarce.[5] According to Hamburg, many young women in such circumstances try to cope as best they can with their disadvantaged social environment by postponing work (since there are no jobs anyway) and instead having children. By having babies, they mobilize their families to support them. Then, when the children are more able to care for themselves, and when their relatives are lined up to provide help with child care, they go back to school or begin working. Odd as it may seem, then, for some teenage girls, getting pregnant may be an adaptive way of coping with a difficult sociocultural environment—and indeed of *changing* that environment in order to achieve personal goals.

For further information on the studies "Riegel" referred to, see Thompson and Spanier (1978),[1] Chilman (1986),[2] Lancaster and Hamburg (1986),[3] Hamburg (1986),[4] and Mosher and McNally (1991).[5]

Thus a contextual perspective will prove to be important to us as we examine specific aspects of development in later chapters.

But perhaps you have noticed that the contextual-dialectical perspective does not give us a very clear picture of the course of human development. Indeed, there is no full-blown contextual or dialectical theory as yet. Up to this point, Riegel and others have mainly alerted us to the need to examine how personal and environmental factors interact over time to produce developmental change. We could, therefore, criticize contextual-dialectical theory for being only partially formulated at this point. But a more serious criticism can also be made: The contextual-dialectical perspective may never provide any coherent developmental theory. Why? Suppose we really take seriously the idea that development can take a wide range of forms owing to the influence of a wide range of factors both within and outside the person. How can we ever state generalizations about development that will hold up for most people? Must we develop separate theories for different subgroups of people—one theory for black women born in 1920 and living in Kenya, another for white men born in 1960 and living in the southeastern United States, and so on? If change over a lifetime depends on the ongoing transactions between a unique person and a unique environment, is each life span unique?

Some theorists worry that the contextual-dialectical perspective will never lead us to a coherent view of human development (Baltes, 1983; Dixon & Lerner, 1992). As an alternative, they suggest that we combine the contextual perspective with the best features of stage theories that propose universal developmental paths (Lerner & Kauffman, 1985). We might then see humans as moving in orderly directions in some aspects of their development, yet we could also try to understand how that developmental course can be altered by contextual factors. We might view developmental attainments such as formal-operational thinking not as inevitable achievements but as attainments that are more or less *probable* depending on the individual's life experiences (Lerner & Kauffman, 1985).

Whether contextual theorists will be able to develop useful theories of human development is not yet clear, but in the meantime they are responsible for an increased awareness that individual development must be studied in its larger social and historical context.

THEORIES AND WORLD VIEWS

That completes our survey of some of the "grand" theories of human development. But these theories can be grouped into even grander categories, for each is grounded in a broader world view, or set of philosophical assumptions that guide scientific thought. By examining the fundamental assumptions that underlie different theories of development, we can better compare them and appreciate how deeply some of their disagreements run. We can also appreciate how perspectives on human development have evolved over the 20th century. Three broad models or world views can be delineated: the *organismic model,* the *mechanistic model,* and the *contextual model* (Overton, 1984; Pepper, 1942; Reese & Overton, 1970; also see Dixon & Lerner, 1992; Lerner, 1986).

The Organismic Model

The **organismic model** likens humans to plants and other living organisms. In this view, human beings are organized wholes or systems; they cannot be understood piece by piece, or behavior by behavior, because they are greater than the sum of their parts. In addition, humans are active in the developmental process; forces springing from within themselves, rather than environmental events, are primarily responsible for their development. True, just as plants need sun, rain, and soil in order to flourish, humans need a supportive environment in order to develop in healthy directions. However, they "unfold," much as a rose unfolds, according to a "master plan" carried in their genes. Finally, the organismic model holds that humans evolve through distinct or discontinuous stages as they reorganize over time; these stages are universal and lead to the same final state of maturity.

The study of human development had its start under the influence of the organismic world view. Charles Darwin's evolutionary theory inspired scholars to look for an orderly "evolution" of the human organism from conception on and to view development as a process of biological maturation (Dixon & Lerner, 1992). Prominent among the early theorists, for example, was Arnold Gesell (1880–1961), an American physician and psychologist who collected some of the first systematic data on normal milestones in child development and influenced many parents with his still-popular books on child rearing (Gesell & Ilg, 1949). He believed that psychological development after birth, like the growth of the embryo before birth, was genetically controlled and highly predictable. Children simply "bloomed" according to a timetable laid out in their genes; how their parents raised them had relatively little impact.

Freud, too, was powerfully influenced by Darwin's work and can be considered a subscriber to the organismic world view. And Jean Piaget, even though he rejected Gesell's position that biological maturation was *everything* in favor of an interactionist position on the nature/nurture issue, is a classic example of an organismic theorist. We might imagine parents who subscribe to this world view as supportive but not "pushy" in their efforts to enhance their children's development. They would tend to trust their children to seek out the learning opportunities they most need at a given stage in their growth. They would respond to their children's changing needs and interests but would not attempt to structure their life experiences for them.

The Mechanistic Model

The **mechanistic model** likens human beings to machines. More specifically, this model assumes that humans (1) are a collection of parts (for example, they can be analyzed behavior by behavior, much as machines can be taken apart piece by piece); (2) are relatively passive in the developmental process, changing mainly in response to outside stimulation (much as machines depend on outside energy sources to operate); (3) change gradually or continuously as "parts," or specific behavior patterns, are added or subtracted; and (4) can develop along a number of different paths, depending on environmental influences.

Learning theorists such as Watson and Skinner clearly express a mechanistic world view, for they see human beings as passively shaped by external stimuli and they analyze human behavior response by response. Bandura's social learning theory, although it is still primarily mechanistic, does incorporate the organismic assumption that humans are active beings who influence their environment as they are being influenced by it. A mechanistic world view may be guiding parents who attempt to orchestrate every minute of their children's time from an early age—who insist that their children go to the "right" preschools, hear the "right" bedtime stories, and participate in the "right" recreational activities. Such parents may assume that their children will not develop at all (or at least will never be Harvard material) unless they are systematically exposed to the proper stimulation. A mechanistic world view also guides behavior modifiers who attempt to use learning principles to shape desirable behaviors and eliminate undesirable ones.

The Contextual Model

Finally, the **contextual model** offers as a metaphor for human development an ongoing historical event or drama, an ever-changing interplay of forces. The focus is on the dynamic relationship between person and environment; person and environment are inseparable and form a unit. People are active in the developmental process (as in the organismic model), *and* the environment is active as well (as in the mechanistic model). The potential exists for both qualitative and quantitative change, and development can proceed along many different paths depending on the intricate interplay of internal and external influences.

Parents who adopt a contextual model of development are likely to realize that their children are influencing them just as much as they are influencing their children. The mother of Carlos and Elena, for example, may notice that she often makes polite requests when interacting with cooperative Carlos but that stubborn Elena drives her to bark orders. Parents who fall in the contextual camp are likely to view themselves as *partners* with their children in the development process—not fans watching from the wings (as in the organismic model) and not heavy-handed directors either (as in the mechanistic model). Out of the "dialectic" or dialogue between child and parent (and between child and the rest of the broader social environment) will come change.

It is because different theories rest on different world views that they sometimes seem to offer such drastically different pictures of human development and its causes (see Table 2.3). Each world view contains unquestioned assumptions that determine what "facts" are considered important and how they are interpreted. Consequently, theorists who view the world through different lenses are likely to continue disagreeing even when the same "facts" are set before them. This is the very nature of science. And it means that our understanding of human development has changed and will continue to change as one prevailing world view gives way to another.

Changing World Views

Early in the study of human development, psychoanalytic theory, guided by organismic assumptions, had its day. Then behavioral learning theories, guided by mechanistic assumptions about development, came to the fore. And today the stands on key developmental issues taken by contextual-dialectical theorists are the stands that most developmentalists have adopted. The field has moved beyond the extreme, black-or-white positions taken by many of its pioneers. We now appreciate that human beings have the potential to develop in good *and* bad directions, that human development is always the product of nature *and* nurture, that humans *and* their environments are active in the developmental process, that development is both continuous *and* discontinuous in form, and that development has both universal aspects *and* aspects particular to certain cultures, times, and individuals. In short, the world views and theories that guide the study of human development have become increasingly complex as the incredible complexity of human development has become more apparent.

To illustrate this point (and to show you where we are heading next in this book), we'll consider two contemporary and very influential developmental theories, one of which emphasizes the role of nature in development, the other of which highlights the role of nurture. *Ethological theorists* (see Chapters 3 and 13) adopt a biological perspective on development, claiming that humans come to the world genetically equipped to engage in certain behaviors (for exam-

TABLE 2.3 The organismic, mechanistic, and contextual models or world views compared.

	Model		
	Organismic	*Mechanistic*	*Contextual*
Guiding metaphor for humans	Plant	Machine	Historical event
Nature of humans	Coherent, organized whole	Collection of "parts" (specific behaviors)	Part of changing person/environment relationship
Role of person in development	Active	Passive	Active
Role of environment in development	Passive	Active	Active
Form of development	Discontinuous, stagelike	Continuous, gradual	Discontinuous and continuous
Direction of development	One universal direction of growth	Multidirectional	Multidirectional
Examples	Psychoanalytic theory: Freud, Erikson (Chap. 10) Cognitive-developmental theory: Piaget, Kohlberg (Chap. 12) Ethological theory (Chaps. 3, 13)	Learning theories: Watson, Skinner, Bandura	Dialectical theory: Riegel Ecological approach: Bronfenbrenner (Chap. 4) Life-span perspective (Chap. 1)

ple, following after their caregivers when they are about 1 year of age) that have aided the human species in adapting to its environment over the course of evolution. Yet ethologists know full well that environmental factors (such as the responsiveness of parents to their infants) interact with genetic makeup to shape development.

By contrast, another modern perspective on development, Urie Bronfenbrenner's *ecological approach* (see Chapter 4), emphasizes the "nurture" side of the nature/nurture issue. It describes a series of environmental systems, ranging from the home to the wider society, that influence the developing person. Yet Bronfenbrenner is keenly aware that people influence their environments, just as environments influence people. Today, then, biologically oriented and environmentally oriented theorists can agree: Nature and nurture are *both* critical in the developmental process.

APPLICATIONS: THERE'S NOTHING AS USEFUL AS A GOOD THEORY

As we noted at the start of the chapter, one of the main functions of theories in any science is to guide attempts to gain knowledge through research. Thus Freud stimulated researchers to study inner personality conflicts, Skinner inspired them to analyze how behavior changes when its consequences change, and Piaget inspired them to explore children's thinking about every imaginable topic. Different theories stimulate different kinds of research and yield different kinds of "facts."

Theories also guide practice. As we have seen, each theory of human development represents a particular way of defining developmental issues and problems. Often how you define a problem determines how you attempt to solve it. To illustrate this point, let's take one last look at teenage pregnancy, which is clearly defined as a social problem in society today. As we have seen, different theorists hold radically different opinions about the causes of teenage pregnancy. How do you suppose each would go about trying to *reduce* the rate of teenage pregnancy?

Psychoanalytic theorists are likely to locate the "problem" within the person. Freud might want to identify teenagers who have especially strong ids and weak egos and superegos or are experiencing extremes of anxiety and strained relationships with their parents. "High-risk" teenagers might then be treated through psychoanalysis; the aim would be to help them resolve the inner conflicts that might "get them in trouble." This approach to solving the problem follows naturally from a psychoanalytic view of the causes of the problem. And it might well work with teenagers who are indeed emotionally disturbed. The only catch is that most pregnant girls are not psychologically disturbed; they are quite similar psychologically to girls who do not get pregnant (Furstenberg et al., 1981; Phipps-Yonas, 1980).

Adopting Piaget's cognitive-developmental perspective might make us somewhat pessimistic about the chances of getting young teenagers to engage in long-term planning and rational decision making about sexual issues until they are solidly into the formal operations stage of cognitive development. However, Piaget would want us to identify the kinds of faulty "cognitive structures" or misunderstandings that adolescents have about their risks of pregnancy and about contraceptive methods; we could then attempt to correct their mistaken ideas. Presumably the solution is improved sex education courses that teach teenagers accurate information and help them think clearly about the consequences of their sexual decisions. And, instead of just *telling* concrete-operational thinkers about the consequences of early pregnancy, we might make those consequences concrete instead of abstract for them (Proctor, 1986), perhaps by having students talk to teenage mothers and fathers about their lives or tend infants in a day-care center.

Most researchers concerned about teenage sexuality and pregnancy do indeed agree that improved sex education is an important part of the solution. And yet, even when sex-education courses impart knowledge, they only sometimes succeed in convincing adolescents to postpone sex or to use contraception and only rarely lower pregnancy rates (Eisen, Zellman, & McAlister, 1990; Kirby, Waszak, & Ziegler, 1991). So perhaps we need to consider solutions that locate the problem in the *environment* rather than in the individual's psychological weaknesses or cognitive deficiencies.

Learning theorists strongly believe that changing the environment will change the person. In support of this belief, Douglas Kirby (1985) found that only one of the sex-education projects he studied resulted in an increase in birth-control use and a decrease in the rate of unintended pregnancies. It involved a major change in the school environment: the establishment of a health clinic where students who were already sexually active could, in the strictest confidence, obtain specific guidance about how to use birth-control devices and where to obtain them. This program reflects a Skinnerian philosophy. In the face of the AIDS epidemic, more and more school systems seem to be trying to encourage and reinforce abstinence and safer sex practices and to reduce the "punishment" associated with obtaining condoms by distributing them free of charge at school.

Albert Bandura's cognitive social learning theory gives us some additional ideas about how to change the environment. Parents might be taught how to be better role models of responsible sexual behavior and how to communicate to their children about sex. Peers might be mobilized to serve as models of the advantages of postponing sex or engaging in safer sex. Television programs might focus less on the joys of sex and more on its unwanted consequences. Through observational learning experiences, teenagers might develop more sexually responsible habits, especially if they come to believe that the consequences of more responsible sex will be to their liking (Balassone, 1991).

Contextual-dialectical theorists would insist even more strongly than Bandura that changing *both* the person and the environment is essential. The ultimate solution might require changing the broader social context in which today's adolescents are developing. Perhaps teenage pregnancy in poverty areas will not be significantly reduced until schools do more to motivate students, until jobs are made available, and until more disadvantaged young people gain hope that they can climb out of poverty if they pursue an education and postpone parenthood (Furstenberg, Brooks-Gunn, & Morgan, 1987). In the meantime, it would not hurt to help adolescents understand the pros and cons of different life choices and appreciate that they have the power to shape their own development.

We see, then, that the theoretical position that one takes has a tremendous impact on how one goes about attempting to optimize development. Yet, as we have also seen, each theory may have only a partial solution to the problem being addressed. In all likelihood, multiple approaches will be needed to make a serious dent in complex problems such as the high rate of teenage pregnancy—or to achieve the larger goal of understanding human development.

REFLECTIONS

More than all else, we hope that reading this chapter has made you realize that theories are not just useless ideas. Developmentalists need theories to guide their work. And *people in general* need theories to guide their behavior. Human beings simply cannot make sense of life unless they impose some order on it by making assumptions and forming generalizations. Every parent, teacher, human service professional, and observer of human beings is guided by *some* set of beliefs about how human beings develop and why they develop as they do. Moreover, their beliefs inform their behavior (McGillicuddy-DeLisi, 1985; Miller, 1988). All things considered, it is better to be conscious of one's guiding beliefs than to be unaware of them. We hope that reading this chapter will stimulate you to clarify your own theories of human development. One way to start is by completing the exercise that appears in Box 2.6 and seeing which theorists' views are most compatible with your own.

You need not choose one theory and reject others. Indeed, because different theories often highlight different aspects of development, one may be more relevant to a particular issue or to a particular age group than another. Today many developmentalists are theoretical **eclectics**: individuals who rely on

BOX 2.6 Compare Yourself with the Theorists on Developmental Issues

In Box 2.1, before you read this chapter, you were asked to indicate your positions on basic issues in human development by answering six questions. If you transcribe your answers below, you can compare your stands to those of the theorists described in this chapter (and also review the theories). With whom do you seem to agree the most?

	Question 1	2	3	4	5	6
Your pattern of answers:	__	__	__	__	__	__

Freud's Psychoanalytic Theory

a b b a a a

Freud held that biologically based sexual instincts motivate behavior and steer development through five psychosexual stages. He believed that (1) the child's urges are basically selfish and aggressive; (2) biological changes are the driving force behind psychosexual stages (though he believed that parents influence how well these stages are negotiated); (3) children are passively influenced by forces beyond their control; (4) development is stagelike rather than continuous; (5) traits established in early childhood definitely carry over into adult personality traits; and (6) the psychosexual stages are universal.

Learning Theory: Skinner's Version

b e b c b b

Skinner maintains that development is the result of learning from the consequences of one's behavior. In his view, (1) children are inherently neither good nor bad; (2) nurture or environment is far more important than nature; (3) people are passively shaped by environmental events; (4) development is gradual and continuous, as habits increase or decrease in strength; (5) early behavior may change dramatically later if the environment changes; and (6) development can proceed in many different directions depending on the individual's learning experiences.

Learning Theory: Bandura's Version

b d a c b b

Bandura's social learning theory states that humans change through cognitive forms of learning, especially observational learning. He argues that (1) children are inherently neither good nor bad; (2) nurture is more important than nature; (3) people influence their environments and thus are active in their own development; (4) development is continuous rather than stagelike; (5) traits are unlikely to be stable if the person's environment changes; and (6) development can proceed in many directions depending on life experiences.

Piaget's Cognitive-Developmental Theory

c b a a b a

Piaget described four distinct stages in the development of intelligence that result as children attempt to make sense of their experience. He suggested that (1) we are born with positive tendencies such as curiosity; (2) maturation guides all children through the same sequence of stages, although experience is necessary as well and can influence the rate of development; (3) we are active in our own development as we "construct" more sophisticated understandings; (4) development is stagelike; (5) cognitive abilities change dramatically, and (6) everyone progresses through the same sequence of stages.

Contextual-Dialectical Theory

b c a b b b

Riegel and similar theorists believe that development results from the "dialogue" between a changing person and a changing physical and sociocultural context. These theorists appear to believe that (1) humans are inherently neither good nor bad; (2) nature and nurture, interacting continually, make us what we are; (3) people are active in their own development; (4) development probably involves some continuity and some discontinuity, some stagelike changes and some gradual ones; (5) early traits may be replaced by different traits if the environment changes; and (6) although some aspects of development may be universal, development also varies widely from individual to individual.

many theories, recognizing that none of the major theories of human development can explain everything but that each has something to contribute to our understanding. In many ways, the emerging contextual-dialectical perspective on development is the broadest point of view yet proposed. It is also compatible with the life-span perspective on development introduced in Chapter 1. There is no reason why many of the insights offered by Freud, Piaget, Bandura, and others cannot be incorporated within this perspective to help us understand changing people in changing worlds.

In the remainder of this book, we take an eclectic and contextual approach to human development, borrowing from many theories in trying to draw a systematic and unified portrait of the developing person. We will also explore theoretical controversies, for these squabbles often produce some of the most exciting breakthroughs in the field. We invite you to join us in examining not just the specific "facts" of development but also the broader perspectives that have generated those facts and that give them larger meaning.

SUMMARY POINTS

1. A theory is a set of ideas proposed to describe and explain certain phenomena; it provides a perspective that helps organize a wide range of facts and is valuable to the extent that it is parsimonious, falsifiable, and valid.

2. Theories of human development address issues concerning assumptions about human nature, nature/nurture, activity/passivity, continuity/discontinuity, and universality/particularity in development.

3. According to Freud's psychoanalytic theory, humans are driven by inborn instincts of which they are largely unconscious. The id, which is purely instinctual, rules the infant; the rational ego emerges during infancy; and the superego, or conscience, takes form in the preschool years. Five psychosexual stages—oral, anal, phallic, latency, and genital—unfold as the sex instinct matures; each is characterized by conflicts that create the need for ego defense mechanisms and have lasting effects on the personality.

4. Learning theorists hold that we change gradually through learning experiences and that we can develop in many different directions. Behaviorist John Watson advocated attention to overt behavior and environmental influences on development. B. F. Skinner advanced the behavioral perspective by demonstrating the importance of operant conditioning and reinforcement. Albert Bandura's cognitive social learning theory differs from behavioral learning theories in emphasizing cognitive processes, observational learning, and a reciprocal determinism of person and environment.

5. Jean Piaget's cognitive-developmental theory stresses universal, invariant stages in which children actively construct increasingly complex understandings by interacting with their environments. These stages are: sensorimotor, preoperational, concrete-operational, and formal-operational.

6. The emerging contextual-dialectical perspective on development, illustrated by Riegel's dialectical theory, emphasizes the study of the relations between a changing person and a changing world. Development results from the "dialectics" among the inner-biological, individual-psychological, outer-physical, and cultural-sociological dimensions of development.

7. Theories can be grouped into families based on the broad world views that underlie them. The contextual model or world view differs from the mechanistic model that guides learning theories and the organismic model that underlies stage theories.

8. Theories of human development guide not only research but also practice; psychoanalytic, cognitive-developmental, learning, and contextual-dialectical theorists would each propose different approaches to the problem of teenage pregnancy.

9. From an eclectic perspective, no single theoretical viewpoint offers a totally adequate account of human development, but each contributes in important ways to our understanding.

KEY TERMS

accommodation
activity/passivity issue
anal stage
assimilation
behaviorism
concrete operations stage
constructivism
contextual-dialectical theories
contextual model
continuity/discontinuity issue
defense mechanisms
developmental stage
dialectical theory
eclectic
ego
Electra complex
fixation
formal operations stage
genital stage
id
identification
instinct
latency period
libido
mechanistic model
nature/nurture issue
observational learning
Oedipus complex
operant conditioning
oral stage
organismic model
phallic stage
preoperational stage
psychoanalytic theory
punisher
reciprocal determinism
regression
reinforcer
repression
sensorimotor stage
social learning theory
superego
tabula rasa
unconscious motivation
universality/particularity issue

3

THE GENETICS OF LIFE-SPAN DEVELOPMENT

Oscar Stohr and Jack Yufe, one a Catholic Czech who had been loyal to the Nazis in World War II, the other raised in the Caribbean by his Jewish father and taught to despise Nazism, quickly discovered that they shared a passion for spicy food, a habit of flushing the toilet both before and after using it, and an enjoyment of sneezing loudly to scare people (Begley, 1979).

Perhaps the influence of **genes** on development must be taken seriously.

Imagine discovering that you have a long-lost identical twin somewhere in the world and preparing to meet this twin face-to-face for the first time. This is a fantasy that many people have, but it has been a reality for many of the participants in a study of twins separated at birth being conducted at the University of Minnesota by Dr. Thomas Bouchard, Jr., and his associates (Bouchard, 1984; Bouchard et al., 1990). Although the research team expected to observe similarities in the ways twins responded to a large battery of tests, they probably were not prepared for the number of eerie coincidences that occurred when these twins were reunited:

Jim Lewis and Jim Springer, together again after spending all but the first 4 weeks of their 39 years apart, had both married women named Linda—and then women named Betty. They named their first sons James Alan and James Allan, respectively, and had dogs named Toy (Begley, 1987).

Bridget Harison and Dorothy Lowe, when they arrived at the University of Minnesota after 34 years of separation, each wore a watch, bracelets on both wrists, and rings on seven fingers (Begley, 1987).

Jim Springer and Jim Lewis were unaware of each other's existence until they were reunited at age 39 as part of a study of identical twins reared apart.

What are the roles of heredity and environment in shaping the many physical and psychological characteristics that each of us possesses? That is the puzzle to be grappled with in this chapter. Before you read further, take the brief quiz on heredity in Box 3.1. We suspect that many of you have studied genetics and heredity before—and have also been exposed to some misconceptions about heredity that circulate in our society. Answers to the quiz will become clear as you read the chapter.

Most students we have taught are environmentalists at heart. They tend to believe that there is no such thing as a "bad seed," that proper parenting and a stimulating environment can make the development of virtually any child go well, and that most of the psychological differences between people are due to differences in their experiences over the course of a lifetime. We hope that reading this chapter will increase your appreciation of genetic contributions to development without diminishing your belief in the importance of environmental influences.

We will begin by considering some ways in which genes make human beings alike in their characteristics and in their development. Then we will look at what the individual inherits at conception and at how this genetic endowment can influence his or her traits. At that point we will be ready to ask how genes and environment make individuals different from one another in such aspects of behavior as intelligence and personality. This will put us in a position to draw some general conclusions about heredity and environment from a life-span perspective. Let's start by focusing on the genes that all humans share.

SPECIES HEREDITY, EVOLUTION, AND HUMAN DEVELOPMENT

Most discussions of heredity focus on its role in creating differences among people. Some individuals inherit blue eyes, others brown eyes; some individuals inherit blood type O, others blood type A or B. But isn't it remarkable that just about every one of us has two eyes and that we all have blood coursing through our

BOX 3.1 What Do You Know about Heredity?

Answer each question true or false.

1. Children born of the same two parents share exactly one-half of their genes in common.
2. Two brown-eyed parents cannot have a blue-eyed child.
3. It is the father's genetic contribution that determines whether a child is a boy or a girl.
4. If a boy is color blind when it comes to distinguishing red and green, he can blame his mother.
5. Similarities in personality between brothers and sisters are usually due more to their growing up in the same family environment than to similarities in their genetic makeups.
6. Characteristics that are highly influenced by genes cannot be altered by environmental forces.
7. A child whose mother or father has the severe psychological disorder schizophrenia has at least a 50% chance of becoming schizophrenic.
8. Height is genetically influenced, but weight is not.

(Answers: 1—F, 2—F, 3—T, 4—T, 5—F, 6—F, 7—F, 8—F. You might want to return to this quiz after you read the chapter to make sure that you understand the answers.)

veins? And that virtually all of us develop in similar ways at similar ages—walking and talking at about 1 year, maturing sexually at about 12 to 14, watching our skin wrinkle in our 40s and 50s? These similarities are not coincidental. They are due to **species heredity**—the genetic endowment that members of a particular species have in common, including genes that govern maturation and aging processes. Humans can feel guilty but cannot fly; birds can fly but cannot feel guilty. Humans and birds each have their own distinct species heredity.

Species heredity, in collaboration with early experience, is responsible for maturational processes that all normal children undergo. Many years ago, Conrad Waddington (1966) coined the term **canalization** to refer to ways in which genes work to limit or restrict development to a small number of possible outcomes. Some aspects of development are more highly canalized than others. For example, all infants, even deaf ones, babble around the middle of their first year of life. Assuming that babies are not severely deprived of stimulation or traumatized, variations in their environments have little effect on such highly canalized attributes as babbling. Although normal experience is just as essential if a child is to develop normally (Gottlieb, 1991a), species heredity acts to ensure that all of us experience universal milestones in development and are not destroyed by less-than-perfect parenting or other less-than-optimal life experiences. Less highly canalized attributes such as verbal ability and the capacity for empathy can be deflected away from their normal developmental pathways by life experiences. As a result, they vary more from person to person and from culture to culture.

Species heredity, then, is very important to our understanding of *universal* patterns of development and aging. And where did we get this common species heredity? That's a question evolutionary theory can help answer.

Darwin's Theory of Evolution

The theory of evolution proposed by Charles Darwin (1809–1882), and modified somewhat over the years, attempts to explain how the characteristics of any species change over time and how new species can evolve from earlier ones (Darwin, 1859). The main arguments are these:

1. *There is genetic variation in a species.* Some members of the species have different genes (and different genetically influenced characteristics and behaviors) than others do. If all members of the species were genetically identical, there would be no way for the genetic makeup of the species to change over time.

2. *Some genes aid in adaptation more than others do.* Suppose that some members of a species have genes that make them strong and intelligent, whereas others have genes that make them weak and dull. Surely those with the genes for strength and intelligence would be better able to adapt to their environment—for example, to win fights for survival or to figure out how to obtain food.

3. *Those genes that aid their bearers in adapting to the environment will be passed on to future generations more frequently than those genes that do not.* This is the principle of **natural selection**—the idea that nature "selects," or allows to survive and reproduce, those members of a species whose genes permit them to adapt to their environment. By contrast, those genes that somehow reduce the chances that an individual will survive and reproduce will become rarer and rarer over time because they will not be passed on to many offspring. Through natural selection, then, the genetic makeup of a whole species can slowly change over time.

Consider a classic example of speeded-up evolution. H. B. D. Kettlewell (1959) carefully studied moths in England. There is genetic variation among moths that makes some of them dark in color and others light in color. By placing light and dark moths in a number of different sites, Kettlewell found that, in rural areas, light-colored moths were more likely to survive than dark-colored moths. Just the opposite was true in the industrial areas of Birmingham: Dark moths were more likely to survive than light moths. The explanation? In rural areas, light-colored moths blended in well with light-colored trees and were better protected from predators by their camouflage. Natural selection favored them. However, in sooty industrial areas, light-colored moths were easy pickings against the darkened trees, whereas dark moths were well disguised. When industry came to England, the proportion of dark moths increased; as pollution was brought under control in some of the highly industrialized areas of the nation, the proportion of light-colored moths increased again (Bishop & Cooke, 1975).

Notice, then, that evolutionary theory is not just about genes. It is about the *interaction* between genes and environment. A particular genetic makeup may enhance survival in one kind of environment but prove maladaptive if the environment changes dramatically. Which genes are advantageous and therefore become more common in future generations depends on what traits the environment demands.

If we take the evolutionary perspective seriously, we begin to appreciate that humans, like any other species, are as they are and develop as they do partly because they have a shared species heredity that has passed the test of natural selection. As long as some people are more likely than others to survive and to have children, biological evolution is slowly at work (Scarr & Kidd, 1983). Perhaps the most significant legacy of human evolution, though, is a powerful brain that allows us to learn from our experiences and to master a complex language so that we can communicate virtually anything to others. What could be more adaptive? Humans have not had to wait for biological evolution to give them furrier bodies as protection from the cold; they have been able to use their brains to invent better and better clothing and heating systems and to communicate what they know to future generations (Scarr & Kidd, 1983). Most of the changes we see over the course of history are due to this kind of *cultural evolution* rather than to biological evolution. What evolutionary biologists would want us to remember is that the ability to learn and the ability to teach others are themselves the products of biological evolution.

Modern Evolutionary Perspectives on Development

Darwin's evolutionary theory was influential as the scientific study of human development began and is being appreciated anew today (see Charlesworth, 1992). It has been the foundation for the work of ethologists, psychobiologists, and other scholars who attempt to understand relationships between biology and behavior.

Ethology is a discipline concerned with understanding the evolved behavior of various species in their natural environments (see Archer, 1992; Hinde, 1983). Noted ethologists such as Konrad Lorenz and Niko Tinbergen have asked how behaviors that are specieswide (or at least universal in a segment of a species, such as males or females or infants) might be adaptive in the sense that they contribute to survival. Because behavior is adaptive only in relation to a particular environment, ethologists prefer naturalistic observation as a method of study. So, for example, they have recorded bird songs in the wild, analyzed the features of these songs carefully, explored how male birds learn the songs characteristic of their species, and attempted to understand how songs aid birds in reproducing and surviving.

Ethologists suggest that humans, too, display species-specific behaviors that are the products of our evolutionary history. In Chapter 13 we will encounter an influential ethological theory that views the tendency of human infants to form close attachments and to cry for, cling to, and follow after their caregivers — like the tendency of baby birds to follow behind their mothers — as a pattern of behavior that has evolved because it increases the odds that the young will survive. Other ethologists have observed that preschool children, like many other primates, form "dominance hierarchies," or pecking orders, in which each group member has a ranking. These social hierarchies serve the adaptive function of reducing aggression by making it clear when an individual should submit to a more dominant member of the group rather than start what is likely to be a costly fight (Strayer, 1980; see also Gandelman, 1992).

Ethologists and other modern evolutionary theorists do not claim that humans are robots that simply act out "instinctive" behaviors dictated by their genes. Instead, they believe that humans have evolved in ways that allow them to *learn* which patterns of social behavior are most biologically adaptive in the culture, subculture, and particular circumstances they encounter (Archer, 1992; Belsky, Steinberg, & Draper, 1991). Indeed, it is has become clear that innate, specieswide tendencies in both animals and humans can often be altered dramatically by early learning experiences. A growing cadre of developmental psychobiologists are attempting to understand just how biological factors such as genes and hormones interact with experience, starting in the womb, to guide development (see Gandelman, 1992).

Consider, for example, that young mallard ducklings clearly prefer their mothers' vocal calls to those of other birds such as chickens — a behavior that appears to be innate and certainly has adaptive value for the species. Yet Gilbert Gottlieb (1991b) has shown that duckling embryos that were prevented from vocalizing and were exposed to chicken calls before hatching come to prefer the call of a chicken to that of a mallard mother! The ducklings' prenatal experiences apparently overrode their genetic predisposition, which suggests that even seemingly "instinctive" patterns of behavior will not emerge unless the individual has not only normal genes but also *normal early experiences.* Because humans have a greater capacity for learning than ducks do, it is reasonable to think that many of the behavior patterns called for by our human species heredity may or may not emerge depending on the individual's learning experiences.

At this point, many evolutionary hypotheses about human development and behavior are speculative (Lerner & von Eye, 1992). Much remains to be learned about the roles of genes, hormones, and other biological influences on human development. Ethologists and psychobiologists have already made an important point, though: Humans, like other animals, may behave and develop as they do partly because their species heredity, the product of natural selection over the course of evolution, predisposes them to behave and develop as they do. Yet these scientists' work also tells us that genes do not *determine* anything; instead, genes are partners with the environment in directing all humans along many of the same developmental pathways (Gandelman, 1992; Gottlieb, 1991b).

But human beings are not all alike, partly because they have different genetic makeups and partly because they are influenced by the often very diverse environments in which they develop. Let's now turn to the ways in which genes contribute to *differences* among us.

THE WORKINGS OF INDIVIDUAL HEREDITY

To understand individual heredity, we must start at **conception,** the moment when a woman's egg is fertilized by a man's sperm. Once we have established what is inherited at conception, we can examine the mechanisms through which genes translate into traits.

Conception and the Genetic Code

About once every 28 days, roughly midway between menstrual periods, human females ovulate. An ovum or egg cell ripens, leaves the ovary, and enters the fallopian tube. If a woman has sexual intercourse with a fertile male during or a few days before or after ovulation, the 300 to 450 million sperm cells contained in her partner's seminal fluid begin to swim, tadpole-style, in all directions. Of the 5000 to 20,000 sperm that survive the long journey into the fallopian tubes, one may meet and penetrate the ovum on its descent from the ovary. A biochemical reaction occurs that repels other sperm, preventing them from repeating the fertilization process. Within a few hours the sperm cell begins to disintegrate, releasing its genetic material. The nucleus of the ovum releases its own genetic material, and a new cell nucleus is created from the genetic material provided by mother and father. This new cell, called a **zygote,** is the beginning of a human being. Conception has occurred.

What is this genetic material contained in the new zygote? It is 46 threadlike bodies called **chromosomes,** which function as 23 pairs. Each member of a chromosome pair influences the same characteristics as the other member of the pair. Each chromosome is made up of thousands of genes, the basic units of heredity. Genes are actually stretches of DNA, the "double helix" molecule that provides a chemical "code" for development. Like chromosomes, genes function as pairs, the two members of each gene pair being located at the same sites on their corresponding chromosomes.

The sperm cell and the ovum each contributed 23 chromosomes to the zygote. Thus of each chromosome pair—and of each pair of genes on corresponding chromosomes—one member came from the father and one member came from the mother. Once formed, the single-celled zygote becomes a multiple-celled organism through a process of cell division called **mitosis.** During mitosis a cell (and each of its 46 chromosomes) divides to produce two identical cells, each containing the same 46 chromosomes (see Figure 3.1). As the zygote moves through the fallopian tube toward its prenatal home in the uterus, it first divides into two cells, and the two then become four, the four become eight, and so on. Except for sperm and ova, all cells in the individual's body contain copies of the 46 chromosomes provided at conception. Mitosis continues throughout life, creating new cells that enable us to grow and replacing old cells that are damaged.

How is it that sperm and ova have only 23 chromosomes? It is because they are produced through a different process of cell division, called **meiosis.** A reproductive germ cell in the ovaries of a female or the testes of a male contains 46 chromosomes, but it splits to form two 46-chromosome cells, and then these two cells split again to form four cells, each with 23 chromosomes. Each resulting sperm cell or ovum thus has only one member of each of the parent's 23 pairs of chromosomes.

Genetic Uniqueness and Relatedness

To understand how we are different from but like others genetically, consider those 46 chromosomes that contain the blueprint for the development of a new individual. When a pair of parental chromosomes moves apart during meiosis, it is a matter of chance which of the two chromosomes will end up in a particular sperm or ovum. And, because each chromosome pair segregates independently of all other

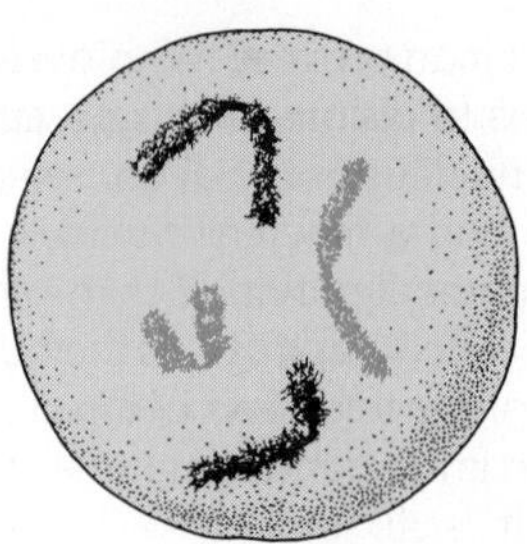

Step 1
Original parent cell (for illustrative purposes this cell contains but four chromosomes).

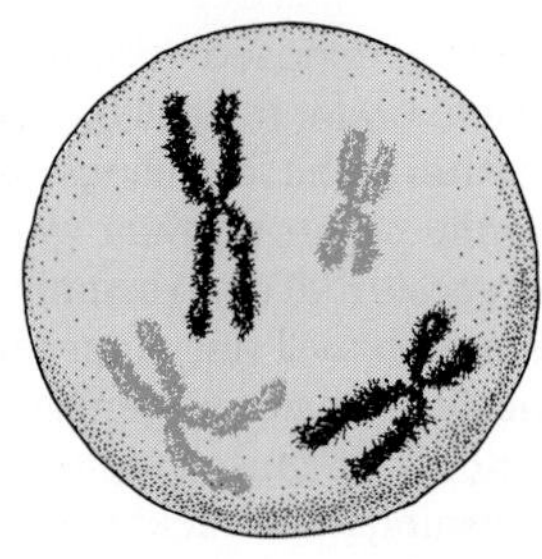

Step 2
Each chromosome splits lengthwise, producing a duplicate.

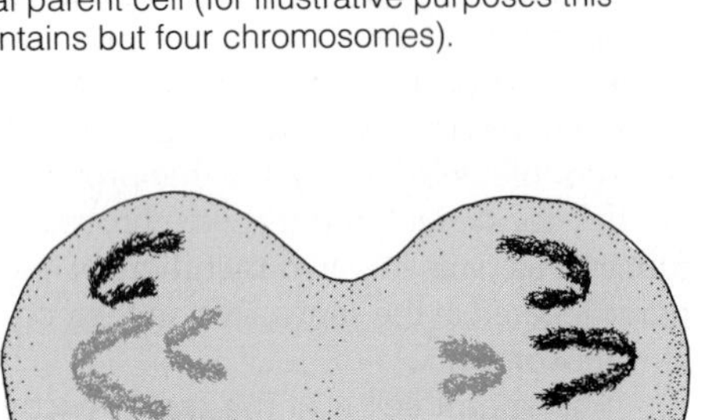

Step 3
The duplicate sets of chromosomes move to opposite ends of the parent cell, which then begins to divide.

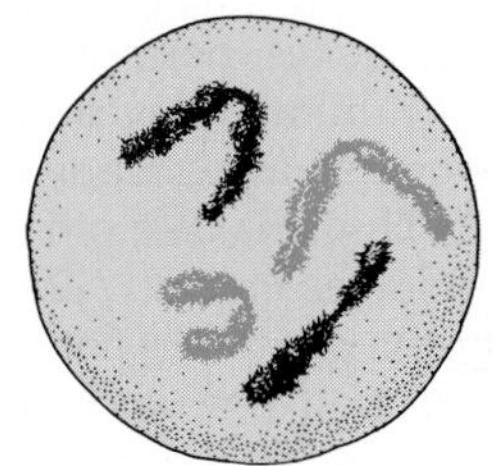

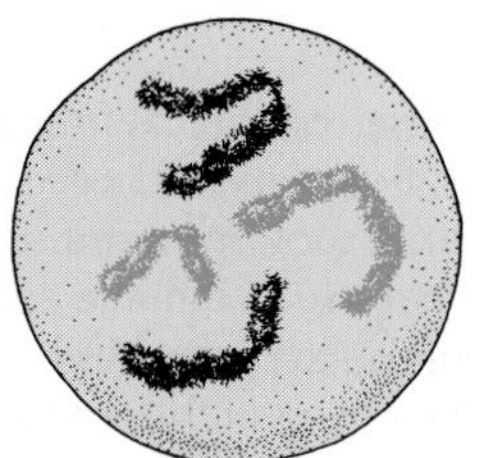

Step 4
The cell completes its division, producing two daughter cells that have identical sets of chromosomes.

FIGURE 3.1 Mitosis: The way cells reproduce themselves.

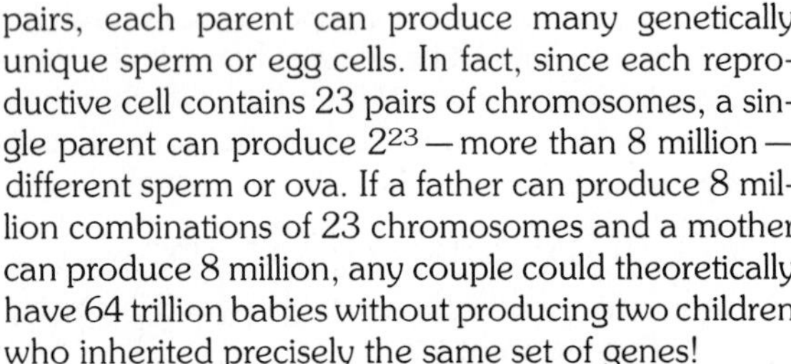

pairs, each parent can produce many genetically unique sperm or egg cells. In fact, since each reproductive cell contains 23 pairs of chromosomes, a single parent can produce 2^{23} — more than 8 million — different sperm or ova. If a father can produce 8 million combinations of 23 chromosomes and a mother can produce 8 million, any couple could theoretically have 64 trillion babies without producing two children who inherited precisely the same set of genes!

In fact, the genetic uniqueness of children of the same parents is even greater than this because of a quirk of meiosis known as **crossing over.** When pairs of chromosomes line up before they separate, they cross each other and parts of them are exchanged, much as if you were to exchange a couple of fingers with a friend after a handshake. This crossing-over phenomenon increases still further the number of distinct sperm or ova that an individual can produce. In short, it is incredibly unlikely that there ever was or ever will be another human exactly like you genetically. The one exception is **identical twins** (or identical triplets, and so on). They result when one fertilized ovum later divides to form two or more genetically identical individuals, as happens in about 1 of every 250 births (Plomin, 1990). Identical twins thus share 100% of their genes.

How genetically alike are parent and child, or brother and sister? You and either your mother or your father have 50% of your genes in common, because you received half of your chromosomes (and genes) from each parent. But, if you have followed our mathematics, you will see that siblings may have many genes in common or very few, depending on the luck of the draw of chromosomes during meiosis. Indeed, we've all seen that some siblings are almost like twins, whereas others don't even seem to belong in the same family. Siblings do receive half of their genes from the same mother and half from the same father, so their genetic resemblance is 50%, like that of parent and child. The critical difference is that siblings share half of their genes *on the average*, with some sharing more and others sharing less.

The same applies to **fraternal twins** — pairs that result when two ova are released at approximately the same time and each is fertilized by a different sperm, as happens in about 1 of every 125 births. Fraternal twins are no more alike genetically than brothers and sisters born at different times and need not even be of the same sex. Grandparent and grandchild, as well as half-brothers or half-sisters, have 25% of their genes in common on the average. Thus each of us (with the exception of identical twins) is genetically unique, but each of us also has genes in common with kin — genes that contribute to family resemblances.

Determination of Sex

Of the 23 pairs of chromosomes that each individual inherits, 22 (called *autosomes*) are similar in males and females. Sex is determined by the 23rd pair, the sex chromosomes. A male child has one long chromosome called an **X chromosome** (based on its shape) and a short, stubby companion called a **Y chromosome.** Females have two X chromosomes. Figure 3.2 shows chromosomes that have been photographed through a powerful microscope and then arranged in pairs and rephotographed in a pattern called a **karyotype.**

Which parent determines the child's sex, then? Since mothers have only X chromosomes to give, while a father's sperm cell will have either an X or a Y chromosome (depending on how chromosomes sort out during meiosis), it is the father who determines a child's gender. If an ovum (with its one X chromosome) is fertilized by a sperm bearing a Y chromosome, the product is an XY zygote, a genetic male. If a sperm carrying an X chromosome reaches the ovum first, the result is an XX zygote, a genetic female. Yet women throughout history have been criticized, tortured, divorced, and even beheaded for failing to bear their husbands male heirs.

So, we now have a genetically unique boy or girl with about 500,000 genes in all on his or her 46 chromosomes. How do these genes influence the individual's characteristics and development? It is still a mystery, but we'll first offer a solution that focuses on the nature of genes themselves.

Translation of the Genetic Code

Genes provide instructions for development. Specifically, they call for the production of chemical substances, such as enzymes and other proteins, that act on each other in such a way that cells are formed and begin to function. For example, genes set in motion a process that results in the laying down of a pigment called melanin in the iris of the eye. Some people's genes call for much of this pigment, and the result is brown eyes; other people's genes call for less of it, and the result is blue eyes. Genes also guide the formation of cells that become the brain, potentially influencing intelligence in the process. It is clear that genes do not singlehandedly orchestrate development; instead, they influence and in turn are influenced by the biochemical environment surrounding them (Gottlieb, 1991b). No one, however, completely understands the remarkable process that transforms a single cell into millions of diverse cells—blood cells, nerve cells, skin cells, and so on—all organized into a living, breathing human being.

Nor does anyone fully understand how genes help to bring about certain developments at certain points in the life span. Some genes clearly direct the production of proteins that are in turn responsible for how the body's organs are constructed and how they function. Other genes apparently have the task of *regulating* the first set of genes. Current thinking is that specific gene pairs with specific messages to send are "turned on" or "turned off" by regulatory genes at different points in the life span (Scarr & Kidd, 1983). Thus, regulatory genes might "turn on" genes responsible for the growth spurt we experience as adolescents or shut down the action of these genes in adulthood.

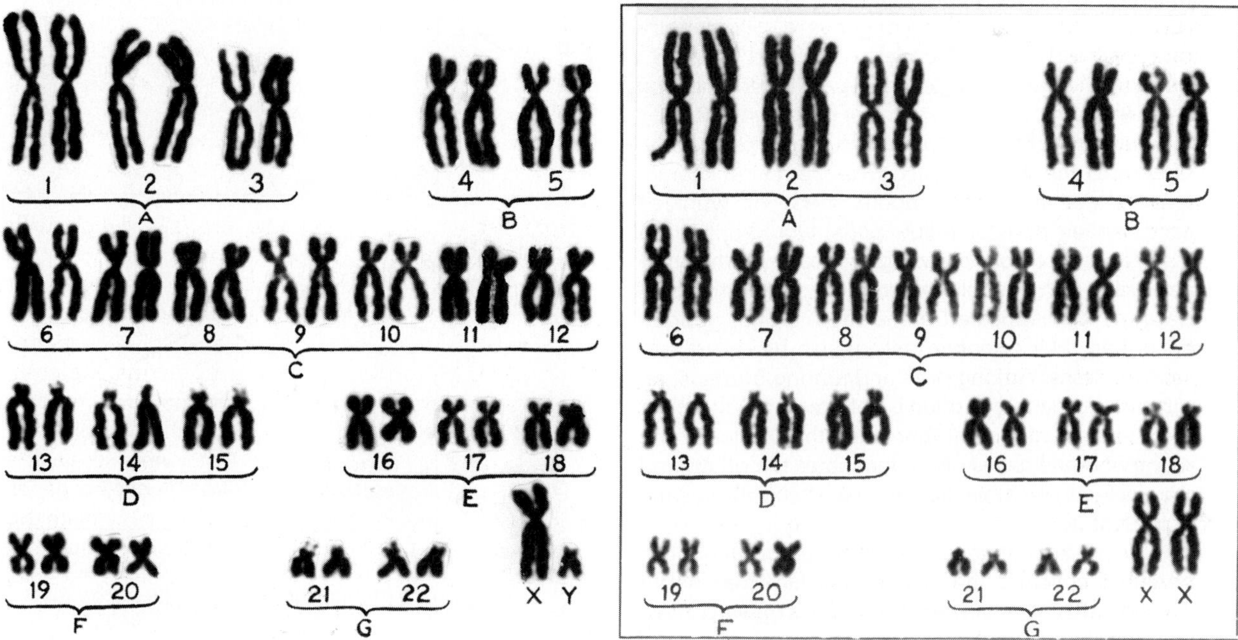

FIGURE 3.2 The male karyotype (left) shows the 22 pairs of autosomal chromosomes and the 2 sex chromosomes—an elongated X and a shorter Y chromosome. The photographic arrangement of a female's chromosomes (right) shows two X chromosomes.

We cannot emphasize this message enough: *Environmental factors influence how the messages specified by the genes are carried out.* Consider the genes that influence an individual's height. One's genetic makeup is called one's **genotype;** some people inherit genes calling for exceptional height while others inherit genes calling for a short stature. But genotype is different from **phenotype,** or the actual characteristic or trait a person eventually has (for example, a height of 5 feet 8 inches). The significant point here is that an individual whose genotype calls for exceptional height may or may not be tall. A child who is severely malnourished from the prenatal period on may have the genetic potential to be a basketball star but may well end up too short to make the team. So environmental influences combine with genetic influences to determine how a genotype is translated into a particular phenotype—the way a person actually looks, thinks, feels, and behaves.

Another way to approach the riddle of how genes influence us is to consider the major mechanisms of inheritance: the ways in which parents' genes influence their children's traits.

Mechanisms of Inheritance

There are three main mechanisms of inheritance: single gene-pair inheritance, sex-linked inheritance, and polygenic (or multiple gene) inheritance.

Single Gene-Pair Inheritance

Through **single gene-pair inheritance,** some human characteristics are influenced by only one pair of genes: one from the mother, one from the father. Although he knew nothing of genes, a 19th-century monk named Gregor Mendel contributed greatly to our knowledge of single gene-pair inheritance by cross-breeding different strains of peas and watching the outcomes. His major discovery was a predictable pattern to the way in which two alternative characteristics (for example, smooth seeds or wrinkled seeds, green pods or yellow pods) would appear in the offspring of cross-breedings. He called some characteristics (for example, smooth seeds) "dominant" because they appeared more often in later generations than their opposite traits, which he called "recessive" traits. Among peas and among humans, an offspring's phenotype often is not simply a "blend" of the characteristics of mother and father. Instead, one of the parental genes often dominates the other, and the child will resemble the parent who contributed the dominant gene.

As an illustration of the principles of Mendelian heredity, consider the remarkable fact that about three-fourths of us can curl our tongues upward into a tubelike shape, whereas one-fourth of us cannot. Although the ability to curl one's tongue is of dubious value, this trait is determined by a single gene pair. It happens that the gene associated with tongue curling is a **dominant gene.** A weaker gene calling for the absence of tongue-curling ability is said to be a **recessive gene.** The person who inherits one "tongue-curl" gene and one "no-curl" gene would be able to curl his or her tongue (that is, would have a tongue-curling phenotype) because the tongue-curl gene overpowers the no-curl gene.

Let's label the dominant, tongue-curl gene T and the recessive, no-curl gene t. We can now calculate the odds that parents with different genotypes for tongue curling would have children who can or cannot curl their tongues. Figure 3.3 shows two examples. In each part we see that a father will contribute one or the other of his two genes to a sperm, and the mother will contribute one or the other of her two genes to an ovum. Each child inherits one of the mother's genes and one of the father's, so the four cells of each grid represent the four possible kinds of children that two parents, given their genotypes, could have.

Part A of Figure 3.3 shows that dominant genes triumph over recessive genes. If a father with the ge-

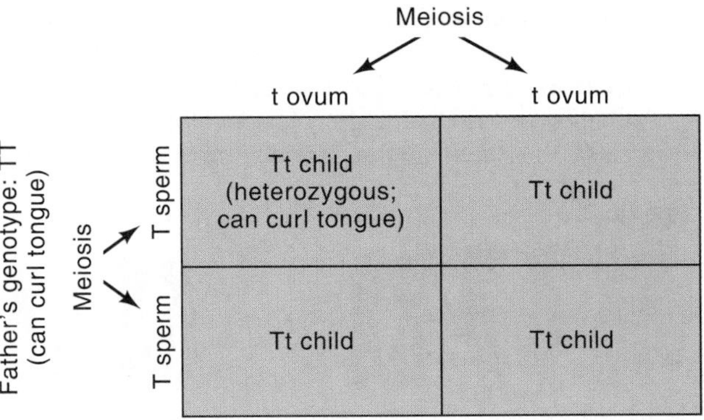

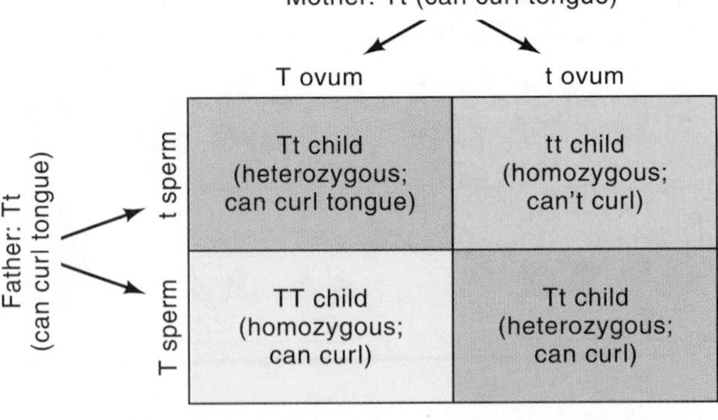

FIGURE 3.3 Two examples of the inheritance of the ability (or lack of ability) to curl one's tongue.

notype TT (a tongue-curler) and a mother with the genotype tt (lacking the ability to curl her tongue) have children, each and every child they produce will necessarily have one gene for tongue curling and one for a lack of tongue curling (genotype Tt). Because the tongue-curl gene dominates, we can say that this couple has a 100% chance of having a tongue-curling child. Notice that two different genotypes—TT and Tt—both make for the same phenotype: an acrobatic tongue.

Part B of Figure 3.3 tells us that a tongue-curling man and a tongue-curling woman can surprise everyone and have a child who lacks this talent. These two parents both have the Tt genotype. If the father's recessive gene and the mother's recessive gene happen to unite in the zygote, a non-tongue-curling child (with the genotype tt) will be born. The chances are 25%—one out of four—that this couple will have such a child. Of course, the laws of conception are much like the laws of cards. This couple could either beat the odds and have a whole family of non-tongue-curling children or have no such children at all. Since people who cannot curl their tongues must have the tt genotype, two non-tongue-curling parents will have only non-tongue-curling (tt) children.

Table 3.1 lists a number of other examples of dominant and recessive traits associated with single gene-pair inheritance. In truth, many of the physical characteristics in this table (such as eye color and hair color and curliness) are actually influenced by more than the workings of a single pair of genes. However, it turns out that many genetically linked diseases and defects are entirely due to inheriting two recessive genes, one from each parent. Consider a common example: **sickle-cell disease.**

Individuals with sickle-cell disease have sickle-shaped blood cells that tend to cluster together and distribute less oxygen through the circulatory system than normal cells do. People with this disease have great difficulty breathing and exerting themselves, experience painful swelling of their joints, and often die by adolescence from heart or kidney failure. About 9% of African Americans in the United States are heterozygous for this attribute (we'll call their genotype Ss); they carry one gene that calls for round blood cells and one that calls for sickle-shaped blood cells (Thompson, 1975). Such people are also called **carriers** of the sickle-cell disease because, although they do not have the disease, they can transmit the gene for it to their children. The child who inherits two recessive sickle-cell genes (ss) has sickle-cell disease. As Part B of Figure 3.3 shows, an Ss father and an Ss mother (two carriers) have a 25% chance of having a child with sickle-cell disease.

An interesting feature of the sickle-cell trait is that the dominant gene associated with round blood cells shows **incomplete dominance**—that is, it does not totally mask all the effects of the recessive sickle-cell

TABLE 3.1 Examples of dominant and recessive traits.

Dominant Traits	*Recessive Traits*
Brown eyes	Gray, green, hazel, or blue eyes
Dark hair	Blond hair
Nonred hair	Red hair
Curly hair	Straight hair
Normal vision	Nearsightedness
Farsightedness	Normal vision
Roman nose	Straight nose
Broad lips	Thin lips
Extra digits	Five digits
Double-jointedness	Normal joints
Pigmented skin	Albinism
Type A blood	Type O blood
Type B blood	Type O blood
Normal hearing	Congenital deafness
Normal blood cells	Sickle-cell disease*
Huntington's disease*	Normal physiology
Normal physiology	Cystic fibrosis*
Normal physiology	Phenylketonuria (PKU)*
Normal physiology	Tay-Sachs disease*

*This condition is discussed elsewhere in the chapter.

SOURCES: Data from Burns & Bottino (1989) and McKusick (1989).

gene. Thus carriers of the sickle-cell gene actually have many round blood cells and some sickle-shaped cells (see Figure 3.4). When they are at high altitudes, are given anesthesia, or are otherwise deprived of oxygen, carriers may experience symptoms of sickle-cell disease—very painful swelling of the joints and severe fatigue (Burns & Bottino, 1989). But under normal circumstances carriers do not experience these problems.

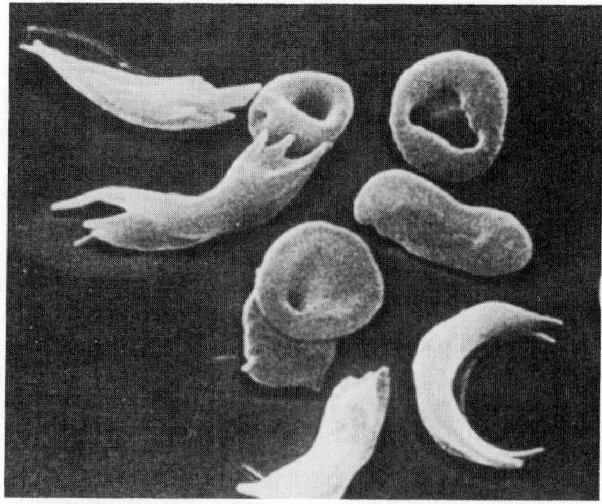

FIGURE 3.4 "Sickled" (elongated) and normal (round) blood cells from a carrier of the sickle-cell gene.

In still other cases of single gene-pair heredity, two distinct genes influence a trait but neither dominates the other. This is called **codominance** because the person's phenotype is an exact compromise between the two genes that he or she has inherited. For example, the genes for blood types A and B each dominate the gene for blood type O, but neither dominates the other. The person who inherits one of each has both A antigens and B antigens in his or her blood. If you have the blood type AB, you illustrate this principle of genetic codominance. Similarly, black/white interracial marriages often produce children with light-brown skin, a compromise between genes calling for heavily pigmented skin and genes calling for lightly pigmented skin. Single gene-pair inheritance is obviously a bit more complex than it looks at first glance.

Several genetic defects besides sickle-cell disease can be traced to a single pair of genes. Most of them are associated with recessive genes (we will examine some additional examples at the end of the chapter). All of us carry genes for several recessive genetic defects. However, there are more than 2000 such genes, and a couple will not be at risk for having a child with such a defect unless *both of them are carriers of the same defective gene.*

Why, then, do most societies have taboos against incest or laws against marriage between first cousins? It is because relatives who mate share a common genetic heritage and run an especially high risk that the defective genes they possess will be the *same ones* their relative possesses. Perhaps for this genetic reason, many species of animals have evolved in ways that enable them to recognize their relatives so they will not make the mistake of mating with them (Bateson, 1985).

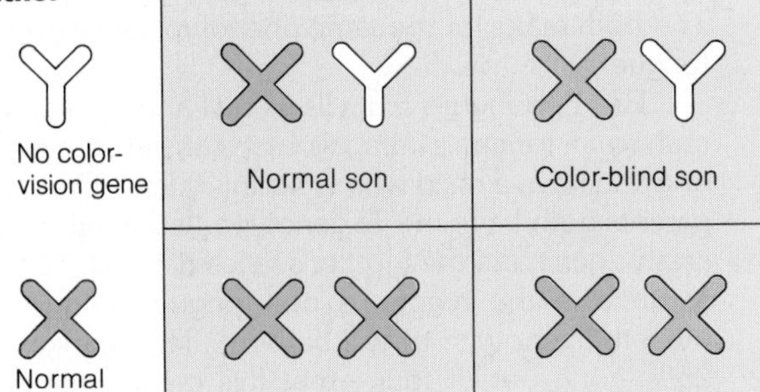

FIGURE 3.5 The workings of sex-linked inheritance of red/green color blindness. Notice that a son has a 50% chance of being color blind, whereas a daughter has a 0% chance. A girl will be color blind only if her father is color blind *and* her mother is at least a carrier of the color-blindness gene.

Sex-Linked Inheritance

Some traits are called **sex-linked characteristics** because they are influenced by single genes located on the sex chromosomes rather than on the other 22 pairs of chromosomes. Indeed, we could say "X-linked" rather than sex-linked because the vast majority of these sex-linked attributes are produced by genes located only on X chromosomes.

Let's ask why far more males than females display *red/green color blindness.* This inability to distinguish red and green is caused by a recessive gene that appears only on X chromosomes. If you'll recall, Y chromosomes are shorter than X chromosomes and have fewer genes. If a boy inherits the recessive color-blindness gene on his X chromosome, there is no color-vision gene on the Y chromosome that could potentially dominate the color-blindness gene. He will be color blind. By contrast, a girl who inherits the gene will usually have a normal color-vision gene on her other X chromosome that will dominate the color-blindness gene (see Figure 3.5). She would have to inherit two of the recessive color-blindness genes (one from each parent) to be color blind herself. Who, then, should a boy blame if he is color blind? Definitely his mother, for she is the source of his X chromosome. *Hemophilia,* a disease in which the blood's ability to clot is deficient, is also far more common among males than females because it too is associated with a gene on X chromosomes. Other sex-linked traits include the Duchenne type of muscular dystrophy and certain forms of deafness and night blindness.

Polygenic Inheritance

So far we have considered only the influence of single genes or gene pairs on human traits. However, most important human characteristics are influenced by *multiple* pairs of genes; that is, they are **polygenic traits.** Examples of polygenic traits include height and weight, intelligence, temperament, susceptibility to cancer, and a host of others (Plomin, 1990). Let's say that intelligence is influenced by three pairs of genes and that the gene pairs AA, BB, and CC would tend to make for genius, whereas the genotype aa bb cc would make for extremely low intelligence. Without going into the mathematics, there are 27 distinct genotypes that could result if we calculated all possible children that one couple of average intelligence (each with an Aa Bb Cc genotype, for example) could produce. Gene combinations that call for average intelligence would be more likely to occur than combinations associated with either very high or very low intelligence. When a trait is influenced by multiple genes, we would therefore expect many degrees of the trait in a population; we would also expect many people to be near the average and few to be extreme. This is exactly the way intelligence and most other measurable human traits are distributed in a large population.

We have no idea exactly how many gene pairs influence intelligence or other polygenic traits. At this point all we can say is that unknown numbers and combinations of genes, interacting with environmental factors, create a wide range of individual differences in most important human traits.

Mutations

We have now examined the three major mechanisms by which the genes inherited at conception influence traits: single gene-pair, sex-linked, and polygenic inheritance. Occasionally, however, a new gene appears out of nowhere; it is not passed on by a parent. A **mutation** is a change in the structure or arrangement of one or more genes that produces a new phenotype. Experts believe that the recessive gene for the sex-linked disorder hemophilia was first introduced into the royal families of Europe by Queen Victoria. Since no cases of hemophilia could be found in Queen Victoria's ancestry, the gene may have been a mutation that she then passed on to her offspring. New cases of hemophilia, then, can be due either to spontaneous mutations or to sex-linked inheritance. The odds that mutations will occur are increased by environmental hazards such as radiation, toxic industrial waste, and agricultural chemicals in food (Burns & Bottino, 1989).

Some mutations have beneficial effects and become more and more common in a population through the process of natural selection. The sickle-cell gene is a good example. It probably arose originally as a mutation but became more prevalent in Africa, Central America, and other tropical areas over many generations because it protected those who had it from malaria and allowed them to produce more children than people without the protective gene. Unfortunately, the sickle-cell gene is not advantageous (and can be harmful) in environments where malaria is no longer a problem. Thus mutations can be either beneficial or harmful, depending on their nature and on the environment in which their bearers live.

Chromosome Abnormalities

A final way in which genetic endowment can influence human characteristics is through the occurrence of **chromosome abnormalities** — cases in which a child receives too many or too few chromosomes (or abnormal chromosomes) at conception. Most chromosome abnormalities are due to errors in chromosome division during meiosis. Through an accident of nature, an ovum or sperm cell may be produced with more or fewer than the usual 23 chromosomes. In most cases a zygote with the wrong number of chromosomes is spontaneously aborted, but approximately 1 child in 200 is born with either more or, more rarely, fewer chromosomes than the normal 46 (Plomin, 1986).

One of the most familiar chromosome abnormalities is **Down syndrome**, a chromosome disorder also known as *trisomy 21* because children with it receive three rather than two 21st chromosomes. Children with Down syndrome have distinctive eyelid folds, short stubby limbs, and thick tongues (see Figure 3.6). They vary widely in their levels of intellectual functioning, but they are typically mentally retarded to some degree and therefore develop and learn at a slower pace than most children do.

What determines who has a Down syndrome child and who does not? Part of the answer is sheer chance. The errors in cell division responsible for Down syndrome can occur in any man or woman. However, the odds also increase dramatically as the age of the mother increases. The chances of having a baby with the syndrome are about 1 in 1000 for mothers under 30 but climb to as high as 1 in 25 for mothers age 45 or older (Pueschel & Goldstein, 1983). Mothers who have already borne one Down syndrome child have an even higher risk, presumably because they are more susceptible to producing defective eggs than most women are.

Why is the older woman at high risk for producing a child with chromosome abnormalities? Two explanations have been advanced. First, since ova

FIGURE 3.6 Children with Down syndrome can live rich lives if they receive appropriate educational opportunities and support.

actually begin to form during the prenatal period, it is possible that they degenerate and become abnormal over the years. Second, older women may have had more opportunities to become exposed to environmental hazards such as radiation, drugs, chemicals, and viruses that can damage ova. There is some support for both of these hypotheses (Strigini et al., 1990). Most cases of Down syndrome can be traced to the mother's egg, but one-fourth of these children received their extra 21st chromosome from their fathers rather than from their mothers (Magenis et al., 1977). A father's age has some bearing on the odds of a Down syndrome birth, but not nearly as much as the mother's age. The risk of such a birth is also greater if a father has been exposed to environmental hazards that can damage his chromosomes—for example, radiation associated with repeated abdominal X rays (Strigini et al., 1990).

Most other chromosome abnormalities involve cases in which a child receives either too many or too few sex chromosomes. These *sex chromosome abnormalities,* like Down syndrome, can be attributed mainly to errors in meiosis that become increasingly likely in older parents and parents whose chromosomes have been damaged by environmental hazards. One well-known example is **Turner syndrome,** in which a female (about 1 in 3000) is born with a single X chromosome (XO) in each of her cells. These girls remain small and often have stubby fingers and toes, a "webbed" neck, a broad chest, and underdeveloped breasts. They are unable to reproduce and typically favor traditionally feminine activities. Although they score about average on tests of verbal intelligence, their spatial and mathematical reasoning abilities are often deficient and they tend to underachieve in school (Downey et al., 1991).

Another example is **Klinefelter syndrome,** in which a male (1 in 200) is born with one or more extra X chromosomes (XXY). Klinefelter males tend to be tall and generally masculine in appearance, but they are sterile and at puberty develop feminine sex characteristics such as enlarged breasts. Most have normal general intelligence test scores, but many are below average in language skills and school achievement (Mandoki, Sumner, Hoffman, & Riconda, 1991).

We have now outlined the fundamentals of heredity. Each person has a unique genetic makeup, or genotype, contained in his or her 23 pairs of chromosomes. Combinations of the parents' genes are passed on at conception and influence people's traits (phenotypes) through the mechanisms of single gene-pair, sex-linked, and polygenic inheritance. A minority of individuals are also powerfully affected by genetic mutations or chromosome abnormalities. We turn our attention now to exploring the extent to which important psychological differences among humans are influenced by their hereditary endowments and their experiences.

STUDYING GENETIC AND ENVIRONMENTAL INFLUENCES

Behavioral genetics is the scientific study of the extent to which genetic and environmental differences among people or animals are responsible for differences in their traits (Plomin, DeFries, & McClearn, 1990). To behavioral geneticists it is impossible to say that one person's intelligence test score is the result of, say, 80%, 50%, or 20% heredity and the rest environment. The individual would have no intelligence at all without *both* a genetic makeup and experiences. However, behavioral geneticists do estimate the **heritability** of measured intelligence (IQ) and of other traits or behaviors. Heritability is the proportion of all the variability in a trait *within a large group of people* that can be linked to genetic differences among those individuals. To say that measured intelligence is "heritable" is to say that differences among people in their tested IQ scores are to some degree attributable to the fact that different individuals have different genes.

Individual differences in psychological traits are usually the product of both hereditary and environmental influences. When behavioral geneticists tell us that a trait is or is not heritable, they also tell us about the extent to which differences in experience create psychological or behavioral differences among people. They can, therefore, provide us with important evidence about the relative contributions of genetic and environmental factors to existing human differences (see Plomin, 1990). However, even when a trait proves to be highly heritable in a population, that does not in any way mean that the environment can have no impact on the trait or that special intervention programs are doomed to fail. Some children may currently be performing poorly on IQ tests partly because of their genetic makeup, but they can still be stimulated to higher levels of intellectual performance if their environment is improved (Scarr & Carter-Saltzman, 1983; Wachs, 1992).

To study the influence of genes on animal behavior, behavioral geneticists have set up breeding experiments. Studies of human genetics must examine resemblances between pairs of people who have a high or low degree of genetic relatedness.

Experimental Breeding of Animals

Deliberately manipulating the genetic makeup of animals to study genetic influences on behavior is much like what Gregor Mendel did to discover the workings of heredity in plants. One of the most commonly used breeding experiments is **selective breeding**—attempting to breed a trait selectively in animals. A classic example is R. C. Tryon's (1940) attempt to show that maze-learning ability is a heritable or genetically influenced attribute in rats. Tryon first tested a large number of rats for the ability to run a complex maze. Rats that made few errors were labeled "maze bright"; those that made many errors were termed "maze dull." Then, across several generations, Tryon mated bright rats with bright rats and dull rats with dull rats. If differences in experience rather than differences in genetic makeup had accounted for the initial differences between bright and dull rats, this selective breeding would have had no impact. Instead, across generations the differences in learning performance between the maze-bright and maze-dull groups of rats became increasingly larger. Tryon had shown that maze-learning ability in rats is influenced by genetic makeup.

Selective-breeding studies have also shown that genes contribute to such attributes as activity level, emotionality, aggressiveness, and sex drive in rats, mice, and chickens (Plomin, DeFries, & McClearn, 1990). Because people don't take kindly to the idea of being selectively bred by experimenters, research on genetic influence in humans relies instead on determining the extent to which people who are genetically similar are also psychologically similar.

Twin Studies

Twins have long been recognized as very important sources of evidence about the effects of heredity. One type of twin study involves determining whether identical twins reared together are more similar to each other in traits of interest than fraternal twins reared together. If genes matter, identical twins should be more similar, for they have 100% of their genes in common, whereas fraternal twins share only 50% on the average.

This method assumes that the environments experienced by identical twins are no more similar than those experienced by fraternal twins. Is that really a safe assumption? After all, identical twins are often dressed and treated alike. Yet there is little relationship between how similarly twins are treated and how similar they are, which suggests that the twin method is fundamentally sound (Loehlin, 1992; Lytton, 1977).

Today's most sophisticated twin studies include not only identical and fraternal twin pairs raised together but also identical and fraternal twins reared apart—four groups in all, differing in both the extent to which they share the same genes and the extent to which they share the same home environment. Identical twins separated near birth and brought up in very different environments—like the twins introduced at the beginning of the chapter— are particularly fascinating and informative in their own right, of course, because any similarities between them cannot be attributed to their common family experiences.

In the study of twins reared apart, a critical issue is whether their environments are actually different. If twins are separated early in life but are selectively placed into homes very similar to the one they left, any similarity in their psychological traits could be environmental rather than genetic in origin. Again, though, checks on this assumption suggest that the extent to which separated twins experience similar environments is largely unrelated to how similar the twins are psychologically (Bouchard et al., 1990).

Adoption Studies

Much can also be learned about heredity and environment by studying individuals who are adopted early in life. Are adopted children similar to their biological parents, whose genes they share, or are they similar to their adoptive parents, whose environment they share? If adopted children resemble their biological parents in intelligence or personality, even though those parents did not raise them, genes must be influential. If they resemble their adoptive parents, even though they are genetically unrelated to them, a good case can be made for environmental influence. Like the twin method, the adoption method has proven useful to researchers as a way to estimate the relative contributions of heredity and environment to individual differences.

Estimating the Contributions of Genes and Environment

Behavioral geneticists rely on some simple and some not so simple mathematical calculations to tell them whether or not a trait is genetically influenced and to estimate the degree to which heredity and environment can account for individual differences in the trait. When they study traits that a person either has or does not have (for example, a smoking habit or diabetes), researchers calculate and compare **concordance rates**—the percentage of pairs of people (for example, identical twins or adoptive parents and children) in which *both* members display the trait of interest if one member has it. Suppose we are interested in whether becoming a homosexual man is genetically influenced. We might locate gay men who have twins, either identical or fraternal, and then track down their twin siblings to determine whether they too are gay. In one study of this type (Bailey & Pillard, 1991), the concordance rate for identical twins was 52% (29 of the 56 co-twins of gay men were also gay), whereas the concordance rate for fraternal twins was 22% (12 of 54 co-twins were also gay). This finding suggests that genetic makeup does contribute to a man's sexual orientation. Since identical twins are *not* perfectly concordant, however, we can also conclude that their *experiences* must have something to do with how their sexual orientations evolve. After all, in 48% of the identical twin pairs, one twin was gay and the other was not, despite their identical genes.

When a trait can assume many values (for example, height or intelligence), *correlation coefficients* rather than concordance rates are calculated (see Chapter 1). In a behavioral genetics study of IQ scores, a correlation would indicate whether the IQ scores of twins are systematically related to the IQ scores of their co-twins, such that, if one twin is bright, the other is bright and, if one is not-so-bright, the other is not-so-bright. The larger the correlation for a group of twins, the closer the resemblance between members of each twin pair.

As we noted earlier, behavioral genetics studies have something to tell us about *both* genetic and environmental influences on development. Consider a hypothetical example. Suppose we give a scale measuring "social sensitivity" to many pairs of identical twins and fraternal twins, some pairs raised together, others separated near birth and raised apart. Hypothetical correlations, reflecting the degree of similarity between twins, are presented in Table 3.2. From such data, behavioral geneticists can estimate the contributions of three factors to individual differences in social sensitivity: genes, shared environmental influences, and nonshared environmental influences.

1. *Genes.* In our example, genetic influences are clearly evident, for identical twins are consistently more similar in social sensitivity than fraternal twins are. The correlation of +.50 for identical twins reared apart, in and of itself, also testifies to the importance of genetic makeup. If identical twins grow up in different families, any similarity in their psychological traits must be due to their genetic similarity. Thus these data suggest that social sensitivity is heritable; some of the variation in social sensitivity within the sample studied can be linked to variations in genetic endowment.

2. *Shared environmental influences.* **Shared environmental influences** are experiences that individuals living in the same home environment share and that work to make them similar to one another. As you can see from our hypothetical correlations, both identical and fraternal twins are more similar in social sensitivity if they are raised together than if they are raised apart. (Compare, for example, the .60 correlation for identical twins reared together to the .50 correlation for identical twins reared apart.) Growing up in the same family and neighborhood apparently makes twins somewhat more similar than they become if they grow up in different homes. Perhaps sets of twins who grow up with parents who strongly encourage sensitivity to other people become especially sensitive, whereas twin pairs who live with selfish, insensitive parents become highly insensitive themselves.

TABLE 3.2 Hypothetical correlations from a twin study of the heritability of social sensitivity.

	Raised Together	*Raised Apart*
Identical twin pairs	.60	.50
Fraternal twin pairs	.30	.20

An effect of *genes* is evident: .60 is greater than .30, and .50 is greater than .20. An effect of *shared environment* is evident: .60 is greater than .50, and .30 is greater than .20. And an effect of *nonshared environment* is evident: .60 is less than 1.00; if identical twins raised in the same home are not identically sensitive, the differences between them must be due to their unique, nonshared experiences.

3. *Nonshared environmental influences.* **Nonshared environmental influences** are experiences that are unique to the individual, that are *not* shared by other members of the family, and that make members of the same family different from one another (Rowe, 1993; Rowe & Plomin, 1981). Where is the evidence of nonshared environmental influence in Table 3.2? Notice that identical twins raised together are not perfectly similar, even though they share 100% of their genes and the same family environment; a correlation of +.60 is less than a perfect correlation of +1.00. Differences between identical twins raised together must be due to differences in their experiences. Perhaps identical twins are treated differently by their parents, friends, and teachers, or perhaps one twin seeks out or receives more social learning opportunities than the other, and this results in differences in their degrees of social sensitivity. Anyone who has a brother or sister can attest to the fact that different children in the same family are not always treated identically by their parents—and they do not have the same experiences outside the house either.

Consider once more the four possible correlations in Table 3.2. If *genes* were all that mattered, the correlations for identical twins would be +1.00 (regardless of whether they were raised together or apart) and the correlations for fraternal twins would be .50 (because they share 50% rather than 100% of their genes). If *shared environmental influences* were all that mattered, we would see correlations of +1.00 for both identical and fraternal twins raised together but no similarity at all (correlations of .00) between twins raised in different environments. Finally, if *nonshared environmental influences*, or unique experiences, were all that mattered, pairs of twins—whether identical or fraternal, raised together or raised apart—would be no more alike than pairs of strangers plucked at random from a street corner. Their characteristics would depend entirely on their idiosyncratic experiences in life, and all the correlations in the table would be .00. Keep these predictions in mind as we see what researchers have discovered about the actual contributions of genes, shared environment, and nonshared environment to the many similarities and differences among human beings.

GENES, ENVIRONMENT, AND INDIVIDUAL DIFFERENCES IN TRAITS

Information from twin and adoption studies has dramatically changed the way we think about human development, as we shall now see. We will sample what these studies say about the contributions of genes, shared environment, and nonshared environment to differences among people in intellectual abilities, aspects of personality, psychological problems, and aging (see Plomin, 1986, 1990, for excellent reviews).

Intellectual Abilities

How do genes and environment contribute to differences in intellectual functioning, and how do their relative contributions change over the life span? Consider the average correlations between the IQ scores of different types of relatives presented in Table 3.3. These averages are from a review by Thomas Bouchard and Matthew McGue (1981) of studies involving 526 correlations based on 113,942 pairs of children, adolescents, or adults. Clearly, these correlations become higher when pairs of people are more closely related genetically and are highest when the pairs are identical twins.

Can you also detect the workings of environment? Notice that (1) pairs of family members reared together are somewhat more similar in IQ than pairs reared apart; (2) fraternal twins, who should have especially similar family experiences because they grow up at the same time, are often more alike than siblings born at different times; and (3) the IQs of adopted children are related to those of their adoptive parents. All of these findings suggest that *shared environmental influences* tend to make individuals who live together in the same family somewhat more alike than they would be if they lived separately. Notice too, though, that identical twins reared together, who share the same genetic makeup and the same family environment, are not perfectly similar. This is evidence that their unique or *nonshared* experiences have made them different from each other.

Because the correlations in Table 3.3 are averages based on studies of children and studies of adults, they do not tell us whether the contributions of genes and environment to differences in intellectual ability change over the life span. Could it be that genes are important early but that individual differences in experiences at home, in school, and elsewhere increasingly account for differences among us in intellectual performance as we get older? Sensible as that sounds, it does not seem to be the case. Genes actually appear to become *more* rather than less important with age as a contributor to similarities and differences in intellectual performance (McCartney, Harris, & Bernieri, 1990).

TABLE 3.3 Average correlations between the intelligence scores of different pairs of individuals.

	Reared Together	*Reared Apart*
Identical twins	.86	.72
Fraternal twins	.60	.52
Biological siblings	.47	.24
Biological parent and child	.42	.22
Half-siblings	.31	—
Adopted siblings	.34	—
Adoptive parent and adopted child	.19	—

Note: All but one of these averages were calculated by Bouchard and McGue (1981) based on studies of both children and adults. The correlation for fraternal twins reared apart was based on data reported by Pedersen, McClearn, Plomin, and Friberg (1985).

Consider a longitudinal study of the intellectual development of identical and fraternal twins from infancy to adolescence conducted by Ronald Wilson (1978, 1983). Identical twins scored no more similarly than fraternal twins on a measure of infant mental development during the first year of life. Generally, neither differences in genetic makeup nor differences in experience account very well for the many behavioral and psychological differences among very young infants (Plomin, 1986). This may be due to the workings of species heredity; all infants share a powerful maturational program that channels them along the same course of development, despite their unique hereditary endowments and despite variations in their early life experiences (McCall, 1981).

However, in Wilson's study the influence of individual heredity began to show itself at about 18 months of age. Now the correlation between the mental development scores of identical twins was higher than the correlation between the scores obtained by fraternal twins. Moreover, at about this same age the profiles of change from one testing to the next became more similar for identical twins than for fraternal twins. If one identical twin had a big spurt in mental development between 18 and 24 months of age, the other twin was likely to show the same spurt at the same time. Importantly, then, the *course* of mental development was shown to be genetically influenced.

Figure 3.7 shows what happened as these twins continued to develop. Identical twins stayed highly similar throughout childhood and into adolescence (the average correlation between the IQ scores of identical twins was about .85). Meanwhile, fraternal twins were most similar in IQ at about age 3 and became *less* similar over the years. By age 15 the correlation between their IQ scores dropped to .54. During childhood, identical twins' IQ scores also continued to change in similar directions at similar times. By contrast, members of fraternal twin pairs took their own distinct developmental paths, guided in part by their different genetic makeups. As a result, the heritability of IQ scores in this sample actually increased from the infant years to adolescence.

A similar message comes from adoption studies. The intellectual performance of adopted children is correlated with the intellectual performance of both

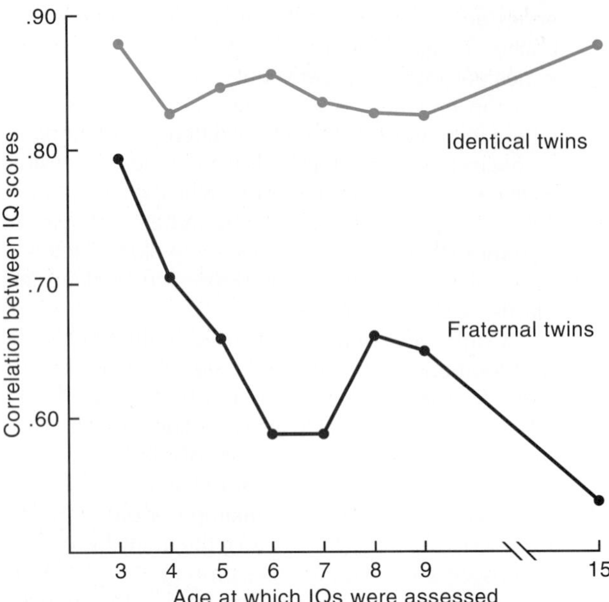

FIGURE 3.7 Changes in the correlations between the IQ scores of identical and fraternal twins over childhood. (Data from Wilson, 1983.)

their biological parents (suggesting effects of genetic makeup) and their adoptive parents (suggesting effects of family environment). By adolescence the resemblance to biological parents remains evident, but adopted children no longer resemble their adoptive parents intellectually (Scarr & Weinberg, 1978). This is true even though we might expect highly intelligent adoptive parents to provide more intellectually stimulating homes for adolescents than less intellectually inclined adoptive parents do.

In sum, *shared environmental influences* on intelligence test performance become less significant as children get older (Dunn & Plomin, 1990; McCartney et al., 1990). Why? Very possibly, it is because children raised in the same home become more independent of their parents as they get older and increasingly go their own ways, becoming influenced by environmental factors outside the home such as the peer groups they join and the teachers they have in school (Scarr & Weinberg, 1978). These *nonshared environmental influences* on intellectual development—influences unique to the individual and not shared by other family members—become more significant with age from infancy to adolescence, as does the influence of individual heredity.

Do the relative contributions of genetic makeup and environment to individual differences in intellectual functioning change in adulthood? Not really. Thomas Bouchard and his colleagues (1990) reported a correlation of +.69 between the IQ scores obtained by pairs of identical twins reared apart and reunited in middle age. This suggests that genetic influences on intellectual performance are still very evident in middle adulthood; however, the correlation is not a perfect +1.00, and some identical twin pairs differ considerably in IQ due to the effects of *nonshared* experiences. Identical twins continue to perform more similarly on IQ tests than fraternal twins do in old age (Kallmann & Jarvik, 1959). What's more, if one identical twin experiences a major drop in intellectual performance in later life, the other twin often does too (Jarvik & Bank, 1983). Overall, it now appears that at least 50% of the variability in IQ scores among individuals can be credited to genetic differences among these individuals (Chipuer, Rovine, & Plomin, 1990). The remaining half can be attributed to differences in their life experiences.

A common mistake is to interpret evidence of the heritability of IQ scores as evidence that we cannot improve the developing person's intellectual functioning by enriching his or her environment. This is absolutely not the case. Even though the IQs of adopted children are ultimately correlated more strongly with the IQs of their biological parents than with the IQs of their adoptive parents, the *level* of intellectual performance that these children reach can still increase dramatically if they are adopted into intellectually stimulating homes. For example, Sandra Scarr and Richard Weinberg (1976, 1983; Weinberg, Scarr, & Waldman, 1992) have studied disadvantaged African-American children adopted into the homes of white, middle-class, highly educated parents. These children's IQs were positively correlated with measures of the intellectual abilities of their biological parents, indicating once more that IQ is heritable. At the same time, though, these children as a group scored about 20 points higher on IQ tests than would be expected if they had remained in the lower socioeconomic environments provided by their biological parents. Their actual IQ scores, in other words, were closer in value to those of their adoptive parents than to those of their biological parents. Possibly, then, providing children with stimulating home environments helps them realize whatever genetically based potential they have (Wilson, 1983).

In sum, about half of the variation in the scores individuals obtain on IQ tests, and tests of a number of more specific mental abilities as well, can be tied to differences in genetic makeup (Plomin, 1990). Although experiences shared by members of the same family appear to be influential in childhood, the most important environmental influences in the long run are *nonshared,* or unique to the individual, and tend to make brothers and sisters different from each other rather than similar.

Temperament and Personality

As parents well know, different babies have different personalities. In trying to describe infant personality, researchers have focused on aspects of **tempera-**

ment: tendencies to respond in predictable ways that can be considered the building blocks of later personality. (See Chapter 10 for a fuller discussion of temperament.) Although different researchers have defined infant temperament in different ways, one useful scheme (Buss & Plomin, 1984) focuses on individual differences in *emotionality* (the tendency to become upset by events), *activity* (the infant's typical vigor and pace of behavior), and *sociability* (a preference to be with others versus a tendency toward shyness and withdrawal).

At birth it's difficult to detect influences of individual heredity on babies' temperaments. Twins are similar in such traits as irritability, but this is apparently due to environmental factors, for identical twins are no more similar than fraternal twins (Riese, 1990). Individual genetic makeup shows itself more and more as infants get older (Loehlin, 1992). In their longitudinal study of twins, for example, Ronald Wilson and Adam Matheny (1986) found that identical twin infants were more similar than fraternal twin infants in emotionality—in whether they were easily upset and irritable or happy and animated, as reported by their parents and as observed in the laboratory. This became evident only during the second year of life. After 1 year of age, identical twins also showed similar ups and downs in emotional tone from testing to testing, much as they show similar patterns of mental growth. Meanwhile, fraternal twins were beginning to take their own distinct developmental paths and were becoming *less* similar.

Genes also help to create individual differences in the aspect of temperament called sociability. For example, identical twins are more alike than fraternal twins in the extent to which they show negative emotional reactions when a stranger approaches them (Goldsmith & Campos, 1986), and adopted infants who are shy tend to have biological parents who are relatively shy as well (Plomin & DeFries, 1985). An infant's activity level, whether rated by parents or actually measured with a motion recorder, is also genetically influenced (Saudino & Eaton, 1991).

In a review of twin studies of these three aspects of temperament in infancy and beyond, Arnold Buss and Robert Plomin (1984) reported average correlations for pairs of identical twins of .63 for emotionality, .62 for activity, and .53 for sociability. The corresponding correlations for fraternal twins were not much greater than zero. Think about that: A zero correlation is what you would expect if these children were pairs of strangers living in different homes rather than twins who share half of their genes and the same home! It does not seem to matter whether we look at fraternal twin pairs or ordinary siblings or unrelated children adopted into the same family; living in the same home does little to make children similar in many aspects of personality (Ahern et al., 1982; Dunn & Plomin, 1990). *Nonshared* environmental factors have at least as much to do with individual differences in temperament as genes do, though (Braungart, Plomin, DeFries, & Fulker, 1992; Goldsmith & Campos, 1986).

Similar conclusions have been reached about the contributions of genes and environment to adult personality. Much of the attention has centered on two broad and important personality dimensions. One is **extraversion/introversion,** or the extent to which a person is outgoing and socially oriented or shy, retiring, and uncomfortable around other people—a trait dimension that corresponds closely to the dimension of early temperament called sociability. The second is **neuroticism,** or the extent to which a person is psychologically stable or unstable, anxious, and easily upset—a trait that can be likened to the aspect of infant temperament called emotionality.

In a large-scale study of twins in Sweden, correlations reflecting the likenesses between identical twin pairs on these two traits were around .50 (Floderus-Myrhed, Pedersen, & Rasmuson, 1980). Obviously, identical genes do not make for identical personalities; the unique experiences of identical twins must have contributed to differences in their levels of extraversion and neuroticism. However, the correlations for fraternal twins were quite low (about .20), suggesting that adult personality, like infant temperament, is genetically influenced (see also Rose et al., 1988). Overall, it has been estimated that, of all the differences among adults in major dimensions of personality, about 40% of the variation may be due to genetic differences (Loehlin, 1985). Only 5% of the variation reflects the effects of shared family environment—ways in which living in the same home makes children similar to each other and different from children in other families. Identical twins are about as similar in personality when they are raised apart all their lives as when they grow up in the same home (Bouchard et al., 1990). Finally, the remaining 55% of the variability in adult personalities is due largely to nonshared environmental influences—experiences that are not shared with other family members. (See Figure 3.8.)

Contributions to personality of both genes and nonshared environmental influences remain evident even in later life, although genetic contributions may become somewhat weaker (Loehlin, 1992). For instance, elderly identical twins, even those separated all their lives, continue to be more alike than fraternal twins in sociability, emotionality, and activity level (Plomin et al., 1988). We are probably safe in concluding that there is no point in adulthood at which one's genetic makeup ceases to affect one's psychological characteristics—just as there is no point at which the effects of life experiences cease to matter.

The big question raised by behavioral genetics findings of this sort is this (Dunn & Plomin, 1990): Why do fraternal twins and other biological brothers

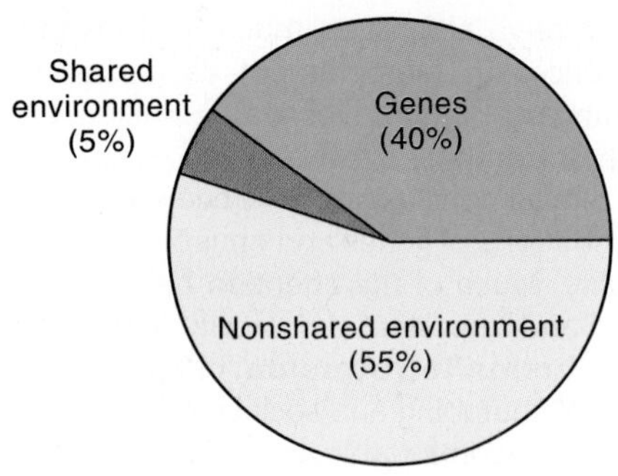

FIGURE 3.8 Estimated contributions of genes, shared environment, and nonshared environment to individual differences in personality.

and sisters, despite sharing 50% of their genes and growing up in the same home, have such very different personalities? On average, the correlation between their scores on personality scales is only .15 (Dunn & Plomin, 1990). It is becoming increasingly clear that siblings simply do not have the same experiences, even though they are raised by the same parents in the same home in the same neighborhood. They are treated differently by their parents, they experience their relationships with one another differently, and they often go their separate ways outside the home as well (Dunn & Plomin, 1990).

Herein lies a very significant message: The family environment *is* important in personality development, but not because it has some standard effect on all family members that makes them alike. True, there are some areas of socialization in which parents treat all their children similarly and contribute to similarities among them (Hoffman, 1991). For example, they may model and seek to foster the same moral, religious, and political values, attitudes, and interests in all their children. For these and many other psychological characteristics, shared environmental influences are often as important as genes in creating similarities among brothers and sisters (Hoffman, 1991; Plomin, 1990). Yet behavior geneticists are discovering that the family environment is also important because it creates *differences* among family members (Dunn & Plomin, 1990; Rowe, 1993). When it comes to the shaping of many basic personality traits, *nonshared* environmental influences—interacting with genetic influences—seem to be most significant. As we see in Box 3.2, researchers are now trying to learn more about how differences in the experiences of brothers and sisters might actually be contributing to differences in their personalities.

Psychological Problems

Both genes and environment also contribute to psychological problems across the life span. For example, some children, due to the genes they inherited at conception, are predisposed to be *hyperactive;* they are likely to be irritable infants and to have difficulty paying attention in school (Morrison & Stewart, 1973; Stevenson, 1992; see also Chapter 16 on *attention deficit disorder with hyperactivity*). Similarly, genes may predispose a child to be a bully and to get in trouble at school (O'Connor, Foch, Sherry, & Plomin, 1980), or to be highly fearful of such things as animals, accidents, and the unknown (Stevenson, Batten, & Cherner, 1992). And genes contribute to the tendency to engage in delinquent behavior as an adolescent (Rowe, 1983): The correlation between the rates of delinquent behavior reported by identical twins (.71) is higher than that for fraternal twin pairs (.47). The fact that identical twins are not perfectly similar in any of these problem behaviors tells us again that nonshared or unique experiences are important. However, shared environmental influences matter too; for instance, even fraternal twins show similar levels of delinquent behavior and, indeed, often carry out their misdeeds together (Rowe, 1983).

In short, we now know that children may inherit predispositions to develop a number of problems and disorders and that children's experiences, interacting with their genetic makeup, have a good deal of impact on how well adjusted they turn out to be. One implication is clear: It is overly simple and often wrong to assume that any behavior problem a child displays must be the result of "bad" parenting.

Now consider a psychological disorder of adulthood, **schizophrenia.** Schizophrenia is a serious mental illness that involves disturbances in logical thinking, emotional expression, and social behavior and that typically emerges in late adolescence or early adulthood. The average concordance rate (instances in which both twins have schizophrenia if one twin does) for identical twins averages about 46% across studies, whereas the concordance rate for fraternal twins is only 14% (Gottesman & Shields, 1982). In addition, children who have one or more biological parent who is schizophrenic have an increased risk of schizophrenia, even if they are adopted away early in life (Heston, 1970). Thus it is genes, not the unusual family environment that a schizophrenic parent might provide, that place the children of schizophrenics at risk.

But let's put this evidence of the heritability of schizophrenia in perspective. It is easy to mistakenly conclude that any child of a schizophrenic is doomed to become a schizophrenic. The rate of schizophrenia in the general population is about 1%. By comparison, about 10–14% of children who have one schizophrenic parent develop schizophrenic symptoms themselves (Kessler, 1975). Although this figure does suggest that children of schizophrenics are at greater risk for schizophrenia than other children, notice that

BOX 3.2 Mom Always Liked You Best: Nonshared Environmental Influences in the Family

Whenever he was irritated at his brother, Tommy Smothers of the comedy team the Smothers Brothers had a standard comeback: "Mom always liked you best!" If you think back to your own family experiences, you, too, may recall ways in which your parents treated you and your brothers or sisters differently. You may also recall that you and your siblings had lopsided relationships, with one more dominant or one more giving, and that you and your siblings traveled in different circles outside the home. Adolescent brothers and sisters do indeed report that they have very different experiences (Daniels & Plomin, 1985; Dunn & Stocker, 1989).

What's more, differences in the experiences of siblings are systematically associated with differences in their personalities. Denise Daniels (1986), for example, surveyed biological and adoptive sibling pairs ranging in age from 12 to 18 about the extent to which their relationships with their parents, siblings, and peers were similar or different. For instance, they were asked whether their mother had been more strict with them, more strict with their sibling, or equally strict with both of them. These adolescents also completed several personality scales.

The more different the experiences of sibling pairs were, the more different their personality traits were. For example, the sibling in a pair who was more emotional than the other also experienced more antagonism and jealousy in the sibling relationship, and the sibling who was more sociable experienced more sibling closeness and belonged to more popular peer groups. Moreover, the adolescent who experienced more affection from his or her father had higher vocational aspirations than the sibling who experienced less paternal love.

In another study, Laura Baker and Denise Daniels (1990) asked identical and fraternal twins ranging in age from 18 to 75 to recall their childhood experiences. Again, siblings who reported the greatest differences in experience were likely to be the most different in personality. Here the twin who reported that his or her mother had been stricter was likely to be more depressed and to have a lower sense of well-being than his or her co-twin. And, as in the study by Daniels (1986), the twin who affiliated with a more popular peer group as a youth was more outgoing as an adult. Interestingly, twins generally agreed (though by no means perfectly) about which twin had the better or worse time of it; it was rare for both to feel shortchanged or for both to feel favored.

Although correlational studies of this sort cannot firmly establish that differences in experience *cause* differences in personality, they do suggest that some of the most important environmental influences on development may be nonshared experiences unique to each member of the family (Dunn & Plomin, 1990). This is a tremendously important insight. Developmentalists have long assumed that parents treat all their children much the same and steer them along similar developmental paths—that shared environmental influences within the family are what matter most in the developmental process. Increasingly, this appears to be a wrong assumption. Instead, it seems sounder to assume that different children in the same family experience *different* relationships with their mothers and fathers—and with siblings, peers, grandparents, teachers, coaches, and pets, for that matter. If we can learn more about the unique experiences of children growing up in the same home, we are likely to learn a good deal about which experiences contribute most to healthy development.

86–90% of the children of one schizophrenic parent *do not* develop the disorder. Even if you are an identical twin whose co-twin develops the disorder, the odds are only about 1 in 2 that you too will become schizophrenic. Clearly an individual's experiences must also be an important contributor to this mental illness. People do not inherit psychological disorders; instead, they inherit *predispositions* to develop disorders. Assuming that a person has inherited a genetic susceptibility to schizophrenia, it may take one or more stressful experiences (for example, hostile, rejecting parents; an abusive marriage) to trigger the illness.

The same can be said for the many other problems of adulthood that appear to have some genetic basis. For instance, some men and women inherit a predisposition to become involved in criminal behavior, though not all of them actually become criminals (Baker, Mack, Moffitt, & Mednick, 1989; Carey, 1992). Similarly, heredity contributes to predispositions toward alcohol and drug abuse, depression and other affective disorders, eating disorders such as anorexia nervosa, and a number of other psychological disorders, but it hardly makes those problems inevitable (Plomin, 1990).

More and Less Heritable Traits

You may have the impression by now that individual differences in virtually any human trait one cares to examine are significantly influenced by genes. Although there is truth to this, some traits are more heritable than others. Observable physical characteristics—from eye color to height—are very strongly associated with individual genetic endowment (Plomin, 1990). Even weight is heritable; adopted children resemble their biological parents but not their adoptive parents in weight, and identical twins are quite similar in weight, whether they grow up together or apart (Grilo & Pogue-Geile, 1991). Certain aspects of physiology are highly heritable, too. For example, identical twins have strikingly similar patterns of measured brain activity, about as similar as readings taken from the same brain at different times

(Lykken, Tellegen, & Iacono, 1982). Their bodies also react much the same to alcohol (Martin et al., 1985; Neale & Martin, 1989).

The fact that individual differences in these physical and physiological characteristics are strongly heritable does *not* necessarily mean that environmental forces have no effect on them. If, for example, one identical twin were well fed and the other starved throughout life, the first twin would be taller than the second. Saying that height is a heritable trait means only that the differences among individuals in a group of people studied—people who have grown up in whatever environments they have grown up in—can be accounted for to some extent by differences in their genetic makeups.

If physical and physiological characteristics can be described as strongly heritable, general intelligence seems to be moderately heritable. As we saw, about half of the variability among people in tested intelligence can be traced to genetic endowment and the other half to differences in experience. Somewhat less influenced by genes are aspects of temperament and personality and susceptibility to a number of psychological disorders; here genetic differences may account for about 40% of the variability among people, environmental factors for the remainder. Finally, it has become clear that genetic endowment modestly influences even attitudes and interests—for example, a person's vocational interests and degree of commitment to his or her religion, though not what that religion is (Bouchard et al., 1990). Figure 3.9 presents some of the correlations obtained in the Minnesota Twin Study between the traits of identical twins raised apart and reunited later in life. It is clear that heredity influences physical traits more than psychological ones, but a broad range of psychological traits are heritable to some extent.

Is there any trait that is *not* influenced by heredity? From one perspective, we should answer "no." *All* human traits depend on having both a genotype and an environment. In this sense, genes and environment are both "100% important" (Hebb, 1970). But it is also the case that individual differences in some traits seem to have little relationship to genetic endowment. For example, identical twins are not much more alike with respect to how well or how poorly they perform on tests of creativity than fraternal twins are (Plomin, 1990; Reznikoff et al., 1973). Twins of both types are similarly creative (or uncreative), but their similarity is apparently related to their shared experiences in the family. Thus some mental abilities are more heritable than others are.

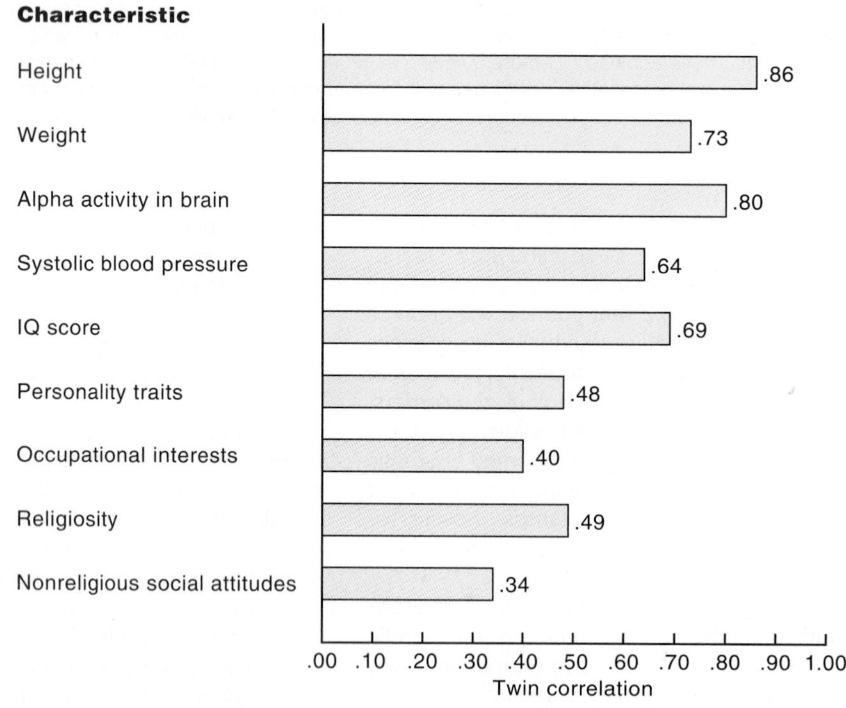

FIGURE 3.9 Correlations between the traits of identical twins raised apart in the Minnesota Twin Study. The number of pairs of twins on which a correlation is based ranges from 31 to 56, depending on the quality being measured. Correlations for personality traits, occupational interests, and so on are average correlations based on administering multiple self-report scales to twins. (Adapted from Bouchard et al., 1990.)

Moreover, genes influence some aspects of personality more than others. Genes seem to have a good deal to do with how sociable or extraverted or emotional or neurotic a person is. However, having a "masculine" or "feminine" self-concept and being able to tolerate ambiguous situations are not as heritable (Loehlin, 1982). Finally, many social and political attitudes seem to be more heavily influenced by life experiences than by genetic makeup (Loehlin & Nichols, 1976; Truett et al., 1992). Thus the balance of genetic and environmental contributions to human diversity is somewhat different for different traits.

Genes, Environment, and Aging

Some people age and die much earlier than others. What can behavioral genetics research tell us about influences on aging? Many years ago, Franz Kallmann and Gerhard Sander (1949) repeatedly assessed both identical and fraternal twins as they aged and discovered that identical twins show visible signs of aging—graying and thinning of the hair, wrinkling, physical disabilities—at similar times. Identical twins are also more similar than fraternal twins in self-reported health and in the extent to which they suffer from chronic illnesses, even when they were separated early in life and brought up in different environments (Harris et al., 1992). Moreover, the identical twins in the Kallmann study died 4 years apart, on average, whereas the fraternal twins died 5½ years apart (Kallmann & Jarvik, 1959). This finding suggests that individual genetic makeup, perhaps by influencing one's susceptibility to major diseases, has a bearing on how long a person lives. Life events such as HIV infection or a car accident can change one's odds considerably, of course.

It seems quite likely that there is also a *specieswide* genetic program that calls for *all of us* to age and die. The maximum human life span is somewhere between 110 and 120 years, and it has not changed much over history, despite improvements in living conditions and health care that have increased the average length of life. Gerontologists agree that there must be some genetic basis for aging and dying; the only puzzle is what it is. No specific "aging genes" have yet been identified. It could be that there are no such genes and that, instead, the genetic program that maintains life may simply run out (McClearn & Foch, 1985).

Researchers hope eventually to discover the genetic basis of aging and death by studying genetic defects that produce the symptoms of aging early in life. Certainly one of the most frightening of these disorders is **progeria**, a syndrome that involves premature aging starting in infancy (see Figure 3.10). As F. L. DeBusk (1972) describes the condition, growth slows down starting in infancy, hair loss and balding occur,

Identical twins age similarly, as retired dentists Leon (left) and Leo (right) Viall illustrate.

the skin becomes covered with "age spots," joints stiffen, fat is lost, and bones degenerate and become fragile. Victims die on the average at age 13—some as early as 7, some as late as 27—often from the heart diseases that strike elderly people. Progeria appears to be associated with a single dominant gene that arises as a new mutation in each case of the disease (Brown, 1985).

Although research on progeria may tell us something about the genetics of aging, this disease does not perfectly mimic the normal aging process (Brown, 1985; Mills & Weiss, 1990). For example, victims' bodies certainly age, but their nervous systems show none of the deterioration that occurs in many older adults very late in life. It is as if the normally developing mind of a child were trapped in the deteriorating body of an aged adult. The chromosomal abnormality Down syndrome may more closely mimic aging (Brown, 1985). Individuals with Down syndrome show several symptoms of premature aging, including early graying and loss of hair, cardiovascular problems, and the early onset of *Alzheimer's disease*—the degenerative brain disease that is the leading cause of "senility." As we will see in Chapter 16, some cases of this disease can be traced to a dominant gene on Chromosome 21, the same chromosome that people with Down syndrome have in triplicate.

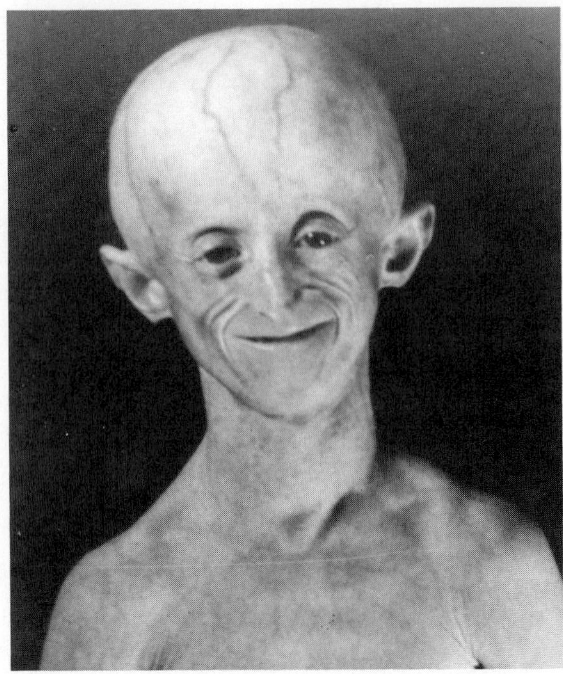

FIGURE 3.10 Progeria. This boy was a roly-poly, normal infant at 10 months but soon began to show the symptoms of premature aging associated with progeria. Fortunately, only about 1 in 8 million people has this genetic disorder.

None of the disorders that trigger premature aging includes *all* of the symptoms of normal aging, but it is possible that increased understanding of *several* of these "early aging" disorders will eventually help us unravel a very great mystery—why we age and die. There is no question that our human genes contribute to these final "developments," but there are many questions left unanswered about how they do so.

A LIFE-SPAN PERSPECTIVE ON HEREDITY AND ENVIRONMENT

What should we conclude overall about the influences of genes and environment and about the ways in which these two great forces in development conspire to make us what we are? Let's try to tie things together.

Genes and Environment Are at Work over the Entire Life Span

It should be clear that genes do not just orchestrate our growth before birth and then leave us alone. Instead, they are "turning on" and "turning off" in patterned ways throughout the life span, and they are partly responsible for attributes and behavior patterns that we carry with us throughout our lives. Our shared species heredity makes us similar in the way we develop and age. Our unique individual genetic makeups cause us to develop and age in our own special ways. Similarly, environmental influences impinge on us from conception to death.

As we have also seen, the extent to which individual differences in traits can be attributed to genetic makeup, shared environmental influences, and nonshared environmental influences is greater at some points of the life span than at others. Most likely because of strong specieswide maturational forces in early infancy, identical twins are often no more similar than fraternal twins at first. Later in infancy, and increasingly through childhood and adolescence, children's unique genetic blueprints seem to show themselves more and more in their behavior; identical twins remain similar, but fraternal twins, like brothers and sisters generally, go their own ways and become more and more dissimilar. Although we need to know more about the behavioral genetics of old age, there seems to be little change over the adult years in the proportions of variation among us that can be linked to differences in our genetic makeups or environments.

Meanwhile, shared environmental influences—the forces that make children in the same family alike—are stronger early in life than they are later in life (McCartney et al., 1990). Nonshared environmental influences—those unique experiences that make members of the same family *different*—often tend to be more important than the shared environmental influences that make siblings similar. They remain important, along with genetic endowment, throughout the life span. In short, as we move out of the home and into the larger world, we seem to become, more and more, products of our unique genes and our unique experiences.

Genes and Environment Interact

The goal of much of the research discussed in this chapter has been to establish how much of the variation we observe in human traits (such as intelligence) can be attributed to individual differences in genetic makeup and how much can be attributed to individual differences in experience. Useful as that research is, it does not take us very far in understanding the complex interplay between genetic and environmental influences over the life span. As Ann Anastasi (1958) asserted many years ago, instead of asking how much is due to genes and how much is due to environment, we should be asking *how* heredity and environment interact to make us what we are.

It is clear that genes do not *determine* anything; instead, they provide us with potential that is realized or not depending on the quality of our experiences. Figure 3.11 illustrates this view. We see evidence that genetic endowment matters: Children with high genetic potential to be intelligent will generally outperform children with below-average potential on IQ

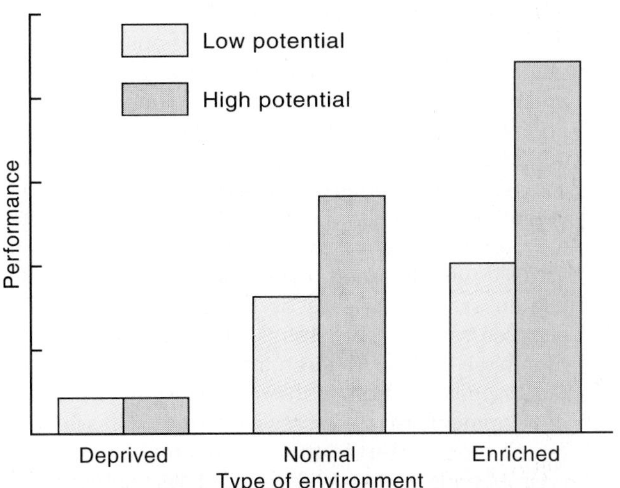

FIGURE 3.11 An example of a gene/environment interaction. The effect of whether a child has high or low genetic potential depends on what kind of environment he or she is raised in. By the same token, the effect of the environment on a child depends on his or her genetic endowment.

tests. It is equally clear that environment matters: Regardless of their genetic potential, children generally obtain higher IQ scores if they are brought up in enriched, intellectually stimulating environments than if they are raised in restricted, intellectually impoverished ones.

The most important message in the figure, however, is embodied in the concept of **gene/environment interaction:** *How our genotypes are expressed depends on what kind of environment we experience, and how we respond to the environment depends on what kind of genes we have.* In Figure 3.11 we see that growing up in a deprived environment can make children with the genes to be geniuses perform as poorly as children with far less genetic potential, even though this high-potential genotype will be expressed as far more intelligent behavior if children are brought up in more stimulating environments. Also, children with high genetic potential are more able than children with low genetic potential to benefit from enriching experiences, although both groups of children benefit to some extent. It works both ways: The effect of one's genes depends on one's environment, and the effect of one's environment depends on one's genes.

Genes and Environment Are Correlated

Appreciating that genes and environment interact is a good start, but heredity and environment are even more intimately intertwined than the concept of gene/environment interaction implies. Each person's genetic makeup influences the kinds of experiences that he or she seeks out and actually has, and these experiences then strengthen or weaken genetically based tendencies.

Sandra Scarr and Kathleen McCartney (1983), drawing on the theorizing of Plomin, DeFries, and Loehlin (1977), have proposed three kinds of **gene/environment correlations,** or ways in which one's genes and one's environment are systematically interrelated: passive, evocative, and active genotype/environment correlations. The concept of gene/environment *interactions* tells us that people with different genes react differently to the environments they encounter. The concept of gene/environment *correlations* says that people with different genes *encounter* different environments (Loehlin, 1992). As an illustration, let's imagine one child with a genetic potential to be highly sociable and a second child whose genes make for shyness and withdrawal.

Passive Genotype/Environment Correlations

The kind of home environment that parents provide for their children is influenced in part by the parents' own genotypes. And, since parents also provide their children with genes, it turns out that the rearing environments to which children are exposed are correlated with (and are likely to suit) their own genotypes. This kind of correlation between genes and environment is termed "passive" because it is not the result of any deliberate action on the part of parents or children.

For instance, sociable parents not only transmit their "sociable" genes to their children but also, because they have "sociable" genes, create a very social home environment, inviting their friends over frequently and taking their children to many social events. These children inherit genes for sociability, but they also receive an environment that matches their genes and that may make them even more sociable than they would otherwise be. By contrast, the child with shy parents is likely to receive genes for shyness *and* an environment without much social stimulation. When genotype and environment are correlated in this way, it is almost impossible to determine whether genes or home experiences have a greater influence on sociability.

Evocative Genotype/Environment Correlations

A child's genotype also evokes certain kinds of reactions from other people. The smiley, sociable baby is likely to get more smiles and social stimulation than the withdrawn, shy baby does. Similarly, the sociable child may be sought out more often as a playmate by other children, the sociable adolescent may be invited to more parties, and the sociable adult may be given more job assignments involving public relations. In short, genetic makeup may affect the reactions of other people to a child and, hence, the kind of social environment that the child will experience.

Active Genotype/Environment Correlations

Finally, a child's genotype influences what kinds of environments he or she actively seeks out. The individual with a genetic predisposition to be extraverted is likely to seek out parties, invite friends to the house, join organizations, and otherwise build a "niche" that is highly socially stimulating. The child with genes for shyness may actively avoid large-group activities and instead develop interests in activities that can be engaged in alone.

Scarr and McCartney go on to suggest that the balance of passive, evocative, and active genotype/environment correlations shifts during development. Because infants are at home a good deal, their environment is largely influenced by their parents through passive genetic influences. Evocative influences continue to operate in much the same way throughout life; our characteristic traits consistently prompt characteristic reactions in other people. As children develop, however, they become increasingly able to build their own niches, so active gene influences become more important. Scarr and McCartney believe that this is one reason why fraternal twins, siblings, and adopted children in the same family become less alike as they get older. They share an early home environment, but, because they are genetically different, they increasingly build different niches as they get older and more independent. Identical twins, by contrast, may stay alike, even when separated, because their similar genes make them continue to seek out similar experiences.

Summarizing their argument, Scarr and McCartney suggest that we are the products of "cooperative efforts of the nature/nurture team, directed by the genetic quarterback" (1983, p. 433). In effect, genes influence human development by influencing the experiences we have, which in turn affect our development. Not all developmentalists would agree that genetic endowment is the "quarterback" of the "nature/nurture team" (see Wachs, 1992, for example). However, most would agree that the genes people inherit and the experiences they have are intimately intertwined and therefore difficult, if not impossible, to untangle.

Is there any evidence supporting Scarr and McCartney's contention that one's genes are correlated with and perhaps even influence one's experiences in life? Increasingly, there is. Behavioral geneticists are discovering that identical twins are more similar than fraternal twins, and biological siblings are more similar than adoptive siblings, with respect to a wide range of measures of the "environment"—for example, in the degree of warmth their mothers show toward them (Plomin & Bergeman, 1991), the time they spend watching television (Plomin, Corley, DeFries, & Fulker, 1990), the number of negative life events they report experiencing as adults (Plomin, Corley, et al., 1990), and even the likelihood that they will divorce (McGue & Lykken, 1992). If our genetically influenced personality traits affect how others treat us and what experiences we seek out on our own, these findings make perfect sense.

However, such findings also challenge some of our most fundamental assumptions about human development. After all, what they really say is that things we regard as purely "environmental" influences may actually reflect, in part, the workings of heredity. To use an example offered by Robert Plomin (1990), suppose we find that parents who read to their children have brighter children than parents who do not read to their children. In the not-so-distant past, most developmentalists would have interpreted this finding as still more evidence that parents make important contributions to their children's intellectual development. Without denying the importance of parents, suppose we offer this alternative interpretation: Parents and children whose genes predispose them to be highly intelligent are more likely to seek out opportunities to read stories than parents and children who are less intellectually inclined. If this is the case, can we be so sure that reading to children *causes* them to be brighter? The concept of gene/environment correlations reminds us that humans, partly guided by their genetically based predispositions, actively shape the environments that in turn influence them. As a result, genetic makeup may contribute to what appear to be links between experiences and developmental outcomes. We simply must view genes and environment as partners in the developmental process.

In sum, both genes and environment are at work over the entire life span, and the relative contributions of these two forces change somewhat with age. But we are missing the full story unless we appreciate both gene/environment interactions and gene/environment correlations. Environmental forces help determine whether we achieve our genetic potential, and our genetic potential helps determine how we respond to experiences—and, indeed, what experiences we have. Now you can understand why today's developmentalists regard it as foolish to ask whether nature *or* nurture is responsible for human development. We are shaped by an incredibly complex interplay of genetic and environmental influences from conception to death.

APPLICATIONS: GENETIC DEFECTS AND THEIR DETECTION AND TREATMENT

What use is genetic research to parents who run the risk of having a child with some genetically linked disorder? To set parents-to-be at ease, let's note that about 95%

of babies will *not* have genetic defects (Baird et al., 1988). However, there are a couple of thousand genetic defects associated with a single gene or gene pair, several kinds of chromosome disorders, and many polygenic susceptibilities to diseases and disorders such as schizophrenia. **Genetic counseling** is a service that offers relevant information to people who suspect that they or their unborn children are at risk for some genetically based problem. Today's genetic counselors have access to more information than ever about the nature, detection, and treatment of genetic defects (see Nightingale & Goodman, 1990). To illustrate this, we will focus on four disorders: Tay-Sachs disease, Huntington's disease, PKU, and cystic fibrosis.

Tay-Sachs Disease

Suppose that a Jewish couple is planning to have a child and has heard that **Tay-Sachs disease** is especially common among Jewish children. This disease causes a degeneration of the nervous system and usually kills its victims by the age of 5. The couple might seek out a genetic counselor, usually a medical researcher, geneticist, or physician. The genetic counselor will likely obtain a complete family history from each partner—one that includes information about the diseases and causes of death of relatives, the countries of origin of relatives (particularly since Tay-Sachs disease strikes most frequently among Jewish people of Eastern European ancestry), and any previous problems in the child-bearing process. For some defects and disorders, especially those influenced by multiple gene pairs, family histories of this sort are the only basis for calculating the odds that a problem might occur.

However, tests are available to determine conclusively whether prospective parents are carriers of the genes associated with many hereditary defects. The number of such tests is increasing at a staggering rate due to remarkable advances in genetic science (Bishop & Waldholz, 1990). For example, blood tests can determine whether a prospective parent carries the recessive gene for Tay-Sachs disease, as well as sickle-cell disease, hemophilia, and many other conditions.

Suppose our couple learns from a blood test that they are both carriers of the gene for Tay-Sachs disease. A genetic counselor would explain that there is a 1-in-4 chance that any child they conceive would inherit a recessive gene from each of them and have Tay-Sachs disease. There is also a 1-in-4 chance that the child would inherit two dominant (and normal) genes and a 2-in-4 chance that any child would, like the parents themselves, be a carrier. After providing the couple with this information, the genetic counselor would inform them about screening procedures that can detect many genetic abnormalities (including Tay-Sachs disease) in the fetus. Three widely used techniques—**amniocentesis, chorionic villus biopsy,** and **ultrasound**—are described in Table 3.4.

For the parents whose tests reveal a normal fetus, the anxiety of undergoing the tests and waiting for the results gives way to relief. For those who learn that their fetus has a serious defect, the experience can be agonizing, especially if their religious or personal beliefs argue against the option of abortion. In the case of Tay-Sachs disease, for example, the choice is between terminating the pregnancy and watching one's baby deteriorate and die, because no cure for this condition has been discovered.

TABLE 3.4 Methods of detecting chromosomal and genetic abnormalities prenatally.

Method	*Description*	*Strengths and Weaknesses*
Amniocentesis	Needle is inserted into the abdomen, and sample of amniotic fluid is withdrawn. Fetal cells can be analyzed to determine sex of fetus, presence of chromosomal abnormalities such as Down syndrome, and presence of many genetic defects.	Despite complications about 1% of the time and a slight risk of miscarriage, method is considered safe (Nightingale & Goodman, 1990). Commonly recommended for mothers over 35. Cannot be performed before the 14th–16th week of pregnancy, however, and involves a two-week wait for results.
Chorionic villus biopsy	Catheter is inserted through vagina and cervix and into membrane called the *chorion*, which surrounds the fetus, to extract tiny hair cells containing the genetic code of the fetus.	Permits same tests as amniocentesis but can be performed as early as the 9th week (Nightingale & Goodman, 1990), allowing parents more time to consider the pros and cons of continuing the pregnancy if an abnormality is detected. Appears to involve little more risk than amniocentesis (Nightingale & Goodman, 1990).
Ultrasound	Womb is scanned with sound waves to create a visual image of the fetus on a monitor screen.	Can detect only those genetic defects that produce visible physical abnormalities. Safer than X rays; very safe overall. Prospective parents often enjoy "meeting" their child.

Huntington's Disease

Occasionally a genetic defect is associated with a single *dominant* gene. **Huntington's disease** is a famous (and terrifying) example that typically strikes in middle age. The nervous systems of its victims steadily deteriorate; among the effects are motor disturbances such as slurred speech, an erratic, seemingly drunken walk, grimaces, and jerky movements; personality changes involving increased moodiness and irritability; and dementia or loss of cognitive abilities (Bishop & Waldholz, 1990; Swavely & Falek, 1989). Any child of a parent with Huntington's disease will have the disease if he or she receives the dominant Huntington's gene rather than its normal counterpart gene at conception; the risk is therefore 1 out of 2, or 50%. Fortunately the gene is very rare; 5 to 10 people in 100,000 develop the disease (Gusella et al., 1983).

In 1983, James Gusella and his colleagues were able to apply a then-brand-new technique of locating specific genes on the chromosomes to trace the gene for Huntington's disease to Chromosome 4. This breakthrough was made possible in part by the efforts of Nancy Wexler, a psychologist whose mother had developed Huntington's disease and who therefore stood a 50-50 chance of developing it herself (Bishop & Waldholz, 1990). Wexler assembled a team to collect blood samples from a large family in Venezuela in which Huntington's disease ran rampant. Gusella and his team were then able to pinpoint how the genetic "fingerprints" of family members who had Huntington's differed from those of family members who did not. This achievement is one of many occurring at an unprecedented rate under the auspices of the Human Genome Project, an effort sponsored by the National Institutes of Health to map the locations of all the human genes (Little, 1992).

Once the genes responsible for a genetic defect are located, work can begin to develop a test for the presence of those genes and, perhaps ultimately, to understand how such genes work their damage and how their effects can be treated or cured. The discovery of the location of the Huntington's gene led, in 1986, to the development of a test to enable the relatives of Huntington's victims to find out whether or not they had inherited the gene. Before the test became available, children of a Huntington's disease victim had to wonder about that for a good part of their lives. The slightest signs of clumsiness, mood swings, or personality changes aroused fear that the disease had struck (Bishop & Waldholz, 1990). Some sons and daughters of victims were afraid to marry or to have children in case they might later prove to have the Huntington's gene (Omenn, 1983).

Now that the test for the gene is available, not all individuals at risk for Huntington's want to take it; but many who do take it feel better knowing one way or the other what the future holds (Wiggins et al., 1992). Their remaining hope is that increased knowledge about the Huntington's gene will lead to a treatment or even a cure in the near future.

Phenylketonuria (PKU)

Some genetic defects *are* curable. One of the greatest success stories in genetic research involves **phenylketonuria,** or **PKU,** a disorder caused by a pair of recessive genes. Affected children lack a critical enzyme needed to metabolize phenylalanine, a component of many foods (including milk) and the main ingredient in aspartame, the sweetener used in many diet foods and beverages. As phenylalanine accumulates in the body, it is converted to a harmful acid that attacks the nervous system and causes children to be mentally retarded and hyperactive.

The great breakthroughs came in the mid-1950s, when scientists developed a special diet low in phenylalanine, and in 1961, when they developed a simple blood test that could detect PKU soon after birth, before any damage had been done. Newborn infants are now routinely screened for PKU, and affected children are immediately placed on the special (and, unfortunately, quite distasteful) diet. Children with PKU must adhere to some form of the special diet until they are at least 8 or so years of age to avoid brain damage (Holtzman et al., 1986). Here, then, is a way to prevent one of the many causes of mental retardation. And here we also have a wonderful example of the interaction between genes and environment: A child will develop the condition and become mentally retarded only if he or she inherits the PKU genes *and* eats a normal (rather than special) diet.

Cystic Fibrosis

Cystic fibrosis (CF), a serious genetic disease affecting about 1 in 1000 babies, is still another defect that is caused by a pair of recessive genes and that is being conquered by genetic researchers. CF results when the child lacks an enzyme that prevents mucus from obstructing the lungs and digestive tract (Ayala & Kiger, 1984). Children with CF experience chronic lung infections and must be slapped on the back by their parents for several minutes a couple of times a day so that they will cough up mucus. Damage to the pancreas causes them to develop serious digestive problems, which in turn may cause them to become malnourished (Bishop & Waldholz, 1990). Because of medical advances, far more CF patients are living into adulthood today than in the past. However, their average age at death is still 26, and few live beyond 40 (Seligmann, 1990). About 1 in 20 people in the United States is a carrier of the recessive gene responsible for cystic fibrosis (Bishop & Waldholz, 1990), making it the most common genetic defect. As is true of other recessive hereditary conditions, two carriers would run a 25% risk of conceiving a child with cystic fibrosis.

The story of cystic fibrosis illustrates well the remarkable speed with which genetic researchers are gaining the knowledge they need to combat genetic diseases. In 1985 genetic researchers identified the approximate location of the gene responsible for CF on Chromosome 7 (Bishop & Waldholz, 1990). This made possible a test to determine whether a fetus has inherited two of the recessive genes. In 1989 researchers isolated the cystic fibrosis gene itself, and only a year later two research teams demonstrated in the laboratory that they could neutralize the damaging effects of the CF gene (Denning, Kagan, Mueller, & Neu, 1991; Seligmann, 1990). Soon thereafter came the development and testing of a gene replacement therapy that involves inserting normal genes, carried by genetically engineered cold viruses, into the noses and lungs of patients with cystic fibrosis in hopes that these imported genes can override the effects of the CF genes ("Gene Therapy," 1993).

Treatments and cures for genetic conditions are not always easy to come by. The basic cause of sickle-cell disease has been known for many years, for example, but there is still no effective cure for it. And the children of adults with Huntington's disease can find out whether they will develop the disease but cannot do anything to keep from getting it.

Yet many potentially devastating effects of genetic and chromosomal abnormalities can at least be minimized or controlled, if not cured. Children with Turner syndrome or Klinefelter syndrome can be given sex hormones to make them more normal in appearance; individuals with sickle-cell disease can be given transfusions of blood containing the normal red blood cells they lack; and so on. And, inspired by experimentation with gene replacement therapies for cystic fibrosis and other conditions, geneticists are hopeful that many serious genetic defects will become treatable in the near future through techniques that involve replacing genes that cause disorders with normal genes.

Meanwhile, society as a whole will have to grapple with the ethical issues that have arisen as geneticists have gained the capacity to identify the carriers or potential victims of diseases and disorders, to give parents information that might prompt them to decide on an abortion, and even to experiment with techniques for altering the genetic code.

It's no surprise that identical twins look alike and that parents dress them alike. The surprise in this photo is that the identical twins—without any instructions—unconsciously put their hands in similar positions.

REFLECTIONS

It is impossible to study genetic influences on development without being struck by the remarkable similarities between identical twins. Perhaps the most compelling evidence of the power of genes in human development is the fact that parents tend to become stronger believers in hereditary influences after they have a second child and see for themselves that what they do as parents affects each child differently (Himelstein, Graham, & Weiner, 1991). Learning theorists have had difficulty explaining why different individuals raised in similar environments sometimes turn out so differently (Scarr, 1991). In those strands of DNA we carry may lie part of the explanation.

Genetic research has always been controversial, however. Some respected researchers continue to question the validity of the kinds of studies that we have surveyed in this chapter and doubt that the influences of genes and environment on individual differences can ever be cleanly separated (for example, Hoffman, 1991; Lewontin, Rose, & Kamin, 1984). Then there are those who resist the messages that this research contains. They want to believe that all people are created equal in all respects. Or they don't want to think that they're doomed to resemble their parents or limited in their potential to achieve anything they choose. Or it bothers them to think that parents, teachers, or government programs cannot achieve everything they might want to achieve by improving the environments in which children develop. Perhaps you fall somewhere in this camp of skeptics and resisters.

If you do, let us lay out a more positive way of thinking about the implications of genetic research. First, it is quite possible to believe that people deserve equal rights and equal opportunities while still recognizing that they have different potentials sketched in their genetic codes. Indeed, it can be argued that society is richer when its members are diverse, when each has unique strengths to contribute. Second, as we have stressed repeatedly, the fact that individual differences in behavior in a group of people are partly or even largely due to differences in their genetic makeups does not mean that those traits are unalterable. Being born into a family of alcoholics hardly means that one must become an alcoholic or that one cannot be treated successfully if one *does* become an alcoholic. In fact, efforts to prevent alcoholism might well become more effective if we can identify individuals who are at risk and target preventive efforts at them. Genetic research led to a cure for mental retardation caused by PKU, and it is likely to contribute to future efforts to optimize human development. Of course, providing children with optimal experiences depends on knowing which kinds of environments stimulate growth and which kinds of environments do not. It is fitting, then, that our next chapter takes a closer look at environmental influences on development.

SUMMARY POINTS

1. As humans, we share a species heredity that is the product of natural selection and that makes some aspects of our development and aging strongly canalized and universal. Ethologists and other modern evolutionary theorists believe that normal development must be understood as the product of both specieswide genes and experiential factors.

2. Each human also has an individual heredity provided at conception, when sperm and ovum, each having retained 23 chromosomes at meiosis, unite to form a single-cell zygote that contains 46 chromosomes (23 from each parent). The result is that each child of the same parents (other than identical twins) is genetically unique.

3. A child's sex is determined by the sex (X and Y) chromosomes; since genetic males have an X and a Y chromosome whereas genetic females have two X chromosomes, the father determines the child's sex.

4. The genetic basis for development is not completely understood, but we do know that genes provide an instructional "code" that influences how cells are formed and how they function and that regulator genes turn these genes "on" and "off" throughout the life span. Environmental factors influence how one's genotype (genetic makeup) is translated into a phenotype (actual traits).

5. There are three main mechanisms of inheritance: single gene-pair inheritance, sex-linked inheritance, and polygenic (multiple gene) inheritance. Most important human traits are influenced by polygenic inheritance. Some children are also affected by noninherited changes in gene structure (mutations), and others, because of errors in meiosis, have chromosome abnormalities (such as Down syndrome) or sex chromosome abnormalities (such as Turner and Klinefelter syndromes).

6. Behavioral genetics is the study of genetic and environmental contributions to individual differences in psychological traits and behaviors. Human behavioral geneticists, by conducting twin and adoption studies, describe resemblances between pairs of people using concordance rates and correlation coefficients. They then estimate the heritability of traits (the proportion of variation in a trait in a group linked to genetic differences among those individuals), as well as the contributions of shared and nonshared environmental influences.

7. Performance on measures of intelligence is a heritable trait. Infant mental development is strongly influenced by a specieswide, genetically programmed, maturational plan, but, over the course of childhood and adolescence, individual differences in mental ability become more consistent and more strongly reflect both individual genetic makeup and environmental influences. Shared environmental influences that make members of the same family alike become less significant with age, whereas the effects of genes and nonshared or unique environmental influences remain evident throughout the adult years.

8. Aspects of infant temperament such as emotionality, sociability, and activity, as well as adult personality traits such as extraversion and neuroticism, are also genetically influenced. Sharing a home environment influences some psychological characteristics, but members of the same family often develop distinct personalities owing to nonshared aspects of their experiences.

9. Many psychological disorders and problems, including hyperactivity, delinquency, and schizophrenia, have some genetic basis, but environmental factors have a good deal of influence on whether or not a genetic predisposition to develop a problem is realized.

10. Overall, physical and physiological characteristics are more strongly influenced by individual genetic endowment than intellectual abilities and personality traits are. Certain traits (creativity and some social attitudes) appear to be more strongly influenced by environmental factors than genetic ones.

11. Just as genetic makeup influences development, it influences how individuals age and when they die. The genetic basis of aging is not yet understood, but the study of early aging disorders such as progeria may provide clues.

12. Overall, both genes and environmental influences (either shared or not shared with other family members) are influential over the entire life span, although shared environmental influences are sometimes modest and become less important with age. Most important, gene/environment interactions show that environment influences how genes are expressed, and genes influence how people react to the environment. Moreover, passive, evocative, and ac-

tive gene/environment correlations suggest that we experience and seek out environments that match and further reinforce our genetic predispositions.

13. Genetic conditions such as Tay-Sachs disease, Huntington's disease, PKU, and cystic fibrosis can have profound effects on development. Genetic counseling can help people calculate the risks that their unborn children may have a genetic disorder. Blood tests can identify the carriers of many single gene-pair disorders, and abnormalities in the fetus can be detected through amniocentesis, chorionic villus biopsy, and ultrasound. As knowledge of the genetic code increases, many more genetic disorders are likely to become predictable, detectable, and treatable.

KEY TERMS

amniocentesis
behavioral genetics
canalization
carrier
chorionic villus biopsy
chromosome
chromosome abnormalities
codominance
conception
concordance rate
crossing over
cystic fibrosis (CF)
dominant gene
Down syndrome
ethology
extraversion/introversion
fraternal twins
gene
gene/environment correlation
gene/environment interaction
genetic counseling
genotype
heritability
Huntington's disease
identical twins
incomplete dominance
karyotype
Klinefelter syndrome
meiosis
mitosis
mutation
natural selection
neuroticism
nonshared environmental influences
phenotype
phenylketonuria (PKU)
polygenic trait
progeria
recessive gene
schizophrenia
selective breeding
sex-linked characteristic
shared environmental influences
sickle-cell disease
single gene-pair inheritance
species heredity
Tay-Sachs disease
temperament
Turner syndrome
ultrasound
X chromosome
Y chromosome
zygote

Environmental Influences on Life-Span Development

In 1970 a neglected and abused child named Genie came to the attention of authorities in Los Angeles, California. Her incredible story is well known to developmentalists (see Curtiss, 1977; Pines, 1981; Rymer, 1993). Genie had been locked away in a back room as a toddler and had remained in solitary confinement until she was rescued at age 13. During her captivity she had been tied down in a potty chair during the day and "caged" at night in a crib covered with wire. Genie's mother, who was nearly blind, would spend a few minutes with her every day as she fed the child. However, Genie's abusive father, who apparently hated children, would not permit anyone to talk to her. Nor would he tolerate television or any other noise-making appliances. In fact, whenever Genie made a sound, her father was likely to come into her room and beat her while barking and growling like a wild dog.

What were the effects of this dreadful environment on Genie's development? About as disastrous as you might guess. Although she showed some signs of having experienced puberty, she weighed less than 60 pounds, walked haltingly, and could not chew solid food when she was freed. Her vision and hearing were normal, but her intellectual performance was at roughly the level of a normal 1-year-old. She understood only a few words and spoke only a couple of negatives such as "stopit" and "nomore" (Rymer, 1993). As you might expect, she was quite emotionally disturbed as well.

Now, what do you suppose happened once she was given her first chance at a stimulating environment—special education classes, help from a speech therapist after school, and nurturance in one therapist's family? Genie surprised everyone with her progress. A mere eight months after her rescue, she had a vocabulary of 200 words and was already putting together the two-word sentences that are typical of young language learners. Her intelligence test scores climbed steadily over the years. At the age of 19 she could use public transportation and was functioning quite well in both her foster home and her special classes at school.

And yet she was far from a normal young woman. Her speech was still less sophisticated than that used by a normal 5-year-old, as evidenced by sentences such as "M. say not lift my leg in dentist chair" (Curtiss, 1977). And her intelligence test performance was still near the cutoff for mental retardation. Moreover, she regressed after being subjected to a series of foster placements, including an abusive one, and having to endure the loss of adults she had come to love (Rymer, 1993). At last report she was living in a home for mentally retarded adults and visiting her mother once a month (Rymer, 1993).

Obviously, environmental influences on development—for bad and for good—demand our serious attention. In Chapter 3 we emphasized genetic influences on development. We also stressed that genes and environment interact throughout the life span to make us what we are. If sharing a common genetic heritage can make different human beings alike in some respects, so can sharing similar environments. If having unique genes can make one person different from another, so can having unique experiences. But what is "environment," really? And what are some of the specific ways in which environmental factors influence development? In this chapter we address those questions, in the hope that you will carry through the remainder of your study of life-span development an understanding of the workings of genes and environment.

First we will attempt to conceptualize what the environment is. Then we will examine some of the critical impacts of environmental factors on very early development—development before birth and in the period surrounding birth. Finally, we will turn to interrelationships between development and environment after birth, emphasizing that individual development always occurs in a cultural and historical context. We will, of course, be examining environmental influences on development throughout this text. Our mission here is to grasp the concept of environment and to examine a few fascinating and important examples of how much one's environment can matter.

WHAT IS THE ENVIRONMENT?

Let's start off with a modern definition of environment offered by Urie Bronfenbrenner and Ann Crouter (1983): **Environment** is "any event or condition outside the organism that is presumed to influence, or be influenced by, the person's development" (p. 359). The physical environment includes everything from the molecules that reach the fetus's bloodstream before birth to the architectural design of one's home to the climate outside it; the social environment includes all the people who can potentially influence and be influenced by the developing person. Older concepts of environment tended to view it as a set of forces that shape the individual, as though the person were just a lump of clay to be molded. Now we understand that people also shape their physical and social environments and are, in turn, affected by the environments they have helped create. In other words, the relationship between person and environment is one of *reciprocal influence*.

For example, a pregnant woman may take a drug such as cocaine, which makes her newborn extraordinarily fussy. Environment has affected development. But a fussy baby is likely to affect the environment— for example, by irritating his mother. The mother now expresses her tenseness and irritability in her interactions with him, and this makes him all the more irritable and fussy, which of course aggravates his mother even more, which of course makes him even more cranky. Understanding the ongoing transactions between a changing person and a changing environment is quite a challenge, but theorist Urie Bronfenbrenner has offered a useful way of conceptualizing the environment, as we'll now see.

We are affected by the physical as well as the social environments in which we develop.

Bronfenbrenner's Ecological Approach to Development

According to the **ecological approach** to development set forth by Urie Bronfenbrenner (1979, 1989), the developing person is embedded in a series of environmental systems that interact with one another and with the individual to influence development. Closest to the person is what Bronfenbrenner calls the **microsystem,** which consists of the immediate environments in which the person functions. The primary microsystem for a first-born infant is likely to be the family—perhaps infant, mother, and father interacting with one another. This infant may also experience other microsystems, such as a day-care center or grandmother's house. Within any microsystem, infants contribute to their own development by affecting their companions, who in turn influence them in new ways. Indeed, even before they are born, infants can shape their future environment—for example, by causing their parents to become worried about finances or even to break up or to marry. Thus a microsystem like the family is indeed a system in which each person influences and is influenced by every other person.

Understanding the complex reciprocal influences of infant, mother, and father would be enough of a challenge, but Bronfenbrenner insists that we cannot understand child development or family relations unless we also understand what he terms the **mesosystem**—the interrelationships or linkages between microsystems. Unpleasant experiences at the day-care center (one microsystem) could certainly upset an infant and, in turn, disturb relationships within the family (another microsystem) and ultimately interfere with the infant's development. By the same token, a crisis in the family could make a child withdraw from staff members and other children at the day-care center so that his or her experience there becomes less stimulating. On the other hand, a loving and stimulating home environment is likely to allow a child to benefit more from experiences in the day-care center, or later in school.

According to Bronfenbrenner, the environment also includes the **exosystem**—social settings that the individual never experiences directly but that can still influence his or her development. Thus, children can be affected by whether or not their parents enjoy supportive social relationships, as well as by whether their parents' work is satisfying or stressful. In support of this notion, Cotterell (1986) discovered that mothers have difficulty providing a stimulating home environment when they have few friends to turn to for information and support and when their husbands work unusual shifts and are away from home a great deal. Similarly, children's experiences in school can be affected by their exosystem—by a racial integration plan adopted by the school board or by a plant closing in their community that results in a cut in the school system's budget.

Finally, we reach the broadest context in which development occurs: the **macrosystem,** or the larger subcultural and cultural contexts in which the microsystem, mesosystem, and exosystem are embedded. As we will illustrate in this chapter, this broader social environment can indeed have important effects on development. **Culture** can be defined as a system of meanings shared by a population of people and transmitted to future generations

(Rohner, 1984). Those shared understandings include views about the nature of human beings at different points in the life span, about what children need to be taught to function in society, and about how one should lead one's life as an adult. Because culture changes or evolves over time, and because people developing in particular historical periods are affected by societal events (such as wars or technological breakthroughs), each generation (or *cohort*) of individuals in a particular society develops in a distinct social context. We cannot simply assume that development is the same in all cultures and historical periods. Moreover, we must adopt what anthropologist Ruth Benedict (1934) termed the principle of **cultural relativity**—the concept that human behavior cannot be properly understood unless it is interpreted within its larger cultural context. Adolescent sexual experimentation may be strongly encouraged in one society but punished severely in another; laughter during a funeral may be regarded as outrageously inappropriate in one cultural context but entirely fitting in another.

The environmental systems proposed by Bronfenbrenner—each of them shaping and being shaped by the developing person—are diagramed in Figure 4.1. Each of us functions in particular microsystems that are linked to one another through the mesosystem and embedded in the larger context of the exosystem and the macrosystem. As we develop, settings such as the family or the broader culture evolve and change. Moreover, we move into new settings, as when a child progresses from preschool to elementary school to junior high school and also becomes involved in new peer groups and social organizations. As our environments change, we are likely to change.

We are now ready to examine some specific examples of the workings of environment over the life span. We will concentrate first on the physical environment and its crucial effects on development before birth; then we will see how the social environments associated with different cultures—that is, how different "macrosystems"—affect development from birth to death.

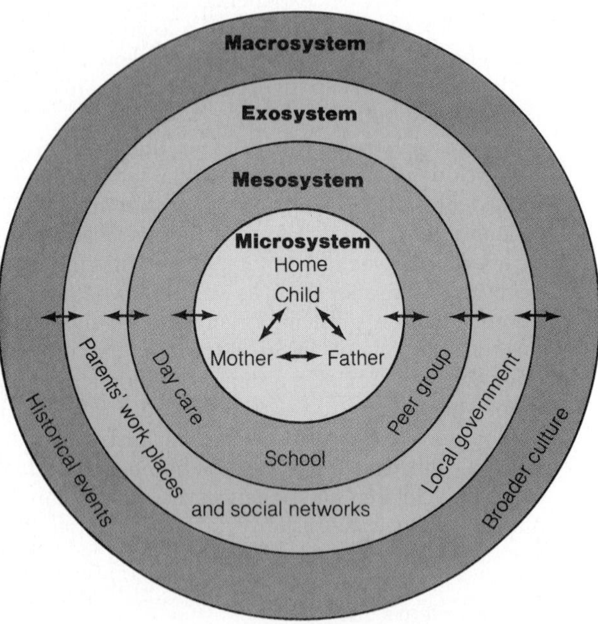

FIGURE 4.1 Bronfenbrenner's ecological model of the environment as a series of nested structures. The microsystem refers to relations between the child and the immediate environment, the mesosystem to connections among the child's immediate settings, the exosystem to settings that affect but do not contain the child, and the macrosystem to the broader cultural context in which development takes place. (Adapted from Kopp & Krakow, 1982.)

PRENATAL DEVELOPMENT AND THE PRENATAL ENVIRONMENT

Perhaps at no time in the life span is development occurring faster—or is the environment more potentially important—than in the period between conception and birth. To understand how the **prenatal environment,** the physical environment of the womb, can affect development, we must first understand the maturational process that is occurring before birth.

Stages of Prenatal Development

As we saw in Chapter 3, the product of conception, a *zygote*, works its way down the fallopian tube. It will take about 266 days (or about 9 months) for this one-celled zygote to become a fetus of some 200 billion cells that is ready to be born. Prenatal development is divided into three periods: the germinal period, the period of the embryo, and the period of the fetus.

The Germinal Period

The **germinal period** lasts about 8 to 14 days, from conception until the **blastula**—a hollow ball of cells about the size of the head of a pin—is implanted in the wall of the uterus. The zygote first divides into two cells through mitosis; this cell division is then repeated many times, forming the blastula. When the blastula reaches the uterus, tendrils in its outer layer burrow into the blood vessels of the uterine wall. Actually this is quite an accomplishment in itself, as only about half of all fertilized ova are successfully implanted in the uterus (Roberts & Lowe, 1975). In addition, as many as half of all implanted embryos are abnormal in some way or burrow into a site incapable of sustaining them; they are miscarried (spontaneously aborted) and expelled (Adler & Carey, 1982). Apparently, then, only about 1 zygote in 4 will survive the initial phases of prenatal development.

The Period of the Embryo

The **period of the embryo** lasts from implantation at the end of the second week after conception to the end of the eighth week of prenatal development. In this short time, virtually all the major organs of the body take shape in at least a primitive form. Soon after implantation, the embryo secretes a hormone that prevents the mother from menstruating; this helps ensure its survival. The presence of this hormone in a woman's urine is taken as evidence of pregnancy in common pregnancy tests.

The layers of the embryo differentiate to form structures necessary for sustaining development. The outer layer becomes the **amnion** (a watertight membrane that surrounds the embryo and fills with fluid that cushions and protects the embryo) and the **chorion** (a membrane that surrounds the amnion and becomes attached to the uterine lining to gather nourishment for the embryo). The side of the chorion that has rootlike villi for gathering nourishment from the uterine tissues eventually becomes the lining of the **placenta,** a tissue that is fed by blood vessels from the mother and the embryo and is connected to the embryo by means of the embryo's lifeline, the **umbilical cord.** Through the placenta and umbilical cord, the embryo receives oxygen and nutrients from the mother while eliminating carbon dioxide and metabolic wastes into the mother's bloodstream. A membrane called the *placental barrier* allows these small molecules (as well as more dangerous substances that we will discuss shortly) to pass through, but it prevents the quite large blood cells of embryo and mother from mingling (see Figure 4.2).

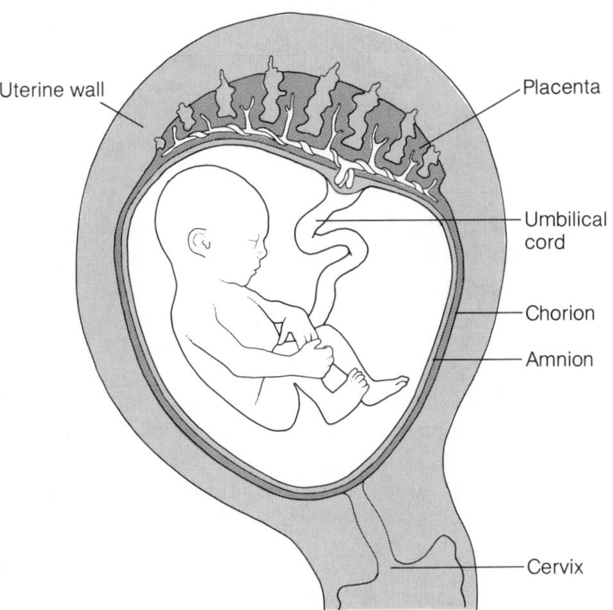

FIGURE 4.2 The embryo and its prenatal environment.

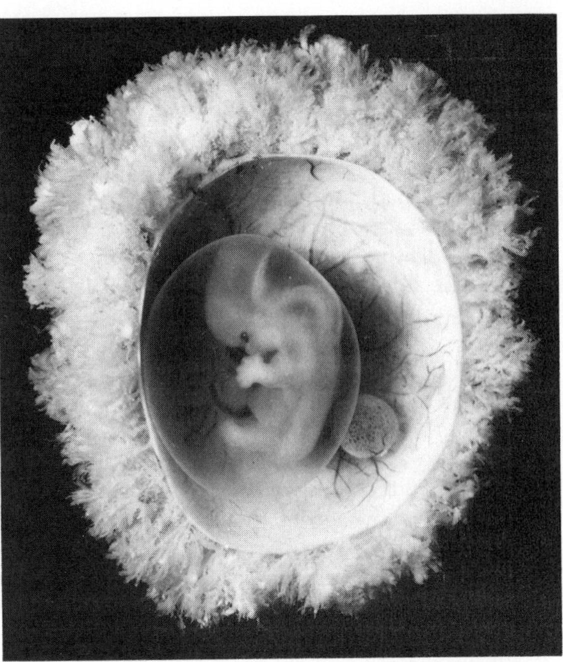

FIGURE 4.3 The embryo at 40 days, with yolk sac in the lower right. Even though it does not look very human, the embryo already has a beating heart.

Meanwhile, the inner layers of the germinal cell mass are also differentiating. Cells, influenced by their environment of neighboring cells, cluster into groups, take on specialized functions, and become distinct organ systems (Sameroff, 1983). Development proceeds at a breathtaking pace (see Figure 4.3). By only the fourth week after conception, a tiny heart not only has formed but has begun to beat. After the head forms, the eyes, ears, nose, and mouth rapidly take shape, and buds that will become arms and legs appear. During the second month a very primitive nervous system is making newly formed muscles contract. At only 60 days after conception, at the close of the period of the embryo, the organism is a little over an inch long and has a distinctly human appearance.

In the seventh and eighth prenatal weeks, the important process of sexual differentiation begins. First, an undifferentiated tissue will become either the male testes or the female ovaries: If the embryo inherited a Y chromosome at conception, a gene on it will call for the construction of testes; in a genetic female with two X chromosomes, ovaries will form instead. The testes of a male embryo will then secrete **testosterone,** the primary male sex hormone and the hormone that will stimulate the development of a male internal reproductive system, as well as another hormone that inhibits the development of a female internal reproductive system. In the absence of these hormones, the embryo will develop the internal reproductive system of a female. Clearly the period of the embryo is a dramatic and highly important phase of development:

the period when the structures that make us "human" evolve and take shape.

The Period of the Fetus

The **period of the fetus** lasts from the ninth week of pregnancy until birth. Organ systems that were formed during the period of the embryo continue their growth and begin to function. In the third month, distinguishable external sex organs begin to appear. If testosterone is secreted by the testes of a male, a penis and scrotum appear; without testosterone, female genitalia form. The bones and muscles also develop, and the fetus becomes quite active. By the end of the third month, it is moving its arms, kicking its legs, making fists, and even turning somersaults (Apgar & Beck, 1974). It is only about three inches long but can swallow, digest food, and urinate.

During the *second trimester* (the fourth, fifth, and sixth months), even more refined activities (such as thumbsucking) appear, and by the end of this period the sensory organs are apparently functioning. We know this is so because premature infants as young as 25 weeks of age will become alert in response to a loud bell and blink in response to a bright light (Allen & Capute, 1986). At about 24 weeks of age, midway through the fifth month, the fetus reaches the **age of viability,** the point at which survival outside the uterus *may* be possible. Survival is "iffy" at this point, but the brain and respiratory system are well enough developed to make it possible in some cases. As medical techniques for keeping fragile babies alive have improved, the age of viability has decreased.

During the *third trimester* (the seventh, eighth, and ninth months), the fetus is gaining weight at a tremendously rapid rate (see Figure 4.4). This is also a critical time in the development of the brain, for brain cells are multiplying at an astonishing rate. By the middle of the ninth month, the fetus is so large that its most comfortable position in its cramped quarters is a head-down posture with the limbs curled in the so-called fetal position. At irregular intervals over the last month of pregnancy, the mother's uterus will contract. When these contractions become stronger, more frequent, and regular, the mother is entering the first stage of labor and the prenatal period is drawing to a close. Under normal circumstances, birth will occur in a matter of hours.

The developing embryo or fetus is a vulnerable little creature. How can its development be optimized? What hazards does it face? A number of odd ideas about the effects of the prenatal physical environment on growth have been offered by "experts" throughout history and well into the 20th century. For example, it was once believed that pregnant women could enhance their chances of bearing sons if they exercised (thereby stimulating the muscle development of their fetuses!) and that sexual activity during pregnancy (now recommended until a couple of weeks before delivery) would cause the child to be sexually precocious (MacFarlane, 1977). And until the early 1940s it was widely—and very wrongly—believed that the placenta was a marvelous screening device that protected the embryo or fetus from nicotine, viruses, and all kinds of other hazards.

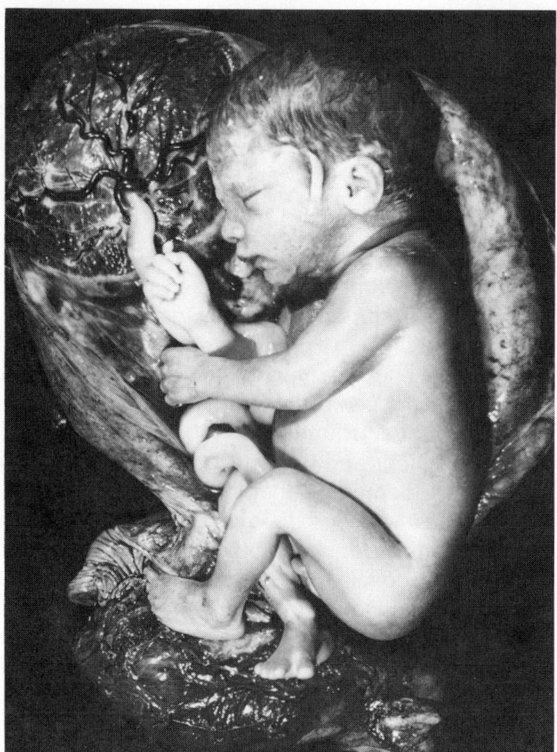

FIGURE 4.4 A human fetus at 8 months of age. By this age, survival outside the womb is possible.

The Mother's Age, Emotional State, and Nutrition

Age

The safest time to bear a child appears to be from about age 17 or 18 to age 35 (Kessner, 1973). One reason for increased rates of complications and fetal and infant mortality among teenage mothers is that the reproductive system of the very young teen may not be physically mature enough to sustain a fetus. However, the greater problem appears to be that teenagers often do not receive prenatal care (Abma & Mott, 1991). Teenage mothers and their babies are usually *not* at risk when they do receive appropriate prenatal care and medical treatment during the birth process (Baker & Mednick, 1984).

As for mothers over 40, they run a higher-than-average risk that their fetus will have chromosome abnormalities and may be spontaneously aborted as a result (see Chapter 3). The risks of complications during pregnancy and delivery are also higher in older women, perhaps in part because they, like adolescents, are less likely than women in their 20s and 30s to seek prenatal care early in their pregnancies (Brown, 1988). Even so, the vast majority of older women have normal pregnancies and healthy babies (Leroy, 1988).

Emotional State

Does it matter how the mother feels about her pregnancy or about her life situation while she is pregnant? Although most women are happy about conceiving a child, the fact remains that over half of all pregnancies are unplanned or unintended ("Half Our Pregnancies," 1983). Even mothers who want their babies are likely to experience at least some symptoms of anxiety and depression during their pregnancies (Kaplan, 1986). What effects might these negative emotions, as well as more severe emotional stresses, have on the fetus?

When a mother becomes emotionally aroused, her glands secrete powerful hormones such as adrenaline (also called epinephrine). These may cross the placental barrier and enter the fetus's bloodstream. At the very least, these hormones temporarily increase the fetus's motor activity (Sontag, 1941). However, a temporarily stressful experience such as falling or receiving a scare will generally not damage mother or fetus (Stott & Latchford, 1976). It is only when mothers experience *prolonged and severe* emotional stress and anxiety during their pregnancies that damage may be done. Chronically stressed mothers are at risk for such complications as miscarriage (spontaneous abortion), prolonged and painful labor, and premature delivery (Sameroff & Chandler, 1975). Moreover, Stott and Latchford (1976) discovered that infants whose mothers had experienced such prolonged stresses as marital problems, relocations, and economic worries were at risk for both physical and behavioral abnormalities. Other researchers have found that the babies of highly stressed mothers tend to be small, hyperactive, irritable, and quite irregular in their feeding, sleeping, and bowel habits (Sameroff & Chandler, 1975; Vaughan et al., 1987). However, it is difficult to establish that these difficulties are really caused by the mother's prolonged stress during pregnancy. It is possible that the baby of an emotional mother is genetically predisposed to have a "difficult" temperament—or that the mother's emotional tensions affect her care of the infant *after* birth. Nonetheless, mothers experiencing chronic stress during pregnancy might want to seek counseling: In one study, the babies of stressed mothers who received counseling weighed more at birth than the babies of stressed mothers who did not get help (Rothberg & Lits, 1991).

Nutrition

Forty years ago, doctors often advised mothers to gain no more than 2 pounds a month while pregnant and believed that a total gain of 15 to 18 pounds was quite sufficient. Today doctors are more likely to advise a gain of 3 to 4 pounds during the first three months of pregnancy and about a pound a week thereafter—a total increase of 24 to 28 pounds. Obstetricians now know that inadequate prenatal nutrition can be harmful and that severe malnutrition of the mother, as often occurs during famine, increases infant mortality and makes for small, underweight babies (Stein & Susser, 1976; Stein, Susser, Saenger, & Marolla, 1975). Such babies also tend to have fewer and smaller brain cells than babies born to well-nourished women and, in some cases (though by no means all), have lasting intellectual deficiencies (Gorman & Pollitt, 1992; Winick, 1976). These harmful effects are most likely when the malnutrition occurs in the last trimester of pregnancy, for this is when the fetus is putting on most of its weight and when new brain cells are rapidly forming (Tanner, 1990). Yet there is hope: Much depends on whether a child receives adequate diet *post*natally. Dietary supplements, especially when combined with stimulating day care, can go a long way toward heading off the potentially damaging effects of prenatal malnutrition (Super, Herrera, & Mora, 1990; Zeskind & Ramey, 1981).

Teratogens

A **teratogen** is any disease, drug, or other environmental agent that can harm a developing fetus (for example, by causing deformities, blindness, brain damage, or even death). The list of teratogens has grown frighteningly large over the years, and there are many more potential teratogens in the environment whose effects on development have still not been assessed. Before considering the effects of some major teratogens, let's emphasize that over 90% of babies are normal and that many of those born with defects have mild, temporary, or reversible problems (Baird, Anderson, Newcombe, & Lowry, 1988; Heinonen, Slone, & Shapiro, 1977). We'll also lay out a few generalizations about the effects of teratogens so that we can then illustrate these larger themes with examples (Abel, 1989; Spreen et al., 1984):

1. The effects of a teratogenic agent on an organ system are worst during the critical period when that organ system grows most rapidly.
2. Not all embryos and fetuses are affected, or affected equally, by a teratogen.
3. Susceptibility to harm is influenced by the unborn child's genetic makeup as well as by the mother's genetic makeup and the quality of the prenatal environment she provides.

4. The same defect can be caused by different teratogens.
5. A variety of defects can result from a single teratogen.
6. The higher the "dose" of a teratogen, the more likely it is that serious damage will be done.

Let's look more closely at the first generalization, for it is particularly important. A period of rapid growth in an organ system can be viewed as a **critical period** for that organ system: a time during which the developing organism is especially sensitive to environmental influences, positive or negative. As you'll recall, the organs take form during the period of the embryo (weeks 3 to 8 of prenatal development). As Figure 4.5 shows, it is during this time—before a woman is even likely to know she is pregnant—that most organ systems are most vulnerable to damage. Moreover, each organ has a critical period that corresponds to its own time of most rapid development. Once an organ or body part is fully formed, it often becomes less susceptible to damage. However, some organ systems (the nervous system, for example) can be damaged throughout pregnancy. For that reason, it might be better to speak of "sensitive periods" of prenatal development than of critical periods.

Diseases

The disease **rubella** (German measles) illustrates several principles of teratology. Women affected by this single teratogen during their pregnancies often bear children who have one or more of a variety of defects, including blindness, deafness, heart defects, and mental retardation. Rubella is most dangerous during the first trimester of pregnancy, a critical period in which the eyes, ears, heart, and brain are rapidly forming. Yet not all babies whose mothers had rubella, even during the most critical period of prenatal development, will have problems. Birth defects occur in 60–85% of babies whose mothers had the disease in the first eight weeks of pregnancy, in about 50% of those infected in the third month, and in only 16% of those infected in weeks 13 to 20 (Kelley-Buchanan, 1988). Consistent with the critical-period

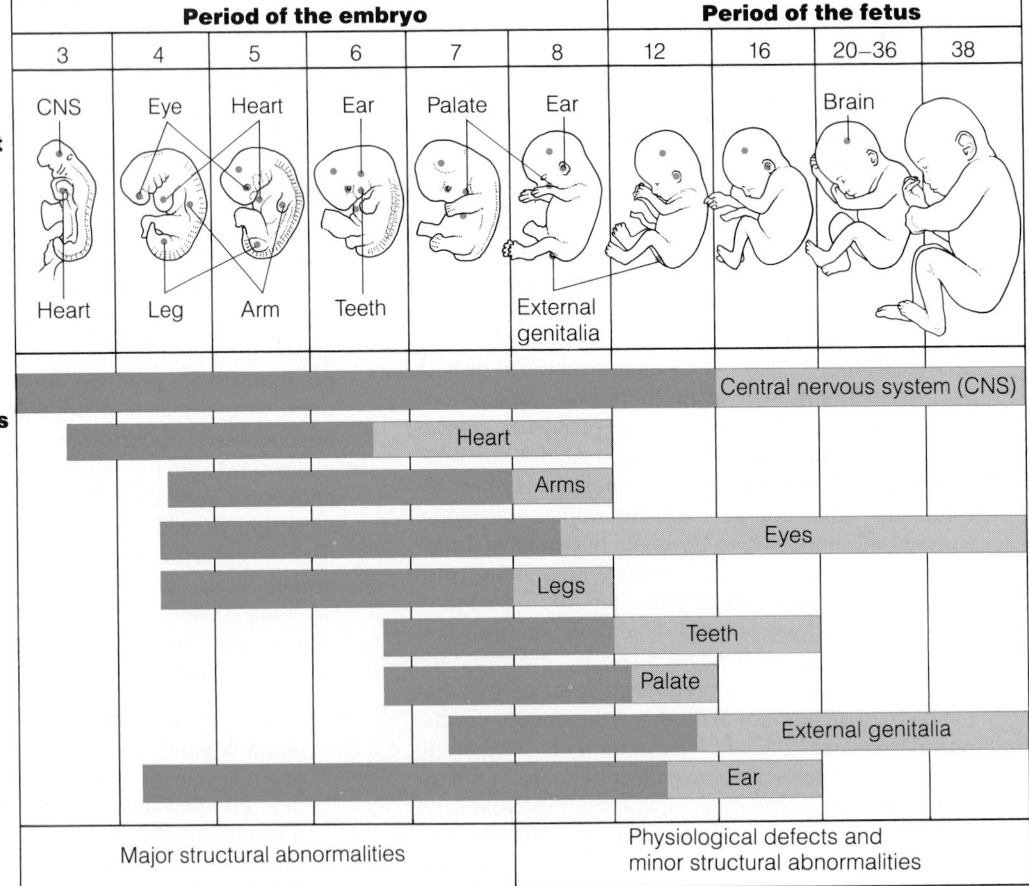

FIGURE 4.5 The critical periods of prenatal development. Teratogens are more likely to produce major structural abnormalities during the third through the eighth prenatal weeks. Note, however, that many organs and body parts remain sensitive to teratogenic agents throughout the nine-month prenatal period. (Adapted from Moore, 1977.)

principle, damage to the eyes and heart is most likely in the first eight weeks, when these organs are forming, whereas deafness is more common if the mother contracts rubella in weeks 6 to 13 of the pregnancy. Today doctors stress that a woman should not try to become pregnant unless she has already been immunized against this disease or has had it.

Now consider another teratogen, the sexually transmitted disease **syphilis.** Assuming that they live long enough to be born, the babies of mothers who have syphilis, like the babies of mothers who have rubella, often suffer from blindness, deafness, heart problems, or brain damage (Miller, 1976). Here is an illustration of the principle stating that different teratogens can be responsible for the same problem. The difference is that syphilis has its most damaging effects in the middle and later stages of pregnancy, because syphilitic organisms cannot cross the placental barrier until the 18th prenatal week. This means that a mother-to-be who finds out she has the disease can be treated with antibiotics long before the disease could harm her fetus. Table 4.1 describes a number of maternal conditions that may affect prenatal development.

TABLE 4.1 Maternal diseases and conditions that may affect an embryo, fetus, or newborn.

Disease or Condition	*Effects*
Sexually transmitted diseases	
Acquired immune deficiency syndrome (AIDS)	If transmitted from mother to child, lowers defenses against disease and typically leads to death. Mothers can acquire it through sexual contact or the use of blood-contaminated drug needles (see text).
Gonorrhea	Attacks the eyes of the child during birth; blindness is prevented by administering silver nitrate eyedrops to newborns.
Herpes simplex (genital herpes)	May cause eye damage, serious brain damage, or death unless mothers with active herpes undergo cesarean deliveries to avoid infecting their babies through contact with the vaginal tract (Hanshaw, Dudgeon, & Marshall, 1985).
Syphilis	Untreated, can cause miscarriage or serious birth defects such as blindness and mental retardation (see text).
Other maternal conditions or diseases	
Chicken pox	Can cause spontaneous abortion or premature delivery, though not malformations. Premature infants who are infected are weak and at risk of dying.
Diabetes mellitus	Increases risks of stillbirth, death, and malformations, though the vast majority of babies of diabetic women survive.
Hepatitis	Can be transmitted from mother to child, most likely during the birth process if the fetus swallows maternal blood.
Hypertension (chronic high blood pressure)	Increases chances of miscarriage and infant death.
Influenza (flu)	More powerful strains can cause spontaneous abortions or neural abnormalities early in pregnancy.
Mumps	Although a relatively mild disease, kills some fetuses if contracted in the first trimester.
Rubella	May cause blindness, deafness, mental retardation, and heart defects (see text).
Toxemia	Affecting about 5% of mothers in the third trimester, its mildest form, *preeclampsia*, causes high blood pressure and rapid weight gain in the mother. Untreated, preeclampsia may become *eclampsia* and cause maternal convulsions as well as coma and death of mother and/or unborn child. Surviving infants may be brain damaged.
Toxoplasmosis	Caused by a parasite present in raw meat and cat feces; can produce serious eye or brain damage or even death in the unborn child.

SOURCES: Based in part on information from Edelman & Mandle (1990), Evans, Fletcher, Dixler, & Shulman (1989), and Kelley-Buchanan (1988).

The sexually transmitted disease of even greater concern today is **acquired immune deficiency syndrome (AIDS),** the fatal disease that is caused by the virus HIV, destroys the immune system, and makes victims susceptible to rare, "opportunistic" infections that eventually kill them. HIV-infected mothers can transmit the virus to their babies (1) prenatally, if the virus passes through the placenta; (2) during birth, when there may be an exchange of blood between mother and child as the umbilical cord separates from the placenta; or (3) after birth, if the virus is passed through the mother's milk during breast feeding (Task Force on Pediatric AIDS, 1989). Despite all these possibilities for infection, it appears that only around 25% of babies born to HIV-infected mothers are infected (Gabiano et al., 1992). Although these infants are living longer today than they did at the outset of the AIDS epidemic, thanks to the development of appropriate treatments, they live only about three years on average (Jones et al., 1992). Mother-to-child transmission of HIV in the United States is especially common among inner-city minority women who take drugs intravenously or have sexual partners who do (Mitchell, 1989). These families often need many services in addition to competent medical care.

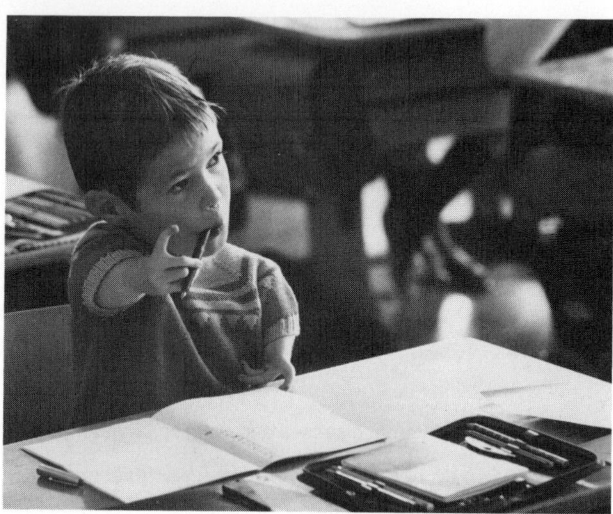

This boy has the flipper-like arms and deformed hands produced by the drug thalidomide.

Drugs

Surveys suggest that up to 60% of pregnant women take at least one prescription or over-the-counter drug during pregnancy (Schnoll, 1986). In 1960 a West German drug company began to market one such drug, an over-the-counter tranquilizer, that was said to relieve morning sickness (the periodic nausea that many women experience during the first trimester of pregnancy). Presumably the drug was perfectly safe, for it had no ill effects in tests on pregnant rats. The medication was **thalidomide,** the drug that more than any other alerted the world to the dangers of taking drugs during pregnancy.

Thousands of women who used thalidomide during the first two months of pregnancy were suddenly giving birth to babies with tragic defects — most notably, babies with all or parts of their limbs missing and with the feet or hands attached directly to the torso like flippers. Eyes, ears, noses, and hearts were also often badly deformed. It soon became clear that there were critical periods for different deformities. If the mother had taken the drug on or around the 35th day after her last menstrual period, her baby was likely to be born without ears; if she had taken it on the 39th through 41st day after last menstruation, the baby often had grossly deformed arms or no arms at all; if thalidomide had been taken between the 40th and 46th day, the child might have deformed legs or no legs. But, if the mother waited until the 52nd day before using thalidomide, her baby was usually not affected (Apgar & Beck, 1974). Interestingly enough, thalidomide now shows promise as a drug that slows the replication of the HIV virus (Makonkawkeyoon et al., 1993).

Pregnant women today do not take thalidomide, of course, but many of them do use another drug that is clearly teratogenic: alcohol (Vorhees & Mollnow, 1987). It was not so long ago — in 1973 — that a cluster of symptoms dubbed **fetal alcohol syndrome (FAS)** was identified (Jones, Smith, Ulleland, & Streissguth, 1973). The most noticeable physical symptoms are a small head and malformations of the heart, limbs, joints, and face. Affected newborns are likely to display excessive irritability, hyperactivity, seizures, or tremors. They are smaller and lighter than normal, and their physical growth lags behind that of their agemates. The majority of children with fetal alcohol syndrome score well below average on intelligence tests throughout childhood and adolescence, and many are mentally retarded (Abel, 1981; Streissguth, Herman, & Smith, 1978; Streissguth, Randels, & Smith, 1991). Hyperactive behavior and attention deficits are also common among these children (Nanson & Hiscock, 1990).

How much drinking must a mother do to risk harming her baby? In keeping with the dosage principle of teratology, the symptoms of fetal alcohol syndrome are most severe when the "dose" of alcohol is highest — that is, when the mother is clearly an alcoholic. Heavy drinkers (those who consume five or more drinks a day) run a 30% or higher risk of having a child with FAS (Vorhees & Mollnow, 1987). However, even moderate alcohol consumption or "social drinking" (1–3 ounces a day) can lead to a set of less serious problems, called "fetal alcohol effects," in some babies. Such effects include retarded physical growth and minor physical abnormalities, as well as

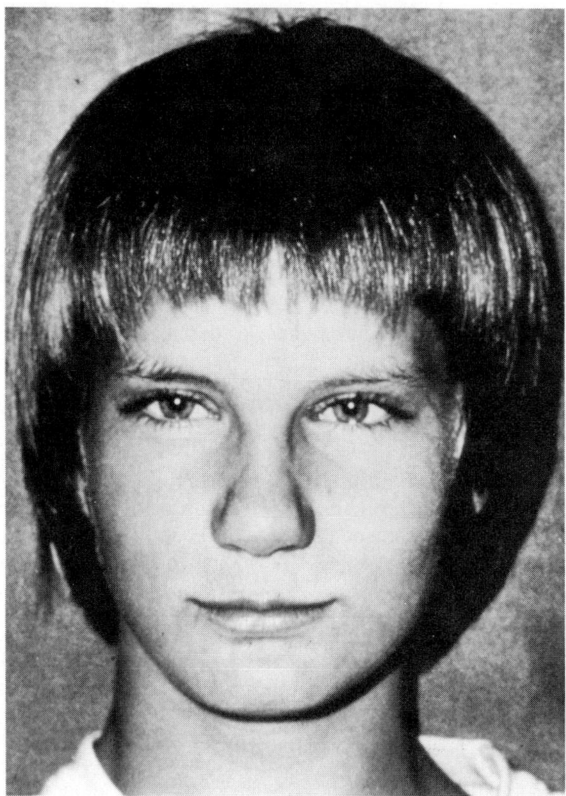

This girl's widely spaced eyes, flattened nose, and underdeveloped lip are three of the common physical symptoms of fetal alcohol syndrome (FAS).

such problems as poor fine and gross motor skills, difficulty paying attention, and low IQ and mental performance scores (Jacobson et al., 1993; Streissguth, Barr, & Sampson, 1990; Vorhees & Mollnow, 1987). There really seems to be no amount of drinking that is entirely safe. Even a mother who drinks less than an ounce a day is likely to have a sluggish or placid newborn (S. W. Jacobson et al., 1984) and may have an infant whose mental development is slightly below average (Jacobson et al., 1993). What's more, there is no well-defined critical period before or after which fetal alcohol effects cannot occur; drinking late in pregnancy can be as risky as drinking soon after conception (Jacobson et al., 1993).

Why do some babies of drinking mothers suffer ill effects while others do not? The chances of damage depend in part on the mother's physiology—for example, on how efficiently she metabolizes alcohol and, therefore, how much alcohol is passed on to the fetus (Abel, 1989). Complicating the picture is the fact that problem drinkers often have other problems that can aggravate the effects of alcohol on the fetus or cause damage in their own right—among them malnutrition, use of drugs other than alcohol, cigarette smoking, and lack of prenatal care (Abel, 1989). In addition, the embryo's genetic makeup and physical condition will influence its ability to resist and recover from damage. So, for example, one fraternal twin may show all the physical abnormalities associated with FAS whereas the other twin, though exposed to the same prenatal environment, may show virtually none (Christoffel & Salafsky, 1975). As our third principle of teratology states, both the child's and the mother's characteristics can influence the extent to which a given teratogen proves damaging.

Today much concern centers on the risks associated with cocaine use and the characteristics of "crack babies." In one study of low-income inner-city women, 18% were estimated to have used cocaine during pregnancy (Zuckerman et al., 1989). Because cocaine use constricts the blood vessels, it reduces the flow of oxygen to the fetus; because it suppresses appetite, it may contribute to fetal malnourishment (Zuckerman et al., 1989). At birth some babies born to cocaine users appear to experience tremors, irritability, and respiratory difficulties (Neuspiel & Hamel, 1991; Singer, Farkas, & Kliegman, 1992). Their cries are either frequent and high pitched or infrequent and more subdued, suggesting that exposure to cocaine has caused them to be either extremely irritable or extremely sluggish (Lester et al., 1991). About a third of these babies also experience retarded growth in the womb and are born prematurely with low birth weights and small heads (Hawley & Disney, 1992). As a result, they may be at risk for later learning and behavior problems. However, we really know very little about the longer-term development of the babies of cocaine and crack cocaine users or about whether any problems they do display are due to prenatal exposure to cocaine or to any of a host of other prenatal or postnatal risk factors they may experience as the children of substance-abusing parents (Hawley & Disney, 1992).

Table 4.2 catalogs a number of other drugs and chemical substances and their known or suspected effects on the child. What should we make of these findings? Perhaps Virginia Apgar summarized it best: "A woman who is pregnant, or thinks she could possibly be pregnant, should not take any drugs whatsoever unless absolutely essential—and then only when prescribed by a physician who is aware of the pregnancy" (Apgar & Beck, 1974, p. 445).

Environmental Hazards

A mother can control what she ingests, but sometimes she cannot control the physical environment surrounding her or her exposure to the thousands of chemicals used in industry and agriculture. Radiation is one potential environmental hazard. After atomic bombs were dropped on Hiroshima and Nagasaki in 1945, not one pregnant woman who was within one-half mile of the blasts gave birth to a live child, and 75% of those who were within a mile and a quarter of

TABLE 4.2 Some drugs that affect the fetus or newborn.

Drug	*Effects*
Alcohol	Small head, facial abnormalities, heart defects, low birth weight, and intellectual retardation (fetal alcohol syndrome; see text).
Antibiotics	Heavy use of streptomycin by mothers can produce hearing loss. Terramycin and tetracycline may be linked to premature delivery, retarded skeletal growth, cataracts, and a staining of the baby's teeth.
Aspirin	Used in large quantities, aspirin and other salicylates may cause neonatal bleeding and gastrointestinal discomfort. There is preliminary evidence that aspirin may be associated with low birth weight and lower intelligence test scores and with mild motor skill deficits (Barr, Streissguth, Darby, & Sampson, 1990; Vorhees & Mollnow, 1987).
Barbiturates	In clinical doses, barbiturates cause the fetus or newborn to be sluggish. Large doses may cause anoxia (oxygen starvation) or interfere with breathing.
Hallucinogens	Heavy use of marijuana has been linked to premature birth, low birth weight, and behavioral abnormalities at birth, but it does not appear to have long-lasting effects on most children (Fried, 1982; Fried, O'Connell, & Watkinson, 1992; Zuckerman et al., 1989). LSD use may cause chromosome damage in prospective parents (Estop et al., 1991), although the evidence remains controversial (Schardein, 1985).
Narcotics	Addiction to heroin, codeine, methadone, or morphine increases the risk of premature delivery. The newborn is often addicted and experiences potentially fatal withdrawal symptoms (for example, vomiting, convulsions) unless increasingly smaller doses of the addictive drug are given after birth.
Sex hormones	Birth-control pills containing female hormones have been known to produce heart defects and cardiovascular problems (Heinonen et al., 1977; Schardein, 1985), but today's pill formulas are safer. Progesterone in drugs used to prevent miscarriage may masculinize the fetus. Diethystilbestrol (DES), once also prescribed to prevent miscarriage, has been linked to reproductive problems and cervical cancer in exposed daughters (Hamm, 1981).
Stimulants	Caffeine use has been linked to prematurity, abnormal reflexes, and irritability at birth (S. W. Jacobson et al., 1984) but does not seem to have longer-lasting effects on development (Barr & Streissguth, 1991). Cocaine use slows fetal growth and may result in later learning and behavior problems (see text).
Tobacco	Babies of smokers tend to be small and premature and sometimes show long-term lags in physical and/or intellectual growth (Fried et al., 1992; U.S. Department of Health, Education and Welfare, 1979), although most children seem to overcome early problems (Lefkowitz, 1981). "Passive smoking" is risky as well; babies weigh less if their fathers smoke (Rubin et al., 1986).
Tranquilizers	May produce respiratory distress in newborns. Valium may also produce poor muscle tone and lethargy.
Vaccines	Immunization with live-virus vaccines should be avoided during pregnancy unless essential, for many of these viruses (for example, mumps, measles, smallpox) are powerful teratogens.
Vitamins	Yes, even vitamins can be risky. Large amounts of vitamin A can cause cleft palate, heart malformation, and other serious defects. Vitamin D is suspected of causing birth defects as well.

SOURCES: Based in part on information from Abel (1989), Anderson & Golbus (1989), and Kelley-Buchanan (1988).

the blasts had stillborn infants or seriously handicapped children who died soon after birth (Apgar & Beck, 1974). Surviving children of these mothers proved to have a higher than normal rate of mental retardation (Vorhees & Mollnow, 1987). Even clinical doses of radiation (such as those used in X rays and cancer treatment) seem to be capable of causing mutations, spontaneous abortions, and a variety of birth defects, especially if the mother is exposed during the first trimester of pregnancy. For this reason, expectant mothers are routinely advised to avoid X rays unless it is absolutely essential to their own survival, and women who work with X-ray equipment must take proper precautions.

Then there are the pollutants in the air we breathe and the water we drink. For example, "heavy metals," such as lead, are discharged by smelting operations and other industries and may be present in paint or water pipes. Children who are exposed to lead prenatally show various degrees of impaired intellectual functioning (Bellinger et al., 1987; Rutter, 1980). The polluting chemicals called PCBs, now outlawed but still present in the environment, represent another hazard. Joseph Jacobson and his colleagues found that newborns exposed to low levels of PCBs, due to their mothers' eating fish from Lake Michigan during pregnancy, were neurologically immature and that some were also born small or prematurely (J. L. Jacobson et al., 1984). At age 4 these children showed deficiencies in short-term memory, and the extent of their deficits corresponded to the doses of PCBs they received prenatally (Jacobson, Jacobson, & Humphrey, 1990). The principle of critical periods was also borne out: Although larger quantities of PCBs are passed through breast feeding than via the placenta, exposure to PCBs after birth through nursing had no relationship to cognitive performance.

Finally, a *father's* exposure to environmental toxins can also affect children. How? It seems that a father's prolonged exposure to radiation, anesthetic gases used in operating rooms, pesticides, and other environmental toxins can damage the chromosomes in his sperm and cause genetic defects in his children (Gunderson & Sackett, 1982; Stone, 1992; Strigini et al., 1990). Clearly, there is a critical need for more research aimed at identifying a potentially huge range of chemicals, wastes, and other environmental hazards that could affect unborn children.

Summing Up

The message is clear: The chemistry of the prenatal environment can often determine whether an embryo or fetus survives and how it looks and functions if it does survive. By becoming familiar with the material discussed here, and by staying abreast of new knowledge as it becomes available, parents-to-be can do much to increase the already high odds that their unborn child will be normal as it approaches its next challenge: the birth process.

THE PERINATAL ENVIRONMENT

The **perinatal environment** is the environment surrounding birth; it includes influences such as drugs given to the mother during delivery, delivery practices, and the social environment shortly after birth. Like the prenatal environment, the perinatal environment can greatly affect human development.

The Birth Process

Childbirth is a three-stage process. The first stage begins as the mother experiences *contractions* of the uterus spaced at 10-minute to 15-minute intervals and ends when her cervix has fully dilated so that the fetus's head can pass through. This phase of labor lasts an average of 8 to 14 hours for firstborn children and 3 to 8 hours for later-borns. The second stage of labor is *delivery,* which begins as the fetus's head passes through the cervix into the vagina and ends when the baby emerges from the mother's body. This is the time when the mother is often told to bear down (push) with each contraction in order to assist her baby through the birth canal. A quick delivery may take a half-hour, whereas a long one may take more than an hour and a half. Finally, the third stage of the birth process is the *afterbirth,* or the expulsion of the placenta a few minutes after delivery.

The second stage of labor ends when the baby has emerged from the mother; in the third stage the placenta will be expelled.

When the birth process is completed, the mother (and often the father too, if he is present) is physically exhausted and relieved to be through the ordeal of giving birth. Meanwhile, the fetus has been thrust from its quite carefree existence into a strange new world.

Possible Hazards during the Birth Process

In the large majority of births the entire process goes smoothly, and parents and newborn quickly begin their relationship. Occasionally, however, problems arise.

Anoxia

One clear hazard during the birth process is **anoxia**, or oxygen shortage. Anoxia can occur for any number of reasons — for example, because the umbilical cord becomes pinched or tangled during birth, because sedatives given to the mother reach the fetus and interfere with the baby's breathing, or because mucus lodged in the baby's throat prevents normal breathing. Why is anoxia dangerous? Largely because brain cells die if they are starved of oxygen for more than a few minutes. Severe anoxia can result in *cerebral palsy,* a motor disability in which the affected individual has difficulties controlling muscles of the arms, legs, or head (Vaughn, McKay, & Behrman, 1984). Brain damage that results in mental retardation is also possible when anoxia is severe.

Milder cases of anoxia make some infants irritable at birth or delay their motor and cognitive development (Sameroff & Chandler, 1975). However, many victims, especially those whose environments after birth are optimal, function perfectly normally later in childhood (Sameroff & Chandler, 1975). In one study, for example, children who suffered from relatively brief anoxia scored below normal as a group on measures of intellectual development at age 3 but had average intelligence test scores by age 7 (Corah et al., 1965). Only a minority of these children showed persisting problems. Thus, prolonged anoxia can cause permanent disabilities, but the effects of milder anoxia are typically overcome as a child gets older.

Another bit of good news is that the incidence of anoxia has been greatly reduced by the use of fetal monitoring procedures during labor and delivery. Doctors are now alert to the risk of anoxia if the fetus is not positioned in the usual head-down position, for then the birth process takes longer. If the baby is born feet or buttocks first (a **breech presentation**), delivery becomes more complex, although the vast majority of breech babies are normal. A vaginal delivery is nearly impossible for the 1 fetus in 100 lying sideways in the uterus. The fetus must be turned to assume a head-first position or be delivered by **cesarean section,** a surgical procedure in which an incision is made in the mother's abdomen and uterus so that the baby can be removed. And that leads us to the potential hazards associated with delivery procedures and technologies themselves.

Delivery Methods

During the 19th century, many doctors believed that the routine use of *forceps* (an instrument resembling an oversized pair of salad tongs) was the best way to deliver babies (Edwards & Waldorf, 1984). Unfortunately, the use of forceps on the soft skull of the fetus sometimes caused serious problems, including cranial bleeding and brain damage. Now forceps are used with great care only when a baby is in danger.

As for the cesarean section (or C-section), it, too, has been controversial. Use of this alternative to normal vaginal delivery has prevented the death of many babies—for example, when the baby is too large or the mother is too small to permit normal delivery, when a fetus out of position cannot be repositioned, or when fetal monitoring reveals that a birth complication is likely. Medical advances have made cesarean sections about as safe as vaginal deliveries, and few ill effects on mothers and infants have been observed (Kochanevich-Wallace, McCluskey-Fawcett, Meck, & Simons, 1988). However, mothers who have C-sections do take far longer to recover from the birth process (Gottlieb & Barrett, 1986), and newborns born this way sometimes experience respiratory difficulties. Moreover, some observers question why cesarean deliveries have become so much more common over the years, now accounting for almost a quarter of all births in the United States (Taffel, Placek, Moien, & Kosary, 1991). Some evidence hints that obstetricians rely heavily on this procedure because it protects them from the costly malpractice suits that might arise from complications in vaginal deliveries (Localio et al., 1993).

Medications

Finally, concerns have also been raised about medications given to mothers during the birth process—analgesics and anesthetics to reduce their pain, sedatives to relax them, and stimulants to induce or intensify uterine contractions. Yvonne Brackbill and her associates (1985) have found that babies whose mothers receive large doses of obstetrical medication smile infrequently, are generally sluggish and irritable, and are difficult to feed or cuddle during the first few weeks of life. In short, they act as though they were drugged, which can make it hard for their parents to become emotionally attached to them (Murray, Dolby, Nation, & Thomas, 1981). Some babies of heavily medicated mothers even show deficits in motor and cognitive development for at least a year after birth (Brackbill, 1979). Doses of medication large enough to affect mothers can have much greater impacts on newborns who weigh only 7 pounds and have immature circulatory and excretory systems that cannot get rid of drugs for days or even weeks.

So, should mothers avoid obstetric medications at all costs? That advice is perhaps too strong. For example, some women are at risk of experiencing birth complications because of their size or body shape or because their babies are large. For such women, sedatives in appropriate doses can actually *reduce* the chances of complications such as anoxia (Myers, 1980; Myers & Myers, 1979).

It is also important to recognize that there are many drugs—each with its own potential effects, some safer than others. The infants most negatively affected by drugs have often been those whose mothers inhaled general anesthetics such as nitrous oxide (Brackbill et al., 1985). More alert to the potentially negative effects of such medications, doctors today are more likely than doctors of the past to use drugs only when clearly necessary and to use the least toxic drugs in the lowest effective doses at the safest times (Finster, Pedersen, & Morishima, 1984). Thus, taking obstetric medications is not as risky a business today as it once was, but it is still a decision that requires weighing the pros and cons carefully.

TABLE 4.3 The Apgar test.

Characteristic	Score 0	1	2
Heart rate	Absent	Slow (under 100 beats per minute)	Over 100 beats per minute
Respiratory effort	Absent	Slow or irregular	Good; baby is crying
Muscle tone	Flaccid; limp	Weak; some flexion	Strong; active motion
Color	Blue or pale	Body pink, extremities blue	Completely pink
Reflex irritability	No response	Frown, grimace, or weak cry	Vigorous cry

Identifying High-Risk Newborns

In the end, a small minority of infants are in great jeopardy at birth because of genetic defects, prenatal hazards, or perinatal damage. It is essential to these infants' survival and well-being that they be identified as early as possible. Although much more sophisticated methods of evaluating the health and functioning of newborns exist (Molfese, 1989), the **Apgar test** is routinely used to assess the newborn's heart rate, respiration, color, muscle tone, and reflexes immediately after birth and then five minutes later (see Table 4.3). Scores for each factor in this simple test range from 0 to 2, with a total possible score of 0 to 10. Infants who score 7 or higher are in good shape. However, infants scoring 4 or lower are at risk—their heartbeats are sluggish or nonexistent, their muscles are limp, and their breathing (if they are breathing) is shallow and irregular. These babies will immediately experience a different postnatal environment than the normal baby experiences, for they require medical intervention in intensive-care units to survive, as we will see at the end of the chapter.

The Social Environment Surrounding Birth

The birth of a baby is a dramatic experience for the whole family. However, it was not that long ago that most hospitals barred fathers from the delivery room and snatched babies away from their mothers soon after delivery to place them in nurseries. Let's look briefly at the birth experience from a family perspective.

The Mother

It is now clear that psychological factors such as the mother's attitude toward her pregnancy, her knowledge about the birth process, and the support she receives from her partner and other people are important determinants of her experience of delivery and of her new baby. When the father, or another supportive person whose main role is to comfort the mother, is present during labor and delivery, women experience less pain, use less medication, are less likely to have cesarean sections, and feel more positive about the whole birth process (Hodnett & Osborn, 1989; Kennell et al., 1991).

The first minutes after birth can be a special time in which the mother begins to love her newborn—provided she is allowed to get to know this little stranger. Marshall Klaus and John Kennell believe that the first 6 to 12 hours after birth are a sensitive period for the emotional *bonding* of a mother to her infant, a time when the mother is especially ready to develop a strong affection for her baby and when her baby is especially alert and responsive (Kennell, Voos, & Klaus, 1979). In a study testing their hypothesis, Klaus and Kennell (1976) had half of a group of new mothers follow what was then a traditional hospital routine: They saw their babies briefly after delivery, visited with them 6 to 12 hours later, and then had half-hour feeding sessions every four hours during their three-day stay in the hospital. Mothers in an "extended contact" experimental group were allowed five "extra" hours a day to cuddle their babies, including an hour of skin-to-skin contact within three hours of birth.

A month later, mothers who had had extended contact with their infants appeared to be more involved with them and held them closer during feeding sessions. A year later these mothers were still more nurturing, and their 1-year-olds outperformed control infants on tests of physical and mental development. Apparently, then, extended early contact promoted early mother/infant bonding, which may in turn have motivated mothers to interact in stimulating ways with their babies. However, subsequent research has indicated that "early contact" effects are not as large or as lasting as Klaus and Kennell found them to be (Goldberg, 1983). Such contact can be a pleasant experience for both mother and baby, and it can help a mother *begin* to form an emotional bond to her child. However, attachments between infants and caregivers are not formed in a matter of minutes or hours. They develop slowly, through social interactions taking place over many weeks and months, and can develop even when there is no early contact at all between parent and infant.

In most cases a secure and loving attachment will grow (Rode, Chang, Fisch, & Sroufe, 1981; see also Chapter 13). However, as Box 4.1 reveals, the mother/child relationship may get off to a rocky start if the new mother experiences postpartum depression.

BOX 4.1 The "Down Side" of New Parenthood: Postpartum Depression

For some new mothers the experience of giving birth is anything but joyful; it is a time of profound sadness and hopelessness. Valerie Whiffen (1992) points out that there are actually three distinct depressive states that sometimes affect new mothers. A mother experiencing the *maternity blues* is tearful, irritable, moody, anxious, and depressed within the first ten days after birth. This condition is relatively mild, passes quickly, and is probably linked to the steep drops in hormone levels that normally occur after delivery, as well as to the stresses associated with delivering a child and taking on the responsibilities of parenthood. As many as half of new mothers may experience the maternity blues (Kraus & Redman, 1986). A second, and far more serious, condition is *postpartum psychosis;* a very small minority of new mothers who have had previous histories of psychological disorder experience hallucinations and other symptoms of severe psychopathology after giving birth and require hospitalization. In between these extremes is the condition of primary interest to us here, **postpartum depression,** or an episode of clinical depression that lasts for a matter of months rather than days in a woman who has just given birth.

Postpartum depression affects about 13% of new mothers (Whiffen, 1992). Most of the affected women have histories of depression, and many were depressed during pregnancy as well. It is very rare for a woman who has never had significant emotional problems to become clinically depressed for the first time after giving birth (Whiffen, 1992). Moreover, women who are vulnerable to depression are more likely to actually become depressed if they are experiencing other life stresses besides the stress of becoming a mother (O'Hara, Schlechte, Lewis, & Varner, 1991). Lack of social support—especially a poor relationship with one's partner—also increases the odds (Gotlib, Whiffen, Wallace, & Mount, 1991). Researchers have not been able to detect any simple or straightforward connection between hormonal changes in the postpartum period and postpartum depression (O'Hara et al., 1991), so at this point environmental factors such as marital conflict seem more important than hormonal factors.

Is postpartum depression a unique form of depression? Although some would argue that the hormonal changes accompanying it make it unique, Whiffen (1992) concludes that it is basically no different from any other kind. She suggests that we may not really need to speak of "postpartum depression" any more than we need to speak of "post-breakup depression" or "postretirement depression." Postpartum or not, depression tends to occur when a vulnerable individual experiences overwhelming stress (see Chapter 16). In this case the stresses simply center around the transition to new parenthood.

Whether it is a unique syndrome or not, postpartum depression has significant implications for the parent/infant relationship. In a study comparing 70 mothers experiencing postpartum depression and 59 nondepressed mothers over a 24-month period, Susan Campbell and her associates (1992) found that depressed women often did not want their babies in the first place and perceived them as difficult babies. These depressed women also interacted less positively with their infants and in some cases seemed hostile toward them. Other studies suggest that, when mothers are depressed, withdrawn, and unresponsive, the mother/infant attachment is likely to be insecure, and infants may develop depressive symptoms and behavior problems of their own (Field et al., 1985; Murray, 1992; Radke-Yarrow, Cummings, Kuczynski, & Chapman, 1985). For their own sake and for the sake of their infants, then, mothers experiencing more than a mild case of the "maternity blues" should seek professional help in overcoming their depression.

The Father

The birth process is also a significant event in the life of a father. He, too, may experience anxiety during his partner's pregnancy and during the birth process, and he, too, may find early contact with his baby special. Like the mother, he often shows an **engrossment** with the baby—an intense fascination and a desire to touch, hold, caress, and talk to this new member of the family (Greenberg & Morris, 1974; Peterson, Mehl, & Liederman, 1979). One young father put it this way: "When I come up to see [my] wife . . . I go look at the kid and then I pick her up and then I put her down. . . . I keep going back to the kid. It's like a magnet. That's what I can't get over, the fact that I feel like that" (Greenberg & Morris, 1974, p. 524). Some studies find that fathers who handle and help care for their babies in the hospital later spend more time with them at home than fathers who have not had these early interactions (Greenberg & Morris, 1974). Other studies fail to find these long-term effects on the father/infant relationship but suggest that early contact with the newborn makes a father feel closer to his partner and more a part of a "family" (Palkovitz, 1985). Like mothers, however, fathers have much time later to learn to love their children even if they do not have much contact shortly after birth.

Risk and Resilience: Do Negative Effects of the Prenatal and Perinatal Environments Endure?

We have now encountered many examples of what can go wrong during the prenatal and perinatal periods of development. Certainly some damaging effects are irreversible: The thalidomide baby will never grow normal arms or legs, and the child who is mentally retarded from fetal alcohol syndrome will always be mentally retarded. And yet there are countless adults walking around today whose mothers, unaware of many risk factors that concern us now, smoked and drank during their pregnancies, or received heavy doses of medication during delivery, and yet had children who turned out fine. As we have already emphasized, not all embryos, fetuses, or newborns exposed to hazards are affected by them. Is it also possible that some babies who are exposed and who are clearly affected recover from their deficiencies later in life?

Indeed it is, and we now have longitudinal follow-up studies to tell us so (Kopp & Kahler, 1989). Consider these findings: Monroe Lefkowitz (1981) reported that, 9 to 11 years after they were born, the children of mothers who smoked during pregnancy were no smaller, no less intelligent, no less achievement oriented, and no less socially adjusted than the children of nonsmokers. Zela Stein and her associates found that, as young adults entering the military, Dutch males whose mothers experienced famine during their pregnancies scored no lower on a test of intelligence than males who received adequate prenatal nutrition (Stein & Susser, 1976; Stein et al., 1975).

And then we have the results of major longitudinal studies of babies who were "at risk" at birth—for example, who had low birth weights, had been exposed to prenatal hazards, or suffered poor health (Baker & Mednick, 1984; Werner, 1989; Werner & Smith, 1982, 1992). These studies indicate that babies at risk—particularly those whose problems at birth are severe—have more intellectual and social problems as children and as adolescents than normal babies do. And yet many of these at-risk babies outgrow their problems with time. Emmy Werner and Ruth Smith (1982), in reporting on their longitudinal study of all babies born in 1955 on the island of Kauai in Hawaii, went so far as to title their book *Vulnerable but Invincible*, so impressed were they by the **resilience** of young human beings—the "self-righting" tendencies that allow many of them (about a third) to recover from early disadvantages (such as prenatal and perinatal difficulties, poverty, and disorganized families) and to get back on a normal course of development. The Kauai babies have now been followed into their early 30s, and it is clear that their outcomes in life have had more to do with their experiences since birth—including their experiences as adults—than with any problems they experienced at birth (Werner & Smith, 1992).

The interesting question, then, is this: Why do some children recover from early deficiencies while others continue to have problems later in life? Two sets of "protective factors" have proven important (Garmezy, 1987; Werner, 1989). First, some children, in part because of their genetic makeup, may have greater personal strengths and recuperative powers than others do. For example, Werner and Smith (1982, 1992) found that some children who seemed to have everything working against them had qualities, such as intelligence, sociability, and communication skills, that helped them to choose or create more nurturing and stimulating environments and to cope with challenges. And that leads us to a second answer: The children who display resilience usually have favorable *postnatal* environments, whereas the children who do not recover often encounter multiple stresses after they are born (Baker & Mednick, 1984; Werner & Smith, 1992). More specifically, resilient children receive the social support they need, within or outside the family, and—most importantly—they are able to find at least one person who loves them unconditionally (Werner & Smith, 1992).

Consider one at-risk group of babies: those with low birth weight. The 8–9% of infants who weigh less than 2500 grams (5½ pounds) at birth are especially likely to have difficulty if they not only arrive prematurely (more than 3 weeks before their due dates) but also are smaller than they should be considering the time they have been in the womb (Kopp & Parmelee, 1979).

As we have seen, the mother's smoking or drinking, fetal malnutrition, and a number of other factors can contribute to prematurity and low birth weight. Low-birth-weight babies are clearly at risk. They must first be helped to survive, for they are likely to develop infections, respiratory difficulties, and other problems. As Table 4.4 illustrates, the smaller these babies are, the lower their odds of survival. Assuming they do survive, they may be difficult to love because they are often tiny and wrinkled, as well as both unresponsive and irritable. What's more, they may be stereotyped by those around them as intellectually and socially limited (Stern & Hildebrandt, 1986).

It doesn't sound good. And yet researchers are learning that the fates of premature and low-birth-weight babies depend considerably on the quality of their postnatal environments (Beckwith & Parmelee, 1986; Brooks-Gunn et al., 1993; Greenberg & Crnic, 1988; Wilson, 1985). Consider what Ronald Wilson (1985) found in his study of twins who were especially small at birth (weighing under 1750 grams, or less than about 3¾ pounds) and who were also small for their (short) gestation ages. These babies were deficient in mental development as infants, but they caught up over time. Indeed, those whose families had high socioeconomic status caught up *completely* to the average child by age 6. Problems were more lasting among at-risk twins who grew up in lower-income homes, but they, too, showed self-righting tendencies. It seems that premature, low-birth-weight babies display normal intellectual functioning during childhood when they live in middle-class homes, when their mothers are relatively well educated, and when their mothers are attentive and responsive when interacting with them; but these children continue to show intellectual deficits if they grow up in less favorable environments (Beckwith & Parmelee, 1986; Cohen, Parmelee, Beckwith, & Sigman, 1986).

TABLE 4.4 Infant mortality as a function of birth weight.

	Birth weight		Percentage of babies who die
	In grams	*In Pounds*	
Very low birth weight	500–749	1 lb, 9 oz or less	67
	750–999	1 lb, 10 oz–2 lb, 3 oz	33
	1000–1249	2 lb, 4 oz–2 lb, 12 oz	16
Low birth weight	1249–1499	2 lb, 13 oz–3 lb, 4 oz	9
	1500–2500	3 lb, 5 oz–5 lb, 8 oz	6
Average birth weight	2500–3000	5 lb, 9 oz–6 lb, 9 oz	2
	3001–4500	6 lb, 10 oz–9 lb, 14 oz	1

Studies like these raise a larger issue about the importance of early experience. Some developmentalists take seriously the concept of critical (or sensitive) periods in early development (MacDonald, 1986). Others stress the resilience of human beings—their ability to rebound from early disadvantages and to respond to environmental influences throughout their lives rather than only during so-called critical periods (Kagan, 1986). Which is it?

We have encountered evidence in favor of both positions. Hazards during the important prenatal and perinatal periods *can* leave lasting scars, and yet many children show remarkable resilience. Isn't this the lesson we learn from the case of Genie described at the beginning of the chapter? Yes, she was permanently affected by extreme deprivation during sensitive periods of development early in life. But even she showed considerable resilience when her environment improved. There *do* seem to be some points in the life span, especially early on, when both positive and negative environmental forces have especially strong impacts. Yet, at the same time, *environment matters throughout life*. Certainly, it would be a huge mistake to assume that all children who have problems at birth are doomed. In short, early experience by itself rarely makes or breaks the developing person; later experience counts too. It is time, then, to turn our attention to the *postnatal* environment.

THE POSTNATAL ENVIRONMENT

In chapters to come, we will have much to say about a wide range of environmental influences on development: parents, peers, schools, workplaces, and so on. Here we merely want to make the point that human development is influenced by the broader social context in which it occurs—by cultural factors, or what Urie Bronfenbrenner terms the *macrosystem*. Through cross-cultural research, developmentalists are able to answer some critical questions: Which aspects of development are universal—evident across cultures despite often startling differences in cultural values, beliefs, lifestyles, and child-rearing practices? Which developmental processes and outcomes are instead more strongly shaped by environmental forces unique to the particular culture in which an individual develops?

Culture and Socialization Goals for Infants and Children

Parents are products of their broader culture, and they in turn transmit that culture to their offspring. **Socialization** is the process by which individuals acquire the beliefs, values, and behaviors judged important in their society. By socializing the young, society controls their undesirable behavior, prepares them to adapt to the environment in which they must function, and ensures that cultural traditions will be carried on by future generations. Parents, siblings, peers, schools, churches, and many other people and institutions all contribute to the socialization process. How much do children's socialization experiences differ from society to society? A good deal.

Think about the traits that you would most want to instill in your children. There is much disagreement within our own society, and much variation from society to society, in specific socialization goals. The parents of an Eskimo boy might want him to learn hunting skills and to be strong; the parents of a Chicago boy might want him to learn computer skills and to be smart. Yet Robert LeVine (1974, p. 230; see also LeVine, 1988) maintains that parents everywhere share three very broad goals for their children:

1. The *survival goal*—to promote the children's physical survival and health, ensuring that they will live long enough to have children of their own.
2. The *economic goal*—to foster the skills and traits children will need for economic self-maintenance as adults.
3. The *self-actualization goal*—to foster capacities for maximizing other cultural values (for example,

morality, religion, achievement, wealth, prestige, and a sense of personal satisfaction).

LeVine also maintains that these universal goals of parenting form a hierarchy. Until parents are confident that their children will survive, higher-order goals (such as teaching them to talk, count, or follow moral rules) are put on the back burner. And only when parents and other caregivers believe that their children have acquired the basic attributes that will eventually contribute to their economic self-sufficiency will they encourage such goals as self-actualization or self-fulfillment.

Because different peoples must adapt to different environments, they sometimes emphasize different parenting goals, and their child-rearing practices differ accordingly. In societies where infant mortality is high, the survival goal of parenting is emphasized. Babies may not even be named or viewed as persons until they seem likely to survive (Nsamenang, 1992). Parents keep infants nearby 24 hours a day to protect them. Among the !Kung, a hunting and gathering society of the Kalahari Desert in southern Africa, for example, babies are carried upright in slings during the day, and they sleep in bed with their mothers at night (Konner, 1981). They are breastfed, suckling several times an hour as desired, and may not be weaned until the ripe old age of 4. In general, infants in hunter/gatherer societies are indulged considerably, at least until their survival is assured.

Infant-care practices are considerably different in modern, industrialized societies, where infant mortality is lower. Babies typically sleep apart from their parents; they breastfeed, if at all, for only a few months before being switched to the bottle and then to solid food; and they generally must learn to accommodate their needs to their parents' schedules (Konner, 1981). Not surprisingly, Mayan mothers in Guatemala, whose babies sleep in the same bed with them until they are toddlers, express shock at the American practice of leaving infants alone in their own bedrooms (Morelli, Rogoff, Oppenheim, & Goldsmith, 1992). American mothers, of course, believe that this practice is perfectly appropriate and serves the goal of fostering independence.

Parenting practices are also influenced by specific cultural belief systems. Amy Richman and her associates (1988) have observed mothers interacting with their babies in five societies, two agrarian and three industrial. Figure 4.6 shows some striking differences between how Gusii mothers in Kenya and white middle-class mothers in Boston interact with their 9- to 10-month-old infants (see also Richman, Miller, & LeVine, 1992). Gusii mothers hold their infants and make physical contact to soothe them far more, but they look at and talk to their babies far less.

Why the differences? Like so many parents in non-Western societies with high infant mortality rates, Gusii mothers emphasize the survival goal of parenting, keeping their offspring comfortable and safe by holding them close. In addition, the Gusii believe that babies cannot understand speech until about age 2. No wonder, then, that they rarely converse with their young charges. And, because cultural norms in their society demand that they avert their gaze during conversations, they rarely make eye contact with their babies either, even during lengthy breastfeeding sessions. In Boston, by contrast, playpens and infant seats are available as substitutes for mothers' arms, and their use probably reflects the value American

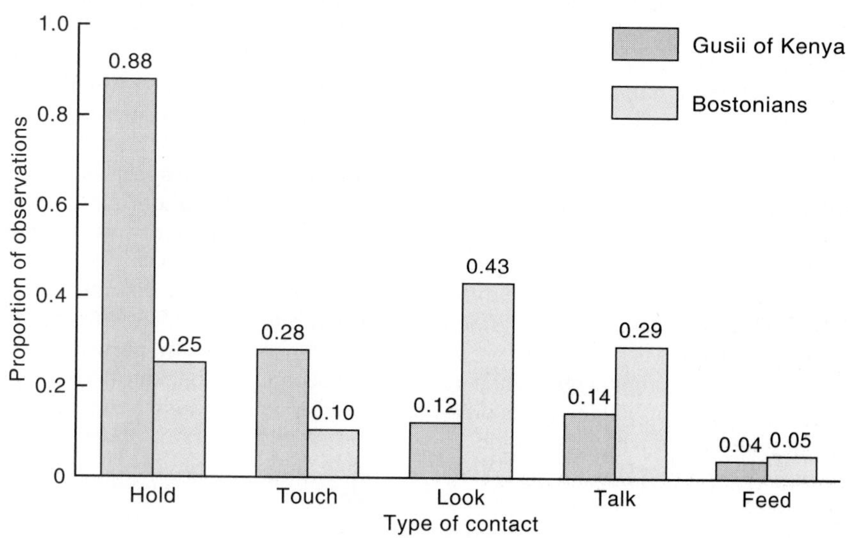

FIGURE 4.6 Gusii parents in Africa hold and touch their infants more, but look at and talk to them less, than parents in the United States do. (Based on data from Richman et al., 1988.)

In many cultures, parents attempt to achieve the survival goal of parenting by keeping their babies close at all times.

parents place on teaching their children to be autonomous. Moreover, American mothers believe that babies *can* understand speech and that they should get an early start on developing language skills in order to succeed in school; as a result, these mothers chat away while they interact with their babies.

Although we do not know what long-term effects these divergent parenting practices may have, it is clear that infants respond to the parenting they receive. Thus, for example, Gusii babies cry less often and are generally quieter than Boston babies are (Richman et al., 1988). Of special significance for development, however, may be the *goodness of fit* between an infant's temperament and the culture's demands. Charles Super and Sarah Harkness (1981) found that in Boston, where mothers establish regular schedules for their infants, with planned nap times, feeding times, and bedtimes, a baby who could not learn to sleep through the night was labeled a "problem baby." In Kokwet, a rural farming community in Kenya, the same baby would not be viewed as difficult at all. Because mothers sleep with their infants, it is easy to feed them whenever they are hungry. What disturbs a Kokwet mother is a baby who fusses when handed to another caregiver for a short time while the mother attempts to go about her work. The baby whose temperament is mismatched to its cultural "niche" is likely to have a more difficult experience of infancy than the baby who is more temperamentally suited to meet cultural demands.

Once a child's survival is assured and parents turn their attention to the economic goal of parenting, they emphasize the values and skills that are most necessary to make a living in their society (Barry, Child, & Bacon, 1959; Ogbu, 1981; Whiting & Edwards, 1988). A cross-cultural study of 122 traditional societies by Godfrey Ellis and Larry Petersen (1992) makes this point well. In agricultural societies, where people generally work as part of organized teams and must be able to accept supervision by others, parents tend to stress conformity and obedience in raising their children and make heavy use of control tactics, including physical punishment, to bring them into line. By contrast, in hunting, gathering, and fishing societies, adults typically go out on their own to find food. Accordingly, parents stress independence, assertiveness, and self-reliance in raising children, and they are much more permissive than parents in agricultural societies are, allowing their children to make many decisions on their own.

Variation within Cultures: Socioeconomic and Ethnic Diversity

Important as cross-cultural variation in development can be, diversity within societies is greater than variation among societies (Konner, 1991). Consider first variations associated with **socioeconomic status (SES),** the position people hold in society based on such factors as income, education, occupational status, and the prestige of their neighborhoods (Brislin, 1993). In our society it is meaningful to distinguish among upper, middle, and lower socioeconomic groups, the latter including both working-class people and families living in poverty. For about one in five children in the United States, poverty is a way of life (Garbarino, 1992). African-American, Hispanic-American, and Native-American children are especially likely to live in poverty and to experience the health problems and social stresses that accompany poverty. They are especially likely to suffer ill effects if living in poverty undermines their parents' ability to be involved with them and to provide consistent guidance (McLoyd, 1990).

Parents from different socioeconomic backgrounds typically differ in their socialization goals and parenting styles. In particular, parents from lower socioeconomic backgrounds emphasize conformity, obedience, neatness, and respect for power and tend to use authoritarian, power-assertive forms of discipline such as physical punishment (Kohn, 1969; Maccoby, 1980). Middle- and upper-SES parents stress such traits as self-reliance, ambition, creativity, and independence and tend to be more permissive. They are more likely than lower-SES parents to explain their rules and less likely to say "Do it because I say so."

These differences in child-rearing values and styles can be linked to the kinds of jobs parents have (Kohn, 1969). Lower-SES, blue-collar workers expect that their children, like themselves, will have to work for a boss and defer to his or her authority, whereas middle-SES professionals and business owners expect that their children, like themselves, will be self-employed or will manage other people and will therefore need to be independent, self-assertive, creative, and so on. Being able to aid their children in achieving economic security goals, middle- and upper-class parents may also feel freer to turn to LeVine's self-actualization goals, encouraging their children to pursue whatever interests them. Notice that the differences in parenting observed between parents of higher and lower socioeconomic status in our society exactly parallel the differences we discussed earlier between parents in agricultural societies and those in hunter/gatherer societies (Barry et al., 1959; Ellis & Petersen, 1992). The type of work that parents perform influences the kinds of values they seek to instill in their children and the ways they go about doing so (see Figure 4.7). Indeed, what appear to be cultural differences among societies sometimes turn out to stem from lower levels of education or income in one society than in another and disappear when socioeconomic status is properly controlled (Brislin, 1993).

Our society is not only socioeconomically but also racially and ethnically diverse. African-American, Hispanic-American, Native-American, and Asian-American children are likely to have different developmental experiences than white children of European backgrounds do. Within each of these broad racial/ethnic groups, of course, there are also immense variations associated with such factors as specific national origin, length of time in North America, degree of integration into mainstream society, language usage, and socioeconomic status.

Although scholars who conduct cross-cultural research have long been sensitive to the need to avoid imposing their own values on people from other cultures, the same cannot be said of scholars studying racial and ethnic diversity within the United States and other industrialized countries. For many years, minority group children and adults have been judged according to white middle-class standards and found to be "deficient" (Helms, 1992; Ogbu, 1981). More and more researchers today are adopting a contextual perspective on development and appreciate the importance of understanding the distinctive cultural contexts in which children from different racial and ethnic backgrounds develop.

To cite just one example: It has often been assumed, based on research with white middle-class families, that *the* critical relationship in a child's life is the mother/child relationship. Yet in many cultural groups around the world, as well as among African Americans in the United States, child-care responsibilities are shared with grandmothers, older siblings, aunts and uncles, and other relatives so that mothers can earn a living (Tronick, Morelli, & Ivey, 1992; Wilson, 1989). From a white middle-class perspective, it might seem that black children are neglected by their mothers, but a closer look reveals that these children often have a whole team of parent figures at their disposal and that their maternal grandmothers in particular are often central figures in their lives. After much dissecting of the "problems" of disadvantaged minority groups, developmentalists are now beginning to uncover some of the strengths of their cultural traditions.

Developmentalists have also tended to regard the child-rearing style used by white middle-class parents as a particularly good one. But, as John Ogbu (1981) emphasizes, that style may do more harm than good in an environment that demands attributes other than self-reliance. If, for example, a family cannot survive unless children are obedient, it would be foolish to encourage children to "do their own thing." There is no one "right" way to socialize children. Instead, the definition of a competent parent depends on the particular qualities needed for success in a given culture or subculture. And that definition may also change as society changes. The broad goals of

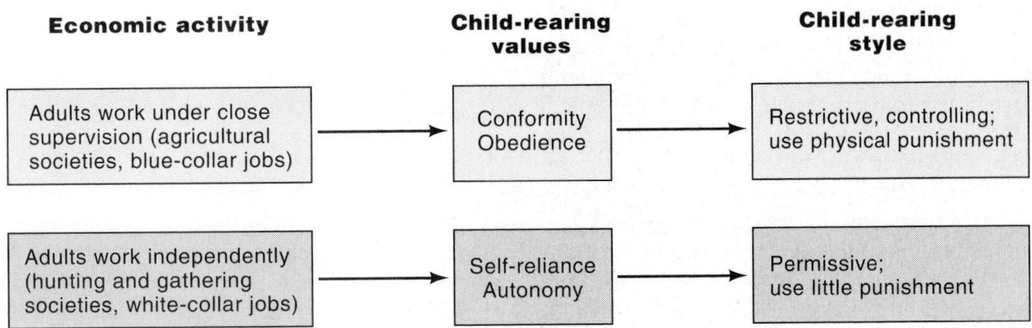

FIGURE 4.7 The ways in which adults make a living influence their child-rearing values and practices.

Children of different racial and ethnic backgrounds, although similar in most respects, often learn different cultural traditions.

parenting may be universal, but the specific goals of socialization and the practices used by parents to achieve those goals differ widely from place to place, time to time, and individual to individual.

Cultural Variation and Our Understanding of Child Development

What differences do all these variations in socialization really make? Perhaps it has occurred to you that, if children are raised differently in different cultures and subcultures, our understandings of development might depend on which culture or subculture we study. This is the case, and here are some examples.

1. *Culture affects the behavior shown by children of a particular age.* Children in many industrialized countries such as the United States are more competitive and less cooperative and helpful than their agemates in agricultural societies such as Mexico (Kagan & Masden, 1972; Whiting & Whiting, 1975). This is probably because Americans socialize children to be independent and assertive, whereas agrarian cultures often teach children to cooperate within the family for the good of all.

2. *Culture affects the rate of development.* !Kung infants walk earlier than Western babies do, perhaps because they spend a good deal of time in slings that keep them upright and give them considerable freedom of movement (Konner, 1976). A Ugandan baby, who is rarely parted from the mother early in life, begins to protest separations from her at only 5 or 6 months of age (Ainsworth, 1967); in our society, separation anxiety is rare before 7 months of age. There are many differences across cultures in the ages at which developmental milestones are attained.

3. *Culture affects the very direction of development.* Research in our society indicates that, as children get older and more intelligent, they are more and more able to pass up a small reward immediately and wait for a larger reward in the future (Mischel & Metzner, 1962). This ability to delay gratification is believed to indicate "maturity." Yet, among the Aborigines of Australia, older and more intelligent children are *less* likely to delay gratification than younger and less intelligent ones (Bochner & David, 1968). For nomadic hunters who move frequently, like the Aborigines, it is maladaptive to be burdened by hoarded goods; older children have learned the value of consuming goods immediately.

Or consider this example: As children in the United States get older, they increasingly understand that dreams are not real, that they are only internal mental phenomena. However, among the Atayal, an aboriginal group in Taiwan, children give up the belief that dreams are real but revert back to this "immature" belief at about age 11 (Kohlberg, 1966). It is at this age that they are socialized into their culture's belief that the soul leaves the body during a dream and goes on a real journey through the spiritual world. Examples like this are relatively rare, but they provide tantalizing hints that development *can* proceed in one direction in one society and in the very opposite direction in another society.

4. *Culture affects our understanding of positive and negative influences on development.* One team of investigators (Johnson, Teigen, & Davila, 1983) sought to determine whether a high level of anxiety in children is associated with a restrictive parenting style (in which parents set many rules and strictly enforce them) or a more permissive parenting style. In Mexico, where restrictive parenting is common, children whose parents were permissive were the most anxious. In Norway, where parents are generally permissive, children whose parents were *restrictive* were the most anxious. It appears that children become anxious when their parents use a style that is atypical in their particular society. Such findings obviously make it difficult to state general rules of good parenting that will be valid in all societies.

The broader message is clear: We simply must view development in its cultural context. Most of the research reported in this textbook has been conducted with children and adults in North America and may not hold up in other societies. To be sure, there are many universal aspects of human development—many ways in which all children develop along similar paths despite variations in their experiences. However, as Christine Fry (1985) puts it, "If you want your pet theory vetoed, ask an anthropologist" (p. 236).

The Adolescent Transition

In all societies, children who have been socialized for adult life ultimately *become* adults. The process of "dying" as a child and being "reborn" as an adult appears to be a universal experience (Schlegel & Barry, 1991). However, the adolescent "coming of age" experience varies greatly and occurs at widely different ages across cultures.

Most societies in the world have developed rituals to clearly mark the transition from childhood to adulthood—rituals called adolescent **rites of passage** (van Gennep, 1908/1960). Alice Schlegel and Herbert Barry (1991) report that 68% of nonindustrialized societies hold such initiation ceremonies for boys, and 79% hold them for girls, often when they reach puberty (Schlegel & Barry, 1991). Box 4.2 shows how the rites of passage occur for boys and girls in one society in eastern Africa. In societies with such rituals, there is no prolonged period of adolescence, no struggling for years to attain adult status in the eyes of society. These rites also serve political purposes—for example, ensuring that boys become loyal to their male elders or allowing a father to advertise his daughter's maturity so he will obtain suitable compensation when he transfers this valuable reproductive "property" to another man (Paige & Paige, 1981). Although many societies do not grant the adolescent full adult status until he or she marries, or even marries and produces children (Nsamenang, 1992; Schlegel & Barry, 1991), puberty rites at least serve to mark a clear end to childhood and start the adolescent on the way to adulthood.

Now let's examine our society as an anthropologist might. When are you an adult? For some adolescents a Bar or Bas Mitzvah or a confirmation ceremony signifies a sort of passage to adulthood, but these ceremonies do not apply to all and do not confer full adult status on youth. High school graduation is an important marker perhaps. Then again, our society has devised *many* legal ages—16 and up for driving, 18 for voting, and typically 21 for drinking—rather than one clear boundary between childhood and adulthood. Must one assume a full-time job or marry to fully establish one's credentials as an adult? Western industrialized societies seem to put adolescents through a prolonged period—often lasting from age 10 or 12 to the early 20s—in which they are in limbo between childhood and adulthood, unsure what their status is (McKinney, 1984). Although conflicts between parents and adolescents are not unheard of in nonindustrialized societies, they are more common when youth must struggle for years to define themselves as individuals and to find their own niche in society (Schlegel & Barry, 1991).

Clearly, then, adolescence is not just a matter of physical and cognitive maturation; it is a *social* pro-

BOX 4.2 Rites of Passage among the Kaguru

Witness coming of age among the Kaguru of eastern Africa, as described by T.O. Beidelman (1971). As a group, boys as young as 10 to 12 are led into the bush, stripped of their clothes, and shaved of all hair, symbolically losing their previous status as children. They then undergo the painful experience of being circumcised without benefit of anesthesia. Their elders make animal noises to warn them that they will be eaten by wild animals if they ever reveal the secrets of their initiation. The boys also learn about sexual practices and are taught ritual songs and riddles that instruct them in the ways of adulthood. After this transitional period, they wash off the white ashes intended to "cool" them down during their circumcision and are "anointed" with red earth, visually displaying their new status as adults. They are led back to the village and reintegrated into society with celebrations and feasts. They are even given new names as members of the community bless them. Now each youth is ready for sexual activity and marriage and is viewed as a morally responsible adult.

The Kaguru girl is initiated by herself whenever she experiences her first menstruation. Unlike a boy, she does not become a more morally worthy person in the community's eyes when her rite of passage is completed; the prevailing view is that women are tainted creatures throughout life. The goal is to teach a girl to control her strong sexuality so that she will use it in appropriate ways to bear many children. The Kaguru do not surgically remove the clitoris, as some societies do, but they do cut the girl's genital area as a mark of her new status. She, too, is separated from the community so that she can be properly instructed in the ways of adulthood, often by her grandmother. One of the songs that both she and the boys learn goes: "The mouth of the wildcat is always open; let it be so, for it will never fill up" (p. 110). The message is that women (wildcats) are sexually insatiable and must remain so. After her instruction is completed, the girl, like the boy, enjoys celebrations and feasts as she reenters society.

Circumcision is part of a boy's coming of age in some societies.

However these rites of passage may strike us, they serve a clear purpose for the Kaguru. A child dies and an adult is born; the conversion is evident to the individual and to the whole community. Moreover, the child is given clear guidance regarding how to play the role of an adult in Kaguru society. Unlike adolescents in our society, Kaguru youth need not struggle for years to find their place in the social order.

cess. The experience of adolescence and its impacts on later development and adjustment are influenced by how a particular society defines childhood and adulthood, by what demands and pressures it places on adolescents, and by what opportunities it provides them as they make their passage into adulthood.

Living Out Adult Lives: Age Norms and Life Transitions

The experience of adulthood is dramatically different for men and women who work in high-rise buildings and eat microwave dinners than it is for men and women who spend their days hunting game and gathering fruit in the rain forest. Moreover, the cultural and historical context in which adults develop influences the timing of major life events such as marrying, having children, and becoming a grandparent. Each society, through its *age grades* and *age norms* (see Chapter 1), informs its members what they should be doing when during their adult years and what they can expect of life when they become old.

One sensible way to study environmental influences on adult development (or on development at any age, for that matter) is to assess the effects on short-term adaptation and long-term development of specific life events or transitions. Some life events can be classified as **normative transitions,** or transitions that a majority of people in a particular society experience (see Datan & Ginsberg, 1975). Transitions such as starting school as a child, graduating from high school, marrying, becoming a parent, and retiring from work are normative in our society.

Age norms tell us when it is appropriate to pass through such normative transitions: We "should" become parents, for example, when we are in our 20s; age 13 is too early, and age 53 is too late. Normative transitions can be described as "on time" or "off time," depending on whether they occur when age norms say they should. Life events that are idiosyncratic to the individual or that only a minority of people experience — becoming infected with the HIV virus, being sexually abused, or inheriting a million dollars, for example — are called **nonnormative transitions** (see Callahan & McClusky, 1983). Experiencing the death of a child is certainly not a normative transition, but it just as certainly can have devastating effects on parents and alter their future development.

Bernice Neugarten, Joan Moore, and John Lowe (1965) tried to identify prevailing age norms in the United States of the 1960s by asking middle-class, middle-aged adults in Chicago questions about the "best ages" for major life transitions. They found that there was a great deal of consensus about when certain life transitions should ideally occur. Age norms in Japan in the 1970s (Plath & Ikeda, 1975) and in New Zealand in the 1990s (Byrd & Breuss, 1992) have been found to be quite similar (see Figure 4.8). However, in nonindustrialized countries where people marry young, do not retire from productive roles unless they fall ill, and die at relatively early ages, quite different age norms often prevail.

Members of different groups within a society may also subscribe to different age norms. In some lower-income African-American communities in the United States, for example, age norms suggest that it is appropriate to become a parent in one's mid-teens rather than in one's 20s and a grandparent in one's mid-30s rather than in one's 40s or 50s (Burton, 1990). Generally, adults from lower socioeconomic backgrounds believe that normative adult transitions such as finishing school and marrying should occur earlier in adulthood than white-collar adults believe they should (Zepelin, Sills, & Heath, 1986–1987).

It appears, then, that members of any particular culture or subculture share a set of expectations about how adult lives should be led. More important, age norms influence how people lead their lives. Once age norms have been internalized, they serve as a **social clock,** a personal sense of when things should be done and when one is ahead of or behind the schedule dictated by age norms (Neugarten, 1968). Influenced by her social clock, for example, a 25-year-old woman in our society might begin to feel that, although her career is progressing right on schedule, she needs to think about getting married before she is "too old." Once she is married, her social "alarm clock" might go off in her mid-30s if she has not had children yet, prompting her to think about having a baby. Age norms, as embodied in the social clock, also affect how easily people adjust to life transitions. Such life changes as having children or retiring typically have more negative psychological impacts on us when they occur "off time" than when they occur "on time" (McLanahan & Sorensen, 1985).

As societies change, so do their age norms. Neugarten and her colleagues repeated their 1965 survey of age norms in the United States 20 years later (Passuth, Maines, & Neugarten, cited in Neugarten & Neugarten, 1986). Whereas almost 90% of the respondents in the 1960s thought the best age for a woman to marry was between 19 and 24, only 40% of the 1980s sample chose a "best" age in that narrow range. In the 1960s study a "young man" was generally believed to be 18 to 22 years old; in the 1980s study a young man meant anyone from 18 to 40. Based on such findings, Neugarten (1975; Neugarten & Neugarten, 1986) has argued that we are becoming an increasingly **age-irrelevant society,** a society in which age norms have loosened, boundaries between periods of the life span have become blurred, and people are experiencing major life transitions at a wider variety of ages.

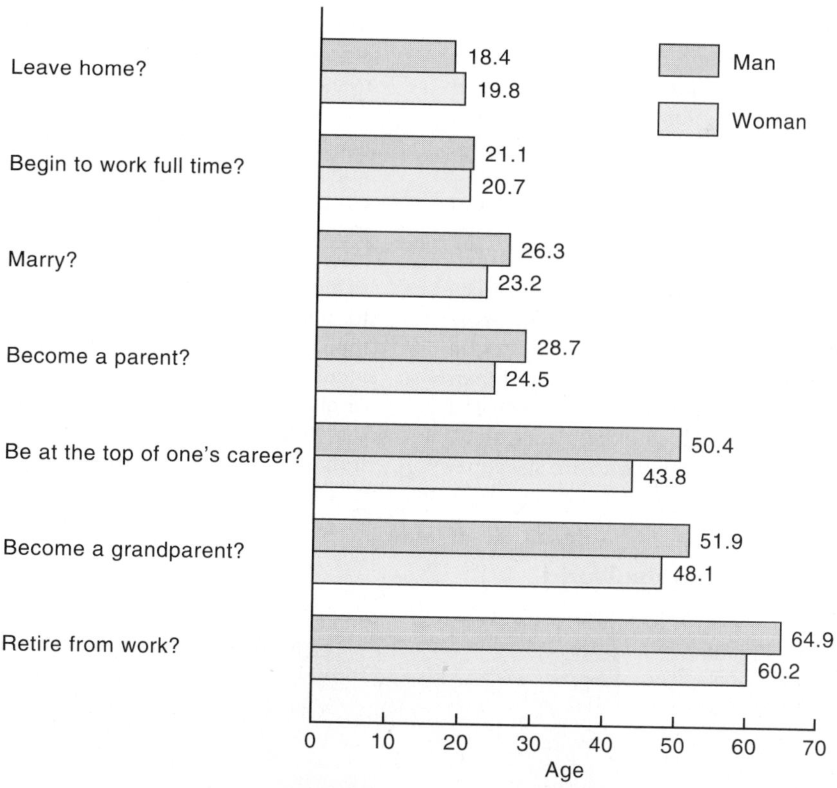

FIGURE 4.8 Age norms: Mean ages at which adults in New Zealand believe that a man and a woman should experience various normative transitions. *Do you agree with them?* (Adapted from data reported by Byrd & Breuss, 1992.)

We *do* see some women today marrying in their early teens and others waiting until their 30s or 40s, until their careers are firmly established—or forgoing marriage entirely. We also see mandatory retirement ages being abolished and older adults working, going back to college, jogging, and doing a variety of other things that seem inconsistent with more traditional age norms. Although age is not yet entirely irrelevant in our society, the age norms that guide adult lives are indeed becoming less rigid (Roscoe & Peterson, 1989; Zepelin et al., 1986–1987).

If our society is moving in the direction of becoming age irrelevant, theories that describe age-related stages of adult development may need to be revised. Why? Because if adults today truly are experiencing major life transitions at diverse ages, age alone will increasingly tell us less and less about what an adult is like. We would have to focus instead on how adults are affected by whatever major life events and role changes they experience, *whenever they occur*. In other words, if age were irrelevant in society, it might also become irrelevant in developmental theories! More generally, patterns of adult development can be expected to differ depending on what age norms prevail in a society and how rigid or loose these norms are—another illustration of the importance of the social environment in which development occurs.

Growing Old in a Changing World

What can adults in different cultural settings look forward to when they become old? A few aspects of the aging experience may be universal. As we saw in Chapter 1, all societies seem to define some portion of the life span as old age, although they disagree about when old age begins (Amoss & Harrell, 1981). Moreover, many biological changes and diseases that eventually lead to frailty and dependence are common to all cultures. Other than that, the experience of being an old person varies dramatically from society to society and changes over time as a society changes.

In some societies, to be old is to be honored and respected. In rural Taiwan, for example, birthday celebrations are held only when there is something worth celebrating—namely, the 60th, 70th, 80th, 88th (rather than 90th, because 9's are considered unlucky), and 100th birthdays (Harrell, 1981). The word for "old" (*lau*) is sometimes applied to middle-aged or even young adults to signify that they are as worthy of respect as the aged (Harrell, 1981). How many middle-aged adults do you know who would be delighted to be called "old"?

Is it true, then, that elderly people have higher status in traditional societies than in modernized societies? There is at least a grain of truth to this (Finley, 1982; Fry, 1985; Keith, 1990). However, we can also find many examples of hunter/gatherer and agricultural societies in which the old have low status and modern industrialized societies in which they have high status (Sokolovsky, 1990; see also Box 4.3).

What, then, determines the status of older people in a society? Two factors may be critical (Amoss & Harrell, 1981). First, old people will be valued to the extent that their contributions to society exceed their costs to society. Most societies distinguish between the frail elderly and the healthy elderly and show more respect for those older adults who are still capable of pulling their weight (Barker, 1990). Second, old people are valued to the extent that they control resources. When they own property and can leave inheritances to their children, or when they fill leadership roles in the community, their status is likely to be high.

What often (but not always) happens as a society first undergoes the rapid social changes of modernization is that older people, unable to make as many contributions to society as they once did, lose some of their power. Young adults turn to schools rather than to old people for the knowledge they need to fill jobs in industry; they give up traditional rituals; they move to cities and support themselves without help from their elders (Amoss, 1981). Yet social changes that increase the contributions of the elderly to society or give them new powers can also increase their status. In the 1970s, for example, younger Coast Salish Indians in Washington State and British Columbia be-

BOX 4.3 Aging around the World

There is no universal experience of old age. Even among traditional hunter/gatherer societies we see great variation. Among the !Kung in Botswana about 30 years ago, people hunted and gathered foods from a bountiful land. Older people were respected, and, if they were in good health, they showed a great deal of playfulness and vigor after they were relieved of their work roles (Biesele & Howell, 1981). As owners of water holes and organizers of systems for sharing food, the elderly had leadership roles. They were valued for their knowledge about local wildlife, kinship lines, and rituals, and they played a key role in preparing their grandchildren for adulthood. As one young person said of an elderly woman, "She is an old person and knows everything" (p. 88). Today the !Kung have largely given up hunting and gathering for raising animals and gardening, but aging individuals can continue to count on help from their families and communities (Draper & Keith, 1992).

Among the Inuit Eskimo of Alaska, who must survive in a cold and barren environment, life for the frail is cruel indeed. Men lose whatever status they had once they become too weak to hunt (Guemple, 1983). The childless old are often verbally abused and fed only grudgingly. Even elderly people with children have sometimes been abandoned or "helped" to die. Similarly, on

the Polynesian island of Niue, where survival is also difficult, frail older adults may be mocked if they foolishly let themselves be hit by falling coconuts or may be left to lie in their own waste if they are too ill to get up (Barker, 1990). Anthony Glascock (1990) found that half of the traditional societies he studied neglected, abandoned, or even killed frail elders, although many of these very same societies showed considerable respect for healthy and vigorous elders.

Just as we can find variation in the status of the old among hunter/gatherer societies, we can find it among modernized nations—or even within our own society. For example, in both Japan and China, children have long been taught to hold their aging parents in high esteem and to provide for them. Most elders live with their children—typically their eldest sons—and laws actually punish those who fail to care properly for aging parents (Goodstein & Goldstein, 1986; Kiefer, 1990). In the United States, older Japanese Americans are apparently experiencing some problems as their children become more Americanized, but the traditional Japanese value of respect for aging parents has largely survived (Osako & Liu, 1986). Mexican-American and African-American elders also seem to enjoy especially strong family ties (Markides, Boldt, & Ray, 1986; Taylor & Chatters, 1991), and Native-American elders often serve as storehouses of cultural knowledge, spiritual leaders, and teachers of the young (Weibel-Orlando, 1990). Thus, older members of minority groups are better off than older Anglo-Americans in some respects. Yet it is important to recognize that they are also more likely than Anglo-Americans to experience such problems as poverty, poor living conditions, and poor health (Dowd & Bengtson, 1978; Markides, Liang, & Jackson, 1990). In this sense, many minority group members carry into old age disadvantages they have experienced all their lives.

Obviously the aging experience is shaped by the social context in which it occurs. The quality of life experienced by older adults can be high or low in both traditional and modern societies. Moreover, the aging experience can vary widely across and within the various racial, ethnic, and socioeconomic groups that make up a society.

gan to want to rediscover their heritage (Amoss, 1981). Suddenly old people, who knew that heritage thoroughly, regained much of the respect they had lost when the tribe first experienced modernization. Older people actively took advantage of this happy turn of events by reviving the old dances, leading them every winter weekend, and recruiting young people to the "old ways." They aggressively helped to create a social environment that was more favorable to them.

In short, modernization in itself is not necessarily bad for the elderly (Sokolovsky, 1990). Much depends on whether social changes involve a loss or a gain in their ability to contribute to society and in their control over resources. Older people sometimes do lose status as their societies begin to modernize but may regain it if industrialization brings with it a higher standard of living and better health care (Finley, 1982; Keith, 1990). As Jennie Keith (1990) notes, modernization has, in a sense, made old age possible for many people; they need not die simply because they can no longer chase prey or chew meat.

Mainly, there is no one experience of old age, any more than there is one experience of any other phase of the life span. Comparing human development in different cultures and subcultures is the only way to determine which developmental processes and pathways are universal and which are peculiar to our own society.

APPLICATIONS: GETTING LIFE OFF TO A GOOD START

The more we learn about important environmental influences on human development, the better able we are to optimize the environment and therefore to optimize development. Although the nature and quality of an individual's environment matter throughout the life span, it seems sensible to do as much as possible to get a baby's life off to a good start. Developmentalists have learned a good deal about how to optimize development in the important prenatal and perinatal periods.

Before Birth

For starters, it would be good for babies if more of them were planned and wanted. Once a woman is pregnant, she should seek good prenatal care so that she can learn how to optimize the well-being of both herself and her unborn child and so that any problems during the pregnancy can be managed appropriately. As we have seen, the guidelines for pregnant women are not that complicated, though they are often violated. They boil down to such practices as eating an adequate diet, protecting oneself against diseases, and avoiding drugs.

Today many couples are also enrolling in classes that prepare them for childbirth. The "natural childbirth" movement arose from the work of Grantly Dick-Read in England and Fernand Lamaze in France. These two obstetricians discovered that many women could give birth painlessly, without medication, through what has come to be called the **Lamaze method** of prepared childbirth. This method teaches women to associate childbirth with pleasant feelings and to ready themselves for the process by learning exercises, breathing and pushing methods, and relaxation techniques that make childbirth easier (Dick-Read, 1933/1972; Lamaze, 1958). Parents typically attend Lamaze classes for six to eight weeks before the delivery. The father (or another supportive person) becomes a coach who helps the mother train her muscles and perfect her breathing for the event that lies ahead. He will usually be there to help his partner during delivery as well. Women who regularly attend Lamaze or similar childbirth classes are indeed more relaxed during labor, experience less pain, less often need medication, have an easier time delivering, and have more positive attitudes toward themselves, their families, and the childbirth process than do women without such training (Wideman & Singer, 1984). Childbirth education can be made even more effective if it is supplemented with effective pain-management techniques such as hypnosis (Harmon, Hynan, & Tyre, 1990).

Giving Birth

Women today have more choices about how and where they want to give birth than women did 20 years ago. Gone are the days when almost all women gave birth in a hospital, on their backs, with their legs in stirrups, and under the influence of medication. For some years there has been a movement to return to the time when birth was a natural family event that occurred at home rather than a medical problem to be solved with high technology (Edwards & Waldorf, 1984).

Today, more and more couples are opting for home deliveries, often with the aid of a certified nurse/midwife who is trained in nonsurgical obstetrics. Those who favor this approach argue that the relaxed atmosphere of the home setting calms the mother, making her delivery quicker and easier. Although the mothers who choose home delivery are usually those who expect an easy childbirth, the fact that mortality is low for infants born at home suggests that the risks of home deliveries are not great for healthy mothers who have received good prenatal care and are at low risk for birth complications (MacFarlane, 1977).

Obstetricians in the United States have resisted the home-birth movement, partly because they fear birth complications and partly because home births threaten their monopoly in the childbirth field (Edwards & Waldorf, 1984). In response to the growing home-birth movement and to criticisms of conventional delivery practices, many hospitals have developed birthing rooms, or **alternative birth centers,** that provide a homelike atmosphere but still make medical technology available (Klee, 1986). Other alternative birth centers have been developed independently of hospitals and place the task of delivery in the hands of certified nurse/midwives, typically registered nurses who have taken additional coursework in obstetrics. In either case, mates or other close companions (and often even the couple's other children) can be present during labor, and healthy infants can remain in the same room with their mothers (rooming-in) rather than spending their first days in the hospital nursery. So far, the evidence suggests that delivery in low-risk birth centers is no more risky to mothers and their babies than delivery in a hospital and is less likely to involve interventions such as anesthesia, intravenous transfusions, and cesarean sections (Fullerton & Severino, 1992). Linnea Klee (1986) has found that mothers who choose alternative birth centers often want access to medical technologies "in case something goes wrong," whereas mothers who choose home delivery more often distrust the medical establishment. Today the woman whose pregnancy is going smoothly has considerable freedom to give birth as she chooses.

After the Birth

So now that you have a baby, what do you do? New parents are often uncertain about how to relate to their babies and may find the period after birth stressful. T. Berry Brazelton (1979) has devised a way to help parents appreciate their baby's competencies and feel competent themselves as parents. He developed a newborn assessment technique, the *Brazelton Neonatal Behavioral Assessment Scale,* that assesses the strength of 20 infant reflexes as well as the infant's responses to 26 situations (for example, reactions to cuddling, general irritability, and orienting response to the examiner's face and voice). This test teaches parents to understand their babies as individuals and to appreciate many of the pleasing competencies that they possess. During "Brazelton training," parents observe the test being administered and also learn how to administer it themselves to elicit smiles and other heart-warming responses from their babies.

Mothers of high-risk (and sometimes difficult-to-love) infants who receive Brazelton training become more responsive in their face-to-face interactions with their babies than mothers who do not, and their infants score higher on the Brazelton test one month later (Widmayer & Field, 1980). In addition, compared to untrained parents, trained parents are more knowledgeable about infant behavior, more confident of their caretaking abilities, and more satisfied with their infants (Myers, 1982). Although this brief intervention does not always accomplish wonders (Belsky, 1985; Worobey & Brazelton, 1986), it is a good way to help parents and babies get started right.

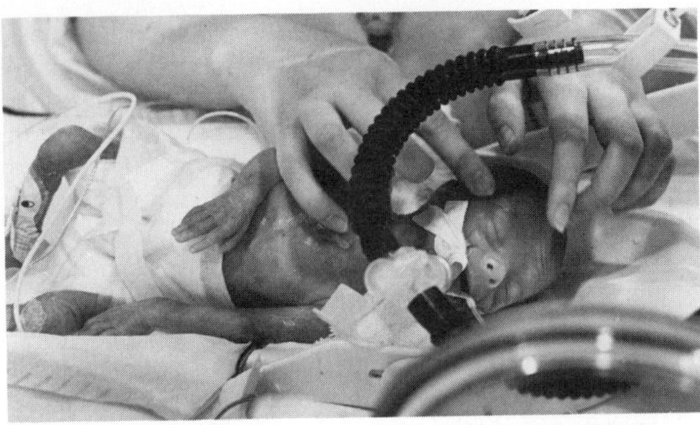

Premature, low-birth-weight babies experience the rather bizarre environment provided by modern incubators, hooked up to the many machines that monitor them and keep them alive.

Giving the seriously premature or low-birth-weight infant a good start is a more difficult undertaking. Neonatal intensive-care units, with their high-tech life-sustaining machines and computerized monitoring systems, have greatly increased the odds that babies who are at high risk will survive the perinatal period (Kopp & Krakow, 1983). Yet much is still being learned about how to optimize the rather abnormal environment in which these infants spend their first several weeks of life.

Not long ago these babies simply lay in their isolettes receiving little stimulation and little human contact. They were, in effect, deprived of the sensory stimulation they would have received either in the womb or in a normal home environment. Today their perinatal sensory environment is much improved, thanks to research on the effects of sensory-stimulation programs. Many of these programs have centered on the "body senses" because much bodily stimulation is provided in the womb. So preterm infants have been stroked, held upright, rocked, and even put on waterbeds (Schaefer, Hatcher, & Barglow, 1980). For example, Frank Scafidi and his colleagues (1986, 1990) provided premature infants with just three 15-minute stimulation sessions a day over 10 days. These babies' bodies were massaged and their limbs were flexed and extended. In the latest test, stimulated babies gained 21% more weight per day, showed more mature behaviors on the Brazelton scale, and were able to leave the hospital five days earlier than control infants (Scafidi et al., 1990). Kathryn Barnard and Helen Bee (1983) found that preterm babies exposed to a combination of bodily and auditory stimulation in the hospital—15-minute doses of a rocking bed and a heartbeat sound—showed lasting benefits, for they scored higher than control infants on a measure of infant mental development at age 2. It appears that fairly simple and inexpensive environmental changes and special stimulation programs can help the high-risk infant develop normally.

High-risk infants can also benefit from programs that teach their parents how to provide them with responsive care and appropriate intellectual stimulation once they are home. Home visits to advise parents, combined with a stimulating day-care program, can teach mothers of low-birth-weight toddlers to be better teachers of their young children and to stimulate the children's cognitive development (Brooks-Gunn et al., 1993; Spiker, Ferguson, & Brooks-Gunn, 1993). One program that taught mothers to recognize and respond appropriately to their babies' cues allowed low-birth-weight children to fully catch up to normal-birth-weight children in mental development by the age of 7 (Achenbach et al., 1990). It is just as important to keep development on track after the perinatal period comes to a close as it is to get it started on the right track from the beginning.

REFLECTIONS

We hope that, after reading Chapters 3 and 4, you have a fuller appreciation of how both nature and nurture contribute to human development. We have emphasized what can go wrong—the genetic defects, the prenatal risk factors, the birth complications, and so on. These sorts of problems show that the wrong genes or the wrong early environment can have profound impacts on development, but they make for depressing reading. Let's now emphasize the positive.

First, we know more about these problems today than ever before and can better prevent and treat them to allow more and more children to survive and thrive. Second, we can only marvel at the strengths of the human organism. The vast majority of us come into existence with an amazingly effective genetic program to guide our development. Most of us, whether we grow up in !Kung or Japanese or Native-American families, also receive the benefits of a normal human environment, an environment that joins forces with this genetic program to promote normal development. Perhaps most remarkably, it seems to take very adverse conditions over a long period of time—conditions like those experienced by Genie—to *keep* us from developing normally. Special interventions or a favorable home environment later in life can often get abnormal infants back on course, and even children who suffer all sorts of insults and indignities during their early years sometimes manage to become competent adults nonetheless. It's almost as if nature defies us to spoil her plan.

At the same time, we are clearly influenced by our experiences throughout the life span. Being a developing person in the Kalahari Desert is not like being a developing person in downtown Manhattan, because development is embedded in a social and cultural context. We will encounter numerous examples in the remainder of this text of the positive and negative impacts that environmental forces can have on development, but we will also want to bear in mind throughout that each person's genetic endowment affects what experiences he or she has and how he or she is affected by them.

SUMMARY POINTS

1. The environment of human development includes all events or conditions outside the person that affect or are affected by the person's development, including both the physical and the social environment. As Bronfenbrenner's ecological model emphasizes, development depends on the ongoing *reciprocal* transactions between a changing person and a series of ever-changing environmental systems.

2. Environmental influences on development begin at conception as the zygote starts its passage through three stages of prenatal development: (a) the germinal period, (b) the period of the embryo, and (c) the period of the fetus.

3. The prenatal physical environment, as influenced by the age of the mother, her health, and a variety of teratogens, can significantly affect development, especially during sensitive periods when the embryo's organs are rapidly forming.

4. The perinatal environment (the environment surrounding birth) is also important. Childbirth is a three-step process consisting of the contractions of labor, the delivery, and the afterbirth (expulsion of the placenta). Risks to the baby include anoxia and the effects of medications given to the mother.

5. Early emotional bonding, though pleasant, does not seem necessary for loving attachments to form.

6. Some problems created by prenatal and perinatal hazards are long-lasting, but many babies at risk show remarkable resilience and outgrow their problems, especially if they have personal strengths such as sociability and grow up in stimulating postnatal environments.

7. After birth, humans are affected by the cultural context in which they develop. Survival, economic, and self-actualization goals of parenting are universal, but parents in each culture or subculture emphasize the specific traits and skills most necessary for adult life in their particular societal context.

8. Because child-rearing practices differ from society to society, findings regarding human development are influenced by the culture and historical period in which the research is conducted. Socioeconomic and ethnic diversity within a society is also significant in understanding development.

9. During adolescence, children are socially redefined as adults, sometimes through rites of passage. In our society the passage to adulthood is prolonged and ill defined.

10. The timing of normative life transitions during adulthood is guided by the age norms that prevail in a society, norms internalized in the form of the social clock. However, Bernice Neugarten theorizes that our society is becoming an age-irrelevant one with weaker age norms.

11. The experience of growing old also varies widely across cultures and historical periods. The status of older adults depends largely on their contributions to society (relative to their costs) and on their control of resources. Their status sometimes, though not always, decreases when a society first modernizes, but it may rebound later on.

12. Ways of getting human lives off to a good start today include prepared-childbirth classes, alternative birth centers, neonatal intensive-care units, and training for parents of high-risk infants.

KEY TERMS

acquired immune deficiency syndrome (AIDS)
age-irrelevant society
age of viability
alternative birth centers
amnion
anoxia
Apgar test
blastula
breech presentation
cesarean section
chorion
critical period
cultural relativity
culture
ecological approach
engrossment
environment
exosystem
fetal alcohol syndrome (FAS)
germinal period
Lamaze method
macrosystem
mesosystem
microsystem
nonnormative transition
normative transition
perinatal environment
period of the embryo
period of the fetus
placenta
postpartum depression
prenatal environment
resilience
rites of passage
rubella
social clock
socialization
socioeconomic status (SES)
syphilis
teratogen
testosterone
thalidomide
umbilical cord

5

THE PHYSICAL SELF

When you are very young, each of your cells, based on its individual personality and aptitude, selects an area of specialization, such as the thigh, in which to pursue its career. As you grow, the cell multiplies, and it teaches its offspring to be thigh cells also. . . . Thus the proud thigh-cell tradition is handed down from generation to generation, so that by the time you're a teenager, you have an extremely competent, efficient, and hard-working colony down there, providing you with thighs so sleek and taut that they look great even when encased in Spandex garments that would be a snug fit on a Bic pen. But as your body approaches middle age, this cellular discipline starts to break down. The newer cells . . . become listless and bored, and many of them, looking for "kicks," turn to cellulite. Your bodily tissue begins to deteriorate, gradually becoming saggier and lumpier, until one day you glance in the mirror and realize, to your horror, that you look as though for some reason you are attempting to smuggle out of the country an entire driveway's worth of gravel concealed inside your upper legs [Barry, 1990, pp. 19-20].

Such is humorist Dave Barry's view of physical development and aging — a more dismal view, we think, than the one we are about to present. This chapter traces changes in the body's size and proportions as well as changes in the functioning of selected body systems. The nervous system and the endocrine system are emphasized because humans could not function at all without them. We will also look at the reproductive system: its maturation during adolescence and the changes it undergoes during adulthood. And we will examine the physical self in action: the development of motor skills during childhood and changes in physical fitness and motor behavior during adulthood. As we go, we will be trying to identify influences on physical development and aging, so that we can better understand why some children develop — and why some older adults age — more rapidly than others. To lay the groundwork for all of this, let's briefly consider the nature of the human body.

THE BODY'S SYSTEMS AND DEVELOPMENT

The human body is a marvelously complex system of organs working together to make the full range of human behavior possible. As we saw in Chapter 4, all the major organs of the body take shape during the prenatal period. Each bodily system — the digestive system, the circulatory system, the nervous system, the reproductive system, and so on — has its own orderly timetable of development. For example, the nervous system develops very rapidly, completing most of its important growth by the end of infancy. The reproductive system, by contrast, is slower to develop than most of the body's organs and systems and does not reach its time of rapid growth until adolescence (see Figure 5.1).

If we want to understand physical growth and sexual maturation, we must understand the workings of the endocrine (hormonal) system. And, if we want to know why adults are both physically and mentally more competent than infants, we must understand the nervous system.

The Endocrine System

How *does* the human body grow? All humans have a distinctly human genetic makeup that makes them develop physically in similar directions and at similar rates. Individual heredity also influences the individual's rate of physical development and final size — in interaction, of course, with environmental factors such as whether a child's diet includes milk and other nutritious foods.

But how are genetic messages translated into action? It is here that the endocrine system plays its role. **Endocrine glands** secrete chemicals called *hormones* directly into the bloodstream. Perhaps the most critical of the endocrine glands is the **pituitary gland,** the so-called master gland located at the base of the brain. Directly controlled by the *hypothalamus* of the brain, it triggers the release of hormones from all other endocrine glands by sending hormonal messages to those glands. Moreover, the pituitary produces **growth hormone,** which stimulates the rapid growth and development of body cells. Children who lack this hormone are unlikely to exceed 4 feet (or 130 cm) in height as adults (Tanner, 1990).

The *thyroid gland* also plays an important role in growth and development, as well as in the development of the nervous system. Babies born with a thyroid deficiency soon become mentally handicapped if their condition goes unnoticed and untreated (Tanner, 1990). Children who develop a thyroid defi-

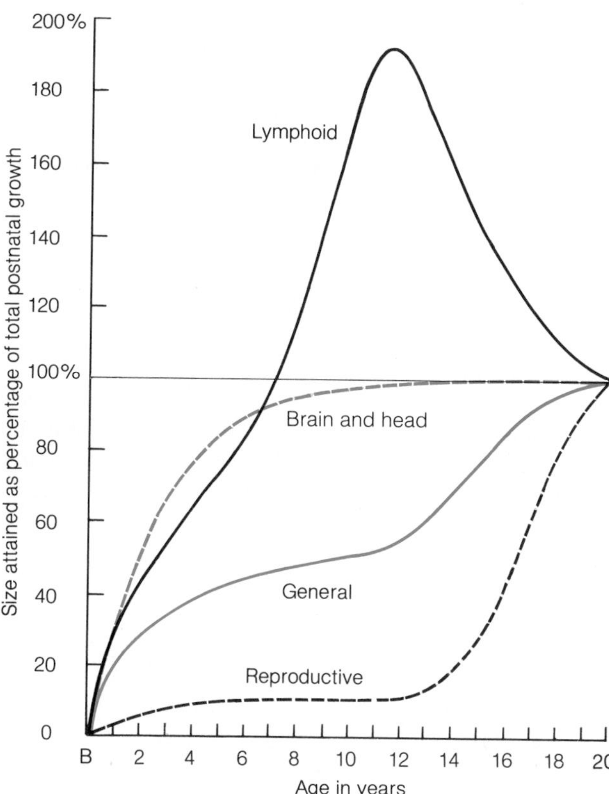

FIGURE 5.1 Growth curves for different body systems. Each curve plots the size of a group of organs or body parts as a percentage of their size at age 20 (which is the 100% level on the vertical scale). The "general" curve describes changes in the body's size as well as the growth of respiratory and digestive organs and musculature. The brain and head grow more rapidly than the body in general, and the reproductive organs are the slowest to reach adult size. (The lymph nodes and other parts of the lymphoid system, which function as part of the immune system, also grow rapidly and actually exceed adult size during late childhood and adolescence.) (From Tanner, 1962.)

ciency later in life will not suffer brain damage, since most of their brain growth has already occurred, but their physical growth will slow down drastically.

In Chapter 4 we encountered still another critical role of the endocrine system. A male fetus will not develop male reproductive organs unless (1) a gene on his Y chromosome triggers the development of the testes (which are endocrine glands), and (2) the testes secrete the most important of the male hormones, *testosterone.* Male sex hormones become highly important again during adolescence. When people speak of adolescence as a time of "raging hormones," they are quite right. The testes of a male secrete large quantities of testosterone and other male hormones (called **androgens**). These hormones stimulate the production of growth hormone, which in turn triggers the adolescent growth spurt. Androgens are also responsible for the development of the male sex organs and contribute to sexual motivation during adulthood (Tanner, 1990).

Meanwhile, in adolescent girls, the ovaries (also endocrine glands) produce larger quantities of the primary female hormone, **estrogen,** and of progesterone. Estrogen increases dramatically at puberty, stimulating the production of growth hormone and the adolescent growth spurt, much like testosterone in males. It is also responsible for the development of the breasts, pubic hair, and female sex organs, as well as for the control of menstrual cycles throughout a woman's reproductive years. Finally, the *adrenal glands* secrete androgenlike hormones that contribute to the maturation of the bones and muscles in both sexes (Tanner, 1990). The roles of different endocrine glands in physical growth and development are summarized in Table 5.1.

In adulthood, endocrine glands continue to secrete hormones, under the direction of the hypothalamus and the pituitary, to regulate bodily processes (Andres & Tobin, 1977). For example, thyroid hormones help the body's cells metabolize (break

TABLE 5.1 Hormonal influences on growth and development.

Endocrine Gland	*Hormones Produced*	*Effects on Growth and Development*
Pituitary	Growth hormone (GH)	Regulates growth from birth through adolescence; triggers adolescent growth spurt.
	Activating hormones	Signal other endocrine glands (such as the ovaries and testes) to secrete their hormones.
Thyroid	Thyroxine	Affects growth and development of the brain and helps to regulate growth of the body during childhood.
Testes	Testosterone	Is responsible for development of the male reproductive system during the prenatal period; directs male sexual development during adolescence.
Ovaries	Estrogen Progesterone	Responsible for regulation of menstrual cycle; estrogen directs female sexual development during adolescence.
Adrenal glands	Adrenal androgens	Play a supportive role in the development of muscle and bones.

down) foods into usable nutrients, and the adrenal glands help the body cope with stress. Throughout the life span, then, the endocrine system works together with the nervous system to keep the body on an even keel. As we will see in Chapter 17, some theorists even believe that changes in the functioning of the endocrine glands late in life bring about aging and death.

In short, the endocrine system, in collaboration with the brain, is centrally involved in growth during childhood, physical and sexual and maturation during adolescence, functioning over the entire life span, and aging later in life.

The Nervous System

None of the physical or mental achievements that we regard as human would be possible without a functioning nervous system. Briefly, the nervous system consists of the brain and spinal cord (central nervous system) and neural tissue that extends into all parts of the body (peripheral nervous system). Its basic unit is a **neuron.** Although neurons come in many shapes and sizes, they have some common features. Branching, bushy *dendrites* receive signals from other neurons, and the long *axon* of a neuron transmits signals — to another neuron or, in some cases, directly to a muscle cell. The point at which the axon of one neuron makes a connection with another neuron is called a **synapse.** By releasing *neurotransmitters* stored at the ends of its axons, one neuron can either stimulate or inhibit the action of another neuron. During development, axons become covered by a waxy material called **myelin,** which acts like insulation to speed the transmission of neural impulses.

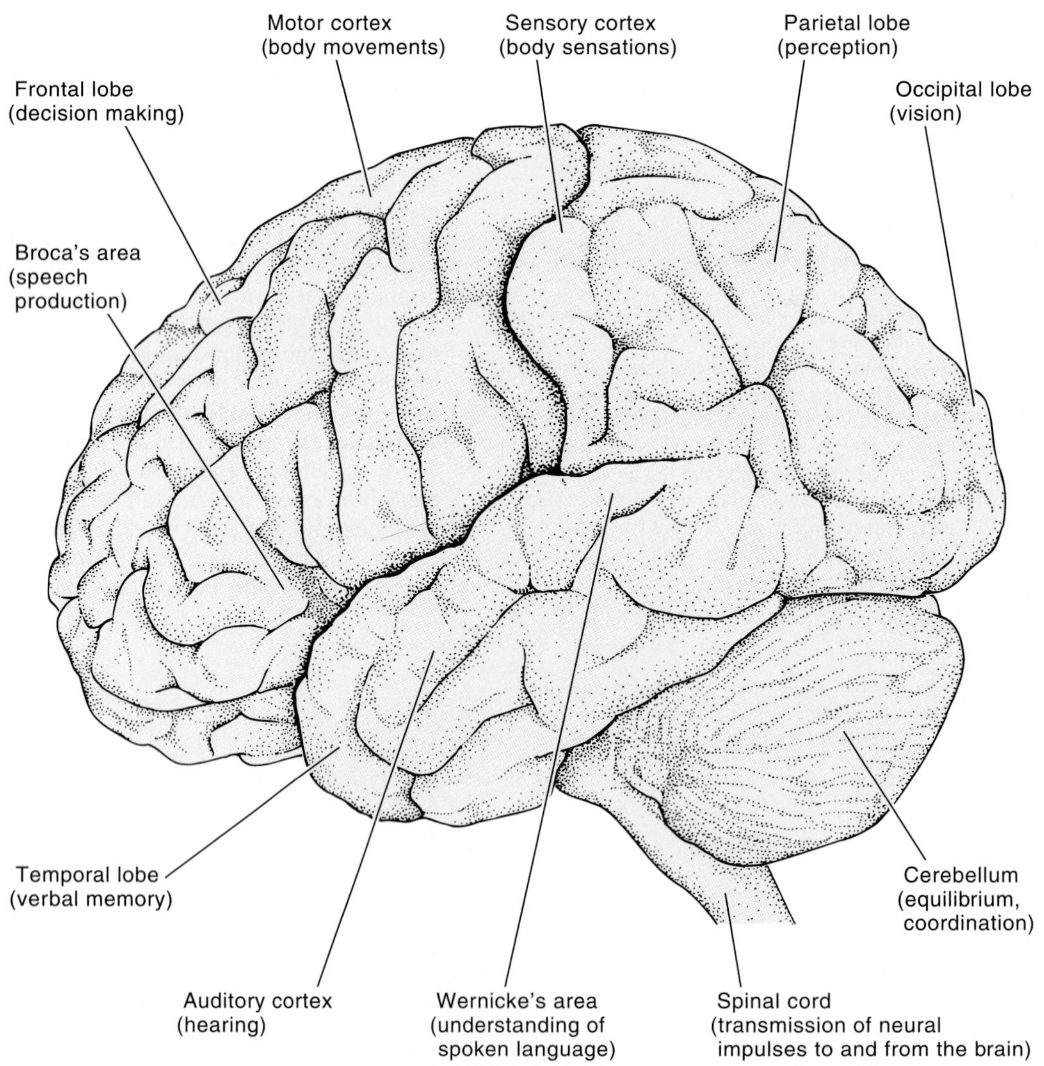

FIGURE 5.2 A side view of the left cerebral cortex and some of the functions it controls. The cerebellum and the spinal cord, though not part of the cortex, serve important functions as well.

Now imagine a brain with as many as 100 billion neurons, each communicating through synapses to thousands of others (Cowan, 1979). During development the brain becomes organized into complex systems of interconnected neurons. At birth the most fully developed areas of the brain are the more primitive or "lower" portions, such as the spinal cord, brain stem, and midbrain. These portions of the brain are adequate to control the infant's states of waking and sleeping, to permit simple motor reactions, and to regulate such biological functions as digestion, respiration, and elimination, making life possible. However, we would be little different from snakes if the higher centers of the brain did not develop. It is the convoluted outer covering of the brain—the **cerebral cortex**—that is organized into areas that control voluntary body movements, perception, and higher intellectual functions such as learning, thinking, and speaking (see Figure 5.2).

So why are young infants less physically and mentally capable than adults? Is it that adults have more neurons than infants do? Do they have more synapses connecting neurons or a more organized pattern of connections? Finally, what happens to the brain in later life? We address these and other questions as we now examine three aspects of the physical self in each phase of the life span: the body (its size, composition, and functioning), the brain, and the use of body and brain in physical activities such as locomotion and finely controlled movements.

THE INFANT

Tremendous amounts of growth, brain development, and physical development occur during the two years of infancy. Understanding the newborn's capacities and limitations brings a fuller appreciation of the dramatic changes that take place between birth and adulthood.

A Profile of the Newborn

Newborns used to be viewed as helpless little organisms unprepared to cope with the world outside the womb. We now know that they are far better equipped for life than that. What *are* the capabilities of the newborn?

One of the newborn's greatest strengths is a full set of useful **reflexes.** A reflex is an unlearned and automatic response to a stimulus, as when the eye automatically blinks in response to a puff of air. Reflexes can be contrasted with the newborn's spontaneous arm waving, leg kicking, and thrashing—movements that have no obvious stimulus. Table 5.2 lists some reflexes that can be readily observed in all normal newborns. These seemingly simple reactions are actually quite graceful, varied, and complex patterns of behavior (Prechtl, 1981).

Some reflexes are called *survival reflexes* because they have clear adaptive value. Examples include the breathing reflex (useful for obvious reasons), the eye-blink reflex (which protects against bright lights or foreign particles), and the sucking reflex (needed to obtain food). The so-called *primitive*

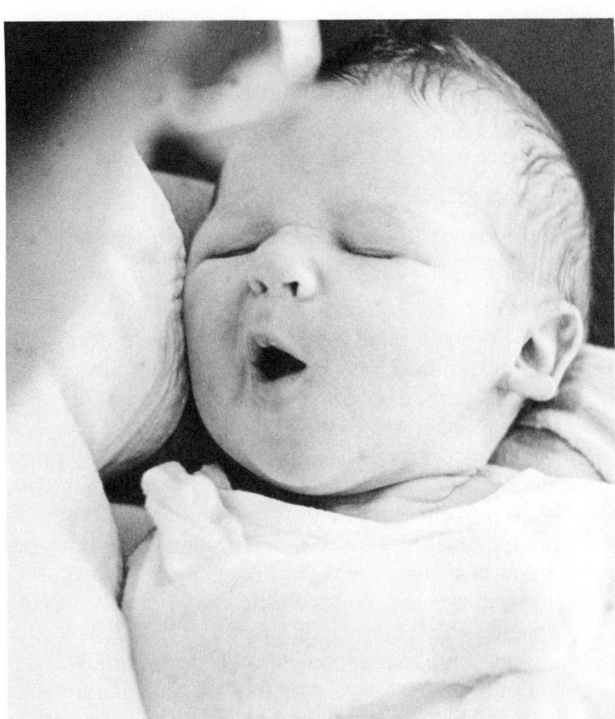

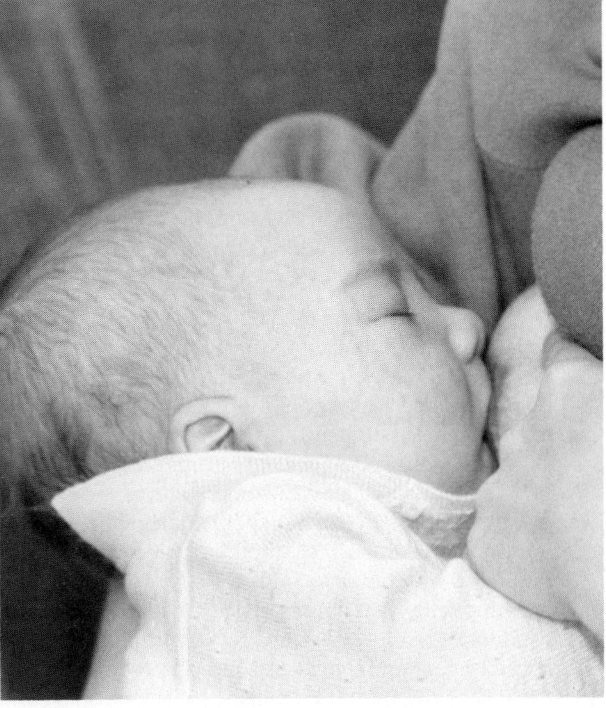

The rooting reflex (left) and the sucking reflex (right) are two of the newborn's adaptive reflexes. The infant will turn in the direction of a touch on the cheek, searching for something to suck, and then *will* suck an object placed in its mouth.

TABLE 5.2 Major reflexes present in full-term newborns.

Reflexes	*Developmental Course*	*Significance*
Survival reflexes		
Breathing reflex	Permanent	Provides oxygen and expels carbon dioxide
Eyeblink reflex	Permanent	Protects eyes from bright light or foreign objects
Pupillary reflex: Constriction of pupils to bright light; dilation to dark or dimly lit surroundings	Permanent	Protects against bright lights; adapts visual system to low illumination
Rooting reflex: Turning of cheek in direction of a tactile (touch) stimulus	Gradually weakens over the first 6 months of life	Orients child to breast or bottle
Sucking reflex: Sucking on objects placed (or taken) into mouth	Is gradually modified by experience over the first few months of life	Allows child to take in nutrients
Swallowing reflex	Is permanent but modified by experience	Allows child to take in nutrients and protects against choking
Primitive reflexes		
Babinski reflex: Fanning and then curling toes when bottom of foot is stroked	Usually disappears within the first 8 months to 1 year of life	Presence at birth and disappearance in first year indicate normal neurological development
Grasping reflex: Curling of fingers around objects (such as a finger) that touch baby's palm	Disappears in first 3–4 months; is replaced by a voluntary grasp	Presence at birth and later disappearance indicate normal neurological development
Moro reflex: Loud noise or sudden change in position of baby's head will cause baby to throw arms outward, arch back, and then bring arms toward each other as if to hold onto something	Disappears over the first 6–7 months; however, child continues to react to unexpected noises or a loss of bodily support by showing a startle reflex (which does not disappear)	Presence at birth and later disappearance (or evolution into the startle reflex) indicate normal neurological development
Swimming reflex: Infant immersed in water will display active movements of arms and legs and involuntarily hold breath (thus staying afloat for some time)	Disappears in first 4–6 months	Presence at birth and later disappearance indicate normal neurological development
Stepping reflex: Infants held upright so that their feet touch a flat surface will step as if to walk	Disappears in first 8 weeks unless infant has regular opportunities to practice it	Presence at birth and later disappearance indicate normal neurological development

Note: Preterm infants may show little or no evidence of primitive reflexes at birth, and their survival reflexes are likely to be irregular or immature. However, the missing reflexes will typically appear soon after birth and will disappear a little later than they do among full-term infants.

reflexes are not nearly as useful; in fact, many are believed to be remnants of our evolutionary history that have outlived their purpose. The *Babinski reflex* is a good example. Why would it be adaptive for infants to fan their toes when the bottoms of their feet are stroked? We don't know. Other primitive reflexes may have some use, at least in some cultures. For example, the grasping reflex may help infants who are carried in slings or on their mothers' hips to hang on. Finally, other primitive reflexes—for example, the grasping reflex and the stepping reflex—may be forerunners of useful voluntary behaviors that develop later in infancy (Fentress & McLeod, 1986). Alternatively, they may have little relation to later grasping and walking but may have evolved because they help newborns adapt to their environment (Oppenheim, 1980).

Primitive reflexes typically disappear during the early months of infancy. They are controlled by the lower, "subcortical" areas of the brain and are lost as the higher centers of the cerebral cortex develop and begin to control behavior. Even though many primitive reflexes are not very useful to infants, they have proven to be extremely useful in diagnosing infants' neurological problems. If such reflexes are *not* present at birth—or if they last too long in infancy—we know that something is wrong with a baby's nervous system. The existence of reflexes at birth tells us that infants come to life ready to respond to stimulation in adaptive ways. The disappearance of certain reflexes tells us that the nervous system is developing normally.

Another strength of newborns is their senses. As we saw in Chapter 4, the sensory systems are developing before birth, and (as we shall see in Chapter 6) all of the major senses are functioning reasonably well at birth. Newborns do indeed see and hear, and they respond to tastes, smells, and touches in predictable ways too.

Still another strength of newborns is that they are capable of learning from their experiences. They can, for example, learn to suck faster if sucking produces a pleasant-tasting sugary liquid rather than plain water (Kron, 1966; Lipsitt, 1990). In other words, they can change their behavior according to its consequences (see Chapter 8 on learning capacities).

Finally, the fact that newborns have organized patterns of daily activity is another sign that they are well equipped for life. **Infant states** are the different levels of consciousness that newborns experience in a typical day; these range from sleeping to crying (see Table 5.3). Their existence suggests that infants' physiological processes are well organized from birth (Thoman & Whitney, 1989). Infants rarely have problems establishing regular sleep cycles, for example, unless their nervous systems are abnormal in some way (Willemsen, 1979). Research on infant states also makes it clear that newborns have a good deal of individuality (Thoman & Whitney, 1989). In a study by Brown (1964), one newborn was observed to be in an alert state only 4% of the time, whereas another was alert 37% of the time. Similarly, one newborn cried only 17% of the time, but another spent fully 39% of its time crying. Such variations among infants have obvious implications for parents. It is likely to be far more pleasant to be with a baby who is often alert and who rarely cries than it is to interact with a baby who is rarely attentive and frequently fussy.

During the first few days of life, newborns average about 70% of their time (16–18 hours a day) sleeping and only two to three hours in a state of alert inactivity in which they are actively taking in what is going on around them (Berg, Adkinson, & Strock, 1973; Hutt, Lenard, & Prechtl, 1969). They normally take seven to ten daily naps of about 45 minutes to 2 hours each. Somewhere between 3 and 7 months of age, infants reach a milestone that parents appreciate—they begin to sleep through the night (Berg & Berg, 1979).

It seems that young infants make good use of all their sleep time. At birth, babies spend about half of their sleeping hours in a state of active, irregular sleep called **REM sleep** (for the rapid eye movements that occur during it). Infants older than 6 months spend only 25–30% of their total sleep in REM sleep, and the percentage drops to about 20% over the rest of the life span. During REM sleep, brain activity is more typical of wakefulness than of regular (non-REM) sleep, and adults awakened from REM sleep usually report that they were dreaming. Why, then, do young infants spend so much time in REM sleep? It has been suggested that REM sleep provides young infants with abundant internal stimulation that allows their nervous systems to mature (Boismier, 1977; Roffwarg, Muzio, & Dement, 1966).

Newborn infants are indeed competent and ready for life. They have a wide range of reflexes, functioning senses, a capacity to learn, and an organized pattern of waking and sleeping. But think for a moment about newborns in comparison to adults: Newborns are also quite limited beings. Their brains are not nearly as developed as they will be by the end of infancy. They do move spontaneously and display a wide range of adaptive reflexes. They even reach in the direction of a moving object that they are watching, showing a primitive form of eye/hand

TABLE 5.3 Infant states described by Wolff (1966).

State	*Characteristics*
Regular sleep	Babies lie still with their eyes closed and unmoving. Breathing is regular, and the skin is pale. The infant does not respond to mild stimuli such as soft voices or flashing lights.
Irregular sleep	Babies breathe irregularly, and their eyes may move underneath their closed eyelids (in rapid eye movements, or REMs). The infant often grimaces, jerks, and twitches and may stir a bit in response to soft sounds or flashes of light.
Drowsiness	Drowsy babies who are just waking or falling asleep will intermittently open and close their eyes. They are fairly inactive, and their eyes have a glazed look when open. Breathing is regular but more rapid than in regular sleep.
Alert inactivity	Here we have a baby who scans the environment with interest. Head, trunk, and lip movements may occur, and breathing is fast and irregular. This is the state in which infants are most susceptible to learning.
Waking activity	Hungry or otherwise uncomfortable babies may wake suddenly and show sudden bursts of vigorous activity in which they twist their bodies and kick their legs. Their eyes are open, but they are not actively attending to their surroundings as they are in a state of alert inactivity. Breathing is irregular.
Crying	Babies often move from waking activity into a crying state in which they first whimper and then burst into loud, agitated cries accompanied by strong kicks and arm movements.

coordination (Hofsten, 1982, 1984). However, their capacity to move *voluntarily and intentionally*—for example, to grasp objects and bring them to their mouths—is limited, and they are obviously not yet mobile. Consequently, they cannot meet their most basic needs. Although their senses are working, they certainly cannot *interpret* something like the patterns of light on a television screen in the way an older individual can. They can learn, but they are slow learners compared to older children, often requiring many learning trials before they make the connection between stimulus and response. And, while we're faulting them, we may as well note that having a repertoire of cries is a far cry (so to speak) from having command of a human language that can express an infinite number of ideas. Newborns are clearly lacking important social and communication skills.

In short, newborns have *both* strengths and limitations. The strengths indicate that newborns are actively taking in what is happening around them, are able to adapt to their environments, and possess capacities that can serve as building blocks for later development. However, the limitations of the newborn tell us that *much* remains to be accomplished during development.

The Body: Physical Growth

Newborns are typically about 20 inches long and weigh 7–7½ pounds. They do not remain tiny for long, for in the first few months of life they are gaining nearly an ounce of weight a day and an inch in length each month. By age 2, they have already attained about half of their eventual adult height and weigh 27 to 30 pounds. If they continued at their rapid pace of growth until age 18, they would stand about 12 feet 3 inches high and weigh several tons!

You have probably noticed that young infants also seem to be all head. That is because growth proceeds in a **cephalocaudal direction**: literally, from the head to the tail. This pattern is clear in Figure 5.3: The head is far ahead of the rest of the body during the prenatal period and accounts for about 25% of the newborn's length. But the head accounts for only 12% of an adult's height. During the first year after birth, the trunk grows the fastest; in the second year, the legs are the fastest-growing part of the body.

While infants are growing from the head downward, they are also growing from the center outward to the extremities. This **proximodistal direction** of development can be seen during the prenatal period, when the chest and internal organs form before the arms, hands, and fingers. During the first year of life, the trunk is rapidly filling out while the arms remain short and stubby until they undergo their own period of rapid development. Overall, then, physical growth is orderly, obeying both the cephalocaudal and proximodistal principles of development.

Meanwhile, the bones and muscles are developing quickly. At birth most of the infant's bones are soft, pliable, and difficult to break. They are too small and flexible to allow newborns to sit up or balance themselves when pulled to a standing position. The soft cartilage-like tissues of the young infant gradually ossify (harden) into bony material as calcium and other minerals are deposited into them. In addition, more bones develop, and they become more closely inter-

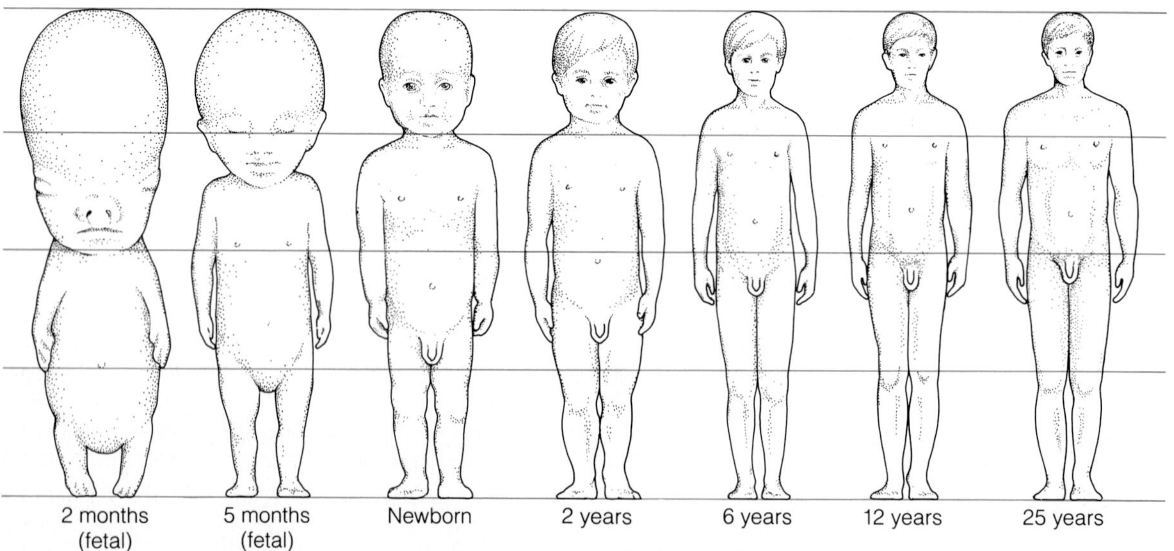

FIGURE 5.3 Changes in the proportions of the human body from the fetal period through adulthood. The head represents 50% of body length at two months after conception but only 12–13% of adult height. By contrast, the legs constitute only about 12–13% of the length of a 2-month-old fetus but 50% of an adult's height.

connected. As for muscles, young infants are relative weaklings. They have all the muscle cells they will ever have, but their strength will increase as their muscles grow larger. Muscular development also proceeds in cephalocaudal and proximodistal directions.

The rapid physical and muscular growth that occurs during infancy helps make possible the tremendous advances in motor development that we see during these two years. The other necessary ingredient is a more fully developed brain.

The Brain

The brain develops at its fastest rate prenatally and in the early months after birth (Kolb & Fantie, 1989; Rakic, 1991; Tanner, 1990). Indeed, the last three months of prenatal life and the first two years after birth have been termed the period of the **brain growth spurt,** for several reasons. First, new neurons are being formed rapidly during the prenatal period. Second, neural cells are increasing in size and weight both before and after birth. At birth a baby's brain is only 25% of its eventual adult weight; by age 2 it has already reached 75% of its adult weight. Third, the neurons are rapidly being covered with the waxy myelin that increases their ability to transmit signals effectively. Fourth, levels of neurotransmitters are increasing. Finally, neurons are organizing themselves into intricately interconnected groups that take on specialized functions, such as the control of motor behavior or visual perception.

Amazingly, neurons are also dying in massive numbers during this same period of rapid brain development. Researchers estimate that almost *half* of the neurons produced in early life also die in early life (Janowsky & Finlay, 1986). Neurons are also sprouting many dendritic branches and forming many synapses, or connections, with other neurons that later disappear. In one study the number of synapses between cortical neurons grew to a peak at about age 1 or 2 and then declined thereafter (Huttenlocher, 1979). If we liken the developing brain to a house under construction, we must imagine that the builder decides to build many rooms and many hallways between rooms and later goes back and knocks about half of them out!

What is happening? The brain of the fetus and young infant has a great deal of **plasticity**, meaning that its cells are highly responsive to the effects of experience, both normal and abnormal, both growth-producing and damaging. As William Greenough and his colleagues (Greenough, Black, & Wallace, 1987) explain, the immature brain has evolved so that it produces an excess of neural synapses in preparation for receiving early sensory and motor stimulation of the sort available to all developing humans (see also Cowan, 1979; Rakic, 1991). The genetic code supplies only a rough sketch of the wiring of the brain; it is up to experience, during sensitive periods for brain development early in life, to finalize and fine-tune the neural circuitry. The neural connections most often activated by the infant's early experiences will survive; the synapses that are used infrequently will disappear.

Assuming that the infant does indeed have normal opportunities to explore and experience the world through his or her senses and motor activities, the result will be a normal brain and normal perceptual and motor development. To return to our house-building analogy, it is like waiting to see which rooms and hallways get the most traffic before deciding which to retain in the final house. (Not a bad idea at all.) In sum, the development of the brain early in life is not due entirely to the unfolding of a maturational program; it is the handiwork of both a genetic program and early experience.

The immature brain is also plastic in the sense that it is highly responsive to each individual's unique experiences (Gandelman, 1992; Greenough et al., 1987). On the negative side, the developing brain is highly vulnerable to damage if it is exposed to drugs or diseases or if it is deprived of the sensory and motor experiences necessary for normal growth. On the positive side, though, this highly adaptable brain can often recover successfully from injuries. Neurons are not yet fully committed to their specialized functions and can often take over the functions of neurons that are damaged (Kolb & Fantie, 1989; Rakic, 1991). Moreover, the immature, plastic brain is in a particularly good position to benefit from stimulating experiences. Rats that grow up in enriched environments with plenty of sensory stimulation develop larger, better functioning brains with more synapses than rats that grow up in barren cages (Bennett, Diamond, Krech, & Rosenzweig, 1964; Greenough et al., 1987). Brain plasticity is greatest early in development. However, the organization of synapses within the nervous system continues to change in response to experience throughout life (Greenough, 1986).

How are early developments in the brain linked to infant development? We have seen that one of the strengths of newborns is a set of reflexes. These reflexes are made possible by the lower centers of the nervous system (the spinal cord, brain stem, and so on), which are relatively well developed at birth. Additionally, in the higher centers of the brain (the cortex), the sensory areas develop more rapidly than the portions of the cortex involved in thought and language (Greenough et al., 1987). Thus the senses of newborns are in good working order, but newborns do not learn, remember, or think as effectively as they will later in life. Moreover, the steady development of the motor areas of the cerebral cortex, combined with early sensory and motor experience, converts the infant from a being who is not very capable of moving voluntarily or deliberately to achieve goals into a 1- or 2-year-old who most definitely can.

Physical Behavior

The motor behaviors of newborns are far more organized and sophisticated than they appear to be at first glance (Prechtl, 1981). Yet newborns are not ready to dance or thread needles. By age 2, however, immobile infants have become toddlers, walking up and down stairs by themselves and using their hands to accomplish simple self-care tasks and to operate toys. How do the gross motor skills involved in walking and the fine motor skills involved in manipulating toys develop?

Basic Trends in Locomotor Development

Examine the motor milestones listed in Table 5.4. Column 2 shows the age at which 50% of U.S. infants master each skill. This average age of mastery is called the **developmental norm** for a skill. Column 3 indicates when almost all infants (90%) have mastered each milestone. Children who master a skill somewhat earlier or somewhat later than the developmental norm still fall within the normal range of development. Only significantly delayed achievement of new skills is cause for concern. Can you recognize the workings of the cephalocaudal and proximodistal principles of development in these milestones?

Early motor development does proceed in a *cephalocaudal* direction, because the neurons between the brain and the muscles myelinate in a head-to-tail manner. Thus infants can lift their heads before they can control their trunks enough to sit, and they can sit before they can control their legs to walk. The *proximodistal* principle of development is less obvious in Table 5.4 but is also evident in early motor development. Activities involving the trunk are mastered before activities involving the arms and legs, and activities involving the arms and legs are mastered before activities involving the hands and fingers or feet and toes. Therefore, infants can roll over before they can walk or bring their arms together to grasp a bottle, and children generally master "gross motor skills" (such as drawing large circles) before mastering "fine motor skills" (such as writing their names). Long ago, Mary Shirley (1933) concluded that locomotor development is a predictable maturational phenomenon. As the nerves and muscles mature in a downward and outward direction, infants gradually gain control over the lower and the peripheral parts of their bodies.

Life changes dramatically for infants and their parents when the infants begin to crawl or creep at about 7 months of age. With this new mobility they are better able to explore the objects around them and to interact with other people. Experience in moving through the spatial world contributes to cognitive, social, and emotional development. For example, crawlers—as well as noncrawlers who are made mobile with the aid of special walkers—are more able to search for and find hidden objects than are infants of the same age who are not mobile (Kermoian & Campos, 1988). Crawling also contributes to more frequent social interactions with parents (Gustafson, 1984) and to the emergence of a healthy fear of heights (Campos, Bertenthal, & Kermoian, 1992).

Although parents must be on their toes when their infants first begin walking, at about 1 year of age, they take great delight in witnessing this new milestone in motor development. According to Esther Thelen (1984), the basic motor patterns required for walking are present at birth. They are evident in the newborn's stepping reflex and in the spontaneous kicking that infants do when they are lying down. But infants must develop more muscle and become less top-heavy before walking is possible. Even when they do begin to walk, they lack good balance because of their big heads and short legs. Steps are short; legs are wide apart; and hips, knees, and ankles are flexed. There is much teetering and falling, and a smooth gait and good balance will not be achieved for some time. Thelen's point is that we would walk funny too if we, like infants, were "fat, weak, and unstable" (Thelen, 1984, p. 246).

TABLE 5.4 Age norms (in months) for important motor milestones (based on Anglo-American, Hispanic, and African-American children in the United States).

Skill	*Month When 50% of Infants Have Mastered the Skill*	*Month When 90% of Infants Have Mastered the Skill*
Lifts head 90° while lying on stomach	2.2	3.2
Rolls over	2.8	4.7
Sits propped up	2.9	4.2
Sits without support	5.5	7.8
Stands holding on	5.8	10.0
Walks holding on	9.2	12.7
Stands alone momentarily	9.8	13.0
Stands alone well	11.5	13.9
Walks well	12.1	14.3
Walks up steps	17.0	22.0
Kicks ball forward	20.0	24.0

SOURCE: Adapted from Frankenburg & Dodds, 1967.

Manipulating Objects

When we look at what infants can do with their hands, we also see a progression from reflexive activity to more voluntary, coordinated behavior. As we saw, newborns come equipped with a grasping reflex. It weakens at 2 to 4 months of age, and for a time infants cannot aim their grasps very well. They take swipes at objects, but they often miss or close their hands too early or too late (Bower, 1982). By the middle of the first year, infants can once again grasp objects well, although they use a rather clumsy, clawlike

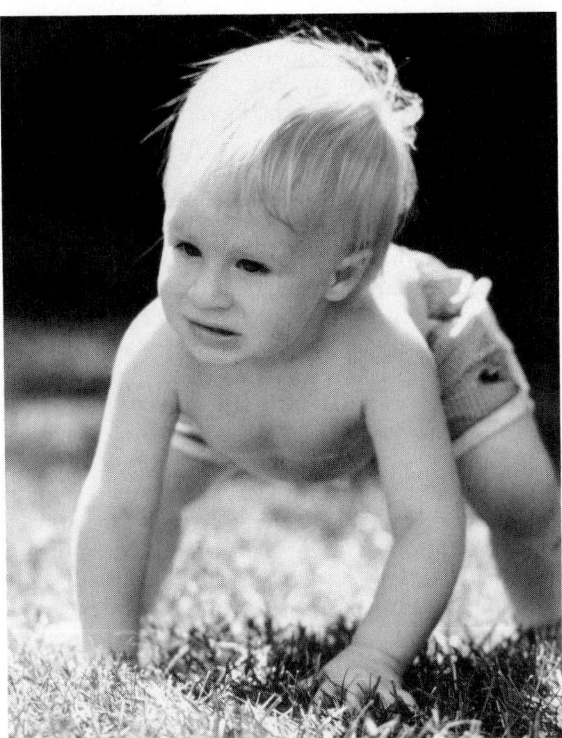

Young toddlers have difficulty maintaining their balance because of their large, heavy heads and torsos and their weak muscles.

grasp in which they press the palm and outer fingers together. Their eyes and hands are better coordinated than the younger infant's; they reach for an object along a straighter path and can correct their reach, if necessary, to obtain the target (Hofsten, 1991; Mathew & Cook, 1990). The workings of the proximodistal principle of development can be seen when infants who could control their arms and then their hands finally become able to control the individual fingers enough to use a **pincer grasp.** Involving only the thumb and the forefinger (or another finger), the pincer grasp appears at about 9 to 12 months (Halverson, 1931).

By 16 months of age infants can scribble with a crayon, and by the end of the second year they can copy a simple horizontal or vertical line and even build towers of five or more blocks. They are rapidly gaining control of specific, differentiated movements and then *integrating* those movements into whole, coordinated actions (Fentress & McLeod, 1986). Thus infants can use a pincer grasp as part of a meaningful sequence of movements — for example, reaching for a block, snatching it with a pincer grasp, laying it precisely on a tower of blocks, and releasing it. They use their new locomotor and manipulation skills to get to know the world around them. By cornering bugs and turning the dials on the television set, they develop their minds.

Nature, Nurture, and Motor Development

Motor development during infancy is truly impressive. As the cortex of the brain develops to allow voluntary and coordinated actions, primitive reflexes disappear and skilled, deliberate movements take their place. And, as body proportions change and the muscles develop, infants become able to balance themselves enough to walk, though with difficulty. Infants do not need to be taught these motor skills. Motor development depends in part on the maturation of body and brain, and infants all over the world progress through the same motor milestones in just about the same order and at just about the same times.

What role does experience play in motor development, then? For one thing, it affects the rate at which infants progress through the sequence of motor milestones. For example, infants who are given opportunities to practice their stepping reflex early in life walk at an earlier age than infants who do not receive this early training (Zelazo, Zelazo, & Kolb, 1972).

Moreover, cross-cultural studies tell us that the ages at which infants attain milestones in motor development are influenced by their parents' beliefs about motor development and by the opportunities available to practice motor skills. For example, Brian Hopkins (1991) compared the motor development of white infants in England to that of black infants whose families immigrated to England from Jamaica. As in several other comparisons of black and white infants, the black infants developed motor skills at earlier ages. This did not appear to be a genetic difference between the races, however, for black babies were especially likely to acquire motor skills early if their mothers adhered to traditional Jamaican practices for handling infants and nurturing motor development. These handling routines involve massaging infants, stretching and rotating their limbs, eliciting their stepping responses, holding them by the arms and shaking them gently up and down, throwing them into the air, and even holding them by the ankles upside down. Jamaican mothers expect early motor development, work to achieve it, and get it.

Yet infants who do not receive nearly so much opportunity to practice their motor skills still develop perfectly normal motor skills. Why? Consider this surprising finding: Wayne and Marsena Dennis (1940) found that Hopi Indian infants who were tightly swaddled and bound to cradleboards for the first nine to ten months of life were no slower to walk than other Hopi infants whose parents declined to follow this tribal custom.

It seems that infants do not need special motor training, but they *do* need normal opportunities to move around, if genetically programmed maturational changes are to unfold properly. Hopi infants, though restricted to cradleboards early in infancy, had some months to "catch up" on practicing their motor skills before they finally began to walk. However,

Babies who are swaddled tightly and kept on cradleboards for much of the day will still develop normal motor skills as long as they have reasonable opportunities to move about.

Wayne Dennis (1960) also studied infants in institutional settings who had no toys and spent most of their time lying on their backs, often on hollowed-out mattresses that made it impossible for them even to roll over onto their stomachs. Of all infants aged 1 to 2, only 42% could sit alone, and *none* could walk. In fact, only 8% of the 2- and 3-year-olds and 15% of the 3- and 4-year-olds could walk alone! As Dennis concluded, maturation is certainly necessary for motor development, but it is not sufficient. Infants also need normal opportunities to practice and perfect their motor skills as they pursue their goals and explore the interesting world around them (see Goldfield, 1989).

THE CHILD

Development of the body, brain, and motor behavior during childhood is slower than it was during infancy, but it is steady. One need only compare the bodies and the physical feats of the 2-year-old and the 10-year-old to be impressed by how much change occurs over childhood.

The Body

From age 2 until puberty, children gain about 2 to 3 inches in height and 6 to 7 pounds in weight every year. During middle childhood (ages 6–11), children may *seem* to grow very little, probably because the gains are small in proportion to the child's size (4–4½ feet tall and 60–80 pounds) and therefore harder to detect (Eichorn, 1979). The cephalocaudal and proximodistal principles of growth continue to operate. As the lower parts of the body and the extremities fill out, the child takes on more adultlike body proportions. The bones are continuing to grow and harden, and the muscles are becoming stronger.

The Brain

Although new neurons are no longer forming during childhood, the brain is still developing. By a child's fifth birthday the brain has achieved fully 90% of its adult weight. The myelination of neurons continues throughout childhood, and different areas of the brain are becoming more specialized.

One important example of the developing organization of the brain is the **lateralization,** or specialization, of the two hemispheres of the cerebral cortex. In most people the left cerebral hemisphere controls the right side of the body and is specially equipped to process language, whereas the right hemisphere controls the left side of the body and specializes in processing music and in carrying out such spatial activities as mentally visualizing designs. Because of lateralization, we come to rely more on one hand or side of the body than on the other. About 90% or so of us rely on our right hands (or left hemispheres) to write and perform other motor activities. When exactly does the brain become lateralized?

It was once thought that lateralization took place gradually throughout infancy and childhood and was not complete until adolescence (Lenneberg, 1967). Now, however, it is believed that brain lateralization originates in the prenatal period and is clearly evident at birth. For example, about two-thirds of all fetuses end up positioned in the womb with their right ears facing outward; this may give them a right ear advantage and result in the left hemisphere's specialization in language processing (Previc, 1991). From the first day of life, speech sounds stimulate more electrical activity in the left side of the cerebral cortex than in the right (Molfese, 1977). In addition, most newborns turn to the right rather than to the left when they lie on their backs, and these same babies later tend to reach for objects with their right hands (Michel, 1981).

It is true that hand preferences usually do not stabilize until after infancy. Nonetheless, the early preference for the right hand that most infants show indicates that their young brains are already organized in a lateralized fashion (Kinsbourne, 1989). Then, as children develop, they come to rely more and more consistently on one hemisphere or the other to carry out various tasks. This developmental trend involves a change in how the two sides of the brain are *used* rather than a fundamental change in the brain's structure (Kinsbourne, 1989; Witelson, 1987).

Children *do* rely increasingly on one hemisphere or the other to perform certain tasks as they get older. For example, Stanley Coren, Clare Porac, and Pam Duncan (1981) have shown that preferences for using one side of the body or the other become stronger between the preschool years and the high school years. They asked 3- to 5-year-olds and high school students to do such things as pick up a crayon, kick a ball, look into an opaque bottle to identify what was inside, or put an ear close to a box to hear sounds coming from it. In this way they could see which hand, foot, eye, or ear each child favored. Although most preschoolers already preferred their right hands and feet, right eyes and ears were preferred more clearly by high school students than by the young children. Moreover, only about 32% of the preschoolers consistently demonstrated preference for the right side of the body on all tasks, whereas about 52% of the adolescents did.

Overall, then, the brain appears to be structured very early in life so that the two hemispheres of the cortex will be capable of specialized functioning. As we develop, the large majority of us come to rely more on the left hemisphere to carry out language activities and more on the right hemisphere to do such things as perceive shapes and listen to music. We also come to rely more consistently on one hemisphere—usually the left—to control many of our physical activities.

Physical Behavior

Have you ever watched 3-year-olds try to catch a ball? Often their little arms clap together well after the ball has already bounced off their stomachs and dropped to the ground. Infants and toddlers are quite capable of controlling their movements in relation to a stationary world. What they will master during childhood is the ability to move capably in a *changing* environment—when a ball is moving toward them, or when they must navigate on a crowded sidewalk (Keough & Sugden, 1985). They will also refine many motor skills. For example, young children throw a ball only with the arm, but older children learn to step forward as they throw. Thus, older children can throw farther than younger ones—not just because they are bigger and stronger but also because they use more refined and efficient techniques of movement (Haywood, 1986).

The toddler in motion appears awkward compared to the older child, who takes steps in more fluid and rhythmic strides and is better able to avoid obstacles. And children quickly become able to do more than just walk. By age 3, they can walk or run in a straight line, though they cannot easily turn or stop while running. Four-year-olds can skip, hop on one foot, and run much farther and faster than they could a year earlier (Corbin, 1973). By age 5, children are becoming rather graceful. With each passing year, school-age children can run a little faster, jump a little higher, and throw a ball a little farther (Herkowitz, 1978; Keough & Sugden, 1985).

Preschool children are not as coordinated as they will be in a few years.

At the same time, eye/hand coordination and control of the small muscles are improving rapidly, giving children more and more sophisticated use of their hands. Three-year-olds find it difficult to button their shirts, tie their shoes, or copy simple designs. By age 5, children can accomplish all of these feats and can even cut a straight line with scissors or copy letters and numbers with a crayon. By age 8 or 9, they can use household tools such as screwdrivers and have become skilled performers at games such as soccer and Pacman that require eye/hand coordination.

Finally, older children have quicker reactions than young children do. When basketballs suddenly fly toward their heads or when dogs run in front of their bikes, they can do something about it. In studies of *reaction time*, a stimulus, such as a light, suddenly appears, and the subject's task is to respond to it as quickly as possible—for example, by pushing a button. These studies reveal that reaction time improves steadily throughout childhood (Thomas, Gallagher, & Purvis, 1981; Wilkinson & Allison, 1989). Indeed, as children get older, they can carry out any number of cognitive processes more quickly (Kail, 1991; Kail & Park, 1992). This speeding of neural responses with age may have a lot to do with the steady improvements in memory and other cognitive skills we observe from infancy to adolescence (see Chapter 8).

In short, no matter what aspect of physical growth and motor behavior we consider, we see steady and impressive improvement over the childhood years. But these changes are not nearly so dramatic as those that will occur during the adolescent years, as the child becomes an adult.

THE ADOLESCENT

The Body: Physical and Sexual Maturation

Think back to the dramatic physical changes of adolescence and your reactions to them. You rapidly grew taller during the **adolescent growth spurt** and took on the body size and proportions of an adult. Moreover, you experienced **puberty,** the point in life when an individual attains sexual maturity and becomes capable of producing a child. The term *puberty*, by the way, is derived from a Latin word meaning "to grow hairy." Sprouting hair here and there is at least part of what it means to be an adolescent.

The Adolescent Growth Spurt

Typically, a girl's rapid growth begins at age 10½ and reaches a peak at age 12 (Tanner, 1981). Boys lag behind girls by about two years, so that their growth spurt typically begins at age 13 and peaks at age 14. As a result, there is a period in early junior high school when many boys appear "shrimpy" compared to many girls. Both sexes return to a slower rate of growth after the peak of their growth spurts.

Different parts of the body grow at different rates. One of the most disturbing aspects of growth for many adolescents is that the extremities of the body enlarge before the trunk and central areas do. Thus, adolescents may be embarrassed by having monstrous feet or protruding noses before the rest of their bodies have caught up. This direction of growth is the opposite of the proximodistal (center to extremities) direction that characterizes early physical development.

Muscles also develop rapidly in both sexes, with boys normally gaining a higher proportion of muscle mass than girls do. Girls must be content with gaining extra fat, primarily in the breasts, hips, and buttocks. Total body weight increases in both sexes, but it is distributed differently: The hips broaden in young women, the shoulders in young men.

Sexual Maturation

For most girls the first visible sign of sexual maturation is the accumulation of fatty tissue around their nipples, forming small "breast buds" at about age 11. Straight, soft pubic hair usually begins to appear a little later, although as many as one-third of all girls develop some pubic hair before their breasts begin to develop (Tanner, 1990). As a girl enters her growth spurt, the breasts grow rapidly and the internal sex organs begin to mature. The most dramatic event in the sexual maturation process is the achievement of **menarche**—the first menstruation—normally between the ages of 11 and 15, with an average of 12½ in the United States (Tanner, 1990). Young girls often menstruate without ovulating, so they *may* not actually be capable of reproducing for 12 to 18 months after menarche (Tanner, 1990). In the year after menarche, the breasts and kinky pubic hair also complete their development, and axillary (underarm) hair grows—only to be shaven off by most females in our society.

For the average boy the sexual maturation process begins at about age 11 to 11½ with an initial enlargement of the testes and scrotum (the saclike structure that encloses the testes). Unpigmented, straight pubic hair appears soon thereafter, and about six months later the penis grows rapidly at about the same time that the adolescent growth spurt begins. The marker of sexual maturation that is most like menarche in girls is a boy's first ejaculation—the emission of seminal fluid in a "wet dream" or while masturbating. It typically occurs at about age 13 or 14. Just as girls often do not ovulate until some time after menarche, boys often do not produce viable sperm until some time after their first ejaculation.

Somewhat later, boys begin to sprout facial hair, first at the corners of the upper lip and finally on the chin and jawline. Increased glandular activity makes for body odor and pimples in both boys and girls—a cruel fate indeed when one longs to be attractive to potential dating partners. As the voice lowers, many boys have the embarrassing experience of hearing their voices "crack" uncontrollably up and down between a squeaky soprano and a deep baritone, sometimes within a single sentence. Boys may not see the first signs of a hairy chest until their late teens or early twenties, if at all.

Variations in the Timing of Physical and Sexual Maturation

So far we've been describing developmental norms, or the average ages when adolescent changes take place. But, as Figure 5.4 suggests, there are great individual differences in the timing of physical and sexual maturation. An early-maturing girl may develop breast buds at age 8, start her growth spurt soon thereafter, and reach menarche at age 10½. Meanwhile, a late-developing boy may not begin to experience a growth of the penis until age 14½ or a height spurt until age 16. Within a junior high school, then, one will find a wide assortment of bodies, ranging from those that are entirely childlike to those that are fully adultlike. No wonder adolescents are self-conscious about their appearance!

What determines an adolescent's rate of development? In part, it is a matter of genetic influence.

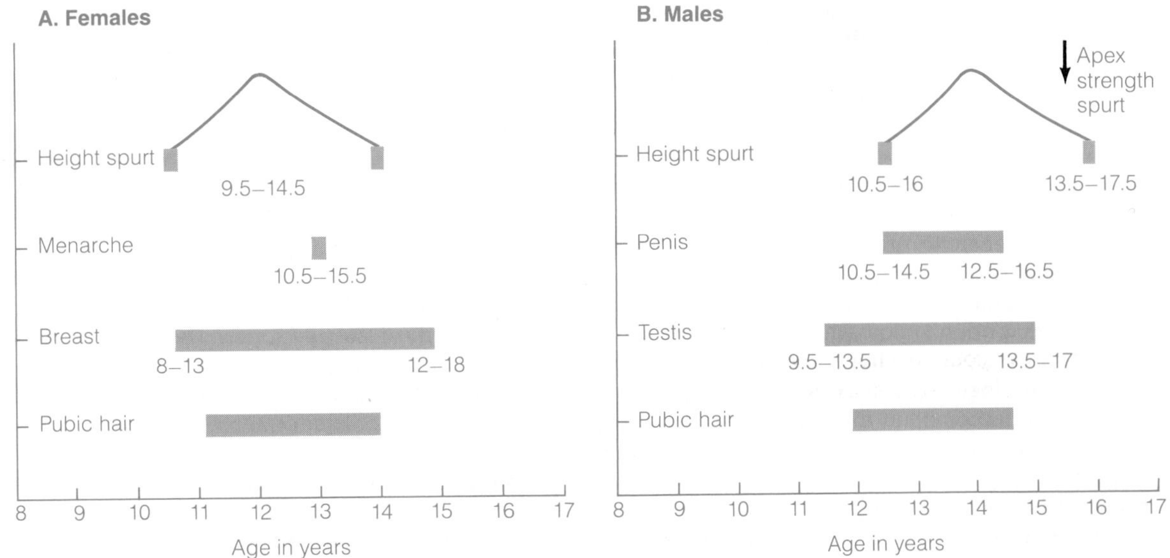

FIGURE 5.4 Sequence of events in the sexual maturation of females (A) and males (B). The numbers represent the variation among individuals in the ages at which each aspect of sexual maturation begins or ends. For example, we see that the growth of the penis may begin as early as age 10½ or as late as age 14½. (Adapted from Marshall & Tanner, 1970.)

Identical twins typically experience changes at similar times, and early or late maturation tends to run in families (Tanner, 1990). In both sexes the changes involved in physical and sexual maturation are triggered when the hypothalamus of the brain stimulates activity in the endocrine system (see discussion at start of chapter). Boys and girls have similar levels of both male and female sex hormones during childhood. However, by the time sexual maturation is complete, males have larger quantities of male hormones (androgens, including testosterone) circulating in their blood than females do, while females have larger quantities of female hormones (estrogen, progesterone, and others).

Physical and sexual maturation, then, are processes set in motion by the genes and executed by hormones. But environment also plays its part in the timing of maturation. This is dramatically illustrated by the **secular trend,** a historical trend in industrialized societies toward earlier maturation and greater body size. In 1880, for example, the average girl reached menarche at about age 16. In 1900 the average was down to about 14 to 15, and by the 1980s it was down to 12½ (Tanner, 1981). In addition, people have been growing taller and heavier over the past century: Many adolescents are taller than their grandparents, although the secular trend now appears to be leveling off in our society (Tanner, 1981). One can still find cultures where sexual maturity is reached much later than it is in industrialized nations. For example, in one part of New Guinea the average girl does not reach menarche until age 18 (Tanner, 1990). Many of the more prosperous Third World countries are now experiencing the secular trend.

What explains the secular trend? Better nutrition and advances in medical care seem to be most responsible (Tanner, 1990). Today's children are more likely than their parents or grandparents to reach their genetic potentials for maturation and growth because they are better fed and less likely to experience growth-retarding illnesses. Even within our own relatively affluent society, poorly nourished adolescents mature later than well-nourished ones do. Whereas overweight girls tend to mature early, girls who engage regularly in strenuous physical activity and girls who suffer from *anorexia nervosa* (the life-threatening eating disorder that involves dieting to the point of starvation) may begin menstruating very late or stop menstruating after they have begun (Frisch, Wyshak, & Vincent, 1980; Hopwood et al., 1990). One 11-year-old with a fear of weight gain overzealously dieted and exercised until age 18, finally changed her ways, and then did not reach menarche until age 21 (Hopwood et al., 1990). Similarly, undernourished boys grow more slowly and are likely to produce fewer viable sperm than their well-fed peers do (Frisch, 1983). Truly, then, physical and sexual maturation are the products of an *interaction* between heredity and environment.

The Psychological Effects of Adolescent Development

What effects do the many changes associated with puberty really have on adolescents? In our culture, girls typically become quite concerned about appearance and worry about how others will respond to them (Greif & Ulman, 1982). One adolescent girl may think she is too tall, another that she is too short. One may try to pad her breasts, whereas another may hunch her shoulders to hide hers. Yet most girls do feel better about their bodies, their relationships with peers, and their abilities after they first develop breasts (Brooks-Gunn & Warren, 1988). Their emotional reactions to menarche are mixed (Greif & Ulman, 1982). Girls are often a bit excited, but they are somewhat scared and confused as well, especially if they mature early or don't know what to expect (Ruble & Brooks-Gunn, 1982). Some develop poor body images because they are bothered by the weight gains that typically accompany menarche (Duncan et al., 1985). Few girls are traumatized by menarche, but at the same time few express delight at becoming a woman (Ruble & Brooks-Gunn, 1982).

What about boys? Their body images are more positive than those of girls, and they are more likely to welcome their weight gain (Richards et al., 1990). But they hope to be tall, hairy, and handsome, and they may become preoccupied with the aspects of body image that center on physical and athletic prowess (Berscheid, Walster, & Bohrnstedt, 1973). Whereas menarche is a memorable event for girls, boys are often only dimly aware of the physical changes they are experiencing (Zani, 1991). When Alan Gaddis and Jeanne Brooks-Gunn (1985) interviewed a small sample of boys about their first ejaculation, they found that few boys had told anyone. These boys seemed to react more positively to their first ejaculation than girls react to their first menstruation, feeling "excited" and "grown up." Yet, like girls, boys were also surprised by the experience and sometimes a bit scared. It seems, then, that sexual maturation provokes mixed reactions in both males and females, but stronger reactions in females.

Adolescents who are maturing physically and sexually not only come to feel differently about themselves but come to be viewed and treated differently by other people. Laurence Steinberg (1981, 1988) has examined changes in family relations. Around age 11 to 13, when pubertal changes are peaking, adolescents become more independent, less close to their parents, and more likely to experience conflicts with their parents, especially with their mothers (see also Hill, 1988). This conflict with parents is rarely severe; it more often involves bickering about unmade beds, late hours, and loud music than arguments about core values. But it can be unpleasant nonetheless. Fortunately, parent/child relationships become warmer again once the pubertal transition is completed (Hill, 1988; Paikoff & Brooks-Gunn, 1991).

Higher and more variable levels of sex hormones in early adolescence also contribute to increased sexual motivation (Udry, 1990) and may help to explain increased conflict with parents, increased moodiness, bouts of depression, lower or more variable energy levels, and restlessness during this period (Buchanan, Eccles, & Becker, 1992). Overall, biological changes and accompanying changes in the social environment interact to influence how adolescence is experienced by each individual (Paikoff & Brooks-Gunn, 1991).

Early or Late Development

If "timely" maturation has psychological implications, what is it like to be "off time" — to be an especially early or late developer? The answer depends on whether we are talking about males or females and also on whether we examine their adjustment during adolescence or later on.

Let's first consider the short-term impacts of being an early-developing or late-developing boy. Other things being equal, the early-developing boy should be at an advantage during the years when he is developed and other boys are not. He is likely to star on the athletic field, impress the girls, and have his way in fights, if nothing else. Mary Cover Jones and Nancy Bayley (1950) followed the development of early- and late-maturing boys over a six-year period. Early maturers were indeed at an advantage. They were poised and confident in social settings, were judged to be attractive, and often won athletic honors and student elections. By comparison, late-maturing boys tended to be more anxious and attention seeking. Perhaps because they are the only ones in their peer groups who have not matured, late-maturing boys tend to feel unsure of themselves and inferior (Livson & Peskin, 1980). As a group they even score lower than other students do, at least in early adolescence, on school achievement tests (Dubas, Graber, & Petersen, 1991).

Now consider early- and late-maturing girls. Traditionally, physical prowess has not been as important in girls' peer groups as in boys', so it is not a given that the early-developing girl will gain status from being larger and more muscled. In addition, since girls develop about two years earlier than boys do, she will be somewhat of a "freak" for a time — the only one in her grade who is developed and thus the target of some teasing. Perhaps for some of these reasons, early maturation appears to be more of a disadvantage than an advantage for girls. In the sixth grade, when most girls are not yet developed, the early-maturing girl tends to be *less* popular than her prepubertal classmates (Faust, 1960; Jones & Mussen, 1958) and is likely to report more symptoms of depression (Rierdan & Koff, 1991). Later in adolescence the picture is reversed somewhat, with the early maturer enjoying more status among peers than the late maturer (Faust, 1960). However, the early-maturing girl is nonetheless more likely than her on-time or late-developing peers to rebel against parents and to become involved in the "teen scene" of dating, drinking, having sex, and engaging in minor troublemaking (Simmons & Blyth, 1987; Stattin & Magnusson, 1990). Additionally, involvement with older friends, including boyfriends, may hurt her school achievement (Stattin & Magnusson, 1990; see also Box 5.1). Late-maturing girls (like late-maturing boys) may experience some anxiety as they wait to mature, but they are not nearly as disadvantaged as late-maturing boys. Indeed, whereas later-developing boys tend to perform poorly on school achievement tests, later-developing girls outperform other students (Dubas et al., 1991).

Do these differences between early and late developers persist into adulthood? In general, they fade over time. By 12th grade, for example, differences in academic performance between early and late maturers have already disappeared (Dubas et al., 1991). Yet there are some interesting twists in the plot. Jones (1965) found that early-maturing boys were still somewhat more sociable, confident, and responsible in their 30s than their peers who had matured later in adolescence. So some of the advantages of early maturation had carried over into adulthood. But these early maturers were also more rigid and conforming than the late maturers, who as men seemed more able to be playful and innovative and to cope with ambiguous situations. Possibly their need to struggle with the problems of late maturation created some strengths in late-maturing boys. By contrast, early-maturing boys may have been pushed into adult roles before they really had much time to experiment.

There are similar hints that struggle stimulates growth in girls. Although early-maturing girls have adjustment difficulties for a time during adolescence, they are no less well adjusted than late maturers as young adults (Stattin & Magnusson, 1990). Some evidence even suggests that they are more self-directed and better able to cope with challenges than late-developing women (Peskin, 1973). In short, those individuals who have a relatively difficult time coping with physical and sexual maturation — late-developing boys and early-developing girls — may learn through their struggles to cope with adversity and respond flexibly to change (Livson & Peskin, 1980).

Overall, then, both the advantages of maturing early and the disadvantages of maturing late are greater for males than for females. Late-maturing boys and early-maturing girls are especially likely to find the adolescent period disruptive. However, psychological differences between early- and late-maturing adolescents become smaller and more mixed in nature by adulthood. Finally, let's note that differences between early and late maturers are relatively small and that many other factors besides the timing of maturation influence whether this period of life goes smoothly or not.

The Brain

Adolescents experience not only observable physical changes but also mental changes as they develop. Through the ages, adults have noticed that teenagers suddenly begin to ask hypothetical "what if" questions and to reason about weighty abstractions such

BOX 5.1 Struggling through Puberty

Research suggests that late-maturing boys and early-maturing girls have the most difficulty adjusting to puberty and all its accompanying physical and social changes, perhaps because they stand out as different from their peers for a time. Here, two college students reflect on their experiences.

Late-Maturing Boy:
I didn't grow until I was almost 16 years old. Even after that growth spurt of six inches in six months, I was only 5'6" tall. I still had baby fat around my waist, barely had hair under my arms, and was years away from even thinking about shaving. The fact that everyone around me was developing and I wasn't made me stay home, become less autonomous. I would come home from school, plop myself on the couch, and watch TV for the rest of the day.

Things really started to change in college. I grew to about 5'11" and lost my baby fat. With my maturity, my self-confidence grew.

Early-Maturing Girl:
Suddenly my entire world was drastically and permanently altered by my first outward sign of sexual maturation, the budding of my breasts at age 8. Other girls in my class would make fun of me or isolate me and make me feel different from them. They would tease me by telling the boys that I wore a bra. Although this does not seem like a big deal now, in the fourth grade it was a very emotionally painful experience.

By the end of fifth grade, I had begun menstruating. It was at this point that older boys became interested in me. Naturally, I was at first flattered by all of their attention, but I quickly realized what it was that they were after and once again felt very alone. From the day of my first menstruation on, though, I honestly feel that my mom began to give me more responsibility and listen to me.

as truth and justice. Can these shifts in thinking be tied to developments within the brain? Perhaps so, for the brain is completing its development from ages 12 to 20. By about age 16 the brain reaches its full adult weight (Tanner, 1990). Myelination of its neural pathways, including those that allow us to concentrate for lengthy periods of time, continues during adolescence (Benes, 1989; Tanner, 1990). This may help explain why infants, toddlers, school-aged children, and even young adolescents have shorter attention spans than do older adolescents and adults (Tanner, 1990). The speed at which the nervous system processes information also continues to increase during adolescence (Kail, 1991).

There appear to be a few systematic spurts in brain development over the years of infancy, childhood, and adolescence that occur at roughly the ages at which children are believed by Jean Piaget and others to acquire new cognitive abilities (Case, 1992; Fischer, Kenny, & Pipp, 1990; Thatcher, 1992). Particularly important during adolescence may be a reorganization of the neural circuitry of the frontal lobes, which are involved in higher-level cognitive activities such as strategic planning. The frontal lobes continue to develop up to the age of 20 or so (Stuss, 1992). Twelve-year-olds, even those who are intellectually gifted, appear to be "clever" but not "wise"—that is, they are capable of solving many problems correctly but not as skilled as older individuals at showing foresight or adopting broad perspectives on problems (Segalowitz, Unsal, & Dywan, 1992). Although changes in the brain are far less dramatic during adolescence than earlier in life, it is quite likely that some of the cognitive growth we observe during the teenage years becomes possible only after adolescents' brains undergo a process of reorganization and fine-tuning.

Physical Behavior

The dramatic physical growth that occurs during adolescence makes teenagers stronger and more physically competent than children. By age 14 adolescents can perform many motor activities as well as adults can (Keough & Sugden, 1985). Where they still often fall short compared to adults is in activities that require strength. Rapid muscle development over the adolescent years makes both boys and girls (but especially boys) noticeably stronger than they were as children (Faust, 1977). Their performance of large-muscle activities continues to improve: An adolescent can throw a ball farther, cover more ground in the standing long jump, and run much faster than a child can (Keough & Sugden, 1985). However, as the adolescent years progress, the physical performance of boys continues to improve, while that of girls often levels off—or, worse yet, *declines* (Thomas & French, 1985; see also Figure 5.5).

It is easy to see that their larger muscles enable boys to outperform girls in activities that require strength. By the mid-20s, muscle accounts for 40% of the average man's body weight, compared to 24% of the average woman's (Marshall, 1977). But biological differences cannot entirely explain sex differences in physical performance (Smoll & Schutz, 1990). After all, young women *do* experience physical and muscular growth, so why would they perform *worse* on some physical tests in later adolescence than they did in earlier adolescence? Gender-role socialization may be responsible (Herkowitz, 1978). As girls mature sexually and physically, they are often encouraged to be less "tomboyish" and to become more interested in traditionally "feminine" (and, often, more sedentary) activities. Let's note, however, that studies of world records in track, swimming, and cycling suggest

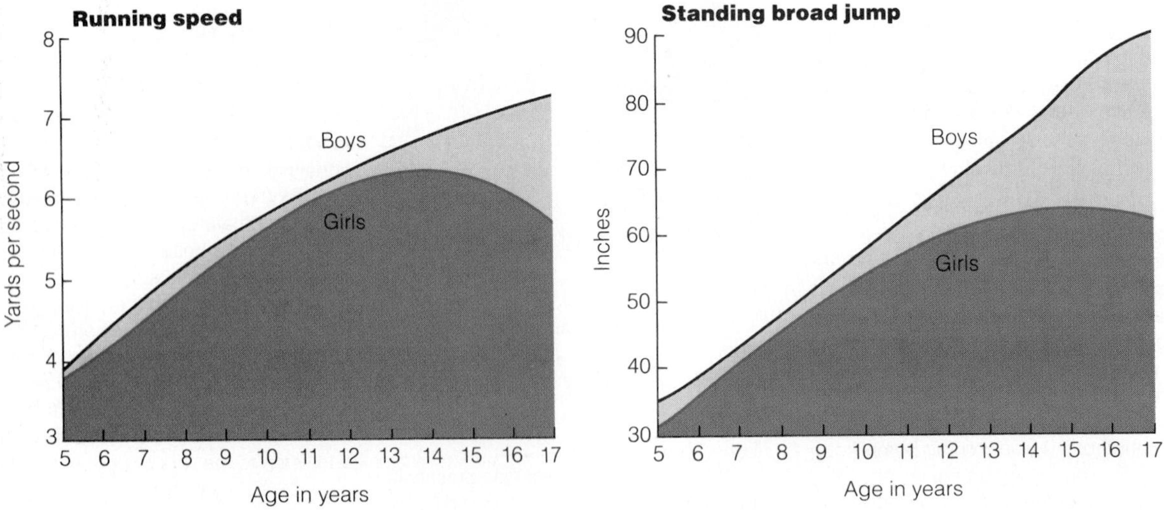

FIGURE 5.5 Age and sex differences in performance on two tests of large-muscle activity. (From Johnson & Buskirk, 1974.)

that, as gender roles have changed in the past few decades, women have been improving their performances, and the male/female gap in physical performance has narrowed dramatically (Dyer, 1977; Whipp & Ward, 1992). As today's girls participate more often in sports and other strenuous physical activities, their performance on tests of large-muscle activity is likely to improve during adolescence rather than decline. Then both young women and young men will be likely to enter adulthood in peak physical condition.

THE ADULT

Although the adolescent becomes physically, sexually, and neurologically mature, changes in the physical self continue during the adult years. We'll now examine the changes in body and brain that are part of the aging process.

The Body

The body of the mature adolescent or young adult is at its prime in many ways. It is strong and fit; its organs are functioning efficiently. But it is aging. Physical aging occurs slowly and steadily over most of the life span. It begins to have noticeable effects on physical appearance and functioning in middle age and has had an even more significant impact by the time old age is reached.

Physical Appearance and Structure

Only minor changes in physical appearance occur in the 20s and 30s, but many people do notice signs that they are aging as they reach their 40s. The skin wrinkles, and the hair thins and turns gray (and may drop out by the handfuls in balding men). Middle-age spread may strike as people put on extra weight around the midsection (and have the "love handles" and potbellies to prove it). Some people find these changes difficult to accept, for they equate "old" with "unattractive."

The body shows additional effects of aging in old age. After gaining weight from their 20s to their 50s, people typically begin to lose it starting in their 60s (Shephard, 1978). Loss of weight in old age is usually coupled with a loss of muscle over the entire span of adulthood (Montoye & Lamphiear, 1977; Murray et al., 1985). The result may be sagging flesh. "Age spots" also appear on the skin, which wrinkles and thins. The bones lose tissue so that the vertebrae collapse a bit, and many people get shorter as they age, though only by a half-inch for the average man and an inch for the average woman (Adams, Davies, & Sweetnam, 1970). Older people may *seem* to shrink more than that as they age, but recall the secular trend: Old people today were *always* relatively short; they grew up in a time when people did not grow as tall as younger people do today.

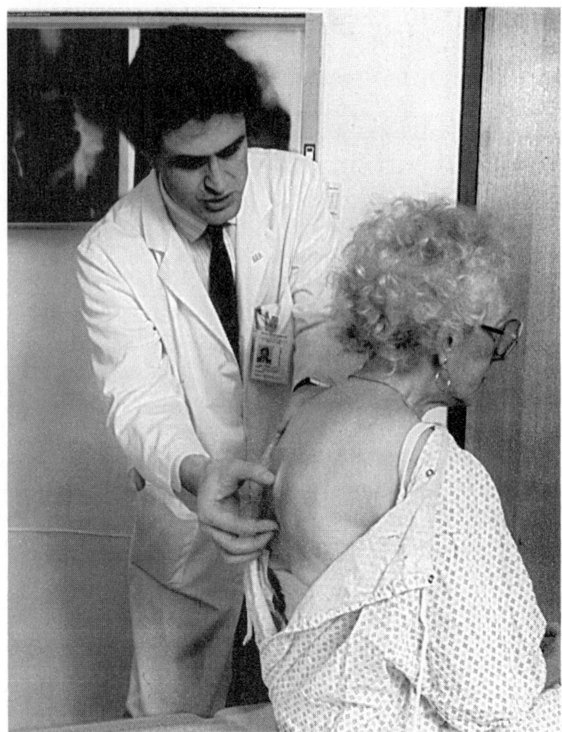

FIGURE 5.6 The "dowager's hump" associated with osteoporosis.

Extreme bone loss in later life results from the disease called **osteoporosis**, a serious loss of minerals that leaves the bones fragile and easily fractured. It is a special problem for older women, who never had as much bone mass as men to start with and whose bones tend to thin rapidly after menopause (Johnston et al., 1985). Women with osteoporosis often have the so-called dowager's hump, a noticeably rounded upper back (see Figure 5.6). Increased calcium intake, exercise, and hormone replacement therapy (taking estrogen and progesterone to compensate for hormone loss due to menopause) have all been recommended to help prevent or slow osteoporosis (Soules & Bremner, 1982). Hormone replacement therapy may also relieve the physical symptoms of menopause and protect against the increased risk of coronary heart disease associated with the loss of estrogen (Matthews, 1992).

The joints are also aging over the adult years. The cushioning between bones wears out, and the joints become stiffer. In its extreme this normal aging process takes the form of *osteoarthritis*, a common disability in old age. The older person who can no longer fasten buttons, stoop to pick up dropped items, or even get into and out of the bathtub may easily feel incompetent and dependent (Whitbourne, 1985).

Bodily Functioning and Health

Aging also involves a gradual decline in the efficiency of most bodily systems from the 20s on (Christofalo, 1988; Whitbourne, 1985). No matter what physical function we look at—strength, the capacity of the heart or lungs to meet the demands of exercise, the ability of the body to control its temperature, or the ability of the immune system to fight disease—the gradual effects of aging are evident.

Each system of the body seems to have its own timetable of development and aging. However, most systems increase to a peak sometime between childhood and early adulthood and decline slowly thereafter (Bafitis & Sargent, 1977; see also Figure 5.7). During the peak years of physiological functioning, death rates are lower than they are in either infancy or later adulthood (Bafitis & Sargent, 1977). Neither the infant nor the old person is well equipped to cope with such stresses to the body as pneumonia, extreme temperature changes, or exhausting activity. Finally, individual differences in physiological functioning grow larger as age increases (Bafitis & Sargent, 1977; Harris et al., 1992). One finds more differences in aerobic capacity and other physiological measures among 70-year-olds than among 20-year-olds. In other words, not all older people have poor physiological functioning, even though the average old person is less physiologically fit than the average young person.

Another fact of physical aging is a decline in the **reserve capacity** of many organ systems—that is, their ability to respond to demands for extraordinary output, as in emergencies (Goldberg & Hagberg, 1990). For example, old and young do not differ much in resting heart rates, but older adults, unless they are completely disease-free, will have lower *maximal* heart rates (Lakatta, 1990). This means that older adults who do not feel very old at all as they go about their normal routines may feel very old indeed if they try to run up mountains.

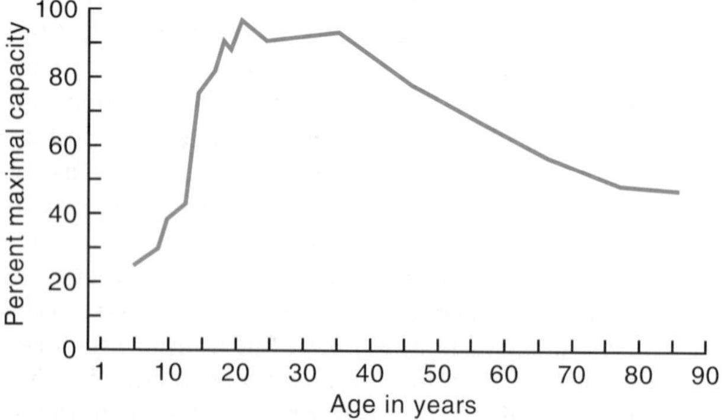

FIGURE 5.7 Changes in vital capacity (the volume of air that can be moved in and out of the lungs when a person breathes) over the life span. (Data from Bafitis & Sargent, 1977.)

By the time people are 65 or older, it is hard to find many of them who do not have something or other wrong with their bodies. National health surveys indicate that 86% of the 65-and-older age group have at least one chronic impairment, whether it is a sensory loss, a physical disability, or a degenerative disease (Harris, 1978). Arthritis alone affects 38%. About 20% have hypertension (high blood pressure), and about the same percentage have a heart condition (Harris, 1978). These data imply that older adults are not healthy. Yet, despite their impairments, about two-thirds of people 65 and older are, according to their own reports or those of people who know them well, in "good" or "excellent" health (National Center for Health Statistics, 1990). Similarly, over 80% of old people are well enough to engage in major life activities such as work inside or outside the home (Harris, 1978). By their own standards, then, the majority of older people are able to retain their sense of well-being and ability to function despite minor impairments. Among minority-group members who live in poverty, health problems and difficulties in day-to-day functioning are likely to be more severe than average, however (Clark & Maddox, 1992; National Center for Health Statistics, 1990).

The Reproductive System

The levels of sex hormones secreted during adolescence help ensure interest in sexual behavior during adulthood and have other effects on emotions and behavior as well. Like the rest of the body, though, the reproductive system ages.

Hormones and Adult Life

Although hormone levels fluctuate up and down in both sexes over time, hormone changes influence the lives of women more than men. Hormone levels shift drastically each month as women progress through their menstrual cycles. Estrogen and progesterone levels rise to a peak at midcycle, when a woman is ovulating, and decline as she approaches her menstrual period. Many women feel at their best in the middle of the menstrual cycle, when they are ovulating, and experience more negative moods as their menstrual period approaches and during menstruation (Asso, 1983; McFarlane & Williams, 1990). Much attention has recently been focused on **premenstrual syndrome (PMS),** which is characterized by irritability, moodiness, and physical symptoms such as breast tenderness and headaches during the days just before the menstrual flow. Cramps and other symptoms during menstruation are also of concern.

How much is the typical woman bothered by premenstrual and menstrual symptoms? Most women are far from incapacitated. Indeed, quite a few studies reveal little mood fluctuation at all over the menstrual cycle when women don't know that their menstrual cycles are being studied and are simply asked to complete mood surveys every day (Englander-Golden et al., 1986; McFarlane & Williams, 1990). We can quickly dispense with the sexist notion that a woman could not be president because she might fall apart if an international crisis occurred at the wrong time of the month. Yet, for a small minority of women, the symptoms are severe and life is disrupted each month (see Table 5.5).

Some women experience more severe hormonal fluctuations than other women do, or their systems may react more strongly to them. We now know that genetic endowment influences the extent to which a woman experiences both premenstrual and menstrual distress—and not just because some women are more genetically predisposed to be emotionally unstable than others are (Kendler et al., 1992). But social factors also affect the experience of menstrual-cycle changes. Learned societal stereotypes of what women "should" experience at different phases of the menstrual cycle appear to influence what women do experience and report (Ainscough, 1990; Englander-Golden et al., 1986). Perhaps because they are especially influenced by these traditional negative stereotypes, women who are housewives or who hold traditional female jobs outside the home experience more negative emotions during their premenstrual and menstrual phases of the month than do women in non-traditional occupations (Brown & Woods, 1986). Most likely, then, biological, psychological, social, and cultural factors all contribute to a woman's experience of the menstrual cycle (McFarlane & Williams, 1990).

What about men? Their hormone levels also fluctuate, but more on a daily than a monthly basis. For example, testosterone levels are higher in the morning than in the afternoon, vary from day to day, and are high when a man is under stress (Harman & Talbert, 1985). Men with high testosterone levels tend to be more sexually active than those with lower testosterone levels (Davidson et al., 1983; Schiavi et al., 1991), as well as more aggressive (Archer, 1991). However, both sexual behavior and aggression are influenced by many factors besides hormone levels, and it is not clear whether changes in men's moods are associated with changes in their hormone levels.

TABLE 5.5 Percentage of women reporting premenstrual symptoms.

Symptom	*Mild/ Moderate*	*Severe/ Disabling*
Weight gain	40.2	5.6
Crying	19.6	4.5
Lowered work or school performance	11.7	3.4
Napping	17.3	1.1
Headache	27.4	7.3
Skin disorders	32.4	6.7
Cramps	24.6	6.1
Anxiety	27.0	3.4
Backache	16.8	5.0
Fatigue	28.5	3.9
Painful breasts	27.9	7.6
Swelling	39.5	5.2
Irritability	44.2	12.2
Mood swings	46.5	4.7
Depression	29.7	7.0
Tension	34.3	7.6

SOURCE: Data from Woods, Most, & Dery, 1982.

Menopause

The ending of a woman's menstrual periods in midlife is called **menopause**. Humorist Dave Barry (1990) calls it the stage of life when a woman's body senses that "her furniture is much too nice for her to have a baby barfing on it" (p. 89). Consider the basic facts of this "change of life" (see Matthews, 1992; Soules & Bremner, 1982; Unger & Crawford, 1992). The average woman experiences menopause at age 51, and the usual age range is from 42 to 58. The process actually takes place over about four years, as periods become either more or less frequent and less regular (McKinlay, Brambilla, & Posner, 1992). Levels of estrogens and other female hormones decline, so that the woman who has been through menopause has a hormone mix that is less "feminine" and more "masculine" than that of the premenopausal woman. When menopause is completed, a woman is no longer ovulating, no longer menstruating, and no longer capable of conceiving a child.

The age at which a woman reaches menopause is unrelated to the age at which she reached menarche (Treloar, 1982). Although the age of menarche has declined over history as part of the secular trend, the age of menopause does not appear to have changed much and is similar from culture to culture (Greene, 1984). What *has* changed is that women are now living long enough to experience a considerable period of postmenopausal life.

What is your image of a "menopausal woman"? The stereotyped image is this: She is even worse than the woman experiencing premenstrual syndrome; she is irritable and will scream at you or burst into tears without provocation; she is depressed and emotionally unstable. How much truth is there to this stereotype? Not much at all. Only two menopausal symptoms have been directly tied to decreases in female hormone levels; both are physical rather than psychological and can be successfully treated with hormone replacement therapy (Greene, 1984; Unger & Crawford, 1992). The first symptom, affecting about two-thirds of menopausal women in many studies, is **hot flashes**. These are sudden experiences of warmth and sweating, usually centered around the face and upper body, that occur at unpredictable times, last for a few seconds or minutes, and are often followed by a cold shiver. The other symptom is *vaginal dryness*. The walls of the vagina become thinner and dryer, and some women experience irritation or pain during intercourse as a result.

What about the psychological symptoms — the irritability and depression? Once again, we discover that there is wide variation among menopausal women — and not much truth at all to the negative stereotypes. In a particularly well-designed study, Karen Matthews and her associates (Matthews, 1992; Matthews et al., 1990) studied 541 women who were initially premenopausal over a three-year period, comparing those who subsequently experienced menopause with women of similar ages who did not become menopausal. The typical woman entering menopause initially experienced some physical symptoms such as hot flashes. Some women also reported mild depression and temporary emotional distress, probably in reaction to their physical symptoms, but only about 10% could be said to have become seriously depressed in response to menopause. As a general rule, menopause had no effect whatsoever on women's levels of anxiety, anger, perceived stress, or job dissatisfaction. It seems that, when women *do* experience severe psychological problems during the menopausal transition, those problems often are ones that existed well before the age of menopause (Greene, 1984).

Women who have been through menopause generally claim that it did little to change them and even improved their lives (Neugarten et al., 1963; Unger & Crawford, 1992). For most women, menopause also has no major effect one way or the other on sexual interest and activity, although sexual activity does gradually decline over the adult years (Greene, 1984). A minority of women may feel less feminine and desirable, but another minority find sex more enjoyable once they are free from the worry of becoming pregnant. Despite all the negative stereotypes, menopause seems to be "no big deal" for most women.

Why do some women experience more severe menopausal symptoms than others do? Perhaps because some women undergo greater biological changes. But psychological and social factors are also involved, just as they are in women's reactions to sexual maturation and to their menstrual cycles. For example, women who expect menopause to be a negative experience are likely to get what they expect, whereas those who have more positive expectations report fewer symptoms (Matthews, 1992). There is also a good deal of variation across cultures in how menopause is experienced (see Box 5.2). It would seem that the impact of menopause is affected by the meaning it has to a woman, as influenced by her society's prevailing views of menopause and by her own personal characteristics.

The Male Climacteric

Despite popular references to the "male menopause," men cannot experience menopause, since they do not menstruate. What they can experience is captured by the term **climacteric** — meaning "critical time" or, more specifically, the loss of reproductive capacity in either sex in later life. Women experience their climacteric within a relatively narrow age range around age 50. Men, however, may lose the ability to father children around then, much later, or even never: Men in their 90s have been known to father children. The sperm produced by older men may not be as active as those produced by younger men. Levels of testosterone also decrease very gradually over the adult years in most men (Schiavi et al., 1991), although not in extremely healthy men (Harman & Tsitouras, 1980). In sum, the changes associated with the climacteric in men are more gradual, more variable, and less complete than those in women (Soules & Bremner, 1982).

What are the psychological impacts of these changes? There are few. Because they occur gradually, changes in the reproductive system cannot really explain the "midlife crisis" that some men experience. As we'll see in Chapter 15, whether a man experiences a midlife transition period in his 40s is related more to events in his career and personal life than to any changes in his hormones. Frequency of sexual activity does decline as men age, but this trend cannot easily be tied to decreased hormone levels either. Older men may need a minimum level of testosterone to remain sexually active, but their sexual activity may decline over the years even if their testosterone levels remain high (Tsitouras, Martin, & Harman, 1982; see also Chapter 11 on sexuality).

For both sexes, then, changes in the reproductive system are a normal part of aging. Yet neither women nor men seem to suffer much as their ability to have children wanes or disappears. Sexual activity becomes less frequent, but it remains an important part of life for most older adults.

The Aging Brain

Many people fear that aging means losing one's brain cells and ultimately becoming "senile." As we'll see in Chapter 16, Alzheimer's disease and other conditions that cause dementia are *not* part of normal aging, and they affect only minorities of older people. What *does* normally happen to the brain as we age?

Normal aging *is* associated with *degeneration* within the nervous system — a loss of neurons, diminished functioning of many remaining neurons, and potentially harmful changes in the tissues surrounding and supporting neurons (Selkoe, 1992). As people age, more and more of their neurons atrophy or shrivel, transmit signals less effectively, and ultimately die (Bondareff, 1985). Just as brain weight and vol-

BOX 5.2 Cultural Differences in the Experience of Menopause

Menopause is universal, but the experience of it is not. In one study, for example, 69% of a sample of Canadian women reported experiencing at least one hot flash during the menopausal period, but only 20% of Japanese women recalled having had any (Lock, 1986). Psychological symptoms vary even more widely from culture to culture (Unger & Crawford, 1992). For instance, Marcha Flint (1982) surveyed women of a high and socially advantaged caste in India and found that very few of these women experienced any symptoms at all. Women who had not reached menopause looked forward to it, and women who had reached it were pleased that they had. Why? According to Flint, menopause brought social rewards to these Indian women. They were freed from the taboos associated with menstruation that had kept them veiled and segregated from male society as younger women. They could now mingle with men other than their husbands and fathers and even drink the local brew with the fellows. Moreover, they still had meaningful work roles and were seen as wise by virtue of their years. In our society, by comparison, aging tends to mean loss of status to older women.

This example tells us that social attitudes can influence adjustments to biological change. Yet Ann Wright (1982) warns us that adjustment to menopause is influenced by more than a society's views of this phase of life. For example, she expected Navajo women in the United States to have an easy time adjusting to menopause because postmenopausal Navajo women are freed from menstrual taboos, have meaningful roles in society, and become eligible to take on ceremonial roles. Instead, she found that menopausal complaints were about as common among Navajo women as they are among Anglo-American women. Why? Unlike Flint's advantaged women in India, Native-American women living on the reservation had low incomes and poor health and had to cope with hard physical labor. Other studies also suggest that women from lower socioeconomic backgrounds have more difficulty with menopause than more affluent women do (Unger & Crawford, 1992). Within any cultural or socioeconomic group, of course, individual women will also differ tremendously in their responses to this universal transition. Biological, psychological, and social factors all play a part.

ume increase over the childhood years, they decrease over the adult years, especially after age 50 (Yamaura, Ito, Kubota, & Matsuzawa, 1980). Elderly adults may end up with 5–30% fewer neurons, depending on the brain site studied, than young adults have (Selkoe, 1992). Neuron loss seems to be greater in the areas of the brain responsible for sensory and motor activities than in either the association areas of the cortex, which are involved in thought, or the brain stem and lower brain, which are involved in basic physiological functions such as breathing (Whitbourne, 1985).

Other signs of brain degeneration include (1) declines in the levels of important neurotransmitters; (2) the formation of "senile plaques," or hard areas in the tissue surrounding neurons that may interfere with neuronal functioning; and (3) reduced blood flow to the brain, which may starve neurons of the oxygen and nutrients they need in order to function (Bondareff, 1985). One of the main implications of such degeneration, as we will see shortly, is that older brains typically process information more slowly than younger brains do.

However, recent research suggests that there is more to aging than degeneration; *plasticity* and neural growth also occur in the aging nervous system. The brain apparently can change in response to experience and develop new capabilities *throughout the life span* (Black, Isaacs, & Greenough, 1991; Greenough, 1986). Consider the landmark findings of Paul Coleman, Stephen Buell, Dorothy Flood, and their colleagues (Buell & Coleman, 1979; Flood et al., 1987; Flood & Coleman, 1990). They compared brain tissue collected from autopsies of middle-aged adults, normal elderly adults, and elderly adults who had *Alzheimer's disease*. Like other researchers, they found evidence of neural death in old brains. But they also discovered that remaining neurons often grow longer, bushier dendrites and presumably make new connections, or synapses, with other neurons as the person ages. Dendrites tend to grow longer between middle age and early old age but degenerate in advanced old age and among Alzheimer's patients (Coleman & Flood, 1987). These findings suggest that *both* degeneration and plasticity characterize the aging brain.

In part, brain plasticity in later life appears to be a compensation for brain degeneration; surviving neurons seem to step in to carry out the functions of dead or dying neurons (Bondareff, 1985; Flood & Coleman,

Mental "exercise" in later life is likely to contribute to neural growth in the aging brain and compensate for neural degeneration.

1990). This may allow the aging person to maintain abilities quite well despite some normal neural loss. But brain growth in old age is also a direct response to stimulation or experience. William Greenough (1986) and his colleagues have demonstrated in several studies that adult rats that are trained to perform tasks such as running mazes will form new synapses in precisely the brain areas that are most involved in the specific type of learning they are experiencing. Similarly, placing adult rats in environments that are more complex and stimulating than their usual laboratory cages results in measurable neural growth (Black et al., 1989; Connor, Diamond, & Johnson, 1980). The aging brain is clearly less plastic, less influenced by environmental enrichment or deprivation, than the infant brain is (Black et al., 1991). Yet it is now clear that the brain retains some of its plasticity *throughout* the life span.

What does all this mean for older adults? Both degeneration and plasticity—both losses and gains—characterize the aging brain. In some people, degeneration may win out, and declines in intellectual performance will occur. In other people, plasticity may prevail; their brains may form new and adaptive neural connections faster than they are lost so that performance on some tasks may actually *improve* with age (at least until very old age). As we'll see in Chapters 7, 8, and 9, there are wide differences among older adults in how effectively they learn, remember, and think, as well as in how well their intellectual abilities hold up as they age (Morse, 1993). One key to maintaining or even improving performance in old age is to avoid the many diseases that can interfere with nervous-system functioning. Another key is to remain intellectually active—to create an "enriched environment" for one's brain. Certainly we can reject the view that aging involves nothing but a slow death of neural tissue. Old brains *can* learn new tricks!

Physical Behavior

How well can older adults carry out physical activities in daily life? Obviously those who have severe arthritis may have difficulty merely walking or dressing themselves without pain, but here we focus on two more typical changes in physical behavior over the adult years: a slowing of behavior and a decreased ability to engage in strenuous activities.

The Slowing of Behavior

You may have noticed, as you breeze by them on the sidewalk, that older adults often walk more slowly than young people do. Indeed, some of them walk as if they were treading on a slippery surface—with short, shuffling steps and not much arm movement (Murray, Kory, & Clarkson, 1969; see also Figure 5.8). Why is this? For one thing, the sensory systems involved in balance do not function as well in old age as they did in earlier years (Ochs, Newberry, Lenhardt, & Harkins, 1985). Elderly people, like young chil-

FIGURE 5.8 Compared to the young man, the average older man takes shorter strides, does not achieve so large an angle between heel and floor, and swings his arms less widely. He appears to be treading cautiously. (Based on Murray, Kory, & Clarkson, 1969.)

dren, have difficulty performing tests in which they must maintain their balance when they are placed on a moving platform or are given misleading sensory feedback (Stelmach et al., 1989; Woollacott, Shumway-Cook, & Nashner, 1986). Thus many older people may walk slowly to compensate for poor balance.

An older person's slow pace of walking may also be due to reduced cardiovascular functioning. Cunningham, Rechnitzer, Pearce, and Donner (1982) tested men aged 19 to 66 and found that the pace at which men of any age chose to walk and the fastest pace at which they could walk were associated with cardiovascular capacity. Older people with strong hearts may walk very briskly, but those—probably the majority—who have cardiovascular limitations find themselves slowing down.

Older adults actually perform many motor actions more slowly than younger adults do (Stelmach & Nahom, 1992). When we try to account for why older people do so many things slowly, we cannot overlook changes in the brain. James Birren has argued that *the* central change that comes about as we age is a slowing of the nervous system (Birren & Fisher, 1992). This affects not only motor behavior but mental functioning as well, and it impacts a majority of elderly people to at least some degree. We have already seen that young children have slow reaction times. Reaction times improve until the 20s and then gradually decrease over the adult years (Wilkinson & Allison, 1989). Elderly adults are especially slow to react when tasks are complex—when any one of several stimuli might appear, each of which requires a different response (Spirduso & MacRae, 1990). On average, older adults take one and a half to two times longer to respond than young adults do when they perform a wide range of cognitive tasks that require speedy answers (Lima, Hale, & Myerson, 1991).

Some older adults remain quick; physically fit older people and those who are free from cardiovascular diseases have quicker reactions than their peers who lead sedentary lives or have diseases (Spirduso & MacRae, 1990). Aerobic exercise or experience playing video games can speed the reactions of older adults (Dustman et al., 1989, 1992). In addition, experience can help elderly people compensate for the slowing of the nervous system so that they can continue to perform well on familiar motor tasks, as we see in the interesting study of typists reported in Box 5.3. In short, we should not expect all old people to be slow in all situations, although most of them do slow down somewhat.

Performance of Vigorous Activity

The slowing of the nervous system and of motor performance is one important fact of aging. Another is that many people become out of shape. Typically, adults decrease their involvement in vigorous physical activity as they get older—females earlier than males (Shephard & Montelpare, 1988). By late adulthood they may find that they get tired just climbing stairs or carrying groceries; running a marathon would be out of the question. Because of declines in reserve capacity, aging bodies are at a greater disadvantage when they must perform tasks requiring maximal strength, speed, or endurance than when they are asked to perform normal daily activities (Goldberg & Hagberg, 1990). The average older person tires more quickly and needs more time to recover after vigorous activity than the average younger person.

Yet once again there is more diversity among older adults than among younger ones. *Some* older people can perform vigorous physical activities with distinction. Michael Stones and Albert Kozma (1985) cite the examples of the 70-year-old woman who competed in the 1972 Olympic equestrian events and the 98-year-old man who could run a marathon (26 miles) in 7½ hours!

Aging, Disease, Disuse, and Abuse

As we've seen, many aspects of physical functioning typically decline over the adult years. But an important question arises: When we look at the performance of older people, are we seeing the effects of aging alone or the effects of something else? The "something else" could be disease, disuse of the body, abuse of the body—or all three.

For instance, most older people have at least some chronic disease or impairment. How would an elderly person function if he or she could manage to stay completely disease-free? James Birren and his colleagues (1963) addressed just this question in a classic study of men aged 65 to 91. Extensive medical examinations were conducted to identify two groups of elderly men: (1) those who were almost perfectly healthy and had *no* signs of disease at all and (2) those who had slight traces of disease-in-the-making but no clinically diagnosable diseases. Several aspects of physical and intellectual functioning were assessed in these men, and the participants were compared to young men.

The most remarkable finding was that the healthier group of older men hardly differed at all from the younger men. They were equal even in their capacity for physical exercise, and they actually beat the younger men on measures of intelligence requiring general information or knowledge of vocabulary words. Their main limitations were the slower brain activity and reaction times that seem to be so basic to the aging process. Overall, *aging itself in the absence of disease had little effect on physical and psychological functioning.* However, the men with slight traces of impending disease *were* deficient on several measures. Diseases that have progressed to the point of symptoms have even more serious consequences for performance.

BOX 5.3 Are Older Typists Really Slower Typists?

In a very revealing study of aging and the slowing of reaction times, Timothy Salthouse (1984) tested the psychomotor performance of female typists ranging in age from 19 to 72. On average, and in keeping with the results of countless studies, the older women performed more slowly than the younger ones on a "choice" reaction-time task: They had to quickly press one typewriter key when the letter *R* appeared and another when the letter *L* appeared on a screen. In the graph the diagonal line for choice reaction time shows the average performance of women of different ages. Each dot represents the reaction time of a particular woman. Longer reaction times (dots higher on the graph) indicate slower performance. Yet notice that older women typed written material just as fast as the younger women did. Their reaction times during a typing exercise were *not* slowed by age.

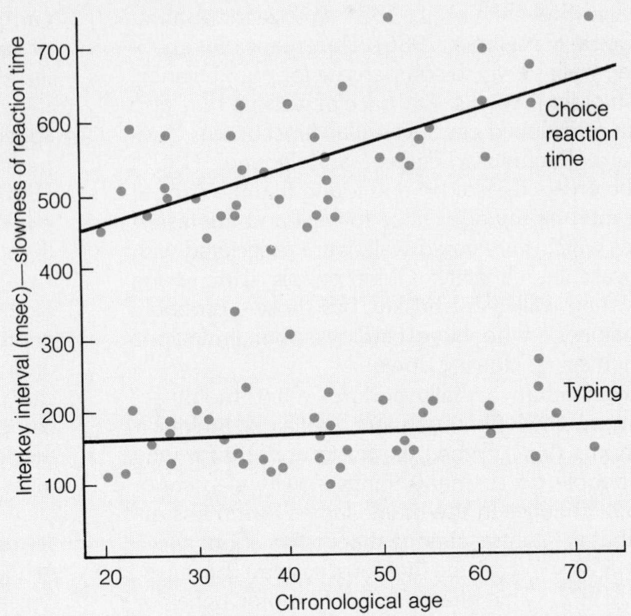

(From Salthouse, 1974.)

How did the older women keep up their typing speed even though their nervous systems' reactions had slowed? Through a careful analysis, Salthouse established that they did exactly what any highly skilled, experienced typist does. As they typed one letter, they were already processing information about the next letters to be typed, giving themselves more time to get ready for any particular stroke of the keys (see also Bosman, 1993). They were planning farther ahead than the younger typists were. Thus, practice at a skill may allow older people who perform quite slowly on reaction-time tasks in the laboratory to perform familiar motor tasks very quickly and effectively in everyday life. This is an excellent example of a common process: compensation for the declines associated with aging.

So it is possible that disease, rather than aging itself, accounts for many declines in functioning in later life (see also Houx, Vreeling, & Jolles, 1991). We must note, however, that Birren and his colleagues had a terrible time finding the perfectly healthy older people whom they studied. Most older people experience *both* aging and disease, and it is difficult to separate the effects of the two. Although aging and disease are distinct, increased vulnerability to disease is one part—and an important part—of normal aging.

Disuse of the body also contributes to steeper declines in physical functioning in some adults than in others (Wagner et al., 1992). Masters and Johnson (1966) proposed a "use it or lose it" maxim to describe the fact that sexual functioning deteriorates if a person engages in little or no sexual activity. The same maxim can be applied to other systems of the body. Muscles atrophy if they are not used, and the heart functions less well if a person leads a sedentary life. The signs of deterioration observed in some aging adults are much like the changes observed in people of any age who are confined to bed for a long time (Goldberg & Hagberg, 1990). The brain also needs "mental exercise" to continue to function effectively in old age (Black et al., 1991). In short, most systems of the body seem to thrive on *use*, but too many people become inactive as they age (Wagner et al., 1992).

Finally, *abuse* of the body contributes to declines in functioning in some people. Excessive alcohol consumption, a high-fat diet, and smoking are all clear examples. Additionally, although elderly adults are not often recreational drug abusers, many do take several prescribed medications. Drugs typically affect older adults more powerfully than they do younger adults; drugs can also interact with one another and with the aging body's chemistry to impair functioning (Cherry & Morton, 1989; Lamy, 1986). Overall, then, poor functioning in old age may represent any combination of the effects of aging, disease, disuse, and abuse. We may not be able to do much to change basic aging processes, but we quite certainly can change our lifestyles to optimize the odds of a long and healthy old age.

APPLICATIONS: OPTIMIZING HEALTHY DEVELOPMENT

Throughout the ages, human beings have searched for the secret to a longer and healthier life. The Spanish explorer Ponce de León searched for a fountain of youth in Florida. Other seekers of immortality, guided by the mistaken theory that decreases in levels of sex hormones were responsible for aging, transplanted ape testicles into old men in an effort to prolong their lives (Walford, 1983). If biologists identify the genes at the root of basic aging processes and figure out how to alter them, we might all live to be 500. In the meantime, the best we can do is try to avoid the diseases and disabilities that can make us function poorly and die young. A nutritious diet, regular exercise, and avoidance of known health risks can have very positive effects on health, especially if healthy lifestyles are adopted in childhood and continued throughout the life span (Margolis, Sparrow, & Swanson, 1989).

Nutrition

As we saw in Chapter 4, adequate nutrition is essential for getting development off to a good start. The baby whose mother is severely malnourished during her pregnancy is likely to be small, to have fewer than the normal number of brain cells, and to be at risk for developmental difficulties and even death. Prenatally malnourished babies can achieve normal intellectual growth if they receive appropriate cognitive and social stimulation after birth (Zeskind & Ramey, 1981), but some such babies remain undernourished and understimulated after they are born. In famine-stricken countries such as Somalia and Ethiopia, many children are ravaged by serious nutrition-related diseases. Even if prolonged malnutrition does not kill them, it may seriously retard the development of their brains and cause them to remain smaller than normal throughout life (Tanner, 1990).

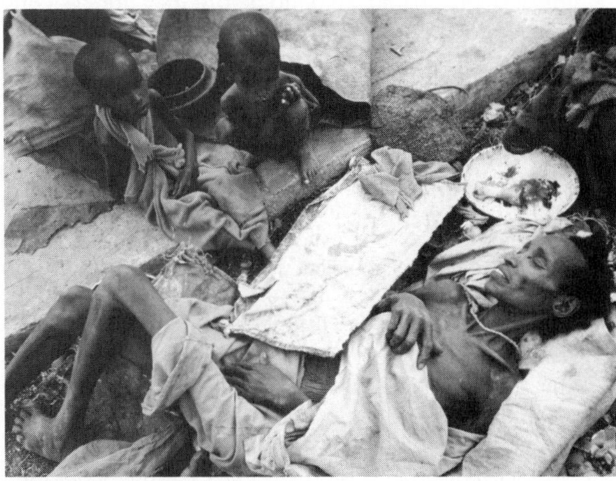

Severe malnutrition, of the kind epidemic in African nations like Somalia, can seriously impair both physical and intellectual development.

Infants and young children seem able to cope with a *temporary* shortage of food. Although their growth is likely to slow down while they are malnourished, they grow much faster than normal when their diets become adequate again (Tanner, 1990). This **catch-up growth** after a period of malnutrition or illness reflects the body's struggle to get back on the growth course that it is genetically programmed to follow.

In the United States and other Western countries, severe malnutrition is relatively rare, but many young children, especially in poverty-stricken areas, are not getting enough vitamins and minerals (Eichorn, 1979). Vitamin and mineral deficiencies may make children irritable and listless and slow their rate of growth. A child who is malnourished in this way is also less resistant to illnesses. Perhaps because they grow so rapidly but often subsist on a diet of junk food, 13- to 16-year-olds are more susceptible to vitamin and mineral deficiencies than either younger children or older adolescents (McGanity, 1976). Inadequate nutrition also becomes a problem for some elderly adults. People typically reduce their total caloric intake in old age (McGandy et al., 1966), in part because they become less physically active. Yet some older adults eat so little that they do not get enough nutrients, especially if they are poor and live alone (Davis, Murphy, & Neuhaus, 1988; Guigoz & Munro, 1985). Older adults who are malnourished may feel unwell, become more susceptible to illnesses, and even begin to show the cognitive impairments associated with Alzheimer's disease and other forms of dementia (Weg, 1983). Programs such as Meals on Wheels that deliver nourishing food to the homes of disabled or ill senior citizens can play an important role in preventing such problems.

There are also health risks associated with being overweight. The term *obesity* is commonly used to describe individuals who are at least 20% above the "ideal" weight for their height, age, and sex. Obesity is clearly a threat to health. Obese people do not live as long as their normal-weight peers, and they are at greater risk for such problems as heart and kidney disease, high blood pressure, diabetes, liver problems, and even arthritis. Obesity is usually the product of both nature and nurture: Heredity is perhaps the most important factor (Grilo & Pogue-Geile, 1991), but overeating and inactivity also contribute. Teenagers face increased risks of obesity because their metabolism rates slow down as they mature physically. Individuals who are overweight as adolescents—even those who slim down as adults—run a greater-than-average risk of coronary heart disease and a host of other health problems some 55 years later (Must et al., 1992). Middle-aged adults also run a risk of gaining weight, especially if they become less physically active but keep eating as much as they did as younger adults (Weg, 1983).

There are reasons to believe that we might be better off being underweight than overweight or even average in weight. Rats placed on diets in which they receive severely restricted amounts of very nourishing food live longer on average and achieve greater maximum ages than rats who are free to eat as much as they choose (Ausman & Russell, 1990; Masoro, 1988). Diet restriction of this sort is the most promising means of extending life discovered to date. Roy Walford (1983) emphasizes that a severely restricted diet must be adopted gradually over a number of years and that it must be exceptionally high in nutritional value. Walford follows such a diet himself, fasting two days a week and eating a very healthy daily diet of about 2100 calories on the remaining five days.

At this point, however, it has not been demonstrated conclusively that severe caloric restriction will actually extend the lives of humans as successfully as it has extended the lives of rats. Nor is it clear exactly what calorie counts or what combinations of nutrients are optimal. Simply going on a starvation diet without knowing what you are doing is a good way to shorten your life, for most evidence tells us that people whose weight is *moderate* live longer than individuals who are either seriously overweight or seriously underweight (Guralnik & Kaplan, 1989). What *is* clear is that humans of all ages can benefit from a nutritious diet that provides an adequate number of calories overall and that contains adequate amounts of protein, vitamins, and fiber—as well as less fat, cholesterol, and salt than most Americans consume (Margolis et al., 1989).

Exercise

What if more people exercised vigorously throughout their lives? If disuse of the body contributes to poor physical functioning, can exercise prevent health problems and slow the aging process? Regular exercise has many beneficial effects on the body at any age and can make an old body function more like a younger body. It can improve cardiovascular and respiratory functioning, slow bone loss, strengthen muscles, and enhance mental functioning and a sense of well-being (Berger & Hecht, 1989). Robert Dustman and his colleagues (1989) were able to improve oxygen uptake capacity, reaction time, memory, and several other aspects of cognitive functioning in elderly adults by giving them four months of aerobic training that involved three one-hour sessions a week of fast walking and occasional jogging.

Roy Shephard (1978, 1990) estimates that regular fitness training at retirement age can delay becoming physically dependent by as many as eight years. What exercise cannot do is halt the inevitable aging process. Even the hearts of long-time athletes lose some of their capacity over time (Heath, Hagberg, Ehsani, & Holloszy, 1981).

Older adults who exercise vigorously and regularly are likely to be in better physical shape than young adults who live the lives of "couch potatoes."

Avoiding Known Health Risks

Finally, we can maintain our health and extend our lives by avoiding known health risks and adopting habits that promote health (Margolis et al., 1989; Walford, 1983). Figure 5.9 shows that adults who had good health practices in middle age were more likely than adults who did not to be in excellent physical shape in old age. It is well known that smoking increases one's risks of coronary heart disease, cancer, emphysema, and a host of other ailments. Because most people begin smoking before they are 20, early prevention efforts can save lives (Margolis et al., 1989). Moderate alcohol consumption—for example, a glass of wine or a beer with dinner at night—appears to protect the heart and reduce the risk of death from cardiovascular disease, whereas heavy drinking is a health hazard (Scherr et al., 1992). Eating breakfast every day, getting seven to eight hours of sleep, and avoiding between-meal snacks are also linked to better physical health and functioning in later life.

James Fries and Lawrence Crapo (1981) have suggested that most of us could live to be about 85—in good health—if we changed our lifestyles. We would then die a "natural" death when our organs no longer have enough reserve capacity left to fight such insults as pneumonia. If today's young people are really getting the message about the effects of lifestyle on health, they should experience a longer and healthier old age than that experienced by today's co-

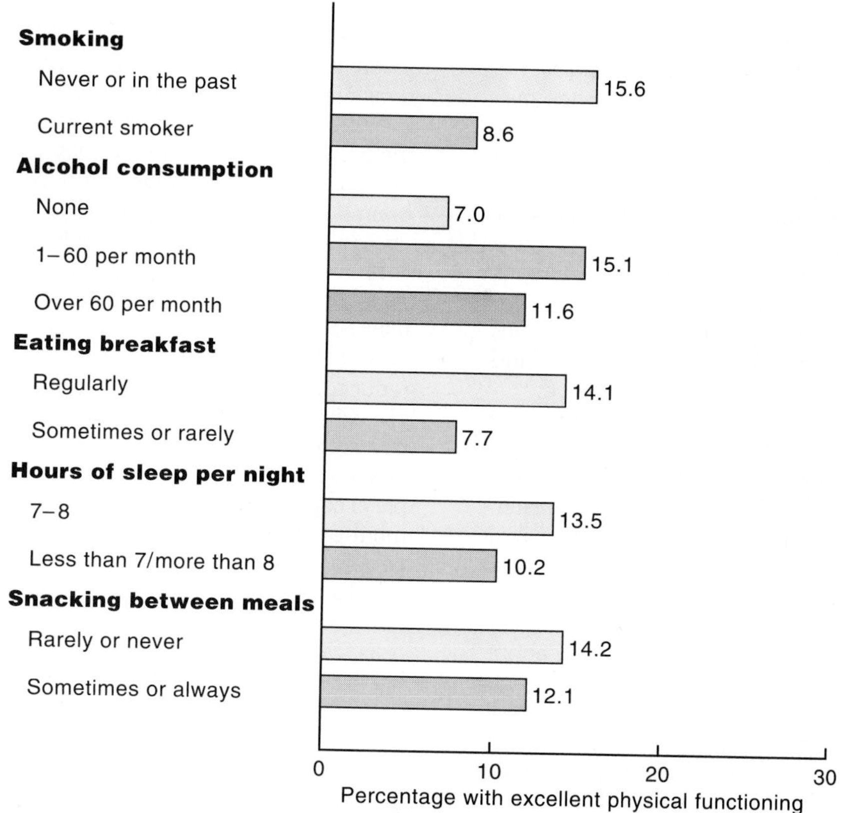

FIGURE 5.9 Percentages of adults with excellent physical functioning in old age as a function of their healthy or unhealthy practices in middle age. Questions about physical functioning assessed the ability to carry out activities of daily living, including vigorous ones. (Adapted from Guralnik & Kaplan, 1989.)

hort of older people. We need not wait until the mysteries of aging are unraveled before doing what we can to avoid dying young.

REFLECTIONS

Have you noticed how hard it is to distinguish between body and mind? "Mind"—the nervous system—is, after all, part of the body, a system of cells interrelated to other systems of cells. Its functioning is affected by the capacity of the heart and lungs to supply it with oxygen and nutrients; at the same time, it regulates the functioning of these organs. It allows us to walk or run, yet it suffers if we do not do so regularly.

Moreover, changes in the body require psychological adjustments and bring psychological change. Newly mobile infants benefit cognitively and emotionally from access to a larger physical and social world; adolescents alter their body images in response to physical and sexual maturation; and aging adults change in response to disease and disability. At the same time, psychological attitudes influence reactions to physical changes. The teenage boy who values physical prowess above all else may be especially discouraged if he matures late, and the woman who expects menopause to be difficult may indeed find it so. In short, we must keep our focus on the *whole person*, body and mind, as we now turn toward the more "psychological" aspects of human development.

SUMMARY POINTS

1. Each of the many systems of the human body develops and ages at its own rate, guided by a genetic program set into action by the brain and hormones released by the endocrine system. The nervous system, billions of neurons communicating by means of neurotransmitter chemicals, is central to all human functioning.

2. Newborns have a wide range of reflexes, working senses, a capacity to learn, and organized sleeping and waking states; they are competent but also limited creatures.

3. Infants grow physically in a cephalocaudal and proximodistal pattern; bones harden, muscles strengthen, and neurons proliferate and organize themselves into interconnected groups. The plasticity of the infant brain allows it to select certain neural

connections over others in response to normal early experiences and to benefit from enriching stimulation.

4. As the motor areas of the brain's cortex mature, motor milestones are achieved in a predictable cephalocaudal and proximodistal order, permitting more controlled motions. Maturation guides early motor development, but normal opportunities to practice motor behaviors are also necessary.

5. During childhood the body steadily grows, neural transmission speeds up, lateralization of various brain functions, though present at birth, becomes more evident in behavior, and both large-muscle and small-muscle control and reaction time improve.

6. The adolescent growth spurt and pubertal changes make adolescence a time of dramatic physical change: Girls reach menarche at an average age of 12½; boys experience their first ejaculation a bit later. Rates of maturation vary widely, in part because of genetic makeup and in part because of nutrition and health status.

7. Most adolescent girls and boys react to the maturation process with mixed feelings, worry about their physical appearance or capabilities, and experience heightened conflict with parents. Advantages of early maturation are greater for boys than for girls, but differences between early and later maturers fade over time.

8. During adolescence the brain continues to develop, permitting sustained attention and strategic planning; physical capabilities of boys improve, whereas those of many girls level off or even decline, perhaps due to gender stereotypes.

9. Most systems of the body reach a peak of functioning between childhood and early adulthood and decline gradually thereafter; decreases in reserve capacity are especially noticeable, but individual differences in physiological functioning become greater with age.

10. During the reproductive years of adulthood, many women experience mood swings during the menstrual cycle, but few women are incapacitated. Men's hormone levels also fluctuate, though not in monthly cycles.

11. Women reach menopause and lose their reproductive capacity at about age 50; most experience hot flashes and vaginal dryness, but few experience severe psychological symptoms. The reproductive systems of men age more gradually and less completely.

12. There is both degeneration and plasticity in the aging brain; neurons atrophy and die, levels of neurotransmitters decrease, and blood flow to the brain decreases, but the aging brain forms new synapses to compensate for neural loss and reorganizes itself in response to learning experiences.

13. As people age, they experience a slowing of their nervous systems, reaction times, and motor behavior; their capacity for vigorous activity is also reduced.

14. Aging, disease, disuse, and abuse of the body all affect performance in later life. Perfectly healthy older people function much like younger people except for their slower reactions, but the development of chronic diseases is a fact of aging for most people.

15. A healthy lifestyle at any age includes proper nutrition, exercise, and avoidance of known health risks. Such a lifestyle can slow, though not halt, the aging process.

KEY TERMS

adolescent growth spurt
androgens
brain growth spurt
catch-up growth
cephalocaudal direction
cerebral cortex
climacteric
developmental norm
endocrine gland
estrogen
growth hormone
hot flashes
infant states
lateralization
menarche
menopause
myelin
neuron
osteoporosis
pincer grasp
pituitary gland
plasticity
premenstrual syndrome (PMS)
proximodistal direction
puberty
reflex
REM sleep
reserve capacity
secular trend
synapse

6

PERCEPTION

You are a newborn, just entering the world. It is bright and noisy. You are sponged, swaddled, and handed to your mother. She says "Oh, look at you," and gently strokes your head and shoulders. What do you make of all this sensory input? And how does your experience of this first encounter differ from your mother's?

Psychologists have long distinguished between sensation and perception. **Sensation** is the process by which sensory receptor neurons detect information and transmit it to the brain. From birth, infants sense the environment. They detect light, sound, odor-bearing molecules in the air, and other stimuli. But do they make "sense" of it? **Perception** is the interpretation of sensory input: recognizing what you see, understanding what is said to you, knowing that the odor you have detected is a sizzling steak, and so on. Does the newborn really perceive the world, or merely sense it? And what happens to sensory and perceptual capacities as we age? Do the senses still work well in later life, or do most older people have difficulty seeing, hearing, and otherwise experiencing the world around them?

Perhaps we should start with a more basic question: Why should you care about the development of sensation and perception? Perhaps because sensation and perception are at the very heart of human functioning. Just try to think of one thing you do that does not depend on your perceiving the world around you. You certainly would have a tough time as a college student if you could neither read the printed word nor understand speech. Indeed, you would not be able to walk to class without the aid of the body senses that control movement. Possibly one of the reasons that sensation and perception may not seem important is that they occur so effortlessly. We simply take them for granted — unless perhaps we are made to imagine what it might be like to be blind or deaf. Then most of us are terrorized.

There is another reason to be interested in sensation and perception. They have been at the center of some fundamental debates among philosophers over the centuries regarding how we gain knowledge of reality. Let's look briefly at two issues that both early philosophers and contemporary developmental theorists have debated.

ISSUES IN PERCEPTUAL DEVELOPMENT

Empiricists such as the 17th-century British philosopher John Locke (1690/1939) believed that infants enter the world as *tabulae rasae* (blank slates) who know nothing except what they learn through their senses and who are therefore the products of nurture rather than nature. Empiricists think infants perceive the world very differently than adults do because they lack perceptual experience. In contrast, *nativists* take the nature side of the nature/nurture issue and argue that we come to the world with knowledge. For example, René Descartes (1638/1965) and Immanuel Kant (1781/1958) believed that we are born with an understanding of the spatial world. Presumably infants don't need to learn that receding objects will appear smaller or that approaching objects will seem larger; perceptual understandings like these are innate or mature very rapidly. According to nativists, these abilities have been built into the human nervous system through the course of evolution, making the infant perceiver quite similar to the adult perceiver.

Today's developmental theorists typically take less extreme stands on the nature/nurture issue. They understand that human beings' innate biological endowment, maturational processes, and experience *all* contribute to perceptual development. Yet they still grapple with nature/nurture issues (Bornstein, 1992). They attempt to determine which perceptual capacities are evident so early in life as to seem innate and to identify the kinds of experiences that are required for normal perceptual development.

Now consider a second issue that philosophers have debated: Is the coherent reality that we experience through the senses actually "out there," or is it something that we create by imposing meaning on otherwise-ambiguous stimulation to the senses? This issue is contested in two modern theories of perceptual development: enrichment theory and differentiation theory.

Enrichment theory, which has been associated with Jean Piaget (1954, 1960), argues that the stimulation received by sensory receptors is actually quite fragmented and confusing. We must add to it, or "enrich" it, if it is to make sense. You may look at a blurry camp photo, for example, and be able to recognize a particular individual because you can draw on your memory of who was at camp and who was friends with whom to mentally construct a recognized face. In this view, then, we bring a good deal of stored knowledge to our perceptual experiences, and this knowledge helps us create order and meaning out of the bits and pieces of sensory stimulation that we receive (see Figure 6.1). Cognition "enriches" sensory experience, and cognitive development makes the adult more able than the infant to construct a meaningful world.

By contrast, **differentiation theory** argues that all the information we could want is "out there" in the stimulation we receive. It is our task to "differentiate" that stimulation—to detect differences that were there all the time. Eleanor Gibson (1969, 1987, 1991) takes this view. Consider the world of dogs. At age 2 children may say "dog" when they see cats, dogs, or any other small furry animals. They have not yet noticed the **distinctive features** of these animals—the critical differences in shape, size, and other qualities that make them distinguishable from one another. Once children have this bit of perceptual learning taken care of, they might begin to differentiate breeds of dogs, noticing that bulldogs have squashed noses and Irish setters have long ones. Through continued perceptual learning, adults who serve as judges in dog shows are able to make fine distinctions among dogs of the same breed that the rest of us miss. Gibson's point is that the pieces of information needed in order to make these fine distinctions were always there in the dogs themselves. Although young infants seem to be sensitive to much of the information contained in the perceptual world, they will be able to extract more and more such information as they get older.

FIGURE 6.1 Expectations influence perception. If you saw this drawing amid drawings of faces, you would be likely to perceive an elderly bald man with glasses. But look again with the idea of finding an animal, and you are likely to see a rat with large ears and its tail circling in front of its body. Cognition has a great deal to do with what we make of sensory stimulation. This is the position taken by enrichment theorists such as Jean Piaget. (Adapted from Reese, 1963.)

Thus enrichment theorists such as Piaget and differentiation theorists such as Gibson disagree about how we come to perceive a more meaningful world as we get older. Either we get better at adding information to sensory stimulation, or we get better at detecting information that is already contained in that stimulation. There is merit in both positions.

Philosophers were discussing the kinds of issues about perception that Gibson and Piaget have raised long before anyone had conducted research on the perceptual capabilities of young infants. Now such research has been conducted, and it has provided some of the most exciting data in all of developmental psychology.

So let us get into it. We will look very closely at sensation and perception in infancy, for this is when most fundamental perceptual capacities emerge. We will also see how much more "intelligent" the senses become during childhood and adolescence. And we will confront the image of old age as a time when sensory capacities are lost in order to determine how much truth there is to this image. As we go, we will see how nature and nurture contribute to perceptual development across the life span.

THE INFANT

The pioneering American psychologist William James (1890) claimed that sights, sounds, and other sensory inputs formed a "blooming, buzzing confusion" to the young infant. James was actually noting that impressions from the several senses are fused rather than separable, but his statement has since been quoted to represent the view that the world of the young infant is hopelessly confusing.

Today the accepted view is that young infants have far greater perceptual abilities than anyone ever suspected. Their senses are functioning even before birth, and in the early months of life they show many signs that they are perceiving a coherent rather than a chaotic world. Why the change in views? It is not that babies have gotten any smarter. It is that researchers have gotten smarter. They have developed more sophisticated methods of studying exactly what infants can and cannot do. Infants, after all, cannot tell us directly what they perceive, so the trick has been to develop ways to let their behavior speak for them. We will see several examples of the ingenuity of modern research methods as we now explore perception in infancy.

Vision

Most of us tend to think of vision as our most indispensable sense. Because vision is indeed important, we'll examine its early development in some detail before turning to the other major senses.

Basic Capacities

The eye functions by taking in stimulation in the form of light and converting it to electricochemical signals to the brain. How well does the newborn's visual system work?

Quite well, in fact. From the first, the infant can detect changes in brightness; the pupils of newborns' eyes constrict in bright light and dilate (expand) in dim light (Pratt, 1954). The ability to discriminate degrees of brightness develops rapidly. By only 2 months of age, infants can distinguish a white bar that differs only 5% in luminance from a solid white background (Peeples & Teller, 1975).

Very young infants also see the world in color, not in black and white, as some early observers had thought. How do we know this? A widely used technique for studying perception relies on the fact that infants will lose interest in a stimulus presented repeatedly over time. This learning to be bored is called **habituation.** If an infant who has habituated to one stimulus regains interest when a somewhat different stimulus is substituted, we know that the two stimuli have been discriminated.

So, suppose we habituate an infant to a blue disk. What will happen if we now present either a blue disk of a different shade or a green disk? As Marc Bornstein and his colleagues established, 4-month-old infants will show little interest in another blue disk but will be very attentive to a green disk—even when the light reflected from these two stimuli differs in wavelength from the original blue stimulus by exactly the same amount (Bornstein, Kessen, & Weiskopf, 1976). Four-month-olds appear to discriminate colors and categorize portions of the continuum of wavelengths of light into the same basic color categories (red, blue, green, and yellow) that adults do (see also Catherwood, Crassini, & Freiberg, 1989). Color vision is present at birth and fully mature by 3 months of age (Banks & Salapatek, 1983).

Are objects clear or blurry to young infants? This is a matter of **visual acuity,** or the ability to perceive detail. By adult standards the newborn's visual acuity is poor. You have undoubtedly heard of 20/20 vision, as measured by the familiar Snellen eye chart with the big *E* at the top. Infants cannot be asked to read eye charts. However, they do prefer to look at a patterned stimulus rather than a blank one—unless it is so fine-grained that it looks no different than a blank. So, by presenting increasingly fine-grained striped patterns to infants, we can find the point at which their acuity for the stripes is lost.

Although estimates differ, the newborn's vision may be as poor as 20/600, which means that the infant sees clearly at 20 feet what an adult with normal vision can see at 600 feet (Banks & Salapatek, 1983). Many sights are blurry to the young infant unless they are bold patterns with sharp light/dark contrasts—the faces of parents, for example (Banks & Salapatek, 1983). The young infant's world is also blurred because of limitations in **visual accommodation,** the ability of the lens of the eye to change shape in order to bring objects at different distances into focus. It is likely to take six months to a year before the infant will see as well as an adult (Banks & Salapatek, 1983).

In short, the eyes of the young infant are not working at peak levels, but they are certainly working. Newborns can perceive light and dark, distinguish colors, and see patterns that are not too finely detailed. But does all this visual stimulation make any sense?

Very Early Pattern Perception

It is one thing to say that young infants (those under 2 months of age) can see, but it is another to say that they can discriminate different patterns of visual stimulation. In the early 1960s, Robert Fantz conducted a number of pioneering studies to determine whether infants can discriminate forms or patterns. Babies were placed on their backs in an apparatus called a looking chamber and shown two or more patterns. An observer then recorded the amount of time the infant spent gazing at each pattern. In this "preferential looking" technique, it is assumed that infants would not gaze longer at one pattern than another unless they could distinguish them.

What did Fantz learn? Babies less than 2 days old could indeed discriminate visual forms (Fantz, 1963). They preferred to look at patterned stimuli such as faces or concentric circles rather than at unpatterned disks. They also seemed to have a special interest in the human face, for they looked at faces longer than at other patterned stimuli such as a bull's-eye or newsprint. However, Fantz (1961) also established that young infants looked only a little bit longer at a face drawing than at a stimulus with facial features in a scrambled array. Here, then, was a hint that human faces are of interest to very young infants not because they are perceived as meaningful faces, but because they have certain physical properties that create interest, whether those properties show up in a real face or a scrambled face.

So the search began for the properties of patterns that "turn infants on." For one thing, young infants are attracted to patterns that have a large amount of light/dark transition, or **contour**; they respond to sharp boundaries between light and dark areas (Banks & Ginsburg, 1985). Since faces and scrambled faces have an equal amount of contour, they are equally interesting.

Second, young infants are attracted to *movement.* Newborns can and do track a moving target with their eyes, although their tracking at first is imprecise and unlikely to occur unless the target is moving slowly (Kremenitzer et al., 1979). And they look longer at moving objects than at stationary ones (Slater et al., 1985).

Finally, young infants seem to be attracted to *moderately complex* patterns. They are likely to prefer a clear pattern of some kind (for example, a bold checkerboard pattern) to either a blank stimulus or a very elaborate one like a page from the *New York Times* (Fantz & Fagan, 1975). As infants mature, they come to prefer more and more complex stimuli.

In sum, we know that infants under 2 months of age have visual preferences, and we also know something about the physical properties of stimuli that attract their attention. They seek out contour, movement, and moderate complexity. As it happens, human faces have all of these physical properties. Martin Banks and his colleagues have offered a very simple explanation for these early visual preferences: *Young infants seem to prefer to look at whatever they can see well* (Banks & Ginsburg, 1985). Based on a very complex mathematical model, Banks has been able to predict what different patterns might look like to the eye of a young infant. Figure 6.2 gives an example. The young eye sees a highly complex checkerboard as a big dark blob. A moderately complex checkerboard still has pattern to it by the time it is processed by the infant's eye. Less-than-perfect vision would therefore explain why young infants prefer moderate complexity to high complexity. Indeed, limited vision can account for a number of the infant's visual preferences. Young infants seem to actively seek out exactly the visual input that they can see well and that will stimulate the development of the visual centers of their brains (Banks & Ginsburg, 1985; Haith, 1980).

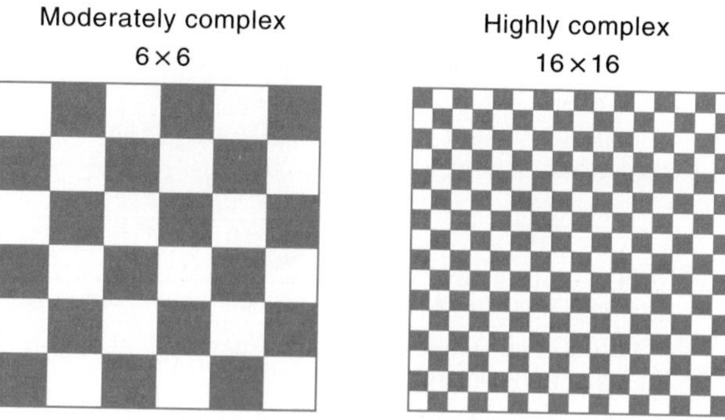

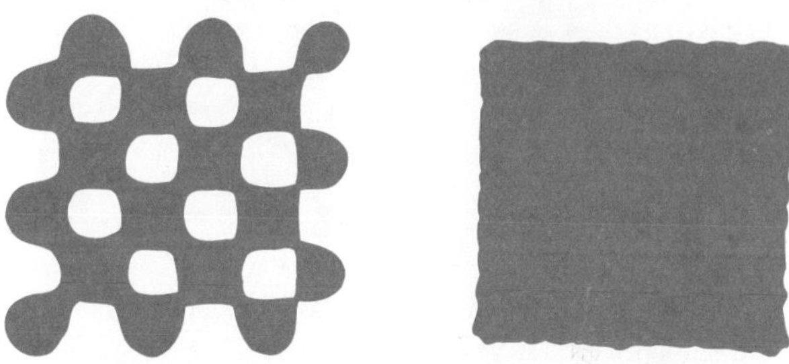

FIGURE 6.2 What the young eye sees. By the time these two checkerboards are processed by eyes with undeveloped vision, only the checkerboard on the left may have any pattern remaining. Blurry vision in early infancy helps to explain a preference for moderately complex rather than highly complex stimuli. (From Banks & Salapatek, 1983.)

Later Pattern Perception: Perceiving Faces

To this point we have established that, from birth, infants discriminate patterns and prefer some over others. But do they really perceive *forms*? For example, do they just see an angle or two when they view a triangle, or do they see a whole triangular form that stands out from its background as a distinct shape? Some research suggests that newborns and 1-month-olds are sensitive to information about whole shapes or forms (Slater et al., 1991; Treiber & Wilcox, 1980). But most studies point to an important breakthrough in the perception of forms starting at about 2 or 3 months of age.

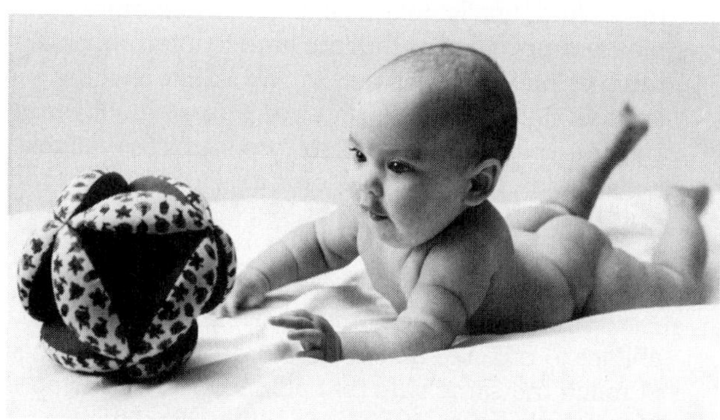

Young infants are attracted to visual stimuli with well-defined contours (or areas of light/dark contrast), to movement, and to bold patterns that are neither too simple nor too complex.

Part of the story is told in Figure 6.3, which shows what Philip Salapatek (1975; Maurer & Salapatek, 1976) discovered about the eye movements of 1-month-olds and 2-month-olds when they look at geometric figures or faces (see also Bronson, 1991). Starting at about 2 months of age, infants no longer focus on some external boundary or contour, as 1-month-olds do. Instead, they explore the interiors of figures thoroughly (for example, looking at a person's facial features rather than just at the chin, hairline, and top of the head). It is as though they are no longer content to locate where an object starts and where it ends, as 1-month-olds tend to do; they seem to want to know *what it is*.

Around 2 or 3 months of age, infants also begin to prefer looking at a normal face rather than at a scrambled face (Dannemiller & Stephens, 1988; Kagan, 1971). James Dannemiller and Benjamin Stephens (1988) demonstrated that at 3 months of

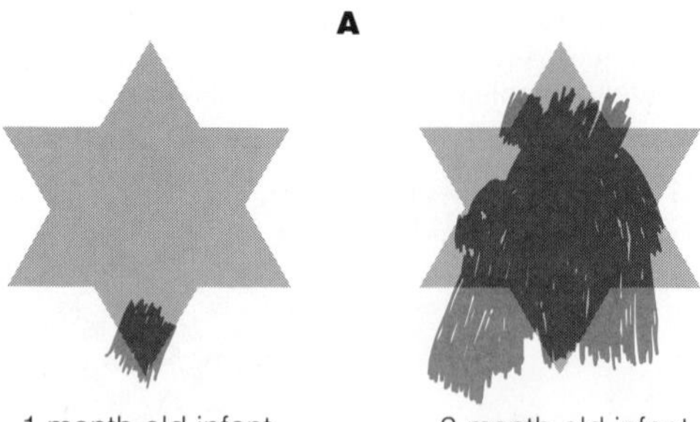

Visual scanning of a geometric figure by 1- and 2-month-old infants

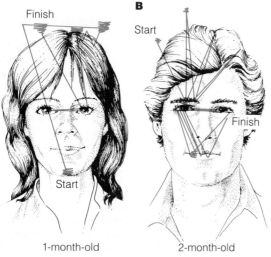

Visual scanning of the human face by 1- and 2-month-old infants

FIGURE 6.3 Visual scanning in early infancy. The 1-month-old seems to be trying to locate where an object begins and ends, whereas the 2-month-old seems to be on the way to figuring out what an object is by exploring it inside and out. (Adapted from Salapatek, 1975.)

age, but not at 6 weeks, infants even prefer a normal face drawing to an otherwise identical pattern in which areas that are normally dark on a face (facial features, hair) were made light and areas that are normally light (the cheeks, for example) were made dark. Why does the human face seem to take on special significance at this age?

Jerome Kagan (1971) proposed that infants are beginning to form mental representations or recipes—schemata—for familiar objects. The infant who has by now had some weeks of experience looking at human faces forms a schema, or mental image, of what faces generally look like. After about 2 or 3 months of age, the infant is in a position to compare new sights to schemata for familiar objects and will take special interest in sights that are *moderately discrepant* from an existing schema—that is, neither highly familiar (and therefore boring) nor highly novel (and therefore impossible to interpret, like a scrambled face drawing). By 2 to 3 months of age, then, infants truly perceive a *face form,* not just an appealing patterning of light and dark. And now it is not just the physical properties of stimuli that matter; it is their *familiarity*.

Interestingly, it is also at about the age of 2 to 3 months that infants seem to recognize their parents' faces. Maria Barrera and Daphne Maurer (1981) have shown that 3-month-old infants recognize photographs of their mothers' faces and prefer to look at their mothers rather than at strangers. Even more amazingly, 2- to 3-month-olds will look longer at faces that adults rate as attractive than at faces that adults rate as unattractive (Langlois et al., 1987; Samuels & Ewy, 1985). So, by the tender age of 12 weeks, infants seem to have formed schemata to represent the human face in general and some faces in particular and even find some faces more appealing than others.

Another milestone in form perception is achieved around 1 year of age. Now, for example, infants often show more interest in a scrambled face than in a normal face. What has changed? According to Jerome Kagan (1971), infants now become interested in understanding stimuli that are highly discrepant from existing schemata. By now, he argues, their existing schemata are well developed, and they have the cognitive capacity to try to "explain" things that are very different from what they have come to expect. In fact, 2-year-olds who can talk show that they are actively forming theories about a scrambled face. They say things like "Who hit him in the nose?" or "Who that, Mommy? A monster, Mommy?" (Kagan, 1971).

According to Kagan, experience with the visual world makes possible the meaningful interpretation of forms such as faces. Infants are at first attracted to objects on the basis of their physical properties. Then they are attracted to them because they are familiar enough that they can be matched to perceptual schemata. And, finally, infants take interest in more complex and novel forms that are hard to interpret on the basis of previous knowledge. We could say that infants at first *sense* the physical properties of forms such as faces, then *perceive* those forms as recognizable wholes, and finally become able to interpret even novel sights intelligently.

Organizing a World of Objects

From an early age, infants also show remarkable abilities to organize and impose order on visual scenes in much the same way that adults do. Decades ago, Max Wertheimer (1923) and other practitioners of **Gestalt psychology** argued that human perception is guided by principles for imposing order and wholeness on sensory input. Shown arrays of numbers and letters, for example, adults will perceive as "belonging together" those that are near one another or that are similar in form. If they are viewing letters arranged in the form of a triangle, adults will organize what they see into a well-formed, whole triangle, even if one or two letters are missing.

It seems that infants, at least by 3 or 4 months of age, operate according to some of these very same Gestalt organizing principles (Aslin, 1987; Bornstein, Ferdinandsen, & Gross, 1981; Van Giffen & Haith, 1984). For example, Katherine Van Giffen and Marshall Haith (1984) reported that 3-month-olds, though not 1-month-olds, will focus their attention on a small irregularity in an otherwise well-formed circle or square pattern, as if they appreciated that it *is* a deviation from an otherwise well-formed and symmetrical pattern. Early Gestalt psychologists believed that principles for organizing the perceptual world were innate, and findings like this support them.

Additional evidence of the young infant's ability to make sense of the visual world comes from studies of their ability to perceive a world of distinct objects separated from other objects and to understand some of the basic properties of objects. Start with this problem: How would an infant know that a glass of milk in front of a cereal box on the kitchen table is not just part of the box? How does an infant know where one object ends and another begins? After studying this issue, Elizabeth Spelke and her colleagues (Kellman & Spelke, 1983; Spelke, 1990) concluded that young infants are sensitive to a number of cues about the wholeness of objects, especially cues available when an object moves. For example, 4-month-olds seem to expect all the parts of an object to move in the same direction at the same time, and they therefore use common motion as an important cue in determining what is or what is not part of the same object (Kellman & Spelke, 1983). It takes infants longer to determine the boundaries of objects that are stationary (Spelke, 1990; Spelke, Hofsten, & Kestenbaum, 1989). Thus babies appear to have an unlearned ability to organize a visual scene into distinct objects, especially if those objects are moving.

But that's not all. Recently, researchers have been exploring infants' understandings of the physical laws that govern the motion of objects and of abstract properties of objects such as their number. Their findings, as Box 6.1 illustrates, are making it clearer than ever that young infants know a good deal more about the world around them than anyone imagined.

Perception of Three-Dimensional Space

Another important aspect of visual perception involves perceiving depth and knowing when objects are near or far away. Do young infants perceive a three-dimensional spatial world?

Very young infants have some intriguing abilities to interpret spatial information. For example, they react defensively when objects move toward their faces; blinking in response to "looming" objects first appears at about 3 weeks of age and becomes much more consistent over the next three months (Nanez, 1987; Yonas, 1981).

Somewhat later in infancy, babies also seem to operate by the principle of **size constancy,** or the tendency to perceive an object as the same size despite changes in its distance from the eyes. We do not perceive friends as shrinking when they walk away from us, nor do we perceive them as swelling in size when they approach. Yet, as distance changes, the size of the image cast on the retina changes. So, if infants perceive an object as constant in size even when it is moved closer or farther away, this would suggest that their perception is three-dimensional. By 4 to 5 months of age, infants clearly recognize that a model of a human head is still the same old head when it is moved closer or farther away, but they treat a larger head substituted for the original head as novel and stare at it intently (Day & McKenzie, 1981). Size constancy is just one example of a number of early-developing perceptual constancies involving such dimensions as form, color, brightness, and shape.

Does this evidence of early spatial perception mean that infants know enough about space to avoid crawling off the edges of beds or staircases? The first attempt to examine depth perception in infants was carried out by Eleanor Gibson and Richard Walk (1960) using an apparatus called the **visual cliff.** This cliff (see Figure 6.4) consists of an elevated glass platform divided into two sections by a center board.

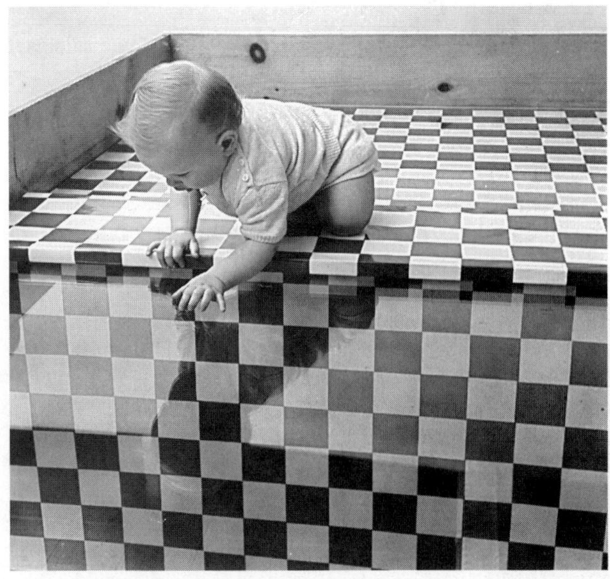

FIGURE 6.4 An infant on the edge of a visual cliff.

BOX 6.1 Babies Know Math and Physics

Although the title of this box may seem ridiculous to you, developmentalists have discovered that very young infants have some pretty impressive understandings of the physical world. Consider first the infant's grasp of mathematics. Prentice Starkey, Elizabeth Spelke, and Rochel Gelman (1990) reported a series of interesting experiments in which they sought to determine whether 6- to 8-month-old infants could recognize one-to-one correspondences between sets of objects and sounds. In one demonstration they showed infants a pair of visual displays, one with two objects, the other with three objects. As the infants watched the displays, the experimenter sounded either two or three drumbeats. Remarkably, infants looked longer at the two-object display when two drumbeats were sounded and longer at the three-object display when three drumbeats were struck. Young infants are known to prefer that any sound effects they hear be consistent with the events they are viewing. It seems, then, that infants possess an abstract concept of number that allows them to detect one-to-one correspondences between sets of entities (in this case, between objects and sounds).

Building on this research, Karen Wynn (1992) investigated whether 5-month-old infants could add and subtract numbers. Her test procedure, summarized in the figure at the right, involved showing the infants a display area with a single Mickey Mouse doll in it, raising a screen in order to hide the doll, and having the infant watch as a hand placed a second doll in the display area and came out empty. Infants then were observed to see how long they looked at each of two outcomes when the screen was dropped again: a correct outcome in which two dolls were in the display area when the screen was removed (1 + 1 = 2), or an incorrect outcome in which only one doll was present (1 + 1 = 1).

Which of these two events attracted more attention? Infants looked longer at the incorrect outcome, as though surprised by the mathematical error it represented. They also looked longer at a 1 + 1 = 3 scenario than at the correct 1 + 1 = 2 outcome. In other words, they did not merely expect there to be some greater number of dolls present after the addition of one doll; they expected precisely one more doll. These 5-month-olds also seemed to excel at subtraction: They were surprised when two dolls minus one doll resulted in two dolls rather than one.

Elizabeth Spelke and her colleagues have been testing infants to determine what they know of Newtonian physics—specifically, whether they know some of the basic laws of object motion (Spelke, Breinlinger, Macomber, & Jacobson, 1992). Do young infants know, for example, that a falling object will move downward along a continuous path until it encounters an obstruction? Spelke's studies suggest that infants only 4 months of age seem surprised when a ball that is dropped behind a screen is later revealed to have ended up *below* a shelf rather than resting upon it (Spelke et al., 1992). They look longer at this "impossible" event than at the comparison event in which the ball's motion stops when it reaches a barrier. By 6 months of age, infants also seem surprised when a ball drops behind a screen and then, when the screen is lifted, appears to be suspended in midair rather than lying at the bottom of the display unit (Kim & Spelke, 1992; Spelke et al., 1992). At very tender ages, then, babies somehow know a good deal about laws of physical motion and gravity.

And what does this research add up to? Although we cannot always be sure why infants look more at one outcome than at another, these studies tend to support the nativist argument that many fundamental perceptual abilities are innate or mature very early in life. The findings also suggest that young infants perceive and reason about the physical world in much the same ways adults do. This may mean that coming to know the physical world is a matter of fleshing out understandings that we have had all along rather than devising radically different new ones (Spelke et al., 1992). True, infants have quite a bit left to learn, but they may have a decent head start on passing their college math and science courses!

On the "shallow" side a checkerboard pattern is placed directly under the glass. On the "deep" side the pattern is several feet below the glass, creating the illusion of a dropoff or "cliff." Infants are placed on the center board and coaxed by their mothers to cross both the "shallow" and the "deep" sides. Testing infants 6½ months of age and older, Gibson and Walk found that 27 of 36 infants would cross the shallow side to reach Mom, but only 3 of 36 would cross the deep side. Most infants of crawling age (typically 7 months or older) clearly perceive depth and are afraid of dropoffs.

But the testing procedure used by Gibson and Walk depended on the ability of infants to crawl. Would younger infants who cannot yet crawl be able to perceive a dropoff? Joseph Campos and his colleagues (Campos, Langer, & Krowitz, 1970) figured that the heart rates of young infants might tell them. So they lowered babies over the shallow and deep sides of the visual cliff. Babies as young as 2 months of age had a slower heart rate on the deep side than on the shallow side. Why slower? When we are afraid, our hearts beat faster, not slower. A slow heart rate is a sign of interest. So 2-month-old infants *perceive a difference* between the deep and shallow sides of the visual cliff, but they have not yet learned to *fear* dropoffs.

Fear of dropoffs appears to be learned through experience crawling about—and perhaps falling now and then, or at least coming close to it (Campos, Bertenthal, & Kermoian, 1992). Some beginning crawlers will shuffle right off the ends of beds or the tops of stairwells if they are not watched carefully (Campos et al., 1978). However, Joseph Campos,

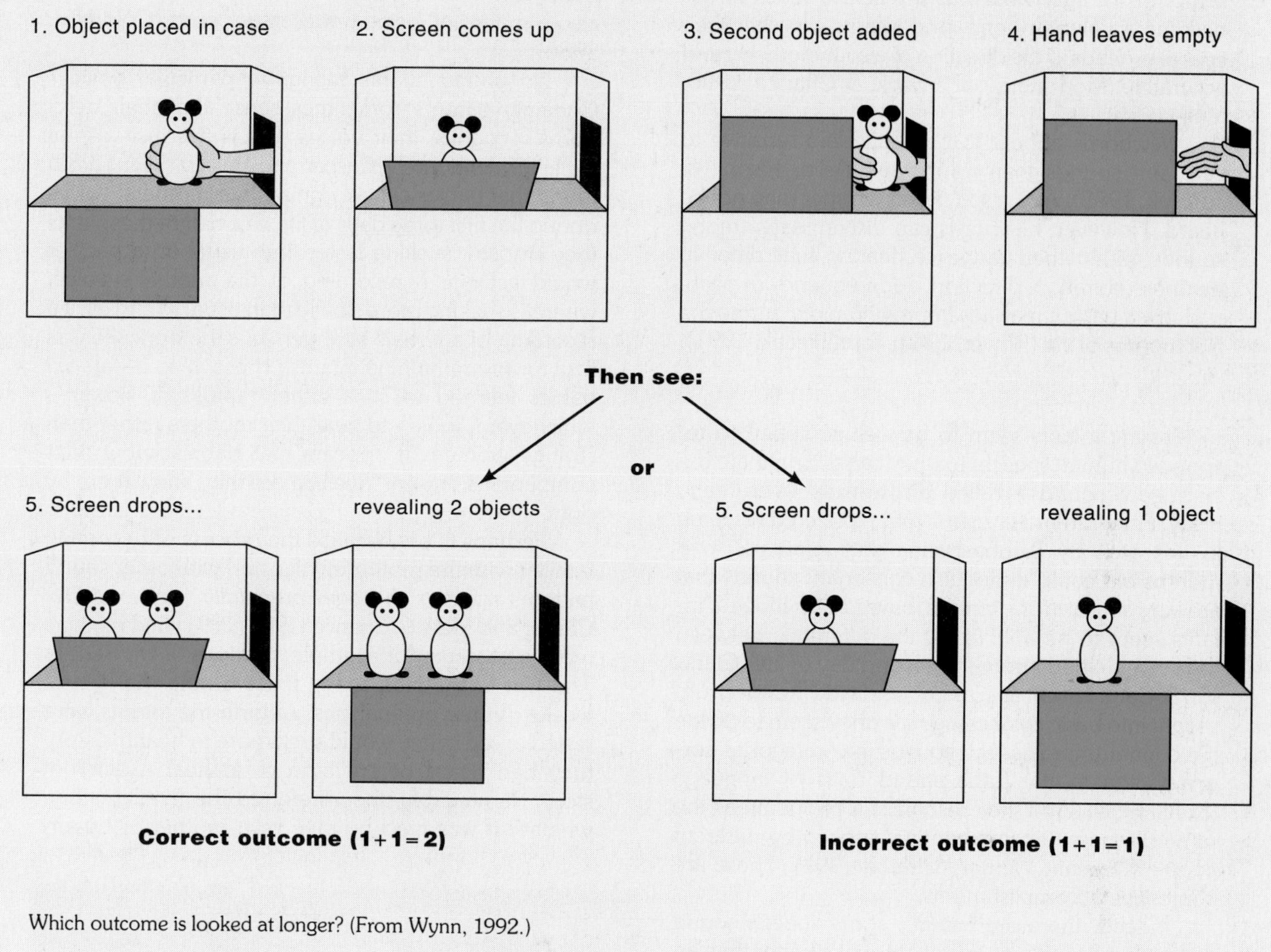

Which outcome is looked at longer? (From Wynn, 1992.)

Bennett Bertenthal, and Rosanne Kermoian (1992) have established that fear of dropoffs is stronger in infants who have logged a few weeks of experience crawling than in infants of the same age who do not yet crawl; also, providing infants who do not crawl with walkers that allow them to move about hastens the development of a healthy fear of heights. Both maturation and normal experiences moving about contribute to the perception and interpretation of depth, it seems. Motor development and perceptual development are also closely linked; infants rely on their senses in order to move about and explore the world, and their explorations and actions contribute to further advances in their ability to perceive a meaningful world (Bertenthal, 1993).

In summary, perception of space develops rapidly in early infancy. The ability to see that an object is looming toward the face emerges within the first month of life. The perception of size constancy despite variations in distance emerges by 4 or 5 months of age. By about 2 months of age, infants also seem to perceive some difference between an apparent dropoff and a solid surface. However, it is only in the second half of the first year that infants come to *fear* dropoffs through a combination of maturation and experience from crawling.

Hearing

Hearing is at least as important to us as vision, especially since we depend on it to communicate with others through spoken language. Sound striking the ear creates vibrations of the eardrum, which are transmitted to the cochlea in the inner ear and converted to signals to the brain. Newborns can hear quite well—

better than they can see (Lewkowicz, 1988). They can also localize sounds: They are startled by loud noises and will turn away from them, but they will turn in the direction of softer sounds (Field et al., 1980). By 4 months of age, what was a reflexive reaction has become a voluntary one, and infants can shift their eyes and heads in the direction of a sound quickly and accurately (Morrongiello, Fenwick, & Chance, 1990; Muir, 1985).

Newborns appear to be a little less sensitive to very soft sounds than adults are (Aslin, Pisoni, & Jusczyk, 1983). As a result, a soft whisper may not be heard. However, newborns can discriminate among sounds within their range of hearing that differ in loudness, duration, direction, and frequency or pitch, and these basic capacities improve rapidly during the first months of life (Bower, 1982; Trehub et al., 1991).

Perceiving Speech

Young infants seem to be well equipped to respond to human speech, for they can discriminate basic speech sounds—called **phonemes**—very early in life. Peter Eimas (1975b, 1985) pioneered research in this area by demonstrating that infants 2 to 3 months old could distinguish consonant sounds that are very similar (for example, *ba* and *pa*). Indeed, infants seem to be able to tell the difference between the vowels *a* and *i* from the second day of life (Clarkson & Berg, 1983). Just as babies divide the spectrum of light into basic color categories, they seem to divide the continuum of speech sounds into categories corresponding to the basic sound units of language (Kuhl, 1991). And they recognize a phoneme as the same phoneme even when it is spoken by different people (Marean, Werner, & Kuhl, 1992). These are impressive accomplishments.

Indeed, there are actually some speech sound discriminations that an infant can make better than an adult (Werker & Tees, 1992). We begin life biologically prepared to learn any language humans anywhere speak. As we mature, we normally become especially sensitive to the sound differences that are significant in our own language and less sensitive to sound differences that are irrelevant to our own language. For example, infants can easily discriminate the consonants *r* and *l* (Eimas, 1975a). So can adults who speak English, French, Spanish, or German. However, Chinese and Japanese make no distinction between *r* and *l*, and adult native speakers of those languages cannot make this particular auditory discrimination as well as infants can (Miyawaki et al., 1975). Similarly, infants raised in English-speaking homes can make discriminations that are important in Hindi but nonexistent in English, but English-speaking adults have trouble doing so (Werker et al., 1981).

By the end of the first year, as infants begin to master their first words, they are already becoming insensitive to sound contrasts that are irrelevant in their native language (Werker & Tees, 1984). In other words, the effects of their auditory experiences are starting to show. Interestingly, then, perceptual development, like so many aspects of life-span development, is not just a matter of adding new abilities; it is also a matter of *losing* unnecessary ones (Colombo, 1986).

Do young infants recognize particular voices? Certainly parents sometimes sense that their newborns recognize their voices, but is this just wishful thinking? Anthony DeCasper and William Fifer (1980) found that babies can recognize their mothers' voices during the first three days of life. For half of the infants they studied, sucking faster than usual on a pacifier would activate a recording of the mother's voice, whereas sucking more slowly than usual would elicit a recording of a female stranger. Just the opposite was true for the remaining infants. These 1- to 3-day-old babies learned to suck either rapidly or slowly—whichever it took—to hear their mothers rather than strange women. It appears that babies know their companions "by ear" well before they know them by sight.

Perhaps this is because the process of becoming familiar with the mother's voice and with other sound patterns appears to begin *prenatally*. Anthony DeCasper and Melanie Spence (1986, 1991) had mothers recite a passage (for example, portions of Dr. Seuss's *The Cat in the Hat*) many times during the last six weeks of their pregnancies. At birth the infants were tested to see if they would suck more to hear the story they had heard before birth or to hear a different story. Remarkably, they preferred the familiar story, whether it was read by their own mother or by an-

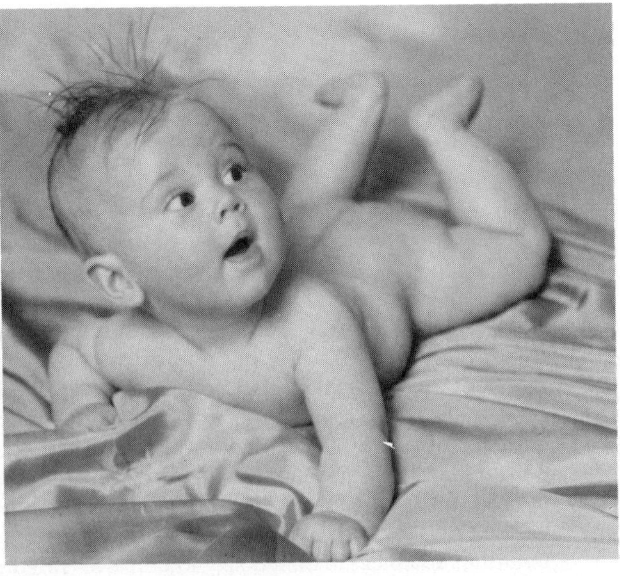

From birth, infants will look in the direction of an interesting sound. This ability to localize sound improves and becomes more voluntary by 4 months of age.

IT'S TYPICAL FOR WOMEN WHO HAVE BEEN REAL GO-GETTERS IN BUSINESS TO TURN THAT SAME PASSION ONTO THE EXPERIENCE OF PARENTING.
© 1986 Universal Press Syndicate

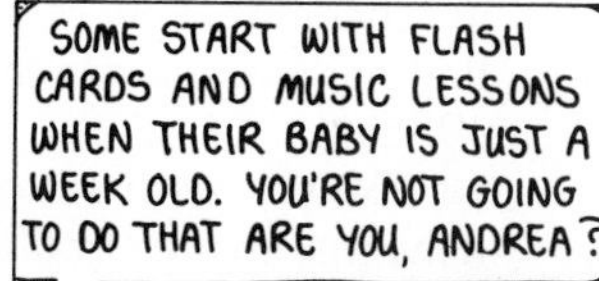

SOME START WITH FLASH CARDS AND MUSIC LESSONS WHEN THEIR BABY IS JUST A WEEK OLD. YOU'RE NOT GOING TO DO THAT ARE YOU, ANDREA?

START EDUCATING THE BABY A WEEK AFTER BIRTH ?? DON'T BE RIDICULOUS.

WE WOULD HAVE MISSED THE WHOLE NINE MONTHS OF PREGNANCY!
..THIS NEXT SELECTION IS FROM VIVALDI, LITTLE ONE...
2.4
Guisewite

CATHY, copyright 1986, Universal Press Syndicate. Reprinted with permission. All rights reserved.

other baby's mother. Somehow these infants were able to recognize the distinctive sound pattern of the story they had heard in the womb. Auditory learning before birth could also explain why newborns prefer to hear their mothers' voices to those of unfamiliar women (DeCasper & Spence, 1986). Before we get carried away with the notion of educating youngsters before they are even born, however, we should bear in mind that the acoustics of the womb are poor and the nervous systems of fetuses are immature. Although some parents today seem willing to try almost anything to get their children's education off to an early start, it is doubtful that factual information can be instilled prenatally.

Perceiving Music

The evidence that we have presented thus far suggests that infants have an innate readiness to perceive speech. Yet we now know that young infants are similarly sensitive to the features of musical sounds (Aslin et al., 1983; Krumhansl & Jusczyk, 1990). For one thing, newborns seem to like music. They will learn either to suck or to refrain from sucking a pacifier to have folk music played, and they will learn to do whatever it takes to *avoid* hearing nonrhythmic noise (Butterfield & Siperstein, 1972). By a few months of age, infants are also quite skilled at discriminating between melodies and at recognizing the same tune despite changes in tempo or pitch (Chang & Trehub, 1977; Trehub, 1985). They even perceive the structure of musical pieces, preferring to listen to Mozart appropriately segmented into natural musical phrases rather than to the same Mozart piece stopped inappropriately in the middle of natural phrases (Krumhansl & Jusczyk, 1990). It is not yet clear whether infants prefer Mozart to Muzak or Madonna, but it *is* clear that they are well equipped to perceive both speech sounds and musical sounds and to detect patterns in the sounds they hear.

In sum, hearing is more developed than vision at birth. Infants can distinguish between speech sounds, recognize familiar sound patterns such as their mothers' voices, and discriminate between music and nonrhythmic noise soon after birth. Within the first year they lose sensitivity to sound contrasts that are not significant in the language they are starting to learn, and they refine their auditory perception skills.

Taste and Smell

Can newborns detect different tastes and smells? The sensory receptors for taste — taste buds — are located mainly on the tongue. In ways not fully understood, taste buds respond to chemical molecules and give rise to perceptions of sweet, salty, bitter, or sour tastes. We are apparently born with a sweet tooth, for shortly after birth babies will suck faster and longer for sweet (sugary) liquids than for bitter, sour, salty, or neutral (water) solutions (Crook, 1978). Different taste sensations also produce distinct facial expressions in the newborn. Jacob Steiner and his colleagues (Ganchrow, Steiner, & Daher, 1983; Steiner, 1979) have found that newborns lick their lips and sometimes smile when they are tasting a sugar solution but purse their lips and even drool to get rid of the foul taste when they are given bitter quinine. Their facial expressions become increasingly pronounced as a solution becomes sweeter or more bitter, suggesting that newborns can discriminate different concentrations of a substance.

The sense of smell, or **olfaction,** depends on sensory receptors in the nasal passage that react to chemical molecules in the air. It, too, is working well at birth. Newborns react vigorously to unpleasant smells such as vinegar or ammonia. At only a few hours of age they will turn their heads away from an unpleasant odor (Rieser, Yonas, & Wilkner, 1976). Even more remarkable is evidence that babies who are breastfed can recognize their mothers solely by the smell of their breasts or underarms within a week or two of birth (Cernoch & Porter, 1985; Porter et al., 1992). Thus the sense of smell we often take for

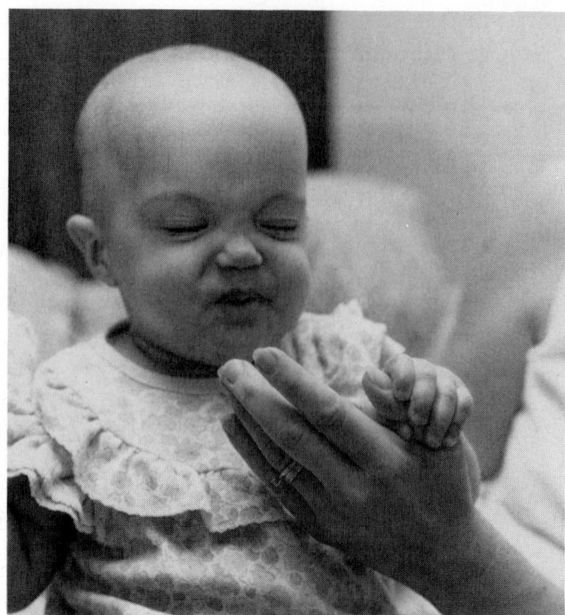

Young infants clearly respond to tastes. In response to a sugar solution, they part their lips, lick their upper lips, make sucking movements, and sometimes smile. In response to bitter tastes, they purse their lips or open their mouths with the corners down and drool. This baby does not like the garlic on her mother's hand.

granted may help babies and their parents get to know each other right from the start.

In sum, both the sense of taste and the sense of smell are working very well at birth. Later development is mainly a matter of learning to recognize what it is that is being tasted or smelled. As wine tasters illustrate, these senses can become highly educated indeed.

Touch, Temperature, and Pain

Receptors in the skin detect touch or pressure, heat or cold, and painful stimuli. We saw in Chapter 5 that newborns respond with reflexes if they are touched in appropriate areas. Even in their sleep, newborns will habituate to strokes of the same spot on the skin but respond again if the tactile stimulation is shifted to a new spot—from the ear to the lips, for example (Kisilevsky & Muir, 1984). In fact, the sense of touch seems to be operating quite nicely well before birth and may, along with the body sense that detects motion, be the first sense to develop (Field, 1990).

Later, infants become able to discriminate an object solely on the basis of their experience touching it. At 5 months of age, for example, babies will become habituated to a plywood shape after they have held it and explored it with their hands for a time without being allowed to see it. They then show more interest in touching a new shape than in touching the shape that has become familiar to them (Streri & Pecheux, 1986a).

Newborns are also sensitive to warmth and cold. If the milk in their bottle is too hot, they will refuse it; if the room temperature suddenly drops, they become more active, for this helps maintain body heat (Pratt, 1954).

Finally, babies clearly respond to painful stimuli. Even 1-day-old infants experience pain from pin pricks like those administered in blood tests (Fletcher, 1987). For obvious ethical reasons, researchers have not exposed infants to severely painful stimuli. However, analyses of boys' cries as they undergo circumcisions leave no doubt that these surgical procedures are painful (Porter, Miller, & Marshall, 1986). Such research challenges the medical wisdom of giving babies who must undergo major surgery little or no anesthesia. It turns out that infants are more likely to survive heart surgery if they receive deep anesthesia that keeps them unconscious during the operation and for a day afterward than if they receive light anesthesia that does not entirely protect them from the stressful experience of pain (Anand & Hickey, 1992).

We have now seen that each of the major senses is operating in some form at birth and that perceptual abilities that rely on each sense increase dramatically during infancy. Let's ask one final question about infant perception: Can infants meaningfully integrate information from the different senses?

Integrating Sensory Information

It would obviously be useful for the infant who is attempting to understand the world to be able to put together information gained from viewing, fingering, sniffing, and otherwise exploring objects. It now seems clear that the senses do indeed function in an integrated way at birth. For instance, the fact that newborns will look in the direction of a sound they hear suggests that vision and hearing are linked (Bower, 1982). Moreover, infants 8 to 31 days old expect to feel objects that they can see and are frustrated by a visual illusion that looks like a graspable object but proves to be nothing but air when they reach for it (Bower, Broughton, & Moore, 1970). Thus vision and touch, as well as vision and hearing, seem to be interrelated early in life.

A somewhat more difficult task is to recognize through one sense an object that is familiar through another; this is called **cross-modal perception.** This capacity is tapped in children's games that involve feeling familiar objects placed in a bag and identifying what they are by touch alone. A vivid demonstration of cross-modal perception in early life involved familiarizing infants with an object through touch and then determining if they could recognize the object by sight (Meltzoff & Borton, 1979). One-month-old infants were given one of two pacifiers to suck without being allowed to see what they were sucking. One pacifier was round and smooth, and the other had hard nubs on it. Infants then saw two styrofoam forms, one shaped like the smooth pacifier and the other like the nubbed pacifier. They tended to look more at the pacifier they had sucked than at the unfamiliar one, suggesting that they recognized by sight a stimulus that was familiar only through touch (see also Gibson & Walker, 1984).

Although this oral-to-visual cross-modal transfer may be evident very early, other forms of cross-modal perception are not consistently or reliably displayed until about 4 to 6 months of age (Gibson & Spelke, 1983; Rose, Gottfried, & Bridger, 1981; Streri & Pecheux, 1986b). Performance on more complex cross-modal perception tasks continues to improve with age during childhood and even adolescence (Botuck & Turkewitz, 1990).

Overall, it seems that the senses are integrated at birth; infants react to incongruities between what one sense tells them and what another sense tells them. Then, as the separate senses continue to develop and each becomes a more effective means of exploring objects, babies become more skilled at cross-modal perception and are able to coordinate information gained through one sense with information gained through another. As it turns out, those infants who are adept at integrating their sensory experiences later tend to score higher than their peers on IQ tests, suggesting that cross-modal perceptual ability is an early indicator of intellectual ability (Rose, Feldman, Wallace, & McCarton, 1991).

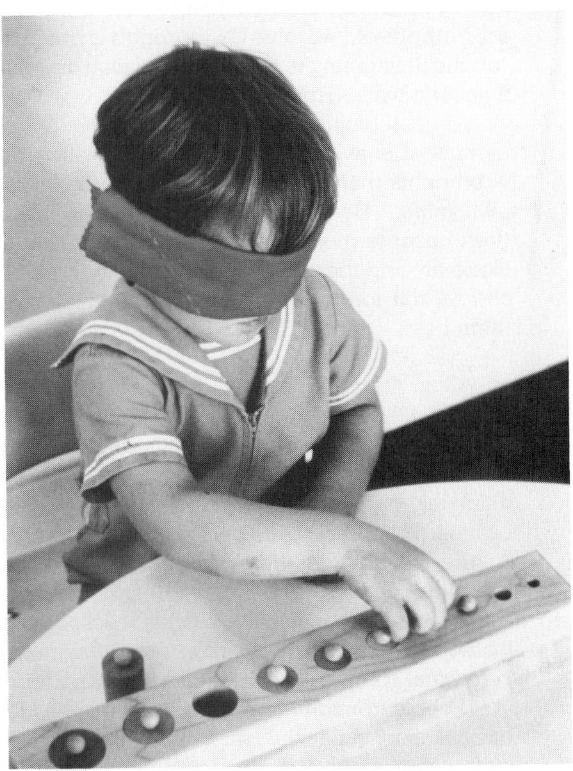

Intersensory perception. The ability to recognize through one sense (here, touch) what has been learned through another (vision) increases with age during infancy and childhood.

Nature, Nurture, and Early Perceptual Development

What remarkable perceptual competencies even the very young infant has, and what remarkable progress is made within the first few months of life! All of the major senses begin working before birth and are clearly functioning at birth. Many perceptual abilities — for example, the ability to perceive depth or to distinguish melodies — then emerge within just a few months after birth. Gradually, basic perceptual capacities are fine-tuned, and, importantly, infants become more and more able to *interpret* their sensory experiences — to recognize a pattern of light as a face, for example. By the time infancy ends, the most important aspects of perceptual development are complete (Bornstein, 1992). The senses and the mind are working to create a meaningful world of recognized objects, sounds, tastes, smells, and bodily sensations.

The fact that perceptual development takes place so quickly can be viewed as support for the "nature" side of the nature/nurture debate. Many basic perceptual capacities appear to be innate or to develop rapidly in all normal infants. What, then, is the role of early sensory experience in perceptual development?

Early Experience, the Brain, and Perceptual Development

We can start by asking what visual perception would be like in an infant who was blind at birth but later had surgery to permit vision. Sensory-deprivation research involving animals gives us some clues (see Gandelman, 1992). In such studies, young animals are temporarily deprived of sensory stimulation. If they later show a perceptual deficit, the experiences that they did *not* have are judged to have been necessary for normal development.

Nearly half a century ago, Austin Riesen and his associates discovered that chimpanzees raised in the dark experience a degeneration of the optic nerve that seriously restricts their vision (Riesen et al., 1951). If the chimps spent no more than seven months in the dark, the damage could be reversed; otherwise it was permanent. In chimps exposed to diffuse, unpatterned light for brief periods every day, damage to the optic nerves did not occur. Yet animals deprived of patterned stimulation later had difficulty discriminating forms such as circles and squares — a task that normal chimps easily master (Riesen, 1965).

In short, the visual system requires stimulation early in life, including *patterned* stimulation, to develop normally—in humans as well as in chimpanzees. Some babies are born with cataracts that make them nearly blind. Once surgery restores their sight, they (like Riesen's chimps) have difficulty, at least initially, discriminating common forms such as spheres and cubes (Walk, 1981). Full and lasting recovery of perceptual abilities after a period of early visual deprivation is sometimes very difficult to achieve (Mitchell, 1988).

It is now clear that specific forms of visual stimulation are necessary if neurons in the visual areas of the brain are to develop properly (Gandelman, 1992; Greenough, Black, & Wallace, 1987). For example, specific neural cells respond to either horizontal, vertical, or oblique (slanted) lines. If a kitten is fitted with goggles that allow it to view only vertical stripes, it develops an abundance of "vertical" cells but loses some of the cells that would enable it to detect horizontal and oblique lines (Stryker et al., 1978). Similarly, humans who have severe *astigmatism*—misshapened lenses that distort images—often have lasting difficulty seeing lines equally well in all orientations even after their vision is corrected (Mitchell et al., 1973).

Suppose that infants receive visual stimulation but are tied to cradleboards (as is done in some cultures) so that they cannot actively move about in their environment. Would this interfere with their visual development? An early study of kittens suggested that it would (Held & Hein, 1963). However, Richard Walk (1981) suspected that young animals may not need to move independently if objects in the environment move. His research showed that (1) kittens who grew up in restraining holders with no interesting movement to watch tended to doze off and showed no more depth perception than kittens raised entirely in the dark, whereas (2) kittens who grew up in restraining holders but watched cars streak around a racetrack, approaching and receding, had depth perception equal to that of a third group of kittens that were free to move around in a lighted environment.

These findings imply that infants kept on cradleboards and physically disabled infants who cannot move about independently should suffer no perceptual deficits as long as they are regularly exposed to moving objects and pay attention to them (see also Arterberry, Yonas, & Bensen, 1989). Fortunately, most babies seek out and receive just the visual experiences they need in order to develop normal visual perception. The same message applies to the sense of hearing. That is, exposure to auditory stimulation early in life affects the architecture of the developing brain, which in turn influences auditory perception skills (Finitzo, Gunnarson, & Clark, 1990). The conclusion is clear: *Maturation alone is not enough; normal perceptual development also requires normal perceptual experience.*

The Child's Active Role in Perceptual Development

Parents need not worry about arranging just the right sensory environment for their children; young humans actively seek just the stimulation they need in order to develop properly. Eleanor Gibson (1988) sees infants as active explorers and stimulus seekers from the start; they orchestrate their own perceptual, motor, and cognitive development through their exploratory behavior.

According to Gibson, infants proceed through three phases of exploratory behavior: (1) from birth to 4 months they explore their immediate surroundings by looking and listening, and they learn a bit about objects by mouthing them and watching them move; (2) from 5 to 7 months, once the ability to voluntarily grasp objects has developed, babies pay far closer attention to objects and explore them with their hands; and (3) by 8 or 9 months of age, after they have begun to crawl, infants extend their explorations out into the larger environment and carefully examine the objects they encounter on their journeys, learning all about their properties. Whereas a young infant may merely mouth a new toy and look at it now and then, a 12-month-old will give it a thorough examination—turning it, fingering it, poking it, and watching it intently all the while (Ruff et al., 1992).

By combining perception and action in their exploratory behavior, infants actively create sensory environments that meet their needs and develop their own minds (Bertenthal & Campos, 1987). As children become more able to attend selectively to the world around them, they become even more able to choose the forms and levels of stimulation that suit them best.

Cultural Influences on Perceptual Development

Do infants who grow up in different cultural environments encounter different sensory stimulation and ultimately perceive the world in different ways? Perceptual preferences obviously differ from culture to culture. In some cultures, people think hefty women are more beautiful than slim ones, or relish eating sheep's eyeballs or chicken heads, or delight in music that sounds to us like disorganized noise. Are more basic perceptual competencies also affected by socialization?

People from different cultures only rarely differ in basic sensory capacities, such as the ability to discriminate degrees of brightness or loudness (Berry et al., 1992). However, their perceptions and interpretations of sensory input can vary considerably. For example, we have already seen that children become insensitive, starting at the end of the first year of life, to

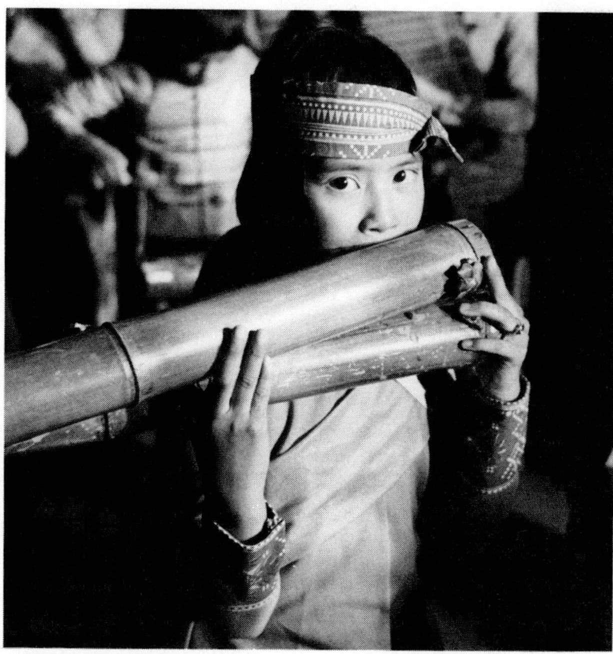

Perceptions of music are shaped by the learning experiences available in one's culture.

speech sound contrasts that are not important in their culture's language. Michael Lynch and his associates (1990) have shown that the same is true with respect to perceptions of music. Infants from the United States, they found, noticed equally well notes that violated either Western musical scales or the Javanese pelog scale. This suggests that humans are born with the potential to perceive music from a variety of cultures. However, American adults were less sensitive to bad notes in the unfamiliar Javanese musical system than to mistuned notes in their native Western scale, suggesting that their years of experience with Western music had shaped their perceptual skills. Many other examples of the effects of cultural learning experiences on visual and auditory perception can be cited (Berry et al., 1992).

In sum, a common biological heritage *and* common sensory experiences combine to ensure that all normal humans develop the same basic perceptual abilities. However, perceptual development is also shaped by specific sensory experiences that only some children have, as influenced by their own explorations of the world and by the cultural context in which they develop.

THE CHILD

If most sensory and perceptual development is complete by the end of infancy, what is left to accomplish during childhood? Mostly it is a matter of learning to use the senses more intelligently. As a result, it becomes hard to separate perceptual development from cognitive development (Bornstein, 1992). For example, children rapidly build knowledge of the world so that they can recognize and label what they sense, giving it greater meaning. In addition, much of perceptual development in childhood is really a matter of the development of **attention**, the focusing of perception and cognition on something in particular. In other words, youngsters become better able to use their senses deliberately and strategically to gather the information most relevant to a task at hand. They also become more skilled at making the kinds of perceptual discriminations that are so important in complex cognitive tasks, such as learning to read.

The Development of Attention

From the start, infants actively use their senses to explore their environment, and they prefer some sensory stimuli to others (Gibson, 1987). Still, we can characterize the attention of the infant or very young child as "captured by" something and that of the older child as "directed toward" something. Selective as they are, 1-month-old infants do not really deliberately choose to attend to a face; instead, a face attracts their attention. Similarly, toddlers and preschoolers often seem to be caught up by one event and then quickly caught up by another. As children get older, their attention spans become longer, they become more selective in what they attend to, and they are better able to plan and carry out systematic strategies for using their senses to achieve goals.

Increased Attention Span

Young children do have short attention spans. Researchers know that they should limit their experimental sessions with young children to a few minutes, and nursery school teachers often switch classroom activities every 15 to 20 minutes. Even when they are doing things they like, such as watching a television program or playing with a toy, 2- and 3-year-olds spend far less time actually concentrating on the program or the toy than older children do (Anderson et al., 1986; Ruff & Lawson, 1990). In one study of sustained attention, children were asked to put strips of colored paper in appropriately colored boxes (Yendovitskaya, 1971). Children aged 2½ to 3½ worked for an average of 18 minutes and were easily distracted; children aged 5½ to 6 often persisted for an hour or more. Further improvements in attention span occur later in childhood.

More Selective Attention

Although infants clearly deploy their senses in a selective manner, they are not very good at controlling their attention — deliberately concentrating on one thing while ignoring something else. With age, attention becomes more selective.

Consider what George Strutt and his associates (1975) found when they had 6-, 9-, 12-, and 20-year-olds sort cards into piles as quickly as possible according to the geometric design printed on them (for example, a circle or a square). In some trials the cards also contained distracting information (for example, a star above or below the form). Six-year-olds were slightly slower than older children when only the target design was on the card, but they were considerably slower when the distracting, irrelevant information was present. They were apparently less able than the older children to *selectively* focus their attention on the critical information and disregard the irrelevant information. Four- and 5-year-olds have even more trouble attending selectively (Enns & Akhtar, 1989). As children get older, they also become better able to tune in one speaker while ignoring another who is talking at the same time—or to monitor two conversations at the same time and recall what was said (Maccoby, 1967). These findings should suggest to teachers of young children that performance will be better if distractions in task materials and in the room are kept to a minimum.

More Systematic Attention

Finally, as they get older, children become more able to plan and carry out systematic perceptual searches. We have already seen that older infants are more likely than younger ones to thoroughly explore a pattern, both its exterior and its interior. Research with children in the former Soviet Union reveals that visual scanning becomes considerably more detailed or "exhaustive" over the first six years of life (Zaporozhets, 1965). But the most revealing findings come from studies of how children go about a *visual search*. Elaine Vurpillot (1968) recorded the eye movements of 4- to 10-year-olds who were trying to decide whether two houses, each with several windows containing various objects, were identical or different. As Figure 6.5 illustrates, children aged 4 and 5 were not at all systematic. They often looked at only a few windows and as a result came to wrong conclusions. In contrast, children older than 6½ were highly systematic. They checked each window in one house with the corresponding window in the other house, pair by pair.

In summary, learning to control attention is an important part of perceptual development during childhood. Infants and young children are without question selectively attentive to the world around them, but they haven't fully taken charge of their attentional processes. With age, children become more able to concentrate on a task for a long period, to focus on relevant information and ignore distractions, and to use their senses in purposeful and systematic ways to achieve goals.

Perception and Learning to Read

One of the most challenging perceptual tasks that children face in our culture is learning to read. How do they come to realize that the print on the page represents spoken words, and how do they then learn to translate print into spoken language?

Eleanor Gibson and Harry Levin (1975) have identified three phases in learning to read. First, children equate reading with storytelling: They may pick up a storybook and "read" very sensible sentences—most of which have no relation to the words on the page.

Next, children recognize that the squiggles on the printed page represent words. They may try to match the spoken words of a familiar story to the symbols on the page, often incorrectly (Smith, 1977). Thus a 3-year-old who knows that the title of her storybook is *Santa Is Coming to Town* might try to "read" the cover by touching each letter and uttering a word or syllable, as illus-

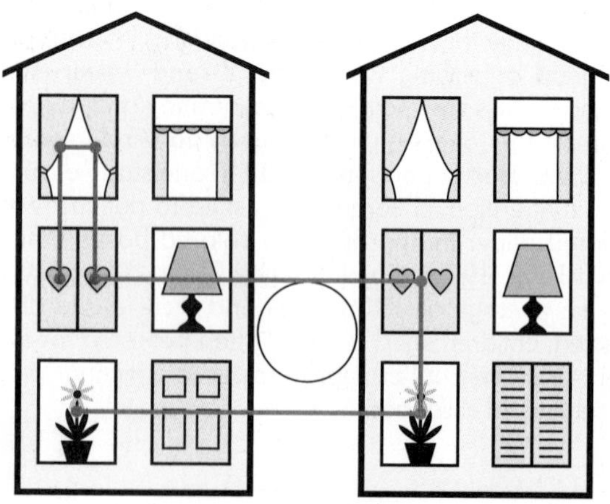

Five-year-old: "The same"

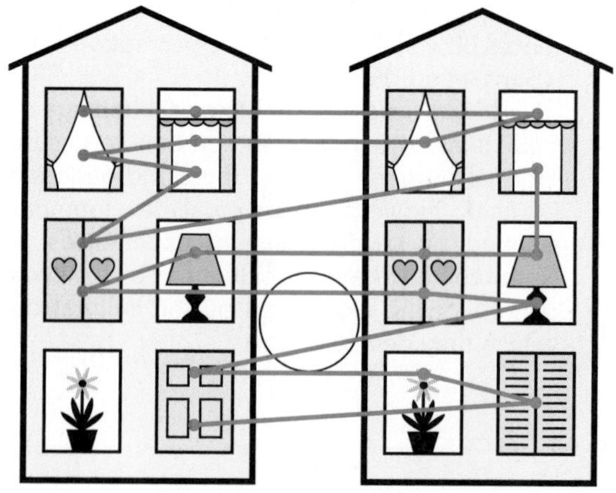

Eight-year-old: "Not the same"

FIGURE 6.5 Are the houses in each pair exactly the same or different? Preschool children often guess incorrectly because they do not systematically compare all the pairs of windows as school-aged children do. (Based on Vurpillot, 1968.)

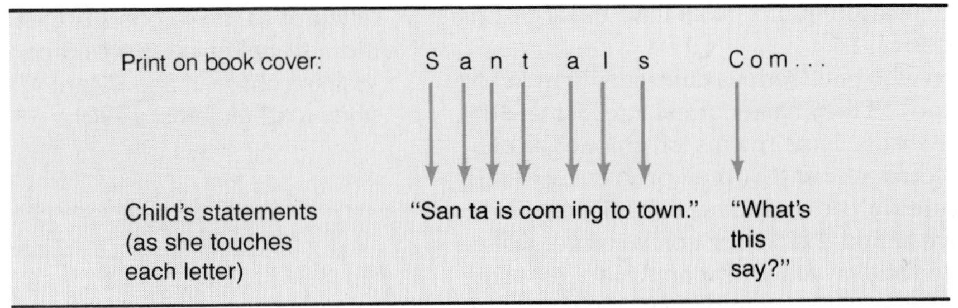

FIGURE 6.6 One step in the development of reading is to recognize that the letters on the page of a book correspond to words and parts of words. This 3-year-old does not yet have the letter/sound correspondences right, however.

trated in Figure 6.6. This kind of activity sets the stage for learning that each letter is related to a particular sound and that combinations of letters (and sounds) make up printed words.

In the third and final phase of learning to read, children have become quite skilled at decoding letters; they can "sound out" unknown words by breaking them into individual sounds or syllables. Children gain solid mastery of the rules for translating letters into sounds by the third or fourth grade (Morrison, 1984). However, the complexities of letter/sound correspondences in English can give even older readers problems. For example, the *c* in *circle* is pronounced very differently from the *c* in *cannery*, and the *gh* in *ghetto* does not sound a bit like the *gh* in *rough*.

In part, reading is an exercise in visual form perception. As Eleanor Gibson (1969) puts it, readers must learn to recognize the *distinctive features* of letters—the specific elements (such as straight and curved lines) that distinguish one letter from another. Gibson and her colleagues tested for this skill by showing children aged 4 to 8 a "standard" letterlike form and asking them to select those identical to the standard from among a set of similar forms (Gibson, Gibson, Pick, & Osser, 1962; see also Figure 6.7). The 4- and 5-year-olds often mistakenly selected stimuli that were not identical to the standard. Similarly, many preschoolers have trouble learning to notice the subtle differences between *b* and *d* or *m* and *w* (Chall, 1983). Perhaps this is why serious reading instruction normally begins at age 6 in many countries: The 6- to 8-year-olds in Gibson's study were far more able than younger children to detect the distinctive features that differentiated the variations from the standard form.

To make sense of all those squiggles on the page, of course, children must not only differentiate among them but also learn how they correspond to sounds in spoken language. To do so, they first must acquire what is called **phonological awareness**; that is, they must realize that spoken words can be decomposed into basic sound units, or *phonemes*. Children who have phonological awareness can recognize that *cat* and *trouble* both have the phoneme /t/ in them and can tell you how many distinct sounds there are in the word *bunch*. Once they are aware of the phonemes in spoken language, children are in a position to detect correspondences between sounds and printed letters. Poor readers are usually those who have had difficulty mastering the complex rules of letter/sound correspondence and their many exceptions (Morrison, 1984; Vellutino, 1991). These children must devote so much mental effort to decoding the words on the page that they have little attention to spare for interpreting and remembering what they have read. By contrast, good readers quickly and automatically decode letters and words so that they can direct their attention to comprehension. Learning to read may well be an easier task for children who speak Japanese, Finnish, and other languages with more regular

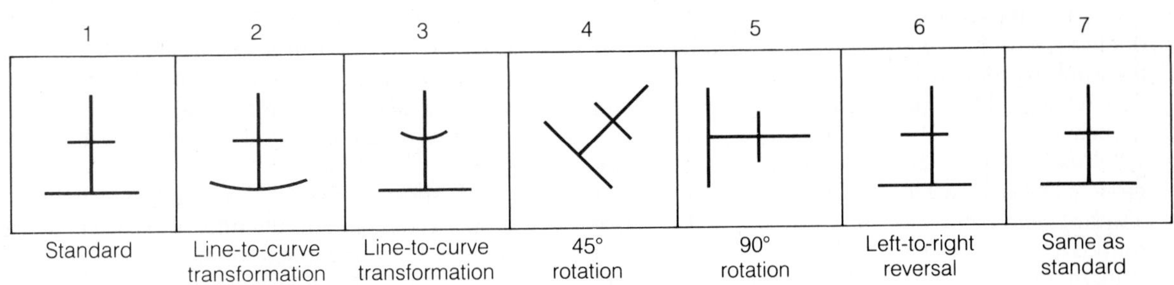

FIGURE 6.7 Examples of figures used to test children's ability to detect the distinctive features of letterlike forms. (Adapted from Gibson, Gibson, Pick, & Osser, 1962.)

letter/sound correspondence rules than those of English (Morrison, 1984).

Children who have serious difficulties learning to read, even though they have normal intellectual ability and no sensory impairments or emotional difficulties that could account for their problem, are said to have **dyslexia,** or a reading disability. Dyslexic children have varied disabilities; some cannot distinguish between letters with similar appearances, some have trouble associating sounds with letters, a few read words backward (*top* might become *pot*), and many have difficulties that cannot be pinpointed easily. In at least some dyslexic children, the brain is not fully lateralized (Gross-Glenn et al., 1991; Witelson, 1977). As dyslexic individuals read material aloud, both the left and right hemispheres of the cerebral cortex are active, whereas normally one or the other hemisphere (usually the left) plays a dominant role (Gross-Glenn et al., 1991).

Children who become dyslexic readers often show deficiencies in language learning, including deficiencies in phonological awareness, well before they enter school (Bruck, 1992; Scarborough, 1990). Partly because these youngsters have difficulty analyzing the sounds in speech, they also have trouble detecting sound/letter correspondences, which in turn impairs their ability to recognize printed words automatically and effortlessly (Bruck, 1990; Vellutino, 1991). Dyslexic children continue to perform very poorly on tests of phonological awareness and tests of word recognition as adults, even if they have managed to become decent readers (Bruck, 1990, 1992). This suggests that dyslexia is a lifelong disability, not just a developmental delay that is eventually overcome (Bruck, 1992).

What does all this suggest about teaching children to read? For years there has been debate over the merits of two broad approaches to reading instruction: the phonics approach and the whole-language approach. The phonics or "code-oriented" approach teaches children to analyze words into their component sounds—that is, it systematically teaches them letter/sound correspondence rules (Vellutino, 1991). By contrast, the whole-language approach emphasizes reading for meaning and teaches children to recognize specific words by sight or to figure out what they mean using clues in the surrounding context. This latter approach assumes that the "parts" of printed words (the letters) are not as meaningful as the whole words and that children can learn to read as effortlessly and naturally as they learn to understand speech.

Research most strongly supports the phonics approach. Data indicate that children must, somehow or another, learn that spoken words are made up of sounds and that the letters of the alphabet correspond to these sounds (Adams, 1990; Vellutino, 1991). There is no reason, though, why reading programs cannot attempt to make good use of both forms of instruction, teaching letter/sound correspondences but also helping children find meaning and enjoyment in what they read (Adams, 1990).

THE ADOLESCENT

There is little to report about perception during adolescence, unless we perhaps talk of preferences for loud music and junk food and their implications for hearing and health. Some of the developments that occur during childhood are not quite completed until adolescence. For example, portions of the brain that help regulate attention are not fully myelinated until adolescence (Tanner, 1990). Perhaps this helps explain why adolescents and young adults have incredibly long attention spans on occasion, as when they spend hours cramming for tests or typing term papers into the wee hours of the morning.

In addition, adolescents become still more efficient at ignoring irrelevant information so that they can concentrate on the task at hand. Not only do they learn more than children do about material they are supposed to master, but they learn *less* about distracting information that could potentially interfere with their performance (Miller & Weiss, 1981). Similarly, adolescents can divide their attention more systematically between two tasks. For instance, Andrew Schiff and Irwin Knopf (1985) watched the eye movements of 9-year-olds and 13-year-olds during a two-part visual search task. Children were to push a response key when particular symbols appeared at the center of a screen and also remember letters flashed at the corners of the screen. The adolescents developed an efficient strategy for switching their eyes back and forth from the center to the corners at the right times. The 9-year-olds had an unfortunate tendency to look at blank areas of the screen or to focus too much attention on the letters in the corners of the screen, thereby failing to detect the symbols in the center.

Finally, adolescents are more skilled than children at integrating information from two or more senses. For example, Shelly Botuck and Gerald Turkewitz (1990) asked 7-, 13-, and 17-year-olds to indicate whether the pattern in a sequence of sounds and the pattern in a sequence of light flashes were the same or different. Performance on this intersensory perception task continued to improve between the ages of 13 and 17.

In short, adolescence appears to be a time when basic perceptual and attentional skills are perfected. Adolescents are capable of allocating their attention very strategically and using their senses efficiently and effectively to solve problems.

Adolescents are skilled at dividing their attention between two tasks.

THE ADULT

What becomes of sensory and perceptual capacities during adulthood? There is good news and bad news, and we might as well dispense with the bad news first: Sensory and perceptual capacities decline with age in the normal person. Often these declines begin in early adulthood and become noticeable in one's 40s, sometimes giving middle-aged people a feeling that they are getting old. Further declines take place in later life, to the point that one would have a hard time finding a person aged 65 or older who does not have a sensory or perceptual impairment of some kind. The good news (or the not-so-bad news) is that these changes are gradual and usually minor. As a result, we can often compensate for them, making small adjustments such as turning up the volume on the TV set or adding a little extra seasoning to food. Because losses are not severe, and because of the process of compensation, only a minority of old people develop serious problems such as blindness and deafness.

The losses we are talking about take two general forms. First, sensation is affected, as indicated by increases in **sensory thresholds.** The threshold for a sense is the point at which low levels of stimulation can be detected — a dim light can be seen, a faint tone can be heard, a slight odor can be detected, and so on. Stimulation that is below the threshold cannot be detected, so a raising of the threshold with age means that sensitivity to very low levels of stimulation is lost. (We saw that the very young infant is also insensitive to some very low levels of stimulation.)

Second, perceptual abilities also decline in some aging adults. Even when stimulation is intense enough to be well above the detection threshold, older people may have difficulty processing or interpreting sensory information. As we'll see, they may have trouble searching a visual scene, understanding rapid speech in a noisy room, or recognizing the foods that they are tasting.

So, sensory and perceptual declines (with compensation) are typical during adulthood, although they are far steeper in some individuals than in others. These declines involve both a raising of thresholds for detecting stimulation and a loss of some perceptual abilities.

Vision

Several changes in the eye and in the parts of the nervous system related to vision take place over the adult years, leading to vision problems in later life (see Corso, 1981; Fozard, 1990; Kline & Schieber, 1985). You may have noticed that the eyes of old people are often slightly discolored and dull. However, the more significant changes take place *within* the eye. The pupil of an old person normally is smaller than that of a young adult and does not change in size as much when lighting conditions change. The lens that focuses light to cast a sharp image on the retina has been gaining new cells from childhood on, making it denser and less flexible later in life: It cannot change shape, or accommodate, as well to bring objects at different distances into focus. The lens is also yellowing, and both it and the gelatinous liquid behind it are becoming less transparent. Finally, the sensory receptor cells in the retina and the complex nerves leading from the retina to the visual areas of the brain do not function as efficiently as they once did. What impacts do these physical and neural changes have on visual sensation and perception?

Basic Changes in Visual Capacities

Gradual changes in the eye are often not noticeable until middle age. In their 40s many people notice a nearly universal problem — a loss of near vision. This change is related to a decreased ability of the lens to accommodate to objects that are close to the eye. Over the years an adult may, without even being aware of it, gradually move newspapers and books farther from the eye to make them clearer — a form of compensation for decline. Eventually, however, the arms may simply be too short to do the trick any longer. So middle-aged adults cope by getting reading glasses (or, if they also have problems with distance vision, bifocals). In one study only 4% of adults in their 20s and 30s wore glasses or contact lenses to correct their *near* vision; this figure jumped to 51% of adults in their 40s and 50s and about 80% of adults aged 60 or older (Kosnik et al., 1988). Even with their corrective lenses, older adults report more difficulty "reading the small print" than younger adults do (Kosnik et al., 1988).

Because older people also have higher visual detection thresholds than younger adults do (Kline & Schieber, 1985), they are less sensitive to dim lights and may have trouble making things out in the dark (Kosnik et al., 1988). This can make night driving and navigating in a dark house difficult. In addition, when younger individuals suddenly find themselves in the dark, their eyes adapt and quickly become more sensitive to even low levels of light. But for the older person this process of **dark adaptation** occurs more slowly. Thus the older person who is driving at night may have special problems when turning onto a dark road from a lighted highway.

It might seem that avoiding the dark would be the way to compensate, but, ironically, many older adults also have difficulty with glare from bright lights (Kline & Schieber, 1985). The glare from headlights or from the lights in a very brightly lit room may interfere with clear vision, and old people may take some time to recover from sudden glares (for example, popping flashbulbs). In short, older people are in a bind: They cannot make things out well when illumination is low, but glare interferes with their vision when illumination is high.

For most of us the heart of vision is visual acuity—the ability to see a clear image rather than a blur. Visual acuity, as measured by standard eye charts, increases in childhood, peaks in the 20s, remains quite steady through middle age, and steadily declines in old age (Pitts, 1982). The implications for the average adult are fairly minor. For example, in one major study, 69% of 75- to 85-year-olds had corrected vision between 20/10 and 20/25 (Kahn et al., 1977). At worst, then, most of them could see at 20 feet what a person with standard acuity could see at 25 feet. Only 3.3% of them had corrected vision of 20/200 or worse—a cutoff commonly used to define legal blindness. We probably needn't fear becoming blind in old age, though most of us will indeed wear corrective lenses (see Figure 6.8).

The minority of elderly people who experience serious declines in visual acuity typically suffer from pathological conditions of the eye that become more prevalent in old age but are not part of aging itself (Pitts, 1982). For example, **cataracts,**—opaque areas of the lens—are the leading cause of blindness in old age, affecting 5%–7% of people over 65 (Corso, 1981; Greenberg & Branch, 1982). A contributing factor is lifelong heavy exposure to sunlight and its damaging ultraviolet rays (Kline & Schieber, 1985). Fortunately, cataracts can often be corrected surgically.

Even older adults who have good visual acuity may have difficulty perceiving moving objects (Sivak, Olson, & Pastalan, 1981). Older adults have difficulty reading street signs while they are driving (Kosnik et al., 1988), and they are less able than younger adults to judge the speed of other vehicles (Scialfa et al., 1991). They also have a smaller field of vision, so objects off to the side (cars coming from intersecting streets?) may not be detected until there is little time to react (Owsley et al., 1991). In addition, depth perception may decrease slightly by old age—although so many cues are available to help us judge distance and depth that the damage may not be great (Kline & Schieber, 1985; Pitts, 1982).

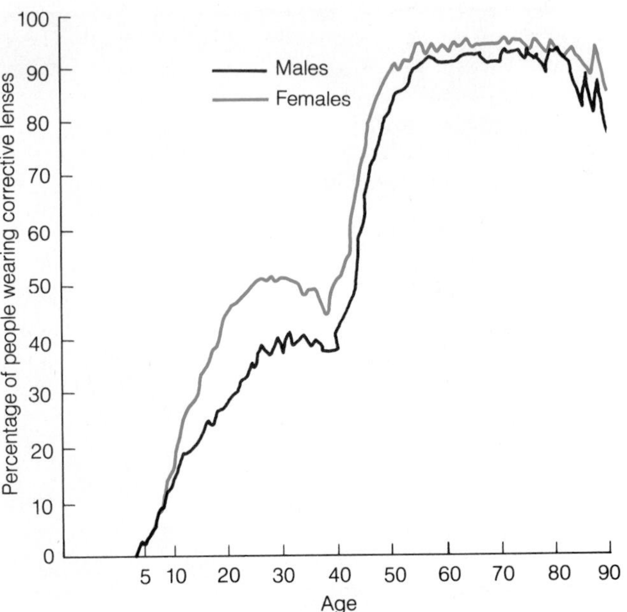

FIGURE 6.8 Percentage of Americans with corrective lenses. The percentage of people wearing glasses or contact lenses rises from less than 1% among 3-year-olds to 92% of those aged 75 or older! Notice the steep rise during childhood and adolescence—and then another steep rise during the 40s, when many people find they need reading glasses because the lenses of their eyes become less able to change shapes. (From National Center for Health Statistics, 1983.)

In case you have formed the impression that old people should not be allowed to drive, let's quickly note that the drivers who cause the most accidents are those under 25. When we take into account the fact that young people do more driving than elderly people do, it turns out that both elderly drivers and young drivers have more accidents *per mile driven* than middle-aged drivers do (Williams & Carsten, 1989). The kinds of accidents elderly adults tend to have—ones that involve failing to heed signs, failing to give up the right-of-way at intersections, and the like—are closely related to the difficulties in visual perception that they most often experience (Kline et al., 1992). At the same time, the driving records of older adults are not as bad as might be expected, because many of them compensate for visual losses and slower reactions by driving less frequently, especially at night and during rush hour—or by being more cautious when they do drive (Kline et al., 1992). So, young drivers might try to be patient the next time they find themselves behind a slow-moving elderly driver: He or she is doing everyone a favor by compensating for losses rather than denying them and driving like a young maniac!

Attention and Complex Visual Perception

As we saw when we examined perceptual development during infancy and childhood, perception is more than just seeing: It is using the senses intelligently and allocating attention efficiently. Young children have more difficulty performing complex visual search tasks and ignoring irrelevant information than older children do. Do older adults also have more difficulty than younger adults?

Older people perform worse than younger ones on a number of tests that require dividing one's attention between two tasks or selectively attending to certain stimuli while ignoring others (Hartley, 1992; McDowd & Birren, 1990). In everyday life this may translate into difficulty carrying on a conversation while driving or problems locating the Bird's Eye asparagus amid all the frozen vegetables at the supermarket.

In one test of visual search skills, Dana Plude and William Hoyer (1981) asked young adults and elderly adults to sort cards containing from one to nine letters into two bins, depending on whether or not they contained specific target letters. Older adults were apparently more distracted by irrelevant information, for they were especially slow compared to young adults when the number of distractor letters on the cards was high. In many situations, elderly people appear to have difficulty inhibiting responses to irrelevant stimuli in order to focus their attention more squarely on relevant stimuli (Hartley, 1992; Hasher, Stoltzfus, Zacks, & Rypma, 1991).

Yet the older adults in Plude and Hoyer's study had difficulty only when the letters to be hunted for changed from session to session. When sorters got to practice over all six sessions with the same target letters, older adults were no longer especially bothered by having to search through many distractors. Similarly, older adults search more effectively when they know in advance where to look for a target in a larger display than when the location of a target is unpredictable (Farkas & Hoyer, 1980; Nissen & Corkin, 1985).

On the basis of findings like these, Plude and Hoyer (1985) conclude that older adults have their greatest difficulties in processing visual information when the situation is *novel* (they're not sure exactly what to look for or where to look) and when it is *complex* (there's a great deal of distracting information to search through, or two tasks must be performed at once). By contrast, they have fewer problems if they have clear expectations about what they are to do and if the task is not overly complex. Thus an older factory worker who has inspected radios for years may be just as speedy and accurate as a younger worker at this well-practiced, familiar task, but he or she might perform relatively poorly if suddenly asked to inspect pocket calculators and look for a much larger number of possible defects—a novel and complex task.

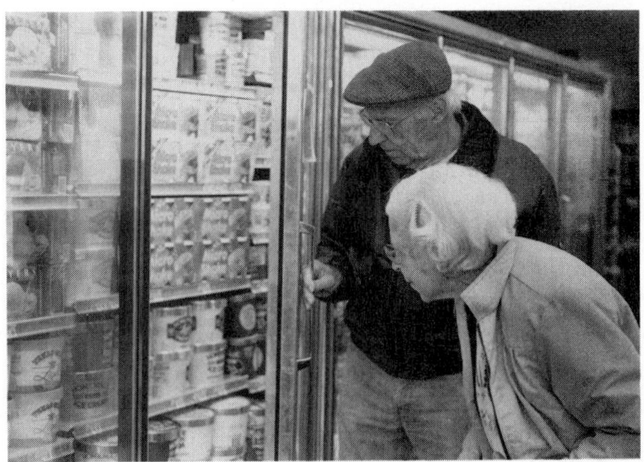

An older adult is likely to find the ice cream as efficiently as a younger adult in a familiar supermarket but may have difficulty with this visual search task if the supermarket is unfamiliar.

In summary, it is normal for adults to experience a gradual loss of vision as they age and to encounter special problems when they are in either darkness or bright light and when they are viewing moving objects. Performance on novel and complex visual perception tasks may also suffer in old age, partly because older adults are less able than younger people to filter out distracting information.

Hearing

There is some truth to the stereotype of the hard-of-hearing older person. The older the age group, the greater the percentage of people who have at least a mild hearing loss: about 20% in the 45–54 age group and as many as 75% in the 75–79 age group (Butler & Lewis, 1977). In England almost half of a sample of people aged 75 or older reported difficulty understanding what is said when someone whispers to them in a quiet room (Davis, 1983). The good news is that most older people experience only mild hearing impairments.

Basic Capacities

Sources of hearing problems range from excess wax buildup in the ears to a sluggish nervous system. Most age-related hearing problems seem to originate in the inner ear, however (Olsho, Harkins, & Lenhardt, 1985). The cochlear hair cells that serve as auditory receptors, their surrounding structures, and the neurons leading from them to the brain degenerate gradually over the adult years. The most noticeable result is a loss of sensitivity to high-frequency or high-pitched sounds. Thus the older person may have difficulty hearing a child's high voice or the flutes in an orchestra but may have less trouble with deep voices or tubas. After age 50, lower-frequency sounds also become increasingly difficult to hear (Fozard, 1990). To be heard by the average older adult, then, a sound—especially a high-pitched sound but, ultimately, any sound—must be louder than it needs to be to exceed the hearing threshold of a younger adult.

Insensitivity to high-frequency sounds is more noticeable in men than in women (Corso, 1963). This could be because men age faster than women do, but it could also occur because men tend to experience more noise during their lives than women do. Although the problem seems to affect older people everywhere to some extent, men who have lived and worked in noisy industrial environments experience more hearing loss than those exposed to lower levels of noise, and people in "noisy" cultures experience more loss than people in "quiet" societies (Bergman, 1980; McFarland, 1968, cited by Baltes, Reese, & Nesselroade, 1977). Fans of loud rock music, beware!

Speech Perception

Perhaps the most important thing we do with our ears in everyday life is listen to other people during conversations. The ability to hear is one requisite for understanding speech, but this complex auditory perception task also depends on cognitive processes such as attention and memory. How well do aging adults do?

Under ideal listening conditions, older adults typically have somewhat more difficulty discriminating words that are read to them than younger adults do, perhaps because of degeneration within the ear (Fozard, 1990; Olsho et al., 1985). However, these problems are minor compared to those that many (though certainly not all) older adults experience under *poor listening conditions*. Here the functioning of the brain is probably more important than the functioning of the ear (Fozard, 1990). For example, when you are trying to understand what someone is saying in the presence of loud background noise, you must keep your attention focused and "hear between the lines," inferring what a word is from context when you cannot make it out completely. If you want to remember what you have heard, you must devote some mental effort to doing so. Because aging brains tend to process information more slowly than younger brains do, older adults sometimes have difficulty getting and remembering all of a speaker's message (Fozard, 1990; Tun et al., 1992).

Older adults are especially likely to have problems understanding speech if there is a great deal of background noise (Bergman, 1980; Hutchinson, 1989). The performance gap between them and younger adults is also greater when the speech signal is "degraded" in other respects—for example, when it is fast, when it reverberates in a room, or when some of its frequencies are filtered out or distorted, as is the case when listening to a voice on the telephone or on a videocassette (Bergman et al., 1976; Fozard, 1990; see also Figure 6.9). Problems in understanding speech under these difficult conditions often become noticeable after about age 50 and more serious thereafter (Olsho et al., 1985). Moreover, these problems can occur even in older people who do not have significant measured hearing losses (Bergman, 1980).

But let's note that some messages are easier to understand than others. Like visual perception tasks, auditory perception tasks are more difficult for older people when they are novel and complex (McDowd & Craik, 1988). In familiar, everyday situations, older adults are able to make good use of contextual cues to interpret what they hear (Fozard, 1990; Hutchinson, 1989). In one study, for example, elderly adults were about as able as young adults to recall meaningful sentences they had just heard (Wingfield, Poon, Lombardi, & Lowe, 1985). However, they had serious dif-

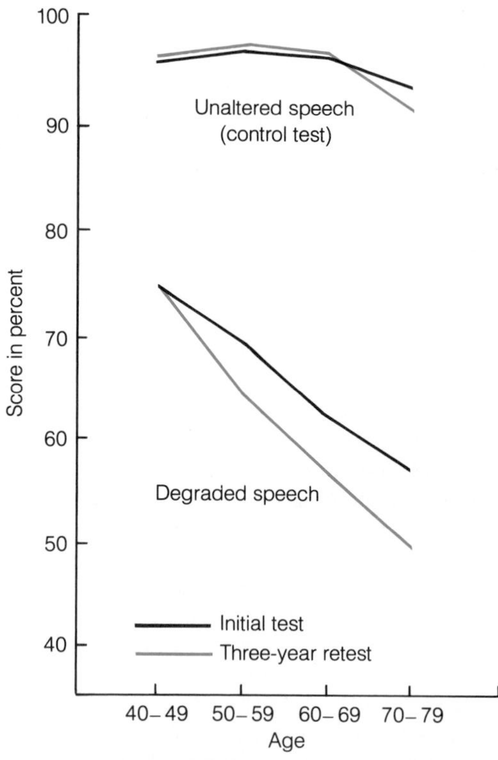

FIGURE 6.9 Age differences in hearing speech. Older adults have little difficulty understanding "unaltered speech"—sentences read aloud to them under excellent listening conditions. But, compared with younger adults, they do have difficulty in making out different forms of "degraded speech." In this study they also experienced steeper declines in the accuracy of their speech perception over a three-year period, especially when they listened to degraded speech. (From Bergman et al., 1976.)

ficulties in repeating back grammatical sentences that made no sense or random strings of words, especially when these meaningless stimuli were spoken rapidly. So an older person may be able to follow an ordinary conversation but not a technical presentation on an unfamiliar topic—especially if the speaker makes the task even harder by talking too fast.

Overall, then, most older adults have only mild hearing losses and only minor problems understanding everyday speech, and they can compensate for their difficulties quite successfully—for example, by reading lips and relying on contextual cues. Novel and complex speech heard under poor listening conditions is likely to cause more trouble. For those rarer older people who develop a significant hearing loss, the psychological effects can be far more serious, as we'll see at the end of this chapter.

Taste and Smell

Does the aging of sensory systems also mean that older people become less able to appreciate tastes and aromas? Studies designed to measure taste thresholds suggest that, with increasing age, many of us have more difficulty detecting weak taste stimulation—for example, a little bit of salt or citric acid in water (Corso, 1981; Whitbourne, 1985). In addition, both middle-aged and older adults sometimes have difficulty consistently discriminating among tastes that are detectable but that differ in intensity. In one study, for example, older adults (aged 70 to 88) were less able than young adults (aged 23 to 39) to reliably judge one solution to be saltier, or more bitter, or more acidic than another (Weiffenbach, Cowart, & Baum, 1986). Interestingly, older adults did not have difficulty distinguishing degrees of sweetness; we don't seem to ever lose the sweet tooth we are born with.

The ability to perceive odors also declines with age. Sensitivity to faint odors increases from childhood to early adulthood and then declines starting in middle age (Cain & Gent, 1991; Doty et al., 1984). Similarly, the ability to distinguish among odors of different intensities improves during childhood and declines during late adulthood (Rovee, Cohen, & Shlapack, 1975; Stevens & Cain, 1987). Older adults also experience particular odors differently than younger adults do and do not label them in the same ways (Russell et al., 1993). All things considered, age takes a greater toll on the sense of smell than on the sense of taste (Bartoshuk & Weiffenbach, 1990). However, differences between age groups are usually small, and many older people retain their sensitivity to both taste and smell quite well.

How do declines in the senses of taste and smell affect the older person's ability to recognize and enjoy food? Susan Schiffman (1977) blindfolded young adults and elderly adults and asked them to identify blended foods by taste and smell alone. As Table 6.1 reveals, the older people were less often correct than the college students. But was this due to a loss of taste sensitivity or to a loss of smell sensitivity? Or was it instead a cognitive problem—recalling the right name for a food that was in fact perceived?

Claire Murphy (1985) attempted to shed light on these questions by presenting young and elderly adults with 12 of the blended foods used by Schiffman. She observed that older people often came up with the wrong specific label but the right idea (identifying sugar as fruit or salt as peanuts, for example). Thus at least some of their difficulty might have been cognitive in nature. Murphy also tested women whose nostrils were blocked and found that *both* young and elderly women did very poorly when they could not smell and had to rely on taste alone. This finding suggests that reduced ability to identify foods in old age is due less to losses in the sense of taste than to losses in the sense of smell (see also Schiffman & Pasternak, 1979). Declines in the cognitive skills required to remember and name what one has tasted also contribute.

How might losses in the senses of taste and smell affect an older person, then? Susan Whitbourne (1985)

TABLE 6.1 Age differences in recognition of foods.

	Percentage Recognizing Food	
Pureed Food Substance	*College Students (ages 18–22)*	*Elderly People (ages 67–93)*
Apple	93	79
Banana	93	59
Pear	93	86
Pineapple	93	86
Strawberry	100	79
Walnut	33	28
Broccoli	81	62
Cabbage	74	69
Carrot	79	55
Celery	89	55
Corn	96	76
Cucumber	44	28
Green bean	85	62
Green pepper	78	59
Potato	52	59
Tomato	93	93
Beef	100	79
Fish	89	90
Pork	93	72
Rice	81	55

Elderly adults have more difficulty than young college students identifying most blended foods by taste and smell alone. Percentages of those recognizing food include reasonable guesses such as "orange" in response to "apple." Notice that some foods (for example, cucumber) are very difficult for people of any age to identify by taste and smell alone. Appearance and texture are important to our recognition of such foods.

Source: From Schiffman, 1977.

summarizes several implications. If foods do not have much taste, interest in eating may decline and nutritional problems could result. Another possible response is overuse of seasonings such as salt, which would threaten health in still another way. (One of our students was horrified to witness her grandmother dumping most of a box of salt into the mashed potatoes one Thanksgiving Day!) Decreased sensitivity to odors can not only decrease enjoyment of food but also make older adults oblivious to dangerous odors such as gas leaks.

Touch, Temperature, and Pain

By now we've seen numerous indications that older adults are often less able than younger adults to detect weak sensory stimulation, and this holds true regarding the sense of touch as well. The detection threshold for touch increases and sensitivity is gradually lost from middle childhood on (Kenshalo, 1977; Verrillo & Verrillo, 1985). It is not clear that minor losses in touch sensitivity have many implications for daily life, however.

Similarly, older people may be less sensitive to changes in temperature than younger adults are (Verrillo & Verrillo, 1985). For example, some elderly people keep their homes too cool because they are unaware of being cold. They are then in danger if their already-too-cold bodies experience a temperature drop (Corso, 1981). Others may fail to notice if the temperature becomes uncomfortably hot. Since older bodies are also less able than younger ones to maintain an even temperature, elderly people face an increased risk of death in heat waves or cold snaps (Rango, 1985; Whitbourne, 1985).

Finally, consider the perception of pain. It seems only fair that older people should also be less sensitive to painful stimulation. They are less likely to report weak levels of stimulation as painful, although the age differences in pain thresholds are not large or totally consistent (Kenshalo, 1977; Verrillo & Verrillo, 1985). The more important question is whether older adults have more tolerance for pain that exceeds the threshold for detection. Apparently they do not (Verrillo & Verrillo, 1985). For example, Stephen Harkins, Donald Price, and Michael Martelli (1986) subjected young (age 20–36), middle-aged (45–60), and older (65–80) adults to painful heats of different temperatures. Middle-aged and older adults judged the least intense heats to be less hot than the young adults did, reconfirming the finding that older adults are relatively insensitive to very weak pain stimuli. Yet they also tended to judge the hottest of the stimuli to be especially hot, suggesting that they definitely experienced highly painful stimuli as intense. In addition, judgments of the *unpleasantness* of these painful stimuli barely differed across age groups. Thus the researchers concluded that there are more similarities than differences among age groups in the experience of pain.

For older adults with arthritis, osteoporosis, cancer, and other diseases, chronic pain can clearly interfere with effective daily functioning and can decrease psychological well-being (Moss, Lawton, & Glicksman, 1991). Although this may be little comfort to them, it is quite possible that humans are biologically designed to remain sensitive to pain across the entire life span, because pain protects them (Whitbourne, 1985). The infant who cries will bring an adult running; the elderly person who feels a stab of pain may turn down the hot water in the bath, stop lifting heavy boxes, or even go to the doctor.

The Adult in Perspective

Of all the changes in sensation and perception during adulthood that we have considered, those involving vision and hearing appear to be the most important and the most nearly universal. Not only are these senses less keen, but they are used less effectively in such complex perceptual tasks as searching a cluttered room for a missing book or following rapid conversation in a noisy room. Declines in the other senses seem to be less serious and do not affect as many people.

Still, the vision and hearing of most elderly adults remain reasonably good. It is the minority of older adults with severe or multiple losses that we must worry about. In our complex society, difficulties in driving, watching television, reading newspapers, and getting around can limit satisfaction and social interaction in old age. Sensory impairments may even increase the risks of death, especially when deficits in vision and balance conspire to cause life-threatening falls (Ochs, Newberry, Lenhardt, & Harkins, 1985). So what can be done to help optimize the development of individuals with sensory impairments?

APPLICATIONS: AIDING HEARING-IMPAIRED PEOPLE, YOUNG AND OLD

Although sensory impairments can change the course of normal life-span development, much can be done to help even individuals who are born totally deaf or blind to develop in positive directions and function effectively in everyday life. We close this chapter by briefly examining interventions for children and adults who have hearing impairments.

It is critical for babies born with impaired hearing to be identified as early as possible. A committee of the National Institutes of Health recently noted that the average hearing-impaired child is not identified until the age of 2½, usually when it becomes clear that his or her language skills have not developed normally (Associated Press, 1993). Because children who receive no special intervention before the age of 3 usually have lasting difficulties with speech and language skills, the committee recommended that all newborns in the United States be given hearing tests soon after birth. How do you test the hearing of newborns? The recommended testing procedure involves making clicking sounds in the infant's ear and then determining with sensors attached to the head whether the brain is responding appropriately (Associated Press, 1993).

Once hearing-impaired infants are identified, interventions can be planned. Most programs attempt to capitalize on whatever residual hearing children have by equipping them with hearing aids (or, these days, more advanced devices such as cochlear implants) and involving their parents in efforts to develop their language and communication skills (Maxon & Brackett, 1992). In describing one successful program for hearing-impaired children, Fred Bess and Freeman McConnell (1981) note that infants are first fitted with hearing aids that are carefully matched to their problems. Much effort is invested in helping both parents and children get used to the idea and in periodically checking to see that the aids are functioning properly. Then teachers go to the home to show parents how to make their children more aware of the world of sound. For instance, on hearing the screech of a car's brakes outside, parents might put their hands to their ears, rush their child to the window, and talk about the noise. Similarly, parents are urged to slam doors, deliberately rattle pots and pans, and create other such opportunities for the child to become alert to sounds. All the while, parents are using words to describe everyday objects, people, and events.

This combination of the right hearing aid and auditory training in the home has proven quite effective in improving the ability of hearing-impaired infants and preschoolers to hear speech and learn to speak. Some experts make the learning of sign language part of early intervention for more severely hearing-impaired children. The earlier these children acquire *some* language system, whether spoken or signed, the better their command of language is likely to be later in life (Mayberry & Eichen, 1991).

And what about the other end of the life span? Most hearing-impaired adults were not born that way but became hearing impaired during their lives. Many are reluctant at first to admit that they have a hearing problem and to seek help because they associate their problem with "getting old" (Goffinet, 1992). Some individuals become depressed and withdrawn because of the strains they experience when they cannot understand what is being said, misinterpret what is said, or have to keep asking people to repeat what they said. One 89-year-old woman became extremely depressed and isolated as she lost her hearing entirely: "There is an *awfulness* about silence . . . I am days without speaking a word. It is affecting my voice.

Hearing-impaired children master language best if they receive early training in oral language, sign language, or both. These children use sign language but also wear amplification devices that help them make use of their residual hearing. (Photograph provided by Telex Communications, Inc., Minneapolis, MN.)

I fear for my mind. I can't hear the alarm clock, telephone ring, door bell, radio, television—or the human voice" (Meadows-Orlans & Orlans, 1990, pp. 424–425). At the other extreme, some individuals cope very well with their hearing impairments and maintain active, satisfying lifestyles (Meadows-Orlans & Orlans, 1990).

Most hearing aids cannot really restore normal hearing; they tend to distort sounds and to magnify background noise as well as what one is trying to hear. In addition, many older people have hearing aids that are of poor quality or that are poorly matched to their specific hearing problems (Corso, 1981).

However, there are many simple ways to help people with hearing losses to compensate. For one thing, the environment can be altered to facilitate hearing; furniture can be arranged to permit face-to-face contact, and noisy appliances can be moved away from areas where conversations normally take place (Olsho et al., 1985). Then there are simple guidelines we can follow to make ourselves more understandable to the hearing-impaired person. Most importantly, don't shout! Shouting not only distorts speech but raises the pitch of the voice—and higher-pitched speech is more difficult for elderly people to hear. Several other recommendations for communicating effectively with hearing-impaired elderly people are presented in Box 6.2. With modern technology, appropriate education, effective coping strategies, and help from those of us who hear, hearing-impaired individuals of all ages can thrive.

BOX 6.2 Guidelines for Talking to Hearing-Impaired People

Raymond Hull (1980) has recommended 13 simple steps we can take to make it easier for hearing-impaired elderly people to understand speech. Most of these measures are equally applicable to hearing-impaired people of any age.

1. Speak slightly louder than usual.
2. Use a normal rate of speech; avoid fast talk.
3. Be within 3 to 6 feet of the listener.
4. Make sure there's enough light so that the listener can see your lips and gestures well.
5. Don't bother speaking if you're in the next room or otherwise not visible.
6. Don't try if there is a great deal of background noise.
7. Don't speak right into the person's ear. You won't be visible, and your speech will be distorted if it is too loud.
8. Reword what you said if it is not understood; don't just repeat the same words.
9. *Don't* use exaggerated articulations.
10. Arrange the seating in a room so that conversants are close to each other and visible.
11. Include hearing-impaired people in discussions concerning them.
12. At meetings, make sure speakers use a microphone, even if no one asks.
13. Above all, treat elderly persons as adults. They, of anyone, deserve that respect.

REFLECTIONS

What are some of the larger messages that emerge from our survey of perceptual development over the life span? For one thing, researchers have identified perceptual competencies in the very young infant that no one—except perhaps observant parents—even suspected were there. Have you ever noticed that Olympic records seem to be broken every time a competition is held? Well, it often seems that each new study of infant perception tells us that this or that perceptual capacity emerges earlier than previous researchers had reported. The lesson for developmentalists seems to be that the quality of knowledge gained in science depends on what researchers are looking for and what methods they use to look for it. The lesson for parents is that they should assume that their babies are making the most of their everyday sensory experiences.

Recent research also provides us with a more optimistic picture of perception in old age. It's true that modest declines in the functioning of the senses seem to be part of normal aging. However, the declines are neither so steep nor so common as was once believed. In addition, researchers have identified positive phenomena related to sensory and perceptual changes. They have shown, for example, that older adults are adept at compensating for gradual declines in perceptual abilities and that they perform familiar perceptual tasks quite effectively by relying on expectations gained through experience.

We are about to turn our attention to cognitive development across the life span. Let's reemphasize, then, that perception is our primary means of obtaining knowledge about the world. How *would* infants gain knowledge of teddy bears, spoons, or videocassettes without being able to see them, finger them, and pop them into their mouths? How would we know anything at all without the input that our senses provide? Perception is truly at the heart of human cognitive development.

SUMMARY POINTS

1. *Sensation* is the detection of sensory stimulation; *perception* is the interpretation of what is sensed. Developmentalists and philosophers differ about whether basic knowledge of the world is innate (the nativist position) or must be acquired through the senses (the empiricist position) and about whether sensory information needs to be embellished (enrichment theory) or is rich as it is (differentiation theory).

2. From birth the visual system is working reasonably well. Infants under 2 months of age discriminate brightness and colors and are attracted to contour, moderate complexity, and movement. Starting at 2 or 3 months of age, they more clearly perceive whole patterns such as faces and seem to understand a good deal about objects and their properties. Spatial perception also develops rapidly, and by about 7 months infants not only perceive but also fear dropoffs.

3. Young infants can recognize their mothers' voices, distinguish speech sounds that adults cannot discriminate, and analyze features of musical sounds.

4. The senses of taste and smell are also well developed at birth. Newborns avoid unpleasant tastes and enjoy sweet tastes, and they soon recognize their mothers by odor alone. Newborns are also sensitive to touch, temperature, and pain.

5. The senses are interrelated at birth but, as children develop, performance on cross-modal perception tasks improves.

6. Although many basic perceptual abilities unfold early in life and may be innate, early perceptual development also requires normal sensory stimulation and can take somewhat different forms depending on the sensory experiences available in one's culture.

7. During childhood we learn to sustain attention for longer periods of time, to direct it more selectively (filtering out distracting information), and to plan and carry out more systematic perceptual searches. Children must develop phonological awareness, detect distinguishing features of letters, and grasp letter/sound correspondence rules in order to read. During adolescence, sensation and perception are at their peaks.

8. Over adulthood, sensory and perceptual capacities gradually decline in most individuals, though many changes are minor and can be compensated for. Visual difficulties include a loss of near vision starting in middle age, problems perceiving motion, and difficulty performing novel and complex visual searches.

9. Hearing difficulty associated with aging most commonly involves loss of sensitivity to high-frequency (high-pitched) sounds. Even elderly people without significant hearing losses may experience difficulty understanding novel and complex speech.

10. Many older people have difficulty recognizing or enjoying foods, largely because of declines in the sense of smell and cognitive skills; touch, temperature, and pain sensitivity also decrease slightly.

11. The development of individuals with hearing impairments can be optimized through diagnosis early in infancy and help in compensating for hearing loss throughout life.

KEY TERMS

attention
cataracts
contour
cross-modal perception
dark adaptation
differentiation theory
distinctive feature
dyslexia
enrichment theory
Gestalt psychology
habituation
olfaction
perception
phoneme
phonological awareness
sensation
sensory threshold
size constancy
visual accommodation
visual acuity
visual cliff

COGNITION AND LANGUAGE

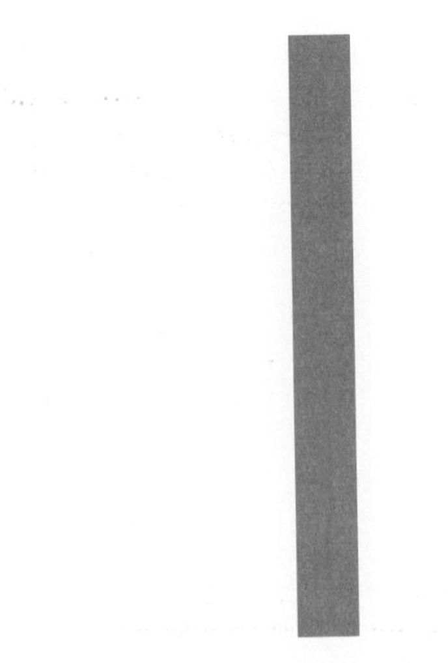

Three-year-old: Mommy, I always ask why. Why do I always ask why?
Mother: Because you are curious about things.
Three-year-old: What is curious?
[Callanan & Oakes, 1992, p. 222]

We now begin an examination of the development of **cognition**—that is, the activity of knowing and the processes through which knowledge is acquired and problems are solved. Human beings are cognitive beings throughout the life span, but their minds change in important ways. This chapter concentrates on the very influential theory of cognitive development proposed by Jean Piaget, tracing growth in cognitive capacities during infancy, childhood, and adolescence and then asking what becomes of these capacities during adulthood. In addition, it traces the development of language and the ways in which language development is related to the development of the mind.

Cognitive development is viewed primarily through one lens here: that of Jean Piaget and his cognitive-developmental perspective. Chapter 8 introduces an *information-processing approach* to the mind that focuses on specific mental activities such as paying attention, perceiving, storing relevant information in memory, weighing decisions, and so on. Chapter 9 considers the mind from the perspective of intelligence testers and describes changes and individual differences in intellectual performance over the life span.

PIAGET'S APPROACH TO COGNITIVE DEVELOPMENT

As Chapter 2's introduction to Jean Piaget indicated, he at one time worked on the development of standardized intelligence tests but quickly became disenchanted with an approach that seemed to be concerned only with determining the ages at which children could correctly answer certain questions. Piaget became intrigued by children's *mistakes*, for he noticed that children of the same age often made similar kinds of mistakes—errors that were typically quite different from those made by younger or older children. Could these age-related differences in error patterns reflect developmental steps, or stages, in intellectual growth? Piaget thought so, and he devoted his life to studying how children think, not just what they know (Flavell, 1963).

His studies began with close observation of his own three children as infants: how they explored new toys, solved simple problems that he arranged for them, and generally came to understand themselves and their world. Later Piaget studied larger samples of children through what has become known as the **clinical method,** a flexible question-and-answer technique used to discover how children think about problems. Many contemporary researchers consider the method imprecise because it does not involve standardized questions to all children tested, but Piaget (1929) believed that the investigator should have the flexibility to pursue an individual child's line of reasoning so as to fully understand the child's mind. From his naturalistic observations of his own children and through use of the clinical method to explore children's understandings of everything from the rules of games to the concepts of space and time, Piaget formulated his view of the development of intelligence.

What Is Intelligence?

Piaget defined intelligence as a basic life function that helps the organism adapt to its environment. We observe adaptation as we watch the toddler figuring out how to work a jack-in-the-box, the school-aged child figuring out how to divide candies among friends, or the adult figuring out how to program a video recorder. The newborn enters an unfamiliar world with few means of adapting to it other than working senses and reflexes. But Piaget viewed infants as active agents in their own development—learning about the world of people and things by observing, investigating, and experimenting (Cowan, 1978).

Knowledge gained through active exploration takes the form of one or another **scheme** (sometimes called a *schema* in the singular, *schemata* in the plural). Schemes are cognitive structures: organized patterns of action or thought that we construct to organize or interpret our experience (Piaget, 1952, 1977). For example, the infant's grasping actions and sucking responses are early schemes, for both are patterns of action used to "adapt to" or deal with different objects. During their second year, children develop symbolic schemes, or concepts. They use internal mental symbols such as images to represent or stand for aspects of experience, as when a young child sees a

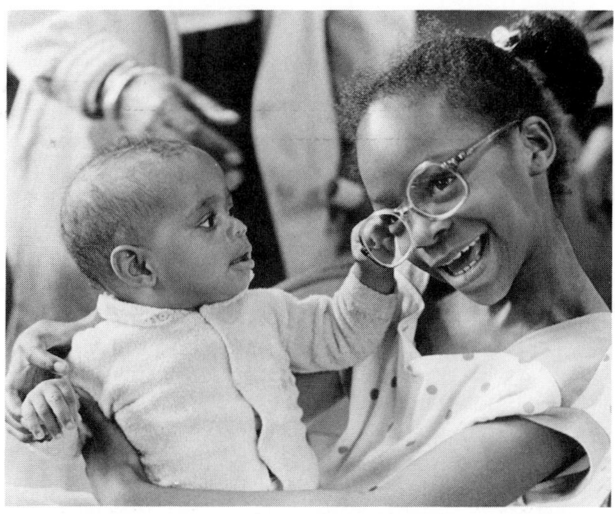

The grasping scheme. Infants have a range of behavioral schemes that allow them to explore new objects. Each scheme is a general pattern of behavior that can be adjusted to fit specific objects.

funny dance and carries away a mental model or image of how the dance was done. This capacity is clearly involved in early language development, for words are symbols for things. Older children become able to manipulate symbols in their heads to help them solve problems.

As children develop more sophisticated schemes, or cognitive structures, they become increasingly able to adapt to their environments. Because they gain new schemes as they develop, children of different ages will deal with or understand the same stimuli differently. The infant may get to know a shoe mainly as a "thing-to-chew," the preschooler may decide to let the shoe symbolize or represent a telephone and put it to his or her ear, and the school-aged child may mentally count its shoelace eyelets.

How Does Intelligence Develop?

Piaget believed that all schemes — all forms of understanding — are created through the operation of two inborn intellectual functions, which he called organization and adaptation. Through **organization,** children combine existing schemes into new and more complex ones. For example, the young infant who gazes, reaches, and grasps will organize these simple schemes into a complex structure, *visually directed reaching,* that permits him or her to actively seek out objects for closer examination. Complex cognitive structures in older children grow out of reorganizations of more primitive structures.

Adaptation is the process of adjusting to the demands of the environment. It occurs through two complementary processes, assimilation and accommodation. Imagine that you are a 2-year-old, that the world is new, and that you see your first horse. What will you make of it? In all likelihood you will try to relate it to something familiar. **Assimilation** is the process by which we interpret new experiences in terms of existing schemes or cognitive structures. Thus, if you already have a scheme that mentally represents your knowledge of dogs, you may label this new beast "doggie." Through assimilation we deal with the environment in our own terms, sometimes bending the world to squeeze it into our existing categories. Throughout the life span we rely on our existing cognitive structures to understand new events.

But what if you notice that this "doggie" is bigger than most dogs and has a mane and an awfully odd "bark"? You may then be prompted to change your understanding of the world of four-legged animals. **Accommodation** is the process of modifying existing schemes to better fit new experiences. Perhaps you will need to invent a new name for this horse or ask your mother what it is and revise your concept of four-legged animals accordingly.

If we always assimilated new experiences, our understandings would never advance. Piaget believed that all new experiences are greeted with a mix of assimilation and accommodation. Once we have schemes, we apply them to make sense of the world, but we also encounter puzzles that force us to modify our understandings through accommodation. According to Piaget, when new events seriously challenge old schemes, or prove our existing understandings to be inadequate, we experience cognitive conflict. This cognitive "disequilibrium" then stimulates cognitive growth and the formation of more adequate understandings (Piaget, 1985).

Intelligence, then, develops through the *interaction of the individual with the environment.* Piaget takes an interactionist position on the nature/nurture issue that has come to be called **constructivism.** He believes that children "construct reality," or actively create knowledge of the world, from their experiences. They are neither born with innate ideas nor programmed with knowledge by adults.

In sum, Piaget views human beings as active creators of their own intellectual development. Their knowledge of the world, which takes the form of cognitive structures or schemes, changes as they organize and reorganize their existing knowledge and adapt to new experiences through the complementary processes of assimilation and accommodation. Through the interaction of biological maturation and experience, all normal human beings progress through four distinct stages of cognitive development:

1. the *sensorimotor* stage (birth to 2 years)
2. the *preoperational* stage (2 to 7 years)
3. the stage of *concrete operations* (7 to 11 years)
4. the stage of *formal operations* (11 years or later and beyond)

These stages represent qualitatively different ways of thinking and occur in an *invariant sequence*—that is, in the same order in all children. However, depending on their experiences, children may progress through the stages rapidly or slowly; the age ranges associated with the stages are only averages.

THE INFANT

Piaget's **sensorimotor stage**, spanning the two years of infancy, involves coming to know the world through one's senses and actions. The dominant cognitive structures are *behavioral schemes*—patterns of action that evolve as infants begin to coordinate sensory input and motor responses (for example, by seeing and then grasping what is seen). Because infants solve problems through their actions rather than in their heads, their mode of thought is qualitatively different from that of older children.

Substages of the Sensorimotor Stage

At the start of the sensorimotor period, infants do not seem very intelligent, but we see increasing signs of intelligent behavior as they pass through the six substages of this stage. Infants are transformed from *reflexive* creatures who do not seem capable of deliberate actions to *reflective* ones who can plan solutions to simple problems and carry them out.

Substage 1: Reflexive Activity (Birth to 1 Month)

During the first month of life, infants actively exercise and refine their innate reflexes such as sucking and grasping. New objects are assimilated to reflexive schemes; for example, the baby who initially sucks only nipples begins to suck blankets, fingers, and toys. The sucking reflex is altered in subtle ways as the infant accommodates it to different objects. Granted, this is not high intellect, but these primitive adaptations represent the beginning of cognitive growth.

Substage 2: Primary Circular Reactions (1 to 4 Months)

Increasingly, the infant seeks pleasurable stimulation. **Primary circular reactions** are pleasurable actions, centered on the infant's own body, that are discovered by chance and performed over and over. Piaget's son, Laurent, brought his thumb to his mouth and sucked, apparently found it satisfying, and formed a habit of doing it. Repeatedly kicking one's legs or blowing bubbles is also a primary circular reaction—primary because it involves the body, circular because the pleasure it brings stimulates its repetition. Notice that the infant is actively exercising behavioral schemes and making things happen.

Substage 3: Secondary Circular Reactions (4 to 8 Months)

Secondary circular reactions are like primary circular reactions, except that they are centered on objects and events in the external environment. An infant may, for example, discover that a shake of the hand grasping a rattle results in an interesting noise. The shaking action is then repeated over and over. Although this behavior seems intentional, Piaget argued that it is not. There was no purposeful goal of making noise when the action was first performed; an interesting outcome just happened to occur.

Substage 4: Coordination of Secondary Schemes (8 to 12 Months)

True intentional behavior is seen when the infant can coordinate previously unrelated acts so that one serves as a *means* to achieving another. At 9 months of age, for example, Piaget's son, Laurent, was able to use a lifting scheme as the means for using his familiar grasping scheme: He lifted a cushion and then grasped the cigar case beneath it with his other hand (Piaget, 1952). It was evident to Piaget that the lifting action was intentional—that it served as a means to an end.

Substage 5: Tertiary Circular Reactions (12 to 18 Months)

Notice that infants are gradually learning a great deal about the effects of their actions on the world. In Substage 5 the infant blossoms as a curious investigator of cause-and-effect relationships. **Tertiary circular reactions** involve devising *new* means of acting on objects to produce interesting results. The Substage-3 infant may find it satisfying to repeatedly squeeze a rubber duck to produce a quack (a secondary circular reaction). The Substage-5 infant may explore novel means to the same end: What happens if I step on the duck, or drop it, or bang it with my fist? What if I squeeze gently instead of firmly? Such tertiary circular reactions are trial-and-error schemes

One-year-olds in the stage of tertiary circular reactions delight in making their toys respond in new and interesting ways.

TABLE 7.1 Summary of the substages and intellectual accomplishments of the sensorimotor period.

Substage	*Ways of Adapting*	*Object Concept*
1. Reflex activity (0–1 month)	Exercise and accommodation of inborn reflexes	Tracks moving object but ignores its disappearance
2. Primary circular reactions (1–4 months)	Repetition of interesting acts centered on one's own body	Looks intently at the spot where an object disappeared
3. Secondary circular reactions (4–8 months)	Repetition of interesting acts on external objects	Searches for partly concealed object
4. Coordination of secondary schemes (8–12 months)	Combining of actions to solve simple problems (first evidence of intentionality)	Searches for and finds concealed object, but may err by searching site of last success
5. Tertiary circular reactions (12–18 months)	Experimentation to find new ways to solve problems or produce interesting outcomes	Searches for and finds object where it was last seen
6. Beginning of thought (18–24 months)	First evidence of insight; can solve problems mentally, using symbols	Object concept is complete; searches for and finds objects that have been hidden through *invisible* displacements

that reflect an active curiosity about the way the world works. Parents may be less than thrilled by this exciting cognitive advance when their infant explores new ways to drop food off the highchair tray!

Substage 6: Beginning of Thought (18 Months to 2 Years)

The crowning achievement of the sensorimotor stage involves internalizing behavioral schemes to construct mental symbols, or images, that can then guide future behavior. Now the infant can experiment *mentally* and may therefore show a kind of "insight" into how to solve a problem. For example, Piaget (1952) placed a bread crust out of reach on a table and laid a stick nearby to challenge his son, Laurent. Laurent was about to give up on reaching the bread, but then he "again looks at the bread, and without moving, looks very briefly at the stick, then suddenly grasps it and directs it toward the bread" (p. 335). This was not trial-and-error experimentation; Laurent's "problem solving" occurred at an internal, symbolic level as he perhaps visualized the stick being used to obtain the distant bread. This new **symbolic capacity**—the ability to use images, words, or gestures to represent or stand for objects and experiences—will show itself not only in more sophisticated problem solving but also in the language explosion and the enjoyment of pretend play that are so evident in the preschool years.

The advances in problem-solving ability reflected in the six substages of the sensorimotor period bring with them other important changes. Consider the quality of infants' play activities. They are not really interested in manipulating toys until the substage of secondary circular reactions (4 to 8 months), when they may repeat an action like sucking or banging a toy over and over. When they reach the substage of tertiary circular reactions (12 to 18 months), they experiment in varied ways with toys, exploring them thoroughly and learning all about their properties. Reaching the final substage, the beginning of thought, opens up the possibility of letting one object represent or stand for another, so that a cooking pot can become a hat, or a shoe can become a telephone. Such **symbolic play** (or pretend play) flourishes once infants acquire the capacity for representational thought. It is also in this stage, according to Piaget, that infants can imitate models who are no longer present, mainly because the infants can now create and later recall mental representations of what they have seen.

Table 7.1 summarizes the six substages of the sensorimotor period and also indicates parallel developments in the understanding that objects exist even when the infant is not experiencing them (the topic to which we turn next).

The Development of Object Permanence

According to Piaget, infants are born lacking the concept of **object permanence.** This is the very fundamental understanding that objects continue to exist when they are no longer visible or otherwise detectable to the senses. It probably doesn't occur to you to wonder whether your coat is still in the closet after you shut the closet door (unless perhaps you have taken a philosophy course). But very young infants, because they rely so heavily on their senses, seem to operate as though objects exist only when they are perceived or acted on. According to Piaget, the infant must "construct" the notion that reality exists apart from one's experience of it.

Piaget believed that the concept of object permanence develops gradually over the entire sensorimotor period. Up through Substage 3, or roughly 4–8 months, infants will not search for a toy that has been fully covered by a cloth. In Substage 4 they master that trick but still rely very much on their perceptions and actions to "know" an object (Piaget, 1954). After his 10-month-old daughter, Jacqueline, had repeatedly retrieved a toy parrot from one hiding place, Piaget put it in a new spot while she watched him. Amazingly, she looked in the original hiding place. She seemed to assume that her behavior determined where the object would appear; she did not treat the object as if it existed apart from her own actions. This tendency of 8- to 12-month-olds to search for an object in the place where they last had success finding it is called the ***A*, not *B*, error.**

In Substage 5 the young 1-year-old overcomes this error but continues to have trouble with invisible displacements—as when you hide a toy in your hand, move your hand under a pillow, and remove the hand. The infant will search where the object was last seen, seeming confused when it is not in your hand and failing to look under the pillow where it was deposited. Finally, by Substage 6 the infant is capable of *mentally representing* such invisible moves and conceiving of the object in its final location. According to Piaget, the concept of object permanence is fully mastered at this point. However, recent research suggests that infants may develop at least some understandings of object permanence far earlier than Piaget claimed (see Box 7.1).

All in all, children's intellectual achievements during the sensorimotor period are truly remarkable. By its end, they have become planful thinkers who can solve some problems in their heads and who have developed not only object permanence but many other concepts as well.

THE CHILD

No one has done more to make us aware of the surprising turns that children's minds can take than Jean Piaget, who described how children enter the preoperational

BOX 7.1 Hiding Games: Early Understanding of Object Permanence

Are very young infants really as bound to their perceptions as Piaget believed? Do they really fail to grasp that objects exist even when they are out of sight? Some researchers doubt it, and their studies echo a theme that is heard in much of the research inspired by Piaget: Young infants seem to be more competent than Piaget believed.

Thomas Bower (1982) suggested that the young infants tested by Piaget had failed to demonstrate object permanence merely because Piaget equated searching for an object with understanding that it still exists. So, Bower had infants aged 1 to 4 months watch as a screen blocked a toy from view. A few seconds later the screen was removed, revealing either the toy or an empty space where the toy had been. If these infants did not realize that the toy still existed once it was hidden from view, they should have been surprised when it was still there. Instead, they were puzzled when the toy was *not* there. Research now tell us that infants have a basic understanding of object permanence by 3 or 4 months of age—long before they are capable of searching for and finding hidden objects—and that Piaget therefore underestimated their understanding (Baillargeon & DeVos, 1991).

Similarly, recent research suggests that 8-month-olds who make the "*A*, not *B*, error," looking for an object where they last found it rather than in its new hiding place, may know more than their seemingly misguided searching behavior reveals. Renee Baillargeon and Marcia Graber (1988) had 8-month-old infants watch as screens were moved in front of two placemats, one of which had an interesting object sitting on it (see figure to the right). After a 15-second delay a hand appeared and retrieved the object from either the place where it had been hidden (the "possible event") or the other location (the "impossible event").

Were infants surprised to see the object snatched from a place that was empty before the screens were put in place? Indeed they were, as evidenced by their tendency to look longer at the seemingly impossible event than at the possible event. This and other evidence suggests that infants who err in object permanence tasks by searching in spot A (the site of previous success) rather than in spot B (a new hiding location) can remember, at least for several seconds, that the object is now in B. However, they may not yet be able to act appropriately on this knowledge by searching in B (Baillargeon & Graber, 1988; Diamond, 1985). This may be because they cannot inhibit a tendency to reach for the spot they last searched. Indeed, Adele Diamond (1985) has observed that some of the infants who reach for spot A hardly look there, as though they know it is not the right place to be looking but cannot stop themselves.

In sum, it seems that babies sometimes know a good deal more about object permanence than they reveal through their actions when they are given the kinds of search tasks Piaget devised. Gradually they become more skilled at acting on their knowledge and searching in the right spot, so that by the end of the sensorimotor period they are masters of even very complex "hide and seek" games (Wishart & Bower, 1985).

stage of cognitive development in their preschool years and progress to the concrete-operational stage as they enter their elementary school years.

The Preschool Child: Piaget's Preoperational Stage

The **preoperational stage** of cognitive development extends from roughly 2 to 7 years of age. Recall that the sensorimotor stage ended with the emergence of the symbolic capacity. This capacity runs wild in the preschool years and is the greatest cognitive strength of the preschooler compared to the infant. Imagine the possibilities: The child can now use words to refer to things, people, and events that are not physically present. Instead of being trapped in the immediate present, the child can refer to both past and future. Pretend or fantasy play flourishes at this age; blocks can stand for telephones, cardboard boxes for trains. Some children even invent imaginary friends and elaborate make-believe worlds. Although parents may worry about such flights of fancy, imaginative uses of the symbolic capacity contribute to both cognitive and social development (as we'll see in Chapter 15).

Yet the young child's mind is limited compared to that of an older child, and it was the limitations of preoperational thinking that Piaget explored most thoroughly. Preschoolers are freer of the immediate present than infants, but they are still highly influenced by their perceptions and thus easily fooled by appearances. We can best illustrate this reliance on perceptions by considering Piaget's classic tests of conservation.

Lack of Conservation

One of the many understandings about the physical world that children must develop is the concept of **conservation,** the idea that certain properties of an object or substance do not change when its appearance is altered in some superficial way. So, find yourself a 4- or 5-year-old and try Piaget's conservation-of-liquid-quantity task. Pour equal amounts of water into two identical glasses, and get the child to agree that they have the "same amount of water to drink." Then, *as the child watches,* pour the water from one

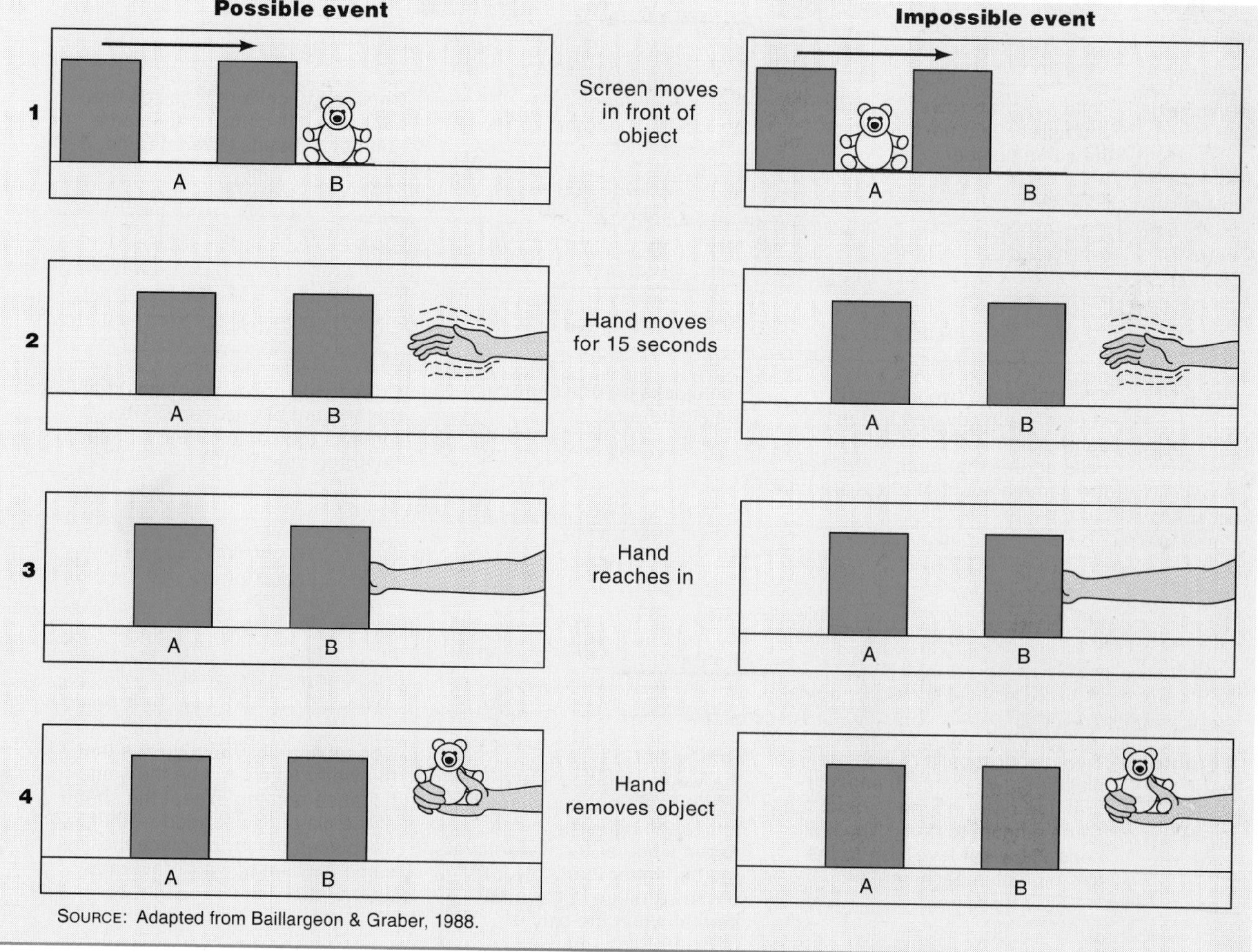

SOURCE: Adapted from Baillargeon & Graber, 1988.

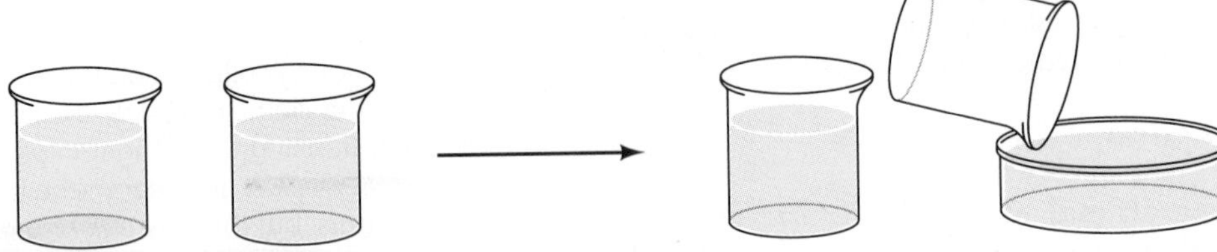

Liquids: Two identical beakers are filled to the same level, and the child agrees that they have the same amount to drink.

Contents of one beaker are poured into a different-shaped beaker so that the two columns of water are of unequal height.

Conserving child recognizes that each beaker has the same amount to drink (on the average, conservation of liquids is attained at age 6–7 years).

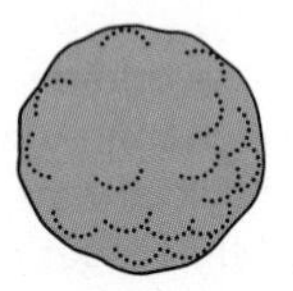
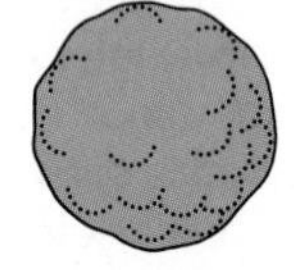
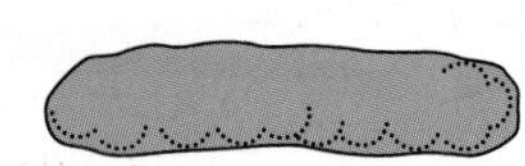
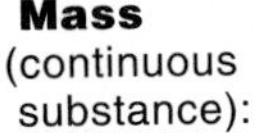

Mass (continuous substance): Two identical balls of playdough are presented. The child agrees that they have equal amounts of dough.

One ball is rolled into the shape of a sausage.

Conserving child recognizes that each object contains the same amount of dough (average age, 6–7).

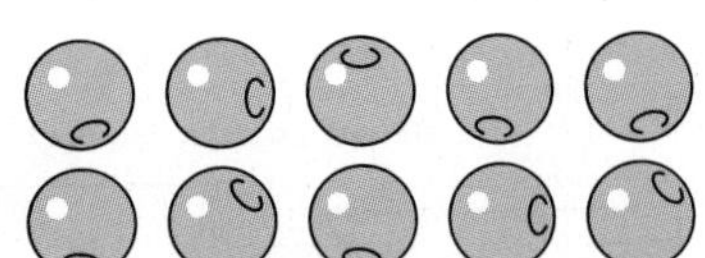
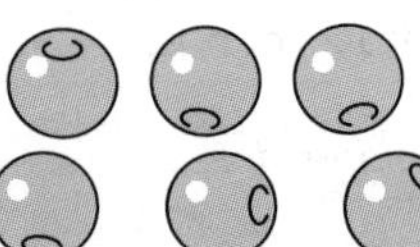

Number: Child sees two rows of beads and agrees that each row has the same number.

One row of beads is increased in length.

Conserving child recognizes that each row still contains the same number of beads (average age, 6–7).

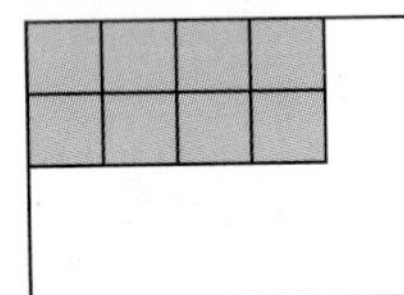
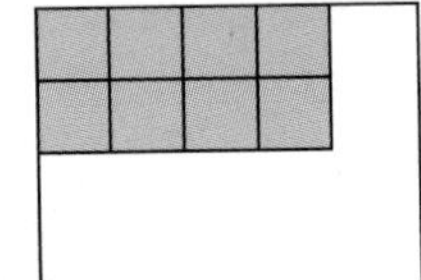
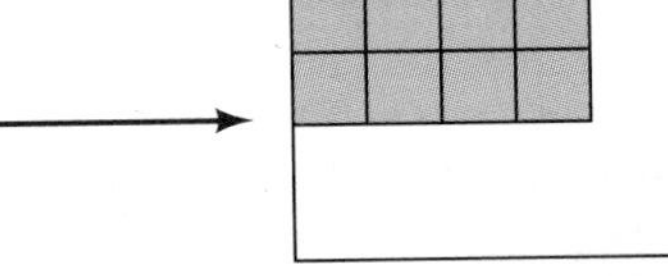
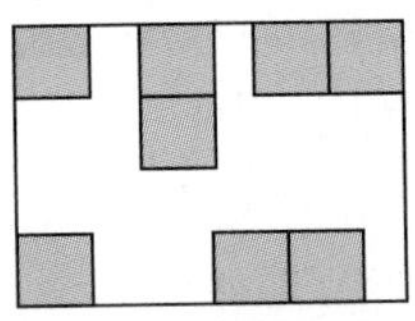

Area: The child sees two identical sheets, each covered by the same number of blocks. The child agrees that each sheet has the same amount of uncovered area.

The blocks on one sheet are scattered.

Conserving child recognizes that the amount of uncovered area remains the same for each sheet (average age, 9–10).

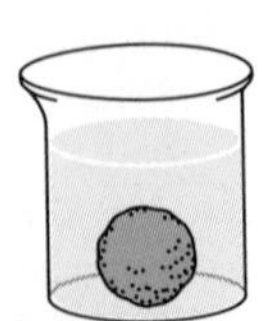

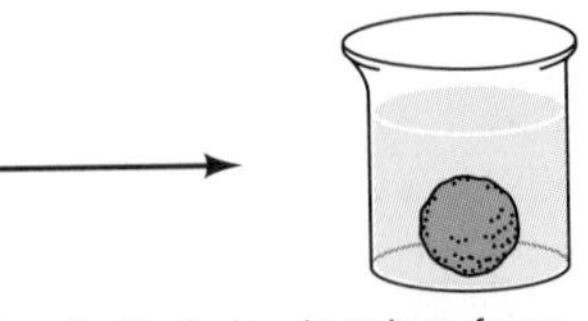

Volume (water displacement): Two identical balls of clay are placed in two identical beakers that had been judged to have the same amount to drink. The child sees the water level rise to the same point in each beaker.

One ball of clay is taken from the water, molded into a different shape, and placed above the beaker. Child is asked whether the water level will be higher than, lower than, or the same as in the other beaker when the clay is reinserted into the water.

Conserving child recognizes that the water levels will be the same because nothing except the shape of the clay has changed — that is, the pieces of clay displace the same amount of water (average age, 9–12).

FIGURE 7.1 Some common tests of the child's ability to conserve.

glass into a shorter, wider glass. Now ask whether the two containers—the tall, narrow glass or the shorter, broader one—have the same amount of water to drink or whether one has more water. Children younger than 6 or 7 will usually say that the taller glass has more water than the shorter one (see Figure 7.1). Thus they lack the understanding that the volume of liquid is *conserved* despite the change in the shape it takes in different containers.

How can preschoolers be so easily fooled by appearances? According to Piaget, the preschooler is unable to engage in **decentration,** the ability to focus on two or more dimensions of a problem at one time. Consider the conservation task: The child must focus on height and width simultaneously and recognize that the increased width of the short, broad container compensates for its lesser height. Preoperational thinkers engage in **centration**—the tendency to center on a single aspect of the problem. They focus on height alone and conclude that the taller glass has more liquid; or, alternatively, they focus on width and conclude that the short, wide glass has more. In other ways as well, preschoolers seem to have one-track minds. They may have trouble, for example, understanding that you can love and be angry at someone at the same time (Harter, 1982).

A second contributor to success on conservation tasks is **reversibility**, the process of mentally undoing or reversing an action. Older children often display mastery of reversibility by suggesting that the water be poured back into its original container to prove that it is still the same amount. The young child shows *irreversibility* of thinking and may insist that the water would overflow the glass if it were poured back.

Finally, preoperational thinkers fail to demonstrate conservation because they have trouble conceptualizing *transformations*, or processes of change from one state to another, as when water is poured from one glass to another (see Figure 7.2). As a result, preoperational thinking is sometimes called *static thought*.

Preoperational children do not understand the concept of conservation, then, because they engage in centration, irreversible thought, and static thought. The older child, in the stage of concrete operations, has mastered decentration, reversibility, and transformational thought. The correct answer to the conservation task is now a matter of logic; there is no longer a need to rely on perceptions as one's guide. Indeed, a 9-year-old tested by one of our students grasped the logic so well and thought the question of which glass had more water so stupid that she asked "Is *this* what you do in college?!"

Egocentrism

Piaget believed that preoperational thought also involves **egocentrism**—a tendency to view the world solely from one's own perspective and to have difficulty recognizing other points of view. For example, he asked children to indicate what a display of three mountains would look like from several different vantage points. Young children often chose the view from their own position (Piaget & Inhelder, 1956). Similarly, young children often assume that, if they know something, other people do too (Ruffman & Olson, 1989). The same holds for desires: The 4-year-old who wants to go to McDonald's for dinner may say that Mom and Dad want to go to McDonald's too, despite the fact that Mom's on a diet and Dad prefers Pizza Hut.

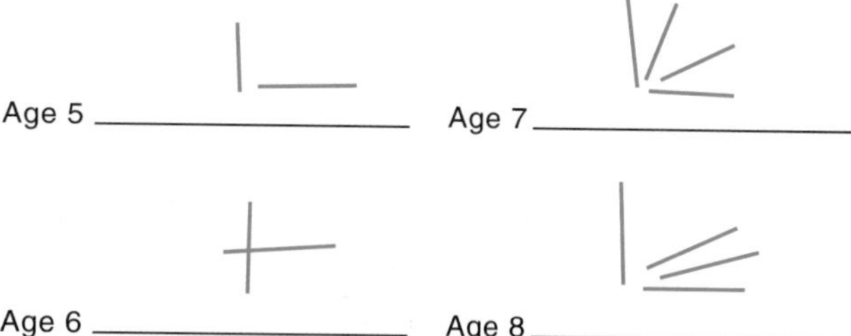

FIGURE 7.2 Preoperational thought is static. Slowly and repeatedly drop a pencil in front of a preschooler, and then ask the child to draw the falling of the pencil (or give the child a number of strips of paper to be arranged to show the falling of the pencil). Preoperational thinkers (the 5- and 6-year-olds) generally show you the before and after but nothing in between. Older children are better able to conceptualize transformations like the falling of the pencil.

Difficulty with Classification

The limitations of relying on perceptions and intuitions are also apparent when preoperational children are asked to classify objects and think about classification systems. When 2- or 3-year-old children are asked to sort objects on the basis of similarities, they make interesting designs or change their sorting criteria from moment to moment. Older preoperational children can group objects systematically on the basis of shape, color, function, or some other dimension of similarity (Inhelder & Piaget, 1964). However, even children aged 4 to 7 have trouble thinking about relations between classes and subclasses, or wholes and parts. Given a set of wooden beads, most of which are brown but a few of which are white, preoperational children do fine when they are asked if all the beads are wooden and if there are more brown beads than white beads. That is, they can conceive of the whole class (wooden beads) or of the two subclasses (brown and white beads). However, when the question is "Which would make the longer necklace, the brown beads or the wooden beads?" they usually say "The brown beads." They cannot *simultaneously* relate the whole class to its parts; they lack what Piaget termed the concept of **class inclusion,** or the logical understanding that the parts are included within the whole. Notice that the child *centers* on the most striking perceptual feature of the problem—the fact that brown beads are more numerous than white ones—again being fooled by appearances.

Did Piaget Underestimate the Preoperational Child?

Are preschool children really as illogical and egocentric as Piaget proposed? Actually, Piaget recognized that older preschool children are making important progress toward logical thought (see Davidson, 1992). True, 2- to 4-year-olds were said to be in a *preconceptual period* and were described as quite illogical in most ways. However, 4-year-olds were said to have entered an *intuitive period*; less egocentric and perception-bound than younger children, they have many sound intuitions about the world and simply lack the ability to justify these intuitions on logical grounds. But, despite Piaget's descriptions of this intuitive period within the preoperational stage, many developmentalists believe that Piaget seriously underestimated the competencies of preschool children by giving them very complex tasks to perform. Consider a few examples of the strengths uncovered by researchers using simpler tasks.

Rochel Gelman (1972) simplified Piaget's conservation-of-number task (which was shown in Figure 7.1) and discovered that children as young as 3 have some grasp of the concept that number remains the same even when items are rearranged spatially. She first got children to focus their attention on number by playing a game in which two plates, one with two toy mice and one with three toy mice, were presented; the plate with the larger number was always declared the "winner." Then Gelman started introducing changes, sometimes adding or subtracting mice but sometimes just bunching up or spreading out the mice. Young children were not fooled by spatial rearrangements; they seemed to understand that number remained the same. However, they showed their limitations when they were given larger sets of numbers that they could not count.

Similarly, several researchers have demonstrated, by reducing tasks to the bare essentials, that preschool children are not as egocentric as Piaget claimed. In one study, 3-year-olds were shown a card with a dog on one side and a cat on the other (Flavell, Everett, Croft, & Flavell, 1981). The card was held vertically between the child (who could see the dog) and the experimenter (who could see the cat). When children were asked what the experimenter could see, these 3-year-olds performed flawlessly. In another study, 2½- to 5-year-olds were introduced to a puppet named Tony, shown how he could hide a "treasure" under one of four containers, given a chance to find the treasure by following the white footprints Tony left, and shown that the telltale footprints could be erased with a sponge (Chandler, Fritz, & Hala, 1989). When given a chance to help Tony hide the treasure so that a second player seated outside the room would not be able to find it, even 2½-year-olds delighted in misleading the second child. They destroyed Tony's footprints after the treasure had been hidden, laid down false trails of footprints, and blatantly lied by directing the second player to containers they knew to be empty. In short, these young preschoolers attempted to create false beliefs in another child and, in the process, revealed a keen awareness that other people do not necessarily share their own knowledge and beliefs (see also Hala, Chandler, & Fritz, 1991; Lewis & Osborne, 1990).

Finally, preschool children seem to have a good deal more understanding of classification systems than Piaget believed (Markman, 1989; Taylor & Gelman, 1989; Waxman & Hatch, 1992). Sandra Waxman and Thomas Hatch (1992) asked 3- and 4-year-olds to teach a puppet all the different names they could think of for certain animals, plants, articles of clothing, and pieces of furniture. The goal was to see if children knew terms associated with familiar classification hierarchies—for example, if they knew that a rose is a type of flower and is also a member of the larger category of plants. Children performed quite well, largely because a clever method of prompting responses was used. Depending on which term(s) the child forgot to mention (rose, flower, or plant), he or she was asked (about the rose): "Is this a dandelion?" "Is this a tree?" "Is this an animal?" Very often children came up with the proper terms in response (for example, "No, silly, [it's not an animal] it's a plant!"). If children had merely been asked "Is it a plant?" they might very well have said "No, it's a flower," and been judged ignorant of the plant classification hierarchy. Even though young children typically fail the tests of class inclusion that Piaget devised, then, they appear to have a fairly good grasp of familiar classification hierarchies.

Studies like these have raised important questions about the adequacy of Piaget's theory and have led to a more careful consideration of the demands placed on children by cognitive assessment tasks. Simplified tasks that focus youngsters' attention on relevant aspects of the task and do not place heavy demands on their memories or verbal skills tend to reveal that young children develop sound understandings of the physical world earlier than Piaget thought. Yet Piaget was right in arguing that preschool children are more intuitive, egocentric, and illogical than elementary school children are. Preschool children still seem to have difficulty grasping the logic behind concepts such as conservation, and they have difficulty applying their emerging understandings consistently to a wide range of tasks, especially to complex tasks that demand some mental gymnastics.

The School-Aged Child: Piaget's Stage of Concrete Operations

About the time children start elementary school, their minds undergo a transformation. Piaget's third stage of cognitive development extends from roughly 7 to 11 or more years of age. The **concrete operations stage** involves mastering the **logical operations** that were missing in the preoperational stage—that is, becoming able to perform *mental* actions on objects, such as mentally adding and subtracting Halloween candies, classifying dinosaurs, or ordering dolls from largest to smallest. For every limitation of the preoperational child, we can see a corresponding strength of the concrete-operational child.

Conservation

Given the conservation-of-liquid task (Figure 7.1), the preoperational child centers on either the height or the width of the glasses, ignoring the other dimension. The concrete-operational child can *decenter* and juggle two dimensions at once. *Reversibility* now allows the child to mentally reverse the pouring process and imagine the water in its original container. *Transformational thought* allows the child to better understand the process of change involved in pouring the water. Overall, armed with logical operations, the child now *knows* that there must be the same amount of water after it is poured into a different container; he or she has logic, not just appearances, as a guide.

Looking back at the conservation tasks in Figure 7.1, you will notice that some forms of conservation (for example, mass and number) are understood years earlier than others (area or volume). Piaget maintained that operational abilities evolve in a predictable order as simple skills that appear early are reorganized into increasingly complex skills. Some studies support Piaget's view (Tomlinson-Keasey et al., 1979), but others challenge his notion that different concrete-operational skills are mastered in the same predictable order by all children (Case, 1985; Kuhn, 1992).

Relational Logic and Transitivity

To appreciate the nature and power of logical operations, consider the child's ability to think about relative size. A preoperational child given a set of sticks of different lengths and asked to arrange them in order from biggest to smallest is likely to struggle along, awkwardly comparing one pair of sticks at a time. Concrete-operational children are capable of the logical operation of **seriation,** which enables them to arrange items *mentally* along a quantifiable dimension such as length or weight. Thus they perform this seriating task quickly and correctly.

Concrete-operational thinkers also master the related concept of **transitivity**, which describes the necessary relations among elements in a series. If, for example, John is taller than Mark, and Mark is taller than Sam, who is taller—John or Sam? It follows *logically* that John must be taller than Sam, and the concrete operator grasps the transitivity of these size relationships (see Figure 7.3). Lacking the concept of

Question	**Answer**
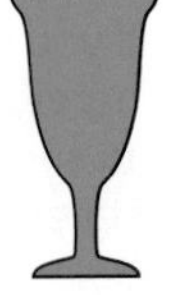  1. Show one pair of items: Which is taller, the red vase or the pink vase?	The red vase is taller than the pink vase.
 2. Show second pair of items: Which is taller, the pink vase or the gray vase?	The pink vase is taller than the gray vase.
3. Show nothing: Which is taller, the red vase or the gray vase?	Therefore, the red vase *must* be taller than the gray vase.

FIGURE 7.3 A transitivity problem. In Step 3 the concrete-operational child recognizes the logical necessity of the conclusion that the red vase is taller than the gray vase. The preoperational child may want to see the two vases next to each other before answering.

transitivity, the preoperational child will need to rely on perceptions to answer the question; he or she may insist that John and Sam stand next to each other in order to determine who is taller. Preoperational children probably have a better understanding of such transitive relations than Piaget gave them credit for (Gelman, 1978; Trabasso, 1975), but they still have difficulty grasping the logical necessity of transitivity (Chapman & Lindenberger, 1988).

Other Advances in Cognition

The school-aged child overcomes much of the egocentrism of the preoperational period, becoming better and better at adopting other people's perspectives. Classification abilities improve as the child comes to grasp the concept of *class inclusion* and can bear in mind that subclasses (brown beads + white beads) are included in a whole class (wooden beads). Mastery of mathematical operations improves the child's ability to solve arithmetic problems and results in an interest in measuring and counting things precisely (or even fury if companions don't keep accurate score in games). Overall, school-aged children appear more logical than preschoolers because they now possess a powerful arsenal of "actions in the head."

But surely, if Piaget proposed a fourth stage of cognitive development, there must be some limitations to concrete operations. Indeed there are. This mode of thought is applied to objects, situations, and events that are real or readily imaginable (thus the term *concrete* operations). As we'll see later, concrete operators have difficulty thinking about abstract ideas and hypothetical propositions that have no basis in reality.

THE ADOLESCENT

Although tremendous advances in cognition occur from infancy to the end of childhood, still other transformations of the mind are in store for the adolescent. If teenagers become introspective, question their parents' authority, dream of perfect worlds, and contemplate their futures, cognitive development may help explain why.

The Formal Operations Stage of Cognitive Development

Piaget set the beginning of the **formal operations stage** of cognitive development at age 11 or 12, or possibly later. Recall that concrete operations are mental actions on *objects* (tangible things and events), as when an individual mentally classifies animals into categories. Formal operations are mental actions on *ideas*. Thus the adolescent who acquires formal operations can mentally juggle and think logically about ideas that cannot be seen, heard, tasted, smelled, or touched. In other words, formal-operational thought is more hypothetical and abstract than concrete-operational thought; it also involves more systematic and scientific approaches to problem solving (Keating, 1980).

Hypothetical and Abstract Thinking

If you could have a third eye and put it anywhere on your body, where would you put it, and why? That question was posed to 9-year-old fourth-graders (i.e., concrete operators) and to 11- to 12-year-old sixth-graders (the age when the first signs of formal operations often appear). In their drawings, all the 9-year-olds placed the third eye on their foreheads between their existing eyes; many thought the exercise was "stupid." The 11- and 12-year-olds were not as bound by the realities of eye location. They could invent ideas that were contrary to fact (for example, the idea of an eye in one's palm) and think logically about the implications of such ideas (see Figure 7.4). Thus, concrete operators deal with realities, whereas formal operators can deal with *possibilities*, including those that contradict known reality. This may be one reason why adolescents come to appreciate absurd humor, as we see in Box 7.2.

Formal-operational thought is also more abstract than concrete-operational thought. The school-aged child might define the justice system in terms of police and judges; the adolescent might define it more abstractly as a branch of government concerned with balancing the rights of different interests in society. Also, the school-aged child might be able to think logically about concrete and factually true statements, as in this syllogism: If you drink poison, you will die. Fred drank poison. Therefore, Fred will die. The adolescent can engage in such if–then thinking about either contrary-to-fact statements ("If you drink milk, you will die") or symbols (If *P*, then *Q*. *P*. Therefore, *Q*).

Problem-Solving Strategies

Formal operations also permit systematic and scientific thinking about problems. One of Piaget's famous tests for formal-operational thinking is the pendulum task. The child is given a number of weights that can be tied to a string to make a pendulum and is told that he or she may vary the length of the string, the amount of weight attached to it, and the height from which the weight is released in order to find out which of these factors alone or in combination determines how quickly the pendulum makes its arc. How would you go about solving this problem?

The concrete operator is likely to jump right in without much advanced planning, using a *trial-and-error* approach. That is, the child may try a variety of things but fail to test out different hypotheses systematically—for example, the hypothesis that, the shorter

FIGURE 7.4 Where would you put a third eye? Tanya (age 9) did not show much inventiveness in drawing her "third eye." But Ken (age 11) said of his eye on top of a tuft of hair: "I could revolve the eye to look in all directions." John (also 11) wanted a third eye in his palm: "I could see around corners and see what kind of cookie I'll get out of the cookie jar." Ken and John show early signs of formal-operational thought.

the string is, the faster the pendulum swings, all other factors remaining constant. Concrete operators are therefore unlikely to solve the problem. What they *can* do is draw proper conclusions from their observations—for example, from watching as someone else demonstrates what happens if a pendulum with a short string is compared to a pendulum with a long string.

What will the formal-operational individual do? In all likelihood, he or she will first sit and think, or *plan* an overall strategy for solving the problem. To begin with, *all* the possible hypotheses should be generated; after all, the one that is overlooked may be the right one. Then it must be determined how each hypothesis can be tested. This is a matter of **hypothetical-deductive reasoning,** or reasoning from general ideas to their specific implications. In the pendulum problem it means starting with a hypothesis and tracing the specific implications of this idea in an if–then fashion: "If the length of the string matters, then I should see a difference when I compare a long string to a short string while holding other factors constant." The trick in hypothesis testing is to vary each factor (for example, the length of the string) while holding all the others constant (the weight, the height from which the weight is dropped, and so on). (It is, by the way, the length of the string that matters; the shorter the string, the faster the swing.)

In summary, formal-operational thought involves being able to think systematically about hypothetical ideas and abstract concepts. It also involves mastering the hypothetical-deductive approach to problems that scientists use—forming many hypotheses and systematically testing them through an experimental method.

Progress toward Mastery of Formal Operations

Are 11- and 12-year-olds really capable of all these sophisticated mental activities? In most cases, no. Piaget (1970) himself described the transition from concrete operations to formal operations as taking place gradually over several years. Many researchers have found it useful to distinguish between early and late formal operations. For example, 11- to 13-year-olds just entering the formal operations stage are able to consider simple hypothetical propositions such as the three-eye problem. But most are not yet able to devise an overall game plan for solving a problem or to systematically generate and test hypotheses. These achievements are more likely later in adolescence.

Consider the findings of Suzanne Martorano (1977), who gave 80 girls in grades 6, 8, 10, and 12 a battery of ten Piagetian tasks. She included the pendulum problem in order to assess the ability to test hypotheses systematically. Other tasks included

BOX 7.2 Children's Humor and Cognitive Development

Where does the fish keep its money?

Answer: In the riverbank.

Do you remember going through a phase in early elementary school of telling terrible jokes like this one? A preschooler hearing this joke may laugh at the silly idea of a fish having money. But, if asked to rephrase the joke, the child is likely to say the answer was "In the bank." A child of this age misses the whole idea that the humor of the joke depends on the double meaning of "bank." Anything that looks or sounds silly may amuse preschoolers—calling a "shoe" a "floo" or a "poo," for example. Once children realize that everything has a correct name, mislabeling things becomes funny (McGhee, 1979).

With the onset of concrete-operational thought and advances in awareness of the nature of language, children come to appreciate jokes and riddles that involve linguistic ambiguities. The riverbank joke boils down to a classification task: There is a large category of banks, with at least two subclasses, financial institutions and the banks of streams. School-aged children who have mastered the concept of class inclusion can keep the class and subclasses in mind at once and move back and forth mentally between the two meanings of bank. Appreciation of such puns is high among second-graders (7- to 8-year-olds) and continues to grow until fourth or fifth grade (McGhee & Chapman, 1980; Yalisove, 1978).

Children's tastes in humor change again when they enter the stage of formal operations at about age 11 or 12 (Yalisove, 1978). Simple riddles and puns are no longer cognitively challenging enough, it seems, and are likely to elicit loud groans (McGhee, 1979). Adolescents do, however, appreciate jokes that involve an absurd or contrary-to-fact premise and a punchline that is quite logical if the absurd premise is accepted. The humor in "How do you fit six elephants into a Volkswagen?" depends on appreciating that "Three in the front and three in the back" is a perfectly logical answer only if one accepts the hypothetical premise that multiple elephants could fit into a small car (Yalisove, 1978). Reality-oriented school-aged children might simply judge this joke stupid; after all, elephants *can't* fit into cars. Clearly, then, children cannot appreciate certain forms of humor until they have the required cognitive abilities. Research on children's humor seems to suggest that children and adolescents are most attracted to jokes that challenge them intellectually by requiring them to use the cognitive skills they are just beginning to master (McGhee, 1979).

identifying all the possible combinations of chemicals that could produce a chemical reaction; figuring proportions in order to analyze how the behavior of a balance beam is affected by the heaviness of weights on the beam and their distances from the fulcrum, or center; and thinking about correlations between variables. The 6th- and 8th-graders (ages 11–12 and 13–14) passed only two or three of the ten tasks on the average, and the 10th- and 12th-graders (ages 15–16 and 17–18) passed an average of five or six. Thus even the 12th-graders did not consistently show formal operations across tasks; indeed, only 55% of them passed the pendulum problem, and they typically used concrete operations on some tasks and formal operations on others.

Progress toward mastery of formal operations is obviously slow, at least as measured by Piaget's scientific tasks. These findings have major implications for secondary school teachers, who are often trying to teach very abstract material to students with a wide range of thinking patterns. Teachers may need to give concrete thinkers extra aid by using specific examples and demonstrations to help clarify general principles. Even at the college level, many students have yet to gain a solid command of formal operations and may have a hard time learning potentially difficult subjects such as statistics (Hudak & Anderson, 1990).

Implications of Formal Thought

Formal-operational thought contributes to other changes in adolescence—some good, some not so good. First the good news: As we'll see in upcoming chapters, formal-operational thought may pave the way for gaining a sense of identity as an individual, thinking in more complex ways about moral issues, and understanding other people. Advances in cognitive development help to lay the groundwork for advances in many other areas of development.

Now the bad news: Formal operations may also be related to some of the more painful aspects of the adolescent experience. Children tend to accept the world as it is and to heed the words of authority figures. The adolescent armed with formal operations can think more independently, imagine alternatives to present realities, and raise questions about everything from why parents set down the rules they do to why there is injustice in the world. A sometimes-painful implication of formal operations is *confusion* bred of questioning. *Rebellion* is also more likely in the formal-operational period. The ability to detect logical inconsistencies and flaws in the world as it is may generate rebellious anger at parents or the government. In addition, some adolescents get carried away with *idealism*. They invent perfect worlds or envision perfectly logical solutions to problems they detect in the world around them, sometimes losing sight of practical considerations and real barriers to social change. Just as infants flaunt the new schemes they develop, adolescents may go overboard with their new cognitive skills, irritate their parents, and become frustrated when the world does not respond to their flawless logic.

One other potentially troubling change that may accompany formal operations is worth considering. David Elkind (1967) has proposed that formal-operational thought leads to **adolescent egocentrism,** a difficulty in properly differentiating one's own thoughts and feelings from those of other people. The young child's egocentrism is rooted in an unawareness that different people have different perspectives, but the adolescent's is rooted in an enhanced ability to reflect about one's own and others' thoughts. Elkind identified two types of adolescent egocentrism: the imaginary audience and the personal fable.

The **imaginary audience** phenomenon involves confusing your own thougthts with those of a hypothesized audience for your behavior. Thus the teenage girl who spills Pepsi on her dress at a party may feel extremely self-conscious: "They're all thinking what a slob I am! I wish I could crawl into a hole." She assumes that everyone else in the room is as preoccupied with the stain as she is. Or, a teenage boy may spend hours in front of the mirror getting ready for a date and then concern himself so much with how he imagines his date is reacting to him that he hardly notices her: "Why did I say that? . . . She looks bored. . . . Did she notice my pimple?" (She, of course, is equally preoccupied with how she is "playing" to her audience. No wonder teenagers are often awkward and painfully aware of their every slip on first dates!)

The second form of adolescent egocentrism is the **personal fable,** a tendency to think that you and your thoughts and feelings are unique or special (Elkind, 1967). If the imaginary audience is a product of the failure to differentiate between self and other, the personal fable is a product of differentiating too much. Thus the adolescent who is in love for the first time imagines that no one in the history of the human race has ever felt such heights of emotion. When the relationship breaks up, of course, no one—least of all a parent—could possibly understand the crushing agony. The personal fable may also lead adolescents to feel that rules that apply to others do not apply to them. Thus *they* won't be hurt if they speed down the highway without wearing a seatbelt or drive under the influence of alcohol. And *they* won't become pregnant if they engage in sex without contraception, so why bother with contraception (see Arnett, 1990)?

Elkind hypothesized that the imaginary audience and the personal fable phenomena should increase when formal operations are first being acquired and then decrease as adolescents get older, gain fuller control of formal operations, and assume adult roles

An adolescent may feel that everyone is as preoccupied with her appearance as she is, a form of adolescent egocentrism known as the imaginary audience phenomenon.

that require fuller consideration of others' perspectives. Indeed, both the self-consciousness associated with the imaginary audience and the sense of specialness associated with the personal fable are most evident in early adolescence and decline with age (Elkind & Bowen, 1979; Enright, Lapsley, & Shukla, 1979; Lechner & Rosenthal, 1984).

However, a clear relationship between the onset of formal operations and adolescent egocentrism is not always found (Gray & Hudson, 1984; O'Connor & Nikolic, 1990). Very possibly, adolescent egocentrism is more closely linked to the emergence of advanced social perspective-taking abilities that allow adolescents to contemplate how other people might perceive them and react to their behavior (Jahnke & Blanchard-Fields, 1993; Lapsley et al., 1986). The truth is that researchers have not yet figured out precisely why young adolescents often feel that the whole world is watching them or that not one person in the world can truly understand them. We can conclude, though, that the acquisition of formal operations brings with it both new competencies and new challenges.

THE ADULT

Do adults think any differently than adolescents do? Does cognition change over the adult years? Until recently, developmentalists have not asked such questions. After all, Piaget indicated that the highest stage of cognitive development, formal operations, was fully mastered by most people by age 15 to 18. Why bother studying cognitive development in adulthood? As it turns out, it has been well worth the effort. Research has revealed limitations in adult performance that must be explained, and it also suggests that at least some adults progress beyond formal operations, to more advanced forms of thought.

Limitations in Adult Cognitive Performance

If many high school students are shaky in their command of formal operations, do most of us gain fuller mastery after the high school years? Gains are indeed made between adolescence and adulthood (Blackburn & Papalia, 1992), but, still, only about half of all college students show firm and consistent mastery of formal operations on Piaget's scientific-reasoning tasks (Neimark, 1975). Similarly, sizable percentages of American adults do not solve scientific problems at the formal level, and there are some societies in which *no* adults solve formal-operational problems (Neimark, 1975).

Why don't more adults do well on Piagetian tasks? It does seem to take at least an average level of performance on standardized intelligence tests to reason at the formal level (Inhelder, 1966), but most college students meet this criterion. What seems more important than basic intelligence is formal education (Neimark, 1979); in cultures in which virtually no one solves Piaget's problems, people do not receive advanced schooling. But lack of formal education is not a problem for college students, either. Perhaps a better explanation is that thinking in a formal-operational way requires *expertise in a domain of knowledge.*

Piaget (1972) himself suggested that adults are likely to use formal operations in a field of expertise but to use concrete operations in less familiar areas. There is some support for this idea. For example, hunters in preliterate societies who fail Piagetian scientific-reasoning tasks will often reason at a formal level when tracking prey, perhaps because this is an important and well-learned activity (Tulkin & Konner, 1973). Or consider this finding: Richard De Lisi and Joanne Staudt (1980) gave three kinds of formal-operational tasks — the pendulum problem, a political problem, and a literary criticism problem — to college students majoring in physics, political science, and English. As Figure 7.5 illustrates, each group of majors did very well on the problem relevant to their field of expertise. On problems outside their fields, however, about half the students failed. Very possibly, many adolescents and adults fail to use formal reasoning on Piaget's scientific problems simply because these problems are unfamiliar to them (see also Ward & Overton, 1990).

As Kurt Fischer (1980; Fischer, Kenny, & Pipp, 1990) maintains, each person may have an optimal level of cognitive performance that will show itself in familiar and well-trained content domains. However, performance is likely to be highly inconsistent across content areas unless the person has had a chance to build knowledge and skills in all these domains. More often, adults may use and strengthen formal modes of thinking *only in their areas of expertise.* By adopting a contextual perspective on cognitive development, we can appreciate that the individual's experience and the nature of the tasks he or she is asked to perform

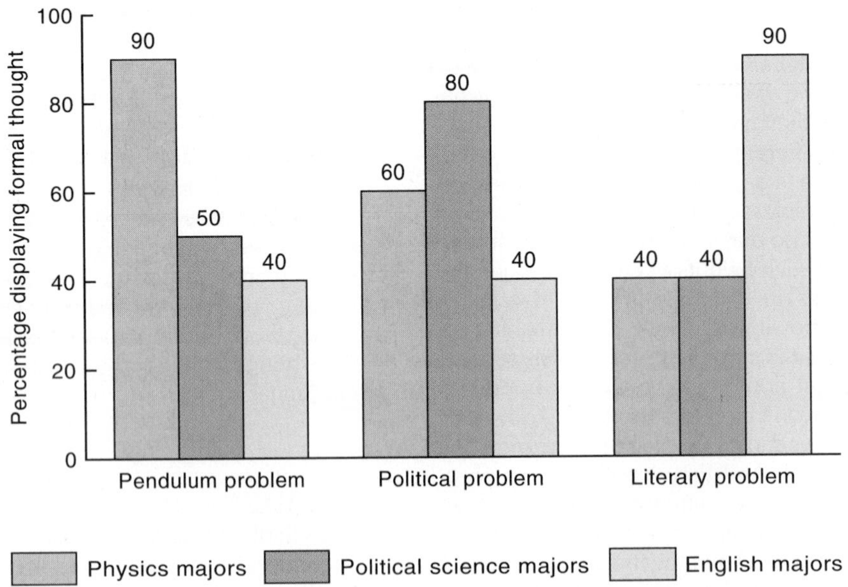

FIGURE 7.5 Expertise and formal operations. College students show the greatest command of formal-operational thought in the subject area most related to their major. (Data from De Lisi & Staudt, 1980.)

influence cognitive performance across the life span (Salthouse, 1990).

Growth beyond Formal Operations?

While some researchers have been asking why adults sometimes perform so poorly on cognitive tasks, others have been asking why certain adults sometimes perform so well. Take Piaget himself. Was his ability to generate a complex theory of development no more than the application of formal-operational thought? Or are there advances in cognitive development during adulthood that would better explain the remarkable cognitive achievements of some adults?

At this point there are several intriguing ideas about what may lie beyond formal operations—that is, about "postformal" modes of thought (see Commons, Richards, & Armon, 1984; Labouvie-Vief, 1992). First consider a rather negative profile of the adolescent who has attained formal operations. This adolescent—Wally, we'll call him—is carried away with his new powers of logical thinking. He does beautifully on a Piagetian problem in which everything is given in the problem and the only task is to generate logically possible solutions and identify the one correct one. But he insists that there is a logically correct answer for every question—that, if you simply apply logic, you'll arrive at absolute truths. Perhaps formal-operational adolescents like Wally are not fully equipped for a real world in which there are many ways to look at an issue and often no one right answer (Cavanaugh et al., 1985; Labouvie-Vief, 1992). Let's consider some of the ways in which adults may outperform adolescents cognitively.

Relativism in the college years. As one student said, "I am the type of person who would never tell anyone that their idea is wrong—if they searched, well, even if they hadn't searched, even if they just believed it—that's cool for them" (Kitchener & King, 1981, p. 96). Many of these students later decide that there are sound reasons for preferring some beliefs to others.

Relativistic Thinking

Several researchers have suggested that adults are more likely than adolescents to see knowledge as relative rather than absolute (Labouvie-Vief, 1984; Sinnott, 1989). **Relativistic thinking** in this sense means understanding that knowledge depends on the subjective perspective of the knower. An *absolutist* assumes that truth lies in the nature of reality and that there is only one truth; a *relativist* assumes that one's own starting assumptions influence the "truth" that is discovered and that there are multiple ways of viewing a problem.

Consider a logic problem given to preadolescents, adolescents, and adults by Gisela Labouvie-Vief and her colleagues (Labouvie-Vief, Adams, Hakim-Larson, & Hayden, 1983):

> John is known to be a heavy drinker, especially when he goes to parties. Mary, John's wife, warns him that if he gets drunk one more time she will leave him and take the children. Tonight John is out late at an office party. John comes home drunk [p. 5].

Does Mary leave John? Most preadolescents and many adolescents quickly and confidently said "yes." They did not question the assumption that Mary would stand by her word; they simply applied logic to the information they were given. Adults were more likely to realize that different starting assumptions were possible and that the answer depended on which assumptions were chosen. One woman, for example, noted that, if Mary had stayed with John for years, she would be unlikely to leave him now. This same woman said "There was no right or wrong answer. You could get logically to both answers" (p. 12).

In a study of cognitive growth over the college years, William Perry (1970) found that beginning college students often assumed that there were absolute, objective truths to be found if only they applied their minds or sought answers from their professors. As their college careers progressed, they often became frustrated in their search for absolute truths. They saw that many questions seemed to have a number of alternative answers, depending on the perspective of the answerer. Taking the extremely relativistic view that any opinion was as good as any other, several of these students said they weren't sure how they could ever decide what to believe. Eventually, many of them understood that some opinions can be better supported than others; they were then able to commit themselves to specific positions while being fully aware that they were choosing among relative perspectives. Between adolescence and adulthood, then, many people start out as absolutists, then become relativists, and finally are able to make commitments to positions despite their more sophisticated awareness of the nature and limits of knowledge (see also Kitchener & King, 1981; Kitchener et al., 1989; Labouvie-Vief, 1992).

Dialectical Thinking

Adults may also achieve advances in **dialectical thinking** (Basseches, 1984; Kramer, 1989; Riegel, 1973), which involves the ability to uncover and resolve contradictions between opposing ideas (recall Chapter 2's discussion of Klaus Riegel's dialectical perspective on development). Real-world issues like health-care reform and educational planning are filled with inconsistencies that may be ignored by formal-operational adolescents seeking logical truths. But consider the college student asked by Michael Basseches (1984) to reflect on higher education. This student first stated a *thesis*— that college is a place where a special kind of exchange of knowledge goes on. He then detected an opposing idea, an *antithesis*—that people could exchange views as well at a cafe in Paris as at a college. Finally, he pulled the thesis and antithesis together into a *synthesis*, arguing that people at college were more qualified to give opinions on certain subjects than people in a cafe were. Thus he reached a more sophisticated understanding by resolving one idea and its opposite. Basseches found that such dialectical thinking was more common among faculty than among college seniors, and more common among college seniors than among freshmen (see also Irwin & Sheese, 1989).

Basseches, Riegel, and others hold that dialectical thinkers do not ignore practical realities in order to apply formal logic to problems. Instead, they thrive on detecting inconsistencies and paradoxes and then formulating new syntheses from their theses and antitheses—only to repeat the process of changing their understandings again and again. According to Piaget, formal-operational thinkers have reached a state of cognitive balance, or equilibrium, in which all the pieces of the puzzle fit and the world makes sense. By contrast, dialectical thinkers are in a never-ending state of *disequilibrium* (Riegel, 1973).

Systematic Thinking

Advanced thinkers also seem to engage in **systematic thinking,** or thinking about abstract systems of knowledge (Commons, Richards, & Kuhn, 1982; Fischer et al., 1990; Richards & Commons, 1990). If the concrete-operational thinker operates on concrete *objects,* and the formal-operational thinker performs mental actions on *ideas,* the postformal thinker manipulates whole *systems* of ideas. Thus, when a professor asks you to compare and contrast theories—or, worse yet, to uncover overall principles behind several theories or to form a supertheory based on several theories—you are being asked to reason about systems.

Kurt Fischer and his associates have found that systematic thinking improves considerably in early adulthood. In one study (Kenny & Fischer, cited by Kenny, 1983), they asked individuals aged 8 to 20 to explain the basic mathematical operations of addition, subtraction, multiplication, and division. At about age 16, students became able to *compare* math operations in an abstract way—for example, to recognize that addition and multiplication both involve combining numbers to produce larger ones and that multiplication is really addition repeated a specified number of times ($8 + 8 + 8$ and 8×3 both yield 24). Only older students were able to engage in even more abstract thinking about the system of mathematics—for example, to compare and contrast dissimilar operations like addition and division or to identify abstract principles that underlie all four math operations and account for their similarities and differences.

So, What Lies beyond Formal Operations?

It is not yet entirely clear whether any of these advanced cognitive abilities—relativistic thinking, dialectical thinking, or systematic thinking—might really qualify as a new and higher stage of cognitive development that evolves out of formal-operational thinking. Some of these skills may instead develop alongside formal-operational thought but not replace it (Chandler & Boutilier, 1992). It does seem, though, that these types of thinking are most evident among adults who have received advanced education, are open to rethinking issues, and live in a culture that nourishes their efforts to entertain new ideas (Irwin, 1991). It is also clear that cognitive development does not end in adolescence. During adulthood many people become better able to define and think through "real-life" problems that require resolution of contradictory and ambiguous information, that can be viewed from several perspectives, and that do not have one right answer.

Cognitive development during adulthood also involves learning to think in more efficient ways as one gains expertise. Indeed, as adults become experts in their areas of specialization, they often develop mental shortcuts that enable them to bypass formal methods of thought (Scribner, 1984). A truck loader, for example, may simply know from experience how many boxes will fit in a truck and can dispense with any mathematical calculations. Overall, age does not tell us much about how an adult thinks; life circumstances and the demands placed on people to think at work, in the home, and in the community often tell us more.

Aging and Cognitive Performance

What becomes of cognitive capacities in later adulthood? Some mental abilities decline as the average person ages, and it appears that older adults often have

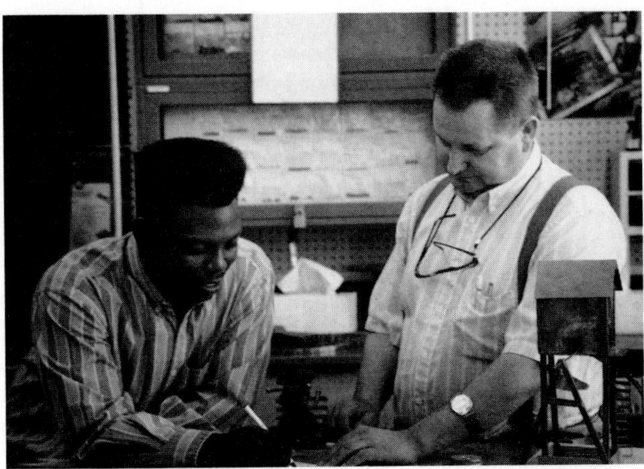

Adults come to think very efficiently once they gain expertise on the job.

trouble solving Piagetian tests of formal-operational thinking (Blackburn & Papalia, 1992). Indeed, elderly adults sometimes perform more poorly than young and middle-aged adults even on *concrete*-operational tasks assessing conservation and classification skills (Blackburn & Papalia, 1992; Denney, 1982).

Does this really mean that elderly adults regress to immature modes of thought, perhaps as a result of brain degeneration? Probably not (Blackburn & Papalia, 1992). For one thing, these studies have involved cross-sectional comparisons of different age groups. The poorer performance of older groups does not necessarily mean that cognitive abilities are lost as one ages. It could be due to a cohort effect, for the average older adult today has had less formal schooling than the average younger adult has had. Level of education is usually far more predictive of success on Piagetian tasks than age is (Blackburn & Papalia, 1992), and older adults who are attending college tend to perform just as well as younger college students on tests of formal operations (Blackburn, 1984; Hooper, Hooper, & Colbert, 1985). Moreover, very brief training can quickly improve the performance of older adults long out of school, which suggests that the necessary cognitive abilities are there but merely need to be reactivated (Blackburn & Papalia, 1992).

Questions have also been raised about the relevance of the skills assessed in Piagetian tasks to the lives of older adults (Labouvie-Vief, 1985). Not only are these problems unfamiliar to many older adults, but they resemble the intellectual challenges that children confront in school, not those that most adults encounter in everyday contexts. Thus, older people may not be very motivated to solve them. Also, older adults may rely on modes of cognition that have proved useful to them in daily life but that make them look cognitively deficient in the laboratory (Salthouse, 1990).

Consider this example. Kathy Pearce and Nancy Denney (1984) found that elderly adults, like young children but unlike other age groups, often group two objects on the basis of some functional relationship between them (for example, putting a pipe and matches together because matches are used to light pipes) rather than on the basis of similarity (for example, putting a pipe and a saxophone together because they are similar in shape). In school and in some job situations, Pearce and Denney suggest, people are asked to group objects on the basis of similarity, but in everyday life it may make more sense to associate objects that are commonly used together.

Such findings suggest that what appear to be deficits in older people may merely be differences in style. Similar stylistic differences in classification skills have been observed cross-culturally and can, if researchers are not careful, lead to the incorrect conclusion that uneducated adults from non-Western cultures lack basic cognitive skills. A case in point: Kpelle adults in Africa, when asked to sort foods, clothing, tools, and cooking utensils into groups, sorted them into pairs based on functional relationships. "When an exasperated experimenter asked finally, 'How would a fool do it,' he was given back sorts of the type that were initially expected—four neat piles with foods in one, tools in another, and so on" (Glick, 1975, p. 636).

In sum, today's older adults appear not to perform concrete- and formal-operational tasks as well as their younger contemporaries do. Planners of adult education for senior citizens might bear in mind that some of their students (though by no means all) may benefit from more concrete forms of instruction. However, these age differences may be related to factors other than age, such as education and motivation; an actual age-related decline in operational abilities has not been firmly established. Most importantly, older adults who perform poorly on unfamiliar problems in laboratory situations often perform very capably on the sorts of problems that they encounter in everyday contexts (Cornelius & Caspi, 1987; Salthouse, 1990).

PIAGET IN PERSPECTIVE

Now that we have examined Jean Piaget's theory of cognitive development, it is time to evaluate it. Let's start by giving credit where credit is due. Then we'll consider challenges to Piaget's version of things.

Piaget's Contributions

Piaget is a giant in the field of human development. As one scholar quoted by Harry Beilin (1992) put it, "assessing the impact of Piaget on developmental psychology is like assessing the impact of Shakespeare on English literature or Aristotle on philosophy—impossible" (p. 191). It is hard to imagine that we would know even a fraction of what we know about intellectual development without his ground-breaking work. One sign of a good theory is that it stimulates research, and Piaget's cognitive-developmental perspective has now been applied to almost every aspect of human development.

We can credit Piaget with some major insights into development. He showed us that infants are active in their own development—that from the start they seek to master problems and to understand the incomprehensible. Similarly, Piaget taught us that young humans do indeed think differently than older humans and that there is great value in finding out how people of different ages reason, not just whether they give right or wrong answers.

Finally, and quite importantly, Piaget was largely right in his basic description of cognitive development. The *sequences* he proposed seem to describe quite well the course and content of intellectual development for children and adolescents from the hundreds of cultures and subcultures that have now been studied (Bjorklund, 1989; Flavell, 1985). Although cultural factors do influence the *rate* of cognitive growth, the direction of development is always from sensorimotor thinking to preoperational thinking to concrete operations and, for many, to formal operations.

Challenges to Piaget

Partly because Piaget's theory has been so enormously influential, it has gotten more than its share of criticism. We will focus on four major criticisms here.

Underestimating Young Minds

One frequent charge is that Piaget was incorrect about when individuals can be expected to master a concept or enter a particular stage of development. Most notably, Piaget seems to have underestimated the cognitive abilities of infants and young children. When researchers have used more familiar problems than Piaget used and have reduced tasks to their essentials, the hidden competencies of young children—and of adolescents and adults too—have been revealed.

Failing to Distinguish Competence from Performance

Piaget was concerned with identifying the cognitive structures, or underlying competencies, that influence performance on cognitive tasks. The age ranges Piaget proposed for some stages may have been off target in part because he largely ignored the many factors besides competence that can influence task performance: everything from the individual's motivation, verbal abilities, and memory capacity to the nature, complexity, and familiarity of a specific task. Piaget assumed that children who failed one of his tasks lacked the underlying concept he was testing. Yet researchers keep finding that individuals who fail one task often perform well on a slightly different task designed to assess the same cognitive ability (Kuhn, 1992).

Claiming That Broad Stages of Development Exist

According to Piaget, each new stage of cognitive development is a coherent mode of thinking that is applied across a wide range of specific problems. Yet our review suggests that transitions in cognitive growth occur gradually; there is often little consistency in the individual's performance on different tasks that presumably measure the abilities defining a given stage. For example, it may be years before a 7-year-old who can conserve number will be able to conserve volume; a 15-year-old who shows an advanced understanding of mathematical concepts may take considerably longer to move through a sequence of steps in understanding scientific hypothesis testing. More and more researchers are arguing that cognitive development is *domain specific*—that is, it is a matter of building skills in particular content areas, and growth in one domain may proceed much faster than growth in another (Fischer et al., 1990; Flavell, 1985).

Studies of adult cognitive development also raise questions about Piaget's stages. Specifically, critics have charged that Piaget may not have chosen the right model of mature thought when he described the formal-operational stage of development (Labouvie-Vief, 1992). Mature minds seem to be able to do more than think formally, and critics maintain that Piaget stopped too soon, and possibly headed in the wrong direction, in describing adult thought.

Failing to Adequately Explain Development

Several critics suggest that Piaget did a better job of describing development than of explaining how it comes about (Brainerd, 1978; Kuhn, 1992). To be sure, Piaget did present his interactionist position on the nature/nurture issue. Presumably humans are always assimilating new experiences in ways that their level of maturation allows, accommodating their thinking to those experiences, and reorganizing their cognitive structures into increasingly complex modes of thought. The problem is that this explanation is rather vague. We need to know far more about links between milestones in neurological development and cognitive change, as well as about the specific kinds of experiences that contribute to important cognitive advances.

Giving Limited Attention to Social Influences on Cognitive Development

Piaget may have paid too little attention to the ways in which children's minds develop through their social interactions with more competent individuals. Piaget's child often resembles an isolated scientist exploring the world alone, when in fact children develop their minds through interactions with parents, teachers, and more competent peers and siblings. As we will see shortly, a belief in the significance of social interaction for cognitive development is a cornerstone of the sociocultural perspective on cognitive development offered by one of Piaget's early critics, Lev Vygotsky.

So, Piaget's theory of cognitive development might have been stronger if he had devoted more attention to designing tasks that could better reveal the competencies of infants and young children; if he had explored the many factors besides underlying competence that influence actual performance; if he had been able to provide more convincing evidence that his stages are indeed coherent stages; if he had been more specific about *why* development proceeds as it does; and if he had more fully considered social influences on the development of thought. It may be unfair, however, to expect an innovator who achieved so much to have accomplished everything.

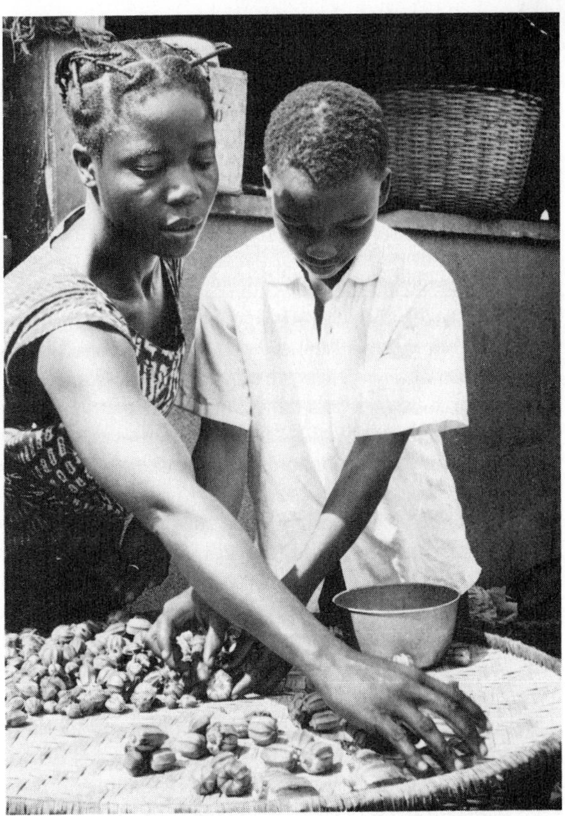

According to Vygotsky's theory, cognitive development is shaped by the culture in which children live and by the kinds of problem-solving strategies that parents and other knowledgeable guides pass on to them.

VYGOTSKY'S SOCIOCULTURAL PERSPECTIVE

In order to view Piaget's work from a new vantage point and to lay the groundwork for a discussion of language development, we'll now consider a perspective on cognitive development that has been arousing much interest recently: that offered by Lev Vygotsky (1934/1962, 1930–1935/1978; see also Wertsch & Tulviste, 1992). This Russian psychologist was an active scholar in the 1920s and 1930s, when Piaget was formulating his theory. Vygotsky died at the age of 38, before his views were fully formulated, but his main theme was this: *Cognitive growth occurs in a sociocultural context and evolves out of the child's social interactions.*

Consider this scenario: Annie, a 4-year-old, receives a jigsaw puzzle, her first, for her birthday. She attempts to work the puzzle but gets nowhere until her father comes along, sits down beside her, and gives her some tips. He suggests that it would be a good idea to put the corners together first. He points to the pink area at the edge of one corner piece and says "Let's look for another pink piece." When Annie seems frustrated, he places two interlocking pieces near each other so that she will notice them. And when she succeeds, he offers words of encouragement. As Annie gets the hang of it, he steps back and lets her work more and more independently. This kind of social interaction, claimed Vygotsky, fosters cognitive growth.

How? First, Annie and her father are operating in what Vygotsky called the **zone of proximal development** — the difference between what a learner can accomplish independently and what he or she can accomplish with the guidance and encouragement of a more skilled partner. It is the zone in which sensitive instruction should be aimed and in which new cognitive growth can be expected to occur. Annie obviously becomes a more competent puzzle-solver with her father's help than without it. More importantly, she will internalize the problem-solving techniques that she uses in collaboration with him and will ultimately use them on her own, rising to a new level of independent mastery. In short, Vygotsky rejects Piaget's view of children as independent explorers in favor of the view that they learn more sophisticated cognitive strategies from their interactions with more mature thinkers.

In Vygotsky's view, language is the primary vehicle through which adults pass culturally valued modes of thinking and problem solving on to their children. Whereas Piaget maintained that cognitive development influences language development, Vygotsky argued that language shapes thought in important ways. Piaget and Vygotsky both noticed that preschool children often talk to themselves as they go about their daily activities, almost as if they were play-by-play sports announcers ("I'm putting the big piece in the corner. Now I'll find a pink one. Not that one—this one.") Two preschool children playing next to each other sometimes carry on their own separate monologues rather than truly conversing.

Piaget (1926) regarded such speech as egocentric, as further evidence that preoperational thinkers cannot yet take the perspectives of other people (in this case, their conversation partners). He did not believe that egocentric speech played any useful role in cognitive development. Vygotsky, however, called this nonsocial speech **private speech**—speech for the self that guides the individual's thought and behavior. Rather than viewing it as a sign of cognitive immaturity, he saw it as a critical step in the development of mature thought and as the forerunner of the silent thinking-in-words that we adults engage in every day.

Studies conducted by Vygotsky and other researchers (see Berk, 1992) support his claim. *Social speech* (for example, the conversation between Annie and her father as they jointly worked a puzzle) gives rise to *private speech* (Annie's talking aloud, much as her father talked to her, as she then tries to work the puzzle on her own), which in turn goes "underground" to become first mutterings and lip movements and then *inner speech* (Annie's silent verbal thought). Use of private speech increases during the early preschool years and decreases during the early elementary school years as children become capable of inner speech. Intellectually capable children rely more heavily on private speech in the preschool years and make the transition to inner speech earlier in the elementary school years than their less academically capable peers do (Berk, 1992; Berk & Landau, 1993; Kohlberg, Yaeger, & Hjertholm, 1968). This suggests that the preschool child's self-talk is indeed a sign of cognitive maturity, as Vygotsky claimed, rather than a sign of immature egocentrism, as Piaget claimed.

In further support of Vygotsky's views, it has been found that young children rely most heavily on private speech when they are struggling to solve difficult problems (Berk, 1992). Indeed, even adults sometimes revert to thinking aloud when they are stumped by a problem (John-Steiner, 1992). In addition, heavy use of private speech contributes to effective problem-solving performance—if not immediately then later, when children encounter similar problems in the future (Behrend, Rosengren, & Perlmutter, 1989; Bivens & Berk, 1990). Thus, private speech not only helps children think their way through challenging problems but also allows them to incorporate into their own thinking the problem-solving strategies that they learned initially during their collaborations with adults.

In sum, Vygotsky's sociocultural perspective stresses social influences on cognitive development that Piaget largely ignored: Children's minds develop as they engage in social interactions with skilled partners on tasks that are within their zone of proximal development and as they incorporate what skilled partners say to them into what they say to themselves. As social speech is transformed into private speech and then inner speech, the culture's preferred methods of problem solving work their way from the language of competent guides into the thinking of the individual.

Vygotsky made a good case that language shapes thought. Perhaps no one appreciates that point more than deaf people who are introduced to sign language after years without any language; suddenly they can express thoughts that they could barely formulate before (Sacks, 1989). As Oliver Sacks (1989) demonstrates in his book *Seeing Voices*, deaf individuals who are denied access to American Sign Language or some other true language system are likely to show delayed cognitive development and underachievement in school compared to those who have access to language as a tool of thought. Language does shape the nature of thought, and yet Piaget was also right to point out that children's cognitive skills influence their progress in mastering language. With that in mind, we turn to language development and further consider the relationships between language development and cognitive development.

MASTERING LANGUAGE

Although language is one of the most intricate bodies of knowledge we will ever acquire, all normal children master a language very early in life. Indeed, many infants are talking before they can walk. Can language be all that complex, then? It certainly can be. Linguists (scholars who study language) have yet to fully describe the rules of English (or of any other language), and so far computers cannot understand speech as well as most 5-year-olds can. What exactly is the task facing young language learners?

What Must Be Mastered

Linguists define **language** as a communication system in which a limited number of signals—sounds or letters (or gestures, in the case of the sign language used by deaf people)—can be combined according to agreed-upon rules to produce an infinite number of messages. As Vygotsky appreciated, any human language is both a marvelously versatile means of social communication and an essential tool of thought. Whether based on sounds or signs, language allows us to convey to our fellow humans (or to ourselves) virtually any thought or feeling we might have. To master a spoken language such as English, a child must know what basic sounds are used to form words, what words mean, how to combine words to form meaningful statements, and how to use language effectively in their social interactions. That is, the child must master four aspects of language: phonology, semantics, syntax, and pragmatics.

Phonology is the sound system of a language, and the basic units of sound in any given language are its **phonemes.** The child in an English-speaking country must come to know the 45 phonemes used in English (which correspond roughly to the familiar vowel and consonant sounds) and must also learn which ones can be combined in English and which ones cannot (for example, *st-*, but not *sb-*). Other languages have other basic sounds (or, in a sign language, basic hand shapes and motions). Children must learn to hear and to pronounce the phonemes of their language in order to make sense of the speech they hear and to be understood when they speak.

Semantics is the aspect of language that concerns meanings. Words stand for, or symbolize, things, and the child must map the proper relationships between words and things. Grasping semantics obviously depends on understanding the world and thus on cognitive development. The basic meaningful units of language are called **morphemes,** which include words and grammatical markers (such as the *-ed* for past tense, the *-s* to signal a plural noun, and other prefixes and suffixes). Knowledge of semantics is also required to interpret whole sentences or speeches or paragraphs.

The language system also involves **syntax,** or the rules that specify how words are to be combined to form sentences. Consider these three sentences: (1) Fang Fred bit, (2) Fang bit Fred, and (3) Fred bit Fang. The first, as even very young children recognize, violates the rules of English sentence structure or syntax, although this word order would be perfectly acceptable in French. The second two sentences are grammatical English sentences that have very different meanings conveyed by their different word orders. Children must master rules of syntax to understand or use simple declarative sentences like these and then must master complex sentences with many phrases.

Finally, language learners must also master what has been termed **pragmatics** — rules specifying how language is to be used appropriately in different social contexts. That is, children have to learn when to say what to whom. They must learn to communicate effectively by taking into account who the listener is, what the listener already knows, and what the listener needs or wants to hear. "Give me that cookie" may be grammatical English, but the child is far more likely to win Grandma's heart (not to mention a cookie) with a polite "May I please try one of your yummy cookies, Grandma?"

In short, mastering a human language is an incredible challenge, for it requires learning phonology, semantics, syntax, and pragmatics. Moreover, human communication involves not only language use but also *nonverbal communication* (facial expressions, intonation, tone of voice, gestures, and so on). Children must also learn these nonverbal signals, which often clarify the meaning of a verbal message and are important means of communicating in their own right. Let's look at the course of language development and then ask how nature and nurture contribute to the child's remarkable accomplishment.

The Course of Language Development

For the first 10 to 13 months of life, infants are not yet capable of speaking meaningful words, but they are building up to that achievement.

Before the First Words

As we learned in Chapter 6, newborns seem to "tune in" to human speech immediately. Very young infants can even distinguish between phonemes such as *b* and *p* or *d* and *t* (Eimas, 1975). Indeed, 7-month-old infants from homes where English is spoken are better than English-speaking adults at differentiating certain phonemes that are *not* used in English (Werker, Gilbert, Humphrey, & Tees, 1981).

What about producing sounds? Prelinguistic vocalizations develop in a stagelike manner related to the maturation of motor control over the muscles involved in articulating sound (Sachs, 1985). At birth, infants produce at least three kinds of cries: a "hunger" cry, a "mad" cry, and a "pain" cry (Wolff, 1969). By the third week of life, they also produce a "fake" cry, which may be what Piaget would call a primary circular reaction — the repeating of an interesting noise for the sheer pleasure of making it (Wolff, 1969).

The next milestone in vocalization, at about 3 to 5 weeks of age, is **cooing**: repeating vowel-like sounds such as "oooooh" and "aaaaah." Babies coo when they are contented. At about 3 to 4 months of age, infants expand their range of sounds considerably as they begin to produce consonant sounds. They then enter a period of **babbling** between about 4 and 6 months of age, repeating consonant/vowel combinations such as "baba" or "dadadada" over and over (again, a primary circular reaction in Piaget's terminology). Interestingly, deaf infants whose parents are deaf and communicate through sign language "babble" in sign language. They experiment with gestures in much the same way that hearing infants experiment with sounds in preparation for their first meaningful communications (Petitto & Marentette, 1991).

Up to about 6 months of age, infants all over the world, even deaf ones, sound pretty much alike, but the effects of experience soon become apparent. At roughly this age, deaf infants fall behind hearing infants in their ability to produce well-formed syllables (Oller & Eilers, 1988). By the time infants are about 8 months old, they babble with something of an accent; adults can often tell from their babbling whether babies have been listening to French, Chinese, or Arabic (de Boysson-Bardies, Sagart, & Durand, 1984). These advanced babblers increasingly restrict their sounds to those that are phonemes in the language they are hearing, and they pick up the intonation patterns of that language as well (de Villiers & de Villiers, 1979). Apparently, then, babies are "learning the tune before the words" (Bates, O'Connell, & Shore, 1987, p. 157). As their babbling progresses, infants also begin to use certain babbling sounds selectively in certain situations; thus a baby named Jeanette used the *m* sound when requesting objects but not when manipulating objects and used vowel sounds when manipulating objects but not when requesting them (Blake & de Boysson-Bardies, 1992). Possibly, then, babbling sounds begin to take on specific meanings to infants (if not to their conversation partners), and this readies them to attach meanings to words.

As they attempt to master the semantics of language, infants come to understand many words before they can produce them. That is, *comprehension is ahead of production, or expression, in language development*. Before they really understand the specific words in a command, they will obey commands (e.g., "Get the ball") in familiar contexts, probably by interpreting tone of voice and context cues (Benedict, 1979). Shortly before speaking their first true words, however, as they approach a year of age, they really seem to understand familiar words. If their mothers name a familiar toy, they will look at it rather than at other nearby objects (Thomas et al., 1981). From infancy on, we generally understand more words than we are able to control in our own speech or writing.

In their first year, infants are also learning basic lessons about the pragmatics of language. For example, during the first six months they are most likely to coo or babble *while* a partner is speaking (Freedle & Lewis, 1977; Rosenthal, 1982). After that point, however, they seem to have mastered the rule of conversational turn-taking, for they vocalize when a partner has stopped talking. This marks a basic, highly important step in learning to use language appropriately in social interactions. Indeed, infants are learning a great deal about how to communicate before they ever utter a meaningful word.

The First Words: Holophrastic Speech

An infant's first meaningful word, spoken at about a year of age, is a special event for parents. First words have been called **holophrases** because a single word sometimes conveys an entire sentence's worth of meaning. These single-word "sentences" can serve different communication functions depending on the way they are said and the context in which they are said (Greenfield & Smith, 1976). For example, 17-month-old Shelley used the word *ghetti* (spaghetti) in three different ways over a five-minute period. First she pointed to the pan on the stove and seemed to be asking "Is that spaghetti?" Later the function of her holophrase was to name the spaghetti when shown the contents of the pan, as in "It's spaghetti." Finally, there was little question that she was requesting spaghetti when she tugged at her companion's sleeve as he was eating and used the word in a whining tone.

Although there are limits to the amount of meaning that can be packed into a single word and its accompanying tone of voice and gestures, 1-year-olds in the holophrastic stage of language development do seem to have mastered such basic language functions as naming, questioning, requesting, and demanding. They also show a new ability to use symbols — not just words, but gestures (behavioral schemes, in Piaget's terminology) such as pointing, raising their arms to signal "up," or panting heavily to say "dog" (Acredolo & Goodwyn, 1988; Bates et al., 1987).

What do 1-year-olds talk about? They talk about objects and the actions on objects featured in Piaget's sensorimotor stage. Katherine Nelson (1973) studied 18 infants as they learned their first 50 words and found that nearly two-thirds of these early words referred to objects, including familiar people. Moreover, these objects were nearly all either manipulatable by the child (bottles, shoes) or capable of moving themselves (animals, trucks). Toddlers' first words also include many references to familiar actions (Nelson, Hampson, & Shaw, 1993). In other words, toddlers are talking a lot about the "sensorimotor schemes" that Piaget believed were so important in cognitive development.

Initial language acquisition proceeds literally one word at a time. Three or four months may pass before the child has a vocabulary of 10 words (Nelson, 1973). Then the pace quickens dramatically at around 18 months of age, so that by 24 months of age children are producing an average of 186 words (Nelson, 1973). During this vocabulary spurt, toddlers seem to arrive at the wonderful realization that everything has a name; they then want to learn all the names they possibly can (Reznick & Goldfield, 1992).

But how do toddlers figure out what words mean? They accomplish this feat by using several strategies that help them narrow down the possible meanings that a new word could have (de Villiers & de Villiers, 1992; Markman, 1989; Taylor & Gelman, 1988). For example, they tend to assume that a new word refers to a whole object rather than to some part of the object and to a class of similar objects (eyeglasses in general) rather than to one specific object (Mommy's reading glasses). They also assume that each word has a unique meaning (Clark, 1983). As a result, when they hear the new word *macaroon*, they are likely to conclude that it does not mean exactly the same thing as the more familiar word *cookie* and most likely refers to a particular kind of cookie (Taylor & Gelman, 1989). Finally, young language learners infer word meanings by paying close attention to the contexts in which unfamiliar words are used (Nelson et al., 1993). This includes noticing how a word is used in sentences. The child who hears a new word, *zav*, used as a noun to refer to a toy ("This is a zav") concludes that this new word refers to a kind of toy. However, the child who hears *zav* used as an adjective ("This is a zav one") will infer that *zav* is some attribute of a toy, such as its color (Taylor & Gelman, 1988).

Despite the soundness of their strategies for inferring word meanings, children do not always succeed at first. Two kinds of semantic errors are common. First, there is **overextension,** or using a word to refer to too wide a range of objects or events, as when a 2-year-old calls all furry, four-legged animals "doggie." The second, and opposite, error is **underextension,** as when a child initially uses the word "doggie" to refer only to basset hounds like the family pet. Getting semantics right seems to be mainly a matter of discriminating similarities and differences—for example, categorizing animals on the basis of size, shape, the sounds they make, and other perceptual features (Clark & Clark, 1977).

But might children know more about the world than their semantic errors suggest? Yes. Two-year-olds who call all four-legged animals "doggie" can often point out a dog in a set of animal pictures when asked to do so (Thompson & Chapman, 1977). They may overextend the meaning of "doggie" merely because they have no better word yet for new animals such as horses and goats and want to communicate nonetheless (Baron, 1992).

From Holophrases to Simple Sentences: Telegraphic Speech

The next step in language development, normally taken at about 18 to 24 months of age, is combining two words into a simple sentence. Toddlers all over the world use two-word sentences to express the same basic ideas (see Table 7.2). Early combinations of two, three, or more words are sometimes called **telegraphic speech** because, like telegrams, many of these sentences contain critical content words and omit frills such as articles, prepositions, and auxiliary verbs.

Now, it is ungrammatical in adult English to say "No wet" or "Where ball." However, these two-word sentences are not just random word combinations or mistakes; they reflect children's *own* systematic rules for forming sentences. Psycholinguists have approached early child language as though it were a foreign language and have tried to describe the rules that young children seem to be using to form sentences. At first, psycholinguists such as Martin Braine (1963) focused on the order of the two words in two-word sentences, believing that children followed predictable rules of syntax. Now the emphasis has shifted to the *meanings* that children are attempting to convey.

Two-word sentences, like holophrases, serve several communication functions: naming, demanding, negating, and so on. Lois Bloom (1970) and others feel that it is therefore appropriate to describe early language in terms of a **functional grammar**—one that emphasizes the semantic relations between words, or the meanings being expressed. For example, young children often use the same word order to convey different meanings. "Mommy sock" might mean "The sock is Mommy's" in one context and "Mommy is putting on my sock" in another. Word order sometimes does play a role: "Billy hit" and "Hit Billy" may mean different things. Body language and

TABLE 7.2 Similarities in children's spontaneous two-word sentences in several languages.

	Language			
Function of Sentence	*English*	*German*	*Russian*	*Samoan*
To locate or name	There book	Buch da (book there)	Tosya tam (Tosya there)	Keith lea (Keith there)
To demand	More milk Give candy	Mehr milch (more milk)	Yesche moloko (more milk)	Mai pepe (give doll)
To negate	No wet Not hungry	Nicht blasen (not blow)	Vody nyet (water no)	Le'ai (not eat)
To indicate possession	My shoe Mama dress	Mein ball (my ball) Mamas hut (Mama's hat)	Mami chashka (Mama's cup)	Lole a'u (candy my)
To modify or quality	Pretty dress Big boat	Armer wauwau (poor dog)	Papa bol'shoy (Papa big)	Fa'ali'i pepe (headstrong baby)
To question	Where ball	Wo ball (where ball)	Gde papa (where Papa)	Fea Punafu (where Punafu)

SOURCE: Adapted from Slobin, 1979.

tone of voice also communicate meanings, as when a child points and whines to emphasize a request for ice cream and not merely a noting of its existence. As it turns out, children from different cultures, and even different children within a particular society, differ considerably in how they construct their two-word sentences and what sorts of words they include in them (Bates et al., 1987). Their communication goals may be much the same, but individual children devise their own ways of achieving them.

Overall, children learn to make combinations of words, accompanied by body language, perform basic communication functions as they interact with others. By the age of 2, they are typically understanding quite a bit, are using many words appropriately either alone or in two-word telegraphic sentences, and are positioning themselves for the language explosion that will occur during the preschool years.

The Language Explosion of the Preschool Years

In the short period from age 2 to 5, children come to speak sentences that are remarkably complex and adultlike. Table 7.3 gives an inkling of how fast things move in the particularly important period from age 2 to age 3. From the two-word stage of language acquisition, children progress to three-word telegraphic sentences and then to still longer sentences, beginning to add the little function words like articles and prepositions that were often missing in their early telegraphic sentences (de Villiers & de Villiers, 1992). They infer more and more of the rules of adult language. It does not seem to matter whether they are deaf children learning a sign language or hearing children learning an oral language; they progress through roughly the same stages and make the same kinds of errors on their way to mastering grammatical rules (Bellugi, 1988).

TABLE 7.3 Samples of Kyle's speech at 24 months and 11 months later. At 24 months, Kyle speaks in telegraphic sentences no more than three words long; by 35 months, his sentences are much longer and grammatically complex, though not error-free, and he is far more able to participate in the give-and-take of conversation (if not to heed his mother and respect the dignity of potato bugs).

Age 24 Months (His second birthday party)	*Age 35 Months (Playing with a potato bug)*
Want cake now. Boons! Boons! [pointing to balloons] They mine! [referring to colors] I wan' see. See sky now. Ow-ee [point to knee]	Mother: Kyle, why don't you take the bug back to his friends? Kyle: After I hold him, then I'll take the bug back to his friends. Mommy, where did the bug go? Mommy, I didn't know where the bug go. Find it. Maybe Winston's on it [the family dog]. Winston, get off the bug! [Kyle spots the bug and picks it up.] Mother: Kyle, *please* let the bug go back to his friends. Kyle: He does not want to go to his friends. [He drops the bug and squashes it, much to his mother's horror.] I stepped on it and it will not go to his friends.

How do we know when children are mastering new rules? Oddly enough, their progress sometimes reveals itself in new "mistakes." Consider the task of learning grammatical markers for plurals of nouns and past tenses of verbs (Brown, 1973; Mervis & Johnson, 1991). Typically this happens sometime during the third year. But a child who has been saying "feet" and "went" may suddenly start to say "foots" and "goed." Does this represent a step backward? Not at all. The child was probably using the correct irregular forms at first by imitating adult speech, without really understanding the meaning of plurality or verb tense. The use of "foots" and "goed" is a breakthrough: He or she has now inferred the rule of adding *-s* to pluralize nouns and adding *-ed* to signal past tense. At first, however, the youngster overapplies the rules to cases in which the proper form is irregular—an important process in language acquisition known as **overregularization.** When the child masters exceptions to the rules, he or she will say "feet" and "went" once more. The grammatical morphemes used most frequently in English are mastered in the order in which they appear in Table 7.4 (Brown, 1973; de Villiers & de Villiers, 1973).

Children must also master rules for creating variations of the basic declarative sentence; that is, they must learn the rules for converting a basic idea such as "I am eating pizza" into such forms as questions ("What am I eating?"), negative sentences ("I am not eating pizza"), and imperatives ("Eat the pizza!"). The prominent linguist Noam Chomsky (1968, 1975) drew attention to the child's learning of these rules by proposing that language be described in terms of a **transformational grammar,** or rules of syntax for transforming basic sentences into other forms.

How, for example, do young children learn to phrase the questions that they so frequently ask? The earliest questions often consist of nothing more than two- or three-word sentences with rising intonation ("See kitty?"). Sometimes "wh" words like *what* or *where* appear ("Where kitty?"). During the second stage of question asking, children begin to use auxiliary, or helping, verbs, but their questions are of this form: "What Daddy is eating?" "Where the kitty is going?" Their understanding of transformation rules is still incomplete (Dale, 1976). Finally, they learn the transformation rule that calls for moving the auxiliary

TABLE 7.4 Order of acquisition of English grammatical morphemes.

Morpheme	*Example*
1. Present progressive: *-ing*	He is sitt*ing* down.
2. Preposition: *in*	The mouse is *in* the box.
3. Preposition: *on*	The book is *on* the table.
4. Plural: *-s*	The dog*s* ran away.
5. Past irregular: for example, *went*	The boy *went* home.
6. Possessive: *-'s*	The girl*'s* dog is big.
7. Uncontractible copula *be:* for example, *are, was*	*Are* they boys or girls? *Was* that a dog?
8. Articles: *the, a*	He has *a* book.
9. Past regular: *-ed*	He jump*ed* the stream.
10. Third person regular: *-s*	She run*s* fast.
11. Third person irregular: for example, *has, does*	*Does* the dog bark?
12. Uncontractible auxiliary *be:* for example, *is, were*	*Is* he running? *Were* they at home?
13. Contractible copula *be:* for example, *-'s, -'re*	That*'s* a spaniel.
14. Contractible auxiliary *be:* for example, *-'s, -'re*	They*'re* running very slowly.

SOURCE: Adapted from Clark & Clark, 1977.

verb ahead of the subject (as in the adultlike sentence "What is Daddy eating?").

By the end of the preschool period (age 5–6), children's sentences are very much like those of adults, even though they have never had a formal lesson in grammar. It's an amazing accomplishment. Yet there is still more to accomplish.

Later Language Development

Not only do school-aged children improve their pronunciation skills, produce longer and more complex sentences, and continue to expand their vocabularies, but they also begin to think about and manipulate language in ways that were previously impossible.

Listening to preschool children talk, we notice that many of them have difficulty articulating certain phonemes; *spaghetti* may come out as *pasketti*, *elephant* as *effalunt*. Most early articulation problems disappear during the elementary school years (Owens, 1984). School-aged children also acquire many complex syntactical rules, such as those for forming and interpreting passive sentences like "Goofy was liked by Donald" (Sudhalter & Braine, 1985) and conditional sentences like "If Goofy had come, Donald would have been delighted" (Boloh & Champaud, 1993). And not until the middle elementary school years do children master certain subtle differences in sentence construction, such as the distinction between "Ask Ellen what to feed the doll" and "Tell Ellen what to feed the doll" (C. S. Chomsky, 1969). Preschoolers often treat *ask* as if it meant *tell* and reply "hamburgers" or "eggs" instead of asking Ellen a question. Command of grammar continues to improve through adolescence; teenagers' spoken and written sentences become increasingly long and complex (Clark & Clark, 1977; Hunt, 1970).

School-aged children and adolescents are also expanding their knowledge of semantics. Thanks to the remarkable vocabulary spurt of the preschool period, 6-year-olds already understand some 8000 to 14,000 words (Carey, 1977) and will continue to expand their vocabularies at a rate of about 15 words a day for many years to come. During adolescence, with the help of formal-operational thought, children become better able to understand and define abstract terms (McGhee-Bidlack, 1991). They also become better able with age to infer meanings that are not explicitly stated (Beal, 1990). This includes being able to recognize sarcasm, as when a teacher says to a noisy 8-year-old "My, but you're quiet today" (Capelli, Nakagawa, & Madden, 1990).

Finally, children become increasingly able to communicate effectively because they are less cognitively egocentric and more able to take the perspective of their listeners. Although the preschool child is not so egocentric as Piaget claimed, when the communication task is challenging, the limitations of the younger child become apparent. Robert Krauss and Sam Glucksberg (1977), for example, had children from ages 4 to 10 describe blocks with unfamiliar graphic designs on them to a peer on the other side of a screen so that the peer could identify them. As shown in Table 7.5, kindergartners described designs in egocentric and idiosyncratic ways that could not mean

TABLE 7.5 Typical idiosyncratic descriptions offered by preschool children when talking about unfamiliar graphic designs in the Krauss and Glucksberg communication game.

Form	Child Responding # 1	# 2	# 3	# 4	# 5
	Man's legs	Airplane	Drape holder	Zebra	Flying saucer
	Mother's hat	Ring	Key hold	Lion	Snake
	Daddy's shirt	Milk jug	Shoe hold	Coffee pot	Dog

SOURCE: Krauss & Glucksberg, 1977.

much to their listeners. Third- and fifth-graders gave far less egocentric and more informative descriptions.

Older children are also more able to *evaluate* their messages and recognize when the content is ambiguous or uninformative, as well as to recognize that someone else's message is ambiguous and request clarifying information (Beal, 1987; Beal & Belgrad, 1990). Throughout childhood and adolescence, advances in cognitive development are accompanied by advances in language and communication skills.

Language in Adulthood

Clearly, language skills improve steadily throughout childhood and adolescence, but what happens during adulthood? Adults simply hold on to the knowledge of phonology they gained as children. They also retain their knowledge of grammar, although older adults tend to use less complex sentences than younger adults do (Bromley, 1991; Kemper, 1992). Meanwhile, knowledge of the semantics of language *expands* during adulthood, at least until people are in their 70s or 80s (Obler & Albert, 1985; Schaie, 1983). After all, adults gain experience with the world from year to year, so it is not surprising that their vocabularies continue to grow. Although older adults more often have the "tip-of-the-tongue" experience of not being able to come up with a term or a person's name when they need it (Burke, MacKay, Worthley, & Wade, 1991), this problem is a matter of not being able to retrieve information stored in memory rather than a matter of no longer knowing words. Overall, command of semantics holds up very well in later life (Kemper, 1992; Light, 1990).

True, hearing impairments limit the ability of some older adults to understand speech; and, as we saw in Chapter 6, many older adults have trouble comprehending rapid speech under poor listening conditions. Moreover, brain disorders such as Alzheimer's disease destroy the linguistic abilities of a small minority of older people (Obler & Albert, 1985), and even mild memory impairments can interfere with the comprehension of speech and written material (Light, 1990). All things considered, though, language abilities, perhaps because they are so important and so well exercised in everyday life, survive over the life span much better than less-practiced cognitive skills (Berg & Sternberg, 1985).

In sum, we cannot help but be awed by the pace at which children master the fundamentals of a human language during their first five years of life, but we must also appreciate the continued growth that occurs in childhood and adolescence and the maintenance of language skills throughout the life span. It is time to ask how these remarkable skills are acquired.

How Language Develops: Three Theories

What abilities must young children bring to the language-learning task, and what help must their companions provide them? Theorists attempting to explain language acquisition have differed considerably in their positions on the nature/nurture issue (Bohannon & Warren-Leubecker, 1989), as illustrated by the learning, nativist, and interactionist perspectives on language development.

The Learning Perspective

How do children learn language? Most adults would say that children imitate what they hear, receiving praise when they get it right and being corrected when they get it wrong. Different learning theorists emphasize different aspects of this broad process. Social-learning theorist Albert Bandura (1971) and others emphasize observational learning—learning

Language competencies are typically well maintained in old age.

by listening to and then imitating older companions. Behaviorist B. F. Skinner (1957) and others emphasize the role of reinforcement. As children achieve better and better approximations of adult language, parents and other adults praise meaningful speech and correct errors. Children are also reinforced by getting what they want when they speak correctly (Dale, 1976). In general, learning theorists consider the child's social environment to be critical to what and how much he or she learns.

How well does the learning perspective account for language development? Certainly it is no accident that children end up speaking the same language that their parents speak, down to the regional accent. Children do learn the words that they hear spoken by others—even on television programs (Leonard, Chapman, Rowan, & Weiss, 1983; Rice & Woodsmall, 1988). In addition, young children are more likely to start using new words if they are reinforced for doing so than if they are not (Whitehurst & Valdez-Menchaca, 1988). And, finally, children whose caregivers frequently encourage them to converse by asking questions, making requests, and the like are more advanced in early language development, and even in later reading proficiency, than those whose parents are less conversational (Huttenlocher et al., 1991; Norman-Jackson, 1982; Valdez-Menchaca & Whitehurst, 1992; Whitehurst et al., 1988).

However, learning theorists have had an easier time explaining the development of phonology and semantics than accounting for how syntactical rules are acquired. For example, after analyzing conversations between mothers and young children, Roger Brown, Courtney Cazden, and Ursula Bellugi (1969) discovered that a mother's approval or disapproval depended on the truth value or semantics of what was said, *not* on the grammatical correctness of the statement. Thus, when a child looking at a cow says "Him cow" (truthful but grammatically incorrect), Mom is likely to provide reinforcement ("That's right, darling"), whereas if the child were to say "There's a dog, Mommy" (grammatically correct but untruthful), Mom would probably correct the child ("No, silly—that's a cow"). Similarly, parents seem just as likely to reward a grammatically primitive request ("Want milk") as a well-formed version of the same idea (Brown & Hanlon, 1970). Such evidence casts doubt on the idea that the major mechanism behind syntactic development is reinforcement.

Could imitation of adults account for the acquisition of syntax? We have already seen that young children produce many sentences that they are unlikely to have heard adults using ("Allgone cookie," overregularizations such as "It swimmed," and so on). These kinds of sentences are not imitations. Also, an adult is likely to get nowhere in teaching syntax by saying "Repeat after me" unless the child already has at least some knowledge of the grammatical form to be learned (Baron, 1992; McNeill, 1970). Young children *do* frequently imitate other people's speech, and this may help them get to the point of producing new structures themselves. But it is hard to see how imitation and reinforcement alone can account for the learning of grammatical rules (Slobin, 1979).

The Nativist Perspective

Nativists have made little of the role of the language environment and much of the role of the child's biologically programmed capacities in explaining language development. Noted linguist Noam Chomsky (1968, 1975) proposed that humans have an inborn mechanism for mastering language called the **language acquisition device (LAD).** The LAD contains knowledge of certain universal features of language and has the capacity to figure out the specific rules of any particular language. To learn to speak, children need only hear other humans speak; using the LAD, they quickly grasp the rules of whatever language they hear (see Figure 7.6).

What evidence supports a nativist perspective on language development? First, children do acquire an incredibly complex communication system very rapidly. (Indeed, as Box 7.3 illustrates, they can acquire *two* languages with little difficulty.) Second, they all progress through the same sequences at roughly similar ages, and they even make the same kinds of errors, which suggests that language development is guided by a specieswide maturational plan. Third, these universal aspects of early language development occur despite cultural differences in the styles of speech that adults use in talking to young children. In

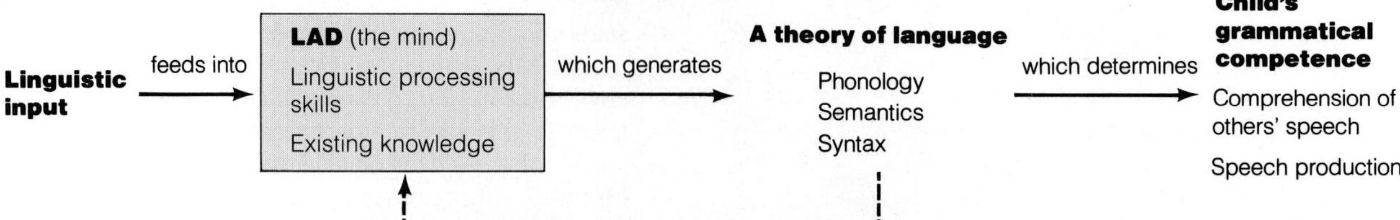

FIGURE 7.6 The language acquisition device (LAD).

some cultures parents do not even talk directly to children under 2, believing that babies are incapable of understanding speech (Richman, Miller, & LeVine, 1992; Schieffelin & Ochs, 1983).

Last but not least, we have evidence that the capacity for acquiring language has a genetic basis. The fact that some of our linguistic competencies are shared with chimpanzees and other primates suggests that they arose during the course of evolution and are part of our genetic endowment as humans (Greenfield & Savage-Rumbaugh, 1993). The fact that certain speech and language disorders run in families suggests that individual heredity also influences the course of language development (Lewis & Thompson, 1992). To cite a dramatic example, Myrna Gopnik and Martha Crago (1991) studied one three-generation family in which several members were hopelessly incapable of learning the rules of morphology for forming plurals and past tenses. Because half of them had the problem and half did not, it appeared that their disorder was due to a single dominant gene that half of them inherited.

There are two major problems with the nativist perspective. First, attributing language development to a built-in language acquisition device does not really explain it. Explanation would require knowing *how* such an inborn language processor sifts through language input and infers the rules of language (Moerk, 1989). Second, nativists, in focusing on the defects of learning theories of language development, tend to underestimate the contributions of the child's language environment. The nativists base much of their argument on two assumptions: (1) that the only thing children need to develop language is exposure to speech, and (2) that the speech children hear is so incredibly complex that only a highly powerful brain could possibly detect regularities in it. Both assumptions now seem to be inaccurate, and most researchers currently believe that language development depends on an interaction of nature and nurture.

The Interactionist Perspective

Theorists such as Elizabeth Bates (Bates & MacWhinney, 1982) and Neil Bohannon (Bohannon & Warren-Leubecker, 1989) believe that *both* learning theorists and nativists are correct: Children's biologically based competencies *and* their language environment interact to shape the course of language development.

Interactionists emphasize that the acquisition of language skills depends on and is related to the acquisition of many other capacities: perceptual, cognitive, motor, social, and emotional. They point out that the capacity for acquiring language is not unique (as nativists who speak of the LAD claim); the same mind that acquires language acquires other cognitive skills as well (Bates et al., 1987). For example, young children first begin to use words as meaningful symbols at a time when they are also displaying other new symbolic capacities, such as the ability to engage in pretend play and to use tools to solve problems. The interactionists' position is not unlike that taken by Piaget (1970), for he believed that milestones in cognitive development pave the way for progress in language development and that maturation and environment interact to guide both cognitive development and language development. Like Piaget (but unlike learning theorists), many interactionists argue that children can benefit from exposure to speech only if they are maturationally ready.

However, the interactionist position also emphasizes—as Vygotsky did but Piaget did not—ways in which social interactions with adults contribute to cognitive and linguistic development. Interactionists stress that the "universals" in language development reflect an interplay among biological maturation, cognitive development, and the language environment. Language is primarily a means of communicating—one that develops in the context of social interactions as children and their companions strive to get their messages across, one way or another.

Long before infants use words, their caregivers are showing them how to take turns in conversations—even if the most these young infants can contribute when their turn comes is a laugh or a bit of babbling (Bruner, 1983). As adults converse with young children, they create a supportive learning environment that helps the children grasp the regularities of language (Bruner, 1983; Harris, 1992). For example, parents may go through their children's

BOX 7.3 Bilingualism: The Challenges and Consequences of Learning More than One Language

Some toddlers acquire not one but two languages. What can these bilingual individuals tell us about the capacity of human beings to acquire language? One question of interest centers on whether young children are better at learning languages than adults are. If so, that would suggest that there may be a critical (or at least sensitive) period for language acquisition. Eric Lenneberg (1967) claimed that there is such a critical period and that it lasts until puberty, when the lateralization of language functions in the left hemisphere of the brain is completed. Elissa Newport and her colleagues (Newport, 1991) have been attempting to determine whether there is a critical period for second-language learning as well.

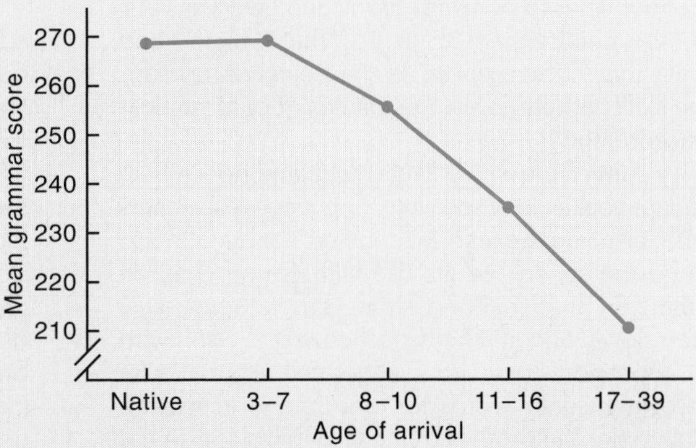

The relationship between age of arrival in the United States and score on the test of English grammar. (From Johnson & Newport, 1989.)

In one study (Johnson & Newport, 1989), native speakers of Korean or Chinese who had come to the United States between the ages of 3 and 39 were tested for mastery of English grammar. Among the subjects who began learning English before puberty, those who learned it earliest learned it best. Among those who arrived in the United States after puberty, performance was generally poor, regardless of age of arrival (see figure above). The number of years of experience with English an individual had had was not as important as when he or she first encountered English. Similarly, deaf adults showed fuller mastery of sign language if they were exposed to American Sign Language as young children than if they first encountered it later in life (Newport, 1991). Although we would want a good deal more evidence before accepting the critical-period hypothesis, this research does suggest that young children are very capable of learning not only a first language but a second one.

But could learning two languages early in life confuse children and ultimately interfere with their mastery of language skills? Could it even slow their intellectual development? Early studies suggested that bilingual children scored well below their monolingual peers on tests of language ability and general intelligence (Hakuta, 1988). However, these studies were fatally flawed: The bilinguals were often immigrant children from lower socioeconomic backgrounds who were tested in English (rather than in the language they had most fully mastered) and who were then compared to middle-class, English-speaking monolinguals (Diaz, 1983).

Recent research makes it clear that children exposed to two languages before age 3 have little difficulty becoming highly proficient in both. Bilingual 2-year-olds do mix elements of both languages in their speech, almost as though they believed they were learning one language. By age 3 or possibly even earlier, though, bilingual children are well aware that the two languages they are learning are distinct and know which language to use in which context (Lanza, 1992; Reich, 1986). They can, for example, speak Spanish with one parent and English with the other without many slips. Even when children do not start learning a second language until after age 3, they often take no more than a year to achieve near-native levels of mastery (Reich, 1986).

Moreover, comparisons of bilingual and monolingual children carefully matched for socioeconomic status and other factors suggest that there are cognitive *advantages* to bilingualism. Bilingual children outperform monolingual children on measures of linguistic awareness; they are, for example, more able to identify and correct grammatical errors (Galambos & Goldin-Meadow, 1990). They also excel on tests of concept formation and nonverbal intellectual ability (Diaz, 1985).

Despite these positive findings and increased federal support for bilingual education in the United States, many nonnative English speakers receive no classroom instruction in their native tongue. They are instead asked to give up their native language in favor of English and to learn basic academic skills in a foreign tongue. Even children enrolled in bilingual education programs often do not receive sufficient encouragement to master both languages (Baron, 1992). Judging from the research, however, it might make sense to provide *all* children with instruction in two languages—a strategy that might not only improve language proficiency and cognitive growth but also foster a greater appreciation of ethnic diversity and help meet our society's increasing need for a bilingually competent workforce (Hakuta & Garcia, 1989).

favorite picture books at bedtime asking "What's this?" and "What's that?" This gives their children repeated opportunities to learn that conversing involves taking turns, that things have names, and that there are proper ways to pose questions and give answers. Soon the children are asking "What's this?" and "What's that?" themselves. As children gain new language skills, adults adjust their styles of communication accordingly.

Try conversing with a 2-year-old, and notice how you adapt your style of speaking. Language researchers use the term **motherese** (also called "baby talk") to describe the speech adults use with young children (Gelman & Shatz, 1977): short, simple sentences, spoken slowly and in a high-pitched voice, often with much repetition, and with exaggerated emphasis on key words (usually words for objects and activities). For example, the mother trying to get her son to eat his peas might say "Eat your peas now. Not the cracker. See those *peas*? Yeah, eat the *peas*." Calling this speech style "motherese" is actually sexist, for fathers use it as well. Indeed, it seems to be used by adults in the large majority of language communities that have been studied (Fernald et al., 1989). And infants, from the earliest days of life, seem to pay more attention to the high-pitched sounds and varied intonational patterns of motherese than to the "flatter" speech adults use when communicating with one another (Cooper & Aslin, 1990; Pegg, Werker, & McLeod, 1992). Indeed, infants may pick up messages carried by their parents' intonation patterns ("I approve," "Pay attention") before they can understand a word of what is being said (Fernald, 1989).

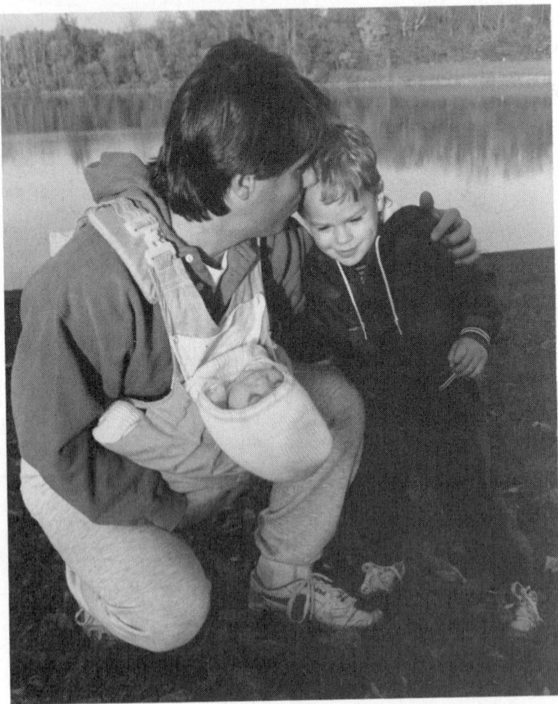
Motherese is used by fathers, too. Both mothers and fathers adapt their speech to young language learners.

Would children learn language just as well if adults talked to them in an adultlike style? Perhaps not. The nativists seem to have underestimated the contributions of environment to language development, for mere exposure to speech is not enough. Catherine Snow and her associates, for example, found that a group of Dutch-speaking children, despite the fact that they watched a great deal of German television, did not acquire any German words or grammar (Snow et al., 1976). True, there are cultural groups (the Kaluli of New Guinea, the natives of American Samoa, and the Trackton people of the Piedmont Carolinas) in which motherese does not seem to be used, and children in these societies seem to acquire language without noticeable delays (Gordon, 1990; Ochs, 1982; Schieffelin, 1986). Yet even these children participate in *conversations* with speakers of the language they are learning, and that is what seems to be required in order to master a human language (Bohannon, MacWhinney, & Snow, 1990). Those parents who do use motherese further simplify the child's task of figuring out the rules of language (Harris, 1992; Kemler Nelson, Hirsh-Pasek, Jusczyk, & Cassidy, 1989). They provide children with a rich language-learning environment in which they and other adults converse with the children daily in attention-getting and understandable ways about the very objects and events that have captured the youngsters' attention.

Adults speaking to young children also use specific communication strategies that foster language development. For example, if a child says "Doggie go," an adult may respond with an **expansion**—a more grammatically complete expression of the same thought ("Yes, the dog is going away"). Adults use conversational techniques like expansions mainly to improve communication, not to teach grammar (Penner, 1987). However, these techniques also serve as a subtle form of correction after children produce grammatically incorrect sentences (Bohannon & Stanowicz, 1988). Moreover, they expose children to new, more grammatically correct forms in contexts in which these forms are highly likely to be understood and built into the child's own grammar (Bohannon & Stanowicz, 1988; Farrar, 1992; Penner, 1987).

How can adults best facilitate young children's language learning? What cognitive capacities enable children to learn how language works? Much remains to be learned about language development, but it does seem to require the interaction of a biologically prepared child with at least one conversational partner, ideally one who tailors his or her own speech to the child's level of understanding.

APPLICATIONS: IMPROVING COGNITIVE FUNCTIONING

Having examined both Piaget's and Vygotsky's theories of cognitive development, we might ask what each has to contribute to the goal of optimizing mental functioning. As Piaget's views first became popular in the United States and Canada, psychologists and educators designed studies to determine whether they could speed cognitive development and help children and adults solve problems more effectively. Some researchers had a different motive: to challenge Piaget's view that concepts like conservation cannot be mastered until the child is intellectually ready.

What has been learned from these training studies? Generally, they suggest that many Piagetian concepts can be taught to children who are slightly younger than the age at which the concepts would naturally emerge. Training is sometimes difficult, and it does not always generalize well to new problems, but progress can be achieved. Dorothy Field (1981), for example, demonstrated that 4-year-olds could be trained to recognize the identity of a substance like a ball of clay before and after its appearance is altered—that is, to understand that, although the clay looks different, it is still the *same* clay and has to be the same amount of clay. Field found that nearly 75% of the children given this identity training could solve at least three out of five conservation problems 2½ to 5 months after training.

Similar training studies have demonstrated that children who function at the late concrete operations stage can be taught formal operations (Adey & Shayer, 1992). Researchers have had even more luck improving the cognitive performance of older adults, sometimes with very simple interventions (Blackburn & Papalia, 1992; Denney, 1982). Such studies suggest that many elderly individuals who perform poorly on Piagetian problem-solving tasks simply need a quick "refresher course" to show their underlying competence. Make no mistake: *No one* has demonstrated that 2-year-olds can be taught formal operations. But at least these studies establish that specific training experiences can somewhat speed a child's progress through Piaget's stages or bring out more advanced capacities in an adult who is performing at a less advanced level.

Piaget himself sneered at attempts by Americans to speed children's progress through his stages (Piaget, 1970). He believed that parents should simply provide young children with opportunities to explore their world and that teachers should use a discovery approach in the classroom that allows children to learn by doing. Given their natural curiosity and normal opportunities to try their hand at solving problems, children would construct ever more complex understandings on their own. Many educators began building Piaget's ideas about discovery-based education into school curricula, especially in science classes (see Gallagher & Easley, 1978). Teachers have also taken seriously Piaget's notion that children best understand material that they can assimilate into their existing understandings. Finding out what the learner already knows and teaching accordingly is in the spirit of Piaget.

And what would Lev Vygotsky recommend to teachers who want to stimulate cognitive growth? As you might guess, Vygotsky's theoretical orientation leads to a very different approach to education than Piaget's does—a more social one. Whereas students in Piaget's classroom would most likely be engaged in independent exploration, students in Vygotsky's classroom would be interacting with and learning from teachers and more knowledgeable peers. The role of teachers and other more skillful collaborators would be to organize the learning activity and to make it more manageable by providing hints and suggestions carefully tailored to the child's current abilities and by gradually turning over more and more of the mental work to the student. According to Vygotsky's sociocultural perspective, the guidance provided by a skilled partner will then be internalized by the learner, first as private speech and eventually as silent inner speech.

Is there any evidence that Vygotsky's guided-learning approach might be superior to Piaget's discovery approach? Consider what Lisa Freund (1990) found when she had 3- to 5-year-old children help a puppet decide which furnishings (sofas, beds, bathtubs, stoves, and so on) should be placed in each of six rooms of a dollhouse that the puppet was moving into. First the children were tested to determine what they already knew about proper furniture placement. Then each child worked at a similar task, either alone (as might be the case in Piaget's discovery-based education) or with his or her mother (Vygotsky's guided learning). Finally, to assess what they had learned, Freund asked the children to perform a final, rather complex, furniture-sorting task. The results were clear: Children who had sorted furniture with help from their mothers showed dramatic improvements in sorting ability, whereas those who had practiced on their own showed little improvement, even though they had received some corrective feedback from the experimenter. Similarly, collaborating with a competent peer can produce cognitive gains that a child might not achieve working alone (Azmitia, 1992; Gauvain & Rogoff, 1989).

So children do not always learn the most when they function as solitary scientists, seeking discoveries on their own; often, conceptual growth springs more readily from children's interactions with other people—particularly with competent people who provide an optimal amount of guidance. Yet it would seem that many children might benefit most from the best of both worlds: opportunities to explore on their own *and* supportive companions to offer help when it is needed.

REFLECTIONS

Pause for a moment and consider the truly remarkable accomplishments that we have described in this chapter. The capacities of the human mind for thought and language are truly awesome. We can marvel at how an infant with no capacity for solving problems "in the head" and no ability to talk can grow into an adult like Piaget or Chomsky who can invent abstract theories and communicate them to the rest of us—or into a typical adult who uses thought and language very effectively in everyday life. Imagine not even grasping the fundamental concept that the rest of the world exists even when you are not directly experiencing it. Imagine being able later in life to conceptualize hypothetical worlds that you have never experienced. Imagine progressing from a "vocabulary" of cries to a capacity to express an infinite number of ideas in language. Imagine, as you watch your next television program, how differently family members of different ages interpret that same program, each with his or her own cognitive structures for interpreting events, each with his or her own vocabulary and language competencies.

Because the human mind is so complex, we should not be surprised that it is not yet understood. Piaget attacked only part of the puzzle, and he only partially succeeded. Despite challenges to Piaget's theory, however, we urge you to learn it well and to give it a chance to change the way you view infants, young children, and adolescents. If nothing else, try some conservation tasks on a preschooler: Seeing it is believing it!

SUMMARY POINTS

1. Jean Piaget, through his clinical method, formulated four stages of cognitive development, in which children construct increasingly complex schemes through an interaction of maturation and experience. Children adapt to the world through the processes of organization and adaptation (assimilating new experience to existing understandings and accommodating existing understandings to new experience).

2. According to Piaget, infants progress through six substages of the sensorimotor stage by perceiving and acting on the world: from reflexes, to repeated actions (primary and secondary circular reactions), to experimentation (tertiary reactions), and finally to the ability to engage in symbolic or representational thought. This symbolic capacity permits full mastery of the concept that objects exist apart from our perceptions.

3. In Piaget's preoperational stage (ages 2–7), children make many uses of their symbolic capacity but are limited by their dependence on appearances, lack of logical mental operations, and egocentrism. They fail to grasp the concept of conservation because they engage in centration, irreversible thinking, and static thought. Recent research suggests that preschool children's capacities are greater than Piaget supposed.

4. School-aged children enter the stage of concrete operations (ages 7–11) and begin to master conservation tasks; they can think about relations, grasping seriation and transitivity, and they understand the concept of class inclusion.

5. Adolescents often show the first signs of formal operations at 11 or 12 and later master the hypothetical-deductive reasoning skills required to solve scientific problems. Cognitive changes result in other developmental advances and may also contribute to confusion, rebellion, idealism, and adolescent egocentrism (the imaginary audience and personal fable).

6. Adults are most likely to display formal-operational skills in their areas of expertise. Some adults, especially well-educated ones, may advance beyond formal operations to display relativistic, dialectical, and systematic thinking. Although aging adults often perform less well than younger adults on Piagetian tasks, factors other than biological aging may explain this.

7. Piaget has made huge contributions to the field of human development but has been criticized for underestimating the capacities of infants and young children, not considering factors besides competence that influence performance, failing to demonstrate that his stages have coherence, offering vague explanations of development, and underestimating the role of language and social interaction in cognitive development.

8. Vygotsky's sociocultural perspective emphasizes social influences on cognitive development more than Piaget's theory does. Children internalize problem-solving techniques shown to them by knowledgeable partners sensitive to their zone of proximal development; language shapes their thought as social speech becomes private speech and later inner speech.

9. To acquire language, children must master phonology (sound), semantics (meaning), and syntax (sentence structure), as well as learn how to use language appropriately (pragmatics) and to understand nonverbal communication.

10. Infants begin to discriminate speech sounds and progress from crying, cooing, and babbling to one-word holophrases and then to telegraphic speech guided by a functional grammar that allows them to name things, make requests, and achieve other communication goals.

11. Language abilities improve dramatically in the preschool years, as illustrated by the appearance of overregularizations and new transformation rules. School-aged children and adolescents refine their language skills and become less egocentric communicators. Knowledge of semantics continues to expand during adulthood, and language abilities hold up well in old age.

12. Theories of language development include learning theories, nativist theories, and interactionist theories that emphasize both the child's biologically based capacities and experience conversing with adults who speak in motherese and use strategies that simplify the language-learning task.

13. Attempts to teach cognitive skills suggest that development can be speeded up, though with some difficulty and with limits, and that older adults can be helped to use their cognitive competencies more effectively. Piaget advocated a discovery approach to learning, whereas Vygotsky's followers emphasize guided learning involving collaboration between the learner and a more capable adult or peer.

KEY TERMS

A, not *B*, error
accommodation
adaptation
adolescent egocentrism
assimilation
babbling
centration
class inclusion
clinical method
cognition
concrete operations stage
conservation
constructivism
cooing
decentration
dialectical thinking
egocentrism
expansion
formal operations stage
functional grammar
holophrase
hypothetical-deductive reasoning
imaginary audience
language
language acquisition device (LAD)
logical operation
morpheme
motherese
object permanence
organization
overextension
overregularization
personal fable
phoneme
phonology
pragmatics
preoperational stage
primary circular reaction
private speech
relativistic thinking
reversibility
scheme (schema)
secondary circular reaction
semantics
sensorimotor stage
seriation
symbolic capacity
symbolic play
syntax
systematic thinking
telegraphic speech
tertiary circular reaction
transformational grammar
transitivity
underextension
zone of proximal development

LEARNING AND INFORMATION PROCESSING

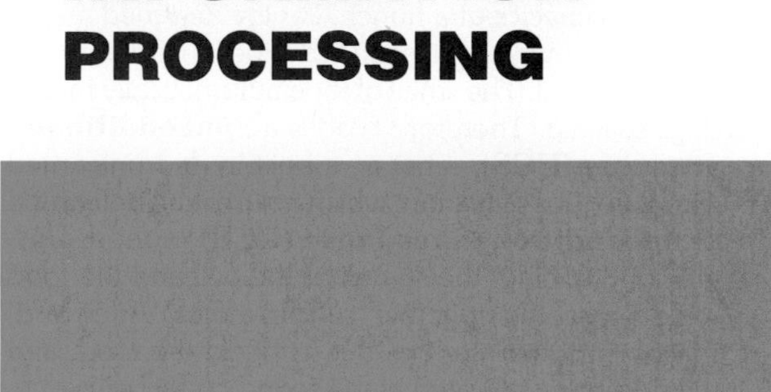

"What did you learn in school today?"
"Where did you learn *that*?"
"I can't believe I remembered that."
"It's on the tip of my tongue."
"Sorry, I forgot."

Lines like these appear often in our conversations; learning and remembering, failing to learn and forgetting—these are all important parts of our daily lives. Moreover, individuals develop as they do partly because of what they have learned and remembered from their experiences. In this chapter our examination of cognitive development continues, but from a different perspective than Piaget's. We first introduce traditional learning theories that describe the basic learning mechanisms important at all ages. Then the chapter turns to an information-processing perspective on the mind that is useful in analyzing more complex forms of learning, memory, and problem solving. Finally, it examines how the capacities to learn, remember, and use stored information to solve problems change over the life span.

BASIC LEARNING PROCESSES

Learning is typically defined as a relatively permanent change in behavior (or behavior potential) that results from one's experiences. It is change—in thoughts, perceptions, or reactions to the environment—that is neither programmed by the genes nor due to maturation (Domjan, 1993). The capacity to learn is in place even before birth and strongly affects development and adaptation throughout the life span.

In Chapter 6 we introduced one very simple and often-overlooked form of learning called **habituation,** or learning *not* to respond to a stimulus that is repeated over and over. Habituation might be thought of as learning to be bored by the familiar (for example, the continual ticking of a clock or the flickering of a fluorescent light). We might soon be overloaded if we reacted to everything in our environments, even after seeing it countless times before. It seems adaptive to reserve attention for novel experiences. From birth, humans habituate to repeatedly presented lights, sounds, and smells; such stimuli are somehow recognized as "old hat" (Willemsen, 1979). Here we will consider three fundamental types of learning featured in major learning theories of human development: classical conditioning, operant conditioning, and observational learning.

Classical Conditioning

In **classical conditioning,** a stimulus that initially had no effect on the individual comes to elicit a response through its association with a stimulus that already elicits the response. That is, a new association between stimulus and response is learned. As an illustration, consider how the Russian physiologist Ivan Pavlov originally discovered classical conditioning. In the course of his work on digestive processes in dogs, Pavlov noticed that his dogs would often salivate at the appearance of a caretaker who had come to feed them. To check out a hunch, Pavlov designed an experiment in which he sounded a bell just before the dogs were fed. The smell of food automatically makes dogs salivate. Therefore food is an **unconditioned stimulus (UCS)**—that is, a built-in and unlearned stimulus—for salivation, which in turn is an unlearned or **unconditioned response (UCR)** to food. During conditioning, the stimuli of the bell and the food were presented together several times. Afterward, Pavlov sounded the bell but withheld the food, and the dogs now salivated at the sound of the bell alone. Their behavior had changed as a result of their experience. Specifically, an initially neutral stimulus, the bell, was now a **conditioned stimulus (CS)** for a **conditioned response (CR),** salivation. (See Figure 8.1.)

What role does classical conditioning play in human development? It is highly involved in the learning of emotional responses and attitudes. In a classic study, John Watson, founder of behavioral psychology, and Rosalie Raynor (1920) set out to demonstrate that fears can be learned—that they are not necessarily inborn, as was commonly thought at the time. These researchers presented a gentle white rat to a now-famous infant named Albert, who showed no fear of it whatsoever. However, every time Albert reached for the white rat, Watson would slip behind him and bang a steel rod with a hammer. In this situation the loud noise was the unconditioned stimulus for fear, which was the unconditioned response (because infants are naturally upset by loud

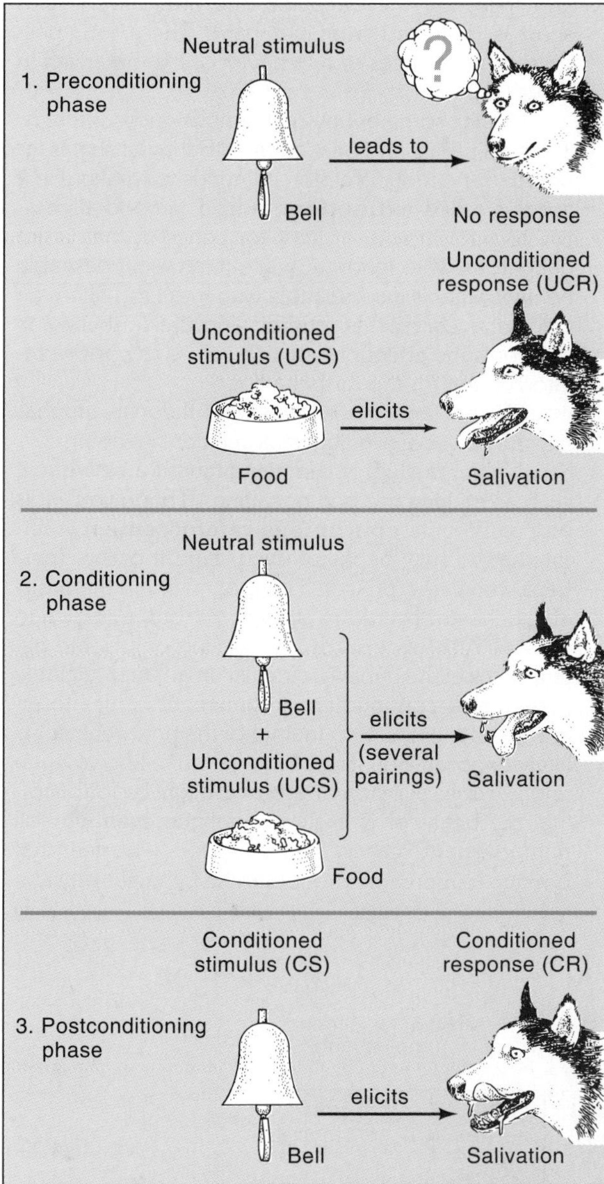

FIGURE 8.1 The three phases of classical conditioning. In the preconditioning phase, the unconditioned stimulus (UCS) always elicits an unconditioned response (UCR), whereas the conditioned stimulus (CS) never does. During the conditioning phase, the CS and UCS are paired repeatedly and eventually associated. At this point the learner passes into the postconditioning phase, in which the CS alone will elicit the original response (now called a conditioned response, or CR).

noise). Through learning, the white rat became a conditioned stimulus for a conditioned fear response. By today's standards, this experiment would be viewed as unethical, but Watson had made his point: Emotional responses can be learned.

Perhaps you can identify a fear or phobia you learned when an object or event that is not fearsome in itself became associated with a frightening experience. To this day, one of the authors shivers at the sight (or even the thought) of antiseptic cotton, undoubtedly because cotton just happened to be there when the iodine swabbed on a skinned knee caused painful shivers.

Fortunately, responses that are learned through classical conditioning can be unlearned through the same process, in this case called **counterconditioning.** Mary Cover Jones (1924) demonstrated that a 2-year-old named Peter overcame his fear of furry animals after being exposed to a rabbit (for him, a CS for fearful responses) while he ate some of his favorite food (a UCS for pleasant feelings). Peter gradually came to associate the rabbit with pleasurable rather than fearful feelings. Classical conditioning is undoubtedly involved when infants learn to love their parents, who at first may be neutral stimuli but who become associated with the positive sensations of receiving milk, being rocked, and being comforted. And classical conditioning helps explain why adults find that certain songs on the radio, scents, or articles of clothing "turn them on."

Operant (Instrumental) Conditioning

Another highly important form of basic learning is **operant conditioning.** In classical conditioning, responses are elicited or provoked by a stimulus. In operant conditioning, a learner first *emits* a response, or behaves in some way, and then comes to associate this action with the positive or negative consequences that ensue. B. F. Skinner (1953) made this form of conditioning famous. The basic principle makes a good deal of sense: We tend to repeat behaviors that have pleasant consequences and cut down on behaviors that have unpleasant consequences. Through operant conditioning, we learn new skills and a range of habits, both good and bad.

In the language of operant conditioning, *reinforcement* occurs when a consequence *strengthens* a response, or makes it more likely to occur in the future. If a child cleans his room and then receives a hug, the hug will probably provide **positive reinforcement** for room cleaning and make the behavior more likely in the future. *Positive* here means that something has been *added* to the situation, and *reinforcement* means that the behavior is strengthened. Thus a positive reinforcer is an event that, when introduced following a behavior, makes that behavior more probable in the future. **Negative reinforcement** also involves the strengthening of some behavioral tendency, but the behavior is strengthened because something negative or unpleasant is *removed* from the situation, or is escaped or avoided, after the behavior occurs. Have you been in a car in which an obnoxious buzzer sounds until you fasten your seatbelt? The idea is that your "buckling up" behavior will become a habit through *negative reinforcement,* because buckling up allows you to escape the unpleasant buzzer. No candy or hugs follow the buckling up, so it is not positive reinforcement that makes you likely to perform this behavior. It is negative reinforcement.

We are likely to keep doing things that allow us to escape or avoid unpleasantness, so we learn many habits through negative reinforcement. If a teenager finds that lying to Mom is the secret to avoiding long lectures, she will keep right on lying. If a man finds that a few beers allow him to escape his feelings of anxiety, he'll keep right on drinking. In each case a behavior is strengthened through negative reinforcement—through the removal or elimination of something unpleasant.

The point about negative reinforcement has been labored because there is a common—and absolutely incorrect—tendency to think that the term *negative reinforcement* is a fancy name for punishment. Contrast reinforcement, whether it is positive or negative, with punishment: Whereas reinforcement increases the strength of the behavior that preceded it, **punishment** decreases the strength of that behavior. There are two forms of punishment paralleling the two forms of reinforcement. Either an unpleasant event can be added to the situation following the behavior (for example, a cashier is criticized for coming up short of cash at the end of the day), or something pleasant can be removed from the situation following the behavior (the amount she was short is deducted from her pay). These four possible consequences of a behavior are summarized in Figure 8.2.

Finally, some behavior is simply ignored; that is, it has no particular consequence. Behavior that is ignored, or no longer reinforced, tends to weaken, in a process called **extinction.** Indeed, a good alternative to punishment, at least for behavior that is not dangerous, is to ignore it while reinforcing desirable behavior that is incompatible with it. All too often the well-behaved child is ignored and the misbehaving child gets the attention—which serves as positive reinforcement for the misbehavior.

Skinner and other behavioral theorists emphasize the power of positive reinforcement in raising children. When a child is first being taught a new habit, such as making the bed or saying "Thank you," it is best to provide **continuous reinforcement,** reinforcing the new behavior every time it occurs (perhaps with warm praise). Then, to maintain the desirable behavior over long periods, it is best to switch to **partial reinforcement,** reinforcing only some occurrences of the behavior, ideally on an unpredictable schedule. If continuous reinforcement comes to an abrupt end, extinction (fading) of the new behavior is likely to occur. But, if a child never quite knows when another dose of parental approval might be forthcoming, the behavior is likely to continue even after all reinforcement ceases. Those parents who feel that positive reinforcement of desirable behavior must be

	Positive stimulus (pleasant)	Negative stimulus (unpleasant)
Administered	**Positive reinforcement** (strengthens the behavior) Dad gives in to the whining and lets Moosie play Nintendo, making whining more likely in the future.	**Punishment** (weakens the behavior) Dad calls Moosie a "baby." Moosie does not like this at all and is less likely to whine in the future.
Withdrawn	**Punishment** (weakens the behavior) Dad confiscates Moosie's favorite Nintendo game to discourage whining in the future.	**Negative reinforcement** (strengthens the behavior) Dad stops joking with Lulu. Moosie gets very jealous when Dad pays attention to Lulu, so his whining enables him to bring this unpleasant state of affairs to an end.

FIGURE 8.2 Possible consequences of behavior. Moosie comes into the TV room and sees his father talking and joking with his sister, Lulu, as the two watch a football game. Soon Moosie begins to whine, louder and louder, that he wants them to turn off the television so he can play Nintendo games. Here are four possible consequences of his behavior. Consider both the type of consequence—whether it is a positive or negative stimulus—and whether it is administered ("added to" the situation) or withdrawn.

supplemented by punishment of bad behavior can use the guidelines in Box 8.1 to make punishment more effective.

Observational Learning

The form of basic learning we will consider last is **observational learning,** which results from observing the behavior of other people. Almost anything can be learned by watching (or listening to) other people. In imitation of parents the child may learn how to speak a language and tackle math problems, as well as how to swear, snack between meals, and smoke. As we saw in Chapter 2, this form of learning takes center stage in Albert Bandura's social learning theory (1977, 1986, 1989).

Bandura set out to demonstrate that people could learn a response that was neither elicited by a conditioned stimulus (classical conditioning) nor performed and then strengthened by a reinforcer (operant conditioning). His classic experiment involved the learning of aggressive behavior by nursery school children (Bandura, 1965). Children watched a short film in which an adult *model* attacked an inflatable "Bobo" doll, hitting the doll with a mallet while shouting "Sockeroo," throwing rubber balls at the doll while shouting "Bang, bang, bang," and so on. There were three experimental conditions:

1. Children in the *model-rewarded* condition saw a second adult give the aggressive model some candy and a soft drink for a "championship performance."

BOX 8.1 Using Punishment Effectively

Although operant researchers emphasize positive reinforcement of good behavior, most parents use punishment at least occasionally. They can use it more effectively by following these guidelines, derived from the research literature (Domjan, 1993; Parke, 1977):

• **Punish as soon as possible.** It is best to punish as the child prepares to misbehave or at least during the act. Postponing punishment ("Wait 'til Daddy comes home!") is bad practice. Young children may conclude that Daddy is punishing them for whatever they are doing at the moment—for example, putting toys back in the toy box. Delayed punishment can be effective with older children if the punisher explains why the child is being punished (Verna, 1977).

• **Punish with intensity (but not too much intensity).** Laboratory research with young children suggests that intense punishment, in the form of loud buzzers or noises, is more effective than mild punishment. That is, a loud "No" is likely to be more effective than a soft "No." But we should not be misled into thinking that severe physical punishment is a good idea. Severe spankings have several disadvantages: They create high anxiety, which can interfere with "learning one's lesson," and they may make the child learn to fear and avoid the punisher. Harsh physical punishment also teaches the child to rely on aggression as a way of dealing with problems (Weiss, Dodge, Bates, & Pettit, 1992). So, intense punishment can be effective as long as it is not so intense that it has these sorts of negative side effects.

One negative side effect of physical punishment is that it teaches children through observational learning to be aggressive.

• **Punish consistently.** Acts that are punished only now and then persist. After all, the child is being reinforced part of the time for the (usually fun) misbehavior.

• **Be otherwise warm.** Children respond better to punishment from a person who is otherwise affectionate than from someone who is usually cold.

• **Explain yourself.** Explaining why the behavior was wrong and is being punished helps children learn to control their own behavior in the future (for example, to recall why the behavior would be unwise). Older children and, in particular, adolescents want and benefit from explanations that point out the social consequences of misbehavior.

• **Reinforce alternative behavior.** Since punishment alone tells a child only what *not* to do, it makes sense to strengthen acceptable alternatives to the misbehavior. The parent who does not want a toddler to play with an expensive vase might punish that behavior but also reinforce play with an unbreakable plastic pot.

• **Consider alternative responses to the misbehavior.** Although spanking seems to be the first thing many parents think of when a child misbehaves, punishment can also involve taking away desirable stimuli (for example, TV privileges). And a highly effective alternative to punishment is a procedure called *time out,* which involves removing children from the situation in which their misbehavior is positively reinforced. The boy who is throwing toys around the room might be sent for a few minutes to a quiet room where he is cut off from the pleasure of creating havoc. When misbehavior is no longer reinforced, it weakens through extinction.

2. Children in the *model-punished* condition saw a second adult scold and spank the model for beating up on Bobo.
3. Children in the *no-consequences* condition simply saw the model behave aggressively.

After the film ended, it was the children's turn to be in a playroom with the Bobo doll and many of the props the model had used to work Bobo over. What did children in the three conditions learn from observing the model in the film?

As the left side of Figure 8.3 shows, children in the model-rewarded condition and the no-consequences condition imitated more of the model's aggressive acts than children who had seen the model punished for aggression. But Bandura also devised a learning test, in which he encouraged children to reproduce all of the model's behavior they could remember. The results of this test, which appear in the right-hand portion of Figure 8.3, indicate that all the children learned about the same amount from observing the model regardless of the experimental condition they were in. Apparently the children who had seen the model punished imitated fewer of the model's behaviors on the initial "performance" test because they had learned from the film that they might be punished for striking Bobo. Nonetheless, these children learned a great deal about how to behave aggressively—knowledge that could be acted upon in the future if their expectation and fear of punishment were not so great.

This study demonstrates that children can indeed learn new behavior simply through observing a model—even though they have not tried out the aggressive behaviors before and have not been reinforced for performing them. Moreover, the study points out an important distinction between *learning* and *performance*: Children can learn from observation without imitating (performing) the learned responses. Whether they will perform what they learn depends in part on whether the model was reinforced or punished for his or her actions—a process called *vicarious reinforcement.* In addition, although children can learn by observing even without being reinforced, reinforcing them directly for imitating will increase the chances that they will continue to perform what they have learned.

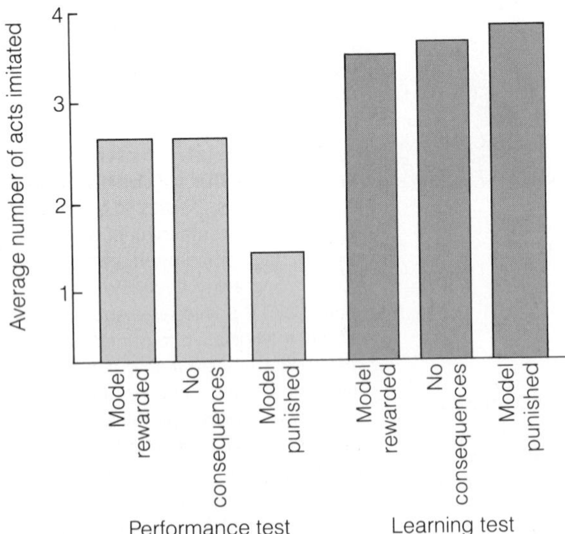

FIGURE 8.3 Average number of aggressive responses imitated during the performance test and the learning test for children who had seen a model rewarded, punished, or receiving no consequence for his actions. (Adapted from Bandura, 1965.)

Social learning theorists such as Albert Bandura are far more cognitively oriented than behavioral theorists such as John Watson and B. F. Skinner. Observational learning, unlike classical and operant conditioning, requires a mind that attends to, remembers, and interprets information about other people's behavior. To learn anything, the learner must first pay attention to a model. In real life, some models are more influential than others because they capture more attention. People who are warm and nurturant and/or powerful and competent are most likely to be imitated by children (Bandura, 1977). Parents, teachers, older siblings, and popular peers often fit these descriptions. As people mature, they prefer models who are similar to themselves in some way. These models might include friends, or people in the same occupation, ethnic group, or political party (Bandura, 1986).

Cognitive processes are also involved in storing information about what was observed. Somehow the learner must mentally represent or symbolize what the model did or said. These symbolic representations might be *images* of the model's action or *words* that describe and summarize what was seen. Finally, learners also process information about the consequences of behavior, form expectations about the likelihood of reinforcement or punishment in the future, and even *mentally* reinforce or punish their own actions—all very cognitive activities.

Basic Learning Processes and Development

Many of the changes in behavior that occur as people develop result from basic learning processes. Humans of all ages learn positive and negative emotional associations to a wide range of stimuli (classical conditioning). They form habits, good and bad, by being influenced by the reinforcing or punishing consequences of what they do (operant conditioning). And they change their own understandings and behaviors after watching other people behave (observational learning). Later we will see how basic learning capacities change as people get older. Yet many psychologists have concluded that learning theories do not

In Bandura's classic experiment, children who had watched an adult model show aggression toward a Bobo doll in several unusual ways (*top row*) performed similar acts themselves (*middle and bottom rows*), even though they hadn't been reinforced for committing such acts.

adequately explain how humans learn complex material, remember it, and use it to solve problems. Let's look now at an approach that addresses these issues.

THE INFORMATION-PROCESSING APPROACH

As the behavioral perspective on learning gained a firm hold among psychologists, it became unfashionable to study mental events that could not be directly observed. According to Howard Gardner (1985), the "cognitive revolution" in psychology could not have occurred without (1) a demonstration of the inadequacies of the behaviorist approach and (2) the rise of computer technology.

Showing deficiencies in the behaviorist approach was easiest in relation to complex learning and memory tasks. Consider learning from this textbook. Obviously some very complex processes occur between your registering of the pattern of print on this page and your writing of an essay about it. To account for these processes, behaviorists would have to talk about chains of mental stimuli and responses between an external stimulus (for instance, the printed page) and an overt response. This approach proved cumbersome at best.

Then came computers, with their capacity for systematically converting input to output. The computer seemed to provide a good analogy to the human mind (Gardner, 1985; Newell & Simon, 1961). Any computer has a limited capacity, associated with its hardware and software, for processing information. The computer's *hardware* is the machine itself— its keyboard (or input system), its storage capacity, and so on. The mind's "hardware" is the nervous system, including the brain, the sensory receptors, and their neural connections. The computer's *software* consists of the programs used to manipulate stored and received information: word-processing and statistics programs and the like. The mind, too, has its "software," or mental "programs" that represent the ways information is registered, interpreted, stored, retrieved, and analyzed.

The computer, then, was the model for the **information-processing approach** to human cognition, which emphasizes the basic mental processes involved in attention, perception, memory, and decision making. When the information-processing approach began to guide studies of development, the challenge became one of determining how the hardware and software of the mind change over the life span. Just as today's more highly developed computers have greater capacity than those of the past, maturation of the nervous system plus experience presumably enable adults to remember more than young children can and to perform more complex cognitive feats with greater accuracy (Kail & Bisanz, 1992; Klahr & Wallace, 1976).

Figure 8.4 presents one influential conception of the human information-processing system. If your history professor says that the U.S. Constitution was ratified in 1789, this statement is an environmental stimulus. Assuming that you are not lost in a daydream, your **sensory register** will log it, holding it for a fraction of a second as a kind of afterimage (or, in this example, a kind of echo). Much that strikes the sensory register quickly disappears without further processing. Attentional processes (see Chapter 6) have a good deal to do with which sensory stimuli enter the sensory register in the first place and which are processed even further. If you think you may need to remember 1789, it will be moved into **short-term (or working) memory,** which can hold a limited amount of information (perhaps only about seven items or chunks of information) for several seconds. For example, short-term memory can hold on to a telephone number while you dial it. Short-term memory (called working memory when its active quality is being emphasized) temporarily stores information so that it can be operated on. It is what is "on one's mind," or in one's consciousness, at any moment.

To be remembered for any length of time, information must be moved from short-term memory into **long-term memory,** a relatively permanent store of information that represents what most people mean by memory. More than likely, you will hold the professor's statement in short-term memory just long enough to record it in your notes. Later, as you study your notes, you will rehearse the information or use other memory strategies to move it into long-term memory so that you can retrieve it the next day when you are taking the test.

This simplified model shows what you must do to learn and remember something. The first step is **encoding** the information: getting it into the system, learning it, moving it from the sensory register to short-term memory and then to long-term memory while organizing it in a form suitable for storage. If it never gets in, it cannot be remembered. Then there is **storage,** or the holding of information in the long-term memory store. Memories fade over time unless they are appropriately stored in long-term memory. And, finally, there is **retrieval,** or the process of getting information out again when it is needed.

If you are asked a multiple-choice question about when the Constitution was ratified, you need not actively retrieve the correct date; you merely need to recognize it among the options. This is an example of **recognition memory.** But assume you were asked "When was the Constitution ratified?" This would be a test of **recall memory,** which requires active retrieval without the aid of cues. In between recognition and recall memory is **cued recall memory,** in which one is given a hint or cue to facilitate retrieval (for example, "When was the Constitution ratified? It's the year the French Revolution began and rhymes with *wine*."). Most people find questions requiring recognition memory easier to answer than those requiring cued recall, and those requiring cued recall are easier than those requiring pure recall. This is true

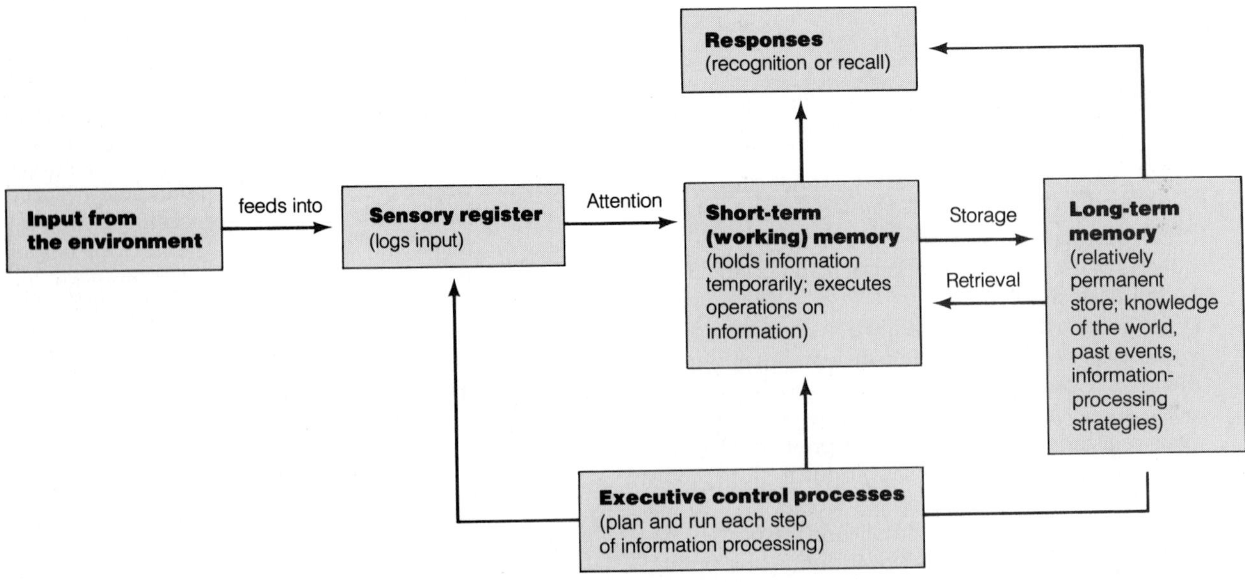

FIGURE 8.4 A model of information processing. (Adapted from Atkinson & Shiffrin, 1968.)

across the life span, which suggests that many things that we have apparently encoded or learned are "in there someplace," although we have trouble retrieving them without cues. Breakdowns in remembering can involve difficulties in initial encoding, storage, or retrieval.

Now imagine that you are asked how many years passed between the signing of the Declaration of Independence (1776, remember?) and the ratification of the Constitution. Here we have a simple example of **problem solving,** or use of the information-processing system to achieve a goal or to arrive at a decision (in this case, to answer the question). Here, too, the information-processing model describes what happens between stimulus and response. The question will move through the memory system. You will need to draw on your long-term memory to understand the question, and then you will have to search long-term memory for the two relevant dates. Moreover, you will need to locate your stored knowledge of the mathematical operation of subtraction. You will then transfer this stored information to short-term memory so that you can use your subtraction "program" (1789 minus 1776) to derive the correct answer.

Notice that processing information successfully requires both knowing what you are doing and making decisions. This is why the information-processing model includes **executive control processes** involved in planning and monitoring what is done. These control processes run the show, guiding the selection, organization, manipulation, and interpretation of information all the way along. Stored knowledge about the world and about information processing guides what is done with new information.

The information-processing approach to cognition has the advantage of focusing attention on *how* people remember things or solve problems, not just on what they recall or what answer they give. A young child's performance on a problem could break down in any number of ways: The child might not be paying attention to the relevant aspects of the problem, might be unable to hold all the relevant pieces of information in short-term memory long enough to do anything with them, might lack the strategies for transferring new information into long-term memory or retrieving information from long-term memory as needed, might simply not have enough stored knowledge to understand the problem, or might not have the executive control processes needed to manage the steps in problem solving. If we can identify how information processes in the younger individual differ from those processes in the older person, we will have gained much insight into cognitive development.

Many processes involved in learning, memory, and problem solving improve between infancy and adulthood and then decline somewhat in old age, although this pattern is not uniform for all processes or all people. Our task in this chapter is to describe these age trends and, more interestingly, to try to determine why they occur.

THE INFANT

We have already seen that infants explore the world thoroughly through their senses. But are they learning from their sensory experiences and remembering anything?

Can Young Infants Learn?

Infants *can* learn at birth and indeed before birth (Lipsitt, 1990; Rovee-Collier, 1987). After they are repeatedly exposed to a stimulus, newborns show habituation to it, ceasing to be interested any longer and preferring something novel (Friedman, 1972). Newborns can also be classically conditioned, although not always easily (Fitzgerald & Brackbill, 1976). Lewis Lipsitt and Herbert Kaye (1964) paired a musical tone with the presentation of a nipple (an unconditioned stimulus for sucking). After several of these conditioning trials, 2- to 3-day-old infants began to suck at the sound of the tone, which had become a conditioned stimulus (CS) for the sucking response. Operant conditioning is also possible. At the tender age of 1 day, infants will learn to suck faster on a nipple if their sucking is positively reinforced by sugary rather than plain water (Kron, 1966).

Whether true observational learning exists at birth is controversial. Newborns apparently can imitate certain facial expressions, such as surprise and sadness, and certain actions, such as sticking out the tongue or pursing the lips, as long as they are already capable of these behaviors (Field, Woodson, Greenberg, & Cohen, 1982; Meltzoff & Moore, 1983, 1989; see also Figure 8.5). However, this imitative response is probably quite different from the older child's ability to imitate a novel act or store a representation of what a model did. Eugene Abravanel and Ann Sigafoos (1984) were able to get 1-month-old infants to imitate tongue protrusion reliably, but older infants in the study (up to 5 months of age) did not do so. This suggests that imitation in the newborn may be an involuntary, automatic, reflexlike action that disappears with age (just as many of the newborn's reflexes do), to be replaced later by more voluntary imitation as the cortex of the brain develops (see also Kaitz et al., 1988; Vinter, 1986).

So newborns can learn. But are they competent learners? In some respects they are, especially when they are learning responses that produce food or are otherwise significant biologically (Rovee-Collier, 1987). However, they are less competent learners than they will be later in infancy. For one thing, newborns are often slow to learn. They may need nearly 200 conditioning trials to learn to turn their heads at the sound

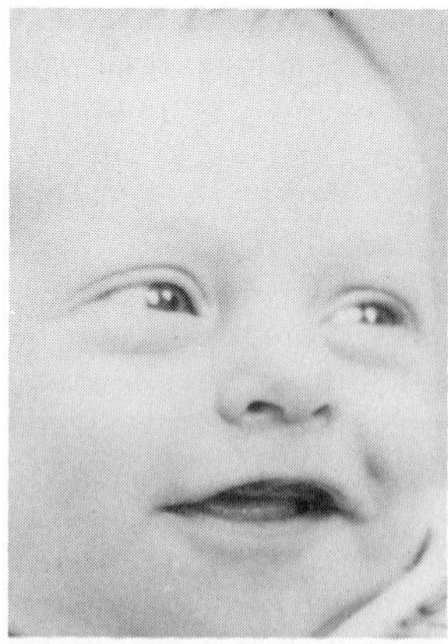

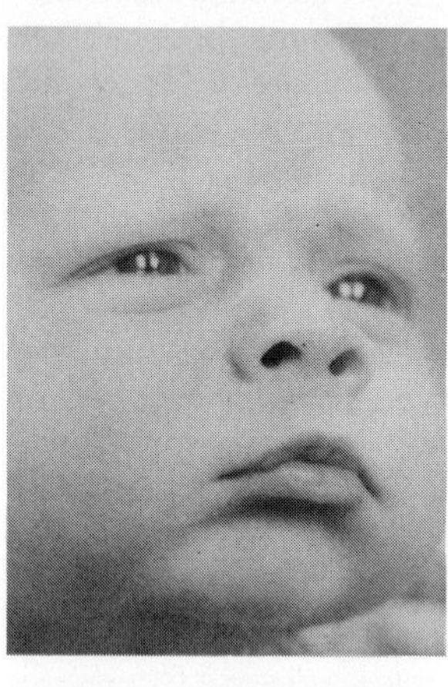
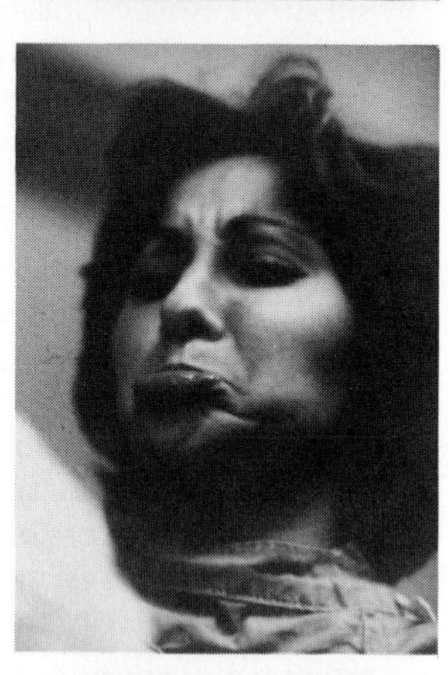
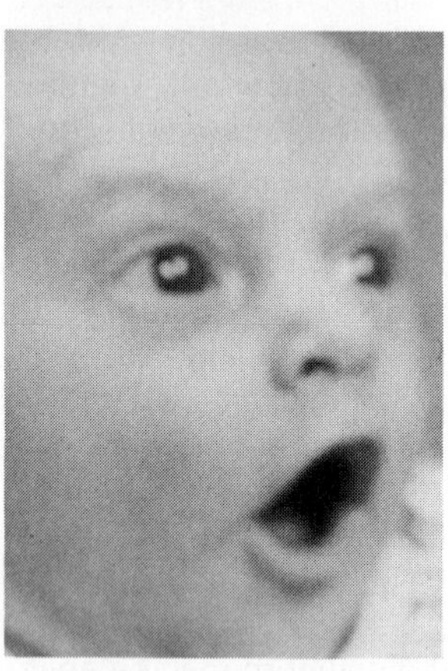

FIGURE 8.5 Newborns can imitate facial expressions—here, happy, sad, and surprised expressions. (From Field, Woodson, Greenberg, & Cohen, 1982.)

of a bell in order to be reinforced with milk (Papoušek, 1967). By 3 months of age, infants need only about 40 trials to learn the same response, and by 5 months they need fewer than 30. Second, the range of responses that a newborn can learn and perform is quite limited. Only a few reflexes can be classically conditioned, and only behaviors already within the newborn's repertoire can be learned through operant conditioning or observation. Entirely novel behaviors cannot be learned. As infants develop, they rapidly become able to learn more kinds of responses, and to learn them faster.

How Well Do Infants Remember What They Have Learned?

Assessing infant memory has required ingenuity, since infants cannot just tell us what they recall. An infant's habituation to a repeatedly presented stimulus, for example, tells us that the stimulus is recognized as something experienced before. Newborns do show recognition memory, preferring a new sight to something they have seen many times (Fagan, 1984) and showing a reduced interest in a word they heard spoken repeatedly 24 hours earlier (Swain, Zelazo, & Clifton, 1993). As they get older, infants need less "study time" before a stimulus becomes old hat, and they can *retain* what they have learned longer (Fagan, 1984).

Another method of establishing the existence of memory in early infancy has relied on operant-conditioning techniques and has been used extensively by Carolyn Rovee-Collier (1984, 1987) and her colleagues to explore infant memory capacities. If a ribbon is run between a baby's ankle and an attractive mobile, as shown in Figure 8.6, the infant will soon learn that kicking its leg brings about a very reinforcing consequence: the jiggling of the mobile. Then the mobile is removed and presented at a later time to see if the infant will kick again. To succeed at this task, the infant must recognize the mobile and "recall" that the thing to do is to kick, a feat that seems to require a simple form of cued recall. Infants 2 months old remember how to make the mobile move for up to three days, whereas infants 3 months old can remember for more than a week.

What if stronger cues to aid recall were provided? Janet Davis and Rovee-Collier (1983) brought 2-month-old infants who had learned the kicking response back to the laboratory 18 days later and "reminded" them of the response by rotating the mobile. These infants kicked up a storm as soon as the ribbon was attached to their ankles, whereas infants who were not reminded showed no sign of remembering to kick. It seems, then, that cued recall (in this case, memory cued by the mere presence of the mobile or, better yet, its rotation by the experimenter) may emerge during the first couple of months of life. However, this research also suggests that young infants have difficulty *retrieving* what they have learned if they are not given sufficient cues or if the context in which they are tested is even slightly different from the context in which they learned a response (Howe & Courage, 1993; Rovee-Collier et al., 1992; Singer & Fagen, 1992). In short, these early memories are fragile.

When, then, are infants capable of actively retrieving information from memory when no cues are

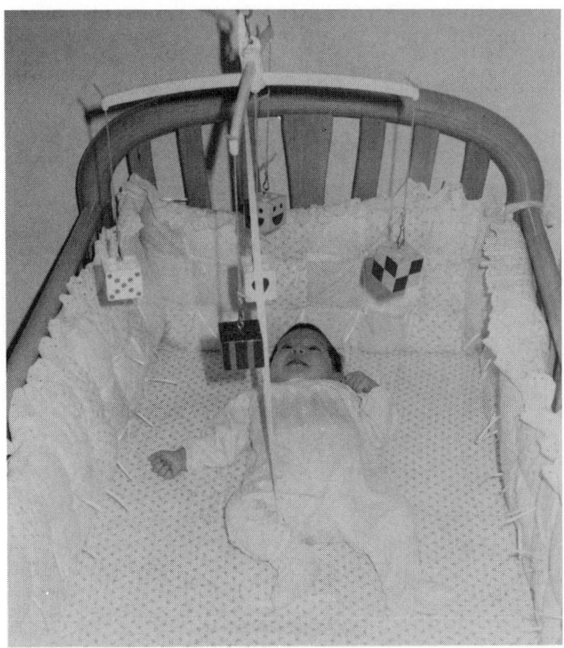

FIGURE 8.6 When ribbons are tied to their ankles, young infants soon learn to make a mobile move by kicking their legs. Carolyn Rovee-Collier has made use of this operant-conditioning paradigm to find out how long infants will remember the trick for making the mobile move.

available? At about 8 to 9 months of age, infants will search for and find a hidden toy in tasks like those used to test for Piaget's concept of object permanence (Sophian, 1980). This is evidence of recall. **Deferred imitation,** or the ability to imitate a novel act after a delay, also provides evidence of recall memory. As early as 9 months of age, many infants can imitate novel actions (for example, pushing a button on a box to produce a beep) after a 24-hour delay (Meltzoff, 1988). More and more of them will be able to imitate single actions by 18 months of age, when they also start to imitate combinations of novel actions (Abravanel & Gingold, 1985).

By age 2, infants seem to be able to recall events that happened months earlier and can even relate them in story form (Howe & Courage, 1993). Katherine Nelson (1984), for example, relates how Emily, at only 24 months of age, reconstructed a trip to the library with her grandmother that took place four months earlier: "Go library. I sat in Mormor's lap. I went to the library. Probably that's what we did. Probably we did in the *bus*!" (p. 122).

What remarkable progress is made during the two years of infancy! Babies begin with an ability to learn only certain kinds of associations, often very slowly, but soon become more and more polished learners. They show recognition memory for familiar stimuli at birth and cued recall memory by about 2 months of age. As they get older, they can retain information longer and longer. Recall memory, which requires actively retrieving an image of an object or event that is no longer present, appears to emerge toward the end of the first year. And by age 2 infants seem able to consciously and deliberately recall an event that happened long ago. By then they are beginning to do what you and I do when we speak of "remembering." And yet, although infants clearly store memories, the infant years are a blank for most of us. Box 8.2 explores this mystery.

Basic Learning Processes after Infancy

The basic learning processes that develop in infancy continue to operate throughout the life span in much the same way. True, learning capacities change. For example, the older child's ability to learn through observation is greater than the younger child's, partly because older children can use words to describe what they have seen and this helps them retain more information (Coates & Hartup, 1969). In addition, learning efficiency declines somewhat later in life; it takes older adults longer to learn classically conditioned responses, for example (Woodruff-Pak, 1990).

For the most part, however, basic forms of learning are both evident and important at *all* ages. The young adult habituates to the familiar. He or she also might develop a classically conditioned fear of flying after a very rough flight, might cease to work hard on the job after receiving the punishment of a pay cut, or might learn a new method of de-boning chicken by watching *The Frugal Gourmet*. In addition, many older adults become increasingly dependent because the people around them unknowingly reinforce dependent behavior (M. Baltes & Wahl, 1992); they could be helped to become more independent through systematic reinforcement of independence. Changes in all of us are partly the result of learning experiences.

THE CHILD

The 2-year-old is already a highly capable information processor, as evidenced by the rapid language learning that takes place at this age. But dramatic improvements in learning, memory, and problem solving occur throughout the childhood years, as children learn everything from how to flush toilets to how to work advanced math problems.

Learning and Memory over the Childhood Years

In countless learning situations, older children learn faster and remember more than younger children do (Kail, 1990). For example, 2-year-olds can repeat back about two digits immediately after hearing them, 10-year-olds about six digits. But *why*? Here are four major hypotheses about why learning and memory

BOX 8.2 Where Did Our Early Childhood Memories Go?

Although infants are quite capable of remembering their experiences, most people recall almost nothing that happened to them before the age of about 3—or, if they do have memories, some of them turn out to be pure fiction. This lack of memory for the early years of life has been termed **infantile amnesia**. Recently JoNell Usher and Ulric Neisser (1993) asked college students who had experienced (1) the birth of a younger sibling, (2) hospitalization, (3) the death of a family member, or (4) a family move early in life to answer questions about those experiences (for example, who told them their mothers were going to the hospital to give birth, what they were doing when she left, and where they were when they first saw the new baby). As the figure below shows, the percentage of memory questions successfully answered increased dramatically as age at the time of the experience increased. Based on this evidence, Usher and Neisser concluded that the earliest age of recall was age 2 for the birth of a sibling and hospitalization and age 3 for the death of a family member and a move. In an earlier study, only 3 of 22 college students who were younger than 3 at the time of a sibling's birth remembered anything at all about the event (Sheingold & Tenney, 1982).

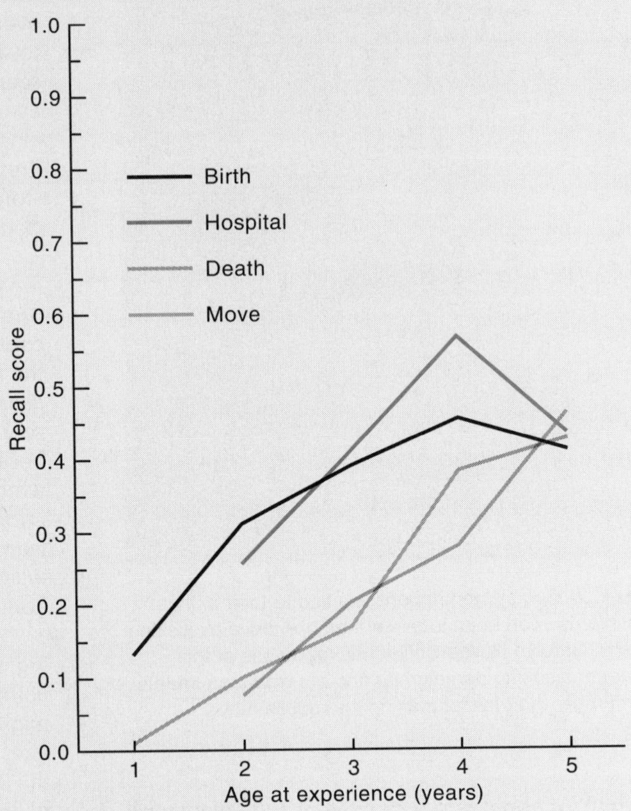

College students' recall of early life events increases as a function of how old they were at the time of the event. (From Usher & Neisser, 1993.)

Is the problem that the infant brain is incapable of forming lasting memories? This idea is flatly contradicted by research (Howe & Courage, 1993). Two-year-olds seem to be able to remember, at least in a fragmentary way, events that occurred when they were months younger (Fivush, Gray, & Fromhoff, 1987; Perris, Myers, & Clifton, 1990). Indeed, the 2½-year-olds in one study retained information about an experience they had had at 6½ months of age that involved searching for a noise-making toy in a totally dark laboratory room (Perris et al., 1990). Why, then, can't we adults remember?

Sigmund Freud thought infantile amnesia was a matter of blocking out or repressing from consciousness highly emotional events, but contemporary researchers have developed more cognitive explanations. For example, infants do not use language and adults do, so it is possible that early memories are stored in some nonverbal code that we cannot retrieve once we are verbal adults (Sheingold & Tenney, 1982; White & Pillemer, 1979). Or possibly we must gain the capacity to create verbal narratives of our experiences in order to remember them (Nelson, 1992).

Another possibility is that infants do not have enough space in working memory to hold the multiple pieces of information about actor, action, and setting that are needed to encode a coherent memory of an event (White & Pillemer, 1979). Or, as Mark Howe and Mary Courage (1993) suggest, maybe what is lacking is not cognitive or language ability but a sense of self around which memories of personally experienced events can be organized. Once an infant gains a sense of self at about 18 to 24 months of age, Howe and Courage suggest, he or she can encode experiences as "events that happened to *me*." We still cannot pinpoint the reasons for infantile amnesia, but it is clear that a period of life that is highly important to later development is a blank for most of us (Perlmutter, 1986).

improve, patterned after those formulated by John Flavell and Henry Wellman (1977):

1. *Changes in basic capacities.* Older children have higher-powered "hardware" than young children do; their brains have more "working memory space" for manipulating information and can process information faster.
2. *Changes in memory strategies.* Older children have better "software"; they have learned and

consistently use effective methods for getting information into long-term memory and retrieving it when they need it.
3. *Increased knowledge about memory.* Older children know more about memory (for example, about how long they must study to learn things thoroughly, which kinds of memory tasks take more effort, which strategies best fit each task, and so on).
4. *Increased knowledge about the world.* Older children know more about the world in general than young children. This knowledge, or expertise, makes material to be learned more familiar, and familiar material is easier to learn and remember than unfamiliar material.

Do Basic Capacities Change?

Since the nervous system continues to develop in the early years of life, it seems plausible that older children remember more than younger children do because they have a better "computer"—a larger or more efficient information-processing system. However, we can quickly rule out the idea that the storage capacity of long-term memory enlarges. There is no consistent evidence that it changes after the first month of life (Perlmutter, 1986). In fact, both young and old alike have more room for storage than they could ever possibly use. Nor does the capacity of the sensory register to take in stimuli seem to change much (Bjorklund, 1989; House, 1982). It does seem, however, that more short-term memory space becomes available with age, which would allow older children and adults to perform more mental operations at once than young children can.

This idea has been featured in revisions of Piaget's theory of cognitive development proposed by two neo-Piagetian theorists, Juan Pascual-Leone (1970, 1984) and Robbie Case (1985, 1992). Both seek to build on Piaget's insights into cognitive development, but both have also been strongly influenced by the information-processing approach. They propose that more advanced stages of cognitive development are made possible by increases in the capacity of short-term (working) memory to operate on some information while simultaneously storing other information relevant to a problem. For example, Piaget stressed the preschooler's tendency to *center* on one aspect of a problem and lose sight of another (for example, to attend to the height of a glass but ignore its width, or vice versa). Perhaps, say the neo-Piagetians, this is not a matter of lacking certain cognitive structures; perhaps young children simply do not have enough working memory capacity to keep both pieces of information in mind at once and coordinate them. Similarly, young children may do poorly on memory tasks because they cannot keep the first items on a list in mind while processing newer ones. And they may fail to solve mathematical problems correctly because they cannot keep the facts of the problem in mind while they are performing calculations.

The *total* capacity of short-term memory for storing and operating on information does not seem to change with age (Dempster, 1985). However, older children appear to have more working-memory space available for constructive *use* (Case, 1985; Kail, 1990). As children develop, they become faster and more efficient at executing basic mental processes, such as identifying numbers or words to be learned (Kail, 1991); these processes become *automatized* so that they can be done with little mental effort. This, in turn, frees space in working memory for other purposes, such as storing the information needed to solve a problem (see Figure 8.7). Improvements in operating speed and working-memory efficiency could be due to maturational changes in the brain (Case, 1992) or could reflect the older child's greater familiarity with numbers, letters, and other stimuli (Bjorklund, 1989). There is general agreement, though, that older children can process more information in working memory and process it faster than younger children can, and this is one reason why memory improves over childhood.

Do Memory Strategies Change?

A good sign of the memory limitations of young children is the fact that their recognition memory is way ahead of their recall memory. If 4-year-olds were shown the 12 items in Figure 8.8, they would *recognize* nearly all of them if asked to select the objects they had seen from a larger set of pictures (Brown, 1975). But, if asked to *recall* the objects, they might remember only 2 to 4 of them—a far cry from the 7 to 9 items that an 8-year-old would recall or the 10 to 11 an adult would recall several minutes later. What specific strategies evolve during childhood to permit this dramatic improvement in performance?

Even though children as young as 2 can deliberately remember to do "important" things, such as

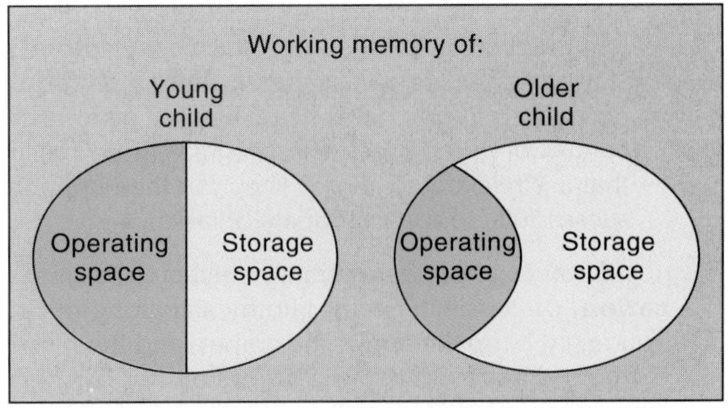

FIGURE 8.7 As they age, children come to carry out mental operations much faster and more efficiently, thus using up less operating space and leaving more storage space in working memory. (From Case, 1985.)

reminding Mom to buy candy at the grocery store (Somerville, Wellman, & Cultice, 1983), preschoolers have not mastered effective strategies for moving information from short-term to long-term memory. For example, when instructed to remember toys they have been shown, 3- and 4-year-olds will look very carefully at the objects and will often label them once, but only rarely do they use the memory strategy called **rehearsal,** the repeating of items one is trying to learn and remember (Baker-Ward, Ornstein, & Holden, 1984). To rehearse the objects in Figure 8.8, you might simply say over and over "Apple, truck, grapes, ..."

John Flavell and his associates (Flavell, 1985; Flavell, Beach, & Chinsky, 1966) have found that the use of rehearsal—as indicated by talking aloud and moving the lips— increases dramatically with age: Whereas only 10% of 5-year-olds repeated the names of pictures they were asked to recall, more than half of 7-year-olds and 85% of 10-year-olds used this strategy. By about age 7, most children use rehearsal effectively on many memory tasks, typically rehearsing each item presented to them one at a time. Older children discover that it is even more effective to rehearse clusters of words, repeating, for example, the first and second words in a list as they are rehearsing the third (Ornstein, Naus, & Liberty, 1975).

Flavell (1985) has concluded that rehearsal and other memory strategies develop through three stages:

1. *Mediation deficiency.* At this stage the child lacks the basic cognitive skills to execute or benefit from the strategy; attempts to coach the child in its use will be ineffective.
2. *Production deficiency.* Now the child can use the strategy and can benefit from its use—but does not often use it. This is what is meant by the term **production deficiency.** At this stage, prompting or coaching the child to employ the strategy may pay off in more effective recall.
3. *Mature strategy use.* Finally the strategy is used *spontaneously* and effectively to aid learning and memory. Now coaching is a waste of time. It may take children awhile to derive much benefit from a strategy they are just acquiring (Miller, Woody-Ramsey, & Aloise, 1991), but, as they gain fuller control of it, they seem to recognize more easily that it is relevant to a task. They can then apply it successfully to a wider variety of tasks.

Another important memory strategy is **organization,** or classifying items into meaningful groups. You might lump the apple, the grapes, and the hamburger in Figure 8.8 into a category of "foods" and form other categories for "animals," "vehicles," and "baseball equipment." You would then rehearse each category and recall it as a cluster. Another organizational strategy, *chunking,* is used when we break a long number (6065551843) into manageable subunits (606-555-1843, a phone number).

FIGURE 8.8 A memory task. Imagine that you have 120 seconds to learn the 12 objects pictured here. What tricks or strategies might you devise to make your task easier?

Use of organization develops through the same three stages as rehearsal but is mastered a bit later in childhood. Until about age 9 or 10, children are not much better at recalling lists of items that lend themselves readily to grouping than they are at recalling lists of unrelated words (Flavell & Wellman, 1977). Coaching in organization, like coaching in rehearsal, may increase use of the strategy among 6- to 8-year-old children who are in the production-deficiency stage of mastery (Kee & Bell, 1981).

Finally, there is the strategy of **elaboration,** or the active creation of meaningful links *between* items to be remembered. Elaboration is achieved by adding something to the items, in the form of either words or images. Creating and utilizing a sentence like "The apple fell on the horse's nose" would help you remember two of the items in Figure 8.8. Elaboration is especially helpful in learning foreign languages. For example, one might link the Spanish word *pato* (pronounced pot-o) to the English word *duck* by imagining a duck in a pot of boiling water. This is the most mentally taxing of the three memory strategies and is rarely used spontaneously before adolescence (Pressley, 1982).

Using effective memory strategies to learn material is only half the battle. *Retrieval strategies* can influence how much is ultimately recalled, even when effective memory strategies were used to learn the material initially. Indeed, retrieving something from memory can often be a complex adventure in problem solving, as when you try to remember when you went on a trip by searching for cues that might trigger your memory ("Well, I still had long hair then, but it was after Muffy's wedding, and . . .").

Consider this example of the young child's problem with retrieval. Michael Pressley and Joel Levin (1980) prompted 6- and 11-year-olds to use the elaboration strategy to learn pairs of items. When it was time for the recall test, half the children were told to use their elaborate images to help them remember, and the other half were given no special instructions. The 11-year-olds recalled more of the items than the younger children did, and they performed well regardless of whether they were told to use their images as an aid. In contrast, the 6-year-olds recalled nearly twice as many items when given retrieval instructions than when left to their own devices. Strange as it may seem, it apparently did not occur to these young children to use the images they had worked so hard to create as part of their retrieval strategy. The message here is important: Even when younger schoolchildren are shown how to use effective memory strategies such as organization and elaboration, they still may do less well than older children because they fail to exploit the results of those strategies during retrieval.

Does Knowledge about Memory and Other Cognitive Processes Change?

The term **metamemory** refers to knowledge of memory and memory processes. It is knowing, for example, what one's memory limits are, which memory strategies are more or less effective, and which memory tasks are more or less difficult (Flavell, 1985). Metamemory is one aspect of **metacognition,** or knowledge of the human mind and of the whole range of cognitive processes. Your store of metacognitive knowledge might include an understanding that you are better at geometry problems than at algebra problems, that it is harder to pay attention to a task when there is distracting noise in the background than when it is quiet, and that it is wise to check out a proposed solution to a problem before concluding that it is correct.

When do children first show evidence of metamemory? If instructed to remember where the *Sesame Street* character Big Bird has been hidden so that they can later wake him up, even 2- and 3-year-olds will go stand near the hiding spot, or at least look or point at that spot; they do not do these things as often if Big Bird is visible and they don't need to remember where he is (DeLoache, Cassidy, & Brown, 1985). By age 2, then, children have acquired at least one simple bit of knowledge about memory: To remember something, you have to work at it!

Children learn a good deal more about memory during their preschool years (Cunningham & Weaver, 1989; Schneider & Sodian, 1988; Wellman, 1977), but they have much left to learn. In one study (Yussen & Levy, 1975), preschoolers, third-graders, and adults were asked to estimate whether they would be able to recall sets of pictures of varying sizes. Preschoolers' estimates were highly unrealistic—as if they believed they could perform any memory feat imaginable—and they were unfazed by information about how another child had done on the task. Only by age 7 or so do most children realize that related items or those that can be organized into categories are easier to recall than unrelated items (Kreutzer, Leonard, & Flavell, 1975). And, although 7- and 9-year-olds realize that rehearsing and categorizing are more effective strategies than merely looking at items or naming them, only 11-year-olds know that organization is more effective than rehearsal (Justice, 1985).

Are increases in metamemory a major contributor to improved memory performance over the childhood years? The evidence is mixed. Metamemory and memory performance are positively correlated, but usually quite weakly (Cavanaugh & Perlmutter, 1982). Good metamemory apparently is not required for good recall (Bjorklund & Zeman, 1982). Moreover, children who know what to do may not always do it, so good metamemory is no guarantee of good recall (Salatas & Flavell, 1976). It seems that children must not only know *that* a strategy is effective but know *why* it is effective in order to be motivated to use it (Fabricius & Cavalier, 1989). Overall, there seem to be at least some links between metamemory and memory performance—enough to suggest the merits of teaching children more about how memory works and how they can make it work more effectively for them.

Does Increased Knowledge of the World in General Contribute to Improvements in Memory?

Ten-year-olds obviously know considerably more about the world in general than 2-year-olds do. The individual's knowledge of a content area to be learned, or **knowledge base,** as it has come to be called, clearly affects learning and memory performance. Think about the difference between reading about a topic that you already know well and reading about a new topic. In the first case, you can read quite quickly because you are able to link the information to the knowledge you have already stored. All you really need to do is check for any new information or information that contradicts what you already know. Learning about a highly unfamiliar topic is more difficult. You may even sigh "It's Greek to me" and learn almost nothing.

Perhaps the most dramatic illustration of the powerful influence of knowledge base on memory was provided by Michelene Chi (1978). She demonstrated that children could outperform adults at a memory task—something that children virtually never do. How? She simply recruited children who were expert chess players and compared them to adults who were familiar with the game but lacked expertise. On a test of memory for sequences of digits, the children recalled fewer than the adults did, as is typical. But on a test of memory for the locations of *chess pieces,* the children clearly beat the adults (Figure 8.9). Because they were experts, these children were able to form more and larger meaningful mental "chunks" or groups of chess pieces, and that was what allowed them to remember more.

Pause to consider the implications: On most tasks, young children are the novices and older children or adults are the experts. Perhaps older children and adults recall longer strings of digits only because they are more familiar with numbers than young children are. Perhaps they recall more words in word lists because they have more familiarity with language. Or perhaps memory improves over childhood simply because older children know more about all kinds of things than younger children do (Bjorklund, 1989).

In their areas of expertise, whether the topic is math or dinosaurs, children appear to develop highly specialized and effective strategies of information processing, just as the young chess players studied by Chi apparently had (Chi, Hutchinson, & Robin, 1989). Indeed, children with low general intellectual ability but high expertise sometimes understand and remember more about stories in their area of expertise than children with higher intellectual ability but less expertise (Schneider, Korkel, & Weinert, 1989). It seems that the more one knows, the more one *can* know. It also seems that how well a child does on a memory task depends not only on age but also on familiarity with the specific task at hand.

A Summing Up

We can now draw four conclusions about the development of learning and memory:

1. Older children have a greater information-processing *capacity* than younger children do, particularly in the sense that they have automatized certain basic information processes to leave room in working memory for other cognitive processes.
2. Older children use more effective *memory strategies* in encoding and retrieving information.
3. Older children know more about memory, and their *metamemory* may allow them to choose more appropriate strategies and to control and monitor their learning more effectively.
4. Older children know more in general, and their larger *knowledge base* improves their ability to learn and remember.

Can we choose a best hypothesis? Probably not at this point. All these phenomena may contribute something to the dramatic improvements in learning and memory that occur over the childhood years. They may also interact. For example, the automatization of certain information processes may leave the child with enough working-memory space to use effective memory strategies that were just too mentally demanding earlier in childhood (Bjorklund, 1989; Miller et al., 1991). Or, increased knowledge may permit faster information processing. We will return to these same four hypotheses when we consider changes in learning and memory in adulthood.

Problem Solving in Childhood

To solve any problem, one must process information about the task, as well as use stored information, to achieve a goal. How do problem-solving capacities change during childhood? Piaget provided one answer to this question by proposing that children progress through broad stages of cognitive growth, but

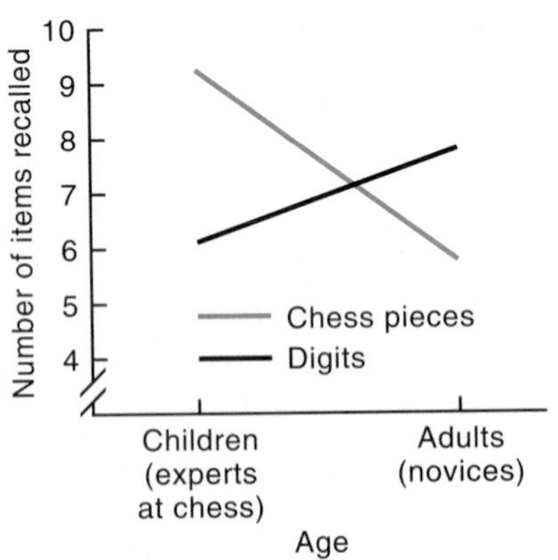

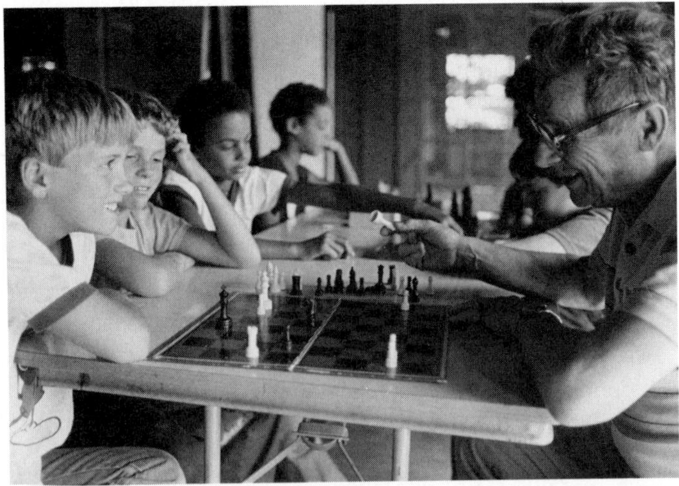

FIGURE 8.9 Effects of expertise on memory. Michelene Chi found that child chess experts outperformed adult chess novices on a test of recall for the location of chess pieces (though, in keeping with the usual developmental trend, these children could not recall strings of numbers as well as adults could). (Adapted from Chi, 1978.)

information-processing theorists were not satisfied with this explanation. They sought to pinpoint more specific reasons why problem-solving prowess improves so dramatically as children get older.

Consider the problem of predicting what will happen to the balance beam in Figure 8.10 when weights are put on each side of the fulcrum, or balancing point. The goal is to decide which way the balance beam will tip when it is released. To judge correctly, one must take into account both the number of weights and their distances from the fulcrum. Piaget believed that concrete-operational thinkers can appreciate the significance of either the amount of weight or its distance from the center but will not grasp the inverse relationship between the two factors until they reach the stage of formal operations. Then new cognitive structures allow them to understand that balance can be maintained by decreasing a weight but moving it farther away from the fulcrum or by increasing a weight but moving it closer to the fulcrum (Piaget & Inhelder, 1966/1969). Still, Piaget did not provide a very satisfying account of how children approach this problem and why they typically fail to solve it before their adolescent years.

Robert Siegler (1981) proposed that the information-processing perspective could provide a fuller analysis. His "rule assessment" approach determines what information about a problem children take in and what rules they then formulate to account for what they have observed. This approach assumes that children's problem-solving attempts are rule governed rather than hit-or-miss, and that children fail to solve problems because they fail to encode all the critical aspects of the problem and therefore are guided by faulty rules.

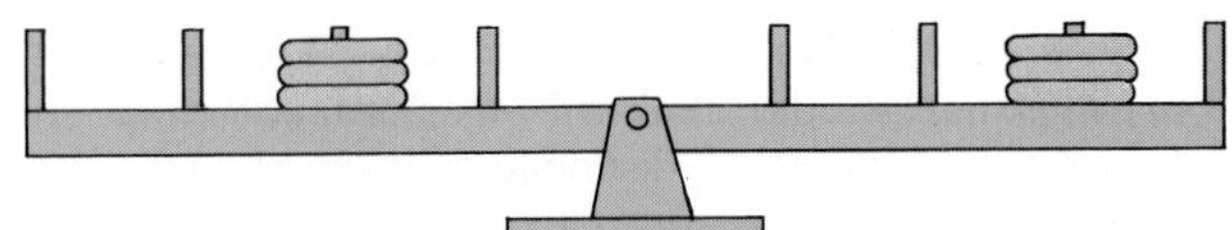

FIGURE 8.10 The balance-scale apparatus used by Siegler to study children's problem-solving abilities.

Siegler proposed that four rules were possible in the balance-beam problem:

Rule 1. The child predicts that the arm with more weight will drop, totally ignoring information about the distance of weights from the center.

Rule 2. Weight is still the most important factor, but, if the weights on each arm are equal, the child will consider the distance of the weights from the fulcrum to break the tie.

Rule 3. Both weight and distance are considered, but, if one side has more weight while the other has its weights farther from the fulcrum, the child is confused and will simply guess.

Rule 4. Using this mature rule, the child knows that the pull on each arm is a function of weight times distance. For example, if there are three weights on the second peg to the left and two weights on the fourth peg to the right, the left torque is $3 \times 2 = 6$ and the right torque is $2 \times 4 = 8$, so the right arm will go down.

Table 8.1 presents six problems that Siegler devised to identify exactly which of the four rules each problem solver was using. For example, children using rule 1 and encoding only weight should be able to solve problems 1, 2, and 4 but will think the arms should balance in problem 3, even though one set of

TABLE 8.1 Six balance-scale problems and the patterning of answers that follows from using each of four rules for solving problems.

		Siegler's Rule			
Problem	*Correct Answer*	*1*	*2*	*3*	*4*
1.	Balance	100% correct	100% correct	100% correct	100% correct
2.	Left down	100% correct	100% correct	100% correct	100% correct
3.	Left down	0% correct (will say balance)	100% correct	100% correct	100% correct
4.	Left down	100% correct	100% correct	33% correct (chance responding)	100% correct
5.	Left down	0% correct (will say right down)	0% correct (wil say right down)	33% correct (chance responding)	100% correct
6.	Balance	0% correct (will say right down)	0% correct (will say right down)	33% correct (chance responding	100% correct

SOURCE: Adapted from Siegler, 1981.

weights is farther from center than the other. Similarly, they should think the right arm will drop on problems 5 and 6. A distinctive pattern of successes and failures is associated with each of the other possible rules.

When Siegler (1981) administered these tasks to individuals aged 3 to 20, he found that 91% appeared to be using one or the other of the four rules, but with pronounced age differences. Almost no 3-year-olds used any kind of rule, suggesting that the very young child has limited problem-solving skills and tends to proceed in a haphazard rather than logical way when solving problems (see also Klahr & Robinson, 1981). By contrast, 4- and 5-year-olds were rule governed, more than 80% of them using rule 1 and encoding weight but ignoring distance. By age 8, children were generally using rule 2 or 3; by 12, the vast majority had settled on rule 3. And, although most 20-year-olds continued to use rule 3, 30% of them had discovered the weight-times-distance principle reflected in rule 4.

Imagine how effective teachers might be if they, like Siegler, could accurately diagnose the information-processing strategies of their learners to know exactly what each child is noticing (or failing to notice) about a problem and exactly what rules or strategies each child is using. This same rule assessment approach has in fact been used to identify exactly why individual children make errors on arithmetic problems (see Mayer, 1985). For example, the child who works the subtraction problem 24 − 18 and gets 16 rather than 6 is not just making a random mistake but is using a faulty rule—one that does not yet include a procedure for "borrowing." Helping this child requires instruction quite different from that appropriate for the child who gets the answer 7 and understands borrowing just fine but thinks 14 − 8 is 7.

Much remains to be learned about how and why children progress from one problem-solving rule to another as they get older (Siegler & Crowley, 1991). However, the rule assessment approach gives us a fairly specific idea of what children are doing (or doing wrong) as they attack problems and illustrates how the information-processing approach to cognitive development has helped to fill in some of the gaps in Piaget's account.

THE ADOLESCENT

Although parents who are in the midst of reminding their adolescent sons and daughters about household chores may wonder whether teenagers process any information at all, learning, memory, and problem solving continue to improve considerably during the adolescent years. How exactly?

First, new learning and memory strategies emerge; it is during adolescence that the memory strategy of elaboration is mastered (Pressley, 1982). Adolescents also develop and refine advanced learning and memory strategies that are highly relevant to school learning—for example, note-taking and underlining skills. Ann Brown and Sandra Smiley (1978) asked students from the 5th grade (age 11) to 12th grade to read and recall a story. Some learners were asked to recall the story immediately; others were given an additional five minutes to study it before they were tested. Amazingly, 5th-graders gained almost nothing from the extra study period, except for those few who used the time to underline or take notes. Junior high school students benefited to an extent, but only in senior high school did most students use underlining and note taking effectively to improve their recall. When some groups of students were told that they could underline or take notes if they wished, 5th-graders still did not improve, largely because they tended to underline everything rather than highlighting the most important points.

As they get older, adolescents also make more deliberate use of strategies that younger children use more or less unconsciously (Bjorklund, 1985). For example, they may deliberately organize a list of words instead of simply using any natural organization or grouping that happens to be there already. And they use existing strategies more selectively (Bray, Hersh, & Turner, 1985; Bray, Justice, & Zahm, 1983; Miller & Weiss, 1981)—for example, memorizing the material on which they know they will be tested and deliberately forgetting the rest. Patricia Miller and Michael Weiss (1981) asked children to remember the locations of animals that had been hidden behind small doors, ignoring the household objects hidden behind other doors. As Figure 8.11 shows, 13-year-olds recalled more than 7- and 10-year-olds about where the animals had been hidden, but they remembered *less* about task-irrelevant information (the locations of the household objects). Between the ages of 7 and 11, children get better at distinguishing between what is relevant and what is irrelevant information; during adolescence they advance even farther by selectively using their memory strategies only on the relevant material (Bray et al., 1985). If it's not going to be on the test, forget it!

Other strides are made in adolescence besides these changes in *memory strategies*. *Basic capacities* continue to increase; adolescents can remember more digits or words in memory-span tests than children can (Dempster, 1981), and they perform any number of cognitive operations more speedily than children do (Kail, 1991). Of course, adolescents also continue to expand their *knowledge base*, so they may do better than children on some tasks simply because they know more about the topic. *Metamemory* and *metacognition* also improve (Brown, Bransford, Ferrara, & Campione, 1983). For example, adolescents become better able to tailor their reading strategies to different

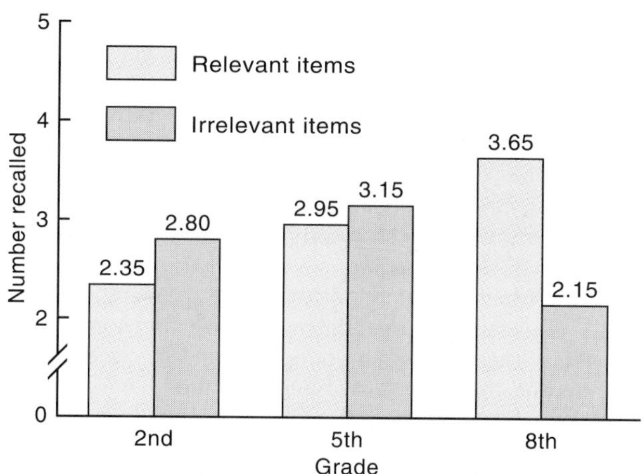

FIGURE 8.11 Adolescents are better able than children to concentrate on relevant material and to ignore irrelevant material. (Data from Miller & Weiss, 1981.)

purposes (studying versus skimming) and better able to realize when they don't understand something (Baker & Brown, 1984). Growth in strategies, basic capacities, knowledge base, and metacognition probably also helps explain the growth in everyday problem-solving ability that occurs during the adolescent years (Berg, 1989). Teenagers perfect a number of information-processing skills and become able to apply them *deliberately and spontaneously* across a wide variety of tasks (Brown et al., 1983).

THE ADULT

If you are about age 20, you will be pleased to know that the young adult college student has served as the standard of effective information processing against which all other age groups are compared. Although information processes are thought to be most efficient in young adults, some growth does occur during the adult years before aging begins to take its toll on some memory and problem-solving capacities.

Developing Expertise

Young adults still have some mental skills to learn. Comparisons of people who are new to their chosen fields of study with those who are more experienced make this clear. At Piaget's highest stage of cognitive development, formal operations, adults often perform better in their areas of specialization than in unfamiliar areas. Similarly, adults often learn, remember, and solve problems best in their areas of expertise. Experts process information differently than novices do; that is, knowledge base influences both the nature and the effectiveness of information processing.

Consider first the effects of knowledge base on memory. How might adults who are baseball experts and adults who care little for baseball perceive and remember the same game? George Spilich and his associates (1979) had baseball experts and novices listen to a tape of a half inning of play. Experts recalled more of the information that was central to the game—the important plays and the fate of each batter, in proper order—whereas novices were caught up by less central facts such as the threatening weather conditions and the number of people attending the game. Experts also recalled more central details—for example, noting that a double was a line drive down the left-field line rather than just a double. At any age, experts in a field are likely to remember new information in that content domain more fully than novices do (Morrow, Leirer, & Altieri, 1992).

Now consider the impact of increased expertise in one's career on problem-solving ability. Alan Lesgold (1984) and his associates observed how radiologists at different stages of career development interpret X rays and make diagnoses based on them. These physicians were developing organized knowledge bases to guide their perceptions of X rays and their ultimate decisions about treatment. Resident radiologists recently out of medical school seemed to rely on general, relatively simple rules of diagnosis (for example, noting all the abnormalities one can and then looking for a disease that fits). These novices often did not consider such additional information as the patient's medical condition or the exact location of a dark spot on the film—factors that could mean the difference between seeing a collapsed lung and seeing a tumor. Experienced physicians did consider these sorts of complexities. They had more elaborately organized and complete knowledge bases and could quickly, surely, and almost automatically call up just

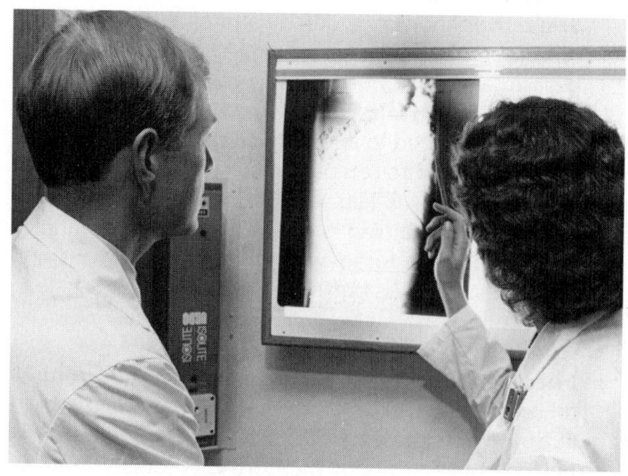

Adults who have gained proficiency in their chosen fields can draw from their well-organized knowledge bases to find just the right information to fit the problem at hand. Solving problems is automatic and effortless for experts.

the specific knowledge they needed to make an accurate diagnosis.

Are the benefits of expertise content-specific, or does gaining expertise in one domain carry over into other domains and make one a more generally effective learner or problem solver? That is an interesting question. One research team (Ericsson, Chase, & Faloon, 1980) put an average college student to work at improving the number of digits he could recall. He practiced for about an hour a day, three to five days a week, for more than a year and a half—over 200 hours in all. His improvement? He went from a memory span of 7 digits to one of 79 digits! His method involved forming meaningful associations between strings of digits and running times—for example, seeing 3492 as "3 minutes and 49 point 2 seconds, near world-record mile time" (p. 1181). It also involved chunking numbers into groups of three or four and then organizing the chunks into large units.

Did all this work pay off in a better memory for information other than numbers? Not really. When he was given letters of the alphabet to recall, this young man's memory span was unexceptional (about six letters). Clearly the expertise he developed was *domain-specific*. Similarly, Rajan Mahadevan, a man with an exceptional memory for arrays of numbers, turns out to possess no special ability at all for remembering the positions and orientations of objects (Biederman et al., 1992), and Shakuntala Devi, a woman who can solve complex mathematical problems in her head at amazing speeds, is apparently no faster than average at performing other cognitive operations (Jensen, 1990). Each of these experts apparently relies on stored knowledge and specialized information-processing strategies peculiar to numbers to achieve these cognitive feats.

In sum, experts know more than novices do, their knowledge base is more organized, and they are able to use their knowledge quickly and effectively to learn, remember, and solve problems in their areas of expertise, although not in other domains (Bedard & Chi, 1992; Chi, Glaser, & Rees, 1982). In effect, experts do not need to think much; they are like experienced drivers who can put themselves on "autopilot" and carry out well-learned routines very quickly and accurately. By gaining expertise over the years, adults can compensate for losses in information-processing capacities, which is our next topic.

Learning, Memory, and Aging

Many older adults feel that they are becoming forgetful (Loewen, Shaw, & Craik, 1990; Sunderland et al., 1986). No less an expert on learning than B. F. Skinner complained about memory problems: "One of the more disheartening experiences of old age is discovering that a point you have just made—so significant, so beautifully expressed—was made by you in something you published a long time ago" (Skinner, 1983, p. 242). When young and elderly adults were asked to keep diaries of their problems with memory in everyday life, the older adults reported more such problems, especially when it came to remembering names, routines like filling the car with gas, and items they would need later (Cavanaugh, Grady, & Perlmutter, 1983). Older adults were also more upset by their memory lapses, perhaps because they viewed them as signs of aging.

Much research indicates that, on average, older adults learn new material more slowly and sometimes learn it less well than young and middle-aged adults do and that they remember what they have learned less well. However, the following qualifications are important:

- Most of the research is based on cross-sectional studies comparing age groups, which suggests that the age differences detected could be related to factors other than age.
- Declines, when observed, typically do not become noticeable until the late 60s and the 70s.
- Difficulties in remembering affect elderly people more noticeably as they continue to age and are most severe among the oldest old.
- Not all older people experience these difficulties.
- Not all kinds of memory tasks cause older people difficulty.

Studies of memory skills in adulthood suggest that the aspects of learning and memory in which older adults look most deficient in comparison with young and middle-aged adults are some of the same areas in which young children compare unfavorably to older children (for reviews, see Guttentag, 1985; Hultsch & Dixon, 1990; Light, 1991; Perlmutter, 1986; Poon, 1985). Here are some of the major weaknesses—and, by implication, strengths—of the older adult:

Timed Tasks. On the average, older adults are slower than younger adults to learn and retrieve information; they may need to go through the material more times to learn it equally well and may need more time to respond when their memory is tested. Thus they are hurt by time limits. Allowing them to set their own pace during learning or testing sometimes helps them close the gap between themselves and younger adults (Botwinick, 1984; Canestrari, 1963).

Unfamiliar Tasks. Older adults fare especially poorly compared to younger adults when the material to be learned is unfamiliar or meaningless—when they cannot tie it to their existing knowledge. In a convincing demonstration of how familiarity influences memory, Barrett and Wright (1981) had young and elderly adults examine modern words likely to be more familiar to young adults (for example, *dude, disco,* and *bummer*) and words from the past likely to be more familiar to older adults (for example, *pompadour*, *gramophone*, and *vamp*). Sure enough, young adults outperformed older adults on the "new" words, but older adults outperformed young adults on the "old" words. Many laboratory tasks involve learning material that is unfamiliar and thus do not allow older adults to make use of their knowledge base (Poon, 1985).

Unexercised Skills. Older adults are also likely to be at a disadvantage when they are required to use learning and memory skills that they rarely use in daily life. They hold their own when they can rely on well-practiced skills that have become effortless and automatic with practice. For example, Lynne Reder, Cynthia Wible, and John Martin (1986) found that elderly adults were just as good as young adults at judging whether sentences presented to them were plausible based on a story they had read. Judging whether something makes sense in the context of what one has read was a well-exercised ability. However, older adults were deficient when it came to judging whether specific sentences had or had not appeared in the story—a skill that is seldom used outside school (see Figure 8.12). Quite sensibly, older adults read to get the gist or significance of a story and do not bother with the details (Adams, 1991; Adams, Labouvie-Vief, Hobart, & Dorosz, 1990). In other ways as well, age differences are smaller when well-practiced skills are assessed than when less-practiced skills are assessed (Denney, 1982).

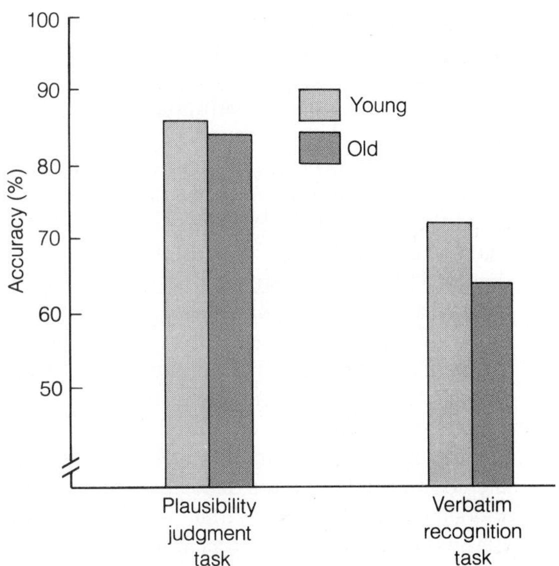

FIGURE 8.12 Older people don't always do worse than younger people on tests of learning and memory. Comparing college students and college alumni of retirement age, Reder, Wible, and Martin (1986) found that the old performed just as well as the young at judging whether statements were plausible according to a story they had read. This may be a well-practiced and automatic cognitive activity. Older adults did do worse at judging whether statements had actually appeared in the story, a less well-practiced task for adults who have been out of school for years. (Adapted from Reder, Wible, & Martin, 1986.)

Recall versus Recognition. Older adults are likely to be more deficient on tasks requiring recall memory than on tasks requiring only recognition of what was learned. In one study of memory for high school classmates (Bahrick, Bahrick, & Wittlinger, 1975), even adults who were almost 35 years past graduation could still recognize which of five names matched a picture in their yearbook about 90% of the time. However, the ability to actively recall names of classmates when given only their photos as cues dropped considerably as the age of the rememberer increased. A large gap between recognition and recall tells us that older people have encoded and stored the information but cannot retrieve it without the help of cues. Sometimes older adults fail to retrieve information because they never thoroughly encoded or learned it in the first place, but at other times they simply cannot retrieve information that is "in there."

Deliberate, Effortful Memory Tasks. Finally, older adults seem to have more trouble with tasks that require conscious or deliberate information processing (for example, recalling lists of words) than with tasks that involve more automatic, unconscious, or unintentional memory (Hasher & Zacks, 1979, 1984; Mitchell, 1989). Consider this example of automatic learning: You know, without ever having tried to learn it, that the word *result* appears more frequently in speech and writing than the word *insult.* Lynn Hasher and Rose Zacks (1979) discovered that young children, young adults, and older adults are about equally accurate at estimating how frequently they have encountered objects or words presented to them (see also Ellis, Palmer, & Reeves, 1988). By contrast, actively recalling the specific items in a list of unrelated words requires "effortful" use of memory strategies and is more easily accomplished by young adults than by elderly adults or children.

Memory researchers now distinguish between **implicit memory,** which occurs unintentionally and without consciousness, and **explicit memory,** which involves conscious recollection of the past (Roediger, 1990; Schacter, 1992). Explicit memory is tested through traditional recognition and recall tests. When implicit memory is tested, learners do not even know that their memory is being assessed. For example, individuals might be exposed to a list of words (without being asked to memorize them) and then given word stems such as TAB____ and asked to complete them with the first word that comes to mind. People who were exposed to the word *tablet* in the initial task are likely to come up with the word *tablet* rather than *table* or *tabby* to complete the word stem, demonstrating that they retained something from their earlier experience.

On tests of implicit memory, as on tests of the automatic learning of frequency information, young children often do no worse than older children, and elderly adults often do no worse than younger adults (Graf, 1990; Mitchell, 1989; Parkin & Streete, 1988). Even when age differences in implicit memory can be detected, they are far smaller than age differences in explicit memory (Hultsch, Masson, & Small, 1991). Young and old alike retain a tremendous amount of information without any effort at all, but older adults struggle more than young adults when they must deliberately try to remember things.

Overall, these findings suggest that older adults, like young children, have difficulty with tasks that are *cognitively demanding*—that require speed, the learning of unfamiliar material, the use of unexercised abilities, recall rather than recognition, or deliberate and effortful rather than automatic or implicit memory. Yet older adults and young children have difficulty for different reasons, as we will now see.

Explaining Declines in Learning and Memory in Old Age

In asking *why* some older adults struggle with some learning and memory tasks, we can first return to the same hypotheses we used to explain childhood improvements in performance: changes in (1) basic processing capacities, (2) strategy use, (3) metamemory, and (4) knowledge base. Then we will consider some additional possibilities.

The Knowledge-Base, Metamemory, and Memory-Strategy Hypotheses. Let's start with the hypothesis that differences in *knowledge base* explain differences between older and younger adults. We immediately encounter a problem: Young children may be ignorant, but elderly adults are not. Older adults are generally at least as knowledgeable as young adults (Camp, 1989). They often equal or surpass younger adults on measures of vocabulary and knowledge of word meanings (Light, 1991; West, Crook, & Barron, 1992). Moreover, they know a lot about the world. For example, Leonard Poon and his associates tested recognition memory for public events occurring from the 1910s to the 1970s (Poon, Fozard, Paulshock, & Thomas, 1979). People ranging in age from their 30s to their 60s recognized events from the 1950s, 1960s, and 1970s about equally well. Adults also retain a surprising amount of information they learned in high school Spanish, algebra, and geometry courses taken as many as 50 years earlier (Bahrick, 1984; Bahrick & Hall, 1991). So, deficiencies in knowledge base are probably not the source of most of the memory problems that older adults display. On the contrary, gains in knowledge probably help older adults compensate

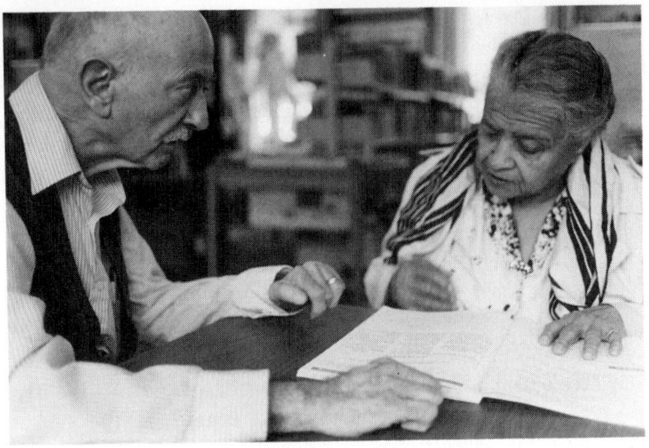

Many adults continue to expand their knowledge bases well into old age.

for losses in information-processing efficiency (Salthouse, 1993).

Could elderly adults, like young children, be deficient in the specific knowledge called metamemory? Is their knowledge of some of the strategies that prove useful in school learning—and in laboratory memory tasks—a bit rusty? This theory sounds plausible, but research shows that older adults seem to know as much as younger adults about which memory strategies are best and which memory tasks are hardest (Light, 1991). However, older adults *do* express more negative beliefs about their memory skills than younger adults do (Hultsch & Dixon, 1990). Moreover, those older adults who believe that their memories are failing or that they can do nothing to prevent memory loss in old age tend to perform poorly on memory tests (Cavanaugh & Poon, 1989; Dixon & Hultsch; 1983a; Hertzog, Hultsch, & Dixon, 1989). Although it could be that memory loss causes lack of confidence in memory skills rather than vice versa (Lachman & Leff, 1989), *motivational aspects of metamemory*, such as the belief that one is hopelessly forgetful, may be significant in old age.

What about the hypothesis that failure to use effective *memory strategies* accounts for deficits in old age? Many older adults do show production deficiencies; that is, they do not spontaneously use strategies such as organization and elaboration, even though they know them and are capable of using them (Light, 1991; Poon, 1985). This may indeed be an important part of the problem when older adults are asked to deliberately memorize something. But *why* do many older adults fail to use effective strategies?

Declines in Basic Processing Capacities. The answer may lie in our fourth hypothesis—the notion that *basic processing capacities* change with age. Which capacities? Much attention has focused on declines in the capacity of working memory to actively operate on information while simultaneously storing other information relevant to a task (Light, 1991; Salthouse, 1992). In one test of working-memory capacity, the individual reads a series of sentences while trying to hold in mind one underlined key word from each sentence in order to form a new sentence from the key words (Hultsch, Hammer, & Small, 1993). Working-memory capacity, then, involves being able to do a lot at once with one's mind. It declines during adulthood, after having increased during childhood and adolescence. Moreover, an adult's working-memory capacity predicts how well she or he will perform on a wide range of cognitive tasks (Light, 1991; Salthouse, 1992).

Both young children and older adults, it seems, need to devote more space in working memory than older children or young adults do to carrying out basic mental operations such as recognizing stimuli (Guttentag, 1985). This leaves less space for other purposes, such as thinking about or rehearsing material. We have seen that both younger children and older adults do relatively well when learning and remembering can take place automatically—when mental effort is *not* required—but struggle when they must exert a great deal of mental effort or carry out several mental operations at once.

Limitations in working-memory capacity could be rooted in the slow functioning of the nervous system both early and late in life (Cerella, 1990; Kail, 1991; Salthouse, 1992; see also Chapter 5). That is, a sluggish "computer" may not be able to keep up with the processing demands of complex learning and memory tasks. Another possibility is inefficient inhibition of irrelevant thoughts both early and late in life (Bjorklund & Harnishfeger, 1990; Dempster, 1992; Hasher & Zacks, 1988). According to this view, both young children and elderly adults are distractible and have difficulty keeping task-irrelevant thoughts from popping into their minds while they perform cognitive tasks (see Chapter 6 on selective attention). If irrelevant thoughts and associations consume precious working-memory space that could otherwise be devoted to the task at hand, this could explain why children and elderly adults seem to have too little working-memory space to, say, execute a demanding memory strategy like elaboration and store the products of their efforts. It may be that both slow neural transmission and difficulty in inhibiting irrelevant responses contribute to limitations in working memory in childhood and old age (Dempster, 1992).

To this point, then, we might conclude that many older adults, although they have a vast knowledge base and a good deal of knowledge about learning and memory, experience declines in basic processing capacity that make it difficult for them to carry out memory strategies that will drain their limited working-memory capacity. But the basic-processing-capacity hypothesis cannot explain everything about age differences in memory (Light, 1991). We must consider some additional hypotheses—ones suggesting that age differences in learning and memory are not so much the result of biological decline as of a variety of contextual factors.

Contextual Contributors. Our first contextual hypothesis is that *cohort differences in education, health, and lifestyle* can explain the apparent decline of some learning and memory skills in old age. Elderly people today are less educated, on average, than younger adults are, and they are further removed from their school days. In some cultures, *only* those individuals who have had formal schooling use memory strategies such as verbal rehearsal (Kuhn, 1992; Wagner, 1978). Moreover, education can compensate for aging. Older adults who are highly educated or who have strong verbal skills sometimes perform just as well as younger adults do (Cavanaugh, 1983; West et al., 1992). And adults who are presently in college outperform those who have been out of school for years and may have become rusty at the sorts of learning and memory skills required in school (Zivian & Darjes, 1983).

Similarly, older adults are more likely than younger adults to have chronic or degenerative diseases, and even mild diseases can impair memory performance (Houx, Vreeling, & Jolles, 1991; Hultsch et al., 1993). Older adults are also likely to lead less active lifestyles and to perform fewer cognitively demanding activities than younger adults do. These age-group differences in lifestyle also contribute to age differences in cognitive performance (Hultsch et al., 1993). The implication of such cohort effects is clear: Declines in information-processing skills are not inevitable or universal. Older adults may be able to maintain their memory skills quite well if they are relatively well educated, manage to stay healthy, and exercise their minds.

Second, older adults may perform poorly on some cognitive tasks not because of deficient abilities but because of *motivational factors*. Motivation is important at all ages, but older adults seem to be especially likely to ask whether information is potentially useful to them before they invest energy in learning it (Schaie, 1977/1978). In one study in which adults were to learn nonsense syllables, fully 80% of the elderly subjects simply dropped out of the study; they saw no point in learning such nonsense (Hulicka, 1967)! A quite different motivational problem experienced by some older adults is anxiety (Kausler, 1990). Anxiety, depression, and other negative emotional states may hurt the performance of older adults more than that of younger adults (Deptula, Singh, & Pomara, 1993).

Finally, we must consider the hypothesis that older adults display learning and memory deficits mainly because the *kinds of tasks* that have typically been presented to them are so far removed from the everyday contexts in which they normally learn and remember. Think about the difference between remembering a list of food terms in the laboratory and remembering what to buy at the grocery store. In learning a list, the person may have no choice but to use mental memory strategies such as organization and elaboration. But in everyday life both young and old adults rely far less on such internal strategies than on *external memory aids*—notes, lists, and the like (Cavanaugh et al., 1983; see also Box 8.3). After all, why conjure up images to help you remember what to buy at the supermarket when you can simply write out a shopping list? You can even use other people as an aid to memory (Dixon, 1992); for example, you can ask your spouse to remind you to get soy sauce and have a grocery clerk help you find it!

In the everyday task of grocery shopping, the job of remembering where to find the brown sugar or the cream cheese is simplified immensely because we can draw on our previous experience in the store (our knowledge base). Moreover, items are embedded in a meaningful context (such as the baking section or the dairy section), so cues are available in the store to help us remember. In one demonstration of the importance of such contextual cues, Kathryn Waddell and Barbara Rogoff (1981) showed that elderly adults did just as well as middle-aged adults at remembering the locations of objects (toy cars, pieces of furniture, and so on) that had been placed in a meaningful landscape consisting of a parking lot, houses, a church, and other landmarks. They had difficulty only when these items were stripped of a meaningful context and were placed in cubicles (see Figure 8.13). In everyday situations, then, elderly adults can place new information in the context of what they already know and can make use of situational cues to help them remember. As a result, they sometimes, though not always, remember as well as or better than younger adults (Hultsch & Dixon, 1990; Poon, 1985).

Summing Up. Impressed by the influence of such factors as cohort differences, motivation, and task char-

BOX 8.3 Everyday Memory: Remembering to Take One's Medications

"Which one is the muscle relaxant?" A middle-aged man one of us knows has had some difficulty keeping straight the four different drugs he was prescribed recently for back pain. One wonders, then, how elderly adults who sometimes take a dozen or more different medications daily possibly keep up with them all. Do declines in information-processing skills make it difficult for these adults to understand a doctor's instructions and to remember to take their medications at the prescribed times? Here is an area in which memory lapses can mean life or death.

Roger Morrell, Denise Park, and Leonard Poon (1989) attempted to determine how well young and elderly adults can comprehend and remember information about medications. In one of their studies they presented young adults (aged 18 to 24) and elderly adults (aged 60 to 87) with information about several medications actually prescribed for one elderly man and then allowed them to study the information for as long as they wished. Participants were tested for comprehension and recall of the critical information (the reason for each prescription, the times of day to take it, the amount to take, and any special instructions on the label).

How did these adults do? Older adults had a lot more trouble making

sense of the prescription information and remembering it; their rate of memory errors was 53%, compared to 25% for the young adults. Moreover, both young and elderly adults had more trouble understanding these real prescriptions than understanding prescriptions made up by the researchers for the purposes of the research.

What can health-care professionals do to increase the odds that older patients will grasp and comply with medication instructions? By writing clear, organized instructions and spending more time explaining to older patients what they are to do, health-care professionals can simplify the learning task (Morrell et al., 1989). For example, older adults seem to understand "Take at 8 A.M. and 8 P.M." better than "Take every 12 hours."

Alternatively, older adults can be given external memory aids. Denise Park and her colleagues (1992) explored the benefits of two such aids—an organization chart (a poster or pocket-sized table giving an hour-by-hour account of when drugs should be taken) and a medication organizer (a dispenser with columns for different days of the week and pill compartments for times of the day). Young-old adults (those 70 or under) adhered to their medication schedules 94% of the time and got no benefit from aids. But old-old adults (those 71 and older) had an adherence rate of 85%, mainly because they forgot to take medications. This group complied more fully with instructions when they were given both the chart and the organizer than when they were given one or the other or neither. Because we know that poor health is one contributor to poor memory functioning, it makes awfully good sense to reduce the cognitive demands on old and ailing patients by having external memory aids do the mental work for them.

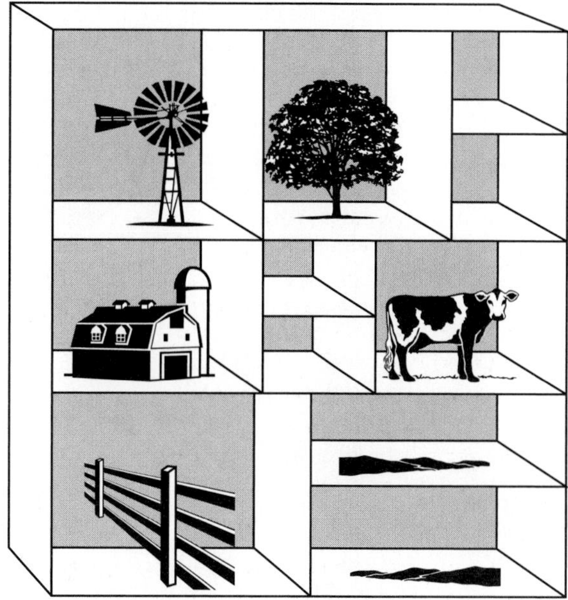

FIGURE 8.13 Older adults remember the locations of items better when they are placed in the context of a meaningful landscape than when they are placed in cubicles. The contextual perspective on information processing reminds us that older adults can perform well or poorly depending on the nature of the task they confront. (Adapted from Waddell & Rogoff, 1981.)

acteristics on the performance of elderly adults, many researchers are adopting a *contextual perspective* on learning and memory (Dixon, 1992; Hultsch & Dixon, 1984). They emphasize that performance on learning and memory tasks is the product of an interaction among (1) characteristics of the learner, such as goals, motivations, and abilities; (2) characteristics of the particular task at hand; and (3) characteristics of the broader context, including the cultural context, in which a task is performed. They are not convinced that there is a universal biological decline in basic learning and memory capacities, for older individuals often perform very capably in certain contexts.

Perhaps the truth lies somewhere between the basic-processing-capacity view, which points to a general decline in cognitive resources that affects performance on many tasks, and the contextual view, which stresses variability from person to person and task to task. Most adults, at least if they live to an advanced old age, may well experience some loss of basic processing resources such as working memory. However, they may also have developed specialized knowledge and strategies that allow them to compensate for these losses as they carry out the everyday cognitive activities most important to them (P. Baltes, Smith, & Staudinger, 1992).

Problem Solving and Aging

We know that problem-solving skills improve steadily from early childhood through adolescence, but what becomes of them in adulthood? On the one hand, we might expect to see a decline in problem-solving prowess paralleling the decline in learning and memory performance. But, if adults also increase their knowledge bases and develop expertise as they get older, might not older adults outwit younger novices on many problem-solving tasks?

When they are given traditional problem-solving tasks to perform in the laboratory, young adults typically perform better than middle-aged adults, who in turn outperform older adults (Denney, 1989; Offenbach, 1974). However, consider research using the Twenty Questions task (see Denney, 1985). Subjects are given an array of items and asked to find out, in as few yes/no questions as possible, which item the experimenter has in mind (see Figure 8.14). The soundest problem-solving strategy is to ask **constraint-seeking questions**—ones that rule out more than one item (for example, "Is it an animal?"). Young children and older adults tend to pursue specific hypotheses instead ("Is it a pig?" "Is it a pencil?"). Consequently, they must ask more questions to identify the right object. However, older adults do far better if the task is altered to make it more familiar; they then draw on their knowledge base to solve the problem. For example, when Denney (1980) used an array of playing cards, older adults asked plenty of constraint-seeking questions ("Is it a heart?" "Is it a face card?"). Thus older adults are capable of using effective problem-solving strategies but do not use them in some contexts, especially when given unfamiliar tasks in a laboratory.

FIGURE 8.14 A Twenty Questions game. You can try it on a young child or a friend by thinking of one item in the group and asking your testee to find out which it is by asking you yes/no questions. Look for constraint-seeking questions (for example, "Is it animate?"), and note the total number of questions required to identify the correct item.

What if adults are asked to deal with real-life problems like grease fires in the kitchen, warm refrigerators, or family squabbles? Nancy Denney and Kathy Pearce (1989) asked elderly adults to help them devise everyday problems that would be meaningful and familiar to older individuals. One problem was to generate ideas about how a 65-year-old recently widowed woman could improve her social life; another was to advise an elderly couple living on Social Security what to do when they were unable to pay their heating bill one winter. On these everyday problems, performance increased from early adulthood to middle age and declined thereafter.

Other findings echo this one: When given everyday problems to which they can apply the expertise they have gained through experience, middle-aged adults often outperform young adults; elderly adults, too, perform far more competently than they do when they are given unfamiliar problems in the laboratory (Cornelius & Caspi, 1987; Denney, 1989; Salthouse, 1990). Ultimately, declines in basic capacities may limit the problem-solving skills of many elderly adults not only in the laboratory but in real life as well (Denney, 1989; Kasworm & Medina, 1990). We should bear in mind, though, that there is wide variation in cognitive competence among older adults. For example, the amount of education a person has had is at least as important as age in determining success at problem solving in the adult years (Denney, 1985).

In sum, we get much the same message about problem-solving skills that we got about memory capacities. Although performance on unfamiliar, meaningless laboratory tasks often appears to decline after early adulthood, the ability to perform more familiar, everyday information-processing tasks often improves through middle age and is maintained until quite late in life. Once again, this supports a contextual view of cognition: The gap between age groups can be wide or nonexistent, depending on what a problem-solving task demands and whether it allows the problem solver to make use of his or her expertise (Denney, 1989; Reese & Rodeheaver, 1985).

Some cognitive researchers now feel that what appear to be cognitive deficits in old age may actually reflect cognitive adaptation and growth (Dixon, 1992; Perlmutter, 1986; Poon, 1985). It may make good sense for older adults to let some little-needed cognitive skills grow rusty in order to maintain and strengthen those skills that are most useful to them in everyday life. Gains in knowledge or expertise in important domains may help compensate for losses in basic processing capacities (P. Baltes et al., 1992; Dixon, 1992). Children improve their ability to do all kinds of things; older adults may improve their ability to perform relevant learning, memory, and problem-solving tasks and forget the rest!

APPLICATIONS: IMPROVING MEMORY

Have you noticed that the material in this chapter has great potential value to teachers? Skinner's operant-conditioning principles have long been widely applied in behavior modification programs to improve classroom learning and motivation. The information-processing perspective has yielded better methods for diagnosing learning problems and improving instruction. Here we'll focus on interventions aimed at boosting the memory skills of young children and older adults. Just how much can be achieved through training?

Garrett Lange and Sarah Pierce (1992) recently took on the challenge of teaching the memory strategy of organization (grouping) to 4- and 5-year-olds. Using pictures of objects and animals as the stimuli, they taught these preschoolers a "group-and-name trick" that involved sorting items to be learned into groups based on similarity, naming the group, naming the items within the group, and, at recall, naming the group before calling out the items within that group. Because such memory-training programs have not always been successful, these researchers also attempted to increase motivation through encouragement and praise. They even included training in metacognition: They made sure children understood the rationale for the sorting strategy, knew when it could be used, and could see firsthand that it could improve their performance.

How successful was the training? These children did virtually no sorting of items to be learned before they were trained, but they did a good deal of it after training, even seven days later. They clearly learned to use the organization strategy they were taught. They also outperformed untrained control children on measures of recall. However, the gains in recall were fairly small compared to the much larger gains in strategy use that occurred. These young children apparently could not derive full benefit from the memory strategy they were taught, possibly because they could not carry out the strategy *and* store the items to be learned in working memory. Older children are likely to gain more from training in memory strategies and to transfer what they have learned to new tasks (Bjorklund, 1989).

How well do older adults respond to attempts to teach them more effective memory strategies? Although a number of studies have shown that such training can be very effective (Verhaeghen, Marcoen, & Goossens, 1992), there are limits. Consider the interesting work of Paul Baltes and his colleagues (P. Baltes et al., 1992; P. Baltes & Kliegl, 1992; Kliegl, Smith, & Baltes, 1989). In one study (Kliegl et al., 1989) these researchers trained young adults (aged 19–29) and elderly adults (aged 65–83) in a mnemonic technique called the **method of loci.** It involves devising a mental map of a route through a familiar place (such as one's home) and then creating images linking items to be learned to landmarks along the route. For example, the German adults in the study were taught to associate words on word lists with 40 well-known landmarks in West Berlin, and they continued to practice for many sessions so that their maximal level of performance could be assessed.

The accomplishments of these adults were quite remarkable, as Figure 8.15 shows. Older adults improved from recalling fewer than 3 words in correct order after hearing a 30-word list only once to recalling over 10 words, and young adults upped their performance even more, from 6 to over 20 words. These findings tell us that there is a great deal of cognitive plasticity and potential throughout the life span. As Baltes and his colleagues put it, older adults have considerable "reserve capacity" (though less than young adults) that can be tapped through intensive training. Indeed, despite limitations in basic processing capacity, older adults who master powerful memory techniques

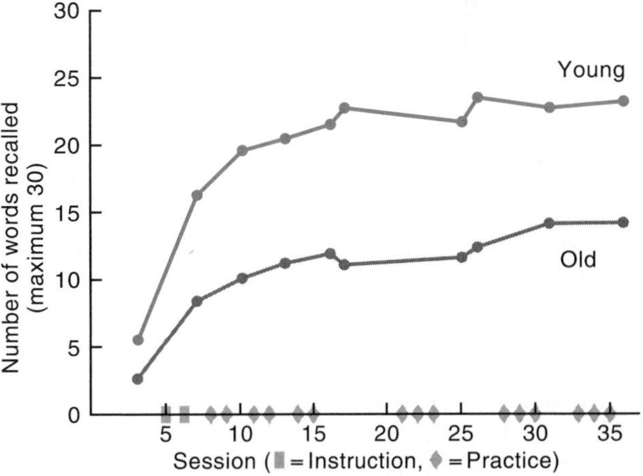

FIGURE 8.15 Trained to use the method of loci and then given many practice sessions, younger adults improved their recall of word lists more than older adults did, suggesting that aging places limits on maximal performance. Still, elderly adults benefited considerably from this memory training. (From P. Baltes & Kliegl, 1992.)

can outperform young adults who have not learned and practiced these techniques.

Although coaching children and elderly adults in memory strategies can be effective, the strategies learned often are not applied in new learning situations (Bjorklund, 1989; Pressley et al., 1985; Storandt, 1992). Both age groups may find that these strategies demand too much mental effort (Guttentag, 1985). When the elderly adults in one training study were retested after three years, fewer than a third of them still used the mnemonic techniques they had learned, and the group as a whole had reverted to the level of memory performance it had displayed before training (Scogin & Bienias, 1988).

What, then, is the solution? If some memory strategies are too mentally taxing for many young children and elderly adults, it may make more sense to change the learning environment than to change the learner (Pressley, 1983). If, for example, young children or some older adults do not spontaneously organize the material they are learning to make it more meaningful, one can organize it for them. Indeed, giving children practice at learning highly organized material can help them master the grouping strategy on their own (Best, 1993). Similarly, if the material to be learned is unfamiliar, one can use examples or analogies that will help learners relate it to something that *is* familiar (for example, teaching a senior citizens' group about the federal budget by likening it to their personal budgets). If young children and older adults need more time, let them set their own pace. Surely the best of all possible worlds for the learner would be one in which these two approaches are combined: Materials and teaching techniques are tailored to the learner's information-processing capacities, *and* training is offered in how to stretch those capacities.

REFLECTIONS

We have covered a lot of ground in this chapter. Reflecting on the development of learning and information-processing capacities, it strikes us that the information-processing approach can provide a rich account of why people of different ages succeed or fail in their efforts to learn, remember, and think. This approach is popular among developmentalists today, and its potential is just being realized.

It also strikes us that research on information processing does not paint a very pretty picture of either the very young child or the elderly adult. Both are said to be lacking in basic information-processing capacities; both come up short when their learning, memory, and problem-solving skills are tested in the laboratory. But perhaps the deeper message is that the laboratory and the real world are not the same. An "incompetent" preschooler is, after all, acquiring language in no time at all and absorbing knowledge like a sponge. Surely the more deliberate and organized information-processing strategies can wait until later in childhood! And those "less competent" older adults also have many things down quite nicely. They've become experts at living their lives—able to draw on stored knowledge and automatized processing routines to perform everyday tasks skillfully. Any losses in brain power they experience are often matched by gains in know-how. In short, humans seem well adapted to do with their minds exactly what they need to do at each stage of the life span, and the human mind is remarkable at every age.

SUMMARY POINTS

1. Learning, a relatively permanent change in behavior resulting from experience, is the process by which new information, attitudes, abilities, and habits are acquired. Forms of learning include habituation (learning not to respond to a repeated stimulus), classical conditioning, operant conditioning, and observational learning.

2. In classical conditioning, an initially neutral stimulus is repeatedly paired with an unconditioned stimulus that always elicits an unconditioned response; consequently, the neutral stimulus becomes a conditioned stimulus for the response. Many emotional responses are acquired this way.

3. In operant conditioning, what is learned is an association between a response or behavior and the consequences that it produces. In reinforcement (positive or negative), consequences strengthen behavior. Punishment decreases the strength of behavior, and extinction occurs when no consequences follow the behavior.

4. In observational learning, the individual learns from observing another person (a model). Learning may occur in the absence of reinforcement even if performance (imitation) does not. However, the consequences of the action for the model or the learner can affect the likelihood of performance. Observational learning is cognitive learning, involving selective attention and symbolic representation of what was seen.

5. The behaviorist perspective has given way to the more cognitive information-processing approach. The human "computer" takes in information into a sensory register, short-term (working) memory, and long-term memory during encoding; stores it; retrieves it (demonstrating recognition, cued recall, or recall memory); and uses it to solve problems.

6. Infants are capable of learning from the start. They show recognition memory at birth, simple recall in the presence of cues at 2 or 3 months, recall in the absence of cues toward the end of the first year, and

deliberate attempts to retrieve memories by age 2. Basic learning processes improve considerably over infancy and into childhood and continue to operate throughout the life span.

7. Learning and memory continue to improve during childhood: (a) Basic information-processing capacity increases as the brain matures and fundamental processes are automatized to free working-memory space; (b) memory strategies such as rehearsal, organization, and elaboration improve, leading finally to their spontaneous use; (c) metamemory improves; and (d) general knowledge base grows, improving the processing of new information in areas of expertise.

8. Even young children use rules to solve problems, but their problem-solving skills improve as they replace faulty rules with ones that incorporate all the relevant aspects of the problem.

9. Adolescents master advanced learning strategies such as elaboration, note taking, and underlining; use their strategies more deliberately and selectively; and use their increased metacognitive abilities to guide their learning and remembering.

10. As adults gain expertise in a domain, they develop large and organized knowledge bases as well as highly effective, specialized, and automatized ways of using their knowledge.

11. Many older adults, though not all, perform less well than young adults on learning and memory tasks that require speed, the learning of unfamiliar or meaningless material, the use of unexercised abilities, recall rather than recognition memory, and deliberate, effortful memory rather than automatic or implicit memory.

12. Older adults retain their knowledge base well and have only limited deficiencies in metamemory. A late-life decrease in basic working-memory capacity may limit the use of memory strategies and hurt performance. According to the contextual perspective, factors such as cohort differences, low motivation, and the irrelevance of many laboratory tasks to everyday life also contribute to age differences in learning and memory.

13. On average, older adults also perform less well than younger adults on laboratory problem-solving tasks, but everyday problem-solving skills are likely to improve from early adulthood to middle adulthood and to be maintained well in old age.

14. Basic learning theories and the information-processing approach can be applied to improve education. Memory-skills training can benefit both young children and elderly adults. However, since transfer to new situations does not always occur, altering instruction to better match the capacities of the learner is also appropriate.

KEY TERMS

classical conditioning
conditioned response (CR)
conditioned stimulus (CS)
constraint-seeking questions
continuous reinforcement
counterconditioning
cued recall memory
deferred imitation
elaboration
encoding
executive control processes
explicit memory
extinction
habituation
implicit memory
infantile amnesia
information-processing approach
knowledge base
learning
long-term memory
metacognition
metamemory
method of loci
negative reinforcement
observational learning
operant conditioning
organization (as a memory strategy)
partial reinforcement
positive reinforcement
problem solving
production deficiency
punishment
recall memory
recognition memory
rehearsal
retrieval
sensory register
short-term (or working) memory
storage
unconditioned response (UCR)
unconditioned stimulus (UCS)

9 INTELLIGENCE, CREATIVITY, AND WISDOM

At the age of 35, Michael lives in an institution for the mentally retarded. He has been labeled profoundly retarded and has an IQ score of 17, as nearly as it can be estimated. Michael responds to people with grins and is able to walk haltingly, but he cannot feed or dress himself and does not use language.

When he was 3 years old, the 19th-century English philosopher John Stuart Mill began to study Greek under his father's direction. At age 6½ he wrote a history of Rome. He tackled Latin at age 8, and before age 9 he was reading original Latin works. At 8 he also began his study of geometry and algebra. Mill's IQ score has been estimated at 190, on a scale on which 100 is average (Cox, 1926).

Some gifted children as young as 10 thrive as college students (Robinson & Robinson, 1982). Some minds develop faster and further than others.

As these examples indicate, the range of human cognitive abilities is immense. So far, our exploration of cognitive development has focused mainly on what human minds have in common, not on how they differ. Piaget, after all, was interested in identifying *universal* stages describing the ways in which thought is structured or organized by all normal humans as they develop. Similarly, the information-processing approach has been used mainly to understand the basic cognitive processes all people rely on to learn, remember, and solve problems.

In this chapter we continue our exploration of how the human mind normally changes over the life span, but with a greater emphasis on individual differences in cognitive abilities. We introduce still another approach to the study of the mind: the *psychometric,* or testing, approach to intelligence, which led to the creation of intelligence tests. We examine how performance on intelligence tests changes over the life span, touching on the hereditary and environmental influences that make one person more "intelligent" than another. We'll also view both the gifted and the mentally retarded individual from a life-span perspective. Finally, we'll consider forms of intellectual ability that are not typically measured by intelligence tests, especially creativity and wisdom.

WHAT IS INTELLIGENCE?

There is no clear consensus about what intelligence is (Weinberg, 1989). Piaget defined intelligence as "adaptive thinking or action" (Piaget, 1950). Other experts have offered different definitions, many of them centering in some way on the ability to think abstractly or to solve problems effectively (Sternberg, 1991; Sternberg & Berg, 1986). Early definitions of intelligence tended to reflect the assumption that intelligence is innate intellectual ability, genetically determined and thus fixed at conception. But it has now become clear that intelligence is *not* fixed. Instead, it is changeable and subject to environmental influence, for an individual's intelligence test scores may vary—often considerably—over a lifetime. Bear in mind that understandings of this complex human quality have changed since the first intelligence tests were created at the turn of the century—and that there is still no single, universally accepted definition of intelligence.

The Psychometric Approach to Intelligence

The research tradition that spawned the development of standardized tests of intelligence is the **psychometric approach** (see Gardner & Clark, 1992; Horn & Hofer, 1992). According to psychometric theorists, intelligence is a trait or a set of traits that characterizes some people to a greater extent than others. The goals, then, are to identify these traits precisely and to measure them so that differences among individuals can be described. But, from the start, experts could not agree on whether intelligence is one general cognitive ability or many specific abilities.

Is Intelligence a Single Attribute or Many Attributes?

One way of trying to determine whether intelligence is a single ability or many abilities is to ask people to perform a large number of mental tasks and then to analyze their performance using a statistical procedure called **factor analysis.** This technique identifies clusters of tasks or test items (called *factors*) that are highly correlated with one another and unrelated to other items. Suppose, for example, that the items given to a group of people include many that require verbal skills (for example, defining words) and many that require mathematical skills (solving arithmetic puzzles). Now suppose that people who do well on any verbal item also do well on other verbal items, and those who do well on any math problem also do well on other math problems. Further suppose that people who do well on verbal problems may or may not perform well on math problems, and vice versa. In this case, math performance does not correlate highly with verbal performance, and factor analysis would reveal a "verbal ability factor" that is distinct from a "math ability factor." If, by contrast, correlations among the items revealed that those people who do well on any item in the test tend to do well on others as well, it would seem that one general ability factor is involved in performance on both verbal and math problems.

Charles Spearman (1927) was among the first to use factor analysis to try to determine whether intelligence is one or many abilities. He concluded that a general mental ability (called *g*) contributes to performance on many different kinds of tasks. However, he also noticed that a student who excelled at most tasks might also score very low on a particular measure (for example, memory for words). So he proposed that intelligence has two aspects: *g*, or general ability, and *s*, or special abilities, each of which is specific to a particular kind of task.

When Louis Thurstone (1938; Thurstone & Thurstone, 1941) factor-analyzed test scores obtained by eighth-graders and college students, he identified seven fairly distinct factors that he called *primary mental abilities*: spatial ability, perceptual speed (the quick noting of visual detail), numerical reasoning (arithmetic skills), verbal meaning (defining of words), word fluency (speed in recognizing words), memory, and inductive reasoning (formation of a rule to describe a set of observations). Thus Thurstone concluded that Spearman's general ability factor should be broken into several distinct mental abilities.

The controversy was not over. J. P. Guilford (1967, 1988) proposed that there are as many as 180 distinct mental abilities. According to his **structure-of-intellect model,** there are five kinds of intellectual *contents* (things that people can think about, such as sights, ideas, or the behaviors of other people); six types of mental *operations* or actions that can be performed on these contents (such as recognizing, remembering, or evaluating); and six kinds of intellectual *products* or outcomes of thinking (such as a concept or an inference). Simple multiplication tells us that there are $5 \times 6 \times 6 = 180$ possible combinations of the contents, operations, and products (see Figure 9.1).

Obviously the use of factor analysis did not exactly settle the question of what intelligence is. The specific methods of factor analysis used by various researchers have differed, and the results of a factor analysis depend on how many different kinds of tasks are included in the group of tasks given to test takers.

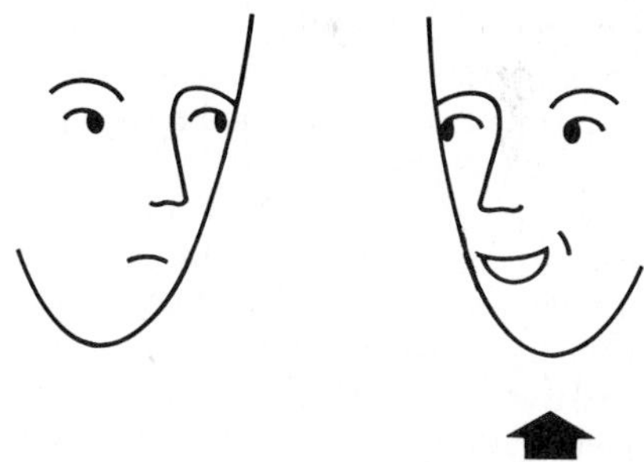

1. I'm glad you're feeling a little better.
2. You make the funniest faces!
3. Didn't I tell you she'd say "No"?

FIGURE 9.1 An item from one of Guilford's tests of social intelligence. The task is to read the characters' expressions and decide what the person marked by the arrow is probably saying to the other person. (The correct answer appears below.) In terms of Guilford's structure-of-intellect model, this item involves thinking about a behavioral *content* (the figure's facial expression) and using the *operation* of cognition to yield the *product* of the likely implication of that facial expression. (Adapted from Guilford, 1967.)

Answer: 3

Moreover, the researcher's own interpretations of the resulting patterns of correlations influence how factors are labeled. There does, however, seem to be a consensus today that intelligence can be viewed as a combination of (1) a general ability factor that influences how well people do on a wide range of cognitive tasks and (2) a number of more specific ability factors that influence how well people do on particular types of tests (for example, on tests of numerical reasoning or vocabulary; see Carroll, 1992; Gardner & Clark, 1992).

A Contemporary Psychometric View of Intelligence

Raymond Cattell and John Horn have greatly influenced current thinking concerning intelligence by proposing that Spearman's *g* and Thurstone's seven major mental abilities can be divided into two major dimensions of intellect: fluid intelligence and crystallized intelligence (Cattell, 1963; Horn & Cattell, 1967; Horn & Hofer, 1992). **Fluid intelligence** is the ability to use one's mind actively to solve novel problems—for example, to solve verbal analogies, remember unrelated pairs of words, or recognize relationships among geometric figures. The skills involved are not taught and are believed to be relatively free of cultural influences. **Crystallized intelligence,** in contrast, is the ability to use knowledge acquired through schooling and other life experiences. Tests of general information ("At what temperature does water boil?"), word comprehension ("What is the meaning of *duplicate*?"), and numerical abilities are all measures of crystallized intelligence. Thus, fluid intelligence involves using one's mind in new and flexible ways, whereas crystallized intelligence involves using what one has already learned through experience.

The concepts of fluid and crystallized intelligence have proved useful, but there are those who believe that none of the psychometric theories of intelligence have fully described what it means to be an intelligent person. Let's examine a way of thinking about intelligence that is quite different from regarding it as some specified number of intellectual factors. Doing so will help us capture the nature of intelligence—and help us appreciate the limitations of the IQ tests used to measure it.

A Modern Information-Processing Theory of Intelligence

Robert Sternberg (1985, 1988) has proposed a **triarchic theory of intelligence** that emphasizes three aspects of intelligent behavior: context, experience, and information-processing components.

First, Sternberg argues that what is defined as intelligent behavior depends on the sociocultural *context* in which it is displayed. Intelligent people adapt to the environment they are in (for example, a job setting), shape that environment to make it suit them better, or find a better environment. Such people have "street smarts." Psychologists, according to Sternberg, must begin to understand intelligence as behavior in the real world, not as behavior in taking tests.

This perspective views intelligent behavior as varying from one culture or subculture to another, from one period in history to another, and from one period of the life span to another. For example, Sternberg describes attending a conference in Venezuela and showing up at 8:00 A.M. sharp, only to find that he and four other North Americans were the only ones there. A behavior that is "intelligent" in North America proved to be rather "dumb" in a culture where expectations about punctuality are different. Each culture or subculture defines intelligence in its own way (Jayanthi & Rogoff, 1985). Sternberg also notes that what is intelligent can change over time. Numerical abilities once played an important role in intelligent behavior in our own society but may no

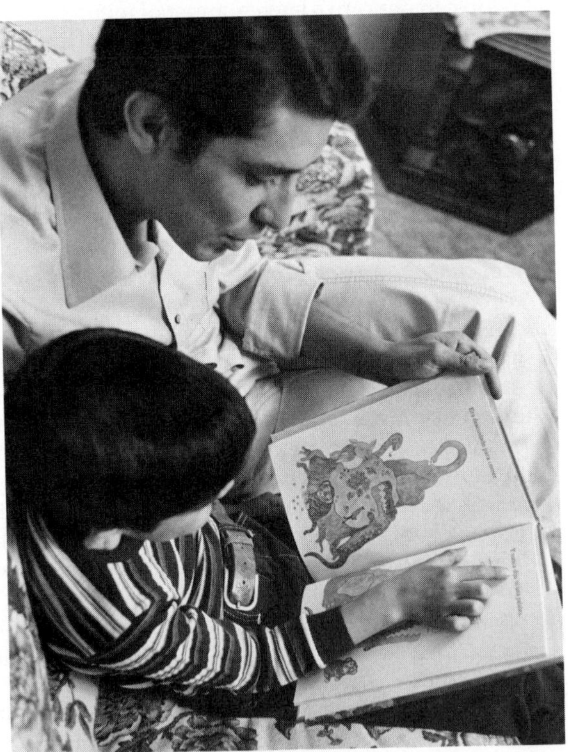

How would you define an intelligent child? Mexican-American parents, like Cambodian, Filipino, and Vietnamese parents, say that the intelligent child is motivated, socially skilled, and able to manage his or her own behavior, whereas Anglo-American parents place less emphasis on these noncognitive aspects of intelligence (Okagaki & Sternberg, 1993). Each cultural group defines intelligence in its own way.

longer be so important now that calculators and computers are widely used. And certainly the infant learning how to master new toys shows a different kind of intelligence than the adult mastering a college curriculum. Thus our definition of the intelligent infant must differ from our definition of the intelligent adult.

The second aspect of the triarchic theory focuses on the role of *experience* in intelligence. What is intelligent when one first encounters a new task is not the same as what is intelligent after extensive experience with that task. The first kind of intelligence, *response to novelty,* requires active and conscious information processing. Sternberg believes that relatively novel tasks provide the best measures of intelligence because they tap the individual's ability to come up with good ideas or fresh insights.

In daily life, however, people also perform more or less intelligently on tasks they have done over and over (reading the newspaper, for example). This second kind of intelligence reflects **automatization,** or an increased efficiency of information processing with practice. It is intelligent to develop little "programs in the mind" for performing common everyday activities efficiently and unthinkingly. Most importantly, says Sternberg, it is crucial to know how familiar a task is to a person in order to assess that person's behavior fairly. For example, giving people of two different cultural groups an intelligence test whose items are familiar to one group and novel to the other introduces **culture bias,** making it difficult to obtain a fair assessment of the groups' relative abilities.

The third aspect of the triarchic theory focuses on *information-processing components.* As an information-processing theorist, Sternberg believes that the theories of intelligence underlying the development of IQ tests ignore *how* people produce intelligent answers. He argues that the components of intelligent behavior range from identifying the problem to carrying out strategies to solve it; a full picture of intelligence includes not only the number of answers people get right but also the processes they use to arrive at their answers and the efficiency with which they use those processes.

So, fully assessing how intelligent Harry and Huang are requires consideration of the *context* in which they perform (their age, culture, and historical period); their previous *experience* with a task (whether their behavior reflects response to novelty or automatized processes); and the *information-processing* strategies they use. Individuals who are intelligent according to this model are able to carry out logical thought processes efficiently and effectively in order to solve both novel and familiar problems and adapt to their environment. Unfortunately, today's widely used tests of intelligence do not reflect this sophisticated view of intelligence.

HOW IS INTELLIGENCE MEASURED?

When psychologists first began to devise intelligence tests at the turn of the century, their concern was not with defining the nature of intelligence but with the more practical task of determining which schoolchildren were likely to be slow learners. Consequently, many tests had no precisely defined theory of intelligence behind them and were originally intended to assess intelligence in children, not in adults.

Alfred Binet and the Stanford-Binet Test

Alfred Binet and a colleague, Theodore Simon, produced the forerunner of our modern intelligence tests. In 1904 they were commissioned by the French government to devise a test that would identify "dull" children who might need special instruction. Binet and Simon devised a large battery of tasks measuring the skills believed to be necessary for classroom learning: attention, perception, memory, reasoning, verbal comprehension, and so on. Items that discriminated between normal children and those described by their teachers as slow were kept in the final test.

The test was soon revised to make the items *age graded.* For example, a set of "6-year-old" items could be passed by most 6-year-olds but few 5-year-olds; "12-year-old" items could be handled by most 12-year-olds but not by younger children. This approach permitted the testers to describe a child's **mental age (MA),** the level of age-graded problems that the child is able to solve. Thus a child who passes all items at the 5-year-old level but does poorly on more advanced items—regardless of her actual age—is said to have an MA of 5.

Binet's influence is still with us in the form of the modern *Stanford-Binet Scale.* In 1916 Lewis Terman of Stanford University translated and published a revised version of Binet's test for use with American children. It contained age-graded items for ages 3 to 13. Moreover, Terman made use of a procedure that had been developed for comparing mental age to chronological age. It is one thing to have a mental age of 10 when one is chronologically only 8, but another thing entirely to have that same mental age when one is 15. The **intelligence quotient,** or **IQ,** was originally calculated by dividing mental age by chronological age and then multiplying by 100:

$$IQ = MA/CA \times 100$$

An IQ score of 100 indicates average intelligence, regardless of a child's age: The normal child passes just the items that agemates typically pass, and mental age increases each year but always equals chronological age. The child of 8 with a mental age of 10 has experienced rapid intellectual growth and has a high IQ (specifically, 125); the child of 15 with a mental age of 10 has an IQ of only 67 and is clearly below average compared to children of the same age.

A revised version of the Stanford-Binet is still in use (Thorndike, Hagen, & Sattler, 1986). Its **test norms**—standards of normal performance expressed as average scores and the range of scores around the average—are based on the performance of a large and representative sample of people (2-year-olds through adults) from many socioeconomic and racial backgrounds. The concept of mental age is no longer used to calculate IQ; instead, individuals receive scores that reflect how well or how poorly they do as compared with others of the same age. An IQ of 100 is still average, and, the higher the IQ score an individual attains, the better the performance is in comparison to agemates.

The Wechsler Scales

David Wechsler constructed a set of intelligence tests that is also in wide use. The Wechsler Preschool and Primary Scale of Intelligence (WPPSI) is for children between the ages of 3 and 8 (Wechsler, 1989). The Wechsler Intelligence Scale for Children (WISC-III) is appropriate for schoolchildren aged 6 to 16 (Wechsler, 1991), and the Wechsler Adult Intelligence Scale–Revised (WAIS-R) is used with adults (Wechsler, 1981). The Wechsler tests yield a *verbal IQ* score based on items measuring vocabulary, general knowledge, arithmetic reasoning, and the like, as well as a *performance IQ* based on such nonverbal skills as the ability to assemble puzzles, solve mazes, reproduce geometric designs with colored blocks, and rearrange pictures to tell a meaningful story. As with the Stanford-Binet, a score of 100 is defined as average performance for one's age. A person's *full-scale IQ* is a combination of the verbal and performance scores.

The Distribution of IQ Scores

To more fully interpret an IQ score of 130 or 85, it helps to know how IQ scores are distributed in the population at large. Scores for large groups of people form a **normal distribution,** or a symmetrical, bell-shaped spread around the average score of 100 (see Figure 9.2). Scores around the average are common; the more distant the score from 100 on either side, the rarer it is. Over two-thirds of us have IQs between 85 and 115. Fewer than 3% have scores of 130 or above, a score that has often been used as one criterion of giftedness. John Stuart Mill, with his estimated IQ of 190, was very rare indeed! Similarly, fewer than 3% have IQs below 70, a cutoff that is commonly used today to define mental retardation.

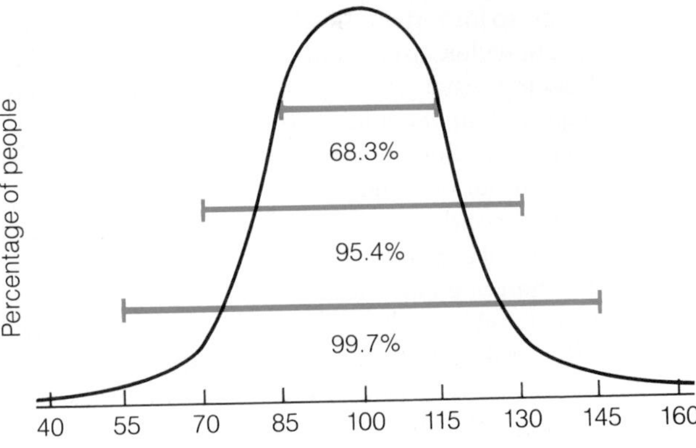

FIGURE 9.2 The approximate distribution of IQ scores.

Intelligence Testing Today

Traditional IQ tests continue to be used, and new ones are continually being developed. However, some scholars, disenchanted with the way in which intelligence has traditionally been defined and measured, have sought to develop entirely new approaches to intellectual assessment.

One promising approach, called **dynamic assessment,** attempts to evaluate how well children actually learn new material when an examiner provides them with competent instruction (Campione, Brown, Ferrara, & Bryant, 1984; Frisby & Braden, 1992). Reuven Feuerstein and his colleagues (1979), for example, have argued that, even though intelligence is often defined as a *potential* to learn from experience, IQ tests typically assess only *what has been learned,* not what can be learned. This approach may be biased against children from culturally different or disadvantaged backgrounds who lack opportunities to learn what the tests measure. Feuerstein's *Learning Potential Assessment Device* asks children to learn new things with the guidance of an adult who provides increasingly helpful cues. This test interprets intelligence as the ability to learn quickly with minimal guidance.

Robert Sternberg (1985, 1991) uses a similar approach in a test he has constructed based on his triarchic theory of intelligence. To better understand the information processes involved in verbal ability, for example, Sternberg does not ask people to define words they learned in the past, as IQ testers so often do. Instead, he places an unfamiliar word in a set of sentences and asks people to learn, from context, what the new word means, just as they must do in real life.

Despite their vast influence, IQ tests have been roundly criticized. A single IQ score derived from a test that assesses only some of the many kinds of intelligence that humans can display certainly does not do justice to the complexity of human mental functioning (Gardner, 1983; Sternberg, 1992). And, as Sternberg (1992) and others note, it is high time to bring modern information-processing theory to bear on the testing of intelligence in order to understand *how* highly intelligent individuals succeed where others fail. In sum, the nature of intelligence is still poorly understood. We do, however, have a vast store of information about how IQ scores change over the life span and about the implications for development and achievement of having a low or high IQ.

THE INFANT

As we saw in Chapters 7 and 8, the mind develops very rapidly in infancy. But how can an infant's intellectual growth be measured? Is it possible to identify infants who are more or less intelligent than their agemates? And does high (or low) intelligence in infancy predict high (or low) intelligence in childhood and adulthood?

Developmental Quotients

None of the standard intelligence tests can be used with children much younger than 3, because the test items require verbal skills and attention spans that the infant does not have. Some developmentalists have tried to measure infant intelligence by assessing the rate at which infants achieve important developmental milestones. Perhaps the best known and most widely used of the infant tests is the *Bayley Scales of Infant Development* (Bayley, 1969, 1993). This test, designed for infants aged 2 to 30 months, has three parts:

1. The *motor scale,* which measures the infant's ability to do such things as grasp a cube and throw a ball.
2. The *mental scale,* which includes adaptive behaviors such as reaching for a desirable object, searching for a hidden toy, and following directions.
3. The *infant behavioral record,* a rating of the child's behavior on dimensions such as goal-directedness, fearfulness, and social responsivity.

On the basis of the first two scores, the infant is given a **DQ,** or **developmental quotient,** rather than an IQ. The DQ summarizes how well or how poorly the infant performs in comparison to a large norm group of infants of the same age.

Infant Intelligence and Later Intelligence

As they grow older, infants do progress through many developmental milestones of the kind assessed by the Bayley Scales, so such scales are useful in charting infants' developmental progress. They are also useful in diagnosing neurological problems and mental retardation—even when these conditions are fairly mild and difficult to detect through standard pediatric or neurological examinations (Escalona, 1968; Honzik, 1983). But developmentalists have also been interested in the larger issue of continuity versus discontinuity in intellectual development: Can we predict which infants are likely to be gifted, average, or mentally retarded during the school years?

Apparently not, based on their DQs. Correlations between infant DQ and child IQ are very low—sometimes close to zero. The infant who does well on the Bayley Scales or other infant tests may or may not obtain a high IQ score later in life (Honzik, 1983; McCall, 1983; Rose, Feldman, Wallace, & McCarton, 1989). True, the infant who scores very low on an infant test often turns out to be mentally retarded, but otherwise there seems to be a good deal of discontinuity between early and later scores until a child is 4 or older.

Why don't infant development scales do a better job of predicting children's later IQs? Perhaps the main reason is that infant tests and IQ tests tap qualitatively different kinds of abilities (McCall, Eichorn, & Hogarty, 1977). Piaget would undoubtedly approve of this argument. Infant scales focus heavily on the sensory and motor skills that Piaget believed are so important in infancy; IQ tests such as the Stanford-Binet and WISC emphasize more abstract abilities, such as verbal reasoning, concept formation, and problem solving.

Robert McCall (1981, 1983) offers a second explanation, arguing that the growth of intelligence during infancy is highly influenced by powerful and universal maturational processes. Maturational forces pull infants back on course if environmental influences cause them to stray. For this reason, higher or lower infant test scores are likely to be mere temporary deviations from a universal developmental path. As the child nears age 2, McCall argues, maturational forces become less strong, so individual differences become larger and more stable over time. Consistent differences related to both individual genetic makeup and environment now begin to emerge.

Should we give up on trying to predict later IQ on the basis of development in infancy? Perhaps not yet. The information-processing approach has given new life to the idea that there is continuity in intelligence from infancy to childhood. Several researchers have found that certain measures of infant attention predict later IQ better than infant intelligence tests do (Bornstein & Sigman, 1986; Fagan & McGrath, 1981; McCall & Carriger, 1993; Rose, Feldman, & Wallace, 1992; Thompson, Fagan, & Fulker, 1991). Specifically, *speed of habituation* (the speed with which an infant loses interest in a repeatedly presented stimulus) and *preference for novelty* (the infant's tendency to prefer a novel stimulus to a familiar one), assessed in the first year of life, have an average correlation of about +.45 with IQ in childhood, particularly with verbal IQ and memory skills (Bornstein & Sigman, 1986; McCall & Carriger, 1993).

Perhaps, then, we can characterize the "smart" infant as one who quickly gets bored by the same old thing, seeks out novel experiences, and soaks up information quickly—in short, as an efficient information processor. There seems to be some continuity between infant intelligence and childhood intelligence after all. Such Bayley Scale accomplishments as throwing a ball are unlikely to carry over into vocabulary learning or problem-solving skills in childhood. However, the extent to which the young infant processes information quickly can predict the extent to which he or she will learn quickly and solve problems efficiently later in childhood.

THE CHILD

Over the childhood years, children become able to answer more questions, and more difficult questions, on IQ tests. That is, their mental ages increase. What about a child's IQ score, which reflects how that child compares with peers? And what does an IQ really tell us about a child?

How Stable Are IQ Scores during Childhood?

It was once assumed that a person's IQ reflected his or her genetically determined intellectual capacity and therefore would remain quite stable over time. In other words, a child with an IQ of 120 at age 5 was expected to obtain a similar IQ at age 10, 15, or 20. Is this idea supported by research? As we have seen, infant tests do not predict later IQ test scores well at all. However, starting at about age 4 there is a fairly strong relationship between early and later IQ, and the relationship grows even stronger by middle childhood. Table 9.1 summarizes the results of a longitudinal study of more than 250 children (Honzik, Macfarlane, & Allen, 1948; see also Sameroff et al., 1993): The shorter the interval between two testings, the higher the correlation between children's IQ scores. Even when a number of years have passed, IQ seems to be a very stable attribute: The scores that children obtain at age 6 are clearly related to those they obtain 12 years later, at age 18.

TABLE 9.1 Correlations of IQs measured during the preschool years and middle childhood with IQs measured at ages 10 and 18.

Age of Child	*Correlation with IQ at Age 10*	*Correlation with IQ at Age 18*
4	.66	.42
6	.76	.61
8	.88	.70
10	—	.76
12	.87	.76

SOURCE: From Honzik, Macfarlane, & Allen, 1948.

There is something these correlations are not telling us, however. They are based on a large *group* of children, and they do not necessarily mean that the IQs of *individual children* will remain stable over the years. As it turns out, many children show sizable ups and downs in their IQ scores over the course of childhood. Robert McCall and his associates looked at the IQ scores of 140 children who had taken intelligence tests at regular intervals from age 2½ to age 17 (McCall, Applebaum, & Hogarty, 1973). The average difference between a child's highest and lowest scores was a whopping 28.5 points. About one-third showed changes of more than 30 points, and one child changed by 74 IQ points!

How do we reconcile the conclusion that IQ is relatively stable with this clear evidence of instability? We can still conclude that, within a group, children's standings (high or low) in comparison with peers stay quite stable from one point to another during the childhood years. But, at the same time, many individual children experience drops or gains in IQ scores over the years. Apparently IQ is reasonably stable for some children but highly variable for many others.

Some wandering of IQ scores upward or downward over time is just random fluctuation—a good day at one testing, a bad day at the next. Yet it is interesting to note that children whose scores fluctuate the most tend to live in unstable home environments—that is, their life experiences had fluctuated between periods of happiness and turmoil (Honzik et al., 1948). Moreover, some children are likely to gain IQ points over childhood and others are likely to lose them. Who are the gainers, and who are the losers?

Gainers seem to have parents who foster achievement and are neither too strict nor too lax in child rearing (McCall et al., 1973). On the other hand, noticeable drops in IQ with age often occur among children who live in poverty. Otto Klineberg (1963) proposed a **cumulative-deficit hypothesis** to explain this: Impoverished environments inhibit intellectual growth, and these negative effects accumulate over time. There is some support for the cumulative-deficit hypothesis, especially when a child's parents are not only poor but low in intellectual functioning themselves (Jensen, 1977; Ramey & Ramey, 1992).

How Well Do IQ Scores Predict School Achievement?

If the original purpose of IQ tests was to estimate how well children would do in school, have these tests achieved their purpose? Yes, fairly well. The correlations between children's IQ scores and their grades, their scores on achievement tests, and other indicators of learning average from +.50 to +.70 (Fraser et al., 1987; Minton & Schneider, 1980), making general intellectual ability one of the best predictors of school achievement available (Fraser et al., 1987). Yet an IQ score does not tell us everything about a student. Factors such as work habits, interests, and motivation to succeed also affect academic achieve-

BOX 9.1 Cognitive Styles and IQ

Cognitive differences among children include more than differences in their IQ scores. For one thing, individuals differ in their **cognitive styles**—their characteristic and preferred ways of approaching problems and processing information. One way of characterizing an individual's cognitive style is along a dimension of reflectivity/impulsivity (Kagan et al., 1964). Children high in **impulsivity** seem to respond to problems quickly, favoring the first hypothesis they think of. Those high in **reflectivity** have a slower conceptual tempo; they take their time and evaluate many possible hypotheses before arriving at an answer.

The illustration (at right) is from the *Matching Familiar Figures Test,* which is used to assess reflectivity/impulsivity. The child is to select the figure among six alternatives that exactly matches the "standard" figure at the top. An individual may be slow or fast, accurate or inaccurate. Typically, a child who is fast and inaccurate is identified as impulsive; one who is slow and accurate is identified as reflective.

A reflective style would seem superior; for many problems, accuracy is valued, regardless of speed. Also, regardless of cultural background, children become more reflective (slower but more accurate) as they get older, suggesting that reflectivity is more developmentally mature than impulsivity (Salkind & Nelson, 1980; Smith & Caplan, 1988). Therefore, some researchers are convinced that reflective individuals are simply more competent than impulsive individuals at processing information and that what has been called cognitive "style" boils down to cognitive "ability" (Block, Gjerde, & Block, 1986; McKenna, 1990).

However, there is still considerable debate about whether tests of reflectivity/impulsivity measure differences in ability or differences in style—or both (Kogan, 1983; Smith & Kemler Nelson, 1988). If impulsive children are just developmentally slow compared to their more reflective peers, there should be some point in development at which everyone becomes reflective. But there is no such point; differences along this dimension can be found even among adults (Zelniker & Jeffrey, 1979). And, although impulsive children do poorly on tasks (like the matching-figures task) that require careful analysis of detail, they sometimes outperform reflective children on tasks that require global analysis—for example, the task of quickly determining if one overall shape matches another (Zelniker & Jeffrey, 1976, 1979). This would suggest that both impulsive and reflective children have their strengths and that impulsive children should be viewed as intellectually different rather than intellectually inferior. Given evidence on both sides of the issue, it may be best to conclude that cognitive style is probably a matter of *both* style and ability (Smith & Kemler Nelson, 1988).

Still, given the demands of our schools for accuracy, reflective children generally have an easier time with reading, memorizing, and other academic activities and do better in school as a result (Messer, 1976). Impulsive children are not lacking in general intellectual ability, but they invest too little effort in their work and make careless errors, sometimes even on tasks on which their global style of processing is appropriate (Smith & Kemler Nelson, 1988). They might benefit from training that helps them adopt a more reflective approach to many of the learning tasks they confront in the classroom.

Answer to sample problem: The first bear in the first row matches the standard.

ment. In addition, children who have similar IQ scores often have quite different styles of problem solving that influence their school achievement (see Box 9.1).

THE ADOLESCENT

Intellectual growth is very rapid during infancy and childhood. What happens during adolescence?

Continuity between Childhood and Adulthood

Intellectual growth continues its rapid pace in early adolescence and then slows down in later adolescence (Bayley, 1968). By the teen years, IQ scores have become even more stable and predict IQ in middle age very well (Eichorn, Hunt, & Honzik, 1981). This does not mean that individuals no longer show changes in their scores from testing to testing, though. They do.

IQ scores also continue to predict school achievement. Adolescents with higher IQs obtain higher grades in junior and senior high school (Fraser et al., 1987). They are also less likely to drop out of high school and more likely to go on to college than their peers with lower IQs (Brody & Brody, 1976). However, IQ scores do not predict college grades as well as they predict high school grades (Brody & Brody, 1976). This is probably because most college students have at least the average intellectual ability needed to succeed in college. Actual success is therefore more influenced by personal qualities such as motivation.

So far, no surprises. Patterns that emerged in childhood continue in adolescence. However, some interesting research has explored whether pubertal changes during adolescence influence intellectual growth.

The Timing of Puberty and Mental Abilities

Research on sex differences in mental abilities suggests that females tend to outperform males on measures of verbal ability, whereas males tend to outperform females on tests of mathematical and spatial abilities (Maccoby & Jacklin, 1974). These differences often are not evident until early adolescence. Could pubertal changes somehow affect the mental development of girls and boys?

Consider spatial ability (for example, the ability to recognize a complex geometric figure that has been rotated in three-dimensional space, as in Figure 9.3, or to navigate using a map). Both late-maturing girls and late-maturing boys often outperform early maturers on measures of spatial ability, though not by much (Newcombe & Bandura, 1983; Sanders & Soares, 1986; Waber, 1977). Why is this? It has proved difficult to explain this finding or to use it as an explanation for sex differences in spatial ability, but we have some clues (Newcombe, Dubas, & Baenninger, 1989).

Deborah Waber (1977) once proposed that the earlier physical maturation of girls cuts short the process by which the two sides of the brain take on specialized functions such as spatial reasoning. However, most evidence contradicts this hypothesis. First, the expected differences in brain lateralization between early and late maturers have not always been found (Linn & Peterson, 1985). Second, sex differences in spatial ability often show up *before* puberty, weakening the argument that the timing of puberty is the critical factor (Kerns & Berenbaum, 1991; Linn & Petersen, 1985). Finally, we have reason to think that sex differences in spatial ability are partly the product of sex differences in socialization. Females who excel on spatial ability tasks are more likely than other females to perceive themselves as having traditionally "masculine" traits and interests and to participate in the sorts of masculine-stereotyped activities that

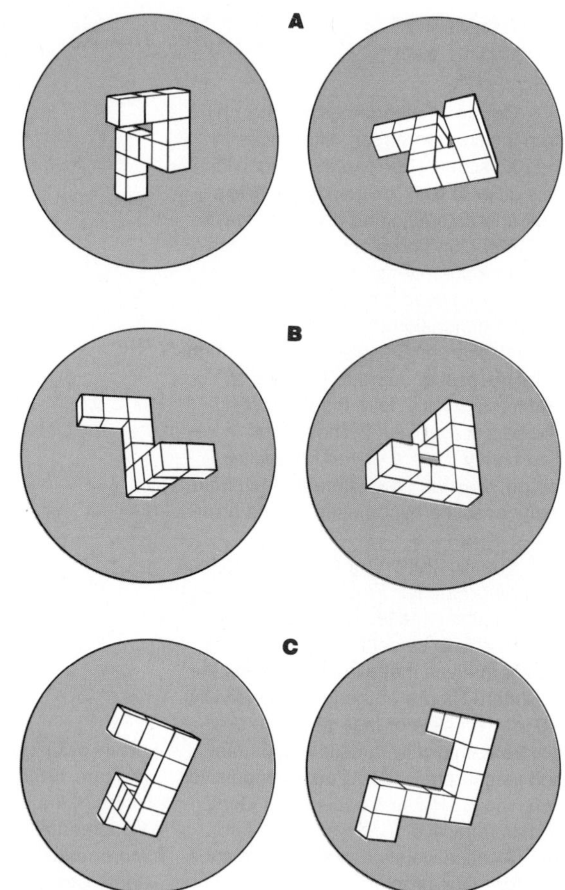

FIGURE 9.3 A spatial ability task. Decide whether the two figures in each pair are alike or different. (From Shepard & Metzler, 1971.)

Answer: The two figures in items A and B are the same, but the two in item C are different.

sharpen spatial skills (Newcombe & Bandura, 1983; Newcombe & Dubas, 1992; Signorella, Jamison, & Krupa, 1989). Females who adopt a more traditional, feminine self-concept may be less motivated to become involved in "masculine" activities like model building, carpentry, and soccer (Newcombe & Dubas, 1992).

In sum, individual differences in at least one important mental ability, spatial skills, do seem to be related to the timing of puberty, with late maturers outperforming early maturers. However, it is not at all clear that girls' earlier puberty accounts for the male edge in spatial ability. Having a "masculine" self-concept and engaging in masculine pursuits may be more important.

THE ADULT

Do IQ scores predict achievement after people have left school? Does performance on IQ tests change during the adult years? And do IQ scores decline in old age, as performance on Piagetian cognitive tasks and performance on many memory tasks appear to do?

Does IQ Affect Occupational Success in Adulthood?

There is indeed a relationship between IQ and occupational status. This was demonstrated in an early study of World War II military personnel (Harrell & Harrell, 1945). Table 9.2 shows the rank order (from most prestigious to least prestigious) of civilian occupations these men had had. The average IQ score for an occupation increases as the prestige of the occupation increases (see also Gottfredson, 1986). The reason for this relationship is clear: It undoubtedly takes more intellectual ability to complete law school and become a lawyer than it does to be a farmhand. But notice also the "Range of IQs" column. There were some very bright men working in low-status occupations. Apparently a high IQ is no guarantee that one will be working in a prestigious job.

Now a second question: Are bright lawyers, electricians, or farmhands more successful or productive than their less intelligent colleagues? The answer here is also "yes." The correlation between scores on tests of intellectual ability and such measures of job performance as supervisor ratings is about +.50 (Gottfredson, 1986; Hunter & Hunter, 1984). General intellectual ability seems to predict job performance in a wide range of occupations better than any other indicator yet devised, and it predicts likelihood of success as accurately for members of racial and ethnic minority groups as for whites (Hunter & Hunter, 1984). The more intellectually capable adults are better able to learn what they need to know about their occupations and to solve the problems that arise day by day.

TABLE 9.2 Average IQs and range of IQs for enlisted military personnel who had worked at various civilian occupations.

Occupation	*Average IQ*	*Range of IQs*
Accountant	128.1	94–157
Lawyer	127.6	96–157
Engineer	126.6	100–151
Chemist	124.8	102–153
Reporter	124.5	100–157
Teacher	122.8	76–155
Pharmacist	120.5	76–149
Bookkeeper	120.0	70–157
Sales manager	119.0	90–137
Purchasing agent	118.7	82–153
Radio repairman	115.3	56–151
Salesman	115.1	60–153
Artist	114.9	82–139
Stock clerk	111.8	54–151
Machinist	110.1	38–153
Electrician	109.0	64–149
Riveter	104.1	50–141
Butcher	102.9	42–147
Bartender	102.2	56–137
Carpenter	102.1	42–147
Chauffeur	100.8	46–143
Cook and baker	97.2	20–147
Truck driver	96.2	16–149
Barber	95.3	42–141
Farmhand	91.4	24–141
Miner	90.6	42–139

SOURCE: From Harrell & Harrell, 1945.

In sum, IQ does have some bearing on occupational success, predicting both what kind of occupation an individual chooses and how well he or she performs in it. At the same time, an IQ score does not tell the whole story; personal qualities such as motivation and environmental factors such as social support for one's aspirations also affect vocational outcomes (see Chapter 15).

How Do Intellectual Abilities Change with Age?

Perhaps no question about adult development has been studied as thoroughly as that of how intellectual abilities change with age. Early cross-sectional studies comparing different age groups of adults yielded disturbing findings — disturbing, at least, to anyone over 20. For example, extensive testing during World War I using the *Army Alpha Test* showed that scores on this IQ-type test steadily decreased from the young groups of 20 years of age or less to the older groups of up to 50 and 60 years of age (Yerkes, 1921). Does this finding mean that we're brightest at 20 and it's downhill from there? Not really. In longitudinal follow-up studies, the scores a group of middle-aged people obtained on the Army Alpha Test were compared to the scores these same adults had obtained when they were college freshmen. The middle-age scores were *higher* on every subtest except the one dealing with arithmetic (Owens, 1953). This finding, along with longitudinal evidence that IQs decline only modestly in old age, startled psychologists who had long assumed that intellectual performance peaked at about age 20 (Cunningham & Owens, 1983).

Why the big discrepancy? As noted in Chapter 1, both cross-sectional and longitudinal studies have their problems. Cross-sectional studies compare people of different cohorts who have had different levels of education and life experiences because they were born at different times. Yet longitudinal studies are also flawed. People die or drop out of such studies. Those who are left — those whose scores can be charted across the years — tend to be individuals with better health and higher intellectual functioning, the very people who may be most likely to improve their abilities in earlier adulthood and maintain them in old age (Schaie, 1983).

So neither kind of study is entirely adequate in determining how IQ test performance changes with age, though both have value. For example, cross-sectional studies *do* tell us that the average older person today performs worse on IQ tests than the average younger person. This information may be useful in planning adult education programs. And the longitudinal studies have told us a great deal about change over time (in at least a select segment of the population) and have revealed that individual differences in IQ scores are quite stable over the adult years. Still, the best information about changes in intellectual abilities has come from a sophisticated *sequential study* directed by K. Warner Schaie that combines the cross-sectional and the longitudinal approaches (see Schaie, 1983, 1989a; Schaie & Hertzog, 1983, 1986; Schaie & Willis, 1993).

Schaie's study began in 1956 with a sample of members of a health maintenance organization ranging in age from 22 to 70. They were given a revised test of primary mental abilities that yielded scores for five separate mental abilities (see Box 9.2). Seven years later, as many of them as could be found were retested. In addition, a new sample of adults ranging in age from their 20s to their 70s was tested. These two samples made it possible to determine how the performance of the same individuals changed over a period of seven years *and* to compare the performance of people who were 20 years old in 1956 with that of a different cohort of people who were 20 in 1963. This same strategy was repeated in 1970, 1977, and 1984, giving the researchers a wealth of information about different cohorts, including longitudinal data on some of the same people over a 28-year period.

What has this study revealed? First, it seems that when a person is born has at least as much influence on intellectual functioning as age does. In other words, cohort or generational effects on performance exist. This evidence confirms the suspicion that cross-sectional comparisons of different age groups yield too grim a picture of declines in intellectual abilities during adulthood. Specifically, recently born cohorts (the youngest people in the study were born in 1959) have tended to outperform earlier generations (the oldest were born in 1889) on most tests. Yet on the test of numerical ability, people born between 1903 and 1924 actually performed better than both earlier and later generations. So different generations may have a special edge in different areas of intellectual performance, showing that when one is born *does* affect one's intellectual abilities.

What happened to the mental abilities of these individuals as they aged? Table 9.3 charts average performance in five areas at various ages as a percentage of performance at age 25. These data have been corrected to eliminate some of the problems that can make longitudinal data misleading. Numbers higher than 100 indicate that performance exceeded that at age 25. For the most part, modest gains in abilities occur in the 30s, 40s, and even 50s; scores level off in the late 50s and early 60s; and declines begin to occur in the late 60s and 70s — far later than was previously thought. By the age of 80, significant declines in several abilities are evident. Before that age, however, the average older person functions within the normal range of ability for young adults.

But another important message of Schaie's study, and of other research as well, is that patterns of aging differ for different abilities. For one thing, *fluid intelligence* (those abilities requiring active thinking and reasoning applied to novel problems, as measured by tests like the primary mental abilities tests of reasoning and space) usually declines earlier and more steeply than *crystallized intelligence* (those abilities involving

BOX 9.2 The Primary Mental Abilities Measured in Schaie's Seattle Study

• *Verbal meaning:* One must recognize the meaning of a word by identifying the best synonym for it from a list of four words. This ability comes in handy in reading and understanding speech.

• *Space:* This is the ability to imagine how an object would look if it were rotated in space. Given one figure (an *F*, for example), one must quickly determine whether six other figures are or are not the *F* at another angle (for example, upside down). Spatial ability would aid in reading maps or assembling pieces of equipment.

• *Reasoning:* The test of reasoning involves foreseeing the pattern in a series of letters. Given the pattern *"b c r c d r d e r,"* one would have to figure out that the next letter should be *e*. Reasoning enters into solving problems in real life, as when one analyzes a situation on the basis of past experience and plans an appropriate future course.

• *Number:* This is the ability to deal with basic arithmetic problems quickly. Given an addition problem that has been worked to yield a sum, one must decide whether it has been worked correctly. Although mathematics abilities may be less useful today now that we have calculators, they still play a role in daily life.

• *Word fluency:* Finally, the word-fluency test measures the quick recall of words. During a five-minute period one must write down as many words as possible that begin with the letter *s*. Presumably this ability enters into talking and reading easily.

SOURCE: These descriptions are based on those provided by Schaie (1983, pp. 73–74) of the following test: Thurstone, L. L., & Thurstone, T. G. (1948). *SRA Primary Mental Abilities, Ages 11–17, Form AM.* Chicago: Science Research Associates, Inc.

TABLE 9.3 Mental abilities at different ages as a percentage of performance at age 25[a].

Age	Verbal Meaning	Space	Reasoning	Number	Word Fluency	Overall Intellectual Ability
32	105	103	100	107	105	105
39	109	105	103	110	105	108
46	109	107	102	120	104	109
53	113	106	103	122	94	111
60	111	105	101	126	90	110
67	107	103	91	122	83[a]	104
74	97	90	81[a]	109	81[a]	92
81	87	79	73[a]	90	62[a]	80[a]

[a]These average performances fall in the lowest 25% of the distribution for 25-year-olds. Thus they represent the most substantial declines in performance in old age.

SOURCE: Modified from Schaie, 1983.

the use of knowledge acquired through experience, as in answering the verbal-meaning test used by Schaie). Consistently, older adults appear to lose some of their ability to grapple with new problems, but they maintain their "crystallized" general knowledge and vocabulary quite well and sometimes even improve on them (Dixon, Kramer, & Baltes, 1985; Horn & Hofer, 1992; Wang & Kaufman, 1993). An overall IQ score obscures this important fact of cognitive aging.

Similarly, performance IQ scores on the Wechsler adult IQ test (which often involve nonverbal items posing novel problems) decline earlier than verbal IQ scores do (Busse & Maddox, 1985). In addition, both tests of fluid intelligence and tests of performance IQ are often timed, and performance on timed or speeded tests declines more in old age than performance on unspeeded tests does (Jarvik & Bank, 1983). Fluid, performance, and speeded IQ test items may be less familiar to older adults who have been out of school for years than to younger adults; in this sense, the tests may be subtly biased against older adults (Cornelius, 1984; Labouvie-Vief, 1985). However, declines in these fluid aspects of intelligence seem to be due primarily to the slowing of response that most people experience as they age (Hertzog, 1989; Salthouse, 1993; Schaie, 1989b).

We seem to be discovering that speed of information processing is related to intellectual functioning across the life span. Not only is rapid information processing in infancy associated with high IQ scores in childhood, but young adults with quick reaction times outperform their more sluggish agemates on IQ tests, and adults who lose information-processing speed in later life lose some of their ability to think through complex and novel problems as well (Jensen, 1993). It is not just that older adults can't finish tests that have time limits, for declines in fluid intelligence in later life occur even on untimed tests (Wang & Kaufman, 1993). The problem is that the slower information processor cannot keep in mind and process simultaneously all relevant aspects of a complex problem.

We now have an overall picture of intellectual functioning in adulthood. Age-group differences in performance suggest that older adults today are at a disadvantage on many tests compared to younger adults, partly because of deficiencies in the quality of education they received early in life. But actual declines in intellectual abilities associated with aging are generally minor until people enter their 60s or 70s. Even in old age, declines in performance on fluid intelligence, performance intelligence, and speeded tests are more apparent than declines in crystallized intelligence, verbal intelligence, and performance on untimed tests.

One last message of this research is worth special emphasis: *Declines in intellectual abilities are not universal.* Even among the 81-year-olds in Schaie's study, only about 30–40% had experienced a significant decline in intellectual ability in the previous seven years (Schaie, 1990). Moreover, although few 81-year-olds maintained all five mental abilities, almost all retained at least one ability from testing to testing, and about half retained four out of five (Schaie, 1989a). So the range of differences in intellectual functioning in a group of older adults is extremely large (Morse, 1993), and anyone who stereotypes all elderly adults as intellectually limited is likely to be wrong most of the time.

What Factors Are Associated with Declining Intellectual Abilities in Old Age?

What is most likely to affect declines in intellectual performance in old age? *Poor health,* not surprisingly, is one risk factor. People who have cardiovascular diseases or other chronic illnesses show steeper declines in mental abilities than their healthier peers.

Diseases (and most likely the drugs used to treat them as well) also contribute to a rapid decline in intellectual abilities within a few years of death (Johansson, Zarit, & Berg, 1992; Kleemeier, 1962; White & Cunningham, 1988). This phenomenon has been given the depressing label **terminal drop.** Perhaps there really is something, then, to the saying "Sound body, sound mind."

A second factor in decline is an *unstimulating lifestyle.* Schaie and his colleagues found that the biggest intellectual declines were shown by elderly widows who had low social status, engaged in few activities, and were dissatisfied with their lives (Gribbin, Schaie, & Parham, 1980; Schaie, 1984). These women were alone, having apparently disengaged themselves from life. Individuals who maintain their performance or even show gains tend to have above-average socioeconomic status, advanced education, intact marriages, intellectually capable spouses, and physically and mentally active lifestyles (Jarvik & Bank, 1983; Schaie, 1990).

The moral is "Use it or lose it!" This rule, which usually refers to muscular strength or sexual functioning, seems also to apply to intellectual functioning in later life (Schaie, 1983). The plasticity of the nervous system throughout the life span enables elderly individuals to benefit from intellectual stimulation and training, to maintain the intellectual skills most relevant to their activities, and to compensate for the loss of less-exercised abilities (Dixon et al., 1985). There is still much to learn about how health, lifestyle, and other factors shape the individual's intellectual growth and decline. What is certain is that most of us can look forward to many years of optimal intellectual functioning before *some* of us experience losses of *some* mental abilities in later life.

FACTORS THAT INFLUENCE IQ SCORES

Now that we have surveyed changes in intellectual functioning over the life span, let's address a different question: Why do children or adults who are *the same age* differ in IQ? As usual, our best answer is that genetic and environmental factors interact to make us what we are.

Genes

The pioneers of the IQ testing movement believed that individual differences in IQ exist simply because some people inherit better genes at conception than others do. Even though IQ scores are now known *not* to be determined entirely by genes, heredity does influence intelligence. As we saw in Chapter 3, identical twins obtain more similar IQ scores than fraternal twins do, even when they have been raised apart all their lives. About half of the variation in IQ scores within a group of children or adults is associated with genetic differences among them (Plomin, 1990). This leaves about half of the variation attributable to differences in the environments in which people develop. So let's examine the home environment in infancy and early childhood to detect factors that stimulate or inhibit intellectual development. Then we will see how far this information can take us in explaining differences in IQ scores associated with socioeconomic status and race or ethnicity.

Home Environment

A recent study by Arnold Sameroff and his colleagues (1993) provides a broad overview of some of the environmental factors that put children at risk for having low IQ scores—and, by implication, some of the factors associated with higher IQs. These researchers assessed the 10 risk factors shown in Table 9.4 at age 4

TABLE 9.4 Ten environmental risk factors associated with low IQ and mean IQs at age 4 of children who did or did not experience each risk factor.

	Mean IQ at Age 4 If:	
Risk Factor	*Child Experienced Risk Factor*	*Child Did Not Experience Risk Factor*
Child is member of minority group	90	110
Head of household is unemployed or low-skilled worker	90	108
Mother did not complete high school	92	109
Family has four or more children	94	105
Father is absent from family	95	106
Family experienced many stressful life events	97	105
Parents have rigid child-rearing values	92	107
Mother is highly anxious/distressed	97	105
Mother has poor mental health/diagnosed disorder	99	107
Mother shows little positive affect toward child	88	107

SOURCE: Data and descriptions compiled from Sameroff et al., 1993.

and again at age 13. Every one of these factors was related to IQ at age 4, and most also predicted IQ at age 13. In addition, the greater the number of these risk factors affecting a child, the lower his or her IQ. Which particular risk factors a child experienced was less important than how many he or she experienced. Clearly it is not good for intellectual development to grow up in a disadvantaged home with an adult who is unable to provide much intellectual nurturance.

In what specific ways do parents influence their children's intellectual development? Bettye Caldwell and Robert Bradley have developed a widely used instrument for determining how intellectually stimulating or impoverished a home environment is (Caldwell & Bradley, 1984; Bradley & Caldwell, 1984). Sample items from the preschool version of their **HOME inventory** (*H*ome *O*bservation for *M*easurement of the *E*nvironment) are shown in Table 9.5 (Caldwell & Bradley, 1984). Bradley and his colleagues (1989) have found that scores on the HOME predict children's cognitive functioning quite well. Moreover, gains in IQ from age 1 to age 3 are likely to occur among children from stimulating homes, whereas children from families with low HOME scores often experience drops in IQ over the same period. All of this is truer for Anglo- and African-American children than for Mexican-American children, however. The early IQ scores of Mexican-American children are not very closely related to their families' HOME scores, suggesting that the HOME inventory may not be capturing the ways in which Hispanic parents foster their children's intellectual development.

What particular aspects of the home environment best predict high IQs? Studies using the HOME inventory indicate that the most important factors are parental involvement with the child, provision of appropriate play materials, and opportunities for a variety of stimulation (Gottfried, 1984). Other researchers (e.g., Crockenberg, 1983) would add that the sheer amount of stimulation parents provide to their young children may not be as important as whether that stimulation is responsive—that is, whether it is in reaction to the child's own behavior (a smile in return for a smile, an answer in return for a question). Also, stimulation should be matched to the competencies of the child—neither too simple nor too challenging—which depends on the parent's knowing the child's capacities well (Hunt & Paraskevopoulos, 1980; Miller, 1986). In short, an intellectually stimulating home is one in which parents are eager to be involved with their children and are responsive to their developmental needs and behavior (MacPhee, Ramey, & Yeates, 1984).

Do differences in stimulation in the home really *create* individual differences in IQ? We know that bright parents are likely to provide intellectually stimulating home environments (Coon et al., 1990; Longstreth et al., 1981). But could it be that any correlation between the quality of the home environment and

TABLE 9.5 Subscales and sample items from the HOME inventory.

Subscale 1: Emotional and Verbal Responsivity of Parent (11 items)	
Sample items:	Parent responds verbally to child's vocalizations or verbalizations
	Parent's speech is distinct, clear, and audible
	Parent caresses or kisses child at least once
Subscale 2: Avoidance of Restriction and Punishment (8 items)	
Sample items:	Parent neither slaps nor spanks child during visit
	Parent does not scold or criticize child during visit
	Parent does not interfere with or restrict child more than three times during visit
Subscale 3: Organization of Physical and Temporal Environment (6 items)	
Sample items:	Child gets out of house at least four times a week
	Child's play environment is safe
Subscale 4: Provision of Appropriate Play Materials (9 items)	
Sample items:	Child has a push or pull toy
	Parent provides learning facilitators appropriate to age—mobile, table and chairs, highchair, playpen, and so on.
	Parent provides toys for child to play with during visit
Subscale 5: Parental Involvement with Child (6 items)	
Sample items:	Parent talks to child while doing household work
	Parent structures child's play periods
Subscale 6: Opportunities for Variety in Daily Stimulation (5 items)	
Sample items:	Father provides some care daily
	Child has three or more books of his or her own

SOURCE: Adapted from Caldwell & Bradley, 1984.

children's IQ scores simply reflects the fact that bright parents transmit genes for high intelligence to their offspring? Keith Yeates and his colleagues (Yeates, MacPhee, Campbell, & Ramey, 1983) evaluated this hypothesis in a longitudinal study of 112 mothers and their children aged 2 to 4. They measured the mothers' IQs, the children's IQs from age 2 to age 4, and the families' HOME environments. The best predictor of a child's IQ at age 2 was the mother's IQ, just as a genetic hypothesis would suggest; home environment had little effect. But the picture changed by the time children were 4 years old, when the quality of the home environment *did* correlate significantly with IQ. Moreover, the researchers established statistically that differences in the quality of the home environment influenced children's IQs regardless of the IQs of their mothers. This continues to be true as children get older, although the genetic hypothesis has some truth to it too (Luster & Dubow, 1992). Finally, we know that adopted children's IQ scores rise considerably when they are moved from less stimulating to more stimulating homes (Turkheimer, 1991). In sum, the argument that genetic influences can fully explain the apparent effects of home environment on IQ does not hold up.

Social-Class Differences in IQ

Children from lower- and working-class homes average some 10 to 20 points below their middle-class agemates on IQ tests. As socioeconomic conditions have improved in developed countries during the 20th century, average IQ scores have increased accordingly (Flynn, 1987). Similarly, improving the economic conditions of children's homes can improve their IQs. For example, Sandra Scarr and Richard Weinberg have charted the intellectual growth of black and white children adopted before their first birthdays (Scarr & Weinberg, 1983; Weinberg, Scarr, & Waldman, 1992). Many of these children came from disadvantaged family backgrounds and had biological parents who were poorly educated and somewhat below average in IQ. They were placed in middle-class homes with adoptive parents who were highly educated and above average in intelligence. Throughout childhood and adolescence, these adoptees have posted average or above-average scores on standardized IQ tests—higher scores than they would have obtained if they had stayed in the disadvantaged environments offered by their natural parents.

Could social-class differences in IQ be due to differences in the quality of the home environment that parents of different socioeconomic levels provide? Yes, at least partially. Scores on the HOME inventory are higher in middle-class homes than in lower-class homes, indicating that middle-class homes tend to be more intellectually stimulating (Bradley et al., 1989; Gottfried, 1984). Poor nutrition, drug abuse, disruptive family experiences, and other factors associated with poverty may also contribute to the social-class gap in IQ (Gottfried & Gottfried, 1984).

Racial and Ethnic Differences in IQ

Racial and ethnic differences in IQ scores have also been observed. In the United States, for example, African-American, Native-American, and Hispanic-American children tend to score below Anglo-American children on IQ tests (Minton & Schneider, 1980). Different subcultural groups sometimes also show distinctive profiles of mental abilities; for example, black children may do particularly well on verbal tasks, Hispanic children on nonverbal items that test spatial abilities (Saccuzzo, Johnson, & Russell, 1992; Taylor & Richards, 1991).

A good deal of research has compared African-American and Anglo-American children. Black children living in the southeastern United States seem to do especially poorly, but even black children living in the North or in metropolitan areas of the South have tended to attain average IQs about 12 to 15 points lower than those of their white agemates (Loehlin, Lindzey, & Spuhler, 1975). Of course, it is essential to keep in mind that these are differences in *group averages*. Like the IQ scores of white children, those of black children run the whole range, from the mentally retarded zone to the gifted zone, and many black children have higher IQs than most white children do. We certainly cannot predict an individual's IQ merely on the basis of racial or ethnic identity.

Having said that, we must ask why these average group differences exist. If you are thinking about the social-class differences we just described, your answer is likely to be that minority-group children simply grow up in less advantaged environments. This is true. But, before we consider this environmental explanation for racial and ethnic differences, let's consider the following alternative ideas: (1) bias in testing hurts members of minority groups, (2) minority-group members are not highly motivated in testing situations, and (3) group differences in IQ may have a hereditary basis.

Culture Bias

There may be *culture bias* in testing; that is, IQ tests may be more appropriate for children from white middle-class backgrounds than for those from other subcultural groups (Helms, 1992). Low-income African-American children who speak a different dialect of English than that spoken by middle-class Anglo children, as well as Hispanic children who hear Spanish rather than English at home, may not understand the test instructions or items very well. Their experiences may not allow them to become familiar with some of the information that is called for on the tests (for example, "What is a 747?").

It is true that minority-group children often do not have as much exposure to the culture reflected in the tests as nonminority children do. If IQ tests assess

Differences in intellectual functioning within any racial or ethnic group are far greater than differences among groups.

"proficiency in white culture," minority children are bound to look deficient (Helms, 1992). But, even though standardized IQ test items sometimes have a white middle-class flavor, group differences in IQ probably cannot be traced solely to test bias. *Culture-fair IQ tests* include items that should be equally unfamiliar (or familiar) to people from all ethnic groups and social classes. Still, racial and ethnic differences emerge on such tests (Jensen, 1980). In addition, IQ tests seem to predict future school achievement as well for blacks and other minorities as they do for whites (Anastasi, 1988; Oakland & Parmelee, 1985).

Motivational Factors

Another possibility is that minority children are not highly motivated in testing situations (Moore, 1986; Zigler, Abelson, Trickett, & Seitz, 1982). They may be wary of strange examiners, may see little point in trying to do well, and may shake their heads as if to say they don't know the answer before the question is ever completed. Disadvantaged children do indeed score some 7 to 10 points better when they are given time to warm up to a friendly examiner or are given a mix of easy and hard items so that they do not become discouraged by a long string of difficult items (Zigler et al., 1982). Even though most all children do better with a friendly examiner (Sacks, 1952), it still seems that black children, even those from middle-class homes, are often less comfortable in testing situations than white middle-class children are (Moore, 1986).

Genetic Influences

Perhaps no idea in psychology has sparked more heated debate than the suggestion that racial and ethnic differences in IQ scores are due to group differences in genetic makeup. The strongest proponent of this view has been Arthur Jensen (1969, 1980). Based on evidence that differences in genetic makeup contribute, along with environment, to IQ differences *within* either the white or the black population, Jensen went on to suggest that IQ differences *between* whites and blacks may be due to genetic differences between the races.

However, most psychologists do not think that the evidence that heredity contributes to within-group differences says much at all about the reasons for between-group differences. Richard Lewontin (1976) makes this point with an analogy. Suppose that corn seeds with different genetic makeups are randomly drawn from a bag and planted in two fields — one that is barren and one that has fertile soil. Since all the plants within each field were grown in the same soil, their differences in height would have to be due to differences in genetic makeup. A genetic explanation would fit. But, if the plants in the fertile field are generally taller than those in the barren field, this *between-field* variation must be entirely due to environment. Similarly, even though genes partially explain individual differences in IQ *within* black groups and white groups, the average difference *between* the racial groups may still reflect nothing more than differences in the environments they typically experience (Plomin, 1990). There is currently no basis for concluding that differences in genetic makeup between the races account for average group differences in IQ.

Environmental Influences

It is time to return to an environmental hypothesis about racial and ethnic differences in IQ. Many of the intellectual and academic differences that have been attributed to race or ethnicity probably reflect racial and ethnic differences in socioeconomic status instead (Patterson Kupersmidt, & Vaden, 1990). Research on adopted children is very relevant here. Placement in more advantaged homes has allowed lower-income black children to equal or exceed the average IQ in the general population and to exceed the IQs of comparable black children raised in more disadvantaged environments by 20 points (Moore, 1986; Scarr & Weinberg, 1983; Weinberg et al., 1992). As Scarr and Weinberg (1983) conclude, this could not have happened if black children were genetically deficient.

The major message of this research is that children, whether they are black or white, perform better on IQ tests when they grow up in intellectually stimulating environments with involved, responsive parents and are exposed to the "culture of the tests and the schools" (Scarr & Weinberg, 1983, p. 261). There are signs, though, that the IQ gap between black and white children has been decreasing in recent years as educational and economic opportunities for African Americans have improved (Vincent, 1991). Perhaps the issue of racial and ethnic differences in IQ will largely disappear as life conditions for minority-group families improve further. Unfortunately, more African-American than white children continue to live in poverty, and socioeconomic differences between the races continue to explain part of the average IQ difference between the races.

THE EXTREMES OF INTELLIGENCE

Although we have identified some of the factors that contribute to individual differences in intellectual performance, we cannot fully appreciate the magnitude of these differences without considering people at the extremes of the IQ continuum. Just how different are gifted individuals and mentally retarded individuals? And how different are their lives?

Giftedness

The gifted child used to be identified solely by an IQ score—one that was at least 130 or 140. Programs for gifted children still focus mainly on those with very high IQs, but there is increased recognition that some children are gifted because they have special abilities rather than because they have high general intelligence. So today's definitions emphasize that **giftedness** involves having a high IQ *or* showing special abilities in areas valued in our society, such as creativity, mathematics, the performing and visual arts, or even leadership (Coleman, 1985).

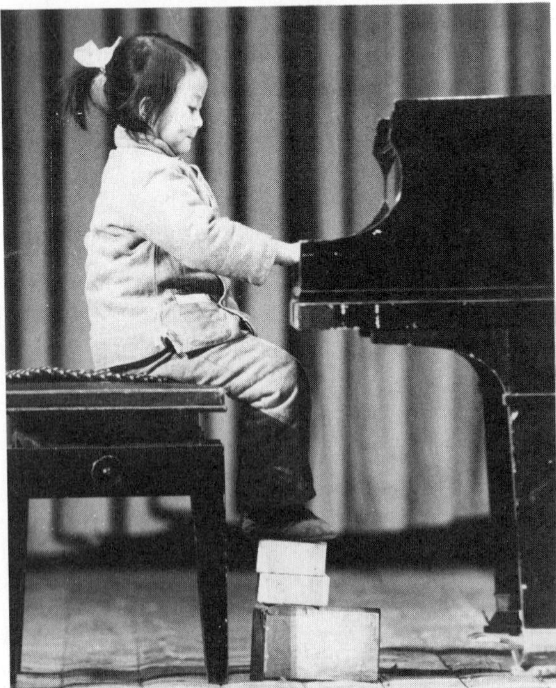

Gifted children have either high IQ scores or special abilities. This four-year-old Chinese girl is already entering musical competitions in Beijing.

None other than Lewis Terman, developer of the Stanford-Binet test, launched a major longitudinal study of gifted children back in 1922 (Fincher, 1973; Terman, 1954; Terman & Oden, 1959). The subjects were more than 1500 California schoolchildren who were nominated by their teachers as gifted and who had IQs of 140 or higher. Like other scholars of his era, Terman assumed that intelligence was fixed at birth; therefore he expected gifted children to remain gifted throughout their lives (Cravens, 1992).

It soon became apparent that these high-IQ children were exceptional in many other ways as well. For example, they had weighed more at birth and had learned to walk and talk sooner than most toddlers. They reached puberty somewhat earlier than average and had better-than-average health. Their teachers rated them as better adjusted and more morally mature than their less-intelligent peers. And, although they were no more popular than their classmates, they were quick to take on leadership responsibilities. Taken together, these findings destroy the stereotype that most gifted children are frail, sickly youngsters who are socially inadequate and emotionally immature.

Another convincing demonstration of the personal and social maturity of most gifted children comes from a study by Nancy Robinson and Paul Janos (1986) of high-IQ children who skipped high school entirely and entered the University of Washington as part of a special program to accelerate their education. Contrary to the common wisdom that gifted children will suffer socially and emotionally if they skip grades and are forced to fit in with much older students, these youngsters showed no signs at all of maladjustment (see also Noble, Robinson, & Gunderson, 1993; Richardson & Benbow, 1990). Indeed, on several measures of psychological and social maturity and adjustment, they equaled their much older college classmates, as well as similarly gifted students who attended high school. Many of them thrived in college, for the first time finding friends like themselves—friends who "got their jokes" (Noble et al., 1993, p. 125).

What becomes of gifted children as adults? Most of Terman's gifted children remained remarkable in many respects. Fewer than 5% were rated as seriously maladjusted, and their rates of such problems as ill health, mental illness, alcoholism, and delinquent behavior were but a fraction of those observed in the general population (Terman, 1954). They were also more satisfied with their marriages and less likely to divorce.

The occupational achievements of the men in the sample were impressive. The vast majority (86%) were working in professional or semiprofessional jobs by age 40. As a group they had taken out more than 200 patents and written some 2000 scientific reports, 100 books, 375 plays or short stories, and more than 300 essays, sketches, magazine articles, and critiques.

And gifted women? Due to the influence of gender-role expectations during the period covered by the study, gifted women were less likely than gifted men to pursue their education beyond college and often sacrificed their career goals, raising families and performing community service instead (Schuster, 1990; Tomlinson-Keasey & Little, 1990). More recent cohorts of gifted women, however, are pursuing careers more vigorously and seem to have a greater sense of well-being than the women who took part in Terman's study (Schuster, 1990; Subotnik, Karp, & Morgan, 1989).

Overall, most of Terman's gifted children moved through adulthood as healthy, happy, and highly productive individuals. Yet some fared better than others (see Box 9.3). In an analysis of some of the factors that predicted the paths these adults' lives took over a 40-year period, Carolyn Tomlinson-Keasey and Todd Little (1990) concluded that, even within this elite group, the quality of the individual's home environment was important. The most well-adjusted and successful adults had highly educated parents who offered them both love and intellectual stimulation. They were also individuals who were especially determined to achieve.

Mental Retardation

What about the other extreme of the IQ continuum? **Mental retardation** is currently defined by the American Association on Mental Retardation (1992) as significantly below-average general intellectual functioning associated with limitations in adaptive behavior and originating during childhood or adolescence. Specifically, to be diagnosed as mentally retarded, an individual must obtain an IQ score below 70 *and* have difficulties meeting age-appropriate expectations in important areas of everyday functioning.

Four levels of mental retardation have traditionally been recognized, each of them representing a portion of the IQ range below 70: mild, moderate, severe, and profound (Grossman, 1983). A *mildly retarded* adult (IQ 55–69 on the Wechsler tests) is likely to have a mental age comparable to that of an 8- to 12-year-old child. Mildly retarded persons can learn both academic and practical skills in school, and they can potentially work and live independently or with occasional help as adults. *Moderately retarded* individuals (IQ 40–54) can also learn basic academic skills and many life skills, but they are more likely than mildly retarded people to need supervision and support in order to hold jobs and live in the community.

BOX 9.3 What Became of the Child Prodigies?

Books in the popular literature have added to the insights that Terman's study gave us about gifted children. One, *Whatever Happened to the Quiz Kids?,* was written by Ruth Feldman (1982) about the later lives of children who, like her, had appeared on the program *Quiz Kids* in the 1940s and 1950s, awing radio (and later TV) audiences with their knowledge. Feldman interviewed some former Quiz Kids and sent questionnaires to as many others as she could trace. They were highly successful—even more so than Terman's group. The most famous of them was James Watson, winner of the Nobel Prize for his part in unlocking the structure of the genetic material DNA. Nearly all were college graduates, and many had advanced or professional degrees. Perhaps because they were of a later generation, a larger percentage of female Quiz Kids than female "Termites" (as Terman's subjects were nicknamed) worked outside the home for most of their adult lives. Failure was rare.

Yet failure can come even to the most gifted of prodigies. In *Terman's Kids*, Joel Shurkin (1992) describes several less-than-happy life stories of some of Terman's Termites. A woman who graduated from Stanford at age 17 and was headed for success as a writer became a landlady instead; an emotionally disturbed boy took cyanide at age 18 after being rejected in love.

But no failed genius is more notorious than William Sidis. According to Amy Wallace's (1986) biography *The Prodigy,* Sidis was the son of a brilliant Harvard psychologist and the godson of the pioneering psychologist William James. From infancy, "Billy" was the subject of an experiment designed by his father to prove that magnificent talents can be developed in any child. Given the most enriched of early environments (and probably some good genes as well), Billy could read the newspaper at 18 months of age and had learned eight languages by the time he reached school age. His school years were brief, however, for he entered Harvard at age 11 and was teaching mathematics at Rice University by age 17.

Unfortunately, his parents invested so much energy in developing his mind that they apparently neglected his social and emotional development. His social incompetence and odd habits were as widely publicized as his intellectual feats, and finally William Sidis had apparently had enough of it all. He quit the academic life, took a series of menial jobs, and lived as a hermit, writing about obscure topics and jumping at every opportunity to show children his prodigious collection of streetcar and subway tickets. Sidis seemed content with his life of obscurity, but he certainly did not achieve the greatness that might have been predicted. He died of a stroke at age 46.

William Sidis was clearly the exception to all we know about gifted children and their outcomes. Nonetheless, his story reminds us that early blooming is no guarantee of later flowering. And it works the other way, too: Late blooming does not rule out eminence in adulthood. We need only cite the case of Albert Einstein, whose name is synonymous with genius. Einstein didn't speak until age 4, could not read until age 7, and was judged by his teachers to have little future at all (Feldman, 1982)!

Severely retarded persons (IQ 25–39) typically can learn many basic self-help skills and communication skills, but they typically master few academic skills and need a good deal of continuing training and support as adults. Finally, *profoundly retarded* persons, with IQs below 25 and mental ages below 3 years, show major delays in all areas of development and require basic care, sometimes in institutional settings. They, too, can benefit considerably from training, though. Obviously, then, there are important differences among these subgroups of mentally retarded individuals, and there are differences within each subgroup as well.

Mental retardation has many causes. The more severely retarded persons are often affected by what is called **organic retardation**; that is, their retardation is due to some identifiable biological cause associated with hereditary factors, diseases, or injuries. *Down syndrome*, the condition associated with an extra 21st chromosome, is a familiar example of organic retardation (see Chapter 3). Many other forms of organic retardation are associated with prenatal risk factors—an alcoholic mother, exposure to rubella, and so on (see Chapter 4). Such children, because they are seriously delayed and often have physical defects, can often be identified at birth or during infancy. However, the most common form of mental retardation, **cultural-familial retardation,** is not usually recognized until a child performs poorly on an IQ test in school. It appears to be related to some combination of low genetic potential and a poor environment. Culturally-familially retarded children are generally mildly retarded, come from poverty areas, and have a parent or sibling who is also retarded (Westling, 1986). From one-half to three-quarters of mental retardation is of the cultural-familial type: exact cause unknown (Zigler & Hodapp, 1991).

What becomes of mentally retarded children as they grow up? As a general rule, they proceed along the same paths and through the same sequences of developmental milestones as other children do (Zigler & Hodapp, 1991). Because they are developing at a slower-than-normal pace, their mental ages continue to increase well into adulthood, whereas normally mental growth levels off in adolescence (Fisher & Zeaman, 1970). Their IQs remain low, of course, because they do not achieve the same level of growth that others do.

As for their outcomes in life, consider a follow-up study of individuals who had been put in segregated special education classes for the mentally retarded during the 1920s (the time when Terman began his study of the gifted) and 1930s (Ross et al., 1985). These individuals had a mean IQ of 67 (most were either mildly retarded or had IQs from 70 to 80). They were compared with their siblings and with nonretarded peers about 35 years later. Generally, these mentally retarded adults had poor life outcomes in middle age in comparison with nonretarded groups (see also Schalock, Holl, Elliott, & Ross, 1992). About 80% of the retarded men were employed, but they usually held semiskilled or unskilled jobs that required little education or intellectual ability. (As was true in Terman's gifted sample, women tended to marry and become homemakers.) Compared with nonretarded peers, retarded men and women fared worse on other counts as well. For example, they had lower incomes, less adequate housing, poorer adjustment in social relationships, and a greater dependency on others.

Yet the authors of the study still found grounds for optimism. These individuals had done much better during adulthood than stereotyped expectations of mentally retarded persons would predict. After all, most of them worked and had married, and about 80% reported having had no need for public assistance in the 10 years before they were interviewed. This study, like others before it, suggests that many children who are labeled mentally retarded by the schools—and who do indeed have difficulty with the tasks demanded of them in school—"vanish" into the general population after they leave school. Apparently they can adapt to the demands of adult life. As the authors put it, "It does not take as many IQ points as most people believe to be productive, to get along with others, and to be self-fulfilled" (Ross et al., 1985, p. 149).

CREATIVITY AND SPECIAL TALENTS

Despite their happy outcomes, not one of Terman's high-IQ gifted children became truly eminent. Recall that teachers had nominated the bright children for the study. Is it possible that they had overlooked some children who were gifted with special talents but who had IQs below 140 and were not "teachers' pets" (Fincher, 1973)? As we've seen, recent definitions of giftedness take into account not only a high IQ but also the ability to do outstanding work in a particular area such as music, art, or writing. The word *creativity* comes to mind. Creativity may be more important than IQ in allowing a Michelangelo or a Mozart to break new ground. But what is creativity, and what do we know about its development?

What Is Creativity?

Definitions of creativity have provoked as much controversy as definitions of intelligence (see Mumford & Gustafson, 1988). However, **creativity** is most often defined as the ability to produce *novel* responses that are not simply outlandish but are appropriate in context and valued by others. In his structure-of-intellect model, J. P. Guilford (1967, 1988) captured the idea of creativity by proposing that it involves divergent rather than convergent thinking. **Divergent thinking** requires coming up with a variety of ideas or solutions to a problem when there is no one right answer.

Indeed, the most common measure of creativity, at least in children, is what is called **ideational fluency,** or the sheer number of different (including novel) ideas that one can generate—for example, when asked to think of all the possible uses for a cork or to list all the words that can be made from the letters in *baseball* (Kogan, 1983). **Convergent thinking** involves "converging" on the one best answer to a problem and is precisely what IQ tests measure.

Research suggests that creativity and divergent thinking truly are distinct from general intelligence and convergent thinking. For example, Getzels and Jackson (1962) gave more than 500 students, in grades 6 to 12, intelligence tests and five creativity tests:

1. A word-association test in which students were asked to give as many definitions as possible for fairly common words.
2. A test of alternative uses, in which students were asked to think of as many uses as they could for familiar objects.
3. A hidden-shapes test that required them to find geometric figures hidden in more complex figures.
4. A fables test in which they furnished the last line for an unfinished fable.
5. A make-up-problems test in which they were to make up a variety of mathematical problems from a large amount of numerical information.

Scores on these creativity measures and scores on IQ tests correlated very little. Thus creativity seems to be largely independent of general intelligence as defined by IQ tests (Kogan, 1983). At the same time, highly creative people rarely have below-average IQs, so a *minimum* of intelligence is probably required for creativity (Runco, 1992; Wallach, 1971). Among people with above-average IQs, however, an individual's IQ score is unrelated to his or her level of creativity. (Test yourself on Figure 9.4.)

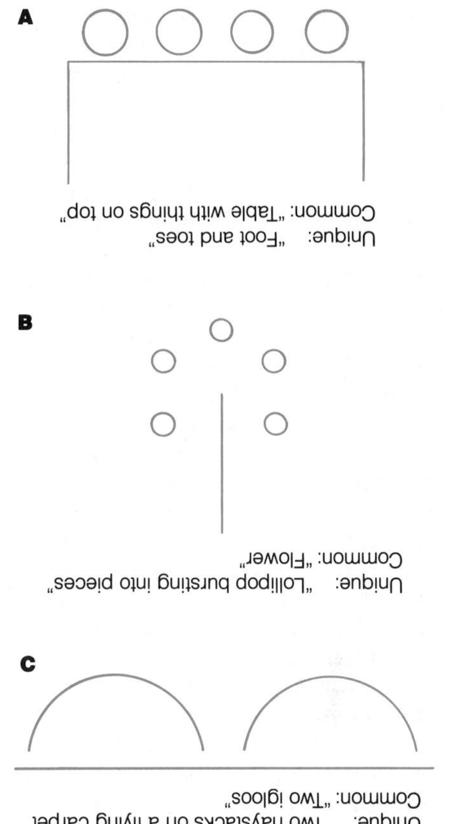

FIGURE 9.4 Are you creative? Indicate what you see in each of the three drawings. Below each drawing you will find examples of unique and common responses, drawn from a study of creativity in children. (From Wallach & Kogan, 1965.)

Creativity in Childhood and Adolescence

What is the child who scores high on tests of creativity like? Getzels and Jackson (1962) compared children who had high creativity scores but normal-range IQ scores with children who scored high in IQ but not in creativity. Personality measures suggested that the creative children showed more freedom, originality, humor, violence, and playfulness than the high-IQ children. Perhaps as a result, the high-IQ children were more success oriented and received more approval from teachers. Compared with their less creative peers, creative children also engaged in more fantasy or pretend play (Kogan, 1983). Such play often involves inventing new uses for familiar objects and new roles for oneself.

Although IQ scores vary across racial and socioeconomic groups, scores on creativity tests do not (Kogan, 1983). Moreover, genetic influences (a source of individual differences in IQ) have little to do with performance on tests of creativity; twins are similar in the degree of creativity they display, but identical twins are no more similar than fraternal twins (Plomin, 1990; Reznikoff et al., 1973). This suggests that certain qualities of the home environment tend to make brothers and sisters alike in their degree of creativity. What qualities? Although we have little research to go on, parents of creative children and adolescents tend to value nonconformity and independence, accept their children as they are, encourage their curiosity and playfulness, and grant them a good deal of freedom to explore new possibilities on their own (Getzels & Jackson, 1962; Harrington, Block, & Block, 1987; Runco, 1992). In some cases the parent/child relationship is even distant; a surprising number of eminent creators seem to have experienced rather lonely, insecure, and unhappy childhoods (Ochse, 1990). Out of their adversity may have come a strong desire to excel. Overall, then, creative abilities are influenced by factors quite distinct from those that influence the cognitive abilities measured on IQ tests.

How does the capacity to be creative change with age? We really are not sure (Kogan, 1983). Overall, performance on tests of creativity seems to increase over the childhood and adolescent years, but there appear to be certain ages along the way when it drops off. Summarizing his cross-cultural research, Paul Torrance (1975) has suggested that creativity declines temporarily during periods when children experience societal pressures to conform, as when they enter school, and that the ages at which creativity flourishes or is stifled vary from culture to culture (see also Smith & Carlsson, 1985). Howard Gardner (Gardner, Phelps, & Wolf, 1990) suggests that preschool children are highly original, playful, and uninhibited but that school-aged children become restricted in their creative expression as they attempt to master their culture's rules for art, music, dance, and other creative endeavors so that they can do things the "right" way. During adolescence, Gardner believes, some individuals give up the desire to express themselves creatively because they feel their work is not original enough. Other adolescents regain some of the innovativeness and freedom of expression they had as preschoolers and put it to use, along with the technical skills they gained as children, to produce highly creative works. Overall, the developmental course of creativity is not so predictable or steady as the increase in mental age seen on measures of IQ. Instead, creativity seems to wax and wane with age in response to developmental needs and cultural demands.

How well does performance on tests of creativity predict actual creative accomplishments such as original artwork or outstanding science projects? There are some links (Runco, 1992). For example, Harrington, Block, and Block (1983) found that the quality of preschoolers' answers on a test of ideational fluency predicted their teachers' ratings of their creativity in sixth grade. More important, some researchers have found that scores on creativity tests administered in either elementary or secondary school predict actual creative achievements, such as inventions and novels, in adulthood (Howieson, 1981; Torrance, 1988).

However, just as it is a mistake to expect IQ to predict creative accomplishments, it may also be a mistake to expect tests of creativity to do so with any great accuracy (Kogan, 1983; Wallach, 1985). Why? Because both kinds of tests attempt to measure *general* cognitive abilities. In actuality, there are many *specific talents,* and each of them (artistic, mathematical, musical, and so on) requires distinct skills and experiences (Gardner, 1983; see also Box 9.4).

So researchers are now looking at individuals who do indeed show exceptional talent in a particular field and are trying to determine the basis of their accomplishments. David Feldman (1980, 1982, 1986), for example, has studied children who are "prodigies" in such areas as chess, music, and mathe-

BOX 9.4 The Many Sides of Intelligence

Howard Gardner is one psychologist who is not fond of describing people with a single IQ score. In his book *Frames of Mind*, Gardner (1983) argues that there are many intelligences, not one; he proposes the following intellectual abilities as distinctive: *linguistic intelligence* (shown by the poet's facility with words), *musical intelligence* (based on an acute sensitivity to sound patterns), *logical-mathematical intelligence* (the kind of abstract thinking shown by mathematicians and scientists and emphasized by Piaget), *spatial intelligence* (most obvious in great artists who can perceive things accurately and transform what they see), *bodily-kinesthetic intelligence* (the "intelligent" movement shown by dancers and athletes), and at least two forms of *personal intelligence* (the ability to understand one's own inner life and exceptional sensitivity to other people, which is also called social intelligence). Notice that traditional IQ tests emphasize linguistic and logical-mathematical intelligence but ignore most of the other forms.

Gardner does not claim that this is *the* definitive list of intelligences. But he does make his case that each ability is distinct. He argues, for example, that a person can be exceptional in one ability but poor in others. Indeed, this is dramatically clear in **idiot savants,** people who have an extraordinary talent but are otherwise mentally retarded. Leslie Lemke is one such individual (*Lexington Leader*, November 21, 1980). He is blind, has cerebral palsy, and is mentally retarded, and he could not talk until he was an adult. Yet he can hear a musical piece once and play it flawlessly on the piano or imitate songs in perfect German or Italian even though his own speech is still primitive. Other idiot savants, despite IQs below 70, can draw well enough to gain admittance to art school or calculate on the spot what day of the week January 16, 1909, was (O'Connor & Hermelin, 1991).

Gardner also notes that each intelligence has its own distinctive developmental course. Many of the great composers, for example, revealed their genius in childhood, whereas logical-mathematical intelligence often shows up later in life. Finally, each of Gardner's intelligences can be linked to a specific area of the brain.

It perhaps says something about our culture that we seem to value some of Gardner's intelligences far more than others. We provide gifted programs to nurture the abilities of children who score high in traditional IQ tests or who show talent in math or science. But do we try to identify and nurture the talents of children who show exceptional social skills and sensitivity to other people? Perhaps when we learn more about such abilities as personal, musical, and bodily-kinesthetic intelligence, we will do more to foster these talents as well.

matics. These individuals were generally similar to other children in areas outside their fields of expertise. What contributed to their special achievements? They were, of course, talented, but they also seemed to have a powerful motivation to develop their special talents—a real passion for what they were doing. The Olympic gymnast Olga Korbutt put it well: "If gymnastics did not exist, I would have invented it" (Feldman, 1982, p. 35). Moreover, these achievers were blessed with an *environment* that nurtured their talent and motivation (see also Hennessey & Amabile, 1988; Monass & Engelhard, 1990). They were strongly encouraged and supported by their families and intensively tutored or coached by experts. According to Feldman, the child with creative potential in a specific field must become intimately familiar with the current state of the field if he or she is to advance or transform it, as the ground-breaking artist or musician does. As Howard Gruber (1982) puts it, "Insight comes to the prepared mind . . ." (p. 22). To further emphasize the importance of environment, Feldman notes that child prodigies must be lucky enough to live in a culture and time that recognizes and values their special abilities. Olga Korbutt's talent might not have bloomed if gymnastics had not been highly valued in the Soviet Union when she was growing up.

In summary, there are many forms of giftedness, many "intelligences." Studies of creativity have revealed that performance on creativity tests is distinct from performance on IQ tests. Yet neither tests of general intelligence nor tests of general creativity are very good at predicting which children will show exceptional talent in a *specific* field. Instead, that kind of talent seems to be related to characteristics of the individual, including exceptional motivation, *and* characteristics of the environment, especially support and prolonged training in the field.

Creative Achievement during Adulthood

Studies of creativity during the adult years have focused on a very small number of so-called eminent creators in such fields as art, music, science, and philosophy. The big question has been this: *When* in adulthood are such individuals most productive and most likely to create their best works? Is it early in adulthood, when they can benefit from youth's enthusiasm and freshness of approach? Or is it later in adulthood, when they have fully mastered their field and have the experience and knowledge necessary to make a breakthrough in it? And what becomes of the careers of eminent creators in old age?

Early studies by Harvey Lehman (1953) and Wayne Dennis (1966) provided a fairly clear picture of how creative careers unfold (see also Simonton, 1990). In most fields, creative production increases steeply from the 20s to the late 30s and early 40s and then gradually declines thereafter, though not to the

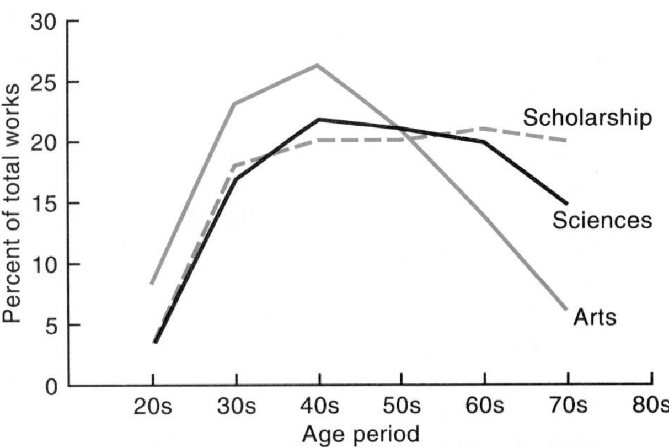

FIGURE 9.5 Percentage of total works produced in each decade of the lives of eminent creators. The "scholarship" group includes historians and philosophers; the "sciences" category includes natural and physical scientists, inventors, and mathematicians; and the "arts" creators include architects, musicians, dramatists, poets, and so on. (Data from Dennis, 1966.)

same low levels that characterized very early adulthood. Peak times of creative achievement also vary from field to field. As Figure 9.5 shows, the productivity of scholars in the humanities (for example, historians and philosophers) continues well into old age and actually peaks in the 60s, possibly because creative work in these fields often involves integrating knowledge that has "crystallized" over many years. By contrast, productivity in the arts (for example, music or drama) peaks in the 30s and 40s and declines quite steeply thereafter, perhaps because artistic creativity depends on a more "fluid" or innovative kind of thinking. Scientists seem to be intermediate, peaking in their 40s and declining only in their 70s. Even within the same general field, differences in peak times have been noted. For example, poets reach their peak before novelists do, and mathematicians peak before other scientists do (Dennis, 1966; Lehman, 1953).

Still, in many fields (including psychology, by the way), creative production rises to a peak in the late 30s or early 40s, and there are some declines in both total number of works and number of high-quality works thereafter. This same pattern can be detected across different cultures and historical periods (Simonton, 1975). Even so, the percentage of a creator's works that are major, significant ones does not change much at all over the years (Simonton, 1990). This means that many creators are still producing outstanding works in old age—sometimes their greatest works—not just rehashes of earlier triumphs (Lehman, 1953; Over, 1989; Simonton, 1989). Michelangelo, for instance, was in his 70s and 80s when he worked on St. Peter's Cathedral, and Goethe was polishing *Faust* at 83. Indeed, the most eminent among the eminent seem to start early and finish late (Simonton, 1990).

How can we account for changes in creative production over the adult years? One explanation, proposed long ago (Beard, 1874, cited by Simonton, 1984), is that creative achievement requires both enthusiasm and experience. In early adulthood the enthusiasm is there, but the experience is not; in later adulthood the experience is there, but the enthusiasm or vigor has fallen off. People in their 30s and 40s have it all.

Dean Simonton (1984, 1990, 1991) has offered another theory: Each creator may have a certain potential to create that is realized over the adult years; as the potential is realized, less is left to achieve. According to Simonton, creative activity involves two processes: *ideation* (generating creative ideas) and *elaboration* (executing ideas to produce actual poems, paintings, or scientific publications). After a career is launched, some time elapses before any ideas are generated or any works actually completed. This would explain the rise in creative achievement between the 20s and 30s. Also, some kinds of work take longer to formulate or complete than others, which helps explain why a poet (who can generate and carry out ideas quickly) might reach a creative peak earlier in life than, say, a historian (who may need to devote years to the research and writing necessary to complete a book once the idea for it is hatched).

Why does creative production eventually begin to taper off? Simonton (1990, 1991) suggests that older creators may simply have used up much of their total stock of potential ideas. They never totally exhaust their creative potential, but they have less of it left to realize. Simonton argues, then, that changes in creative production over the adult years have more to do with the nature of the creative process than with a loss of mental ability in later life. A creator who starts his or her career late is likely to experience the very same rise and fall of creative output that others do, only later in life. And the creators with immense creative potential to realize will keep right on producing great works until they die.

What about mere mortals like us? Here, researchers have fallen back on tests designed to measure creativity. In one study, Robert McCrae and his colleagues found that scores on a test of divergent-thinking abilities decreased at least modestly after about age 40 and decreased even more steeply starting at about 70 (McCrae, Arenberg, & Costa, 1987; see also Alpaugh & Birren, 1977). It seems that elderly adults do not differ much from younger adults in the originality of their ideas; the main difference is that they generate fewer of them (Jaquish & Ripple, 1981). Generally, then, these studies agree with the studies of eminent achievers: Creative behavior becomes less frequent in later life, but it remains possible throughout the adult years.

WISDOM: DOES IT COME WITH AGE?

Most people believe that adults become wiser as they get older. Indeed, this belief been expressed in many cultures throughout history (Clayton & Birren, 1980; Holliday & Chandler, 1986). It is also featured in Erik Erikson's influential theory of life-span development. Erikson claims that some older adults gain wisdom as they face the prospect of death and attempt to find meaning in their lives (Erikson, 1982; see also Chapter 10). Notice, too, that the word *wise* is never used to describe children, adolescents, or even young adults (unless perhaps it is to call one of them a "wise guy"). Is it possible that the declines in cognitive ability that occur as we age are accompanied by intellectual growth in the form of increased wisdom?

But what is wisdom, and how could one go about measuring it? There is no consensus as yet, and very little research (see Sternberg, 1990). Paul Baltes and his colleagues offer this definition of **wisdom**: "good judgment and advice about important but uncertain matters of life" (Staudinger, Smith, & Baltes, 1992, p. 272). In this view, the wise person has exceptional insight into what life is all about.

Does wisdom typically increase with age, or are one's life experiences more important than one's age in determining whether or not one is wise? Ursula Staudinger, Jacqui Smith, and Paul Baltes (1992) took up this question in a study that can serve to illustrate how research on the development of wisdom is

We tend to believe that age brings wisdom. It can—but does not do so often.

being done. These researchers interviewed young (ages 25–35) and elderly (ages 65–82) women who were either clinical psychologists or similarly well-educated professionals in other fields. The goal was to assess the relative contributions of age and specialized experience to wisdom, based on the assumption that clinical psychologists stand to gain special sensitivity to human problems from their professional training and practice.

These women were interviewed about a person named Martha, who had chosen to have a family but no career and who met up with an old friend who had chosen to have a career but no family. The women were asked to talk about how Martha might review and evaluate her life after this encounter. Answers were scored for five qualities judged to be indicators of wisdom: (1) knowledge of the human condition (for example, of the concerns of mothers and professional women); (2) sound strategies for analyzing life problems and determining the costs and benefits of different decisions; (3) awareness of the relevance of contextual factors, such as norms regarding women's roles, in shaping the developmental paths people take; (4) awareness that life goals differ depending on the culture and the individual; and (5) insight into the unpredictability of life.

What was found? First, wisdom proved to be rare (see also Smith & Baltes, 1990, who found that only about 5% of the responses given by the adults they tested qualified as "wise"). Second, expertise proved to be more relevant than age to the development of wisdom. That is, clinical psychologists, whether they were young or old, displayed more signs of wisdom than other women did. Older women were generally no wiser — or less wise — than younger women.

So far, research does not support the common belief that wisdom is acquired *only* in old age. However, it does seem that the knowledge and analytic skills that contribute to wisdom hold up very well later in life, like other crystallized intellectual abilities. In addition, older adults, like younger ones, may be able to acquire a capacity for wisdom as long as they have the kinds of life experiences that sharpen their insights into the human condition. It may also take a certain kind of personality and a desire to benefit humanity (Baltes & Smith, 1990; Orwoll & Perlmutter, 1990). At this early stage in the study of wisdom, though, there is much disagreement about what it is, how it develops, and how it is related to other mental abilities.

APPLICATIONS: BOOSTING INTELLECTUAL PERFORMANCE ACROSS THE LIFE SPAN

How much can special training improve performance on tests of intelligence? Is such training effective only early in life, when intellectual growth is most rapid, or can it also work later in life? Intervention studies have explored how plastic, or moldable, intelligence is in early childhood, adolescence, and old age. Most of these interventions have been offered to those most in need of them — disadvantaged infants and preschoolers, mentally retarded individuals, and adults whose intellectual abilities are declining in old age.

Early Intervention for Preschool Children

During the 1960s a number of programs were launched to enrich the early learning experiences of disadvantaged preschoolers. *Project Head Start* is perhaps the best known of these interventions. The idea was to provide a variety of social and intellectual experiences that might better prepare these children for school. At first, Head Start and similar programs seemed to be a smashing success; children in the programs were posting average gains of about 10 points on IQ tests. But then discouragement set in: By the time children reached the middle years of grade school, their IQs were no higher than those of control-group children (Gray, Ramsey, & Klaus, 1982). Such findings led Arthur Jensen (1969, p. 2) to conclude that "compensatory education has been tried and it apparently has failed."

But that was not the end of it. Children in some of these programs have now been followed into their teens and even 20s. Irving Lazar and Richard Darlington (1982) reported on the long-term effects of 11 early intervention programs in several areas of the United States. Other follow-up studies of Head Start and similar early education programs for disadvantaged children have been conducted since then (Berrueta-Clement et al., 1984; Darlington, 1991; Lee, Brooks-Gunn, & Schnur, 1988; Lee et al., 1990). These long-term studies indicate the following:

1. Children who participate in early intervention programs show immediate gains on IQ and school achievement tests, whereas nonparticipants do not. However, the gains rarely last for more than three or four years after the program has ended. Impacts on measures other than IQ are more encouraging.
2. Compensatory education improves both children's and mothers' attitudes about achievement. When asked to describe something that has made them feel proud of themselves, program participants are more likely than nonparticipants to mention scholastic achievements or (in the case of 15- to 18-year-olds) job-related successes. Mothers of program participants tend to be more satisfied with their children's school performance and to hold higher occupational aspirations for their children.
3. Program participants are more likely to meet their school's basic requirements than nonparticipants are. They are less likely to be assigned to special education classes, to be retained in a grade, or to drop out of high school.

4. There is even some evidence (though not in all studies) that teenagers who have participated in early compensatory education are less likely than nonparticipants to become pregnant, to require welfare assistance, and to be involved in delinquent behavior.

In sum, longitudinal evaluations suggest that compensatory education has been tried and works. Programs seem most effective if they start early and last long. For example, Craig Ramey and his colleagues (see Ramey & Ramey, 1992) reported outstanding success with the Abecedarian program, an early intervention for extremely disadvantaged, primarily African-American, children that involved an intellectually stimulating day-care program, home visits, and medical and nutritional care from birth to kindergarten entry. At age 12, program participants were still outperforming nonparticipants by 5 to 10 points on IQ tests and were doing better in school. At age 15, their IQ advantage had disappeared, but they continued to perform better on academic achievement tests and were less likely to need special education services (Campbell & Ramey, 1993).

These findings are indeed encouraging, but is it too late to intervene after the years of infancy and early childhood have passed? Not at all, says Israeli psychologist Reuven Feuerstein.

Enrichment for Low-IQ Adolescents

Early in this chapter we described Feuerstein's dynamic assessment approach, which involves testing intelligence by directly testing the potential to learn with guidance. He has also developed cognitive training programs for culturally different, learning disabled, and mentally retarded adolescents and young adults (Feuerstein et al., 1981). According to Feuerstein, such individuals are not absorbing as much from their experiences as more advantaged learners are, mainly because they have not had many opportunities to learn thinking skills from more competent thinkers. What they need, then, is a "mediator," a guide who structures and interprets the environment for them at first. They will then come to learn more from their experiences on their own. (This approach should remind you of Lev Vygotsky's theory, described in Chapter 7, that children acquire new ways of thinking through their social interactions with more experienced problem solvers; it is based in part on Vygotsky's work.)

Feuerstein's "Instrumental Enrichment" program leads students through several cognitive tasks, teaching them the concepts and cognitive strategies they need to perform well. It also attempts to increase their motivation to learn. Participants in one intervention study were 12- to 15-year-old mentally retarded and nearly mentally retarded adolescents who were three to four years behind their peers academically (Feuerstein et al., 1981). Compared to a control group that received a general enrichment program, participants in Feuerstein's special program showed immediate gains on intellectual and cognitive measures. Moreover, participants were still ahead of nonparticipants two years later, when they took both a military intelligence test and the Primary Mental Abilities test. Even more impressively, benefits of the training appeared to *increase* over this two-year period, rather than fading away as the gains of intervention programs often do. This kind of cumulative effect is precisely what Feuerstein expected, for the whole idea of his approach is to help students learn more in the future from their own experiences. Although not all attempts to implement Feuerstein's curriculum have worked this well (Blagg, 1991; Frisby & Braden, 1992), it is clear that cognitive interventions need not occur in infancy to be successful.

Raising the IQs of Aging Adults

But can you teach old dogs new tricks? And can you reteach old dogs who have suffered declines in mental abilities the old tricks they have lost? K. Warner Schaie and Sherry Willis (1986) sought to find out by attempting to train elderly adults in spatial ability and reasoning, two of the fluid mental abilities that are most likely to decline in old age. Within a group of older people ranging in age from 64 to 95 who participated in Schaie's longitudinal study of intelligence, they first identified individuals whose scores on one of the two abilities had declined over a 14-year period, as well as individuals who had remained stable over the same period. The goal with the decliners would be to restore lost ability; the goal with those who had maintained their ability would be to improve it. Participants took pretests measuring both abilities, received five hours of training in either spatial ability or reasoning, and then were given posttests on both abilities. The spatial training involved learning how to rotate objects in space, at first physically and then mentally. Training in reasoning involved learning how to detect a recurring pattern in a series of stimuli (for example, musical notes) and to identify what the next stimulus in the sequence should be.

Figure 9.6 shows the effects of the training. Those who were trained in an ability clearly showed greater gains in that ability than did those who were not. And both those who had suffered ability declines and those who had maintained their abilities prior to the study improved, though decliners showed significantly more improvement in spatial ability than nondecliners did. Schaie and Willis estimated that 40% of the decliners gained enough through training to bring them back up to the level of performance they had achieved 14 years earlier, before decline set in.

The larger messages? You *can* teach old dogs new tricks—and reteach them old tricks—in very little

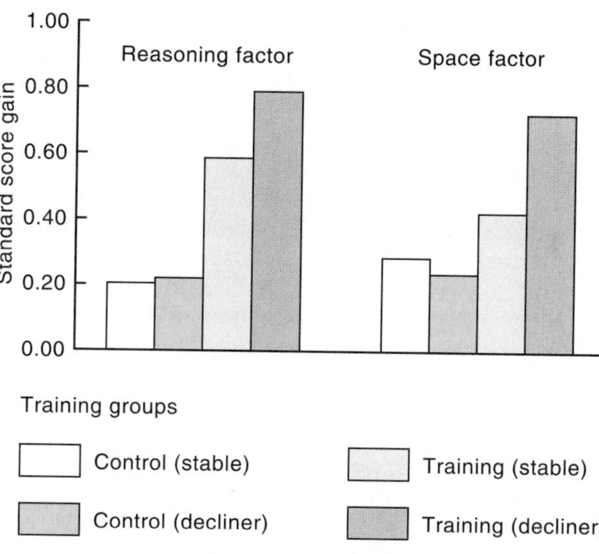

FIGURE 9.6 Effects of training on the spatial ability and reasoning of elderly adults. Elderly adults trained in either reasoning or spatial ability outperformed similar controls who received no training. Those whose abilities had declined before the training study gained more than those whose abilities had remained stable. (Adapted from Schaie & Willis, 1986.)

time. Similar studies suggest that the benefits of training persist (Hayslip, 1989; Schaie, 1990) and that older adults can even improve on their own by practicing relevant skills (Baltes, Sowarka, & Kliegl, 1989). This research does not mean that cognitive abilities can be restored in elderly people who have Alzheimer's disease or other brain disorders, but it does suggest that many older adults can revive rusty intellectual skills with a little coaching and practice. In sum, we are delighted to conclude that the human mind has a good deal of plasticity over the entire life span.

REFLECTIONS

Our account of cognitive development over the life span is now complete. We hope you appreciate that each of the three major approaches to the mind that we have considered—the Piagetian cognitive-developmental approach discussed in Chapter 7, the information-processing approach discussed in Chapter 8, and the psychometric or testing approach discussed here—offers something of value. Perhaps we can summarize it this way: Piaget has shown us that comparing the thought of a preschooler to the thought of an adult is like comparing a tadpole to a frog. Modes of thought change qualitatively with age. The information-processing approach has put the thinking process under a microscope so that we can understand more precisely why the young child cannot remember as much information or solve problems as successfully as the adult can. Finally, the psychometric approach has told us that, if we look at the wide range of tasks to which the mind can be applied, we can recognize distinct mental abilities that each person consistently displays in greater or lesser amounts. We need not choose one approach and reject the others. Our understanding of the mind is likely to be richer if all three approaches continue to thrive.

Indeed, the three approaches have led to several identical conclusions. No matter how we have looked at cognitive development, we've seen that dramatic cognitive growth in infancy, childhood, and adolescence is followed by relative stability during early adulthood and middle age and, finally, by modest decline in old age for at least some individuals. We have also seen that there is a good deal of plasticity in the nervous system and that cognitive performance can be improved at any age. Finally, we've seen that *cognition becomes specialized*. Adults are most likely to use Piaget's formal-operational thought in their areas of specialization. They develop specialized knowledge bases and information-processing strategies that allow them to think most effectively in the areas they know best. And, as we've seen here, they may have plenty of one mental ability but little of another, or they may gain ground in one ability over time while losing ground in another. One's age, immediate environment, and larger cultural and historical contexts influence which abilities prosper and which do not.

There are truly many "intelligences." From today's vantage point it seems foolish indeed to think that a single IQ score can possibly describe the complexities of human cognitive development. Besides, there is more to psychological development than the development of the mind. We now turn our attention to the personal, social, and emotional aspects of life-span development.

SUMMARY POINTS

1. The psychometric or testing approach to cognition defines intelligence as a set of traits that allows some people to think and solve problems more effectively than others. It consists of a general factor *g* along with more specific fluid and crystallized abilities. Sternberg's contemporary triarchic theory of intelligence, with its contextual, experiential, and information-processing components, offers an alternative view.

2. Intelligence tests such as the Stanford-Binet and the Wechsler scales compare an individual's performance on a variety of cognitive tasks with the average performance of agemates. Scores on these tests in a large population form a normal or bell-shaped distribution, with an average score of 100. Some

testers are experimenting with dynamic assessment methods that determine how well individuals learn new material with guidance.

3. In infancy, mental growth is rapid and is measured by developmental quotients derived from tests such as the Bayley Scales. However, infant scores do not predict later IQ as well as rapid habituation and preference for novelty do.

4. During childhood, mental growth continues, and IQs at one age predict IQs at later ages quite well. However, many individuals show wide variations in their IQ scores over time. Those who gain IQ points often have favorable home environments, whereas disadvantaged children often show a cumulative deficit.

5. In adolescence, IQs continue to be relatively stable over time and to predict school achievement. The timing of puberty is related to performance on measures of spatial ability but may not explain sex differences in this intellectual skill.

6. IQ is related to the status or prestige of an adult's occupation, as well as to his or her success within that occupation. Both cross-sectional studies and longitudinal studies tend to distort the picture of age-related change. Sequential studies suggest that (a) date of birth (cohort) influences test performance, (b) no major declines in mental abilities occur until the 60s or 70s, (c) some abilities (especially fluid ones) decline more than others (especially crystallized ones), and (d) not all people's abilities decline. Decline is most likely in those who have poor health and unstimulating lifestyles.

7. Individual differences in IQ at a given age are linked to genetic factors and to intellectually stimulating qualities of the early home environment. The low average scores of some minority groups on IQ tests may be explained better by culture bias in testing, low motivation, and low socioeconomic status than by genetic differences. Minority children perform much better when they grow up in intellectually stimulating homes.

8. Children identified as gifted on the basis of a high IQ score have been found to be above average in virtually all ways; mentally retarded individuals show varied levels of functioning, depending on their IQs and the causes (organic or cultural-familial) of their retardation. Mildly retarded individuals appear to meet the demands of adult life better than the demands of school.

9. Creativity, the ability to produce novel and socially valued works, is a distinct mental ability that demands divergent rather than convergent thinking; it is largely independent of IQ once a minimum IQ is exceeded, increases with age during childhood, and is fostered in homes where independence is valued. Eminent creators are typically more productive during their late 30s and 40s than before or after. Performance on creativity tests declines in later life, but creative capacities clearly survive into old age.

10. Wisdom, or exceptional insight into the human condition, can emerge in later life, or earlier in adulthood as well, if an individual has life experiences that nurture it.

11. Attempts to boost performance on IQ tests suggest that mental abilities are plastic throughout the life span.

KEY TERMS

automatization
cognitive style
convergent thinking
creativity
crystallized intelligence
cultural-familial retardation
culture bias
cumulative-deficit hypothesis
developmental quotient (DQ)
divergent thinking
dynamic assessment
factor analysis
fluid intelligence
giftedness
HOME inventory
ideational fluency
idiot savant
impulsivity
intelligence quotient (IQ)
mental age (MA)
mental retardation
normal distribution
organic retardation
psychometric approach
reflectivity
structure-of-intellect model
terminal drop
test norms
triarchic theory of intelligence
wisdom

10

SELF-CONCEPTIONS, PERSONALITY, AND EMOTIONAL EXPRESSION

Who am I?

> I'm a person who says what I think . . . not [one] who's going to say one thing and do the other. I'm really lucky. I've never [drunk or] done drugs, but I'm always high. I love life. I'm about five years ahead of my age. I've got a lot of different business interests . . . a construction company, oil wells, land. . . . I'm trying everything. I travel a lot . . . it's difficult to be traveling and in school at the same time. [People] perceive me as being unusual . . . very mysterious, and I hope they see me as being a competitor, because I do all my talking on the field.
>
> —Herschel Walker, former college student and Olympic bobsledder, and currently running back for the Philadephia Eagles (as quoted in Blount, 1986)

How would you answer the "Who am I?" question? If you are like most adults, you would probably respond by mentioning some of your noteworthy personal characteristics (honesty, friendliness), some roles you play in life (student, hospital volunteer), your religious or moral views, and perhaps your political leanings, your main accomplishments, and your interests. In doing so, you would be describing that elusive concept that psychologists call the personality. This chapter is about the ways in which our personalities, and our perceptions of those personalities, change—and remain the same—over the life span.

CONCEPTUALIZING THE SELF

Personality can be defined as the organized combination of attributes, motives, values, and behaviors that is unique to each individual. Most people describe personalities in terms of *personality traits*—dispositions such as sociability, independence, dominance, anxiety, and so on, which are assumed to be relatively consistent across different situations and over time. Thus, if you peg a classmate as insecure, you expect this person to behave insecurely at school and at work, now and next year. Similarly, psychologists who adopt the *psychometric approach* to personality, and who therefore attempt to measure aspects of personality through the use of tests and scales, also assume that personality consists of traits and that these traits do not change from day to day. Whether or not our personality traits do in fact remain highly consistent across situations and times is a question that this chapter examines in some detail.

Theories of Personality Development

How does the personality develop? Is it formed in childhood and stable from then on, or does it continue to evolve and change throughout our lives? To get some feel for current debates about the nature of personality development, let's examine some striking differences between two major theoretical perspectives on the nature of personality and personality development: psychoanalytic theory and social learning theory.

Psychoanalytic Theory

As you recall from Chapter 2, Freud was concerned with the development and inner dynamics of three parts of the personality: the selfish id, the rational ego, and the moralistic superego. He strongly believed that biological urges residing within the id push all children through universal stages of psychosexual

Erik Erikson's eight stages of psychosocial development allow for personal growth throughout the life span.

development, starting with the oral stage of infancy and ending with the genital stage of adolescence when sexual maturity is attained. Freud did not propose any stages of adult psychosexual growth; in fact, he believed that the personality was formed in infancy and early childhood—during the first five years of life, essentially—and changed little thereafter. Anxieties arising from harsh parenting or other unfavorable early experiences, he claimed, would leave a permanent mark on the personality and reveal themselves in adult personality traits.

Erik Erikson (1902–1994), a neo-Freudian theorist whose work we highlight in this chapter, also concerned himself with the inner dynamics of personality and proposed that the personality evolves through systematic stages (Erikson 1963, 1968, 1982). Erikson studied with Freud's daughter, Anna, and emigrated to the United States when Hitler rose to power in Germany. Based on his clinical work and on studies of such diverse groups as victims of combat fatigue, civil rights workers, and American Indians, Erikson came to believe that social and cultural influences are critically important in shaping the personality. Compared to Freud, Erikson placed: (1) less emphasis on sexual urges as the drivers of development and more emphasis on social influences such as peers, teachers, schools, and churches; (2) less emphasis on the irrational, selfish side of human nature and more emphasis on the rational ego and its adaptive powers; and (3) less emphasis on the lasting imprint of early experience and more emphasis on the potential for growth and change throughout the life span.

Erikson believed that human beings everywhere face eight major psychosocial crises, or conflicts, during their lives, as shown in Table 10.1. Whether the conflict of a particular stage is successfully resolved or not, the individual is pushed by both biological maturation and social demands into the next stage. For example, the first conflict, **trust versus mistrust,** revolves around whether or not an infant becomes able to trust other people to be responsive to his or her needs. To develop a sense of trust, infants must be able to count on their primary caregivers to feed them, relieve their discomfort, and come when beckoned. If caregivers neglect, reject, or respond inconsistently to the infant, he or she will mistrust others. A healthy balance between the terms of the conflict must be struck for development to proceed optimally.

TABLE 10.1 The eight stages of Erikson's psychosocial theory.

Stage/Age Range	*Description*	*Resulting Ego Virtue*
1. *Trust versus mistrust* (birth to 1 year)	Infants must learn to trust their caregivers to meet their needs. Responsive parenting is critical.	Hope
2. *Autonomy versus shame and doubt* (1 to 3 years)	Children must learn to be autonomous—to assert their wills and do things for themselves—or they will doubt their abilities.	Will (a sense of self)
3. *Initiative versus guilt* (3 to 6 years)	Preschoolers develop initiative by devising and carrying out bold plans, but they must learn not to impinge on the rights of others.	Purpose (goal setting)
4. *Industry versus inferiority* (6 to 12 years)	Children must master important social and academic skills and feel competent when they compare themselves to their peers, or they will suffer feelings of inferiority.	Competence
5. *Identity versus role confusion* (12 to 20 years)	Adolescents must grapple with the question "Who am I?" They must establish social and vocational identities by exploring their possibilities or else remain confused about the roles they should play as adults.	Fidelity (ability to commit self)
6. *Intimacy versus isolation* (20 to 40 years)	Young adults seek to form an intimate relationship (or a shared identity) with another person, but they may fear intimacy or may not want to give up their independence and may experience loneliness and isolation instead.	Love
7. *Generativity versus stagnation* (40 to 65 years)	Middle-aged adults must feel that they are producing something of value—something that will outlive them—either by successfully raising their children or by contributing to society through their work; otherwise, they will become stagnant and self-centered.	Care (investment in future generations)
8. *Integrity versus despair* (65 and older)	Older adults must come to view their lives as meaningful in order to face death without worries and regrets over unfulfilled goals and frustrations.	Wisdom

Trust should outweigh mistrust, but an element of skepticism is needed as well: An infant who is overindulged may become too trusting (a gullible "sucker"). As individuals successfully resolve the central conflict of each stage of psychosocial development, they gain new personality strengths (or ego virtues) — for example, a sense of purpose as a preschooler, life goals as an adolescent, or a greater concern for future generations as a middle-aged adult. Individual differences in personality presumably reflect the different experiences individuals have as they struggle to cope with the challenges of each life stage.

Erikson, then, did not agree with Freud that the personality is essentially "set in stone" during early childhood. Yet he, like other psychoanalytic theorists, believed that people everywhere progress through systematic stages of development, undergoing similar personality changes at similar ages.

Social Learning Theory

Social learning theorists such as Albert Bandura (1986) and Walter Mischel (1973) reject the whole notion of universal stages of personality development. Instead, they emphasize that we can change at any time in life if our environments change. An aggressive boy can become a warm and caring man if his aggression is no longer reinforced; a woman who has been socially withdrawn can become more outgoing if she begins to interact closely with friends who serve as models of outgoing, sociable behavior. From this perspective, personality is a set of behavior tendencies shaped by our interactions with other people in specific social situations.

Social learning theorists believe strongly in situational influences on behavior. They doubt that people have enduring traits that show themselves consistently in a wide range of situations over long stretches of the life span. True, this kind of consistency could occur if the individual's social environment remained the same. If Rick the rancher continues to do the same ranching on the same ranch in the same small town for a lifetime, he might well stay the "same old Rick." But most of us experience a series of changes in our social environments as we become older. Just as we behave differently when we are in a library than when we are at a party, we become "different people" as we take on new roles in life, develop new relationships, or move to new locations. To the social learning theorist, then, personality development is a very individual process whose direction depends on each person's social experiences. Theorists who adopt the contextual-dialectical perspective (introduced in Chapter 2) make similar assumptions. Indeed, contextual theorists are likely to say that personality traits, considered apart from the social contexts that shape and give meaning to our actions, are meaningless abstractions.

Obviously stage theorists (represented by Freud, Erikson, and other psychoanalytic theorists) and nonstage theorists (social learning theorists and contextual-dialectical theorists) do not see eye to eye about how the personality develops. Stage theorists propose universal, age-related personality changes, whereas nonstage theorists propose that change may occur at any time in life and can proceed in many directions. Moreover, some theorists agree with Freud that personality development is essentially completed early in life and that our traits remain largely stable thereafter, whereas other theorists suspect that we never stop changing as individuals. We will be examining whether research supports Erikson's theory of psychosocial development and whether personality traits expressed in childhood continue to be evident in adulthood.

Self-Concept and Self-Esteem

When you describe yourself, you may not be describing your actual personality so much as you are revealing your **self-concept** — your *perceptions* of your unique attributes and traits. We all know people who seem to have unrealistic self-conceptions — the fellow who thinks he is "God's gift to women" (who don't agree) or the woman who believes she is a dull plodder but is actually quite brilliant. A closely related aspect of self-perception is **self-esteem** — your overall evaluation of your worth as a person, high or low, based on all the positive and negative self-perceptions that make up your self-concept. Like self-concept, self-esteem may or may not be closely related to how objectively desirable a person's characteristics are.

This chapter is concerned with the development of objective personality traits and more subjective self-conceptions and evaluations. When do infants become aware of themselves as distinct individuals, and when do they begin to display their unique personalities? How do children perceive and evaluate themselves, and to what extent do their personalities predict what they will be like as adults? How do adolescents go about "finding themselves" as individuals? Do people's personalities and self-perceptions systematically change over the adult years, or do they remain essentially the same? After answering some of these questions, we will take a closer look at the development of one important and particularly fascinating facet of personality: the way we experience and express emotions.

THE INFANT

Do infants have any awareness that they exist or any sense of themselves as distinct individuals? Let's explore this issue and then see if it makes any sense to say that infants have unique "personalities."

The Emerging Self

Many developmental theorists believe that infants are born without a sense of self. Margaret Mahler (Mahler, Pine, & Bergman, 1975) likens the newborn to a "chick in an egg" whose needs are met and who has no reason to differentiate itself from the surrounding environment. It is not easy to determine when infants first gain a sense of themselves as beings separate from the world around them, but the first glimmers of this capacity can be detected in the first two or three months of life (Samuels, 1986; Stern, 1983). For example, 8- to 12-week-old infants whose arms and legs are connected by strings to mobiles and audiovisual equipment delight in producing interesting sights and sounds by kicking and pulling (Lewis, Alessandri, & Sullivan, 1990; Rovee-Collier, 1987). When the strings are disconnected and they can no longer produce such effects, they pull or kick all the harder and become frustrated and angry (Lewis et al., 1990). This suggests that they have a sense of agency and recognize that they exist apart from and can act upon other people and objects.

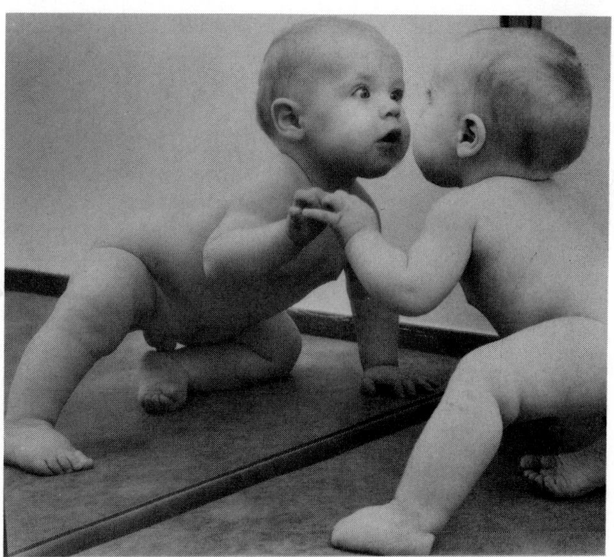

Does this boy really know that the tot in the mirror is him? Probably not if he is younger than 18 months of age, for that is when self-recognition is mastered by most toddlers.

Once babies know that they *are* (that they exist independently of other entities), they are in a position to find out *who* or *what* they are (Harter, 1983). When, for example, do infants recognize themselves as distinct individuals and become able to tell themselves apart from other infants? To find out, Michael Lewis and Jeanne Brooks-Gunn (1979) used an ingenious technique first used with chimpanzees: Mother daubs a spot of rouge on the infant's nose and then places the infant in front of a mirror. If infants have some mental image of their own faces and recognize their mirror images as themselves, they should soon notice the red spot and reach for or wipe their own noses rather than the nose of the mirror image. When infants 9 to 24 months old were given this rouge test, the youngest infants showed no self-recognition: They seemed to treat the image in the mirror as if it were "some other kid." Only among 18- to 24-month-olds did a large majority of infants show clear signs of self-recognition, touching their noses because they apparently realized that they had a strange mark on their faces that warranted investigation. They knew exactly who that kid in the mirror was!

To learn to recognize their own facial features, infants have to categorize the people they encounter in daily life and then place themselves into the social categories they are forming. According to Lewis and Brooks-Gunn, babies begin to form a **categorical self** as they classify themselves along socially significant dimensions such as age and sex, figuring out what is "like me" and what is "not like me." By the end of the first year, infants are already able to distinguish between strange babies and strange adults or between strange women and strange men (Brooks-Gunn & Lewis, 1981; Lewis & Brooks-Gunn, 1979). Before they are 18 months old, toddlers can tell themselves apart from toddlers of the other sex or from older individuals but are less able to distinguish between photos of themselves and photos of other infants of the same sex. As they approach age 2, they also master this task. By 18 to 24 months of age, then, most infants definitely have an awareness of who they are—at least as a physical self with a unique appearance and as a categorical self belonging to specific age and gender categories.

To what can we attribute this emerging self-awareness? First, the ability to recognize the self depends on cognitive development (Bertenthal & Fischer, 1978). Children who are mentally retarded are slow to recognize themselves in a mirror but can do so once they have attained a mental age of at least 18 to 20 months (Hill & Tomlin, 1981). Second, self-awareness depends on social experiences. Chimpanzees who have been raised in complete isolation, unlike those who have had contact with other chimps, fail to recognize themselves in a mirror (Gallup, 1979). Human toddlers who have formed secure attachments to their parents seem to be better able to recognize themselves in a mirror and know more about their names and genders than do toddlers whose relationships are less secure (Pipp, Easterbrooks, & Harmon, 1992).

The critical role of social interaction in the development of the self was appreciated long ago by Charles Cooley (1902) and George Herbert Mead (1934). Cooley used the term **looking-glass self** to emphasize that our understanding of self is a reflection of how other people respond to us; that is, our self-concepts are the images cast by a social mirror. Through their actions and words, parents and other companions communicate to infants that they are babies and are also either girls or boys. Later, social feedback helps children determine what they are like and what they can and cannot do well. Throughout life we forge new self-concepts through our social interactions. Thus the development of the self and social development, as well as cognitive development, are closely intertwined, beginning in infancy.

Early Temperament

Even though it takes infants some time to become aware of themselves as individuals, they *are* individuals with their own distinctive personalities from the very first weeks of life. The study of infant personality has centered on dimensions of **temperament,** or tendencies to respond in predictable ways to events. These tendencies serve as the building blocks of personality by influencing the kinds of interactions the individual has with his or her environment. Although temperament has been defined and measured in a number of different ways, there is much agreement that babies differ in their temperaments from an early age (Goldsmith et al., 1987).

Arnold Buss and Robert Plomin (1984) have focused on three dimensions of temperament: *emotionality, activity,* and *sociability.* They have found that some babies are more emotionally reactive (or easily and intensely irritated by events) than others are; that some are highly active while others are quite sluggish; and that some are very sociable, or interested in and responsive to people, while others are standoffish. Twin and adoption studies tell us that these aspects of temperament are partly influenced by genetic endowment, and this is true in infancy as well as in childhood, adolescence, and adulthood (Braungart et al., 1992; Plomin, 1986).

Jerome Kagan and his colleagues have been investigating another aspect of early temperament that they believe is highly significant—**behavioral inhibition,** or the tendency to be extremely shy and restrained in response to unfamiliar people and situations (Kagan, 1989; Kagan et al., 1988; Kagan, Snidman, & Arcus, 1992; Reznick et al., 1986). Inhibited children might be considered extremely high in emotionality and low in sociability. Kagan (1989) estimates that about 15% of toddlers have this inhibited temperament.

At 4 months of age, infants who will later be recognized as inhibited children wriggle and fret more than most infants in response to new sights and sounds. At 21 months their inhibition is clear: They take a long time to warm up to a strange examiner, retreat from unfamiliar objects such as a large robot, and fret and cling to their mothers. In follow-up tests at ages 5½ and 7½, about three-fourths of the highly inhibited and highly uninhibited children still displayed the same temperament they showed at 21 months of age. Those who had been inhibited as toddlers were more likely than children who had been uninhibited to be shy with peers and to be afraid of trying out a balance beam.

Kagan and his colleagues have also found that inhibited youngsters show distinctive physiological reactions to novel events; they become highly aroused (as indicated by high heart rates) in situations that barely faze other children. A recent twin study suggests that behavioral inhibition is genetically influenced (Robinson et al., 1992). Very possibly, then, genes affect temperament by influencing the development of the nervous system and the way it responds to environmental stimuli.

Still another useful way of describing infant temperament comes from the work of Alexander Thomas, Stella Chess, and their colleagues (Chess & Thomas, 1984; Thomas & Chess, 1977, 1986; Thomas, Chess, & Birch, 1970). These researchers gathered information about five main dimensions of infant behavior: typical mood, regularity or predictability of biological functions such as feeding and sleeping habits, tendency to approach or withdraw from new stimuli, intensity of emotional reactions, and adaptability to new experiences and changes in routine. Most infants could be placed into one of three categories based on the overall patterning of these temperamental qualities:

1. **Easy temperament.** Easy infants are even tempered, typically content or happy, and quite open and adaptable to new experiences such as the approach of a stranger or their first taste of strained plums. They have regular feeding and sleeping habits, and they tolerate frustrations and discomforts well.
2. **Difficult temperament.** Difficult infants are active, irritable, and irregular in their habits. They often react very negatively (and vigorously) to changes in routine and are slow to adapt to new people or situations. They cry frequently and loudly and often have tantrums when they are frustrated by such events as being restrained or having to live with a dirty diaper.
3. **Slow-to-warm-up temperament.** Slow-to-warm-up infants are quite inactive, somewhat moody, and only moderately regular in their daily schedules. Like difficult infants, they are slow to adapt to new people and situations, but they typically respond in mildly, rather than intensely, negative ways. For example, they may resist cuddling by looking away from the cuddler rather than by kicking or screaming. They do eventually adjust, showing a quiet interest in new foods, people, or places.

Of the infants in Thomas and Chess's New York Longitudinal Study, 40% were easy infants, 10% were difficult infants, 15% were slow-to-warm-up infants, and the remaining third could not be clearly placed in one category or another because they shared qualities of two or more categories. Thomas and Chess went on to study the extent of continuity and discontinuity in temperament over the years from infancy to early adulthood (Chess & Thomas, 1984; Thomas & Chess, 1986). Difficult infants who had fussed when they could not have more milk often became children who fell apart if they could not work math problems correctly. But by adulthood an individual's adjustment had little to do with his or her temperament during infancy, suggesting a good deal of discontinuity over this long time span. However, being difficult (or easy) in temperament as a 3- or 4-year-old did predict being difficult (or easy) in temperament and being poorly or well adjusted as a young adult.

Even so, the relationship between early and later temperament was far from perfect. For example, 39% of the individuals tested were in the same temperamental category as young adults that they had been in as 4-year-olds, but the rest changed (Korn, 1984). Apparently, many easy children turned into maladjusted adults, and many difficult children outgrew their behavior problems. So what determines whether or not temperamental qualities persist? Much may depend on what Thomas and Chess call the **goodness of fit** between child and environment—the extent to which the child's temperament is compatible with the demands and expectations of the social world to which the child must adapt (see also Lerner et al., 1989). A good example comes from observations of the Masai of East Africa (DeVries, 1984). In most settings an easy temperament is likely to be more adaptive than a difficult one, but among the Masai during a famine babies with *difficult* temperaments outlived easy babies, probably because they clamored louder for attention and food. In other words, a temperament that is a good fit to the demands of one environment may not be adaptive under other circumstances. The goodness-of-fit concept is another example of how individual predispositions and the environment interact to influence developmental outcomes.

In their longitudinal study, Chess and Thomas (1984) found that difficult children often continued to display difficult temperaments later in life if the person/environment fit was bad—if their parents were impatient, inconsistent, and demanding with them. However, difficult infants whose parents adapted more successfully to their temperaments and gave them more time to adjust to new experiences enjoyed a good fit to the environment and became able to master new situations effectively and energetically (see Box 10.1). It seems, then, that there is both continuity and discontinuity in those aspects of temperament first expressed in infancy. Although certain temperamental dispositions seem to be sketched in our genes at conception, early temperamental qualities *may or may not* carry over into childhood and adulthood, depending on the goodness of fit between the individual's predispositions and his or her social environment.

In sum, by the end of the first two years of life, infants have become very aware of themselves as individuals. Toddlers recognize themselves in a mirror, refer to themselves by name, and understand that they are physically distinct from other human beings. Cognitive development and experiences with the social looking glass make this new self-awareness possible. Moreover, each toddler has his or her own

BOX 10.1 The Case of Carl: Goodness of Fit

The case of Carl illustrates the importance to later personality development of the match between a child's temperament and his or her social environment. Early in life, Carl was one of the most difficult children Stella Chess and Alexander Thomas had ever encountered: "Whether it was the first bath or the first solid foods in infancy, the beginning of nursery and elementary school, or the first birthday parties or shopping trips, each experience evoked stormy responses, with loud crying and struggling to get away" (1984, p. 188). Carl's mother became convinced that she was a bad parent, but his father accepted and even delighted in Carl's "lusty" behavior and patiently and supportively waited for him to adapt to new situations. As a result, Carl did not develop serious behavior problems as a child. His difficult temperament did come out in force when he entered college and had to adapt to a whole new environment. He became extremely frustrated and thought about dropping out but eventually reduced his course load and got through this difficult period successfully. By age 23 he was no longer considered by the researchers to have a difficult temperament. How different his later personality and adjustment might have been had the fit between his difficult temperament and his parents' demands and expectations been poor! When children have difficult temperaments and grow up with parents who cannot control their behavior effectively, they are likely to have serious behavior problems as adolescents (Maziade et al., 1990).

Clearly, healthy personality development depends on the goodness of fit between child and parent and on the mutual influences of parents and child on one another (see also Doelling & Johnson, 1990, and Lerner et al., 1989, for evidence that children's adjustment to foster homes and students' adjustments to school are influenced by the fit between the child's temperament and the environment's demands). The moral for parents is clear: Get to know your baby as an individual, and allow for his or her special personality quirks.

personality, based in part on temperamental qualities that are sketched in the genetic code and expressed from the first days of life. However, the personality is by no means set in infancy. There is continuity in development in the sense that early temperamental traits sometimes carry over into later life, but there is discontinuity as well, and much depends on the goodness of fit between person and environment.

Preschool children emphasize the "active self" in their self-descriptions, noting things they can do but saying little about their psychological traits.

THE CHILD

Children's personalities continue to take form, and children acquire much richer understandings of themselves as individuals, as they continue to experience cognitive growth and interact with other people. Ask children of different ages to tell you about themselves. You'll find their responses amusing, and you'll learn something about how children come to know themselves as individuals.

Elaborating on a Sense of Self

Once toddlers begin to talk, they can and do tell us about their emerging self-concepts. By age 2 some toddlers are already using the personal pronouns *I*, *me*, *my*, and *mine* (or their names) when referring to the self and *you* when addressing a companion (Lewis & Brooks-Gunn, 1979; Stipek, Gralinski, & Kopp, 1990). This linguistic distinction suggests that 2-year-olds have a firm concept of "self" and "others." Toddlers also show us that they are developing a categorical self when they describe themselves in terms of age and sex ("Katie big girl").

Preschool children even become aware that different racial and ethnic categories exist, although it takes a while before they can classify themselves correctly. For example, 3- to 5-year-old Native American children can easily discriminate American Indians from Anglos in photographs but are less often able to correctly indicate which category they most resemble (Spencer & Markstrom-Adams, 1990). African-American preschoolers also sometimes misidentify themselves as white (Spencer, 1988). These responses could mean that young children are uncertain of their racial or ethnic identity. However, minority children are more likely demonstrating both an early awareness that minority groups are devalued in society and a desire to be part of what they think is the most desirable group (Spencer & Markstrom-Adams, 1990).

The preschool child's self-concept is very concrete and physical (Damon & Hart, 1982, 1988). When asked to describe themselves, preschoolers dwell on their physical characteristics ("I have brown hair"), their possessions ("I have a bike"), and the physical actions they can perform ("I can jump"). In one study (Keller, Ford, & Meachum, 1978), 3- to 5-year-olds were asked to say ten things about themselves and to complete the sentences "I am a ________" and "I am a boy/girl who ________." Fully half of the children's responses were *action* statements such as "I play baseball" or "I walk to school." Very few of these young children made any mention of their psychological traits or inner qualities. Young children do sometimes use global terms such as "nice" or "mean," "good" or "bad," to describe themselves and others (Livesley & Bromley, 1973). And, claims Rebecca Eder (1989, 1990), their descriptions of their characteristic behavior patterns and preferences ("I like to play by myself at school") may provide the foundation for later trait descriptions ("I'm shy").

By the age of 8 or so, children are more capable of describing their enduring inner qualities (Livesley & Bromley, 1973), and their self-descriptions are filled with personality-trait terms ("I'm friendly," "I'm funny," "I'm curious," and so on). Moreover, they now describe not just what they typically do or what they can do but how their abilities compare with those of their companions (Secord & Peevers, 1974). The preschooler who claimed to be able to hit a baseball now becomes the third-grader who claims to be a better batter than any of her classmates. What has changed? For one thing, children have gained the cognitive capacity to infer from regularities in their behavior that they have certain consistent traits. For another, they are more capable of **social comparison**—of noticing how they stack up compared to other individuals and using that information to judge themselves. They then define and evaluate themselves in terms of whether they are more or less competent than other children.

Young children often seem to be rather oblivious to information about how they compare to others and have difficulty processing such information when they receive it (Butler, 1990; Ruble, 1983). They have a delightful tendency to believe that they are the greatest, even in the face of direct evidence that they have been outclassed by their peers. Karin Frey and Diane Ruble (1985) report that kindergartners do watch their classmates and make social comparisons ("Same lunchbox—we're twinsies!"). However, they usually do this to be sociable or to find out how to do their classwork rather than to evaluate themselves. By contrast, first-grade children begin to seek information that will tell them whether they are more or less competent than their peers; they glance at each other's papers, ask "How many did you miss?" and say things like "I got more than you did." Older elementary school children are more politically astute and avoid making potentially embarrassing social comparisons out loud. Yet they most certainly sneak looks at other children's papers and are highly attentive to information about where they stand in the classroom pecking order. Interestingly, this preoccupation with evaluating oneself in comparison to others is not nearly as evident among children raised in communal kibbutzim in Israel, perhaps because cooperation and teamwork are so strongly emphasized there (Butler & Ruzany, 1993).

Social comparisons help school-aged children understand both how they are like others and how they are different from others. On the one hand, elementary school children are more likely than preschoolers to define themselves as part of social units ("I'm a Kimball, a second-grader at Brookside School, a Brownie Scout"). They are forming a social identity that ties them to similar others (Damon & Hart, 1988). On the other hand, school-aged children also take special notice of how they differ from others. An African-American girl in a largely white school, for example, is more likely to mention her race when she is asked to tell about herself than is a black girl in an all-black school (McGuire et al., 1978). Why? Simply because children do attempt to discover the ways in which they can distinguish themselves from their peers.

Self-Esteem

As children amass a wide range of perceptions of themselves and engage in social comparisons, they begin to evaluate their overall worth. Susan Harter (1982, 1986, 1990a) has developed a self-perception scale that assesses children's overall self-worth by asking them to evaluate their *scholastic competence* (for example, feeling smart, doing well in school), *social acceptance* (being popular, feeling liked), *behavioral conduct* (not getting in trouble), *athletic competence* (being good at sports), and *physical appearance* (feeling good-looking). When an early version of this scale was given to third- through ninth-graders, even third-graders showed that they had well-defined positive or negative feelings about themselves. Moreover, children make important distinctions between their competency in one area and their competency in another; they do not just have generally high or generally low self-esteem.

The accuracy of self-evaluations increases steadily over the elementary school years (Butler, 1990; Harter, 1982). Young children (4- to 7-year-olds) can be accused of having inflated egos; their self-esteem scores may reflect their *desires* to be liked or to be "good" at various activities as much as their actual competencies (Eccles et al., 1993; Harter & Pike, 1984). However, starting at about age 8, children's self-evaluations become more realistic and accurate. For example, those with high scholastic self-esteem are rated as intellectually competent by their teachers, and those with high athletic self-esteem are frequently chosen by peers in sporting events. At the same time, children are increasingly realizing what they "should" be like and are forming an ever-grander "ideal self." As a result, the gap between the real self and the ideal self increases with age, and older children run a greater risk than younger children do of thinking that they fall short of what they should be (Glick & Zigler, 1985).

Why do some children have higher self-esteem than others? One answer is that some children are in fact more competent and socially attractive than others; they therefore receive more positive feedback when they observe their own performance and when they engage in social comparison. But parents, teachers, and other important sources of feedback can also play a critical role. Children with high self-esteem tend to have parents who are warm and democratic (Coopersmith, 1967; Isberg et al., 1989; Lamborn, Mounts, Steinberg, & Dornbusch, 1991). These parents are loving and supportive, and they enforce clearly stated rules of behavior while allowing their children to express their opinions and participate in decision making. The relationship between high self-esteem and this nurturing parenting style is much the same in Taipei and Canberra as it is in Phoenix and Winnipeg (Scott, Scott, & McCabe, 1991).

Parents who frequently communicate approval and acceptance are likely to help their children think positively about themselves (Felson, 1990; Isberg et al., 1989). Saying, whether through words, looks, or actions, "You're not important" or "Why can't you be more like your older brother?" is likely to have the opposite effect on self-esteem. This is the concept of the looking-glass self in action: Children will form self-concepts that reflect the evaluations of significant people in their lives. Consistent discipline provided in a spirit of democracy may also contribute to self-esteem by giving children a firm basis for evaluating whether their behavior is good or bad and by sending them the message that their opinions are respected.

Teachers, peers, and other significant individuals probably contribute to self-esteem in much the same way that parents do. The judgments of other people, along with all the information that children gain by observing their own behavior and comparing it with that of their peers, shape their overall self-evaluations. Once self-esteem has been established, it tends to remain quite stable over the grade school years and is positively correlated with good adjustment (Coopersmith, 1967).

The Personality Stabilizes

Although some aspects of an infant's temperament carry over into later personality, we cannot always be confident that the sociable or irritable infant will remain that way as a child or adult. Many important dimensions of personality do not "gel" until the elementary school years (Moss & Susman, 1980; Ozer & Gjerde, 1989). As the years then go by, some of our behavior patterns become even more strongly rooted because of the kinds of interactions with the social environment they set in motion and because of the reactions they evoke from other people (Caspi, Elder, & Bem, 1987, 1988).

Consider the results of a major longitudinal study of development from birth to early adulthood reported by Jerome Kagan and Howard Moss (1962). Many personality traits did not stabilize until childhood. Some then remained evident in adulthood, whereas others changed considerably from childhood to adulthood (see Figure 10.1). Achievement orientation, sex-typed (or sex-appropriate) activity, and spontaneity were reasonably stable over time in both males and females. For example, both girls and boys who were highly achievement oriented became achievement-oriented adults, whereas their less academically oriented peers grew into adults with little drive. By contrast, tendencies toward anger or aggression and initiation of activities with the other sex were stable for males but not for females, whereas tendencies to react passively in stressful situations and to be dependent on other people were much more stable for females.

How can we explain this pattern of results? Kagan and Moss (1962) suggest that the stability of a personality trait over time depends on its being valued by society and consistent with society's prescribed gender roles (that is, on its goodness of fit to social expectations). Only then will it be reinforced. Parents, peers, teachers, and other agents of socialization value achievement in both sexes, so early socialization experiences encourage both boys and girls to remain achievement oriented. Society also encourages sex-typed activities for both boys and girls. But aggressive tendencies may persist less in girls, and passivity and dependence may be less stable in boys, because our society has traditionally not tolerated aggressive girls (see also Asendorpf & Van Aken, 1991; Bornstein, 1992). Thus traits that conflict with cultural norms may be discouraged and may fail to endure.

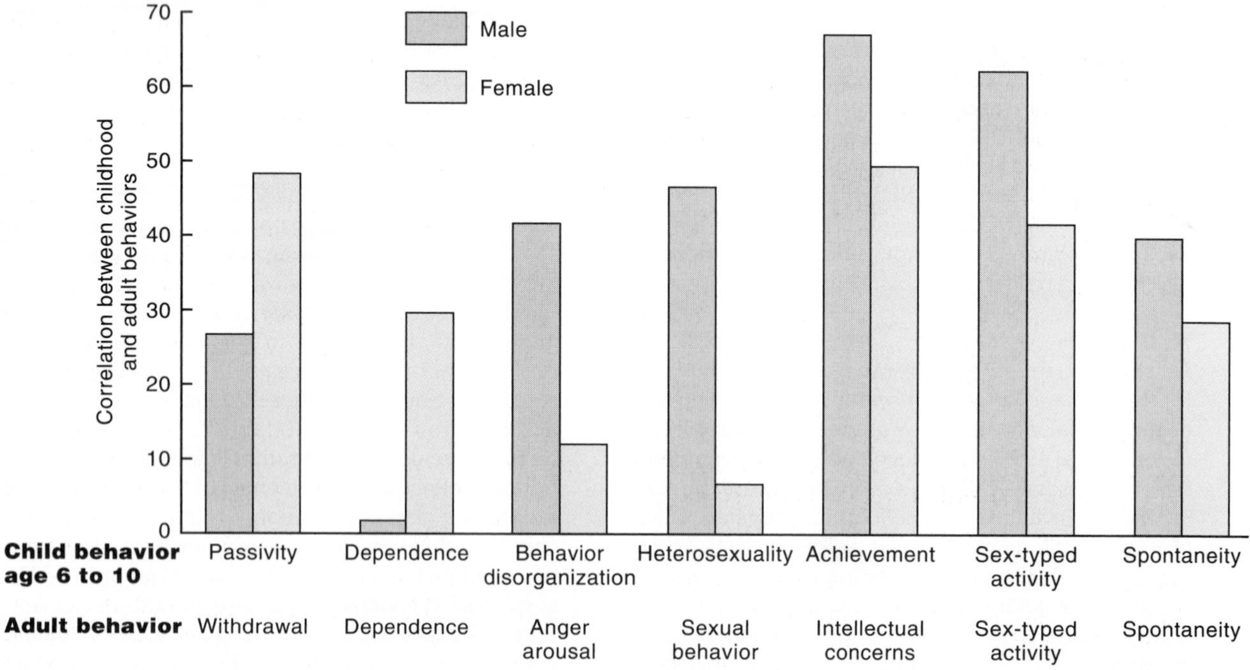

FIGURE 10.1 Stability and change in seven classes of behavior between childhood and early adulthood. *Note:* Each bar shows the correlation between child behavior and adult behavior. The higher the correlation, the more the individual's standing within the group on that trait remains consistent over time. (Adapted from Kagan & Moss, 1962.)

Culture, then, as expressed in others' reactions to a child's behavior, influences which of their distinctive personality traits children are most likely to carry with them into later life.

The Self and Erikson's Stages of Psychosocial Development

Erik Erikson's (1963, 1982) theory of personality development gives us new insights into some of the changes in self-conceptions and self-evaluations that occur during childhood. As we saw earlier, Erikson proposed that infants face the psychosocial conflict of basic *trust versus mistrust*. During this period they begin to recognize that they are separate from the caregivers who respond to their needs, and infants do indeed learn to distinguish self from other (typically the mother).

Toddlers, or those "terrible" 2-year-olds, acquire an even clearer sense of themselves as individuals as they struggle with the psychosocial conflict of **autonomy versus shame and doubt.** They are determined to do things themselves to demonstrate their independence and their control over their parents. They say "me, me, me" and "no" even when they really mean "yes," loudly proclaiming that they have a will of their own. If their parents humiliate or punish them when they have toileting accidents or spill their milk, they may end up doubting their competence or even believing that they are fundamentally bad people. Notice that the toddler's quest for autonomy is happening at the very age when children first recognize themselves in the mirror.

Four- and 5-year-olds who have achieved a sense of autonomy enter Erikson's stage of **initiative versus guilt,** in which they develop a sense of purpose by devising bold plans but must also learn not to step on other people in the process. In the preschool years of imaginative play, children acquire new motor skills, plot and plan to build sand castles and conquer the "bad guys" in their fantasy play, and take great pride in accomplishing the goals they set. Isn't it understandable, then, that these preschoolers would define themselves in terms of their physical activities and abilities?

A sense of initiative, Erikson believed, will pave the way for success when elementary school children face the conflict of **industry versus inferiority.** To gain a sense of industry, children must master the important cognitive and social skills—reading, writing, cooperative teamwork, and so on—that are necessary to win the approval of both adults and peers (Kowaz & Marcia, 1991). It seems natural that they would measure themselves against their peers to determine how competent they are becoming—that is, that they would use social comparison to evaluate themselves and would acquire a sense of inferiority if those comparisons turned out unfavorably. According to Erikson, children who successfully master each of these psychosocial conflicts gain new ego strengths—a trust in themselves and the future, a strong and independent will, a sense of purpose and adventure, and a feeling of basic competence. Moreover, they put themselves in a position to pose the question "Who am I?"—and, if all goes well, to answer it—during adolescence.

THE ADOLESCENT

Perhaps no period of the life span is more important to the development of the self than adolescence. Adolescence is truly a time for "finding oneself," for getting to know very intimately the person one has become, and for struggling to determine the person one will be.

The Self-Concept: Becoming a Personality Theorist

Raymond Montemayor and Marvin Eisen (1977) learned a great deal about the self-concepts of children and adolescents from grades 4 to 12 by asking students to write 20 different answers to the question "Who am I?" Box 10.2 shows the answers of a 9-year-old, an 11-year-old, and a 17-year-old.

What age differences can you detect? There are several (see also Damon & Hart, 1988; Harter, 1990b; Livesley & Bromley, 1973). First, self-descriptions become *less physical and more psychological* as children get older. Second, these self-portraits become *less concrete and more abstract.* Recall Piaget's theory that children begin to shift from concrete-operational to formal-operational thinking at about age 11 or 12. Although 9- to 10-year-olds are capable of describing their psychological traits, they often do so in fairly concrete terms ("I love! food"). Children entering adolescence (11- to 12-year-olds) more often generalize about their broader personality traits ("I am a truthful person"). High school students' self-descriptions are even more abstract, focusing not only on personality traits but also on important values and ideologies or beliefs ("I am a pseudoliberal").

Third, adolescents reflect more about what they are like; they are *more self-aware* than children are (Selman, 1980). Their new cognitive ability to think about their own and other people's thoughts and feelings can make them painfully self-conscious. Finally, perhaps because they are capable of reflecting on their personalities, older adolescents seem to be able to paint a *more integrated, coherent self-portrait* than children or younger adolescents can. Instead of merely listing traits, they organize their self-perceptions, including those that seem contradictory, into a coherent

BOX 10.2 **Three Children Answer the Question "Who Am I?"**

9-year-old

My name is Bruce C. I have brown eyes. I have brown hair. I love! sports. I have seven people in my family. I have great! eye site. I have lots! of friends. I live at. . . . I have an uncle who is almost 7 feet tall. My teacher is Mrs. V. I play hockey! I'm almost the smartest boy in the class. I love! food. . . . I love! school.

11½-year-old

My name is A. I'm a human being . . . a girl . . . a truthful person. I'm not pretty. I do so-so in my studies. I'm a very good cellist. I'm a little tall for my age. I like several boys. . . . I'm old fashioned. I am a very good swimmer. . . . I try to be helpful. . . . Mostly I'm good, but I lose my temper. I'm not well liked by some girls and boys. I don't know if boys like me. . . .

17-year-old

I am a human being . . . a girl . . . an individual. . . . I am a Pisces. I am a moody person . . . an indecisive person . . . an ambitious person. I am a big curious person. . . . I am lonely. I am an American (God help me). I am a Democrat. I am a liberal person. I am a radical. I am conservative. I am a pseudoliberal. I am an Atheist. I am not a classifiable person (i.e., I don't want to be).

SOURCE: From Montemayor & Eisen, 1977, pp. 317–318.

picture—a theory of what makes them tick (Bernstein, 1980; Harter, 1986; Harter & Monsour, 1992).

As an illustration, consider an interesting study by Susan Harter and Ann Monsour (1992) in which 13-, 15-, and 17-year-olds were asked to describe themselves when they are with parents, with friends, in romantic relationships, and in the classroom. These adolescents were then asked to sort through their self-descriptions, identify any opposites or inconsistencies, and indicate which opposites confused or upset them. The 13-year-olds were quite unaware of inconsistencies within themselves. If they did detect any, they were not especially bothered by them. By age 15, students identified many more inconsistencies and were clearly confused by them. Consider the ninth-grade girl who filled out the chart in Figure 10.2. She noted several inconsistencies within her personality; she was both attentive and lazy in school, talkative and nervous in romantic relationships, smart at school and fun-loving with friends, and so on. In talking about her tendency to be happy with friends but depressed at home, she said "I really think of myself as a happy person, and I want to be that way with everyone because I think that's my true self, but I get depressed with my family and it bugs me because that's not what I want to be like" (Harter & Monsour, 1992, p. 253). These 15-year-olds, especially the girls, seemed to feel that there were several different selves inside them and were concerned about finding the "real me."

It was not until their later high school years that adolescents were able to both detect conflicting self-perceptions and integrate them into a more coherent view of themselves. Thus a 17- or 18-year-old boy might conclude that it is perfectly understandable to be relaxed and confident in most situations but nervous on dates if one has not yet had much dating experience or that "moodiness" can explain being cheerful with friends on some occasions but irritable on others. Harter and Monsour believe that cognitive development—specifically the ability to compare abstract trait concepts and ultimately integrate them through higher-order concepts like "moodiness"—is behind this change in self-perceptions.

In sum, self-understandings become more psychological, abstract, and integrated, and self-awareness increases, from childhood to adolescence and over the course of adolescence. Truly, the adolescent becomes a sophisticated personality theorist who reflects upon and understands the workings of his or her personality (and who also has a richer understanding of other people).

Adolescent Self-Esteem

The founder of developmental psychology, G. Stanley Hall, characterized adolescence as a time of emotional turmoil and psychological *storm and stress.* By this account, adolescents might be expected to experience low, or at least very unstable, self-esteem. Does research support this view?

To some extent it does. For instance, Roberta Simmons and her colleagues (Simmons, Rosenberg, & Rosenberg, 1973) assessed the self-perceptions of children who were aged 8 to 11, 12 to 14, and 15 or older. Self-image problems were greatest among the 12- to 14-year-olds. These early adolescents had relatively low self-esteem, were highly self-conscious, and reported that their self-perceptions were highly changeable. Leaving elementary school as the oldest and most revered of students and entering the larger world of junior high school as the youngest and least competent will damage self-esteem temporarily (Simmons et al., 1987; Wigfield et al., 1991). This dip in self-esteem is likely to be greatest when multiple stressors pile up—for example, when adolescents are not only making the transition to junior high school

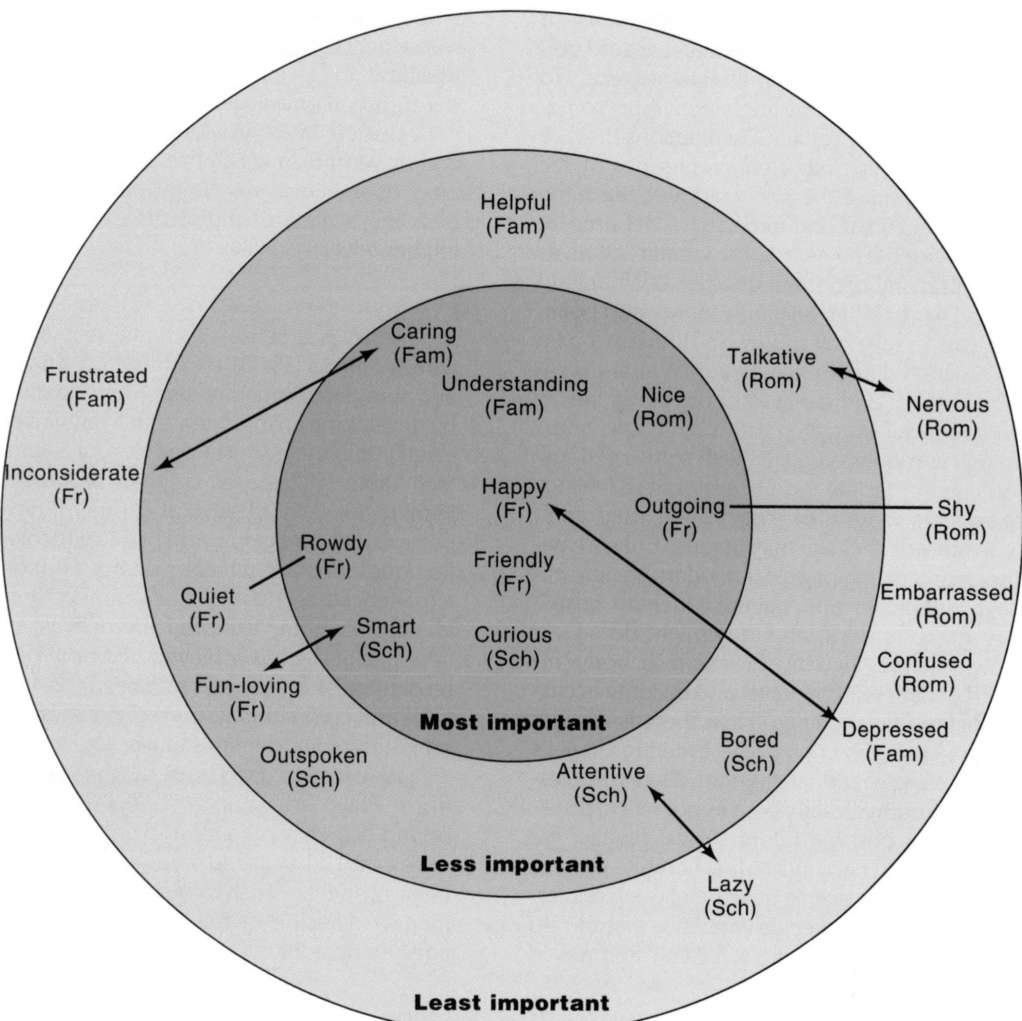

FIGURE 10.2 Self-description by a ninth-grade girl. Adolescents were asked to describe what they are like in four contexts: Fam = family, Rom = romantic relationships, Fr = friends, and Sch = school. They were to put traits central to their self-concept in the center of the circle, less important traits in the outer circles. Traits linked by lines with arrowheads were perceived to be in conflict or at war; lines without arrowheads mark trait inconsistencies thought to be of little consequence. This girl is aware of several inconsistencies between pairs of traits she attributes to herself. (From Harter & Monsour, 1992.)

but also coping with pubertal changes, beginning to date, and perhaps dealing with a family move all at the same time (Simmons et al., 1987). Some of us do indeed remember seventh grade as a year we would like to forget!

But, before we conclude that adolescence is hazardous to the self, we should note that most adolescents emerge from this period with essentially the same degree of self-esteem they had at the outset (Dusek & Flaherty, 1981). Apparently they revise their self-concepts in fairly minor ways as they experience the physical, cognitive, and social changes of adolescence. In addition, even though some young people do experience self-doubts as they enter adolescence, gradual, modest increases in self-esteem occur in later adolescence (Marsh, 1989; Mullis, Mullis, & Normandin, 1992; Savin-Williams & Demo, 1984). Temporary "ripples" in self-esteem smooth out, making Hall's characterization of adolescence as a stormy time for the self inaccurate for most adolescents (Offer, Ostrov, & Howard, 1984).

Forming a Sense of Identity

Like G. Stanley Hall, Erik Erikson believed that adolescence is a time of major changes in the self. It was Erikson (1968) who characterized adolescence as a critical period in the lifelong process of forming one's identity as a person and who proposed that adolescents experience the psychosocial conflict of **identity versus role confusion.** The concept of **identity** is slippery, but it refers mainly to a self-definition—a firm and coherent sense of who you are, where you are heading, and where you fit into society. To achieve a sense of identity, the adolescent must somehow integrate the many separate perceptions that are part of the self-concept into a coherent sense of self and must feel that he or she is, deep down, the same person yesterday, today, and tomorrow—at home, at school, or at work. The search for identity involves grappling with many important questions: What kind of career do I want? What religious, moral, and political values can I really call my own? Who am I as a man or woman and as a sexual being? Where do I fit in the world? What do I really want out of my life?

Can you recall struggling with such issues yourself? Are you currently struggling with some of them? If so, you can appreciate the uncomfortable feelings that adolescents may experience when they can't seem to work out their identity issues. Erikson believed that many young people in modern society experience a full-blown and painful "identity crisis." There are many reasons why they might do so. As their bodies change, they must revise their body images (a part of their self-concepts) and become accustomed to being sexual beings. Then there is the fact that they are changing cognitively. Entering Piaget's stage of formal-operational thought allows adolescents to think systematically about hypothetical possibilities, including possible future selves. Finally, we cannot ignore social demands. Most notably, parents and other socialization agents quite bluntly ask adolescents to "grow up"—to decide what they want to do in life and to get on with it. According to Erikson (1968), our society supports youth by providing them with a period when they are relatively free of responsibilities and can experiment with different roles in order to find themselves—a so-called moratorium period. Society even provides settings such as colleges and universities in which this experimentation can take place (sometimes resulting in a missed term-paper deadline, a citation for disorderly conduct, or a crashing hangover).

Developmental Trends in Identity Formation

When is a sense of identity actually achieved? James Marcia (1966) expanded on Erikson's theory and stimulated much research on identity formation by developing an interview that allows investigators to classify adolescents into one of four *identity statuses* (see Table 10.2) based on their progress toward an identity in each of several domains (for example, occupational, religious, and political/ideological). The key questions are whether or not an individual has experienced a *crisis* (or has seriously grappled with identity issues and explored alternatives) and whether or not he or she has achieved a *commitment* (that is, a resolution of the questions raised). On the basis of crisis and commitment, the individual is classified into one of the four identity statuses shown in the table.

We can get a good sense of when identity is formed from Philip Meilman's (1979) study of college-bound boys between 12 and 18, 21-year-old college males, and 24-year-old young men (see Figure 10.3). Most of the 12- and 15-year-olds were in either the identity diffusion or the foreclosure status. At these ages many adolescents simply have not yet thought

TABLE 10.2 The four identity statuses, as shown by current religious beliefs.

	No Crisis Experienced	*Crisis Experienced*
No Commitment Made	*Diffusion Status* The person has not yet thought about or resolved identity issues and has failed to chart directions in life. *Example:* "I haven't really thought much about religion, and I guess I don't know what I believe exactly."	*Moratorium Status* The individual is currently experiencing an identity crisis and is actively raising questions and seeking answers. *Example:* "I'm in the middle of evaluating my beliefs and hope that I'll be able to figure out what's right for me. I like many of the answers provided by my Catholic upbringing, but I've also become skeptical about some teachings and have been looking into Unitarianism to see if it might help me answer my questions."
Commitment Made	*Foreclosure Status* The individual seems to know who he or she is but has latched on to an identity prematurely, without much thought (e.g., by uncritically becoming what parents or other authority figures suggest he or she should). *Example:* "My parents are Baptists and I'm a Baptist; it's just the way I grew up."	*Identity Achievement Status* The individual has resolved his or her identity crises and made commitments to particular goals, beliefs, and values. *Example:* "I really did some soul-searching about my religion and other religions too and finally know what I believe and what I don't."

about who they are— either they have no idea or they know that any ideas they do have are likely to change (the **diffusion status,** with no crisis and no commitment). Other adolescents may say things like "I'm going to be a doctor like my dad" and appear to have their acts together. However, it becomes apparent that they have never really thought through *on their own* what suits them best and have simply accepted identities suggested to them by their parents or other people (the **foreclosure status,** involving a commitment without a crisis).

As Figure 10.3 indicates, progress toward identity achievement becomes more evident starting at age 18. Notice that more individuals now begin to fall into the **moratorium status,** in which the individual is currently experiencing a crisis or is actively exploring identity issues. Presumably, entering the moratorium status is a good sign; if the individual can find answers to the questions raised, he or she will move on to the identity achievement status. Yet notice that only 20% of the 18-year-olds, 40% of the college students, and slightly over half of the 24-year-olds in Meilman's study had achieved a firm identity based on a careful weighing of alternatives (the **identity achievement status**).

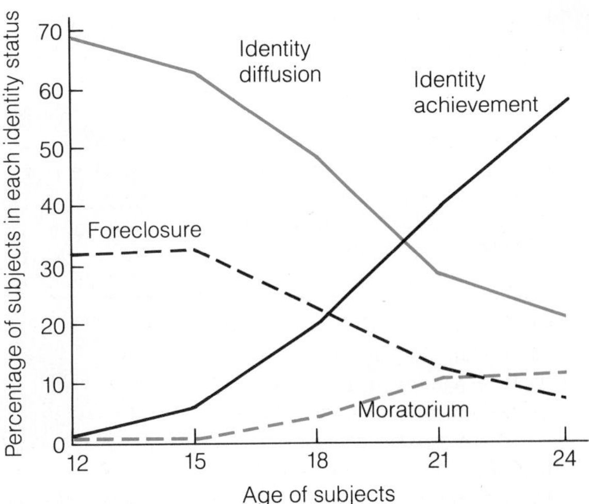

FIGURE 10.3 Percentages of subjects in each of Marcia's four identity statuses as a function of age. Note that only 4% of the 15-year-olds and 20% of the 18-year-olds had achieved a stable identity. (Based on Meilman, 1979.)

Is the identity formation process different for females than it is for males? In most respects, no (Archer, 1992). Females progress toward achieving a clear sense of identity at about the same rates that males do (Streitmatter, 1993). However, one intriguing sex difference has been observed: Although today's college women are just as concerned about establishing a career identity as men are, they attach greater importance to the aspects of identity that center on interpersonal relationships, gender role, and sexuality (Bilsker, Schiedel, & Marcia, 1988; Kroger, 1988; Patterson, Sochting, & Marcia, 1992). They are also more concerned than males with the issue of how to balance career and family goals (Archer, 1992; Matula et al., 1992). Perhaps it is the continuing influence of traditional gender roles we see here.

Judging from such research, identity formation takes quite a bit of time. Not until the late teens and early 20s do many young men and women move from the diffusion or foreclosure status into the moratorium status and then achieve a sense of identity (Waterman, 1982). But this is by no means the end of the identity formation process. Many adults are *still* struggling with identity issues or have reopened the question of who they are after thinking they had all the answers earlier in life (Waterman & Archer, 1990). A divorce, for example, may cause a woman to rethink what it means to be a woman and reraise questions about other aspects of her identity as well.

The process of achieving identity is also quite uneven (Archer, 1982; Kroger, 1988). For example, Sally Archer (1982) assessed the identity statuses of 6th- to 12th-graders in four domains: occupational choice, gender-role attitudes, religious beliefs, and political ideologies. Only 5% of the adolescents were in the same identity status in all four areas, and more than 90% were in two or three categories across the four areas. Apparently, then, some aspects of identity may take shape earlier than others. The process may be even more complex for members of racial and ethnic minority groups. As Box 10.3 indicates, they face the additional task of forming a positive ethnic identity.

Influences on Identity Formation

The adolescent's progress toward achieving identity is a product of at least four factors: cognitive growth, parenting, social experiences outside the home, and the broader cultural context. *Cognitive development* seems to enable adolescents to imagine and contemplate possible future identities. Adolescents who have achieved solid mastery of formal-operational thought and who think in complex and abstract ways are more likely to raise and resolve identity issues than adolescents who are less cognitively mature (Boyes & Chandler, 1992; Slugoski, Marcia, & Koopman, 1984; Waterman, 1992). Michael Berzonsky (1992) finds that adolescents in the moratorium and achievement statuses also adopt an information-processing style that involves actively seeking out relevant information rather than relying on others for guidance (as foreclosed adolescents tend to do) or putting off decisions and making impulsive choices at the last minute (as diffused adolescents tend to do). Adolescents in the moratorium status also seem to be especially open to the playful and creative experimenting that is so critical to identity formation (Bilsker & Marcia, 1991).

BOX 10.3 Forging a Positive Ethnic Identity

The process of forming an identity may well be more challenging for members of racial and ethnic minorities than for other adolescents. For one thing, they face an extra task—that of forming an **ethnic identity,** a sense of personal identification with an ethnic group and its values and cultural traditions (Phinney & Rosenthal, 1992). Forming a positive ethnic identity seems to proceed through the same steps as forming a vocational or religious identity, even though we don't choose our racial or ethnic heritage in the way we choose our occupations (Phinney & Rosenthal, 1992). Children and young adolescents either say that they identify with their racial or ethnic group because their parents and other members of the group influenced them to do so (foreclosure status) or have not given the issue much thought (diffusion status). As we noted earlier, some minority-group children even identify at first with the majority group, wanting to affiliate themselves with the group that has the most status in society (Spencer & Markstrom-Adams, 1990). One Hispanic adolescent who did so said "I remember I would not say I was Hispanic. My friends . . . were White and Oriental and I tried so hard to fit in with them" (Phinney & Chavira, cited in Phinney & Rosenthal, 1992, p. 158).

Between the ages of 16 and 19, many minority youths move into the moratorium and achievement statuses with respect to ethnic identity (Phinney & Chavira, 1992; Phinney & Rosenthal, 1992). Identity questioning is sometimes triggered by being discriminated against or by having one's group loyalty questioned. According to Signithia Fordham and John Ogbu (1986), for example, many low-income African-American adolescents who perform well in the classroom experience a good deal of ambivalence about their accomplishments because they run the risk of being accused of "acting white" by their black peers if they try to succeed by white standards. Virtually all North American minorities have a term for community members who identify too closely with the mainstream white culture, be it the "apple" (red on the outside, white on the inside) for Native Americans, the "coconut" for Hispanics, the "banana" for Asians, or the "Oreo" for African Americans. Minority adolescents must decide what *they* are inside. Biracial adolescents sometimes face even greater dilemmas: For example, pressured to choose between black and white peer groups, they may not be allowed to achieve an identity as *both* African American and Anglo (Kerwin, Ponterotto, Jackson, & Harris, 1993). Interestingly, Erik Erikson had firsthand experience with ethnic identity struggles; he was the blond, blue-eyed son of a Danish mother and a Jewish stepfather and was nicknamed "the goy" (non-Jew) by the Jewish boys in his neighborhood (Coles, 1970).

Somehow, minority adolescents must work out a resolution to these sorts of conflicts between their own culture and the majority culture. They are likely to do so more successfully if their parents support their efforts. Asian-, African-, and Mexican-American adolescents who have achieved a positive ethnic identity tend to have parents who tried to prepare them to live in a culturally diverse society (Phinney & Nakayama, 1991). Parents can also help by teaching children about their group's cultural traditions (Knight et al., 1993). And, as holds true for other identity domains, parents can foster ethnic pride by simply being warm and democratic parents (Rosenthal & Feldman, 1992). If minority youth succeed at the task of forming an ethnic identity, they are likely to feel better about themselves more generally (Phinney & Rosenthal, 1992).

Yet, even if they achieve a healthy ethnic identity, minority adolescents may encounter extra challenges in settling other identity issues. According to Margaret Spencer and Carol Markstrom-Adams (1990), Native-American, Mexican-American, and African-American youth often take longer to achieve an identity than their Anglo peers do. Why might this be? Spencer and Markstrom-Adams suggest several possibilities. For one thing, minority adolescents may come to realize that prejudice and discrimination in society may limit their vocational prospects, forcing them to rethink their goals (Ogbu, 1988). In addition, confronted with conflicts between the values of their subculture and the values of the majority culture, minority youths may find it more adaptive to "foreclose" identity and adopt the beliefs of their own group than to work out these difficult issues on their own.

How well do minority adolescents cope with these special challenges in the identity formation process? Quite well indeed. Most of them do form a positive ethnic identity, resolve other identity issues successfully, and end up no lower in self-esteem than Anglo youth (Phinney & Rosenthal, 1992). Still, schools and communities might make things easier for minority adolescents by nurturing ethnic pride and continuing efforts to ensure that educational and economic opportunity extend to all.

Second, adolescents' *relationships with parents* affect their progress in forging an identity (Markstrom-Adams, 1992; Waterman, 1982). Youth in the diffusion status of identity formation are more likely than those in the other categories to be neglected or rejected by their parents and to be distant from them. Perhaps it is difficult to forge one's own identity without first having the opportunity to identify with respected parental figures and to take on some of their desirable qualities. At the other extreme, adolescents categorized as being in the foreclosure status appear to be extremely close—possibly too close— to their

Adolescents sometimes experiment with a variety of looks in their search for a sense of identity.

relatively controlling parents. Foreclosed adolescents may never question parental authority or feel any need to forge a separate identity.

By comparison, students who are classified in the moratorium and identity achievement statuses appear to have a solid base of affection at home combined with considerable freedom to be individuals in their own right (Campbell, Adams, & Dobson, 1984; Grotevant & Cooper, 1986). In family discussions, for example, these adolescents experience a sense of closeness and mutual respect while feeling free to disagree with their parents; they are encouraged to compare their perspectives to those of other family members (Grotevant & Cooper, 1986). Notice that this is the same warm and democratic parenting style that seems to help children gain a strong sense of self-esteem.

A third influence on identity formation is *social experiences outside the home*. For example, adolescents who go to college are exposed to diverse ideas and encouraged to think issues through independently. Although college students may be more confused for a time about their identities than peers who begin working after high school (Munro & Adams, 1977), going to college provides the kind of "moratorium period" that Erikson felt was essential to identity formation.

Finally, identity formation is influenced by *the broader social and historical context* in which it occurs—a point that Erikson himself strongly emphasized. The whole notion that adolescents should choose a personal identity after carefully exploring many options may well be peculiar to industrialized Western societies in the 20th century (Cote & Levine, 1988). As in past centuries, adolescents in many traditional societies today—and even in some segments of our own society—simply adopt the adult roles they are expected to adopt, without any soul searching or experimentation. For many of the world's adolescents, what Marcia calls identity foreclosure is probably the most adaptive route to adulthood (Cote & Levine, 1988). In addition, the specific life goals that adolescents choose will also depend on what options are available and valued in their society.

All signs suggest that, in Western society at least, the adolescent who is able to raise serious questions about the self and answer them—that is, the individual who achieves identity—is better off for it. Identity achievement is associated with psychological well-being and high self-esteem, complex thinking about moral issues and other matters, a willingness to accept and cooperate with other people, and a variety of other psychological strengths (Waterman, 1992). By contrast, those individuals who fail to achieve a sense of identity may find themselves lacking self-esteem and drifting aimlessly, trapped in the identity diffusion status. Alternatively, they may take on what Erikson calls a **negative identity** as a "black sheep," "delinquent," or "loser" because it seems better to become everything that one is not supposed to be than to have no identity at all. Erikson recognized that identity issues can and do crop up later in life even for those people who form a positive sense of identity during adolescence. Nonetheless, he quite rightly marked the adolescent period as the key time in life for defining who we are.

THE ADULT

As we enter adulthood, having gained a great deal of understanding of what we are like as individuals, we most definitely have our own unique personalities. What happens during the adult years? Are self-conceptions and personality traits highly changeable, or do they remain much the same?

Self-Perceptions in Adulthood

Let's first ask whether self-concepts and levels of self-esteem change over the adult years. On the one hand, we might expect that many people would gain self-esteem as they cope successfully with the challenges of adult life. On the other hand, we might guess that aging, disease, and losses of roles and relationships in later life could undermine self-esteem. As it turns out, neither view is accurate. Most researchers find no evidence at all that young, middle-aged, and elderly adults differ in self-esteem or in the ways they describe themselves (Bengtson, Reedy, & Gordon, 1985; McGue, Hirsch, & Lykken, 1993; Veroff, Douvan, & Kulka, 1981). There is little truth at all to the stereotyped view that older adults suffer from a poor self-image.

Culture may be more important than age in shaping adults' self-perceptions. For example, Americans say "The squeaky wheel gets the grease," but in Japan "The nail that stands out gets pounded down" (Markus & Kitayama, 1991). Because they have been brought up in an individualistic culture, Americans describe themselves by emphasizing their unique personal traits. By contrast, people from Japan (and similar cultures), having been socialized to define themselves in relation to the larger group, emphasize their social roles and find it difficult to think about their personal qualities apart from the context of specific social relationships (Cousins, 1989). Regardless of their age, then, adults in different cultures are likely to react differently to the "Who am I?" question.

However, adults of different ages *do* differ in their views of what they could or should be in the future. For example, Carol Ryff (1991) asked young, middle-aged, and elderly adults to assess their (1) ideal, (2) likely future, (3) present, and (4) past selves. As Figure 10.4 shows, favorable ratings of the present self actually increased modestly from age group to age group, which is further evidence that older adults do not suffer from low self-esteem. More striking was the tendency of older adults to scale down their visions of what they could ideally be and what they will be in the future (and to judge more positively what they had been in the past). Perhaps, then, we give up some of our bold dreams of fame and perfection as we age and become more content to stay the way we are (Cross & Markus, 1991). The gap between ideal self and real self that grows larger during childhood and adolescence apparently closes again in later life.

In sum, adults of different ages appear to feel equally good about themselves and to describe themselves in similar ways, but older adults tend to perceive a smaller gap between their real and ideal selves. Each adult also maintains much the same level of self-esteem over time, although positive and negative life events can certainly bring about changes in self-perception (Mortimer, Finch, & Kumka, 1982; Tran, Wright, & Chatters, 1991). Could it be that, needing to believe that we are basically the same people over the years, we distort our self-perceptions to maintain such an image? Or is it that we actually don't change much and therefore have no reason to change our self-perceptions? Let's see.

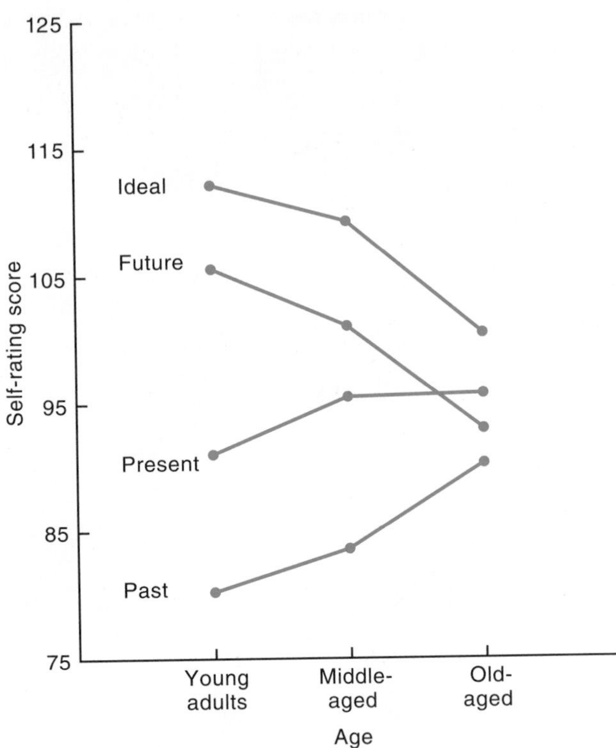

FIGURE 10.4 Favorability of ratings of ideal, likely future, present (real), and past selves by young, middle-aged, and elderly adults. The gap between ideal and real self that widens during childhood and adolescence shrinks during adulthood, as indicated by the converging lines in the graph. As they age, adults become more comfortable with the idea of remaining as they are and have been in the past. (Adapted from Ryff, 1991.)

Stability and Change in Adult Personality

Is there some point in childhood or adolescence at which our personalities become set, to change little thereafter? Or do personality traits change significantly as people launch careers and families in young adulthood, deal with major responsibilities in middle age, face threats to health in old age, and encounter various other crises along the way?

The question is really whether there is continuity (stability) or discontinuity (change) in the personality. And the issue is more complex than it may appear at first glance, partly because there are two senses in which we can be stable or changeable. First, continuity in personality can mean **stability of individual differences,** or lack of change in individuals' rankings within a group on a personality trait dimension. It is indicated by positive correlations between early and later traits. If the most sociable children turn into the most sociable adults, and the least sociable children turn into the least sociable adults, then each person's standing on the dimension of sociability would be stable from childhood to adulthood. But, if knowing how sociable or unsociable a person is early in life provided no basis for predicting how sociable he or she will be in later life, instability of individual differences is evident.

The second indicator of continuity or change involves whether there is **stability of mean levels** of a trait as people age. Level of sociability would be stable during adulthood, for example, if elderly adults were no more or less sociable than younger people on the average. It would be changeable if most people became less (or more) sociable as they aged, making the group's average sociability level drop (or rise). Stability in individual rankings and stability in average trait levels are clearly distinct; one can exist without the other. Figure 10.5 graphs the patterns of stability and change that could potentially be found. Let's see what *has* been found.

Do People Retain Their Rankings on Trait Dimensions over the Years?

Paul Costa, Robert McCrae, and their colleagues have closely studied personality change and continuity by giving adults from their 20s to their 90s personality tests and administering these tests repeatedly over the years (Costa & McCrae, 1992; McCrae & Costa, 1990). They have focused on five major dimensions of personality believed by many theorists to capture the essential ways in which personalities differ. These "big five" personality dimensions—neuroticism, extraversion, openness to experience, agreeableness, and conscientiousness—are shown in Table 10.3. Extraversion and neuroticism have been studied the most; extraversion, you might notice, is related to the aspect of infant temperament called sociability, and neuroticism is the adult counterpart to infant emotionality.

Are individual rankings on these personality dimensions stable over the years? Yes—surprisingly so (Costa & McCrae, 1988, 1992; Costa, McCrae, & Arenberg, 1980, 1983). The adult who tends to be

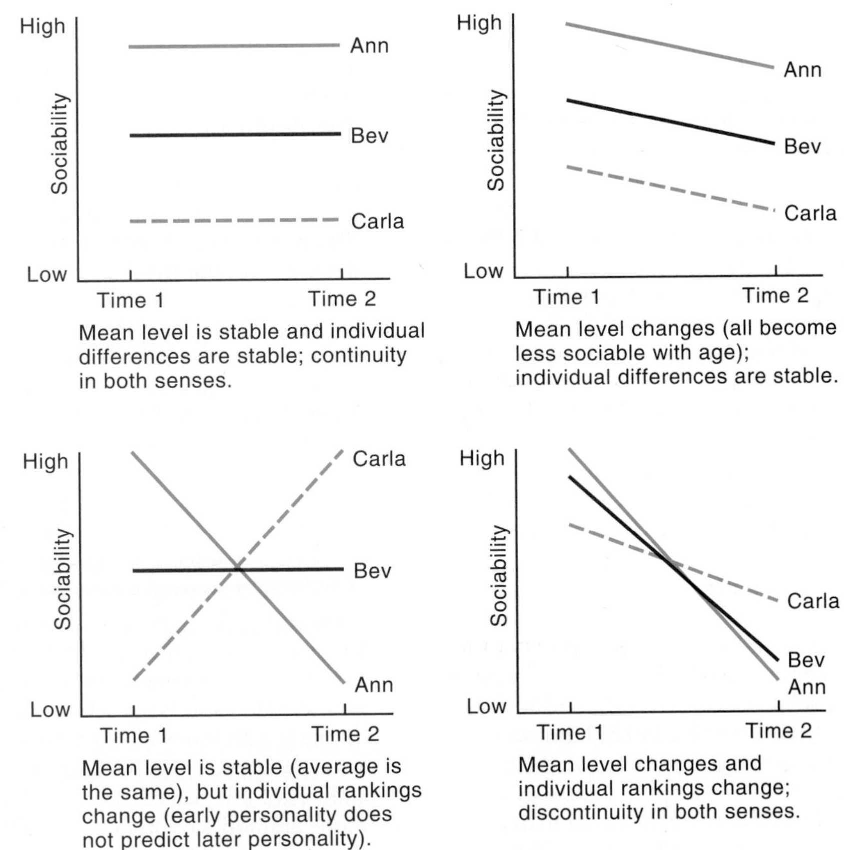

FIGURE 10.5 Possible patterns of stability and change in the personality trait of sociability: The simple case of Ann, Bev, and Carla. Whether there is stability of individual differences is a different issue from whether there is stability in mean levels of traits from one age to another.

TABLE 10.3 The "big five" personality dimensions.

Dimension	*Basic Definition*	*Key Characteristics*
Neuroticism	Emotional instability vs. stability	Anxiety, hostility, depression, self-consciousness, impulsiveness, vulnerability
Extraversion	Sociability vs. introversion	Warmth, gregariousness, assertiveness, activity, excitement seeking, positive emotions
Openness to experience	Curiosity and interest in variety vs. preference for sameness	Openness to fantasy, esthetics, feelings, actions, ideas, values
Agreeableness	Compliance and cooperativeness vs. suspiciousness	Trust, straightforwardness, altruism, compliance, modesty, tender-mindedness
Conscientiousness	Discipline and organization vs. lack of seriousness	Competence, order, dutifulness, achievement striving, self-discipline, deliberation

SOURCE: Adapted from Costa & McCrae, 1992.

extraverted or emotionally stable today is likely to remain extraverted or emotionally stable compared to peers years from now. Correlations between personality trait scores on two occasions 20 to 30 years apart range from about .60 to .80, suggesting some room for change in many individuals, but also considerable consistency over time (Costa & McCrae, 1992).

It seems that personalities are still fairly unsettled in adolescence and early adulthood but then become more firmly established by the time adults are in their 30s (Costa & McCrae, 1992; Kogan, 1990). For example, Stephen Finn (1986) found that college students tested in their 20s had changed quite a bit by age 50, whereas the personalities of middle-aged adults tested in their 40s and then tested again in their 70s were considerably more stable. Stability of individual differences, or consistency over time, is the rule for most adults 30 and older (Costa & McCrae, 1992).

We should note that Costa and McCrae have found greater stability of personality traits than many other researchers have found (for example, Connolly, 1991; Finn, 1986; Haan, 1981; Leon et al., 1979). When stability coefficients are in the neighborhood of .50 or less, as they often are after many years have passed, they are open to varying interpretations. Overall, major personality traits such as extraversion and neuroticism show less stability over the years than intelligence but more stability than such aspects of personality as self-esteem, attitudes, and interests (Bengtson et al., 1985; Connolly, 1991). Moreover, this consistency is not due simply to a desire on the part of adults to *think* they remain the same, for it also shows up when their spouses are asked to rate them over the years (Connolly, 1991; Costa & McCrae, 1988).

In sum, research has confirmed the notion that relatively enduring personality traits exist. Perhaps this explains why we often perceive ourselves as being the same basic people we used to be and why people we have not seen for years often seem not to have changed much at all. If this is bad news for people who are dissatisfied with their current personalities, it is good news for those who want to predict what they and other people will be like in the future or how they will respond to life events. Whether the event is marriage, retirement, or the death of a loved one, for example, individuals who score high on measures of neuroticism may consistently have more difficulty coping than will more emotionally stable individuals (McCrae & Costa, 1990).

Even if individuals' rankings on many personality dimensions remain quite stable during adulthood, it is still possible that most people systematically change in certain common directions. You may be consistently more extraverted than I over the years, and yet both of us, along with our peers, could become less extraverted at age 70 than we were at age 20. So let's examine the second major aspect of continuity in personality: *stability of mean levels* of traits.

Do the Personalities of Adults Change Systematically?

Do older adults, as a group, have different personalities than younger adults do? Cross-sectional studies suggest that they do, in some respects. For example, Bernice Neugarten and her colleagues, in pioneering studies of adult personality, found that elderly men and women were more introverted, introspective, and in touch with inner feelings than middle-aged adults were (Neugarten, 1977). They seemed less concerned with demands placed on them by other people and more attuned to voices within themselves (see also Costa et al., 1983, 1986).

Of course, some age-group differences are generational, or cohort, differences rather than true maturational changes; people's personalities are considerably affected by when they were born and by what sorts of experiences they had in their formative years (Schaie & Parham, 1976). For example, today's older men are more restrained about expressing their feelings and less assertive than today's young men. Yet, when men are assessed repeatedly over the years, there is no sign that they *become* more emotionally restrained or less assertive as they get older (Douglas & Arenberg, 1978). Possibly, then, elderly people grew up in a time when self-expression was less strongly encouraged than it has been in more recent times.

Only longitudinal studies can tell us whether people's personalities actually become different *as they age*. Consider first some evidence of personality growth from adolescence to middle age. Norma Haan (1981) has reported many of the key findings of two long-term longitudinal studies of development conducted in Oakland and Berkeley, California. Professional judges rated men's and women's traits on the basis of their responses to lengthy interviews and tests administered during adolescence and then again when these individuals were in their 30s and 40s. Both men and women in these studies became more cognitively invested in life (more intellectual and interested in achievement), more open to the self (self-aware and introspective), more self-confident (satisfied with themselves, assertive), and more nurturant toward others (giving, sympathetic). Other studies also suggest that both men and women typically become more achievement oriented, confident of their abilities, assertive, and autonomous between their 20s and their 40s and 50s (Helson & Moane, 1987; Helson & Wink, 1992; Stevens & Truss, 1985). These changes make a great deal of sense when we realize that, whereas adolescence is a somewhat unsettled period that involves many life changes, adults have opportunities to become more confident and independent as they actually get their lives off the ground and settle into specific work and family roles.

What about the period from middle age to old age? There are only a few signs that most people change in similar ways during this period. Adults' activity levels (their tendencies to be energetic, fast working, and action oriented) begin to decline in the 50s and continue declining through the 80s and 90s (Costa & McCrae, 1992; Douglas & Arenberg, 1978; Field & Millsap, 1991). Longitudinal studies also reinforce the idea that people become somewhat less extraverted and more introspective in old age (Field & Millsap, 1991; Leon et al., 1979). The remarkable thing is that signs of personality change can be detected even among the "oldest old"—those individuals who are 85 and older (Field & Millsap, 1991). This is a blow to the stereotype that the personality becomes rigid and set in stone in later life. Still, most personality traits do *not* seem to change in systematic directions in old age (Costa & McCrae, 1988, 1992).

Where do we stand, then? Most evidence suggests this:

1. Different generations of people often have somewhat distinctive personality profiles as groups, indicating that the historical context in which people grow up affects their personality development.
2. There is some personality growth from adolescence to middle adulthood—a strengthening of qualities such as self-confidence, autonomy, and nurturance; evidently we do not stop developing as individuals once we turn 20.
3. There are very few ways in which the personality traits of adults systematically change in similar directions as they progress from middle adulthood to later adulthood, although some decreases in activity level and increases in introspectiveness may be observed.

Overall, then, whether we look at individuals' relative positions on trait dimensions (stability of individual differences) or at the average levels of different traits expressed by younger and older adults (stability of mean levels), there seems to be substantial stability in personality during adulthood—along with some change, especially in very early adulthood but at older ages as well.

Why Do People Change or Remain the Same?

Having figured out that there is both stability and change in personality traits over the life span, developmentalists are beginning to ask why people stay the same and why they change. What makes a personality stable? First, the influence of genetic inheritance might be at work (McGue, Bacon, & Lykken, 1993; see also Chapter 3). Heredity appears to influence early temperamental qualities that give rise, in interaction with experience, to enduring personality traits such as extraversion and neuroticism (Loehlin, 1992; Plomin, 1990). Second, childhood experiences may have lasting effects that promote stability of personality. We have seen that at least some personality traits take shape in childhood and adolescence and persist into adulthood and that children's experiences within the family can leave lasting imprints on their personalities (Chess & Thomas, 1984; Loehlin, 1992).

Third and finally, traits remain stable because our environments remain stable. Here the argument is not just that early experiences have lasting effects—it is that *both early and later experiences* promote personality stability because we consistently seek out and have experiences that suit and reinforce our personalities. Imagine that Thelma, because of some mix of genes and early experience, shows an early tendency to be extraverted, whereas Louise is a shy introvert from the start. Thelma's friendliness is likely to elicit friendliness from other people throughout her life.

Moreover, as an extravert, she will seek out and create environments to her liking—placing herself in crowds, at parties, and in jobs where she can socialize. In these environments, Thelma is likely to maintain or even strengthen her initial tendency to be extraverted. Louise, meanwhile, might go out of her way to avoid parties, keep to herself, and therefore remain an introverted individual, comfortable with herself and her lifestyle. Each will be exposed to and will actively seek experiences that are likely to sustain and strengthen their early personality predispositions.

As Avshalom Caspi, Glen Elder, and Daryl Bem (1987, 1988) suggest, our early temperamental qualities lead us to have certain kinds of experiences, and the consequences of those experiences accumulate over the years. Thus the child with an explosive temper may alienate more and more people and get into more and more serious trouble as the years go by. Early traits also evoke from other people reactions that tend to reinforce the traits, as when friends encourage a "party animal" to continue being the life of the party. The result is often considerable continuity of such traits as shyness and emotional instability over the years. This is much like the message Sandra Scarr and Kathleen McCartney (1983) stress when they talk of *gene/environment correlations*: Genetic endowment influences the kinds of experiences we have, and those experiences, in turn, strengthen our genetically based predispositions (see Chapter 3).

What might be responsible for the significant *changes* in personality that some adults experience? Biological factors such as disease could contribute, but a more likely possibility is that adults change in response to changes in their social environments or in response to major life events (Wells & Stryker, 1988). To cite but one example, adults who land good jobs with high incomes and much freedom to make decisions either maintain their initial sense of competence or gain confidence after college, whereas those who face job insecurity and unemployment in their early careers lose some of their sense of competence (Mortimer et al., 1982). In this way, life events help determine whether traits evident in early adulthood will persist or change. If their lives change dramatically enough, adults can become very different people than they were earlier in life.

Finally, change may be more likely when the fit between person and environment is poor. Consider some fascinating research conducted by Florine Livson (1976), using data from the Oakland longitudinal study. She identified two groups of women, both of whom were mentally healthy at age 50. "Traditional" women were conventional and fit well into the stereotypically feminine role. They had been outgoing and popular as teenagers and continued to show these same traits in adulthood, changing little at all. By contrast, "independents" did not fit traditional feminine roles as well. As teenagers they had tended to be unconventional, introspective, and motivated to achieve. During adulthood these nontraditional women, like most women of their era, abandoned careers to pursue the lives of housewives and mothers. They then found themselves confronting a midlife crisis in their 40s: They were depressed and up in the air about what to do with their lives as their children prepared to leave the nest. Yet by age 50 these independent women were able to redirect their lives and rebound toward a level of psychological health equal to that of the traditional woman. Some of the nontraditional women changed dramatically, becoming more like the intellectually alive individuals they had been as teenagers than like the unhappy and irritable women they had become at 40.

The "fit" between the personalities of independent, unconventional women and the traditional wife/mother role can be poor. This may result in dissatisfaction and stimulate positive changes in lifestyle or personality.

Livson (1981) discovered a remarkably similar pattern among men. Mentally healthy men who fit the traditional male role well changed little over the years, whereas "nontraditional" men experienced a difficult time in their 40s, possibly because they were pressured to conform to a traditional masculine role that did not allow them to express their emotional sides. Livson's studies tell us that people are most likely to change when the fit between their personalities and their environments (or lifestyles) is poor. This message about the importance of goodness of fit is the very one that has emerged from research on children with easy, difficult, and slow-to-warm-up temperaments (Chess & Thomas, 1984; Thomas & Chess, 1986). And it supports an important theme of contextual theorists: Personalities unfold through the ongoing transactions between person and environment.

A Summing Up

So, the personality is both stable and changeable during adulthood; although stability tends to prevail. Several basic dimensions of personality, (the "big five" in particular) do tend to remain much the same from one age to another, but other aspects of personality are more changeable. Moreover, there are only a few ways in which most people's personalities shift in the same direction as they get older.

Genes, early childhood experiences, and the tendency to seek out or end up in environments that match and reinforce earlier predispositions all contribute to stability. Change in personality becomes more likely if people's environments change considerably or if they find themselves in situations that are mismatched to the traits they might naturally express. Finally, even if personalities often remain basically the same for long stretches of the life span, this does not mean that they cannot change—as, for example, with the help of a skilled psychotherapist (Costa & McCrae, 1992). Powerful experiences have the capacity to alter us at any stage of life.

One last note: Perhaps significantly, researchers who conclude that adults hardly change at all over the years typically study personality by administering standardized personality scales. These tests were designed to assess enduring traits and may well tell us about the most stable aspects of personality. However, researchers who interview people in depth about their lives often detect considerably more change and growth (Kogan, 1990; Wrightsman, 1988), as we see as we turn to efforts to chart progress through Erikson's stages of psychosocial development during adulthood.

Psychosocial Growth during Adulthood

Erikson was one of the first developmentalists to claim that adults experience stagelike changes in personality during adulthood. Here we ask a simple question: Does research support his ideas?

Establishing Intimacy

As Erikson saw it, young adulthood is a time for dealing with the psychosocial conflict of **intimacy versus isolation.** He theorized that one must achieve a sense of individual identity before becoming able to commit oneself to a *shared identity* with another person—that is, you must know yourself before you can love someone else. The young adult who has no clear sense of self may be threatened by the idea of entering a committed, long-term relationship and being

Early adulthood is the time, according to Erik Erikson, for deciding whether to be intimate with another person or to take a more independent route.

"tied down," or he or she may become overdependent on a partner as a source of identity.

To test Erikson's view that identity paves the way for genuine intimacy, Susan Whitbourne and Stephanie Tesch (1985) measured both identity status and intimacy status among college seniors and 24- to 27-year-old alumni from the same university. The researchers interviewed people about their closest relationships and placed each person in one of six intimacy statuses, ranging from being a social isolate with no close relationships to being involved in a genuinely intimate relationship (see Table 10.4).

TABLE 10.4 Intimacy statuses.

Intimacy Status	*Description*
Isolate	No close relationship
Stereotyped	Shallow relationship with little communication or involvement
Pseudointimate	Relationship is long-lasting but stereotyped or lacking in depth
Preintimate	Relationship rates high on communication and involvement; what is missing is a long-term commitment to one's partner
Merger	Close to intimate, for there is high involvement and open communication, but partners are not co-determining (e.g., one is overdependent on the other and has no separate identity)
Intimate	Has it all—high involvement, open communication, mutual determination, and long-term commitment

SOURCE: Developed by Whitbourne & Tesch (1985) and largely based on the work of Orlofsky, Marcia, & Lesser (1973).

The results were interesting. More alumni than college students fell into either the moratorium (active questioning) or the achievement status of identity formation, indicating that progress toward achieving identity continues to be made *after* college graduation, most likely as young adults face the demands of launching careers and taking on other adult roles. College graduates had also progressed farther than college seniors in resolving intimacy issues; more of them were involved in long-term, committed relationships. Finally, and most important, the college graduates who had well-formed identities were more likely than those who did not to be capable of genuine and lasting intimacy—precisely what Erikson had theorized (see also Matula et al., 1992; Orlofsky, Marcia, & Lesser, 1973; Raskin, 1986).

So far, so good, then. As Erikson claimed, we apparently must know ourselves before we can truly love another person. But does this really work the same way for women as it does for men? Not always. The issues of identity and intimacy seem to be more intertwined for women (Dyk & Adams, 1990; Hodgson & Fischer, 1979; Patterson et al., 1992). Men are likely to become psychologically ready for a serious relationship after they have settled on a career and perhaps even launched it—first graduation, then the wedding. Career-oriented women tend to follow this same identity-before-intimacy route (Dyk & Adams, 1990). Other women resolve intimacy issues before identity issues. They marry, raise children, and only after the children are more self-sufficient ask who they really are as individuals (Hodgson & Fischer, 1979; Schiedel & Marcia, 1985; Whitbourne & Tesch, 1985). Still other women tackle identity and intimacy tasks simultaneously, perhaps forging a personal identity that centers on caring for other people or defining themselves in the context of a love relationship (Dyk & Adams, 1990). In short, Erikson's theory seems to fit men better than it fits women because women find alternative ways of dealing with the issues of identity and intimacy. Sex differences in the paths to identity and intimacy may well diminish as more women postpone marriage to pursue their careers.

Middle Age and Generativity

Is there continuing psychosocial growth in middle age? George Vaillant (1977), a psychoanalytic theorist, has conducted an in-depth longitudinal study of mentally healthy Harvard men from college to middle age, as well as a longitudinal study of blue-collar workers (Vaillant, 1983; Vaillant & Milofsky, 1980). One of his important findings has been that men come to rely on more mature ego defense mechanisms as they get older. As young adults, for example, many men coped with crises in their lives by escaping reality or blaming other people for their deficiencies. In middle age these men were more likely to rely on such mature coping tactics as realistic planning or a healthy sense of humor to get them through difficult times.

What is generativity? It is singer Cissy Houston saying this about her highly successful singing daughter, Whitney: "To be singing with someone you brought into the world, who you cradled in your arms—it's nice. It's wonderful to see something you do that comes out halfway right." (*Newsweek,* January 5, 1987, p. 61).

In addition, Vaillant found that the men he studied did progress through Erikson's stages, although he detected an additional stage between the young-adult stage of intimacy versus isolation and the middle-age stage of generativity versus stagnation. Most men were indeed concerned with intimacy issues in their 20s, but they appeared to enter a new psychosocial stage in their 30s that Vaillant called the **career consolidation stage,** during which they focused most of their energies on advancing in their careers and were not very reflective or concerned about others. Vaillant likened these 30-year-olds to elementary school children in the stage of industry versus inferiority, striving hard to conform to other people's expectations of them and rarely asking themselves if what they were doing was worthwhile. It was as if they had merely traded their lunchboxes for briefcases.

In their 40s, many men then became more concerned with the issue of **generativity versus stagnation,** which involves gaining the capacity to produce something that outlives you and to genuinely care about the welfare of future generations. These men expressed more interest than ever before in passing on something of value, either to their own children or to younger people at work. They reflected on their lives and experienced the kind of intellectual vitality that adolescents sometimes experience as they struggle with identity issues. Few of these men experienced a full-blown and turbulent midlife crisis, just as few had experienced a severe identity crisis as college students. Nonetheless they were growing as individuals, often becoming more caring and self-aware as they entered their 50s. One of these men expressed the developmental progression Vaillant detected perfectly: "At 20 to 30, I think I learned how to get along with my wife. From 30 to 40, I learned how to be a success in my job. And at 40 to 50, I worried less about myself and more about the children" (1977, p. 195).

Thus Vaillant offers evidence that men progress through stages of intimacy, career consolidation, and generativity, in this order. More recently, Dan McAdams and his associates (1993) have found that both middle-aged and older men and women are more likely than young adults to have gained a sense of generativity and to be serving as role models, mentors, and community leaders. Indeed, we now know that women and men alike experience noticeable psychosocial growth in the areas of industry, identity, intimacy, and generativity during early and middle adulthood (Ochse & Plug, 1986; Whitbourne et al., 1992).

Old Age and Integrity

Elderly adults, according to Erikson, confront the psychosocial issue of **integrity versus despair.** They try to find a sense of meaning in their lives that will help them face the inevitability of death. Most older adults, when asked what they would do differently if they had their lives to live over again, say there is little, if anything, they would change (Erikson, Erikson, & Kivnick, 1986; Field & Millsap, 1991). This suggests that most older adults do attain a sense of integrity. But how?

Noted gerontologist Robert Butler (1963, 1975) has proposed that elderly adults engage in a process called **life review,** in which they reflect on unresolved conflicts of the past in order to come to terms with themselves, find new meaning and coherence in their lives, and prepare for death. Do older adults in fact engage in life review, and does it help them achieve a healthy sense of integrity? There is little support for the idea that elderly people spend more of their waking hours thinking about the old days or dwelling in the past than younger people do (Gambria, 1979–1980; Webster & Cappeliez, 1993). However, older adults *are* more likely than younger adults to use their reminiscences to evaluate and integrate the pieces of their lives—that is, to engage in life review (Molinari & Reichlin, 1984–1985).

More importantly, those who use the life-review process to confront and come to terms with their failures display a stronger sense of ego integrity and better overall adjustment than those who do not reminisce or those who obsess about how poorly life has treated them (Taft & Nehrke, 1990; Wong & Watt, 1991). Believing that life review can be beneficial in later life, Butler has used it as a form of therapy, asking elderly adults to reconstruct and reflect on their lives with the help of photo albums and other memorabilia. Participation in life-review therapy can indeed help elderly adults feel less anxious and more content with themselves and their lives (Haight, 1988, 1992).

A Summing Up

On balance, Erikson's theory of psychosocial development during adulthood seems to be partially, though not fully, supported. The evidence is quite convincing that achieving a sense of identity in adolescence paves the way for forming a truly intimate relationship with another person as a young adult. Moreover, gaining a sense of generativity does seem to be an issue for many middle-aged adults, and many older adults seek a sense of integrity through the process of life review. Eriksonian strengths such as identity, intimacy, and generativity do not always emerge in the particular order Erikson proposed (Ochse & Plug, 1986; Whitbourne et al., 1992), but we can certainly agree with Erikson that people are capable of personal growth and change throughout the life span. Personality traits such as extraversion and neuroticism may remain quite consistent over the years, but people do seem to confront new psychological conflicts as they age.

THE EMOTIONAL SELF

Although many aspects of personality development deserve a closer look, one of the most important is the evolution of the emotional self. Emotional development is multifaceted; among other things, it includes acquiring basic capacities for and personal styles of experiencing, expressing, and controlling feelings. When in life do we first experience emotions? How do children come to learn about emotions and about how to express (or hide) them? How do the distinctive emotional "personalities" we form in childhood change during the adult years? Here we will examine only selected aspects of emotional development, saving the important topic of emotional attachments and love until Chapter 13.

Early Emotional Expression

Until fairly recently, most researchers believed that infants did not really have emotional lives—or at least that their emotional expressions were only globally positive or negative in nature. Parents, by contrast, have long felt that their babies' faces reveal a wide range of specific emotions (Johnson et al., 1982). Carroll Izard (1982) and his colleagues have confirmed that parents are basically right. Izard has videotaped infants' responses to such events as grasping an ice cube, having a toy taken away, or seeing their mothers return after a separation. By analyzing specific facial movements (such as the raising of the brows and the wrinkling of the nose) and by asking raters to judge what emotion a baby's face revealed, Izard has established that infants do indeed express distinct emotions in response to different experiences and that adults can readily interpret which emotions they are expressing.

Izard concludes that a number of facial expressions of emotion appear in a predictable order over the first two years. At birth, babies show interest (by staring intently at objects), distress in response to pain, disgust (to foul tastes and odors), and expressions of contentment. Angry expressions appear at 3 to 4 months—about the same time that infants acquire enough control of their limbs to push unpleasant stimuli away. Sadness also emerges at about this same time, with fear making its appearance at age 5 to 7 months. These "primary" emotions seem to be biologically programmed, since they emerge in all normal infants at roughly the same ages and are displayed and interpreted similarly in all cultures (Izard, 1982, 1993; Malatesta et al., 1989).

"Secondary" emotions such as shame, embarrassment, pride, and guilt, involve being self-conscious or evaluating oneself. They appear in the second or third years. Michael Lewis and his colleagues (Lewis, Sullivan, et al., 1989) believe that self-conscious emotions such as embarrassment cannot emerge until children are capable of self-recognition; self-evaluative emotions such as pride and guilt require both self-recognition and a grasp of standards for evaluating one's behavior. Consistent with this view, Lewis and his associates find that the only toddlers who become noticeably embarrassed when they are subjected to lavish praise or asked to "show off" for strangers are those who can recognize themselves in a mirror when given the rouge test. By about age 3, when they are more able to evaluate their performances as good or bad, children begin to show signs of pride (smiling, applauding, shouting "I did it!") when they succeed at a difficult task, as well as shame (a downward gaze with a slumped posture, often accompanied by statements such as "I'm not good at this") when they fail at an easy task (Lewis, Alessandri, & Sullivan, 1992; see also Stipek, Recchia, & McClintic, 1992).

Although the earliest emotional expressions seem to be biologically programmed, the sociocultural environment soon begins to exert its influence. One of the first lessons babies in our culture learn is that positive emotions such as joy and interest are more welcomed than negative emotions. Carol Malatesta and her colleagues have carefully observed the face-to-face interactions of mothers with infants in their first year of life (Malatesta et al., 1986, 1989; Malatesta & Haviland, 1982). They find that young infants display a wide range of positive and negative emotions, changing their expressions with lightning speed (once every 7 seconds) while their mothers do the same. Mothers, however, restrict themselves mainly to displays of interest, surprise, and joy, thus serving as models of positive emotions. What's more, mothers respond selectively to their babies' expressions; over the early months they become increasingly responsive to their babies' expressions of interest and surprise and less responsive to negative emotions (Malatesta et al., 1986, 1989). Through basic learning processes, then, infants are trained to show a pleasant face more frequently and an unpleasant face less frequently—and they do just this over time. They are beginning to learn which emotional expressions are socially acceptable in their culture.

What they learn more specifically may be quite different in one culture than in another, though. For example, American parents love to stimulate their babies until they reach peaks of delight, whereas Gusii mothers in Kenya hardly ever engage in face-to-face play of this sort and seek instead to keep their infants as calm and content as possible (Dixon, Tronick, Keefer, & Brazelton, 1981). Thus American babies learn that intense emotion is okay as long as it is positive, but Gusii babies learn to restrain both positive and negative emotions.

Babies also learn from parents and other companions which emotions are appropriate in particular situations (Denham, 1989; Halberstadt, 1991). One important way in which this may happen is through **social referencing,** the process by which infants monitor others' emotional reactions in ambiguous situations and use this information to regulate their own feelings and behavior (Feinman, 1992; Feinman & Lewis, 1983; Klinnert et al., 1986). The ability to engage in social referencing emerges at about 8 to 10 months of age. For example, Tedra Walden and Tamra Ogan (1988) coaxed mothers to react either positively or fearfully when their infants were introduced to a toy robot. Mothers donned appropriate facial expressions and said either "Oh, look at that! What a nice toy! Oh boy! Oh boy! Nice toy!" or "Oh, look at that scary toy! Ooo, what a scary toy! Ooo, scary toy!" (p. 1232). Compared to younger infants, 10–13-month-olds not only looked more frequently at their mothers' faces for cues but heeded those cues more, reaching for and touching the "scary" toy less often than the "nice" toy. In many everyday situations, then, infants may learn how they should interpret and respond to people, things, and events by studying the emotional responses of their companions.

We still do not know precisely what is going on inside infants' heads as they display emotions. Adults,

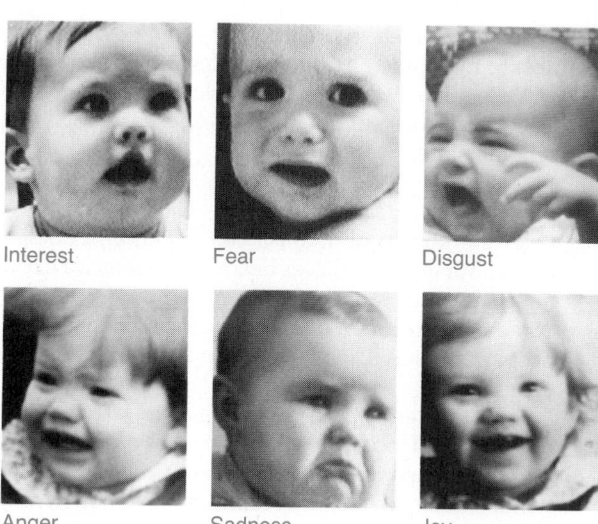

Infants express a wide range of emotions.

after all, think as they feel. But the baby in the doctor's office who displays anger after being given a shot is hardly likely to be thinking "Boy, I'm mad at this lady—she'd better not stick me again." Infants may well need to acquire the capacity for symbolic thought and a sense of self-awareness before they can mentally represent their own emotional experiences and can *consciously* interpret the emotions that their faces and physiological states reveal (Lewis & Michalson, 1983; Lewis, Sullivan, et al., 1989; Stipek, 1983).

Learning about Emotions and How to Control Them

During the preschool and elementary school years, children do become more conscious of their emotions, learn a great deal about how to interpret emotions, and begin to exert more control over their expressive behavior. As soon as they can talk, toddlers converse with family members about the feelings that they and other people experience and often discuss the causes of these emotions (Bretherton et al., 1986; Dunn, Brown, & Beardsall, 1991). By the age of 2, many children tested on their understanding of emotions already show some awareness of which faces are "happy" or "sad" faces and which faces fit which situations. Linda Michalson and Michael Lewis (1985), for example, found that 70% of 2-year-olds could already pick out a happy face as the face that is appropriate at a birthday party. Knowledge of negative emotions comes more slowly, perhaps because these expressions are discouraged and are therefore observed less often than positive emotions. However, such understanding expands rapidly during the preschool years (Gross & Ballif, 1991; Michalson & Lewis, 1985). Children who do well on tests that require interpreting other people's emotions are likely to have had frequent opportunities to discuss emotions with other family members in the home (Dunn et al., 1991).

Nonetheless, young children still have much to learn about emotions. Not until age 8, for example, do children recognize that many situations will elicit different emotional responses from different individuals (Gnepp & Klayman, 1992). Moreover, 8- and 9-year-olds are beginning to understand that a person can experience conflicting emotions (such as excitement and fear) at the same time (Harter, 1986; Wintre, Polivy, & Murray, 1990), and they have become more skilled at integrating facial and situational cues to determine what someone might be feeling (Hoffner & Badzinski, 1989).

From the age of about 2 on, children also begin to use emotional expressions consciously and deliberately as communication signals, as when a child falls but does not burst into tears until Mom is in sight (Cole, 1985). And, although the expressions on infants' faces are usually a true guide to their inner emotional states, preschoolers become capable of controlling or regulating their expressions of emotion. Two-year-olds can be observed to knit their brows and bite or compress their lips in an effort to suppress their sadness or anger (Malatesta et al., 1989). Three-year-olds who peek at a hidden toy after being instructed not to do so lie when asked if they peeked, and they are able to hide their guilt well enough, despite some nervous smiles and body touches, to make it impossible for adult observers to discriminate the liars from the truth tellers (Lewis, Stanger, & Sullivan, 1989). By now inner state and outer expression are not quite so closely matched as they were in infancy (Cole, 1985). Still, preschoolers are quite inept compared with older children at disguising their true feelings; they typically wear their feelings on their faces and express those feelings freely.

It is in elementary school that children truly master the art of emotional deceit! What happens is that children are gradually learning, starting in infancy, a set of **display rules** for emotion—cultural rules specifying what emotions should or should not be expressed under what circumstances (Gross & Ballif, 1991; Harris, 1989). They are also learning the more specific display rules that prevail in their own families, for some parents tolerate outbursts of anger or shrieks of delight more than other parents do (Halberstadt, 1991). As children learn display rules, the gap between what they are experiencing inside and what they express to the world widens (which is a nicer way of saying that they become skilled in the art of deceit).

Consider an interesting study by Carolyn Saarni (1984; see also Saarni, 1990). Children aged 7, 9, and 11 participated in a preliminary research session in which they were rewarded for their labors with an attractive gift—a can of juice, a candy bar, and 50 cents. At the close of a second research session, when they were expecting a nice gift, they instead got a boring

As children learn the emotional display rules of their society, they become more and more skilled at hiding their true feelings and expressing more socially appropriate ones.

baby toy. Here, then, was a situation (not unlike that faced by the countless children given underwear and socks as presents on major holidays and birthdays) in which our culture's display rule reads something like this: "Look pleased about a gift, even if it's disappointing."

Saarni coded the children's behavior into three categories: positive (an enthusiastic "thank you," a broad smile), negative (a failure to say "thank you," a wrinkled nose, an "ugh," a shrug, and so on), and "transitional" (middle-range behaviors reflecting a partial attempt to control one's responses, as in a mumbled "thank you" or a distressed smile). Although even 3- and 4-year-olds will make some attempt to suppress their disappointment in a situation like this (Cole, 1986), the 7-year-olds in Saarni's study, especially the boys, were not very skilled at masking their inner disappointment with grins and gracious thank-yous. Their negative reactions leaked through. Older children, especially girls, were more able to conform to the display rule by pretending to be delighted when they were not.

During childhood and adolescence, individuals continue to sharpen their understanding that there is an inner world of emotional experience that can be quite distinct from outward emotional displays (Harris, Olthof, & Terwogt, 1981). Moreover, they become increasingly able to control their emotional expressions as they learn how they should feel in particular situations and how they should express (or hide) what they feel in accordance with whatever display rules prevail in their culture (Harris, 1989). In all likelihood, this "socialization of emotions" works for the good of society—at least, all societies appear to have established emotional display rules of some kind. We may not like the idea that children become increasingly able to mask and alter their true feelings as they grow older, but life might be unbearable if adults were typically as honest about their feelings as most preschoolers are.

Emotions in Adult Life

Over the course of infancy, childhood, and adolescence, our emotional lives become richer as we experience a wider range of different emotions and become more aware of our emotional experience. How do our emotional lives then change during the adult years?

It has been hypothesized that aging brings with it a blunting of both emotional expression and inner emotional experience (see Malatesta, 1981). The idea is that elderly people do not show much emotion and, in fact, do not react to events with as much emotional intensity as younger and middle-aged adults do. A related view is that, when elderly adults *do* feel emotions, they are often negative ones. Several early studies seemed to support these views, but those studies were flawed. Most notably, they often involved institutionalized elderly people, who are likely to have more restricted and unhappy emotional lives than healthier individuals do (Malatesta, 1981).

It is now clear that the emotional experiences of younger and older adults are far more similar than different. In one study (Malatesta & Kalnok, 1984), young, middle-aged, and older adults were questioned about their emotional experiences and expressions. There was no sign that elderly people experience more negative emotions than younger people do, that emotions are any less important in their lives, or that they experience emotions any less intensely. Moreover, the faces of young, middle-aged, and elderly women were about equally expressive when they recalled events that had provoked various emo-

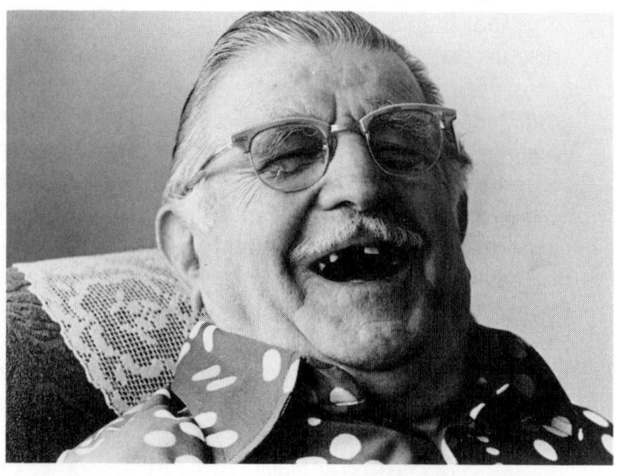

People continue to experience strong emotions in old age.

tions in them (see also Levenson et al., 1991). If there is any difference, it may be that older adults have learned to control and regulate their emotions more effectively and to remain on a more even emotional keel (Lawton et al., 1992).

Thus we would be making a mistake in assuming that most elderly people no longer experience strong emotions or experience mostly negative ones. Older people, like younger people, differ considerably in their emotional "personalities" and lead complex emotional lives.

APPLICATIONS: BOOSTING SELF-ESTEEM THROUGHOUT THE LIFE SPAN

We all know that individuals who lack self-esteem suffer for it. So what possibilities exist for boosting low self-esteem? Earlier in this chapter we noted that parents can do a great deal to foster high self-esteem in their children. Specifically, those who blend love with democratic and consistent discipline nourish self-esteem. Such parents are able to express their disapproval of a child's misbehavior while conveying the message that the child is a valuable and lovable person. They set clear guidelines for behavior and yet allow their children to express their own views and become individuals in their own right. These same parental practices are also associated with the achievement of a solid sense of identity in adolescence.

Susan Rosenholtz (1977, 1985) believes that teachers can also have a major impact on children's self-evaluations. Too often, she argues, educational experiences are set up so that children are ranked on a global dimension of academic competence—placed in high or low reading groups, given grades for academic work, and so on. Children soon come to view themselves as either *generally* competent or *generally* incompetent individuals. The problem, of course, is that half the children in *any* classroom will always end up below average.

Rosenholtz argues that children would be far better off in a *multidimensional* classroom—one in which many different abilities (rather than one general ability dimension) are recognized. She has experimented with a curriculum that teaches children that many abilities are important and that everyone has strengths of some kind. Low-ability students who are exposed to such a curriculum appear to gain confidence; they become more likely than children in traditional classrooms to assert themselves when they work with their classmates (Rosenholtz, 1977). As we discovered in Chapter 9, there are in fact many kinds of intelligence. The child who is deficient in the reading skills that prove so critical to the pecking order in most traditional classrooms may well shine in mechanics, music, art, athletics, or leadership skills. When only generalized academic ability counts in school, it may be difficult indeed for many children to recognize in themselves a talent that could become a source of pride and self-esteem.

And what can be done for those older adults (the minority) who have low opinions of themselves? Could part of the problem be that they have internalized or taken to heart society's negative views of old age? **Ageism** is the term used to describe prejudice against elderly people (Butler, 1975; see also Bodily, 1991). Ageists believe the stereotypes that old people are sickly, cranky, dependent, forgetful, or otherwise incompetent or unpleasant. Although the majority of older adults see themselves as better off than most other older people (Heckhausen & Krueger, 1993), they tend to share society's negative images of old age (Bodily, 1991).

Judith Rodin and Ellen Langer (1980) set out to boost the self-esteem of a particularly vulnerable group: new nursing-home residents. These researchers discovered that 80% of the residents, a week after entering the nursing home, blamed aging for many of the difficulties in functioning that they were experiencing. It did not occur to them that the nursing-home environment could be a source of these problems. In an experiment designed to change their thinking, Rodin and Langer taught one group of residents a new "theory." The fact that they found walking difficult was not because they were old and feeble; it was because the nursing-home floors were tiled and therefore very slippery for people of all ages. The fact that they grew tired in the evening was not due to the weariness of old age; *anyone* would be tired after being awakened at 5:30 in the morning.

Compared to both an untreated control group and a group that was merely given medical information to the effect that physical aging was not the major source of their difficulties, the group that learned to attribute their difficulties to the environment rather than to old age fared well. They became more active and sociable, and even more healthy, than the other groups. The moral? Elderly people who can avoid taking negative stereotypes of old people to heart and who can avoid blaming all their difficulties on the ravages of old age—that is, older adults who can avoid thinking like ageists—appear to have a good chance of feeling good about themselves in later life. Perhaps the worst thing about old age is thinking the worst about old age.

REFLECTIONS

As you can see, there is change *and* stability, discontinuity *and* continuity, in the development of the self across the life span. Before adulthood, considerable change occurs. Infants who only dimly perceive that they exist as separate beings become adolescents or young adults who have developed elaborate theories about the workings of personality and who have forged unique, complex identities. And, despite some stability in temperament and personality, many of the traits we show as infants and children give way to quite different traits later in life.

If children seem like ever-growing seedlings, adults are more like durable oaks. Though capable of growth, adults seem to carry with them through the years fairly consistent self-conceptions, characteristic levels of self-esteem, and stable personality traits. Perhaps there is something to be said for having a stable and consistent sense of who we are and of being able to predict how we will behave in the future. We seem to work hard throughout our lives to maintain a positive view of ourselves, and we take comfort in knowing that there is a link between what we were, what we are, and what we will become. Susan Whitbourne (1986) has shown that adults will use self-deception where necessary to maintain an image of themselves as "loving, competent, and good." It simply is not tolerable to most of us to admit that we don't care about our families, are incompetent at work, or have all the wrong values and priorities. Nor is it tolerable to feel like many different people in the same body (Donahue et al., 1993).

Yet, who wants to be the "same old person" all the time? The individual whose personality is completely stable sounds like a person in a rut — someone whose growth has been stunted. We also want to feel that we are improving, "getting better every day," and that we can overcome any character defects or problems we may have. In a classic demonstration of this, Diana Woodruff and James Birren (1972) had middle-aged adults take a personality test and then complete a second version indicating how they would have responded when they were in college. These adults depicted themselves as quite pitiful creatures in their college years; they genuinely believed that they had gained many personality strengths over the 25 years since their college days. In fact, this personality scale had actually been given to them during college, and they had hardly changed at all over the years (see also McFarland, Ross, & Giltrow, 1992).

In view of our desire to think that we maintain our strengths and also improve on them, the research findings we have discussed in this chapter couldn't be more reassuring. They tell us that we have a sound basis for feeling a sense of continuity between past, present, and future selves, and they tell us that psychological growth can and does occur throughout the life span. Even if we do not yet actually possess all the desirable traits that we would like to have, we can still convince ourselves that we do — or that we soon will!

SUMMARY POINTS

1. Psychoanalytic theorists maintain that we experience similar personality changes at similar ages, although Erik Erikson and other neo-Freudian theorists saw more continued personality growth during adulthood than Freud did. By contrast, social learning theorists and contextual-dialectical theorists maintain that people can change in any number of directions at any time in life if their social environments change. Self-concept (perceptions of one's attributes) and self-esteem (overall evaluations of one's worth) do not always coincide with objective personality traits.

2. Early in their first year, infants acquire some sense that they exist separately from the world around them; by 18 to 24 months of age, they display self-recognition and form a categorical self based on age and sex. Even young infants display distinctive personalities. They differ in emotionality, activity, and sociability; behavioral inhibition; and easy, difficult, and slow-to-warm-up temperaments. Temperament is partially influenced by genetic endowment but also shaped by the goodness of fit between child and environment.

3. The self-concepts of preschool children are very concrete and physical. By about age 8, children begin to describe their inner psychological traits and evaluate their competencies through social comparison processes. Children are most likely to develop high self-esteem if they fare well in social comparisons and if their parents are warm and democratic.

4. During middle childhood, personality traits become more consistent and enduring than they were earlier in life, especially if they are culturally valued. After Erikson's stage of trust versus mistrust in infancy, children progress through the stages of autonomy versus shame and doubt, initiative versus guilt, and industry versus inferiority.

5. During adolescence, self-concepts become more psychological, abstract, and integrated, and self-awareness increases. Most adolescents experience no more than temporary disturbances in self-esteem at the onset of adolescence.

6. The most difficult challenge of adolescence is resolving Erikson's conflict of identity versus role confusion. From the diffusion and foreclosure identity statuses, many college-aged youth progress to the moratorium status and ultimately to the identity achievement status. Identity formation is an uneven process that often continues into adulthood and that is influenced by cognitive development and by social experiences such as interactions with loving parents who encourage individuality.

7. During adulthood, self-conceptions and self-esteem change relatively little, although the gap between the ideal and the real self shrinks with age. Indi-

viduals' rankings on the "big five" dimensions of personality remain quite stable after very early adulthood.

8. From adolescence to middle adulthood, many people appear to gain confidence, autonomy, nurturance, and other personal strengths; from middle age to old age only a few systematic changes occur, notably decreased activity and increased introspectiveness.

9. Stability of personality may be due to genetic makeup, lasting effects of early experience, and the fact that people seek out and encounter experiences that reinforce their earlier personalities. Personality change may be associated with changes in the social environment and lack of goodness of fit between person and environment.

10. Erikson's theory of psychosocial development is supported by evidence that a sense of identity lays a foundation for achieving a sense of intimacy. Vaillant's research suggests stages of intimacy versus isolation, career consolidation, and generativity versus stagnation. The process of life review may help elderly people resolve Erikson's final issue of integrity versus despair.

11. The development of the emotional self begins in infancy. Biologically based primary emotions become socialized in the first year through modeling, reinforcement, and social referencing; secondary emotions emerge in the second and third years. Children rapidly become more knowledgeable about emotions, begin to use emotional expressions deliberately as tools of communication, and learn cultural display rules governing emotional expression.

12. People's emotional personalities are well formed by adulthood, and there is little evidence that elderly people experience fewer or more negative emotions than younger adults do.

13. Children's self-esteem can be strengthened by parents who are warm and democratic and by teachers who establish multidimensional classrooms in which many different abilities are valued. The self-esteem of older adults can be increased by reducing their tendency to internalize ageist attitudes and to blame difficulties on old age.

KEY TERMS

ageism
autonomy versus shame and doubt
behavioral inhibition
career consolidation stage
categorical self
difficult temperament
diffusion status
display rules
easy temperament
ethnic identity
foreclosure status
generativity versus stagnation
goodness of fit
identity
identity achievement status
identity versus role confusion
industry versus inferiority
initiative versus guilt
integrity versus despair
intimacy versus isolation
life review
looking-glass self
moratorium status
negative identity
personality
self-concept
self-esteem
slow-to-warm-up temperament
social comparison
social referencing
stability of individual differences
stability of mean levels
temperament
trust versus mistrust

11

GENDER ROLES AND SEXUALITY

When Rani, a farm laborer in India, returned from the hospital with her newborn daughter, she and her family did not celebrate the blessed event. Instead, she and her mother-in-law mashed up some oleander seeds in oil and forced the poisonous mixture down the baby's throat (Anderson & Moore, 1993). Asked about it afterward, Rani expressed no regret: "There was a lot of bitterness in my heart toward the baby because the gods should have given me a son" (p. A1). In one rural community in India, more than half of the women surveyed admitted to having killed at least one daughter, often with scalding soup; in urban areas, modern technologies such as amniocentesis and ultrasound allow women to rid themselves of unwanted daughters before they are born (Anderson & Moore, 1993). Across India, parents celebrate the birth of a boy and mourn the birth of a girl, mainly because daughters require large dowries when they marry.

It is also estimated that over 5000 Indian women are burned to death with kerosene, driven to suicide, or otherwise murdered each year by their husbands or in-laws because their families cannot deliver sufficient dowry money (Anderson & Moore, 1993). If they are allowed to live, poor Indian women can look forward to hard physical labor for 14 hours a day, eight or nine pregnancies over their reproductive lives, and an early death. In India, as in many other Third World countries, one's biological sex makes a big difference in how life goes, and life can be harsh indeed if one is unfortunate enough to have received two X chromosomes at conception.

In our society, too, gender matters. When proud new parents telephone to announce a birth, the first question friends and family tend to ask is "Is it a boy or a girl?" (Intons-Peterson & Reddel, 1984). Before long, girls discover that they are girls and may acquire a taste for frilly dresses and dollhouses, while boys discover that they are boys and often wrestle each other on the lawn. As adults, we never lose our awareness of being either men or women. We define ourselves partly in terms of our "feminine" or "masculine" qualities, and we play roles that conform to society's view of what a woman or a man should be. In short, being female or male is a highly important aspect of the self throughout the life span.

Gender-role socialization begins very early as parents provide their infants with "gender-appropriate" clothing, toys, and hairstyles.

In this chapter we'll be looking at how the characteristics and life experiences of male and female humans are similar and different—and why. We'll see how girls and boys learn to play their parts as girls or boys and how they are groomed for their roles as women or men. We'll also consider some of the ways in which adult men and women are steered along different developmental paths in our society. In addition, we'll examine the development of sexuality and its implications for relationships between the sexes.

MALE AND FEMALE: SORTING OUT THE DIFFERENCES

What difference does it make whether one is a male or a female? It matters in terms of physical differences, psychological differences, and differences in roles played in society. The physical differences are undeniable. A zygote that receives an X chromosome from each parent is a genetic (XX) female, whereas a zygote that receives a Y chromosome from the father is a genetic (XY) male. Chromosomal differences result in different prenatal hormone balances in males and females, and hormones are responsible for the facts that the genitals of males and females differ and that only females can bear children. Moreover, males typically grow to be taller, heavier, and more muscular than females, although females may be the hardier sex in that they live longer and are less susceptible to many physical disorders. As we'll see later in the chapter, some theorists argue that biological differences between males and females are ultimately responsible for psychological and social differences as well.

However, there is much more to being male or female than biology. Virtually all societies expect the two sexes to adopt different **gender roles,** the patterns of behavior and traits that define how a female or a male should act in a particular society.[1] Characteristics and behaviors viewed as desirable for males or females are specified in **gender-role norms**—that is, society's expectations or standards concerning what males and females *should* be like (Pleck, 1981). Each society's norms generate **gender-role stereotypes,** which are overgeneralized and largely inaccurate beliefs about what males and females *are* like (Pleck, 1981). Through the process of **gender typing,** children not only become aware that they are biological males or females but also acquire the motives, values, and patterns of behavior that their culture considers appropriate for members of their biological sex. Through the gender-typing process, for example, little Susie might learn a gender-role norm stating that women should strive to be good mothers and gender-role stereotypes indicating that women are more skilled at nurturing children than men are. As an adult, Susan might then adopt the traditional feminine role by switching from full- to part-time work when her first child is born and devoting herself to the task of mothering.

We would be very mistaken, then, to credit any differences that we observe between girls and boys (or women and men) to biological causes. They could just as easily be due to differences in the ways males and females are perceived and raised. But, before we try to explain sex differences, perhaps we should find out what these differences are believed to be and what they actually are.

[1]We use the term *sex* when we are referring to the distinction between biological males and biological females and the term *gender* when we are discussing masculine and feminine traits and behavior patterns that develop as social influences interact with biology. Although many developmentalists speak of *sex roles* or *sex-role stereotypes* where we speak of *gender roles* or *gender-role stereotypes,* we believe that it is useful to emphasize through our use of terms that most differences between the sexes are not purely biological but instead are related to socialization experiences.

Gender Norms and Stereotypes

Which sex is more likely to express emotions? To be tidy? To be competitive? To use harsh language? If you are like most people, you undoubtedly have ideas about how men and women differ psychologically and can offer some ready answers to these questions.

The female's role as childbearer has shaped the gender-role norms that prevail in many societies, including our own. Girls have typically been encouraged to assume an **expressive role** that involves being kind, nurturant, cooperative, and sensitive to the needs of others (Parsons, 1955). These psychological traits, it is assumed, will prepare girls to play the roles of wife and mother—to keep the family functioning and to raise children successfully. By contrast, boys have been encouraged to adopt an **instrumental role,** for as a traditionally defined husband and father the male faces the tasks of providing for the family and protecting it from harm. Thus boys are expected to become dominant, independent, assertive, and competitive. Similar norms for males and females apply in many, though certainly not all, societies (Barry, Bacon, & Child, 1957; Whiting & Edwards, 1988; Williams & Best, 1990).

Because cultural norms demand that females play an expressive role and males play an instrumental role, we tend to form stereotypes saying that females possess expressive traits and males possess instrumental traits (Broverman et al., 1972; Eagly, 1987; Williams & Best, 1990). If you're thinking that these stereotypes have disappeared as attention to women's rights has increased and as more women have entered the labor force, think again. Although some change has occurred, adolescents and young adults still endorse most traditional stereotypes about men and women (Bergen & Williams, 1991; Lewin & Tragos, 1987). Might these beliefs about sex differences have a basis in fact, then? Let's see.

Actual Psychological Differences between the Sexes

In a classic review of more than 1500 studies comparing males and females, Eleanor Maccoby and Carol Jacklin (1974) concluded that only four common gender stereotypes are reasonably accurate (that is, consistently supported by research). Here are their conclusions, with some updates and amendments:

1. Females have greater *verbal abilities* than males. According to Maccoby and Jacklin's review, girls tend to develop verbal skills at an earlier age than boys and show a small but consistent advantage on tests of vocabulary, reading comprehension, and speech fluency. However, recent reviewers have concluded that sex differences in verbal ability have all but disappeared,

so Maccoby and Jacklin's conclusion may no longer be valid (Feingold, 1988; Hyde & Linn, 1988).

2. Males outperform females on tests of *visual/spatial ability* (for example, arranging blocks in patterns, identifying the same figure from different angles). Although Maccoby and Jacklin concluded that these differences emerge only in adolescence, they can be detected in childhood and persist across the life span (Kerns & Berenbaum, 1991; Linn & Petersen, 1985).

3. Similarly, males outperform females, on the average, on tests of *mathematical ability,* starting in adolescence. A recent review of the evidence by Janet Hyde and her associates (1990) suggests that girls actually have a slight edge in computational skills and that the sexes do not differ at all in their understanding of math concepts, although males perform better than females on mathematical word problems starting in adolescence and continuing into adulthood. However, within the general population, sex differences in mathematical ability are negligible. The male advantage in mathematical problem-solving skills is evident mainly in samples of high math performers, suggesting that more males than females are mathematically talented. As it turns out, more males than females are also *low* math achievers; on a number of cognitive ability tests, more males than females show up both at the top and at the bottom of the scale (Feingold, 1992).

4. Finally, males are more physically and verbally *aggressive* than females, starting as early as age 2 (see also Eagly & Steffen, 1986).

Since the publication of Maccoby and Jacklin's monumental review, some researchers have argued that there are more true sex differences than Maccoby and Jacklin claimed (for example, Block, 1976; Huston, 1983). Among the additional sex differences suggested are these: (1) boys, starting in infancy, appear to have a higher activity level than girls (Eaton & Enns, 1986; Eaton & Yu, 1989); (2) boys are more developmentally vulnerable to prenatal and perinatal stress, disease, and disorders such as reading disabilities, speech defects, hyperactivity, emotional problems, and mental retardation (Henker & Whalen, 1989; Jacklin, 1989); (3) girls are more compliant with the requests of parents, teachers, and other authority figures (though not with the demands of peers); (4) girls are more likely to use tactful and cooperative, rather than forceful and demanding, tactics when attempting to induce others to comply with them (Cowan & Avants, 1988; Maccoby, 1990); and (5) girls rate themselves higher in the traits of nurturance and empathy (though their behavior does not always differ from that of boys; see Fabes, Eisenberg, & Miller, 1990).

Other researchers take the contrasting view that even the largest of the "real" psychological differences between the sexes are trivial. For example, if

Boys are more aggressive and active than girls and engage in a good deal more rough-and-tumble play.

you imagine all the differences in aggressiveness among children or adults, from the most aggressive to the least aggressive person in a group, it turns out that only 5% of that variation can be traced to whether a person is a male or a female (Hyde, 1984). Apparently the remaining 95% of the variation is due to other differences among people. In other words, *average* levels of aggression for males and females may be noticeably different, but within each sex there are both extremely aggressive and extremely nonaggressive individuals: It is impossible to predict accurately how aggressive a person is simply by knowing his or her gender. Sex differences in other abilities are similarly small (Caplan, MacPherson, & Tobin, 1985; Hyde, 1981; Hyde & Linn, 1988; see also Figure 11.1). Moreover, these sex differences appear to be even smaller today than they used to be (Feingold, 1988; Hyde et al., 1990).

Where is all the evidence that males possess instrumental traits and females possess expressive traits? Where is the evidence that females are more social and more suggestible or that they have lower self-esteem, lack achievement motivation, or are less capable of logical thought? Most of our stereotypes of males and females are just that—overgeneralizations unsupported by fact (Maccoby & Jacklin, 1974). Why do unfounded stereotypes persist? Partly because we, as the holders of male/female stereotypes, are biased in our perceptions. We are more likely to notice and remember behaviors that confirm our beliefs than to

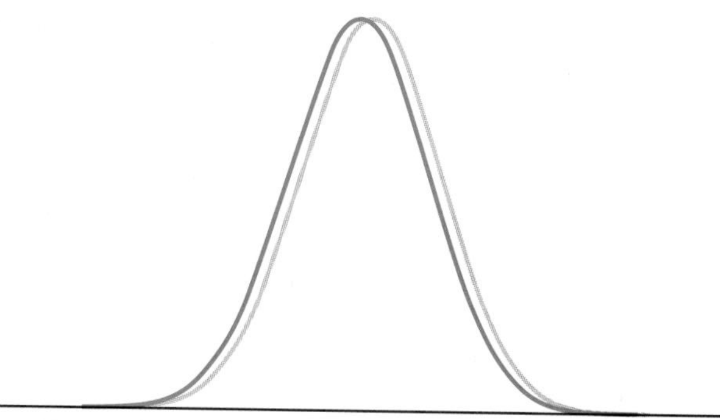

FIGURE 11.1 These two distributions of scores—one for males, one for females—indicate the size of the gap between the sexes in abilities for which sex differences are consistently found. Despite a small difference in average performance, the scores of males and females overlap considerably. (Adapted from Hyde et al., 1990.)

notice exceptions such as independent behavior in a woman or emotional sensitivity in a man (Martin & Halverson, 1981).

Alice Eagly (1987) suggests that differences in the roles that women and men play in society also do a lot to create and maintain gender-role stereotypes. For example, men have traditionally occupied powerful roles in business and industry that require them to be dominant and forceful. Women have more often filled the role of homemaker and therefore have been called upon to be nurturant and sensitive to their children's needs. As a result, we begin to see men as by nature "dominant" and women as by nature "nurturant." We lose sight of the fact that it is differences in the social roles they play that cause men and women to behave differently. It does not occur to us that sex differences in behavior might actually be reversed if women ran companies and men raised children.

As Eagly's social-role hypothesis suggests, we must adopt a contextual perspective on psychological differences between males and females. Sex differences that are evident in one social context often are not evident in another (Deaux & Major, 1990; Maccoby, 1990). For example, women do better on tests of mathematical ability—and sometimes even outperform men—in countries like Israel, where women have excellent occupational opportunities in technical fields (Baker & Jones, 1992). This suggests that sex differences in abilities are not biologically inevitable and that cultural influences on male and female development are significant.

Situational factors can be critical as well. For example, Eleanor Maccoby (1990) has concluded that boys and girls do not differ much at all in psychological traits but that they do behave differently in mixed-sex settings than when they are with members of their own sex. For instance, kindergarten and first-grade girls stay closer to an adult than boys do when they are part of a mixed-sex group (most likely to assure themselves of protection should the boys start any trouble) but stray *farther* from the adult than boys do when they are part of an all-girl group (Greeno, cited in Maccoby, 1990). Girls are not *generally* more dependent on adults than boys, then; it all depends on the social context.

Similarly, women do not *always* lack confidence in their academic abilities, as some researchers have suggested. In one study, college women gave lower estimates of their likely grade-point average than men did *only* when they had to state their predictions publicly—not when the estimates were made privately (Daubman, Heatherington, & Ahn, 1992). These women did not lack confidence; they simply did not want to appear boastful or make others feel inferior. From a contextual perspective, it is really quite silly to speak about the "nature of women" or the "nature of men," for differences between males and females can be large or small depending on the social contexts in which they find themselves.

What should we conclude, then, about psychological differences between the sexes? There is bound to be continuing disagreement among different scholars about which psychological differences are real and which are not. Despite their quibbles, however, most developmentalists can agree on this: *The vast majority of gender stereotypes are not supported by fact.* In truth, males and females are far more psychologically *similar* than they are different, and even the most well-documented differences seem to be modest.

Yet it *does* make a very real difference in our society whether one is a male or a female. First, gender norms and stereotypes, even when they are unfounded, do affect how we perceive ourselves and other people. As long as people expect females to be less competent in math than males, for example, females may well lack confidence in their abilities and perform less competently (Eccles, Jacobs, & Harold, 1990). The fact that many stereotypes are unfounded does not make them any less potent.

In addition, even though males and females are not very different psychologically, they are still steered toward different *roles in society* (Ruble, 1988). In childhood, girls and boys conform to their gender roles by segregating themselves by sex and developing different interests and play activities (Huston, 1985). As adolescents and adults, males and females pursue different vocations and lifestyles. Although more women are entering male-dominated fields today than in the past, men are not often entering female-dominated fields, and most high school students continue to aspire toward occupations that are dominated by members of their own sex (Hannah & Kahn, 1989). If you go to a college graduation ceremony today, you will still see relatively few women among the engineers and few men among the nursing graduates. More men are sharing child-rearing and household responsibilities with their partners today, but most couples still divide the labor along traditional lines, so that she is primarily responsible for child care and housework while he is primarily responsible for income and money management (Zick & McCullough, 1991). When we think about who asks whom out on a date, who stays home from work when a child has the chicken pox, or who sews the buttons back on shirts, we must conclude that traditional gender roles are alive and well, despite significant social change!

In short, we continue to live in a society where, for better or for worse, being male or female *matters*. The psychological differences between the sexes may be few and small, but the physical differences are always visible, and the roles that most men and women play in society continue to differ. So now let's trace how girls and boys master their "gender-role curriculum" and how they apply what they learn throughout their lives.

THE INFANT

At birth there are very few differences, other than the obvious anatomical ones, between males and females (Maccoby & Jacklin, 1974), and even these few differences tend to be small and inconsistent. Nonetheless, it does not take long at all after newborns are labeled as girls or boys for gender stereotypes to affect how they are perceived and treated—and for infants themselves to notice that males and females are different.

Sex Differences and Early Gender-Role Learning

While the baby is still in the hospital delivery room or nursery, parents tend to call an infant son "big guy" or "tiger" and to comment on the vigor of his cries, kicks, and grasps. Girl infants are more likely to be labeled "sugar" or "sweetie" and to be described as soft, cuddly, and adorable (Maccoby, 1980; MacFarlane, 1977). Even when objective examinations reveal no such differences between boys and girls at birth, parents perceive boys as strong, large featured, and coordinated and girls as weaker, finer featured, and more awkward (Rubin, Provenzano, & Luria, 1974; see also Burnham & Harris, 1992; Stern & Karraker, 1989). Soon boys and girls are decked out in either blue or pink and provided with "sex-appropriate" hairstyles, toys, and room furnishings (Pomerleau et al., 1990; Rheingold & Cook, 1975). In one study (Condry & Condry, 1976), college students watched a videotape of a 9-month-old infant who was introduced as either a girl ("Dana") or a boy ("David"). Students who saw "David" interpreted his strong reaction to a jack-in-the-box as "anger," whereas students who watched "Dana" concluded that the very same behavior was "fear." Although stereotyping of boys and girls from birth could be partly the effect of actual differences between the sexes (Burnham & Harris, 1992), it is also likely to be the *cause* of differences between the sexes.

Yet infants are not merely the passive targets of other people's reactions to them; they are actively trying to get to know the social world around them, as well as themselves. By the end of the first year, babies can already distinguish women from men in photographs and perceive them as different kinds of people (Fagot & Leinbach, 1993; Lewis & Brooks-Gunn, 1979). As they begin to categorize other people as males and females, they also establish which of these two significant social categories they themselves belong to. By 18 months of age, most toddlers seem to have a primitive knowledge that they are either like other males or like other females, even if they cannot verbalize it (Lewis & Weinraub, 1979). Almost all children give verbal proof that they have acquired a firm **gender identity,** or an awareness that they are either a boy or a girl, by the age of 2½ to 3 (Thompson, 1975).

As they acquire their gender identities, boys and girls are also beginning to behave differently. Boys aged 14 to 22 months usually prefer trucks and cars to other playthings, whereas girls of this age would rather play with dolls and soft toys (Smith & Daglish, 1977). Many 18- to 24-month-old toddlers will actually refuse to play with toys regarded as appropriate for the other sex—even when there are no other toys to play with (Caldera, Huston, & O'Brien, 1989). As they approach the age of 2, then, infants are already beginning to behave in ways that are considered gender appropriate in our society.

In sum, the two years of infancy lay the groundwork for later gender-role development. Because their sex is important to those around them, and because they see for themselves that males and females differ, infants begin to form categories of "male" and "female," establish a basic gender identity, and pursue "gender-appropriate" pastimes (Lewis & Weinraub, 1979). What's more, they begin the process of becoming sexual beings.

Infant Sexuality

It was Sigmund Freud who made the seemingly outrageous claim that humans are sexual beings from birth onward. We are born, he said, with a reserve of sexual energy that is redirected toward different parts of the body as we develop. Freud may have been wrong about some things, but he was quite right about the fact that infants are sexual beings.

Babies are, of course, biologically equipped at birth with male or female chromosomes, hormones, and genitals. Moreover, young infants in Freud's oral stage of development *do* appear to derive pleasure from sucking, mouthing, biting, and other oral activities. But the clincher is this: Both male babies (Kinsey, Pomeroy, & Martin, 1948) and female babies (Bakwin, 1973) have been observed to touch and manipulate their genital areas, to experience physical arousal, and to undergo what appear to be orgasms (relaxing and turning paler after having been flushed and agitated). Parents in some cultures, well aware of the pleasure infants derive from their genitals, occasionally use genital stimulation as a means of soothing fussy babies (Ford & Beach, 1951).

What should we make of this infant sexuality? Infants feel bodily sensations, but they are hardly aware that their behavior is "sexual." How unfortunate, then, that the mother of one infant girl studied by Bakwin was apparently shocked by this "immoral" behavior and slapped and scolded her innocent child (to no avail). Infants are sexual beings primarily in the sense that their genitals are sensitive and their nervous systems allow sexual responses. They are also as curious about their bodies as they are about the rest of the world. It will not be too long, however, before they begin to learn what human sexuality is about and how the members of their society regard it.

THE CHILD

Because much of the "action" in gender-role development takes place during the toddler and preschool years, we will look closely at what happens then and how different theorists explain it. We'll also discuss how children express curiosity about their bodies and learn about human sexuality.

Gender-Role Development

Very young children rapidly acquire (1) a gender identity—the knowledge that they are boys or girls (and that they will be that way for life); (2) gender stereotypes, or ideas about what males and females are supposedly like; and (3) gender-typed behavior patterns, or tendencies to favor "gender-appropriate" activities and behaviors over those typically associated with the other sex.

Understanding Gender Identity

A critical milestone in gender-role development is acquiring a gender identity. As we have noted, almost all children can accurately label themselves as either boys or girls by the age of 2½ to 3 (Thompson, 1975). It will take longer for them to grasp the fact that a person's biological sex remains the same despite superficial changes. Many 3- to 5-year-olds think that boys can become mommies or girls daddies if they really want to, or that a person who changes hairstyle or clothing can become a member of the other sex (Marcus & Overton, 1978; Slaby & Frey, 1975). Children normally begin to understand that sex is an unchanging quality between the ages of 5 and 7—about when they grasp Piaget's concept of conservation and realize that physical quantities do not change just because their appearance changes. As a result, children enter grade school with a "stable" identity as a male or female.

Acquiring Gender Stereotypes

Remarkable as it may seem, toddlers begin to learn society's gender stereotypes at about the same time they become aware of their basic gender identities. Deanna Kuhn and her associates (Kuhn, Nash, & Brucken, 1978) showed a male doll ("Michael") and a female doll ("Lisa") to children aged 2½ to 3½ and asked each child which of the two dolls would engage in various sex-stereotyped activities. Even among the 2½-year-olds, many boys and girls agreed that girls talk a lot, never hit, often need help, like to play with dolls, and like to help their mothers with chores such as cooking and cleaning. Boys, of course, like to play with cars, help their fathers, build things, and utter comments like "I can hit you." Apparently 2- and 3-year-olds are well on their way to becoming sexists!

Over the next several years, children's heads become filled with considerably more "knowledge" about how males and females differ (Serbin, Powlishta, & Gulko, 1993). As we saw in Chapter 10, during the elementary school years children begin to describe themselves in terms of their underlying psychological traits, rather than just their observable physical characteristics and activities. Similarly, elementary school children begin to understand stereotypes that describe the supposed *psychological traits* of males and females. For example, Deborah Best and her colleagues (1977) found that fourth- and fifth-graders in England, Ireland, and the United States generally agreed that women are weak, emotional, softhearted, sophisticated, and affectionate, whereas men are ambitious, assertive, aggressive, dominating, and cruel.

How seriously do children take the gender-role norms and expectations that they are rapidly learning? William Damon (1977) told children aged 4 to 9 a story about a little boy named George who insists on playing with dolls, even though his parents have told him that dolls are for girls and that boys should play with other toys. Children were then asked a number of questions to assess their impressions of gender roles.

Four-year-olds believed that doll play and other cross-sex behaviors are okay if that is what George really wants to do. As 4-year-old Jack put it, "It's up to him" (Damon, 1977, p. 249). By age 6, about the time they understand that their sex will remain constant, children become extremely rigid in their thinking and intolerant of anyone who violates traditional gender-role standards. These norms now have the force of absolute moral laws and must be obeyed. Consider the reaction of 6-year-old Michael to George's doll play:

> (*Why do you think people tell George not to play with dolls?*) Well, he should only play with things

that boys play with. The things that he is playing with now is girls' stuff. . . . (*Can George play with Barbie dolls if he wants to?*) No sir! . . . (*What should George do?*) He should stop playing with girls' dolls and start playing with G.I. Joe. (*Why can a boy play with G.I. Joe and not a Barbie doll?*) Because if a boy is playing with a Barbie doll, then he's just going to get people teasing him [Damon, 1977, p. 255; italics added].

The oldest children in Damon's sample were more flexible in their thinking and less chauvinistic (see also Martin, 1989; Serbin et al., 1993). Note how 9-year-old James distinguishes between moral rules that we are obligated to obey and gender-role standards or customs that do not have this same moral force:

> (*What if . . . he kept playing with dolls? Do you think [his parents] would punish him?*) No. (*How come?*) It's not really doing anything bad. (*Why isn't it bad?*) Because . . . if he was breaking a window, and he kept on doing that, they could punish him, because you're not supposed to break windows. But if you want to you can play with dolls. (*What's the difference . . . ?*) Well, breaking windows you're not supposed to do. And if you play with dolls, you can, but boys usually don't [Damon, 1977, p. 263; italics added].

Why do 6- or 7-year-olds interpret gender stereotypes as though they were absolute moral rules rather than social conventions? Perhaps it is because they view any rule or custom as a natural law, like the law of gravity, that must always be correct (Carter & Patterson, 1982). Or perhaps these young children must exaggerate gender roles in order to "get them cognitively clear" (Maccoby, 1980). Once their gender identities are more firmly established, they can afford to be more flexible in their thinking about what is "for boys" and what is "for girls."

The Development of Gender-Typed Behavior

Finally, children rapidly come to behave in "gender-appropriate" ways. As we have seen, preferences for gender-appropriate toys are already detectable in infancy. Apparently, babies develop clear preferences for "boy" toys or "girl" toys even before they have established clear identities as males or females or can correctly label toys as "boy things" or "girl things" (Blakemore, LaRue, & Olejnik, 1979; Fagot, Leinbach, & Hagan, 1986). Moreover, children quickly come to favor same-sex playmates. In one study (Jacklin & Maccoby, 1978), pairs of 33-month-old toddlers (two boys, two girls, or a boy and a girl) were placed in a laboratory playroom and observed to see how often they engaged in solitary activities and how often they engaged in social play. As we see in Figure 11.2, both boys and girls were more sociable with same-sex peers than with other-sex peers.

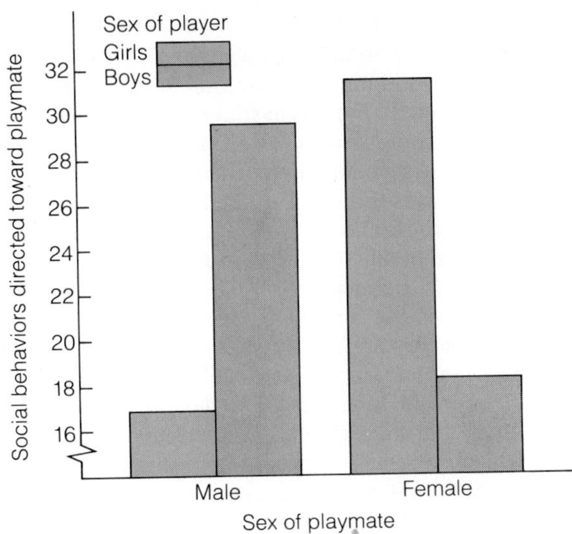

FIGURE 11.2 Do toddlers prefer playmates of their own sex? Apparently so, for boys are much more sociable with boys than with girls, whereas girls are more outgoing with girls than with boys. (Based on Jacklin & Maccoby, 1978.)

During the elementary school years, boys and girls develop even stronger preferences for peers of their own sex and show increased **gender segregation,** separating themselves into boys' and girls' peer groups and interacting far more often with their own sex than with the other sex (Thorne, 1993). Gender segregation occurs in a variety of cultures (Whiting & Edwards, 1988), and Eleanor Maccoby (1988, 1990) suggests that it is due in part to incompatibilities between boys' and girls' play styles. Basically, boys are too rowdy and domineering to suit the tastes of many girls, who prefer less roughhousing and rely on polite negotiations rather than shows of brute force to settle disputes (see also Bukowski et al., 1993). Alan Sroufe and his colleagues (1993) find that those 10- and 11-year-olds who insist most strongly on clear boundaries between the sexes and avoid consorting with "the enemy" tend to be socially competent and popular, whereas children who violate gender segregation rules tend to be less well adjusted.

Boys face stronger pressures to adhere to gender-role expectations than girls do. This may be why they develop stronger gender-typed preferences at earlier ages (Blakemore et al., 1979; Bussey & Bandura, 1992; Lobel & Menashri, 1993). In the early 1980s, John Richardson and Carl Simpson (1982) recorded the toy preferences of 750 children aged 5 to 9 years as expressed in their letters to Santa Claus. As Table 11.1 illustrates, both boys and girls expressed gender-typed preferences, but far more girls than boys asked for "opposite-sex" items. This is still true in the 1990s (Etaugh & Liss, 1992). Just ask your female classmates if they were "tomboys" when they were

TABLE 11.1 Percentages of boys and girls who requested popular "masculine" and "feminine" items from Santa Claus.

Items	*Percentage of Boys Requesting*	*Percenage of Girls Requesting*
Masculine items		
Vehicles	43.5	8.2
Sports equipment	25.1	15.1
Spatial-temporal toys (construction sets, clocks, and so on)	24.5	15.6
Race cars	23.4	5.1
Real vehicles (tricycles, bikes, motorbikes)	15.3	9.7
Feminine items		
Dolls (adult female)	.6	27.4
Dolls (babies)	.6	23.4
Domestic accessories	1.7	21.7
Dollhouses	1.9	16.1
Stuffed animals	5.0	5.4

SOURCE: Based on Richardson & Simpson, 1982.

young, and you're likely to find that most were (Hyde, Rosenberg, & Behrman, 1977). But we defy you to find many male classmates who are willing to admit that they were "sissies" in their youth! The masculine role is very clearly defined in our society, and boys are ridiculed and rejected if they do not conform to it (Martin, 1990). Since girls are given more leeway to engage in cross-sex activities, and since they soon discover that the masculine role has greater status in society and that many "male" activities are fun, it is understandable that many of them are drawn to masculine activities during childhood.

In sum, gender-role development proceeds with remarkable speed. By the time they enter school, children have long been aware of their basic gender identities, have acquired many stereotypes about how the sexes differ, and have come to prefer gender-appropriate activities and same-sex playmates. During middle childhood their knowledge continues to expand as they learn more about gender-stereotyped psychological traits, although they become more flexible in their thinking about gender roles. Yet their *behavior,* especially if they are boys, becomes even more gender-typed, and they segregate themselves even more from the other sex. Now the most intriguing question: How does all this happen?

Theories of Gender-Role Development

Several theories have been proposed to account for sex differences and the development of gender roles. Some theories emphasize the role of biological differences between the sexes, whereas others emphasize social influences on children. Some emphasize what society does to children, others what children do to themselves as they try to understand gender and all its implications. Let's briefly examine a biologically oriented theory and then consider the more "social" approaches offered by psychoanalytic theory, social learning theory, cognitive-developmental theory, and gender schema theory.

Money and Ehrhardt's Biosocial Theory

The biosocial theory of gender-role development proposed by John Money and Anke Ehrhardt (1972) calls attention to the ways in which biological events influence the development of boys and girls. But it also focuses on ways in which early biological developments influence how people *react* to a child and suggests that these social reactions then have much to do with children's assuming gender roles.

Chromosomes, Hormones, and Social Labeling of the Sexes.

Money and Ehrhardt stress that the male (XY) or female (XX) chromosomes one receives at conception are merely a starting point in biological differentiation between the sexes. A number of critical events affect a person's eventual preference for the masculine or feminine role. If a Y chromosome is present, a previously undifferentiated tissue develops into testes as the embryo develops; otherwise it develops into ovaries. At a second critical point, the testes of a male embryo normally secrete the male hormone *testosterone,* which stimulates the development of a male internal reproductive system, and another hormone that inhibits the development of female organs. Without these hormones the internal reproductive system of a female will develop from the same tissues. At a third critical point, three to four months after conception, secretion of testosterone by the testes normally leads to the growth of a penis and scrotum. If testosterone is absent (as in normal females) or if a male fetus's cells are insensitive to the male sex hormones he produces, female external genitalia (labia and clitoris) will form. Finally, testosterone alters the development of the brain and nervous system. For example, it signals the male brain to stop secreting hormones in a cyclical pattern so that males do not experience menstrual cycles at puberty. Clearly, then, fertilized eggs have the potential to acquire the anatomical and physiological features of either sex. Events at each critical step in the sexual differentiation process determine the outcome.

Once a biological male or female is born, social factors immediately enter the picture. Parents and other people label and begin to react to the child on the basis of the appearance of his or her genitalia. If a child's genitals are abnormal and he or she is mislabeled as a member of the other sex, this incorrect label will have an impact of its own on the child's future development. For example, if a biological male were consistently labeled and treated as a girl, he would, by about age 3, acquire the gender identity of

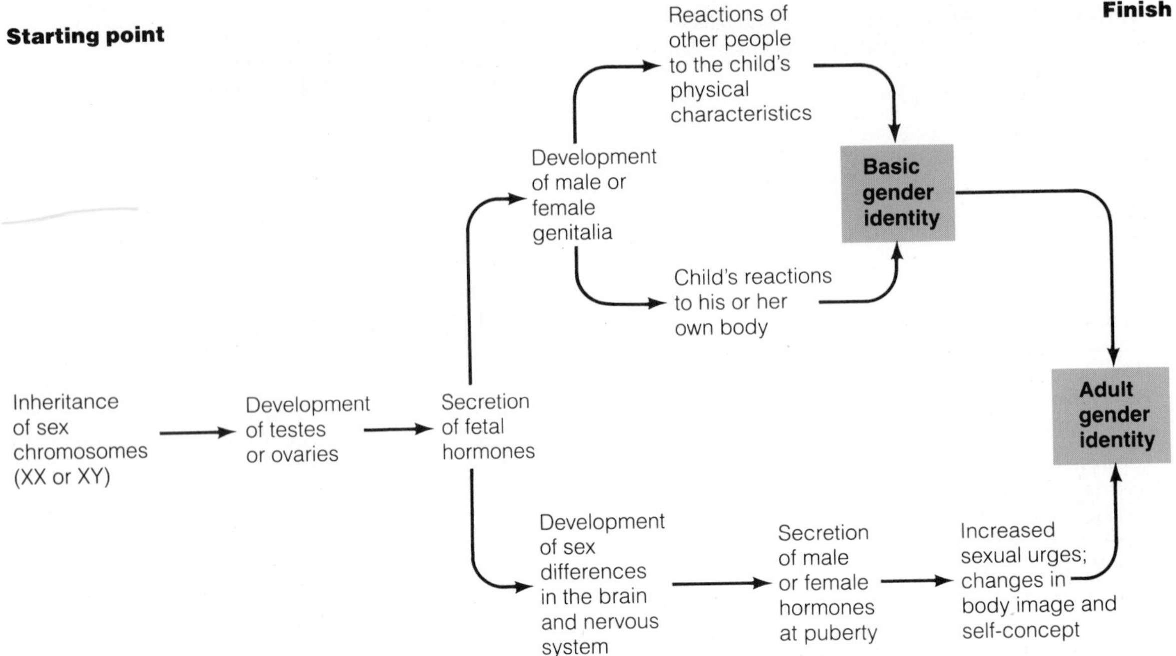

FIGURE 11.3 Critical events in Money and Ehrhardt's biosocial theory of gender typing. (From Money & Ehrhardt, 1972.)

a girl. Finally, biological factors enter the scene again at puberty when large quantities of hormones are released, stimulating the growth of the reproductive system, the appearance of secondary sex characteristics, and the development of sexual urges. These events, in combination with one's earlier self-concept as a male or female, provide the basis for adult gender identity and role behavior. The complex series of critical points that Money and Ehrhardt propose is diagrammed in Figure 11.3.

Evidence of Biological Influences. Biological factors do influence the development of males and females. For example, studies of twins tell us that individual heredity accounts for 20–50% of the variability in the extent to which people describe themselves as having masculine and feminine psychological traits (Loehlin, 1992; Mitchell, Baker, & Jacklin, 1989). The remaining variation in self-perceived masculinity and femininity can be attributed to differences in experience.

Biological influences on development are also evident in studies of children who are exposed to the "wrong" hormones prenatally (Ehrhardt & Baker, 1974; Money & Ehrhardt, 1972; see also Gandelman, 1992). Before the consequences were known, some mothers who had had problems carrying pregnancies to term were given drugs containing progestins, which are converted by the body into the male hormone testosterone. These drugs had the effect of masculinizing female fetuses so that, despite their XX genetic endowment and female internal organs, they were born with external organs that resembled those of a boy (for example, a large clitoris that looked like a penis and fused labia that resembled a scrotum). Several of these **androgenized females** (girls exposed to excess androgens) were recognized as genetic females, underwent surgery to alter their genitals, and were then raised as girls. When Money and Ehrhardt compared them with their sisters and other girls, it became apparent that many more androgenized girls were tomboys and preferred boys' toys and vigorous activities to traditionally feminine pursuits (see also Berenbaum & Hines, 1992). As adolescents they began dating somewhat later than other girls and felt that marriage should be delayed until they had established their careers. A high proportion (37%) described themselves as homosexual or bisexual (Money, 1985; see also Dittman, Kappes, & Kappes, 1992). Androgenized females also perform better than most other females on tests of spatial ability, which is further evidence that early exposure to male hormones has "masculinizing" effects on a female fetus (Kimura, 1992; Resnick et al., 1986).

Finally, male exposure to testosterone and other male hormones may be part of the reason why males are more aggressive and commit more violent acts than females (Archer, 1991; Jacklin, 1989). Evidence from experiments conducted with animals is quite convincing. For example, female rhesus monkeys exposed prenatally to the male hormone testosterone often threaten other monkeys, engage in rough-and-tumble play, and try to "mount" a partner as males do at the beginning of a sexual encounter (Young, Goy, & Phoenix, 1964). Men with high testosterone levels tend to have high rates of delinquency, drug abuse, abusiveness, and violence (Dabbs & Morris, 1990). Because testosterone levels rise as a result of aggressive and competitive activities, it has been difficult to establish unambiguously that high concentrations of male hormones *cause* aggressive behavior in humans (Archer, 1991). Still, there is reason to believe that biological factors contribute to sex differences in sexual aspects of development.

Evidence of Social-Labeling Influences. At the same time, we must also take seriously the *social* aspect of Money and Ehrhardt's biosocial theory. How a child is labeled and treated can also have a considerable impact on gender development. For instance, some androgenized females have been labeled as boys at birth and raised as such until their abnormalities were detected. Money and Ehrhardt (1972) report that the discovery and correction of this condition (by surgery and relabeling as a girl) caused few if any adjustment problems if the sex change took place *before the age of 18 months.* After age 3, sexual reassignment was exceedingly difficult because these genetic females had experienced prolonged masculine gender typing and had already labeled themselves as boys. These findings led Money to conclude that there is a *critical period* (between 18 months and 3 years) for the establishment of gender identity when the label society attaches to the child is likely to "stick." Box 11.1 presents further support for this critical-period concept, as well as evidence that it might better be termed a *sensitive* period.

In sum, Money and Ehrhardt's biosocial theory stresses the importance of early biological developments that influence how parents and other social agents label a child at birth and that possibly also affect behavior more directly. However, the theory also holds that whether children are socialized as boys or girls strongly influences their gender-role development. In short, biological and social factors interact.

Freud's Psychoanalytic Theory

Freud viewed both biology (the sex instinct that is rechanneled toward different parts of the body with age) and environment (especially the ways in which parents treat a child) as responsible for sex-role

BOX 11.1 Is Biology Destiny?

When biological sex and social labeling conflict, which wins out? Consider the fascinating case of a male identical twin whose penis was damaged beyond repair during circumcision (Money & Tucker, 1975). The parents agreed to a surgical procedure that made their 21-month-old boy anatomically a girl. Then they treated him like a girl. By age 5 this boy-turned-girl was quite different from her genetically identical brother. She most certainly knew that she was a girl; had developed strong preferences for feminine toys, activities, and apparel; and was far neater and daintier than her brother. This, then, is a vivid demonstration that the most decisive influence on gender-role development is how a child is labeled and treated. Or is it?

Milton Diamond (1982) describes what was discovered when the BBC attempted to produce a program about this girl after Money and Tucker had completed their study. As a teenager she was quite maladjusted, according to her psychiatrists. She apparently was unhappy, uncomfortable in her female role, and rejected by her peers, who were put off by her masculine appearance and walk and had been known to call her "cavewoman." Perhaps, then, we should back off from the conclusion that social learning is all that matters. Apparently biology matters too.

A second source of evidence is a study of 18 biological males in the Dominican Republic who had a genetic condition that makes the cells insensitive to the effects of male hormones (Imperato-McGinley, Peterson, Gautier, & Sturla, 1979; see also Herdt & Davidson, 1988). They had begun life with ambiguous genitals, were mistaken for girls, and so were labeled and raised as girls. However, under the influence of male hormones produced at puberty, they sprouted beards and became entirely masculine in appearance. How in the world, in light of Money and Ehrhardt's critical-period hypothesis, could a person adjust to becoming a man after leading an entire childhood as a girl?

Amazingly, 16 of these 18 individuals seemed able to accept their late conversion from female to male and to adopt masculine lifestyles, including the establishment of heterosexual relationships. One retained a female identity and sex role, and the remaining individual switched to a male gender identity but still dressed as a female. Obviously this research casts some doubt on the notion that socialization during the first three years is critical to later gender-role development and suggests that hormonal influences may be more important than social influences.

Yet the study has been criticized (see Ehrhardt, 1985). Little information was reported about how these individuals had been raised, for example. It is possible that Dominican adults, knowing that this genetic disorder was common in their society, treated these girls-turned-boys differently from other girls when they were young or that these youngsters recognized on their own that their genitals were not normal. As a result, these "girls" may never have fully committed themselves to being girls. In some areas of New Guinea, boys with this same genetic condition are regarded as members of a "third sex" and are treated differently than either boys or girls (Herdt & Davidson, 1988).

What studies of individuals with genital abnormalities appear to teach us is this: The first three years of life are a *sensitive period* (rather than a critical period) for gender-role development, and *both* biology and society influence a child's gender identity and gender-role development. *Neither* biology nor social labeling is "destiny."

development. More specifically, the 3- to 6-year-old child in the phallic stage of development harbors a biologically based love for the parent of the other sex, experiences internal conflict and anxiety as a result of this incestuous desire, and resolves the conflict through a process of **identification** with the same-sex parent. According to Freud, a boy experiencing his **Oedipus complex** loves his mother, fears that his father will retaliate by castrating him, and ultimately is forced to identify with his father, thereby emulating his father and adopting his father's attitudes and behaviors. Freud believed that a boy would show weak masculinity later in life if his father was inadequate as a masculine model, was often absent from the home, or was not dominant or threatening enough to foster a strong identification based on fear.

Meanwhile, a preschool-aged girl is said to experience an **Electra complex** involving a desire for her father and a rivalry with her mother. However, since she supposedly believes herself to have been castrated already, she is not strongly motivated to identify with her mother. Nonetheless, a girl does identify with her mother and also receives reinforcement from her father for "feminine" behavior resembling that of her mother. Freud believed that a girl would fail to adopt her feminine role if she did not identify with her mother or had a mother who proved inadequate as a feminine model. Thus Freud's theory emphasizes the role of emotions (love, fear, and so on) in motivating gender-role development and argues that children adopt their roles by patterning themselves after their same-sex parents.

We can applaud Freud for identifying the preschool years as a critical time for gender-role development. In addition, his view that boys have a more powerful motivation to adopt their gender role than girls do is consistent with the finding that boys seem to learn gender stereotypes and gender-typed behaviors faster and more completely than girls do. It is also true that boys whose fathers are absent from the home tend to be less traditionally sex-typed than other boys (Stevenson & Black, 1988). Finally, the notion that fathers play an important role in the gender typing of their daughters as well as their sons has now been confirmed (Huston, 1983).

However, on other counts psychoanalytic theory has not fared well at all. Many preschool children are so ignorant of male and female anatomy that it is hard to see how most boys could fear castration or most girls could experience penis envy (Bem, 1989; Katcher, 1955). Moreover, Freud assumed that a boy's identification with his father is based on fear, but most researchers find that boys identify most strongly with fathers who are warm and nurturant rather than overly punitive and threatening (Hetherington & Frankie, 1967; Mussen & Rutherford, 1963). Finally, children are not especially similar psychologically to their same-sex parents (Maccoby & Jacklin, 1974). Apparently other individuals besides parents influence a child's gender-related characteristics. And apparently we must look elsewhere for more complete explanations of gender-role development.

Social Learning Theory

According to social learning theorists such as Albert Bandura (1986) and Walter Mischel (1970), children learn masculine or feminine identities, preferences, and behaviors in two ways. First, through *differential reinforcement,* children are encouraged and rewarded for sex-appropriate behaviors and punished for behaviors considered more appropriate for members of the other sex. Second, through *observational learning,* children adopt the attitudes and behaviors of same-sex models. In this view, a child's gender-role development depends on which of his or her behaviors people reinforce or punish and on what sorts of social models are available. Change the social environment, and you change the course of gender-role development.

Differential Reinforcement.

Parents clearly use differential reinforcement to teach boys how to be boys and girls how to be girls (Lytton & Romney, 1991). Beverly Fagot and Mary Leinbach (1989), for example, have found that parents are already encouraging sex-appropriate play and discouraging cross-sex play during the second year of life, before children have acquired their basic gender identities or display clear preferences for male or female activities. By the tender age of 20 to 24 months, daughters are reinforced for dancing, dressing up (as women), following their parents around, asking for help, and playing with dolls; they are discouraged from manipulating objects, running, jumping, and climbing. By contrast, sons are often reprimanded for such "feminine" behavior as playing with dolls or seeking help and are often actively encouraged to play with "masculine" toys such as blocks, trucks, and push-and-pull toys (Fagot, 1978).

Does this "gender curriculum" in the home influence children? It certainly does. Parents who show the clearest patterns of differential reinforcement have children who are relatively quick to label themselves as girls or boys and to develop strongly sex-typed toy and activity preferences (Fagot & Leinbach, 1989; Fagot, Leinbach, & O'Boyle, 1992). It turns out that fathers are even more likely than mothers to reward children's gender-appropriate behavior and to discourage behavior considered more appropriate for the other sex (Langlois & Downs, 1980; Lytton & Romney, 1991). Women who choose nontraditional professions are more likely than women in traditionally female fields to have had fathers who encouraged them to be assertive and competitive (Coats & Overman, 1992). Fathers, then, seem to be an especially important influence on the gender-role development of both sons and daughters.

Could differential treatment of boys and girls by parents also contribute to sex differences in ability? Possibly so. Jacquelynne Eccles and her colleagues (1990) have conducted a number of studies to determine why girls tend to shy away from math and science courses and are underrepresented in occupations that involve math and science (see also Benbow & Arjmand, 1990). They suggest that parental expectations about sex differences in mathematical ability become self-fulfilling prophecies. The plot goes something like this:

1. Parents, influenced by societal stereotypes about sex differences in ability, expect their sons to outperform their daughters in math. Indeed, before their children have even received math instruction, mothers in the United States, Japan, and Taiwan express a belief that boys have more mathematical ability than girls (Lummis & Stevenson, 1990).
2. Parents attribute their sons' successes in math to ability but credit their daughters' successes to hard work (Parsons, Adler, & Kaczala, 1982). These attributions for performance further reinforce the belief that girls lack mathematical talent and turn in respectable performances only through plodding effort.
3. Children begin to internalize their parents' views, so that girls come to believe that they are "no good" in math (Jacobs & Eccles, 1992).
4. Thinking that they lack ability, girls become less interested in math, less likely to take math courses, and less likely than boys to pursue career possibilities that involve math after high school.

In short, parents who expect their daughters to have trouble with numbers get what they expect. In their research, Eccles and her colleagues have ruled out the possibility that parents (and girls themselves) expect less of girls because girls actually do worse in math than boys do. The negative effects of low parental expectancies on girls' self-perceptions are evident even when boys and girls perform equally well on tests of math aptitude and attain similar grades in math (Eccles et al., 1990). Parental beliefs that girls excel in English and that boys excel in sports contribute to sex differences in interests and competencies in these areas as well (Eccles et al., 1990).

Peers and teachers, like parents, reinforce boys and girls differentially. As Beverly Fagot (1985) discovered, boys only 21 to 25 months of age belittle and disrupt each other for playing with "feminine" toys or with girls, and girls express their disapproval of other girls who choose to play with boys. Teachers, too, provide different kinds of feedback to their male and female students (Jussim & Eccles, 1992; Wilkinson & Marrett, 1985). For example, American and Japanese teachers consistently pay more attention to boys than to girls, giving them both more positive and more negative feedback and possibly conveying the message that they matter more than girls (Brody, 1985; Hamilton, Blumenfeld, Akoh, & Miura, 1991).

Observational Learning. Social learning theorists note that observational learning also contributes in important ways to gender typing. Children see which toys and activities are "for girls" and which are "for boys" and imitate individuals of their own sex. At about the age of 6 or 7 children begin to pay much closer attention to same-sex models than to other-sex models. They will choose toys that members of their own sex prefer even if it means passing up more attractive toys (Frey & Ruble, 1992), and they will stay clear of activities that members of the other sex seem to enjoy (Ruble, Balaban, & Cooper, 1981).

Not only do children learn by watching the children and adults with whom they interact, but they also learn from the media—radio, television, movies, magazines—and even from their picture books and elementary school readers. Although sexism in children's picture books has decreased over the past 50 years, it is still the case that male characters are more likely than female characters to engage in active, instrumental activities such as climbing, riding bikes, and making things, whereas female characters are depicted as passive, dependent, and often helpless, spending their time picking flowers, playing quietly indoors, and "creating problems that require masculine solutions" (Kortenhaus & Demarest, 1993).

It is similar in the world of television: Typically, male characters are dominant individuals who work at a profession, whereas females are passive, emotional creatures who manage a home or work at "feminine" occupations such as nursing (Liebert & Sprafklin, 1988). Children who watch a large amount of television are more likely to choose gender-appropriate

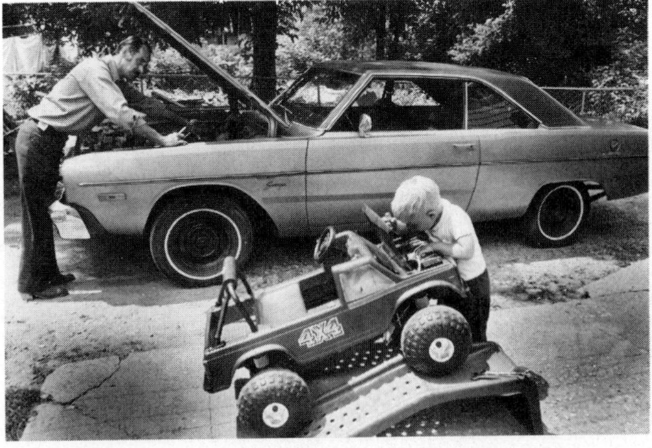

According to psychoanalytic theory, children become appropriately "masculine" or "feminine" through identification with the same-sex parent. Social learning theorists call this same process observational learning.

toys and to hold stereotyped views of males and females than their classmates who watch little television (McGhee & Frueh, 1980; Signorielli & Lears, 1992). As more women play detectives and more men raise families on television, children's notions of female and male roles are likely to change. Indeed, watching *The Cosby Show* and other nonsexist programs is associated with holding *less*-stereotyped views of the sexes (Rosenwasser, Lingenfelter, & Harrington, 1989).

In sum, there is much evidence that both differential reinforcement and observational learning contribute to gender-role development. However, social learning theorists have often portrayed children as the passive recipients of external influences: Parents, peers, television characters, and others show them what to do and reinforce them for doing it. Perhaps this perspective does not put enough emphasis on what children *themselves* contribute to their own gender socialization. Youngsters do not receive gender-stereotyped Christmas presents simply because their parents foist those toys upon them. Instead, parents tend to select gender-neutral and often educational toys for their children, but their boys beg for machine guns and their girls for tea sets (Robinson & Morris, 1986)!

Cognitive-Developmental Theory

Lawrence Kohlberg (1966) proposed a cognitive theory of gender typing that is quite different from the other theories we have considered and helps explain why boys and girls adopt traditional gender roles even when their parents may not want them to do so. Among Kohlberg's major themes are these:

1. Gender-role development depends on cognitive development, for children must acquire certain understandings about gender before they will be influenced by their social experiences.
2. Children actively socialize themselves; they are not merely the passive targets of social influence.

According to both psychoanalytic theory and social learning theory, children first are influenced by their companions to adopt "male" or "female" roles and *then* come to view themselves as girls or boys and to identify with (or habitually imitate) same-sex models. Kohlberg suggests that children *first* come to understand that they are girls or boys and then actively seek out same-sex models and a wide range of information about how to act like a girl or a boy. To Kohlberg, it's not "I'm treated like a boy; therefore I must be a boy." It's more like "I'm a boy; therefore I'll do everything I can to find out how to behave like one."

What understandings are necessary before children will teach themselves to behave like boys or girls? Kohlberg believes that children progress through the following three stages as they acquire an understanding of what it means to be a female or male:

1. *Gender identity.* By age 3 the child recognizes that he or she is a male or a female.
2. *Gender stability.* Somewhat later the child also acquires **gender stability**—that is, comes to understand that this gender identity is stable *over time*. Boys invariably become men, and girls grow up to be women.
3. *Gender consistency.* The gender concept is complete, somewhere between the ages of 5 and 7, when the child achieves **gender consistency,** or realizes that one's sex is also stable *across situations*. Now children know that one's sex cannot be altered by superficial changes such as dressing up as a member of the other sex or engaging in cross-sex activities.

As we saw earlier, 3- to 5-year-olds often do lack the concepts of gender stability and gender consistency; they often claim that a boy could become a mommy if he really wanted to or that a girl could become a boy if she cut her hair and wore a cowboy outfit. As children enter the concrete-operational stage of cognitive development and come to grasp concepts like conservation of liquids, they also realize that gender is conserved despite changes in appearance (Marcus & Overton, 1978). Children have been shown to progress through Kohlberg's three stages in a variety of cultures, which suggests that cognitive maturation is an important influence on the child's emerging understanding of gender (Munroe, Shimmin, & Munroe, 1984).

Criticisms? Sandra Bem (1989) has shown that children need not reach the concrete operations stage to understand gender stability and consistency if they have sufficient knowledge of male and female anatomy to realize that it is one's genitals that make one a male or a female. The most controversial aspect of Kohlberg's theory, though, has been his claim that only when children fully grasp that their biological sex is unchangeable, at the age of 5 to 7, do they actively seek out same-sex models and attempt to acquire values, interests, and behaviors that are consistent with their cognitive judgments about themselves. As we have seen, children do become more attentive to same-sex models at just this age (Ruble et al., 1981). What's more, boys (though not girls) who grasp the concept of gender constancy are more likely than those who do not to pass up a very appealing toy in order to play with an uninteresting one simply because the dull toy was endorsed by same-sex peers (Frey & Ruble, 1992). What is the problem, then? It is that children have already learned many gender-role stereotypes and have developed clear preferences for same-sex activities and playmates long before they master the concepts of gender stability and gender consistency and begin to attend more selectively to same-sex models. It seems that only a rudimentary understanding of gender is required before children will learn gender stereotypes and preferences; knowing how well a child grasps the concept of gender consistency tells us little about how gender-typed that child's behavior is (Bussey & Bandura, 1992; Carter & Levy, 1988; Martin & Little, 1990).

Gender Schema Theory

Carol Martin and Charles Halverson (1981, 1987) have proposed a somewhat different cognitive theory (actually, an information-processing theory) that overcomes the key weakness of Kohlberg's theory. Like Kohlberg, they believe that children are intrinsically motivated to acquire values, interests, and behaviors that are consistent with their cognitive judgments about the self. However, Martin and Halverson argue that this "self-socialization" begins as soon as children acquire a *basic* gender identity, at the age of 2 or 3. According to their *schematic-processing model*, children acquire **gender schemata** — organized sets of beliefs and expectations about males and females that influence the kinds of information they will attend to and remember.

First, children acquire a simple *in-group/out-group schema* that allows them to classify some objects, behaviors, and roles as appropriate for males and others as appropriate for females (for example, cars are for boys, girls can cry but boys should not, and so on). Then they seek out more elaborate information about the role of their own sex, constructing an *own-sex schema*. Thus a young girl who knows her basic gender identity might first learn that sewing is for girls and building model airplanes is for boys. Then, because she is a girl and wants to act consistently with her own self-concept, she gathers a great deal of information about sewing to add to her own-sex schema, largely ignoring any information that comes her way about how to build model airplanes (see Figure 11.4).

Consistent with this schematic-processing theory, children do appear to be especially interested in learning about objects or activities that fit their own-sex schemata. In one study, 4- to 9-year-olds were given boxes of gender-neutral objects (hole punches, burglar alarms, and so on) and were told that the objects were either "girl" items or "boy" items (Bradbard, Martin, Endsley, & Halverson, 1986). Boys explored "boy" items more than girls did, and girls explored "girl" items more than boys did. A week later the children easily recalled which items were for boys and which were for girls; they had apparently sorted the objects according to their "in-group/out-group" schemata. In addition, boys recalled more in-depth information about "boy" items than did girls, whereas girls recalled more than boys about these very same objects if they had been labeled "girl" items. If children's information-gathering efforts are indeed guided by their own-sex schemata in this way, we can easily see how boys and girls might acquire very different stores of knowledge as they develop.

Once gender schemata are in place, children will actually distort new information in memory so that it is consistent with their schemata (Liben & Signorella, 1993; Martin & Halverson, 1983). Martin and Halverson (1983) showed 5- and 6-year-olds pictures of children performing gender-consistent activities (for example, a boy playing with a truck) and pictures of children performing gender-inconsistent activities

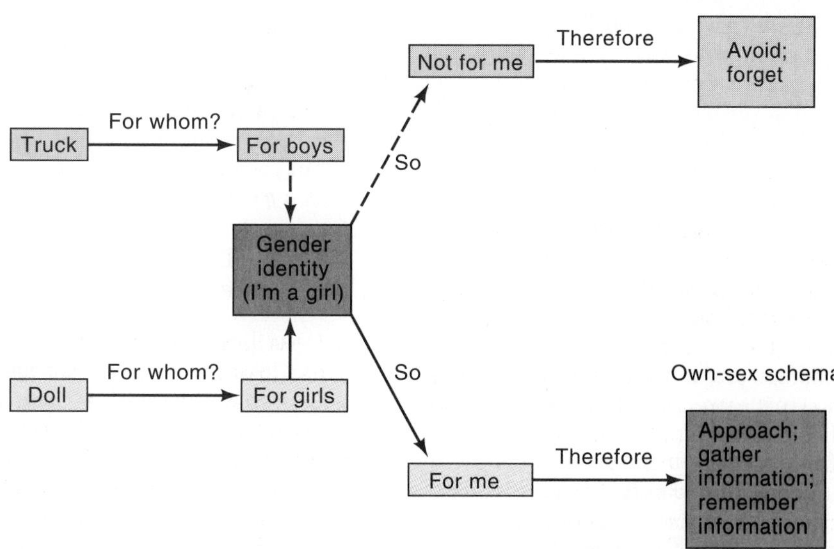

FIGURE 11.4 Gender schema theory in action. A young girl classifies new information according to an "in-group/out-group schema" as either "for boys" or "for girls." Information about boys' toys and activities is ignored, but information about toys and activities for girls is relevant to the self and so is added to an ever-larger "own-sex schema." (Adapted from Martin & Halverson, 1987.)

(for example, a girl sawing wood). A week later the children easily recalled the sex of the actor when activities were gender-consistent; when an actor's behavior was gender-inconsistent, though, children often distorted the scene to make it gender-consistent (for example, by saying that it was a boy, not a girl, who had sawed wood). Thus this research gives us some insight into why inaccurate gender stereotypes persist. The child who believes that women cannot be doctors may be introduced to a female doctor but is likely to remember meeting a nurse and may still insist that women cannot be doctors!

An Attempt at Integration

The biosocial, social learning, cognitive-developmental, and gender schema perspectives all contribute to our understanding of sex differences and gender-role development (Huston, 1983; Serbin et al., 1993). The biosocial model offered by Money and Ehrhardt acknowledges the importance of biological developments that influence how people label and treat a child. Kohlberg's cognitive-developmental theory and Martin and Halverson's gender schema approach convince us that cognitive growth plays a part in early gender-role development. Once children acquire a basic understanding that they are boys or girls and form gender schemata, they become highly motivated to learn their appropriate roles. When they finally grasp, at age 5 to 7, that their sex will never change, they become even more highly motivated and pay special attention to same-sex models. Parents who try hard to avoid teaching their children traditional gender roles are often amazed at how their children seem to become little "sexists" all on their own.

And yet we cannot ignore evidence that socialization agents—parents, as noted by Freud, and siblings, peers, and teachers as well—are teaching children how to be girls or boys well before they even understand that they *are* girls or boys. In other words, social learning theorists were correct in concluding that children behave in gender-consistent ways because of differential reinforcement and observational learning. Differences in social learning experiences may help explain why, even though virtually *all* children form gender concepts and schemata, *some* children are far more gender-typed than others in their preferences and activities (Serbin et al., 1993).

In short, children are born with a male or female biological endowment, are influenced by other people from birth on to become "real boys" or "real girls," and actively socialize themselves to behave in ways that seem consistent with their understandings that they are either boys or girls. All theories of gender-role development would agree that what children actually learn regarding how to be males or females depends greatly on what their particular society offers them in the way of a gender "curriculum." Thus we must view gender-role development from a contextual perspective and appreciate that there is nothing inevitable about the patterns of male and female development that we observe in our own society today. In another era, in another culture, the process of gender-role socialization could produce quite different kinds of boys and girls.

Childhood Sexuality

Although boys and girls spend much of their time in gender-segregated groups, they are nonetheless preparing for the day when they will participate in sexual relationships with the other sex. They are learning a great deal about sexuality and reproduction, are continuing to be curious about their bodies, and are gradually interacting with the other sex in ways that will lead to dating in adolescence.

Knowledge of Sex and Reproduction

As children get older, they learn that sexual anatomy is the key differentiator between males and females and acquire a more correct and explicit vocabulary for discussing sexual organs (Goldman & Goldman, 1982; Gordon, Schroeder, & Abrams, 1990). As Anne Bernstein and Philip Cowan (1975) have shown, their understandings of "where babies come from" also change as they develop cognitively. Young children often seem to assume either that babies are just there all along or that they are somehow manufactured, much as toys might be. According to Jane, aged 3½ "You find [the baby] at a store that makes it. . . . Well, they get it and then they put it in the tummy and then it goes quickly out" (p. 81). Another preschooler, making what he could of a book about reproduction in the animal world, created this scenario:

> (*How would the lady get a baby to grow in her tummy?*) Um, get a rabbit . . . they just get a duck or a goose and they get a little more growned . . . and then they turn into a baby. (*A rabbit will turn into a baby?*) They give them some food, people food, and they grow like a baby. (*If I asked you to tell me just one way that people get babies, what would you say?*) I would say, a store, buy a duck . . . [Bernstein & Cowan, 1975, p. 87; italics supplied].

As these examples illustrate, young children construct their own understandings of reproduction well before they are told the "facts of life." Between the ages of 9 and 11, most children are beginning to understand that sexual intercourse plays a role in the making of babies (Goldman & Goldman, 1982). By 11 or 12 most children have integrated information about sexual intercourse with information about the biological union of egg and sperm (Bernstein & Cowan, 1975). Thus, as children mature cognitively and as they gain access to information, they are able to construct ever-more-accurate understandings of sexuality and reproduction.

Sexual Behavior during Childhood

According to Freud, preschoolers in the *phallic stage* of psychosexual development are actively interested in their genitals and seek bodily pleasure through masturbation. However, Freud assumed that the emotional traumas associated with their Oedipus or Electra complexes would force school-aged children into a *latency period,* during which they repress their sexuality and turn their attention instead to schoolwork and friendships with same-sex peers. It turns out that Freud was half right and half wrong.

Freud was correct that preschoolers are highly curious about their bodies, masturbate, and engage in both same-sex and cross-sex sexual play. He was wrong to believe that such activities occur infrequently among school-aged children. In analyzing interviews with children aged 4 to 14 conducted by Alfred Kinsey and his associates, James Elias and Paul Gebhard (1969) found that: (1) 56% of the boys and 30% of the girls reported that they had masturbated before reaching puberty; (2) 52% of the boys and 35% of the girls had engaged in some form of sexual play with same-sex peers (exhibition of genitals, manipulation of each other's genitals, and so on); and (3) 34% of the boys and 37% of the girls reported similar forms of heterosexual play.

Such sexual experimentation, which is more common among boys than among girls, appears to *increase* with age, rather than declining after the preschool period as Freud claimed (Rosen & Hall, 1984). Perhaps Freud was misled by the fact that preschoolers, often unaware of society's rules of etiquette, are more likely to get caught at their sex play than older children are (Rosen & Hall, 1984). Latency-period children may be more discreet than preschoolers, but they have by no means lost their sexual curiosity.

Freud might also have been misled because the Victorian society in which he lived was especially restrictive about sexuality. Whether children do or do not engage in various forms of sexual experimentation is very much influenced by the cultural context in which they develop. In all societies, children undergo a process of sexual socialization in which they learn which sexual behaviors are and are not permissible in childhood and which are expected in adulthood.

Judging from the anthropological research of Clellan Ford and Frank Beach (1951), the diversity in sexual attitudes and behaviors among cultures of the world is staggering. In *restrictive* societies, children are not allowed to express any sexuality until they reach puberty or sometimes until they marry. In New Guinea, for example, Kwoma boys are not allowed to touch themselves, and a boy caught having an erection is likely to have his penis beaten with a stick! In *semi-restrictive* societies, formal rules prohibiting childhood masturbation and sex play exist; but they are frequently violated, and adults rarely punish children unless the violations are flagrant. How different it is in *permissive* societies, where children are free to express their sexuality and are encouraged to prepare for their roles as mature sexual beings. On the island of Ponape, for example, 4- and 5-year-olds receive a thorough "sex education" from adults and are free to try out what they have learned on one another. Among the Chewa of Africa, parents believe that practice makes perfect and encourage older boys and girls to build huts and play at being husbands and wives in trial marriages.

Preschoolers are naturally curious about the human body.

Where do the United States and other modern Western societies fall on this continuum? Most can be classified as "semirestrictive." There are unspoken rules against childhood masturbation and sex play, but adults ignore many violations. Mainly, grownups leave the task of preparing for adult sexual relations to the children themselves, and children end up learning from their peers how they should relate to the other sex.

As Barrie Thorne's (1993) observations in elementary schools demonstrate, boys and girls may be segregated by gender, but they are hardly oblivious to each other. They talk constantly about who "likes" whom and who is "cute"; they play kiss-and-chase games in which girls attempt to catch boys and infect them with "cooties"; and they have steady boyfriends and girlfriends (if only for a few days). At times boys and girls seem like mortal enemies. But, by loving and hating each other, kissing and running away, they are grooming themselves for more explicitly sexual—but still often ambivalent—heterosexual relationships later in life (Thorne, 1993).

The sexual socialization process does not go as well for those girls and boys who are sexually abused. In Box 11.2 we look at childhood sexual abuse and some of its serious consequences for later development.

BOX 11.2 Child Sexual Abuse

A 26-year-old nursery school teacher stood trial for sexually abusing children at the Wee Care Nursery School: "She was said to have licked peanut butter off children's genitals; played the piano while nude; made children drink her urine and eat her feces; and raped and assaulted them with knives, forks, spoons, and Lego blocks (Ceci & Bruck, 1993, pp. 403–404). We read such stories in the newspaper and are horrified. Yet every day in this country, children, adolescents, and even infants are sexually abused by the adults closest to them.

A more typical scenario for child sexual abuse than the one above would be this: A girl aged 7 or 8—though it happens to boys too—is abused repeatedly by her father, stepfather, or another male relative or family friend (Trickett & Putnam, 1993). Estimates of the percentages of girls and boys who are sexually abused vary wildly, perhaps because so many cases go unreported. In one representative sample of U.S. adults, though, 27% of the women and 16% of the men reported having experienced some form of childhood sexual abuse, ranging from being touched or grabbed in ways they considered abusive to being raped (Finkelhor, Hotaling, Lewis, & Smith, 1989). It is a serious and widespread social problem.

A useful account of the impacts of sexual abuse on the victims is offered by Kathleen Kendall-Tackett, Linda Williams, and David Finkelhor (1993) based on their review of 45 studies. There is no one distinctive "syndrome" of psychological problems that characterizes abuse victims. Instead, these individuals may experience any number of problems commonly seen in emotionally disturbed individuals, including anxiety, depression, low self-esteem, aggression, acting out, withdrawal, and school learning problems. Roughly 20–30% experience each of these problems, and boys seem to experience much the same types and degrees of disturbance as girls do.

Many of these aftereffects boil down to a lack of self-worth and a difficulty trusting others (Cole & Putnam, 1992). A college student of our acquaintance who had been abused repeatedly by her father and by other relatives as well had this to say about her experience:

> It was very painful, emotionally, physically, and psychologically. I wanted to die to escape it. I wanted to escape from my body. . . . I developed a "good" self and a "bad" self. This was the only way I could cope with the experiences. . . . I discovered people I trusted caused me harm. . . . It is difficult for me to accept the fact that people can care for me and expect nothing in return. . . .I dislike closeness and despise people touching me.

Two problems seem to be uniquely associated with being sexually abused. First, about a third of victims engage in "sexualized behavior," acting out sexually by putting objects in vaginas, masturbating in public, behaving seductively, or, if they are older, behaving promiscuously (Kendall-Tackett et al., 1993). One theory is that this sexualized behavior helps victims master or control the traumatic events they experienced (Tharinger, 1990). Perhaps it is not surprising that adults who were sexually abused as children are more likely than nonabused individuals to be sexually abused as adults (Wyatt, Guthrie, & Notgrass, 1992) and to report dissatisfaction with their sexual relationships and disrupted marriages (Finkelhor et al., 1989). Second, about a third of victims display the symptoms of **posttraumatic stress disorder.** This clinical disorder, involving nightmares, flashbacks to the traumatizing events, and feelings of helplessness and anxiety in the face of danger, is usually observed among soldiers in combat and other victims of extreme trauma (Kendall-Tackett et al., 1993).

In a minority of children, sexual abuse may contribute to severe psychological disorders, including multiple-personality disorder, the splitting of the psyche into distinct personalities (Cole & Putnam, 1992; Ross et al., 1991). Yet about a third of children seem to experience no psychological symptoms at all (Kendall-Tackett et al., 1993). It could be that some of these symptomless children will experience problems in later years; long-term follow-up studies simply do not exist. But it could also be that some children are less severely damaged or more able to cope than others are.

Indeed, we know that the effects of abuse are likely to be most severe when the abuse involved penetration and force and occurred frequently over a long period of time; when the perpetrator was a close relative such as the father; and when the child's mother did not serve as a reliable source of emotional support (Beitchman et al., 1991; Kendall-Tackett et al., 1993; Trickett & Putnam, 1993). It is also clear that many symptoms fade within a year or two and that children are likely to recover especially well if their mothers believe their stories and can offer them a stable and loving home environment (Kendall-Tackett et al., 1993). Psychotherapy aimed at treating the anxiety and depression many victims experience and teaching them coping and problem-solving skills so that they will not be revictimized can also contribute to the healing process (O'Donohue & Elliott, 1992). Recovery takes time, but it does take place.

THE ADOLESCENT

After going their separate ways in childhood, boys and girls come together in the most intimate ways during adolescence. How do they prepare for the masculine or feminine gender roles that they will be asked to play in adulthood? And how do they come to grips with their transformation into sexually mature men and women?

Adhering to Gender Roles

We observed earlier that, whereas young elementary school children are highly rigid in their thinking about gender roles, older children become more flexible about gender norms, recognizing that they are not absolute, inviolable laws. Curiously, teenagers once again seem to become highly intolerant of certain role violations and stereotyped in their thinking about the proper roles of males and females. They are more likely than somewhat younger children to make negative judgments about peers who violate expectations by engaging in cross-sex behavior or expressing cross-sex interests (Carter & McCloskey, 1983–1984; Sigelman, Carr, & Begley, 1986; Stoddart & Turiel, 1985).

Consider what Trish Stoddart and Elliot Turiel (1985) found when they asked children aged 5 to 13 questions about boys who wear a barrette or put on nail polish and about girls who sport a crewcut or wear a boy's suit. As Figure 11.5 reveals, both the kindergartners and the adolescents judged these behaviors to be very wrong, whereas third- and fifth-graders viewed them far more tolerantly. Like the elementary school children, eighth-graders clearly understood that gender-role expectations are just social conventions that can easily be changed and do not necessarily apply in all societies. However, these adolescents had also begun to conceptualize gender-role violations as a sign of psychological abnormality and could not tolerate them. Most young adolescents simply want no part of individuals they uncharitably call "fags" or "queers" (Carter & McCloskey, 1983–1984).

Increased intolerance of deviance from gender-role expectations is tied to a larger process of **gender intensification**—a magnification of sex differences associated with increased pressure to conform to gender roles as adolescents reach puberty (Boldizar, 1991; Galambos, Almeida, & Petersen, 1990; Hill & Lynch, 1983). Boys begin to see themselves as more masculine; girls emphasize their feminine side. Why might this gender intensification occur? Phyllis Katz (1979) suggests that adolescents increasingly find that they must conform to traditional gender norms in order to succeed in the dating scene. A girl who was a tomboy and thought nothing of it may find during adolescence that she must dress and behave in more "feminine" ways to attract boys, and a boy may find that he is more popular if he projects a more sharply "masculine" image. Social pressures on adolescents to conform to traditional roles may even help explain why sex differences in cognitive abilities sometimes become noticeable as children enter adolescence (Hill & Lynch, 1983; Roberts et al., 1990). Later in adolescence, teenagers become more comfortable with their identities as men and women and more flexible in their thinking once again (Urberg, 1979).

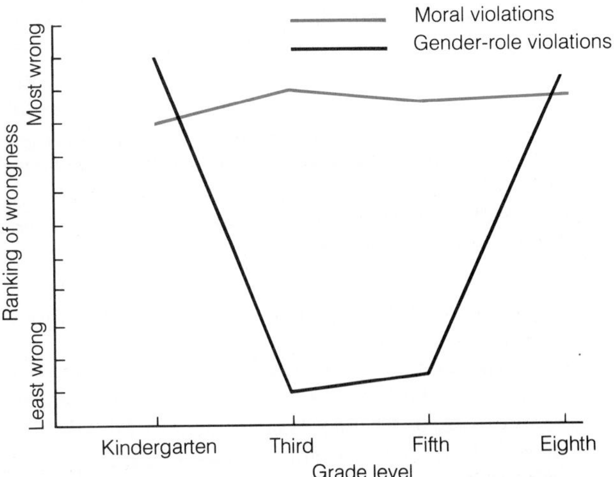

FIGURE 11.5 Children's rankings of the wrongness of gender-role transgressions (such as a boy's wearing nail polish) and violations of moral rules (such as pushing another child from a swing). Notice that children of all ages deplore immoral acts, but only kindergartners and adolescents view gender-role violations as wrong. Elementary school children come to think about gender-role standards more flexibly than they did earlier, but adolescents become concerned about the psychological implications of deviating from one's "proper" role. (Adapted from Stoddart & Turiel, 1985.)

Adolescent Sexuality

Although infants and children are sexual beings, sexuality assumes far greater importance once sexual maturity is achieved. Adolescents must now incorporate into their identities as males or females concepts of themselves as *sexual* males or females. Moreover, they must figure out how to express their sexuality in the context of interpersonal relationships. As part of their search for identity, teenagers raise questions about their sexual attractiveness, their sexual values, and their goals in close relationships. They also experiment with sexual behavior—sometimes with good outcomes, sometimes with bad ones. The psychological aspects of dating relationships are explored further in Chapter 13; here we'll focus on the sexual aspects.

Sexual Orientation

Part of the task of establishing a sexual identity is becoming aware of one's **sexual orientation**—that is, preference for sexual partners of the same or other sex. Sexual orientation exists on a continuum; not all cultures categorize sexual preferences as ours does (Paul, 1993), but we commonly describe people as having primarily heterosexual, homosexual, or bisexual orientations. Most adolescents establish a heterosexual sexual orientation without much soul searching. For youths who are attracted to members of their own sex, however, the process of accepting that they have a homosexual orientation and establishing a positive identity in the face of negative societal attitudes can be a long and torturous one. Often they have an initial awareness of their sexual preference in their early teens but do not accept being gay or lesbian, or gather the courage to "come out," until their mid-20s (Garnets & Kimmel, 1991).

Experimentation with homosexual activity is fairly common during adolescence. Perhaps 20–40% of children and adolescents engage in some form of same-sex sexual experimentation (Masters, Johnson, & Kolodny, 1988; Money, 1988), but few of them become part of the estimated 5–6% of adults who establish an enduring homosexual or bisexual sexual orientation (Smith, 1991). Contrary to societal stereotypes of gay men as effeminate and lesbian women as masculine, gay and lesbian individuals have the same wide range of psychological and social attributes that heterosexual adults do. Knowing that someone prefers same-sex romantic partners tells us no more about his or her personality than knowing that someone is heterosexual.

What influences the development of one's sexual orientation? Part of the answer lies in the genetic code, it seems. Michael Bailey, Richard Pillard, and their colleagues have found that identical twins are more alike in sexual orientation than fraternal twins (Bailey & Pillard, 1991; Bailey et al., 1993). As Table 11.2 reveals, though, in about half the identical twin pairs, one twin is homosexual or bisexual but the other is heterosexual. This means that environment contributes at least as much as genes to the development of sexual orientation.

Other research tells us that many gay men and lesbian women expressed strong cross-sex interests when they were young, despite being subjected to the usual pressures to adopt a traditional gender role (Bell, Weinberg, & Hammersmith, 1981; Green, 1987; Martin, 1990). Richard Green (1987), for example, studied a group of highly feminine boys who didn't just engage in cross-sex play now and then but strongly and consistently preferred female roles, toys, and friends. He found that 75% of these boys (compared with 2% of a control group of gender-typical boys) were exclusively homosexual or bisexual 15 years later. Yet the genetic research by Bailey and Pillard suggests that sexual orientation is every bit as heritable among gay men who were typically masculine boys and lesbian women who were typically feminine girls as among those who showed early cross-sex interests (Bailey & Pillard, 1991; Bailey et al., 1993). All that is clear, then, is that many gay and lesbian adults do know from an early age that traditional gender-role expectations do not suit them.

What environmental factors may help to determine whether or not a genetic predisposition toward homosexuality is actualized? We really do not know as yet. The old psychoanalytic view that male homosexuality stems from having a domineering mother and a weak father has received little support (Bell et al., 1981). Nor is there support for the idea that homosexuals were seduced into a homosexual lifestyle by older individuals. A more promising hypothesis is that hormonal influences during the prenatal period have an important impact (Ellis et al., 1988; Gandelman, 1992). For example, the fact that androgenized females are more likely than most other women to adopt a lesbian or bisexual orientation suggests that high prenatal doses of male hormones may predispose at least some females to homosexuality (Dittman et al., 1992; Money, 1988). However, the fact is that no one yet knows exactly which factors in the prenatal or postnatal environment contribute, along with genes, to a homosexual orientation (Paul, 1993).

TABLE 11.2 If one twin is gay (or lesbian), in what percentage of twin pairs does the other twin also have a homosexual or bisexual sexual orientation? Higher rates of concordance (similarity) for identical twin pairs than for fraternal twin pairs provide evidence of genetic influence on homosexuality, but less-than-perfect concordance points to the operation of environmental influences as well.

	Identical Twins	*Fraternal Twins*
Both male twins are gay/bisexual if one is:	52%	22%
Both female twins are lesbian/bisexual if one is:	48%	16%

SOURCE: Male figures from Bailey & Pillard, 1991. Female figures from Bailey et al., 1993.

Teenage Sexual Morality

Regardless of sexual orientation, adolescents establish attitudes regarding what is and is not appropriate sexual behavior. Have today's teenagers adopted a "new morality" that is radically different from the standards their parents and grandparents held? The sexual attitudes of adolescents have indeed changed dramatically during this century, especially during the 1960s and 1970s. And yet, even before the AIDS epidemic came along, few teenagers had totally abandoned the "old values." In his review of the literature, Philip Dreyer (1982) noted three important changes that have occurred in sexual attitudes (see also Abler & Sedlacek, 1989).

First, most adolescents seem to believe that *sex with affection is acceptable*. They no longer accept the traditional belief that premarital intercourse is always morally wrong, but they don't go so far as to view casual sex as acceptable. They insist that the partners be "in love" or feel a close emotional involvement with each other.

A second important change is the *decline of the* ***double standard.*** According to the double standard, sexual behavior that is viewed as appropriate for males is considered inappropriate for females; there is one standard for males, another for females. Thus in the "old days" a young man was expected to "sow some wild oats," whereas a young woman was expected to remain a virgin until she married. (Apparently there were a few "bad girls" willing to accommodate all those eager young men!) The double standard has not entirely disappeared. For example, fathers still look more favorably on the sexual exploits of their sons than on those of their daughters (Brooks-Gunn & Furstenberg, 1989), and college students still tend to believe that a woman who has many sexual partners is more immoral than an equally promiscuous man (Robinson et al., 1991). However, Western societies have been moving for some time toward a single standard of sexual behavior used to judge both males and females.

The third change might be described as *increased confusion about sexual norms.* As Dreyer notes, the "sex with affection" norm is more than a little ambiguous. Must one be truly in love, or is some degree of liking enough to justify sexual intercourse? It is now up to the individual to answer such questions. But doing so is hard, because adolescents continually receive mixed messages about sexuality (Darling & Hicks, 1982). They are encouraged to be popular and attractive to the other sex, and they watch countless television programs and movies that glamorize sexual behavior. One girl, lamenting the strong peer pressure on her to become sexually active, joked that it had gotten so bad that a "virgin" had come to mean "an awfully ugly third-grader" (Gullotta, Adams, & Alexander, 1986, p. 109). At the same time, teenagers are also told to value virginity and to fear and avoid pregnancy, bad reputations, and AIDS and other sexually transmitted diseases. As a result of these conflicting signals, adolescents are often quite confused about how to behave. The standards for males and females are now more similar, and adolescents tend to agree that sexual intercourse in the context of emotional involvement is acceptable; but teenagers still must forge their own codes of behavior, and they differ widely in what they decide.

Sexual Behavior

If attitudes about sexual behavior have changed over the years, has sexual behavior itself changed? Yes, it has. In fact, it would be difficult to identify aspects of sexual behavior that have *not* changed. Today's teenagers are involved in more intimate forms of sexual behavior at earlier ages than adolescents of the past were. These trends became especially noticeable in the 1960s and have continued through the 1980s and into the 1990s (Dreyer, 1982; Forrest & Singh, 1990; Sonenstein, Pleck, & Ku, 1991). More adolescents report that they masturbate, and more regard it as normal than in past eras (Dreyer, 1982), although many still feel guilty or uneasy about it (Coles & Stokes, 1985). Adolescents also engage in petting at younger ages than previously. Finally, more teenagers are having sexual intercourse and at younger ages.

Figure 11.6 shows the percentages of high school and college students who experienced premarital intercourse in each of four historical periods. Three important messages can be derived from this figure. First, rates of sexual intercourse increase with age over the adolescent years. Recent surveys suggest that about half of high school females and 60% of high school males have engaged in intercourse (Centers for Disease Control, 1992); among college students the rate is now more like 70–80% (Baier, Rosenzweig, &

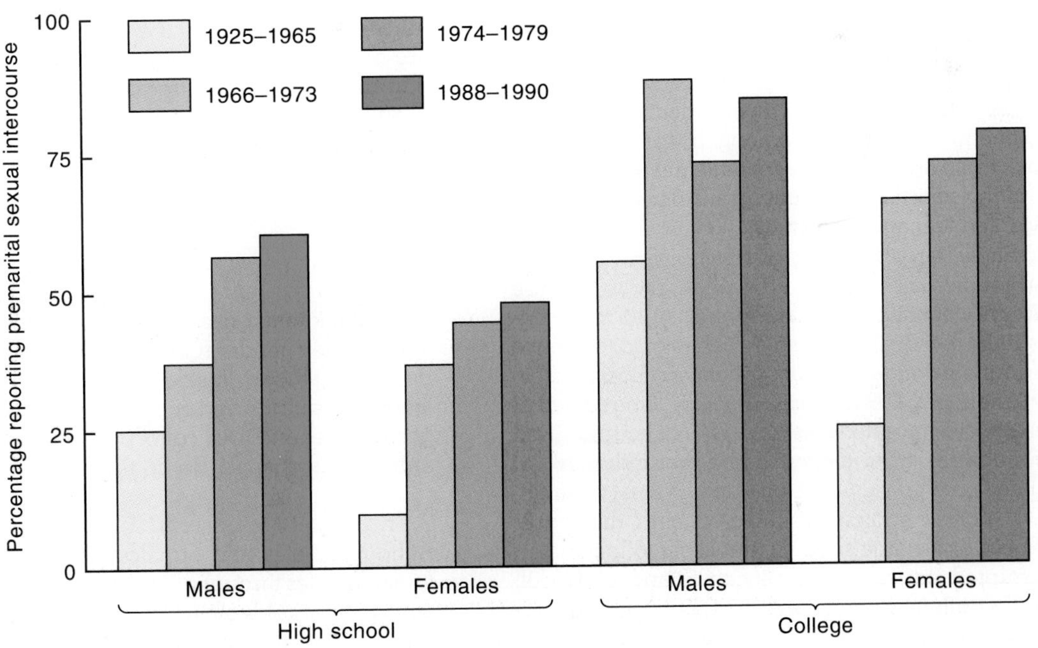

FIGURE 11.6 Historical changes in the percentages of high school and college students reporting premarital sexual intercourse. (Data for first three time periods adapted from Dreyer, 1982; data for most recent period from Baier, Rosenzweig, & Whipple, 1991; Centers for Disease Control, 1992; Reinisch et al., 1992.)

Whipple, 1991; Reinisch et al., 1992). Second, much social change has occurred; the percentages of both males and females who have had intercourse have increased steadily throughout this century (Forrest & Singh, 1990; Sonenstein et al., 1991). Third and finally, notice that the sexual behavior of females has changed much more than that of males; as a result, sex differences in sexual activity have all but disappeared (Darling, Kallen, & VanDusen, 1984; Wielandt & Boldsen, 1989). Apparently, the decline of the double standard reflects changes not only in attitude but in behavior as well.

Yet males and females continue to feel differently about their encounters. For example, females are more insistent than males that sex and love—physical intimacy and emotional intimacy—go together. In one survey, 61% of college women, but only 29% of college men, agreed with the idea "No intercourse without love" (Darling, Davidson, & Passarello, 1992). Females are also more likely than males to have been in a steady relationship with their first sexual partner (Darling et al., 1992). This continuing gap between the sexes can sometimes create misunderstandings and hurt feelings, and it may partly explain why females are less likely to describe their first sexual experience as satisfying (Coles & Stokes, 1985; Darling et al., 1992).

In sum, both the sexual attitudes and the sexual behaviors of adolescents have changed considerably in this century. Sexual involvement is now part of the average adolescent's experience—part of his or her search for identity and emotional fulfillment (Dreyer, 1982). This is true of all major ethnic groups, of rich and poor. In fact, the differences in sexual activity among social groups have been shrinking (Forrest & Singh, 1990). Although most adolescents seem to adjust successfully to sexual involvement, there have also been some casualties among those who are psychologically unready for sex or who end up as a number in the statistics on sexually transmitted disease or unwanted teenage pregnancy.

Sadly, large numbers of sexually active adolescent couples fail to use contraception, partly because they are cognitively immature and fail to take seriously the possibility that their behavior could have unfortunate long-term consequences (Loewenstein & Furstenberg, 1991; Morrison, 1985). One survey of teenage girls revealed that only 47% of couples used a condom at first intercourse and that only 18% of teenage pregnancies were intended (Forrest & Singh, 1990). For the adolescent who gives birth, the consequences of teenage sexuality are likely to include an interrupted education, low income, and a difficult start for both new parent and child (Furstenberg, Lincoln, & Menken, 1981). This young mother's life situation and her child's developmental status are likely to improve later on, especially if she goes back to school and limits her family size, but she is likely to remain economically disadvantaged compared with her peers who postpone parenthood until their 20s (Furstenberg, Brooks-Gunn, & Morgan, 1987).

Many of today's adolescents become involved in sexual activity very early and give little thought to the long-term consequences of their behavior.

What effect has the threat of AIDS had on adolescent sexual behavior? Most studies find some change but not enough. Teens are more likely to use condoms (at least some of the time) than they were a few years ago. However, very few of them (only 1% of college students, by one count) are doing what they would need to do to protect themselves from HIV infection: using a condom (latex, with a spermicide) *every* time (Maticka-Tyndale, 1991). And many adolescents continue to put themselves at risk by having sex with multiple partners (Forrest & Singh, 1990; Maticka-Tyndale, 1991). No wonder many educators are now calling for stronger programs of sex education and distribution of free condoms at school. There is little chance of preventing the unwanted consequences of teenage sexuality unless more adolescents either postpone sex or practice safer sex.

THE ADULT

You might think that, once children and adolescents have learned their gender roles, they simply play them out during adulthood. Instead, as people face the challenges of adult life and enter new social contexts, their gender roles and their concepts of themselves as men and women change. So do their sex lives.

Gender Roles in Adulthood

Although males and females fill their masculine or feminine roles throughout their lives, the specific content of those roles changes considerably over the life span. The young boy may act out his masculine role by playing with trucks or wrestling with his buddies; the grown man may play his role by holding down a

job. Moreover, the degree of difference between male and female roles also changes. Children and adolescents do adopt behaviors consistent with their "boy" or "girl" roles, but the two sexes otherwise adopt quite similar roles in society—namely, those of children and students. Even as they enter adulthood, males' and females' roles do not differ much, because members of both sexes are often single and in school or working.

However, the roles of men and women become more distinct when they marry and, especially, when they have children. Even among newlyweds, for example, the wife typically does the lion's share of the housework, whether or not she is employed, and specific tasks tend to be parceled out along traditional lines: she doing the cooking, he taking out the garbage (Atkinson & Huston, 1984). The birth of a child tends to make even quite egalitarian couples divide their labors in more traditional ways than they did before the birth (Cowan, Cowan, Heming, & Miller, 1991). It is she who becomes primarily responsible for child care and household tasks; he tends to emphasize his role as "breadwinner" and center his energies on providing for the family. Even as men today increase their participation in child care and housework, they still tend to play a "helper" role (Baruch & Barnett, 1986). At least two-thirds of what gets done at home is still done by women (Pleck, 1985; Zick & McCullough, 1991). Moreover, there is still a tendency to view a wife's career as secondary.

What happens after the children are grown? The roles played by men and women become more similar again starting in middle age, when the nest empties and child-care responsibilities end. The similarity between gender roles continues to increase as adults enter old age; as retirees and grandparents, men and women lead similar lives. It would seem, then, that the roles of men and women are fairly similar before marriage, maximally different during the child-rearing years, and more similar again later on.

Do these sorts of shifts in the roles played by men and women during adulthood affect them psychologically? Let's see.

Masculinity, Femininity, and Androgyny

For many years, psychologists assumed that masculinity and femininity were at opposite ends of a continuum. If one possessed highly masculine traits, one must be very unfeminine; being highly feminine implied being unmasculine. Sandra Bem (1974) challenged this assumption by arguing that individuals of either sex can be characterized by psychological **androgyny**—that is, by a balancing or blending of *both* desirable masculine-stereotyped traits (being assertive, analytical, forceful, independent) and desirable feminine-stereotyped traits (being affectionate, compassionate, gentle, understanding). In Bem's model, then, masculinity and femininity are *two separate dimensions* of personality. A male or female who has many desirable masculine-stereotyped traits and few feminine ones is defined as a *masculine sex-typed* person. One who has many feminine- and few masculine-stereotyped traits is said to be *feminine sex-typed.* The androgynous person possesses both masculine and feminine traits, whereas the *undifferentiated* individual lacks both of these kinds of attributes (see Figure 11.7).

Do androgynous people really exist? Bem (1974, 1979) and other investigators (Spence & Helmreich, 1978) have developed self-perception inventories that contain both a masculinity (or instrumentality) scale and a femininity (or expressivity) scale. In one large sample of college students (Spence & Helmreich, 1978), roughly 33% of the test takers were "masculine" men or "feminine" women, about 30% were androgynous, and the remaining individuals were either undifferentiated (low on both scales) or "sex-reversed" (masculine sex-typed females or feminine sex-typed males). Around 30% of children can also be classified as androgynous (Boldizar, 1991;

	Femininity High	Femininity Low
Masculinity High	Androgynous	Masculine sex-typed
Masculinity Low	Feminine sex-typed	Undifferentiated

FIGURE 11.7 Categories of gender-role orientation based on viewing masculinity and femininity as separate dimensions of personality.

Hall & Halberstadt, 1980). So androgynous individuals do indeed exist, and in sizable numbers. Now we can ask whether perceived masculinity, femininity, and androgyny change over the adult years.

Gutmann's Hypothesis about Sex Differences in Adulthood

David Gutmann (1975, 1987) has offered the intriguing hypothesis that gender roles and gender-related traits in adulthood are shaped by what he calls the **parental imperative,** the requirement that mothers and fathers adopt different roles in order to raise children successfully. Drawing on his own cross-cultural research and that of others, he suggests that in many cultures young and middle-aged men must emphasize their "masculine" qualities in order to feed and protect their families, whereas young and middle-aged women must express their "feminine" qualities in order to nurture the young and meet the emotional needs of their families.

According to Gutmann, all this changes dramatically starting in midlife, when men and women are freed from the demands of the parental imperative. Men become less active and more passive, take less interest in community affairs, and focus more on religious contemplation and family relationships. They also become more sensitive and emotionally expressive. Women, meanwhile, are changing in precisely the opposite direction. After being quite passive, submissive, and nurturing in their younger years, they become more active, domineering, and assertive in later life. In many cultures they take charge of the household after being the underlings of their mothers-in-law and become stronger forces in their communities. In short, Gutmann proposes that, over the course of adulthood, psychologically "masculine" men become "feminine" men, while "feminine" women become "masculine" women—that the psychological traits of the two sexes flipflop.

A similar hypothesis is that adults experience a midlife **androgyny shift** in which both men and women retain their gender-typed qualities but add to them qualities traditionally associated with the other sex, thus becoming more androgynous. Ideas along this line were proposed some time ago by the psychoanalytic theorist Carl Jung (1933). Let's see how these ideas have fared.

Does Research Support Gutmann's Hypothesis?

Several studies support Gutmann's hypothesis that women gain masculine-stereotyped strengths as they leave their child-bearing years behind them. Gutmann and other researchers have asked women of different ages in a number of cultures to tell stories about pictures and have scored the stories for themes relating to power. Rather consistently, middle-aged and elderly women are more likely than young women to tell stories about strong, assertive female characters (Friedman & Pines, 1992; Gutmann, 1987; Todd, Friedman, & Kariuki, 1990). This midlife increase in sense of power is evident even among Arab women, despite their low status in society compared to men (Friedman & Pines, 1992).

Other researchers have explored the issue by administering masculinity and femininity scales to both men and women of different ages. In one study, Shirley Feldman and her associates (1981) gave Bem's androgyny inventory to individuals at eight different stages of the family life cycle. Consistent with Gutmann's notion of a parental imperative, taking on the role of parent seemed to lead men to perceive themselves as more masculine in personality and women to perceive themselves as having predominantly feminine strengths (see also Abrahams, Feldman, & Nash, 1978). Moreover, among adults who were beyond their parenting years, especially among grandparents, sex differences in self-perceptions decreased. Contrary to Gutmann's hypothesis, however, grandfathers did not replace their masculine traits with feminine traits and grandmothers did not become less feminine and more masculine. Instead, both sexes experienced an androgyny shift: Grandfathers retained their masculine traits while gaining feminine attributes, and grandmothers retained their feminine traits while taking on masculine attributes as well. This finding is particularly interesting in view of the fact that today's older people should, if anything, be *more* traditionally gender-typed than younger adults who have grown up in an era of more flexible gender norms.

In sum, young adults who are not parents are relatively androgynous, the parenting role brings out traditionally sex-typed traits in both men and women, and androgyny once again emerges when the parenting years are over (but see Fultz & Herzog, 1991). These fluctuations in gender-role orientations during adulthood appear to be related more to changes in the roles men and women play than to age alone (Eagly, 1987). For example, young parents are more psychologically sex-typed than nonparents of the same age (Feldman et al., 1981), and employment outside the home may make at least as much difference as parenthood in determining how sex-typed or androgynous adults are (Cunningham & Antill, 1984). Again, we must adopt a contextual perspective on gender-role development and appreciate that males and females can develop in any number of different directions depending on their social, cultural, and historical context and on the social roles they play.

Children are likely to become androgynous if their parents do not restrict them to stereotypic roles.

Are There Advantages to Being Androgynous?

If a person can be both assertive and sensitive, both independent and understanding, being androgynous sounds psychologically healthy. Is it? Bem (1975, 1978) demonstrated that androgynous men and women behave more flexibly than more sex-typed individuals. For example, androgynous people, like masculine sex-typed people, can display the "masculine," instrumental trait of independence by resisting social pressure to judge very unamusing cartoons as funny just because their companions do. Yet they are as likely as feminine sex-typed individuals to display the "feminine," expressive quality of nurturance by interacting positively with a baby. Androgynous people seem to be highly adaptable, able to adjust their behavior to the demands of the situation at hand (Shaffer, Pegalis, & Cornell, 1992). They also pay less attention to gender and are less likely to discriminate against women than traditionally sex-typed individuals are (Frable, 1989). In addition, androgynous individuals appear to enjoy higher self-esteem and are perceived as more likable and better adjusted than their traditionally sex-typed peers (Allgood-Merten & Stockard, 1991; Boldizar, 1991; Massad, 1981; O'Heron & Orlofsky, 1990). It has also become clear that men can maintain a strong masculine identity and women a strong feminine identity even though they sometimes express traits traditionally associated with the other sex (Spence, 1993).

But, before we jump to the conclusion that androgyny is a thoroughly desirable attribute, let's note some contrary evidence. Apparently it is the possession of "masculine" traits rather than androgyny per se that is most strongly associated with high self-esteem and good adjustment (Boldizar, 1991; Orlofsky & O'Heron, 1987; Whitley, 1983). It may be premature to conclude that one is better off in all respects to be androgynous than to be either masculine or feminine in orientation. Still, we can at least conclude that it is unlikely to be damaging for men to become a little more "feminine" or for women to become a little more "masculine" than they have been traditionally.

Adult Sexuality

We conclude our discussion of gender and adult development by examining changes in sexual interest and behavior over the adult years. Just as adults' sexual orientations are varied, so are their sexual lifestyles. Many adults remain single—some of them actively seeking a wide range of partners, others having one partner at a time, and still others leading celibate lives. Over 9 of 10 Americans marry at some point, and most adults are married at any given time.

What becomes of people's sex lives as they get older? Many young people can barely conceive of their parents or—heaven forbid—their grandparents as sexual beings. We tend to stereotype elderly people as sexless or asexual. But we are wrong: People continue to be sexual beings throughout the life span. Perhaps the most amazing discoveries about sex in late adulthood are those of Bernard Starr and Marcella Weiner (1981), who surveyed 800 elderly volunteers aged 60 to 91. In this group, over 90% claimed to like sex, almost 80% were still sexually active, and 75% said that their sex lives were the same as or better than when they were younger. One 70-year-old widow, asked how often she would like to have sex, was not bashful at all about replying "Morning, noon, and night" (p. 47).

Obviously people can remain highly interested in sex and sexually active in old age. Yet Starr and Weiner's findings are likely to be exaggerated, since only the most sexually active people may have agreed to complete such a survey. More reliable findings are reported by Tom Smith (1991) based on a survey of a representative sample of American adults that asked about many things, including sexual behavior. As

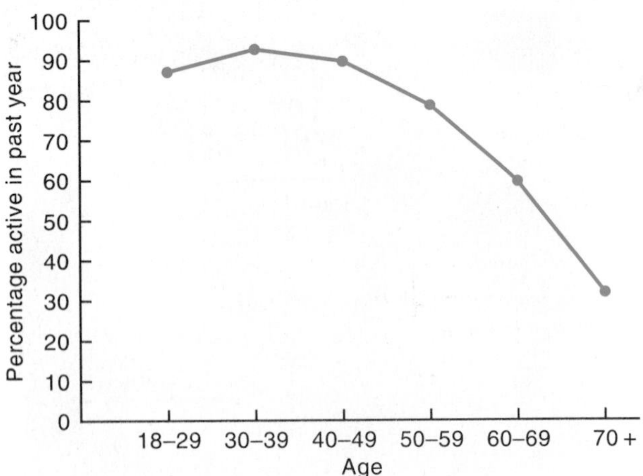

FIGURE 11.8 Percentage of U.S. adults of different ages who reported having at least one sexual partner in the past year. Cross-sectional data like these can be misleading about the degree to which sexual activity declines with age, but longitudinal studies also point to decreased involvement. (Data from Smith, 1991.)

Figure 11.8 shows, the percentage of adults who reported at least some sexual contact in the past year declined quite steadily from age group to age group, although almost a third of adults in their 70s and older were still sexually active. Men were more likely to be sexually active than women, and, as you might expect, adults were more likely to be sexually active if they were married (91%) than if they were separated or divorced (74–80%) or widowed (only 14%).

Among adults who are sexually active, frequency of sexual intercourse declines with age. This is true even among married individuals. In Smith's (1991) sample, for instance, the frequency of intercourse decreased from 105 times a year (twice a week) among adults under age 30 to 16 times a year among people 70 or older. The honeymoon appears to end very quickly; Cathy Greenblat (1983) reported a steep decline in frequency of sex within the first two or three years of marriage. Couples cited such factors as work pressures, children, fatigue, and familiarity with each other as reasons for their diminished activity, although they continued to view sexual activity as important in their marriages. The couples who were most sexually active at the start of their marriages tended to remain relatively active in comparison to other couples later in their marriages (Greenblat, 1983).

In sum, sexual activity declines with age, even among married people and especially among older women. Yet most people do not end their sex lives when they turn 65 (see also George & Weiler, 1981; Marsiglio & Donnelly, 1991). Many older adults continue having sexual intercourse, and many of those who cease having it or have it less frequently continue to be sexually motivated (Kinsey et al., 1948, 1953; Weizman & Hart, 1987).

Explanations for Declining Sexual Activity

How can we explain declines with age in sexual interest and activity? Consider first the physiological changes in sexual capacity that occur with age, as revealed by the pioneering research of William Masters and Virginia Johnson (1966, 1970). Males are at their peak of sexual responsiveness in their late teens and early 20s and gradually become less responsive thereafter. A young man is easily and quickly aroused; his orgasm is intense; and he may have a refractory, or recovery, period of only minutes before he is capable of sexual activity again. The older man is likely to be slower—slower to arouse, slower to ejaculate after being aroused, and slower to recover afterward. In addition, levels of male sex hormones decline gradually with age in many men. This may contribute to diminished sexual functioning among older men (Schiavi et al., 1991), although most researchers do not believe that hormonal factors fully explain the changes in sexual behavior that most men experience.

Physiological changes in women are far less dramatic. Females reach their peak of sexual responsiveness later than men do, often not until their late 30s. Women are capable of more orgasms in a given time span than men are because they have little or no refractory period after orgasm, and this capacity is retained into old age. As we discovered in Chapter 5, menopause does not seem to reduce sexual activity or interest for most women. However, like older men, older women typically are slower to become sexually excited. Moreover, some experience discomfort associated with decreased lubrication.

All things considered, the physiological changes that men and women experience don't really explain why many of them become less sexually active in middle and old age. Masters and Johnson concluded that both men and women are physiologically capable of sexual behavior well into old age. Women retain this physiological capacity even longer than men, yet they are the ones who are less sexually active in old age.

Apparently we must turn to factors other than biological aging to explain changes in sexual behavior. In summarizing these factors, Pauline Robinson (1983) quotes Alex Comfort (1974): "In our experience, old folks stop having sex for the same reason they stop riding a bicycle—general infirmity, thinking it looks ridiculous, and no bicycle" (p. 440).

Under the category of infirmity, any number of diseases and disabilities, as well as the drugs prescribed for them, can limit sexual functioning (Marsiglio & Donnelly, 1991). This is a particular problem for men, who may become impotent if they have high blood pressure, coronary disease, diabetes, or other health problems. *Mental* health problems are also very important: Many cases of impotence among middle-aged and elderly men seem to be attributable to psychological causes such as stress at work and depression rather than to physiological causes (Felstein, 1983; Persson & Svanborg, 1992).

The second source of problems is social attitudes that view sexual activity in old age as "ridiculous," or at least inappropriate. Old people are stereotyped as sexually unappealing and sexless (or as "dirty old men") and are discouraged from expressing sexual interests. These negative attitudes may be internalized by elderly people, causing them to suppress their sexual desires (Purifoy, Grodsky, & Giambra, 1992; Robinson, 1983). Older females may be even further inhibited by the "double standard of aging," which regards aging in women more negatively than aging in men (Arber & Ginn, 1991). More generally, older adults who lack a sense of self-worth and competence are likely to be less sexually active than those who feel good about themselves (Marsiglio & Donnelly, 1991).

Third, there is the "no bicycle" part of Comfort's analogy—namely, the lack of a partner, or at least of a willing and desirable partner. Among older married couples, both husband and wife most frequently attribute declines in their sexual activity to *his* difficulties—impotence, poor health, and so on (Pfeiffer, Verwoerdt, & Davis, 1972). So elderly married women may find themselves without a "bicycle." However, the greater problem is that most older women are widowed, divorced, or single and face grave difficulties in finding partners. The elderly woman searching for a partner confronts the reality that, for every 100 women, there are only 69 men. Moreover, most of these men are married, and those who are single are very often looking for a younger partner (Robinson, 1983). Lack of a partner, then, is *the* major problem for elderly women, many of whom continue to be interested in sex, physiologically capable of sexual behavior, and desirous of love and affection.

Perhaps we should add one more element to Comfort's bicycle analogy: lack of previous cycling experience. Masters and Johnson (1966, 1970) proposed a "use it or lose it" principle of sexual behavior to reflect two findings. First, an individual's level of sexual activity early in adulthood predicts his or her level of sexual activity in later life. The relationship is not necessarily causal, by the way; it could simply be that some people are more sexually motivated than others throughout adulthood. A second aspect of the "use it or lose it" rule may well be causal, however: Middle-aged and elderly adults who experience a long period of sexual abstinence often have difficulty regaining their sexual capacity afterward.

In summary, elderly people can continue to enjoy an active sex life if they retain their physical and mental health, do not allow negative attitudes surrounding sexuality in later life to stand in their way, have a willing and able partner, and can avoid long periods of abstinence. It seems likely that elderly people of the future, influenced by trends toward increased sexual permissiveness during this century, will be freer than the elderly people of today to express their sexual selves.

Most older adults continue to be sexual beings who seek love and affection.

APPLICATIONS: CHANGING GENDER-ROLE ATTITUDES AND BEHAVIOR

Many people believe that the world would be a better place if sexism were eliminated and if boys and girls were no longer socialized to adopt traditional "masculine" or "feminine" roles, interests, and behaviors. Children of both sexes would then have the freedom to be androgynous; women would no longer suffer from a lack of assertiveness in the world of work, and men would no longer be forced to suppress their emotions. Just how successful are efforts to encourage more flexible gender roles and eliminate sexist attitudes?

In a number of projects designed to change gender-role behavior, children have been exposed to nonsexist films, encouraged to imitate models of cross-sex behavior, reinforced by teachers for trying out cross-sex activities, and provided with nonsexist educational materials (Katz, 1986; Katz & Walsh, 1991). For example, Rebecca Bigler and Lynn Liben (1990) reasoned that, if they could alter children's gender stereotypes, they could head off the biased information processing that stereotypes promote. They exposed 6- to 11-year-olds to a series of problem-solving discussions emphasizing that (1) the most important considerations in deciding who could perform well in such traditionally masculine or feminine occupations as construction worker and beautician are the person's interests and willingness to learn and (2) the person's gender is irrelevant. Compared to children who received no such training, program participants showed a clear decline in occupational stereotyping, especially if they had entered the study with firm ideas about which jobs are for women and which are for men. Moreover, this reduction in stereotyping brought about the predicted decrease in biased information processing: Participants were more likely than nonparticipants to remember counterstereotypic information presented to them in stories (for example, recalling that the "garbage man" in a story was actually a woman).

Yet many efforts at change work in the short run but fail to have lasting effects. For example, Marlaine Lockheed (1986) sought to break down the rigid gender segregation of the middle-childhood years by having fourth- and fifth-graders participate in small, mixed-sex work groups in the classroom. Children in the experimental classes did indeed interact more with classmates of the other sex than children in comparison classes did. Yet, when children were asked to name their favorite classmates, they continued to choose children of their own sex almost exclusively. One suspects, then, that, despite their exposure to cross-sex cooperation and interaction, these children were going to go right back to their sex-segregated worlds. Indeed, one group of 4-year-olds who were praised by their teachers for cross-sex play reverted to same-sex play just as soon as the reinforcement program ended (Serbin, Tonick, & Sternglanz, 1977).

Perhaps the greatest obstacle to achieving lasting change is that children have been groomed for their traditional gender roles ever since they were born and continue to be bombarded with traditional gender-role messages every day. A short-term intervention project may have little chance of succeeding in this larger context. It may be that more substantial change in the ways boys and girls view themselves and behave must await further change in society (Etaugh, Levine, & Mennella, 1984). Judith Lorber (1986) sees much hope in her 13-year-old's response when Lorber inquired whether a new mother of their acquaintance had delivered a boy or a girl: "Why do you want to know?" this child of a new era asked (p. 567).

REFLECTIONS

This chapter raises some provocative questions about what it really means, or should mean, to be a male or a female. Clearly the answer depends on many factors —one's culture, the times in which one lives, one's own unique predispositions and experiences, and, of course, one's age and stage of life. In particular, one must wonder about the pressures exerted on all of us to conform to gender-role expectations.

If males and females start out much alike and become more similar again in middle age after experiencing the androgyny shift, why does society devote so much effort in the intervening years to making them different from each other? Certainly we have encountered little support for the notion that gender differences are biologically inevitable. And if, despite considerable social pressure to develop in different directions, males and females are still more psychologically similar than different, why do so many societies demand that they suppress some of their capacities in order to exaggerate others?

Some observers believe that traditional gender roles have done a great deal of damage, not only to women but to men as well (Eisler & Blalock, 1991; Pleck, 1981; Unger & Crawford, 1992). Today's emphasis on androgyny could be a step in the right direction if it helps us overcome the tendency to force girls and boys into narrow molds that represent our ideals of masculinity and femininity. Such ideals only make most of us feel inadequate because we are not "masculine" or "feminine" enough. And yet a new ideal of androgyny may create similar problems—too much pressure on children and adults to live up to an unattainable model of psychological adjustment, this time one in which they must blend masculine and feminine traits (Pleck, 1981). Besides, the concept of androgyny reinforces the false notion that psychological traits *are* either masculine or feminine (Lott, 1985; Unger & Crawford, 1992). Perhaps it is time to see people, regardless of their biological sex, as people. That, surely, would be the most radical social change of all!

SUMMARY POINTS

1. Differences between males and females can be detected in the physical, psychological, and social realms; some gender differences are biological in origin, and others arise as males and females learn their gender roles (including gender-role norms and stereotypes).

2. Research comparing males and females indicates that the two sexes are far more similar than different psychologically. The average male is more aggressive and better at spatial and mathematical problem-solving tasks but less adept at verbal tasks

than the average female. Males may also be more active and developmentally vulnerable, and less compliant, than females, but these and other sex differences are small and becoming even smaller.

3. During infancy, boys and girls are very similar, but adults treat them differently. By age 2, infants have gained a primitive knowledge of their own gender identity and display "gender-appropriate" play preferences. Infants are also sexual beings from the start, even though they have no awareness that their physiological responses are "sexual."

4. Gender typing progresses most rapidly during the toddler and preschool years, with 2- and 3-year-olds already learning gender stereotypes; school-age children know that sex is unchanging, are at first quite rigid and then more flexible in their thinking about gender norms, and segregate themselves by sex.

5. The biosocial theory proposed by Money and Ehrhardt emphasizes prenatal biological developments but also stresses the importance of how a child is labeled and treated during a critical period for gender identity information.

6. From Freud's psychoanalytic perspective, gender-role development results from the child's identification with the same-sex parent; social learning theorists focus on differential reinforcement and observational learning; Kohlberg's cognitive-developmental theory emphasizes self-socialization once children master gender identity, stability, and consistency concepts; and gender schema theory holds that children socialize themselves as soon as they have a basic gender identity and can construct gender schemata.

7. Contrary to Freud's theory, sexual curiosity continues into the latency stage. Societies vary from restrictive to permissive in how they prepare children for mature sexual relationships, and much is learned from peers.

8. Through gender intensification, adolescents show increased concern with conforming to gender norms. Forming a positive sexual identity is an important task of adolescence and can be difficult for youth with a homosexual orientation. During this century the view that sex with affection is acceptable has come to prevail, the double standard has weakened, and conflicting norms have increased confusion among teenagers. In addition, more adolescents are engaging in sexual behavior at earlier ages than in the past, despite the AIDS threat.

9. Adults are influenced by the changing demands of gender roles. Marriage and parenthood appear to cause men and women to adopt more traditionally sex-typed roles. Freed from the parental imperative, middle-aged and elderly adults tend to experience a shift toward androgyny, blending desirable masculine-stereotyped and feminine-stereotyped qualities (though not switching personalities). Androgyny tends to be associated with good adjustment and adaptability in young and old.

10. Most adults marry and become less sexually active over the course of their marriages. Declines in the physiological capacity for sex cannot fully explain declines in sexual activity; poor physical or mental health, lack of a partner, negative societal attitudes, and periods of sexual abstinence also contribute.

11. Attempts to change the gender-role attitudes and behaviors of children have been partially successful but often fail to have lasting effects, perhaps because socialization into traditional roles is so pervasive. Yet societal pressure to adopt narrowly defined gender roles appears to be lessening.

KEY TERMS

androgenized females
androgyny
androgyny shift
double standard
Electra complex
expressive role
gender consistency
gender identity
gender intensification
gender role
gender-role norms
gender-role stereotypes
gender schema (plural: schemata)
gender segregation
gender stability
gender typing
identification
instrumental role
Oedipus complex
parental imperative
posttraumatic stress disorder
sexual orientation

12

CHOICES: THE DEVELOPMENT OF MORALITY AND MOTIVATION

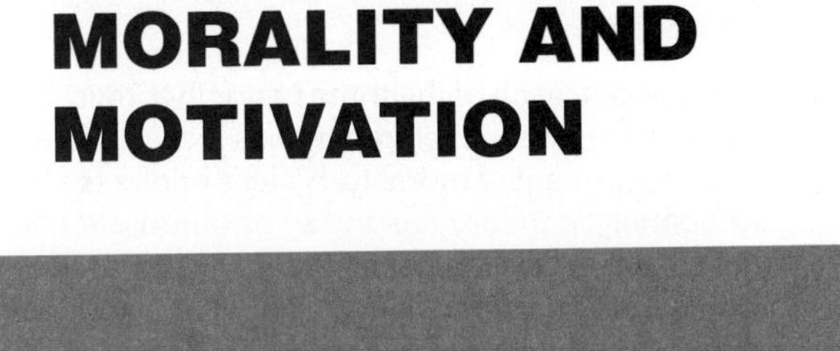

Jennifer Ertman and Elizabeth Pena called their parents to say they were on their way home from the pool party they had attended and took a shortcut through a heavily wooded area. They were spotted by six gang members, ages 14 to 18, who had been drinking beer and fistfighting as part of an initiation ritual for two new recruits. The bodies of the girls were found four days later; they had been raped repeatedly and strangled. One gang member, appearing on a television program about gangs just the day before the murders, had said it all: "Human life means nothing" [Ingrassia, 1993].

Roger Lindsay was fishing when he spotted a man in the middle of the lake starting to go under. Without thinking, Roger jumped in and swam out after him, dragged him back to shore, and resuscitated him. What makes his act particularly heroic is that he was wearing a heavy artificial limb, having lost his leg in a motorcycle accident years earlier [Kreutz, 1991].

Both Roger Lindsay and the teenagers who killed Jennifer Ertman and Elizabeth Pena made choices—choices that reflected the ways in which they were raised and the kinds of people they had become. How, we wonder, can human beings be capable of such good and yet such bad? In this chapter we continue our examination of the development of the self by exploring how we come to acquire the characteristic moral outlooks and motivations that help define us as individuals. When and how do children acquire a sense of right and wrong, a set of moral standards? How do our ways of dealing with moral choices change over the life span? How do children acquire motives such as a strong need for achievement, and how do motivations change over the life span? We will begin by looking at the development of a sense of morality.

PERSPECTIVES ON MORAL DEVELOPMENT

During the course of development, most of us somehow acquire a desire to behave in responsible and moral ways, to think of ourselves and to be thought of by others as moral individuals (Blasi, 1984; Hoffman, 1988). Moreover, we must sometimes choose between gratifying our own needs and doing what is "right," as when a student who is strongly driven to achieve nonetheless refrains from cheating on an exam.

Although we could debate endlessly about what **morality** really is, most of us might agree that the term implies an ability (1) to distinguish right from wrong, (2) to act on this distinction, and (3) to experience pride when one does the right thing and guilt or shame when one does not. Accordingly, three basic components of morality have been identified:

1. An *affective*, or emotional, component, consisting of the feelings (guilt, concern for others' feelings, and so on) that surround right or wrong actions and that motivate moral thoughts and actions.
2. A *cognitive* component, centering on the way we conceptualize right and wrong and make decisions about how to behave.
3. A *behavioral* component, reflecting how we actually behave when, for example, we experience the temptation to cheat or are called upon to help a needy person.

As it turns out, each of the three major theoretical perspectives on moral development has focused on a different component of morality. So let's briefly see what psychoanalytic theory has to say about moral affect, what cognitive-developmental theory has to say about moral cognition or reasoning, and what social learning theory can tell us about moral behavior.

Moral Affect: Psychoanalytic Theory

What kinds of **moral affects,** or emotions, do you feel if you contemplate cheating or lying? Chances are you experience such negative feelings as shame, guilt, anxiety, and fear of being detected—feelings that keep you from doing things you know are wrong. **Empathy,** the vicarious experiencing of another person's feelings (for example, smiling at the good fortune of another or experiencing another person's distress), is another important moral affect; empathizing with individuals who are suffering can motivate prosocial behavior such as helping. Positive emotions like pride and self-satisfaction when one has done the right thing are also an important part of morality. We will generally be motivated to avoid negative moral emotions and experience positive ones by acting in moral ways.

Assuming that young infants are unlikely to feel these sorts of moral emotions, when do they arise?

Learning to resist temptation is an important part of moral development.

Freud's (1935/1960) psychoanalytic theory offered an answer (see Chapter 2). Freud believed that the mature personality has three components: the selfish and irrational id, the rational ego, and the moralistic superego. The *superego,* or conscience, has the important task of ensuring that any plans formed by the ego to gratify the id's urges are morally acceptable. Infants and toddlers, Freud claimed, lack a superego and are essentially "all id." They will therefore act on their selfish motives unless their parents control them.

During the phallic stage (ages 3–6), when children are presumed to experience an emotional conflict over their love for the other-sex parent, the superego is formed. To resolve his *Oedipus complex,* Freud claimed, a boy identifies with and patterns himself after his father, particularly if the father is a threatening figure who arouses fear. Not only does he learn his masculine role in this manner, but he takes on as his own, through the process called **internalization,** his father's moral standards. Similarly, a girl resolves her *Electra complex* by identifying with her mother and internalizing her mother's moral standards. However, Freud believed that girls, because they do not experience the intense fear of castration that boys experience, develop weaker superegos than males do.

Having a superego, then, is like having a parent inside your head—always there, even when someone else isn't, to tell you what is right or wrong and to arouse emotions such as shame and guilt if you so much as think about violating the rules. We can applaud Freud for pointing out that emotion is a very important part of morality, that parents contribute in important ways to moral development, and that children must somehow internalize moral standards if they are to behave morally even when no authority figure is present to detect and punish them.

However, the specifics of Freud's theory are largely unsupported. Cold, threatening, and punitive parents (as we shall see later) do *not* raise morally mature youngsters, and males do *not* appear to have stronger superegos than females. Moreover, moral development begins well before the phallic stage, and children who are 6 or 7 years old, and who have presumably achieved moral maturity by resolving their Oedipal conflicts, have *not* completed their moral growth. Although Freud's broad themes have merit, it may be time to lay the particulars of his theory of moral development to rest. Modern psychoanalytic theorists are discovering instead that the learning of moral emotions and standards of behavior begins in infancy as children who have formed loving (rather than fear-provoking) attachments to their parents begin to notice their parents' emotional reactions to their good and bad behavior (Emde et al., 1991; Kochanska, 1993).

Moral Reasoning: Cognitive-Developmental Theory

Cognitive developmentalists study morality by looking at the development of **moral reasoning**—the thinking process that occurs when we decide whether an act is right or wrong. These theorists assume that moral development depends on cognitive development. Moral reasoning is said to progress through an *invariant sequence,* or a fixed and universal order, of stages, each of which represents a consistent way of thinking about moral issues that is different from the stage preceding or following it. To cognitive-developmental theorists, what is really of interest is *how we decide* what to do, not what we decide or what we actually do. A young child and an adult might both decide not to steal a pen that is there for the taking, but the reasons they give for their decision might be entirely different.

Piaget's View

A cognitive-developmental perspective on moral development was first outlined by Jean Piaget (1932/1965). He studied children's concepts of the nature of rules by asking Swiss children about their games of marbles, and he explored children's concepts of justice by presenting them with moral dilemmas to ponder. For example, he told children about two boys, John and Henry. John, after being called to dinner, went through the door to the dining room. Although he could not have known it, there was a chair with a tray holding 15 cups on it behind the door. When the door swung open, all 15 cups broke. Henry, by contrast, was trying to reach some jam in the cupboard when his mother was out and knocked over and broke a single cup. Having heard the two stories, children were asked "Are these children equally guilty?" and "If not, which child is naughtier? Why?"

From the ways in which children answered such questions, Piaget formulated a theory of moral development that includes a **premoral period** and two moral stages. During the premoral period (the preschool years), children show little concern for or awareness of rules and are not considered to be moral beings. Between the ages of 6 and 10, Piaget claimed, they are usually in the stage of **heteronomous morality** ("heteronomous" meaning "being under the rule of another"). Children of this age believe that rules come from parents and other authority figures and are sacred and unalterable. They also believe that rule violations are wrong to the extent that they have damaging consequences, even if the violator had good intentions (as the boy who broke 15 cups did). Finally, at the age of 10 or 11, most children enter the stage of **autonomous morality.** They now view rules as agreements between individuals—agreements that can be changed through a consensus of those individuals. In judging actions, they pay more attention to whether an actor's intentions were good or bad, seeing Henry, the misbehaving boy who broke one cup, as naughtier than John, the well-intentioned boy who broke 15. According to Piaget, progress through these stages depends on cognitive maturation and social experience. Specifically, he believed that peers contribute more to moral development than parents do because peers are equals and must learn to take one another's perspectives and resolve disagreements among themselves fairly. Several features of Piaget's two stages of moral development are summarized in Table 12.1.

Kohlberg's Theory

Inspired by Piaget's pioneering work, Lawrence Kohlberg (1963, 1981, 1984; Colby & Kohlberg, 1987) formulated the cognitive-developmental theory that has come to dominate the study of moral development.[1] He began his work by asking 10-, 13-, and 16-year-old boys questions about various moral dilemmas to assess how they were thinking about these issues. Careful analysis of the responses led Kohlberg to conclude that moral growth progresses through a universal and invariant sequence of three broad moral levels, each of which is composed of two distinct stages. Each stage grows out of the preceding stage and represents a more complex way of thinking about moral issues. Kohlberg insists that a person cannot skip any stages; moreover, once a person has reached a higher stage, he or she will not regress to earlier stages.

Think about how you would respond to the following moral dilemma posed by Kohlberg and his colleagues:

> There was a woman who had very bad cancer, and there was no treatment known to medicine that would save her. Her doctor, Dr. Jefferson, knew that she had only about 6 months to live. She was in terrible pain, but she was so weak that a good dose of a pain killer like ether or morphine would make her die sooner. She was delirious and almost crazy with pain, and in her calm periods she would ask Dr. Jefferson to give her enough ether to kill her. She said she couldn't stand the pain and she was going to die in a few months anyway. Although he knows that mercy killing is against the law, the doctor thinks about granting her request [Colby, Kohlberg, Gibbs, & Lieberman, 1983, p. 79].

What do you think? Should Dr. Jefferson give her the drug that would make her die? Why or why not? Should the woman have the right to make the final decision? Why or why not? These are among the questions that people are asked after hearing the dilemma. Remember, Kohlberg's goal is to understand *how* an individual thinks, not whether he or she is for or against providing the woman with the drug. Individuals at each stage of moral reasoning might well endorse *either* of the alternative courses of action, but for different reasons. Kohlberg's three levels of moral reasoning, and the two stages within each level, are as follows:

Level 1: Preconventional Morality.

At the level of **preconventional morality,** rules are really external to the self rather than internalized. The child conforms to rules imposed by authority figures in order to avoid punishment or to obtain personal rewards. The perspective of the self dominates: What is right is what one can get away with or what is personally satisfying.

Stage 1: Punishment-and-obedience orientation. The goodness or badness of an act depends on its consequences. The child will obey authorities to avoid punishment but may not consider an act wrong if it will not be punished. The greater the harm done or the more severe the punishment, the more "bad" the act is.

Stage 2: Instrumental hedonism. A person at the second stage of moral development conforms to rules in order to gain rewards or satisfy personal needs. There is some concern for the perspectives of others, but it is ultimately motivated by the hope of benefit in return. "You scratch my back and I'll scratch yours" is the guiding philosophy.

[1]Lawrence Kohlberg was born in 1927 and died in 1987. He put his own moral principles into action as a youth by helping to transport Jewish refugees from Europe to Israel after World War II. He devised his theory of moral development as a doctoral student at the University of Chicago and then spent most of his career at Harvard studying moral development and promoting moral education (Green, 1989).

TABLE 12.1 Piaget's two major stages of moral development.

	Stage of Moral Reasoning	
Aspect of Morality	*Stage of Heteronomous Morality (ages 6 to 10)*	*Stage of Autonomous Morality (ages 10 or 11 and up)*
Conception of rules	*Rules are moral absolutes.* Heteronomous children develop a strong respect for rules and believe they must be obeyed at all times. Rules are laid down by authority figures such as God, the police, or parents. They are sacred and unalterable.	*Rules are agreements among individuals.* Children now realize that the rules of games are not handed down from adult authority figures but are constructed through a consensus of players and can therefore be changed through consensus. Similarly, laws in society are agreements that can be changed with the consent of the people they govern.
Basis for judging acts	*Consequences matter more than intentions.* An act is wrong to the extent that it has damaging consequences. Thus John, who accidentally broke 15 cups while performing a well-intentioned act, is often judged naughtier than Henry, who broke 1 cup while stealing jam.	*Intentions matter more than consequences.* Children's judgments of right or wrong now depend more on the actor's intent to deceive, cause harm, or violate rules than on the magnitude of the damage done. Ten-year-olds reliably say that Henry, who broke 1 cup while stealing jam, is naughtier than the well-intentioned John, who broke 15 cups accidentally. And, unlike an inflexible 6-year-old, a 10-year-old might allow that it is morally defensible to break the speed limit when one is rushing to the hospital in a medical emergency.
View of punishment	*Punishment is for the sake of punishment.* Heteronomous children favor punishment for its own sake rather than as a means of helping the rule violator understand the implications of the transgression. Thus a 6-year-old might favor spanking a boy who has broken a window rather than making him pay for the window from his allowance.	*The punishment should fit the crime.* Autonomous children try to tailor punishments to the act. Making a boy who deliberately breaks a window pay to have it replaced teaches him that windows cost money and that wrongs should be righted.
Nature of justice	*Justice is immanent in the world.* Heteronomous children believe in **immanent justice**—the idea that rule violations will invariably be punished. So, if a 7-year-old girl were to fall and skin her knee shortly after stealing cookies, she might conclude that this injury was the punishment she deserved for her crime. The forces of justice reside in the universe and will get you one way or another!	*Justice is less than perfect.* Perhaps because they have learned from experience that wrongdoing often goes undetected and unpunished, autonomous children no longer believe in immanent justice.

Level 2: Conventional Morality. At the level of **conventional morality,** the individual *has* internalized many moral values. He or she strives to obey the rules set forth by others (parents, peers, the government) in order to win their approval and recognition for good behavior or to maintain social order. The perspectives of other people are clearly recognized and given serious consideration.

Stage 3: "Good boy" or "good girl" morality. What is right is now that which pleases, helps, or is approved by others. People are often judged by their intentions, "meaning well" is valued, and being "nice" is important.

Stage 4: Authority and social-order-maintaining morality. Now what is right is what conforms to the rules of legitimate authorities. The reason for conforming is not so much a fear of punishment as a belief that rules and laws maintain a social order that is worth preserving. Doing one's duty and respecting law and order are valued.

Level 3: Postconventional Morality. At the third and final level of moral reasoning, **postconventional morality,** the individual defines what is right in terms of broad principles of justice that have validity apart from the views of particular authority figures. The individual may distinguish between what is morally right and what is legal, recognizing that some laws—for example, the racial segregation laws that Dr. Martin Luther King, Jr., challenged—violate basic moral principle. Thus the person transcends the perspectives of particular social groups or authorities and begins to take the perspective of *all* individuals.

Stage 5: Morality of contract, individual rights, and democratically accepted law. At this "social contract" stage, there is an increased understanding of the underlying purposes served by laws and a concern that rules be arrived at through a democratic consensus so that they express the will of the majority or maximize social welfare. Whereas the person at Stage 4 is unlikely to challenge an established law, the Stage-5 moral reasoner might call for democratic change in a law that compromises basic rights. The principles embodied in the U.S. Constitution illustrate stage-5 morality.

Stage 6: Morality of individual principles of conscience. At this "highest" stage of moral reasoning, the individual defines right and wrong on the basis of self-chosen principles that are broad and universal in application. The Stage-6 thinker does *not* just make up whatever principles he or she happens to favor but instead arrives at abstract principles of respect for all individuals and their rights that *all* religions or moral authorities might view as moral. Kohlberg (1981) described Stage-6 thinking as a kind of "moral musical chairs" in which the person facing a moral dilemma is able to take the perspective or "chair" of each and every person or group that could potentially be affected by a decision and arrive at a solution that would be regarded as just from every "chair." Stage 6 is Kohlberg's vision of ideal moral reasoning, but it is so rarely observed that Kohlberg stopped attempting to measure its existence.

In Box 12.1 we present examples of how people at the preconventional, conventional, and postconventional levels might reason about the mercy-killing dilemma. Progress through Kohlberg's stages of moral reasoning depends in part on the development of perspective-taking abilities (Selman, 1980; see also Chapter 13). Specifically, as individuals become more able to consider perspectives other than their own, moral reasoning progresses from a rather egocentric focus on personal welfare at the preconventional level, to a concern with the perspectives of other people

BOX 12.1 **Sample Responses to the Mercy-Killing Dilemma at Kohlberg's Three Levels of Moral Reasoning**

Preconventional Morality

Give the drug:

Stage 1: Dr. Jefferson should give the terminally ill woman a drug that will kill her because there is little chance that he will be found out and punished and he would not have to live with her agony anymore.

Stage 2: Dr. Jefferson should give her the drug because he might benefit from the gratitude of her family in the long run if he does what she wants. He should think of it as the right thing to do if it serves his purposes.

Do not give the drug:

Stage 1: The doctor runs a big risk of losing his license and being thrown in prison if he gives her the drug.

Stage 2: Besides, he really has little to gain personally by taking such a big chance. If the woman wants to kill herself, that's her business, but why should he help her if he stands to gain little in return?

Conventional Morality

Give the drug:

Stage 3: Most people would understand that the doctor was motivated by concern for the woman rather than by self-interest. They would be able to forgive him for what was essentially an act of kindness. (*Note:* Many Stage-3 thinkers would be likely to disapprove of mercy killing, however.)

Stage 4: The doctor should give the woman the drug because of the Hippocratic oath, which spells out a doctor's duty to relieve suffering. This oath should be taken seriously by all doctors.

Do not give the drug:

Stage 3: Most people are likely to disapprove of mercy killing. Dr. Jefferson would clearly lose the respect of his colleagues and friends if he administered the drug. A good person simply would not do this.

Stage 4: Mercy killing is against the laws that we as citizens are obligated to uphold. The Bible is another compelling authority, and it too says "Thou shalt not kill." Dr. Jefferson simply can't take the law into his own hands; instead, he has a duty to uphold the law.

Postconventional Morality

Give the drug:

Stage 5: Although most of our laws have a sound basis in moral principle, laws against mercy killing do not. The doctor's act is morally justified in that it relieves the suffering of an agonized human being. Yet, if Dr. Jefferson breaks the law in the service of a greater good, he should still be willing to be held legally accountable because society would be damaged if everyone simply ignored laws they do not like.

Stage 6: One must consider the effects of this act on everyone concerned—the doctor, the dying woman, other terminally ill people, all people everywhere. Basic moral principle dictates that all people have a right to dignity and self-determination, as long as others are not harmed by their decisions. Assuming that no one else will be hurt, then, the dying woman has a right to live and die as she chooses. The doctor is doing right by respecting her integrity as a person and saving her, her family, and all of society from needless suffering.

Do not give the drug:

Stage 5: The laws against mercy killing protect citizens from harm at the hands of unscrupulous doctors and should be upheld. If the laws were to be changed through the democratic process, that might be another thing. But right now the doctor can best serve society by adhering to them.

Stage 6: If we truly adhere to the principle that human life should be valued above all else and all lives should be valued equally, it is morally wrong to "play God" and decide that some lives are worth living and others are not. Before long we would have a world in which no life has value.

(parents, friends, and even members of the society in which one lives) at the conventional level, and, ultimately, to a concern with what is right from the perspective of *all* people at the postconventional level.

Moral Behavior: Social Learning Theory

Social learning theorists such as Albert Bandura (1986, 1991) and Walter Mischel (1974) have been primarily interested in the behavioral component of morality—in what we actually *do* when faced with temptation. These theorists claim that moral behavior is learned in the same way that other social behaviors are learned: through reinforcement and punishment and through observational learning. They also consider moral behavior to be strongly influenced by the nature of the specific situations in which people find themselves. That is, a person may behave morally in one situation but transgress in another or proclaim that nothing is more important than honesty but then lie.

To highlight the difference between social learning theory and other perspectives, let's see how different theorists might attempt to predict whether a teenager (Bubba, we'll call him) will cheat on his upcoming math test. Freud would certainly want to know whether Bubba identified strongly with his father in early childhood. If he did, presumably he has developed a strong superego as part of his personality and therefore will be less likely to cheat, lie, or steal than a child with a weak superego (unless, of course, his father had a weak superego).

Kohlberg, meanwhile, would be interested in Bubba's level of cognitive development and, specifically, in the stage at which he reasons about moral dilemmas. Although Kohlberg insists that one's level of moral reasoning does not necessarily predict which decision one will make, Kohlberg would at least expect Bubba's mode of decision making to be consistent across many moral situations. Moreover, since Kohlberg believes that each higher stage permits a more adequate way of making moral decisions, he might expect the child whose moral reasoning is advanced to be less likely to cheat than the child who still thinks at the preconventional level. Notice, then, that both the psychoanalytic perspective and the cognitive-developmental perspective view morality as a kind of personality trait—a quality that each of us possesses and that consistently influences our judgments and actions.

What might social learning theorists say about Bubba? They would be curious about the moral habits he has learned and the expectations he has formed about the probable consequences of his actions. If Bubba's parents, for example, have consistently reinforced him when he has behaved morally and punished him when he has misbehaved, he will be more likely to behave in morally acceptable ways than a child who has not had adequate moral training. Bubba will also be better off if he has been exposed to many models of morally acceptable behavior rather than brought up in the company of liars, cheaters, and thieves.

And yet social learning theorists are skeptical of the notion that morality is a single highly consistent trait or mode of thinking that will show itself in all situations. Even if Bubba's parents have taught him to be honest, for example, that learning may not generalize well to the math class when Bubba faces an opportunity to cheat. Moreover, *situational* influences in the math class might have more influence on Bubba's behavior than his prior learning. What if it is obvious to him that he stands no chance of being caught and punished? What if his friend Willard promises to get him a date on Friday night (a powerful reinforcer) if he enters into a cheating conspiracy? What if he observes his classmates cheating on the test and sees that they are getting away with it?

In sum, the social learning perspective on moral development holds that morality is *situation-specific behavior* rather than a generalized trait such as a strong superego or a postconventional mode of moral reasoning. Influenced by specific learning experiences, we do acquire moral (or immoral) habits that express themselves in situations in which it is possible to cheat, lie, steal, help a person in need, and so on. And yet each specific moral situation we encounter also affects our behavior.

We are now ready to trace the development of morality from infancy to old age. Our coverage charts the development of the self as a moral being, examining moral affect, cognition, and behavior as they have been conceptualized by psychoanalytic, cognitive-developmental, and social learning theorists.

THE INFANT

Do infants have any sense of right or wrong? If a baby takes a toy that belongs to another child, would you label the act stealing? If an infant hits another child in the head with a toy, would you insist that the infant be put on trial for assault? Of course not. Adults in our society, including psychologists, tend to view infants as **amoral**—that is, lacking in any sense of morality. Since we do not believe that infants are capable of evaluating their behavior in the light of moral standards, we do not hold them morally responsible for any wrongs they commit (although we certainly attempt to prevent them from harming others). Nor do we expect them to be "good" when we are not around to watch them.

Yet, even though infants are initially quite amoral, it is now clear that they begin to learn important moral lessons during their first two years of life (Emde et al., 1991; Gralinski & Kopp, 1993). Roger Burton (1984) provides a delightful example of the moral socialization of his 1½-year-old daughter Ursula. It seems that

Ursula was so taken by the candy that she and her sisters had gathered on Halloween that she snatched some from her sisters' bags. The sisters immediately said "No, that's mine," and conveyed their outrage in the strongest terms. A week later the sisters again found some of their candy in Ursula's bag and raised a fuss, and it was their mother's turn to explain the rules to Ursula. The problem continued until finally Burton himself came upon Ursula in a sister's bedroom looking at some forbidden candy. Ursula looked up and said "No, this is Maria's, not Ursula's" (p. 199).

Burton and others believe that it is through such social learning experiences, accumulated over the years, that children come to understand the meaning of stealing. Moreover, they learn from being reprimanded to associate the act of stealing with negative emotional responses. As they near the age of 2, children are already beginning to show clear signs of distress when they break things or otherwise violate standards of behavior (Cole, Barrett, & Zahn-Waxler, 1992; Emde et al., 1991; Kagan, 1981; Kochanska, 1993). This means they are beginning to anticipate disapproval when they fail to comply with the rules that parents and other authority figures have set for them. So moral learning begins in infancy as children encounter rules, experience other people's positive or negative reactions to their rule-breaking behavior, test the limits to see what they can get away with, and work out, in interaction with their caregivers, understandings of what is acceptable and what is not (Emde et al., 1991; Gralinski & Kopp, 1993). If parents are firm but not harsh as they attempt to get toddlers to comply with their demands, these young children are likely to become cooperative rather than defiant and eventually will be able to control their own behavior even when parents are not around (Crockenberg & Litman, 1990).

It is also becoming clear that infants are not quite so selfish, egocentric, and unconcerned about other people as Freud, Piaget, Kohlberg, and many other theorists have assumed. Perhaps the strongest evidence that infants have something akin to a moral sense comes from studies of empathy and **prosocial behavior,** positive social acts such as helping or sharing that reflect a concern for the welfare of others. Even newborns display a very primitive form of empathy: They become distressed by the cries of other newborns (Hoffman, 1988; Martin & Clark, 1982). It is unlikely that they really distinguish between another infant's distress and their own, though. Moreover, they are not yet capable of acting on their primitive empathy by behaving altruistically to relieve another's distress (Hoffman, 1981).

The capacity to act prosocially emerges in the second year of life. Carolyn Zahn-Waxler and her colleagues (1992) report that over half of the 13- to 15-month-old infants they studied were observed to engage in at least one act of prosocial behavior—helping, sharing, expressing concern, comforting, and so on. These behaviors became increasingly common from age 1 to age 2, when all but one child in their study acted prosocially. Consider the reaction of 21-month-old John to his distressed playmate, Jerry:

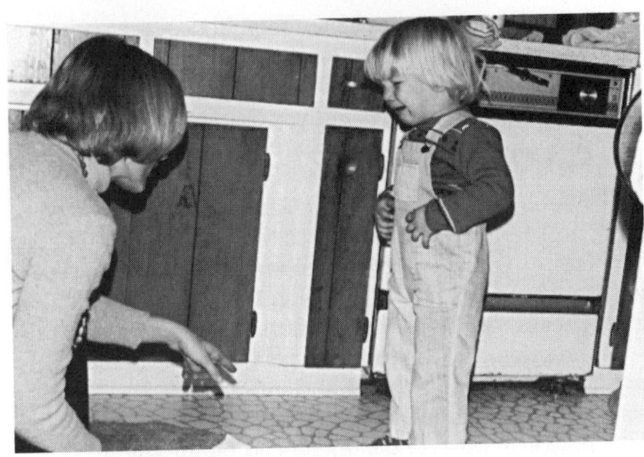

Children learn very early that some acts have negative consequences.

> Today Jerry was kind of cranky; he just started . . . bawling and he wouldn't stop. John kept coming over and handing Jerry toys, trying to cheer him up. . . . He'd say things like "Here, Jerry," and I said to John "Jerry's sad; he doesn't feel good; he had a shot today." John would look at me with his eyebrows wrinkled together like he really understood that Jerry was crying because he was unhappy . . . [Zahn-Waxler, Radke-Yarrow, & King, 1979, pp. 321–322].

Overall, then, infants are amoral in some senses, particularly when it comes to making judgments of right and wrong or resisting temptations to engage in prohibited behaviors. Yet at the same time their "moral socialization" has begun, they are learning standards of conduct, and they already show the rudiments of concern for other people. Drawing on this evidence, Martin Hoffman (1981, 1993) has argued that empathy is built into the very nature of human beings and serves as an important motivator of moral behavior. It is empathy, Hoffman argues, that compels us to set aside our own selfish motives to help other people—and to avoid harming them.

THE CHILD

During the years from age 2 to age 12, children's standards of morality and their motivation to live up to these standards grow out of their social experiences in the family, peer group, and wider society. Research on moral development during childhood has explored how children of different ages think about moral issues. It has also told us a good deal about how children actually behave when their moral values are tested.

Kohlberg's View of the Child's Moral Reasoning

The hypothetical moral dilemmas that Lawrence Kohlberg devised to assess stages of moral reasoning (for example, the mercy-killing dilemma presented earlier) are too complex for preschool children to understand. How do school-aged children do? They generally reason at the preconventional level, taking an egocentric perspective on morality and defining as right those acts that are rewarded and as wrong those acts that are punished (Colby et al., 1983). At best, they are beginning to make the transition to conventional moral reasoning by displaying a Stage-3 concern with being a "good boy" or a "good girl" who gains the approval of others.

In short, from Kohlberg's perspective most children, and especially young children, are not really moral beings yet, for they have not yet internalized conventional societal values as their own. Kohlberg's stages seem to be more useful in describing the moral reasoning of adolescents and adults than in describing that of young children. However, other researchers have looked more closely at the moral reasoning of young children and find that they engage in some fairly sophisticated thinking about right and wrong.

Research on Piaget's Theory of Moral Reasoning

Piaget claimed that children progress from a premoral period to a stage of heteronomous morality and then to a stage of autonomous morality at about age 10. Consistent with his view, young children are more likely than older children to display such aspects of heteronomous morality as a belief in *immanent justice* and a tendency to emphasize consequences more than intentions when judging how wrong an act is (Jose, 1990; Surber, 1982). Moreover, a child's level of moral reasoning does depend, in part, on his or her level of cognitive development. At the same time, however, it has become clear that Piaget, like Kohlberg, badly underestimated the moral sophistication of preschool and young grade-school children.

Consider first Piaget's claim that young children judge acts as right or wrong on the basis of their consequences rather than the intentions that guided them. He found that children in the heteronomous stage of moral reasoning (ages 6 to 10) usually judged John, the well-intentioned boy who broke 15 cups accidentally, to be naughtier than Henry, who broke one cup while reaching for some forbidden jam. The problem is that this moral-decision story confused the issue by asking if the individual who causes a small amount of harm in the service of bad intentions is naughtier than the person who causes a large amount of damage despite good intentions.

Sharon Nelson (1980) overcame this flaw in an interesting experiment with 3-year-olds. Each child listened to stories in which a character threw a ball to a playmate. The actor's motive was described as *good* (his friend had nothing to play with) or *bad* (the actor was mad at his friend), and the consequences of his act were either *positive* (the friend caught the ball and was happy to play with it) or *negative* (the ball hit the friend in the head and made him cry). To make the task even simpler, Nelson showed children drawings of what happened (see Figure 12.1 for an example).

How did these 3-year-olds judge the "goodness" or "badness" of the actor's behavior? As we see in

FIGURE 12.1 Examples of drawings used by Nelson to convey an actor's intentions to preschool children. Here we see negative intent and a negative consequence. (From Nelson, 1980.)

Figure 12.2, they did judge acts that had positive consequences more favorably than acts that had negative consequences. Yet the more interesting finding was that the well-intentioned child who had wanted to play was evaluated much more favorably than the child who intended to hurt his friend, *regardless of the consequences of his actions.* Apparently, then, even very young children can base their moral judgments on an actor's intentions (see also Bussey, 1992; Nelson-Le Gall, 1985). Indeed, young children frequently attempt to escape punishment by pleading "I didn't mean it! I didn't mean it!" Overall, Piaget was correct to conclude that young children assign more weight to consequences and less weight to intentions than older children do, but he was wrong to conclude that young children are incapable of weighing both factors at once when they evaluate others' conduct (Olthof, Ferguson, & Luiten, 1989; Surber, 1982).

Piaget also claimed that children in the heteronomous stage of moral development view rules as sacred prescriptions laid down by respected authority figures. These moral absolutes cannot be questioned or changed. However, Elliot Turiel (1978, 1983) observed that children actually encounter two kinds of rules in daily life: (1) **moral rules,** or standards that focus on the welfare and basic rights of individuals, and (2) **social-conventional rules,** standards determined by social consensus that tell us what is appropriate in a particular social setting. Moral rules include rules against hitting, stealing, lying, and otherwise harming others or violating their rights. Social-conventional rules are more like rules of social etiquette and include the rules of games as well as school rules that forbid eating snacks in class or using the restroom without permission.

Children are already beginning to learn during their preschool years that moral and social-conventional rules are different and that moral rules are more compelling and unalterable (Nucci & Nucci, 1982; Smetana, 1989; Smetana, Schlagman, & Adams, 1993). Judith Smetana (1981), for example, discovered that preschool children as young as age 2½ regard moral transgressions such as hitting, stealing, or refusing to share as much more serious and deserving of punishment than social-conventional violations such as not staying in one's seat in nursery school or not saying grace before eating. Even more remarkable is what these youngsters said when asked if a violation would be okay if there were no rule against it: They claimed that it was *always* wrong to hit people or commit other moral transgressions, rule or no rule, but they felt that it would be perfectly okay for children to get out of their seats at nursery school or violate other social conventions in the absence of any explicit rules.

Moreover, 6- to 10-year-old children, who should be in Piaget's heteronomous stage of morality and should therefore be even more likely than younger children to regard the laws laid down by adults as "sacred," are very capable of questioning adult authority (Tisak, 1986; Tisak & Tisak, 1990). These children claim that it is perfectly fine for parents to enforce rules against stealing and other moral violations, but they believe that it can be inappropriate and unjustifiable for parents to arbitrarily restrict their children's friendships. It turns out that school-aged children will not blindly accept any dictate offered by an adult as legitimate.

Overall, then, children younger than about 10 years are considerably more sophisticated in their moral thinking than Piaget believed. They are quite capable of judging acts as right or wrong according to whether the actor's intentions were good or bad, even though they do often place more weight on an act's consequences and less weight on the motives behind the act than older children do. In addition, they do not view *all* rules as absolute, sacred, and unchangeable. Instead, they realize that social-conventional rules are far more arbitrary and less binding than moral rules,

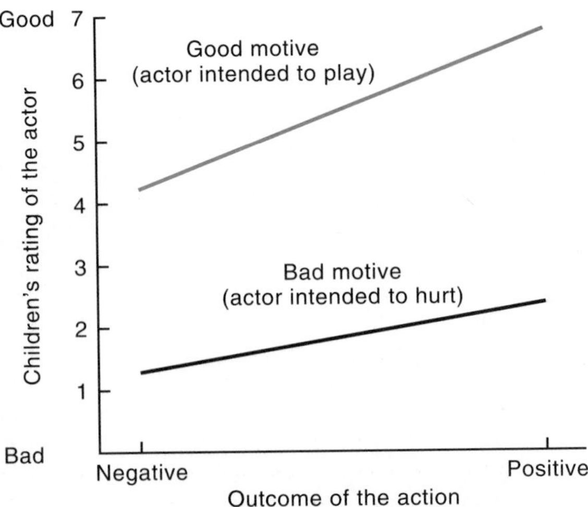

FIGURE 12.2 Average ratings of an actor's behavior for actors who had either good or bad intentions and produced either positive or negative outcomes. (From Nelson, 1980.)

and they challenge adult authority when they believe it is illegitimate.

It seems that both Piaget and Kohlberg failed to appreciate how much moral growth takes place in early childhood. Both regarded young children as selfish and amoral creatures who have not yet internalized rules of moral conduct and cannot be expected to behave morally. Yet we now appreciate that even toddlers are capable of feeling empathy, showing concern for the welfare of others, and behaving in prosocial ways (Hoffman, 1988; Zahn-Waxler et al., 1992). What's more, we know that 5- and 6-year-olds have already formed concepts of fairness and will act fairly by dividing rewards equally among everyone who is entitled to them (Damon, 1977; Sigelman & Waitzman, 1991). Young children have by no means completed their moral growth, but they are well on their way to becoming moral beings long before late childhood and early adolescence, the periods that Piaget and Kohlberg mark as the time of substantial moral growth.

Although it is often difficult to tell whether children are working together or using each other's work, most youngsters can be tempted to cheat if the situational factors are right. Children's moral conduct is fairly inconsistent from situation to situation.

Resisting Temptation: Children's Moral Behavior

To many people, the ultimate goal of moral socialization is to produce a child who can resist the temptation to violate moral rules even when there is little chance of detection and punishment (Hoffman, 1970). This individual not only has internalized moral values but is motivated to abide by them. Can children be trusted to abide by rules? Will they cheat if they think they can get away with it? What factors influence whether or not a child will behave morally? These are just the sorts of questions that social learning theorists have asked, and their findings add greatly to our understanding of moral development and how it can be fostered.

Consider a classic study of moral behavior reported by Hugh Hartshorne and Mark May (1928–1930). Their purpose was to investigate the moral character of 10,000 children (aged 8–16) by tempting them to lie, cheat, or steal in a variety of situations. It readily became apparent that almost all children espoused "sound" moral values, claiming that honesty was good, cheating and stealing were wrong, and so on. Yet the most noteworthy findings of this massive investigation were that (1) children who cheated or violated other moral rules in a particular situation were just as likely as those who did not to state that cheating is wrong, and (2) most children *did* violate their own moral rules in at least one situation. In other words, Hartshorne and May had a tough time finding children who not only espoused the right values but consistently acted according to those values. Most children's moral behavior was quite inconsistent from situation to situation.

Reanalyses of these data and new investigations suggest that children are somewhat more consistent in their behavior than Hartshorne and May had concluded (Burton, 1963; Nelson, Grinder, & Mutterer, 1969; Rushton, 1980). Across a set of situations, some children tend to be more honest, more likely to resist temptation, or more helpful than other children. Still, moral thought, affect, and behavior are not as closely interrelated in childhood as they will be by adolescence or adulthood (Blasi, 1980).

Why are children relatively inconsistent in their moral behavior? One explanation may be that they are reasoning at Kohlberg's preconventional level. When punishment and reward are the primary considerations in defining acts as right or wrong, perhaps it is not surprising that the child may see nothing wrong with cheating when the chances of detection and punishment are slim. In addition, moral inconsistency results from *situational* influences on behavior: the importance of the goal that can be achieved by transgressing, the probability of being detected, and the amount of encouragement provided by peers (Burton, 1976). Social learning theorists have identified many important situational influences on moral behavior, so let's see what they have learned that might aid parents and other socialization agents in raising a child who can be counted on to behave morally.

How Does One Raise Moral Children?

Social learning theorists would advise parents who want to foster moral maturity in their children to reinforce moral behavior, punish immoral behavior, and serve as models of moral behavior. Reinforcement can be used to strengthen prosocial behaviors such as sharing or to teach children acceptable alternatives to acts one wants to discourage (Fischer, 1963;

Perry & Parke, 1975). Punishment of misdeeds can also contribute to moral growth if it is not overly harsh, if it teaches children to associate negative emotions with their wrongdoing, if it is accompanied by an explanation of why the forbidden act is wrong and should be avoided, and if it is supplemented by efforts to encourage and reinforce more acceptable behavior (Perry & Parke, 1975; see also Chapter 8). The problem with punishment, especially severe physical punishment, is that it may have undesirable side effects (such as making children resentful or overly anxious or teaching them that aggression is an appropriate means of solving problems).

Social learning theorists also emphasize that parents should serve as models of moral behavior. Children will follow the example of an adult who resists temptation (Toner, Parke, & Yussen, 1978). Moreover, they are especially likely to do so if models state the rule they are following and a rationale for not committing the prohibited act (Grusec, Kuczynski, Rushton, & Simutis, 1979). Finally, the explanations or rationales offered by adults seem to work best when they are tailored to the child's level of moral development (Toner & Potts, 1981). Thus a girl who reasons at the preconventional level might respond well to the argument that swiping other children's belongings will get her in big trouble with the teacher, whereas a conventional thinker might be swayed by an argument that focuses on the rights and feelings of classmates. In disciplining children who have not yet internalized conventional moral standards, it may be necessary to point out what *they* stand to gain or lose by behaving or misbehaving.

The important work of Martin Hoffman (1970, 1983, 1988) has provided additional insights into how to foster not only moral behavior but moral thought and affect as well. Several years ago, Hoffman (1970) reviewed the child-rearing literature to determine which parental approaches were associated with high levels of moral development. Three major approaches were compared:

1. **Love withdrawal**: withholding attention, affection, or approval after a child misbehaves—or, in other words, creating anxiety by threatening a loss of reinforcement from parents.
2. **Power assertion**: using power to administer spankings, take away privileges, and so on—in other words, using punishment.
3. **Induction**: explaining to a child why the behavior is wrong and should be changed by emphasizing how it affects other people.

Suppose that little Ronnie has just put the beloved family cat through a cycle in the clothes dryer. Using love withdrawal, a parent might say "How could you do something like that? I can't even bear to look at you!" Using power assertion, a parent might say "Get to your room this minute; you're going to catch it." Using induction, a parent might say "Ronnie, look how scared Fluffy is. You could have killed her, and you know how sad we'd all be if she died." Induction, then, is a matter of providing rationales or explanations that focus special attention on the consequences of wrongdoing for other people (or cats, as the case may be).

Which approach best fosters moral development? As you can see in Table 12.2, induction is more often positively associated with children's moral maturity than either love withdrawal or power assertion (Brody & Shaffer, 1982). The use of power assertion is actually more often associated with moral *immaturity* than with moral maturity. Love withdrawal has been found to have positive effects in some studies but negative effects in others. Why is induction particularly effective? By explaining *why* an act was wrong through induction, parents can (1) communicate standards and provide children with cognitive rationales that they can use to evaluate their own behavior, (2) help children empathize with the individuals they may have hurt and associate moral emotions such as guilt and shame with their wrongdoing, and (3) point out what the child should have done instead. In short, induction calls attention to the cognitive, affective, and behavioral aspects of morality and may help children to integrate them.

Hoffman (1983) realizes that parents often combine power assertion, love withdrawal, and induction

TABLE 12.2 Relationships between parents' use of three disciplinary strategies and children's moral development.

	Type of Discipline		
Direction of Relationship between Parents' Use of a Disciplinary Strategy and Children's Moral Maturity	*Power Assertion*	*Love Withdrawal*	*Induction*
Positive correlation	7	8	38
Negative correlation	32	11	6

Note: Table entries represent the number of occasions on which a particular disciplinary technique was found to be associated (either positively or negatively) with a measure of children's moral affect, reasoning, or behavior.

SOURCE: Adapted from Brody & Shaffer, 1982.

rather than using a single approach. In fact, he believes that prudent use of power assertion or love withdrawal as an accompaniment to induction can help motivate the child to pay attention to the message being communicated. Still, children must be taught why immoral acts are wrong if they are ever to truly internalize the moral values that adults would like them to acquire. Hoffman's work provides a fairly clear picture of how parents can best contribute to the moral growth of their children.

Yet we must appreciate that some children are more morally trainable than others. As Grazyna Kochanska (1993) emphasizes, a child's temperament influences how he or she responds to socialization efforts. Some children are, by temperament, more emotionally arousable than others and therefore more likely to become appropriately anxious and distressed when they are disciplined. Some children are also less impulsive than others, which enables them to inhibit their urges to engage in wrongdoing. Those who are relatively high in emotionality and low in impulsivity should be relatively easy to socialize using positive disciplinary techniques such as induction. However, children who are not easily led to associate guilt and other negative emotions with their wrongdoings or who have difficulty controlling their impulses to repeat forbidden acts may drive parents to use more power-assertive (and ineffective) discipline (Anderson, Lytton, & Romney, 1986; Lytton, 1990). In other words, parents affect children, but children also affect their parents as moral socialization proceeds and children prepare to resist the temptations of adolescence.

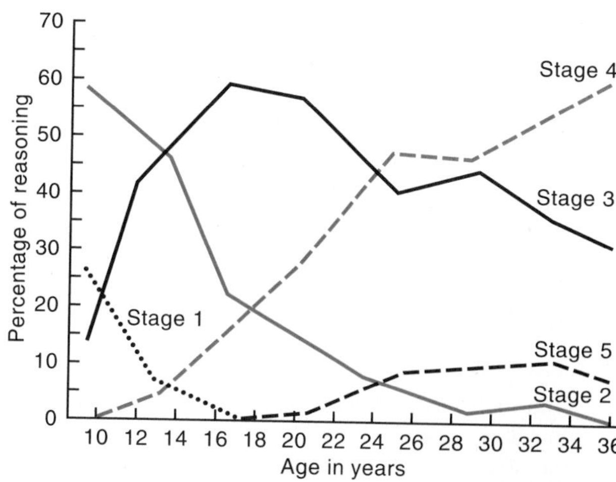

FIGURE 12.3 Average percentage of moral reasoning at each of Kohlberg's stages for males from age 10 to age 36. (From Colby et al., 1983.)

THE ADOLESCENT

As adolescents gain the capacity to think about abstract and hypothetical ideas, and as they begin to chart their future identities, many of them reflect a great deal on their values and moral standards. Others do not reflect enough, it seems, and end up behaving in antisocial ways.

Changes in Moral Reasoning

Although most teenagers break the law now and then, adolescence is actually a period of considerable growth in moral reasoning and a time when many individuals become increasingly motivated to behave morally. Consider first the results of a 20-year longitudinal study that involved repeatedly asking the 10-, 13-, and 16-year-old boys originally studied by Kohlberg to respond to moral dilemmas (Colby et al., 1983). Figure 12.3 shows the percentage of judgments offered at each age that reflected each of Kohlberg's six stages.

A number of interesting developmental trends can be seen here. Notice that the preconventional reasoning (Stage-1 and -2 thinking) that dominates among 10-year-olds decreases considerably during the teen years. During the adolescent years, conventional reasoning (Stages 3 and 4) is becoming the dominant mode of moral thinking. So, among 13- to 14-year-olds, most moral judgments reflect either a Stage-2 (instrumental hedonism) approach—"You scratch my back and I'll scratch yours"—or a Stage-3 ("good boy"/"good girl") concern with being nice and earning approval. Over half of the judgments offered by 16- to 18-year-olds embodied Stage-3 reasoning, but about a fifth were scored as Stage-4 (authority and social-order-maintaining morality) arguments. These older adolescents were beginning to take a broad societal perspective on justice and were concerned about acting in ways that would help maintain the social system.

Where are all the postconventional moral reasoners? Kohlberg's work suggests that postconventional reasoning does not appear until early adulthood. In short, the main developmental trend in moral reasoning during adolescence is a shift from preconventional thinking to more conventional reasoning. It is during adolescence that most individuals seem to rise above a concern with external rewards and punishments and begin to express a genuine concern with living up to the moral standards that parents and other authorities have taught them and ensuring that laws designed to make human relations orderly and fair are taken seriously and maintained.

William Damon and Daniel Hart (1992) have observed another important breakthrough in moral development during adolescence: many teens begin to view morality as an important part of their identity. Because adolescents are more sensitive than children are to the expectations of those around them, they are more motivated to portray and view themselves as honest, fair, and caring individuals. Many come to feel that they would lose self-respect if they selfishly ignored others' needs (Eisenberg et al., 1991). A few even become moral leaders who devote their lives to achieving social justice (Colby & Damon, 1992).

In short, most adolescents have clearly internalized conventional moral values, and many are highly motivated to be the kinds of moral beings that people around them want them to be. But what about those adolescents who seem to have no moral values at all?

Antisocial Behavior

Although most adolescents are law abiding most of the time, a small minority of youth, like the gang members mentioned at the beginning of this chapter, are involved in serious antisocial conduct—muggings, rapes, armed robberies, knifings, drive-by shootings. Might adolescents who engage repeatedly in aggressive, antisocial acts be cases of arrested moral development who have not internalized the conventional values of society? Studies do suggest that juvenile offenders are more likely than nondelinquents to engage in preconventional, relatively egocentric, moral reasoning (Blasi, 1980; Gibbs, Basinger, & Fuller, 1992; Trevethan & Walker, 1989). Some offenders clearly lack a sense of right and wrong and feel little remorse about their criminal acts. Yet the relationship between moral reasoning and antisocial behavior is weak; a sizable number of delinquents are capable of conventional moral reasoning but commit illegal acts anyway (Blasi, 1980). This suggests that we must consider a wider range of factors in order to understand the origins of antisocial conduct.

Kenneth Dodge has advanced our understanding by offering a social information-processing model of aggressive behavior (Dodge, 1980, 1986, 1993; Dodge & Frame, 1982). Imagine that you are walking down the aisle in a classroom and trip over a classmate's leg. As you fall to the floor, you really have little information about why this incident occurred, but you are already emotionally aroused. Dodge and other social information-processing theorists believe that the individual's reactions to frustration, anger, or provocation depend not so much on the social cues present in the situation as on the ways in which the person processes and interprets this information.

An individual who is provoked (as by being tripped) will progress through five steps in information processing: (1) *encoding* (taking in information), (2) *interpretation* (making sense of it), (3) *response search* (thinking of possible actions), (4) *response evaluation* (weighing the pros and cons of possible actions), and (5) *enactment* (doing something). Highly aggressive youth, including adolescents incarcerated for violent crimes (Slaby & Guerra, 1988), show deficient or biased information processing at every step of the way—or they skip steps entirely and act impulsively, "without thinking" (Dodge, 1993; Slaby & Guerra, 1988).

For example, a highly aggressive adolescent who is tripped by a classmate is likely to (1) process relatively few of the available cues in the situation and show a bias toward information suggesting that the tripping was deliberate rather than accidental (for example, noticing a fleeting smirk on the classmate's face); (2) infer, based on the information gathered, that the classmate did indeed have a hostile intent; (3) think of only a few possible ways to react, mostly aggressive ones; (4) conclude, after evaluating alternative actions, that an aggressive response will have favorable outcomes (or perhaps not think about the consequences of possible actions at all); and (5) carry out the particular aggressive response selected (see Table 12.3).

One distinctive characteristic of highly aggressive youth is that they tend to see the world as a hostile place; if a situation is ambiguous (as a tripping or bumping incident is likely to be), they are more likely than nonaggressive youth to attribute hostile intent to whoever harms them. It is likely that emotions come into play at this point, for the anger individuals experience

TABLE 12.3 The five steps in Dodge's social information-processing model and likely responses of a highly aggressive youth to provocation.

Step	*Behaviors*	*Likely Responses of Aggressive Youth*
1. Encoding	Search for, attend to, and register cues in the situation	Focus on cues suggesting hostile intent; ignore other relevant information
2. Interpretation	Interpret situation; infer other's motive	Infer that provoker had hostile intent
3. Response Search	Generate possible responses	Generate few options, most of them aggressive
4. Response Evaluation	Assess likely consequences of responses generated; choose the best	See advantages in responding aggressively rather than nonaggressively (or fail to evaluate consequences at all; act impulsively)
5. Enactment	Produce chosen response; act	Behave aggressively

Note: See Dodge (1993) for further details and relevant research.

when they believe they have been harmed deliberately is likely to motivate aggressive action (Graham, Hudley, & Williams, 1992). This in turn could trigger counteraggression, which is likely to reinforce the belief that other people are hostile. In addition, aggressive youth tend to evaluate the consequences of aggression far more positively than other adolescents do. They expect their aggressive acts to achieve the desired results, view being "tough" and controlling others as important to their self-esteem, and feel morally justified in acting because they believe they are only retaliating against individuals who are "out to get them" (Boldizar, Perry, & Perry, 1989; Coie et al., 1991; Quiggle et al., 1992).

In one recent study (Guerra & Slaby, 1990), a group of incarcerated violent juveniles were coached (1) to look for situational cues other than those suggesting hostile intentions, (2) to control their impulses, and (3) to generate nonaggressive solutions to conflicts. These adolescents showed dramatic improvements in social information-processing skills, began to place less value on aggression, and behaved less aggressively in their interactions with authority figures and other inmates. Trained offenders were only somewhat less likely than untrained offenders to violate their paroles after release, though, suggesting that they may have reverted to their antisocial ways when they returned to the environments in which their aggressive tendencies originated. Indeed, for many young African-American and Hispanic males in gang-dominated inner-city neighborhoods, being quick to detect others' hostile intentions and defend oneself against assault may well be an important survival skill (Hudley & Graham, 1993).

And that leads us to an important point: Dodge's social information-processing model is helpful in understanding why children and adolescents might be provoked to behave aggressively in particular situations, but it does not fully explain how aggressive and nonaggressive individuals came to have such different information-processing styles in the first place (Dodge, 1993). Severe antisocial behavior is most likely the product of an interplay between genetic predisposition and social learning experiences. Twin studies suggest that some individuals are genetically predisposed to have hostile, irritable temperaments and to engage in aggressive, delinquent, and criminal behavior (Plomin, 1990; Rushton et al., 1986). This does *not* mean that they are doomed to become antisocial individuals, however, for the social environments in which they are raised play a crucial role in determining their actual conduct.

What social influences are important? Some cultural contexts are especially likely to breed aggression; the United States happens to lead all industrialized countries in rapes and murders (Wolff, Rutten, & Bayer, 1992). In addition, rates of violent crime are

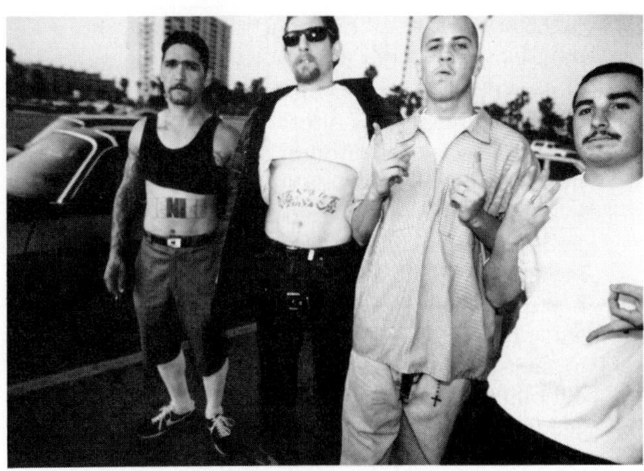

Aggressive tendencies nurtured in coercive family environments can be further strengthened in antisocial peer groups or gangs.

over three times higher in lower socioeconomic areas than in middle-class ones (Elliott & Ageton, 1980).

Then there are family influences on aggression. Gerald Patterson and his colleagues have found that highly antisocial children and adolescents often come from **coercive family environments** in which family members are locked in power struggles, each trying to control the others through coercive tactics such as threatening, yelling, and hitting (Dishion et al., 1991; Patterson, 1982; Patterson, DeBaryshe, & Ramsey, 1989). In such families, parents increasingly lose control over their children's behavior, until even the loudest lectures and hardest spankings have little effect. The next steps in the making of an antisocial adolescent are predictable: The child (1) ends up performing poorly in school and being rejected by other children; (2) becomes involved in a peer group made up of other low-achieving, antisocial, and unpopular youths; and (3) is steered even further in the direction of a delinquent career by these colleagues in crime (Dishion et al., 1991; see also Cairns et al., 1988).

In sum, the severe antisocial behavior that some adolescents display is more than a matter of immature moral reasoning, although many delinquent youth do reason at Kohlberg's preconventional level. Antisocial behavior can also be traced to deficiencies in social information-processing skills that make youngsters quick to attribute hostile intentions to other people and convinced of the value of aggression. This information-processing style, in turn, may be rooted both in genetically influenced temperamental traits and in social learning experiences in the family, peer group, and wider society. All these factors help to determine whether youth enter adulthood as model citizens or menaces to society.

THE ADULT

Most adults assume the responsibilities of parents, employers or work supervisors, or community leaders, so their moral decisions affect not only their own lives but those of people around them as well. How does moral thinking change during adulthood?

As we have discovered already (see Figure 12.3, p. 341), Kohlberg's postconventional moral reasoning appears to emerge *only* during the adult years (if it emerges at all). In Kohlberg's 20-year longitudinal study (Colby et al., 1983), the large majority of adults in their 30s still reasoned at the conventional level, although many of them had shifted from Stage 3 to Stage 4. A minority of individuals—one-sixth to one-eighth of the sample—had begun to use Stage-5 postconventional reasoning, showing a deeper understanding of the basis for laws and distinguishing between just and unjust laws. Clearly there is moral growth in early adulthood (Walker, 1989). Do these trends continue into later adulthood, or do older adults instead revert to less mature forms of moral reasoning?

Previous chapters have shown that elderly people do not perform as well as young and middle-aged adults do on many cognitive tasks. Yet most studies suggest that there are no real age differences in stage of moral reasoning, at least when relatively educated adults are studied and when the age groups compared have similar levels of education (Chap, 1985–1986; Pratt et al., 1991; Pratt, Golding, & Hunter, 1983; Pratt, Golding, & Kerig, 1987). Older adults seem to reason as complexly as younger adults do, whether they are given Kohlberg's hypothetical dilemmas to ponder or asked to discuss real-life situations in which they were "unsure about the right thing to do" (Pratt et al., 1991). Although no long-term longitudinal studies are available, these cross-sectional comparisons suggest that moral thinking does not deteriorate in old age.

Indeed, some researchers have uncovered evidence that elderly adults (and, to a lesser extent, middle-aged adults as well) may be somewhat *more* morally sophisticated than young adults. Older adults appear to have firmer opinions about what is morally right and wrong (Chap, 1985-1986). They reformulate the issues raised by moral dilemmas in their own ways (Pratt, Golding, Hunter, & Norris, 1988), and they show more coherence and consistency in their moral reasoning (Pratt et al., 1983).

In short, most older people seem to maintain the level of moral reasoning they attained earlier in adulthood, and some may even integrate their thinking into a more coherent moral philosophy. Kohlberg (1973) himself argued that experience in confronting moral issues and taking responsibility for one's decisions over a lifetime may help adults form more coherent moral outlooks (see also Gibbs, 1979). Certainly the possibility that moral growth continues not only in early adulthood but throughout the life span deserves more attention.

For many adults, moral decisions are intimately related to religious values and beliefs. In Box 12.2 we briefly examine religious development across the life span and the contributions that religious involvement may make to the well-being of elderly individuals.

KOHLBERG'S THEORY OF MORAL DEVELOPMENT IN PERSPECTIVE

Kohlberg's theory of moral development has dominated research in this area for many years. We have now seen that children think about hypothetical moral dilemmas primarily in a preconventional manner, that adolescents adopt a conventional mode of moral reasoning, and that a minority of adults progress to the postconventional level. Kohlberg appears to have discovered an important developmental progression in moral thought. But let's now complete our discussion of moral development by evaluating Kohlberg's influential theory, examining both its supporting evidence and its criticisms.

Evidence Supportive of Kohlberg's Stage Sequence

As you'll recall, Kohlberg claims that his stages form an invariant and universal sequence of moral growth. Do all people progress through the stages in precisely the order Kohlberg specified? It appears that they do, to a point. Longitudinal studies of moral growth in Turkey, Israel, and the United States demonstrate this (see Colby & Kohlberg, 1987; Snarey, 1985; Walker, 1989). Regardless of their culture, individuals do not skip stages. Moreover, only about 5% of them regress from a higher stage to a lower stage from one testing to the next, and these instances of regression are so few that they probably reflect scoring errors. However, the idea that everyone progresses through Stages 1 to 4 in order is better supported than the idea that people continue to progress from Stage 4 to Stages 5 and 6. Stage 3 or 4 is the end of the developmental journey for most individuals worldwide (Snarey, 1985).

Factors That Promote Moral Growth

How much support is there for Kohlberg's thinking about the factors that contribute to moral growth? Basically, he has argued, as Piaget did, that two influences are most important: cognitive growth and relevant social experiences.

Cognitive Growth

What kind of cognitive growth is necessary? The preconventional reasoner adopts an egocentric, very concrete perspective on moral issues. To reach the

BOX 12.2 The Development of Religious Faith

James Fowler (1981, 1991) believes that religious development closely parallels moral development. He has attempted to describe the development of **faith**—by which he means the ways in which we make or find meaning in our lives, whether within or outside the context of organized religion. His six stages of faith are based on the developmental theories of Piaget, Erikson, and Kohlberg, as well as on interviews with individuals ranging in age from 3 to 84. Notice that they are strikingly similar to Kohlberg's stages of moral reasoning.

1. *Intuitive-projective faith* (early childhood). The development of faith actually begins before this stage, Fowler argues, when infants learn trust in their interactions with caregivers (Fowler, 1991). Soon young preoperational children, with their great imaginative capacities, pick up fragments of religious stories and invent their own intuitive images of good and evil forces in the world. Their descriptions of God are very concrete: "He has a light shirt on, he has brown hair, he has brown eyelashes" (Fowler, 1981, p. 127; see also Hyde, 1990). They do the best they can to make sense of religious teachings. Yet we must wonder what it all means to the young child—for example, to the young girl from Connecticut whose version of the Lord's Prayer went "Our Father who art in New Haven, Harold be they name" (Fischer & Lazerson, 1984, p. 332).

2. *Mythic-literal faith* (later childhood). As they gain capacities for logical thought (concrete operations), children develop more coherent, but still very concrete, ways of ordering the world. Religious teachings are interpreted literally, and God is often likened to a parent figure—a loving disciplinarian who rewards the good and punishes the bad.

3. *Synthetic-conventional faith* (adolescence). As they acquire formal-operational cognitive abilities, adolescents take what they have been taught and synthesize it into a coherent belief

system that expresses their identity and ties them to other people. Although synthetic-conventional faith is more abstract than earlier forms, the individual is largely conforming to the values of significant others and has not yet seriously reflected about alternative ideologies. Most adults remain in this stage.

4. *Individuative-reflective faith* (early adulthood). Some adults progress to the particularly important stage of **individuative-reflective faith,** in which they engage for the first time in serious questioning of the conventional beliefs they learned as children and adolescents and attempt to fashion a belief system that is uniquely their own. Some adults continue to accept many of the beliefs they grew up with after careful deliberation; others reject those beliefs and create personal philosophies more to their liking. According to Fowler, the transition to individuative-reflective faith is unlikely unless a person achieves solid command of formal-operational thought and has life experiences that force new thinking (going off to college?).

5. *Conjunctive faith* (middle age). A few adults go on to establish a belief system that allows them to interpret reality in multiple ways and make sense of paradoxes. A 78-year-old woman interviewed by Fowler expressed this complex world view: "Whether you call it God or Jesus or Cosmic Flow or Reality or Love, it doesn't matter what you call it. It is there. And what you learn directly from that source will not tie you up in creeds . . . that separate you from your fellow man" (Fowler, 1981, p. 192).

6. *Universalizing faith* (middle age or beyond). Finally, just as Kohlberg believes that there is an ideal form of moral reasoning described by his sixth stage (Universal Principle), Fowler believes that a few individuals, such as Mahatma Gandhi or Mother Teresa, somehow transcend specific belief systems and life's mysteries to achieve a sense of oneness with all beings and a commitment to breaking down the barriers that divide people. You'll have to read Fowler's fascinating book to get the full flavor of this stage!

We tend to think of religion as especially central in the lives of elderly adults. Although many older individuals are indeed highly religious, there is actually little change from middle age to late old age in the tendency to view religion as important and as greatly comforting (Blazer & Palmore, 1976; Palmore, 1981). In other words, research offers no support for the idea that people "get religion" or cling to it more strongly as they approach death. Poor health actually forces some elderly people to cut back on their participation in organized religious activities, although many of them compensate with increased involvement in private religious activities such as prayer and Bible study (Ainlay & Smith, 1984; Young & Dowling, 1987).

As it turns out, those older adults who *do* remain highly involved in religion appear to be happier and better adjusted than those who do not (Blazer & Palmore, 1976; Coke, 1992). This seems to be especially true among elderly African Americans (Hatch, 1991). Although we cannot be sure that the relationship between religious involvement and well-being is causal, old and young alike may have a greater sense of well-being if they believe that life has purpose and meaning than if they do not (Reker, Peacock, & Wong, 1987).

conventional stage of moral reasoning and become concerned about living up to the moral standards that significant others transmit, an individual must be capable of taking other people's perspectives (Walker, 1980). Gaining the capacity for postconventional or "principled" moral reasoning requires still more cognitive growth—namely, a solid command of formal-operational thinking (Tomlinson-Keasey & Keasey, 1974; Walker, 1980). The person who bases moral judgments on abstract principles must be able to reason abstractly and take all possible perspectives on a moral issue. Both perspective-taking abilities and more general cognitive abilities appear to be *necessary but not sufficient* for moral growth, however. In other words, not all proficient role takers have reached the conventional level of moral reasoning, and not all formal operators progress to the postconventional level. It is just that these milestones in moral development cannot be achieved without the requisite cognitive skills (see also Stewart & Pascual-Leone, 1992).

Relevant Social Experience

The second major influence on moral development proposed by Kohlberg is relevant social experience. What social experiences matter? Kohlberg stressed the need for experiences that require people to take the perspectives of others so that they can appreciate that they are part of a larger social order and that moral rules are a consensus of individuals in society. Interacting with people who hold views different from one's own also creates *cognitive disequilibrium,* or a conflict between existing cognitive structures and new ideas, which in turn stimulates new ways of thinking.

Like Piaget, Kohlberg felt that interactions with peers—in which children experience differences between their own and others' perspectives—probably contribute more to moral growth than one-sided interactions with adult authority figures—in which children are expected to defer to the adults (however, see Kohlberg & Diessner, 1991, on the importance of the child's identification with parents). But, it is now clear that parents play a highly significant role, not only by using inductive discipline but by encouraging children to think about moral issues. Lawrence Walker and John Taylor (1991), for example, have found that the children who show the most moral growth over a period of two years have parents who, during discussions of moral dilemmas, encourage them to clearly state their positions, paraphrase those positions in a warm and supportive way, and offer more advanced moral arguments that the children can compare to their own arguments. Children who show little moral growth have parents who tend to challenge the child's judgments and present higher-stage reasoning in a lecture-like way as lessons to be learned.

Despite this evidence of parental contributions, however, Piaget and Kohlberg were right to call attention to the role of peers in moral development. Children do seem to think more actively and deeply about their own and their partners' moral ideas in discussions with peers than in talks with their mothers or other adults; moreover, discussions with peers are more likely to stimulate moral growth (Kruger, 1992; Kruger & Tomasello, 1986). There seems to be something special about hashing out disagreements with one's equals and having to take their perspectives. Presumably college students' many "bull sessions" with their friends, in which they debate the pros and cons of the burning issues of the day, are contributing to their moral growth.

Another important kind of social experience is advanced schooling. Consistently, adults who go on to college and receive many years of education think more complexly about moral issues than those who are less educated (Boldizar, Wilson, & Deemer, 1989; Pratt et al., 1991; Rest & Thoma, 1985). Advanced educational experiences not only contribute to cognitive growth but also provide exposure to the diverse ideas and perspectives that produce cognitive conflict and soul searching.

Finally, simply living in a complex, diverse, and democratic society can stimulate moral development. Just as we learn the give-and-take of mutual perspective taking by discussing issues with our friends, we learn in a diverse democracy that the opinions of many groups must be weighed and that laws reflect a consensus of the citizens rather than the arbitrary rulings of a dictator. Indeed, cross-cultural studies suggest that postconventional moral reasoning emerges primarily in Western democracies; people in rural villages in underdeveloped countries show no signs of it (Harkness, Edwards, & Super, 1981; Snarey, 1985; Tietjen & Walker, 1985). Individuals in these homogeneous communities may have less experience with the kinds of political conflicts and compromises that take place in a more complex society and so may never have any need to question conventional moral standards. By adopting a contextual perspective on development, we can appreciate that the conventional (mostly Stage-3) reasoning typically displayed by adults in these societies is adaptive and mature within their own social systems (Harkness et al., 1981).

In sum, Kohlberg not only devised a stage sequence that appears to have universal applicability but he also correctly identified some of the major factors that determine how far an individual progresses in the sequence. Advanced moral reasoning is most likely if the individual has acquired the necessary cognitive skills (particularly perspective-taking skills and, later, the ability to reason abstractly). Moreover, an individual's moral development is highly influenced by social learning experiences, including interactions with parents, discussions with peers, exposure to higher education, and participation in democracy.

Is Kohlberg's theory of moral development sound, then? Not entirely, say the critics. Whenever a theory arouses the enormous interest that Kohlberg's has aroused, you can bet that it will also provoke an enormous amount of criticism. Many of the criticisms have centered on the possibility that Kohlberg's theory is

Adults in many rural societies seem to have no need for postconventional moral reasoning because they share the same moral perspective.

biased against certain groups of people and on the fact that it says much about moral reasoning but little about moral affect and behavior.

Is Kohlberg's Theory Biased?

Some critics have charged that Kohlberg's theory reflects a cultural bias, a liberal bias, and/or a sexist bias. That is, it has been said that the stage theory unfairly makes people from non-Western cultures, people with conservative values, or the half of the human race that is female appear to be less than morally mature.

Although research indicates that children and adolescents in all cultures proceed through the first three or four stages in order, we have seen that postconventional reasoning as Kohlberg defines it simply does not exist in some societies. Critics charge that Kohlberg's highest stages reflect a Western ideal of justice, making the stage theory biased against people who live in non-Western societies or who do not value individualism and individual rights highly enough to want to challenge society's rules (Gibbs & Schnell, 1985; Shweder, Mahapatra, & Miller, 1990). People in societies that emphasize social harmony and place the good of the group ahead of the good of the individual may be viewed as conventional moral thinkers in Kohlberg's system but may actually have very sophisticated concepts of justice (Snarey, 1985; Tietjen & Walker, 1985). The theme that moral development can vary considerably from society to society is explored further in Box 12.3.

Similarly, critics charge that a person must hold liberal values—for example, opposing capital punishment or supporting civil disobedience in the name of human rights—in order to be classified as a postconventional moral reasoner. In one study (de Vries & Walker, 1986), 100% of the college students who showed signs of postconventional thought opposed capital punishment, whereas none of the men and only a third of the women who were transitional between Stage-2 and Stage-3 moral reasoning opposed capital punishment. As de Vries and Walker (1986) note, it could be that opposition to capital punishment is a more valid moral position than support of capital punishment in that it involves valuing life highly. However, it could also be that the theory is unfair to conservatives who emphasize law-and-order principles (Lapsley et al., 1984).

These criticisms may have some merit. However, no criticism of Kohlberg has stirred more heat than the charge that his theory is biased against women. Carol Gilligan (1977, 1982, 1993) has been disturbed by the fact that Kohlberg's stages were based on interviews with males; also, in some studies, women seemed to be the moral inferiors of men, reasoning at Stage 3 when men usually reasoned at Stage 4. She hypothesizes that females develop a distinctly *feminine* orientation to moral issues—one that is no less mature than the orientation adopted by most men and incorporated into Kohlberg's theory. Gilligan suggests that boys, who are traditionally raised to be independent, assertive, and achievement oriented, come to view moral dilemmas as inevitable conflicts between the rights of two or more parties and to view laws and other social conventions as necessary for resolving these conflicts (a perspective reflected in Kohlberg's Stage-4 reasoning). Girls, Gilligan argues, are brought up to be nurturant, empathic, and concerned with the needs of others and to define their sense of "goodness" in terms of their concern for other people (a perspective that approximates Stage 3 in Kohlberg's scheme). What this boils down to is the difference between a "masculine" **morality of justice** (in which laws defining individual rights prevail) and a "feminine" **morality of care** (in which one's responsibility for the welfare of other people is most central).

At this point there is little support for Gilligan's claim that Kohlberg's theory is systematically biased against females. Most studies indicate that women reason just as complexly about moral issues as men do when their answers are scored by Kohlberg's criteria (Pratt et al., 1991; Thoma, 1986; Walker, 1984, 1989). Nor is it clear that women think entirely differently about moral dilemmas than men do (Ford & Lowery, 1986; Lyons, 1983; Walker, 1989). Perhaps the only reliable sex difference discovered so far is that women are more likely than men, when asked to discuss moral issues they have actually faced, to cite problems that arose in their personal relationships (Pratt et al., 1988, 1991; Walker, 1989). These real-life interpersonal dilemmas tend to elicit care-oriented reasoning from both men and women.

BOX 12.3 Cultural Differences in Moral Thinking

Is each of the following acts wrong? If so, how serious a violation is it?

1. A young married woman is beaten black and blue by her husband after going to a movie without his permission despite having been warned not to do so again.
2. A brother and sister decide to get married and have children.
3. The day after his father died, the oldest son in a family gets a haircut and eats chicken.

These are three of 39 acts presented by Richard Shweder, Manamohan Mahapatra, and Joan Miller (1990, pp. 165–166) to children aged 5 to 13 and adults in India and the United States. You may be surprised to learn that Hindu children and adults rated the son's having a haircut and eating chicken after his father's death as among the most morally offensive of the 39 acts they rated, and the husband's beating of his disobedient wife was not considered wrong at all. American children and adults, of course, viewed beating one's wife as far more serious than breaking seemingly arbitrary rules about appropriate mourning behavior. Although Indians and Americans could agree that a few acts, like brother/sister incest, were serious moral violations, they did not agree on much else.

Moreover, Indian children and adults viewed the Hindu ban against behavior disrespectful of one's dead father as a universal moral rule; they thought it would be best if everyone in the world followed it, and they strongly disagreed that it would be acceptable to change the rule if most people in their society wanted to change it. For similar reasons, they believed that it is a serious moral offense for a widow to eat fish or wear brightly colored clothes or for a woman to cook food for her family or touch her children during her menstrual period. To orthodox Hindus, rules against such behavior are required by natural law; they are not just arbitrary social conventions created by members of society. Hindus also regard it as morally necessary for a man to beat his disobedient wife in order to uphold his obligations as head of the family.

What effects do cultural beliefs of this sort have on moral development? The developmental trend in moral thinking detected in India was very different from that observed in the United States, as the figure below shows. With age, Indian children saw more and more issues as matters of universal moral principle, whereas American children saw fewer and fewer issues as matters of universal principle (and more and more as matters of arbitrary social convention that can legitimately differ from society to society). Moreover, even the youngest children in both societies expressed moral outlooks very similar to those expressed by adults in their own society and very different from those expressed by either children or adults in the other society.

Based on these cross-cultural findings, Shweder calls into question Kohlberg's claims that all children everywhere construct similar moral codes at similar ages and that certain universal moral principles exist. In addition, Shweder questions Turiel's claim that children everywhere distinguish from an early age between moral rules and social-conventional rules, for Shweder found that the concept of social-conventional rules was simply not very meaningful to Indians of any age.

Overall, then, these findings challenge the cognitive-developmental position that important aspects of moral development are universal. They tend instead to support a social learning or contextual perspective on moral development, suggesting that children's moral judgments are shaped by the social context in which they develop (see also Haidt, Koller, & Dias, 1993). Perhaps children all over the world think in more and more complex ways about moral issues as they get older, as Kohlberg claimed, but at the same time adopt quite varied notions about what is right and what is wrong, as Shweder claims.

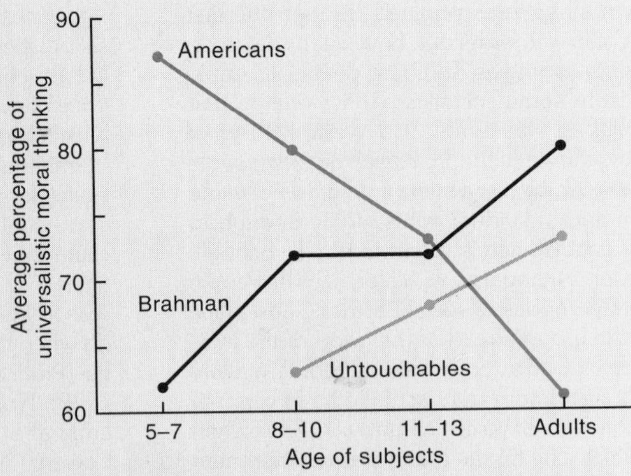

Universalistic moral thinking—the tendency to view rules of behavior as universally valid and unalterable—increases with age among Hindu children in India but decreases with age in the United States. The course of moral development is likely to be different in different societies. (From Shweder et al., 1990.)

Although her hypothesis about sex differences in moral reasoning has not received much support, Gilligan's work *has* increased our awareness that both men and women often think about moral issues—especially real-life as opposed to hypothetical moral issues—in terms of their responsibilities for the welfare of other people. Kohlberg emphasized only one way—a very legalistic way—of thinking about right and wrong. There seems to be merit in tracing the development of *both* a morality of justice and a morality of care in *both* males and females (Brabeck, 1983; Gilligan, 1993).

Is Kohlberg's Theory Incomplete?

Another major criticism of Kohlberg's theory is that it focuses so much on moral reasoning that it almost entirely ignores moral affect and moral behavior (Gibbs & Schnell, 1985; Haan, Aerts, & Cooper, 1985). For example, Norma Haan and her colleagues (1985) point out that moral dilemmas in everyday life arouse powerful emotions. We care about moral issues and about the people who will be affected by our decisions; we agonize about what to do; we very much want to feel that we are moral beings, and our egos are threatened when we act immorally. Such emotions play a central role in morality by motivating our actions, and any theory that overlooks the role of emotions and motivations in morality is therefore incomplete (see also Haidt et al., 1993; Hart & Chmiel, 1992). Moreover, Haan argues, what we should ultimately be interested in when studying morality is how people actually behave in specific situations.

There is no question that Kohlberg has been concerned primarily with moral reasoning, rather than with moral affect or behavior. Also, as already noted, a person might decide to uphold or to break a law at any of the stages of moral reasoning. What distinguishes one stage from the next is the complexity or structure of a person's reasoning, not the specific decisions he or she reaches. Nonetheless, Kohlberg has argued that more advanced moral reasoners are more likely to behave in accordance with widely accepted moral standards than less advanced moral reasoners are. He would predict, for example, that the preconventional thinker might readily decide to cheat on a test if the chances of being detected were small and the potential rewards high. The postconventional thinker would be more likely to appreciate that cheating is wrong in principle, regardless of the chances of detection, because it infringes on the rights of others and undermines social order.

How well *does* a person's stage of moral reasoning predict his or her behavior? Many researchers have found that the moral judgments of young children do *not* predict what they will do when they are given a chance to cheat or violate other moral norms (Nelson, Grinder, & Biaggio, 1969; Toner & Potts, 1981). Studies of older grade-school children, adolescents, and adults often do find some consistency between moral reasoning and conduct. Individuals at higher stages of moral reasoning are more likely than individuals at lower stages to behave altruistically and conscientiously and are less likely to cheat or engage in delinquent and criminal activity (Blasi, 1980; Colby & Kohlberg, 1987; Linn, 1989; Rest, 1993). Kohlberg (1975), for example, found that only 15% of students who reasoned at the postconventional level cheated when given an opportunity to do so, compared with 55% of the students at the conventional level and 70% of those at the preconventional level. Yet the relationship between stage of moral reasoning and moral behavior is typically weak. This suggests that many personal qualities besides level of moral reasoning, and many situational or contextual factors as well, also influence whether a person will behave morally or immorally in daily life (Kurtines, 1986; Thoma, Rest, & Davison, 1991).

In sum, Kohlberg's theory of moral development has become prominent for good reason. It does indeed describe a universal sequence of changes in moral reasoning extending from childhood through adulthood. Moreover, the evidence supports Kohlberg's view that both cognitive growth and social experiences contribute to moral growth. However, there is also some merit to the critics' positions. The theory may not be entirely fair to people who live in non-Western societies, who hold values other than liberal, democratic ones, or who emphasize a morality of care rather than a morality of justice. Furthermore, because Kohlberg's theory focuses entirely on moral reasoning, we must rely on other perspectives (such as social learning theory) to understand how moral affect and moral behavior develop and how thought, emotion, and behavior interact to make us the moral beings we ultimately become.

THE DEVELOPMENT OF ACHIEVEMENT MOTIVATION

Just as our moral outlooks help define us as individuals, so do our characteristic motivations. To illustrate, we'll take a look at achievement motivation. David McClelland and his associates (McClelland, Atkinson, Clark, & Lowell, 1953; see also McClelland, 1985) defined the **need for achievement (n Ach)** as a "learned motive to compete and to strive for success whenever one's behavior can be evaluated against a standard of excellence" (p. 78). In other words, people with strong achievement motivation take pride in their ability to meet high standards and are motivated by this sense of self-fulfillment to work hard, be successful, and outperform others when faced with new challenges. What are the origins of this achievement motive, how does it typically evolve over the life span, and what experiences strengthen or weaken it?

The Early Origins of Achievement Motivation

Some time ago, psychoanalyst Robert White (1959) proposed that human beings are intrinsically motivated from infancy onward to master their environment. He called this **effectance motivation** — a desire to have an effect on or to successfully control the world of objects and people. This effectance, or mastery, motive can be seen in action when infants struggle to open kitchen cabinets, take their first steps, or figure out how new toys work — and derive great pleasure from their efforts (MacTurk, McCarthy, Vietze, & Yarrow, 1987; Mayes & Zigler, 1992). White argued that it is the very nature of human beings to seek out challenges just for the joy of attempting to master them.

Much evidence supports the claim that infants are curious, active explorers who are constantly striving to understand and to exert control over the world around them. This, you'll recall, was one of Jean Piaget's major themes. A striving for mastery or competence appears to be inborn, then, and will display itself in the behavior of all normal infants without any prompting from parents. Even so, some infants appear to be more mastery oriented than others. Given a new push toy, one baby may simply look at it, while another may mouth it, bang it, and push it back and forth across the floor; presented with a toy behind a screen, one baby may simply look at it and another will figure out a way to get it (Yarrow et al., 1984). Why might some infants have a stronger effectance motive than others?

Early Influences on Mastery Motivation

Three influences on mastery motivation appear to be important: appropriate stimulation, a responsive environment, and a secure relationship with a caregiver. First, parents whose infants are highly mastery oriented frequently provide *sensory stimulation* designed to arouse and amuse their babies, tickling them, bouncing them, playing games of pat-a-cake, and so on (Yarrow et al., 1984). Second, mastery motivation will blossom if infants grow up in a *responsive environment* and have plenty of opportunities to see for themselves that they can control their environments (Ford & Thompson, 1985). Parents who return smiles and coos or respond promptly to cries show infants that they can affect people around them. Similarly, when young infants see that their actions can make a brightly colored mobile rotate, they smile and coo and take far more interest in the mobile than infants who

Babies come equipped with an innate effectance, or mastery, motive.

have no control over its movements (Watson & Ramey, 1972). When babies see that they can no longer have this kind of effect on the environment, they become angry (Lewis, Alessandri, & Sullivan, 1990).

Third and finally, a *secure and loving attachment* to parents seems to promote mastery motivation. Infants who are securely attached to their mothers at 12 to 18 months of age are more likely than those who are insecurely attached (1) to venture away from their mothers to explore a strange environment (Cassidy, 1986), (2) to persist until they master new challenges (Frankel & Bates, 1990), and (3) to display a strong sense of curiosity, self-reliance, and eagerness to solve problems four years later in kindergarten (Arend, Gove, & Sroufe, 1979; see also Chapter 13).

Does an infant's level of effectance, or mastery, motivation affect his or her later achievement behavior? Apparently it does. Babies who actively attempt to master challenges at 6 and 12 months of age have been found to score higher on tests of mental development at age 2½ than their less mastery-oriented peers (Messer et al., 1986).

In short, infants are intrinsically motivated to master challenges; parents may help strengthen this inborn motive by stimulating their infants appropriately, responding to their actions, and developing a secure relationship with them; and the strength of an infant's mastery motivation may influence how much the child learns from experiences and how well he or she functions intellectually later in childhood.

From Mastery to Achievement Motivation

How, though, does the baby's effectance motivation evolve into the school child's achievement motivation? Deborah Stipek and her associates (Stipek, Recchia, & McClintic, 1992) have conducted an interesting series of studies with 1- to 5-year-olds to find out when children develop the capacity to evaluate themselves according to standards — a capacity central to achievement motivation (and central to morality as well, as we saw). In this research, children were observed as they engaged in activities that had clear-cut achievement goals (for example, hammering pegs into pegboards, working puzzles, knocking down plastic pins with a bowling ball). Some tasks were structured so that children either could or could not master them, which enabled the researchers to observe reactions to success or failure. Based on this research, Stipek and her colleagues suggest that children progress through three stages in learning to evaluate their performances in achievement situations, stages we will call joy in mastery, approval seeking, and internalized standards.

Stage 1: Joy in Mastery. Before the age of 2, infants are visibly pleased to master challenges, displaying the effectance motivation White (1959) wrote about. However, they do not call other people's attention to their triumphs or otherwise seek recognition. Also, rather than being bothered by failures, they simply shift goals and attempt to master other toys. They are not yet evaluating their outcomes in relation to performance standards that define success and failure.

Stage 2: Approval Seeking. As they near age 2, toddlers begin to anticipate how others will evaluate their performances. They seek recognition when they succeed and expect disapproval when they fail. For example, children as young as 2 who succeeded on a task often smiled, held their heads and chins up high, and made such statements as "I did it" as they called the experimenter's attention to their feats. Meanwhile, 2-year-olds who failed would often turn away from the experimenter as though they wanted to avoid disapproval. It seems, then, that 2-year-olds are already appraising their outcomes as successes or failures and have already learned that they can expect approval after successes and disapproval after failures (see also Bullock & Lutkenhaus, 1988).

Stage 3: Internalized Standards. Another important breakthrough occurs around age 3, as children begin to react more independently to their successes and failures. They seem to have truly internalized standards of performance and are not as dependent on others to tell them when they have done well or poorly. The Stage-3 children in the study seemed capable of experiencing true *pride* (rather than mere pleasure) in their achievements and true *shame* (rather than mere disappointment) in their failures.

In sum, infants are guided by an effectance or mastery motive and take pleasure in their everyday accomplishments; 2-year-olds begin to anticipate others' approval or disapproval of their performances; and children 3 and older internalize standards of performance and experience true pride or shame, depending on how successfully they meet those standards.

Achievement Motivation during Childhood and Adolescence

Researchers exploring the development of achievement motivation in childhood and adolescence initially assumed that behavior in achievement settings could be understood as the product of the individual's need for achievement. They soon discovered that achievement behavior is considerably more complex as that.

Need for Achievement

In their pioneering studies of achievement motivation, David McClelland and his colleagues (1953) gave children or adults pictures and asked them to compose stories about the pictures. It was assumed that people would project their own motives onto the pictured situation and that the number of achievement-related themes in the stories would provide a measure of an individual's need for achievement. What story would you tell about the scene portrayed in Figure 12.4? A person with a high need for achievement might say that the men have been working for months on a new scientific breakthrough that will revolutionize medicine, whereas a person with a low need for achievement might say that these fellows are glad the day is over so that they can go home and watch television. Children who score high in need for achievement based on measures like this do indeed tend to

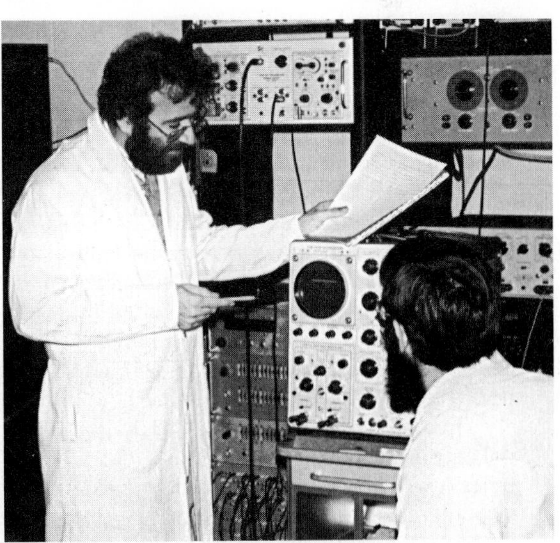

FIGURE 12.4 Scenes like this one were used by David McClelland and his associates to measure achievement motivation.

receive better grades in school than those who score low (McClelland et al., 1953).

Yet it has become clear that achievement motivation is too complex to be reduced to a single, global motive. Among the other important factors to be considered are the value placed on achieving a particular goal, the individual's perceived competence and expectancies of success, and the individual's beliefs concerning the causes of success or failure.

The Value Placed on Achievement in a Particular Situation

John Atkinson (1964) insisted that the *value* of success to the individual (as well as the aversiveness of failing) is an important influence on achievement outcomes (see also Wigfield & Eccles, 1992). We are more likely to pursue and strive hard to achieve goals we really care about than goals that are unimportant, so a strong need for achievement predicts success only when the value placed on achievement is high (Raynor, 1970).

Perceived Competence and Expectancies of Success

We are also more likely to work hard when we think we are capable and have a reasonable chance of succeeding than when we see no hope of attaining a goal (Atkinson, 1964; Mac Iver, Stipek, & Daniels, 1991). In fact, children with high IQs and low expectancies of academic success often earn poorer grades than their classmates who have lower IQs but higher expectancies (Battle, 1966; Crandall, 1967). Children who perceive themselves as competent and expect to achieve often do succeed, whereas those who expect to fail may spend little time or effort pursuing goals that they believe are out of reach.

Attributions for Success and Failure

Researchers have also discovered that children's achievement behavior depends on how they interpret their successes and failures and whether they think they can control these outcomes. Bernard Weiner (1974, 1986) has proposed an **attribution theory** of motivation, in which the explanations (causal attributions) we offer for our outcomes influence our future expectancies of success and our future motivation to succeed. Weiner has emphasized four causes of success or failure: ability (or lack thereof), effort, task difficulty, and luck (either good or bad).

Two of these causes, ability and effort, are internal causes or qualities of the individual, whereas the other two, task difficulty and luck, are external or environmental factors. In other words, Weiner proposes that causal attributions can be grouped along a locus dimension (internal versus external). Here Weiner's thinking corresponds to earlier work on a dimension of personality called **locus of control** (Crandall, 1967, 1969). Individuals with an *internal locus of control* assume that they are personally responsible for what happens to them. For example, they might credit an *A* grade on a paper to superior writing ability or hard work. Individuals with an *external locus of control* believe that their outcomes depend more on luck, fate, or the actions of others than on their own abilities and efforts. They might say that their *A*'s are due to luck ("The teacher just happened to like my paper topic"), indiscriminate grading, or some other external cause. Children with an internal locus of control earn higher grades and higher scores on academic achievement tests than children with an external locus of control do (Findley & Cooper, 1983), perhaps because they believe their efforts will pay off and therefore work harder.

But Weiner claims that causes also differ along a *stability* dimension. Ability and task difficulty are reasonably stable or unchangeable. If one has low math ability today, one is likely to have the same low ability tomorrow; if algebra problems are difficult today, similar algebra problems are likely to be difficult tomorrow. By contrast, the amount of effort one expends and the workings of luck are highly unstable or variable from situation to situation (see Table 12.4).

Why is it useful to categorize causes of success and failure along both a locus of causality and a stability dimension? Mainly because it is not *always* adaptive to attribute what happens to internal causes, as research on locus of control would lead us to believe. It is indeed healthy to conclude that your successes must be due to high ability; this not only will make you feel proud but will lead you to expect more successes in the future, since ability is relatively stable and should therefore continue to affect future performance. But is it healthy to conclude after a failure that you are hopelessly incompetent, miserably lacking in ability? Hardly! Low ability may be an internal cause of poor performance, but because it is also a

TABLE 12.4 Weiner's classification of the causes of achievement outcomes (and examples of how you might explain a terrible test grade).

	Locus of Causality	
	Internal Cause	*External Cause*
Stable Cause	*Ability* "I'm hopeless in math."	*Task difficulty* "That test was incredibly hard and much too long."
Unstable Cause	*Effort* "I should have studied more instead of going out to play."	*Luck* "What luck! Every question seemed to be about the one day of class I missed."

stable cause, attributing failure to low ability is saying that you can do little to improve on your lousy performance. Not only would you have low expectancies of future success and little motivation to strive, but you would also lose self-esteem by admitting that you are "dumb."

Carol Dweck and her colleagues (Dweck & Elliott, 1983; Dweck & Leggett, 1988) find that high achievers tend to attribute their successes to internal and stable causes such as high ability. However, they blame their failures either on external factors beyond their control ("That test was impossibly hard." "That professor's grading is biased") or—and this is even more adaptive—on internal causes that they can overcome (particularly insufficient effort). They do *not* blame the internal but stable factor of low ability ("I'm terrible at this and will never do any better"). Students with this healthy attributional style have a **mastery orientation**; they thrive on challenges and persist in the face of failure, believing that their increased effort will pay off (Dweck & Leggett, 1988).

Children who tend to be low achievers often attribute their successes either to the internal cause of hard work or to external causes such as luck or the easiness of the task. Thus they do not experience the pride and self-esteem that come from viewing oneself as highly capable. Yet they often attribute their failures to an internal and stable cause—namely, lack of ability. As a result, they have low expectancies of success and tend to give up (Dweck & Elliott, 1983). Carol Dweck describes children with this attributional style as having a **learned helplessness orientation**, a tendency to avoid challenges and to cease trying when one experiences failure based on the belief that one can do little to improve (Dweck, 1978; Dweck & Leggett, 1988).

A helpless orientation to learning is especially likely to develop in students with learning disabilities and attention deficits (Ayres, Cooley, & Dunn, 1990; Milich & Okazaki, 1991). Yet even many high-ability students adopt this unhealthy learning style (Dweck, 1978; Phillips, 1984). Teachers and parents may foster it by praising children for being neat or working hard when they succeed but criticizing them for lacking intelligence or understanding when they fail.

Unfortunately, girls receive this helplessness-producing pattern of feedback more often than boys do (Dweck et al., 1978; Dweck & Elliott, 1983). This may help explain why girls sometimes display signs of learned helplessness in subject areas like mathematics. Both parents and teachers seem to believe that males have more mathematical ability than females do and that whatever successes females achieve in math class are the product of hard work (Eccles, Jacobs, & Harold, 1990; Jussim & Eccles, 1992). Influenced by these gender stereotypes, girls are more likely than boys to judge their math ability as low, to expect to do poorly on math exams, to attribute their poor math performances to lack of ability, to express little confidence that they can improve their performance by trying harder, and to seek to avoid rather than master mathematics (Stipek & Gralinski, 1991).

Developmental Trends in Achievement Motivation

Interestingly, much of what we have said about the importance of attributions regarding one's successes and failures may not apply to very young children. Before the age of 7 or so, children seem to bounce back from failure rather well. Even after repeated poor performances, they almost invariably think that they have high ability and that they will do well in the future (Dweck & Elliott, 1983; Stipek & Mac Iver, 1989). Nor do they typically give up or become helpless in the face of failure, as older children often do (Miller, 1985), although even 5- and 6-year-olds can be induced to become helpless if they are pointedly criticized for their mistakes as they attempt to master a task (Heyman, Dweck, & Cain, 1992).

Now consider what Deborah Stipek (1984) concluded after reviewing studies on the development of achievement motivation from early childhood to adolescence:

> On the average, children value academic achievement more as they progress through school, but their expectations for success and self-perceptions of competence decline, and their affect toward school becomes more negative. Children also become increasingly concerned about achievement outcomes and reinforcement (e.g., high grades) associated with positive outcomes and less concerned about intrinsic satisfaction in achieving greater competence [p. 153].

Many of the negative trends Stipek describes become especially apparent during the junior high school years. More and more teenagers become alienated from school and display little motivation for academic tasks. Many other adolescents continue to work hard at their studies but adopt what Susan Harter (1981) calls an *extrinsic* rather than an intrinsic orientation toward achievement: They work to obtain good grades, parent or teacher approval, and other external rewards rather than because they find learning itself gratifying.

What is behind this disturbing developmental trend? It is partly the result of cognitive growth. Young children engage in egocentric, wishful thinking; the more they want to succeed, the more they believe they *will* succeed, even if they have failed in the past (Stipek, Roberts, & Sanborn, 1984). In addition, young children are protected from damaging self-perceptions because they do not yet fully understand the concept of ability (Nicholls, 1978; Nicholls &

Miller, 1984). Not recognizing that some failures may be due to a relatively enduring lack of talent or that low ability can prevent even the hardest worker from succeeding, they believe that they can become smarter if they try harder (Dweck & Leggett, 1988; Stipek & Mac Iver, 1989). It is not until age 10 or so that children come to view ability as a stable trait—and become more vulnerable to feelings of helplessness after repeated failures.

As they get older, children become increasingly capable of analyzing the causes of events, interpreting feedback from teachers, making social comparisons, and inferring enduring traits such as high or low ability from their behavior (Stipek & Mac Iver, 1989). The result is that they come to view their abilities more realistically—and lose some academic self-esteem in the process (Benenson & Dweck, 1986; Stipek & Mac Iver, 1989).

But declines in achievement motivation may also be caused by educational practices and an accumulation of feedback in school about one's deficiencies (Eccles, Lord, & Midgley, 1991; Stipek & Mac Iver, 1989). Preschool teachers often praise their young charges merely for trying and do not hand out much criticism. As Deborah Stipek (1984) notes, it would be unthinkable for an adult to say to a 5-year-old exhibiting a drawing "What an ugly picture. You sure can't draw very well" (p. 156). The positive feedback young children receive for their efforts may contribute to their sense that hard work can overcome any barrier (Rosenholtz & Simpson, 1984). By contrast, elementary and secondary school teachers increasingly reserve praise, high grades, and other forms of approval for children who turn in high-quality products. As they progress through school, then, children receive more and more feedback telling them precisely what capabilities they have and what capabilities they lack. Due to both cognitive growth and changes in the feedback provided at school, some exuberantly confident youngsters turn into adolescents who are fully aware that they lack academic ability in certain areas and are less motivated to achieve.

Parents have a lot to do with why some children and adolescents remain more achievement oriented than others. As we saw earlier, parents can foster mastery motivation in infancy by providing their babies with appropriate sensory stimulation, being responsive, and building a secure attachment relationship. Parents can then strengthen their children's need for achievement by stressing and reinforcing independence and self-reliance at an early age—by encouraging children to do things on their own (Grolnick & Ryan, 1989; Winterbottom, 1958). They can also emphasize the importance of doing things *well*, or meeting high standards of performance (Rosen & D'Andrade, 1959).

What works best, it seems, is the same warm and democratic but firm parenting style that we associated in Chapter 10 with the development of high self-esteem during childhood and a clear sense of identity during adolescence. This parenting style is related to high achievement in both Western societies (Baumrind, 1973; Lamborn et al., 1991; Steinberg, Elmen, & Mounts, 1989) and Asian ones (Lin & Fu, 1990). If children are encouraged and supported in a positive manner as they do their schoolwork, they are likely to enjoy new challenges and feel confident about mastering them. As Golda Ginsburg and Phyllis Bronstein (1993) have found, parents can undermine a child's school performance and intrinsic motivation to learn if they (1) are uninvolved and offer little in the way of guidance or (2) are highly controlling and do such things as nag continually about homework, offer bribes for good grades, and criticize bad grades.

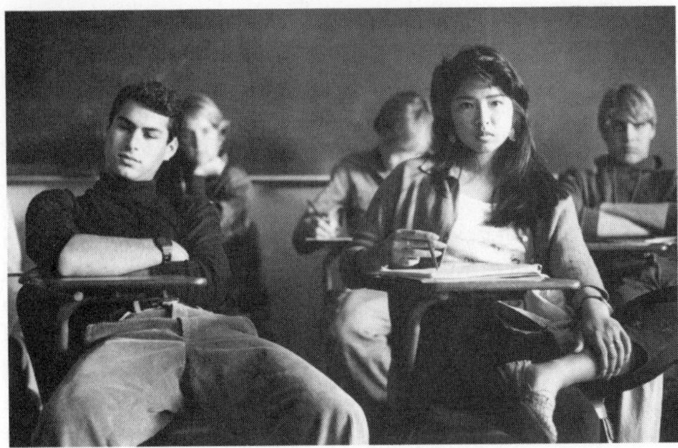

By adolescence, some students have little motivation to achieve in the classroom.

Finally, peers are an important influence on children and adolescents and can sometimes undermine parents' efforts to encourage school achievement. When James Coleman (1961) asked high school students how they would like to be remembered, only 31% of the boys and 28% of the girls wanted to be remembered as bright students. They were more concerned with having the athletic and social skills that lead to popularity. Since peer acceptance is highly important to most adolescents, perhaps it is not surprising that some of them emphasize academic goals less and social goals more than they did as children, particularly if they attend schools where few students are highly achievement oriented.

The problem of peer pressures that interfere with academic achievement motivation may be especially acute for many lower-income African-American and Hispanic students and may help explain why they often lag behind Anglo-American and Asian-American students in school achievement (Slaughter-Defoe et al., 1990; Tharp, 1989). Lawrence Steinberg and his colleagues (Steinberg, Dornbusch, & Brown, 1992) note that the African-American and Hispanic peer cultures in many low-income areas actively discourage academic achievement, whereas Anglo- and Asian-American peer groups tend to value and encourage it. High-achieving African-American students in some inner-city schools actually run the risk of being rejected by their African-American peers if their academic accomplishments cause them to be perceived as "acting white" (Fordham & Ogbu, 1986).

A Summing Up

It should be clear by now that achievement motivation involves far more than just a global need for achievement. Children do differ in their characteristic motives to achieve, but the *value* of success to the individual must also be considered: Why act on any motive to achieve if the goal seems unimportant or irrelevant to your other goals? Moreover, an individual's perceived competence and *expectancies* of success also count, for there may be little point in striving if you lack confidence that you can meet the challenge. Finally, drawing on attribution theory, we must recognize that achievement behavior is very much affected by the ways in which an individual interprets successes and failures and whether he or she develops a mastery-oriented or helpless approach to challenges. Due to both cognitive development and changes in the feedback they receive at school, children typically lose some of their intrinsic motivation to achieve as they get older. But the extent to which they are achievement oriented as adolescents will also depend considerably on how much parents, peers, and other important social agents value achievement.

Achievement Strivings during the Adult Years

Highly achievement-oriented children tend to become highly achievement-oriented adults (Kagan & Moss, 1962), and achievement-oriented young adults tend to remain relatively achievement oriented in middle age (Stevens & Truss, 1985). The characteristic motives that we acquire in childhood and adolescence and carry into adulthood influence our decisions and life outcomes. For instance, women who have a strong need to achieve are more likely to work outside the home than women who are less achievement oriented (Krogh, 1985), and adults with strong achievement needs are more competent workers than adults who have little concern with working hard and mastering challenges (Helmreich, Sawin, & Carsrud, 1986; Spence, 1985). What happens to achievement motivation in later life? Is there any support for the common belief that older adults lose some of their drive to excel?

Joseph Veroff, David Reuman, and Sheila Feld (1984) explored this question by analyzing motivational themes in stories that American adults, some surveyed in 1957 and the others in 1976, told in response to pictures like the one shown in Figure 12.4.

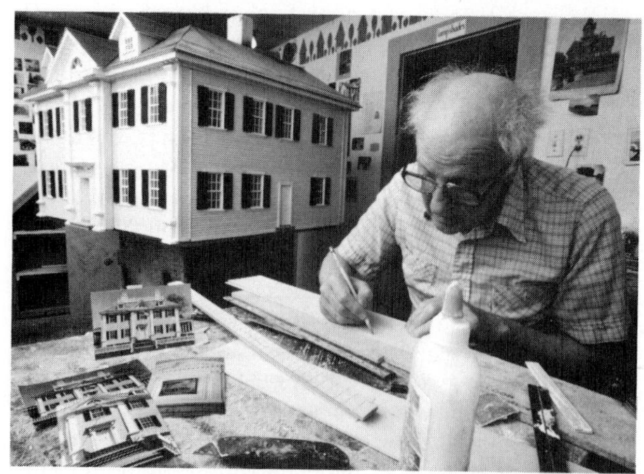

Most elderly adults continue to be motivated to achieve important goals.

Older men displayed only slightly lower levels of achievement motivation than young or middle-aged men did. Here, then, we find no support for the stereotyped idea that older adults are "unmotivated" or have ceased to pursue goals (see also Costa & McCrae, 1988; McAdams, de St. Aubin, & Logan, 1993). Some researchers have detected increases in achievement motivation from young adulthood to middle adulthood (Stevens & Truss, 1985; Veroff, Atkinson, Feld, & Gurin, 1960) and declines in later middle age and old age (Veroff et al., 1960). However, most evidence suggests that older and younger men are far more similar than different in their need for personal achievement (Kausler, 1990). More importantly, different individuals often show quite different patterns of change, depending on whether their efforts meet with success or failure and whether they are able to formulate new goals once old ones are attained (Raynor, 1982).

How do women's achievement motives change over the years? Veroff and his associates (1984) found that need for achievement declined fairly steeply from age group to age group among women (see also Mellinger & Erdwins, 1985). However, this age trend pertains mainly to *career-related* motivation and an interest in striving for success in competitive situations. Older women seem to be every bit as concerned as younger women with performing everyday tasks competently (Maehr & Kleiber, 1981; Veroff et al., 1984).

Many women set aside career-achievement goals after they have children and make nurturing those children their top priority (Krogh, 1985). However, highly educated women appear to regain a strong motive to achieve outside the home once the children are older and they can invest more energy in outside work (Baruch, 1967; Malatesta & Culver, 1984). Apparently, then, women are especially likely to be motivated to achieve career success when they have the educational background that would allow them to pursue attractive career goals and when they are not preoccupied by other needs.

All things considered, it appears that adults' achievement-related motives are far more affected by their life situations or social contexts than by the aging process. Adults of different ages are often more alike than they are different, and people tend to retain their characteristic levels of achievement motivation over the years, much as they retain many personality traits. There is certainly little evidence that elderly people inevitably lose their motivation to pursue important goals. Moreover, those elderly adults who do have a strong sense of purpose and direction and feel they are achieving their goals enjoy greater physical and psychological well-being than those who do not (Hooker & Siegler, 1993; Rapkin & Fischer, 1992; Reker et al., 1987). Throughout the life span, then, we seem to derive great satisfaction from setting and achieving goals, large and small.

APPLICATIONS: FOSTERING ACHIEVEMENT MOTIVATION AND MORAL MATURITY IN THE SCHOOLS

Most educators would agree that their job is not only to motivate students to learn but also to teach them basic values such as honesty, fairness, and respect for other people. The research discussed in this chapter has a lot to say about how schools might best go about producing motivated learners and good citizens.

Fostering Achievement Motivation and Combating Learned Helplessness

Elaine Elliott and Carol Dweck (1988) set out to determine whether children might become less susceptible to learned helplessness if they were encouraged to adopt learning goals rather than performance goals in the classroom. That is, children were encouraged to view difficult tasks as opportunities to *improve* their abilities, not just to display whatever abilities (or inabilities) they currently possess.

In the study, fifth-graders were asked to perform a novel task. They were led to believe that they had either low or high ability and were warned that they would soon be performing similar tasks that would prove quite difficult. Half the children worked under a *performance goal* (not unlike the goals emphasized in many classrooms): They were told that their performance would be compared to that of other children and evaluated by an expert. The remaining children were induced to adopt a *learning goal*: Although they would make some mistakes, they were told, working at the tasks would "sharpen the mind" and help them at school.

As expected, the only children who displayed the telltale signs of helplessness (that is, deteriorating performance and attribution of failure to low ability) were those who believed they had low ability and were pursuing a performance goal. For them, working on the task meant demonstrating again and again that they were stupid. By contrast, even "low ability" students who pursued a learning goal persisted despite their failures and showed remarkably little frustration, possibly because they were convinced that they could grow from their experience. Perhaps, then, teachers undermine achievement motivation by distributing gold stars and grades and frequently calling attention to how students stand in comparison to one another. Children might be better off if teachers nurtured their intrinsic motivation to master challenges (see also Boggiano & Katz, 1991; Butler, 1990; Stipek & Kowalski, 1989). Then slow learners could view their mistakes as a sign that they should change strategies to improve their competencies rather than as further proof that they lack ability.

Teachers can also help students who are prone to learned helplessness by coaching them in more adaptive attribution styles. For example, Carol Dweck (1975) exposed children who had become helpless in the face of repeated failures on math problems to a simple "attribution retraining" treatment. Over 25 sessions these children experienced some successes and were told after each of several prearranged failures that they had not worked fast enough and should have tried harder. Through this retraining, they learned to attribute their failures to lack of effort rather than to low ability (the mastery-oriented attribution pattern). They also performed much better on the math problems than they had initially. By contrast, helpless children who were given nothing but success experiences during their treatment sessions never learned to cope with failure and retained their helpless ways.

In sum, teachers (and parents as well) can do much to foster a mastery-oriented approach to learning by helping children to view learning situations as opportunities to gain competence ("You'll learn a lot by working on this"), to see themselves as having the competence to master challenging work ("You're pretty smart, you know"), and to believe that they can overcome incompetence through effort ("C'mon—you'll get it if you keep trying").

Moral Education

How might schools best foster basic moral values and encourage prosocial behavior such as sharing, cooperation, and helping? If, as both Piaget and Kohlberg claim, peers are at least as important as parents in stimulating moral growth, perhaps the most sensible technique schools can use is to harness "peer power." This is precisely what many psychologists and educators have attempted to do. They have put children or adolescents together in pairs or small groups to discuss hypothetical moral dilemmas. The rationale is quite simple: Exposure to forms of moral reasoning more mature than their own will create cognitive disequilibrium, which motivates children to devise more mature modes of thinking.

Does participation in group discussions of moral issues produce more mature moral reasoning? It appears so (Schlaefli, Rest, & Thoma, 1985). Average changes that are the equivalent of about four to five years of natural development can be achieved in programs lasting only 3 to 12 weeks. Moreover, researchers have learned what kinds of discussion are most helpful. For example, it is indeed important that students be exposed to reasoning that is slightly more mature than their own (Berkowitz, 1985). Even more interesting is evidence that moral growth is most likely to occur when students actively transform, analyze, or otherwise act upon what their conversation partners have said—when they say things like "You're missing an important difference here" or "Here's something I think we can agree on" (Berkowitz & Gibbs, 1983).

Although discussion of moral issues can indeed stimulate moral growth, Kohlberg and his colleagues attempted to achieve more significant and lasting changes by altering the entire moral atmosphere of a school to create a democratically governed and caring community (Kohlberg, 1985; Power, Higgins, & Kohlberg, 1989). In this **just-community approach** to moral education, high school students and teachers jointly decide on school rules, discuss pressing moral issues facing the school community (such as drug use, cheating, and race relations), and democratically decide how to handle discipline cases. The program has been tried in a low-income area of Cambridge, Massachusetts, as well as in the wealthy suburb of Scarsdale, New York. The just-community experience seems to be as effective as discussions of moral issues in raising levels of moral reasoning (Power et al., 1989). More importantly, perhaps, the approach changes the "moral culture" of the school so that students come to feel a sense of responsibility to the school community and to understand that cheating and other immoral acts harm everyone concerned. Demonstrations like these suggest that schools can indeed push students not only to higher levels of academic achievement but to higher levels of moral awareness as well.

REFLECTIONS

We hope that this chapter has stimulated you to think about your own priorities—about whether you are studying right now for the sake of learning or for the sake of a grade and about what moral values guide your decisions. We'll leave you to your own reflections—though we do hope you'll go out and engage your friends in some stimulating discussion of the moral issues of our time!

We have now completed our series of chapters on the development of the self, or the person as an individual. In Chapter 10 we looked at the development of self-conceptions and distinctive personality traits, noting both continuity and change over the years. In Chapter 11 we focused on our identities as males or females, exploring the many implications of gender for human development. In the present chapter, of course, we have concentrated on the ways in which our identities as individuals partly reflect our characteristic moral outlooks and motives.

But individual development does not occur in a vacuum. Repeatedly, we have seen that the individual's development may take different paths depending on the social context in which it occurs. Our task in upcoming chapters will be to put the individual even more squarely into a social context. We will examine the development of social relationships in the next chapter, starting with the infant's formation of an attachment to a parent. In Chapter 14 we'll put the individual in a family context, exploring what it means to be a family member during each phase of the life span and how the family itself develops and changes over time. Finally, Chapter 15 will provide an opportunity to view the individual in interaction with other individuals in play, school, and work settings. It should become clear that throughout our lives we are both independent and interdependent—separate from and connected to other developing persons.

SUMMARY POINTS

1. Morality has cognitive, affective, and behavioral components; it is the ability to distinguish between right and wrong, to act on that distinction, and to experience appropriate moral emotions.

2. Freud's psychoanalytic theory describes moral development in terms of the formation of the superego and a sense of guilt. Cognitive-developmental theorist Jean Piaget proposed that children's moral thinking progresses through premoral, heteronomous, and autonomous stages. Lawrence Kohlberg proposed three levels of moral reasoning—preconventional, conventional, and postconventional—each with two stages. Social learning theorists have focused on how moral behavior is influenced by past learning and situational pressures.

3. Although infants are amoral in some respects, they begin learning about right and wrong through their early disciplinary encounters and already display primitive forms of empathy and prosocial behavior.

4. Most children operate at the preconventional level of moral reasoning, but both Kohlberg and Piaget may have underestimated the moral sophistication of young children (for example, their ability to

consider both intentions and consequences in judging acts and to distinguish between moral and social-conventional rules). Situational influences contribute to moral inconsistency. Reinforcement, modeling, and the disciplinary approach of induction can foster moral growth.

5. During adolescence, a shift from preconventional to conventional moral reasoning is evident, and many adolescents incorporate moral values into their sense of identity as an individual.

6. Some adults progress from the conventional to the postconventional level of moral reasoning; elderly adults typically do not "regress" in their moral thought, and some may even form more coherent moral philosophies.

7. Kohlberg's stages of moral reasoning form an invariant sequence, with progress through them influenced by cognitive growth and social experiences that involve taking others' perspectives. It has been charged that Kohlberg's theory is biased against people from non-Western cultures, people who do not share his values, and women who express a morality of care rather than a morality of justice. Critics also claim that the theory says too little about moral affect and behavior.

8. Early in life, infants display an effectance, or mastery, motivation that can be strengthened by appropriate sensory stimulation, a responsive environment, and a secure parent/child attachment. At about age 2, children become sensitive to approval and disapproval of their performances, and by 3 they evaluate themselves according to internalized standards.

9. During childhood and adolescence, some children develop a stronger need for achievement than others do, but achievement is also influenced by the value placed on success, expectancies of success, and attributions for successful and unsuccessful outcomes. High achievers tend to have a mastery-oriented rather than a helpless attributional style. Cognitive development and changes in teacher feedback may both contribute to declines in intrinsic achievement motivation as children become adolescents, and both parents and peers influence the individual's achievement strivings.

10. Adults of different ages are quite similar in their levels of achievement motivation, although women who turn their attention to child rearing may lose some of their career-oriented achievement motivation.

11. Attempts to combat learned helplessness by emphasizing learning (rather than performance) goals and retraining attributions to emphasize the need for greater effort have been successful, as have attempts to foster moral development through group discussions of moral dilemmas and the just-community approach.

KEY TERMS

amoral
attribution theory
autonomous morality
coercive family environment
conventional morality
effectance motivation
empathy
faith
heteronomous morality
immanent justice
individuative-reflective faith
induction
internalization
just-community approach
learned helplessness orientation
locus of control
love withdrawal
mastery orientation
moral affect
morality
morality of care
morality of justice
moral reasoning
moral rules
need for achievement (n Ach)
postconventional morality
power assertion
preconventional morality
premoral period
prosocial behavior
social-conventional rules

13

PARTICIPATION IN THE SOCIAL WORLD

She is greeted by doctor, nurse, mother, and father as her life begins. As an infant she becomes very attached to her parents, following them around the house—first crawling, then toddling—whimpering if they leave her. As a child she plays kickball and tag with the other children in the neighborhood and becomes friends with the little girl who lives at the end of the block. As a teenager she begins to have crushes on boys, goes on dates, breaks up, and tells her best friend about all of it. After finishing college, she finds the man for her, marries, has two children, and divides her time between them and the troubled families she counsels. At age 50 she and her husband enjoy camping with their children and grandchildren and going to football games and flea markets with their friends. At 75 she is a widow, but she continues to enjoy spending time with her family and friends and reminiscing about all the people who have been important to her during her life.

This is not an unusual life story, although we could have built in a bit more of the pains that come from worrying about relationships or seeing them end. What would make this life story or any life story unusual is to remove the people from it—to picture an infant unattached to any adult, a child who has no friends and rarely plays with other children, or an adult who lives alone, sees no one, and loves no one. Indeed, it is impossible to conceive that a human being could develop normally in a social vacuum. As the poet John Donne wrote, "No man is an island, entire of itself." We might add that no human being can *become* entire without interacting with other human beings.

This chapter traces our development as social beings, centering attention on questions such as these: What sorts of social relationships are especially important during different phases of the life span, and what is the character of these relationships? When and how do we develop the social competence it takes to interact smoothly with other people, to understand them as individuals, and to enter into intimate relationships with them? What are some of the developmental implications of being deprived of close relationships? We begin with some broad perspectives concerning the significance of social relationships for human development.

PERSPECTIVES ON THE SIGNIFICANCE OF RELATIONSHIPS IN LIFE-SPAN DEVELOPMENT

What is it, really, that social relationships contribute to our development? And what relationships are especially significant? Let's briefly see what developmental theorists have had to say.

What Do We Gain from Social Relationships?

No doubt you have your own ideas about why you value your relationships with family and friends. One thing we surely gain from relationships is sheer pleasure. However, close relationships also contribute to development by providing learning opportunities and social support.

The *learning experiences* social interactions provide affect virtually all aspects of our development—physical, cognitive, social, and emotional. This has been one of the major messages of social learning theory. We acquire language as young children, for example, because people converse with us, serving as models of how to communicate and reinforcing our communication attempts. Similarly, we learn everything from physical skills to gender roles and problem-solving techniques from our interactions with parents, teachers, siblings, friends, and others. And of course it is other people who teach us social skills and patterns of social behavior. The infant learns from face-to-face interactions with a parent how to take turns with a social partner, the child learns through other children that expressing interest in what someone is doing is a better way to make friends than grabbing their toys, and the adult continues to look to other people for guidance about how to behave as a lover, parent, worker, or group leader.

A second major function of close relationships is to provide **social support,** or emotional and practical help that bolsters us as individuals and protects us from stress. Robert Kahn and Toni Antonucci (1980) have described three important forms of social support: *affect* (love and affection), *affirmation* (expressions of approval and agreement, acknowledgment of one's worth, and so on), and *aid* (direct assistance in the form of information, advice, assistance, money, and so on). For example, after Hugh is in a minor car accident, his wife may give him a hug (affect), agree with him that it was the other driver's fault (affirmation), and phone the insurance company (aid). As Kahn and Antonucci see it, having reliable sources of social support benefits us both by increasing our sense of well-being and by protecting us from the potentially negative effects of stressful life events.

Although many researchers use the term *social network* to describe the array of significant individuals who serve as sources of social support, Kahn and Antonucci prefer to describe these significant people as a **social convoy,** conveying the idea that the composition of the social support system changes over the life span. An infant's convoy may consist only of parents, but the social convoy enlarges over the years as friends, supportive teachers, colleagues, and other people join it. As new members are added, some members drift away. Others remain in the convoy, but we learn to interact with them in new ways, as when the infant son who is thoroughly dependent on his mother becomes the adolescent son clamoring for his independence—and later the middle-aged son who helps his mother manage her money and care for her lawn. An individual's social convoy, then, is an ever-changing source of social support with those closest to the person at its center (see also Levitt, 1991).

In sum, other people are important to us for an endless range of reasons, but their most critical roles in the developmental process are as teachers and as sources of social support. We could not learn our culture's patterns of social behavior without them, and we could not meet life's challenges nearly so well without the affection, affirmation, and aid provided by our social convoys.

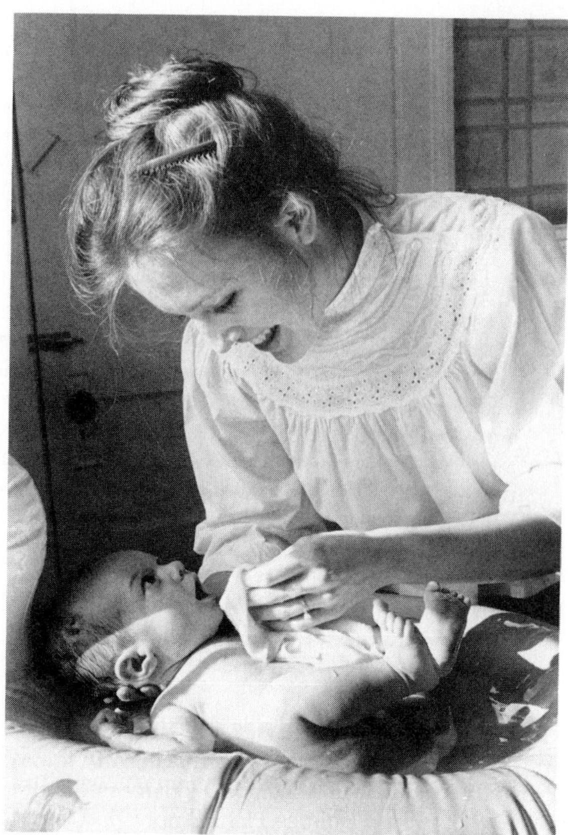

Relationships with caregivers start us on our way as social beings.

Which Relationships Are Most Critical to Development?

Many noted developmental theorists have felt that no social relationship is more important to human development than the very first: the bond between parent and infant. Sigmund Freud (1905/1930) left no doubt about his opinion: A stable mother/child relationship is essential for normal personality development. His follower Erik Erikson tended to agree. So has ethological theorist John Bowlby (1969), whose influential theory of parent/infant attachments we will examine later. Bowlby, for instance, has claimed that the caregiver/infant relationship sets the pattern for later intimate relationships by teaching us whether we can rely on other people to truly care about us. The parent/infant relationship *is* important and has been studied extensively for good reason.

Yet some theorists argue that relationships with peers are equally significant. These researchers think that there are "two social worlds of childhood," one involving adult/child relationships and the other involving peer relationships, and that these two worlds contribute differently to development (Youniss, 1980). Who is a **peer**? Someone who is one's social equal, someone who functions at a similar level of behavioral complexity, and often, though not always, someone of similar age (Lewis & Rosenblum, 1975). As Jean Piaget (1932/1965) observed, relationships with peers are quite different from relationships with parents. Parent/child relationships are lopsided: Because parents have more power than children do, the children are in a subordinate position and must defer to adult authority. By contrast, two children have equal power and influence and must learn to appreciate each other's perspectives, to negotiate and compromise, and to cooperate with each other if they hope to get along. Thus Piaget believed that peers can make a unique contribution to child development that adult authority figures cannot make.

Another theorist who believed that peer relationships contribute significantly to development was neo-Freudian Harry Stack Sullivan (1953; see also Buhrmester & Furman, 1986; Youniss, 1980). He believed that interpersonal needs are important throughout life but that these needs change with age and are gratified through different kinds of social relationships at different ages. According to Sullivan, the parent/child relationship is indeed central up to about age 6;

infants need tender care and nurturance from their parents, and preschool children need their parents to serve as playmates and companions. From about age 6 on, however, peers become increasingly important in children's lives. At first children need peers as companions or playmates; then they need to be accepted by peers; then, around age 9 to 12, they begin to need intimacy in the form of a close friendship.

Indeed, Sullivan placed special emphasis on the developmental significance of **chumships,** or close friendships with peers of the same sex that emerge at about age 9 to 12. It is with their close chums, he believed, that children become capable of truly caring about another person and learn the importance of trust, loyalty, and honesty in relationships. In fact, Sullivan believed that a close chumship could do much to make up for any insecurities caused by a poor parent/child relationship. Moreover, the lessons about intimacy learned in the context of same-sex chumships would then carry over into the intimate romantic relationships formed during adolescence and adulthood. Sullivan believed that a child who never had a chum would be poorly adjusted later in life. As we will see, he was right.

Debates about the relative significance of parents and peers for later development continue to rage, with some developmentalists agreeing with Freud and Bowlby that the quality of an infant's attachment to an adult is the most significant influence on later personality and social development, and others sharing the belief of Piaget and Sullivan that relationships with peers are at least as significant.

THE INFANT

Human infants are social beings from the start, but the nature of their social relationships changes dramatically as they form close attachments to parents or other companions and as they develop the social skills that allow them to coordinate their own activities with those of other infants.

Attachment: The Emergence of the First Relationship

According to John Bowlby (1969), an **attachment** is a strong affectional tie that binds a person to an intimate companion. For most of us the first attachment we form is to a parent. How do we know when baby Michael is attached to his mother? He will try to maintain proximity to her—crying, clinging, approaching, following, doing whatever it takes to maintain closeness. Moreover, he will prefer her to other individuals, reserving his biggest smiles for her and seeking her out when he is upset, discomforted, or afraid. In short, he will show many of the same symptoms that we might observe in an adult who is "in love." True, close emotional ties are expressed in somewhat different ways, and serve somewhat different functions, at different points in the life span. Adults, for example, do not usually feel compelled to follow their mates around the house, and they look to their loved ones for more than comforting hugs and smiles. Nonetheless, there are basic similarities among the infant attached to Mother, the child attached to a best friend, and the adult attached to a mate or lover. Throughout the life span, the objects of our attachments are special people with whom we are motivated to maintain contact and from whom we derive a sense of security (Ainsworth, 1989).

Like any relationship, the parent/child attachment is reciprocal. Parents become attached to their infants; infants become attached to their parents.

The Caregiver's Attachment to the Infant

Parents have an edge on infants: They can begin to form an emotional attachment to their babies even before birth. As we saw in Chapter 4, Marshall Klaus and John Kennell (1976) found that mothers who have an opportunity for skin-to-skin contact with their babies during the first few hours after birth form a special bond to them. Researchers have since discovered that the effects of such early contact are not so large or long lasting as Klaus and Kennell believed (Eyer, 1992; Goldberg, 1983). Moreover, adoptive parents and parents whose babies are premature or ill and must be separated from them during their stay in intensive care still form close attachments to their infants (Levy-Shiff, Goldshmidt, & Har-Even, 1991; Rode, Chang, Fisch, & Sroufe, 1981). Parents *can* become highly emotionally involved with their infants during the first few hours after birth, but early contact is neither crucial nor sufficient for the development of strong parent-to-infant attachments. Instead, these attachments seem to build during parent/child interactions that take place over many weeks and months.

What makes parents become attached to their infants? For starters, babies are "cute"; their chubby cheeks and rounded profiles appeal to adults (Alley, 1981). Moreover, babies behave in ways that are endearing. Early reflexive behaviors such as sucking, rooting, and grasping may help convince parents that their infants enjoy their company (Bowlby, 1969). Smiling may be an especially important signal. It is initially a reflexive response to almost any stimulus but can be triggered by voices at 3 weeks of age and by faces at 5 or 6 weeks of age (Bowlby, 1969; Wolff, 1963). Finally, when infants begin to coo and babble, their parents can enjoy back-and-forth "conversations" with them (Keller & Scholmerich, 1987; Stevenson et al., 1986).

Over the weeks and months, caregivers and infants develop **synchronized routines** much like dances, in which the partners take turns responding to each other's leads (Stern, 1977; Tronick, 1989). These smooth interactions are most likely to develop

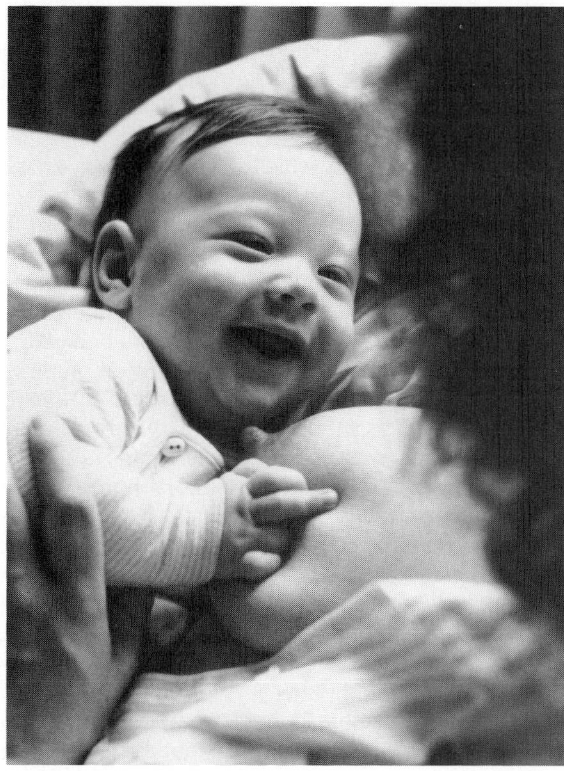

Smiling is one of the behaviors that help to ensure that adults will fall in love with babies.

if the caregiver limits her social stimulation to those periods when the baby is alert and receptive and avoids pushing things when the infant's message is "Cool it—I need a break from all this stimulation." Edward Tronick (1989, p. 112) described one very synchronous "dance" as a mother played peek-a-boo with her infant:

> The infant abruptly turns away from his mother as the game reaches its "peak" of intensity and begins to suck on his thumb and stare into space with a dull facial expression. The mother stops playing and sits back watching . . . . After a few seconds the infant turns back to her with an inviting expression. The mother moves closer, smiles, and says in a high-pitched, exaggerated voice, "Oh, now you're back!" He smiles in response and vocalizes. As they finish crowing together, the infant reinserts his thumb and looks away. The mother again waits. [Soon] the infant turns . . . to her and they greet each other with big smiles.

In sum, infants play an active role in persuading adults to love them. Babies are physically appealing, come equipped with a number of reflexes that promote the formation of an attachment, and are highly responsive to people and capable of synchronizing their behavior with that of their "dance partners." As caregiver and infant perfect their interaction routines, the parent/infant relationship normally blossoms into a strong reciprocal attachment (Isabella & Belsky, 1991).

Yet not all parents become closely attached to their infants. In the first place, some babies are hard to love. Parents may have a difficult time establishing stable and synchronized routines with irritable or unresponsive infants (Field, 1987; Greene, Fox, & Lewis, 1983). Babies born to cocaine users, for instance, are sometimes extremely agitated, irritable, and susceptible to overarousal; at other times they are withdrawn, sluggish, and unresponsive (Lester et al., 1991). Even the most sensitive caregiver may have trouble predicting their reactions and keeping them content.

Second, some adults have difficulty responding to infants. Parents who were themselves unloved, neglected, or abused as children often start out with the best intentions, but then, when their babies are irritable or inattentive (as all infants are at times), these parents may back off from the relationship, sometimes to the point of neglecting or abusing their babies (Biringen, 1990; Crowell & Feldman, 1991; Steele and Pollack, 1974)). Mothers who are depressed may also have difficulty responding sensitively to their babies' signals and forming close attachments (Lyons-Ruth et al., 1990; Radke-Yarrow et al., 1985).

In addition, the broader social context surrounding caregiver and infant can affect how they react to each other. For example, mothers who must care for several small children with little or no assistance may find themselves unwilling or unable to devote much attention to their newest baby, particularly if the infant is at all irritable or unresponsive (Belsky, 1980; Crockenberg, 1981). Also, parents who are unhappy in their marriages may have difficulty interacting responsively with their infants (Cox et al., 1989; Howes & Markman, 1989). The cultural context in which caregiver and baby interact may also matter. For instance, German parents strongly encourage independence and discourage clingy behavior in their children, which may explain why German infants are more likely than infants in many other societies to ignore or avoid their parents when they are reunited with them after a separation (Grossmann et al., 1985). Intense distress over separations is far more common in cultures such as Japan, where mothers and babies are rarely separated early in life (Takahashi, 1990; van IJzendoorn & Kroonenberg, 1988). In short, although most new parents quickly fall in love with their infants, various characteristics of the baby, the caregiver, and the surrounding social environment can clearly affect the nature of parents' attachments to their children.

The Infant's Attachment to the Caregiver

Infants require some time before they are developmentally ready to form a genuine attachment to another human being. They progress through the following phases as they develop close ties with their caregivers (Ainsworth, 1973; Bowlby, 1969):

1. *Undiscriminating social responsiveness* (birth to 2 or 3 months). Very young infants are responsive to voices, faces, and other social stimuli, but any human is of interest to them. They do not yet show a clear preference for one person over another.

2. *Discriminating social responsiveness* (2 or 3 months to 6 or 7 months). Now infants are beginning to express preferences for familiar companions. They are likely to direct their biggest grins and most enthusiastic babbles toward those companions, though they are still quite friendly toward strangers.

3. *Active proximity seeking/True attachment* (6 or 7 months to about 3 years). At about 6 or 7 months of age, infants form their first clear attachments, most often to their mothers. Now able to crawl, an infant will follow along behind her mother to stay close, protest when her mother leaves, and greet her mother warmly when she returns. Within weeks after forming their first attachments, most infants become attached to other people as well—fathers, siblings, grandparents, regular babysitters (Schaffer & Emerson, 1964). By 18 months of age, very few infants are attached to only one person, and some are attached to several.

4. *Goal-corrected partnership* (3 years and older). By about the age of 3, partly because they have more advanced social-cognitive abilities, children can take a parent's goals and plans into consideration and adjust their behavior accordingly to achieve the goal of maintaining optimal proximity to the attachment figure. Thus a 1-year-old cries and tries to follow when Dad leaves the house to talk to a neighbor, whereas the 4-year-old child probably understands where Dad is going and can control the need for his attention until he returns. This final, more partner-like, phase of attachment lasts a lifetime.

Infants no sooner experience the pleasures of love than they discover the agonies of fear. One form of fear, **separation anxiety,** is actually an important sign that an attachment has formed. Once attached to a parent, babies often become wary or fretful when separated from that parent and will follow behind the parent to try to avoid separation. Separation anxiety normally appears at the time infants are forming their first genuine attachments, it peaks at 14 to 18 months, and it gradually becomes less frequent and less intense throughout infancy and the preschool period (Kagan, 1976; Weinraub & Lewis, 1977).

A second fearful response that often emerges once an attachment is formed is **stranger anxiety,** a wary or fretful reaction to the approach of an unfamiliar person. Most infants react positively to strangers until they form their first attachment and then become wary of strangers shortly thereafter (Schaffer & Emerson, 1964). Anxious reactions to strangers—often mixed with signs of interest—become common at 8 to 10 months of age, continue through the first year, and gradually decline in intensity over the second year (Sroufe, 1977). Box 13.1 describes the circumstances under which stranger anxiety is most and least likely to occur and suggests how health-care professionals can use this knowledge to head off outbreaks of fear and trembling in their offices.

Finally, the formation of a strong attachment to a caregiver has another important consequence: It facilitates the development of exploratory behavior. Mary Ainsworth (Ainsworth et al., 1978) emphasizes that an attachment figure serves as a **secure base** for exploration, a point of safety from which an infant can feel free to venture away. Thus Wendy, a securely attached infant visiting a neighbor's home with Mom, may be comfortable exploring the living room as long as she can check back occasionally to see that Mom is still there but may be reluctant to explore if Mom disappears into the bathroom (Sroufe, 1977). Paradoxical as it may seem, then, infants apparently need to rely on another person in order to feel confident about acting independently.

The timetable for the formation of attachments is now clear, and we have seen that the emergence of a specific attachment often brings with it both uncertainty (separation and stranger anxiety) and confidence (a willingness to use the attachment figure as a secure base for exploration). It is time to explain *why* attachments form and why an infant might choose one person rather than another as a love object.

Theories of Attachment

Four major theories about the development of parent/child attachments have been offered: psychoanalytic theory, learning theory, cognitive-developmental theory, and ethological theory. Let's examine the main arguments of each theory and then see what each theory contributes to our understanding.

Psychoanalytic Theory: I Love You Because You Feed Me

According to Freud, infants in the oral stage of psychosexual development will become attached to any person who provides oral pleasure. Since mothers usually feed infants, they are typically the objects of infants' affections. A secure attachment will form if a mother is relaxed and generous in her feeding practices. Erik Erikson also believed that a mother's feeding practices influence the security of an infant's attachment. However, he emphasized that a mother's *general responsiveness* to her child, not just her tendency to gratify oral needs, would affect the strength of the attachment formed during the stage of *trust versus mistrust*. According to Erikson, a care-

BOX 13.1 Combating Stranger Anxiety: The Case of the Doctor's Appointment

It is not unusual for 1- or 2-year-olds visiting the doctor's office to break into tears and cling to their parents. Toddlers who remember previous visits may be suffering "shot anxiety" rather than stranger anxiety, but some infants are undoubtedly bothered by nothing more than the approach of strange adults. Stranger-wary infants often stare at the stranger for a moment and then turn away, whimper, and seek the comfort of their parents. Occasionally, infants become terrified and highly upset. Obviously it is in the interests of doctors and nurses—and babysitters and other "strangers" as well—to be able to prevent such negative reactions. What might we suggest?

1. *Keep familiar companions available.* Stranger anxiety is less likely to occur if an attachment figure is nearby to serve as a "secure base." In one study, fewer than one-third of 6- to 12-month-olds were wary of an approaching stranger when they were seated on their mothers' laps (Morgan & Ricciuti, 1969). Yet about two-thirds of these infants frowned, turned away, whimpered, or cried if they were seated only 4 feet from their mothers (see also Bohlin & Hagekull, 1993). Clearly, doctors and nurses would do well to avoid separating parent and child in the doctor's office unless it is unavoidable. If parent and toddler must be separated, a security blanket or beloved stuffed animal can have much the same calming effect as a parent's presence for some infants (Passman, 1977).

2. *Arrange for companions to respond positively to the stranger.* Beginning at about 6 months of age, infants try to read other people's emotional reactions to uncertain situations and are able to use this information to guide their own responses—a process called *social*

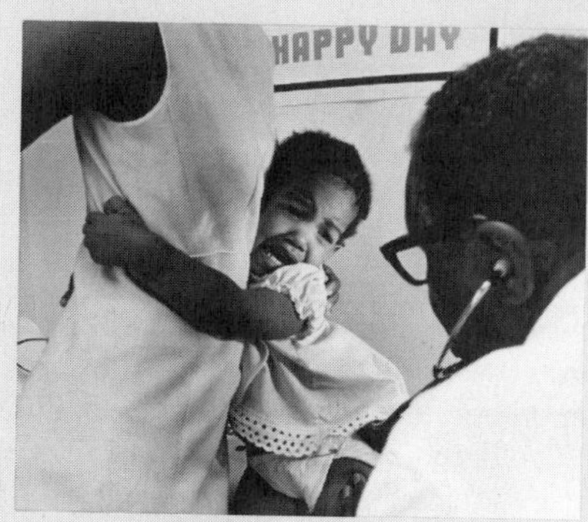

referencing (Feinman, 1992; see also Chapter 10). The result is that infants are likely to respond much more favorably to a stranger's approach if their mothers or fathers greet the stranger warmly than if the parents react neutrally or negatively toward this person. It might not hurt, then, for medical staff to try to start a pleasant exchange with Mom or Dad before directing their attention to the infant.

3. *Make the setting more "familiar."* Stranger anxiety is less likely to occur in familiar settings than in unfamiliar ones. Thus, for example, it may be rare in the home but common in an unfamiliar laboratory (Sroufe, Waters, & Matas, 1974). Although the doctor's office is *not* home, some physicians have deliberately decorated their offices to make them seem more homelike. This should help. Moreover, an unfamiliar environment can become a familiar one if infants are given the time to get used to it. Alan Sroufe and his colleagues (1974) found that over 90% of 10-month-olds became upset if a stranger approached within a minute after they had been placed in an unfamiliar room; only 50% did so when they had had 10 minutes to become accustomed to the room.

4. *Be a sensitive, unobtrusive stranger.* Not surprisingly, an infant's response to a stranger depends on the stranger's behavior (Sroufe, 1977). The meeting is likely to go best if the stranger initially keeps his or her distance and then approaches slowly while smiling, talking, and offering a familiar toy or suggesting a familiar activity (Bretherton, Stolberg, & Kreye, 1981; Sroufe, 1977). It also helps if the stranger, like any sensitive caregiver, takes his or her cues from the infant (Mangelsdorf, 1992). Babies prefer strangers they can control! Intrusive strangers who approach quickly and force themselves on infants (for example, by trying to pick them up before they have time to adjust) probably get the response they deserve.

5. *Try not to look any stranger than you must.* Finally, stranger anxiety is affected by the physical appearance of the stranger. Jerome Kagan (1972) claims that infants form *schemata,* or mental representations, for the faces they encounter in daily life and are most likely to be afraid of people whom they cannot match to their existing schemas. We might infer from this that professionals who have unusual physical features such as beards *or* who dress in unusual outfits might elicit more wariness than those who resemble the people infants encounter every day. Pediatric professionals may not be able to change their physical features, but they can and often have exchanged their starkly white uniforms for more familiar clothing, thus allowing their young patients to more readily recognize them as members of the human race. Babysitters who favor the "punk" or "grunge" look might also heed this advice!

---

giver who consistently responds to an infant's needs breeds in that infant a sense of trust in other people and in the self that is essential to later development.

Learning Theory: I Love You Because You're Reinforcing

For quite different reasons, learning theorists have also assumed that infants will form attachments to the individuals who feed them and meet their other needs. As a caregiver provides food, fresh diapers, tender touches, and other pleasant experiences, the infant comes to associate that person with pleasurable sensations. Through learning, then, caregivers become a source of reinforcement, and infants will do whatever is necessary to attract their attention and remain near these rewarding individuals.

Cognitive-Developmental Theory: I Love You Because I Know You

Proponents of cognitive-developmental theory believe that the ability to form attachments depends in part on the infant's level of intellectual development and knowledge of the surrounding world. Before an attachment can form, the infant must be able to *discriminate* between social and nonsocial stimuli and then among social stimuli (familiar persons versus strangers, one familiar person versus another). Moreover, the infant must recognize that close companions continue to exist even when they are absent; otherwise, there would be no cause for separation anxiety when a caregiver leaves the room (Kohlberg, 1969; Lester et al., 1974). In other words, infants will not form attachments until they have acquired some concept of *person permanence* (a form of the object-permanence concept studied by Jean Piaget and discussed in Chapter 7). So, cognitive-developmental theorists claim that attachments form naturally as infants come to know the social world around them, begin to discriminate familiar companions, and understand that these companions have a permanent existence.

Ethologist Konrad Lorenz demonstrated that goslings would become imprinted to him rather than to their mother if he was the first moving object they encountered during their critical period for imprinting.

Ethological Theory: I Love You Because I Was Born to Love

The most influential theory of attachment today is the ethological theory proposed by John Bowlby (1969, 1973, 1980, 1988) and elaborated on by Mary Ainsworth (1989; Ainsworth et al., 1978). Bowlby, a British psychiatrist who died in 1990, argued that infants (and parents too) are biologically predisposed to form attachments. As we saw in Chapter 3, ethologists assume that all species, including human beings, are born with a number of innate behavioral tendencies that have in some way contributed to the survival of the species over the course of evolution. It makes sense to think, for example, that young birds have tended to survive if they have stayed close to their mothers so that they could be fed and protected from predators—but have starved and been gobbled up, and therefore have failed to pass on their genes to future generations, if they have strayed away. Thus chicks, ducks, and goslings may have gradually evolved so that they engage in **imprinting,** an innate form of learning in which the young will follow and become attached to a moving object (usually the mother) during a critical period early in life. Konrad Lorenz (1937) observed this response in young goslings and noted that imprinting (1) is automatic—young fowl do not have to be taught to follow; (2) occurs only within a *critical period* shortly after the bird has hatched; and (3) is irreversible—once the gosling begins to follow a particular object, whether the object is its mother or Konrad Lorenz, it will remain attached to it. The imprinting response Lorenz observed is a prime example of a species-specific and largely innate behavior that has evolved over time because it has survival value.

What about human infants? Babies may not become imprinted to their mothers in the same way that young fowl do, but they most certainly follow their love objects around. In his theory of human attachment, Bowlby argued that they come equipped with a number of other behaviors besides following that help ensure that adults will love them and tend to them. Among these behaviors are sucking, clinging, smiling, and vocalizing (crying, cooing, and babbling). Moreover, Bowlby argued that adults are biologically programmed to respond to an infant's signals, just as infants are programmed to respond to the sight, sound, and touch of their caregivers. It is difficult indeed for an adult to ignore a baby's cry or fail to warm up to a baby's big grin. In other words, both human infants and human caregivers have evolved in ways that predispose them to form close attachments, and this ensures that infants will receive the care, protection, and stimulation they need to survive and thrive.

If it sounds to you as if ethologists believe that attachments form automatically, we should correct that impression. Bowlby holds that the quality of an attachment will be influenced by the ongoing interaction between infant and caregiver and by the ability of each partner to respond to the other's signals. The infant's preprogrammed signals to other people may eventually wane if they fail to produce favorable reactions because a caregiver is unresponsive to them (Ainsworth et al., 1978). In addition, infants themselves must learn to react sensitively to their caregiver's signals so that they can adjust their own behavior to mesh well with that of their love object. So, although Bowlby believes that humans are biologically prepared to form attachments, he also stresses that mutual learning processes contribute to the unfolding of a secure relationship.

Bowlby strongly believed that the quality of the early parent/infant attachment has important effects on later development. He proposed that, as infants interact with their caregivers, they develop **internal working models**—cognitive representations of themselves and other people—that shape their expectations about human relationships (Bowlby, 1973; see also Bretherton, 1990). Securely attached infants who have received responsive care will form internal working models suggesting that they are lovable individuals and that other people can be trusted to care for them. By contrast, insecurely attached infants subjected to insensitive, neglectful, or abusive care may conclude that they are difficult to love and that other people are unreliable.

How can we assess the quality of the parent/infant attachment in order to test these sorts of theoretical predictions? It is here that Mary Ainsworth made her most notable contribution to Bowlby's attachment theory. She and her associates devised a technique, called the **Strange Situation test** (see Ainsworth et al., 1978), for measuring the quality of an attachment. It consists of a series of eight episodes that gradually escalate the amount of stress infants experience as they react to the approaches of an adult stranger and the departures and returns of their caregivers. On the basis of an infant's pattern of behavior across the episodes, the quality of his or her attachment to a parent is characterized as one of three types: secure, resistant, or avoidant:

1. **Secure attachment.** About 70% of 1-year-olds in our society are securely attached to their mothers (Ainsworth et al., 1978).[1] The securely attached infant actively explores the room when alone with the mother because she serves as a secure base. The infant may be upset by separation but greets the mother when she returns and welcomes physical contact with her. The child is outgoing with a stranger while the mother is present.

2. **Resistant attachment.** About 10% of 1-year-olds show a resistant attachment, or an insecure attachment characterized by ambivalent reactions to their mothers. The resistant infant is quite anxious and unlikely to venture off to play while the mother is present, which suggests that she does not serve as a secure base for exploration. Yet this infant becomes very distressed when the mother departs, often showing much stronger separation anxiety than the securely attached infant. Then, when the mother returns, the infant is ambivalent: He or she may try to remain near the mother but seems to resent her for having left, may resist if she tries to make physical contact, and may even hit and kick her in anger (Ainsworth et al., 1978). Resistant infants are also quite wary of strangers, even when their mothers are present. It seems, then, that resistant or ambivalent infants are drawn to their mothers but lack a sense of trust. When Mom leaves the room, this infant may wonder whether she'll ever come back!

3. **Avoidant attachment.** Avoidant infants (about 20% of 1-year-olds) seem uninterested in exploring, show little distress when separated from their mothers, and avoid contact when their mothers return. These insecurely attached infants are not particularly wary of strangers but sometimes avoid or ignore them in much the same way that they avoid or ignore their mothers. Avoidant infants, then, seem to have distanced themselves from their parents.

Table 13.1 summarizes the features of these three patterns of attachment, which have been the subject of considerable research and have helped to make Bowlby's ethological perspective the leading theory of attachment. Yet the other major theories of attachment—psychoanalytic, social learning, and cognitive-developmental—also have something to contribute to our understanding. Let's examine what research has to say about influences on the quality of the parent/child attachment and then consider the extent to which research has supported claims by both Freud and Bowlby that early attachments have significant implications for later relationships and adjustment.

What Influences the Quality of Early Attachments?

In early investigations of attachment, researchers tested Freud's claim that feeding experiences play a central role in the formation of attachments. In a classic study conducted by Harry Harlow and Robert Zimmerman (1959), monkeys were reared with two surrogate mothers: a wire "mother" and a cloth "mother" wrapped in foam rubber and covered with terrycloth (see Figure 13.1). Half the infants were fed by the cloth mother, and the remaining half by the wire mother. To which mother did these infants become attached? There was no contest, really: Infants strongly preferred the cuddly cloth mother, *regardless of which mother had fed them.* Even if their food came from the wire mother, they spent more time clinging to the cloth mother, ran to "her" when they were upset or afraid, and showed every sign of being attached to her. Harlow's research demonstrated that what he called **contact comfort,** or the pleasurable tactile sensations provided by a soft and cuddly "parent," is a more powerful contributor to attachment in monkeys than feeding or the reduction of hunger.

[1]The percentages of infants falling into each attachment category vary somewhat from culture to culture and from subgroup to subgroup within a particular society (van IJzendoorn & Kroonenberg, 1988). Nonetheless, more babies around the world fall into the secure attachment category than into either of the others.

TABLE 13.1 Behaviors associated with the secure, resistant, and avoidant attachment styles in the Strange Situation test.

Behavior	*Type of Attachment*		
	Secure	*Resistant*	*Avoidant*
Exploration when caregiver is present to provide a "secure base" for exploration?	Yes, actively	No—clings	Yes, but play is not as constructive as that of secure infant
Positive response to stranger?	Yes, comfortable if caregiver is present	No, fearful even with caregiver present	No, often indifferent, as they are to caregiver
Protest when separated from caregiver?	Yes, at least mildly distressed	Yes! *Extremely* upset	No—seemingly unfazed
Positive response to caregiver at reunion?	Yes, happy to be reunited	Yes *and* no. Seeks contact but resents being left; ambivalent	No, ignores or avoids caregiver

We have no reason to believe that feeding is any more important to human infants than to baby monkeys. When Rudolph Schaffer and Peggy Emerson (1964) asked mothers how they scheduled their feedings and when they weaned their infants, it turned out that the generosity of a mother's feeding practices simply did not predict the strength of her infant's attachment to her. In fact, for 39% of these infants, the person who usually fed, bathed, and changed the child (typically the mother) was not even the child's primary attachment figure! In short, we must reject Freud's psychoanalytic theory of attachment, even though we can applaud him for stressing the importance of early emotional attachments to caregivers. Infants do not seem to form an attachment to an adult simply because that person capably satisfies their hunger.

FIGURE 13.1 The wire and cloth surrogate "mothers" used in Harlow's research. This infant has formed an attachment to the cloth mother that provides "contact comfort," even though it must stretch to the wire mother in order to feed.

What *can* parents do to ensure that a secure bond will form? Infants develop secure attachments to mothers and fathers who are responsive to their needs and emotional signals (Ainsworth et al., 1978; Cox et al., 1992; Isabella, 1993; Teti et al., 1991). Thus research supports Erikson's version of psychoanalytic theory, for he claimed that responsive parenting contributes to the development of trust. These findings are also consistent with learning theory, in that a highly responsive adult should be more reinforcing to an infant than a neglectful or aloof one.

Babies who show a resistant rather than secure pattern of attachment sometimes have irritable and unresponsive temperaments (Waters, Vaughn, & Egeland, 1980), but more often they have parents who are inconsistent in their caregiving—reacting enthusiastically or indifferently, depending on their moods, and being unresponsive a good deal of the time (Ainsworth, 1979; Isabella, 1993; Isabella & Belsky, 1991). The infant copes with inconsistent caregiving by trying desperately—through clinging, crying, and other attachment behaviors—to obtain emotional support and comfort and then becomes both saddened and resentful when these efforts fail.

The parents of infants with an avoidant attachment often tend to be impatient, unresponsive to the infant's signals, and resentful when the infant interferes with their own plans; some are even downright rejecting (Ainsworth, 1979; Egeland & Farber, 1984; Isabella, 1993). Or, these parents may be overzealous, chattering endlessly and providing high levels of stimulation even when their babies do not want it (Belsky, Rovine, & Taylor, 1984; Isabella & Belsky, 1991). Infants may be responding quite adaptively by learning to avoid adults who seem to dislike their company or who bombard them with stimulation they do not want and cannot handle. Whereas resistant infants make vigorous attempts to gain emotional support, avoidant infants seem to have learned to do without it (Isabella, 1993).

Infants who have been physically abused or maltreated are highly likely—82% of them in one study (Carlson et al., 1989)—to display what is now recognized as a fourth pattern of attachment: **disorganized/disoriented attachment.** This is a curious combination of features of the resistant and avoidant styles that reflects confusion about whether to approach or avoid the parent (Main & Solomon, 1990). Reunited with their mothers after a separation, these infants may act dazed and freeze; or they may seek contact but then abruptly move away as their mothers approach them; or they may show both patterns in different reunion episodes. Perhaps because abused infants do not know from moment to moment whether their parents will be loving or abusive, they seem uncertain whether to seek out these unpredictable individuals for comfort or to retreat to safety. Unlike secure, resistant, or avoidant infants, they have not been able to devise any coherent strategy for coping with stress. As it turns out, infants who show this disorganized pattern of attachment are at high risk of becoming hostile, aggressive preschoolers (Lyons-Ruth, Alpern, & Repacholi, 1993).

Clearly, the ways in which parents interact with their babies relate in predictable ways to the quality of the attachments that form. Yet the infant's characteristics also have a bearing; after all, attachments are relationships between two people. The baby's temperament is especially important: An attachment is less likely to be secure if the infant is by temperament fearful and easily distressed (Goldsmith & Alansky, 1987; Izard et al., 1991; Vaughn et al., 1992). Which has a stronger bearing on the quality of the attachment, then—the caregiver's style of parenting or the infant's temperament? Both are significant, but longitudinal studies suggest that the caregiver's behavior has more to do with whether or not a secure attachment forms than do characteristics of the infant (Goldberg et al., 1986; Vaughn et al., 1989). In addition, even temperamentally difficult babies are likely to establish secure relationships with caregivers who are patient and adjust their caregiving to the baby's temperamental quirks (Mangelsdorf et al., 1990; van IJzendoorn et al., 1992). These findings are consistent with the *goodness of fit* model introduced in Chapter 10: Secure bonds evolve when parents can respond sensitively to whatever temperamental characteristics their babies display, whereas insecure bonds are more likely when there is a mismatch between caregiving style and infant's temperament (Sroufe, 1985).

How Do Early Attachments Affect Later Development?

From Freud on, almost everyone has assumed that the parent/child relationship is very important in shaping future development. Just how important *is* it? Two lines of research offer us an answer: (1) studies of socially deprived infants and (2) studies of the later development of securely and insecurely attached infants.

The Effects of Social Deprivation in Infancy

What becomes of babies who never have an opportunity to form *any* attachment bond? Studies of infants who grow up in deprived institutional settings give us an idea (Goldfarb, 1943, 1945, 1947; Provence & Lipton, 1962). In the kinds of institutions studied, it was not unusual for one caregiver to be responsible for 8 to 12 infants. Adults rarely saw the infants except to bathe and change them or to prop a bottle against their pillows at feeding times. Often the infants had few or no crib toys and few opportunities to get out and practice motor skills. Thus they were often deprived of sensory as well as social stimulation.

What are such infants like? They seldom cry, coo, or babble; become rigid when they are picked up; have few language skills; and often appear either forlorn and uninterested in their caretakers or emotionally starved and insatiable in their need for affection. Do these negative effects persist? Apparently so. William Goldfarb (1943, 1947) discovered serious deficits in intellectual functioning, language skills, and social competence among children who spent their first three years in an understaffed orphanage. By adolescence many of these children were loners who had a difficult time relating to peers or family members.

Barbara Tizard (1977; Hodges & Tizard, 1989) conducted similar research in institutions that were adequately staffed and apparently provided the stimulation necessary for normal intellectual development. However, because these children had been cared for by 50 to 80 different caregivers in their early years, they rarely became attached to any one adult. The effects? Children who had spent at least four years in these institutions were much less popular and much more restless and disobedient in school at age 8 and more emotionally troubled and antisocial at age 16 than children who left these institutions for adoptive homes early in life.

Why does institutional deprivation have such damaging effects on development? It is probably not just the lack of sensory stimulation, for institutionalized children who lack contact with adult caregivers but have plenty of toys and can see and hear other infants are still developmentally delayed (Provence & Lipton, 1962). Nor is it the lack of a single "mother figure." In *adequately staffed* institutions in the People's Republic of China and in Israel, infants cared for by several responsive caregivers appear to be quite normal in all respects (Kessen, 1975; Oppenheim, Sagi, & Lamb, 1988; see also Chapter 15 for a discussion of the effects of day-care placement on the parent/infant attachment). Similarly, Efe (Pygmy) infants in Zaire seem to thrive despite being cared for and even nursed by a variety of caregivers besides their mothers

Infants develop normally as long as they have continuing relationships with responsive caregivers—whether one or several.

(Tronick, Morelli, & Ivey, 1992). Apparently, then, normal development requires *sustained interactions with responsive caregivers—whether one or several.*

The Later Development of Securely and Insecurely Attached Infants

Now consider infants raised at home. How much difference does having an early secure or insecure attachment make later in life? Everett Waters and his associates (Waters, Wippman, & Sroufe, 1979) measured the quality of infants' attachments to their mothers at 15 months of age and then observed these children in nursery school at age 3½. Children who had been securely attached as infants were social leaders in the nursery school setting: They often initiated play activities, were sensitive to the needs and feelings of other children, and were popular with their peers. Moreover, securely attached infants became children whose teachers described them as curious, self-directed, and eager to learn. By contrast, children who had been insecurely attached at age 15 months, displaying either resistant or avoidant attachment patterns, became 3½-year-olds who were socially and emotionally withdrawn and were hesitant to engage other children in play activities. These children were also less curious, less interested in learning, and less forceful in pursuing their goals than securely attached children, as if they lacked a secure base for exploration. By age 4 to 5, children who were securely attached as infants continue to be more curious, more responsive to peers, and less dependent on adults than classmates who were insecurely attached as infants (Sroufe, Fox, & Pancake, 1983). And, at age 10 to 11, they are more likely to have close friends and close relationships with their friends (Elicker, Englund, & Sroufe, 1992; Grossmann & Grossmann, 1991).

We see, then, that a secure attachment in infancy may have positive implications for both social and intellectual development in childhood (see also Frankel & Bates, 1990; Pipp, Easterbrooks, & Harmon, 1992). Yet we must avoid concluding that infants who are insecurely attached to their mothers are doomed. First, affectionate ties to *fathers* (or perhaps siblings or grandparents) can compensate for insecure mother/infant relationships. Although over 60% of infants have the same kind of attachment with their mothers that they have with their fathers (Fox, Kimmerly, & Schafer, 1991), many infants who are insecurely attached to one parent are securely attached to the other (Cox et al., 1992; Main & Weston, 1981; Rosen & Rothbaum, 1993). Infants who have a secure relationship with one parent, whether it is the father or the mother, are more socially competent than infants who are not securely attached to either parent; those who are securely attached to *both* parents are best off of all (Biller, 1993; Main & Weston, 1981).

In addition, an initially insecure attachment may have no negative long-term consequences if it becomes a secure attachment later on. Unlike diamonds, attachments are not forever. Although most children do experience the same kind of attachment to their parents in childhood that they experienced in infancy (Main & Cassidy, 1988), changing family circumstances can convert insecure attachments into secure ones—or secure attachments into insecure ones (Thompson & Lamb, 1984). A secure attachment may become insecure if a mother withdraws from caregiving activities because of such stresses as marital problems, financial woes, or a lack of social support from friends and family members. Meanwhile, initially insecure infants are likely to become securely attached if the lives of their close companions become less stressful (Vaughn, Egeland, Sroufe, & Waters, 1979) or if their mothers receive an intervention designed to help them cope with their problems and interact more sensitively with their babies (Lieberman, Weston, & Pawl, 1991; Lyons-Ruth et al., 1990). Clearly, the quality of attachment in infancy is unlikely to have long-range effects on development unless the *same* quality is maintained consistently over a reasonably long period (Lamb, 1987).

Finally, we must appreciate that an individual's social relationships *after* infancy affect his or her ultimate social adjustment (Lamb, 1987). Consider what Arlene Skolnick (1986) discovered when she posed this interesting research question: Does the infant who is securely attached to his or her mother at 21 to 30 months of age become the child who is well liked, warm, socially perceptive, and otherwise socially competent . . . and become the adolescent who is popular and a leader among peers . . . and become the middle-aged adult who is sociable, psychologically healthy, and happily married? Using longitudinal data from the Berkeley Guidance Study, Skolnick found that only about a fourth of the participants in the study had either consistently favorable or consistently poor interpersonal relationships across all four periods of life.

The significance of this finding is clear: "Secure attachment to the mother does not make one invulnerable to later problems and socioemotional difficulties, and poor early relations with the mother do not doom a person to a life of loneliness, poor relationships, or psychopathology" (Skolnick, 1986, p. 193). Security of attachment in infancy did have some implications for the quality of later peer relationships. However, positive social adjustment in adulthood was actually better predicted by healthy peer relations during childhood and, especially, during adolescence than by parent/infant interactions that had taken place many years earlier. Although the quality of parent/child interactions affects the quality of peer relations, peers — as we shall soon see — make contributions of their own to healthy development.

A Last Word on Theories of Attachment

How well does research on contributors to and consequences of parent/infant attachment support the major theories of attachment? Freud's theory about the significance of feeding for the development of parent/child attachments lacks support. Erikson's emphasis on responsive parenting and learning theory's emphasis on the reinforcing qualities of parents are far more relevant to an understanding of why infants form secure relationships with some adults but not others. Cognitive-developmental theory does not have much to say about which adults are most likely to appeal to infants, but it correctly emphasizes that infants need to achieve certain milestones in cognitive development before they can recognize a caregiver and enter into a special relationship with her or him.

The Bowlby-Ainsworth ethological theory of attachment is quite well supported by research evidence, perhaps because it is a broad theory that draws not only on ethological research with animals but on psychoanalytic and cognitive perspectives as well. Although it is difficult to prove that behaviors such as smiling or grasping contribute to the survival of the species, it is likely that many infant behaviors that are innate or maturational in nature do contribute to the formation of attachments. Moreover, Bowlby acknowledges that biological preparedness is not enough to guarantee a firm attachment. The *experiences* of caregivers and infants as they interact strongly influence whether a secure, resistant, or avoidant attachment will form. In sum, psychoanalytic, learning, cognitive-developmental, and ethological theories *all* contribute something to our understanding of why and how parent/infant attachments form.

Meanwhile, studies of the later consequences of early bonds challenge Freud's strong claim that the quality of an infant's relationship with his or her mother establishes a pattern of personality and social behavior that decisively determines the quality of all future relationships. Yet they support Bowlby's less extreme position by suggesting that "internal working models" of self and others formed early in life influence later relationships but also can be modified by later relationships (Bowlby, 1973). Despite the significance of the infant/parent bond for later development, we apparently have plenty of time to learn new social skills and different attitudes toward relationships in our later interactions with peers, close friends, lovers, and spouses. It is time, then, to supplement our discussion of parent/child relations with a look at the "second world of childhood" — the world of peer relations.

Peer Relations during Infancy

Developmentalists have viewed the caregiver/infant relationship as so central to development that they have neglected infants' relationships with agemates until fairly recently. When are babies able to interact meaningfully with other infants? Do infants become as attached to familiar playmates as to caregivers?

Although babies show an interest in other babies from the first months of life, they do not really interact until about the middle of the first year. By then, infants will often smile or babble at their tiny companions, vocalize, offer toys, and gesture to one another (Hay, Nash, & Pedersen, 1983; Vandell, Wilson, & Buchanan, 1980). At first many of these friendly gestures go unnoticed and unreciprocated; interactions between infants and adults are a good deal smoother than interactions between two still-quite-socially-awkward infants (Hay, 1985; Vandell & Wilson, 1987).

Infants then pass through three stages of early sociability from age 1 to age 2 (Mueller & Lucas, 1975; Mueller & Vandell, 1979). At first, in the *object-centered* stage, two infants may jointly focus on a toy but will pay more attention to the toy than to each other. During the second, or *simple interactive* stage, infants more obviously influence one another and respond appropriately to one another's behavior. They seem to treat peers as if they were interesting "toys" that are responsive and can be controlled (Brownell, 1986). Consider this example:

> Larry sits on the floor and Bernie turns and looks toward him. Bernie waves his hand and says "da," still looking at Larry. He repeats the vocalization three more times before Larry laughs. Bernie vocalizes again and Larry laughs again. This same sequence . . . is repeated twelve more times before Bernie . . . walks off [Mueller & Lucas, 1975, p. 241].

By about 18 months of age, infants progress to the third, or *complementary interactive* stage, in which their interactions are even more clearly social and reciprocal. They now delight in imitating each other and turn these rounds of imitation into social

With age, infants' interactions with one another become increasingly skilled and reciprocal.

games (Eckerman & Stein, 1990; Howes & Matheson, 1992). They also adopt roles in their play and can reverse roles. Thus the toddler who receives a toy may immediately offer a toy in return, or the one who has been the "chaser" will become the "chasee" in a game of tag.

Toward the end of the second year, infants have become quite proficient at this kind of turn taking and reciprocal exchange. They are even able to adjust their behavior to the particular characteristics of their partner, acting differently toward toddlers their own age than toward younger or older children (Brownell, 1990). They also learn a lot in their "peer groups," imitating what they see other toddlers do (Hanna & Meltzoff, 1993). And, almost inevitably, they get into more conflicts with their playmates as their social skills improve. These squabbles, often over toys, may help infants learn positive social behaviors such as sharing (Caplan et al., 1991; Shantz, 1987).

Surprising as it may seem, some infants also form special relationships with preferred playmates—friendships (Hartup, 1992; Howes, 1983). On Israeli kibbutzim, where children are cared for in groups, Martha Zaslow (1980) discovered that many pairs of infants as young as 1 year of age became especially attached to each other. Hadara and Rivka, for instance, consistently sought each other out as playmates, mourned each other's absence, and disturbed everyone with their loud babbling "conversations" when they were confined to their cribs.

In sum, the caregiver/infant relationship is not the only important social relationship that develops during infancy, although it is the one that comes first and that has the potential to steer social development in either adaptive or maladaptive directions. Through their interactions with significant adults *and* their interactions with peers, infants begin to acquire the social competencies that will permit them to become even more sociable beings during childhood.

THE CHILD

Children's social relationships change tremendously from infancy to later childhood. In part this is because children are gaining an ever-deeper understanding of other people. Let's look at this cognitive growth and then see how it is reflected in children's actual social relationships over the years: Who are the important members of children's social networks, and with whom do they spend the most time? Why are some children more popular than others? What draws children together as friends? And just how important are children's social relationships to their overall development?

Growth in Social Cognition

The infant comes to know parents, siblings, and other companions by appearance and forms expectations about how familiar companions will behave. However, an infant cannot analyze the personalities of other people or recognize that their companions have their own distinct needs, feelings, and thoughts. These skills are part of the larger domain of **social cognition**—thinking about the thoughts, feelings, motives, and behaviors of the self and other people (Flavell, 1985). We have already touched on some important aspects of social-cognitive development in this book, seeing, for example, that older children think differently than younger children do about what they are like as individuals, about how males and females differ, and about why it is wrong to cheat or steal. Here we'll focus on developmental changes in how well children understand their companions as individuals and in how well they can adopt other people's perspectives.

Person Perception

In studies of *person perception,* children are asked to describe familiar people: parents, friends, disliked classmates, and so on. It is becoming clear that even preschool children are budding psychologists. They are formulating a "theory of mind" that reflects their knowledge that human behavior is guided by mental phenomena such as desires, beliefs, and intentions (Miller & Aloise, 1989; Wellman, 1990; see also Chapter 16). Still, as we discovered in Chapter 10, children younger than 7 or 8 describe themselves in physical rather than psychological ways. Not surprisingly, they describe other people that way too (Livesley & Bromley, 1973; Peevers & Secord, 1973; Rholes, Newman, & Ruble, 1990). Five-year-old Jenny, for example, says "My daddy is big. He has hairy legs and eats mustard. Yuck! My daddy likes dogs—do you?'' Not much of a personality profile there! Young children thus are perceiving others in terms of their physical appearance, possessions, and activities. When psychological terms are used, they are often global terms such as ''nice'' or ''mean'' rather than more specific trait labels (Livesley & Bromley, 1973).

Moreover, traits are not yet viewed as enduring qualities that can predict how a person will behave in the future or explain why a person behaves as he or she does (Rholes et al., 1990; Yuill, 1992). The 5-year-old who describes a friend as ''dumb'' is often using this trait label only to describe that friend's recent ''dumb'' behavior and may well expect ''smart'' behavior tomorrow (Rholes & Ruble, 1984; but see also Droege & Stipek, 1993).

After the age of 7 or 8, children are able to ''get below the surface'' of human beings and describe them in terms of their enduring psychological traits. Ten-year-old Kim describes her friend Tonya: ''She's funny and friendly to everyone, and she's in the gifted program because she's smart, but sometimes she's bossy.'' As children reach the age of 11 or 12, they become more likely to make *social comparisons* on important psychological dimensions, noting that one classmate is smarter or shyer than another (Barenboim, 1981). They also make more use of psychological traits to explain why people behave as they do, claiming, for instance, that Mike pulled the dog's tail *because* he's cruel (Gnepp & Chilamkurti, 1988). Clearly, then, children become more ''psychologically minded'' as their emerging social-cognitive abilities permit them to make inferences about enduring inner qualities from the concrete behavior they observe in the people around them.

Social Perspective Taking

Another important aspect of social-cognitive development involves outgrowing the egocentrism that Piaget believed characterizes young children and developing **role-taking skills**: the ability to assume another person's perspective and understand his or her thoughts and feelings in relation to one's own. Robert Selman (1976, 1980; Yeates & Selman, 1989) studied role-taking abilities by asking children questions about interpersonal dilemmas:

> Holly is an 8-year-old girl who likes to climb trees. She is the best tree climber in the neighborhood. One day while climbing down from a tall tree, she falls . . . but does not hurt herself. Her father sees her fall. He is upset and asks her to promise not to climb trees anymore. Holly promises.
>
> Later that day, Holly and her friends meet Shawn. Shawn's kitten is caught in a tree and can't get down. Something has to be done right away or the kitten may fall. Holly is the only one who climbs trees well enough to reach the kitten and get it down but she remembers her promise to her father [Selman, 1976, p. 302].

To assess how well a child understands the perspectives of Holly, her father, and Shawn, Selman asks: ''Does Holly know how Shawn feels about the kitten? How will Holly's father feel if he finds out she climbed the tree? What does Holly think her father will do if he finds out she climbed the tree? What would you do in this situation?'' Children's responses to these questions led Selman (1976) to conclude that role-taking abilities develop in a stagelike manner.

According to Selman, children aged 3 to 6 years are largely egocentric. Unaware of perspectives other than their own, they assume that they and other people see eye to eye. If young children like kittens, for example, they assume that Holly's father does too and therefore will be delighted if Holly saves the kitten. However, as concrete-operational cognitive abilities emerge, children become better able to consider another person's point of view. By age 8 to 10, for example, they appreciate that two people can have different points of view even if they have access to the same information, they are able to think about their own thoughts and the thoughts of another person, and they realize that their companions can do the same. Thus they can appreciate that Holly may think about her father's concern for her safety but conclude that he will understand her reasons for climbing the tree. Finally, adolescents who have reached the formal-operational stage of cognitive development, roughly at age 12, become capable of mentally juggling multiple perspectives, including the perspective of the ''generalized other,'' or the broader social group. The adolescent might thus consider how fathers *in general* react when children disobey them while also considering whether Holly's father is similar to or different from the typical father.

What implications do these advances in social cognition have for children's actual relationships? Important ones. Experience in interacting with peers seems to sharpen role-taking skills, and, in turn, sophisticated role-taking skills help make a child a more sensitive and desirable companion. As it turns out, children whose role-taking skills are advanced are more likely than agemates who perform poorly on tests of role taking to be sociable and popular and to have established close friendships with peers (Gnepp, 1989; Kurdek & Krile, 1982; LeMare & Rubin, 1987; McGuire & Weisz, 1982). Good role takers are in a position to infer the needs of others so that they can respond appropriately to those needs (Hudson, Forman, & Brion-Meisels, 1982). Moreover, they are skilled at figuring out how to resolve the disagreements that inevitably arise when children play together (Shantz, 1987; Yeates & Selman, 1989). Social-cognitive

cognitive growth does indeed bring about changes in the quality of children's social relationships.

Children's Social Networks

The Parent/Child Attachment

How does the parent/child attachment change during childhood? As John Bowlby (1969) noted, it becomes a "goal-corrected partnership" in which parent and child accommodate to each other's needs and the child becomes more independent of the parent. Older preschoolers still seek attention and approval from their parents, and they certainly rush to their parents for comfort when they are frightened or hurt. But they are also becoming increasingly dependent on *peers* for social and emotional support (Furman & Buhrmester, 1992).

Peer Relations

Over the years from age 2 to age 12, children spend more and more time with peers and considerably less time with adults. This trend is shown vividly in Figure 13.2, which summarizes what Sharri Ellis and her colleagues (Ellis, Rogoff, & Cromer, 1981) found when they observed 436 children playing in their homes and around the neighborhood. Interestingly, this same study revealed that youngsters of all ages spent *less* time with agemates (defined as children whose ages were within a year of their own) than with children who were more than a year older or younger than they were. Apparently we must take seriously the idea that peers are not merely agemates but "social equals."

Another finding of this study is a familiar one: Even 1- to 2-year-olds played more often with same-sex companions than with other-sex companions, and this *gender segregation* became increasingly strong with age (Maccoby, 1990; see also Chapter 11). Segregation of the sexes occurs later in some cultures than in others, but it eventually occurs in most societies (Harkness & Super, 1985; Whiting & Edwards, 1988). Once in their sex-segregated worlds, boys and girls experience different kinds of social relationships. Boys tend to form "packs," whereas girls form "pairs"; that is, a boy often plays competitive games or team sports in groups, and a girl more often establishes a cooperative relationship with one friend (Archer, 1992; Maccoby, 1990).

Overall, then, children spend an increasing amount of time with peers, and those peers are typically *same-sex* children who are only *roughly similar* in age but enjoy the same sex-typed activities.

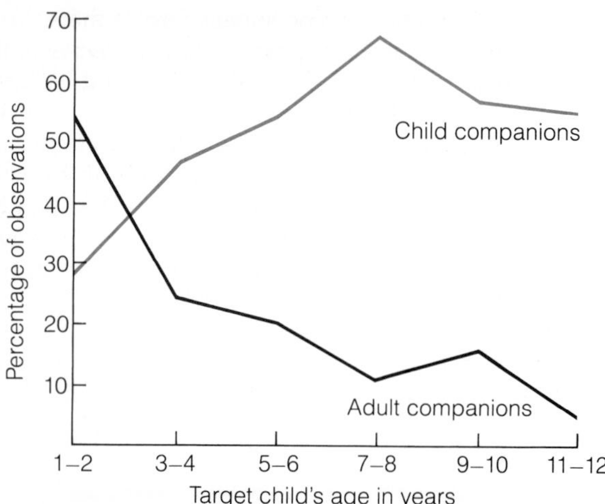

FIGURE 13.2 Developmental changes in the percentage of their time children spend with adults and other children. (From Ellis, Rogoff, & Cromer, 1981.)

Peer Acceptance and Popularity

Typically, researchers study peer-group acceptance through **sociometric techniques**—methods for determining who is liked and disliked in a group. In a sociometric survey, children in a classroom may be asked to nominate several classmates whom they like and several whom they dislike, or they may be asked to rate all of their classmates in terms of their desirability as companions (see Terry & Coie, 1991). According to John Coie and his associates (Coie, Dodge, & Coppotelli, 1982), it is important to find out who is liked *and* who is disliked, for this allows children to be classified into four quite distinct categories of social status: the *popular* (well liked by most and rarely disliked), the *rejected* (rarely liked and often disliked), the *neglected* (isolated children who are neither liked nor disliked but seem instead to be invisible to their classmates), and the *controversial* (children who are liked by many but also disliked by many—for example, the fun-loving child with leadership skills who also has a nasty habit of starting fights).

Why are some children more popular than others, and why are some children rejected by their peers? Popularity is affected by some personal characteristics that a child can do little about. For instance, children with names that are judged to be attractive are more popular than children whose names are unattractive (McDavid & Harari, 1966). Thus Steven or Susan is likely to gain more peer acceptance than Herman, Chastity, or Moon Unit. Moreover, physically attractive children are usualy more popular than physically unattractive children (Langlois, 1986). As early as the preschool years, children have learned a "beauty is good" stereotype convincing them that physically attractive peers are friendlier, nicer, smarter, and better in almost every way than their less attractive counterparts.

A child's *competencies* also influence popularity. For example, children who are relatively intelligent and achieve well in school tend to be more socially accepted than those who are less academically competent (Bukowski et al., 1993; Dishion et al., 1991).

The most important kind of competence, though, may be *social competence*—the ability to apply social-cognitive skills successfully in initiating social interactions, responding positively to peers, resolving interpersonal conflicts, and so on.

As we've seen, children who experienced secure attachments to their parents as infants tend to be popular children, which suggests that they have learned lessons in their earliest relationships that influence the quality of their later relationships. Moreover, we've seen that children who have advanced role-taking skills are likely to be popular. More generally, popular children are socially skilled children—cooperative and responsive rather than argumentative and disruptive (Coie, Dodge, & Kupersmidt, 1990; Ladd, Price, & Hart, 1990). "Rejected" children are usually highly aggressive, although some are socially isolated, submissive children who are overly sensitive to teasing and are seen by others as "easy to push around" (Dodge et al., 1990; Parkhurst & Asher, 1992; Rabiner, Keane, & MacKinnon-Lewis, 1993). By contrast, children who fall into the "neglected" category of sociometric status are usually nonaggressive and have reasonably good social skills but tend to be shy, withdrawn, and unassertive (Coie et al., 1990; Dodge et al., 1990). As a result, no one really notices them.

To appreciate how social skills contribute to popularity, consider what happens when children try to enter and gain acceptance in play groups (Coie & Kupersmidt, 1983; Dodge et al., 1990; Putallaz & Wasserman, 1989). When children who ultimately become popular want to join a group's activity, for example, these socially skilled youngsters first hold back and assess what is going on and then smoothly blend into the group, commenting pleasantly about whatever the other children are discussing. By contrast, children who are eventually rejected by their peers tend to be pushy and disruptive. Jimmy, for example, may sit beside two boys who are playing a Nintendo game and distract them by talking about a TV program he saw the night before. Even worse, he may criticize the way the boys are playing or even threaten to take the game cartridge if he is not allowed to play. Children who end up being neglected by their peers often hover around a group without taking any positive steps to initiate contact and shy away from peers who attempt to make contact with them.

In sum, popularity is affected by many factors. It may help to have a desirable name, an attractive face, or academic skills, but it is probably more important to have advanced social-cognitive skills and to behave in socially competent ways. Definitions of desirable social behavior, of course, vary from culture to culture and change as children get older. Thus, for example, children who are shy are likely to be unpopular in Canada but popular in China, where being quiet and reserved is socially desirable (Chen, Rubin, & Sun, 1992). The ingredients of popularity also change with age: Establishing close relationships with members of the other sex enhances popularity during adolescence, but consorting with "the enemy," and thereby violating norms of gender segregation, *detracts* from popularity during childhood (Sroufe et al., 1993). In short, contextual factors influence who is popular and who is not.

Children in the neglected category of sociometric status are shy and tend to hover on the fringes of a group without daring to enter it.

Do the outcomes of these popularity polls really matter? Yes—especially for children who are actively rejected by their peers. Children who are neglected by their peers often gain greater acceptance later, but those who are rejected, especially because of aggressive behavior, are likely to maintain their rejected status from grade to grade (Cillessen et al., 1992; Coie et al., 1990). More significantly, rejected children are at risk of dropping out of school, engaging in antisocial or delinquent behavior, and displaying psychological and emotional disorders as adolescents or adults (Kupersmidt & Coie, 1990; Morison & Masten, 1991). What's more, these negative outcomes are not solely the result of the aggressive behavior that caused peers to reject these children in the first place; rejection by peers seems to have negative effects of its own on later adjustment (Coie et al., 1992). Whether this means that being rejected by agemates lowers children's self-esteem, causes them to miss out on opportunities for social learning, or forces them to socialize primarily with other antisocial children who reinforce their aggressive tendencies is uncertain (Coie et al., 1992). What *is* clear is that peer acceptance is important to healthy development.

Children's Friendships

Close friends are the most important peers a child has. Through their attachments to friends, children learn how to relate to other people and receive a good deal of emotional support. Having one good friend can go a long way toward reducing loneliness for a child who is excluded from the larger peer group (Parker & Asher, 1993).

What qualifies someone as a friend, though? The answer seems to depend very much on a child's level of social-cognitive development (Selman, 1980). To the preschool child a friend may be "Miguel, who lives next door and plays with me." Before age 8 or so, the principal basis for friendship is *common activity*. Young children form friendships with peers who are similar to themselves in observable characteristics such as age, sex, and racial or ethnic group—and who participate in and enjoy similar activities (Dickens & Perlman, 1981; Hartup, 1992). Even very young friends show emotional closeness and caring (Dunn, 1993). Yet children's descriptions of their friends tend to be egocentric, emphasizing nice things their friends do for them and terrific toys they have.

By contrast, 8- to 10-year-old children, equipped with more sophisticated social perspective-taking skills, begin to see friendships as relationships based on *mutual loyalty* in which two people exchange respect, kindness, and affection (Furman & Bierman, 1983; Selman, 1980): "Miguel and I like each other and stick by each other no matter what." No longer are physical and behavioral similarities sufficient; as children appreciate how their own interests and perspectives and those of their peers are similar or different, they also insist that their friends be *psychologically* similar to themselves. Moreover, they come to appreciate that *each* partner in a friendship must be sensitive to the other's perspective. Perhaps because they rest on a firmer basis, the friendships (or chumships, as Sullivan would call them) of older children are more long lasting than those of younger children (Berndt & Hoyle, 1985).

The Contributions of Peers to Child Development

Developmentalists now know that peers, especially friends, may be every bit as important as parents to child development. Parents may provide a sense of emotional security that enables infants to explore their environment and to appreciate that other people can be interesting companions (Hartup, 1989; Higley et al., 1992). Meanwhile, contact with peers may be especially critical to the learning of social skills and normal patterns of social behavior (Hartup, 1992).

But the influences of peers extend far beyond the realm of social development; peers also contribute to emotional, physical, and cognitive development (Athey, 1984; Hartup, 1992). Peers—especially close friends—contribute to emotional development by teaching children how to participate in emotionally intimate relationships and by offering emotional support and comfort that can help children feel better about themselves, weather stressful events such as a divorce, and feel bolder when faced with new challenges such as the first day of kindergarten (Hartup, 1992; Ladd, 1990). By giving children opportunities to learn and practice new motor skills, peers also contribute to physical development (Athey, 1984). Moreover, social interactions stimulate new cognitive growth; children acquire new knowledge and problem-solving skills from peers and exercise their cognitive and linguistic skills daily in play (Gauvain & Rogoff, 1989; Tudge, 1992). In short, normal child development seems to require both close attachments to adults and close relationships with peers.

THE ADOLESCENT

Although children are already highly involved in peer activities, adolescents spend even more time with peers and less time with parents (Buhrmester & Furman, 1986). As we see in Box 13.2, the quality of the individual's attachment to parents does continue to be highly important throughout adolescence, especially during stressful times. Still, peers begin to rival or surpass parents in importance as sources of intimacy and support (Furman & Buhrmester, 1992; Lempers & Clark-Lempers, 1992). Moreover, the *quality* of peer relations changes. Not only do adolescents begin to form boy/girl friendships and go on dates, but they become more capable of participating in truly deep and intimate attachments.

Social Cognition

Adolescents experience tremendous growth in their ability to understand other people—growth that allows them to form deeper relationships. When asked to describe people they know, adolescents offer personality profiles that are even more psychological than those provided by children (Livesley & Bromley, 1973; O'Mahony, 1986). They see people as unique individuals with distinctive personality traits, interests, values, and feelings. Moreover, they are able to create more integrated, or organized, person descriptions, analyzing how an individual's diverse and often inconsistent traits fit together and make sense as a whole personality. Dan, for example, may notice that Noriko brags about her abilities at times but seems very unsure of herself at other times, and he may integrate these seemingly discrepant impressions by concluding that Noriko is basically insecure and boasts only to hide that insecurity. Some adolescents spend hours psychoanalyzing their friends and acquaintances, trying to figure out what really makes them tick.

Adolescents' role-taking skills are also more sophisticated than those of children (Selman, 1980; Yeates & Selman, 1989). As we saw earlier, many teenagers become mental jugglers, keeping in the air their own perspective, that of another person, *and* that of an abstract "generalized other" representing a larger social group. Suppose that 14-year-old Beth is arguing with her parents about whether she should be

BOX 13.2 College as a "Strange Situation"

Attachments to parents remain highly important during adolescence, despite the increased significance of peers. Just as infants must have a secure base if they are to explore, adolescents seem to need the security provided by supportive parents in order to become more independent and autonomous individuals (Kobak et al., 1993; Rice, 1990). For many youths in our society, going off to college qualifies as a "naturally occurring strange situation" (Kenny, 1987)—a potentially stressful test of one's ability to cope with the unfamiliar. Students who go home on weekends and call home frequently during their first semester are engaging in "attachment behavior" just as surely as the infant who whimpers for his mommy. What role does a secure parent/child bond play in the process of adjusting to college?

In a look at separation distress among first-year college students, William Berman and Michael Sperling (1991) asked freshmen to complete a scale assessing how much they think about and miss their parents. Preoccupation with parents decreased during the first semester as students adjusted to their first extended period of time away from home. Females were more likely than males to miss their mothers in particular and continued to do so at the end of the semester. Yet it was only among males that extreme preoccupation with parents early in the semester predicted depression at the end of the semester. Apparently, then, intense separation anxiety during the transition to college is more common among women than among men but has more negative psychological implications for men than for women.

Mainly, research tells us that college students who are securely attached to their parents are in the best position to pass the "strange situation" test they face when they head off for college. They are likely to display better psychological and social adjustment than students who are insecurely attached to parents (Kenny, 1987; Kenny & Donaldson, 1991; Lapsley, Rice, & FitzGerald, 1990). More generally, the message of research could not be clearer: Adolescents and young adults who enjoy secure attachments with their parents have a stronger sense of identity, higher self-esteem, greater social competence, and better emotional adjustment than their less securely attached peers (Rice, 1990). Having a secure base for exploration is not just kid stuff!

---

allowed to go on single dates. Beth may realize that her parents are motivated by a concern for her welfare *and* imagine how "parents in general" and "teenagers in general" would view the issue. Instead of merely pushing her own perspective, she may be able to integrate her perspective and her parents' into a solution that is best for *the relationship.* Thus she may decide that going on double dates until she demonstrates that she is responsible is the best way to balance her interest in freedom with her parents' concerns for her welfare. Not all 14-year-olds are this mature, but Robert Selman finds that considerable growth in the ability to understand and resolve interpersonal conflicts occurs during the adolescent years (Selman et al., 1986). As adolescents gain new social-cognitive skills, their relationships also change.

Adolescent Friendships

Whereas friendships in early childhood center on common activities, and friendships in late childhood center on mutual loyalty, adolescent friendships increasingly hinge on *intimacy and self-disclosure* (Berndt & Perry, 1990). Teenagers continue to form friendships with peers who are similar to themselves and to express feelings of loyalty toward their friends. However, they increasingly choose friends whose *psychological qualities*—interests, attitudes, values, and personalities—seem to match their own. Now friends are like-minded individuals who can confide in each other.

The transition to intimate friendships based on a sharing of thoughts and feelings occurs earlier among girls than among boys (Berndt & Perry, 1990; Reis et al., 1993). Teenage girls who are best friends are almost like lovers: intensely attached to each other and inseparable—sometimes even possessive, jealous, and outraged by any betrayal of their trust (Douvan & Adelson, 1966). As girls become more autonomous, gain social-cognitive skills, and become more involved in dating toward the end of high school, they become less emotionally dependent on a best friend and more able to accept and even appreciate differences between themselves and their friends (Douvan & Adelson, 1966). Teenage boys do get to know their buddies well by doing things with them, but their friendships are less emotionally intense and they talk less about their feelings than girls who are best friends do (Berndt, 1982; Douvan & Adelson, 1966).

Although same-sex friendships remain important throughout adolescence, teenagers increasingly enter into close cross-sex friendships. How do these other-

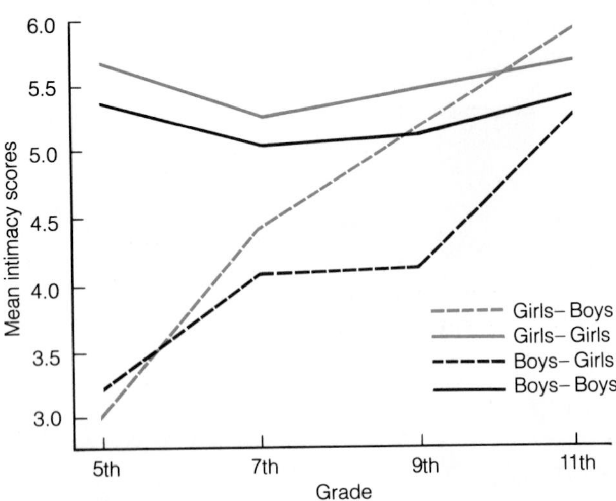

FIGURE 13.3 Changes during adolescence in the intimacy of same-sex and cross-sex friendships. The "Girls–Boys" scores reflect how girls rated the intimacy of their relationships with boys; "Boys–Girls" scores reflect how boys rated their relationships with girls. Cross-sex friendships clearly become more and more intimate during the adolescent years, ultimately achieving the levels of intimacy that characterize same-sex friendships throughout this developmental period. (From Sharabany, Gershoni, & Hofman, 1981.)

sex friendships compare with same-sex friendships? Ruth Sharabany, Ruth Gershoni, and John Hofman (1981) asked 5th- to 11th-graders to assess their same- and cross-sex friendships in terms of such aspects of intimacy as spontaneity, trust and loyalty, sensitivity to the other's feelings, attachment, and so on. As you can see in Figure 13.3, same-sex friendships were highly intimate in most respects throughout this age range, but cross-sex friendships did not attain a high level of intimacy until 11th grade. We can also observe interesting sex differences: All along, girls tended to report higher degrees of intimacy in their friendships than boys did; moreover, girls experienced intimacy in their friendships with boys sooner than boys experienced intimacy in their relationships with girls. These findings offer some support for Harry Stack Sullivan's view that children learn lessons about intimate attachments in their same-sex chumships that they only later apply in their heterosexual relationships. They also confirm that boys are somewhat slower than girls to achieve emotional intimacy in their close relationships.

Social Networks: From Same-Sex Peer Groups to Dating Relationships

Elementary school children are interested in the other sex and are gradually preparing themselves for heterosexual relationships (Thorne, 1993). Still, how do boys and girls who live in their own, gender-segregated worlds arrive at the point of dating "the enemy"? Some time ago, Dexter Dunphy (1963) offered a plausible account of how peer-group structures change during adolescence to pave the way for dating relationships. His five stages, outlined in Figure 13.4, are still relevant today.

The process begins in late childhood, when boys and girls become members of same-sex **cliques,** or small friendship groups, and have little to do with the other sex. Next, members of boy cliques and girl cliques begin to interact with each other more frequently. Same-sex cliques provide what amounts to a secure base for exploring ways to behave with members of the other sex: Talking to a girl when your buddies are there is far less threatening than doing so on your own. In the third stage, the most popular boys and girls form a *heterosexual* clique.

As less popular peers also enter into heterosexual cliques, a new peer group structure, the **crowd,** completes its evolution. The crowd, a collection of up to about four heterosexual cliques, comes into play mainly as a mechanism for arranging organized social activities on the weekend—parties, outings to the lake or mall, and so on. The names may vary, but every school has its crowds of "populars," "jocks," "druggies," and "losers," each consisting of adolescents who are similar to one another in some way (Brown et al., 1993; Brown & Lohr, 1987). Those adolescents who do become members of a mixed-sex clique and a crowd have many opportunities to get to know members of the other sex. Eventually, however, interacting with the other sex in group settings is not enough. Couples form, sometimes double-dating or spending time with other pairs, and the crowd disintegrates after having served its purpose of bringing boys and girls together.

Adolescents in our society go on their first dates at about the age of 14 on average, though there is much variation (Miller, McCoy, & Olson, 1986). Dates have increasingly become a matter of boy and girl informally getting together rather than boy formally asking girl out (Murstein, 1980). Despite changing gender roles, however, both males and females continue to expect boys to take the more active role in dating (Rose & Frieze, 1993).

What were your first dates like? If they were typical, they were probably quite awkward and superficial (Douvan & Adelson, 1966). Boy and girl both want to succeed in the dating scene and may be so concerned with playing a role to impress their partner that they cannot really relax and be themselves. A deeper relationship sometimes evolves as dating partners get to know each other better. Most adolescents do go steady at some time, and these steady relationships, like adult romances, are often based on a genuine emotional attachment rather than mere sexual attraction (Levesque, 1993). The vast majority of "first loves" do not survive, of course; it often takes until

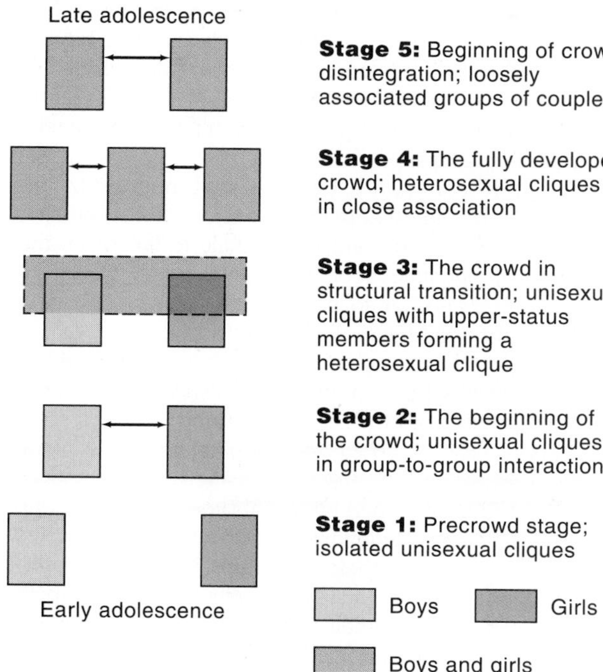

FIGURE 13.4 Stages in the evolution of the peer group during adolescence: from same-sex cliques (*bottom*) to dating couples (*top*). (From Dunphy, 1963.)

later adolescence—or even longer—for dating partners to become ready for more lasting emotional commitment (Levesque, 1993).

Parent and Peer Influence on Adolescents

Should parents worry about the fact that adolescents become more and more involved in both same-sex and cross-sex relationships with peers as they get older? Will they lose influence over their children? Will the values of the peer group replace those that parents have worked so long to instill in their children?

One approach to answering these questions has been to study **conformity,** or the tendency to yield to the opinions and wishes of others. For example, Thomas Berndt (1979) asked children in the 3rd through 12th grades to judge how much they would be likely to bend to parent or peer pressure in a number of hypothetical situations—for example, if parents advocated helping a brother with homework rather than visiting a sick friend or if peers advocated antisocial behavior such as soaping windows on Halloween. Conformity to parents' wishes decreased gradually and steadily with age. Conformity to peers who urged antisocial behavior increased until 9th grade and then declined thereafter (see also Bixenstine, DeCorte, & Bixenstine, 1976; Steinberg & Silverberg, 1986). Apparently, then, parents have some grounds for worrying that their adolescents may get into trouble by going along with the crowd, especially at around the age of 14 or 15. Peer-group norms concerning what is acceptable and what is not are particularly rigid at this age (Gavin & Furman, 1989), and there is nothing worse than being viewed as a "dweeb," "dork," or "geek" who does not fit in (Kinney, 1993).

Why does conformity to peers' misconduct *decrease* by the end of high school? As adolescents progress in their quest for autonomy, they become less dependent on *both* parents and peers for guidance and more able to make their own choices. Laurence Steinberg and Susan Silverberg (1986) argue that increased dependence on peers may even be a necessary step in the development of autonomy. Teenagers who are trying to become more independent of their parents may need the security that peer acceptance provides before they are ready to become truly autonomous in later adolescence. They are unlikely to achieve this acceptance if they conform too closely to adult rules and refuse to "go along with the crowd" to do a little mischief now and then (Allen, Weissberg, & Hawkins, 1989). The parent whose teenager ends up at the police station may not be totally comforted by this thought, but it does seem that a period of heightened conformity to peers is healthy in that it paves the way for later independence.

Parents can also take comfort in the fact that adolescence is typically *not* a time of warfare between parents and peers. One reason why parent/peer conflict is kept to a minimum is that parents and peers sometimes exert their influences in distinct realms. Hans Sebald (1986), for example, asked adolescents whether they would seek the advice of their parents or the advice of their peers on a number of different issues. Peers were more influential than parents when it came to such decisions as what dress styles to wear and which clubs, social events, hobbies, and other social activities to choose. By contrast, adolescents claimed that they would depend more on their parents in deciding which courses to take, whether or not to go to college, which occupations to select, and how to spend money. Apparently, then, peers tend to influence adolescents' social activities and tastes, but parents continue to be the major shapers of their educational and vocational plans and important values (Sebald, 1986; Wilks, 1986). Teenagers are unlikely to be torn between peer and parent pressures as long as peers and parents have different areas of influence.

A second and more important reason why parent/peer warfare is typically kept to a minimum is that parents have a good deal of influence on what kinds of friends their adolescents interact with. Teenagers who have good relationships with their parents are less likely to be exposed to negative peer pressures, and are less susceptible to them, than are those whose family relationships are poor (Brook et al., 1990; Brown et al., 1993; Dishion et al., 1991; Fuligni & Eccles, 1993). For example, Judith Brook and her

It is no accident that teenagers wear the same hairstyles and dress alike. Peers exert more influence than parents in these matters.

colleagues (1990) have found that adolescents whose parents have solid, traditional values form a strong attachment to their parents that leads them to internalize the same values. These youth then associate with friends who share their conventional outlooks and do not engage in such behaviors as taking drugs; they are, as a result, unlikely to use drugs themselves. In other words, a healthy parent/child relationship protects them from unhealthy peer influences.

Problems for youth who *do* "get in with the wrong crowd" and engage in antisocial behavior usually begin at home. One way parents can go wrong is by being too strict, failing to adjust to adolescents' needs for greater autonomy. This may cause teenagers to become alienated from their parents and overly susceptible to negative peer influences — to the point that they would let schoolwork slide or break parental rules to please their friends (Fuligni & Eccles, 1993). Parents can also go wrong by failing to provide enough discipline and by not monitoring their children's activities sufficiently (Brown et al., 1993; Dishion et al., 1991).

Parents who are warm, neither too controlling nor too lax, and consistent in their discipline generally find that their adolescents have internalized their values. Their children also have little need to rebel or to seek acceptance in the peer group that they cannot obtain at home. What's more, this warm, authoritative parenting style is likely to foster the academic and social competencies that gain adolescents entrance into crowds that value academic achievement and disapprove of drug use and other forms of delinquency — crowds that reinforce the very values parents have attempted to instill at home (Brook et al., 1990; Brown et al., 1993). It is when parent/child relationships are stormy that adolescents lack the competencies it takes to be popular, end up by default in peer groups made up of other unpopular, antisocial youth, and become career juvenile delinquents (Dishion et al., 1991). In other words, parents have a good deal of influence over whether their adolescents end up in "good" or "bad" crowds and therefore whether they are exposed to healthy or unhealthy peer influences.

It is commonly believed that many African-American adolescents come from troubled families and are therefore particularly likely to fall under the spell of negative peer influences. Recently, Peggy Giordano and her colleagues (1993) tested this view in a study of African-American and white 12- to 19-year-olds. Contrary to the stereotype, it was *white* adolescents who seemed more determined to distance themselves from their families during the adolescent period. Compared to white teenagers, the African-American teenagers felt closer to their parents and reported that their parents did more to discipline and control them. Meanwhile, black teenagers attached less importance to their friendships, felt less peer pressure, and reported less willingness to give in to peer pressure. True, a small minority of African-American youth become involved in highly antisocial peer groups, but Giordano's findings challenge our stereotypes by suggesting that African-American adolescents are far more parent oriented and less peer oriented than many people believe.

In summary, adolescent socialization is not a continual war of parents *versus* peers; instead, these two important sources of influence *combine* to affect development. As their teenage children become more involved in activities with peers and more susceptible to peer pressures, parents usually continue to be important forces in their children's lives. Parent/peer warfare is kept to a minimum because parents and peers often influence distinct aspects of behavior and decision making and because parents have a hand in ensuring that their children's friends share their views on many important issues. As a result, most adolescents develop healthy peer relationships and acquire social competencies that allow them to form and maintain good relationships as adults.

THE ADULT

Relationships with family and friends are no less important during adulthood than they are earlier in life, but they take on different qualities over the adult years.

Social Cognition

As adults go about the business of interacting with both intimates and acquaintances, they rely on their social-cognitive skills to make sense of other people. *Non*social cognitive abilities, such as those used in testing scientific hypotheses, often improve during early and middle adulthood. Compared with adolescents, who seem to want to force facts into one neat and logical system, adults become better able to accept contradictions in the real world and are more aware that problems can be viewed from a number of different perspectives (see Chapter 7). However, many elderly people seem to perform poorly on tasks that assess nonsocial cognition (Denney, 1982). Do important social-cognitive skills like the ability to analyze other people's personalities or adopt their perspectives change in similar ways during adulthood?

Fredda Blanchard-Fields (1986a) asked adolescents and adults to read stories and judge how responsible the actors in the stories were for their actions. She found that adolescents tend to stick to a single answer based on the facts they are given, whereas adults tend to read between the lines, adopt more than one perspective (for example, a moral perspective and a legal one), and express an awareness that their own perspective on life influences their conclusions and is only one of many that could be taken. Blanchard-Fields (1986b) also presented adolescents, young adults, and middle-aged adults with three dilemmas requiring them to integrate discrepant perspectives: (1) two conflicting historical accounts, (2) a conflict between a teenage boy and his parents over whether he must visit his grandparents with the family, and (3) a disagreement between a man and a woman about an unintended pregnancy. As Figure 13.5 shows, adults—especially middle-aged adults—were better able than adolescents to see both sides of the issues and to integrate the perspectives of *both* parties into a workable solution (Blanchard-Fields, 1986b). Here, then, is evidence that the social-cognitive skills of adults may continue to expand after adolescence. Through a combination of social experience and cognitive growth, adults have the potential to become quite sophisticated students of human psychology.

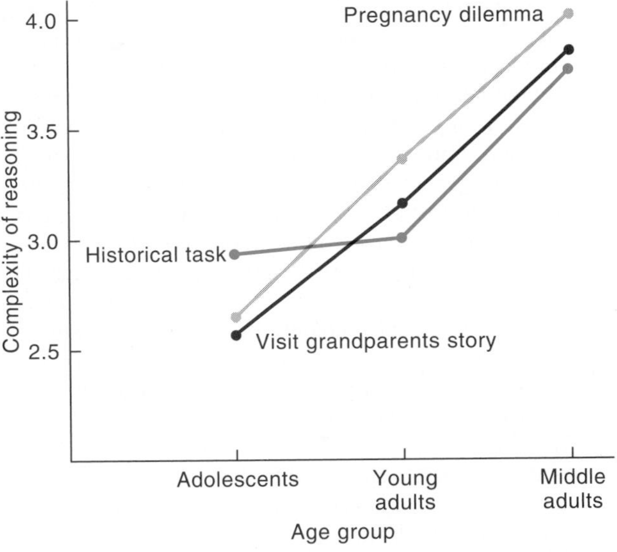

FIGURE 13.5 Increases in social-cognitive skills from adolescence to adulthood. In this study, adolescents had special difficulty applying their social-cognitive skills to the two most emotionally involving tasks (the grandparents and pregnancy vignettes), whereas adults were more able to keep emotional considerations from interfering with their reasoning. (Adapted from Blanchard-Fields, 1986b.)

Do elderly people continue to display these sophisticated social-cognitive skills? For the most part, yes. They perform as well as younger adults on many social-cognitive tasks (Fitzgerald & Martin-Louer, 1983-1984; Pratt et al., 1991). It seems that the social-cognitive abilities of adults depend far more on the extent and nature of their social experiences than on their age. Those elderly adults who have the sharpest social-cognitive skills tend to be socially active; they are deeply involved in meaningful social roles such as those of spouse, grandparent, church member, and worker (Dolen & Bearison, 1982).

So, individuals may actually gain social-cognitive abilities during adulthood that they did not possess as adolescents, and elderly people continue to display sophisticated social-cognitive skills as long as they continue to use those skills every day in their social interactions. It is only when elderly people become socially isolated or inactive that they seem to experience difficulties in reasoning complexly about personal and interpersonal issues.

How many people *do* become socially isolated in old age? Let's find out by examining how people's social networks change over the adult years.

Social Networks

With whom do adults of different ages interact, and how socially active are they? Young adults are busily forming romantic relationships and friendships, typically choosing to associate with people who are similar to themselves in important ways, just as children and adolescents do. Harry Reis and his colleagues (1993), in a 10-year study among college students, found that young adults do more socializing with members of the other sex and less with members of the same sex after college graduation than they did while in college; this was true of both sexes and of unmarried as well as married people. These individuals' relationships also became more intimate, or personally meaningful, over the course of the study. In other words, trends toward greater intimacy with the other sex that began in adolescence continue during early adulthood.

Young singles seem to have more ties to friends than older and/or married adults do (Fischer & Phillips, 1982; Fischer, Sollie, Sorell, & Green, 1989). As adults marry, have children, and take on increasing responsibilities in their jobs, their social networks appear to shrink somewhat. Laura Carstensen (1992) has offered a **selectivity hypothesis** to account for changes in adults' social networks. As we get older,

Carstensen argues, we narrow our range of social partners to those who are most important to us and most likely to meet our emotional needs; we have less desire to meet new people and obtain new social stimulation. This is an adaptive change that involves sacrificing the quantity of our relationships in order to strengthen their *quality*.

What evidence is there to support the selectivity hypothesis? Middle-aged adults interact less frequently with acquaintances and friends than young adults do, but at the same time they interact frequently with spouses and siblings and feel closer emotionally to significant people in their lives than younger adults do (Carstensen, 1992; see also Fischer & Phillips, 1982). And, although elderly adults tend to have fewer friends and smaller social networks overall, particularly if they are men (Connidis & Davies, 1992; Field & Minkler, 1988; Fischer & Phillips, 1982), they have about as many close relationships with relatives as young and middle-aged adults do (Levitt, 1991). It seems that older adults actively *choose* to restrict their interactions to the people who really count (Fredrickson & Carstensen, 1990). Yet they are just as satisfied, if not more satisfied, with their relationships and just as able to count on social support as younger adults are (Antonucci, 1985; Bossé et al., 1993). In other words, adults' social networks do shrink in total size from early adulthood to very old age, but most elderly adults still have emotionally rich and supportive relationships with a small circle of intimates.

But aren't a lot of old people socially isolated and lonely, you ask? This is a common stereotype of older people. But, when U.S. adults aged 65 and older were asked about their problems, only 13% cited loneliness as one of their "very serious problems" (Louis Harris and Associates, 1981). Older people do spend more time alone than younger adults do (Larson, Zuzanek, & Mannell, 1985), but it is *young* adults, not elderly ones, who more often report feelings of loneliness (Parlee, 1979). Perhaps young adults, because they are less secure in their relationships, feel anxious when they are not with other people; elderly adults may have learned that being alone need not mean being lonely and can enjoy their time to themselves. Whatever the reasons, we must rid ourselves of the myth that most older adults suffer from a lack of close attachments. We should focus instead on the fact that their increasing selectiveness makes their social contacts more to their liking.

Romantic Relationships

For many adults the most important member of the larger social network is a spouse or romantic partner. As Erik Erikson has emphasized, early adulthood is an important time for establishing truly intimate and committed relationships—marriages or other enduring emotional attachments.

Partner Selection

Why do we choose the romantic partners we choose? Because we fall in love, you may say. True enough, at least in a society like ours where marriages are not arranged by kin and love between two people is a primary basis for partner choice (see Okonjo, 1992). Yet we do not fall in love with just anyone. Richard Udry (1971) has captured much of what research has to say about why we choose whom we choose in his **filter model of mate selection** (Figure 13.6).

Udry asks us to imagine that mate selection is a process of sifting through all potential partners to find one chosen partner. The first filter in Udry's model, *propinquity,* reflects the truth that we are most likely to become involved with someone who lives nearby. Although your perfect soulmate may be living in Outer Mongolia, there is little chance that you will ever meet this person, much less fall in love! The next filter, the *attractiveness* filter, reminds us of what we have discovered already: People are drawn to physically attractive individuals from an early age. In most cultures of the world, males place more weight on physical attractiveness than females do, possibly to increase the chances that their wives will be healthy and able to bear children; females seem more concerned with qualities like ambition and intelligence, which suggest that a man will be able to provide for the family (Buss, 1989; Feingold, 1992). Because unattractive people face low odds of linking up with attractive people, what typically happens is that we select mates whose level of attractiveness is near our own and who are physically appealing to us. The third filter in Udry's model is *social background*; we favor as romantic partners those who match us in such characteristics as socioeconomic background, education, racial or ethnic group, and religious affiliation.

Assuming that a potential partner passes through these larger, coarser "screens," *consensus,* or similarity with respect to values, attitudes, and interests, may help determine whether the relationship endures or crumbles. If potential mates are psychologically similar, they may then favor a relationship in which there is also *complementarity,* or a meshing of strengths and weaknesses that somehow makes each person more complete. Jerry and Fran, for example, may be similar in most important ways and also find that they complement each other well because Jerry is better at planning social activities than Fran is, while Fran offers Jerry a cool head when he might otherwise become emotionally upset about events at work. Finally, Udry notes that all the compatibility in the world is unlikely to lead to marriage unless both partners possess a *readiness for marriage* (or for a lasting commitment of some kind).

Although Udry concentrated on bases for marital choice, we can readily apply the model to any romantic relationship—heterosexual or homosexual, aimed

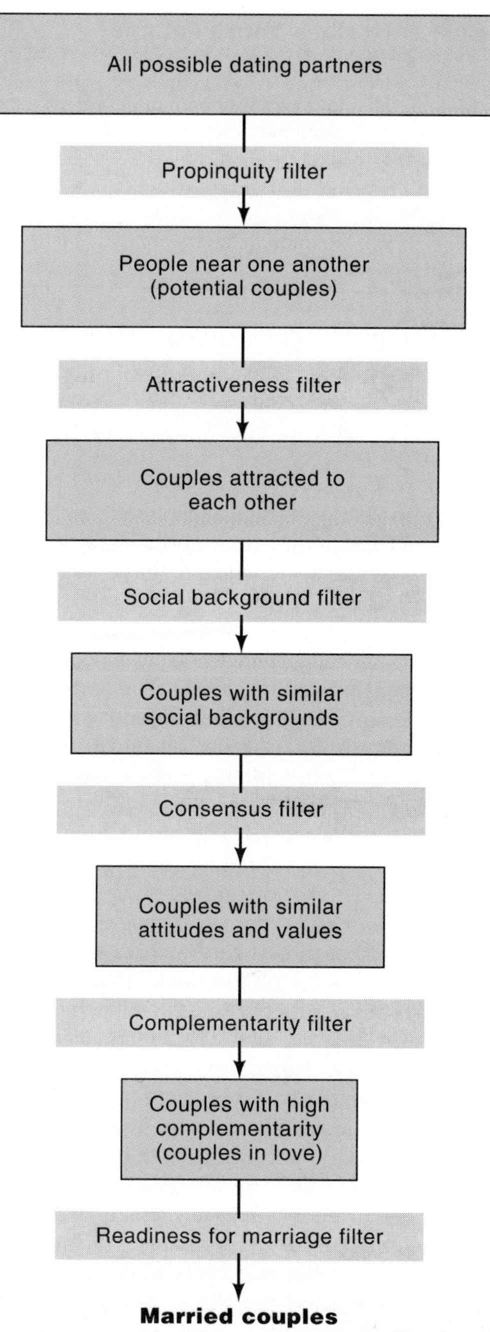

FIGURE 13.6 Udry's filter model of mate selection: Start with all possible partners, and narrow the field down to one. (From Udry, 1971.)

toward marriage or aimed toward a lasting commitment. The model may sound rather "cold and clinical," as if it likens selecting a mate to buying a computer. Nonetheless, the factors that Udry includes in his model *are* very influential in the formation of romantic relationships. The most important theme is that we gravitate toward those who are similar to ourselves in a wide range of important ways (Buss, 1985), just as children do when they select friends. Opposites may attract on occasion, but more often birds of a feather flock together.

Love as Attachment: Styles of Loving

Several researchers, intrigued by the parallels between an infant's attachment to a parent figure and a young adult's love for a romantic partner, have begun to study attachment from a life-span perspective (Ainsworth, 1989; Weiss, 1991). Obviously, parent/infant attachments and adult romantic attachments are not identical. Yet the adult who is in love, like the infant who is attached to a parent, experiences strong affection for his or her partner, wants to be close, and takes comfort from the bond. What's more, married adults who are separated from their spouses due to war or the demands of work experience the same kinds of distress, anger, and, ultimately, depression that infants experience when separated from their mothers and fathers (Vormbrock, 1993).

Cindy Hazan and Phillip Shaver (1987) set out to classify adults into the same three categories of attachment—secure, resistant, and avoidant—that have been used to characterize parent/infant bonds. Box 13.3 shows how Hazan and Shaver translated the three types of infant attachments into adult terms.

What implications do these different styles of attachment have for adults? From studies of college students and of adults who responded to a newspaper ad, Hazan and Shaver concluded that an adult's style of attachment is related to the quality of that individual's romantic relationships (see also Collins & Read, 1990; Levy & Davis, 1988; Senchak & Leonard, 1992). For example, adults with a *secure* attachment style experience a good deal of trust and many positive emotions in their current love relationships, which also tend to last longer than those of adults who fit either of the insecure attachment categories. Both *avoidant* and *resistant* adults report a lot of jealousy and emotional extremes of love and pain in their relationships and are dubious that lasting love can be found. In addition, avoidant lovers seem to fear intimacy, whereas resistant individuals tend to be obsessed by their relationships and overdependent on their partners.

Hazan and Shaver also discovered that there were at least weak correlations between adults' characterizations of their early relationships with their parents and their current attachment styles. Adults with a secure attachment style recalled warm relationships with their parents during childhood, but adults with insecure attachment styles tended to remember their parents as unfair, critical, or cold. Here, then, is support for Bowlby's (1973) hypothesis that we form internal working models of self and other based on our earliest attachments and that these models affect the quality of our later relationships.

BOX 13.3 Three Adult Attachment Types: Which Best Describes Your Feelings?

Secure Attachment (56% of Adults)

I find it relatively easy to get close to others and am comfortable depending on them. I don't often worry about being abandoned or about someone getting too close to me.

Resistant Attachment (19% of Adults)

I find that others are reluctant to get as close as I would like. I often worry that my partner doesn't really love me or won't want to stay with me. I want to get very close to my partner, and this sometimes scares people away.

Avoidant Attachment (25% of Adults)

I am somewhat uncomfortable being close to others; I find it difficult to trust them completely, difficult to allow myself to depend on them. I am nervous when anyone gets too close, and, often, love partners want me to be more intimate than I feel comfortable being.

SOURCE: Adapted from Hazan & Shaver, 1990.

We cannot be certain that the link between early attachments and later romances is causal. Moreover, adults' romantic attachment styles are also shaped by their experiences with romantic partners (Kobak & Hazan, 1991). Still, this and other research suggests that at least some of us may develop cognitive models of relationships as infants and children that affect the quality of our romantic attachments, friendships, and peer relations as adults (see also Bartholomew & Horowitz, 1991; Collins & Read, 1990; Feeney & Noller, 1991; Kobak & Sceery, 1988). What's more, early experiences in the family seem to affect an adult's capacity to be a loving parent: Adults who had secure relations with their parents tend to interact in more sensitive ways with their children and form more secure attachments with them than parents whose early attachments were resistant or avoidant (Biringen, 1990; Crowell & Feldman, 1991; Main & Goldwyn, in press; van IJzendoorn, 1992). In other words, internal working models of relationships may be passed on from one generation to the next.

Relationships with spouses or romantic partners remain central throughout adulthood. These attachments often provide the "secure base" that allows adults to work productively and enjoy their lives (Hazan & Shaver, 1990; Weiss, 1991). We will postpone our discussion of how these relationships evolve and change until Chapter 14. For now, let's consider another attachment that is highly important during adulthood: the friendship bond.

Adult Friendships

Although young adults typically have more friends than older adults do, friends remain an important part of the social convoy throughout the adult years (Blieszner & Adams, 1992). One noteworthy message of research on the quality of adults' friendships is that men and women continue to display the gender-typed differences in styles of friendship that they displayed as children and adolescents. As Paul Wright (1982) puts it, female friends typically interact "face to face," whereas male friends typically interact "side by side." That is, female friends talk about their feelings and problems, while male friends do things together (Roberto & Kimboko, 1989; Winstead, 1986). Perhaps partly for this reason, women seem to find their friendships more intimate and rewarding (Reis et al., 1993; Wright & Scanlon, 1991). The end result is that elderly men are less likely than elderly women to have intimate friendships outside the family (Connidis & Davies, 1992; Field & Minkler, 1988). Often their most important friends are their wives (Kendig et al., 1988).

Elderly adults especially value friendships that have lasted a lifetime (Adams, 1985–1986; Matthews, 1986; Shea, Thompson, & Blieszner, 1988). Imagine having a friend with whom you have shared life experiences for 50 or more years—since, as one man put it, you were "knee-high to a duck" (Matthews, 1986). Almost three-fourths of the women Rebecca Adams interviewed claimed that "old friends are the best friends." Many of these women felt emotionally closer to friends from the past who were geographically distant than to newer friends who lived nearby. However, most elderly people seem to have close friends nearby as well as close friends far away, and they continue to make new friends late in life (Adams, 1985-1986; Matthews, 1986; Shea et al., 1988).

As we get older and begin to develop significant health problems and disabilities, we tend to need more aid and are able to give less aid in return (Silverstein & Waite, 1993). This poses a problem for old friends if one becomes overdependent on the other. Why? Social psychologists have long emphasized the importance of **equity,** or a balance of contributions and gains, in relationships between spouses, friends, and other intimates (Walster, Walster, & Berscheid, 1978). Generally, relationships are perceived as more satisfying when they are equitable than when they are inequitable. A person who receives too much from a relationship is likely to feel guilty; a person who gives a great deal and receives little in return often feels angry or resentful (Walster et al., 1978). We are likely to be more satisfied with our lives in general when our close relationships are equitable than when they are lopsided (Antonucci, Fuhrer, & Jackson, 1990).

How important are equity issues in later-life friendships? Karen Roberto and Jean Scott (1986) report that elderly adults experience less distress in friendships they perceive as equitable than in those they perceive as inequitable. Interestingly, *overbenefited,* or dependent, friends experience more distress than underbenefited, or support-giving, friends. Elderly adults who are unable to contribute equally to a friendship may feel especially uncomfortable in their dependent role, whereas friends who find themselves in the helper role may take some comfort from knowing they are capable of giving. Ultimately, friendships may crumble if they become too inequitable (Allan, 1986). This may be why older adults call on family before friends when they need substantial help or emotional support (Chatters, Taylor, & Jackson, 1986; Felton & Berry, 1992; Kendig et al., 1988). By not overburdening their friends, they stand to keep them longer.

In sum, adults of all ages seem to enjoy close friendships, new and old, and often are able to carry with them throughout life—as part of their social convoy—old friends with whom they share a lifetime of experiences. Just how important is it that adults have these kinds of close relationships?

Adult Relationships and Adult Development

We have emphasized throughout this chapter that close attachments to other people are essential to normal cognitive, social, and emotional development. It should not surprise you to learn, then, that adults are better off in many ways if they enjoy meaningful relationships. Much attention has been centered on the significance of social networks and social support to elderly people—possibly because researchers, like members of the general public, have incorrectly assumed that elderly adults are usually socially isolated. The major generalization that has emerged from this research is this: *It is the quality rather than the quantity of an individual's social relationships that is most closely related to that person's sense of well-being or happiness* (Antonucci & Akiyama, 1991; Arling, 1987; Holahan & Holahan, 1987). We need to perceive whatever relationships we have as satisfying and supportive (Krause, Liang, & Yatomi, 1989; Ward, Sherman, & LaGory, 1984). Just as people can feel lonely despite being surrounded by others, adults apparently can feel deprived of social support even though they receive a lot of it—or they can have quite restricted social networks and yet feel satisfied with their relationships.

The "quality counts" theme is also evidenced by this finding: The size of an adult's social network is not nearly so important as whether it includes at least one

Close friendships that have lasted for years are particularly important to adults.

confidant—a spouse, relative, or friend to whom the individual feels an especially close attachment and with whom thoughts and feelings can be shared (de Jong-Gierveld, 1986; Levitt, 1991). For most married adults, spouses are the most important confidants; for older adults whose spouses have died, children or friends often step in to fill these needs; for single adults, siblings sometimes become especially important (Connidis & Davies, 1992). Elderly adults who have insecure attachments to such significant sources of support as their adult children are likely to be unhappy people (Barnas, Pollina, & Cummings, 1991).

In sum, a small number of close and harmonious relationships can do much to make negative life events more bearable and improve the overall quality of an adult's life. Whatever our ages, it seems, our well-being and development hinge considerably on the quality of our ties to fellow humans—and particularly on our having a close bond with at least one person (Levitt, 1991).

APPLICATIONS: HELPING THE SOCIALLY ISOLATED

Developmentalists naturally have become interested in applying what they have learned about social development to the task of helping socially isolated and lonely individuals to develop richer social relationships. They have been quite successful.

Children who are isolated from their peers typically lack basic social and social-cognitive skills. One popular method of teaching them social skills is called *coaching* (Asher, 1986). An adult therapist models or displays social skills, explains why they are useful, allows children to practice them, and then offers feedback to help children improve on their performances. Sherrie Oden and Steven Asher (1977) coached third- and fourth-grade social isolates in four important social skills: how to participate in play activities, how to take turns and share, how to communicate effectively, and how to give attention and help to peers. Not only did the children who were coached become more outgoing and positive in their social behavior, but a follow-up assessment a year later revealed that they had achieved even further gains in sociometric status within the classroom (see Schneider, 1992, for a review of similar interventions).

Lonely adolescents and young adults are not entirely unlike socially withdrawn children. In many cases they too have social-skills deficits that make it difficult for them to make contact with people, carry on meaningful conversations, and build more intimate relationships (Christopher, Nangle, & Hansen, 1993; Rook, 1984). For instance, Warren Jones and his associates (Jones, Hobbs, & Hockenbury, 1982) discovered that lonely college students are less likely than nonlonely ones to pay positive attention to their conversation partners by referring to them, pursuing topics they bring up, or asking questions. These researchers used a form of coaching to teach a group of lonely college men to be more attentive to female conversation partners. Trainees listened to tapes modeling appropriate conversational behaviors, practiced the skills they observed, and received feedback about their skills. Compared with students who received no coaching or who simply interacted with a partner without benefit of training, the trained students became more able to offer reinforcing attention to women. Moreover, they left the program reporting that they were less lonely, shy, and self-conscious (see Christopher et al., 1993, for a review of similar successful interventions).

However, not all individuals who are lonely and socially isolated are socially incompetent. For some individuals the real problem is a restricted social environment—a lack of opportunities for forming close relationships (Rook, 1984, 1991). Such was the case for the socially isolated elderly people described by Marc Pilisuk and Meredith Minkler (1980). Living in inner-city hotels in San Francisco, these individuals were often prisoners of their rooms because of disability, poverty, and fear of crime. To change things, public health nurses began to offer free blood-pressure checkups in the lobby of one hotel. As the nurses got to know the residents, they were able to draw them into conversations and to link individuals who had common interests. After about a year, the residents formed their own activities club; organized discussions, film showings, and parties; and were well on their way out of their social isolation. The trick was to change their social environment rather than their social skills (see also Heller et al., 1991; Rook, 1991).

Older adults who are lonely often do not need social-skills training as much as they need increased opportunities to interact with people who are similar to them.

Because development is influenced by both individual and environmental factors, it makes sense to think that socially isolated and lonely children and adults can be helped most through efforts to improve their own social skills and confidence in social situations *and* to change their social environments in order to increase opportunities for meaningful interaction with peers. In short, multiple approaches may be needed to enrich social lives and enhance social development across the life span.

REFLECTIONS

We like the notion that each of us travels through life accompanied by an ever-changing social convoy. It's a comforting thought, at least for the majority of us who have rich social networks. It also reminds us that any individual's development is intimately intertwined with that of other individuals. In this chapter we have concentrated mainly on how we as individuals benefit from close attachments—from a secure bond with at least one caregiver as an infant, from close friendships as a child or adolescent, and from intimate romantic relationships and friendships as an adult. Remember, though, that we not only have convoys but also are part of the social convoys of other people. Thus we can contribute to the development of those closest to us by being understanding and supportive friends, warm and responsive parents for our children, and caring supporters of our aging parents.

If we take seriously the idea that each of us affects and is affected by significant members of our social convoys throughout the life span, it becomes necessary to understand the development of *relationships* rather than the development of isolated individuals. In the next chapter we will attempt to determine how relationships within the family change over the life cycle as people play out their roles as children, parents, and grandparents. So far, developmentalists have only scratched the surface in their attempts to understand how relationships change and how partners in relationships shape each other's development as they journey together through time.

SUMMARY POINTS

1. Social relationships contribute immensely to human development, primarily by providing us with critical learning opportunities and social support (affect, affirmation, and aid). The developmental significance of early parent/child relationships was underscored by Freud; that of peer relationships, by Piaget and Sullivan.

2. Because infants have endearing qualities, parents typically become attached to them before or shortly after birth. Then parent and child normally establish synchronized routines, although some parents have difficulty doing so because of characteristics of the baby, parent, or social context.

3. In forming attachments, infants progress through phases of undiscriminating social responsiveness, discriminating social responsiveness, active proximity seeking, and goal-corrected partnership; the formation of attachments at about 6 or 7 months of age is accompanied by separation anxiety and stranger anxiety.

4. Although the Freudian view that infants become attached to those who feed them lacks support, Erik Erikson and learning theorists were correct to emphasize the caregiver's responsiveness and reinforcing qualities, cognitive-developmental theorists to emphasize cognitive requisites for attachment, and ethological theorists John Bowlby and Mary Ainsworth to stress biological predispositions coupled with social experience.

5. Research using Ainsworth's Strange Situation test supports her view that secure attachments are associated with sensitive, responsive parenting; resistant attachments with inconsistent, unresponsive care; and avoidant attachments with rejection or overstimulation. The infant's temperament also affects the quality of the attachment. A secure attachment contributes to later competence, but insecurely attached or socially deprived infants are not inevitably doomed to a lifetime of poor relationships.

6. Infants become increasingly able to coordinate their own activity with that of their small companions to participate in complementary interactive exchanges and form friendships.

7. During the years from 2 to 12, social-cognitive abilities, including person-perception and role-taking skills, improve immensely; children participate in goal-corrected partnerships with their parents and spend increasing amounts of time with peers, especially same-sex ones, forming friendships on the basis of common activity and then mutual loyalty. Physical attributes, academic ability, and social competence contribute to popularity. Children who are rejected by their peers are at risk for future problems, for peer interactions affect all aspects of development.

8. During adolescence, social-cognitive skills improve, same- and cross-sex friendships increasingly involve emotional intimacy and self-disclosure, and heterosexual cliques and crowds facilitate the transition from same-sex peer groups to dating relationships. Although susceptibility to negative peer pressures peaks at about age 14 or 15, adolescence is typically not a continual war of parents versus peers unless poor family relationships result in the adolescent's becoming involved with an antisocial crowd.

9. Adults often have more sophisticated social-cognitive abilities than adolescents do and apparently maintain these skills in old age unless they become socially inactive. Most adults of all ages have high-quality relationships, though social networks shrink with age due to increased social selectivity.

10. In forming romantic attachments, adults screen potential partners through a set of filters, favoring partners similar to themselves. Adults have either secure, resistant, or avoidant attachment styles that may be rooted in their early attachment experiences and that influence their romantic relationships and parenting styles.

11. Although adults are highly involved with their spouses or romantic partners, they continue to value friendships, especially long-lasting and equitable ones. Well-being is influenced more by the quality than by the quantity of relationships. It is especially important to have at least one confidant.

12. Socially withdrawn individuals can be helped through social-skills training and exposure to more social-interaction opportunities.

KEY TERMS

attachment
avoidant attachment
chumship
clique
confidant
conformity
contact comfort
crowd
disorganized/disoriented attachment
equity
filter model of mate selection
imprinting
internal working model
peer
resistant attachment
role-taking skills
secure attachment
secure base
selectivity hypothesis
separation anxiety
social cognition
social convoy
social support
sociometric techniques
stranger anxiety
Strange Situation test
synchronized routines

14

THE FAMILY

When Burnam and Addie Ledford hosted the Ledford family reunion, he was 102, she 93. They had married in 1903 and were nearing their 75th wedding anniversary. They had 13 children, 9 of them still surviving; the oldest was age 69. They also had 32 grandchildren, the oldest age 42; and 39 great-grandchildren—so many that Burnam marveled "It's like planting seeds. . . . They keep coming up." Burnam and Addie clearly valued their bonds to past, present, and future generations of Ledfords (Egerton, 1983).

The Ledfords are an unusual family, but their emphasis on family ties is not at all unusual. We are all bound to families. We are born into them, work our way toward adulthood in them, start our own as adults, and remain connected to them in old age. We are part of our families, and they are part of us. This chapter examines the family and its diverse and important roles in human development throughout the life span. What is a family, and how has the nature of the family changed in recent years? How do infants, children, and adolescents experience family life, and how are they affected by their relationships with parents and siblings? What of adults? How is their development affected by such family transitions as marrying, becoming a parent, watching children leave the nest, and becoming a grandparent? Finally, what are the implications of the diversity that characterizes today's family lifestyles—and of such decisions as remaining childless or divorcing?

Each family has its own developmental tale to tell.

UNDERSTANDING THE FAMILY

The Family as a System

Family theorists conceptualize the family as a social system embedded in larger social systems. To say that it is a system means that the family, like the human body, is truly a whole consisting of interrelated parts, each of which affects and is affected by every other part, and each of which contributes to the functioning of the whole. In the past, developmentalists did not adopt this systems perspective. They typically focused almost entirely on the mother/child relationship, assuming that the only process of interest within the family was the mother's influence on the child's development (Ambert, 1992). Mothers were viewed as shapers and molders, children as lumps of clay. What does this simple view of the "family" leave out? How about the fact that the family system usually includes a man who is husband to his wife and father to his child? That the family usually includes more than one child? That children can affect their parents, just as they are affected by them?

The **nuclear family** consists of husband/father, wife/mother, and at least one child. Jay Belsky (1981) draws our attention to how complex even a simple man, woman, and infant "system" can be. An infant interacting with his or her mother is already involved in a process of *reciprocal* influence: The baby's smile is likely to be greeted by a smile from Mom, and Mom's smile is likely to be reciprocated by the infant's grin. However, the presence of *both* parents "transforms the mother-infant dyad into a *family system* [comprising] a husband-wife as well as mother-infant and father-infant relationships" (Belsky, 1981, p. 17). Every individual and every relationship within the family affects every other individual and relationship through reciprocal influence (see Figure 14.1). You can see why it was rather naive to think that the family could be understood by studying only the ways in which mothers mold their children.

Now think about how complex the family system becomes if we add another child (or two or six) to it—

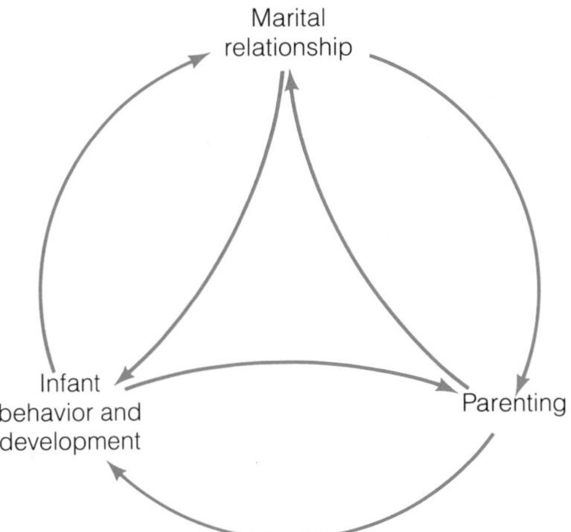

FIGURE 14.1 A model of the family as a social system. Parents affect infants, who affect each parent and the marital relationship. Of course, the marital relationship may affect the parenting the infant receives, the infant's behavior, and so on. Clearly, families are complex social systems. As an exercise, you may wish to rediagram the patterns of influence within a family after adding a sibling or two. (From Belsky, 1981.)

and try to understand the unique relationships between each parent and each of these children, as well as relationships between siblings. Or consider the complexity of an **extended family household,** in which parents and their children live with other kin—some combination of grandparents, siblings, aunts, uncles, nieces, and nephews. Extended family households are very common in many cultures of the world and relatively common among African Americans in the United States (Pearson et al., 1990; Wilson, 1989). This family arrangement is likely to be especially adaptive for economically disadvantaged single mothers, who can obtain needed help with child care and social support by living with their mothers (Burton, 1990). Indeed, there is evidence that both African-American children in the United States and children in the Sudan, where multigeneration families are common, are better adjusted psychologically when they grow up in extended family households with involved grandparents than when they are brought up in two-parent nuclear families (Al-Awad & Sonuga-Barke, 1992; Wilson, 1986). Even when nuclear families do not live in the same household with members of their extended family, they most certainly affect and are affected by these relatives.

Finally, whether a family is of the nuclear or the extended type, we cannot think of it as a unit that exists in a vacuum. As we discussed in Chapter 4, we must adopt an *ecological approach* to the family (Bronfenbrenner, 1979, 1989), viewing it as a system embedded in larger social systems such as a neighborhood, a community, a subculture, and a broader culture. The family experience in our culture is quite different from that in societies where new brides become underlings in the households of their mothers-in-law, or where men can have several wives. There is an almost infinite variety of family forms in the world, and a correspondingly wide range of developmental experiences within the family.

The Family as a Changing System: The Family Life Cycle

It would be difficult enough to study the family as a system if it kept the same members and continued to perform the same activities over and over again for as long as it existed. But, obviously, this is not the case. Family membership changes as new children are born and as grown children leave the nest. Moreover, the individuals within the family are all developing individuals, and the *relationships* between husband and wife, parent and child, and sibling and sibling also develop in systematic ways over time. Since the family is truly a system, changes in family membership or changes in any individual or relationship within the family are bound to affect the dynamics of the whole.

Thus we have to view the family itself as a developing organism. One way to do so is in terms of a **family life cycle,** or sequence of changes in family composition, roles, and relationships that occur from the time people marry until they die. Some time ago, family theorist Evelyn Duvall (1977) outlined eight stages of the family life cycle (see Table 14.1). In each stage, family members play distinctive roles and carry out distinctive developmental tasks—for example, establishing a satisfying relationship as newlyweds, adjusting to the demands of new parenthood in the childbearing phase, and adapting to the departure of children in the "launching" phase. In this chapter we'll look at the impacts of these family transitions on adults, and we'll examine how the child's experience of the family changes as he or she develops. We'll also come to appreciate that an increasing number of people do not experience the traditional family life cycle (Rowland, 1991).

A Changing Family System in a Changing World

Not only is the family a system, and not only is it a developing system, but it exists and develops in a changing world. During the last half of the 20th century, several dramatic social changes have altered the makeup of the typical family and the quality of family experience. Drawing on several analyses of U.S. Census data and other surveys, we will highlight the following trends (see Chadwick & Heaton, 1992; Demo, 1992; Himes, 1992; Norton & Moorman, 1987; Sweet & Bumpass, 1987):

1. *Increased numbers of single adults.* More adults are living as singles today than in the past.

TABLE 14.1 Stages of the family life cycle.

Stage	*Available Roles*
1. Married couple (without children)	Wife Husband
2. Childbearing family (oldest child birth to 30 months)	Wife/mother Husband/father Infant daughter or son
3. Family with preschool children (oldest child 30 months to 6 years)	Wife/mother Husband/father Daughter/sister Son/brother
4. Family with school-aged children (oldest child up to 12 years)	Wife/mother Husband/father Daughter/sister Son/brother
5. Family with teenagers (oldest child 13 to 20 years)	Wife/mother Husband/father Daughter/sister Son/brother
6. Family launching young adults (first child gone to last child gone)	Wife/mother/grandmother Husband/father/grandfather Daughter/sister/aunt Son/brother/uncle
7. Family without children (empty nest to retirement)	Wife/mother/grandmother Husband/father/grandfather
8. Aging family (retirement to death)	Wife/mother/grandmother Husband/father/grandfather Widow or widower

SOURCE: Adapted from Duvall, 1977.

However, don't be deceived into thinking that marriage is out of style, for over 90% of today's young adults can still be expected to marry at some time in their lives (Chadwick & Heaton, 1992).

2. *Postponement of marriage.* Many adults are not rejecting marriage but are simply delaying it while they pursue educational and career goals. Although the average age of first marriage decreased during the first half of the century, it has now risen again, to about 24 for women and 26 for men (Chadwick & Heaton, 1992), despite increased rates of teenage pregnancy among lower-income groups.

3. *Decreased childbearing.* Today's adults are not only waiting longer after they marry to have children, but they are having fewer of them—about two on average. The Baby Boom period after World War II was an unusual departure from an otherwise consistent trend toward smaller family sizes. Increasing numbers of young women are also remaining childless, though few do so by choice (Jacobson & Heaton, 1991).

4. *Increased female participation in the labor force.* In 1950, 12% of married women with children under age 6 worked outside the home; now the figure is 57%, a truly dramatic social change (Chadwick & Heaton, 1992). Although women still carry the lion's share of child-rearing and housework responsibilities, fewer and fewer children have a mother whose full-time job is that of homemaker.

5. *Increased divorce.* It is well known that the divorce rate has been increasing over the past several decades. According to one estimate, up to 60% of newly married couples can expect to divorce (Bumpass, 1990).

6. *Increased numbers of single-parent families.* Partly because of a rising rate of out-of-wedlock births, but mostly because of the rise in divorce rates, it is projected that about half of all children born in the 1980s will spend some time in a single-parent family (Castro Martin & Bumpass, 1989). In 1960 only 9% of children lived with one parent, usually a widowed one; now 24% live with a single parent, usually a never-married or divorced one (Demo, 1992). Father-headed single-parent homes have increased even faster than mother-headed ones, with fathers now heading 15% of all single-parent families (Meyer & Garasky, 1993).

7. *Increased numbers of children living in poverty.* Unfortunately, the higher numbers of single-parent families have contributed to an increase in the proportion of children living below the poverty line; 54% of children living in female-headed homes, compared to 10% of children in two-parent families, live in poverty (Eggebeen & Lichter, 1991). As we'll see, economic stresses have many negative effects on the family.

8. *Increased remarriage.* Simply because more married couples are divorcing, more adults (about 75% of divorced individuals) are remarrying. Often they are forming new, **reconstituted families,** which involve at least a parent, a stepparent, and a child and sometimes blend multiple children from two families into a new family (Glick, 1989). About 25% of American children will spend some time in a reconstituted family (Hetherington, 1989).

9. *Increased years without children.* Because modern couples are compressing their childbearing into a shorter time span, because some divorced individuals do not remarry, and because people are living longer, adults today spend more of their later years as couples—or, especially if they are women, as single adults—without children in their homes (Chadwick & Heaton, 1992).

10. *More multigeneration families.* As a result of these same trends, more children today know their grandparents and even their great-grandparents; the family has been evolving into a "beanpole family" with more generations, but smaller ones, than in the past (Bengtson, Rosenthal, & Burton, 1990). Perhaps the most significant effect of increased longevity, though, is that parent/child relationships last for 50

years or more. As a result, "many more parents and children are finding themselves growing old together" (Aizenberg & Treas, 1985, p. 173).

We should note that many of these trends have affected some ethnic and racial groups more dramatically than others. For example, the rise in mother-headed families has been particularly steep among African Americans; partly as a result, almost half of African-American children now live in poverty (Eggebeen & Lichter, 1991). We'll be looking at the impacts of some of these trends on development later in this chapter. Our main point for now is this: The American family is more diverse than ever before. Our stereotyped image of the family—the traditional *Leave It to Beaver* nuclear family with a breadwinner/father, housewife/mother, and children—is just that: a stereotype. By one estimate, 70% of families in 1960 but only 12% of families in 1980 conformed to this "ideal" (Klineberg, 1984). Although the family is by no means dying, we must broaden our image of it to include the many dual-career, single-parent, reconstituted, and childless families that exist today. Bear that in mind as we begin our excursion into family life at the beginning—with the birth of an infant.

THE INFANT

Children begin to affect their parents even before they arrive, for expectant parents will often plan ahead by selecting names for the infant, decorating a nursery, moving to larger quarters, and changing or leaving jobs (Grossman, Eichler, Winickoff, & Associates, 1980). In a later section we'll see just what effects a new baby has on first-time parents. Here we'll concentrate on the emerging relationships between mothers and fathers and their infants.

The Mother/Infant Relationship

In Chapter 13 we discussed at length the mother/infant attachment and its significance for later development. There is a simple reason why the mother/infant relationship has received far more attention than the father/infant relationship: Mothers have traditionally been the primary caregivers for infants. When mothers are warm, sensitive, and responsive, infants become securely attached to them. By fostering a secure attachment, a parent contributes to other positive outcomes as well—for example, later social competence in interactions with peers, an interest in exploring the world, and rapid intellectual growth (Waters, Wippman, & Sroufe, 1979).

Yet infants also deserve some credit for affecting their mothers. Even a sensitive woman may find it difficult to love a baby who cries endlessly. Indeed, "easy" babies seem to make sensitive and responsive parenting easy, whereas difficult babies who are unresponsive and irritable can sometimes help "produce" rather unaffectionate mothers (Greene, Fox, & Lewis, 1983). Mothers do have considerable influence on infant development. However, the mother/child relationship takes on its distinctive character as a result of the *reciprocal* contributions of mother and infant.

The Father/Infant Relationship

Now that developmentalists have taken seriously the idea that the family is a system, they have discovered that fathers are part of the family too. But how much do fathers interact with their children, and how much do they really contribute to their children's development?

Gender stereotypes would suggest that fathers are not cut out to care for young children. The evidence suggests that they are (Biller, 1993). Overall, fathers and mothers seem to be more similar than different in the ways they interact with infants and young children. In one study, for example, mothers and fathers were observed while they fed their babies (Parke & Sawin, 1976). Fathers were no less able than mothers to perform this caregiving task effectively and to ensure that the milk was consumed; nor were they any less sensitive to the infant's cues during the feeding session. Similarly, fathers, just like mothers, become objects of their infants' love and serve as secure bases for their explorations, especially if these fathers have positive attitudes toward parenting and spend a lot of time with their babies (Cox et al., 1992). We really have no basis for thinking that mothers are uniquely qualified to parent or that men are hopelessly inept around babies. However, the fact that fathers are *capable* of sensitive parenting does not necessarily mean they will play the same roles in their children's lives that mothers do. Fathers and mothers do differ in both the quantity and quality of the parenting they provide (Biller, 1993).

Consider first the matter of quantity. Mothers simply spend more time with children than fathers do, and this seems to be true in most cultures (Demo, 1992; Hewlett, 1992). Fathers in our society are more involved with their children today than they were in the past, especially if their wives work (Barnett & Baruch, 1987). Yet our best estimate is that fathers spend about two-thirds as much time interacting with their children as mothers do (Crouter & McHale, 1993; Demo, 1992).

Now consider the issue of quality: Just how do mothers and fathers differ in their typical styles of interacting with young children? When mothers interact with their babies, a large proportion of their time is devoted to caregiving: offering food, changing diapers, wiping noses, and so on. Although fathers in some societies play an active role in teaching their children, especially their sons, how to perform work activities (Hewlett, 1992), fathers in our society spend much of their time with children in *play*. Specifically, fathers are more likely than mothers to provide playful and rowdy physical stimulation and to initiate unusual or unpredictable games (Biller, 1993; Lamb, 1981). Fathers seem to specialize in tickling, poking, bouncing, and surprising infants, whereas mothers hold, talk to, and play quietly with infants. The tendency for fathers to be less involved overall with children but to spend more of their time in play continues through adolescence (Collins & Russell, 1991).

Fathers also treat boys and girls more differently than mothers do (see Chapter 11). For one thing, fathers often spend more time with sons than with daughters (Barnett & Baruch, 1987; Parke, 1979). In addition, they are more likely than mothers to encourage boys to play with masculine-stereotyped toys, to encourage girls to play with feminine-stereotyped toys, and to discourage play that is considered more appropriate for the other sex (Snow, Jacklin, & Maccoby, 1983). Thus mothers tend to be "equal opportunity" parents, treating girls and boys much the same, while fathers seem to alter their parenting style according to whether they are interacting with sons or daughters (Lytton & Romney, 1991).

In view of the roles that fathers play in their children's lives, what are their unique contributions to child development? Certainly if a mother is for some reason unresponsive or rejecting, a father might be crucial to providing the security that infants need so much (Biller, 1993; Main & Weston, 1981). Babies are also likely to be more socially competent if they are securely attached to *both* parents than if they are securely attached to just one (Biller, 1993; Main & Weston, 1981). In addition, children whose fathers are highly involved with them and sensitive to their needs tend to be enthusiastic and persistent when they are given problems to solve and to be high achievers in school (Biller, 1993; Easterbrooks & Goldberg, 1984). Fathers also have a lot to do with the masculine gender typing of their sons and, to a lesser extent, the feminine gender typing of their daughters (Stevenson & Black, 1988).

In short, fathers richly deserve the increased respect they have been getting from developmentalists lately. They are not only capable of sensitive and responsive parenting, but they can contribute in many positive ways to their children's development when they *use* their competencies and take an active part in child rearing.

Mothers, Fathers, and Infants: The System at Work

So far, we have considered mother/child and father/child relationships without viewing the new family as a *three-person* system. Researchers have begun to show that the mother/child relationship cannot be understood without adding the father to the picture; nor can father/child interactions be understood without examining how mothers influence that relationship. In other words, parents have **indirect effects** on their children through their ability to influence the behavior of their spouses. More generally, indirect effects within the family are instances in which the relationship between two individuals is modified by the behavior or attitudes of a third family member.

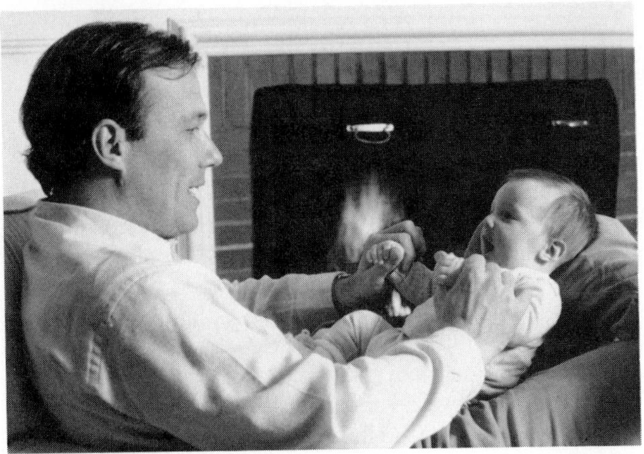

Fathers contribute to the gender-role development of both sons and daughters.

Fathers indirectly influence the mother/infant relationship. Mothers who have close, supportive relationships with their husbands tend to interact more patiently and sensitively with their babies than mothers who are experiencing marital tension and feel that they are raising their children largely without help (Cox et al., 1989, 1992; Howes & Markman, 1989). Meanwhile, mothers indirectly affect the father/infant relationship. For example, fathers tend to be more involved with their infants when their wives believe that a father should play an important role in a child's life (Palkovitz, 1984) and when the two parents talk frequently about the baby (Belsky, Gilstrap, & Rovine, 1984; Lamb & Elster, 1985). In sum, both mothers and fathers can affect their children indirectly through their interactions with their *spouses*. And, overall, children appear to be best off when couples provide *mutual* support and encouragement that allow *both* to be more sensitive and responsive parents (Biller, 1993; Crnic et al., 1983).

Now perhaps you can appreciate that even the simplest of families is a true social system that is bigger than the sum of its parts. Because mothers, fathers, and children all affect one another, both directly and indirectly, socialization within the family is obviously not a one-way street in which influence flows only from parent to child. Indeed, family socialization is not even just a two-way street—it is more like the busy intersection of many avenues of influence.

THE CHILD

As children reach the age of 2 or 3, parents continue to be caregivers and playmates, but they also become more concerned with teaching the youngsters how (and how not) to behave, and they use some approach to child rearing and discipline to achieve this end. Siblings also serve as socialization agents and become an important part of the child's experience of the family.

Dimensions of Child Rearing

How can I be a good parent? Certainly this question is uppermost in most parents' minds. Yet we probably cannot offer any answers that would be good for all times and all social contexts. As John Ogbu (1981) stresses, a "competent" parent in one cultural or subcultural context could well be an incompetent one in another setting where the skills required for success as an adult are quite different. For example, parents in inner-city ghettos are often extremely affectionate with their infants but tend to use harsh and inconsistent punishment with their older children. From a middle-class perspective, such practices are frowned upon; it is better, middle-class parents and many researchers would say, to be warm, to reason with children rather than slap them around, and to enforce rules consistently. Yet Ogbu argues that harsh and inconsistent discipline is likely to foster such traits as assertiveness, self-reliance, and a mistrust of authority figures—traits that are likely to be very useful if a youngster wants to survive in the street culture of the ghetto. So let's bear in mind that "good parenting" is really parenting that prepares children to meet the demands of the specific culture or subculture in which they live.

Having said that, we can nonetheless draw some conclusions about the ingredients of good parenting that will apply in most settings. We can go far in understanding which parenting styles are effective by considering just two factors: the **warmth/hostility dimension** and the **permissiveness/restrictiveness dimension** (Maccoby & Martin, 1983; Schaefer, 1959). Warm parents often smile at, praise, and encourage their children, expressing a great deal of affection, even though they are critical when a child misbehaves. Hostile or rejecting parents are often quick to criticize, belittle, punish, or ignore their children and rarely communicate to children that they are loved and valued. The permissiveness/restrictiveness dimension of parenting relates to how much control over decisions lies with the parent as opposed to the child. Restrictive parents are very controlling; they impose many demands, set many rules, and monitor their children closely to ensure that the rules are followed. Permissive parents make few demands of their children and allow them a great deal of autonomy in exploring the environment, expressing their opinions and emotions, and making decisions about their own activities. By crossing these two dimensions, we actually have four basic patterns of child rearing to consider: warmth combined with restrictiveness, warmth combined with permissiveness, hostility combined with restrictiveness, and hostility combined with permissiveness (Figure 14.2).

We assume that you have no difficulty deciding that warmth or love is preferable to coldness or rejection. Countless studies demonstrate that parental love is a powerful contributor to healthy cognitive, social, and emotional development in childhood (Maccoby & Martin, 1983). As we have seen in this book, warm, responsive parenting is associated with secure attachments to parents, academic competence, high self-esteem, prosocial tendencies (such as cooperativeness), peer acceptance, and a strong sense of morality.

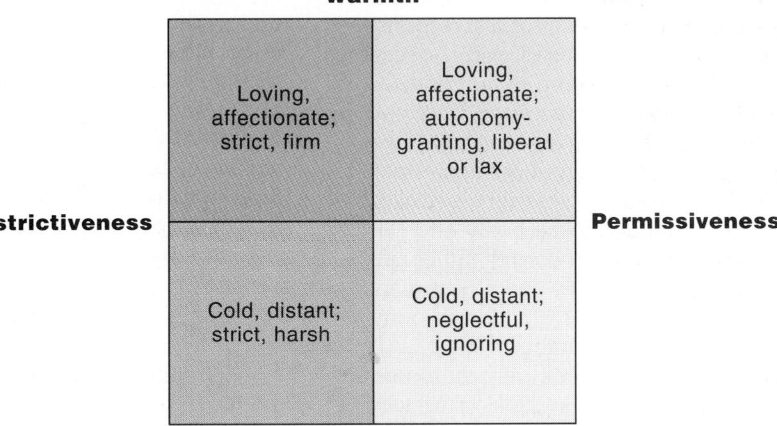

FIGURE 14.2 The dimensions of parenting. Which combination of warmth/hostility and permissiveness/restrictiveness best describes your parents' approach? Which do you think best fosters positive qualities in children?

Children want to please loving parents and so are motivated to do what is expected of them and to learn what their parents would like them to learn. Because youngsters simply do not thrive when they are rejected, Kevin MacDonald (1992) speculates that affection for one's children is an evolved behavior that has allowed parents through the ages to influence their children in any number of adaptive ways.

Now, what about the permissiveness/restrictiveness dimension of parenting: Is it better for parents to be highly controlling or to grant considerable autonomy to their children? Here we need to get more specific about degrees of restrictiveness and permissiveness, and we can do so by considering the three patterns of parental control identified by Diana Baumrind (1967, 1977, 1991):

1. **Authoritarian parenting.** This is a highly restrictive parenting style in which adults impose many rules, expect strict obedience, rarely explain why the child should comply with rules, and often rely on power tactics such as physical punishment to gain compliance.
2. **Authoritative parenting.** Authoritative parents are more flexible. They allow their children a fair amount of freedom but also set clear rules. They explain the rationales for their rules and restrictions, are responsive to their children's needs and points of view, and consistently enforce whatever rules they establish.
3. **Permissive parenting.** This is a lax pattern of parenting in which adults make relatively few demands, encourage their children to express their feelings and impulses, and rarely exert firm control over their behavior.

When Baumrind (1967) linked these three parenting styles to the characteristics of preschool children who were exposed to each style, she found that authoritative parenting was most likely to be associated with positive outcomes for the child. Children of authoritative parents were cheerful, socially responsible, self-reliant, achievement oriented, and cooperative with adults and peers. Children of authoritarian parents tended to be moody and seemingly unhappy, easily annoyed, relatively aimless, and not very pleasant to be around. Finally, children of permissive parents were often impulsive and aggressive, especially if they were boys. They tended to be bossy and self-centered, rebellious, lacking in self-control, rather aimless, and quite low in independence and achievement.

When Baumrind (1977) reassessed these youngsters at ages 8 to 9, children of authoritative parents still had an edge on their peers with respect to both cognitive competence (originality in thinking, achievement motivation, enjoyment of intellectual challenges) and social competence (sociability and leadership). Indeed, the strengths of children exposed to authoritative parenting are still evident in adolescence; they are confident, achievement oriented, and socially competent, and they stay clear of drug abuse and other problem behaviors (Baumrind, 1991). The link between authoritative parenting and positive developmental outcomes is evident in all racial and ethnic groups studied to date in the United States (Lamborn et al., 1991; Steinberg et al., 1991) and in a variety of other cultures as well (Pinto, Folkers, & Sines, 1991; Scott, Scott, & McCabe, 1991).

Now let's put the warmth/hostility and permissiveness/restrictiveness dimensions back together again. In Baumrind's study, most parents were warm and loving rather than hostile. Thus it appears that warmth combined with *moderate* parental control—as opposed to warmth combined with either extreme restrictiveness or extreme permissiveness—is most closely associated with healthy child development. Children apparently need love *and* limits—a set of rules to help them structure their behavior. If they are indulged and given little guidance, they won't learn self-control and may become quite selfish, unruly, and lacking in direction. And if they receive too much guidance? Then, though well behaved, they'll have few opportunities to learn self-reliance and may lack confidence in their own decision-making abilities (Grolnick & Ryan, 1989).

The very least successful parenting styles are those that combine hostility or rejection with either extreme permissiveness *or* extreme restrictiveness (Koestner, Zuroff, & Powers, 1991; Lamborn et al., 1991; Maccoby & Martin, 1983). Children whose parents are rejecting and highly controlling are often extremely withdrawn, inhibited, and low in self-esteem. Sometimes they even show masochistic or suicidal tendencies, possibly because they must bottle up the anxieties and resentments that their harsh and unloving parents have created within them. By contrast, children of permissive and rejecting parents (neglectful parents, really) tend to be hostile and rebellious; as teenagers they are likely to engage in delinquent acts and to abuse drugs (Lamborn et al., 1991; Patterson & Stouthamer-Loeber, 1984). These children have parents who say, in effect, "I don't care about you, and I don't care what you do." It seems quite natural, then, that they would act out their resentments by striking back at authority. In short, the undesirable effects of either extremely restrictive (authoritarian) or extremely permissive parenting are multiplied when parents are also cold, aloof, or unconcerned.

Social Class, Economic Hardship, and Parenting

Parenting styles are shaped in part by socioeconomic factors. Middle-class and lower-class parents often pursue different goals and emphasize different values in raising their children. Compared to middle- and upper-class parents, lower- and working-class parents tend to (1) place more stress on obedience and respect for authority; (2) be more restrictive and authoritarian, more frequently using power-assertive discipline; (3) reason with their children less frequently, and (4) show less warmth and affection (Maccoby, 1980; McLoyd, 1990). Although we find a wide range of parenting styles in any social group (Kelley, Power, & Wimbush, 1992), these *average* social-class differences in parenting have been observed in many cultures and across racial and ethnic groups in the United States (Maccoby, 1980).

Why might they exist? One explanation centers on the stresses associated with low-income living. Vonnie McLoyd (1989, 1990) suggests that poverty or economic hardship makes adults edgy and irritable and diminishes their capacity to be warm, supportive parents. Recently, Rand Conger and his associates (1992, 1993) offered support for this argument by finding a link among economic distress, nonnurturant/uninvolved parenting, and poor adolescent outcomes. The causal scenario, illustrated in Figure 14.3, goes like this: Parents who are experiencing economic pressure, or feeling that they cannot cope with their financial problems, tend to become depressed, which increases marital conflict. Marital conflict, in turn, disrupts each partner's ability to be a supportive, involved parent and therefore contributes to such adolescent problems as low self-esteem, poor school performance, poor peer relations, and adjustment problems such as depression and aggression.

Another explanation for the link between economic factors and parenting styles focuses on the skills needed by workers in white-collar and blue-collar jobs (Kohn, 1969; Ogbu, 1981). Parents from lower socioeconomic groups may quite sensibly emphasize obedience to authority figures if that is what is required in blue-collar jobs like their own. Middle- and upper-class parents may reason with their children and stress individual initiative, curiosity, and creativity more because these are the attributes that count for business executives, professionals, and other white-collar workers. It could be, then, that both middle- and lower-income parents have devised styles of parenting that are well adapted to the distinctive demands of their sociocultural setting.

In sum, the more authoritarian parenting style used by many lower-income parents may reflect *both* (1) the damaging effects of economic stress, particularly of living in poverty or losing one's job, on a parent's ability to parent effectively, and (2) an adaptive attempt to prepare children for jobs in which they will be expected to obey a boss.

Child Effects on Parenting

Child effects in the family are all those instances in which children influence their parents (Ambert, 1992; Lerner, 1993). We need to temper all we have said about parents' effects on children by considering the reciprocal influence of children on parents. One clear example of a child effect is the fact that the style of parenting used with a child depends greatly on the age and competence of the child. For example, infants in their first year of life require and elicit sensitive care, whereas older infants who are asserting their wills and toddling here and there force parents to provide more instruction and discipline (Fagot & Kavanaugh, 1993). Normally, parents then become less restrictive as their children mature and gradually, with parental guidance, become capable of making their own decisions (Amato, 1989; Maccoby, 1984). It makes sense for parents to call many of the shots for 2-year-olds, who are not known for their sound judgment. Ultimately, however, children must learn how to make decisions and govern their own behavior. So, ideally, parents will gradually shift their authoritative approach from a moderately restrictive to a moderately permissive one as a child matures. Indeed, the concept of authoritative parenting implies a sensitivity to the child's changing needs.

Now consider potential effects of a child's personality on parenting. Isn't it possible that easygoing, manageable children *cause* their parents to be warm and authoritative? Couldn't difficult, stubborn, and aggressive children help mold parents who are rejecting and who either rule with an iron hand or throw up

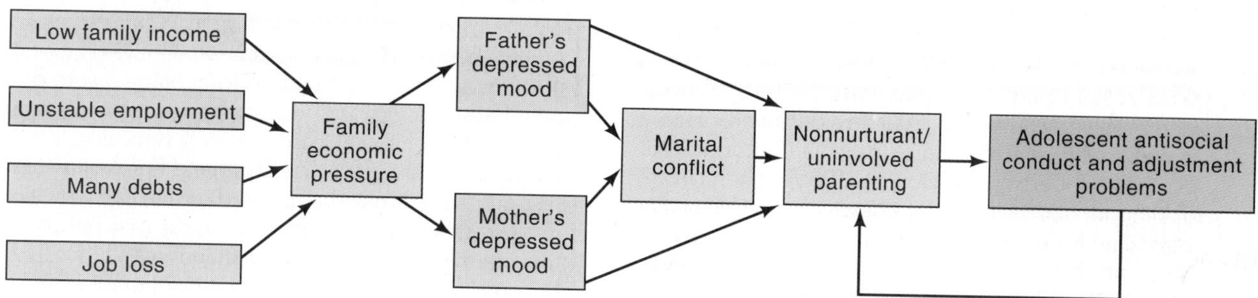

FIGURE 14.3 A model of the relationship among family economic stress, patterns of parenting, and adolescent adjustment. (Adapted from Conger et al., 1992.)

their hands in defeat and become overpermissive? In one demonstration of child effects within the family, Barbara Keller and Richard Bell (1979) challenged the finding (reported in Chapter 12) that a parent's use of the disciplinary technique of *induction* (explanations emphasizing the consequences of a child's behavior for other people) fosters moral maturity in a child. Isn't it possible instead, they reasoned, that children who are already "good" are more likely than less responsive children to elicit inductive explanations from adults?

Keller and Bell had female college students attempt to convince 9-year-old girls to behave altruistically (for example, to spend more time sewing a pillow for a handicapped child than sewing a pillow for themselves). The trick was that the girls had been taught to act either very attentively (looking at the college student's face, smiling, and answering questions promptly) or very inattentively. As expected, students who were confronted with an attentive child used a great deal of induction, pointing out how other children might feel if the child behaved selfishly. By contrast, college students who interacted with an inattentive child were more likely to use power-assertion techniques such as promising rewards for altruism and threatening penalties for selfishness.

In another demonstration of child effects in the family, Kathleen Anderson, Hugh Lytton, and David Romney (1986; see also Lytton, 1990) studied mothers of boys who were officially diagnosed as having conduct disorders—boys who were highly aggressive and had histories of arson, truancy, temper outbursts, and other serious problems. The researchers had each of these mothers interact with her own conduct-disordered son, another mother's conduct-disordered son, and a normal boy. Meanwhile, mothers of normal boys also interacted with their own sons and with both another normal boy and a conduct-disordered boy.

The findings were clear: Boys with conduct disorders were so noncompliant and difficult that they brought out negative, coercive behavior—"bad parenting," in other words—in every mother with whom they interacted. In this study, at least, there was little evidence that the mothers of conduct-disordered boys were any worse disciplinarians than other mothers or that their parenting was the main cause of their sons' aggressive, destructive behavior. Other research tells us that severe antisocial behavior probably results when a child genetically predisposed to be aggressive and unruly becomes caught up in a destructive family process with rejecting, harsh parents (Lytton, 1990; Simons, Robertson, & Downs, 1989). Then, in all likelihood, the child elicits coercive and ineffective parenting from parents at the same time that parents elicit antisocial behavior from the child, and it becomes impossible to say who is more influential.

These demonstrations of child effects within the family are tremendously important. We simply cannot take it for granted that parents have sole responsibility for whether their children are "good" or "bad." It is probably still the case that parents influence children more strongly than children influence them (Baumrind, 1991; Crockenberg & Litman, 1990; Simons et al., 1989). However, we must remind ourselves again that the family is a *system* whose members socialize one another.

Sibling Relationships

A family system consisting of mother, father, and child is perturbed by the arrival of a new baby and becomes a new—and considerably more complex—family system.

A New Baby Arrives

How do children adapt to a new baby in the house? Judy Dunn and Carol Kendrick (1982; see also Dunn, 1993) have studied this question, and the account they provide is not an entirely cheerful one. Mothers typically give less attention to their first-borns after the new baby arrives than before. Partly for this reason, first-borns often find being "dethroned" a stressful experience. They become more difficult and demanding or dependent and "clingy," and they often develop problems with their sleeping, eating, and toileting routines. Most of their battles are with their mothers, but a minority of them are not above hitting, poking, and pinching their younger brothers or sisters. Although positive effects (such as an increased insistence on doing things independently) are also common, it is clear that first-borns are not entirely thrilled to have an attention-grabbing new baby in the house. They resent losing their parents' attention, and their own difficult behavior may alienate their parents even further.

Thus **sibling rivalry**—a spirit of competition, jealousy, or resentment between siblings—often begins as soon as a younger brother or sister arrives. Can it be minimized? The adjustment process is easier if the first-born had positive relationships with both parents before the younger sibling arrived and continues to enjoy close relationships afterward (Dunn & Kendrick, 1982; Volling & Belsky, 1992). Parents are advised to guard against ignoring their first-born, to continue providing love and attention, and to maintain the child's routines as much as possible. They can also encourage older children to become aware of a new baby's needs and feelings and to assist in their new brother or sister's care (Dunn & Kendrick, 1982; Howe and Ross, 1990). Yet Dunn and Kendrick (1981) find that parents may have to walk a thin line between two traps: becoming so attentive to the new baby that they deprive the older child of attention and love, and becoming so indulgent of the first-born that he or she becomes a "spoiled brat" who resents any competition from the younger sibling.

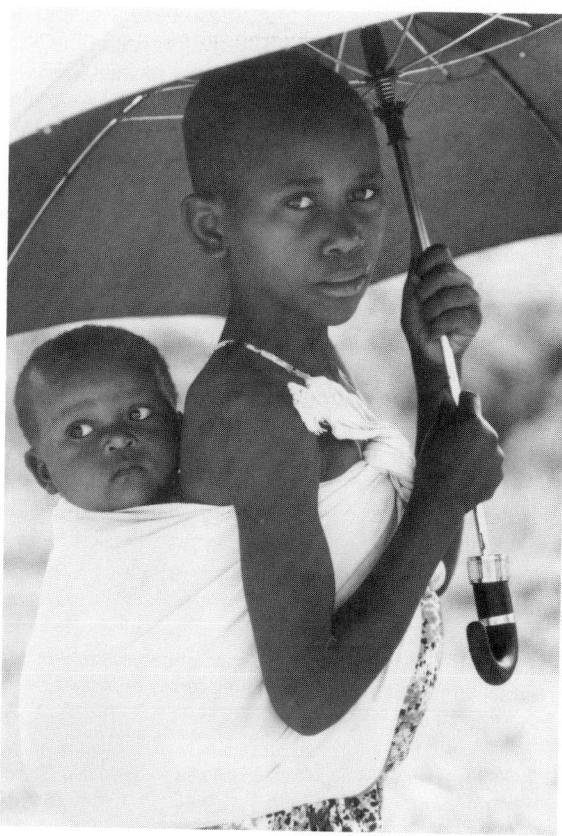

In many societies, older siblings are major caregivers for young children.

Sibling Relationships over the Course of Childhood

Fortunately, most older siblings adjust fairly quickly to having a new brother or sister and stop displaying many of their problem behaviors (Dunn & Kendrick, 1982). Yet, even in the best of sibling relationships, conflict is normal. Judy Dunn (1993) reports that the number of skirmishes between very young siblings can range as high as 56 per hour! Fights, jealousies, bouts of teasing, and shouting matches continue to be part of the sibling relationship throughout childhood, although these conflicts diminish during adolescence as teenagers spend more time away from the family (Buhrmester & Furman, 1990; Furman & Buhrmester, 1992).

Parents can help determine just how smooth or stormy the sibling relationship becomes. Brothers and sisters are likely to get along if their parents get along (Dunn, 1993; MacKinnon, 1989). Sibling relationships are also friendlier and less conflictual if mothers and fathers respond warmly and sensitively to *all* their children and do not consistently favor one child over another (Brody et al., 1992; Stocker, Dunn, & Plomin, 1989). Children pay close attention to what goes on between their siblings and their parents, are acutely sensitive to any hints of favoritism, and may resent it if they think they are being treated less warmly or more strictly than other children in the family (Dunn, 1993).

However, we are dwelling too much on the negative. What is most interesting about sibling relationships is that they are ambivalent; they involve *both* closeness and conflict. For example, Wyndol Furman and Duane Buhrmester (1985a, 1985b) found that school-aged siblings who were similar in age (especially if they were of the same sex) reported more warmth and closeness than other sibling pairs. At the same time, they were most likely to experience friction and conflict (especially if they were of the opposite sex). Moreover, the children in this study perceived their sibling relationships to be more conflict ridden and less satisfying than their relations with parents, grandparents, or friends. And yet siblings were also viewed as more important and more reliable than friends! Acts of kindness and affection between brothers and sisters typically outnumber hateful or rivalrous acts (Abramovitch et al., 1986; Baskett & Johnson, 1982), but the sibling relationship is by nature both close and conflictual.

Contributions of Siblings to Development

What positive roles do siblings actually play in one another's development? One of their important functions is to provide *emotional support*. Brothers and sisters confide in one another and protect and comfort one another in rough times. Even preschoolers jump in to comfort their infant siblings when their mothers leave them or when strangers appear (Stewart & Marvin, 1984). For some children, a secure tie to a favorite sibling can help prevent the anxiety and distress that result from being ignored or neglected by their peers (East & Rook, 1992).

Second, older siblings often provide *caretaking* services for younger siblings. Indeed, in a study of 186 societies, older children were the *principal* caregivers for infants and toddlers in 57% of the cultures studied (Weisner & Gallimore, 1977). In our society as well, older siblings, especially girls, are frequently asked to babysit or tend their younger sibs (McHale & Gamble, 1989).

Finally, older siblings serve as *teachers* of new behavior. Even infants are attentive to older siblings, often imitating their actions or taking over toys that they have abandoned (Abramovitch, Corter, & Pepler, 1980). Older siblings continue to serve as important models later in childhood (Buhrmester & Furman, 1990). Given a problem to master, children are likely to learn more when they have an older sibling available to guide them than when they have access to an equally competent older peer (Azmitia & Hesser, 1993). Not only do older sibs feel a special responsibility to teach, but younger sibs actively seek their guidance. This instruction pays off: When older siblings "play school" with their younger siblings and teach them important lessons such as the ABCs, younger siblings have an easier time learning to read (Norman-Jackson, 1982). What's more, older siblings who tutor their younger sibs may profit as well, for they score higher on tests of academic aptitude and achievement than individuals who have not had these tutoring experiences (Paulhus & Shaffer, 1981; Smith, 1990).

In sum, there is a good deal of reciprocal influence in families that contain preschool or school-aged children. Parents, by adopting particular styles of child rearing with each of their children, are influencing their youngsters' development. Children, meanwhile, influence the extent to which their parents are warm or hostile, restrictive or permissive. And, once a couple has a second child, the family system changes, and sibling relationships take on a life of their own. Although rivalry and conflict seem to be a normal part of such relationships, siblings also provide one another with emotional support, caretaking, and teaching.[1]

THE ADOLESCENT

Conjure up an image of a typical relationship between a teenager and his or her parents. Perhaps you envision a teenage boy who is out all the time with friends, groans when his parents suggest that he do anything with them, and resents the slightest attempt by his parents to cramp his freedom. Or maybe you're seeing a "sassy" teenage girl who thinks her parents don't know a thing and argues with them about virtually everything. Or are you imagining parents wringing their hands in despair and wondering if they'll ever survive their children's adolescent years? Many people believe that the period of the family life cycle during which parents have adolescents in the house is a particularly stressful time, with close parent/child relationships deteriorating into bitter tugs of war. Let's see how much truth there is to these characterizations.

How Do Adolescents Feel about Their Parents?

Although many people believe that adolescents lose respect for their parents and feel less close to them than they did as children, these beliefs simply do not hold up (Galambos, 1992). For example, Daniel Offer, Eric Ostrov, and Kenneth Howard (1981) have found that most high school students, regardless of age and sex, respect their parents and describe their family relationships in positive ways (see Table 14.2). The great majority of teenagers also view their parents as key sources of affection and support (Furman & Buhrmester, 1992; Lempers & Clark-Lempers, 1992).

So far, then, it appears that parent/adolescent relationships are really not very different from parent/child relationships. Yet the parent/child relationship *does* change during adolescence—not so much in its degree of closeness as in the balance of power between parents and adolescents. To understand these changes, we must ask what adolescents are really supposed to achieve as they make the transition to adulthood.

TABLE 14.2 Percentages of adolescents endorsing different statements about their family relationships.

	Percentage Concurring			
Statement	*Males 13–15*	*Males 16–18*	*Females 13–15*	*Females 16–18*
My parents are usually patient with me.	84	79	80	76
I can count on my parents most of the time.	78	76	74	77
I feel I have a part in making family decisions.	71	72	70	73
When my parents are strict, I feel that they are right even if I get angry.	54	54	58	58
Understanding my parents is beyond me.	18	17	21	18
Very often I feel that my father is no good.	16	17	18	16
Very often I feel that my mother is no good.	11	12	12	10

SOURCE: Adapted from Offer, Ostrov, & Howard, 1981.

[1]If siblings play so many important roles in development, you may be wondering if children are damaged by not having them. In the People's Republic of China, where government policy limits families to one child, as well as in North America, only children often outperform later-born children in large families on measures of intelligence and academic achievement; also, their personalities are not much different from those of other children, suggesting that they are not the "spoiled brats" many believe them to be (Falbo & Polit, 1986; Falbo & Poston, 1993). Only children, like children with just one sibling, enjoy the advantages of a good deal of attention and stimulation from their parents, and they apparently gain through friendships outside the home whatever social experiences they may miss by not having brothers or sisters.

The Quest for Autonomy: Renegotiating the Parent/Child Relationship

Most theorists agree that a critical developmental task of adolescence is to achieve **autonomy,** the capacity to make decisions independently and manage life tasks without being overly dependent on other people. If adolescents are to "make it" as adults, they can't be rushing home for reassuring hugs after every little setback or depending on parents to get them to work on time or manage their checkbooks. Parents want their adolescents to become autonomous, and adolescents want the freedom to become autonomous.

What happens within the family system as teenagers become more physically and cognitively mature and more capable of acting autonomously? Conflicts between parents and children become more frequent, at least temporarily, as children reach puberty (Holmbeck & Hill, 1991; Paikoff & Brooks-Gunn, 1991; Steinberg, 1981). These conflicts are usually not severe; most often they are squabbles over such matters as disobedience, homework, or household chores (Montemayor, 1982). As adolescents assert themselves more, though, parents turn over more power to them, and the parent/child relationship changes from one in which parents are dominant to one in which parents and their sons and daughters are on a more equal footing (Steinberg, 1981; Youniss & Smollar, 1985).

In the past, many theorists assumed that achieving autonomy required separating from parents—cutting the cords. Now researchers are appreciating that there is a second important task facing adolescents: *maintaining* a close attachment with their families, even as they are gaining autonomy and preparing to leave the nest (Grotevant & Cooper, 1986; Kobak et al., 1993; Lamborn & Steinberg, 1993). The challenge for parents is really quite similar: to nurture autonomy while still maintaining a positive relationship with their teenagers. Autonomy *and* attachment, or independence *and* interdependence, are the goals. Adolescents are not likely to become confident and independent if they try to distance themselves from their parents (Lamborn & Steinberg, 1993; Ryan & Lynch, 1989).

As it turns out, adolescents are most likely to become autonomous, achievement oriented, and well adjusted if their parents consistently enforce a reasonable set of rules, involve their teenagers in decision making, monitor their comings and goings, *and* continue to be warm and supportive (Brown et al., 1993; Dishion et al., 1991; Lamborn et al., 1991). In other words, the winning combination is a blend of parental warmth and a style of control that is neither too permissive nor too restrictive; it is Baumrind's authoritative style of parenting—the same style that appears to foster healthy child development. This parenting style gives adolescents opportunities to strengthen their independent decision-making skills while still having the benefit of their parents' guidance and advice, and it represents a good "fit" between the adolescent's need for greater freedom and the family environment (Eccles et al., 1993).

It is when parents are rejecting and extremely strict, or rejecting and extremely lax, that teenagers are most likely to be psychologically distressed and get into trouble (Koestner et al., 1991; Lamborn et al., 1991). Then person/environment fit is poor. Of course, it is unfair to blame adolescent problems such as rebelliousness and delinquency entirely on "bad parenting." Instead, it is quite likely that responsible and level-headed adolescents "produce" parents who are loving and reasonable in setting rules and that this positive parenting further contributes to adolescent autonomy. By contrast, parents who are confronted with a teenager who is rude, hostile, and aggressive may become hostile in return and further compound their child's problems. As Box 14.1 reminds us, parents and adolescents exert reciprocal influence on each other during the adolescent transition.

The parent/adolescent relationship is truly a partnership, and its quality depends on what both parents and their children do to renegotiate their relationship. Apparently, most parents and their teenagers maintain positive feelings for each other while reworking their relationship so that it becomes more equal. As a result, most adolescents are able to achieve autonomy and also shift to a more mutual or friendlike attachment to their parents.

THE ADULT

So far we have concentrated on the child's experience of family life. Let's now ask how adults develop and change as they progress through stages of the family life cycle.

Establishing the Marriage

In our society, well over 90% of adults choose to marry, and most choose to marry individuals they love. Parents in colonial America exerted far more influence on when and even whom a child married (Nock, 1987). Even today, marriages in many cultures are not formed on the basis of love but are arranged by leaders of kin groups who are concerned with acquiring property, allies, and the rights to any children produced by a couple. As Corinne Nydegger (1986) puts it, "These matters are too important to be left to youngsters" (p. 111). So, in reading what follows, remember that our way of establishing families is not the only way.

Marrying is a life transition: It involves taking on a new role (as husband or wife) and adjusting to life as a couple. We rejoice at weddings and view newlyweds as supremely happy beings. Yet individuals who have just been struggling to achieve autonomy now find

BOX 14.1 The Growing Pains of Adolescents and Their Middle-Aged Parents

Does watching their children become physically and sexually mature and begin dating affect middle-aged parents? Might it cause parents to reflect on their own loss of youth? Could it even trigger a full-blown "midlife crisis" in which they face their own mortality, evaluate what they have done with their lives, and wonder what to do with themselves as their parenting responsibilities diminish? To find out, Susan Silverberg and Laurence Steinberg (1990) asked the parents of first-born 10- to 15-year-olds to complete scales measuring their self-esteem, satisfaction with life, level of psychological distress, and midlife identity concerns (for example, the extent to which they were reevaluating their life choices and wondering if their lives could have turned out better). The researchers also assessed the degree to which the adolescent of the house had already experienced the physical changes of puberty and become involved in mixed-sex peer activities such as dating.

The findings were quite interesting and point to links between how a youngster is coping with adolescence and how his or her parents are coping with middle age. Parents whose adolescents were highly involved in dating and other mixed-sex peer activities showed more intense midlife concerns, greater psychological distress, and lower life satisfaction than parents whose children were not as heavily into a teenage lifestyle. This was true mainly among parents who were not very invested in their jobs—possibly because their well-being hinged more on what was happening at home than on what was happening at work. Moreover, mothers of daughters were more likely to be experiencing midlife distress if their daughters had matured physically than if they had not. In short, adolescent development was associated with parental unrest. Other studies reinforce the same message: Parents of adolescents are especially likely to experience midlife distress if the parent/adolescent relationship is stormy or if their children are attempting to distance themselves emotionally from their parents (Julian, McKenry, & McKelvey, 1991; Silverberg & Steinberg, 1987).

Here, then, is another example of child effects within the family system. Or is it? If you have absorbed this chapter's message about reciprocal influences within the family, you may be asking yourself whether developmental changes in middle-aged parents couldn't be the cause rather than the effect of developmental changes in adolescents. As Silverberg and Steinberg (1990) note, parents who are psychologically distressed and preoccupied with their own midlife problems may have difficulty giving teenagers the emotional support they need: their sons and daughters may, as a result, seek close relationships elsewhere, perhaps through involvement in dating and peer-group activities.

In sum, teenagers who are experiencing the growing pains of adolescence tend to have parents who are experiencing the growing pains of midlife, but it is unclear who is influencing whom more strongly. Understanding development in its family context becomes more difficult when we appreciate that parents are developing persons too!

that they must compromise with their partners and adapt to each other's personalities and preferences. What happens to couples as they settle into their married lives? Ted Huston and his colleagues find that the honeymoon is short (Huston, McHale, & Crouter, 1986; Huston & Vangelisti, 1991; see also Johnson, Amoloza, & Booth, 1992; Kurdek, 1991a). In their longitudinal study of over 100 newlywed couples, these researchers discovered that several aspects of the marital relationship deteriorated from 3 months to 15 months after the marriage ceremony. For example, couples became less satisfied with the marriage and with their sex lives; they less frequently said "I love you," complimented each other, or disclosed their feelings to each other; and, although they spent only somewhat less time together, more of that time was devoted to getting tasks done and less to having fun or just talking. The couples whose relationships degenerated the most severely were those who had engaged in a great deal of mutual criticism and other negative behaviors from the start.

Huston and his colleagues did find most couples to be far more satisfied than dissatisfied with their relationships after the "honeymoon" was over. Still, their findings illustrate the strains involved in adapting to marriage. Blissfully happy relationships evolve into still happy but more ambivalent ones. Whether it is because couples begin to see "warts" that they didn't notice before marriage, or they stop trying to be on their best behavior, or they simply start to take each other for granted, marital relationships no sooner begin than they change in systematic ways.

New Parenthood and the Child-Rearing Family

Many couples have children within a few years of the marriage ceremony. How does the arrival of a child affect wife, husband, and the marital relationship? One popular view holds that having children draws a couple closer together; other people believe that children introduce additional strains into a relationship. Which is it?

Becoming a Parent

On average, new parenthood is a stressful life transition that involves both positive and negative changes. Most parents claim that having a child improves their lives—that their new "bundle of joy" offers them love, companionship, and enjoyment and makes them feel more self-fulfilled or grown up (Emery & Tuer, 1993; Hoffman & Manis, 1979). But let's analyze the situation more closely. Couples have ad-

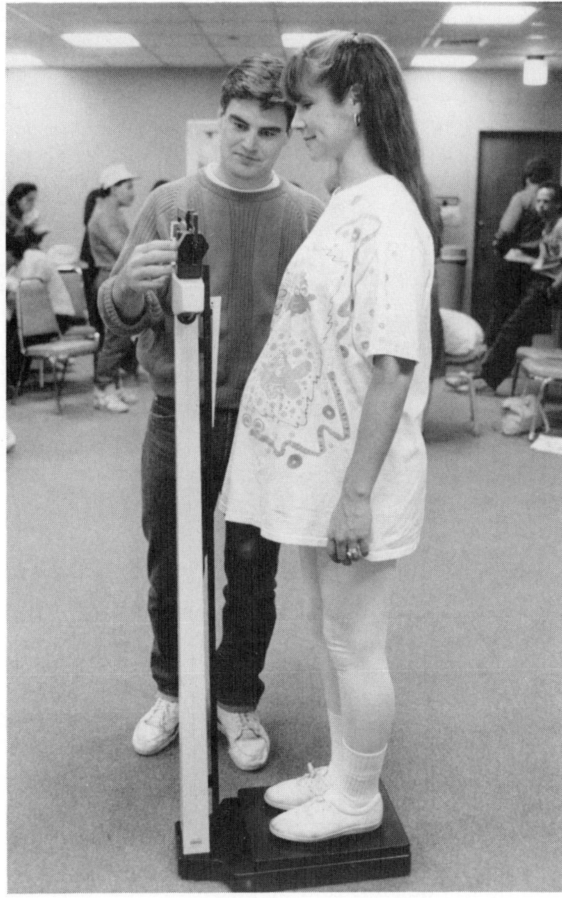

Pregnancy adds to the challenges faced by newlyweds, who are trying to adjust to life as a couple.

ded new roles (as mothers and fathers) to their existing roles (as spouses, workers, and so on) and often find juggling work and family responsibilities stressful. Not only do new parents have an incredible amount of new work to do as caregivers, but they lose sleep, worry about whether they are doing the right things for their baby, find that they have less time to themselves, and often feel a strain on their checking accounts as well. In addition, even egalitarian couples who before becoming parents used to share household tasks begin to divide their labors along more traditional lines. She specializes in the "feminine" role by becoming the primary caregiver and housekeeper, while he is likely to become even more involved in his "masculine" role as provider (Cowan et al., 1991; Emery & Tuer, 1993).

What are the effects of increased stress and of the tendency of husband and wife to establish somewhat separate lifestyles? Marital satisfaction typically declines after a baby is born (Belsky, Lang, & Rovine, 1985; Emery & Tuer, 1993). This decline is usually steeper for women than for men, primarily because the burden of child-care responsibilities typically falls more heavily on mothers and they may resent what they regard as an unfair division of labor (Hackel & Ruble, 1992; Suitor, 1991). It seems that mothers generally experience new parenthood more intensely than fathers do; they not only feel more of the stress, but they enjoy more of the pleasures (Wilkie & Ames, 1986).

However, there are wide individual differences in adjustment to new parenthood: Some new parents experience the transition as a bowl of cherries, others as the pits—as a full-blown crisis in their lives. What might make this life event easier or harder to manage? We can answer that question by focusing on the nature of the event itself, the individual who must cope with it, and the outside resources that the individual has available.

The *event* is the baby, of course. It is clear that infants who are difficult (for example, irritable and fussy) create more stresses and anxieties for parents than infants who are quiet, sociable, responsive, and otherwise easy to love (Sirignano & Lachman, 1985; Wilkie & Ames, 1986).

As for the *person*, some adults are better equipped than others to cope with stress and with conflicts between roles, and they find adaptive ways to restructure their social lives and work roles to accommodate a new baby (Myers-Walls, 1984). In addition, parents who are older, who conceive after the marriage ceremony, and who wait longer once they are married to have children have an easier time than parents who are young and possibly immature or who must adjust to each other at the same time they are adjusting to a new baby (Belsky, 1981). Similarly, parents who have realistic expectations about how parenthood will change their lives tend to adjust more easily than those who expect the experience to be more positive than it turns out to be (Kalmuss, Davidson, & Cushman, 1992). Finally, couples who both recall their own parents as warm and accepting are likely to experience a smoother transition to new parenthood and less marital discord than couples in which either spouse was raised in an aloof or rejecting manner—one of many signs that approaches to the challenges of parenthood are passed from one generation to the next (Belsky & Isabella, 1985; van IJzendoorn, 1992).

Finally, *outside resources* can make a great deal of difference to the new parent. Most important of all is spouse support: Things go considerably better for a new mother when she has a good relationship with her husband and when he shares the burden of childcare and housework responsibilities than when she has no partner or an unsupportive one (Tietjen & Bradley, 1985). Social support from friends and relatives can also help a new parent cope (Stemp, Turner, & Noh, 1986).

In sum, parents who have an easy baby to contend with, who possess positive personal qualities, and who receive reliable support from their spouses and other intimates are in the best position to cope adaptively with the stresses of new parenthood.

The Second Child Arrives

What happens to married couples as they have a second child (or even more) and as their children grow older? The stresses and strains of caring for a toddler are greater than those of caring for an infant (Crnic & Booth, 1991), and the arrival of a second child means additional stress on top of that (Kreppner, Paulsen, & Schuetze, 1982). Parents must not only devote time to the new baby but deal with their first-born child's normal anxieties about this change in lifestyle. Because the workload is heavier, fathers often become more involved with their children (Stewart et al., 1987). But what about the mother who is raising children as a single parent or whose husband is not highly involved in family life? She may find herself without a moment's rest as she tries to keep up with two active, curious, mobile, and needy youngsters.

In view of the strains that a second child creates, it is not surprising that marital satisfaction continues to decline slightly as additional children join the family (Glenn & McLanahan, 1982; Rollins & Feldman, 1970). Marital problems are sometimes particularly acute among low-income working mothers with preschool children — most likely because these mothers are simply overwhelmed with responsibilities (Schumm & Bugaighis, 1986). Again, let's bear in mind that most parents are more satisfied than dissatisfied with their marriages and take great pleasure in their relationships with their children. Still, children complicate their parents' lives by demanding everything from fresh diapers and close monitoring to chauffeuring services and college tuition. By claiming time and energy that might otherwise go into nourishing the marital relationship and by adding stresses to their parents' lives, children do seem to have a negative — though typically only slightly negative — effect on the marital relationship.

The Empty Nest

As children reach maturity, the family becomes a launching pad that fires adolescents and young adults off into the world to work and start their own families. The term **empty nest** describes the family after the departure of the last child. Clearly the emptying of the nest involves changes in role and lifestyle for parents, particularly for mothers who have centered their lives on child rearing. How are parents affected by this transition?

Quite positively, it seems! Just as the entry of children into the family causes modest decreases in marital satisfaction, the departure of the last child causes modest *increases* in marital satisfaction (Glenn, 1975; Lee, 1988; White & Edwards, 1990). After the nest empties, women often feel that their marriages are

Parents can find keeping up with young children draining.

more equitable and that their spouses are more accommodating to their needs (Menaghan, 1983; Suitor, 1991). They, more than their husbands, are likely to feel better about themselves and their lives in general when they no longer have children in the house (Harkins, 1978; McLanahan & Sorenson, 1985). Yet a *minority* of parents — both mothers and fathers — find this transition very disturbing. Women who experience the transition "off-time" — who feel that their departing children are not yet ready to leave — are likely to perceive the event negatively (Harkins, 1978). Fathers who have poor marriages but very close relationships with their children may also find this transition difficult (Lewis, Freneau, & Roberts, 1979). Still, hard as it may be for departing offspring to believe, children appear to cause more stress to their parents when they arrive in the family than when they leave.

Why do parents generally react positively to the empty nest? Possibly it is because they have fewer roles and responsibilities and therefore experience less stress and strain. If parenting is a little like beating one's head against a wall, there is surely some relief when one stops! But we need not view parenthood as self-abuse to understand that empty-nest couples have more time to focus on their marital relationship and to enjoy activities together, as well as more money to spend on themselves. Moreover, parents are likely to view the emptying of the nest as evidence that they have accomplished the ultimate goal of parenting. Expecting and wanting their children to launch adult lives, they take pleasure in having done their job well. Of course, most parents continue to enjoy a good deal of contact with their children after the nest empties, so it is not as if they are really losing this important relationship (White & Edwards, 1990).

To appreciate the positive side of the empty-nest transition, consider 44-year-old LaDonna, a housewife/mother who was constructively preparing for the departure of her last child. She had already taken a job, was considering going back to school to obtain a degree in counseling, and was very much looking forward to the next 20 years. She also expressed what Erik Erikson would call a sense of generativity: "I have five terrific daughters that didn't just happen. It took lots of time to mold, correct, love, and challenge them. . . . It's nice to see such rewarding results." For a parent like LaDonna, the emptying of the nest means the achievement of an important goal and an opportunity to set new goals. No wonder it is typically an easy transition to make.

In recent years an increasing number of adult children have been remaining in the nest or leaving and then "refilling" it, often because of unemployment, limited finances, divorce, or other difficulties in getting their adult lives on track (Ward & Spitze, 1992). Almost 25% of young adults aged 22 to 25 and almost 10% of adults over age 30 live with their parents (Ward, Logan, & Spitze, 1992). Some parents find having adult children in the house distressing (Aquilino, 1991; Umberson, 1992). However, most adapt well to this arrangement, even if they might prefer to see their children out building their own nests (Ward & Spitze, 1992).

Most grandparents prefer and adopt a companionate style of grandparenting.

Grandparenthood

What is your image of grandparents? Are they white-haired, jovial elders offering cookies and hugs? Actually, that image is a bit off the mark. Most adults become grandparents when they are middle-aged, not elderly, and when both Grandma and Grandpa are likely to be highly involved in careers and community activities. But grandparenting styles are diverse, as illustrated by the results of a national survey of grandparents of teenagers conducted by Andrew Cherlin and Frank Furstenberg (1986). These researchers determined the prevalence of three major styles of grandparenting:

1. *Remote.* Remote grandparents (29% of the sample) were symbolic figures seen only occasionally by their grandchildren. Primarily because they were geographically distant, they were emotionally distant as well.

2. *Companionate.* This was the most common style of grandparenting (55% of the sample). Companionate grandparents saw their grandchildren frequently and enjoyed sharing activities with them. They only rarely played a parental role, serving as companions rather than caregivers. Like most grandparents, they operated according to a "norm of noninterference," hesitating to meddle in the way their adult children were raising their children. They were quite happy to leave the child-care responsibilities to their children. As one put it, "You can love them and then say, 'Here, take them now, go on home'" (p. 55).

3. *Involved.* Finally, 16% of the grandparents assumed a parentlike role. Like companionate grandparents, they saw their grandchildren frequently and were playful with them. But, unlike companionate grandparents, they also often helped with child care, gave advice, and played other practical roles in their grandchildren's lives. Some involved grandparents were truly substitute parents who lived with and tended their grandchildren because their daughters were unmarried or recently divorced and worked outside the home.

We see, then, that grandparenting can take many forms but that most grandparents frequently see at least some of their grandchildren and prefer a role that is high in enjoyment and affection but low in responsibility. The vast majority of grandparents find the role very gratifying (Cherlin & Furstenberg, 1986). Remote grandparents are the least satisfied, largely because they wish they lived closer to their grandchildren and could see them more often. The grandparent role may have special significance for Native-American and African-American grandmothers, who often are intimately involved in the upbringing of grandchildren and are looked to as teachers of cultural ways and family traditions (Peterson, 1990; Weibel-Orlando, 1990). Most often, relationships between grandchildren and their maternal grandmothers are the closest (Matthews & Sprey, 1985; Roberto & Stroes, 1992). Traditional gender roles may help explain this, for women often serve as "kin-keepers" in the family, keeping up contacts and ensuring that close, affectionate relationships are maintained (Atkinson, Kivett, & Campbell, 1986; Cherlin & Furstenberg, 1986; Hagestad, 1985).

An important feature of the grandparent role is that it is not entirely voluntary. Adults can decide when to become parents, but they become grandparents, ready or not, when their children have babies. Some women become grandparents in their 30s or even late 20s because their teenage daughters have children. These women often become primary caregivers for their grandchildren and tend to be far less enthusiastic about the role than those who become grandmothers "on time" (Burton & Dilworth-Anderson, 1991; Hagestad & Burton, 1986).

In addition, grandparents' roles can change dramatically if their children's lives change. As Gunhild Hagestad (1985) puts it, grandparents are "the family national guard" (p. 46); they are on alert and come to the rescue when there is a crisis in the family. When a teenage daughter becomes pregnant, grandmother and grandfather may become key parent figures for the baby (Oyserman, Radin, & Benn, 1993). Grandparents may also be drawn into a more highly involved role when a child divorces (Cherlin & Furstenberg, 1986; Clingempeel et al., 1992). Yet if their own child does not obtain custody, grandparents' access to their grandchildren may be reduced or even cut off, causing them much anguish.

In short, grandparenthood is an important role in the lives of middle-aged and elderly adults. It can take a remote, companionate, or involved form, depending on such factors as the grandparents' preferences, the geographical distance between grandparents and grandchildren, and changes in the lives of grandchildren and their parents. And how do grandchildren feel? They typically view their grandparents as important and influential figures in their lives (Furman & Buhrmester, 1985a; Roberto & Stroes, 1992), and they benefit when they have frequent contact with these family elders (Falbo, 1991; Wilson, 1986). Indeed, all three generations seem to benefit from maintaining close ties.

Changing Family Relationships during Adulthood

All relationships develop and change with time. Let's see now what becomes of relationships between spouses, siblings, and parents and their children during the adult years.

The Marital Relationship

What have you concluded about changes in marital relationships over the family life cycle? As we've seen, marital satisfaction, although generally high for most couples throughout their lives together, dips somewhat after the honeymoon period is over, dips still lower in the new-parenthood phase, continues to drop as new children are added to the family, and recovers only when the children leave the nest. These are precisely the trends (see Figure 14.4) discovered by Boyd Rollins and Harold Feldman (1970) when they surveyed adults in the eight phases of the family life cycle about their marital happiness (see also Emery & Tuer, 1993; Levenson, Carstensen, & Gottman, 1993; White & Edwards, 1990). Moreover, Figure 14.4 reinforces another point we have been making: Women, because they have traditionally been more involved than men in rearing children, tend to be more strongly affected by family life transitions — for good or for bad — than men are.

As we've also seen, these average trends fit some families much better than others, depending on such factors as the difficulty of a child's temperament and the extent to which both parents contribute to child rearing. Moreover, the trends are quite weak: Knowing what stage of the family life cycle an adult is in does not allow us to predict very accurately how satisfied that person is with marriage. To do that, we have to consider many additional factors. For example, couples who are happy early in their marriage tend to be happy later, and young couples who are miserable tend to remain that way; marital satisfaction, like many personality traits, tends to be quite stable over the years (Johnson et al., 1992). In addition, happily married people are more likely than unhappily married people to have positive personality traits such as self-confidence, social maturity, and an ability to nurture others (Skolnick, 1981). Moreover, their personalities are *similar* and are likely to remain similar over the years as each partner reinforces in the other the traits that brought them together in the first place (Caspi, Herbener, & Ozer, 1992). It is when "opposites attract" and find their personalities clashing day after day that marital problems tend to arise (Kurdek, 1991a; Russell & Wells, 1991). Finally, happily married partners genuinely like each other and enjoy each other's company; they do not stay together just because it is convenient, because they believe marriage should be a lifelong commitment, or because they think it is "best for the children" (Lauer & Lauer, 1986; Skolnick, 1981).

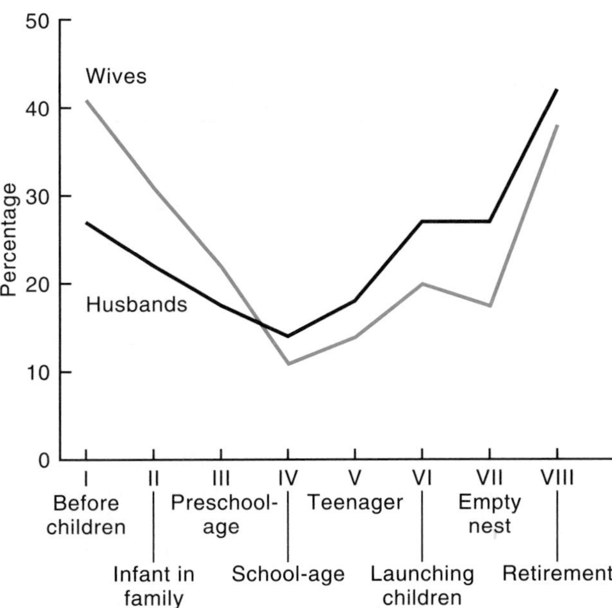

FIGURE 14.4 Percentages of wives and husbands at different stages of the family life cycle who say their marriage is going well "all the time," as opposed to "most of the time" (the most frequent answer) or less often. Marriages tend to be most blissful before children arrive and after they leave, especially for women. (From Rollins & Feldman, 1970.)

Without question, the marital relationship is centrally important to adult development. Indeed, both adults and children seem to thrive when a couple is able to maintain a close and committed partnership over the years (Biller, 1993). And, as we'll see shortly, adults and children alike suffer when a marriage dissolves.

Sibling Relationships

How do the relationships between brothers and sisters change once siblings no longer live together in the same house and have launched their own separate lives? Starting in adolescence, both closeness and conflict between siblings diminish, so that these relationships become less intense and more equal (Buhrmester & Furman, 1990). Contact between siblings then normally decreases as they marry, develop their own friendship networks, and often move away from their hometowns (Goetting, 1986). Victor Cicirelli (1982) finds that adult siblings typically see each other several times a year and communicate through phone calls or letters about how they are getting along. Few of them discuss intimate problems with each other or help each other much, except in times of crisis.

Yet the same ambivalence that characterizes sibling relationships during childhood seems to carry over into adulthood (Cicirelli, 1991). A great deal of caring and emotional closeness persists, despite infrequent contact, and siblings often grow even closer in old age (Cicirelli, 1991). In Cicirelli's 1982 survey, 68% of middle-aged adults and fully 83% of elderly adults described their relationships with siblings as either "close" or "extremely close." The potential for sibling rivalry persists, however. Conflict is far less frequent than during childhood, but old rivalries can and do flare up again during adulthood.

What determines whether these relationships are close or conflictual? Helgola Ross and Joel Milgram (1982) interviewed adults ranging in age from 22 to 93 and discovered that the quality of sibling relationships in adulthood depends on the kinds of life events siblings experience and on their closeness earlier in life. Siblings typically became closer if one moved geographically nearer to the other, became sick, lost a spouse, or divorced. Relationships sometimes deteriorated when one sibling moved away or got married, or when differences between siblings in educational or employment status or values became large. It also turned out that siblings who had enjoyed a close relationship during childhood were likely to be drawn even closer after significant life events such as a parent's illness or death, whereas siblings who had had poor relationships during childhood were likely to become even more rivalrous in response to the same life events (see also Lerner et al., 1991).

The sibling relationship is typically the longest-lasting relationship we have, linking us to individuals who share many of our genes and experiences (Cicirelli, 1991). It is a relationship that can be very close, very tense and conflictual, or, for many people, some of both. When it remains close, older adults are likely to feel better about themselves and their lives (Cicirelli, 1989).

Relationships between the Generations

The different generations in most families are in close contact and enjoy affectionate give-and-take relationships. As young adults leave the nest, they don't sever ties with their parents; instead, they and their parents jointly negotiate a new relationship, often a more intimate one in which they move beyond playing out their roles as "child" and "parent" (Greene & Boxer, 1986; Richards, Bengtson, & Miller, 1989; Rossi & Rossi, 1990). Young adults may begin to see their parents as individuals in their own right rather than merely as parent figures (White, Speisman, & Costos, 1983). Married daughters are especially likely to establish new and more mutual relationships with their mothers.

> I am understanding her now more than I ever did before. I have started to understand that I had to stop blaming her for everything in my life. I felt she had been a lousy parent. Now, I'm more understanding that my mother is a person and that

she has her own problems and her own life. . . . I accepted her as a mother—but she actually is a human being . . . [White et al., 1983, p. 73].

What happens to the parent/child relationship when children become middle-aged and their parents become elderly? In Chapter 13 we challenged the myth that most elderly people are socially isolated and lonely. In large part, they are not lonely because they and their adult children typically continue to care about, socialize with, and help one another late in life (Bengtson et al., 1990; Field et al., 1993). According to national surveys, 80% of people over 65 have living children, about half either live with a child (18%) or live within 10 minutes of at least one child (34%), and about three-fourths see at least one child at least once a week (Shanas, 1980; see also Taeuber, 1990). Aging mothers enjoy closer relations and more contact with their families than aging fathers do (Field et al., 1993; Rossi & Rossi, 1990). And it seems that African-American and Hispanic-American elders often enjoy more supportive relationships with their families than non-Hispanic whites do (Bengtson et al., 1990; Burton & Dilworth-Anderson, 1991; Markides, Liang, & Jackson, 1990). So much for the myth that today's families have abandoned the elderly.

What these findings indicate is that the predominant family form in the United States is neither the isolated nuclear family nor the extended family household; instead, it is what has been called the **modified extended family**—an arrangement in which nuclear families live in their own separate households but have close ties and frequent communication and interaction with their other kin (Litwak, 1960). Most elderly people in our society prefer just this pattern. They do not want to have to live with their children when their health fails (Brody, Johnsen, & Fulcomer, 1984; Okraku, 1987).

Relationships between the generations are not only close and affectionate, but they are generally quite equitable as well. That is, each generation gives something and each generation receives something in return. Among Mexican-American clans, for example, elders receive a great deal of advice and practical help about everything from personal problems to home repairs from their middle-aged children, *and* their middle-aged children turn to them for advice and help as well (Markides, Boldt, & Ray, 1986; Markides et al., 1990). Similarly, different generations within the family mutually influence each other. Parents transmit their values to their children, and adult children also shape their parents' attitudes and values (Axinn & Thornton, 1993; Rossi & Rossi, 1990). Thus relationships within the family system continue to be reciprocally influential throughout the life span.

This means that most aging families do not experience what has been called **role reversal**—a switching of roles late in life such that the parent becomes the needy, dependent one and the child becomes the caregiver (Brody, 1990). However, if aging parents develop serious physical or mental problems, middle-aged adults often *are* called upon to care for them, and the parent/child relationship may then become less reciprocal. Elaine Brody (1985, 1990) uses the term **"middle generation squeeze"** (others call it the "sandwich generation" phenomenon) to describe what middle-aged adults sometimes experience when they are trapped by heavy demands from both the younger and the older generations simultaneously. Imagine that you are a 47-year-old woman immersed in your career, marriage, and social life. You could be forced to cope at the very same time with menopause, a teenage son in the house, a young-adult daughter who needs money for college or help in launching or caring for her own family—*and* a widowed mother who has had a stroke and cannot manage her own home anymore. That is a middle generation squeeze! Box 14.2 demonstrates that middle-aged adults who must foster their children's development while tending to their own development *and* caring for aging parents sometimes find their burdens quite overwhelming.

In sum, generations within a family maintain close relationships throughout adulthood, mutually supporting and influencing each other. Yet the quality of parent/child relationships often changes over the life span. The child who is dependent on parents becomes the adult who can be truly interdependent with them—and in some cases ultimately becomes the person on whom aging parents must depend.

DIVERSITY IN FAMILY LIFE

Useful as it is, the concept of a family life cycle simply does not capture the diversity of adult lifestyles and family experiences (Rowland, 1991). Many of today's adults do not progress in a neat and orderly way through the stages of the traditional family life cycle—marrying, having their children, watching them leave the nest, and so on. A small number never marry; a larger number never have children; and a still larger number move in and out of wedded life by marrying, divorcing, and remarrying. So, let's examine some of these variations in family life.

Singles

Single adults are often pictured as being young and leading an active social life. Because adults are postponing marriage, there is indeed a growing number of young, single adults. Yet it is nearly impossible to describe the "typical" single adult, for this category also includes middle-aged and elderly people who have experienced divorce or the death of a spouse, as well as adults who have never married.

BOX 14.2 The Sandwich Generation: Adults Who Care for Aging Parents

More and more adults with children are finding themselves also caring for their aging parents, "sandwiched" between the younger and older generations and experiencing middle generation squeeze (Brody, 1990). Although spouses and siblings contribute to the care of frail elders, most caregivers are daughters in their 40s and 50s playing out their roles as "kin-keepers"—women whose nests are no sooner emptied of children than they are refilled with aging parents. Daughters are about three times more likely than sons to provide assistance to aging parents (Dwyer & Coward, 1991).

As you might imagine, these caregivers experience many strains: emotional, physical, and financial (Brody, 1990). A woman who is almost wholly responsible for a dependent elder often feels angry and resentful because she has no time for herself and little freedom to pursue her own goals. In addition, she may become socially isolated or experience strain in her other relationships because she has little energy left to give to her husband, employer, or children. Some women are forced to quit their jobs or reduce their work hours in order to cope; some become clinically depressed. Stresses will be especially severe if the elderly parent is mentally impaired and not only has difficulties with memory and judgment but also engages in disruptive and socially inappropriate behavior (Deimling & Bass, 1986) or if the daughter is unmarried and therefore does not have a husband to lean on for practical and emotional support (Brody et al., 1992).

Despite the burdens they experience, most middle-aged caregivers still feel guilty about not doing enough for their parents (Brody, 1985)! Clearly,

adult children today, like those of the past, feel a strong sense of responsibility to care for their ailing parents (Brody et al., 1984; Okraku, 1987; Wolfson et al., 1993). Neither adult children nor aging parents want to have to live together or want to see younger generations overburdened with bills and responsibilities. Yet all generations agree that aging parents deserve emotional support and practical aid. Again, then, we can abandon the myth that today's elderly people are abandoned by their families.

But what really motivates adult children to help? In an interesting attempt to understand caregivers' motives, Victor Cicirelli (1993) assessed whether daughters helped their aging mothers out of love or out of duty. Both daughters highly motivated to help based on a strong attachment to their mothers ("I feel lonely when I don't see my mother often") and daughters motivated by a sense of obligation ("I feel that I should do my part in helping") spent more time helping than women whose motivations to help were weaker. However, those who helped out of love experienced helping as far less stressful and burdensome than those who helped mainly out of a sense of duty. In short, the caregivers most likely to experience psychological distress are those who have highly needy parents, who are not very close to them, and who help only because they feel they must rather than because they love and cherish their parents. These individuals need support and relief from their burden if they are to continue to provide the bulk of the emotional support and care that physically and mentally impaired elders receive (Brody, 1990; Knight, Lutzky, & Macofsky-Urban, 1993).

The problem of caring for an increasingly large number of aging citizens is a worldwide problem. In many other societies, children's responsibilities are much greater than they are in Western nations. After all, aging adults in our society have access to government programs such as Social Security and Medicare, which relieve some of the pressure on children to support aging parents financially. Also, strong norms of independence and individualism make older adults want to live independently and avoid burdening their children. In many Asian societies, however, it would be unthinkable for an aging parent *not* to live with an adult child (Keith, 1992). Among the !Kung of Botswana, an aging adult would likely have no old age at all, much less a satisfying one, without children, for children are the only real source of support (Draper & Buchanan, 1992). So, as the "graying" of the world's population continues, more and more societies have to find ways to help families provide for their oldest members over the years.

It *is* typical to start adulthood as a single person; a majority of adults in the 18-to-29 age range are unmarried (Sweet & Bumpass, 1987). Although young singles are busy preparing for their careers or getting them off the ground, they are also busy building social networks. They are likely to have a wider circle of friends than they will have in later years (Carstensen, 1992). For women, though not for men, postponing marriage and childbearing is likely to pay off in later career success, for it means staying in school longer (Haggstrom, Kanouse, & Morrison, 1986).

Many young singles today live with a romantic partner without being married. Such **cohabitation** is more common than it used to be; about 10% of single adults in their 20s and early 30s cohabitate at present (Sweet & Bumpass, 1987), and an even greater percentage do so at some time during their early adult years (Spanier, 1983). Cohabitation is typically not a substitute for marriage; instead, it is usually a temporary arrangement, sometimes seen as a test of compatibility, that leads either to marriage or to a breakup (Newcomb, 1979; Tanfer, 1987).

It makes sense to think that couples who live together before marrying would have more opportunity than those who do not to determine whether they are truly compatible. Yet couples who live together and then marry seem to be *more* dissatisfied with their marriages (Thomson & Colella, 1992) and *more* likely to divorce (DeMaris & Rao, 1992) than couples who do not live together before marrying. This is especially true of people who have had repeated experiences of living with someone (DeMaris & MacDonald, 1993). Why is this? It is unlikely that the experience of cohabitation itself is responsible (Booth & Johnson, 1988). Instead, it seems that the kinds of people who choose to live together may be somewhat more susceptible to marital problems and less committed to marriage than the kinds of people who do not. They tend, for example, to be less religious, less conventional in their family attitudes, and less committed to the idea of marriage as a permanent arrangement (DeMaris & MacDonald, 1993; Newcomb, 1979). Moreover, cohabiting couples who marry are less similar in age, previous marital status, race, and occupational level than couples who do not live together before marriage (Gwartney-Gibbs, 1986). Possibly, then, their dissimilarities make achieving a harmonious marriage more difficult than it otherwise might be. All in all, there is no support for the notion that cohabitation enables people to select their mates more wisely.

What of the adults who never marry? How do they fare later in adulthood, when most of their peers are married? Not badly at all, it seems, despite stereotypes suggesting that they are miserably lonely and maladjusted. They often manage to make up for their lack of spouse and children by forming close bonds with siblings, friends, or younger adults who become like sons or daughters to them (Rubinstein et al., 1991). They are not a particularly lonely group (Stull & Scarisbrick-Hauser, 1989). As "old-old" people in their 80s and 90s, never-marrieds sometimes do lack relatives who can assist or care for them (Johnson & Troll, 1992). Single adults also tend to have a lower overall sense of well-being or happiness than married adults do (Glenn & Weaver, 1988). Yet it is divorced rather than single adults who tend to be the least happy of all, especially if they live alone (Kurdek, 1991b).

The category of single adults also includes most gay men and lesbian women. Although a minority of homosexual adults marry at some point (Bell & Weinberg, 1978), most remain single throughout their lives and so do not experience the events of the family life cycle. Those gay and lesbian adults who live as couples are likely to have more egalitarian relationships than married couples do; rather than following traditional gender stereotypes, partners tend to work out a division of labor, through trial and error, based on who is especially talented at what or who hates doing what (Blumstein & Schwartz, 1983). Overall, though, gay and lesbian couples seem to be far more similar to heterosexual couples than they are different. Their relationships evolve through the same stages of development, are satisfying or dissatisfying for the same reasons, and are usually just as fulfilling as those of married or cohabiting heterosexuals (Kurdek, 1991a; Kurdek & Schmitt, 1986).

Childless Married Couples

Married couples who remain childless also do not experience all the usual stages of the family life cycle. In 1992, 11% of 40- to 44-year-old women who had married had no children (U.S. Bureau of the Census, 1993). Many childless couples want children but cannot have them, but a growing number of adults, especially highly educated adults with high-status occupations, voluntarily decide to delay having children or avoid having any at all (Kiernan, 1989). A few decades ago, married couples who did not have children were often regarded as selfish or even psychologically disturbed. Although some of that stigma persists, it has become increasingly acceptable to choose a childless (or, as some childless couples prefer to put it, "childfree") life (Veroff, Douvan, & Kulka, 1981).

How are childless couples faring while their peers are having, raising, and launching children? Generally, quite well. Their marital satisfaction is somewhat higher than that of couples with children during the child-rearing years (Emery & Tuer, 1993; Glenn & McLanahan, 1982). And middle-aged and elderly childless couples seem to be no less satisfied with their lives than parents whose children have left the nest (Glenn & McLanahan, 1981; Rempel, 1985). However, elderly women who are childless *and* widowed may find themselves without anyone to help them if they develop health problems (Johnson & Troll, 1992). It seems, then, that childless couples derive a good deal of satisfaction from their marriages but may suffer from a lack of social support very late in life after those marriages end.

Families Experiencing Divorce

Orderly progress through the family life cycle is disrupted when a couple divorces. Divorce is *not* just one life event; rather, it is a series of stressful experiences for the entire family that begins with marital conflict before the divorce and includes a whole complex of life changes afterward. As Mavis Hetherington and Kathleen Camara (1984) see it, families must often cope with "the diminution of financial resources, changes in residence, assumption of new roles and responsibilities, establishment of new patterns of intrafamilial interaction, reorganization of routines and schedules, and eventually the introduction of new relationships into the existing family" (p. 398).

Why do people divorce? What effects does divorce typically have on family members? And how can we explain the fact that some adults and children eventually thrive after a divorce whereas others experience persisting problems?

Before the Divorce

We don't know a lot about the processes within the family that ultimately cause couples to divorce rather than stay together despite dissatisfactions. However, Gay Kitson and her colleagues (1985) have pieced together a portrait of the couples at highest risk for divorce. Generally they are young adults, in their 20s and 30s, who have been married for an average of about seven years and often have young children. They are especially likely to divorce if they married as teenagers, had a short courtship, or conceived a child before marrying—all factors that might suggest an unreadiness for marriage and unusually high financial and psychological stress accompanying new parenthood. Finally, they are more likely to be low in socioeconomic status than high. This profile cannot take us far, however, because all kinds of couples are divorcing today.

Contrary to the notion that today's couples don't really give their marriages a chance to work, research suggests that most divorcing couples experience a few years of marital distress and often try out separations before they make the final decision to divorce (Gottman & Levenson, 1992; Kitson et al., 1985). Although the stated reasons for divorcing are varied, they are no longer restricted to severe problems such as nonsupport, alcoholism, or abuse (Gigy & Kelly, 1992). Instead, couples today typically divorce because they feel their marriages are lacking in communication, emotional fulfillment, or compatibility (see Table 14.3). Wives tend to have longer lists of complaints than their husbands do and often have more to do with initiating the breakup (Gigy & Kelly, 1992; Gray & Silver, 1990).

After the Divorce: Crisis and Reorganization

Most families going through a divorce experience it as a genuine *crisis*—a period of considerable disruption that often lasts for a year or more (Booth & Amato, 1991; Hetherington, 1981, 1989; Hetherington, Cox, & Cox, 1982; Kitson & Morgan, 1990). Typically, both spouses experience emotional as well as practical difficulties. The wife, who usually obtains custody of any children, is likely to be angry, depressed, moody, lonely, and otherwise distressed, although often relieved as well. The husband is also likely to be distressed, particularly if he did not want the divorce and feels shut off from his children. Both individuals must manage the difficult task of revising their identities as single rather than married people. They may both feel socially isolated from former friends and unsure of themselves as they attempt to establish new romantic relationships. Divorced women with children are likely to face the added problem of getting by with less money—about half of the family income they had before, on average (Smock, 1993). Their lives will be especially difficult if they must move to a lower-income neighborhood and try to work and raise young children singlehandedly (Kitson & Morgan, 1990). Because of all these stresses, divorced

TABLE 14.3 Top ten reasons checked by divorcing men and women in California for their divorce. Respondents were given a checklist with 27 items. Notice that incompatibility and lack of emotional fulfillment are strong themes and that more women than men voiced several of these complaints.

Reasons for Divorce Checklist Responses	*Percentage of Males (N = 189)*	*Percentage of Females (N = 212)*
1. Gradual growing apart, losing sense of closeness	79	78
2. Not feeling loved and appreciated by spouse	60	73
3. Sexual intimacy problems	65	64
4. Serious differences in lifestyle or values	57	63
5. Spouse not able/willing to meet my major needs	48	64
6. Frequently feel put down or belittled by spouse	37	59
7. Emotional problems of spouse	44	52
8. Conflict regarding spending and handling of money	44	50
9. Severe and intense conflict; frequent fighting	35	44
10. Problems and conflicts with roles (i.e., divisions of responsibility for household jobs or other chores outside the house)	33	47

SOURCE: Adapted from Gigy & Kelly, 1992.

adults are at high risk for depression, physical health problems, and even death (Stroebe & Stroebe, 1986).

As you might suspect, psychologically distressed adults do not make the best of parents. Moreover, children going through a divorce do not make the best of children, for they are suffering too. They are often angry, fearful, depressed, and guilty, especially if they are preschoolers who fear that they are somehow responsible for what happened (Hetherington, 1981). They are also likely to be whiney and dependent, disobedient, and downright disrespectful. A vicious circle results, in which the child's behavior problems and the parent's ineffective parenting styles feed on each other.

Mavis Hetherington and her associates (1982) find that custodial mothers, overburdened by responsibilities and by their own emotional reactions to the divorce, often become edgy, impatient, and insensitive to their children's needs. In terms of the dimensions of child rearing we have discussed, they become less warm and loving, and they also become more inconsistent in their discipline, sometimes trying to seize control of their children with a heavy-handed, or restrictive, style of parenting but more often failing to carry through in enforcing rules and making few demands that their children behave maturely. Noncustodial fathers, meanwhile, are likely to be overpermissive, indulging their children during visits. This is not the formula for producing well-adjusted, competent children. The behavior problems that children display undoubtedly make effective parenting difficult, but a deterioration in parenting style clearly aggravates these behavior problems.

Mother/child relations, particularly between mothers and sons, are likely to be especially poor about a year after the divorce (Hetherington et al., 1982). For children this breakdown in family functioning is likely to lead not only to behavior problems at home but also to strained relations with peers and academic problems and adjustment difficulties at school (Allison & Furstenberg, 1989; Amato & Keith, 1991b; Hetherington et al., 1982). Although older children and adolescents are in a better position to understand the reasons for their parents' divorce, they seem to suffer no less than young children (Amato, 1993; Hetherington, Clingempeel, & Associates, 1992).

How long do these negative consequences last? Hetherington and her colleagues find that families begin to pull themselves back together about two years after the divorce. Girls normally recover from their social and emotional disturbances by the end of the second year, to the point that they are quite indistinguishable from girls in intact families (Hetherington et al., 1982). Boys improve dramatically during this same period, but many of them continue to show signs of emotional distress and problems in their relationships with parents, siblings, teachers, and peers, even six years after the divorce (Hetherington, 1989).

Indeed, it has become clear that, even after the crisis phase has passed, divorce can leave a residue of negative effects that lasts for years (Amato & Keith, 1991b; Wallerstein, 1991). Judith Wallerstein (1984, 1987; Wallerstein & Blakeslee, 1989), for example, finds that adolescents who are 10 years away from their parents' divorce recall few of the events that transpired when they were preschoolers but often continue to be negative about what the divorce has done to their lives and harbor fantasies that their parents will reconcile. One girl was quite blunt: "I wish my stepfather would go back to his first wife, I wish my stepmother would go back to her first husband, and I would like my mom and dad to get together again" (Wallerstein, 1984, p. 452). Young adults who were school-aged children or adolescents when their parents divorced had painful memories of the divorce and often feared that they would be unable to find happiness in marriage. There may well be some basis for that fear, for adults whose parents divorced are more likely than adults from intact families to experience an unhappy marriage and a divorce themselves (Amato & Keith, 1991a).

In sum, divorce is a difficult experience for all involved. Problems reach crisis proportions about a year after the divorce. Although most of them disappear over the next couple of years, some children have more persistent problems and are still struggling with painful feelings many years later.

But now let's offset this gloomy picture of the typical divorce with more encouraging messages. In the first place, a conflict-ridden two-parent family is clearly more detrimental to a child's development than a stable single-parent family. Indeed, many of the behavior problems that children display after a divorce are actually evident well *before* the divorce and may be related to long-standing family conflict rather than to the divorce itself (Block, Block, & Gjerde, 1986; Cherlin et al., 1991). Take away the marital conflict and the breakdown in parenting often associated with divorce and the experience need not be damaging (Amato, 1993). Indeed, children may *benefit* if the ending of a stormy marriage ultimately reduces the stress they experience and enables either or both parents to be more sensitive and responsive to their needs (Barber & Eccles, 1992; Hetherington, 1989). So much for "staying together for the good of the children."

Moreover, not all families experience all the difficulties we have described. Indeed, some adults and children manage this transition quite well and grow psychologically as a result of it (Bursik, 1991; Hetherington, 1989). What factors, then, might facilitate a positive adjustment to divorce? Box 14.3 addresses this question.

BOX 14.3 "Good" and "Bad" Divorces: Factors Influencing Adjustment

Some adults and children thrive after a divorce, whereas others suffer many negative and long-lasting effects. Of course, an individual's temperament and coping skills are important influences on how well he or she adjusts (Hetherington, 1989). However, other factors can make the individual's task easier:

1. *Adequate financial support.* Families fare better after a divorce if they have adequate finances (Menaghan & Lieberman, 1986; Simons et al., 1993). Adjustment may be more difficult for mother-headed families that fall into poverty and must struggle to survive. Recent efforts to get more noncustodial parents to pay child support may help the cause.

2. *Adequate parenting by the custodial parent.* The custodial parent obviously plays a critical role in what happens to the family. If she or he can continue to be warm, authoritative, and consistent, children are far less likely to experience problems (Hetherington et al., 1992; Kline et al., 1989). It is difficult to be an effective parent when one is depressed and under stress, but parents who understand the stakes involved may be more able to give their children the love and guidance they need.

3. *Emotional support from the noncustodial parent.* If parents continue to squabble after the divorce and are hostile toward each other, both will be upset, the custodial parent's parenting is likely to suffer, and children will feel torn in their loyalties and experience behavior problems (Amato, 1993). Children also suffer when they lose contact with their noncustodial parent. Unfortunately, about a third of children living with their mothers lose all contact with their fathers (Seltzer & Bianchi, 1988). By contrast, regular contact with *supportive* fathers helps children (particularly sons) make a positive adjustment to life in a single-parent home (Amato, 1993; Camara & Resnick, 1988). Ideally, then, children should be able to maintain affectionate ties with both parents and should be protected from any continuing conflict between parents. It may not be as important that parents obtain joint custody as that they both maintain high-quality relationships with their children (Emery & Tuer, 1993; Kline et al., 1989).

4. *Additional social support.* Divorcing adults are less depressed if they have close confidants (Menaghan & Lieberman, 1986). Children also benefit from having close friends to give them social support (Lustig, Wolchik, & Braver, 1992), as well as from participating in peer-support programs in which they and other children of divorce can share their feelings, correct their misconceptions, and learn positive coping skills (Grych & Fincham, 1992; Pedro-Carroll & Cowen, 1985). Adolescents in single-parent homes appear to be less likely to engage in delinquent behavior if a second adult (a grandmother, for example) lives in the home than if one parent bears the sole responsibility for child rearing and supervision (Dornbusch et al., 1985). In short, friends, relatives, peers, school personnel, and other sources of social support outside the family can do much to help families adjust to divorce.

5. *A minimum of additional stressors.* Generally, families respond most positively to divorce if additional disruptions are kept to a minimum—for example, if parents do not have to move, go through court hearings, get new jobs, cope with the loss of their children, and so on (Buehler et al., 1985–1986). Obviously it is easier to deal with a couple of changes than a mountain of stressors. Although families cannot always control events, they can perhaps strive to keep their lives as simple as possible.

Here, then, we have the first steps in the path toward a positive divorce experience—as well as a better understanding of why divorce is more disruptive for some families than others. As Paul Amato (1993) concludes, adjustment to divorce will depend on the "total configuration" of stressors the individual faces and resources he or she has available to aid in coping, including both personal strengths (such as good coping skills) and social supports. This research also serves as still another good example of how the family is a social system embedded in larger social systems. Mother, father, and children will all influence one another's adjustment to divorce, and the family's experience will also depend on its interactions with the surrounding world.

Remarriage and Reconstituted Families

Within three to five years of a divorce, about 75% of single-parent families will experience yet another major change when a parent remarries and the children acquire a stepparent—and sometimes new siblings as well (Hetherington, 1989). Remarriage shortly after divorce contributes further to a "pile-up" of stressors (Fine & Schwebel, 1991; Hill, 1986). And, although most remarried adults are satisfied with their second marriages initially, second marriages are somewhat more likely to end in divorce than first marriages (Booth & Edwards, 1992). Imagine, then, the stresses for adults and children who find themselves in a recurring cycle of marriage, marital conflict, divorce, single status, and remarriage (see Brody, Neubaum, & Forehand, 1988).

How do children fare when their custodial parents remarry? At first there is a period of conflict and disruption as new family roles and relationships are ironed out (Hetherington, 1989; Hetherington et al., 1992). Interestingly, although boys often suffer more than girls when they live with a single-parent mother in the aftermath of divorce, they benefit more than girls when they gain a stepfather. They enjoy higher self-esteem, are less anxious and angry, and overcome most of the adjustment problems they displayed before their mothers remarried (Clingempeel, Ievoli, & Brand, 1984; Hetherington, 1989; Zaslow, 1989). Less is known about the transition from a father-headed single-parent home to a two-parent family with a stepmother, but it appears that this transition is also more difficult for girls, especially if their biological mothers maintain frequent contact with them (Clingempeel & Segal, 1986). Girls, it seems, are often so closely allied with their mothers that they are bothered by either a stepfather competing for their mother's attention or a stepmother attempting to play a substitute-mother role. In sum, the transition from a single-parent family to a reconstituted family requires adjustment and is likely to be more disruptive for girls than for boys.

Even this quick examination of the diverse experiences of single adults, married but childless adults, and divorced and remarried adults should convince us that it is difficult indeed to generalize about the American family. We can gain many insights by tracing the progression of developing human beings through the stages of the traditional family life cycle, but we must also recognize that an increasing number of individuals depart in some way or another from that pattern. Perhaps we should stop talking about *the* family life cycle and start talking about many such cycles (Rowland, 1991).

APPLICATIONS: CONFRONTING THE PROBLEM OF FAMILY VIOLENCE

Just as family relationships can be our greatest source of nurturance and support, they can be our greatest source of anguish. Nowhere is this more obvious than in cases of family violence. Child abuse is perhaps the most visible form of family violence. Every day, infants, children, and adolescents are burned, bruised, beaten, starved, suffocated, sexually abused, or otherwise mistreated by their caretakers. In a national sample of families in the United States, 11% of children had reportedly been kicked, bitten, hit, hit with an object, beaten up, burned, or threatened or attacked with a knife or gun by a parent in the past year (Wolfner & Gelles, 1993). Other children are victims of psychological maltreatment—rejected, verbally abused, and even terrorized by their parents (Emery, 1989; Hart & Brassard, 1987). Still others are neglected and deprived of the basic care and stimulation they need to develop normally.

Abuse of children by their caregivers is only one form of family violence. In all possible relationships within the family, the potential for violence exists. Children and adolescents batter, and in rare cases kill, their parents (Agnew & Huguley, 1989); siblings abuse one another in numerous ways (Straus, 1980; Wiehe, 1990); and spouse abuse, rampant in our society, appears to be the most common form of family violence worldwide. An analysis of family violence in 90 nonindustrial societies by David Levinson (1989) reveals that wife beating occurs in 85% of them; in almost half of these societies it occurs in most or all households, suggesting that it is an accepted part of family

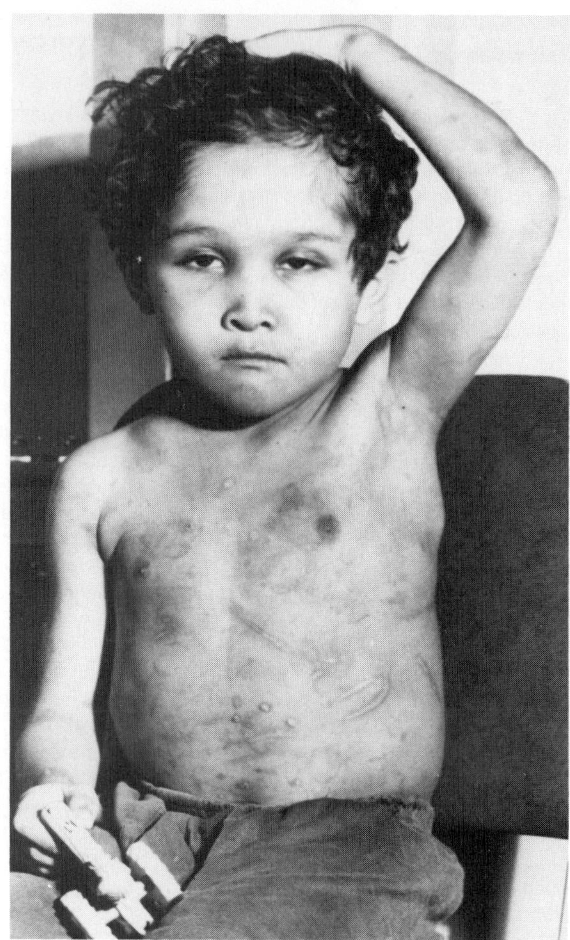

Child abuse is only one of the many forms of family violence that pose a grave problem in our society today. This 5-year-old said of the stepfather who beat, burned, bit, kicked, and punched him, "I guess he doesn't like me."

life. Although spouse abuse is viewed as intolerable in most segments of our society, Murray Straus and Richard Gelles (1986, 1990) nonetheless estimate, based on their surveys, that 16 of 100 married couples in the United States experience some form of marital violence in a year's time—often "only" a shove or a slap, but violence nonetheless. Almost 6% of the couples surveyed reported at least one instance of severe violence (such as kicking or beating). Indeed, dating partners appear to get a head start on marital abuse, for alarmingly high percentages of adolescents and young adults, including college students, experience violence in their dating relationships (Sigelman, Berry, & Wiles, 1984; Stets, 1992).

As Margaret Hudson (1986) has noted, child abuse and neglect, although they have always existed, were "discovered" as social problems in the 1960s; spouse abuse came to the public's attention in the 1970s; and finally, in the 1980s, it became clear that elderly adults are also the targets of family violence. Frail or impaired older people are physically or psychologically mistreated, neglected, financially exploited, and stripped of their rights—typically by adult children or other relatives serving as their major caregivers (Wolf & Pillemer, 1989). No one really knows how many elderly people are abused, but 5% of one sample of elderly adults with Alzheimer's disease had been physically abused by their caregivers in the year since they had been diagnosed (Paveza et al., 1992).

This is not a pretty picture. Here we have a social problem of major dimensions that causes untold suffering and inhibits the development of family members of all ages. What can be done to prevent it or to stop it once it occurs? To answer that applied question, we must first try to gain some insight into why family violence occurs in the first place.

Why Does Family Violence Occur?

Child abuse has been studied the longest, and there are many similarities among the various forms of family violence. Therefore, let's see what has been learned about the causes of child abuse.

Characteristics of the Abuser

Anyone examining a badly beaten child might immediately conclude that the abuser must be a psychologically disturbed individual who needs professional help. Strange as it may seem, though, only about 1 child abuser in 10 appears to have a severe mental illness (Kempe & Kempe, 1978). The abusive parent most often is a young mother with many children who lives in poverty, is unemployed, and often has no spouse to share her load (Gelles, 1992; Wolfner & Gelles, 1993). Yet child abusers come from all races, ethnic groups, and social classes. Many of them appear to be rather typical, loving parents—except for their tendency to become extremely irritated with their children and to do things they will later regret.

There are a few identifiable differences between parents who abuse their children and those who do not. First, although most maltreated children do not abuse their own children when they become parents, roughly 30% do (Kaufman & Zigler, 1989). In other words, abusive parenting, like effective parenting, tends to be passed from generation to generation (Simons et al., 1991; van IJzendoorn, 1992). This "cycle of abuse" is most likely to be broken if abused individuals receive emotional support from parent substitutes, therapists, or spouses and are spared from severe stress as adults (Egeland, Jacobvitz, & Sroufe, 1988; Vondra & Belsky, 1993).

Second, abusive parents seem unable to tolerate the normal behavior of young children. For example, Byron Egeland and his colleagues (1979; Egeland, Sroufe, & Erickson, 1983) have found that, when infants cry to communicate needs such as hunger, nonabusive mothers correctly interpret these cries as signs of discomfort; abusive mothers, however, often infer that the baby is somehow criticizing or rejecting them. Indeed, abusive parents seem to find even an infant's smile unpleasantly arousing (Frodi & Lamb, 1980).

In short, abusive parents not only tend to have been exposed to harsh parenting themselves but also find caregiving more stressful, unpleasant, and ego-threatening than other parents do (Bugental, Blue, & Cruzcosa, 1989; Trickett & Susman, 1988). Still, it has been difficult to identify a particular kind of person who is highly likely to turn into a child abuser. Could some children bring out the worst in parents?

Characteristics of the Child

An abusive parent often singles out only one child in the family as a target; this offers us a hint that child characteristics might matter (Gil, 1970). No one is suggesting that children are to *blame* for being abused, but some children do appear to be somewhat more at risk than others. For example, infants who are emotionally unresponsive, hyperactive, irritable, ill, or premature are more likely to be abused than quiet, healthy, and responsive infants who are easier to care for (Egeland & Sroufe, 1981; Klein & Stern, 1971; Sherrod, O'Connor, Vietze, & Altemeier, 1984). Similarly, defiant children may elicit stronger and stronger forms of physical punishment from their caregivers—until the line between spanking and abuse is crossed (Parke & Lewis, 1981). Yet many difficult children are not mistreated, and many seemingly cheerful and easygoing children are.

Just as characteristics of the caregiver cannot fully explain why abuse occurs, then, neither can characteristics of children. It is quite likely that the *combination* of a high-risk parent and a high-risk child spells trouble (Bugental et al., 1989), but even the match between child and caregiver may not be enough to explain abuse. We should, as always, consider the social context surrounding the family system.

Contextual Factors

Quite consistently, abuse is most likely to occur in families under stress. If, for example, a relatively young, poorly educated mother is overburdened with responsibilities and receives little assistance from the father or any other sources of social support, she stands an increased risk of becoming abusive (Egeland et al., 1983, 1988). Life changes such as the loss of a job or a move to a new residence can also disrupt family functioning and contribute to abuse or neglect (McLoyd, 1989; Wolfner & Gelles, 1993). Moreover, some neighborhoods have higher rates of abuse than other neighborhoods with the same demographic and socioeconomic characteristics. These high-risk areas tend to be deteriorating neighborhoods where families are socially isolated and have little in the way of community services or informal social support (Garbarino, 1992; Garbarino & Sherman, 1980).

Finally, ours is a culture in which many forms of violence are common and in which the use of physical punishment as a means of controlling children's behavior is widely accepted. Cross-cultural studies reveal less child abuse in societies that discourage physical punishment of children and advocate nonviolent ways of resolving interpersonal conflicts (Belsky, 1980; Levinson, 1989).

As you can see, child abuse is a complex phenomenon with a multitude of causes and contributing factors. It is not easy to predict who will become a child abuser and who will not, but abuse seems most likely to result when a vulnerable individual faces overwhelming stress with insufficient support (Wolfner & Gelles, 1993). Much the same is true of spouse abuse, elder abuse, and other forms of family violence.

The Effects of Abuse

As you might imagine, child abuse is not good for child development. Physically abused and otherwise maltreated children tend to have a number of problems. Intellectual deficits and academic difficulties are common (Malinosky-Rummell & Hansen, 1993). John Eckenrode, Molly Laird, and John Doris (1993) have found that children who are neglected are even more likely than those who are physically or sexually abused to obtain low grades and achievement test scores and to have to repeat a grade. Neglected children undoubtedly receive little of the stimulation from nurturing adults that contributes so much to intellectual growth. However, deficits in social behavior are more common among physically abused children than among neglected ones. For example, Eckenrode and his colleagues found that physically abused children were more likely than either other maltreated children or nonmaltreated children to have lengthy records of discipline problems at school. Physically abused children tend to be highly aggressive youngsters who are often rejected by their peers for that reason (Haskett & Kistner, 1991; Salzinger et al., 1993; Trickett et al., 1991).

Not surprisingly, abused and neglected children also tend to have emotional problems, rooted in part in insecure attachments to their caregivers (Cicchetti & Barnett, 1991; see also Chapter 13). They are likely to be fearful, anxious, depressed, and low in self-esteem (Emery, 1989; Trickett et al., 1991). Children of battered women display many of the same social and emotional problems that physically abused children do, which suggests that both witnessing and experiencing violence can cause psychological damage (Fantuzzo et al., 1991; Holden & Ritchie, 1991). Moreover, these social and emotional difficulties are likely to be long-term: Adults who were abused as children tend to be violent, both inside and outside the family, and they show higher-than-average rates of substance abuse, depression, and other psychological problems (Malinosky-Rummell & Hansen, 1993).

One of the most disturbing consequences of physical abuse is a lack of normal empathy in response to the distress of peers. When Mary Main and Carol George (1985) observed the responses of abused and nonabused toddlers to the fussing and crying of peers, they found that nonabused children typically attended carefully to the distressed child, showed concern, or even attempted to provide comfort. As shown in Figure 14.5 , not one abused child showed appropriate concern; instead, abused toddlers were likely to become angry and attack the crying child (see also Klimes-Dougan & Kistner, 1990). In short, abused children react to the distress of peers much as their abusive parents react to their distress:

> . . . Martin (an abused boy of 32 months) tried to take the hand of the crying other child, and when she resisted, he slapped her on the arm with his open hand. He then turned away from her to look at the ground and began vocalizing very strongly, "Cut it out! CUT IT OUT!," each time saying it a little faster and louder. He patted her, but when she became disturbed by his patting, he retreated, hissing at her and baring his teeth. He then began patting her on the back again, his patting became beating, and he continued beating her despite her screams [Main & George, 1985, p. 410].

Without question, child abuse has unfortunate and often long-lasting effects on cognitive, social, and emotional development. The important question then becomes this: Knowing what we know about the causes and effects of abuse, what can be done to prevent it, stop it, and undo the damage?

How Do We Solve the Problem?

The fact that family violence has many causes is discouraging. Where do we begin to intervene, and just how many problems must we correct before we can prevent or stop the violence? Yet, despite the complexity of the problem, progress has been made.

Consider first the task of preventing violence before it starts. This requires identifying high-risk families—a task that is greatly aided by the kinds of studies we have reviewed. For example, once we know that an infant is at risk for abuse because he or she is particularly irritable or unresponsive, it makes sense to help the child's parents appreciate and evoke the baby's positive qualities. Learning how to elicit smiles, reflexes, and other positive responses from premature infants makes parents more responsive to their babies, which in turn helps these at-risk babies develop more normally (Widmayer & Field, 1980).

Other efforts to prevent abuse have been directed at high-risk parents. Steven Schinke and his associates (1986), for example, decided to teach better coping techniques to one high-risk group of

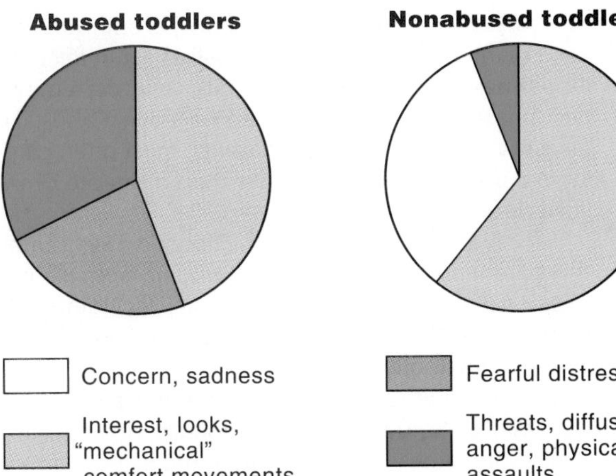

FIGURE 14.5 Responses to distressed peers observed in abused and nonabused toddlers in day care. Abused children distinguish themselves by a lack of concern and a tendency to become upset, angry, and aggressive when other children cry. (Adapted from Main & George, 1985.)

mothers — unwed teenagers who were under a great deal of stress. They conveyed a wide range of stress-management skills: problem-solving strategies, self-praise for handling difficult situations, communication skills (such as refusing unreasonable demands and requesting help), relaxation techniques, and even techniques for building a stronger social-support network. Three months later the mothers who had received the training outperformed the control group on several measures. They had improved their problem-solving skills, had established stronger social-support networks, enjoyed higher self-esteem, and were more confident about their parenting skills. At-risk parents can also benefit from learning effective child management skills (Wolfe et al., 1988). The demonstrated success of these and other interventions has led child welfare agencies in several states to develop family support and education programs aimed at preventing child abuse (Zigler & Finn Stevenson, 1993).

What about the parents who are already abusive? Here the problem is more thorny, largely because our social institutions are very reluctant to intervene in the family unless a child is repeatedly and severely abused. What does seem clear is that a few visits from a social worker are unlikely to solve the problem (Oates, 1986). More promising is Parents Anonymous, a self-help approach based on Alcoholics Anonymous that is available to help caregivers understand their problems and to give them the emotional support they often lack.[2] In extreme cases the abusive parent is prosecuted and the children are taken from the home, although courts have been hesitant to break up families unless the abuse is chronic and severe (Hart & Brassard, 1987). Ultimately, however, a comprehensive approach is likely to be most effective. Abusive parents need emotional support and the opportunity to learn more effective parenting and coping skills (Oates, 1986), and the victims of abuse need day-care programs and training to help them overcome the cognitive, social, and emotional problems associated with abuse (Culp et al., 1991; Fantuzzo, 1990). In short, the ultimate goal in attempting to decrease child abuse and other forms of family violence must be to convert a pathological family system into a healthy one.

REFLECTIONS

James Garbarino (1992) has characterized the family as the "basic unit of human experience" (p. 7). If you do not yet fully appreciate the awesome significance of the family for human development across the life span, think for a moment about how very badly things can go when the family does not fulfill its many important functions. Start with the infant who is neglected and who does not experience anything faintly resembling warm, sensitive, or responsive parenting. How is this infant to form the secure attachments that serve as foundations for later social and intellectual competence? Think about the child or adolescent whose parents are cold or downright hostile — either providing no guidance at all or burying the child in rules and severely punishing every misstep. How will this child learn to care about other people, fit into society, or function as an autonomous adult?

And why stop there? Adults are also developing individuals, and they, too, are greatly affected by their family experiences. Picture the young adult who marries, full of high hopes, only to become the target of unrelenting criticism, anger, and even physical violence. Then there are the trials and tribulations of child rearing. How does a parent thrive as an individual when *nothing* seems to quiet a distressed baby, stop a preschooler's violent outbursts, keep an adolescent off cocaine, or get a 30-year-old "child" away from the television set and out into the world? And how does an elderly parent cope when an adult child never calls or is hateful and abusive?

You get the picture. Fortunately, most of us fare much better than this, and our development is constantly nourished rather than poisoned by our family

[2]Chapters of Parents Anonymous are now located in many cities and towns in the United States. (For locations, one can consult a telephone directory or write to Parents Anonymous, 6733 South Sepulveda Blvd., Suite 270, Los Angeles, CA 90045.) Not only is there no charge for participation in these self-help groups, but many cities and counties provide free family therapy to abusive parents.

relationships. Moreover, most of us seem to appreciate just how important our families are. Children *know* that their parents are their primary sources of affection and aid (Furman & Buhrmester, 1992), and adults who are asked to describe what is most important in their lives almost always speak of their families (Whitbourne, 1986). Although we change, and our families change, as we get older, it seems that we never cease to be affected by, or to affect, those people we call "family."

SUMMARY POINTS

1. The family, whether it is nuclear or extended in form, is best viewed as a changing social system embedded in larger social systems that are also changing. Social trends affecting family life today include greater numbers of single adults; the postponement of marriage; a decline in childbearing; more female participation in the labor force; more divorces, single-parent families, child poverty, and remarriages; more years with an empty nest; and more multigeneration families.

2. Infants affect and are affected by their parents. Compared to mothers, fathers are less involved in caregiving and more involved in rough play. Developmental outcomes are likely to be positive when *both* parents are involved with their children and have positive *indirect* effects on their children by virtue of their influence on each other.

3. Child rearing can be described in terms of the dimensions of warmth/hostility and permissiveness/restrictiveness; generally, children are most socially and cognitively competent when their parents adopt an authoritative style of parenting, combining warmth and moderate control. Lower-income parents generally tend to be more punitive and authoritarian than middle-class parents, due both to the demands of blue-collar jobs and to the negative effects of economic hardship on parenting. "Child effects" in the family remind us that children exert reciprocal influence on their parents.

4. When a second child enters the family system, mothers typically become less attentive to their first-borns, and first-borns find the experience stressful. Sibling relationships are characterized by rivalry *and* affection and provide emotional support, caregiving, and teaching.

5. Parent/child relationships typically remain close in adolescence but are renegotiated; adolescents are most likely to gain autonomy when parents grant more freedom but still serve as loving and supportive guides.

6. Marital satisfaction declines somewhat as newlyweds adjust to each other, declines still further as couples face the stresses of new parenthood and child rearing, and then often increases again after the empty-nest transition. Most adults view the empty-nest phase more positively than negatively and take pleasure in becoming grandparents, most often playing a companionate role rather than a remote or involved role.

7. Although marital satisfaction declines during the parenting years, especially among women, it is affected by many additional factors, including previous satisfaction, personality similarity, and genuine liking for each other.

8. In adulthood, siblings have less contact but normally continue to feel emotionally close. Young adults sometimes establish more mutual and intimate relationships with their parents. Middle-aged adults continue to experience mutually supportive relationships with their elderly parents rather than role reversal, though some do experience the stresses of "middle generation squeeze."

9. Among the adults whose lives are inadequately described by the family life cycle are single adults, some of whom cohabitate, and childless married couples, who usually enjoy high marital and life satisfaction.

10. Divorce significantly disrupts family life for a year or two; some children (especially boys) experience long-lasting social and academic problems, but factors such as financial support, quality of parenting, and social support influence adjustment. Most single-parent families adapt well to becoming part of a reconstituted family, but the transition is often hard for girls.

11. Family violence occurs in all possible relationships within the family. The most recognized form is child abuse; parent characteristics such as a history of abuse and hypersensitivity to child behavior, child characteristics such as a difficult temperament, and social-contextual factors such as low social support all contribute to the problem and must be considered in formulating solutions.

KEY TERMS

authoritarian parenting
authoritative parenting
autonomy
child effects
cohabitation
empty nest
extended family household
family life cycle
indirect effects
"middle generation squeeze"
modified extended family
nuclear family
permissiveness/restrictiveness dimension
permissive parenting
reconstituted family
role reversal
sibling rivalry
warmth/hostility dimension

15

LIFESTYLES: PLAY, SCHOOL, AND WORK

Just for the fun of it, draw a large circle or "pie" to represent all the waking hours available to you in a typical week. Now carve up the pie to show how you allocate your time among different activities. What portion of your time is spent attending classes or studying? Working? Engaging in hobbies, sports, and other recreational activities? Socializing? Performing chores and personal-care tasks? Watching television? Are you satisfied with how you spend your hours, or would you be better off in the long run if you rebudgeted your time?

MAJOR ACTIVITIES ACROSS THE LIFE SPAN

All of us, in each phase of life, have characteristic lifestyles—ways in which we divide our time among major activities such as work, play or leisure, and schooling. Moreover, within any age group there are individual differences in lifestyles, differences that have the potential to shape later development. The central question addressed in this chapter is this: What do we do with our time in different phases of the life span, and how do our activities affect our development?

Infants may not go to school or work, but they do play, and more and more of them spend a good deal of time in day-care settings where they play with other infants. Children continue to spend a lot of time playing, and they are increasingly socialized for the world of work through their learning activities at school and participation in chores at home. In many of the world's cultures (as in earlier times in the United States), children work alongside their parents from an early age and begin to make significant contributions to the family's subsistence at about the age of 6 or 7, when they are given responsibilities for tending younger children, gathering food, or watching herds of cattle (Rogoff et al., 1991; Weisner, 1984). During adolescence, youth in our society are asked to take their schooling seriously and prepare for a career; they often work part time while they attend school, but they also spend a good deal of free time with their friends.

Among adults, a common complaint is that there simply is not enough time for friends and fun because work and family responsibilities consume so many hours. According to Juliet Schor (1991), Americans are working more hours a week than they were 20 years ago, despite increases in economic productivity; by the time work and household activities are done, the typical adult has only about 16 hours a week to spend on leisure activities. We detect what might be viewed as a depressing developmental trend here, then: less play and more work as we get older! Yet the emptying of the nest and retirement offer older adults more leisure time than they had earlier in adulthood—and perhaps new opportunities to play.

So let's look at how our major activities—play, school, and work, in particular—change over the life span. More important, let's examine the ways in which our activities affect our development. Just as children's opportunities for play and classroom learn-

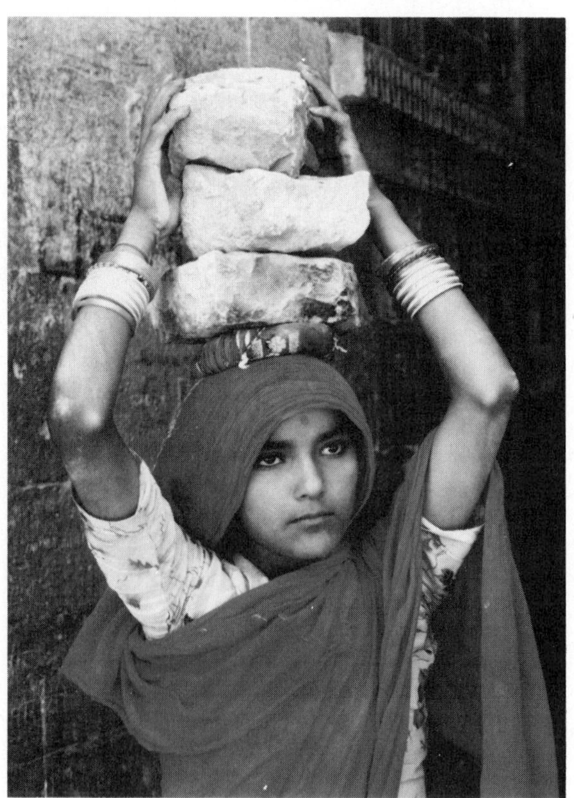

Children in some cultures participate in work at an early age.

ing affect their intellectual and social growth, the daily work experiences of adults influence their development and well-being.

THE INFANT

It may sound odd to speak of an infant's "lifestyle," but infants certainly do have characteristic patterns of daily activity. They log a lot of hours sleeping, but they also spend a good deal of very constructive time exploring the world around them, playing with people and things, and acquiring new competencies in the process. Some infants pursue these activities at home, whereas others today do so in alternative-care settings.

Play

Play can be defined as activity that (1) is enjoyable and absorbing, (2) is intrinsically motivated (done for the sheer enjoyment of doing it rather than to achieve some practical goal), and (3) has an unrealistic or "pretendlike" quality (Rubin, Fein, & Vandenberg, 1983). Young children clearly are playing when they line up the dining-room chairs to create a "boat" and exuberantly make motorboat sounds as they scout for whales. They are caught up in the pleasure of what they are doing, have no intention of producing anything of use, and are quite aware that they are pretending and need not fear drowning in their imaginary ocean. Jean Piaget (1951/1962) was fascinated by the young child's play because he believed it provided a glimpse of the child's emerging cognitive abilities in action. He viewed play as an opportunity for children to practice whatever cognitive competencies they possessed and to strengthen them in the process.

How does the capacity for play evolve as infants progress through the stages of Piaget's sensorimotor period? The sequence is much the same in all cultures (Sigman & Sena, 1993). At first infants play with their own bodies—for example, by kicking their legs or sucking their fingers. At about 4 months of age, they take a greater interest in toys and will repeatedly suck, pat, bang, and shake rattles and toy animals, often inspecting them closely. During these early months they use the behavioral schemes that they have acquired to explore everything in reach and learn a good deal about the world in the process (Ruff & Saltarelli, 1993).

As infants approach their first birthdays, new cognitive capacities allow them to experiment with playthings, performing novel actions rather than merely repeating the same behavior over and over. They also begin to engage in **functional play,** play that involves using objects appropriately to serve the functions they normally serve. Thus 1-year-olds may comb a doll's hair with a comb or turn the dial on a toy phone rather than just sucking or banging it (Belsky & Most, 1981; Sigman & Sena, 1993).

Perhaps the most exciting breakthrough in the infant's play is the emergence of **symbolic play**—pretend play in which one actor, object, or action represents another. Piaget emphasized that the infant's thought changes immensely when he or she acquires the capacity to make one thing stand for another. This **symbolic capacity** is involved in pretend play (where, for example, a clump of mud might symbolize a pie), in language use (where words symbolize or stand for things and events), in delayed imitation (where a mental image symbolizes the behavior that will be imitated), and in problem solving (where solutions can be conjured mentally). As early as 1 year of age, an infant may raise an empty cup to his or her lips, smile, give Mother or Father a knowing glance, and make loud lip-smacking sounds (Nicolich, 1977). This 1-year-old is not merely recognizing that cups are for drinking (as in functional play) but is also quite aware that his or her drinking actions stand for or symbolize real drinking. The earliest forms of symbolic play are actions just like this: The infant pretends to engage in familiar activities such as eating, sleeping, or washing, using appropriate props.

Symbolic play becomes considerably more sophisticated between the ages of 1 and 2 (Corrigan, 1987; McCune-Nicolich & Fenson, 1984). Instead of just pretending to be themselves doing the things they normally do, toddlers get outside the self and pretend to be someone else. They also progress from using objects in familiar ways to using them to stand for things very different from what they are. So, for example, an infant may first pretend to drink from a cup and later pretend to drink from a block. Finally, infants progress from pretending to engage in single acts to pretending to perform multiple acts in meaningful sequences. A young infant may give a doll a drink, whereas an older infant may say "Drink milk," repeatedly raise the cup to the doll's mouth, burp the doll, and wipe its mouth! Interestingly, this ability to combine actions in meaningful ways during pretend play emerges at the same time that 18- to 24-month-olds are becoming capable of combining words into short sentences and imitating two or three actions in a series (Brownell, 1988; Shore, 1986). Toddlers of this age are also beginning to coordinate their actions with those of a play partner, making a social game of imitating each other and sometimes even cooperating to achieve a goal (Brownell & Carriger, 1990; Howes & Matheson, 1992). Advances in cognitive development may be behind all of these breakthroughs.

In sum, play develops during infancy from early exploration of objects, to functional play in which objects are made to perform their usual functions, and finally to ever-more-complex forms of symbolic or pretend play. Parents can foster this development by providing infants with a secure base of affection and by playing along with their little dramas (O'Connell & Bretherton, 1984; O'Reilly & Bornstein, 1993; Slade, 1987).

Alternative-Care Settings and Infant Development

In recent years an important question has arisen about how infants in our society are tended: Should they be cared for at home by a parent, or can they pursue their developmental agendas just as well in a day-care setting? "Infant schools" were quite popular in the early 19th century; however, once women were no longer needed in the labor force, the belief arose that babies must spend their time with a single caregiver—namely, a mother—in order to develop normally (Pence, 1986). With well over half of the mothers in the United States now working outside the home at least part time, more and more infants and young children are receiving alternative forms of care. According to recent U.S. Department of Labor statistics, only 25% of infants and toddlers are cared for by their parents, whereas 27% are with other relatives, 7% are at home with a sitter, 26% are in day-care homes (typically run by a woman who takes a few children into her own home for payment), and 16% are in large day-care centers (Clarke-Stewart, 1993).

Do infants who attend day-care homes or centers suffer in any way compared to infants who stay at home with a parent? Research to date suggests that they are not necessarily damaged by the experience (Clarke-Stewart, 1993; Scarr & Eisenberg, 1993). Jerome Kagan and his associates (Kagan, Kearsley, & Zelazo, 1978), for example, found that infants who attended a high-quality, university-affiliated day-care center were no less securely attached to their mothers than infants who were raised at home. Moreover, day-care infants were generally indistinguishable from home-reared infants on measures of cognitive, linguistic, and social development. In fact, most studies suggest that high-quality day care is often as good for infants and young children as care at home (Clarke-Stewart, 1993; Scarr & Eisenberg, 1993).

However, this broad generalization does not tell the full story. For one thing, we cannot emphasize enough that the *quality* of the day-care setting matters (Clarke-Stewart, 1993; Scarr & Eisenberg, 1993). As Sandra Scarr (1984) puts it, "The who and the where [of early child care] are much less important than the what" (p. 33). Just as some parents are highly nurturant while others are neglecting or abusive, some day-care experiences are actually more beneficial than at-home care and other experiences are dreadful. It is not difficult to see that an infant will suffer in many ways if he or she ends up with an alcoholic babysitter or must compete for adult attention as one of many infants in a large center. Better developmental outcomes are likely in high-quality day care that has (1) a reasonable child-to-caregiver ratio (up to 3 infants, 4 toddlers, or 8 preschoolers per adult); (2) caregivers who are warm, emotionally expressive, and responsive to children; (3) little staff turnover, so that children can feel comfortable with and become attached to their caregivers; and (4) planned activities that are age appropriate (Howes, 1990; Howes, Phillips, & Whitebook, 1992; Zaslow, 1991).

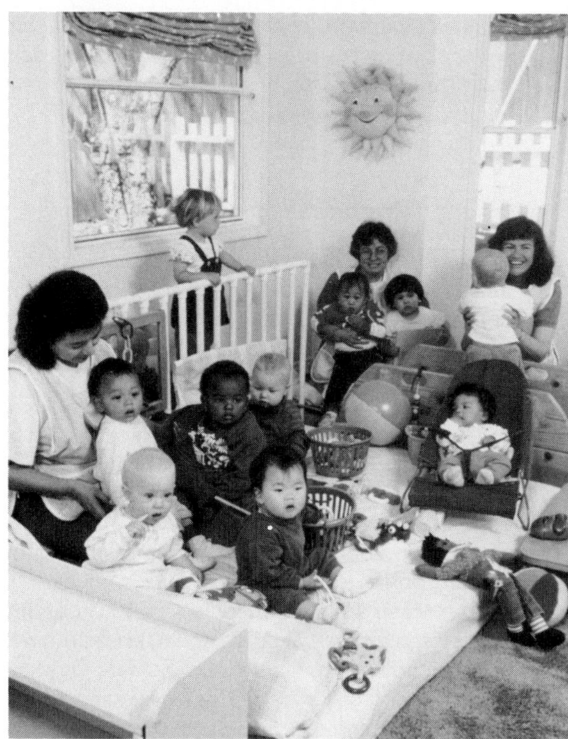

High-quality day care does not necessarily hurt—and sometimes benefits—infants.

Also, some infants fare better in alternative care than others do. First, infants from disadvantaged homes who are at risk of delayed development actually experience *faster* intellectual growth if they attend a high-quality day-care program specially designed to meet their needs than if they stay at home (Ramey & Ramey, 1992). Second, girls are more likely than boys to adapt well to day care (Baydar & Brooks-Gunn, 1991; Belsky & Rovine, 1988). Third, infants and toddlers with easy temperaments are likely to adjust better than children who have "difficult" or "slow to warm up" temperaments (Belsky & Rovine, 1988).

Fourth, infants who have already formed attachments to their parents sometimes fare better than younger infants. Several studies suggest that babies who spend many hours in alternative care before the age of 1 are somewhat less likely to be securely attached to their mothers and fathers than are infants tended primarily by their parents during their first year

(Barglow, Vaughn, & Molitor, 1987; Belsky & Rovine, 1988; Lamb, Sternberg, & Prodromidis, 1992). In their analysis of the research, Michael Lamb and his colleagues (1992) conclude that, on average, 71% of infants cared for exclusively by their mothers, compared to 65% of infants receiving regular alternative care, are securely attached to their mothers. So the difference is small, and most infants in day care do form healthy relationships with their parents, although some researchers continue to be concerned about possible negative effects of too much day care too early in life (Clarke-Stewart, 1993).

Fifth and finally, the effects of alternative care depend greatly on parents' attitudes and behaviors. Outcomes are likely to be better if a mother has positive attitudes about working and about being a mother and if she has the personal qualities it takes to provide warm and sensitive care (Belsky & Rovine, 1988; Crockenberg & Litman, 1991). Ultimately, the quality of parenting that infants receive at home seems to have more to do with their development than with the kind of alternative care they receive when they are not at home (Lamb et al., 1988).

In sum, we cannot draw simple conclusions about the effects of alternative care on infant development, for these effects range from beneficial to damaging. It does seem, however, that alternative care is least likely to disrupt development if infants are old enough to have already formed attachments to their parents and if they interact with *both* responsive substitute caregivers and responsive parents. Infants under age 1, especially boys with difficult temperaments, sometimes do not thrive, especially if they receive low-quality day care and do not have warm, responsive parents.

Meanwhile, many working parents struggle to find and keep competent sitters or high-quality day-care placements. The infants who receive the poorest, most unstable day care are often those whose parents lack the money to pay for child care, are living stressful lives, and are having difficulty providing responsive care themselves (Howes, 1990; Scarr & Eisenberg, 1993). The U.S. government has been far less willing than the governments of many European countries to finance day care (Clarke-Stewart, 1993). Until more options are available, working parents will continue to face the challenges of finding high-quality child care they can afford.[1]

THE CHILD

When infancy is behind them, what do children do with their time? In our society they play, attend school, and watch a good deal of television. All of these activities shape their later development.

Play

So important is play in the life of the child from age 2 to age 5 that these years are sometimes called "the play years." This is when children hop about the room shrieking with delight, don capes and go off on dragon hunts, and whip up cakes and cookies made of clay, sand, or thin air. We can detect two major changes in play between infancy and age 5: It becomes more social, and it becomes more imaginative. After age 5 or so, the exuberant and fanciful play of the preschool years gives way to somewhat more serious play.

Play Becomes More Social

Many years ago, Mildred Parten (1932) devised a useful method for classifying the types of play engaged in by nursery school children of different ages. Her six categories of activity, arranged from least to most social, are as follows:

1. *Unoccupied play.* Children stand idly, look around, or engage in apparently aimless activities such as pacing.
2. *Solitary play.* Children play alone, typically with objects, and appear to be highly involved in what they are doing.
3. *Onlooker play.* Children watch others play, taking an active interest and perhaps even talking to the players, but not directly participating.
4. *Parallel play.* Children play next to one another, doing much the same thing, but they interact very little (for example, two girls might sit near each other, both drawing pictures, without talking to each other to any extent).
5. *Associative play.* Children interact by swapping materials, conversing, or following each other's lead, but they are not really united by the same goal (for example, our two girls may swap crayons and comment on each other's drawings as they draw).
6. *Cooperative play.* Children truly join forces to achieve a common goal; they act as a pair or group, dividing their labor and coordinating their activities in a meaningful way (for example, our two girls collaborate to draw a mural for their teacher).

The major message of Parten's study (and of others like it) is that play becomes increasingly social and socially skilled from age 2 to age 5 (Barnes, 1971; Smith, 1978; see also Howes & Matheson, 1992). Unoccupied and onlooker activities are quite rare at all ages, solitary and parallel play become less frequent with age, and associative and cooperative play (the most social and complex of the types of play) become more frequent with age (see Figure 15.1). However, even though play becomes more social during the preschool years, solitary play still has its

[1]Parents who want practical guidelines for evaluating day-care settings might consult Bradbard and Endsley (1979), Scarr (1984), or Clarke-Stewart (1993).

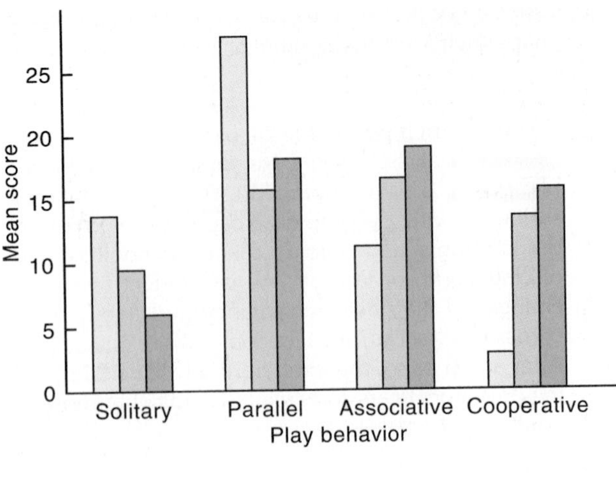

FIGURE 15.1 Frequency of activities engaged in by preschool children of different ages. With age, solitary and parallel play occur less frequently, whereas associative and cooperative play occur more frequently. (Adapted from Barnes, 1971.)

place and should not be considered immature. Indeed, older preschoolers who frequently engage in certain forms of solitary play (for example, constructing things, drawing pictures) tend to be very socially competent (Rubin, 1982).

Play Becomes More Imaginative

By age 2, toddlers readily join in the pretense if you hand them a towel and suggest that they wipe up the imaginary tea you just spilled (Harris & Kavanaugh, 1993). Think about it: Since there is no "tea" in sight, this willingness to clean it up is really quite remarkable. It means that very young children are capable of using their symbolic capacity to construct a mental representation of a pretend event and of acting according to this representation (Harris & Kavanaugh, 1993). Symbolic or pretend play fully blossoms during the preschool years, increasing dramatically in frequency and sophistication (Howes & Matheson, 1992; Rubin et al., 1983).

From age 2 to age 5, pretend play becomes more sophisticated. Children can depict heroes and heroines very different from themselves and can enact elaborate dramas using very few props. Most importantly, they combine their capacity for increasingly social play and their capacity for pretense into *social pretend play* (Howes & Matheson, 1992). Starting at age 2½ or 3, children less often enact scenes on their own using dolls and other toys and more often cooperate with playmates to enact their dramas.

When no playmates are handy, preschoolers may use their symbolic capacity to invent **imaginary companions** (Singer & Singer, 1990; Taylor, Cartwright, & Carlson, 1993). Some are humans, some are animals, and they come with names like Ariel, Nutsy, Little Chop, and Bazooie (Taylor et al., 1993). Donna, age 4, actually invented *five* imaginary husbands who joined her at meals, in conversations on her toy telephone, and on school-bus rides, during which they enjoyed throwing salt at cars (Pines, 1978). A child with imaginary companions may insist that the family wait at restaurants for a table large enough to accommodate their special friends or that the TV be left on while the family is away so that the imaginary companion will not get lonely (Taylor et al., 1993).

Are imaginary friends signs of emotional disturbance or an inability to distinguish between fantasy and reality? Not at all. Marjorie Taylor and her colleagues (1993) found that 4-year-olds with imaginary companions knew full well that their companions were not real and were just as able as other children to keep fantasy and reality straight. What made these children different from children without imaginary companions was their greater capacity for symbolic play. In short, imaginary companions seem to be just another sign of the imaginative powers of young children. Far from being maladjusted, children who invent such companions tend to be happy, playful, and cooperative youngsters (Singer & Singer, 1990).

Play Becomes More Rule Governed

After they enter school, children engage less frequently in symbolic play (Fein, 1981). Now they spend more of their time playing organized games with rules—board games, games of tag or hide-and-seek, organized sports, and so on (Athey, 1984). They also develop individual hobbies, such as building model cars or making scrapbooks, that allow them to develop skills and gain knowledge.

According to Jean Piaget (1932/1965), it is not until children enter the stage of concrete-operational thought, at about age 6 or 7, that they become capable of abiding by the rules of games. They then view rules as sacred and unalterable, and they are quick to accuse one another of cheating if they detect the slightest infraction of the rules. Older children—11- and 12-year-olds who are entering the stage of formal-operational thought—gain a more flexible concept of rules, recognizing that they are arbitrary agreements that can be changed as long as everybody concerned (or at least the majority) agrees to the changes. Partly because of cognitive gains, then, the play of the school-aged child is more organized and rule governed—and less fanciful—than that of the preschool child.

What Good Is Play?

In 19th-century America, child's play was discouraged because it was viewed as a frivolous waste of time (Athey, 1984). Now we know better. Play contributes to virtually all areas of children's development. Indeed, the fact that playful activity occurs among the young of so many species strongly suggests that play is a biologically programmed activity that prepares the young for adult life (Gandelman, 1992).

The contributions of play to physical development are clear enough: Through play, infants can practice body movements, preschoolers get physical exercise and opportunities to improve their manipulation skills and coordination, and school-aged children involved in organized sports and games receive both exercise and skill training (Athey, 1984). Intellectually, play provides a context for using language to communicate and for using the mind to imagine fantasy situations, plan strategies, and solve problems. Children often show more advanced intellectual skills when engaged in pretend play than when they are not at play, suggesting that play helps them develop their minds (Lillard, 1993). Indeed, preschool children who engage in a great deal of symbolic play (or are trained to do so) perform better on tests of Piagetian cognitive development, language skills, and creativity than children who rarely pretend (Fisher, 1992; Johnsen, 1991).

The contributions of play to social development are also important. To carry off a coherent episode of social pretend play, children must adopt different roles, act in character, mesh their own behavior with that of their playmates, and resolve conflicts (Giffin, 1984). It just won't work if one child is saying "We're going to catch the robber now" while another is saying "I'm dying, so go get the doctor." Children may also learn about and prepare for adult roles by "playing house" and stepping into the shoes of their mothers and fathers. Perhaps due to the social experience they gain, preschoolers who engage in a great deal of social pretend play tend to be more popular and socially mature than children who do not (Connolly & Doyle, 1984; Howes & Matheson, 1992). Similarly, playing organized games with rules fosters social development by encouraging children to adopt the perspectives of others and cooperate with them (Piaget, 1932/1965).

Finally, play contributes to healthy emotional development, as psychoanalytic theorists such as Erik Erikson have long emphasized. Through play, children can express bothersome feelings, resolve emotional conflicts, and master challenges that they may not be able to master in real life (Curry & Arnaud, 1984; Fein, 1986). If Danny, for example, has recently been scolded by his mother for drawing on the wall, he may gain control of the situation by scolding his "child" for doing the same thing.

Children who are suffering from emotional disturbances not only reveal their concerns through their play but have difficulty playing in mature and creative ways (Gordon, 1993). For example, Mavis Hetherington and her colleagues (Hetherington, Cox, & Cox, 1979) compared the play of preschool children whose parents were divorcing with that of children from intact families. The children from divorcing families had a restricted style of play: They acted out fewer themes, had difficulty using props in multiple ways or getting by without realistic props, and adopted fewer roles. Moreover, the many aggressive themes in their play reflected their angers and anxieties about divorce. One 6-year-old described by Dorothy and Jerome Singer (1990) dealt with his parents' divorce by repeatedly pretending that Hurricane Gilbert, which had recently struck the southern United States, was destroying a large dollhouse in the play-therapy room where he was being treated. Over and over again, he knocked down furniture and toy people until all was chaos, and then he fixed the damage with his "repair kit." As he came to accept the divorce, he began to act out gentle scenes in which miniature dolls cared for one another and had fun.

Social pretend play during the preschool years contributes to intellectual, social, and emotional development.

Let it never be said, then, that play is useless. Although children play because it is fun, not because it sharpens their skills, they indirectly contribute to their own development—physical, intellectual, social, and emotional—by doing so. In this sense, play truly is the child's work.

School

Today the vast majority of children in our society begin their school careers well before age 6—attending kindergarten as 5-year-olds and, in many cases, going to preschool, nursery school, or day care before that (Clarke-Stewart, 1993). Developmentalists such as Edward Zigler (1987) and David Elkind (1981), author of *The Hurried Child,* fear that the current push for earlier and earlier education may be going too far and that young children today are not given enough time simply to be children — to play and socialize as they choose. Elkind even worries that children may lose their self-initiative and enjoyment of learning when their lives are orchestrated by parents who pressure them to achieve at early ages.

One study seems to confirm Elkind's concerns (Hyson, Hirsch-Pasek, & Rescorla, 1989). Four-year-olds in preschools with a very strong academic thrust gained an initial advantage in basic academic skills such as knowledge of letters and numbers but lost it by the end of kindergarten. What's more, they proved to be *less* creative, *more* anxious in testing situations, and *more* negative toward school than children who attended preschool programs with a social rather than academic emphasis. So, it may well be possible to overdo an emphasis on academics in the preschool years.

However, preschool programs that offer a healthy mix of play and academic skill-building activities can be very beneficial to young children, especially disadvantaged ones. Children who attend high-quality preschool often develop social skills at an earlier age than children who remain at home (Clarke-Stewart, 1993). And, although most children who attend preschool programs are no more or less intellectually advanced than those who remain at home, disadvantaged children who attend programs specially designed to prepare them for school *do* experience more cognitive growth and achieve more success in school than other disadvantaged children (Lee et al., 1990; Ramey & Ramey, 1992). Indeed, as long as preschool programs allow plenty of time for play and social interaction, they can do a lot to help all children acquire social and communication skills, as well as an appreciation of rules and routines, that will help smooth the transition from individual learning at home to group learning in an elementary school (Zigler & Finn Stevenson, 1993).

Getting a Good Education

Elementary and secondary schools can potentially contribute in a variety of ways to child development. Obviously, children acquire a good deal of basic knowledge and many academic skills at school. They also acquire general strategies for learning new information and thinking about problems. Children in developing countries who are exposed to formal education pick up many cognitive skills at school (for example, effective memorization strategies) that children who do not attend school lack (see Rogoff, 1990). In our own society as well, schooling clearly contributes to cognitive growth, both by transmitting information and by teaching children rules, strategies, and problem-solving skills that they can apply to many different kinds of tasks (Ceci, 1991).

Schools also expose children to an **informal curriculum** that teaches them how to fit into their culture. Children learn to obey rules, to cooperate with their classmates, to respect authority, and to become good citizens. Moreover, schools instill basic democratic and social values and are increasingly expected to help combat such social problems as racism, drug abuse, teenage pregnancy, and AIDS (Comer, 1991; Linney & Seidman, 1989). Like families, then, schools serve as socialization agents, potentially affecting children's social and emotional development as well as providing them with knowledge and skills that will allow them to lead productive lives.

In his review of research on education, Michael Rutter (1983) has defined *effective schools* as those that promote academic achievement, social skills, polite and attentive behavior, positive attitudes toward learning, low absenteeism, continuation of education beyond the age at which attendance is mandatory, and the acquisition of skills that will enable students to find and hold jobs. Some schools are clearly more able than others to accomplish these objectives, regardless of students' racial, ethnic, or socioeconomic backgrounds. Indeed, in Rutter's own study of 12 secondary schools, initially low-achieving students in "better" schools ended up scoring just as well on a final test of academic progress as initially high-achieving students in the least effective schools (Rutter et al., 1979). What, then, makes for a good education? You may be surprised by some of the factors that do and do not have a bearing on how "effective" a school is (Fraser et al., 1987; Linney & Seidman, 1989; Reynolds, 1992; Rutter, 1983).

Factors That Have Little to Do with a School's Effectiveness.

Oddly enough, a school's *level of support* has little to do with the quality of education its students receive. Seriously inadequate funding does not make for good education, but, as long as a school has a reasonable level of support, the precise amount of money spent per pupil, the number of books in the school library, teachers' salaries, and teachers' academic credentials play only a minor role in determining student outcomes (Rutter, 1983).

Another factor that has relatively little to do with a school's effectiveness is *average class size* (Rutter, 1983). Within a range of from 20 to 40 students per class, reducing class sizes (from, say, 36 to 24 students) is unlikely to increase student achievement. Even a reduction from 30 students to 15 may have little effect, by itself, on student achievement (Odden, 1990). Tutoring students in grades K (kindergarten) to 3 — especially disadvantaged or low-ability students, one-on-one or in groups no larger than three students — *does* make a big difference in the learning of reading and math (Odden, 1990; Slavin, 1989). However, more modest reductions in the student/teacher ratio do not seem to be worth the large amount of money they cost.

It also does not matter much whether or not a school uses **ability tracking,** in which students are grouped according to ability and then taught in classes or work groups with others of similar academic or intellectual standing. The pros and cons of ability tracking have been debated for years. On one side, we hear that teachers teach best and students learn best when all students are functioning at about the same level; on the other, we are told that tracking undermines the self-esteem of low-ability students and actually contributes to their poor performance. Ability tracking, especially when it involves separate classes for students of different ability, has no clear advantage over mixed-ability grouping for most students (Kulik & Kulik, 1992; Rutter, 1983). It *can* be beneficial, especially to higher-ability students, if it means a curriculum more appropriate to students' learning needs (Kulik & Kulik, 1992). However, low-ability students are unlikely to benefit and may well suffer if they are denied access to the most effective teachers and are stigmatized as "dummies" (Rutter, 1983).

These, then, are examples of school characteristics that do *not* seem to contribute a great deal to effective education. A school that has quite limited financial support (assuming it surpasses a basic minimum), places most students in relatively large classes, and combines students in mixed-ability learning groups or classes is often just as effective as another school that has ample financial resources, small classes, and ability tracking. So what does influence how well children perform?

Factors That Matter. To understand why some schools are more effective than others, we must consider characteristics of the student body, characteristics of the learning environment, and the interaction between student and environment.

First, a school's effectiveness is a function of what it has to work with. On the average, academic achievement tends to be low in schools with a preponderance of economically disadvantaged students, and any child is likely to make more academic progress in a school with a high concentration of intellectually capable peers (Brookover et al., 1979; Rutter, 1983). However, this does *not* mean that schools are only as good as the students they serve. Many schools that serve disadvantaged minority populations are highly effective at motivating students and preparing them for jobs or further education (Reynolds, 1992).

So what is it about the learning environment of some schools that allows them to accomplish so much? Basically, the effective school environment is a comfortable but businesslike setting in which teachers are involved with students and students are motivated to learn (Linney & Seidman, 1989; Rutter, 1983). More specifically, in effective schools teachers:

1. Strongly emphasize academics (they demand a lot from their students and expect them to succeed, regularly assign homework, and work hard to achieve their objectives in the classroom).

In a comfortable and task-oriented classroom, children are motivated to learn.

2. Manage classroom activities effectively to create a task-oriented but comfortable atmosphere (for example, they waste little time on getting activities started or dealing with distracting discipline problems, provide clear instructions and feedback, and encourage and reward good work).
3. Manage discipline problems effectively (for example, they enforce the rules on the spot rather than sending offenders to the principal's office, and they avoid the use of physical punishment, which often only compounds discipline problems and creates a tense, negative atmosphere that is hardly conducive to learning).
4. Work with other faculty as part of a team—one that jointly decides on the curriculum and on approaches to discipline—under the guidance of a principal who provides active, energetic leadership.

One more point must be made: *Characteristics of the student and of the school environment often interact to affect student outcome,* a phenomenon Lee Cronbach and Richard Snow (1977) call **aptitude-treatment interaction (ATI).** Much educational research has been based on the assumption that *one* teaching method, organizational system, or philosophy of education will prove superior for all students, regardless of their ability levels, learning styles, personalities, and cultural backgrounds. This assumption is often wrong. Instead, many educational practices are highly effective with *some* kinds of students but quite ineffective with other students. The secret is to find an appropriate fit between learner and teaching method.

For example, teachers tend to get the most out of high-ability, middle-class students by moving at a quick pace and insisting on high standards of performance—that is, by challenging these students (Brophy, 1979). By contrast, low-ability students react much more favorably to a teacher who motivates them by being warm and encouraging rather than highly demanding and stern. Similarly, highly achievement-oriented students adapt well to unstructured classrooms in which they have a good deal of choice, whereas less achievement-oriented students may prefer more structure (Peterson, 1977). Thus it may be the *goodness of fit* between student and classroom environment that matters most (Lerner et al., 1989). This implies that education that is highly individualized—tailored to suit each student's developmental competencies and needs—is most likely to succeed.

In sum, some students (for example, those from advantaged homes) do typically outperform others, and some learning environments (especially those in which teachers create a motivating, comfortable, and task-oriented setting) are generally more conducive to learning than others. Still, what works best for one kind of student may not work as well with another kind of student. In aptitude-treatment interactions, then, we have another nice example of a recurring theme in this book: the importance of the fit between individuals and their environments.

Meeting the Needs of All Our Children

Public schools in the United States have traditionally been middle-class white institutions staffed by middle-class white instructors who preach middle-class white values. Yet a majority of students in California's schools now belong to various "minority" groups (Garcia, 1993). How well are minority students being served by the schools? And how well are today's schools meeting the needs of students with developmental disabilities and bringing them into the mainstream of education?

Ethnic Differences in School Achievement. Many lower-income African-American, Hispanic, and Native-American students earn poorer grades and achievement test scores than their Anglo-American classmates, whereas Asian Americans (at least Japanese and Chinese Americans) tend to outperform Anglo students (Slaughter-Defoe et al., 1990; Sue & Okazaki, 1990). These racial and ethnic differences exist even after ethnic group differences in family income and other indicators of socioeconomic status are controlled, and they are not merely the product of group differences in ability (Alexander & Entwisle, 1988; Sue & Okazaki, 1990). Why do such differences exist?

Parent and peer influences. One popular hypothesis is that parents in some ethnic and racial groups value education or encourage school achievement more than other parents do. Yet African-American and Hispanic-American parents seem to value education at least as much as Anglo-American parents do (Steinberg, Dornbusch, & Brown, 1992), and they are actually *more* likely to appreciate the value of homework, competency testing, and a longer school day (Stevenson, Chen, & Uttal, 1990).

Despite the important role parents play in their children's school achievement, we cannot understand their contribution without also understanding *peer* influences on school achievement. Laurence Steinberg, Sanford Dornbusch, and B. Bradford Brown (1992) conducted a large-scale study of school achievement among African-, Hispanic-, Asian-, and Anglo-American high school students. They found that academic success and good adjustment are usually associated with *authoritative parenting* (the warm and firm but democratic style discussed in Chapter 14). African-American parents typically value education and provide authoritative parenting. However, their positive influence on school achievement is undermined by peers who devalue education and force many African-American students to choose between academic success and peer acceptance (see also Ogbu, 1990).

Hispanic-American parents tend to be authoritarian, or restrictive, rather than authoritative. As a result, Steinberg and his colleagues suggest, Hispanic-American students may have relatively few opportunities at home to learn self-direction and decision-making skills that would serve them well in school. Moreover, they, like African-American students, tend to associate with peers who do not strongly value education and therefore undercut parents' efforts to stress academic excellence. Anglo-American students are more likely than either African-American or Hispanic students to have *both* authoritative parents and peer support for education working in their favor.

And Asian Americans? Interestingly, many of them, like many Hispanic students, experience strict, authoritarian parenting at home rather than the authoritative style more often associated with school success. Yet Asian-American students' parents have high standards of academic success, and their friends strongly believe in the importance of education, encourage them to succeed, and study with them outside of school. Moreover, although Asian-American students are no more likely than other students to believe that getting an education will pay off in a good job, they more strongly believe that educational *failure* will seriously hurt their vocational prospects. The result? Asian-American students study twice as much as other students, which undoubtedly accounts for much of their success (Steinberg et al., 1992). Because of their group's experiences with racism, many African-American students may not truly believe that their efforts in school will pay off (Ogbu, 1990).

What these findings tell us, then, is that students of any ethnic background are likely to do best when their parents support their school achievement by valuing education and adopting an authoritative style of parenting, when their friends care about school and value scholastic achievement, and when they themselves are motivated to work hard for the sake of their futures.

Teacher expectancies. Finally, we must consider another hypothesis about ethnic differences in school achievement: the possibility that underachievement by some minority students is rooted in stereotyping and discrimination on the part of teachers. According to social stereotypes, Asian-American students are expected to be bright and hard working, whereas African-American and Hispanic students from low-income neighborhoods are expected to perform poorly in school. What happens if teachers believe these stereotypes?

We now know that teachers' expectations can have important effects on students (Minuchin & Shapiro, 1983). As early as the first couple of weeks of kindergarten, and before teachers know much of anything about their students' competencies, many teachers are already placing children into ability groups for reading on the basis of clues to socioeconomic status: grooming, clothing, and mastery of standard English (Rist, 1970). Unfortunately, these ability labels tend to stick; once a child is placed in the "clowns" reading group rather than the "cardinals" reading group, he or she is likely to remain a "clown" and will be expected to perform like one.

In a classic study, Robert Rosenthal and Lenore Jacobson (1968) demonstrated that a teacher's expectancies about a student can influence that student's ultimate achievement through what they called the **Pygmalion effect.** Students actually perform better when they are expected to do well than when they are expected to do poorly, so that teacher expectancies become self-fulfilling prophecies.[2] To demonstrate this, Rosenthal and Jacobson gave each elementary school teacher in their study a list of five students who were supposed to be "rapid bloomers." In fact, the so-called rapid bloomers had been randomly selected from class rosters. Yet planting these high (though false) expectancies in the minds of teachers was sufficient to cause the "rapid bloomers" to show greater gains on measures of IQ and reading achievement than their unlabeled classmates.

By now the Pygmalion effect has been demonstrated in many studies. It is important to note that the positive or negative expectancies most teachers form reflect real ability differences among students. Youngsters expected to perform well (or poorly) in the future have typically performed well (or poorly) in the past (Jussim & Eccles, 1992). Still, even if two students have equal aptitude and motivation, the one whose teacher expects great things is likely to outperform the one whose teacher predicts failure (Jussim & Eccles, 1992).

How exactly does the Pygmalion effect work? It seems that teachers who expect great things of a student are warmer, expose the student to more material and more difficult material, interact with the student more often and give him or her many opportunities to respond, and accept more of the student's ideas (Harris & Rosenthal, 1986). Meanwhile, a Mexican-American or black student from a poverty area might be tagged by a teacher as a low-ability student, might then be treated in ways that do not facilitate learning, and might end up fulfilling the teacher's low expectancies as a result (see Sorensen & Hallinan, 1986).

In sum, parents' values and styles of parenting, peers' support for academic achievement, and teacher expectancies probably all contribute to racial and ethnic differences in school achievement. Some theorists feel that children from lower-income, minority subcultures are at an immediate disadvantage when they enter the middle-class institutions we call schools and that schools must change dramatically if they are to motivate and better educate these children. Among the positive changes we are seeing today are stronger bilingual education programs designed to meet the needs of children from the over 100 distinct language groups in the United States (Garcia, 1993) and multicultural education programs designed to bring the perspectives of many cultural and subcultural groups into the classroom so that all students feel welcome there (Banks, 1993).

Making Integration and Mainstreaming Work. For many African-American students in the past, additional barriers to school success were created by school segregation. Black children in many states were forced to attend "black schools" that were clearly inferior to "white schools." In its landmark decision in the case of *Brown* v. *Board of Education of Topeka* in 1954, the Supreme Court ruled that segregated schools were "inherently unequal" and declared that they must be desegregated. What have we learned since this ruling?

Generally, the effects of school integration on children's racial attitudes, self-esteem, and school achievement have been disappointing (Stephan, 1978). White prejudice toward black students often does not decrease much at all, and the self-esteem of black children in integrated schools is often no higher than that of black children in segregated schools. The most encouraging news has been that minority students tend to achieve more in integrated classrooms, especially if they begin to attend them early in their academic careers (St. John, 1975; see also Entwisle & Alexander, 1992).

Meanwhile, children with developmental disabilities (mental retardation, learning disabilities, physical

[2]According to Greek myth, the sculptor Pygmalion fell so in love with his statue of a beautiful woman that she came to life (with a little divine intervention from the goddess Aphrodite). The myth served as the basis for George Bernard Shaw's play *Pygmalion*, which in turn inspired the musical and movie *My Fair Lady*, in which Henry Higgins's high hopes for the lowly Eliza Doolittle became a reality.

and sensory handicaps, and other special learning needs) have had a somewhat similar history. They used to be placed in separate schools or classrooms — or, in some cases, rejected as unteachable by the public schools — until the U. S. Congress passed the *Education for All Handicapped Children Act* in 1975 and required schools to provide appropriate education for these students. What has been achieved since? Mixed results have come from studies of developmentally disabled children who have been integrated into regular classrooms through a practice called **mainstreaming.** Compared with similar students who attend segregated special education classes, these mainstreamed youngsters sometimes fare better academically and socially but sometimes do not (Buysse & Bailey, 1993; Madden & Slavin, 1983). They rarely show an increase in self-esteem, possibly because their classmates seldom choose them as friends or playmates (Guralnick & Groom, 1988; Taylor, Asher, & Williams, 1987).

What we seem to be learning about both racial integration and mainstreaming is that simply putting diverse students into the same schools and classrooms accomplishes little by itself. Instead, something special must be done to ensure that students do in fact interact in positive ways and also learn what they are supposed to be learning. What techniques for facilitating racial integration and mainstreaming *have* proved successful?

Robert Slavin (1986, 1991) and his colleagues have had much success using **cooperative learning methods,** in which students of different races or ability levels are assigned to work teams and are reinforced for performing well *as a team.* For example, each member of a math team is given problems to solve that are appropriate to his or her ability level. Yet members of a work team also monitor one another's progress and offer one another aid when needed. To encourage this cooperation, the teams that complete the most math units are rewarded — for example, with special certificates that designate them as "superteams." Similarly, the "jigsaw method" of instruction developed by Elliot Aronson and his colleagues (1978) to facilitate racial integration involves giving each member of a small learning team one portion of the material to be learned and requiring him or her to teach it to teammates. In these techniques, then, we see a formula for ensuring that children of different races and ability levels will interact in a context where the efforts of even the least capable team members are important to the group's success.

Elementary school students come to like school better and learn more when they participate in cooperative learning groups than when they receive traditional instruction (Aronson et al., 1978; Slavin, 1986, 1991). Moreover, team members gain self-esteem from their successes, and minority-group members and students with developmental disabilities are more fully accepted by their peers (see also Johnson, Johnson, & Maruyama, 1983; Weinstein, 1991). In short, racial integration and mainstreaming *can* succeed if educators deliberately design learning experiences that encourage students from different backgrounds to pool their efforts in order to achieve common goals.

The Changing Context of Child Development

The lifestyles of children are shaped not only by the schooling they receive but also by the broader cultural context in which they live. Imagine being a child growing up in 18th-century America with heavy work responsibilities, no compulsory schooling, and no TV. As we keep saying, human development takes place in an ever-changing social context. It makes sense to ask, then, how today's children are being affected by some of the major technological changes that have occurred in this century.

In 1946 there were only 10,000 television sets in the United States, but now more than 98% of all households have at least one (Comstock, 1991). Today, children between the ages of 3 and 11 watch an average of two to four hours of TV a day (Huston et al., 1990; Liebert & Sprafkin, 1988). As we see in Figure 15.2, children begin viewing in infancy, gradually increase their time spent in front of the TV until about age 12, and then cut down somewhat during adolescence. By age 18, a child born today will have spent more time watching television than in any other single activity except sleeping (Liebert & Sprafkin, 1988). Minority-group children from lower socioeconomic backgrounds are especially likely to watch a lot of TV (Signorielli, 1991). So, is all this time in

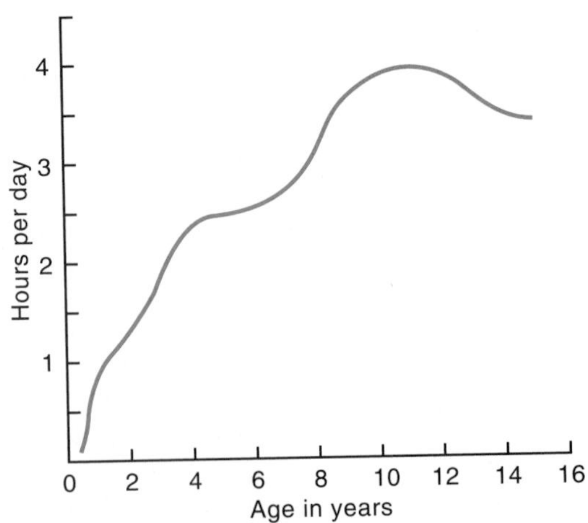

FIGURE 15.2 How many hours per day do children and adolescents in the United States spend watching television? (From Liebert & Sprafkin, 1988.)

front of the tube damaging to children's cognitive, social, and emotional growth?

Television and Children's Lifestyles

One way to answer that question is to find out whether the lifestyles and development of children who have access to television differ from those of children in remote areas who do not have television. As it turns out, children seem to substitute TV viewing for very similar leisure activities such as reading comics, going to movies, or listening to radio (Huston et al., 1992; Schramm, Lyle, & Parker, 1961). They do not necessarily spend any less time playing with peers, doing homework, engaging in leisure reading (excluding comic books), or interacting with their parents. Moreover, the introduction of television into a geographic area does not seem to affect children's cognitive abilities one way or the other (Lonner, Thorndike, Forbes, & Ashworth, 1985). In moderate doses—up to 10 or 15 hours a week—television does not seem to deaden young minds or stunt cognitive development, and it can even be a positive learning experience (Anderson & Collins, 1988). At the same time, children who watch far more television than their peers do tend to perform less well in school (Fraser et al., 1987; Signorielli, 1991). In sum, the overall effects of exposure to television generally are not as negative as some critics have charged—unless children watch so much TV that they have little time left for more growth-inducing pursuits such as play and homework.

But isn't something missing if we focus only on whether or not children have *access* to television? Shouldn't we be asking *what* they are watching? Viewing a steady diet of murder and carnage may have quite different effects from watching *Sesame Street* and other educational programs. Indeed, this is the case.

Television as a Negative Force

The workings of observational learning (as discussed in Chapter 8) suggest that children might learn a variety of antisocial or socially unacceptable behaviors by seeing them performed on television. As it turns out, American television is incredibly violent: By one count, there are over 22 acts of violence an hour on Saturday and Sunday mornings, during "children's" viewing time—more than the 5 or so acts per hour during prime-time viewing hours (Gerbner & Signorielli, cited in Signorielli, 1991). It is estimated that the average 16-year-old has witnessed more than 13,000 killings on television (Gerbner et al., 1986).

Research has clearly established that watching violence on television can cause children to behave more aggressively. Actually, the relationship is reciprocal: Watching violent TV increases children's aggressive tendencies, and being aggressive stimulates interest in violence on television, which promotes further aggression (Eron, 1982; Huesmann et al., 1984).

Heavy exposure to TV violence can blunt children's emotional reactions to real-life violence and convince them that the world is a dangerous place.

Even at age 30, individuals who preferred violent television at age 8 distinguish themselves as more aggressive and more involved in serious criminal activity than other adults (Huesmann, 1986).

Even if children do not act out the aggression they observe on television, they may be influenced by it nonetheless. For one thing, televised aggression desensitizes children to violence—that is, it makes them less emotionally upset by and more tolerant of violent acts in real life (Drabman & Thomas, 1974; Thomas et al., 1977). Also, a steady diet of televised violence can instill "mean world beliefs," making children view the world as a dangerous and downright frightening place (Comstock, 1991).

Parents who are concerned about these negative effects can attempt to restrict their children's viewing of violent programs and encourage their viewing of more educational fare (Huston et al., 1992). They can also watch television with their children and convert viewing sessions into positive learning experiences. For example, they can point out subtleties that young viewers often miss—the aggressor's motives and intentions, and the unpleasant consequences that perpetrators often suffer as a result of their aggressive acts (Collins, Sobol, & Westby, 1981). When adults highlight this kind of information while expressing their disapproval of aggressive behavior—and, even better, when they point out more constructive approaches to solving problems—children are less affected by the violence they view (Singer & Singer, 1990).

Another unfortunate effect that television may have on children is that of reinforcing a variety of social stereotypes (Huston et al., 1992). For example, male characters not only appear two or three times more often than female characters on TV but are portrayed as more powerful, dominant, rational, and intelligent (Signorielli, 1991). The result? Children who watch a lot of commercial television are likely to hold more stereotyped views of masculinity and femininity than their classmates who watch little television (Frueh & McGhee, 1975; Signorielli, 1991). Television can teach children negative stereotypes of minority-group members in much the same manner (Liebert & Sprafkin, 1988). And then there are all those commercials; young children in particular don't understand that the whole idea of commercials is to convince them to buy things. They are highly susceptible to the claims and appeals made by advertisers (Kunkel & Roberts, 1991). In sum, some kinds of television programming clearly foster undesirable attitudes and behaviors in children

Television as a Positive Force

Other kinds of television programs can help parents and educators achieve positive socialization goals. For example, if children watch *prosocial behavior* (positive social acts such as helping and cooperating) on television, they are likely to behave more prosocially themselves (Baran, Chase, & Courtright, 1979; Liebert & Sprafkin, 1988). Moreover, programs designed to counteract gender stereotypes or racial stereotypes by presenting women or minority-group members in positive ways are effective at doing just that (Liebert & Sprafkin, 1988; Rosenwasser, Lingenfelter, & Harrington, 1989). In short, television can work to strengthen children's positive social tendencies and alter their social attitudes for the better.

Television also has the potential to contribute to children's cognitive development and school achievement. This is well illustrated by the success of *Sesame Street,* the immensely popular educational program created by the Children's Television Workshop. Typical episodes combine fast action and humor with a curriculum carefully designed to teach letters of the alphabet, numbers, counting, vocabulary, and many social and emotional lessons. A major evaluation of *Sesame Street* in five areas of the United States during its first season showed that 3- and 5-year-old children who watched *Sesame Street* frequently outperformed other children on an overall test of cognitive skills and academic knowledge and more often knew such things as letters of the alphabet and how to write their names (Ball & Bogatz, 1970, cited in Liebert & Sprafkin, 1988; Bogatz & Ball, 1972). Moreover, disadvantaged children who were regular viewers of *Sesame Street* were later rated by their teachers as better prepared for school and more interested in school activities than their classmates who rarely watched the program (Bogatz & Ball, 1972). A more recent study (Rice et al., 1990) suggests that disadvantaged and advantaged children alike are gaining larger vocabularies and greater command of skills required for reading from the program (Rice et al., 1990).

Is television a positive or a negative force in child development, then? It seems that the medium itself is not so influential as the message. This 20th-century invention has changed the ways in which recent generations of children spend their time, but television viewing, at least in moderate doses, does not seem to be keeping most children from other developmentally important tasks. On the other hand, children are clearly affected by *what they watch.* Television has the capacity to teach children attitudes and behaviors that we would rather not have them learn, but it also has the potential to join forces with parents and educators in helping children to grow in positive directions.

Child Development in the Computer Age

Another technological development that is beginning to affect the lifestyles of children in our society is the computer. Adults who grew up without computers—and are sometimes not sure what to make of them—are now buying them for their children, and schools are increasingly building computers into the educational process. Advertisements on television even hint that parents will ruin their children's futures if they do not rush out to buy a home computer! As Mark Lepper (1985) points out, the computer revolution is raising a host of interesting questions that demand answers: Do computers really help children learn? Do they increase interest in learning or distract young learners? How are they changing children's lifestyles? Is there a danger that more and more children will become "computer nerds," socially isolated and socially inept because they spend hours in front of the computer monitor?

Researchers have begun to ask whether students learn more when they receive **computer-assisted instruction** than when they receive traditional instruction. Some forms of computer-assisted instruction are simply drill exercises (for example, of math problems); more elaborate forms allow students to learn academic material by playing highly motivating and thought-provoking games. After evaluating the research literature, Mark Lepper and Jean-Luc Gurtner (1989) have concluded that computer-assisted instruction is indeed effective—more effective than traditional instruction—and that it may be especially useful in promoting learning among disadvantaged and low-ability students. Moreover, highly involving "tutorials" that encourage thought seem to be more beneficial than simple "drills." What's more, teaching students the computer language Logo and allowing them to use it to figure out how to design graphics on

The computer is altering the experience of childhood and contributing positively to the education and intellectual development of many children.

the computer screen can actually improve their ability to think about their own thinking (called *metacognition*), to attack problems logically, and to come up with creative solutions to problems (Clements, 1990, 1991).

Are there any danger signs? Will children become social isolates who miss out on play with their peers? Probably not. Children simply build the home computer into their play with friends, as if it were any other toy, and classroom research suggests that children who are learning to use the computer engage in *more* collaborative conversations than children who work in a traditional manner (Crook, 1992; Kee, 1986; Weinstein, 1991). So far, there is no indication that involvement with computers inhibits social development. There *is* a danger, though, that, as the computer revolution unfolds, some children will be left behind and will lack the skills required in our increasingly computer-dependent society. Children from economically disadvantaged homes may be exposed to computers in school but are unlikely to have computers at home (Lepper & Gurtner, 1989). Also, boys are far more likely than girls to take an interest in computers and sign up for computer courses and camps, perhaps because computers are often viewed as involving mathematics, a traditionally "masculine" endeavor, and because many of the currently available game programs were designed with boys in mind (Lepper, 1985; Ogletree & Williams, 1990).

Maybe computers, like television sets, will turn out to be either a positive or a negative force in development, depending on how they are used. If children hole up in their bedrooms zapping mutant aliens from space for hours on end, perhaps the effects will be bad. But, if they use computers as tools to help them play with each other and learn in more creative and effective ways, the news may be quite positive.

THE ADOLESCENT

Many of the lifestyle choices of children are made for them by adults. Adolescents must increasingly make their own choices about such matters as how much time to devote to studying, whether to work part time after school, whether to go to college, and, perhaps most significantly, what to be when they grow up. Adolescents become more capable of making these educational and vocational choices as their cognitive and social skills expand; in turn, the choices they make shape their future development.

Adolescent Lifestyles

What do adolescents do with themselves? Some interesting answers come from a study in which Mihaly Csikszentmihalyi and Reed Larson (1984) equipped 75 students in a high school near Chicago with electronic pagers, buzzed them at random times during weekdays and weekends, and had them report on what they were doing and how they felt. Figure 15.3 shows how the average adolescent divided his or her waking hours among productive activities such as schoolwork, maintenance activities such as grooming and chores, and leisure. Surprisingly little time is devoted to schoolwork. On the other hand, U.S. adolescents have a considerable amount of leisure time—more such time than is available to the typical adult—and, not surprisingly, they devote the largest share of it to socializing with friends.

Interestingly, Csikszentmihalyi and Larson (1984) found that adolescents often report being bored when they are doing the very things that are most relevant to preparing for adulthood—doing homework, attending classes, or working. They are most intrinsically motivated and happy when they are engaged in leisure activities away from adult control. However, certain leisure pursuits (such as sports, games, art, and hobbies) seem to combine the best features of leisure and work (Kleiber, Larson, & Csikszentmihalyi, 1986). Not only are adolescents happy and intrinsically motivated when they pursue these activities, but they feel challenged and must exert effort to succeed, just as they must when they are doing schoolwork. Possibly, then, *challenging* leisure activities of this sort help adolescents make the transition from a child's world of play to an adult's world of work (Kleiber et al., 1986).

School

Obtaining an education is the primary "work" of adolescents in our society, though adolescents in many other cultures have already begun their work lives. Teenagers are affected by the school environments they encounter, especially during the transition from elementary school. Moreover, their futures are shaped by their educational experiences.

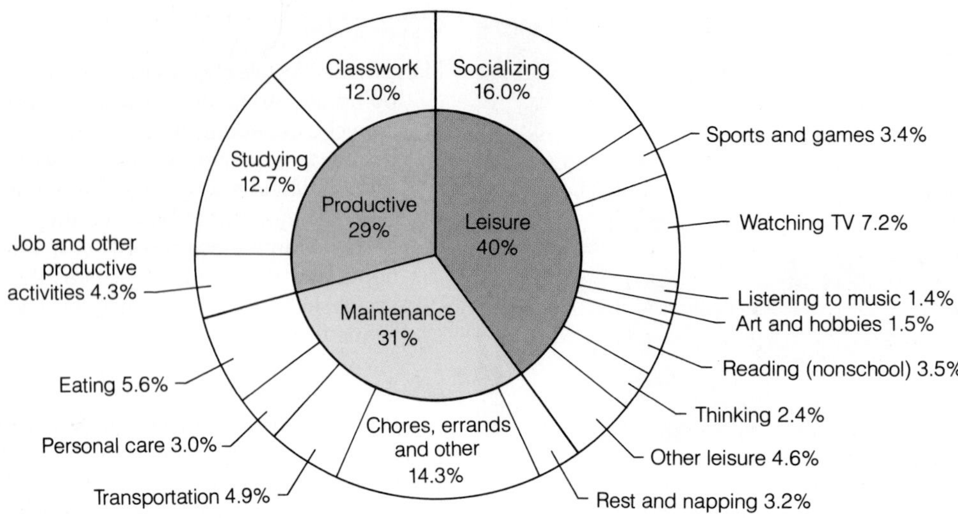

FIGURE 15.3 How high school students divide their waking hours among activities in a typical week. (From Csikszentmihalyi & Larson, 1984.)

Making the Transition from Elementary to Secondary School

For some time now, educators have been concerned about a number of negative changes that often occur when students make the transition from elementary school to junior high school: loss of interest in school, declining grades, and increased troublemaking, to name a few (Eccles et al., 1993). Why is this a treacherous move?

One reason the transition is difficult is because young adolescents are often experiencing major physical and psychological changes at the same time they are being asked to switch schools. Roberta Simmons and Dale Blyth (1987) found that girls who were reaching puberty at the same time they were moving from 6th grade in an elementary school to 7th grade in a junior high school were more likely to experience drops in self-esteem and other negative changes than girls who remained in a K–8 school during this vulnerable period. Could it be, then, that more adolescents would remain interested in school if they didn't have to change schools at the very time they are experiencing pubertal changes? This theory has been part of the rationale for the development of **middle schools,** which serve grades 6 to 8 and are designed to make the transition from elementary school to high school easier for early adolescents. Middle schools are now more common than junior high schools in the United States (Braddock & McPartland, 1993).

Yet Jacquelynne Eccles and her colleagues (Eccles, Lord, & Midgley, 1991; Eccles et al., 1993) have shown that students do not necessarily find the transition to middle school any easier than the transition to junior high school. This has led them to suspect that it is not as important when adolescents make a school change as what their new school is like. Specifically, these researchers have offered a "goodness of fit" hypothesis stating that the transition to a new school is likely to be especially difficult when the new school, whether a junior high or a middle school, is ill matched to the developmental needs of early adolescents.

Eccles and her associates have found that the transition to junior high school often involves going from a small school with close student/teacher relationships, a good deal of choice regarding learning activities, and reasonable discipline to a larger, more bureaucratized environment in which student/teacher relationships are impersonal, good grades are harder to come by, opportunities for choice are limited, assignments are not very intellectually stimulating, and discipline is rigid—all this at a time when adolescents are seeking more rather than less autonomy and have become more rather than less intellectually capable.

Eccles and her colleagues have demonstrated that the fit between developmental needs and school environment is indeed an important influence on adolescent adjustment to school. In one study (Mac Iver & Reuman, 1988), the transition to junior high school brought about a decline in intrinsic interest in learning mainly among students who wanted more involvement in classroom decisions but ended up with fewer such opportunities than they had had in elementary school. In another study (Midgley, Feldlaufer, & Eccles, 1989), students experienced negative changes in their attitudes toward mathematics only if their move from elementary school to junior high resulted in less personal and supportive relationships with math teachers. For those few students whose junior high teachers were more supportive than those they had

had in elementary school, interest in academics actually *increased.*

The message? Declines in academic motivation and performance are not inevitable when children become adolescents. These declines occur primarily when the fit between student and school environment goes from good to poor. Making the transition from a familiar school to a new one is hard enough when adolescents have to cope with pubertal changes at the same time, but it will be even harder when the new school environment is not conducive to growth. Whether they are called middle schools or junior high schools, transitional schools for early adolescents are likely to be most effective if they provide a good fit for adolescents who seek warm, supportive relationships with teachers along with intellectual challenges and increased opportunities for self-direction (Eccles et al., 1993).

Paths to Adulthood

The educational paths and attainments of adolescents are already partially set long before they enter junior high school. Because many individuals' intelligence test scores remain quite stable from childhood on, some children enter adolescence with more aptitude for schoolwork than others (see Chapter 9). Moreover, some students show a stronger need for achievement than others (see Chapter 12). Quite clearly, a bright and achievement-oriented student is more likely to obtain good grades and go on to college and is less likely to drop out of school than a student with less ability and less need to achieve. Even in early elementary school, future dropouts are identifiable by such warning signs as low IQ and achievement test scores, poor grades, aggressive behavior, low socioeconomic status, and troubled homes (Ensminger & Slusarcick, 1992; Lloyd, 1978).

This does *not* mean that adolescents' fates are sealed in childhood; experiences during adolescence still make a difference. Some teenagers make the most of their intellectual abilities, whereas others who have the ability to do well in school drop out or get poor grades. The impacts of school quality or "climate" are the same for adolescents as for children. For example, academic achievement is likely to be greater in schools where most students' peer groups value it highly than in schools where such things as athletics and partying are more important (Brown et al., 1993; Coleman, 1961). Even a highly capable student will find it hard to perform well where scholars are viewed as "nerds" and schoolwork is considered a waste of time. So, ability and motivation are not the only influences on educational achievement during adolescence; the social and intellectual climate of the school also helps to determine which adolescents will succeed and which will not.

The stakes are high. Students who achieve good grades in school are more likely than those who do not to be among the nearly 50% of all adolescents who pursue their schooling after high school. These youth, in turn, are likely to end up in higher-status occupations than their peers who do not attend college or, worse, do not finish high school (Featherman, 1980; McCaul et al., 1992). In a very real sense, then, individuals are steered along "high success" or "low success" routes from childhood on. Depending on their own decisions and the influences of their home and school environments, adolescents are even more distinctly "sorted out" in ways that will affect their adult lifestyles, income levels, and adjustment. Early choices can have far-reaching implications: According to one set of data, the yearly income of elderly men with a grade school education averages $23,000; that of college graduates, $57,000 (Crystal, Shea, & Krishnaswami, 1992).

Careers: Vocational Exploration and Choice

How do adolescents decide what they want to do with their lives? According to a developmental theory of vocational choice proposed by Eli Ginzberg and his colleagues (see Ginzberg, 1972, 1984), vocational choice unfolds through three stages: (1) the fantasy stage, (2) the tentative stage, and (3) the realistic stage.

Children up to about age 10 years, who are in the *fantasy stage* of vocational development, base their choices primarily on wishes and whims, wanting to be zookeepers, pro basketball players, firefighters, rock stars, or whatever else strikes them as glamorous and exciting. These youngsters *are* beginning to narrow their ideas about future careers to those that are consistent with their emerging self-concepts (Gottfredson, 1981). As early as kindergarten, for instance, almost all boys choose traditionally masculine occupations and most girls name traditionally female occupations such as nurse or teacher (Etaugh & Liss, 1992). Indeed, many children, although a long way from making specific and realistic vocational choices, are developing broad vocational interests that will be reflected in their later choices (Trice & McClellan, 1993; Vondracek, Lerner, & Schulenberg, 1986).

According to Ginzberg, it is during the second stage of vocational choice, the *tentative stage,* that adolescents aged 11 to 18 begin to weigh factors other than their wishes and to make preliminary decisions. After considering their *interests* (Would I enjoy counseling people?), they consider their *capacities* (Am I skilled at relating to people, or am I too shy and insecure for this kind of work?) and then also think about their *values* (Is it really important to me to help people, or do I value power, money, or intellectual challenge more?). Adolescents base their vocational choices more on their values and capacities and less on their fantasies and interests as they get older (Kelso, 1977).

As adolescents leave this tentative stage, they also begin to take into account the realities of the job market and the requirements for different occupations (Ginzberg, 1972, 1984). They might now consider the availability of job openings in a field such as psychological counseling, the years of education required, the work conditions, and so on. During this third stage of vocational choice, the *realistic stage*, which spans the ages of about 18 to 22, the individual is likely to narrow things down to a specific choice based on interests, capacities, values, and available opportunities. Now serious preparation for a chosen occupation begins.

The main developmental trend evident in Ginzberg's stages is increasing realism about what one can be. As adolescents narrow down career choices in terms of both personal factors (their own interests, capacities, and values) and environmental factors (the opportunities available and the realities of the job market), they seek the vocation that best suits them. According to influential vocational theorists such as John Holland (1973, 1985) and Donald Super (1980, 1991), vocational choice is just this: an effort to find an optimal fit between one's self-concept or personality and an occupation.

The major criticism of theories of vocational choice is that they place too much emphasis on how the individual's qualities affect his or her decisions and too little on environmental influences (Brooks, 1991). For example, as they get older, adolescents from lower-income families, especially those from minority backgrounds, often make compromises in their career plans (Gottfredson, 1981; Lauver & Jones, 1991). Many such youth come to aspire toward less prestigious occupations than middle-class youth do (Hannah & Kahn, 1989; Henderson, Hesketh, & Tuffin, 1988) and begin to doubt their ability to attain high-status jobs (Lauver & Jones, 1991). When so many minority youth in our society are unemployed, it is little wonder that many are more concerned about finding *any* job than about exploring many careers to find the one that best matches their interests, capabilities, and values (Grotevant & Cooper, 1988).

Similarly, the vocational choices of females have been and continue to be constrained by traditional gender norms. Females, especially college women, are increasingly aspiring toward high-status jobs that have traditionally been male dominated (Fiorentine, 1988; Lauver & Jones, 1991). Yet many young women do not seriously consider masculine-stereotyped jobs, doubt their ability to attain such jobs, and aim instead toward feminine-stereotyped—and often lower-status—occupations (Lauver & Jones, 1991; Reid & Stephens, 1985). Those who come from lower socioeconomic backgrounds, have adopted traditional gender norms, and expect to marry and start families early in adulthood are especially likely to set their vocational sights low (Aneshensel & Rosen, 1980; Hannah & Kahn, 1989). They may feel that they cannot achieve important family goals without scaling down their career ambitions.

In short, societal influences discourage many low-income youth and females from seriously considering options that might well fit their interests, capacities, and values. Those adolescents are not alone, however. Many other teenagers of both sexes simply do not do what vocational theorists advise them to do: explore a wide range of occupations, gather information, and then rationally make a choice (Super, 1991). Those who *do* consider a wide range of options are more likely than those who do not to choose careers that fit their personalities well (Grotevant, Cooper, & Kramer, 1986). Just as Erik Erikson claimed, then, it is through questioning, exploring, and experimenting that adolescents achieve an identity. Yet too often adolescents simply drift into one field or another or make impulsive decisions. And too often they are uninformed about the occupations they do choose (Grotevant & Durrett, 1980).

Would adolescents be able to make more informed and rational choices if they had more experience in the world of work? As things stand, the large majority of adolescents in the United States and Canada do work part time during their high school careers. But, as Box 15.1 demonstrates, there is a negative side to gaining early work experience; adolescents in our complex, technological society may be better off concentrating on their schooling than taking on major job responsibilities.

In sum, as adolescents progress from the fantasy stage through the tentative and realistic stages of vocational development, they make increasingly realistic career choices. The choices of low-income youth and of traditional females are often restricted, but, even when adolescents have considerable freedom in choosing a career, they often do not engage in a thorough process of career exploration and planning. The saving grace is that vocational choice is not a binding decision made in adolescence. We have many opportunities as adults to change our minds and chart new life courses.

THE ADULT

The lifestyles of adults are dominated by work—paid or unpaid, outside the home or within the home. So central is work to an adult's identity that we will want to look very closely at the "work life cycle" and its implications for the development of men and women. But it is the total lifestyle of an adult—the way in which work is intertwined with family life—that often determines how satisfied he or she is with life.

BOX 15.1 Should Adolescents Work?

Most adolescents in North America work part time during the school year for at least a portion of their high school careers. How might these early work experiences influence their development? On the positive side, work experience might be expected not only to boost adolescents' bank accounts but also teach them about the world of work, instill work values such as pride in a job well done, and increase their autonomy and self-reliance. On the negative side, though, some developmentalists have wondered whether long hours at work might not detract from time spent on academics, extracurricular activities, and other pursuits important to adolescent intellectual and social development—or might not result in the freedom and economic means to become heavily involved in deviant activities such as drug and alcohol abuse.

Laurence Steinberg and his associates have attempted to find out just how high school students are affected by their work experiences (Greenberger & Steinberg, 1986; Steinberg, 1984; Steinberg & Dornbusch, 1991; Steinberg, Fegley, & Dornbusch, 1993). The research has involved comparing working and nonworking high school students in terms of such factors as their autonomy from parents, self-reliance, self-esteem, sense of investment in school, academic performance, delinquency, and drug and alcohol use.

Overall, this research contains far more bad news than good news. Although Steinberg's early work suggested that working students gain knowledge about the world of work, consumer issues, and financial management and sometimes greater self-reliance from working, a more recent study (Steinberg & Dornbusch, 1991) points to nothing but negative effects of part-time work, especially for students working more than 20 hours a week. High school students who worked 20+ hours a week had grade-point averages about a third of a letter grade lower than those of students who did not work or who worked only 10 or fewer hours per week (Steinberg & Dornbusch, 1991). Working students were also more likely than nonworkers to be disengaged from school—bored and uninvolved in class and prone to cut class and spend little time on homework. In addition, the more adolescents worked, the more independent they were of parental control, the more likely they were to be experiencing psychological distress (anxiety, depression, and physical symptoms such as headaches), and the more frequently they used alcohol and drugs and engaged in delinquent acts. These negative effects of work generally showed a gradual increase as the number of hours a student worked increased. The effects were evident across socioeconomic and ethnic groups, although the impacts on academic performance were especially negative for Anglo- and Asian-American students, two groups that ordinarily do well in school.

Could it be that students who choose to work or must work long hours already have more problems than other adolescents and that their jobs actually do nothing to worsen their problems? Steinberg and his colleagues (1993) were able to check out this possibility by following students over the course of a year to see what they were like before and after they began working. Students who worked long hours were indeed more disenchanted with school and independent of their parents even before they began working. However, working led to *further* alienation from school and *greater* distance from parents and contributed to *new* problems that had not been apparent before, including increased drug and alcohol use and delinquency and decreased self-reliance. Moreover, students who worked but quit during the course of the study improved their school performance after they stopped working (see also Bachman & Schulenberg, 1993). In short, although problem-prone adolescents may actively choose to work long hours, their development is in turn negatively affected by their heavy involvement in work experiences (Steinberg et al., 1993).

How do we explain these rather gloomy findings? Why doesn't work experience speed up the process of becoming an adult? Perhaps because teenagers typically work in food service jobs (pouring soft drinks behind the counter at McDonald's, scooping ice cream, and the like), perform manual labor (especially cleaning or janitorial work), or serve as clerks or cashiers in stores. These routine and repetitive jobs offer few opportunities for self-direction or decision making and only rarely call on academic skills such as reading and math (Steinberg, 1984). In short, they are simply not the kinds of jobs that "build character" or teach new skills—although they might well motivate some adolescents to stay in school so that they can get better jobs! In addition, working long hours cuts into the time available for schoolwork and school-related activities and provides the money that can purchase a car, greater freedom from parental supervision, and, in some cases, alcohol and drugs.

Steinberg concludes that many adolescents in our complex and rapidly changing society might be better off postponing work if possible so that they can concentrate on obtaining a solid education, growing as individuals in their relationships with family and peers, and exploring the many career options available to them. Interestingly, only 21% of Japanese and Chinese 11th-graders (compared to 74% in the United States) hold jobs; they and their parents agree that their top priority is to do well in school (Stevenson et al., 1993). Steinberg (1984) acknowledges that many adolescents can benefit from vocational training programs in the schools and from *school-based* work experience programs in which students receive classroom instruction that can help them benefit from their trial work experiences. Such programs allow teenagers to blend their roles as students and workers instead of assembling Big Macs when they should be working algebra problems.

Daniel Levinson's Conception of Adult Development

Daniel Levinson (1986, 1990; Levenson et al., 1978) proposed an influential stage theory of adult development that can aid us in organizing our examination of adult career paths and lifestyles. The stages, which were formulated from interviews with 40 men aged 35 to 45 from four occupational groups (executives, biologists, novelists, and factory workers), describe the unfolding of what Levinson called an individual's **life structure.** This is an overall pattern of life that reflects the person's priorities and relationships with other people and the larger society. Central to the life structure are family and work roles. Levinson proposed that adults go through a repeated process of first building a life structure and then questioning and altering it. Structure-building periods, during which the person goes about pursuing goals, alternate with transitional periods, when the person questions his or her life decisions. Box 15.2 outlines Levinson's first six stages.

Although Levinson did not interview men in their 50s and 60s, he speculated that the same alternating periods of structure building and structure questioning continue into later life. Moreover, he claimed that women experience the same stages that men do (Levinson, 1986). In fact, Levinson was convinced that his stages are both maturational in nature and universal. Environmental factors will influence the specifics of an adult's life, but the basic pattern of building, questioning, and rebuilding will still be evident under the surface. Levinson's perspective has gained much attention as a way of conceptualizing how adults progress in their careers and how they change as individuals. Let's see how well the theory fares when we match it up with research on vocational development during the adult years.

Career Paths during Adulthood

Not all research supports Levinson's theory in all its details, but much research suggests that young, middle-aged, and older adults confront different issues in their roles as workers. After engaging in much experimentation as young adults, people settle down into a chosen occupation. Ultimately, they prepare for the end of their careers and make the transition into retirement.

Early Adulthood: Exploration and Establishment

According to Levinson, early adulthood is a time for exploring vocational possibilities, launching careers, making tentative commitments, revising them if necessary, seeking advancement, and establishing oneself firmly in what one hopes is a suitable occupation. Studies of men suggest that most do formulate what Levinson calls a "dream," centering mainly on occupational goals, in their late teens or early 20s (Drebing & Gooden, 1991). They then test out vocational possibilities and ultimately "settle down" into a career.

BOX 15.2 Daniel Levinson's Stages of Adult Development

1. *Early Adult Transition (ages 17 to 22).* Make the transition from adolescence to early adulthood. Try to establish independence from parents and explore possibilities for an adult identity. Form *the dream*, a vision of your life goals.
2. *Entering the Adult World (ages 22 to 28).* Build your first life structure, often by making and testing out a career choice and getting married. Do your best to succeed. Find people who can support your development—a "special woman" (normally a man's wife) and/or a **mentor** (a guide or advisor, perhaps a trusted faculty member or a supervisor at work). Do not question your life; work hard to get off to a good start as an adult, though always with the idea of keeping doors of opportunity open.
3. *Age-30 Transition (ages 28 to 33).* Ask whether what you are doing is really what you want. Are you becoming locked into a poor career choice or an unsatisfying marriage? If any uncomfortable feelings arise from your questioning, either ignore them and plug away, make small adjustments in your life structure, or plan a more major life change (for example, a job change, a divorce, or a decision to return to school).
4. *Settling Down (ages 33 to 40).* Build a new, and often somewhat different, life structure; "make it," or realize your dream. Outgrow your need for a mentor and "become your own man." As in the structure-building period of Entering the Adult World, be ambitious, task oriented, and unreflective.
5. *Midlife Transition (ages 40 to 45).* Begin all over again to question what you have built and where you are heading. If you have been a success, ask whether the dream you formulated as a young adult was really a worthy goal; if you have not achieved your dream, face the fact that you may never achieve it. Confront the facts of aging, and ask what you really want for the future. Consider making major changes in your life structure.
6. *Entering Middle Adulthood (ages 45 to 50).* Create a new life structure appropriate to middle age. If you successfully confronted and resolved midlife issues during the Midlife Transition, you may gain self-understanding, a capacity for mentoring younger adults at work, and a deeper concern for your family—much like the middle-aged adult whom Erik Erikson describes as having acquired a sense of generativity.

(Levinson theorized that this process of building a life structure and then questioning it during a transition period then continues thoughout middle and later adulthood.)

Using data from a longitudinal study of males tracked from adolescence to age 36 (see Super, 1985), Susan Phillips (1982) examined whether men's decisions about jobs at different ages were tentative and exploratory (for example, "to see if I really liked that kind of work") or more final (for example, "to get started in a field I wanted"). The proportions of decisions that were predominantly exploratory were 80% at age 21, 50% at age 25, and 37% at age 36. In other words, young adults progress from wide-open exploration, to tentative or trial commitments, to a stabilization of their choices. Yet notice that, even in their mid-30s, many men were still trying to figure out what they wanted to be when they grew up! The males in this study held an average of seven full-time jobs or training positions between the ages of 18 and 36, and 30% of them not only changed jobs but changed *fields* between ages 25 and 36 (Phillips, 1982).

The situation is very similar for women: They too are highly likely to change their career goals after they leave school and then eventually settle on an occupation in their 30s (Jenkins, 1989; Ornstein & Isabella, 1990). Thus we may make vocational choices as adolescents, but we are obviously very open to making new choices as young adults. It is when the fit between the individual's personality or aptitudes and the demands of the occupation is poor that young adults become dissatisfied and open to exploring other alternatives (Bizot & Goldman, 1993).

Once a person settles on a satisfactory career path, the degree of early success attained greatly affects later outcomes. Douglas Bray and Ann Howard (1983; Howard & Bray, 1988), in longitudinal studies of individuals who started out as beginning managers at AT&T and remained with the company until middle age, found that it was apparent quite early who was on the "fast track" for success and who was not. The successes, those—who rose quickly to higher management levels—tended to be college graduates who were bright, aggressive, and achievement oriented. Their success motivated them all the more, their job satisfaction increased, and their work became more and more central in their lives. Less successful managers continued to be motivated to do their jobs well but lost much of their motivation to advance, perhaps because they realized that they had little chance of doing so. Work became less central in their lives; instead, family, religion, and other nonvocational concerns assumed greater importance (see Figure 15.4). Interestingly, successful and less successful managers were equally satisfied with their lives in general, but they apparently found very different sources of satisfaction.

In sum, the adolescent's initial vocational choices and priorities are by no means the adult's final choices and priorities. As Levinson theorized, adults seem to start out by formulating a career plan (or dream), then engage in much questioning and make trial commitments early in their careers, and eventually settle into a particular career and lifestyle. Apparently, many young adults find that their first jobs are not what they hoped they would be. They then change jobs, or they stay in the same organization but begin to view other aspects of life as more important than work. Other adults achieve early success and become even more committed to advancing their careers.

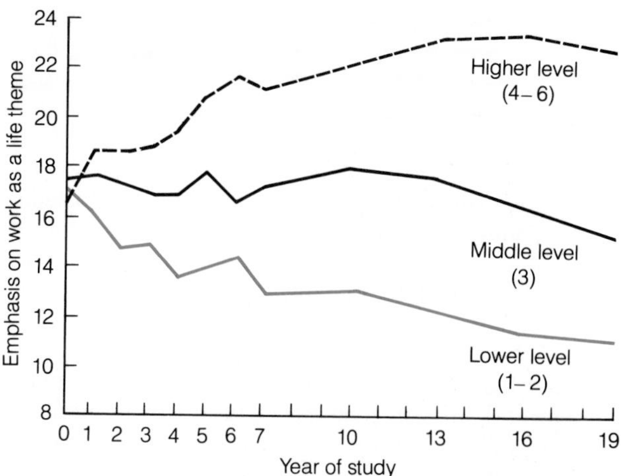

FIGURE 15.4 The extent to which successful ("higher-level") and less successful managers view work as a central theme in their lives over the course of their careers. (From Bray & Howard, 1983.)

Middle Adulthood: Is There a Midlife Crisis?

According to Levinson, the transition period from age 40 to 45 is a developmentally significant time of **midlife crisis**—of questioning one's entire life structure, including one's career, and raising unsettling issues about where one has been and where one is heading. True, most of Levinson's middle-aged men did not seek divorces, quit their jobs, buy red sports cars, and behave like adolescents, as popular images of the midlife crisis might suggest. However, Levinson characterized 80% of the men in his study as having experienced a bona fide crisis—a period of intense inner struggles and disturbing realizations—in their early 40s. What have other researchers concluded about the midlife crisis?

Most everyone seems to agree that middle age is a time when many important issues arise and when men and women *can* find themselves engaged in a painful self-evaluation process (Drebing & Gooden, 1991; Farrell & Rosenberg, 1981; Mercer, Nichols, & Doyle, 1989). Yet many researchers seriously doubt that most adults experience a genuine "crisis" at midlife or that this crisis occurs in such a narrowly defined age range. For example, George Vaillant (1977) found that many of the middle-aged men he studied were evaluating their lives but that virtually none could be described as experiencing a painful upheaval, or crisis.

And Bonnie Hedlund and Peter Ebersole (1983) found that only about 20% of the middle-aged men they studied were reevaluating their dreams or raising questions about the meaning of their lives, which suggests that this sort of soul-searching is far from universal. What's more, midlife questioning was not restricted to the early 40s, as Levinson claimed. Instead, men questioned their lives at a variety of ages, often in response to specific life events such as getting married, changing jobs, or experiencing marital problems.

What about women? Studies aimed at determining whether Levinson's stages apply to females suggest that women's development is more complex and "messy" than men's. Rather than forming a "dream" that centers on career, many young women formulate "split" dreams centering on both career and family (Roberts & Newton, 1987). The "Age-30 Transition" then appears to be an especially important period of reevaluation for many women (Mercer et al., 1989; Roberts & Newton, 1987). Women who had emphasized marriage and family in their 20s sometimes set individual career goals for themselves, whereas career-oriented women sometimes find themselves longing to get married or to have children. In their late 30s or 40s, some women experience a period of midlife unrest in which they seek to define themselves as individuals rather than primarily as wives and mothers (Helson & Wink, 1992; Mercer et al., 1989). Mainly, though, women do not experience distinct stages of the sort Levinson describes so much as *continuous* struggles with the issue of how to balance career and family goals (Mercer et al., 1989; Roberts & Newton, 1987).

If a stage of midlife crisis in the early 40s were widespread, we might expect adults to experience significant personality changes at midlife or to display symptoms of emotional disturbance. This does not seem to be the case for either men or women (Costa, McCrae, & Arenberg, 1983; Costa et al., 1986). Finally, if midlife crises were widespread, we might expect middle-aged adults to be dissatisfied with their work. Instead, middle-aged men and women are generally *more* satisfied with their jobs than younger adults are (Rhodes, 1983; Warr, 1992). In sum, Levinson may have overestimated the extent to which midlife crisis occurs. It would seem more appropriate to call the phenomenon midlife *questioning* than midlife crisis, to recognize that it can occur in response to life events at a variety of ages, and to appreciate that it need not be emotionally wrenching.

How, then, should we evaluate Levinson's theory overall? He certainly stimulated much thought and research by suggesting that people experience stagelike changes in their life structures during adulthood. He also captured the flow of vocational development for both men and women in early adulthood quite well. However, because adults are so varied, it is difficult to fit them into a series of universal stages that unfold at predictable ages. The changes that adults undergo seem to be timed more by the normative and nonnormative life events they experience than by their ages. Thus some 25-year-olds may be entering the adult world and building preliminary life structures, but others may still be wondering what they want to do in life, and still others may be reevaluating their dreams because they dread going to work each morning. The broad themes and developmental trends that Levinson identified are supported by research, but whether most adult lives change in precisely the ways and at precisely the times that he claimed has not been established. And how well Levinson's stages fit women, blue-collar men, and adults in other cultures remains to be determined.

Later Adulthood: Aging Workers

Do we become less able or less motivated to perform well on the job as we enter our 50s and 60s? We can easily think of occupations in which age is a liability. Kareem Abdul Jabbar may have been able to continue the strenuous work of playing pro basketball until age 42, but most pro athletes retire earlier than that. Aging workers who perform heavy physical labor may also find their work increasingly difficult. But do most adults reach a point at which they are simply over the hill?

As it turns out, the job performance of workers in their 50s and 60s is not very different overall from that of younger workers (McEvoy & Cascio, 1989; Rhodes, 1983; Waldman & Avolio, 1986). Age is simply not a very good predictor of how well a person will perform his or her job, and this holds true for both white-collar and blue-collar jobs. Not only are older workers generally as competent as younger workers, but they typically have more positive attitudes toward their work (Rhodes, 1983; Warr, 1992). They are *more* satisfied with their jobs, *more* involved in their work, and *less* interested in finding a new job than younger workers are.

Why is this? Because young adults are often in an exploratory or trial phase of their careers, many of them may not yet feel that they have found the right niche. Young adults are also likely to have less responsible and involving jobs than older workers (Rhodes, 1983). Older workers, by contrast, may have found jobs that suit them well, or they may have settled for less-than-ideal jobs, fearing that it would be difficult for them to find new work. Finally, it could also be that younger and older generations apply different standards when they evaluate their jobs. Whatever the cause, we must conclude from these studies that, on the average, workers in their 50s and 60s equal younger workers in performance and often surpass them in motivation and job satisfaction. The federal government seems to be taking these messages to heart, for it has passed legislation to raise or eliminate mandatory retirement ages and to protect older workers from the age discrimination in hiring and retention that they have too often faced.

Women, Work, and the Family

In our account of the work life cycle to this point, we have had to draw primarily on studies of men. There is a simple reason for this: Traditionally, men have been viewed as the major breadwinners in the family and have dominated the labor force. All that has been rapidly changing, however. Now researchers are looking more closely at *women's* careers to find out whether the same principles that apply to men also apply to women. Most of the trends in vocational development already described are valid for both sexes, but women's careers differ from men's in significant ways.

As we noted in Chapter 14, the employment patterns of women have changed considerably in recent decades. Most women now work outside the home, and the percentage of married women with children under 6 who work has skyrocketed from 12% in 1950 to 57% today (Chadwick & Heaton, 1992). Women are also working for more years and are more often working out of preference than out of necessity (Herring & Wilson-Sadberry, 1993). Finally, women are now entering a wide range of fields that were formerly male dominated or even closed to women: coal mining, truck driving, engineering, and medicine, to name a few.

At the same time, some things have not changed much at all. For example, although the number of female lawyers had risen to about 100,000 by 1984 (about five times as many as there had been a decade earlier), nearly *4 million* women that year were secretaries, and 99% of all secretaries were women (Waldman, 1985). Most women (55%) work in clerical and service occupations, which have traditionally been female dominated and low paying (Unger & Crawford, 1992). Moreover, the gap between women's and men's earnings has narrowed some but has not closed: Across all jobs, a woman averaged about 59 cents for every dollar a man earned in 1978; by 1989 it was 66 cents for every dollar a man earned (Sorensen, 1991). So why aren't women achieving more in the workplace? To answer that question, we must focus on two major barriers to women's career achievement: sex discrimination and conflicts between work and family.

Women today are gradually "breaking through" in traditionally male-dominated fields.

Sex Discrimination

It may be difficult for today's young adults to appreciate that, not very long ago, women were simply barred from entering many occupations or were forbidden to work by their husbands, who viewed a wife's "having" to work as a sign that they had failed as breadwinners. Today, women cannot legally be denied entry into prestigious, male-dominated occupations, but they continue to face discrimination in the labor force. It is no accident, for example, that traditional "female" jobs often pay less than "male" jobs, or that secretaries sometimes earn less than janitors in the same building. There is still a tendency to view "women's work" as less valuable and to assume that a woman somehow needs less money because her husband is the family's major earner. Even when women with the same management degrees as men enter the same kinds of management jobs at the same salaries and obtain equal performance ratings from their supervisors, they do not rise as far in the organization or make as much money as men (Cox & Harquail, 1991).

Moreover, traditional gender roles continue to pervade the workplace. Women are pressured to be "feminine" rather than to display the stereotyped "masculine" behaviors that often lead to career advancement (Gutek, 1985; Unger & Crawford, 1992). Also, one out of two women can expect to experience some form of sexual harassment during her academic career or work life (Fitzgerald & Shullman, 1993). The effects can include anxiety, depression, and stress-related physical ailments, all of which can hurt performance on the job (Gutek & Koss, 1993).

Traditional gender roles also make it difficult for women to obtain the same support for their career ambitions that men receive. For one thing, many women do not receive the mentoring that Daniel Levinson and others have found to be so important to vocational success (Roberts & Newton, 1987). In many companies an "old-boy network" helps promising young men make the right connections and rise quickly to the top. However, since few women have made it to the top in business and industry, a comparable "old-girl network" does not yet exist. Women who identify male mentors may benefit in many ways but are less likely to see their mentors as role models or to socialize with them after work than are women who manage to find female mentors (Gaskill, 1991; Ragins & McFarlin, 1990). In addition, working women generally do not receive as much support for their career goals from their husbands as Levinson's men received from their "special women" (Roberts & Newton, 1987). Even today, over half of all college men are not sure they want their future wives to work if their own income is sufficient to support the family (Spade & Reese, 1991). Clearly, a number of forms of gender-based discrimination make it difficult for women to achieve in the workplace.

Role Conflict

A second major barrier to women's career achievement is **role conflict**—the feeling of being pulled in different directions by the competing demands of different roles (in this instance, family roles and work roles). Role conflict can result when family responsibilities interfere with work performance or when the demands of work interfere with family life (Gutek, Searle, & Klepa, 1991). Many modern women feel they must be "jugglers" (Crosby, 1991), able to feed the children and get them off to school, put in a full day at work, pick up the children, swing by the supermarket, fill the gas tank, fix dinner, throw in a couple of loads of laundry, and still find time for meaningful conversations with their husbands. They are perpetual-motion machines, always, it seems, doing two or three things at once.

Because society continues to view women as the primary keepers of home and hearth, many working wives end up coping with role conflict by subordinating career goals to family responsibilities. Steady movement up the career ladder is most likely to occur when an employee works full time and continuously in the same organization (Sorensen, 1991; Van Velsor & O'Rand, 1984). However, few married women have followed this traditional male route to success. Instead, they have often interrupted their careers to bear and raise children (Moen, 1992; Sorensen, 1983; Waite, Haggstrom, & Kanouse, 1986). In one study of retired elderly women, 55% of the single women but *none* of the married women had worked continuously throughout their adult lives (Keating & Jeffrey, 1983). Today fewer women are dropping out of the labor force while they raise their children (Avioli & Kaplan, 1992; Crosby, 1991; Rexroat, 1992). Yet many women *do* switch from full-time to part-time employment or take less demanding jobs as a means of coping with role conflict (Moen, 1992); in fact, nearly 40% of mothers with preschool children work part time (Folk & Beller, 1993).

Clearly, women who do take part-time jobs or interrupt their careers to raise children damage their chances of rising to highly paid, responsible positions (Sorensen, 1991). Meanwhile, the women who *do* make it to the top of the career ladder, especially in male-dominated fields, sometimes cope with role conflict by limiting their involvement in marriage and parenthood. These highly successful career women are more likely than most working women to be single, divorced, or separated—or, if they are married, to remain childless or have small families (Jenkins, 1989).

Does this mean that it is impossible for women to "have it all"—to combine marriage, family, and a full-time, uninterrupted career? Aren't women who attempt to have it all likely to experience extraordinary role conflict? And won't they be susceptible to the related problem of **role overload**—having too much to do and too little time in which to do it? It has always been assumed—and research supports this assumption—that men are best off psychologically when they participate in multiple roles: when they are workers, husbands, *and* fathers (Baruch, Biener, & Barnett, 1987). Is it different for women?

Grace Baruch and Rosalind Barnett (1986) examined relationships between middle-aged women's lifestyles and their self-esteem, happiness, and level of depression. They compared women who did or did not participate in each of three central roles: worker, spouse, and parent. Moreover, they asked these women about the positive and negative aspects of each of their roles. As it turned out, the sheer number of roles a woman played had little impact on her well-being. Although working outside the home tended to be associated with high self-esteem, women who were wives, mothers, *and* workers were generally neither worse off nor better off than women who played fewer roles and who would be expected to experience less role conflict and overload. Instead, it was the *quality of the individual's experience* in work and family roles that was most closely associated with well-being. Women experienced greater happiness and self-esteem, and less depression, when the rewards they gained from *whatever* roles they played outweighed the hassles. It is now clear that women do not necessarily suffer, and sometimes benefit, when they combine roles as paid workers, wives, and mothers (Crosby, 1991; Moen, 1992). True, some working mothers with young children and unsupportive husbands are under tremendous stress and need relief (Moen, 1992). However, many women gain more than they lose by playing multiple roles, especially if both they and their partners feel good about their working (Spitze, 1988; Vannoy & Philliber, 1992).

Barriers to women's career success caused by sex discrimination and role conflict and overload continue to exist, but women's and men's lives *are* becoming more similar than they used to be (Shelton, 1992). Many women of the 1960s and 1970s experienced a lot of role conflict and overload because both they and their husbands believed that they should continue to fulfill their traditional family responsibilities despite working full time (Pleck, 1985). More recently, role conflict and role overload seem to be decreasing some. Women are spending less time on household tasks and child care, and men are slowly but steadily increasing their involvement in these activities, especially in dual-career families (Dancer & Gilbert, 1993; Moen, 1992). By one estimate, men did 46% as much housework as women in 1975 but 57% as much as women in 1987 (Shelton, 1992). The burdens of mopping and scouring still fall heavier on women than on men, but the division of labor is becoming somewhat more equitable. Husbands are also more supportive than they used to be of the idea that women should have careers (Rexroat, 1992). If present trends continue, we will see more and more families in which *both* men and women are attempting to balance and integrate their central roles as workers, spouses, and parents—and are faring well psychologically because they find gratification in each of these roles.

And what, you might ask, will become of their children? As we saw earlier, the effects on infants and young children of attending day care rather than being cared for at home depend on the quality of care received but are not necessarily negative. More generally, there is no indication that a mother's working—in and of itself—has damaging effects on child development (Hoffman, 1989; Moen, 1992). Indeed, there are signs that children, especially girls, may benefit from the role model a working mother provides, for they tend to be more independent, to set higher educational and vocational goals, and to adopt less stereotyped views of men's and women's roles than children whose mothers do not work (Hoffman, 1989).

Having a working mother *can* be a negative experience, though, especially for young children whose mothers return to full-time work after being at home (Moorehouse, 1991). The key may be whether or not such mothers are able to continue spending "quality time" with their children after they return to work. Martha Moorehouse (1991) found that 6-year-olds whose mothers began working full time were actually more cognitively and socially competent (according to their teachers) than children whose mothers were homemakers *if* these youngsters frequently shared activities such as reading, telling stories, and talking with their mothers. However, they fared worse than children with stay-at-home mothers if they lost out on opportunities for meaningful interaction with their mothers. Similarly, Ann Crouter and her colleagues (1990) discovered that sons of working mothers perform poorly in school if they are not adequately monitored by their parents but perform as well as boys and girls of nonemployed mothers if their parents keep tabs on them and ensure that they pay attention to their school work.

Fortunately, most dual-career couples are able to successfully compensate for lost hours of parent/child interaction during the work week by spending extra time with their children on weekends. Working mothers somehow manage to devote almost as much time as nonworking mothers do to child-centered activities with their children, mainly by giving up personal leisure and housework time (not to mention sleep!), and their husbands pitch in by spending more time with their children than the husbands of stay-at-home mothers do (Nock & Kingston, 1988). The result? Many working couples, though busy and often stressed, are able to enjoy the personal benefits of working without compromising their children's development.

What Does Work Contribute to Adult Development?

Play and schooling clearly contribute to a child's development, but what should we conclude about the effects of work on an adult's adjustment and personal growth? An adult's occupation is a central part of his or her identity. It means a great deal to people to say that they are psychologists, electricians, or nurses. Meanwhile, the experience of being fired or laid off is often highly damaging to an adult's self-esteem, mental health, and family relationships (Price, 1992). Work also provides many personal rewards besides money—for example, opportunities to master challenges, gain status, and form enjoyable relationships (Havighurst, 1982). Just as obviously, work can be a source of stress that spills over into family life and in some cases causes physical or mental disorders (Crouter & McHale, 1993).

Perhaps most interesting is evidence that certain kinds of work stretch the capacities of adults, just as certain kinds of play and schooling stretch children's minds. Melvin Kohn and Carmi Schooler (1982, 1983) have explored the implications for adult development of the **substantive complexity** of a job, or the extent to which it provides opportunities for using one's mind and making independent judgments. For example, a secretary with a substantively complex job would do more than merely perform whatever typing assignments are placed on her desk. She might also handle the department budget, decide what office supplies are needed, interact with the public, assign tasks to clerical helpers, and generally take the initiative for making a number of complex decisions every day.

Kohn and Schooler find that substantively complex or intellectually challenging work is associated with greater intellectual flexibility (an ability to handle intellectual problems adeptly and to keep an open mind about issues) and with greater self-direction (a tendency to be self-confident, independent minded, responsible, and tolerant of others). By contrast, people who engage in intellectually unchallenging work tend to be relatively ineffective thinkers, are negative toward themselves and conforming in relation to others, and are often psychologically distressed as well. People who are already intellectually capable and self-directed, of course, are especially likely to land substantively complex jobs. However, Kohn and his colleagues demonstrate that the quality of one's job in turn influences one's subsequent personal qualities (see also Clausen & Gilens, 1990).

As a rule, the jobs held by middle-class white-collar workers and professionals offer more opportunities for intellectual and personal growth than do working-class jobs. However, Kohn and his colleagues also find that the relationship between substantively complex work and intellectual and personal development holds up at every socioeconomic level. Moreover, mothers whose jobs are substantively complex seem to provide a more stimulating home environment for their children than women who have less intellectually challenging jobs (Menaghan & Parcel, 1991).

So, the way we pass our days as adults can have long-term implications for intellectual and psychological functioning. It seems that those youth who are intellectually challenged in school are likely to develop the intellectual and personal qualities that will allow them to land substantively complex jobs—and that their initial strengths will be further enhanced by their daily work activities. The old idea that work builds character apparently has a good deal of truth to it!

Retirement

Although they are still able to work, the large majority of men and women in our society choose to retire sometime in their 60s. Earlier in this century most people continued working until they simply could not work any longer. Indeed, as late as 1930, over half of all men aged 65 or older were still working (Palmore et al., 1985). The introduction of Social Security in 1934 and the increased availability of private pension plans changed all that, making it financially possible for more men and women to retire. These programs have also reflected society's judgment that older workers *should* retire. The result, as Figure 15.5 shows, is that only about 22% of adults aged 65–74 and 4% of adults aged 75 and older hold regular jobs (Herzog et al., 1989).

How do people adjust to the final chapter of the work life cycle? Robert Atchley (1976) has proposed that adults progress through a series of phases as they make the transition from worker to retiree. The process of adjustment begins with a *preretirement phase* in which workers nearing retirement gather information and plan for the future (Evans, Ekerdt, & Bossé, 1985). As retirement draws closer and workers start to think in terms of time left until the big day, they often begin to separate themselves psychologically from their jobs, coming to view work as a hassle they would just as soon be rid of (Ekerdt & DeViney, 1993).

Just after they retire, workers often experience a *honeymoon phase* when they relish their newfound freedom and perhaps head for the beach, golf course, or camping grounds. Then, according to Atchley, many enter a *disenchantment phase* as the novelty wears off; they feel aimless and sometimes unhappy. Finally, they move on to a *reorientation phase* in which they begin to put together a realistic and satisfying lifestyle. Research supports this view: David Ekerdt and his colleagues (Ekerdt, Bossé, & Levkoff, 1985) found that (1) men who had been retired only a few months were indeed in a honeymoon period in which they were highly satisfied with life and optimistic about the future, (2) men who had been retired 13 to 18 months were rather disenchanted with life, and (3) men who had been retired for longer periods were relatively satisfied once again (see also Williamson, Rinehart, & Blank, 1992).

So, retirement takes getting used to. After retirees have adapted to being retired, though, are they worse off than they were before they retired? Negative images of the retired person abound in our society: He or she supposedly ends up feeling useless, old, bored, sickly, and generally dissatisfied with life. Erdman Palmore and his colleagues (1985) have analyzed seven longitudinal studies of retired men and women. Their main message is that retirement has few effects at all on men and even fewer on women!

Retirement's most consistent effect is a reduction in the individual's income—on average, to about three-fourths of what it was before retirement. The precise financial impact depends on a worker's socioeconomic status (Palmore et al., 1985). Workers who were living below the poverty line before they retired actually have more money after retirement because they become eligible for government programs for the aging poor. High-income individuals have less money after retirement but apparently have enough to satisfy them. Hardest hit are workers whose incomes were below average, but above the poverty line, before they retired; their already-meager incomes drop considerably.

Retired people generally do *not* experience a decline in their health simply because they retire. Their activity patterns don't change much either. About 35–40% of older adults participate in volunteer activities (Chambré, 1993), and retired adults do not alter their involvement in social and leisure activities much at all (Palmore et al., 1985; Parnes & Less, 1985). Indeed, retirement has no noticeable effect on the size of people's social networks, the frequency of their social contacts, or their satisfaction with the social support they receive (Bossé et al., 1993). Finally, retirement does not seem to disrupt marriages (Ekerdt

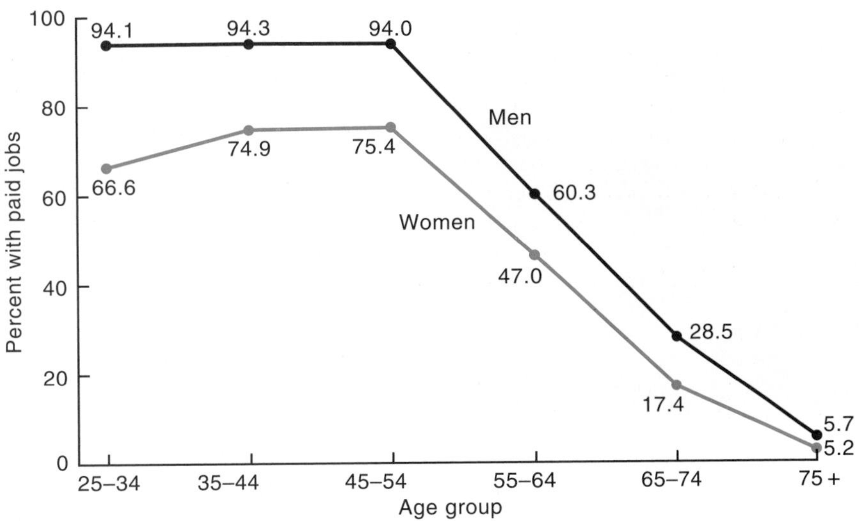

FIGURE 15.5 Percentages of U.S. adults who have regular paid jobs at various ages (not counted are volunteer work and irregularly paid activities). Women are less involved in paid work than men, especially in early adulthood, but they devote more time to unpaid housework, child care, and helping activities. (Based on data from Herzog et al., 1989.)

& Vinick, 1991) or reduce life satisfaction (Palmore et al., 1985).

Overall, then, most retirees adapt quite successfully to retirement and to the drop in income that it typically involves. Yet there are huge individual differences in adjustment. What makes for a favorable adjustment? Adults who (1) retire voluntarily rather than involuntarily, (2) enjoy good health, and (3) have the financial resources to live comfortably typically fare better than those who are forced to retire because of poor health and find themselves with inadequate incomes (Herzog, House, & Morgan, 1991; Palmore et al., 1985). Unfortunately, many widows and minority-group members, after living on limited incomes during their working years, must spend their "golden years" in poverty (Arber & Ginn, 1991; Clark & Maddox, 1992).

The Keys to Successful Aging: Activity or Disengagement?

What makes for a happy and fulfilling old age? One theory of successful aging, **activity theory,** holds that aging adults will find their lives satisfying to the extent that they can maintain their previous lifestyles and activity levels, either by continuing old activities or by finding substitutes—for example, by replacing work with golf, volunteer work, or other stimulating pursuits (Havighurst, Neugarten, & Tobin, 1968; see also Fry, 1992). According to this theory, psychological needs do not really change as people enter old age, and most aging individuals continue to want an active lifestyle.

Other theorists have taken almost precisely the opposite stand on the keys to successful aging. **Disengagement theory** claims that successful aging involves a mutual withdrawal of the aging individual and society (Cumming & Henry, 1961). That is, the aging individual, whose capacities and needs are different from those she or he once had, seeks to leave old roles behind and *reduce* activity. Meanwhile, society both encourages and benefits from the older person's disengagement.

Which is it? Throughout this text we have seen evidence that individuals who remain active in old age benefit from their activity. Those who are physically active maintain their health longer than those who lead sedentary lives (see Chapter 5). Those who are intellectually active are likely to maintain their cognitive functions longer (see Chapter 9 and our earlier discussion of the cognitive benefits of complex work). Finally, those who participate in meaningful social relationships are likely to be more satisfied with life than those who are socially isolated (see Chapter 13). In other words, there is more support for activity theory than for disengagement theory.

But, before we conclude that activity theory tells us all we need to know about successful aging, let's add three qualifications. First, the relationship between sheer level of activity and life satisfaction or well-being is often quite weak (Fry, 1992). Apparently many individuals who are quite inactive are nonetheless satisfied with their lives, and many who are very busy are nonetheless unhappy. This suggests that the *quality* of one's activity is probably more important than its quantity.

Second, some features of disengagement theory have merit. As we saw in Chapter 10, for example, older adults sometimes adopt a more passive stance toward the world around them and become more introspective than they were earlier in life. This sort of psychological withdrawal could be viewed as a kind of

Many older adults subscribe to the activity theory of aging, attempting to find substitutes for lost roles and activities. Others find happiness through disengagement and would just as soon sit and watch.

disengagement. Moreover, most older people today do withdraw voluntarily from certain roles and activities. Most impressively, older adults — and younger members of society as well — are very supportive of the concept of retirement, suggesting that disengagement from work roles is mutually satisfying to the aging person and to society.

But third, and perhaps most important, neither activity theory *nor* disengagement theory adequately allows for individual differences in personality traits and preferences. Activity theorists assume that most people will benefit from maintaining an active lifestyle; disengagement theorists assume that most people will be best off if they disengage. Instead, it appears that people are most satisfied in old age when they can achieve *a good fit between their lifestyle and their individual needs, preferences, and personality* (Fry, 1992; Seleen, 1982). An energetic and outgoing woman might who is denied the opportunity to maintain her active lifestyle in old age may be quite miserable. By contrast, a man who earlier in life found work to be a hassle might like nothing better in his retirement years than to take it easy, do a little fishing, and sit on the porch; he might be extremely unhappy if he were forced to continue working or if he found himself in a nursing home where he was pestered daily to participate in planned recreational activities. Still another older adult may find satisfaction from maintaining a few highly important roles and activities but withdrawing from less central ones (Rapkin & Fischer, 1992).

In short, we cannot assume, as both activity theory and disengagement theory do, that what suits one is likely to suit all. Rather, we should once again adopt an interactional model of development that emphasizes the goodness of fit between person and environment.

APPLICATIONS: IMPROVING THE QUALITY OF EDUCATION

Quite obviously, developmental research has much to contribute to the improvement of education. Educational practices have been greatly influenced by studies of how children of different ages learn and think, what motivates them, and how their achievement and adjustment to school can be enhanced. Today, developmental researchers concerned about the quality of education in North American schools are attempting to learn new lessons about how to educate children by studying what appear to be highly effective schools in Japan and other Asian countries.

Cross-cultural research conducted by Harold Stevenson and his colleagues (Stevenson & Lee, 1990; Stevenson, Lee, & Stigler, 1986; Stevenson, Chen, & Lee, 1993) leaves no doubt that schoolchildren in Taiwan, the People's Republic of China, and Japan outperform students in the United States in math, reading, and other school subjects. The gap in math performance is especially striking; in recent testings of 5th-graders, for example, only 4% of Chinese children and 10% of Japanese students had scores on a math achievement test as low as those of the average American child (Stevenson et al., 1993). Achievement differences of this sort are evident from the time children enter school and increase as children progress from 1st to 5th to 11th grade (Stevenson et al., 1993). Why do these differences exist, and what clues can they provide for improving American education?

The problem is not that American students are "dumber." When they enter school, they perform just about as well on IQ tests as their Asian counterparts (Stevenson et al., 1985), and they score at least as well as Japanese and Chinese students on general-information tests of material *not* typically covered in school (Stevenson et al., 1993). Instead, the achievement gap between American and Asian students seems to be rooted in cultural differences in educational attitudes and practices. For example:

1. Asian students spend more time being educated. Elementary school teachers in Asian countries devote more class time to academics — for example, two to three times as many hours a week on math instruction (see Figure 15.6). The classroom is also a businesslike place where little time is wasted; Asian students spend about 95% of their time at "on task" activities such as listening to the teacher and completing assignments, whereas American students spend only about 80% of their time "on task" (Stigler, Lee, & Stevenson, 1987). Asian students also attend school for more hours per day and more days per year (Stevenson et al., 1986).

2. Asian students, especially Japanese students, are assigned and complete considerably more home-

work than American students (Stevenson & Lee, 1990; see also Figure 15.6).

3. Asian parents are strongly committed to the educational process. They are never quite satisfied with how their children are doing in school or with the quality of education their children are receiving; American parents seem to settle for less (Stevenson et al., 1993). Asian parents also receive frequent communications from their children's teachers in notebooks children carry to and from school each day. They find out how their children are progressing and follow teachers' suggestions for encouraging and assisting their children at home (Stevenson & Lee, 1990).

4. Parents, teachers, and students share a strong belief that hard work or effort will pay off in better learning, whereas Americans tend to put more emphasis on ability as a cause of good or poor performance. The result may be that Americans give up too quickly on a child who appears to have low intellectual ability.

The formula for more effective education is not so mysterious after all, judging from the success of Japanese and Chinese educational systems. The secret is to get teachers, students, and parents working together to make education the top priority for youth, to set high achievement goals, and to invest the day-by-day effort required to attain those goals. Many states and local school districts have begun to respond to evidence that American schools are being outclassed by schools in other countries by strengthening curricula, tightening standards for teacher certification, raising standards for graduation and promotion from grade to grade, and even lengthening the school year. Educational reformers such as James Comer (1988; Anson et al., 1991) have been successful at forging closer ties between inner-city schools and the communities they serve and at involving parents as partners with teachers in the educational process. These educational leaders recognize that improving the academic achievement and vocational preparation of America's youth is crucial if the United States is to maintain a leadership role in an ever-changing and ever-more-competitive world (National Education Goals Panel, 1992).

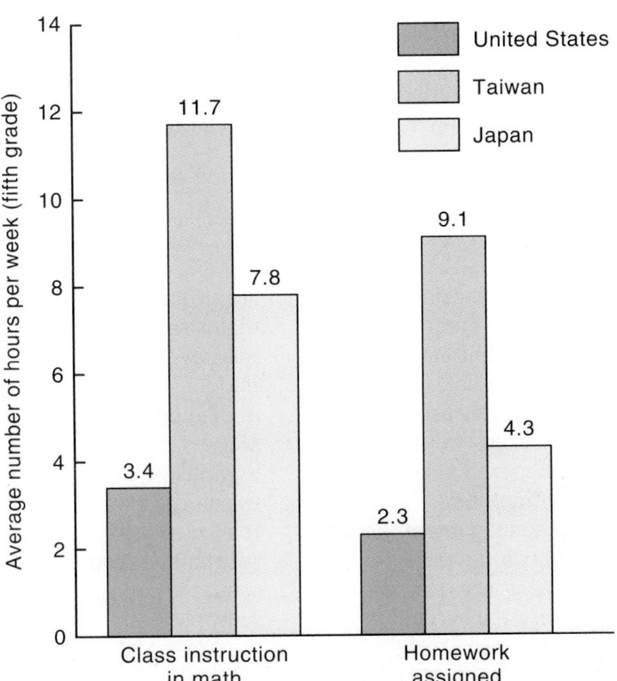

FIGURE 15.6 Average number of hours per week of class instruction in mathematics and of homework (of all kinds) that teachers assign in fifth grade. (Adapted from Chen & Stevenson, 1989; Stevenson & Lee, 1990.)

REFLECTIONS

You've heard the saying "You are what you eat." Perhaps the moral of this chapter is "You are what you *do*." Across the life span, we are clearly affected by the lifestyles that we lead. If all goes well, the developing person moves from a stimulating home (and perhaps stimulating day-care and preschool settings) in which the capacity for play is nurtured through a series of effective schools in which important life skills, values, and goals are acquired. He or she then establishes a satisfying and stimulating blend of work, family life, and leisure as an adult, experiencing still further growth as a result. All along, we seek the good fit between person and environment that is most likely to optimize psychological well-being and growth.

As we go about fashioning our lifestyles, we are often oblivious to the fact that the options we can even contemplate depend on the historical and cultural context in which we live. Like children of the past in our own society, children in some cultures in the world today do not attend school, have never seen television sets or computers, and are content to know that they will work alongside their parents in the fields when they grow up. How different it is to have one's childhood learning experiences structured by professional educators, to live with modern technology, and to face an almost unlimited array of career options as an adolescent. Or consider the differences between the vocational choices available to women today and those available to women of the not-so-distant past. Most girls of the 1940s knew precisely what their future career was to be: that of wife and mother. Today's young women can think about being lawyers or welders. And tomorrow? We can only imagine the opportunities for play, education, and work that may be available in the 21st century.

SUMMARY POINTS

1. Our development is influenced by the play, schooling, and work activities that form our ever-changing lifestyles.

2. As infants' cognitive abilities unfold, their play changes from exploration of objects to functional play. Symbolic play, which emerges at about the age of 1, becomes increasingly complex with age.

3. Infants whose lifestyles include alternative care are likely to be no less competent or well adjusted than infants who are raised at home *if* they receive high-quality substitute care and responsive parenting at home.

4. During the preschool years, play becomes more social (as associative and cooperative play increase) and imaginative (as social pretend play blossoms). Pretend play and the organized games of the school years contribute to physical, intellectual, social, and emotional development.

5. A school's effectiveness is not influenced much by financial support, class size, or use of ability tracking. Instead, elementary and secondary school children perform best when (a) they are intellectually capable and motivated; (b) their teachers create a learning environment that is comfortable, task oriented, and motivating; and (c) there is, as aptitude-treatment interaction research suggests, a good "fit" between their own characteristics and the kind of instruction they receive.

6. Racial and ethnic differences in achievement can be traced to parent and peer influences and teacher expectancies, and the benefits of both racial integration and mainstreaming for developmentally disabled students can be enhanced through cooperative learning methods.

7. Although the availability of television has done little to alter children's participation in developmentally important activities, what children watch can either increase aggressive tendencies and negative social attitudes or foster prosocial behavior, positive social attitudes, and academic learning. Computer-assisted instruction can be beneficial, but the effects of the computer on development may also depend on how this technology is used.

8. Adolescents are likely to benefit from leisure activities that are both enjoyable and challenging and from schools that provide a good fit to their developmental needs and emphasize academics. According to Eli Ginzberg, adolescents become increasingly realistic as they progress through the fantasy, tentative, and realistic stages of vocational choice, but social factors sometimes constrain the choices made by females and low-income youth of both sexes, and many adolescents do not engage in enough systematic career exploration.

9. Daniel Levinson's theory that adults go through a recurring process of building life structures and revising them is supported by evidence that young adults engage in much career exploration. Midlife crisis and upheaval in one's early 40s do not seem to be universal. Older workers are as productive as and more satisfied than younger workers.

10. Despite dramatic changes, most women continue to work in traditionally female and low-paying jobs, owing in part to sex discrimination and role conflict. Yet today's women, like men, typically suffer no damage and can potentially benefit from adding work roles to their other roles, especially if their work is substantively complex.

11. Retiring workers go through an adjustment process that extends from a preretirement phase to honeymoon, disenchantment, and reorientation phases after retirement and typically experience a drop in income but little change in health or psychological well-being. Neither activity theory nor disengagement theory places enough emphasis on the fact that older adults are likely to be most satisfied when their retirement lifestyles suit their individual personalities and preferences.

12. Educational reform in North America can be guided by research suggesting that the success of Asian schools is rooted in more class time spent on academics, more homework, more parent involvement, and a strong belief that hard work pays off.

KEY TERMS

ability tracking
activity theory
aptitude-treatment interaction (ATI)
computer-assisted instruction
cooperative learning methods
disengagement theory
functional play
imaginary companions
informal curriculum
life structure
mainstreaming
mentor
middle school
midlife crisis
play
Pygmalion effect
role conflict
role overload
substantive complexity
symbolic capacity
symbolic play

16

PSYCHOLOGICAL DISORDERS THROUGHOUT THE LIFE SPAN

One-year-old Tanya has not been eating well and is now noticeably small for her age. Tim, age 6, just got in trouble at school again; it seems he can't sit still for more than a few seconds before he's up and into mischief. Just after she turned 16, Laurie came home drunk from a party; her parents don't know it, but it's far from the first time she has been drunk. Beth, a 28-year-old housewife and mother, has become overwhelmed by her responsibilities and has taken to staring out the window, crying, and letting the children fend for themselves. And Alvin, at 73, is getting more than a little forgetful, his wife and children say. The other day he left the water running in the bathtub and flooded the second floor.

It is the rare human being who makes it through the life span without having at least some difficulty adapting to the challenges of living. Each phase of life has its own unique challenges, and some of us inevitably run into trouble mastering them. This chapter is about some of the ways in which human development can go awry. It looks at how development influences psychopathology and how psychopathology alters future development. By applying knowledge of human development to the study of psychological disorders, we can understand them better. And, by learning more about abnormal patterns of development, we can gain new perspectives on the forces that guide and channel—or block and distort—human development more generally.

WHAT MAKES BEHAVIOR ABNORMAL?

It is the job of clinical psychologists, psychiatrists, and other mental health professionals to decide who has a psychological disorder and who does not. How do these professionals—indeed, how do we—define the line between normal and abnormal behavior?

Criteria for Diagnosing Psychological Disorders

Three broad criteria are often applied in diagnosing psychological disorders:

1. *Statistical deviance: Does the person's behavior fall outside the normal range of behavior?* By this criterion, a mild case of the "blahs" or "blues" would not be diagnosed as clinical depression because it is so statistically common, but a more enduring, severe, and persistent case might be.
2. *Maladaptiveness: Does the person's behavior interfere with personal and social adaptation or pose a danger to self or others?* Psychological disorders disrupt functioning and create problems for the individual and/or other people.
3. *Personal distress: Does the behavior cause personal anguish or discomfort?* Many psychological disorders involve a good deal of personal suffering and are of concern for that reason alone.

Although these guidelines provide a start at defining abnormal behavior, they are not very specific. We must ask *which* forms of statistical deviation, *which* failures of adaptation, or *which* kinds of personal distress are significant—and *in what contexts.* To define psychological disorder more precisely, we must start by applying more specific standards of behavior—standards that will differ depending on the individual's sociocultural context and age.

Considering Social Norms and Age Norms

Behaviors are abnormal or normal only within some social context. **Social norms** are the expectations about how to behave that prevail in a particular social context, whether it is a culture, subculture, or everyday setting. Thus, hearing the "spirits" speak or seeing visions is defined as abnormal in the mainstream culture of North America, but among the Plains Indians these "symptoms" have been defined as valued skills (Wrightsman, Sigelman, & Sanford, 1979). Similarly, a child's screaming and shouting may be viewed as quite appropriate on the playground but may raise eyebrows if it occurs in the context of a funeral. Definitions of abnormal behavior vary from culture to culture, from subculture to subculture, and from historical period to historical period. In a very real sense, then, abnormality is in the eye of a particular group of beholders.

In addition—and this point is particularly important from a life-span developmental perspective—abnormal behavior must be defined in relation to **age norms,** or societal expectations about what behavior is appropriate or normal at various ages. The 4-year-old boy who frequently cries, acts impulsively, wets his bed, and talks to his imaginary friend may be perceived as—and may be—perfectly normal. The 40-year-old who does the same things may need help!

We simply cannot define abnormal behavior and development without having a solid grasp of *normal* behavior and development. Box 16.1 reinforces this point.

BOX 16.1 Childhood as a Psychological Disorder

What might happen if we failed to take developmental norms into account in defining what is normal and what is not? With tongue in cheek, Jordan Smoller (1986) throws developmental norms out the window and shows us that we might well view *childhood* as a disorder if we judged children entirely by the yardsticks we use to evaluate adult behavior. How do we know when someone is suffering from the disorder called "childhood"? Says Smoller, we look for the following defining features: congenital onset (one is usually born with the condition), dwarfism (unusually short stature), emotional lability and immaturity (a criterion that leads to the misdiagnosis of many adults as children), knowledge deficits (for example, gross ignorance of politics), and legume anorexia (a refusal to eat vegetables).

The seriousness of "childhood" and the difficulties psychologists face in treating it are illustrated by the case of Billy:

> Billy J., age 8, was brought to treatment by his parents. Billy's affliction was painfully obvious. He stood only 4'3" high and weighed a scant 70 pounds, despite the fact that he ate voraciously. Billy presented a variety of troubling symptoms. His voice was noticeably high for a man. He displayed legume anorexia and, according to his parents, often refused to bathe. His intellectual functioning was also below normal—he had little general knowledge and could barely write a structured sentence. Social skills were also deficient. He often spoke inappropriately and exhibited "whining behavior." His sexual experience was non-existent. Indeed, Billy considered women "icky." . . After years of painstaking treatment, Billy improved gradually. At age 11, his height and weight have increased, his social skills are broader, and he is now functional enough to hold down a paper route [Smoller, 1986, p. 9].

Enough said: We simply cannot define abnormal behavior at any point in the life span without knowing what is normal at that same age.

Specific Diagnostic Criteria

Psychologists and psychiatrists trying to diagnose and treat psychological disorders would need more specific diagnostic criteria than we have outlined thus far. The most widely used diagnostic system is the *Diagnostic and Statistical Manual of Mental Disorders*, published by the American Psychiatric Association. The 1987 version of this manual—known as *DSM-III-R* because it is a revision of the third edition—spells out defining features and symptoms for the whole range of psychological disorders.[1]

Because we will be looking closely at depression in this chapter, we will use it here as an example of how *DSM-III-R* defines disorders. Depression is actually a family of distinct affective or mood disorders, some relatively mild and some severe. One of the most important is **major depression,** which is defined in *DSM-III-R* as at least one episode of feeling profoundly depressed, sad, and hopeless, and/or losing interest in and the ability to derive pleasure from almost all activities, for at least two weeks (American Psychiatric Association, 1987; see also Gotlib & Hammen, 1992). More specifically, a major depressive episode cannot be diagnosed unless the individual experiences at least five of the following symptoms, including one or the other of the first two, persistently during a two-week period:

1. Depressed mood (or irritable mood in children and adolescents) most of the time
2. Greatly decreased interest or pleasure in usual activities
3. Significant weight loss (or weight gain)
4. Insomnia (or too much sleeping)
5. Psychomotor agitation (or sluggishness, slowing of behavior)
6. Fatigue and loss of energy
7. Feelings of worthlessness or extreme guilt
8. Decreased ability to concentrate or indecisiveness
9. Recurring thoughts of death, suicidal ideas, or a suicide attempt

By these criteria, a man suffering from major depression might, for example, feel extremely discouraged; no longer seem to care about his job or even about sexual relations with his wife; lose weight or have difficulty sleeping; speak and move very slowly, as though lacking the energy to perform even the simplest actions; have trouble getting his work done; dwell on how guilty he feels about his many failings; and even begin to think he would be better off dead. Major depression would *not* be diagnosed if this man were merely a little "down" or were going through the normal grieving process after the death of a loved one (although a minority of grieving individuals display major depression in addition to their normal grief reactions). Many more people experience depressive *symptoms* than qualify as having a clinically defined depressive *disorder.*

In sum, diagnosing a psychological disorder such as major depression involves consideration of the broad

[1] *DSM-IV* was about to be released as we wrote this chapter. It uses the same basic classification approach established in *DSM-III-R*.

criteria of statistical deviance, maladaptiveness, and personal distress and also requires the application of specific diagnostic criteria. What's more, it is important to be sensitive to the social norms of the individual's cultural group and to be aware of relevant age norms. Interestingly, *DSM-III-R* takes the position that depression in a child is fundamentally similar to depression in an adult, though acknowledging that children may express their depression somewhat differently than adults do. As we will see shortly, there are still many unanswered questions about whether the symptoms and significance of major depression—and other psychological disorders as well—change over the life span. We do know, though, that many individuals who experience one episode of major depression experience others, which suggests that it is a problem best viewed from a life-span perspective (Coyne & Downey, 1991). Fortunately, there is now keen interest in exploring the relationships between psychopathology and development over the life course.

Developmental Psychopathology

In recent years, psychologists have become increasingly aware of the need to adopt a developmental perspective on abnormal behavior (Cicchetti et al., 1991; Gelfand & Peterson, 1985; Rutter, 1989). As a result, a new field, called **developmental psychopathology,** has emerged. As defined by Alan Sroufe and Michael Rutter (1984), developmental psychopathology is the study of the origins and course of maladaptive behavior. Developmental psychopathologists are well aware of the need to evaluate abnormal behavior in relation to normal development and to attempt to understand how the individual's level of development influences what disorders he or she is likely to display and how those problems are likely to be manifested. They are also interested in finding out how psychological disorders affect later development.

The issues of concern to developmental psychopathologists are the same developmental issues that have concerned us throughout this book—most notably, the nature/nurture issue and the issue of continuity and discontinuity in development. Addressing the nature/nurture issue requires asking important questions such as:

- How do biological, psychological, and social factors interact to give rise to psychological disorders?
- Why do some children who grow up in problem-ridden families develop psychological disorders while others in similar circumstances seem to be invulnerable to the stresses they experience?

Questions about the continuity or discontinuity of maladaptive behavior include:

- Are most childhood problems passing concerns that have no bearing on adult adjustment, or does poor functioning in childhood predict poor functioning later in life?
- How do expressions of psychopathology change as the developmental status of the individual changes?

These are important questions to answer if we want to gain a more complete understanding of the development of psychological disorders—and, indeed, of development more generally—and we address them in this chapter. Specifically, this chapter introduces a small sampling of developmental problems associated with each stage of the life span (for example, infantile autism to illustrate disorders of infancy, anorexia nervosa to illustrate disorders of adolescence, and Alzheimer's disease to illustrate disorders of old age). In addition, we examine research on depression in *every* developmental period in order to see whether this widespread disorder is indeed the same phenomenon at any age or whether its symptoms and significance change over the life span. Finally, we will see that the successful treatment of psychological disorders requires a sensitivity to developmental issues.

THE INFANT

Adults worry about infants who do not eat properly, who cry endlessly, or who seem overly withdrawn and timid. However, because infant development is strongly channeled by biological maturation, very few infants develop severe psychological problems. Yet psychopathology does exist in infancy, and its effects can be tragic.

Infantile Autism

Infantile autism, a disorder first identified and described by Leo Kanner in 1943, seriously disrupts normal infant development. It is an example of what the American Psychiatric Association (1987) calls a "pervasive developmental disorder," a severe disorder associated with gross abnormalities in several areas of development. Fortunately, autism is rare, affecting about 4 or 5 of every 10,000 children and 3 or 4 boys for every girl (American Psychiatric Association, 1987).

To appreciate how very different the autistic child is from the normally developing one, picture the typical infant that we have described in this book: a very social being who responds to others and forms close attachments starting at 6 or 7 months of age, a linguistic being who babbles and later uses one- and two-word sentences to converse, and a curious being who is fascinated by new experiences. Now consider the key features of infantile autism (Rutter & Schopler, 1987; Yirmiya & Sigman, 1991):

Many individuals with infantile autism continue to function poorly as adolescents and adults, but some improve with age. One "improver," Jerry, described his childhood as a reign of "confusion and terror" in which "nothing seemed constant; everything was unpredictable and strange." (Bemporad, 1979, p. 192.)

1. *Early onset.* Autistic children are believed to be autistic from birth and can be distinguished from other severely disordered children who at first develop normally and only later become disturbed.

2. *Deviant social development.* Autistic children seem unable to form normal social relationships or to respond appropriately to social cues; they live in a world of their own. They do not make eye contact, seek other people for comfort, snuggle when held, participate in secure attachment relationships, or make friends. In stark contrast to normal children, autistic children seem to find social contact aversive rather than pleasurable. They also have difficulty reading others' emotions or responding with empathy when others are distressed.

3. *Deviant language and communicative skills.* Many autistic children are mute, whereas others acquire limited language skills but cannot really converse with their companions. Among the unusual features of the autistic child's speech are a very flat, robotlike tone; pronoun reversals (for example, the use of "you" to refer to the self); and **echolalia** (a parroting back of what someone else says). Even those autistic children who have mastered basic sentence structure or grammar have difficulty using language in true give-and-take social exchanges. More generally, autistic children are deficient in their ability to use symbols, not only in language but in gesture and symbolic play (Yirmiya & Sigman, 1991).

4. *Repetitive, stereotyped behavior.* Autistic children have an obsessive need for sameness and can become terribly upset by novelty or change. They engage in stereotyped behaviors such as rocking, flapping their hands in front of their faces, or spinning toys, as though they were seeking sensory stimulation. Yet they also become strongly attached to particular objects and highly distressed when their physical environment is altered (for example, when a chair in the living room is moved a few feet). Very possibly, it is the unpredictability and changeability of human beings that makes interacting with them so unpleasant for autistic children.

The autistic child's development is clearly *deviant* or distorted rather than merely delayed (Rutter & Schopler, 1987). Many people believe that autistic individuals are exceptionally intelligent. Some, like the *Rain Man,* do show special talents such as the ability to quickly calculate days of the week corresponding to dates on the calendar (see Chapter 9's discussion of idiot savants). However, most autistic children are mentally retarded; they display both the deviant behaviors associated with autism and the developmental delays associated with mental retardation. The condition is indeed "pervasive," for it severely impairs cognitive, social, and emotional development (Yirmiya & Sigman, 1991). Yet some researchers now believe that many of the problems autistic children display may be rooted in a lack of understanding of mental states such as feelings, desires, beliefs, and intentions and of their role in human behavior—a lack of what has come to be called a **theory of mind** (see Frith, 1989; Holroyd & Baron-Cohen, 1993; Leslie, 1992).

To understand what the theory-of-mind hypothesis is about, consider the "false belief" task that Simon Baron-Cohen, Alan Leslie, and Uta Frith (1985) presented to autistic, Down syndrome, and normal children who were all of similar mental ages. A doll named Sally puts a marble in her basket and leaves the room; a second doll, Anne, then moves the marble from Sally's basket to her own box while Sally is gone. Where, children are asked, will Sally look for the marble when she returns? Over 80% of normal and Down syndrome children correctly said that she would look in the basket, showing that they understood that Sally had a false belief about where the marble was and that this mental state would guide her actions. However, 80% of the autistic children incorrectly answered that she would look where *they* knew the marble was (in the box) rather than where Sally had every reason to believe it was (in the basket).

Lacking a theory of mind, autistic children simply cannot conceive of someone's having a false belief that contradicts the facts of a situation. Indeed, they do not seem to understand that people have beliefs, false or otherwise. These children are also far behind other children in their ability to engage in symbolic or pretend play because they cannot seem to mentally represent pretend events involving pretend objects (Yirmiya & Sigman, 1991). And think how difficult it must be for them to interpret other people's emotions accurately when they have no idea that people *have* emotions, or to understand and communicate with people when they lack the ability to read people's minds and figure out what others know, intend, or feel.

Whether the cognitive deficit associated with autism will turn out to be a lack of a theory of mind or some broader deficiency in symbolic thinking is unclear at this point (Hughes & Russell, 1993; Yirmiya & Sigman, 1991). What *is* clear is that the social and emotional problems autistic children display may be partly rooted in a cognitive impairment. These children seem to have a kind of "mind-blindness" that makes it hard for them to relate to other people (Frith, 1989).

What causes infantile autism? We are not yet sure. Early theorists suggested that rigid and cold parenting caused the disorder, but this harmful myth has since been put to rest (Achenbach, 1982; see also Donenberg & Baker, 1993). It is now understood that parents and children influence each other and that interacting with an autistic child could easily cause parents to be tense and frustrated. The fact that autism is such a severe disorder present so early in life strongly suggests that it has an organic or physical basis (Rutter & Schopler, 1987). Indeed, autistic children display several neurological abnormalities, but it is not yet clear which of them are most important or how they arise (Volkmar & Cohen, 1988).

There is evidence that genes contribute to autism (Folstein & Rutter, 1977; Steffenburg et al., 1989). Indeed, one research team found that, if one identical twin was autistic, the other was autistic in 91% of the twin pairs studied; the concordance rate for fraternal twin pairs was 0% (Steffenburg et al., 1989). However, the fact that one identical twin can be autistic when the other is not indicates that early environmental influences must also contribute to the disorder. Indeed, some cases of autism have been linked to various prenatal and perinatal complications that can potentially cause brain damage (Lord et al., 1991; Steffenburg et al., 1989). So autism seems to have multiple causes and contributors, both genetic and environmental.

What becomes of autistic children as they get older? The long-term outcome has usually been poor, undoubtedly because autism is such a pervasive and severe disorder and because it is so often accompanied by mental retardation. Most autistic individuals continue to rely on others for help throughout their lives, though a small minority become capable of working and supporting themselves (Gillberg, 1991). Positive outcomes are most likely among those who have normal IQ scores and who can communicate using speech before they are 6 years old (Gillberg & Steffenburg, 1987).

What can be done to treat autistic children? Researchers continue to search for drugs that will correct the suspected brain dysfunctions of these children, but they are a long way from discovering the "magic pill" that will cure autism (Rutter & Schopler, 1987). At present, the most effective treatment approach is intensive behavioral training. O. Ivar Lovaas and his colleagues have pioneered the use of reinforcement principles to shape social and language skills in autistic children. As we'll see at the end of this chapter, Lovaas (1987) has reported remarkably good adjustment among autistic children who received very intensive behavioral training starting early in life. It could well be that the futures of autistic children who have had the benefit of today's more powerful intervention programs may be brighter than those of autistic children of the past.

In sum, infantile autism is one of the most vivid examples we have of human development gone awry. The profound problems that autistic children display in their social interactions, language development, and responses to the physical environment make it clear that their development is deviant and not merely delayed. Moreover, most of them remain disordered, at least to some extent, throughout their lives. Yet we can be encouraged by recent reports of the long-term benefits of early behavioral intervention, and we can also hope that researchers will eventually pinpoint the brain dysfunctions responsible for this disorder and develop effective drug treatments to correct them.

Depression in Infancy

Does it seem possible that an infant could experience major depression as defined by clinicians? Infants are surely not capable of the negative cognitions that are common among depressed adults—the low self-esteem, guilt, worthlessness, hopelessness, and so on (Garber, 1984). After all, they have not yet acquired the capacity for symbolic thought that would allow them to reflect on their experience. Yet infants *can* exhibit some of the behavioral symptoms (loss of interest in activities, psychomotor slowing) and **somatic symptoms** (bodily symptoms such as loss of appetite and disruption of normal sleep patterns) of depression. Researchers are still debating whether true depressive disorders can occur in infancy, but it is clear that babies can and do experience *depression-like* states and symptoms (Garber, 1984; Trad, 1986).

Depressive symptoms are most likely to be observed in infants who lack a secure attachment relationship or who experience a disruption of their all-important emotional bonds (Trad, 1986). Infants permanently separated from their mothers between 6 and 12 months of age are likely to be sad, weepy, listless, unresponsive, and withdrawn and to show delays in virtually all aspects of their development (Spitz, 1946). In addition, infants whose mothers are depressed and therefore emotionally unresponsive begin to adopt an interaction style that resembles that of their depressed caregivers; they vocalize very little and look sad, even when interacting with women other than their mothers (Field, 1992). When Carolyn Zahn-Waxler and her colleagues (1984) repeatedly assessed children of depressed parents from infancy to the age of 5 or 6, they found that many of these children continued to show depression-like symptoms such as apathy and sadness over the years. These youngsters were highly sensitive to the emotional distress of others but kept their own emotions under tight control. Whether due to genes, learning, or — most likely — both, the children of depressed parents are also at increased risk of becoming clinically depressed themselves later in life (Beardslee et al., 1993; Gotlib & Hammen, 1992). Moreover, these children are likely to interact with their own children in a negative manner, increasing the chances that depression will be passed on to still another generation (Whitbeck et al., 1992).

Some infants who are neglected, abused, separated from attachment figures, or otherwise raised in a stressful or unaffectionate manner display a related, and more life-threatening, problem called **failure to thrive.** These youngsters fail to grow normally, lose weight, and become seriously underweight for their age. In some cases an organic or biological cause, such as an illness or heart defect, can be found, but in so-called nonorganic cases the cause seems to be emotional rather than physical. Infants and young children who fail to thrive often show many of the symptoms of depression, as well as delays in their cognitive and social development and bizarre behaviors such as drinking from toilets (Green, 1986).

Lytt Gardner (1972) identified several cases of the failure-to-thrive syndrome, one of which involved twins — a boy and a girl — who grew normally for the first four months of life. Soon afterward their father lost his job, their mother became pregnant with an unwanted baby, and the parents blamed each other for the family's problems. When the father moved out, the mother focused her resentment on her infant son. She fed him and tended to his physical care but became emotionally unresponsive to him. Although his sister continued to grow normally, the boy twin at 13 months of age was about the size of an average 7-month-old.

It is now clear that the mothers of infants with nonorganic failure to thrive are often stressed, depressed, and socially isolated women whose own mothers were emotionally unresponsive or even abusive to them (Gorman, Leifer, & Grossman, 1993). Their babies gain weight and overcome their depression-like emotional symptoms almost immediately when they are removed from their homes (Green, 1986). How can we explain this rapid recovery? Some of these infants have actively resisted feedings by their otherwise-neglectful caregivers and are undernourished as a result (Lozoff, 1989). For others, though, an inadequate diet is not the problem. Current thinking is that emotional traumas inhibit the production of growth hormone by the pituitary gland and that the secretion of growth hormone resumes when these infants (or young children) begin to receive affectionate care (Tanner, 1990). Yet failure-to-thrive infants may relapse if they are returned to parents who have not been helped to become more emotionally responsive; they may then remain smaller than normal and display long-term social and intellectual deficits as well (Brinich, Drotar, & Brinich, 1989; Lachenmeyer & Davidovicz, 1987).

In sum, even babies can display many of the symptoms of depression, although depression in an infant is not the same as depression in an adult (Garber, 1984; Trad, 1986). Most notably, young infants do not have the cognitive capacity to think depressive thoughts but can show many of the behavioral and somatic symptoms of "adult" depression. They can also undergo serious disruptions of their psychological development and failure to thrive if they experience long-term or permanent separation from their attachment figures or are brought up by depressed, unresponsive, or rejecting cargivers.

THE CHILD

Many children experience developmental problems of one sort or another — fears, recurring stomachaches, temper tantrums, and so on. A much smaller proportion are officially diagnosed as having one of the psychological disorders associated with infancy, childhood, or adolescence — or as having a psychological disorder (such as major depression) that can occur at any age. Table 16.1 lists major childhood disorders as categorized in *DSM-III-R.* Many developmental problems can also be placed in one or the other of two broad categories: problems of undercontrol and problems of overcontrol (Achenbach & Edelbrock, 1978).

Undercontrolled disorders are also called *externalizing* problems, for children with these disorders "act out" in ways that disturb other people and place them in conflict with social expectations. Undercontrolled children may be aggressive, disobedient, difficult to control, or disruptive. If their problems are severe enough, they may be diagnosed as having a "conduct disorder" or as being "hyperactive." **Overcontrolled disorders,** or *internalizing* problems, involve inner distress; they are more disruptive to the child than to other people and include anxiety disorders (such as persistent worrying about being separated from loved ones), phobias, severe shyness or withdrawal, and depression.

An important sex difference in childhood disorders has been observed: Undercontrolled disorders are more common among boys, whereas overcontrolled problems are more prevalent among girls (Achenbach et al., 1987; Ostrov, Offer, & Howard, 1989). Moreover, this sex difference is evident in many societies (Lambert, Weisz, & Knight, 1989; Weisz,

TABLE 16.1 Psychological disorders associated with infancy, childhood, or adolescence.

DSM Category	*Major Examples*
Mental retardation	Subaverage general intellectual functioning (mild, moderate, severe, and profound levels)
Pervasive developmental disorders	Autism and similarly severe conditions
Specific developmental disorders	Learning disabilities in the areas of arithmetic, writing, or reading; language and speech disorders; motor-skill disorder
Disruptive behavior disorders	Attention-deficit hyperactivity disorder; conduct disorders (persistent antisocial behavior); oppositional defiant behavior
Anxiety disorders	Separation anxiety disorder, avoidant disorder (extreme fear of strangers), overanxious disorder (diffuse fears)
Eating disorders	Anorexia nervosa, bulimia nervosa, pica (eating nonnutritive substances such as paint or sand)
Gender identity disorders	Confusion concerning gender identity, transsexualism
Tic disorders	Tourette's disorder, chronic motor or vocal tics or involuntary movements
Elimination disorders	Enuresis (inappropriate urination), encopresis (inappropriate defecation)

SOURCE: Based on *DSM-III-R,* American Psychiatric Association, 1987.

Suwanlert, et al., 1993). Yet, as Box 16.2 makes clear, the likelihood that a child will be viewed by parents as having an undercontrolled or overcontrolled behavior problem is very much influenced by cultural factors. To give you a feel for these two categories of childhood disorder, we will now look at one problem of undercontrol—hyperactivity—and one problem of overcontrol—depression.

Attention-Deficit Hyperactivity Disorder

A 5-year-old boy in Florida got up at 5 o'clock one morning and went to the refrigerator. He broke raw eggs on the floor, poured beer on them, and then decided he had better mop up the mess. But, once in the garage, he forgot that he had come for a mop, for he spotted some paint cans and began to paint. The day continued from there (Renner, 1985). Perhaps you can appreciate why the "undercontrolled" behavior of some hyperactive children is disturbing to other people!

When it was first identified, hyperactivity was defined principally as a problem of excess motor activity, and the term was used to describe children who could not seem to sit still or were continually on the go. Now hyperactivity is viewed as first and foremost a problem of *attention.* According to *DSM-III-R* criteria, a child has **attention-deficit hyperactivity disorder (ADHD)** if three symptoms are present:

1. *Inattention* (for example, the child does not seem to listen, is easily distracted, and does not stick to activities or finish tasks)
2. *Impulsivity* (for example, the child acts before thinking and cannot inhibit an urge to blurt something out in class or have a turn in a group activity)
3. *Hyperactivity* (perpetual fidgeting, finger tapping, chattering, and restlessness)

Approximately 3% of children are diagnosable as ADHD, and there are about three ADHD boys for every ADHD girl (American Psychiatric Association, 1987). Many children with ADHD also have diagnosable learning disabilities, and many, because of aggressive, antisocial behavior, also qualify as having conduct disorders (Silver, 1992). As you might expect, ADHD children have difficulty performing well in school. Children diagnosed as having attention-deficit disorders *without* hyperactivity also suffer academically but have fewer of the behavior problems that make ADHD children so hard to tolerate (Cantwell & Baker, 1992; Goodyear & Hynd, 1992). ADHD children irritate adults and become locked in coercive power struggles with their parents, interactions that only aggravate their problems (Barkley et al., 1991; Buhrmester et al., 1992). Because their behavior is so disruptive, they are also rejected by peers (Whalen et al., 1989). In short, ADHD affects cognitive, social, and emotional development in a variety of ways.

Perhaps you have noticed that many of the behaviors displayed by ADHD children can readily be observed in normal preschoolers. We are often struck by how energetic young children are and how quickly their attention flits from one activity to another. Here, then, is a prime example of how critical it is to view abnormal behavior in the context of developmental norms. A child's attention deficits, impulsivity, and hyperactivity must be developmentally inappropriate for a diagnosis of attention-deficit hyperactivity disorder to be justified (American Psychiatric Association, 1987). Otherwise, we might well mistake most average 3- and 4-year-olds for hyperactive children!

Developmental Course

ADHD expresses itself in somewhat different ways at different ages. The condition often reveals itself first in infancy. Many parents of ADHD children report that those youngsters were very active, had difficult temperaments, or had irregular feeding and sleeping patterns as infants (Crook, 1980; Stewart et al., 1966). In the preschool years, perpetual and seemingly haphazard motor activity is the most noticeable sign of this disorder. However, in the grade school

BOX 16.2 Defining the Problem Child: A Cross-Cultural Look

It is parents, teachers, and other important adults in children's lives who decide which children have psychological problems and which do not. But isn't it quite likely that adults in different cultures apply different standards of judgment in deciding when behaviors such as whining or arguing, being fearful or being disobedient, represent serious problems? Isn't it also possible that a culture's characteristic parenting styles and socialization practices affect the kinds of problems children in that culture display? Suppose parents in one culture believe that children should be quiet, obedient, and polite and strongly disapprove of any form of rudeness, aggression, and disrespect, whereas parents in another culture let children run wild. Would parents in the first culture be more likely than parents in the second to view as pathological even the slightest sign of undercontrolled behavior? Would they then overdiagnose aggression and other conduct disorders in their children? Or might these strict and demanding parents successfully teach their children not to act out their frustrations and therefore cause them to have *low* rather than high rates of undercontrolled problems— but perhaps to have high rates of overcontrolled problems such as anxiety, fingernail biting, and shyness?

Intrigued by such questions, John Weisz and his associates have been studying parents' perceptions of their children's behavioral and emotional adjustment in a number of cultures (Lambert et al., 1989, 1992; Weisz, Sigman, et al., 1993; Weisz, Suwanlert, et al., 1993). In one study, Weisz, Marian Sigman, and their colleagues (1993) compared rates of problem behaviors, as reported by parents, among Embu children in Kenya, Thai children in Thailand, and African-American and white children in the United States. Both Embu and Thai parents strongly socialize children to be obedient and self-controlled and are far less tolerant than American parents of rowdy, aggressive, and undercontrolled behavior.

As it turned out, the problems children had (or, more accurately, the problems children were *perceived* to have) varied considerably from culture to culture. Indeed, cultural differences were detected for 62 of the 118 behaviors listed on the child behavior checklist parents completed. Embu parents reported the largest number of overcontrolled problems like fearful behavior, excessive guilt, and somatic symptoms. American parents (white parents more than black) were more likely than other parents to claim that their children often argued, disobeyed, acted cruelly, and engaged in other undercontrolled behaviors. Thai parents' reports of their children's problems were in between those of Embu and American parents. In other research, though, Weisz and his colleagues have found that Thai parents and Jamaican parents, like Embu parents, identify more overcontrolled and fewer undercontrolled problems in their children than parents in the United States do (Lambert et al., 1989; Weisz, Suwanlert, et al., 1993).

These findings suggest that child-rearing values and practices may affect how children express any psychological difficulties they are experiencing. We know from other research that highly restrictive, harsh parenting tends to be associated with the development of overcontrolled problems, whereas permissive parenting tends be associated with the emergence of undercontrolled problems (Achenbach & Edelbrock, 1978). By strictly forbidding any kind of aggression or disobedience, then, Embu, Thai, and Jamaican parents may socialize their children to bottle up negative feelings rather than to express them by throwing temper tantrums or hitting their siblings. The result may be many children with overcontrolled and few with undercontrolled disorders. Meanwhile, more permissive American parents may end up with unruly children because they tolerate unruly behavior.

As Weisz, Sigman, and their colleagues (1993) note, though, there are a number of other possible reasons for cultural differences in rates of child psychopathology. Cross-cultural studies like these often describe interesting cultural differences but cannot fully explain them. Genetic differences between cultural groups could contribute to cultural differences in personality development. Or perhaps Embu, Thai, and Jamaican parents are simply more sensitive to the problems of the quiet, overcontrolled child than American parents are. The living conditions a group experiences may also influence rates of childhood problems. Embu children may have had a large number of somatic symptoms (aches, pains, vomiting, and the like) not because they were prone to overcontrolled behavior problems but because they were suffering from malnutrition and disease.

Whatever the reasons, it is clear that professionals who assess and treat children with problems must understand problem behavior in its cultural context. We must know how parents, teachers, and other adults in a culture judge children's behavior and decide what is or is not a serious problem. We must also understand how a group's child-rearing beliefs and values might foster the development of certain forms of psychopathology and discourage the development of others. Severe childhood problems such as autism may well be recognized as problems the world over, but abnormal development, like normal development, is shaped by the broader sociocultural context in which it occurs.

years the ADHD child may not be overactive so much as fidgety, restless, and inattentive to schoolwork (American Psychiatric Association, 1987).

What becomes of hyperactive children later in life? It used to be thought that hyperactive children outgrew their problems. Now we know that many of them continue to have difficulties adapting throughout the life span, even though they usually do outgrow their overactive behavior (Fischer et al., 1990; Hechtman, Weiss, & Perlman, 1984; Wallander & Hubert, 1985). By one estimate, 50% continue to have problems as adolescents, and at least half of those individuals have problems as adults (Silver, 1992). ADHD adolescents may have difficulty attending to their academic work and may continue to behave impulsively; thus they often perform poorly in school or drop out altogether, and they may commit reckless delinquent acts without thinking about the consequences (Fischer et al., 1990; Wallander & Hubert, 1985).

The picture is somewhat more positive by early adulthood, in that many ADHD individuals seem to adjust better to the workplace than they did to school (Wallander & Hubert, 1985). However, young adults who were diagnosed as hyperactive during childhood are more likely than others to be restless and impulsive, to be involved in more than their share of car accidents and lawbreaking, to lack self-esteem, to abuse alcohol and drugs, and to have emotional problems (Hechtman et al., 1984; Mannuzza et al., 1993; Wallander & Hubert, 1985). Later adjustment is especially poor among hyperactive children who are also aggressive (Fischer et al., 1993; Milich & Loney, 1979).

Suspected Causes

What causes this disorder? We do not yet have a clear answer. We know that some individuals are genetically predisposed to develop it (Stevenson, 1992) and that in 20–30% of families with an ADHD child a parent is also ADHD (Silver, 1992). Environment matters too. For example, prenatal risk factors such as exposure to the disease rubella or to alcohol and drugs are likely contributors to ADHD (Deutsch & Kinsbourne, 1990; Silver, 1992). An intrusive, highly controlling parenting style may also contribute to, or at least aggravate, the problem in some cases (Cunningham & Barkley, 1979; Jacobvitz & Sroufe, 1987). It has also been proposed that hyperactivity is linked to brain damage, food allergies, and high sugar intake. In Box 16.3, though, we see that these particular theories have not been well supported by research. In sum, ADHD remains somewhat of a mystery, but it most likely has both genetic and environmental causes and contributors.

Effective Treatment

What can be done to help hyperactive children? Many of them are given stimulant drugs such as methylphenidate (Ritalin). Stimulants appear to correct an imbalance of neurotransmitter chemicals in the brain and help 70–80% of ADHD children (DuPaul, Barkley, & McMurray, 1991). Although it may seem odd to give overactive children drugs that increase their heart rates and activity levels, stimulants work because they also make ADHD children better able to focus their attention and less distractible and disruptive (DuPaul et al., 1991; Tannock, Schachar, & Logan, 1993). The drugs improve academic performance (Pelham et al., 1993), can help bring aggressive behavior under control (Hinshaw, 1991), and can positively affect classmates' views of ADHD children (Whalen et al., 1989). Moreover, stimulants seem to work effectively with all age groups, from preschoolers to adults who continue to be distractible and impulsive (Wilens & Biederman, 1992).

Why, then, does controversy surround the use of stimulants with ADHD children? Some critics feel that these drugs are prescribed to too many children, including some who are not ADHD, and they are concerned about undesirable side effects. For example, some children taking stimulants experience loss of appetite, difficulty sleeping, and stomachaches or headaches, but these side effects are usually mild (Silver, 1992). Long-term stimulant use can also slow physical growth, although periodic "holidays" from the drug seem to minimize this problem (Wilens & Biederman, 1992).

Critics are also concerned by the absence of convincing evidence that stimulants do anything more than temporarily improve functioning until their effects wear off at the end of the day (DuPaul et al., 1991). As it turns out, ADHD individuals who took stimulants as children are not much better adjusted as adults than those who did not (Hechtman et al., 1984; Wilens & Biederman, 1992). Because of such evidence, and because ADHD is a complex problem affecting all aspects of development, most experts have concluded that drugs should be prescribed with caution and that drugs alone cannot solve all the difficulties faced by ADHD individuals and their families. ADHD children are likely to benefit most from multipronged treatments that involve (1) medication, (2) behavioral programs designed to teach them to stay focused on a task and to control their impulsiveness, and (3) parent training and counseling designed to help parents understand and cope with these often-difficult youngsters (DuPaul & Barkley, 1993; Whalen & Henker, 1991).

In sum, attention-deficit hyperactivity disorder interferes with cognitive, social, and emotional development from the early years of life into the adult years. A difficult infant may become an uncontrollable and overactive preschooler, an inattentive grade school student, a low-achieving and delinquent adolescent, and even an impulsive and restless adult. True, many ADHD children do adapt well later in life, but perhaps even more will do so as we learn more about the causes of this disorder and develop treatments that achieve longer-lasting impacts.

Depression in Childhood

As we saw earlier, the depression-like symptoms displayed by deprived or traumatized infants probably do not qualify as major depressive disorders. When *can* children experience true clinical depression, then? For years many psychologists and psychiatrists, especially those influenced by psychoanalytic theory, argued that young children simply could not be depressed. Feelings of worthlessness, hopelessness, and

BOX 16.3 Clearing Away the Misconceptions about Hyperactivity

We do not fully understand what causes attention-deficit hyperactivity disorder, but researchers are at least weeding out some incorrect ideas about this condition. Initially it was thought that hyperactive children had suffered some sort of "minimal brain damage." The only problem was that researchers could find no evidence of brain damage in most ADHD children, nor could they establish that most children who suffer brain damage become hyperactive (Achenbach, 1982). Researchers are still convinced that the brains of ADHD children process stimulation differently than the brains of other children, but they are now looking for subtle differences in brain chemistry rather than for physical brain damage.

Another hypothesis was that particular foods, food additives, and preservatives cause or at least aggravate hyperactivity. When Dr. Benjamin Feingold (1975) recommended placing hyperactive children on a diet free of chemical food additives, many parents soon became convinced that the diet achieved miracles. But might these parents, expecting good results, have treated their children differently after they launched the special diet than before? We could find out through controlled studies in which children and the adults who are evaluating them do not know whether they are getting the Feingold diet or a diet containing food additives. Such studies clearly indicate that food additives have little apparent effect on the vast majority of ADHD children (Gross, Tofanelli, Butzirus, & Snodgrass, 1987; Harley et al., 1978).

What about sugar, though? Many parents believe that their hyperactive children immediately become worse after they eat sweets, and many teachers advise parents to cut their children's sugar intake to help control their hyperactivity (DiBattista & Shepherd, 1993). Again, however, the research evidence simply fails to support this idea, at least for the vast majority of ADHD children (Milich, Wolraich, & Lindgren, 1986). For example, Richard Milich and William Pelham (1986) had hyperactive boys drink either sugary drinks or ones with the sugar substitute aspartame. Sugar seemed to have no negative effects on these boys' behavior or performance in learning situations. These researchers suggest an interesting explanation for the common observation that sugar makes ADHD children more hyperactive: Perhaps these children simply cannot reorganize their activity after the disruption of stopping to eat a snack—sugary or otherwise.

In short, a very small percentage of ADHD children do seem to have allergic reactions to sugar, food additives, or other foods, but the various "food theories" that have been offered have not proven any better than the "minimal brain damage" theory at explaining the vast majority of cases of ADHD (Silver, 1992). Many other misconceptions are likely to fall by the wayside before research leads us nearer to the truth—and to better ways of preventing and treating ADHD and other serious psychological disorders.

CLOSE TO HOME JOHN McPHERSON

"He does not have a discipline problem! He's just had a little too much sugar, that's all."

self-blame were not believed to be possible until the child formed a strong superego, or internalized moral standards (Garber, 1984).

Once it was appreciated that even very young children *could* become depressed, some researchers argued that childhood depression is qualitatively different from adult depression. Children, it was said, display **masked depression,** or depression in the guise of symptoms other than those we associate directly with depression (Quay et al., 1987). For example, a depressed child would not talk about being sad; instead, he or she might express depression indirectly by behaving aggressively or being very anxious.

Now we know that young children *can* meet the very same criteria for major depression that are used in diagnosing adults—and as early as age 3 (Kashani & Carlson, 1985). Depression in children is rarer than depression in adolescents and adults, but an estimated 2% of children have diagnosable depressive disorders (Gotlib & Hammen, 1992). Many youngsters who show the key symptoms of depression do display aggressive or anxious behavior as well. However, these symptoms of "masked depression" are now understood to be distinct problems; they accompany depression but are not veiled symptoms of it (King, Ollendick, & Gullone, 1991; Ryan et al., 1987).

Although the concept of masked depression in childhood is faulty, there is truth to the idea that depression expresses itself somewhat differently in a young child than in an adult. A depressed preschooler is more likely to display the behavioral and somatic symptoms of depression (losing interest in activities, eating poorly, and so on) than to display cognitive symptoms (hopelessness, excessive guilt) or to talk about being depressed (American Psychiatric Association, 1987; Pataki & Carlson, 1990).

Even school-aged children do not express their depression in precisely the ways that adults or adolescents do, although there are far more similarities than differences. Like preschoolers, they often show their depression more clearly in how they act than in what they say, and they are likely to misbehave, perhaps by getting into fights (Bemporad & Wilson, 1978; Weiss et al., 1992). Later in elementary school, depressed children express more cognitive symptoms such as low self-esteem, hopelessness, and self-blame (McConville, Boag, & Purohit, 1973; Weiss et al., 1992). For example, one 11-year-old who attempted suicide said "The devil is in me"; another claimed "I'm a burden on the family" (Kosky, 1983, p. 459).

The message is clear, then: Parents and other adults need to become more aware that childhood is not always a happy, carefree time and that children *can* develop serious depressive disorders. If you are still not completely convinced that even very young children can suffer from severely depressed moods, consider evidence that children as young as age 2½ or 3 are capable of attempting suicide (Rosenthal & Rosenthal, 1984). At the tender age of 2½, for example, Elizabeth, reacting to her parents' divorce, a string of many different babysitters, and a depressed mother, ate a bottleful of aspirin the day her mother returned from a brief hospital stay. While pretending to feed her doll aspirin, Elizabeth said "The baby is going to the hospital because she died today" (p. 522).

Other children have reportedly jumped from high places, run into traffic, thrown themselves down stairs, and stabbed themselves, often in response to abuse, rejection, or neglect (Pfeffer, 1986; Rosenthal & Rosenthal, 1984). Suicide attempts in childhood are very rare, but the rates are climbing; moreover, some apparent accidents may actually be suicide attempts (Joffe & Offord, 1990). Again the moral is clear: Children's claims that they want to die should be taken seriously.

Do depressed children tend to have recurring bouts of depression, becoming depressed adolescents and adults? Certainly most children get through mild episodes of sadness. However, most clinically depressed children have recurring episodes of serious depression during childhood, adolescence, and even adulthood (Kovacs et al., 1984; Pataki & Carlson, 1990). Their depression disrupts their intellectual development and school achievement as well as their social adjustment (Kovacs & Goldston, 1991). Fortunately, most depressed children respond well to psychotherapy (Petersen et al., 1993; Weisz & Weiss, 1993).

In sum, children, even young ones, can become clinically depressed and even suicidal (though rarely). Moreover, depression in childhood is very similar to depression in adulthood, although it manifests itself somewhat differently as the developing person gains new cognitive capacities. If adults become more sensitive to signs of depression in children, they will be better able to offer appropriate treatment and perhaps reduce the likelihood of recurrences later in life.

Childhood Disorders and the Family

Most of us have a strong belief in the power of the social environment, particularly the family, to shape child development. This belief often leads us to blame parents—especially mothers (Phares & Compas, 1992)—if their children are sad and withdrawn, uncontrollable and "bratty," or otherwise different from most other children. Parents whose children develop problems often draw the very same conclusion, feeling guilty because they assume they are somehow at fault.

It is indeed essential to view developmental disorders from a family systems perspective and to appreciate how emerging problems affect and are affected by family interactions. In a thoughtful analysis of the influence of family environment on a number of childhood disorders, however, Jacob Sines (1987) warns that the power of parents to influence their children's adjustment may not be nearly so great as many of us believe. It is true that youngsters with psychological disorders often come from problem-ridden families. For example, both depressed children and hyperactive children are more likely than children without these disorders to have rejecting or hostile parents. In addition, children with psychological disorders are more likely than other children to have mothers or fathers who have histories of psychologi-

Because parents and children influence each other, it is not always clear whether a parent's hostility is the cause or the effect of a child's misbehavior.

cal disorder themselves—even of the same disorder that affects the child (Phares & Compas, 1992). Youngsters are especially likely to have problems if *both* their parents are troubled (Goodman et al., 1993; Phares & Compas, 1992). Surely this means that children develop problems because they live in disturbed family environments with adults whose own psychological problems and marital conflicts make it difficult for them to parent effectively.

Or are there other interpretations? As Sine notes, we cannot always be sure that unfavorable home environments *cause* childhood disorders. One alternative explanation is a genetic one. We know, for example, that some individuals are predisposed by their genetic makeup—in interaction, as always, with their experiences—to become clinically depressed (Kendler et al., 1992; Moldin, Reich, & Rice, 1991). Perhaps the son of a depressed mother becomes depressed not so much because his mother was unresponsive or rejecting as because he inherited her genetic predisposition to become depressed.

In addition, "poor parenting" could be partly the *effect* of a child's disorder rather than its cause. As we have seen many times in this book, children contribute to their own development by shaping their social environment. Parental rejection may be a factor in the development of behavior problems, but we cannot ignore the possibility that child misbehavior may make loving parents more tense and hostile than they would be if they were interacting with an easy-to-manage child (Anderson, Lytton, & Romney, 1986; Donenberg & Baker, 1993). Both normal and abnormal development are affected by *reciprocal* influences within the family system.

Don't mistake us: Disruption, conflict, and hostility in the family *do* cause and aggravate many childhood problems (Rutter, 1989). But many of these problems may also be rooted partially in genetic endowment and may be the cause as well as the effect of disturbances in parent/child relationships. It is high time to move beyond the simple view that parents are to blame for all their children's problems. We must take seriously the notion that abnormal development, like normal development, is the product of both nature and nurture and of a history of complex transactions between child and social environment.

Do Childhood Problems Persist?

The parents of children who develop psychological problems very much want to know this: Will my child outgrow these problems, or will they persist? Parents are understandably concerned with the issue of continuity versus discontinuity in development. We have already seen that infantile autism, hyperactivity, and clinical depression *do* tend to persist beyond childhood, in many individuals at least. To answer the continuity/discontinuity question more fully, let's consider the entire spectrum of childhood problems. Recall the distinction between undercontrolled (or externalizing) problems and overcontrolled (or internalizing) problems. As it turns out, undercontrolled problems such as aggression are more likely to persist into adolescence and adulthood than are overcontrolled problems such as anxiety, phobias, shyness, and social withdrawal (Robins, 1966, 1979).

Mariellen Fischer and her colleagues (1984) asked parents to complete checklists describing the behavior problems displayed by their children during the preschool years and seven years later, when the children were 9 to 15 years old. The researchers then calculated the probability that a child who did or did not have severe problems during the preschool years would also have severe problems seven years later. As Table 16.2 shows, preschoolers with severe undercontrolled or externalizing problems were almost three times as likely as preschoolers without such problems to be "acting out" later in childhood. Here, then, is evidence of continuity. By contrast, preschoolers who were anxious, shy, and socially withdrawn were really *no more likely* than peers without such internalizing problems to display these same problems seven years later.

Overall, there was more discontinuity than continuity. That is, problems of early childhood were more likely to disappear than to persist. Consider: Even the preschool children with severe problems of undercontrol had only about a 3-in-10 chance of continuing to be severely antisocial and difficult at follow-up. Similarly encouraging news comes from a study of Swedish children (von Knorring, Andersson, & Magnusson, 1987): Only 11% of children who received psychiatric care before age 10 were still receiving psychiatric care in their early 20s. Having serious

TABLE 16.2 Odds of having an externalizing or internalizing problem at ages 9 to 15 if the same problem was or was not evident in preschool.

Status in preschool	Problem later
Externalizing Problems	
Problems	
Boys	25 out of 100
Girls	34 out of 100
No problems	
Boys	10 out of 100
Girls	10 out of 100
Internalizing Problems	
Problems	
Boys	23 out of 100
Girls	14 out of 100
No problems	
Boys	14 out of 100
Girls	10 out of 100

SOURCE: Based on Fischer et al., 1984.

psychological problems as a child clearly does not doom an individual to a life of maladjustment.

Why might we see continuity of problem behavior in some children but discontinuity in others? If children have severe rather than mild psychological problems and continue to live in troubled homes, receiving little help, their difficulties may well persist. However, as Norman Garmezy (1991) and Michael Rutter (1979, 1987) emphasize, many children show remarkable resilience, outgrowing early problems. Such children appear to be protected from lasting damage by their own competencies (especially intellectual ability and social skills) and by strong social support (especially by a stable family situation with at least one caring parent figure). Healthy marriages and stable jobs in adulthood can also help turn maladjusted children into well-adjusted adults (Sampson & Laub, 1993).

What we need to understand is that there is *both* continuity and change in children with psychological disorders. Yes, many outgrow their problems. And yet many adults with serious psychological problems first displayed those problems as children. Again, this is particularly true with respect to antisocial behavior. Most delinquent children do not become criminals, but most criminals were children who behaved antisocially in a variety of ways in a variety of settings, starting at an early age (Loeber, 1982; Sampson & Laub, 1993). Such individuals may trade picking fistfights for stealing wallets, but their underlying pattern of antisocial behavior carries over into later life.

In short, many individuals overcome problems they displayed as children, especially overcontrolled problems. At the same time, many adolescents and adults with severe problems, particularly those who are clearly antisocial, are continuing to act out a pattern of maladaptive behavior that took form much earlier in life.

THE ADOLESCENT

If any age group has a reputation for having problems and causing trouble, it is adolescents. This is supposedly the time when angelic children are transformed into emotionally unstable, unruly, problem-ridden monsters. The view that adolescence is a time of emotional **storm and stress** was set forth by the founder of developmental psychology, G. Stanley Hall (1904). It has been with us ever since.

Is Adolescence Really a Period of Storm and Stress?

Are adolescents really more likely than either children or adults to experience psychological problems? It seems that adolescents have a far worse reputation than they deserve. In daily life, adolescents are no more likely than children to experience the extreme mood swings that might suggest emotional storm and stress, though adolescents do more often experience mildly negative moods (Larson & Lampman-Petraitis, 1989). And it simply is not the case that *most* adolescents are emotionally disturbed or that *most* develop behavior problems such as drug abuse and chronic delinquency. Instead, significant mental health problems—real signs of storm and stress—characterize about 20% of adolescents (Offer & Schonert-Reichl, 1992). Moreover, many of these adolescents were maladjusted before they reached puberty and continue to be maladjusted during adulthood (Strober, 1986). Overall rates of diagnosed psychological disorder are only slightly higher among adolescents than among children or adults (Offer & Schonert-Reichl, 1992).

Yet adolescence *is* a period of heightened vulnerability to some forms of psychological disorder (Kashani et al., 1989). After all, teenagers must cope with physical maturation, the emergence of new cognitive abilities, dating, changes in family dynamics, moves to new and more complex school settings, societal demands to become more responsible and to assume adult roles, and much more (Hill, 1993; Petersen & Hamburg, 1986). Most adolescents cope with these challenges remarkably well and undergo impressive psychological growth, although it is not unusual for them to feel depressed, anxious, and irritable now and then. For a minority, a buildup of stressors during adolescence can precipitate serious psychopathology.

In sum, it can be a mistake to either overestimate or underestimate levels of psychopathology among adolescents. If we cling too strongly to the storm-and-stress view of adolescence and expect most teens to be half crazy, we may dismiss serious and potentially long-lasting problems as simply a normal "phase kids go through," a phase they will "outgrow." Yet, if we think adolescents are too young to have serious psychological problems, we can also fail to provide emotionally troubled youth with the help they need.

What special mental health risks *do* adolescents face? Among females, eating disorders such as anorexia nervosa and bulimia can make the adolescent period treacherous indeed. In addition, many adolescents of both sexes get themselves into trouble by engaging in delinquent behavior, including illegal drug use. Finally, rates of depression do increase dramatically from childhood to adolescence, and suicide rates climb accordingly. These sorts of adolescent problems become far more understandable when we view them in the context of normal adolescent development.

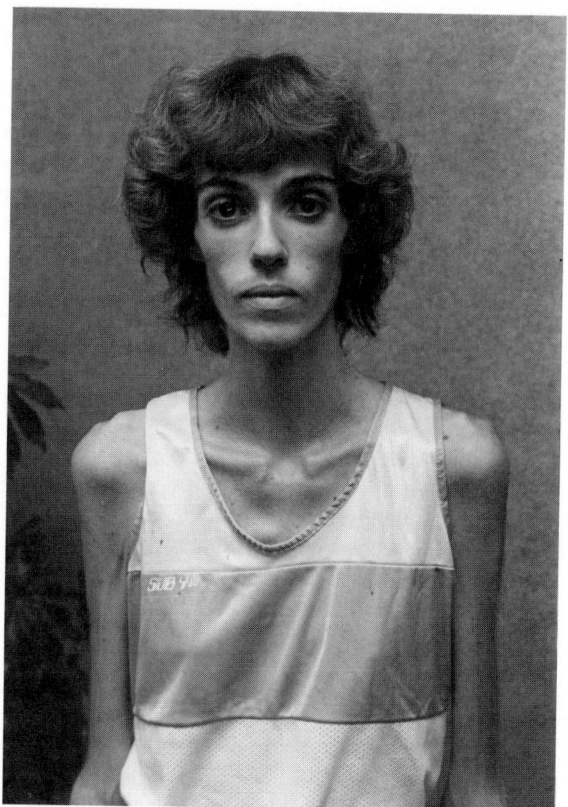

Anorexia can be life threatening.

Eating Disorders

Perhaps no psychological disorders are more associated with adolescence than the eating disorders that afflict adolescent girls and young women. Both anorexia nervosa and bulimia have become more common in recent years in a number of industrialized countries (Gordon, 1990). And both are serious—indeed, potentially fatal—conditions that are difficult to cure (Hsu, 1990).

Anorexia nervosa, which literally means "nervous loss of appetite," has been defined as a refusal to maintain a weight that is at least 85% of the expected weight for one's height and age (American Psychiatric Association, 1987). Anorexic individuals are also characterized by a strong fear of becoming overweight, a distorted body image (a tendency to view themselves as fat even when they are emaciated), and, if they are females, an absence of regular menstrual cycles. The typical anorexic may begin dieting soon after reaching puberty and simply continue, insisting, even when she weighs only 60 or 70 pounds and resembles a cadaver, that she is well nourished and could stand to lose a few more pounds (Hsu, 1990). Up to 1% of adolescent girls suffer from this condition, and 95 out of 100 of its victims are females (American Psychiatric Association, 1987). Between 5 and 20% end up committing suicide or starving themselves to death (Theander, 1985).

Bulimia nervosa, the so-called binge/purge syndrome, involves recurrent episodes of consuming huge quantities of food followed by purging activities such as self-induced vomiting, use of laxatives, or rigid dieting and fasting (American Psychiatric Association, 1987). Like anorexia nervosa, it is rooted in a strong "fear of fat"; its victims believe they are far fatter than they are and want to be far thinner (Williamson et al., 1989). Bulimia is especially prevalent in college populations, affecting few men but as many as 5% of college women (Hsu, 1990). Like anorexia, it is life threatening; laxatives and diuretics used as purging agents can deplete the body of potassium and cause cardiac arrhythmia and heart attacks, and regular vomiting can cause hernias.

A bulimic girl or woman typically binges on the very foods that are taboo to dieters, eating entire half gallons of ice cream, multiple bags of cookies and potato chips, or whole pies and cakes—as much as *55,000 calories* in a single binge session (Johnson et al., 1982). Not surprisingly, bulimic individuals experience a good deal of anxiety and depression in connection with their binge eating. Learning theorists suggest that they learn to engage in purging activities to relieve these negative feelings (Hinz & Williamson, 1987).

Bulimic individuals can be found in all weight ranges (American Psychiatric Association, 1987). Since anorexic females are, by definition, underweight, they are more "successful," in a perverse way, at avoiding fat than bulimic females are. As many as half of anorexic patients are also bulimic, so the two disorders can co-exist (Polivy & Herman, 1985). Other bulimics are overweight. There even seems to be a subgroup of overweight women who resemble bulimics psychologically but do not qualify as bulimic because they do not purge after their binges (Spitzer et al., 1993).

What Causes Eating Disorders?

Eating disorders stem partly from our society's obsession with thinness as the standard of physical attractiveness. Well before they reach puberty, girls in our society associate being thin with being attractive and want to be thinner; 1 out of 4 second-grade girls reports dieting (Thelen et al., 1992). As girls experience pubertal changes, they naturally gain fat and become, in their minds, less attractive (Rodin, Striegel-Moore, & Silberstein, 1990). They have more reason than ever to be obsessed with controlling their weight —or perhaps even to fight the physical and sexual maturation process by dieting (Rodin et al., 1990). As a result, adolescence is a prime time for the emergence of eating disorders (Attie & Brooks-Gunn, 1989).

The dieting that is so common among females in our society can clearly put them at risk for eating disorders. Anorexia nervosa can, of course, be viewed as dieting carried to an extreme. Moreover, attempts to diet may also contribute to binge eating and weight gain (Polivy & Herman, 1985; Rodin et al., 1990). Animals and humans are biologically programmed to compensate for a severe restriction of food intake by storing as much fat as possible; once off a crash diet, the body will continue to do this and will therefore gain weight more easily than before the diet was begun. The bulimic individual desperately attempts to fight biology by controlling her eating, but one little lapse from a rigid diet is enough to loosen this control and precipitate serious binging. Stressful events or depressed moods can also undermine the bulimic individual's usual restraints on eating. In all seriousness, Polivy and Herman (1985) conclude that "perhaps dieting is the disorder that we should be attempting to cure" (p. 200).

Still, we must ask why relatively few adolescent females become anorexic or bulimic, even though almost all of them experience social pressure to be thin. Michael Strober and Laura Humphrey (1987) have pieced together an answer. To begin with, genes predispose some individuals to develop an eating disorder, probably by influencing their personalities (Kendler et al., 1991; Scott, 1986). Anorexic females tend to be introverted young women who worry a good deal and are perfectionists, whereas bulimic females tend to be extraverted and impulsive (Hsu, 1990). Both groups have low self-esteem, a good deal of self-directed anger, and little sense that they can control their lives (Williams et al., 1993). Bulimic women also appear to be particularly vulnerable to other problems such as depression, anxiety disorders, and alcohol or drug abuse (Kendler et al., 1991).

Yet an eating disorder may not emerge unless a susceptible girl experiences disturbed family relationships—that is, unless heredity and environment interact in an unfavorable way. Salvador Minuchin and his colleagues (Minuchin, Rosman, & Baker, 1978) discovered that anorexic females have difficulty with the adolescent task of forming an identity separate from their parents because their families tend to be "enmeshed," or overly interdependent. Their parents are overprotective and do not allow their daughters to argue or to express negative emotions. The result may be a young woman who has not been able to separate herself from her parents and who desperately wants to establish some sense of control over her life, which she can do by dieting (Smolak & Levine, 1993). Bulimic females are more likely than anorexic ones to experience overt conflict and a lack of affection and support in their families; they tend to distance themselves from their parents but are unhappy about it (Scalf-McIver & Thompson, 1989; Smolak & Levine, 1993).

Here, then, is a prime example of how characteristics of the person, family, and wider social environment can interact to produce developmental problems. The young woman who is at risk for eating disorders may be predisposed, partly owing to her genetic makeup, to have difficulty coping with the pressures of adolescence, maintaining self-esteem, and establishing autonomy. However, she may not actually develop an eating disorder unless she also grows up in a culture that overvalues thinness and in a family that makes it hard for her to express her feelings and establish her own identity as an individual.

Can Eating Disorders Be Treated?

Fortunately, both anorexic and bulimic individuals can be successfully treated, although treatment is challenging and at least a third of all clients continue to be anorexic or bulimic after treatment (Zerbe, 1993). Effective therapies for eating-disordered individuals include behavior modification programs designed to bring their eating behavior under control, individual psychotherapy designed to help them understand and gain control over their problem, family therapy designed to help build healthier parent/child relationships, and, for some, antidepressant medication to treat the depression that often accompanies eating disorders (Hsu, 1990). Because only 25–30% of anorexics show any improvement without psychological help (Theander, 1985), and because treatment is likely to be most effective if it begins when the individual is young and has been ill for less than three years (Russell et al., 1987), convincing the individual to seek treatment immediately is extremely important.

Juvenile Delinquency

Another problem that we associate with adolescence is **juvenile delinquency,** or lawbreaking by a minor. Let us ask you a blunt question: Did you, as a minor, ever drink or smoke under age, use an illegal drug such as marijuana, swipe something from a store or from school, deface someone's property, or do anything else that you knew to be illegal? We suspected as much! Virtually all adolescents admit to some sort of wrongdoing (Henggeler, 1989). The peak age for delinquent acts is about 15 or 16, and this seems to be true in a variety of cultures, social classes, and ethnic groups (Shavit & Rattner, 1988). Boys are more involved in delinquent behavior than girls (Steffensmeier & Streifel, 1991). And, although low-income, minority youth are more likely than other adolescents to be arrested and judged delinquent by the courts, self-report surveys suggest that they are really not much more likely to commit delinquent acts (Henggeler, 1989). In short, occasional delinquent behavior appears to be a typical part of the adolescent experience—common among most youth from all sorts of backgrounds, especially in mid-adolescence.

Why is delinquent behavior so common, and why does it peak when it does? The large majority of delinquent acts are committed *with* peers and *for* peers. Age 15 or 16 is not only the peak age for delinquent behavior but is also the age at which youth are especially dependent on peer approval and likely to conform to peer influence (see Chapter 13). Delinquent acts are often carefully chosen so that they will impress peers (Gold & Petronio, 1980); stealing the red flasher off a police car or moving the principal's desk to the gym can make one's reputation! It seems to be entirely normal to engage in minor delinquent acts on occasion in order to "fit in," feel good about oneself, and perhaps ultimately find an identity of one's own. The large majority of youth who commit delinquent acts do not go on to criminal careers as adults; for them, life as a delinquent truly is a phase they pass through.

However, it is *not* normal to engage repeatedly in serious criminal acts—to commit armed robberies, assault people, or otherwise go far beyond the "optimal" range of youthful wrongdoing. The most serious juvenile offenders very often come from troubled homes and have parents who reject them, fail to monitor their activities, and use negative, coercive, power-assertive forms of discipline (Dishion et al., 1991; Sampson & Laub, 1993; Simons, Robertson, & Downs, 1989). These serious offenders often have low IQ scores and, starting in childhood, perform poorly in school and place little value on education (Lynam, Moffitt, & Stouthamer-Loeber, 1993). Moreover, their poor school performance and antisocial acts cause most of their peers to reject them, and they end up by default associating with other antisocial youth, who in turn reinforce their delinquent tendencies (Dishion et al., 1991).

Serious delinquents are likely to continue to be involved in criminal and violent behavior in adulthood and are in need of help (Eron, 1987). Among the most promising approaches to preventing delinquency are early intervention programs based on an ecological model of development. These programs attempt to get high-risk disadvantaged children off to a good start in school, improve their home and community environments, and build the academic and social competencies that can help protect them from becoming involved in antisocial activities later in life (Mulvey, Arthur, & Reppucci, 1993; Zigler, Taussig, & Black, 1992).

Drinking and Drug Use

We can further appreciate just how common delinquent behavior is by looking at the percentages of adolescents who use alcohol and other drugs. The data reported in Figure 16.1, which were collected by Denise Kandel and Mark Davies (1991) in New York

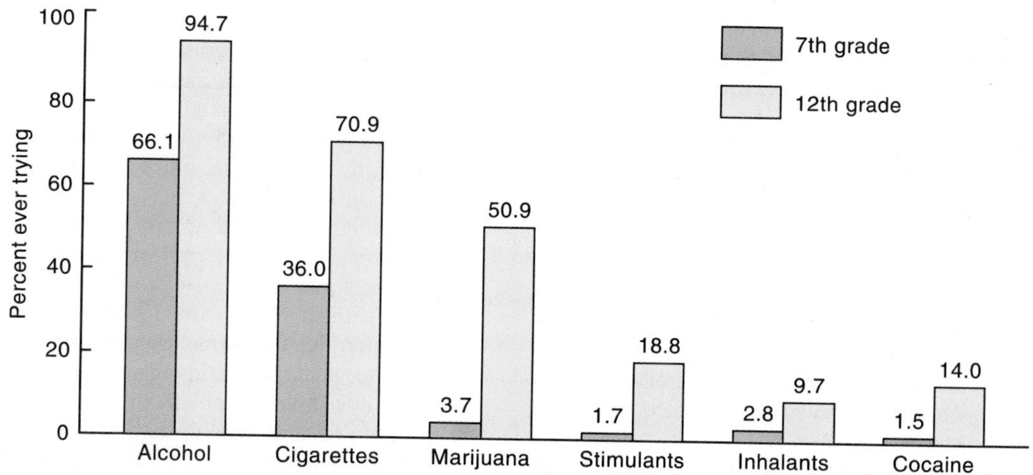

FIGURE 16.1 Percentages of 7th- and 12th-graders in New York State who have tried various drugs. These data, like those collected elsewhere in the United States, show that adolescents begin to experiment with drugs early and that more and more of them do so as they get older. Psychedelics, sedatives, tranquilizers, and heroin are not shown here because they were used by fewer than 5% of the students surveyed. (Based on data from Kandel & Davies, 1991.)

State schools, are typical. Alcohol is by far the most widely used drug among adolescents, and its use begins early. Not only have over 90% of high school seniors tried alcohol, but 39% report at least one episode of "party drinking" (five or more drinks in a row) within the past two weeks (Johnston, O'Malley, & Bachman, 1985). Just over half of all seniors have also tried marijuana, and many have experimented with other illegal substances as well. It is typical for adolescents to try alcohol before they try marijuana, and to try marijuana before they experiment with other illegal drugs (Yamaguchi & Kandel, 1984). Use of virtually all of these substances increased in the 1960s and 1970s. Although alcohol remains as popular as ever today, use of many other substances began to decline in the 1980s (Kandel & Davies, 1991).

In a society in which drug use is widespread, there is nothing particularly abnormal about adolescents who experiment a little with drugs like marijuana. In fact, teenagers who experiment with marijuana are in most ways more well adjusted psychologically and have better family relations than either frequent users or abstainers (Baumrind, 1985; Shedler & Block, 1990). It could well be that experimenting with alcohol and drugs is part of the larger process of experimenting to form an identity and prepare for adult life (Baumrind, 1985). Why, though, do some adolescents go beyond experimenting with drugs and end up abusing them? In offering a model to explain the origins of several adolescent problems, Richard Jessor (1987; Jessor, Donovan, & Costa, 1991) assumes that adolescent problem behaviors are learned ways of achieving important goals, such as independence from parents and peer acceptance. He also believes that the likelihood of problem behavior will depend on the balance between factors that encourage and factors that control against such behavior.

Most adolescents use but do not abuse alcohol, but those who abuse it are often alienated from conventional values, heavily influenced by peers who drink, and prone to other problems.

Jessor and his colleagues have conducted a longitudinal study of problem drinking that started with 13- to 15-year-olds and tracked them until they were age 25 to 27. Problem drinkers were defined as youth who got drunk an average of about 20 times a year and experienced adjustment problems associated with their drinking. As it turned out, three broad factors distinguished problem drinkers from other adolescents: their personal qualities, perceived social environment, and other behavior problems.

With respect to their *personal qualities,* problem drinkers tended to be alienated from conventional values. They placed little value on academic achievement, were not very religious, and generally were not attached to important social institutions such as schools and churches.

Second, problem drinkers perceived their *social environment* differently than other adolescents did. Their parents, they said, were unsupportive and had little impact on them, whereas their peers modeled and reinforced drinking and other problem behaviors. Again and again, researchers find that teenagers who abuse drugs hang out with other teenagers who abuse drugs and do not have very close relationships with their parents (see also Brook et al., 1990; Ellickson & Hays, 1992).

Third, drinking problems occurred within the context of the adolescent's *other behavior problems.* Specifically, problem drinkers were more likely than other adolescents to engage in other rule violations (smoking, using marijuana, committing delinquent acts, and having sexual intercourse) and were less likely to engage in conventional behaviors (studying and attending worship services).

It seems, then, that any particular adolescent problem is likely to be part of a larger *syndrome* of unconventional and norm-breaking behavior (see also Farrell, Danish, & Howard, 1992; Rowe et al., 1989). Consequently, the same personality characteristics and features of the perceived social environment that predict adolescent problem drinking tend to predict other adolescent problem behaviors as well. What's more, these factors predict the continuation of problem behaviors into adulthood (Jessor et al., 1991). In sum, Jessor's model gives us insights into how a wide range of adolescent problems may originate and suggests that preventing and treating such problems may require changing the values of adolescents themselves *and* altering their relationships to parents, peers, schools, and other social institutions (see also Hawkins, Catalano, & Miller, 1992).

Depression and Suicidal Behavior in Adolescence

Children become quite a bit more vulnerable to depression as they enter adolescence, especially if they are girls (Angold & Rutter, 1992). Up to 35% of adolescents experience depressed moods at some time, and as many as 7% have diagnosable depressive disorders (Petersen et al., 1993). Why? Changes in hormone levels have been linked to increases in negative moods during adolescence, but social factors often turn out to be more important than the biological changes of puberty in explaining the rise in depressive symptoms (Angold & Rutter, 1992; Brooks-Gunn & Warren, 1989; Susman, Dorn, & Chrousos, 1991). For one thing, adolescents experience more negative life events and may simply have more to be depressed about than children do (Larson & Ham, 1993). Females may be especially at risk because they are more likely than males to experience stressful life events such as the transition to a middle school or junior high school while they are also going through pubertal changes (Petersen, Sarigiani, & Kennedy, 1991).

We can appreciate that adolescents have one foot in childhood and the other in adulthood when we look at the ways in which depression is manifested during this period. More intellectually mature than children, depressed adolescents display the same cognitive symptoms of depression that adults display. Hopelessness, feelings of worthlessness, suicidal thinking, and other negative cognitions are common (Garber, Weiss, & Shanley, 1993). Yet depressed adolescents, like depressed children, often show other problems along with their depression—substance abuse, eating disorders, anxiety, antisocial behavior, and more (Petersen et al., 1993). Some depressed teenagers look more like budding juvenile delinquents than like victims of depression. Thus, diagnosing depression during adolescence can still be tricky, for depressed adolescents share some of the qualities of both depressed adults and depressed children.

As depression becomes more common from childhood to adolescence, so do suicidal thoughts, suicide attempts, and actual suicides. Moreover, rates of suicide have been increasing in the adolescent age group, especially among white males (McCall, 1991). As a result, suicide has become the third leading cause of death for this age group, far behind accidents and just behind homicides (U. S. Bureau of the Census, 1993). For every adolescent suicide there are many unsuccessful attempts—as many as 50 to 200 by some estimates (Garland & Zigler, 1993). Also, suicidal thoughts that may or may not lead to action are shockingly common during this period (Dubow et al., 1989; Smith & Crawford, 1986). In one survey of high school students, 62.6% reported at least one instance of suicidal thinking, and 10.5% had actually attempted suicide (Smith & Crawford, 1986). In some Native American groups, suicidal thoughts and behaviors are even more widespread (Garland & Zigler, 1993); in one sample of Zuni adolescents, fully 30% had attempted suicide, most of them more than once (Howard-Pitney et al., 1992).

Before we conclude that adolescence is the peak time for suicidal behavior, however, let's consider the suicide rates for different age groups (see Figure 16.2). It is clear that *adults* are more likely to commit suicide than adolescents are. The suicide rate for females peaks in middle age, and the suicide rate for white males climbs throughout adulthood. As a result, elderly white men are the individuals most likely to commit suicide, possibly because they have high status in society as young men but often experience job failure, retirement, reduced income, and illness as they age (McCall, 1991).

Overall, males are more likely to commit suicide than females, by a ratio of about 3 to 1—a difference that holds up across most cultures studied (Girard, 1993). When we look at suicide *attempts*, this ratio is reversed, with females leading males by a ratio of about 3 to 1. Apparently, then, females attempt suicide more often than males do, but males more often

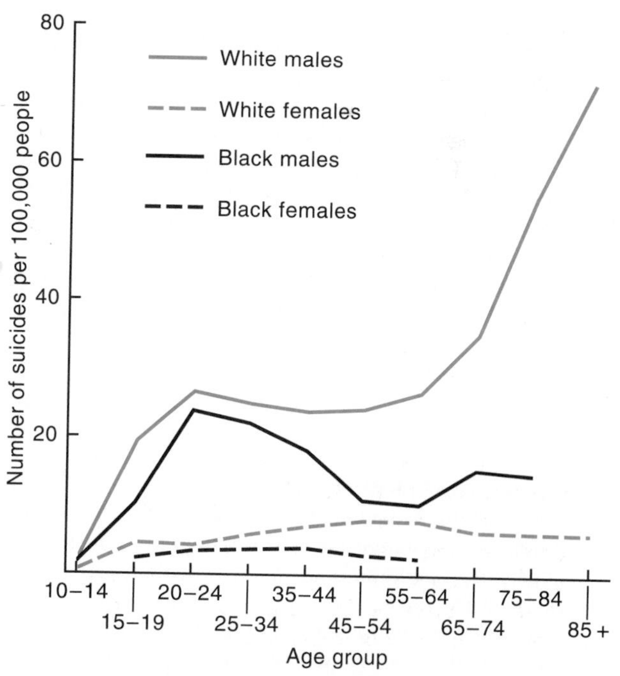

FIGURE 16.2 Number of suicides per 100,000 people by age and sex among whites and African Americans in the United States. Data from the oldest African Americans are not shown because too few cases were studied. (Data from U.S. Bureau of the Census, 1992.)

succeed when they try, probably because they use more lethal techniques (especially guns).

If suicide rates are actually higher in adulthood than in adolescence, why do we hear so much about teenage suicide? Maybe it is because adolescents attempt suicide more frequently than adults do, even though they less often succeed. For this reason, the typical adolescent suicide attempt has been characterized as a "cry for help," a desperate effort to get others to notice and help resolve problems that have become unbearable (Berman & Jobes, 1991). The adolescent who attempts suicide often wants a better life; the adult who attempts suicide is more often determined to end his or her life.

This by no means suggests that adolescent suicide attempts should be taken lightly, though. Their message is clear: "I've got serious problems; wake up and help me!" Suicide attempters often are severely depressed, abuse drugs, or have other psychological disorders (Felts, Chenier, & Barnes, 1992; Garland & Zigler, 1993; Pfeffer et al., 1991). They have often experienced deteriorating relationships with parents and peers, suffered academic and social failures, and begun to feel incapable of coping (Berman & Jobes, 1991; Rubenstein et al., 1989). Lacking effective coping and problem-solving skills, they may see no other way out than suicide (Sadowski & Kelley, 1993). The adolescent who attempts suicide once may try again —and succeed—if he or she receives little help and continues to feel incapable of coping with problems, so professional help is definitely called for after an unsuccessful suicide attempt (Berman & Jobes, 1991).

All in all, adolescence does appear to be a potentially treacherous period of the life span for some individuals. However, let's remind ourselves that the large majority of adolescents, even though they commit an illegal act or think a depressive thought now and then, emerge from this period as well-adjusted and competent young adults. They will face new challenges in adapting to the demands of adult life.

THE ADULT

At any age, psychological problems such as depression and anxiety, as well as physical illnesses, may result when an individual faces overwhelming stress. Because the developmental tasks and daily pressures of adult life *are* stress producing, it is time for us to examine the relationship among stress, coping, and psychopathology. We will also continue our exploration of depression across the life span, delving into the special problems of elderly adults who suffer from Alzheimer's disease and other serious brain disorders.

Stress and Coping in Adulthood

According to Richard Lazarus (1993; Lazarus & Folkman, 1984), **stress** is a state that occurs when we perceive events as straining our coping capacities and threatening our well-being. What determines whether or not an experience is stressful, then, is the person's *appraisal* of the event in relation to his or her coping capacities. From this perspective, Faye may find giving birth to be a very stressful experience, whereas Maria may experience little stress in response to this same event because she is confident that she can manage.

What sorts of life experiences create stress and place the person at risk for developing problems? Most of the attention has focused on major life events, which may be either *normative transitions*—events that are typical at certain ages, such as marrying, becoming a parent, or retiring from work—or *nonnormative transitions*—unusual and unforeseen events that can happen at any age, such as being in a car accident, undergoing surgery, or divorcing. Normative life events, because they can be anticipated, are less likely than nonnormative, unscheduled events to be stressful and to cause psychological problems such as anxiety and depression (Pearlin, 1980). For example, retiring typically has little effect on mental health, but being unexpectedly laid off or demoted at work often takes a psychological toll.

Yet even nonnormative major life events do not seem to have as many implications for mental health as ongoing life strains. Lazarus and his colleagues have focused attention on the significance of **daily hassles**—chronic strains or everyday annoyances that may range in magnitude from repeatedly misplacing one's belongings to facing strong pressures to succeed, being trapped in a conflict-ridden relationship, worrying about bills, or living with a chronic illness (Kanner et al., 1981). An adult's level of psychological distress is actually better predicted by the number of daily hassles he or she is experiencing than by the number of major life events he or she has encountered (Kanner et al., 1981). Morton Lieberman (1983) puts it well: "We are done in more by the drips than by the floods" (p. 133).

In sum, the extent to which people experience stress and its potentially damaging effects depends on both the kinds of events they encounter and the ways in which they appraise them. People generally seem to cope better with major life events that are a normal and expected part of adult development than with life events that they did not expect to occur and are not prepared to manage. Yet the most stress-producing experiences of all may be those "little" daily hassles that, when added up, can make everyday life seem unbearable. The extent to which stress is harmful will then depend in part on the appropriateness and effectiveness of the coping strategies the individual chooses. With this as background, we can look at stress, coping, and psychopathology across the adult years.

Age and Stressful Experiences

When in their lives do you think adults are most likely to experience stressful events? It seems difficult to decide. After all, young adults face the struggles of building a life—of starting careers, finding mates, marrying, and having children. Yet middle-aged adults are involved in many roles and have heavy burdens of responsibility, and elderly adults often experience hardships associated with declining health and lost roles and relationships.

As it turns out, adults experience the greatest number of life changes and strains in early adulthood (McLanahan & Sorensen, 1985; Pearlin, 1980). Life strains decrease from early adulthood to middle adulthood, probably as adults settle into more stable lifestyles. And elderly adults report even fewer hassles than middle-aged adults do, perhaps because they have fewer roles and responsibilities to juggle or because they appraise events differently, no longer perceiving as many things as stressful (Folkman et al., 1987).

Age and Coping Capacities

If young adults have more to cope with than older adults, do they also have more effective coping strategies at their disposal? Some researchers have proposed that coping capacities peak in early and middle adulthood and deteriorate with age. According to this "regression" hypothesis, older adults cope with stressful events less actively and effectively than younger adults do (Pfeiffer, 1977). Other researchers, however, propose a "growth" hypothesis of coping, arguing that coping capacities *improve* with age (Vaillant, 1977).

Which is it? As it turns out, neither the regression hypothesis nor the growth hypothesis is very well supported. Instead, individuals at different ages are typically far more similar than different in their coping styles (Rook, Dooley, & Catalano, 1991). That is, we may each develop distinctive coping styles that we rely on throughout our adult years (Costa, Zonderman, & McCrae, 1991). However, a few signs of *both* growth and regression have been identified, and they carry an interesting message about adult development.

First consider some signs of growth. Robert McCrae (1982), for example, asked adults ranging in age from 24 to 91 to describe their responses to a recent stressful life event. Although few age differences in coping styles were detected, young adults were more likely than middle-aged or elderly adults to use immature and usually ineffective coping techniques, such as expressing anger and hostility or escaping problems through fantasy. Here, then, is some support for the growth hypothesis (see also Felton & Revenson, 1987; Irion & Blanchard-Fields, 1987; Vaillant, 1977).

Now consider some evidence that might be interpreted as regression. Susan Folkman, Richard Lazarus, and their colleagues (1987) compared the coping strategies of middle-aged and elderly adults and found that elderly adults were more passive in some respects (see also Rook et al., 1991). Middle-aged adults were likely to use **problem-focused coping,** attempting to change the stressful situation or eliminate the problem through such tactics as confronting other people, actively planning ways to solve the problem, and seeking social support. Elderly adults relied on more passive, **emotion-focused coping,** changing their appraisal of and emotional response to the problem by trying not to think about it, distancing themselves from it, or making the best of it. An unhappy wife would be using problem-focused coping if she tried to convince her husband to see a marriage counselor with her but emotion-focused coping if she tried to focus on her husband's endearing qualities and live with his faults.

We might be tempted to conclude, then, that middle-aged and elderly adults are showing growth when they manage to deal with stressful events without venting anger or escaping their problems through fantasy, as younger adults more often do. And we might view elderly adults as having regressed when they do not actively try to change their situations but instead decide to live with them. But it may be more accurate to conclude, as Folkman and her colleagues do, that these few age differences in coping styles reflect *neither* growth nor regression. Instead, they may reflect age differences in the kinds of problems people face. It may make sense, for example, for a young or middle-aged woman to confront her misbehaving child or her lazy co-worker if she believes that she can change their behavior (a problem-focused strategy). But it may make just as much sense for an elderly man to accept and make the best of a chronic illness that will not go away (an emotion-focused strategy). If problem-focused strategies best fit problems that are solvable and emotion-focused strategies best fit problems that are not easily fixed, *both* old and young are probably responding adaptively (Brandtstädter & Renner, 1990; Folkman et al., 1987). Indeed, the key to successful coping at any age may be knowing when to try to change distressing situations and when to learn to live with them (Brandtstädter & Renner, 1990).

In sum, both younger and older adults may cope in ways that are appropriate to the kinds of stressful events they are most likely to encounter at their stages of life. Mainly, older and younger adults cope in similar ways with similar problems, casting doubt on both the growth and regression hypotheses (Costa et al., 1991). Yet, if young adults experience more major life events and more ongoing hassles than older adults do, but do not differ greatly from older adults in their coping capacities, shouldn't they also be more susceptible to psychological disorders than older adults?

When Coping Fails: Age and Sex Differences in Psychopathology

When in adulthood *are* people most likely to suffer from psychological disorders? What sorts of disorders predominate in different age groups? The National Institute of Mental Health conducted a major survey of community mental health in New Haven, Baltimore, and St. Louis (Myers et al., 1984; Robins & Regier, 1991). Adults aged 18 or older were interviewed in their homes about the psychological symptoms they were experiencing, and estimates were made of the percentages of respondents meeting the criteria set out in *DSM-III-R* for several psychological disorders.

Overall, a fairly large proportion of adults—15% to 22% of those surveyed in each city—were judged to have suffered from a diagnosable psychological disorder in the previous six months. Figure 16.3 shows how prevalent two very common types of disorders proved to be among men and women of different ages. Notice that both affective disorders (major depression and related mood disorders) and alcohol abuse and dependence affected a larger percentage of young adults than middle-aged or elderly adults. Indeed, the incidence of several other disorders examined in this study, including schizophrenia, anxiety disorders, and antisocial personality, decreased with age. The exception was cognitive impairment, which increased with age in later life, undoubtedly because minorities of older individuals were falling victim to Alzheimer's disease and other organic brain disorders (to be discussed later in this chapter). Otherwise, we must conclude that young adults, because they experience more stress with no better coping resources than older adults possess, are a group at high risk for mental health problems.

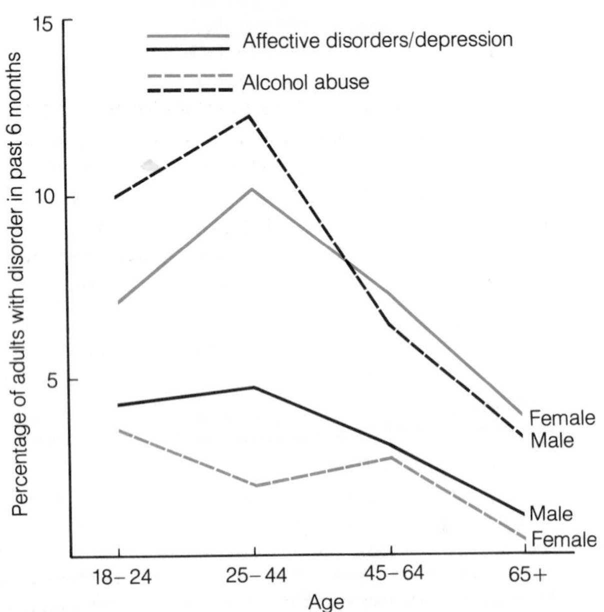

FIGURE 16.3 Percentages of adults of different ages displaying affective disorders or alcohol abuse/dependence in the past six months. (Created from data reported by Myers et al., 1984.)

Figure 16.3 also reveals that men and women are vulnerable to different sorts of problems. Men are far more likely to abuse alcohol (and other drugs) than women are, whereas women are more likely to report symptoms of depression and other affective disorders (and phobias as well). Yet, because some disorders are more prevalent among men whereas others are more prevalent among women, the two sexes have very similar overall rates of diagnosable psychological disorder. Possible reasons for age and sex differences in psychopathology will become clearer as we take a closer look at depression in adulthood.

Depression in Adulthood

It has been estimated that about 8% of adults have experienced a serious diagnosable affective disorder such as major depression at some point in their lives, and many of them have fought repeated episodes of depression; morever, almost 30% of adults have at some time had a period of at least two weeks in which they felt sad or blue (Weisman et al., 1991). But let's examine more closely who is counted in these statistics—and, more interestingly, why.

Age Differences

As Figure 16.3 revealed, some researchers have found that rates of clinical depression decrease from early adulthood to late adulthood (Myers et al., 1984). Other researchers find that rates of diagnosable depression do not differ much across the adult years (Bolla-Wilson & Bleecker, 1989; Feinson & Thoits, 1986). A somewhat different picture emerges when the focus shifts from diagnosable disorders to symptoms experienced: Symptom levels are high among adults under 35, decrease in middle age and early old age, and return to young-adult levels only in late old age (Gatz & Hurwicz, 1990; Kessler et al., 1992; Newmann, 1989). These age differences are usually very small. What is remarkable is that none of these findings supports the stereotyped notion that elderly adults are far more depressed than the rest of the population.

Depression may be especially difficult to diagnose in older adults, however (Allen & Blazer, 1991). Think about it: Symptoms of depression include fatigue, sleeping difficulties, cognitive deficits, and somatic complaints. What if clinicians noted these symptoms in an elderly person but interpreted them as nothing more than normal aging, or as the result of the chronic illnesses that are so common in old age?

Then a case of depression might easily be missed. Elderly adults who are depressed may also "mask" their depression, denying that they are sad and claiming instead that they have medical problems (Allen & Blazer, 1991). This, too, could lead to underdiagnosis of depression in the elderly population. Yet *over*diagnosis of depression in older adults can also occur if bodily complaints attributable to aging and disease are uncritically accepted as evidence of depression (Bolla-Wilson & Bleecker, 1989; Newmann, 1989).

There is currently no reason to conclude that depression in elderly individuals is so different from depression in young and middle-aged adults that entirely different criteria must be developed to detect it (La Rue, Dessonville, & Jarvik, 1985). Still, there seem to be subtle differences across the life span in how depression reveals itself. Clinicians working with elderly adults need to be sensitive to the differences between normal aging processes and psychopathology. Moreover, they should evaluate the health status of elderly individuals, the drugs prescribed for them, and their eating habits to better distinguish between clinical depression and psychological distress stemming from poor health, the side effects of drugs, or poor nutrition (Zarit, Eiler, & Hassinger, 1985). Finally, the fact that relatively few elderly people suffer from severe clinical depression should not blind us to the fact that perhaps a quarter of elderly people are experiencing depressive symptoms and could benefit from treatment (Allen & Blazer, 1991; Gatz & Hurwicz, 1990). The elderly adults most at risk are those who are very old, physically impaired, poor, or socially isolated (Blazer et al., 1991).

Sex Differences

As we have also seen, women are more likely than men to be diagnosed as depressed—by a margin of about two to one (Nolen-Hoeksema, 1990). This gender gap first emerges during adolescence (Petersen et al., 1993). It then reaches a peak in the 30-to-60 age range and becomes less pronounced or even disappears in old age (Nolen-Hoeksema, 1990). How can we explain this trend?

Biological explanations centering on the influence of female hormones are not well supported (Nolen-Hoeksema, 1990). Instead, it could be that young and middle-aged women simply have more to cope with and more to be depressed about than men do, perhaps because they carry the burden of responsibility for raising children and holding their families together (Jorm, 1987; Nolen-Hoeksema, 1990).

Alternatively, women may simply be more likely than men to report their symptoms or seek help (Nolen-Hoeksema, 1990). Or it could be that men and women have been socialized to express their psychological distress in different ways, so that men externalize their problems by behaving antisocially or abusing drugs, whereas women more often internalize their distress (Horwitz & White, 1987; Stapley & Haviland, 1989).

Finally, Susan Nolen-Hoeksema and her colleagues have offered the intriguing hypothesis that women and men differ in the way they cope with their bad moods. When they are depressed, men tend to respond with *distraction* strategies: They engage in enjoyable activities such as sports to get their minds off their problems. Women more often engage in *rumination*: They think a good deal about their problems and try to analyze why they feel the way they do (Nolen-Hoeksema, 1990). Yet ruminating tends to prolong bouts of depression (Nolen-Hoeksema, Morrow, & Frederickson, 1993). By responding as they do, then, men may sidestep or minimize their depression, whereas women may actually aggravate theirs. In sum, any or all of the factors suggested here may contribute to sex differences in rates of depression, but it seems likely that part of the answer lies in the ways males and females have been socialized to respond to stress.

How Does Depression Come About?

A **diathesis/stress model** of psychopathology has proved very useful in explaining how many psychological problems, including depression, arise (see Monroe & Simons, 1991). This model proposes that psychopathology results from the interaction of a predisposition or vulnerability to psychological disorder (diathesis) and the experience of stressful events. As we have seen, certain people are genetically predisposed to become depressed (Kendler et al., 1992, 1993). According to the diathesis/stress model, however, individuals whose families have a history of depression are not likely to become depressed unless they also experience significant losses or other stressful events. Meanwhile, other individuals may experience high levels of stress but not become depressed because they do not have an inherited or learned vulnerability to depression. In short, depression evolves from the interaction of person and environment. To explain more precisely why some individuals become depressed and others do not, we must consider:

1. The individual's *personal resources* (personality traits, coping styles, and the like—whether inherited or learned; the "diathesis" in the diathesis/stress model)
2. The *stressful life events* with which he or she must cope
3. The *social environment* (particularly the availability of social support)

Personal resources include enduring personality traits, styles of interpreting life events, and coping strategies. Individuals who cope effectively with stress typically possess many positive personality traits. They are self-confident and have an easygoing disposition (Holahan & Moos, 1986; Pagel & Becker,

1987). They also tend to be extraverted rather than introverted, and they are even-keeled rather than neurotic or easily upset (McCrae & Costa, 1986). People who are vulnerable to depression lack these protective personality traits. They may even help to bring about more than their share of interpersonal conflicts and other negative life events if they are socially unskilled and emotionally unstable (Gotlib & Hammen, 1992).

Effective copers also have healthy attribution styles, or adaptive ways of explaining good and bad events in their lives. Martin Seligman and his colleagues (see Peterson & Seligman, 1984) have emphasized the importance of attribution styles in their theory of **learned helplessness,** a sense that one cannot control one's outcomes in life that is closely akin to depression. Depression-prone individuals blame themselves rather than external factors when negative life events occur. They also tend to see the internal causes they identify as global ("I'm generally a loser") rather than specific, and as stable ("I'll always be this way") rather than changeable. Children and adults who adopt this pessimistic pattern of internal, global, and stable attributions for bad outcomes *and* experience many stressful life events are likely to become helpless and depressed (Nolen-Hoeksema, Girgus, & Seligman, 1986, 1992; Peterson & Seligman, 1984). Moreover, their experiences with depression make them even more likely to use a pessimistic style of explaining events, which creates a kind of vicious cycle (Nolen-Hoeksema et al., 1992).

Finally, certain coping styles provide better protection against depression than others. Self-confident, easygoing individuals are likely to take constructive action to work out their problems, whereas depression-prone individuals often rely on less effective strategies, such as taking their feelings out on others, denying that they have problems, or trying to escape by drinking or taking drugs (Holahan & Moos, 1986, 1987).

According to the diathesis/stress model, individuals with limited personal resources for coping must experience *stressful life events* before they will become depressed. The odds of becoming depressed increase as the life traumas and stressors experienced by the individual mount (Kendler et al., 1993). One stressful life event (such as the death of a loved one or a divorce) is usually not enough to trigger major depression, but, when negative events pile up or, more important, when everyday strains or hassles become overwhelming, a person may succumb (Lieberman, 1983).

Finally, the individual's *social environment* can affect his or her vulnerability to depression in response to stress. Social support is a powerful contributor to well-being, and supportive family relationships are especially important. Both men and women who face stressful life events are far more likely to become depressed if they lack a partner—or, worse, have a conflict-ridden relationship with a partner—than if they enjoy an intimate and supportive relationship (Coyne & Downey, 1991).

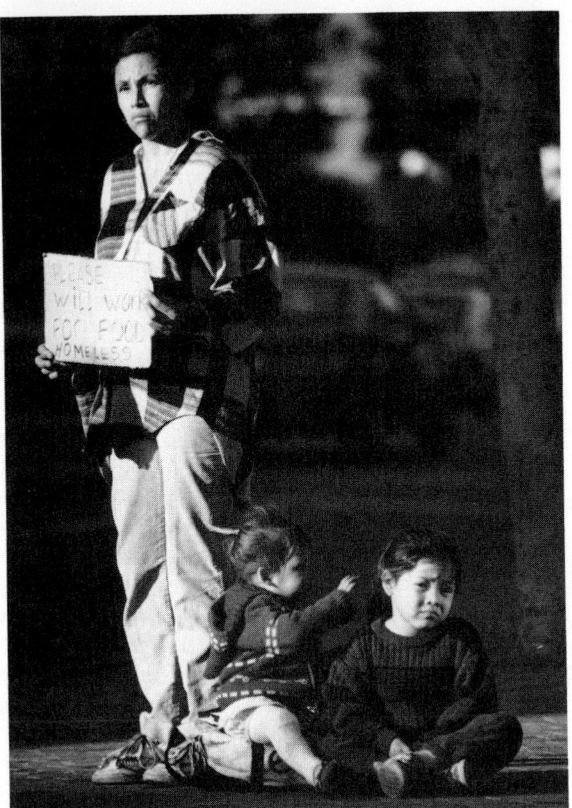

Young women who lack coping resources and must deal with the stresses of life in a crime-ridden neighborhood without adequate social support run a high risk of depression.

In sum, depression is indeed an outgrowth of the ongoing interaction between person and environment, just as the diathesis/stress model of psychopathology suggests. Some people are more vulnerable to depression than others, partly because of their genetic inheritance and partly because of their socialization experiences. These individuals lack the personal resources—the personality traits, attribution styles, and effective coping strategies—that can help them weather stressful times. Yet even these depression-prone individuals are unlikely to become clinically depressed unless they are also bombarded by multiple stress-producing events and must attempt to cope without adequate social support. These same generalizations hold true for children as well as for adults, and for many psychological problems besides depression.

Aging and Dementia

Perhaps nothing scares us more about aging than the thought that we will become "senile." **Dementia,** the technical term for senility, is a progressive loss of cognitive capacities that leads to severe declines in tested intellectual ability, impaired memory, poor judgment, difficulty in thinking abstractly, and, often, personality changes. Becoming "senile" is *not* a normal part of the aging process. Instead, dementia and other severe cognitive impairments affect about 5% of the 65-and-older population overall (Regier et al., 1988). The rate climbs steadily with age, though, from 3% of those 65 to 74 to 16% of those 85 and older (Regier et al., 1988). Thus, although dementia does not accompany normal aging, the odds of it increase the longer one lives.

Dementia is not a single disorder. Indeed, much damage can be done by labeling any older person with cognitive impairments "senile" and then assuming he or she is a lost cause. Many different conditions can produce the symptoms we associate with senility, and some of them are curable or reversible (Heston & White, 1991). It is also a mistake to assume that any elderly person who becomes somewhat forgetful or absentminded — who occasionally misplaces keys or cannot remember someone's name — is becoming senile. As we saw in Chapter 8, small declines in memory capacities in later life are common and usually do not have much effect on daily functioning. If this were all it took to warrant a diagnosis of dementia, many young and middle-aged adults would qualify too! So let's look at some of the specific forms of dementia.

Alzheimer's Disease

The most common cause of dementia is by now a household word — **Alzheimer's disease.** This disease, which can strike in middle age but becomes increasingly likely with advancing age, causes the formation of senile plaques (masses of an abnormal protein called amyloid and dead cell material surrounding neurons) and neurofibrillary tangles (twisted strands of neural fibers within the bodies of neural cells) in the brain. The result is a progressive — and irreversible or incurable — deterioration of neurons and increasingly impaired mental functioning, along with personality changes.

An elderly man with Alzheimer's disease (or dementia of the Alzheimer type, as it is now termed) may at first just experience memory lapses now and then and find this upsetting. As the disorder progresses, he may have trouble coming up with the words he wants during conversations or forget what he is supposed to do next midway through making a sandwich. If tested, he may be unable to answer simple questions about where he is, what the date is, and who the president of the United States is. Eventually he will become incapable of caring for himself, lose all verbal abilities, and die 8 to 10 years after the disease took hold (Heston & White, 1991). Not only do patients with Alzheimer's disease become increasingly unable to function, but they often test the patience of caregivers by forgetting they have left something cooking on the stove, wandering away and getting lost, becoming agitated and uncontrollable, accusing people of stealing the items they have misplaced, experiencing hallucinations, or taking off their clothes in public. Many suffer from depression as well (Teri & Wagner, 1992).

What causes Alzheimer's disease? Many cases, especially those that begin in middle age, appear to have a hereditary basis. Alzheimer's disease does strike repeatedly in some families, affecting about half of all family members (Heston & White, 1991). By analyzing blood samples from such families, genetic researchers were able to locate a gene for the disease on the 21st pair of chromosomes and to conclude that anyone who inherits just one of these apparently dominant genes will eventually develop the disease (St. George-Hyslop et al., 1987). Not coincidentally, individuals with *Down syndrome* — the chromosome disorder that is one of the causes of mental retardation — have three rather than the normal two 21st chromosomes and consistently develop Alzheimer's disease in middle age (Heston & White, 1991). Genes on other chromosomes have also been implicated, and progress continues to be made in explaining how genes may contribute to *some* cases of Alzheimer's disease (Heston & White, 1991).

However, most individuals who fall prey to Alzheimer's disease do so late in old age and have no apparent history of it in their families, so the search for causes continues (see Heston & White, 1991). Much attention has centered on the fact that victims have a deficit in the neurotransmitter acetylcholine, which is essential for normal learning and memory (Heston & White, 1991). The hope is that a drug can be developed to correct this problem. No magic pill has been discovered yet, but a new drug called tacrine, which modestly improves cognitive functioning in some Alzheimer's patients, has recently been approved for use; more such drugs are likely to follow (Associated Press, 1993).

Another hypothesis is that a slow-working virus is responsible for Alzheimer's disease. One study indicated that injecting blood from Alzheimer's patients and their relatives into hamsters can cause degeneration of the hamsters' brains (Manuelidis et al., 1988). It has already been established that a slow-working virus is responsible for Creutzfeldt-Jakob disease, another cause of dementia. If the same proved true of Alzheimer's, it would mean not that the disease could be spread from person to person like the common cold but that the Alzheimer's virus might lie dormant in most people until genes or life experiences somehow activate it in some people later in life (Manuelidis et al., 1988). Still another theory is that the immune system malfunctions and launches an attack on normal brain tissue (Heston & White, 1991). Chances are that Alzheimer's disease will prove to have several causes, some genetic and some environmental; it may even turn out to be a group of distinct diseases, each with a different causality (Heston & White, 1991).

Other Causes of Cognitive Impairment

The second most common type of irreversible dementia is **multi-infarct dementia.** It is caused by a series of minor strokes that cut off the blood supply to areas of the brain. Whereas Alzheimer's disease usually progresses slowly and steadily, multi-infarct dementia often progresses in a steplike manner as each small stroke rather quickly brings about a new deterioration in functioning (American Psychiatric Association, 1987). Huntington's disease (a genetic disorder described in Chapter 3), Pick's disease, Parkinson's disease, Creutzfeldt-Jakob disease, and even AIDS are among the other possible causes of irreversible dementia (Heston & White, 1991). None is as common or as closely linked to old age as Alzheimer's disease (see Figure 16.4).

However, a minority of cases of dementia — perhaps 10–20% — are not related to any of these causes and, more important, are *reversible* or curable (Gurland, 1991). Such problems as alcoholism, toxic reactions to medication, infections, metabolic disorders, and malnutrition can lead to the symptoms of dementia. If these problems are corrected — for example, if the individual is taken off a recently prescribed medicine or is placed on a proper diet — a once-"senile" person can be restored to normal mental functioning. By contrast, if that same person is written off as "senile" or as a victim of Alzheimer's disease, a potentially curable condition may become a progressively worse and irreversible one.

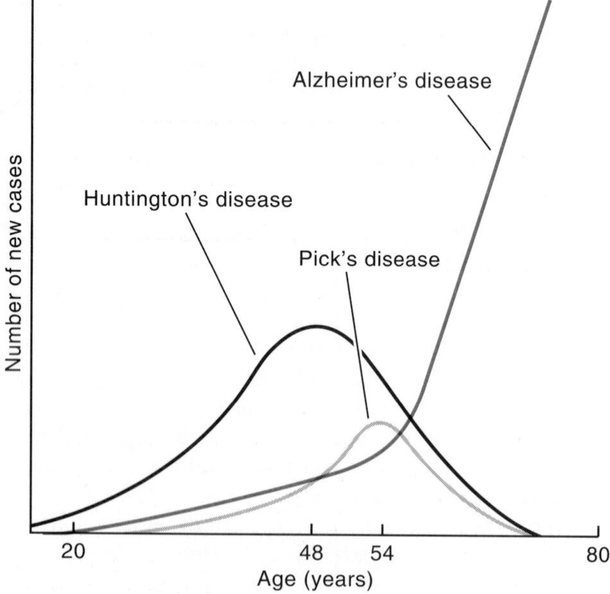

FIGURE 16.4 Most diseases that cause dementia become more prevalent until middle age and then become less prevalent in later life. The odds of developing Alzheimer's disease continue to rise with each passing year, however. (From Heston & White, 1991.)

Similarly, elderly adults may be mistakenly diagnosed as suffering from irreversible dementia when they are actually experiencing **delirium.** This reversible condition develops more rapidly than dementia and is characterized by periods of disorientation, wandering attention, and confusion alternating with periods of coherence over the course of the day (Conn, 1991). Stressful events (such as undergoing surgery) and many of the same factors that can cause reversible forms of dementia can result in delirium, so here, too, it is essential to look carefully for such causes and treat them. Finally, elderly adults who are depressed are all too frequently misdiagnosed as suffering from dementia because they seem forgetful and mentally slow (Esser & Vitaliano, 1988; Kaszniak, 1990). Treatment with antidepressant drugs and psychotherapy can dramatically improve the functioning of such individuals. However, if their depression goes undetected and they are written off as "senile," they are likely to deteriorate further.

The moral is clear: It is absolutely critical to distinguish among irreversible dementias (notably, dementia of the Alzheimer's type and multi-infarct dementia), reversible dementias, delirium, depression, and other conditions that may be mistaken for irreversible dementias — including old age itself. Only after all other causes, especially potentially treatable ones, have been ruled out should a diagnosis of Alzheimer's disease be made. But, even if such a diagnosis is made, and deterioration leading to death must be expected, a great deal can be done to help family members understand and cope with the Alzheimer's patient and to improve his or her functioning using behavioral management techniques (Chiverton & Caine, 1989; Zarit, Orr, & Zarit, 1985).

APPLICATIONS: TREATING PSYCHOLOGICAL DISORDERS

It can be discouraging to read about the countless ways in which human development can go awry. Yet many psychological disorders and developmental problems can be treated successfully, as we have already seen in this chapter. We cannot possibly review all of applied psychology and psychiatry here. Instead, being developmentalists, we will address these questions: What special challenges arise in working with either very young or very old clients? And just how much can be accomplished?

Treating Children and Adolescents

Treating children and adolescents differs in several ways from treating adults. First, children rarely seek treatment on their own (Johnson, Rasbury, & Siegel,

Play therapy can help young children who lack verbal skills to express their feelings. Here it is being used to help a girl deal with her anxieties about being hospitalized.

1986). Instead, they are referred for treatment by adults, usually parents, who are disturbed by their behavior. This means that therapists must view the child *and* his or her parents as the "client." Second, children's therapeutic outcomes often depend greatly on the cooperation of their parents. Whether or not a disturbed family environment has contributed to a child's problem, the participation of parents in treatment will be critical in resolving the problem (Gelfand & Peterson, 1985). Sometimes all members of the family must be treated in order for any enduring change in the child's behavior to occur—a principle underlying the use of family therapy as a treatment approach.

Third—and this is a point very familiar to students of human development—children function at very different levels of cognitive and emotional development than adults do, and interventions for them must be designed accordingly (Gardner, 1993; Johnson et al., 1986). Young children cannot easily participate in therapies that require them to verbalize their problems and gain insight into the causes of their behavior (Gardner, 1993). A more appropriate technique might be play therapy, in which disturbed children are encouraged to act out concerns that they cannot easily express in words. All things considered, then, treating children with psychological disorders is particularly challenging. Treatment must involve the family rather than the client alone, and it must be sensitive to the developmental competencies of that client.

How Well Does Psychotherapy Work?

Recently John Weisz and Bahr Weiss (1993) pulled together analyses of over 200 studies of the effectiveness of psychotherapy in treating problems of childhood and adolescence. Two major categories of psychotherapy were compared: (1) behavioral therapies (e.g., those using reinforcement principles and modeling techniques to alter maladaptive behaviors and teach more adaptive ones) and (2) nonbehavioral therapies (primarily psychoanalytic therapies based on Freudian theory and other "talking cures" in which therapists help clients to express, understand, and solve their problems). These studies examined a wide range of problems (both undercontrolled and overcontrolled) and measured a wide range of outcomes (anxiety, cognitive skills and school achievement, personality and self-concept, social adjustment, and so on).

So, does psychotherapy work with children and adolescents? Indeed it does—at least as well as it works with adults. The average child who received some form of psychotherapy functioned better than over 75% of the untreated children who served as control subjects in the studies, and the benefits of treatment appeared to be lasting. Moreover, undercontrolled, or externalizing, problems (hyperactivity, aggression) proved to be just as responsive to treatment as overcontrolled disorders (phobias, social withdrawal), suggesting that problems of undercontrol need not persist if they are effectively treated (Weisz et al., 1987). Girls tended to respond somewhat better than boys, but age differences in responsiveness to psychotherapy were minimal.

Which therapy approaches work best? Behavioral therapies appear to be more effective with children than nonbehavioral therapies, although these alternative forms of therapy have often proved equally effective in treating adults. Very possibly, this is because children *do,* after all, have limited cognitive skills. Consequently they may have difficulty participating in "talk therapies" but can respond well to direct attempts to alter their behavior or teach them new skills. The only bad news is that the positive effects of therapy demonstrated in controlled experiments are not as evident among children treated in community mental health clinics, which suggests that more may need to be done to extend the use of effective treatment approaches to a wider range of community settings (Weisz & Weiss, 1993).

A Success Story: Behavioral Treatment of Autism

There may be no more stunning example of the power of the behavioral approach in treating childhood disorders than the work of O. Ivar Lovaas and his colleagues with autistic children. As we saw earlier, autistic children have long been considered very difficult to treat and often have severe deficits throughout their lives. Lovaas (1987), who pioneered the use of behavioral therapy with autistic children, has compared two groups of autistic children treated at UCLA. Nineteen children received intensive treatment—more than 40 hours a week of one-on-one treatment for two or more years during their preschool years. Trained student therapists worked with these children using reinforcement principles to reduce their aggressive and self-stimulatory behavior and to teach them developmentally appropriate skills such as how to imitate others, play with toys and with peers, use language, and master academic concepts. Moreover, parents were taught to use the same behavioral techniques at home, and these children were mainstreamed into preschools that served normal children. The children who received this intensive treatment were compared with similarly disturbed children who, because of staff shortages or transportation problems, received a similar treatment program but were exposed to it for only 10 or fewer hours a week.

The intensively trained group and the less intensively trained group were similar in almost all ways before they began the program. In the intensively trained group, for example, all but two children scored in the mentally retarded range on tests of intellectual functioning; none engaged in pretend play; and most were mute. How different these children were at age 6 to 7! Their IQ scores averaged 83—about 30 points higher than the average in the control group. Indeed, 9 of the 19 not only obtained average or above-average IQ scores at follow-up but had been mainstreamed into regular first-grade classes and were adapting well. Eight others were making good progress in classes for children with language disorders, and only two were in classes for autistic/retarded children. The impacts of this early intervention appear to have been lasting: At age 13, 8 of the 19 treated students were still within the normal range of both IQ and school adjustment (Lovaas, Smith, & McEachin, 1989). In contrast, none of the children in the comparison group made similar progress. Instead, these youngsters displayed the usual intellectual deficits of autism, and most attended special classes for autistic and retarded children.

These are truly remarkable and very encouraging findings. They are now supported by other evidence that some autistic children, especially those who are not severely retarded, have a good deal of potential if they receive carefully planned, intensive training starting early in life (see also Harris et al., 1991; but see Schopler, Short, & Mesibov, 1989, for criticisms of the Lovaas research).

Treating Elderly Adults

It can be just as challenging to treat elderly people with psychological problems as it is to treat children. Perhaps the greatest difficulty is that elderly individuals are less likely than younger adults to seek and obtain psychological treatment (Gatz & Smyer, 1992; Lasoski & Thelen, 1987). For example, it is estimated that fewer than one out of four depressed elderly people receive treatment (Klerman, 1983). Possibly these data reflect characteristics of today's elderly generation: They grew up in a time when a social norm of self-reliance was stronger than it is today and when it was considered shameful to have psychological problems (Gatz et al., 1985). Older adults may also believe, wrongly, that problems such as depression and anxiety are just a normal part of getting older or becoming ill (Lazarus, Sadavoy, & Langsley, 1991). Still another barrier to treatment may be *ageism* in the mental health care system: negative attitudes among mental health professionals that cause them to prefer working with younger people, to perceive elderly individuals as untreatable, or to misdiagnose their problems (Gatz & Pearson, 1988).

What happens when elderly adults do seek treatment? Can they benefit from psychotherapy as much as younger adults can? Every bit as much, according to research (Lazarus et al., 1991). Therapists may have to adapt their techniques to be effective with those elders who are cognitively impaired, but these clients, too, can be helped. Research findings underscore the importance of encouraging elderly people with psychological problems to seek treatment. They also show that working with these individuals can be rewarding for mental health professionals. Box 16.4 provides an example of how even a very brief and simple intervention can dramatically improve the mental and physical well-being of elderly adults in nursing homes by making them feel more in control of their lives. Such demonstrations carry an important message: Just as human beings can fall prey to psychological problems at any point in the life span, they have an impressive capacity throughout the life span to overcome problems and to experience new psychological growth.

REFLECTIONS

Analogies are always dangerous, but likening life to a hurdles race seems a good way to put abnormal human development in perspective. The "hurdles" we must jump are the normal developmental tasks of each period of the life span, plus any stressful events that come our way. What is expected of us is fairly clear: We must move along at a good pace, stay on the right course, and avoid stumbling as we cross each hurdle.

Why do some of us set Olympic records whereas others of us cannot even finish the race? The hurdler's success in the race depends on both native endowment and environment (proper nutrition, good training, favorable track conditions, and so on). Similarly, our success in adapting to life's challenges depends on both nature and nurture—on whether we are genetically hardy or genetically predisposed to develop problems and on whether we are nurtured by a supportive social environment or damaged by a destructive one. As we have seen throughout this book, it is naive to assume that either nature or nurture is solely

BOX 16.4 Helping Nursing-Home Residents Achieve a Sense of Personal Control

Some years ago, Ellen Langer and Judith Rodin (1976) began to suspect that declines in physical health and psychological well-being among nursing-home residents might not be entirely due to the ravages of age and illness. Instead, they argued that elderly adults placed in nursing homes lose the feeling that they are in control of their lives and become passive and helpless as a result. In fact, elderly adults often do suffer a loss of perceived control (Arling, Harkins, & Capitman, 1986) and even an increased risk of death (Pastalan, 1983) when they are institutionalized.

Langer and Rodin decided to test out a way of increasing residents' sense of personal control in a Connecticut nursing home. The nursing-home administrator gave different talks to the residents of two floors of the facility. An experimental group (residents of the fourth floor) heard a responsibility-inducing speech. The administrator said it was their responsibility to make their wishes known and to make decisions about how to live their lives. He also offered them plants, made it clear that it was their choice whether they wanted to take one and which one they wanted, and emphasized that the plants were theirs to care for as they would like. Finally, these residents were given a choice about whether and when to see a movie. Residents living on the second

floor served as the control group and received the message that the *staff* was responsible for their well-being and would do everything possible to see to their needs. They were given a plant and were told that the nurses would care for it and that a movie would be scheduled on a particular night.

How much difference did it make whether residents were led to believe that responsibility for their lives lay with them or with their caretakers? A great deal! After three weeks, 93% of the experimental group members were rated as improved by nurses unfamiliar with the experimental manipulation. Judging from the nurses' ratings and the residents' own responses, these residents felt happier, were more mentally alert, and were more involved in activities than the control residents, 71% of whom were judged to have deteriorated during the study period.

Even more impressive were the results of a follow-up study conducted 18 months later (Rodin & Langer, 1977). The personal-control group was still at an advantage compared to the staff-reliant group, for they were rated as more sociable, active, interested in their environment, and self-initiating. They were also judged by a physician to be enjoying better health than they had before the study began. Most significantly, 30% of the control-group members had died in the 18-month period following the experiment, compared with only 15% of those encouraged to feel responsible for their lives.

It seems hard to believe that a brief speech, a plant to care for, and the opportunity to choose to see a movie could have so many beneficial effects on physical health and psychological well-being. Rodin and Langer propose that their treatment fostered a generalized sense of personal control that made residents feel competent to make any number of day-to-day decisions. Subsequent studies agree: Elderly adults fare better when they believe that they are in command of their own life course than when they feel pushed and pulled by external forces (Reich & Zautra, 1989, 1990; Rodin, 1986).

responsible when development proceeds well or poorly; instead, it is the ongoing interaction between heredity and environment that is significant.

The race that developing persons run is a bit odd as hurdles races go: It's not entirely fair, since some of us have more hurdles to cross than others do and have a greater chance of falling as a result. There's another, more heartening, difference between life and a hurdles event: It seems that we can, in the course of living our lives, stumble over a hurdle or two and still win the race in the end. True, a few of us may be destined to falter fairly consistently, and others of us breeze all the way through. That is, there is some continuity over the life span in an individual's ability to adapt to each new developmental challenge. However, discontinuity in adaptation over the life span is also striking. Many of us, it seems, succumb to the challenges of one developmental period or another and yet go on to adapt successfully to later challenges, especially with social support and professional help. Indeed, some of us even *grow* as a result of our experiences with stressful events.

If we take this message seriously, we quickly realize that children and adults with psychological disorders are not all that different from their more "normal" peers. Pick the right moment in the race, and almost any of us might be caught in the act of stumbling.

SUMMARY POINTS

1. To study developmental psychopathology and diagnose many psychological disorders, psychologists and psychiatrists consider the broad criteria of statistical deviance, maladaptiveness, and personal distress and judge behavior in light of social norms and age norms. The *Diagnostic and Statistical Manual*

of Mental Disorders (DSM-III-R) spells out specific diagnostic criteria for a wide range of psychological disorders, including major depression.

2. Infantile autism is characterized by an early onset, deviant social responses, language and communication deficits, and repetitive behavior; it seems to involve the lack of a theory of mind and other deficiencies in symbolic thought. Genetic endowment and prenatal or perinatal hazards contribute to it, and many, but not all, autistic individuals remain impaired in later life.

3. Some infants who have been emotionally starved or separated from attachment figures, including infants whose parents are depressed and infants suffering from failure to thrive, display many depression-like symptoms, if not true clinical depression.

4. Children with attention-deficit hyperactivity disorder, an undercontrolled (externalizing) disorder, display inattention, impulsivity, and hyperactivity; they can be helped through a combination of stimulant drugs and behavioral training but often do not entirely outgrow their problems.

5. Diagnosable depression, an overcontrolled (internalizing) disorder, may exist in childhood, manifests itself somewhat differently at different ages, tends to recur, and can be treated with antidepressant drugs and psychotherapy.

6. It is too simple to view "bad" parenting as the cause of all childhood problems; heredity may also contribute, and children's problems can be partly the cause as well as the effect of disturbed parent/child relationships. Fortunately, most childhood problems, especially problems of overcontrol, are only temporary.

7. Contrary to the "storm and stress" view, adolescents are really not much more vulnerable to psychological disorders than children or adults are. Anorexia nervosa and bulimia, both serious eating disorders, seem to arise when a vulnerable adolescent, typically a girl, is raised in a troubled family and in a society that strongly encourages dieting. Minor delinquent behavior and experimentation with drugs are statistically normal during adolescence, but youth who develop more serious problem behaviors often have unconventional values, perceive their peers as encouraging deviance and their parents as unsupportive, and show a whole syndrome of problems.

8. Risks of depression also rise during adolescence, especially among females; adolescents, in a cry for help, are more likely to attempt but less likely to commit suicide than adults, especially older white men, are.

9. Stressful daily hassles are more likely to cause psychological problems than major life events, even nonnormative ones. Because young adults experience more such life strains than older adults do but have no greater coping capacities, they are therefore more vulnerable to many psychological disorders.

10. Depression, which tends to be most common in early adulthood and among women, results, according to a diathesis/stress model, when a vulnerable individual who lacks personal resources (positive personality traits, a healthy attribution style, and effective coping strategies) experiences multiple stresses without adequate social support.

11. The most common forms of dementia, a progressive loss of cognitive capacities affecting about 5% of the elderly population, are Alzheimer's disease and multi-infarct dementia. These irreversible dementias must be carefully distinguished from correctable conditions such as reversible dementias, delirium, and depression.

12. Treating children and adolescents with psychological problems is especially challenging but often effective; O. Ivar Lovaas has had dramatic success applying intensive behavioral techniques to young autistic children. Elderly adults with psychological disorders also pose special challenges but can benefit just as much as younger adults from psychotherapy.

KEY TERMS

age norm
Alzheimer's disease
anorexia nervosa
attention-deficit hyperactivity disorder (ADHD)
bulimia nervosa
daily hassles
delirium
dementia
developmental psychopathology
diathesis/stress model
echolalia
emotion-focused coping
failure to thrive
infantile autism
juvenile delinquency
learned helplessness
major depression
masked depression
multi-infarct dementia
overcontrolled disorders
problem-focused coping
social norm
somatic symptoms
storm and stress
stress
theory of mind
undercontrolled disorders

17

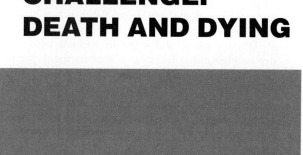

THE FINAL CHALLENGE: DEATH AND DYING

Jessica was 5. She showed her mother the picture she had painted. There were black clouds, dark trees, and large red splashes.

"My," said her mother. "Tell me all about this, Jess." Jessica pointed to the red splashes. "That's blood," she said. "And these are clouds." "Oh," said her mother. "See," said Jessica, "the trees are very sad. The clouds are black. They are sad too." "Why are they sad?" asked her mother. "They are sad because their Daddy has died," said Jessica, the tears slowly running down her cheeks. "Sad like us since Daddy died," said her mother and held her closely, and they wept [Raphael, 1983, p. 138].

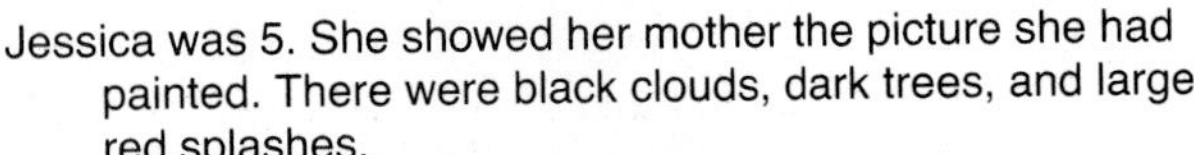

Death hurts. Whether we are 5, 35, or 85 when death strikes a loved one, it still hurts. By adulthood, most of us have experienced a significant loss, even if it was "only" the death of a beloved pet. Even when death is not striking so closely, it is there, lurking somewhere in the background as we go about the tasks of living—in the newspaper, on television, or in our minds. And sooner or later we all face the ultimate developmental task: the task of dying.

This chapter explores death and its place in life-span human development. What is death, and why do we die? How have theorists characterized the experiences of dying and bereaved people? What does death mean, and how is it experienced in infancy, childhood, adolescence, and adulthood? Why do some individuals cope far more successfully with death than others do? We will discover that death is part of the human experience throughout the life span but that each person's experience of it depends on his or her level of development, personality, life circumstances, and sociocultural context. Finally, on a practical note, we'll see what can be done to help dying and bereaved individuals through their ordeals.

LIFE AND DEATH ISSUES

What is death, really? When are we most vulnerable to it, and what kills us? And why is it that all of us eventually die of "old age" if we don't die earlier? These "life and death" questions serve to introduce the topic of death and dying.

What Is Death?

As you have probably noticed, there is a good deal of confusion in our society today about when life begins and when it ends. Proponents and opponents of legalized abortion argue vehemently about when life really begins. And we hear similarly heated debates about whether a person in an irreversible coma is truly alive and whether a terminally ill patient who is in agonizing pain should be kept alive with the help of life support machines or allowed to die naturally. Definitions of death as a biological phenomenon are changing; so are the social meanings attached to death.

Biological Definitions of Death

It used to be easy enough to tell that someone was dead: There was no breathing, no heartbeat, no sign of responsiveness. These criteria of biological death are still useful today. However, technological breakthroughs have forced the medical community to rethink what it means to say that someone is dead. The problem is that biological death is not a single event but a *process*. Different systems of the body die at different rates, and some individuals who have stopped breathing and who lack a heartbeat or pulse can now be revived before their brains cease to function. Moreover, basic bodily processes such as respiration and blood circulation can be maintained by life support machines in patients who have fallen into a coma and whose brains have ceased to function. Is the person whose brain cannot control breathing but who breathes with the aid of a "respirator" (actually a mechanical ventilator) alive or dead?

In 1968 an ad hoc committee of the Harvard Medical School offered a definition of death that it hoped would resolve controversies about when a person is dead—a definition that has since gained widespread acceptance and become the basis for modern legal definitions of death (Berger, 1993). The Harvard group defined biological death as **total brain death**: an irreversible loss of functioning in the entire brain, both the higher centers of the cerebral cortex that are involved in thought and the lower centers of the brain that control basic life processes such as breathing. Specifically, to be judged dead, a person must meet the following criteria:

1. Be totally unresponsive to stimuli, including painful ones.
2. Fail to move for one hour and fail to breathe for three minutes after being removed from a ventilator.

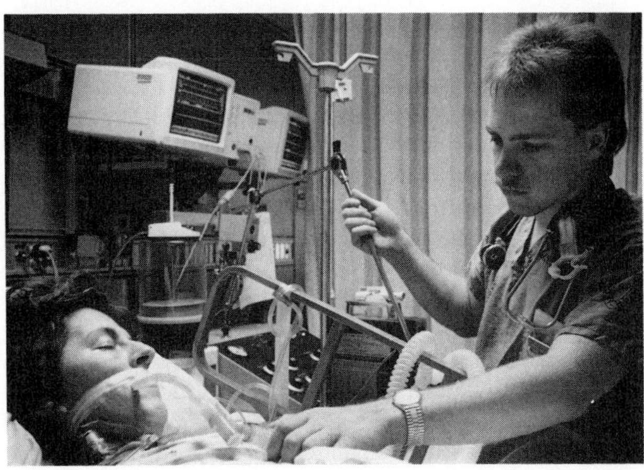

Life support technologies can keep coma victims alive for years, but many people wonder whether it might not be better to let such patients die naturally.

3. Have no reflexes (for example, no eye blink and no constriction of the eye's pupil in response to light).
4. Register a flat electroencephalogram (EEG), indicating an absence of electrical activity in the cortex of the brain.

As an additional precaution, the testing procedure is repeated 24 hours later. Moreover, since coma is sometimes reversible if the cause is either a drug overdose or hypothermia (a body temperature below 90° Fahrenheit), these conditions must be ruled out before a coma victim is pronounced dead.

Now consider some of the life and death issues that have revolved around this definition of biological death. In 1975 Karen Ann Quinlan lapsed into a coma at a party, probably because of the combination of alcohol and drugs she had consumed (Urofsky, 1993). Quinlan was totally unconscious, but her bodily functioning was maintained with the aid of a ventilator and other life support systems. After she had lain wasting away in a fetal position for weeks, her parents finally asked that the devices be turned off. The doctors declined to do so, the case went to court, and the court finally ruled that the respirator could be turned off. Much to everyone's surprise, Quinlan continued to breathe even without the mechanical assistance. She lived on in a vegetative state, lacking all consciousness and being fed through a tube, until she died in 1985.

Then came the case of Nancy Cruzan (see Berger, 1993; Urofsky, 1993). This young Missouri woman was in a car accident one icy night in 1983 and, like Quinlan, fell into a coma and lay for years in a fetal position, lacking consciousness. She had a heartbeat and breathed on her own but could not survive without being fed through a tube. When her parents sought permission to remove the feeding tube in 1988, the judge agreed. However, his decision was appealed by the Missouri attorney general because Cruzan's own desire to terminate medical care had not been demonstrated. The Supreme Court of the United States agreed, essentially ruling that the Constitution does protect an individual's right to refuse unwanted medical treatment but insisting that states can act to preserve life if the individual's wishes are not clear (Urofsky, 1993). Ultimately, Nancy's parents returned to court with new evidence: Some of her friends recalled Nancy's saying that she would not want to be kept alive by artificial means. Based on this testimony, her parents were allowed to remove the feeding tube, and Nancy died the day after Christmas in 1990 (Urofsky, 1993).

These two famous "right to die" cases highlight the fact that we might take three quite different positions on the issue of when a person is dead. First, there is the position laid out in the Harvard definition of total brain death and in most state laws. By these criteria, because the lower portions of their brains were still functioning enough to support breathing and other "vegetative" functions, neither Karen Ann Quinlan nor Nancy Cruzan was dead, even though both were in irreversible comas. Second, there is a more liberal position saying that a person should be declared dead when the cerebral cortex is irreversibly dead, even if bodily functioning is still maintained by the more primitive portions of the brain. After all, is a person really a person if he or she lacks any awareness and if there is no hope that conscious mental activity will be restored? A third position is to favor an even more conservative definition of death than the Harvard definition: Even if a person's brain is totally dead, he or she should not be declared dead until the best medical technology available fails to maintain basic bodily processes. After all, what if we discovered how to revive or cure seemingly hopeless patients?

So there is still plenty of room for debate about when death has occurred. The Harvard total-brain-death definition takes a middle ground between a very strict definition of death in which one is not dead until there is no functioning even with the aid of machines and a more liberal definition in which only the cortex of the brain, rather than the entire brain, must cease to function for the individual to be deemed dead. The very strict definition can mean a prolonged and difficult death for hopeless coma victims—at great expense to society and at great emotional cost to the families involved. But using a more liberal definition of death means that a mistake might occasionally be made; a seemingly irreversible loss of consciousness might turn out to be reversible.

Cases like Quinlan's and Cruzan's also raise issues concerning **euthanasia**—a term meaning "happy" or "good" death that usually refers to hastening the death of someone who is suffering from an incurable illness or injury. Actually there are two very different forms of euthanasia. **Active euthanasia,** or "mercy killing," is deliberately and directly causing a person's death — for example, by administering a lethal dose of drugs to a pain-wracked patient in the late stages of cancer or shooting a spouse who is in the late stages of Alzheimer's disease. **Passive euthanasia,** by contrast, means allowing a terminally ill person to die of natural causes — for example, by withholding extraordinary lifesaving treatments, as happened when Quinlan was removed from her respirator.

In between active euthanasia and passive euthanasia is **assisted suicide** — not killing someone, as in active euthanasia, but making available to a person who wishes to die the means by which *he or she* may do so. Dr. Jack Kevorkian, sometimes known as "Dr. Death," has helped several terminally ill individuals to commit suicide — in some cases by providing them with his "Mercy Machine," a contraption that injects deadly drugs into a patient's veins once he or she pushes a button (Urofsky, 1993). His work has been centered in Michigan, which had no law against assisted suicide until recently, when the doctor's activities prompted the state to pass such a law and prosecute him under it. Extreme as the assisted suicide practiced by Dr. Kevorkian may seem, it is not unlike a practice far more common among today's doctors — writing prescriptions for sleeping pills or other drugs at the request of terminally ill patients who have made known their desire to die, in full knowledge that they will probably take an overdose (Quill, 1993).

Where do we stand as a society on the issue of euthanasia, then? There is overwhelming support among medical personnel and members of the general public for passive euthanasia (Kastenbaum, 1991; Urofsky, 1993). As a result, many states have passed laws making it legal to withhold lifesaving treatments from terminally ill patients and to "pull the plug" on life support equipment when that is the wish of the dying person or the immediate family (Berger, 1993). The "right to die," or "death with dignity," movement has lobbied for such laws. You may be familiar with another product of this movement, the **Living Will,** a document in which a person opposes in writing having any extraordinary medical procedures applied if he or she becomes hopelessly ill (see Figure 17.1). Most states now honor the wishes expressed in such statements. However, several states do not allow the withdrawal of feeding tubes from patients like Nancy Cruzan, and some groups continue to fight Living Will legislation because they maintain that it promotes more active forms of euthanasia (Berger, 1993).

Although passive euthanasia with proper legal safeguards has become widely accepted, active euthanasia is still widely condemned. In fact, the law views it as murder. Opinion is more split on the matter of assisted suicide. Right-to-die advocates believe that the law should be changed so that an incurable patient who is suffering from excruciating pain can ask for and receive assistance in committing suicide. Right-to-life advocates often argue the opposite side of the issue, claiming that everything possible should be done to maintain life and that nothing should be done to cut it short.

Life and death decisions such as these are not easy ones. They are particularly agonizing for people who, like the Quinlans, must confront them personally. Our society will continue to grapple with defining life and death and deciding what forms of euthanasia are or are not morally and legally acceptable. And new issues will undoubtedly arise as new medical technologies are introduced.

Social Meanings of Death

So far we have looked at death from a biological perspective, but it is a psychological and social process as well. The social meanings attached to death vary immensely from historical era to historical era and from culture to culture. Indeed, what we have just discovered is that *society* defines who is dead and who is alive! True, people everywhere die, and people everywhere grieve deaths in some fashion. Moreover, all societies have evolved some manner of reacting to this universal experience — of interpreting its meaning, disposing of corpses, and expressing grief. Beyond these universals, the similarities end.

As Phillippe Ariès (1981) has shown, the social meanings of death have changed over the course of history. In Europe during the Middle Ages, people were expected to recognize that their deaths were approaching so that they could bid their farewells and die with dignity surrounded by loved ones. Since the late 19th century, Ariès argues, Western societies have engaged in a denial of death. We have taken death out of the home and put it in the hospital and funeral parlor; we have shifted responsibility for the care of the dying from family and friends to "experts" — physicians and funeral directors. We have made death a medical failure rather than a natural part of the life cycle. Moreover, we have dispensed with many standard mourning rituals, such as the wearing of armbands or black clothing, and have frowned upon open expressions of grief.

Perhaps this is changing. In the past couple of decades, right-to-die and death-with-dignity advocates have argued forcefully that we should return to some of the old ways, bringing death out into the open rather than avoiding all mention of it, allowing it to occur more naturally, and making it once again an experience to be shared within the family.

If we look at how people in other cultures interpret and manage death, we quickly realize how many alternatives there are to our Western ways (Metcalf & Huntington, 1991; Rosenblatt, 1993; Stroebe, Gergen, Gergen, & Stroebe, 1992). Depending on the

INSTRUCTIONS

CHOICE IN DYING LIVING WILL

PRINT YOUR NAME

I, ______________________________,
being of sound mind, make this statement as a directive to be followed if I become permanently unable to participate in decisions regarding my medical care. These instructions reflect my firm and settled commitment to decline medical treatment under the circumstances indicated below:

I direct my attending physician to withhold or withdraw treatment if I should be in an **incurable or irreversible mental or physical condition with no reasonable expectation of recovery.**

These instructions apply if I am a) **in a terminal condition**; b) **permanently unconscious**; or c) **if I am minimally conscious but have irreversible brain damage and will never regain the ability to make decisions and express my wishes.**

I direct that treatment be limited to measures to keep me comfortable and to relieve pain, including any pain that might occur by withholding or withdrawing treatment.

CROSS OUT ANY STATEMENTS THAT DO NOT REFLECT YOUR WISHES

While I understand that I am not legally required to be specific about future treatments, **if I am in the condition(s) described above I feel especially strongly about the following forms of treatment:**

I do not want cardiac resuscitation.
I do not want mechanical respiration.
I do not want tube feeding.
I do not want antibiotics.

However, I **do want** maximum pain relief, even if it may hasten my death.

ADD PERSONAL INSTRUCTIONS (IF ANY)

Other directions (insert personal instructions):

These directions express my legal right to refuse treatment under federal and state law. I intend my instructions to be carried out, unless I have revoked them in a new writing or by clearly indicating that I have changed my mind.

SIGN AND DATE THE DOCUMENT AND PRINT YOUR ADDRESS

Signed: ______________________ Date: __________

Address: ______________________

____

WITNESSING PROCEDURE

I declare that the person who signed this document is personally known to me and appears to be of sound mind and acting of his or her own free will. He or she signed (or asked another to sign for him or her) this document in my presence.

TWO WITNESSES MUST SIGN AND PRINT THEIR ADDRESSES

Witness: ______________________

Address: ______________________

____

Witness: ______________________

Address: ______________________

____

PAGE 2

FIGURE 17.1 The Living Will. (Reprinted by permission of Choice in Dying.)

society, "funerals are the occasion for avoiding people or holding parties, for fighting or having sexual orgies, for weeping or laughing, in a thousand different combinations" (Metcalf & Huntington, 1991, p. 24). Corpses are treated in a remarkable number of ways too: They "are burned or buried, with or without animal or human sacrifice; they are preserved by smoking, embalming, or pickling; they are eaten—raw, cooked, or rotten; they are ritually exposed as carrion or simply abandoned; or they are dismembered and treated in a variety of these ways" (Metcalf & Huntington, 1991, p. 24). In most societies there is some concept of spiritual immortality. Yet here, too, there is much variety, from concepts of heaven and hell to the idea of reincarnation to a belief in ancestral ghosts who can meddle in the lives of the living (Rosenblatt, 1993).

We need not look beyond the boundaries of the United States and Canada to find considerable variation in the social meanings of death. Different ethnic and racial groups clearly have different rules for expressing grief. It is customary among Puerto Ricans, especially women, to display intense, hysterical emotions after a death (Cook & Dworkin, 1992). Japanese Americans, by contrast, are likely to have been taught to restrain their grief—to smile so as not to burden others with their pain and to avoid the shame associated with losing control of oneself (Cook & Dworkin, 1992). Japanese Americans, Anglo-Americans, and others socialized to restrain their grief might view Puerto Rican mourners as psychologically disturbed when all they are doing is following the rules for emotional display that prevail in their cultural group.

Different subcultural groups also have different mourning rituals and notions of how long a death should be mourned. Irish Americans are likely to believe that the dead deserve a good send-off—a wake with food, drink, and jokes, the kind of party the deceased might have enjoyed (McGoldrick et al., 1991). African Americans share this belief that it is important to go out in style but regard the funeral not as a time for rowdy celebration but as a forum for expressing grief, in some congregations by wailing and singing spirituals (McGoldrick et al., 1991; Perry, 1993). The tradition among the Navajo is to try to forget the loved one as rapidly as possible and resume normal activities after only three or four days of mourning (Cook & Dworkin, 1992). By contrast, Japanese Americans may follow the Japanese tradition of preparing an altar to honor a deceased family member, placing it prominently in their living room, and bowing before it each day so as never to forget (Cook & Dworkin, 1992).

In short, the experiences of dying individuals and of their survivors are very much shaped by the historical and cultural context in which death occurs. Death may be universal, but our experiences of death and dying are not. Moreover, within any society there are subcultural and individual differences in the meanings people attach to death and the ways they deal with it. Death is truly what we humans make of it, which means that we must not presume that there is one "right" way to die or to grieve a death. As Paul Rosenblatt (1993) concludes, "It pays to treat everyone as though he or she were from a different culture" (p. 18).

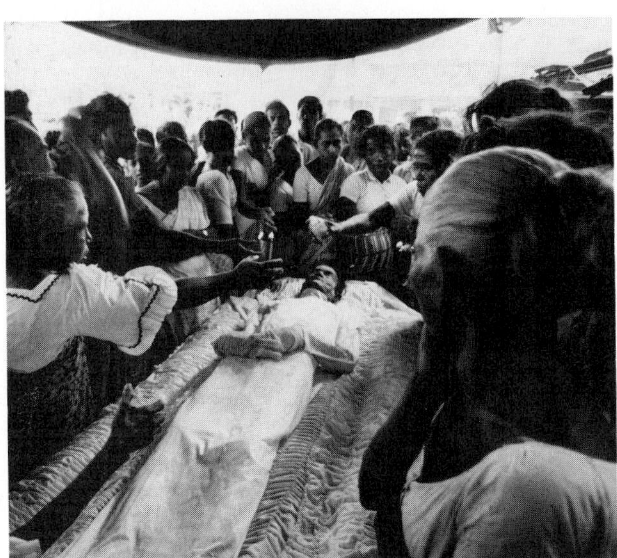

Mourning rituals differ considerably from culture to culture.

What Kills Us and When?

How long are we likely to live? When is death most likely to occur? What are the leading causes of death? In the United States the **life expectancy** at birth—the *average* number of years a newborn can be expected to live—is 75 years (National Center for Health Statistics, 1992). This average life expectancy disguises important differences among males and females and among racial and ethnic groups. The life expectancy for white males is 73, whereas the life expectancy for white females is 79. Female hormones seem to protect women from high blood pressure and heart problems; avoiding health hazards and performing less dangerous work may also help women live longer. Meanwhile, life expectancies for African Americans, many of whom experience the many health hazards associated with poverty, are a good deal lower than those for white Americans: 65 for males, 74 for females. As Figure 17.2 shows, several industrialized nations, led by Japan, have higher life expectancies than the United States. Longevity continues to be far more limited in underdeveloped countries plagued by malaria, famine, AIDS, and other such killers.

Life expectancies have increased dramatically over the course of history. The average life expectancy in ancient Greece is believed to have been around 20 years (Lehr, 1982). In the United States in

1900, the life expectancy at birth was only 49 years (National Center for Health Statistics, 1992). This does not mean that most people at the turn of the century died in their 40s. Rather, many more individuals in the past did not survive infancy and early childhood, and these early deaths pulled the average life expectancy down.

Infants continue to be somewhat vulnerable today, but by 1990 infant mortality in the United States had fallen to 9.2 out of 1000 live births — 7.7 for white infants, 17.0 for African-American ones (U.S. Bureau of the Census, 1993). Assuming that we survive infancy, we have a relatively small chance of dying during childhood, adolescence, or early adulthood.

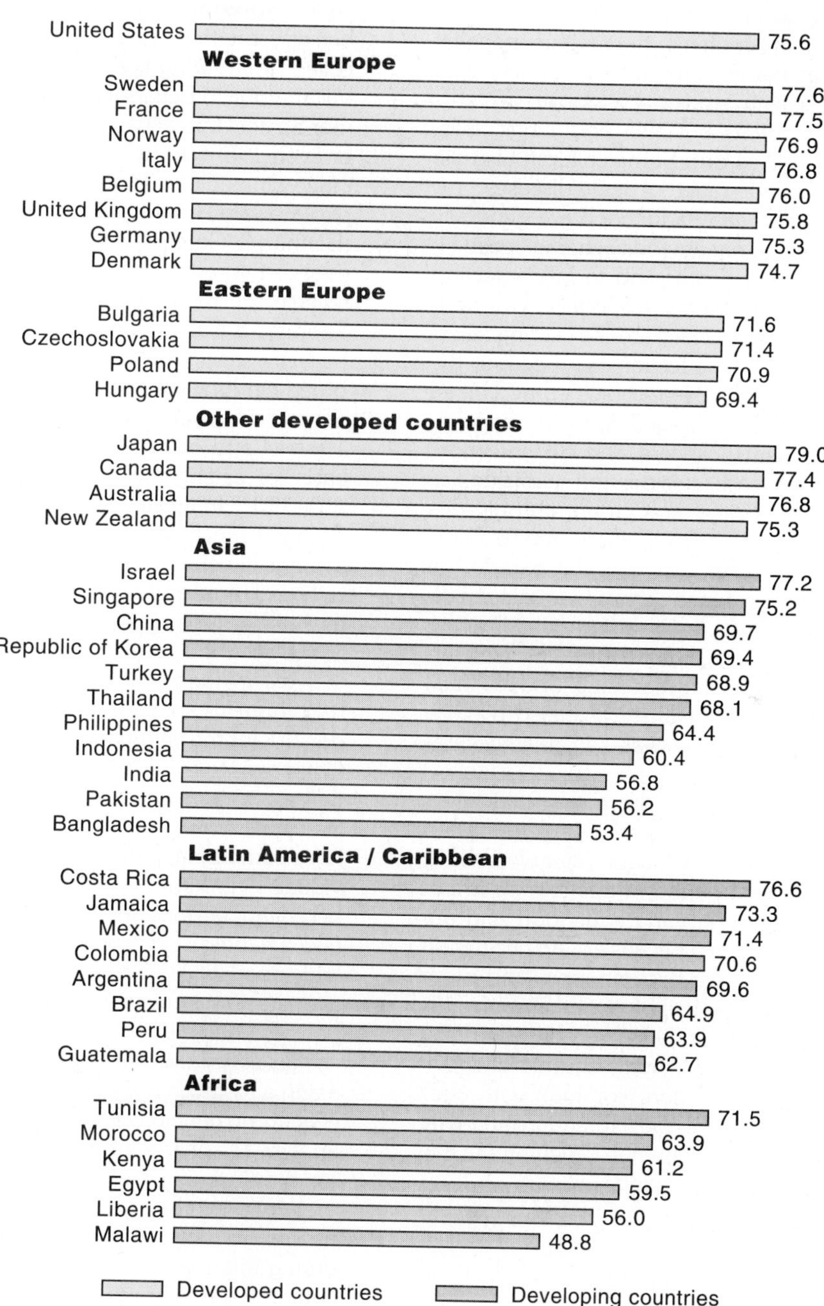

FIGURE 17.2 Life expectancies for an infant born in 1990 in developed and developing countries. The challenge in countries such as Bangladesh and Malawi is to avoid dying in infancy or childhood. (From Kinsella & Taeuber, 1993, based on the International Data Base on Aging, U.S. Bureau of the Census, Center for International Research.)

Death rates then climb steadily throughout middle age and old age. However, just as fewer children are dying today than in the past, more older adults are living longer (National Center for Health Statistics, 1992), thanks primarily to better health care and medical advances.

What kills us? Information collected by the National Center for Health Statistics indicates that the leading causes of death change dramatically over the life span (U.S. Bureau of the Census, 1993). Infant deaths are mainly associated with problems originating in the period surrounding birth or with congenital abnormalities that infants bring with them to life. The leading cause of death among children is accidents (especially car accidents but also poisonings, falls, fires, drownings, and so on). Some children also die from cancer and a wide range of acute diseases.

Adolescence and early adulthood are generally periods of good health but are today characterized by vulnerability to violent deaths and to HIV infection resulting in AIDS. Accidents (especially car accidents), homicides, and suicides are the leading killers of adolescents, and HIV infection has become the sixth leading killer of 15–24-year-olds in the United States. Among young adults aged 25 to 44, the leading killers are accidents, cancers, and HIV infection, followed by heart disease, suicide, and homicide.

Starting in the 45–64 age group, chronic diseases — notably cancers, heart diseases, and stroke — appear at the top of our perverse "hit parade" of leading killers. The incidence of these chronic conditions climbs steadily with age, raising overall death rates considerably. Among adults 65 and older, heart diseases lead the list by far, accounting for 39% of all deaths. Another 22% of deaths are caused by cancers, and 8% are due to strokes and related cerebrovascular causes.

In sum, life expectancies are higher than ever, primarily because fewer people are dying young but also because more are living longer. After we make it through the vulnerable period of infancy, we are at low risk of death through early adulthood and are most likely to die suddenly because of an accident if we do die. As we age, we become more and more vulnerable to death, particularly from chronic diseases. But now a more fundamental question: Why do all of us eventually die? Why do chronic killer diseases become more and more common with age? Why does no one live to be 200? To understand why death is an inevitable part of human development, we need the help of theories of aging.

Theories of Aging: But Why Do We Age and Die?

There is no simple answer to the question of why we ultimately age and die. However, several theories have been proposed, and each of them says something important about the aging process. These theories can be divided into two main categories: **programmed theories of aging,** which emphasize the systematic genetic control of aging processes, and **damage theories of aging,** which emphasize the more haphazard processes that cause cells and organ systems to deteriorate (Walford, 1983).

Programmed Theories of Aging

Human beings, like other species, have a characteristic **maximum life span** — a ceiling on the number of years that anyone lives. For a time it was believed that "long-lived people" in the village of Vilcabamba in Ecuador and in some areas of the former Soviet Union lived to such incredible ages as 165 or even 195. Now we know that these life spans are indeed incredible: They reflect the tendency of people who value long life to greatly exaggerate their ages (Bennett & Garson, 1986; Mazess & Forman, 1979). (Notice that adults in our society more often do the reverse, claiming to be age 39 eternally!) Fanny Thomas, a Californian who was officially verified to be 113 years (and 215 days) old when she died, attributed her long life to eating applesauce three times a day and never marrying (Walford, 1983). Ms. Thomas and others who live about as long are the basis for setting the maximum human life span at 110–120. Interestingly, this maximum has not changed much over the centuries, even though the average life expectancy has been increasing dramatically and more and more individuals today are joining that elite group of people, called **centenarians,** who live to see their 100th birthdays.

We are long-lived compared to most species. The maximum life span for the mouse is 3½ years, for the dog 20, for the chimpanzee 50, and for the long-lived Galapagos tortoise 150 (Walford, 1983). The very fact that each species has its own characteristic maximum life span should convince us that specieswide genes have something to do with controlling how long individuals live. Moreover, we know that an individual's hereditary endowment influences his or her longevity (see Chapter 3 on genetic aspects of aging). In fact, a fairly good way to estimate how long you will live is to average the longevity of your parents and grandparents (Medvedev, 1991).

In short, we have good reason to believe that aging and death are genetically controlled. But how, exactly, do genes control aging? This is what is not yet known. Possibly there is an overall genetic program for development that is responsible for timing both maturational changes and aging. If genes can "turn on" or "turn off" to bring about maturational changes during infancy, or at puberty and menopause, why couldn't genes bring about aging and death in the same way? Alternatively, a genetic program that promotes longevity could eventually just run out (McClearn & Foch, 1985).

The fact that long life tends to run in families is evidence of a programmed, or genetic, theory of aging. These identical twins are celebrating their 100th birthday.

A programmed theory of aging that highlights changes within individual cells was offered some time ago by Leonard Hayflick (1976), who grew cells in cultures, allowed them to divide or double, and measured the number of doublings that occurred. He discovered that cells from human embryos could double only a certain number of times—50 times, plus or minus 10, to be exact—an estimate now referred to as the **Hayflick limit.** Hayflick also demonstrated that cells taken from human adults divide even fewer times, presumably because they have already used up some of their capacity for reproducing themselves. Moreover, the maximum life span of a species is related to the number of cell divisions characteristic of that species: The short-lived mouse's cells can go through only 14 to 28 doublings; the very long-lived Galapagos tortoise's cells can manage 90 to 125. Presumably, cells that are approaching or have exceeded their limit cease to function effectively, die, and ultimately cause the organism to die.

It is not yet certain that Hayflick's limit applies to cells in living organisms in the same way it applies to cells grown in cultures, or that it applies to all kinds of cells, or that we actually run out of viable cells at a very old age (Hart & Turturro, 1983). Still, there does indeed seem to be some kind of genetic "aging clock" operating within cells that may, in interaction with environmental factors, cause cell death later in life (Lockshin & Zakeri, 1990).

Another programmed theory of aging implicates the neuroendocrine system, the complex control system consisting of the brain and the endocrine glands. According to an **endocrine theory** of aging, the genes program hormonal changes that bring about death. Consider Pacific salmon. Shortly after these fish swim back upstream to their place of birth and spawn, their endocrine glands release a massive dose of hormones that causes them to die (Walford, 1983). Could something similar happen to humans? We know that the hypothalamus of the brain, guided by a genetic program, sets in motion the hormonal changes responsible for puberty and menopause (see Chapter 5). Possibly the hypothalamus also serves as an aging clock, systematically altering levels of hormones and brain chemicals in later life so that bodily functioning is no longer regulated properly and we die (Finch, 1976; Rosenfeld, 1985).

Still another programmed theory of aging, the **immune system theory,** focuses on age-related changes in the body's ability to defend itself against potentially life-threatening foreign agents such as infections. The immune system, whose functioning is genetically controlled, undergoes two major changes as we age. First, it becomes less able to detect and fight off foreign "invaders" that can damage the body. Thus an older body is less able than a younger body to mobilize the body's immune defenses against cancer cells, infectious agents, or donated organs (Walford, 1983). Second, the immune system increasingly mistakes normal cells for enemies through what are called **autoimmune reactions.** That is, the immune system actually produces antibodies to attack and kill normal body cells, as illustrated by autoimmune diseases such as rheumatoid arthritis. These age-related changes in immune system functioning do seem to be genetically controlled. For example, hereditary differences among strains of mice in the genes that control the immune system are systematically linked to differences in the longevity of these strains (Smith & Walford, 1977). Thus the immune system theory, like the Hayflick limit and endocrine theories, holds that aging and dying are the inevitable products of our biological endowment as human beings.

Damage Theories of Aging

In contrast to programmed theories of aging, damage theories generally propose that an accumulation of damage to cells and organs over the years ultimately causes death. Aging and death may not be written in the genetic code from conception on; rather, we are the victims of random destructive processes or errors that accumulate while we live.

One early explanation of aging was a "wear-and-tear" theory, proposing that organs simply wear out through use, much as shoes do. We now know that this view is naive. Indeed, using the body (as in regular aerobic exercise) often *improves* rather than diminishes functioning. Nonetheless, more modern versions of the wear-and-tear theory seem to have merit.

According to a **DNA repair theory** of aging, the genetic material DNA is damaged over the years as the cells metabolize nutrients and are increasingly exposed to environmental agents such as pesticides, pollution, and radiation. Cells are equipped to cope with these insults by repairing defective segments of DNA. However, it appears that long-lived species have a greater capacity for repairing DNA than shorter-lived species; also, the cells of younger individuals repair damaged DNA faster than those of older individuals (Hart & Setlow, 1974; Selkoe, 1992). Over time, then, the genetic code contained in the DNA of more and more cells becomes scrambled, and the body's mechanisms for repairing such damage simply cannot keep up with the chaos. More and more cells then function improperly or cease to function, and the organism eventually dies.

A second damage theory of aging is the **cross-linkage theory.** As we age, molecules of the protein collagen, the major connective tissue between cells, become interlinked or coupled. As this cross-linkage of collagen molecules proceeds, the visible result is leathery, wrinkled skin that is not as pliable as the skin of a younger person. Stiff joints and arteriosclerosis ("hardening of the arteries") are also due to cross-linkage. It is possible that this increasing cross-linkage of collagen and other connective tissues interferes with cell functioning. It is even possible that DNA molecules become cross-linked and that the genetic instructions that guide normal cell functioning become error-ridden as a result (Walford, 1983).

Finally, a third damage theory of aging centers on the destructive effects of **free radicals,** or molecules that have an extra or "free" electron, that are chemically unstable, and that react with other molecules in the body to produce substances that damage normal cells (Harman, 1981; Kristal & Yu, 1992). "Age spots" on the skin of older people are one effect of free radicals (Hart & Turturro, 1983). These dangerous chemicals are also suspected of contributing to the cross-linking and deterioration of DNA molecules (Medvedev, 1991; Selkoe, 1992), as well as to Parkinson's disease, Alzheimer's disease, and other forms of brain degeneration (Lohr, 1991).

Unfortunately, we cannot live and breathe without producing free radicals, for they are a byproduct of the metabolism of oxygen. The cells of the body routinely produce enzymes that defend against free radicals, but, as in the case of DNA repair, there may come a time when the body's resources for fighting accumulating damage are no longer up to the task. There is mounting evidence that "antioxidants" such as vitamin E may increase longevity, though not for very long, by keeping the number of free radicals under control (Cesario & Hollander, 1991; Medvedev, 1991).

Theories of Aging and Life Extension

The theories just discussed are some of the most promising explanations of why we age and die. The programmed theories of aging generally claim that aging and dying are as much a part of nature's plan as sprouting teeth or uttering one's first words. The Hayflick limit on cell reproduction, changes in endocrine functioning, and declines in the effectiveness of the immune system all suggest that aging and dying are genetically controlled. The damage theories hold that we eventually succumb to haphazard destructive processes—increasingly faulty DNA that cannot be repaired, cross-linkage of the body's molecules, and an accumulation of free radicals.

None of these specific theories of aging has proved to be *the* explanation; several mechanisms are probably at work (Medvedev, 1991). Biological and environmental factors undoubtedly interact to bring about aging and dying, just as they interact to produce development. For example, genes may well control many aging processes, *including* a decline in the ability of the body to keep environmentally caused damage under control (Walford, 1983).

What does all this say about our prospects for finding the fountain of youth or extending the life span? Genetic researchers are making remarkable progress. It is not at all unthinkable that they might discover the genetic mechanisms behind aging and dying and develop ways of manipulating genes to raise the maximum life span. At present, though, the only technique that has been demonstrated experimentally to extend the life span is dietary restriction: placement on a highly nutritious but severely restricted diet representing a 30–40% cut in normal total caloric intake (Cesario & Hollander, 1991; Masoro, 1988). Laboratory studies involving rats and other animals suggest that dietary restriction extends not only the average longevity but also the maximum life span of a species (Cesario & Hollander, 1991). It may do this by improving the body's ability to defend against free radicals (Kristal & Yu, 1992). But will dietary restriction work as well for humans as it apparently has for rats? What calorie counts and combinations of nutrients are optimal? As yet we don't know.

While we wait for the breakthroughs that might extend the maximum life span of human beings, we can at least reduce our chances of dying young. As suggested in Chapter 5, for example, we can stop smoking, drink only in moderation, eat nutritious food, exercise regularly, and take other steps to ward off the diseases that make us die prematurely. But none of our efforts to delay death will keep us from dying. So let's turn to the question of how humans cope with death and dying.

THE EXPERIENCE OF DYING

People who die suddenly may be blessed, for those who develop life-threatening illnesses face the challenge of coping with the knowledge that they are seriously ill and are likely to die. Perhaps no one has done more to focus attention on the emotional needs of dying patients than psychiatrist Elisabeth Kübler-Ross (1969, 1974), whose "stages of dying" are widely known.

Kübler-Ross's Stages of Dying

In interviews with over 200 terminally ill patients, Kübler-Ross (1969) detected a common sequence of emotional responses to the knowledge that one had a serious, and probably fatal, illness. She believed that similar reactions might occur in response to any major loss, so bear in mind that the family and friends of the dying person might experience some of these same emotional reactions during the loved one's illness and after the death. Kübler-Ross's five stages of dying are as follows:

1. *Denial and isolation*. A common first response to dreadful news is to say "No! It can't be!" **Denial** is a defense mechanism in which anxiety-provoking thoughts are kept out of, or "isolated" from, conscious awareness. A woman who has just been diagnosed as having lung cancer may insist that the diagnosis is wrong—or accept that she is ill but be convinced that she will beat the odds and recover. Denial can be a marvelous coping device: It can get us through a time of acute crisis until we are ready to cope more constructively. Even after dying patients face the facts and become ready to talk about dying, those around them often engage in their own denial, saying such things as "Don't be silly—you'll be well in no time."

2. *Anger*. As the bad news begins to register, the dying person asks "Why me?" Feelings of rage or resentment may be directed at anyone who is handy—doctors, nurses, or family members. Kübler-Ross advises those close to the dying person to be sensitive to this reaction so that they won't try to avoid this irritable person or become angry in return.

3. *Bargaining*. When the dying person bargains, he or she says "Okay—me, but please. . . ." The bargainer asks for some concession from God, the medical staff, or someone else. A woman with lung cancer may beg for a cure—or perhaps simply for a little more time, a little less pain, or a chance to ensure that her children will be taken care of after she dies.

4. *Depression*. When the dying person becomes even more aware of the reality of the situation, depression, despair, and a sense of hopelessness become the predominant emotional responses. Grief focuses on the losses that have already occurred (for example, the loss of the ability to function as one once did) and the losses to come (separation from loved ones, the inability to achieve one's dreams, and so on).

5. *Acceptance*. Assuming that the dying person is able to work through all the complex emotional reactions of the preceding stages, he or she may come to accept the inevitability of death in a calm and peaceful manner. Kübler-Ross (1969) describes the acceptance stage this way: "It is almost void of feelings. It is as if the pain had gone, the struggle is over, and there comes a time for 'the final rest before the long journey,' as one patient phrased it" (p. 100).

In addition to these five "stages of dying," Kübler-Ross emphasizes a sixth response that runs throughout the stages: *hope*. She believes that it is essential for terminally ill patients to retain some sense of hope, even if it is only the hope that they can die with dignity.

Criticisms and Alternative Views

Kübler-Ross deserves immense credit for sensitizing our society to the emotional needs of dying persons and convincing medical professionals to emphasize *caring* rather than curing in working with such persons. At the same time, there are flaws in her account of the dying person's experience (Corr, 1993; Kastenbaum, 1991). Among the most important criticisms are these: (1) Kübler-Ross's use of the term *stages* is inaccurate, (2) she largely ignores the course of the individual's illness, and (3) she makes little of individual differences in emotional responses to dying.

The major problem with Kübler-Ross's "stages" is that they appear not to be stages at all. Research suggests that the dying process is simply not stagelike (Kastenbaum, 1991). Although dying patients usually are depressed as death nears, the other emotional reactions Kübler-Ross describes seem to affect only minorities of individuals (Schulz & Aderman, 1974). Moreover, when these responses do occur, they do not unfold in a set order. Even Kübler-Ross (1974) herself acknowledged that her "stages" do not necessarily follow one another in a lock-step fashion.

As you are by now well aware, developmentalists speak of stages only when most individuals can be shown to proceed through a series of distinct or qualitatively different phases, *in order*. It might have been better if Kübler-Ross had, from the start, described her "stages" simply as common emotional reactions to dying. Unfortunately, some overzealous medical professionals, excited by these "stages," have misused them by trying to push patients through them in

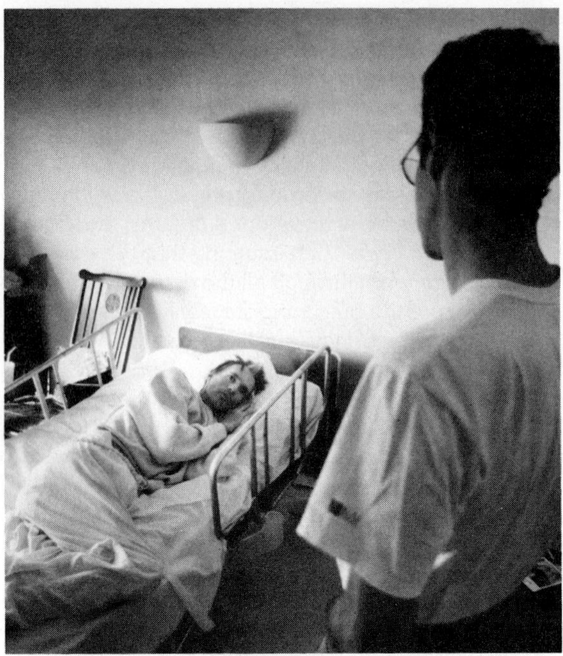

Dying individuals, like this man with AIDS, experience a complex interplay of emotions rather than a stagelike progression toward acceptance.

order, believing that dying patients would never come to accept death unless they experienced the "right" emotions at the "right" times (Kastenbaum, 1991).

Offering an alternative to the idea of stages of dying, Edwin Shneidman (1973, 1980) argues that dying patients alternate between denial and acceptance of death and experience a complex and ever-changing interplay of emotions. One day a patient may seem to accept that death is near; the next day he or she may talk of getting better and going home. Along the way many reactions—disbelief, hope, terror, bewilderment, rage, apathy, calm, anxiety, and others as well—come and go and are even experienced simultaneously. According to Shneidman, then, dying people experience many unpredictable emotional changes rather than distinct stages of dying.

A second major problem in Kübler-Ross's theory is that it pays little attention to how emotional responses are shaped by the course of an illness and the specific events that occur along the way. Barney Glaser and Anselm Strauss (1968), for example, have analyzed the emotional reactions of dying patients and of those around them in relationship to the **dying trajectory**—the perceived shape and duration of the path that the individual is following from life to death. One patient may be on a *lingering* dying trajectory, slowly and gradually worsening over time. The patient, family members, and staff all have a good deal of time to become accustomed to the fact that death lies ahead. Another patient may be following an *erratic* dying trajectory, in which he or she is expected to go through a series of relapses and remissions before dying. Here emotional ups or downs are likely each time the patient's condition takes a turn for better or worse.

It is generally more difficult to cope with surprises than with a course of dying that is predictable. A patient who expects to rebound may become enraged when told that he needs major surgery, whereas a patient who expects steady deterioration may accept the same news more gracefully. According to Glaser and Strauss, then, the perceived dying trajectory, along with actual changes in a patient's condition, will greatly influence the dying person's experiences. Kübler-Ross, by contrast, expects different patients to experience similar responses even if their dying trajectories are different.

Finally, by proposing a set of stages to describe most dying people, Kübler-Ross has overlooked the fact that each individual's personality influences how he or she experiences dying. People cope with dying much as they have coped with the problems of living (Schulz & Schlarb, 1987–1988). For example, John Hinton (1975) found that cancer patients who, according to their spouses, had always faced life's problems directly and effectively, had been satisfied with their lives, and had maintained good interpersonal relationships *before* they became ill displayed less anger and irritability and were less depressed and withdrawn during their illnesses than patients who previously had avoided problems, had been unfulfilled, and had difficulty maintaining good relationships with others (see also Stein, Linn, & Stein, 1989). Depending on their predominant personality traits, coping styles, and social competencies, some dying persons may deny until the bitter end, some may "rage against the dying of the light," some may quickly be crushed by despair, still others may display incredible strength, and most will display combinations of these responses, each in his or her own unique way.

In sum, the experiences of dying persons are far more complex than Kübler-Ross's five "stages" of dying suggest. As Shneidman emphasizes, there is likely to be a complex interplay of many emotions and thoughts, with swings back and forth between acceptance and denial. Moreover, to understand which emotions will predominate and how these emotions will be patterned over time, we must take into account the perceived and actual course of the individual's condition (the dying trajectory) and the individual's prior personality and coping style.

THE EXPERIENCE OF BEREAVEMENT: AN ATTACHMENT MODEL

Most of us know a good deal more about the process of grieving a death than about the process of dying. To describe responses to the death of a loved one, we

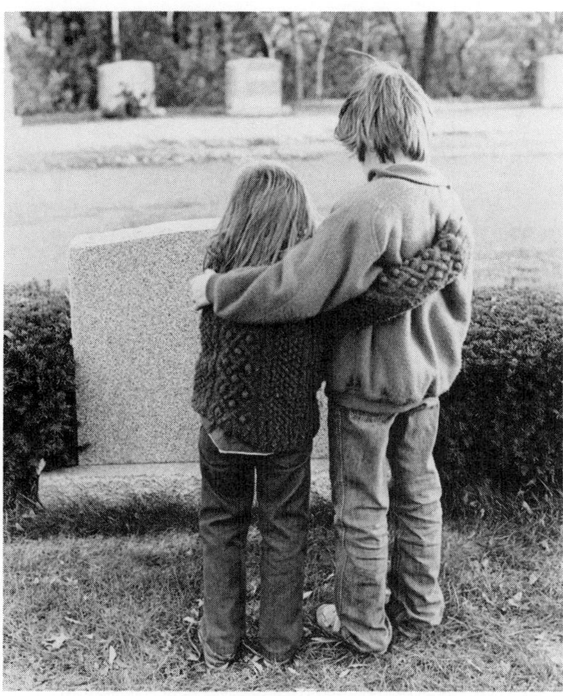

Grief is expressed through mourning behaviors such as visiting the cemetery.

must distinguish among three terms. **Bereavement** is a state of loss, **grief** is the emotional response to loss, and **mourning** consists of culturally prescribed ways of displaying one's reactions. Thus we can speak of a bereaved person who grieves by experiencing such emotions as sadness, anger, and guilt—and who mourns by attending the funeral and laying flowers on the grave each year.

Unless a death is sudden, relatives and friends, like the dying person, have been experiencing many painful emotions *before* the death. They, too, may alternate between acceptance and denial; one day they may express hope that the illness can be halted, and the next day they may despair. Moreover, they often engage in what has been termed **anticipatory grief,** grieving before death occurs for what is happening and for what lies ahead (Rando, 1986).

Yet no amount of preparation and anticipatory grief can eliminate the need to grieve after the death actually occurs. How, then, do we grieve? Much important research on the grieving process has been conducted by Colin Murray Parkes and his colleagues in Great Britain (Parkes, 1986, 1991; Parkes & Weiss, 1983). Parkes and John Bowlby (1980), whose influential ethological theory of attachment was outlined in Chapter 13, have conceptualized grieving in the context of attachment theory as a reaction to separation from a loved one. In other words, the grieving adult can be likened to the infant who experiences separation anxiety when his or her mother disappears from view.

The Parkes-Bowlby model of the grieving process describes four predominant reactions. They overlap considerably and therefore should not be viewed as clearcut "stages," even though the balances among them do change over time. These reactions are numbness, yearning, disorganization and despair, and reorganization.

1. *Numbness.* In the first few hours or days after the death, the bereaved person is often in a daze—gripped by a sense of unreality and disbelief and almost empty of feelings. He or she may make plane reservations, call relatives, or order flowers—all as if in a dream. Underneath this state of numbness and shock is a sense of being on the verge of bursting, and occasionally painful emotions do break through. The bereaved person is struggling to defend himself or herself against the full weight of the loss. The bad news has not fully registered.

2. *Yearning.* As the numbing sense of shock and disbelief diminishes, the bereaved person experiences more and more agony. Grief comes in pangs or waves that typically are most severe from 5 to 14 days after the death. The grieving person has feelings of panic, bouts of uncontrollable weeping, and physical aches and pains. He or she is likely to be extremely restless, unable to concentrate or to sleep, and preoccupied with thoughts of the loved one and of the events leading to the death.

According to Parkes and Bowlby, the reaction that most clearly makes grieving different from other kinds of emotional distress is separation anxiety, the distress of being parted from the object of one's attachment. The bereaved person pines and yearns for the loved one and actually searches for the deceased, as if the finality of the loss has not yet been accepted. A widow may think she heard her husband's voice or saw him in a crowd; she may sense his presence in the house and draw comfort from it; she may be drawn to his favorite chair or wear his bathrobe. Ultimately, of course, the quest to be reunited is doomed to fail.

Both anger and guilt are also common reactions during these early weeks and months of bereavement. Bereaved people often feel irritable and on edge and sometimes experience intense rage—at the loved one for dying, at the doctors for not doing a better job, at almost anyone. To make sense of the death, they seem to need to pin blame somewhere. Unfortunately, they often find reason to blame themselves. It does not take much to trigger guilt feelings in the bereaved. A father may say he should have spent more time teaching his son gun safety; the friend of a young man who dies of AIDS may feel that he was not a good enough friend. One of the London widows studied by Parkes actually felt guilty because she never made her husband bread pudding.

3. *Disorganization and despair.* As time passes, pangs of intense grief and yearning become less

frequent, though they still occur. As it sinks in that a reunion with the loved one is impossible, depression, despair, and apathy increasingly predominate. During most of the first year after the death, and longer in many cases, bereaved individuals often feel apathetic or even defeated. They may have difficulty managing their lives or taking any interest in activities.

4. *Reorganization*. Eventually, bereaved persons begin to pull themselves together again as their pangs of grief and periods of apathy become less frequent. They come to invest less emotional energy in their attachment to the deceased and more in their attachments to the living. If married, they begin to make the transition from being a wife or husband to being a widow or widower, slowly shedding their old identities as married persons and forging new identities as individuals. They begin to feel ready for new activities and possibly for new relationships or attachments.

Figure 17.3 visually portrays the first three phases of the grieving process described by Parkes (see also Jacobs et al., 1987–1988; Shuchter & Zisook, 1993). After a death, numbness and disbelief quickly wane, but we may continue to shake our heads in disbelief occasionally even later on. Yearning and pining in response to separation are most intense in the first few months after the death, but these reactions also continue to plague us now and then in later months. Finally, as we gradually accept the finality of death, despair and depression increasingly overwhelm us, until these reactions too give way and we begin to reorganize or recover.

Some researchers would disagree with the specifics of this view of the bereavement process. However, all agree on one essential point: *It takes a long time to get over the death of a loved one* (Shuchter & Zisook, 1993). We are very sympathetic toward the bereaved immediately after a death—eager to help in any way we can. Too often, though, we quickly grow weary of someone who is depressed, irritable, or preoccupied. We begin to think, sometimes after only a few weeks, that it is time for the bereaved person to cheer up and get on with life. We are wrong! When people suffer a major loss, recovery typically is not evident until a year or two after the death (Murrell & Himmelfarb, 1989; W. Stroebe & Stroebe, 1993). Full recovery can take several years, and some people never fully recover from a crushing loss or give up their attachment to the loved one who died (Klass, 1993; Rubin, 1993; Wortman & Silver, 1989). To be of help to bereaved people, one must understand that their feelings of disbelief, yearning, and despair are likely to linger for a very long time.

We have now presented some of the major theories of how people experience dying and bereavement. However, these theories have been based primarily on the responses of adults. How do infants, children, and adolescents respond to death? What does death even mean to infants and young children? A life-span perspective on death and dying is needed.

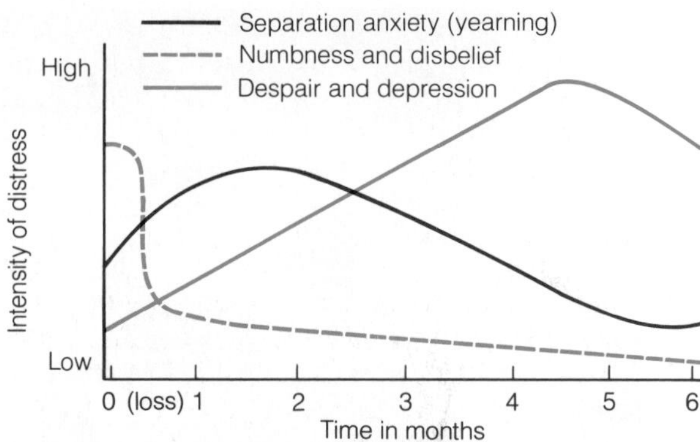

FIGURE 17.3 The overlapping phases of the grieving process over time. (From Jacobs et al., 1987–1988.)

THE INFANT

When in life do we first gain awareness of death? Infants surely do not comprehend death as the cessation of life, but they gain an understanding of concepts that pave the way for an understanding of death. Infants may, for example, come to grasp the concepts of being and nonbeing from such experiences as watching objects and people appear and disappear, playing peek-a-boo, and even going to sleep and "coming alive" again in the morning (Maurer, 1961). As infants begin to acquire the concept of object permanence described by Piaget, they search for missing or hidden objects and can become quite frustrated when those objects are "all gone." Very possibly, then, infants first form a global category of things that are "all gone" and later divide it into subcategories, one of which is "dead" (Kastenbaum, 1985).

The experience that is most directly relevant to an emerging concept of death is the disappearance (for whatever reason) of a loved one. It is here that John Bowlby's theory of attachment is helpful. Infants form their first attachments at about the age of 6 or 7 months, when they begin to display signs of separation anxiety or to protest when their beloved caregivers leave them. They have begun to grasp the concept that persons, like objects, have permanent existence, and they expect a loved one who has disappeared to reappear. According to Bowlby, they are biologically programmed to protest separations by crying, searching for their loved one, and attempting to follow, for these behaviors increase the chances that they will be reunited with a caregiver and protected from harm.

Bowlby (1980) goes on to show that infants separated from their attachment figures display many of the same reactions that bereaved adults do. Whether the cause of separation from a parent is death or a vacation trip, infants first engage in vigorous *protest*—yearning and searching for the loved one and expressing outrage when they fail. One 17-month-old girl said only "Mum, Mum, Mum" for three days after her mother died. She was willing to sit on a nurse's lap but would turn her back, as if she did not want to see that the nurse was not "Mum" (Freud & Burlingham, cited in Bowlby, 1980).

If, after a week or so of protest, an infant has not succeeded in finding the loved one, he or she begins to *despair* and show depression-like symptoms; the baby loses hope, ends the search, and becomes apathetic and sad. Grief may be reflected in a poor appetite (possibly even failure to thrive, as discussed in Chapter 16), a change in sleeping patterns, excessive clinginess, or regression to less mature behavior (Furman, 1984; Raphael, 1983). Ultimately, such infants begin to seek new relationships and will recover from their loss most completely if they can count on an existing attachment figure (for example, the surviving parent) or can attach themselves to someone new.

Clearly, then, infants who are at least 6 months of age or so and who have formed genuine attachment bonds are old enough to experience intense grief and depression-like symptoms when a parent or other loved one dies (see also Chapter 16's discussion of depression in infancy). Moreover, the responses they display—the protest and anger, the yearning and searching, the despair and depression—are the same sorts of responses that bereaved adults display. What is the difference? It is mainly that infants lack the concept that death means permanent separation or loss. Without the cognitive capacity to interpret what has happened, an infant whose mother has died may have little idea why she is gone, where she is, or why she does not return.

THE CHILD

As much as many parents would like to shelter their children from unpleasant life experiences, children do encounter death in their early years. Of college students reflecting on their first encounters with death, 57% recalled the death of a relative, most often a grandparent, and 28% the death of a pet (Dickinson, 1992). How do children come to understand and cope with these experiences of death?

Grasping the Concept of Death

Contrary to what many adults would like to believe, young children are highly curious about death, think about it with some frequency, and are quite willing to talk about it (Kastenbaum, 1991; Stambrook & Parker, 1987). Yet their beliefs about death are often considerably different from those that prevail among adults in Western societies. In our society a "mature" understanding of death has several components (Cotton & Range, 1990; Hoffman & Strauss, 1985; Speece & Brent, 1984, 1992). Death is characterized by:

1. *Finality*—it is the cessation of life and of all life processes, such as movement, sensation, and thought.
2. *Irreversibility*—it cannot be undone.
3. *Universality*—it is inevitable and happens to all living beings.
4. *Biological causality*—it is the result of natural processes internal to the organism, even if external causes set off these internal changes.

Researchers have studied children's conceptions of death by asking them the sorts of questions contained in Table 17.1 or having them draw pictures of their images of death. Research on the topic was pioneered by Maria Nagy (1948), who studied Hungarian children ranging in age from 3 to 10. Nagy and subsequent researchers have found that children between the ages of 3 and 5 are a long way from having a mature concept of death. Rather than viewing death as a final cessation of life functions, they tend to think that the dead retain at least some of their capacities. According to preschoolers, the dead may not be as lively and capable as the living, but they may well be able to move around a bit, hear what is going on outside their coffins, experience hunger, think, and dream (Hoffman & Strauss, 1985).

Preschool-aged children also tend to view death as reversible rather than irreversible. They liken it to a sleep (from which one can awaken) or to a trip (from

TABLE 17.1 Western children's concepts of death and questions pertaining to them.

Concept	*Questions*
Finality	Can a dead person move? Get hungry? Speak? Think? Dream? Do dead people know that they are dead?
Irreversibility	Can a dead person become a live person again? Is there anything that could make a dead animal come back to life?
Universality	Does everyone die at some time? Will your parents die someday? Your friends? Will you die?
Biological causality	What makes a person die? Why do animals die?

SOURCE: Based on Hoffman & Strauss, 1985; Florian & Kravetz, 1985; and other sources.

which one can return). With the right medical care, the proper foods, or a bit of magic, a dead person might be brought back to life (Speece & Brent, 1984). As one youngster put it, "Help them, give them hot food, and keep them healthy so it won't happen again" (Koocher, 1974, p. 408). In addition, young children are not always sure that death is universal; it can be avoided by people who are very clever—or by the child and his or her loved ones (Speece & Brent, 1984). Finally, young children think death is caused by one concrete, external agent or another. One may say that people die because they eat aluminum foil; another may say the cause is eating a dirty bug or a Styrofoam cup (Koocher, 1974; see also Figure 17.4).

Children aged 5 to 7 make considerable progress in acquiring a mature concept of death. The majority of children this age do understand that death is characterized by finality (cessation of life functions), irreversibility, and universality (Speece & Brent, 1992). However, about half do not fully grasp all three of those concepts. In addition, most must still gain a fuller understanding of the biological causality of death. In the early elementary school years, children can catalog a number of concrete causes of death (guns, knives, poison, illness, and so on), but they fail to appreciate that all deaths ultimately involve a failure of internal biological processes (Hoffman & Strauss, 1985; Orbach et al., 1986). Paula, age 12, had mastered this concept: "When the heart stops, blood stops circulating, you stop breathing and that's it . . . there's lots of ways it can get started, but that's what really happens" (Koocher, 1974, pp. 407–408).

Some children have far more sophisticated understandings of death than their agemates. Why might this be? Children's concepts of death appear to be influenced by both their level of cognitive development and their life experiences.

Notice that major breakthroughs in the understanding of death occur in about the 5-to-7 age range—precisely the time that children are making the transition from Piaget's preoperational stage of cognitive development to the concrete-operational stage. Their understandings of death, like their understandings of many other concepts, become more adultlike when they begin to master important logical operations (Cotton & Range, 1990).

Youngsters' concepts of death are also influenced by their specific life experiences, such as the cultural and religious beliefs to which they are exposed (Stambrook & Parker, 1987). Jewish and Christian children in Israel, who are taught our Western concept of death, provide more "mature" answers to questions about death than Druze children, who are taught to believe in reincarnation (Florian & Kravetz, 1985). Obviously, a child who learns that people are reincarnated after they die would be unlikely to view death as a final cessation of all life processes.

FIGURE 17.4 Young children can talk about and draw pictures of death, but they do not yet understand that it is internally caused. This drawing by a 5-year-old boy focuses on one specific external cause of death—a knife. (From Wenestam & Wass, 1987.)

Even within a given society, children's unique life experiences will also affect their understandings of death. For example, preschool children growing up in conflict-torn areas of Belfast, Northern Ireland, where violent deaths are routine, seem to have a more mature concept of death than children in more peaceful neighborhoods of the city (McWhirter, Young, & Majury, 1983). Youngsters' understandings are also influenced by how their parents and other significant individuals communicate with them about death. How is a young child to overcome the belief that death is temporary, for example, if parents and other adults claim that relatives who have died are "asleep"? Isn't it also understandable that such a child might become afraid of going to bed at night?

We must also wonder about statements that liken death to a journey, as in "Grandma has gone away." For all the young child knows, Grandma might be across town or in Chicago and surely could return if she really cared. Experts on death insist that adults are only making death more confusing and frightening to young children when they use such euphemisms (Kastenbaum, 1991). They recommend that parents give children honest but simple answers to the many questions they naturally ask about death. If youngsters are given misleading explanations, they will believe them. If their questions are dodged and they are told nothing, they will actively construct their own ideas—possibly ones that are more disturbing than the truth.

In sum, young children are naturally curious about death and form ideas about it from an early age. During the preschool years, they are likely to view death as only a lessening of life processes rather than a cessation of them; they also see it as reversible, nonuniversal, and attributable to any number of very concrete external causes. By early elementary school, they have mastered the concepts that death is a final, irreversible, and universal cessation of life functions. Later they come to appreciate that death is ultimately due to a failure of internal biological processes. Each child's grasp of death will depend on his or her level of cognitive development and death-related experience. But what does death mean to children who are actually dying?

The Dying Child

Parents and doctors often assume that terminally ill children are unaware that they will die and are better off remaining ignorant. Yet research shows that dying children are far more aware of what is happening to them than adults realize; their tragic experience gives them an understanding of death before their time (Spinetta, 1974; Waechter, 1984). Consider what Myra Bluebond-Langner (1977) found when she carefully observed children ranging in age from 2 to 14 who had leukemia. Even preschool children arrived, over time, at an understanding that they were going to die and that death is irreversible. Despite the secretiveness of adults, these children were closely attuned to what was going on around them. They noticed changes in their treatments and subtle changes in the way adults interacted with them, and—perhaps most important—they learned from the fates of other children who had the same disease and were receiving the same treatments. Over time many of these ill children stopped talking about the long-term future and wanted to celebrate holidays such as Christmas early. A doctor trying to get one boy to cooperate with a procedure said "I thought you would understand, Sandy. You told me once you wanted to be a doctor." Sandy threw an empty syringe at the doctor and screamed "I'm not going to be anything!" (p. 59).

How do terminally ill children cope with the knowledge that they are dying? They are not all the models of bravery that some people suppose them to be. Instead, they experience the same wide range of emotions that dying adults experience—the anger, the depression, and the anxieties over being separated from loved ones, experiencing pain, and wondering what lies ahead. Terminally ill children have higher levels of anxiety—especially about death, mutilation, and loneliness or separation—than either healthy children or chronically ill children who are not expected to die (Waechter, 1984).

Preschoolers respond differently to terminal illness than school-aged children do (Waechter, 1984). For example, preschool children do not often talk about dying. Instead, their behavior reveals their fears; they may have temper tantrums or portray violent acts in their pretend play (see Figure 17.5). By comparison, school-aged children understand more about their situation and can talk about their feelings if they are given an opportunity to do so. They very much want to participate in normal activities so that they will not feel inadequate compared with their peers, and they want to maintain a sense of control or mastery, even if the best they can do is take charge of deciding which finger should be pricked for a blood sample. They also have more sophisticated coping skills than preschoolers do. Whereas preschool children rely on behavioral coping strategies, such as struggling to get away from the nurse with the needle, school-aged children can use such cognitive coping strategies as thinking positive thoughts or distracting themselves while a shot is administered (Worchel, Copeland, & Barker, 1987).

In short, children with terminal illnesses often become painfully aware of the fact that they are dying. They experience a full range of unpleasant emotions and reveal in their behavior, if not in their words, that they are anxious and upset. What, then, can be done

FIGURE 17.5 Young children who are dying seem to understand far more about their situation than we give them credit for, and they often express their awareness through their play and drawings. A 5-year-old boy dying of inoperable heart disease drew this self-portrait featuring a big heart with broken lines drawn through it. He then angrily crossed himself out with a black crayon, shouting "Color me gone!" (From Baker, 1991.)

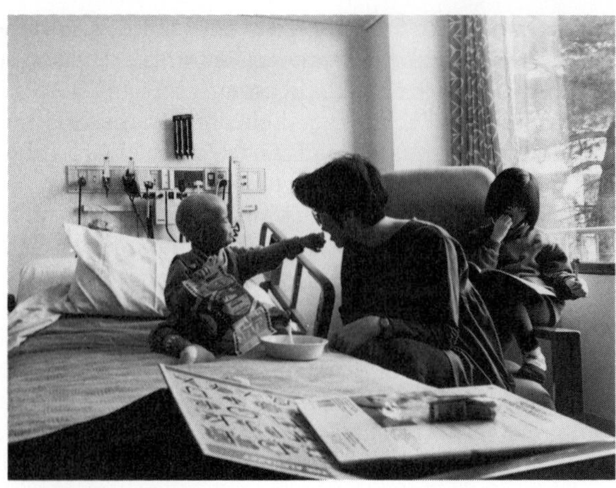

Children who are dying need to know that they are loved and to have opportunities to express their concerns and fears.

to help them cope? Quite obviously, they need the love and support of parents, siblings, and other significant individuals in their lives. Children with cancer who seem to be adjusting well emotionally to their ordeal have a strong sense that their parents are in control of the situation (Worchel et al., 1987). They also have opportunities to talk with adults about their feelings (Waechter, 1984). In other words, they are not the victims of a well-intentioned but ultimately counterproductive conspiracy of silence on the part of parents and medical care providers.

The Bereaved Child

Children's coping capacities are also tested when a parent, sibling, pet, or other loved one dies. Three major messages have emerged from studies of bereaved children:

1. Children most certainly grieve.
2. They express their grief differently than adults do.
3. They are especially vulnerable to long-term negative effects of bereavement (Osterweis, Solomon, & Green, 1984).

Consider some of the reactions that have been observed in young children whose parents have died (Osterweis et al., 1984; Raphael, 1983; Silverman & Worden, 1993). These children often misbehave or strike out in rage at their surviving parent. They ask endless questions: Where is Daddy? When is he coming back? Will I get a new Daddy? Still others go about their activities as if nothing had happened. You can readily see how a parent might be disturbed by some of these behaviors—the seemingly inexplicable tantrums, the distressing questions, or, worse, the child's apparent lack of concern about the death. Yet all of these behaviors indicate that the loss is affecting the child greatly. Even an apparent lack of concern may be the child's attempt to deny and avoid emotions that are simply too overwhelming to face (Osterweis et al., 1984). It is important, then, for adults to recognize that children express their grief in ways that reflect their levels of development.

What grief symptoms do children most commonly experience? The preschooler's grief is likely to manifest itself in problems with sleeping, eating, toileting, and other daily routines. Negative moods, dependency, temper tantrums, and bedwetting episodes are also common (Osterweis et al., 1984; Van Eerdewegh, Clayton, & Van Eerdewegh, 1985). Older children express their sadness, anger, and fear more directly; they often become either withdrawn or aggressive and sometimes experience academic and social difficulties at school (Osterweis et al., 1984). Somatic symptoms such as headaches and other physical ailments may arise (Silverman & Worden, 1993).

Remember, children are highly dependent on their parents. Moreover, they simply do not have the coping capacities that adults do. As a result, *children often take years to recover fully from the death of a parent* (Osterweis et al., 1984). Well beyond the first year after the death, some bereaved children continue to be unhappy, to have difficulty in school, or to engage in delinquent acts. Studies of adults who suffer from chronic depression and related forms of psychopathology suggest that these adults are more likely than others to have experienced the death of a parent in early childhood (Harris & Bifulco, 1991; Osterweis et al., 1984). However, as we will see later, most bereaved children—especially those who have positive coping skills and a good deal of social support—overcome their losses quite successfully.

THE ADOLESCENT

Adolescents typically understand death as the irreversible cessation of biological processes. Once they have attained Piaget's stage of formal operations, they can express abstract concepts of death (Koocher, 1973; see also Figure 17.6). Indeed, some adolescents even use their new cognitive capacities to ponder the meaning of life and death and to grapple with issues like global survival (Wass, 1991). Teenagers are *less* likely than 7-year-olds to view death as nothing but a cessation of life. Instead, most of them, influenced by religious teachings, conceptualize some sort of spiritual continuation after death (McIntyre, Angle, & Struempler, 1972). Similarly, adolescents are more likely than children to say that death is reversible, mainly because they more fully understand modern life-sustaining technologies and the complexities of defining biological death (Brent & Speece, 1993). Thus, adolescence is a time of continued growth in the capacity to conceptualize the complexities of death and to master cultural beliefs about it.

FIGURE 17.6 Compared to children, adolescents often express very abstract concepts of death that are influenced by their religious training. The 16-year-old girl who drew this picture explained: "The water represents the depth of death. The bubbles represent the releasing of the soul. The tree represents the memories we leave behind. The flame represents Hell and the halo represents Heaven." (From Wenestam & Wass, 1987.)

Just as children's reactions to death and dying reflect their developmental capacities and needs, adolescents' reactions to becoming terminally ill are likely to reflect the themes of adolescence (Adams & Deveau, 1986; Corr, 1991). Concerned about their body images as they experience physical and sexual maturation, they may be acutely disturbed if their illness alters their appearance. Wanting to be accepted by peers, they may feel like "freaks" or become upset when friends who do not know what to say or do abandon them (Adams & Deveau, 1986). Eager to become more autonomous, they may be distressed by having to depend on parents and medical personnel and may struggle to assert their wills and maintain a sense of control. Trying to establish their identities and chart future goals, adolescents may be angry and bitter at having their dreams snatched from them.

Similarly, the reactions of an adolescent to the death of a family member or friend are likely to reflect the themes of the adolescent period. For instance, adolescents often suffer more than adults when a parent dies (Harris, 1991; Meshot & Leitner, 1992–1993). Possibly this is because adolescents have so many maturational changes and social pressures to cope with already. Even though teenagers are becoming increasingly independent of their parents, they still depend quite heavily on them for emotional support and guidance. The adolescent whose parent dies may carry on an internal dialogue with that parent for years (Silverman & Worden, 1993). And, given the importance of peers in this developmental period, it is not surprising that adolescents are often devastated when a close friend dies in a car accident, commits suicide, or succumbs to a deadly disease. Unfortunately, the grief of friends often is not taken as seriously as that of family members (Schachter, 1991–1992).

For the most part, adolescents grieve much as adults do. However, they are sometimes reluctant to express their grief for fear of seeming abnormal or losing control (Osterweis et al., 1984). For example, the adolescent who yearns for a dead parent may feel that he or she is being sucked back into the dependency of childhood and may lock these painful feelings inside:

> "When my mother died I thought my heart would break," recalled Geoffrey, age 14. "Yet I couldn't cry. It was locked inside. It was private and tender and sensitive like the way I loved her. They said to me, 'You're cool man, real cool, the way you've taken it,' but I wasn't cool at all. I was hot —hot and raging. All my anger, all my sadness was building up inside me. But I just didn't know any way to let it out" [Raphael, 1983, p. 176].

In sum, by the time children reach adolescence, they have acquired a mature concept of death, understanding it as a final cessation of life that is irreversible, universal, and biologically caused and thinking more abstractly about it. Whereas young children often express their grief indirectly through their behavior (by wetting their beds, throwing tantrums, and so on), older children and adolescents more directly experience and express painful thoughts and emotions and are better equipped to cope with these emotions. In each period of development, children's reactions to bereavement or to the knowledge that they are dying also reflect their major needs. Thus, when a life-threatening illness strikes, the young child may most want reassurance of parental love and protection, the school-aged child may hope to keep up with peers in school, and the adolescent may want to maintain a sense of independence. Infants, children, and adolescents facing death all need their parents and other adults to listen to them and help them cope with their very real emotional reactions.

THE ADULT

How do adults cope with death and dying? We have already introduced models describing adults' experiences of dying and bereavement that partially answer that question. Here we'll elaborate by examining attitudes toward death and dying during the adult years, responses to bereavement in the context of the family life cycle, and factors that determine whether an individual grieves "normally" or pathologically.

Death Anxiety

Adults in our society know full well that death is an irreversible cessation of life processes. However, this by no means suggests that they have mastered their fears of death. **Death anxiety** is a complex set of concerns about death and dying. The person who is highly anxious about death does not want to think about it or be reminded of it, dreads developing a serious illness and facing the pain and stress that dying may entail, and strongly senses that life is too short (Lonetto & Templer, 1986).

Who is most or least anxious about death? On death-anxiety scales, men tend to express less death anxiety than women do, although it is possible that they are just less willing to admit their fears (Hickson, Housley, & Boyle, 1988; Lonetto & Templer, 1986). Strongly religious individuals also tend to be less afraid of death than other people (Bohannon, 1991; Lonetto & Templer, 1986). In addition, personality has a bearing on death anxiety. Those persons who have high self-esteem, a sense of mastery, and a sense of meaning and purpose in their lives are likely to be less anxious about death and dying than individuals who lack confidence, do not have a sense of fulfillment, or show signs of personality disturbance (Lester & Templer, 1992–1993; Rappaport et al., 1993).

The relationship between age and death anxiety is of special interest to us. Do adults become more and more anxious as they reach ages at which death is more probable, or do they become less anxious as they work through their fears and accept the inevitable? Research suggests that death anxiety tends to be lower among elderly adults than among young or middle-aged adults (Gesser, Wong, & Reker, 1987–1988; Lonetto & Templer, 1986). Elderly adults think about their own deaths more frequently than younger adults do but seem to have resolved some of their fears (Kalish & Reynolds, 1977). We should not make too much of this age difference, though; anxieties about death and dying appear to be a fundamental part of the human experience at all ages (Lester & Templer, 1992–1993).

Older adults not only express somewhat less death anxiety than younger adults but also have somewhat different concerns about dying. Richard Kalish and David Reynolds (1977) surveyed members of four ethnic groups in the Los Angeles area. Table 17.2 shows what these adults said they would want to do if they knew they had only six months to live. Notice that young adults seemed to want to "grab all the gusto" they could—to have experiences that would otherwise be forgone—as well as to be with loved ones. Young adults who are dying are especially likely to feel angry that their plans and goals will not be realized (Kalish, 1981). Middle-aged adults were concerned about their relationships. As another study showed, among parents with serious illnesses, concerns about the welfare of family members are often most troublesome (Diggory & Rothman, 1961). Finally, the elderly adults in this survey seemed to have realized enough goals and no longer had children depending on them so much. They wanted to contemplate the meaning of their lives—perhaps to engage in the process of *life review* that we discussed in Chapter 10.

TABLE 17.2 If you were told you had a terminal disease and six months to live, how would you want to spend your time until you died? (N = 434)

Responses	*Young (%)*	*Middled-Aged (%)*	*Old (%)*
Marked change in lifestyle, self-related (travel, sex, drugs, experiences)	24	15	9
Withdrawal (read, contemplate, pray)	14	14	37
Focus concern on others; be with loved ones	29	25	12
Complete projects; tie up loose ends	11	10	3
No change in lifestyle	17	29	31
Other/don't know	5	6	8

SOURCE: From Kalish & Reynolds, 1977.

In sum, death anxiety, though part of the human condition throughout the life span, is likely to be lowest among people who are male, strongly religious, well adjusted, and elderly. Young adults find it especially threatening to be unable to achieve their goals and enjoy important relationships, middle-aged adults are concerned about the welfare of their families, and elderly adults want to make sense of their lives before they die. Notice the echoes of Erik Erikson here: identity and intimacy concerns in early adulthood, issues of generativity and caring for the younger generation in middle adulthood, and a quest for a sense of personal integrity in old age.

Death and the Family Life Cycle

Given the importance of family attachments throughout the life span, it is not surprising that the deaths of family members are typically harder to bear than other deaths. We really cannot understand bereavement unless we adopt a family systems approach and consider the specific relationships and roles that are altered by a death in the family and the ways in which family members affect one another during the grieving process (Lamberti & Detmer, 1993). So let's examine some of the special challenges associated with three kinds of death in the family: the loss of a spouse, the loss of a child, and the loss of a parent.

The Loss of a Spouse

Most of what we know about bereavement is based on studies of widows and widowers. Experiencing the death of a spouse becomes increasingly likely as we age; it is something most women can expect to endure, for women tend to both outlive men on average and marry men who are older than they are. The marital relationship is a central one for most adults, and the loss of a marriage partner can mean the loss of a great deal indeed. Moreover, the death of a spouse often precipitates other changes—the need to move, enter the labor force or change jobs, assume responsibilities that the spouse formerly performed, parent singlehandedly, and so on. Thus widows and widowers must redefine their roles and even their identities (Osterweis et al., 1984). Similar challenges confront anyone, married or not, who loses a romantic attachment figure.

As we noted earlier in this chapter, Colin Murray Parkes, in his extensive research on widows and widowers, has concluded that bereaved adults progress through overlapping phases of numbness, yearning, disorganization and despair, and reorganization. What toll does this grieving process take on the individual's physical, emotional, and cognitive functioning? Table 17.3 shows some of the symptoms that widows and widowers commonly report (Parkes, 1986; see also Shuchter & Zisook, 1993).

Quite clearly, widows and widowers experience many problems. They are at risk for illness and physical symptoms such as loss of appetite, and they tend to overindulge not only in alcohol but in tranquilizers and cigarettes as well. Cognitive functions such as memory and decision making are often impaired. Not surprisingly, their grief creates emotional problems like loneliness and anxiety. Most do not become clinically depressed but display several symptoms of depression in the first months after the death (Harlow, Goldberg, & Comstock, 1991). Many widows and widowers idealize their spouse and marriage, describing both as almost perfect in every way, and those who idealize the most tend to be the most depressed by their loss (Futterman et al., 1990; Lopata, 1979). Although losing a spouse is difficult at any age, young and middle-aged adults appear to suffer somewhat more than elderly adults, perhaps because the death of a spouse at these ages is off-time and therefore unexpected (Parkes, 1986; Zisook & Shuchter, 1991).

TABLE 17.3 Percentages of bereaved and nonbereaved adults reporting various symptoms within the past year.*

Symptoms	*Bereaved*	*Nonbereaved*
Admitted to hospital	18%	6%
Awakening during night	40	12
Changes in appetite	50	29
Increased alcohol consumption	28	3
Sought help for emotional problems	34	7
Wonder if anything is worthwhile	50	26
Worried by loneliness	65	25
Depressed or very unhappy (in past few weeks)	49	29
Restless	49	22
Memory not all right	29	9
Hard to make up mind	53	32
Feel somewhat apart or remote even among friends	34	15

*Responses were gathered in the Harvard Bereavement Study from men and women under the age of 45 who had lost their spouses 14 months before the interviews. Nonbereaved respondents were married adults matched to members of the bereaved sample so that they were similar in age, sex, family size, geographic area, nationality, and socioeconomic status.

SOURCE: Based on Parkes, 1986.

Widows and widowers are even at increased risk of death (M. Stroebe & Stroebe, 1993). In an immense study of 95,647 widowed adults in Finland (Kaprio, Koskenvuo, & Rita, 1987), mortality risks were found to be highest in the weeks immediately following the death and were over twice the expected rate overall. Risks of death from heart problems and violent causes, including suicide, were especially high. And these risks are higher for men than for women, especially if the death was sudden and they do not remarry (M. Stroebe & Stroebe, 1993). Although the stresses of bereavement may undermine the health of both men and women, men often depend particularly heavily on their spouses for social support and must cope with many new responsibilities alone (M. Stroebe & Stroebe, 1993).

We know that the first year after the death is the most difficult, that many widows and widowers begin to show signs of recovery in the second year, and that time tends to heal. Yet grieving and symptoms of distress may continue for years after the death (Lehman, Wortman, & Williams, 1987; Parkes & Weiss, 1983; Thompson et al., 1991). Darrin Lehman, Camille Wortman, and Allan Williams (1987) compared adults whose spouses had died in car accidents four to seven years previously to similar nonbereaved adults. Even this long after their tragedies, bereaved adults showed more depression, hostility, and anxiety; had more worries; and felt less of a sense of psychological well-being than nonbereaved adults. Perhaps because these deaths had been sudden and violent, 62% still had recurring thoughts that the death was unfair or that they had been cheated, and 68% said that they had been unable to find any meaning in the death.

In sum, the loss of a spouse is a painful and damaging experience. During the first weeks and months after the death, the psychological pain is most acute, and the risks of developing serious physical or mental health problems or even dying are at a peak. However, many widows and widowers experience emotional aftereffects for years afterward. If this picture seems too dismal, let us emphasize that the vast majority of bereaved adults *do not* die and do not develop major physical or psychological disorders, even though their risks are higher than average. Instead, most recover from their grief and get on with their lives—and manage to do so without professional treatment (Parkes, 1986).

The Loss of a Child

> My child has died! My heart is torn to shreds. My body is screaming. My mind is crazed. . . . The question is always present on my mind. Why? How could this possibly have happened? The anger is ever so deep, so strong, so frightening [Bertman, 1991, p. 323, citing a mother's reflections on how she reacted to her 16-year-old daughter's death in a car accident after the initial numbness wore off].

Many observers believe that no loss is more difficult for an adult than the death of a child (Osterweis et al., 1984; Rando, 1991). Even when there is forewarning, the loss of a child is experienced as unexpected and untimely; children just aren't supposed to die before their parents do. Many children who die do so suddenly in accidents, which only heightens the shock. And let's not forget that the parent role is a central one for most adults, that their attachment to their children runs deep, and that their own dreams are tied to the fates of their children.

Coping with the death of a child seems to be particularly difficult for mothers (Lang & Gottlieb, 1993). Catherine Sanders (1979–1980) studied adults whose children died at anywhere from age 6 to age 49. Compared with adults who had lost a spouse or a parent, these parents were exceptionally angry, guilty, and depressed, and they had a greater number of physical complaints (see also Leahy, 1992–1993). Understandably, parents experience a raging anger that something so terrible could happen, and they often feel that they were somehow to blame or somehow failed in their role as parent and protector (Rando, 1991). They may continue to feel attached to an internal representation of the lost child many years after the death (Rubin, 1993).

The whole family system is disrupted when a child dies.

The age of the child who dies has relatively little impact on the severity of the grief: Parents can experience severe grief reactions even after a miscarriage, stillborn delivery, or abortion (Hutti, 1992; Peppers, 1987–1988). These crises can be aggravated when friends and relatives fail to appreciate that a real loss has occurred and offer no support (Osterweis et al., 1984). It goes without saying that the death of an infant, child, or adolescent can be devastating. What may be more surprising is the fact that the death of an adult child is usually no less difficult to bear than the death of a younger child (Lesher & Bergey, 1988; Littlefield & Rushton, 1986). The parent/child bond apparently remains very strong throughout adulthood. Finally, the presence of other children in the family does not seem to lessen a parent's grief (Littlefield & Rushton, 1986). Clearly, parents value their children greatly—even before they are born and even after they leave the nest.

The whole family system is altered by the death of a child. Although the odds of divorce do not necessarily rise, the marital relationship is likely to be strained because each partner grieves in his or her own way and is not always able to provide social support to the other (Bohannon, 1990–1991; Rando, 1991). Strains may be especially severe if the marriage was shaky before the death (Bohannon, 1990–1991; Schwab, 1992).

Grieving parents may also have difficulty giving their surviving children the love and support they need to cope with *their* loss. Children are deeply affected when a brother or sister dies, but their grief is often not fully appreciated (Davies, 1991; Rosen, 1986). Siblings of children with cancer, for example, may resent it if they are neglected by their parents, may be anxious about their own health, may feel guilty about some of the unsavory feelings they have, and may feel pressure after the death to replace the lost child in their parents' eyes (Adams & Deveau, 1987).

One 12-year-old boy whose brother died described his experience this way: "My Dad can't talk about it, and my mom cries a lot. It's really hard on them. I pretend I'm O. K. I usually just stay in my room" (Wass, 1991, p. 29). If siblings are isolated from their understandably upset parents or if their grief is not taken seriously, they may have an especially hard time recovering (Rosen, 1986). Bereaved children fare better if their parents are not overwhelmed by grief, remain warm and supportive, and encourage open discussion of feelings (Applebaum & Burns, 1991; Graham-Pole et al., 1989; Sandler et al., 1992).

Finally, grandparents also grieve following the death of a child, both for their grandchild *and* for their child, the bereaved parent (DeFrain, Jakub, & Mendoza, 1991–1992; Ponzetti, 1992). As one grandparent said, "It's like a double whammy!" (DeFrain et al., 1991–1992, p. 178). Clearly, then, those who are attempting to help bereaved families need to include the *whole family* in their efforts.

The Loss of a Parent

Even if we escape the death of a child or spouse, the death of a parent is a normative life transition that the vast majority of us will experience. As noted already, children sometimes experience long-lasting problems after the death of a parent. Fortunately, most of us do not have to face this event until we are middle aged. We are typically less emotionally dependent on our parents by then, and most of us are heavily invested in our own families. Moreover, we expect that our parents will die someday and have prepared ourselves, at least to some degree. Finally, we are likely to share the widespread societal belief that the death of an elderly person is somehow less tragic than that of a young person who has not yet had a chance to live (Kalish & Reynolds, 1976).

Perhaps for all of these reasons, the death of a parent is usually not as emotionally devastating and disruptive as the death of a spouse or child (Leahy, 1992–1993). This is not to say that a parent's death is easy to bear, however. Adult children may feel vulnerable and alone in the world when their parents no longer stand between them and death (Scharlach & Fredriksen, 1993), and they may experience new pressures as the senior generation in the family (Osterweis et al., 1984). Guilt about not doing enough for an aging parent is also common (Moss et al., 1993). Most adult children feel the loss deeply but at the same time gain something in confidence and maturity (Scharlach & Fredriksen, 1993).

Perhaps the best conclusion we can reach about deaths in the family is that *all* of them have the potential to cause great suffering and to put an adult at risk for physical and psychological problems and even death. Still, reactions to the loss of a spouse, child, or parent are also influenced by the special qualities of each of those attachments. The death of a child may be particularly difficult because it is so unexpected, whereas the death of a parent may be easier to bear because it is anticipated.

Who Copes and Who Succumbs?

Why do some individuals cope effectively with grief—and even gain strength from their ordeal—whereas others develop serious psychological disorders after a loss? To answer that question, we must first answer another: Where is the boundary line between normal and abnormal grieving?

Defining Pathological Grief

Beverly Raphael (1983) has identified three forms of pathological (or, as psychologists now prefer to say, "complicated") grief (see also Jacobs, 1993). The victim of *chronic grief* grieves for a longer time than is normal. Years after the death, for example, a widow may still burst into tears at any reminder of her husband, set a place at the table for him, and feel highly anxious and unable to function. These reactions are perfectly normal in the year or so after the death, but they may become abnormal if they persist too long. A second form of pathological grief is *distorted grief,* a tendency to show some grief symptoms in exaggerated form and other symptoms hardly at all. Thus a bereaved person may be intensely angry or overwhelmingly guilty, and this one reaction may completely overshadow or interfere with other responses. Finally, pathology may exist if the person grieves too little—if there is an *absence, inhibition, or delay of grief.* A parent may persist in denying that a child has died long beyond the point at which numbness typically gives way to a fuller awareness of reality, or a widower may find himself unable to cry or to express his painful feelings. In short, either too much or too little of any of the responses that constitute the "normal" bereavement reaction can be a bad sign.

As we discovered in Chapter 16, however, it is not always easy to pin down the dividing line between normal and abnormal behavior. Age norms and social norms must be considered. As we saw earlier, children may express their grief differently than adults do and may be more prone to use denial and acting out as coping mechanisms (Raphael, 1983). In addition, grieving occurs in a cultural context. An Egyptian mother may be conforming to her culture's norms of mourning if she sits alone, withdrawn and mute, for months or even years after a child's death; likewise, a Balinese mother is simply following the rules of her culture if she is calm, composed, and even seemingly cheerful soon after a child's death (Wikan, 1988, 1991). We would certainly be wrong to conclude, based on our society's norms, that the Egyptian mother is suffering from chronic grief or the Balinese mother from absent or inhibited grief.

Another warning: As Camille Wortman and Roxane Silver (1989) argue, some of our society's assumptions about what constitutes normal grieving are not backed very strongly by research (see also Stroebe et al., 1992). For example, we assume that bereaved persons should confront their loss, experience painful emotions, and "work through" those emotions in order to recover. Yet some bereaved individuals never show much depression or distress, and they are often better adjusted months later than those who grieved the hardest after the loss. Particularly in the face of losses as traumatic as those that took place during the Holocaust, repressing painful memories may be more adaptive than reviewing them (Kaminer & Lavie, 1993). Moreover, when evidence shows that significant numbers of bereaved individuals continue to grieve many years after a death, it may not be appropriate to claim that grieving lasting more than a year or two is "pathological." Similarly, because we know that many bereaved people maintain their attachments to lost loved ones indefinitely rather than severing those bonds as they resolve their grief, we should be more cautious about labeling as abnormal individuals who sense the presence of a lost loved one and consult with him or her about important decisions years after a death (Klass, 1993; Stroebe et al., 1992).

With those warnings in mind, we can still ask what distinguishes the people who cope well with loss from those who cope poorly. We will consider some of the factors that may make it especially difficult for adults — and children as well — to cope with the death of a loved one. As is true of coping following any major life event, coping with bereavement is influenced by the resources possessed by the individual, the nature of the event to be coped with, and the surrounding context of support and stressors.

Personal Resources

Just as some individuals are better able to cope with their own dying than others are, some are more equipped to handle the stresses of bereavement. As Bowlby's (1980) attachment theory states, *early experiences in attachment relationships* influence how we later relate to others and handle losses of relationships. If infants and young children receive loving and responsive care, they form *internal working models* of self and others that tell them that they are lovable and that other people can be trusted (see Chapter 13).

Is it pathological to maintain a relationship with one's deceased parent for many years? Probably not. It is common practice in Japan to remember every day during worship family members who have died.

They are later able to cope with the death of loved ones relatively well. By contrast, infants or young children who receive inconsistent care or who suffer the loss of an important attachment figure by death or abandonment may have more difficulty coping with loss later in life. They may, for example, develop a resistant (or ambivalent) style of attachment that leads them to be overly dependent on others and to display extreme grief and anxiety after a loss (Bowlby, 1980; see also Mikulincer, Florian, & Tolmacz, 1990; Parkes, 1991). Or, they may develop an avoidant attachment style that causes them to be "compulsively self-reliant" and to have difficulty accepting a loss and expressing grief.

For some, the loss of an important attachment figure early in life can contribute to chronic depression later. Tirril Harris, Antonio Bifulco, and George Brown find that experiencing the death of a parent as a child is a contributor to serious depression in women, but mainly when the parent's death sets off a whole chain of unfavorable events. This chain usually starts with inadequate, neglectful care after the death and often leads to pregnancy as a teenager and, as a result, involvement in a highly stressful and not very supportive marriage (Bifulco, Harris, & Brown, 1992; Harris & Bifulco, 1991). The depression-prone women who experience this chain of events seem to form internal working models that cause them to be insecure, dependent, and helpless. Still, many other bereaved children receive loving care during childhood and have positive experiences in their later relationships that help them overcome the effects of early loss. So we must consider other influences on how people respond to loss.

Early experiences in the family, as well as genetic endowment, contribute to personality development, and several aspects of *personality and coping style* influence how successfully people cope with death. For example, those individuals who have difficulty coping tend to have low self-esteem (Lund et al., 1985–1986) and lack a sense that they are in control of their lives (Haas-Hawkings et al., 1985). Many had psychological problems such as depression long before they were bereaved (Norris & Murrell, 1990; Zisook & Shuchter, 1991). So, among the bereaved, as among the dying, the enduring capacity of the individual to cope with life's problems is an important influence on outcomes.

The Nature of the Loss

Bereavement outcomes are also influenced by characteristics of the event with which the person must cope. The closeness of one's *relationship to the deceased* is obviously important (Jacobs, 1993; Murrell & Himmelfarb, 1989). Pathological grief after the death of a spouse is more likely when the surviving spouse was highly dependent on the partner than when the spouses were more emotionally independent of each other (Parkes & Weiss, 1983; Sanders, 1993). Pathological grief is also especially likely when the marital attachment was *ambivalent* (or resistant) rather than secure (Parkes & Weiss, 1983; Sable, 1989). As attachment theory would predict, widows and widowers who had mixed feelings about their spouses and felt insecure in their marriages may conclude that they are failures in love and will never achieve the intimacy they so desperately wanted. Bereaved children also fare worse if either they were highly dependent on their deceased parent (as most children are) *or* the parent/child relationship was ambivalent and insecure (Raphael, 1983).

Bereavement reactions are also influenced by the *suddenness or unexpectedness of the death*. Sudden deaths are somewhat more difficult than deaths for which there is forewarning (Parkes & Weiss, 1983; Sanders, 1993). Possibly this is because the survivors have had no opportunity to engage in anticipatory grief. Still, no amount of preparation can eliminate the need to grieve after a death, and the differences in bereavement following sudden death or death after a prolonged illness are surprisingly small. Indeed, there are hints that, when a terminal illness drags on for months and months, the advantages of forewarning are overshadowed by the damaging effects of a prolonged death watch (Rando, 1986; Sanders, 1982–1983).

Finally, the *cause of death* influences bereavement outcomes. One of the reasons why the death of a child is so painful is that children's deaths are often the result of "senseless" events such as car accidents, drownings, or homicides. Parents whose children are murdered have an especially hard time, partly because they become caught up in the search for the murderer and subsequent legal proceedings (Knapp, 1986). Coping with the suicide of a loved one can also be particularly difficult (Gilewski et al., 1991). Suicide survivors may have trouble accepting what happened or figuring out why it happened; they may feel rejected by the deceased and stigmatized by the living (van der Wal, 1989–1990; Van Dongen, 1993). Needless to say, bereavement can also be especially difficult if the bereaved person contributed in some way, even accidentally, to the death (Osterweis et al., 1984).

The Context Surrounding Death: Supports and Stressors

Grief reactions are influenced positively by the presence of a strong social support system and negatively by the presence of additional life stressors. Social support is crucial at all ages. It is especially important for the young child whose parent dies to have adequate substitute parenting. Children tend to have more problems if their surviving parent is crippled by grief and insensitive to their needs than if the surviving parent or substitute caregiver helps them express their grief and maintains a loving home environment (Elizur & Kaffman, 1983; Van Eerdewegh et al., 1985). Too often, adults attempt to protect children from the pain of death and inadvertently isolate them from the rest of the family when they are most in need of support.

Bereaved adults also benefit from social support (Norris & Murrell, 1990; Worden & Silverman, 1993). How can friends and relatives be most supportive? Bereaved individuals do not appreciate people who try to cheer them up or force them out of their grief. Instead, they are helped most by people who serve as confidants and allow them to express their painful feelings freely (Lehman, Ellard, & Wortman, 1986; Pennebaker & O'Heeron, 1984). Bereaved adults who live alone and lack social support run an especially high risk of dying during the bereavement period (Bunch, 1972; Helsing, Szklo, & Comstock, 1981).

Just as social support helps the bereaved, additional stressors hurt. For example, outcomes tend to be poor for widows who must cope with financial problems after bereavement and for widowers who have difficulty managing household tasks without their wives (Umberson, Wortman, & Kessler, 1992). Widows and widowers may have more than the usual difficulty resolving their grief if they must also take on the challenges of caring singlehandedly for young children, finding a new job, or moving (Parkes, 1986; Worden & Silverman, 1993).

By taking into account the person who has experienced a death, the nature of the death, and the context surrounding it, we can put together a profile of the individuals who are most likely to display pathological, or complicated, grief and to develop long-term problems after bereavement. These individuals have had an unfortunate history of interpersonal relationships, perhaps suffering the death of a parent when they were young or insecurity in their early attachments. They have had previous psychological problems and generally have difficulty coping effectively with adversity. The person who died is someone with whom they had either a highly dependent or a highly ambivalent relationship. The death was sudden, untimely, and seemingly senseless. Finally, these high-risk individuals lack the kinds of social support that can aid them in overcoming their loss, and they experience stresses in addition to the bereavement itself. What can be done to help prevent some of these poor outcomes? Let's see.

APPLICATIONS: TAKING THE STING OUT OF DEATH

We as a society are now trying to stop denying and start facing up to the reality of death. A number of efforts are underway to aid children and adults who are dying, who are bereaved, or who simply stand to benefit from knowing more about death and grappling with their feelings about it.

For the Dying

Dramatic changes in the care of dying persons have occurred within the past few decades. In the 1950s, for example, almost 90% of physicians claimed that they would not tell a patient if they discovered a cancer that would probably be fatal (Oken, 1961). In more recent surveys, 80–90% of doctors state that they *would* communicate this sort of news to their patients, or at least that they believe patients should be told of the gravity of their condition (Klenow & Youngs, 1987). This shift suggests that medical personnel have become more sensitive to the needs of dying persons.

However, many observers feel that hospital personnel continue to place too much emphasis on curing people and keeping them alive and do not allow terminally ill patients to "die with dignity." Out of such concerns has arisen a new approach to caring for the dying person: the hospice. A **hospice** is a program that supports dying persons and their families through a philosophy of "caring" rather than "curing." The first such facility was St. Christopher's Hospice near London, opened in 1967 under the direction of Dr. Cicely Saunders (1977). The concept spread quickly to North America, where hospices have now been established in most communities, serving children with cancer, adults with AIDS, and other dying persons (Siebold, 1992). In many hospice programs today, though, there is no care facility like St. Christopher's; instead, dying patients stay at home and are visited by hospice workers.

What makes hospice care different from hospital care? Whether hospice care is provided in a facility or at home, it entails these key features (Butterfield-Picard & Magno, 1982; Corr & Corr, 1992; Siebold, 1992):

1. The dying person and his or her family—not the "experts"—decide what support they need and want.
2. Attempts to cure the patient or prolong his or her life are deemphasized.
3. Pain control is emphasized (powerful "pain cocktails" with such drugs as morphine, cocaine, and alcohol help patients remain pain-free but alert).
4. The setting for care is as normal as possible (preferably the patient's own home, or at least a home-like facility that does not have the sterile atmosphere of many hospital wards).
5. Bereavement counseling is provided to the family before and after the death.

The contrasts between hospice care and traditional hospital care are striking. In the hospital, medical experts have control, efforts are directed at curing the patient or staving off death as long as possible, the setting is sterile and clinical, and family members are too often viewed as a nuisance rather than as the most important of all caregivers. The differences are lessening, though, as more and more hospitals create hospice programs of their own or adopt elements of the hospice philosophy in caring for terminally ill patients (Seale, 1989).

What are the advantages to dying patients and their families of spending their last days together receiving hospice care? In an evaluation of hospice facility care, at-home hospice care, and conventional hospital care in Great Britain, Clive Seale (1991) found that hospice patients spent more of their last days without pain, underwent fewer medical interventions and operations, and received nursing care that was more oriented to their emotional needs. Their families grieved as much as those of hospitalized patients but were more satisfied with the care they received. The hospice approach may not work for all, but for some it does mean an opportunity to die with dignity, free of pain and surrounded by loved ones (Saunders, 1977).

For the Bereaved

Part of the mission of hospice programs is to help family members prepare for and cope with their loss. What other help is available for bereaved individuals? Like anyone with psychological problems, bereaved individuals can benefit from individual or group psychotherapy or counseling (Jacobs, 1993; Piper, McCallum, & Azim, 1992). Those whose grief is chronic and disabling may need help in getting beyond it, whereas those whose grief is inhibited may want help

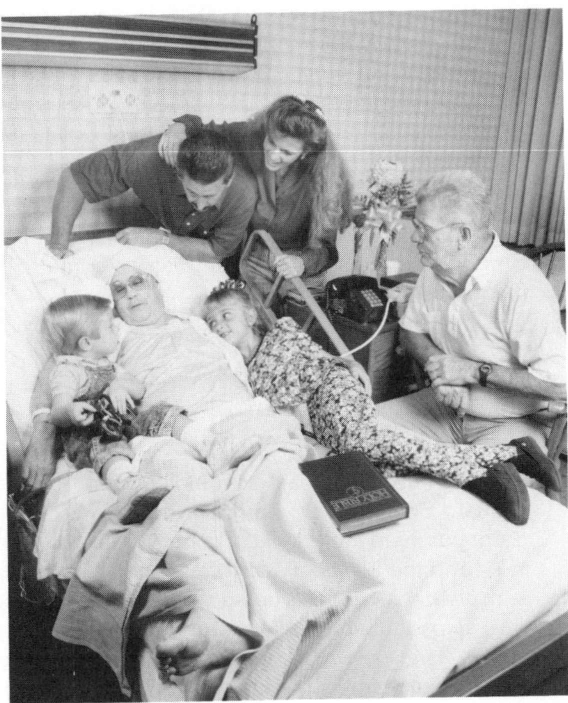
Hospice care helps people live even when they're dying.

expressing their painful emotions (Worden, 1991). Because death takes place in a family context, though, family therapy often makes a good deal of sense. Family therapy can help bereaved parents and children communicate more openly and share their grief, and it can enable parents to maintain the kind of warm and supportive parenting style that will facilitate their children's recovery (Black, 1991; Sandler et al., 1992).

In the United States, still another approach to helping the bereaved has proven popular: the mutual support or self-help group. One such mutual support program is Compassionate Friends, serving parents whose children have died. Another is the Widow-to-Widow program, in which volunteer widows visit new widows to offer them whatever support they need—help and advice in such practical matters as settling finances or finding a job, or simply emotional support and friendship (Silverman, 1969, 1981). Widow-to-Widow members also attend meetings that give them opportunities to learn useful information and to socialize. Participants in such mutual support groups for widows fare better than nonparticipants (Lieberman, 1993; Lund & Caserta, 1992). They tend to be less depressed and anxious, they use less medication, and they have a greater sense of well-being and self-esteem (Lieberman & Videka-Sherman, 1986). Perhaps this is because other widows are in the best position to understand what a new widow is going through and to offer effective social support. One widow summed it up this way: "What's helpful? Why, people who are in the 'same boat.' Unless you've been there you just can't understand" (Bankoff, 1983, p. 230).

For All of Us

Death educators—yes, such professionals exist—maintain that all of us can deal more easily with our own dying and with the deaths of loved ones if we learn more about death and dying and sort through our feelings about it. Death education has a part to play throughout the life span.

Not long ago, most children were sheltered from death by protective adults. One mother interviewed by Robert Kastenbaum (1986) described her "death education" as a child this way: "Nobody prepared me for it, nobody answered my questions, nobody told me one thing or the other. 'I don't want to talk about it,' would be the answer, or, 'I don't know why you ask me such foolish questions'" (p. 247). This mother had vowed that she would communicate more openly with her own children.

Death educators often recommend that parents and teachers adopt a "teachable moments" approach to educating children about death (Leviton & Forman, 1974; Wass, 1991). This means answering children's questions honestly as they arise and capitalizing on events such as the death of a pet, the explosion of the space shuttle *Challenger*, or, increasingly in low-income urban areas, the murder of a relative or neighbor, to teach children about death and to help them understand and express their emotions. Perhaps the most important thing children can learn about death is that adults are willing to discuss it.

Also, death educators insist that death and dying should be part of the school curriculum for all age groups. David Schonfeld and Murray Kappelman (1990) evaluated a death curriculum for prekindergarten to second-grade children that consisted of six 30- to 45-minute lessons, class discussion, and drawing exercises. In three weeks these children achieved gains in their understanding of the irreversibility, universality, and biological causality of death that would normally take a year to achieve. In other words, appropriate learning experiences can help familiarize children with the concept of death and accelerate the development of mature understandings of it. The ultimate goal of such death education is to put children in a better position to cope with this potentially frightening event when the need arises. It is important, of course, to monitor children's reactions to ensure that they are not becoming more fearful of death as they learn about it.

As for adults, they can take advantage of the many courses on death and dying that are now offered at most colleges and universities and in many community education programs. Do adults who take such courses become less anxious about death? Sometimes, but not always. The death education programs that most effectively reduce death anxiety are those that involve the learner not only intellectually but also emotionally—those that include activities in which students must confront and work through their feelings about death (Durlak & Riesenberg, 1991). Death education courses by no means "cure" death anxiety, but they do convey information about death and dying, change attitudes regarding life and death issues, and help people become at least somewhat more comfortable with the realities of death. Each brush we have with death may also bring us closer to an acceptance of this ultimate life transition (Brent et al., 1991).

REFLECTIONS

Needless to say, death is not a happy topic. Indeed, we have seen that coping with the death of a loved one is an extraordinary challenge—one that can leave its mark on people's development for years to come. Yet most of us do survive, through a combination of our own resources and help from those around us. This is encouraging.

Perhaps we can leave you with an even more encouraging message. Most research on bereavement has viewed grief as something like an illness. We catch it, it damages our physical and mental health, and we ultimately return to our normal state. Guided by this model, researchers often fail to look for *positive* effects of death on survivors. Yet bereavement is the very kind of life event that has the potential to foster personal growth (Thomas, DiGiulio, & Sheehan, 1988). Granted, it is a painful way to grow, and we could hardly recommend it as a plan for optimizing human development. Still, the literature on death and dying is filled with testimonials about the lessons that can be learned through suffering. Although it is not always clear that people who claim to have grown from their encounters with death have in fact become better-adjusted individuals, many of them truly believe that they have become more confident, family-oriented, open, and religious people who have a greater appreciation of life (Lehman et al., 1993). Witness these examples:

> A bereaved sibling: "I won't part with anyone in anger; I want to leave them knowing that I care. I think I have become a more caring person because of my experience" [Rosen, 1986, p. 167].
>
> A widow, surprised by how successfully she had built a new and satisfying life: "I'm doing things I never thought I could do. I hate being alone but I have good friends and we care about each other. I'm even traveling. I enjoy my work. I never thought I'd hear myself say that I don't mind being single" [Silverman, 1981, p. 55].
>
> A mother whose infant died: "Now I can survive anything" [DeFrain, Taylor, & Ernst, 1982, p. 57].

So perhaps it is by encountering tragedy that we learn to cope with tragedy, and perhaps it is by struggling to find meaning in death that we come to find meaning in life.

SUMMARY POINTS

1. In defining death as a biological process, the Harvard definition of total brain death is widely applied, but there are still many controversies surrounding it and the issues of active and passive euthanasia and assisted suicide. The social meanings of death vary across cultures, subcultures, and individuals.
2. The average life expectancy for a newborn in the United States has risen to 75 years; death rates decline after infancy and rise dramatically after early adulthood; as we age, accidents give way to chronic diseases as primary causes of death.
3. Programmed, or genetic, theories of aging include the Hayflick limit on cell reproduction, endocrine theory, and immune theory; damage theories of aging focus on an accumulation of random damage to DNA, cross-linkage of molecules, and destructive free radicals. Aging appears to be genetically influenced, but environmental factors also affect longevity.
4. Elisabeth Kübler-Ross stimulated much concern for dying patients by describing five "stages" of dying (denial/isolation, anger, bargaining, depression, and acceptance). However, dying people do not seem to progress through clearcut stages, and their experiences depend on their unique dying trajectories and personalities.
5. Bereavement precipitates grief and mourning, which are expressed, according to Parkes and Bowlby, in overlapping phases of numbness, yearning, disorganization and despair, and, finally, after a year or two, reorganization.
6. Infants do not comprehend death but clearly grieve, protesting and despairing after separations in ways that parallel adults' responses to bereavement.
7. Children are very curious about death and often understand by age 5 to 7 that it is a final cessation of life processes that is irreversible and universal, later realizing that it is ultimately caused by internal biological changes. Terminally ill children often become very aware of their situations and use more cognitive techniques of coping as they get older; bereaved children express their grief differently than adults do and

often experience academic difficulties and behavior problems.

8. Adolescents use their advanced cognitive capacities to understand death more abstractly; they cope with dying and bereavement in ways that reflect the developmental themes of adolescence.

9. Death anxiety appears to be lowest among adults who are male, strongly religious, well adjusted, and elderly. Widows and widowers experience many physical, emotional, and cognitive symptoms; are at increased risk of dying; and often show emotional aftereffects for years. The death of a child is often even more difficult to bear, the death of a parent often easier.

10. Pathological grief that is chronic, distorted, or inhibited is especially likely among individuals who had painful early attachment experiences, suffered the loss of a parent, or lack positive personality traits and coping skills; who had either dependent or ambivalent relationships with individuals who died suddenly and senselessly; and who lack positive social support and face additional stressors.

11. Successful efforts to take the sting out of death have included hospice programs for dying patients and their families, mutual support groups for the bereaved, and death education for all age groups.

KEY TERMS

active euthanasia
anticipatory grief
assisted suicide
autoimmune reactions
bereavement
centenarian
cross-linkage theory
damage theories of aging
death anxiety
denial
DNA repair theory
dying trajectory
endocrine theory
euthanasia
free radicals
grief
Hayflick limit
hospice
immune system theory
life expectancy
Living Will
maximum life span
mourning
passive euthanasia
programmed theories of aging
total brain death

18

EPILOGUE: FITTING THE PIECES TOGETHER

We have now concluded our survey of human development from conception to death and of the many forces that influence it. In this epilogue our goal is to help you integrate what you have learned—to see the "big picture." We begin by summarizing significant trends in physical, cognitive, personal, and social aspects of development, age period by age period. We then pull together the major themes that have emerged from recent theory and research.

MAJOR TRENDS IN HUMAN DEVELOPMENT

Throughout this book we have organized our discussion of development in the different domains of human functioning by age periods. Here, at the risk of oversimplifying, we offer portraits of the developing person in seven periods of life—sketches that show how the strands of development, intertwined, make a *whole person.*

For centuries, artists have rendered their visions of the "seven ages of man" (or, in this 1848 work, the eleven stages of a woman's life). Our understandings of the ages and stages of human development have changed dramatically.

1. Infants (Birth to Age 2)

What is most striking about infant development is the staggering speed with which babies acquire all the basic capacities that make us human. The newborn starts life marvelously equipped to adapt to its environment using reflexes, to take in information through all of its senses, and to learn from and remember its experiences. The rapid growth of body and brain during the first two years of life transforms an otherwise still-helpless neonate into a toddler who is walking, talking, and asserting a newfound sense of self.

As the cortical centers of the brain mature and become organized, many automatic reflexes disappear and are replaced by *voluntary* motor behaviors. In a predictable sequence, infants sit, creep and crawl, and then walk independently, at about 1 year of age; meanwhile, they are becoming better able to manipulate objects with their hands. As their perceptual and motor skills improve, so does their capacity to explore the world around them and to actively contribute to their own cognitive development in the process.

As babies progress through the substages of Piaget's *sensorimotor period,* they develop their minds through their own active efforts to perceive and act upon the world around them. They come to understand that objects have permanent existence, even when they are out of sight. They also acquire *symbolic capacity*—the ability to let one thing stand for another—which is central to intellectual activity throughout the remainder of the life span. By the end of the sensorimotor period, they can *mentally* devise solutions to problems before trying them out. After cooing and babbling, they will utter their first words at the age of 1 and form two-word sentences such as "Go car" by the age of 2.

As their cognitive capacities expand, infants become more aware of themselves as individuals. By age 2 they recognize themselves in the mirror and know that they are girls or boys. In fact, infants are individuals from birth, for they each have distinctive and genetically influenced temperaments that serve as a foundation for later personality.

Infants' temperaments, coupled with their parents' styles of interacting with them, influence how successfully they resolve Erikson's first psychosocial conflict, that of *trust versus mistrust,* and whether they form secure attachments to their caregivers starting at about 7 months of age. The parent/child relationship dominates the social world of the infant and serves as a training ground for later social relationships. Cognitive changes and daily exchanges with attachment figures give rise to more sophisticated social skills that infants then apply in encounters with peers. Equipped with the ability to perceive and act upon the environment, with impressive cognitive and linguistic capacities, with an awareness of self, and with trust in their caregivers, infants are ready to venture out into a larger social world.

2. Preschool Children (Ages 2 through 5)

During the preschool years, 2-year-olds who toddle and teeter along and speak in two-word sentences become young children ready for formal schooling. As their brains continue to mature and as they gain motor experience, preschool children acquire the gross motor control they need to hop and catch balls and the fine motor skills they need to trace letters and use scissors.

During Piaget's *preoperational stage* of cognitive development, young children make wonderful use of their symbolic capacity, mastering all the basic rules of language (with the help of adults willing to converse with them) and joining with other children in imaginative sessions of social pretend play. True, young children often have difficulty with problems that require logical thinking. They fail Piaget's tests of *conservation,* thinking that the juice poured from a stocky glass into a tall, narrow glass somehow becomes "more juice." They are egocentric at times, failing to appreciate differences between their own perspectives and those of other individuals and assuming that their listeners know what they know. They are distractible and lack some of the information-processing skills that allow older children to think about two or more aspects of a problem at once and to learn and remember more efficiently.

Preschoolers' personalities continue to take shape as they struggle with Erikson's conflicts of *autonomy versus shame* and *initiative versus guilt.* If all goes well, they develop the confidence to assert themselves and to carry out bold plans, and their self-esteem is high. They learn a good deal about themselves and other people, although their descriptions of people emphasize physical characteristics and activities and say little about inner qualities such as intentions, motives, and enduring personality traits. Although relatively lacking in self-control, they increasingly become socialized by those around them to control their emotions and behavior and to follow rules of moral conduct. In no time at all, they also learn what they must know to be a boy or a girl in their society.

Preschool children's attachments to their caregivers continue to be central in their social worlds, but they hone their social skills in interactions with peers, learning to take their playmates' perspectives, engage in truly cooperative play, and enter into friendships. All in all, preschoolers are endlessly fascinating: charming and socially skilled but a bit egocentric at times, immensely curious and intellectually alive but sometimes quite illogical, here one moment but off on some new adventure the next.

3. School-Aged Children (Ages 6 through 11)

Compared with preschool children, elementary school children seem considerably more self-controlled, serious, skilled, and logical. Their bodies grow slowly and steadily each year, and they continue to refine their motor skills and use their senses ever more intelligently by directing their attention where it most needs to be directed. As they enter Piaget's *concrete operations stage,* they become able to perform in their heads actions that previously had to be performed with their hands. They can mentally add, subtract, classify, and order objects; grasp conservation problems that fool the preschooler; and draw many logical conclusions about the workings of the physical world. They master the fine points of the rules of language and become better able to take the perspectives of their listeners in conversations. They acquire the memory strategies and other information-processing skills it takes to do schoolwork. And, although their scores on intelligence tests can fluctuate from year to year, their IQs begin to predict fairly well their intellectual standings as adolescents or adults.

The cognitive growth that occurs during the school years, along with social experience, allows children to understand themselves and other people in terms of inner personality traits and underlying motives. School-aged children work through Erikson's conflict of *industry versus inferiority* as they attempt to master new skills, compare their accomplishments with those of their classmates, and absorb feedback about where they stand in their reading groups and where they finish in races. The unrealistically high self-esteem of preschoolers drops as children gain a more accurate view of their strengths and weaknesses. Most children also develop fairly consistent personalities, at least parts of which survive into adulthood.

Under the guidance of parents and teachers, and through their interactions with peers, children also learn the values and moral standards of the society around them. Most are at Kohlberg's level of *preconventional morality,* in which what matters most is whether their acts will be rewarded or punished. Toward the end of elementary school, children begin to understand that rules are cooperative agreements among individuals; this realization sets the stage for their move from preconventional to *conventional morality* in early adolescence. School-aged children also continue to learn about and conform to prevailing social standards regarding how boys and girls should behave.

The social world of school-aged children is more extensive than that of infants and preschool children. Family life is still very important, but more and more

a. Bettie Lou was born in 1914 in Los Angeles and is shown here at 6 months of age with her grandmother.

b. As a young child, she loved going to the beach with her parents.

c. At 12, on the brink of adolescence, Bettie Lou had already become an excellent swimmer. She swam so well in high school that she had a chance to try out for the Olympics. Her father vetoed the idea, however, because he did not want her traveling with the swimming coach. (The strict gender norms of this era limited the opportunities of many females.)

d. As a young adult, Bettie Lou graduated from junior college and began working as a secretary. She married at age 23 but had to keep it a secret for a time because she stood to lose her job if her employers found out. Soon after her husband completed his military service in 1938, the couple had the first of their three children. Bettie Lou immersed herself in parenting, work, and volunteer activities. She had a chance to work as a professional model but turned the offer down, not wanting to be away from her family.

e. At 52, she was a proud grandmother, active in a wide range of volunteer activities as well as work.

f. At 75, Bettie Lou, flanked by her oldest son and his wife, looked and felt much younger than her years. She was back to a heavy schedule of volunteer work, this time centered on her grandchildren, after spending "a little time on myself" for a brief period.

One developing person in the changing historical context of the United States in the 20th century.

time is spent with peers—usually those of the same sex—playing organized games and developing caring friendships with chums. Youngsters who are rejected by their peers and miss out on these important social learning opportunities tend to become maladjusted adults. Teachers, coaches, TV characters, and sports stars all help to socialize children as well. As children go about the business of being children, they are gaining the skills and values they will need to do the serious work of adulthood.

4. Adolescents (Ages 12 through 19)

Adolescence, the passage between childhood and adulthood, is a time of dramatic physical, cognitive, and social change. Adolescents who are adjusting to their growth spurt and to the sexual maturation of their bodies at around age 12 to 14 are naturally preoccupied with their physical appearance and are often more upset by their misshapen noses or gargantuan feet than by any intellectual or character flaws they may possess. Puberty brings with it not only new physical capacities and unfamiliar sexual urges but also new, more adultlike relationships with members of the other sex and with parents.

Meanwhile, the mind is undergoing its own metamorphosis. The child who could reason logically about real-world problems becomes the adolescent who can think systematically about worlds that do not even exist and ideas that contradict reality. Adolescents who fully master Piaget's *formal operations stage* can formulate and test hypotheses to solve scientific problems and can grasp abstract theories and philosophies. These and other new cognitive capacities sometimes leave adolescents thoroughly confused about what to believe, painfully aware of gaps between what is and what should be, and rebellious when their parents or other authority figures are not "logical" enough for their tastes.

Cognitive gains also put adolescents in a position to think about themselves and other people in more sophisticated ways. Teenagers begin to describe themselves in more abstract terms, referring to their core values and philosophies of life. By late adolescence many can integrate their self-perceptions into a coherent sense of who they are, resolving Erikson's conflict of *identity versus role confusion* and charting careers and other life goals. Adolescents have formed fairly stable personalities and are more introspective and self-aware than they were as children. They are also quite astute observers of human behavior, probing the personalities of their companions to figure out what really makes them tick. Conventional moral reasoning is achieved as adolescents first emphasize the importance of being a "good boy" or "good girl," as defined by parents and society, and later appreciate the need for law and order in the social system.

Partly because teenagers become more physically and cognitively mature, and partly because society demands that they take seriously the task of readying themselves for adult roles, social relationships change a good deal during the adolescent years. The balance of power in the family shifts so that adolescents increasingly participate in making decisions about their lives. Adolescents become more and more involved in peer activities, intimate friendships with same- and other-sex peers, and dating relationships. Heightened conformity to peer influence gets many adolescents into a brush or two with the law, but the peer group serves the useful function of helping children who depend heavily on their parents become adults who are less reliant on either parents or peers. Although about 20% of adolescents experience emotional storm and stress during this period of the life span, most teenagers emerge with impressive physical, intellectual, and social competencies, and with at least preliminary notions of who they are and what they will be as adults.

5. Young Adults (Ages 20 through 39)

The years of infancy, childhood, and adolescence are all a preparation for entry into adult life. Physiologically, young adults are at their peak; strength, endurance, reaction time, perceptual abilities, and sexual responsiveness are all optimal, even though the aging process is beginning to take slight, and usually not even noticeable, tolls on the body. Early adulthood is also a period of effective cognitive functioning. Some young adults will solidify and possibly expand upon their command of formal-operational thought, especially in their areas of expertise. Most adults continue to be conventional moral reasoners, but about one in six begins to think at the level of *postconventional morality,* grasping the moral principles underlying society's rules and regulations. If they continue to use their minds, young adults will often improve some on the IQ test scores they obtained as adolescents.

It is fortunate that young adults are physically and intellectually capable, for they face many challenges. They must often continue to work on the adolescent task of identity formation, exploring different options before they settle on a career direction. Meanwhile, they are likely to be working through Erikson's early-adult crisis of *intimacy versus isolation* and, if all goes well, committing themselves to a partner. Young adults are changed by marriage, new parenthood, and other normal events of the family life cycle, just as they are affected by their work experiences. Parenthood tends to lower marital satisfaction and push young husbands and wives into more divergent and traditional gender roles.

In view of the many life changes experienced by young adults, perhaps it is not surprising that this period is characterized by higher divorce rates and more

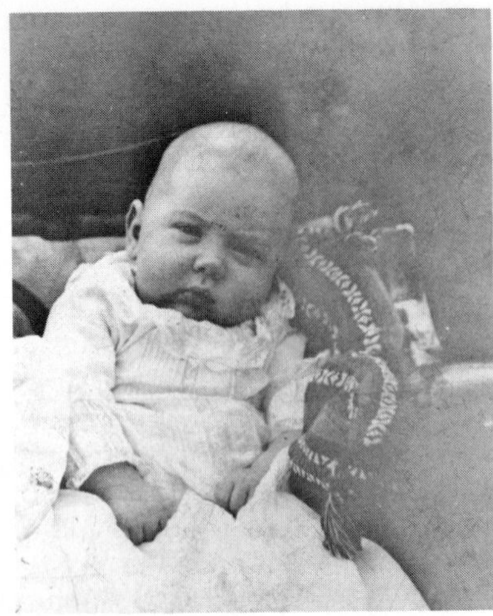

a. Jason ("Jay") was born in 1909 in Columbus, Ohio, and is shown here at 5 months of age.

b. Jay at age 3. He was his parents' first child; two brothers and a sister would eventually join the family.

c. Jay with his grandmother. Just as he was entering adolescence, his father died. Out of financial necessity, his mother moved the family to his grandmother's house in a small town in Ohio. The home had no electricity, and Jay recalls making his own radio at a time when few families had them.

d. After high school, Jay went to business college. He tried out jobs with a couple of banks before he settled in as the credit manager at a company that manufactured garden tools. A devoted hiker, he became the first president of the Central Ohio Hiking Club at age 27. His life changed dramatically when he was drafted at age 34 to fight in World War II. He was wounded and received a Purple Heart and a Bronze Star.

e. Slowed down by limited finances and the war, Jay did not get around to marrying until he was 40. He and his wife had two sons, and Jay continued to work as a credit manager at the same company for 37 years.

f. Jay, shown here at his 80th birthday party, outlived his wife of 32 years. He retired long ago, but he continues to hike with his hiking club every other week, year round. A few years ago he was reelected president of the club—48 years after he had first served!

Another developing person experiences 20th-century America.

stress-related mental health problems than the later adult years. However, for most young adults this is also an exciting and productive time of life, a time when one gains expertise and a good deal of confidence.

6. Middle-Aged Adults (Ages 40 through 64)

Middle adulthood often strikes us as a more settled period than early adulthood, but it is certainly not devoid of change. Gradual declines in the body and its physical capacities that began in the 20s and 30s may now become noticeable. Gray hairs (or no hairs!), a shortness of breath after exercise, and a need for reading glasses proclaim that one is aging. Women experience the changes of menopause around the age of 50; both men and women become more vulnerable to heart diseases and other chronic illnesses. Yet most of the physical changes that middle-aged adults experience occur quite slowly and are not severe, giving people plenty of time to adjust to and compensate for them.

Meanwhile, although intellectual capacities generally remain quite stable, middle-aged adults gradually gain some intellectual capacities and lose others. They are amassing knowledge and often perform better than young adults on measures of crystallized intelligence (vocabulary or general information). Moreover, they have built up expertise that allows them to solve everyday problems very effectively and reach peaks of creative achievement in their careers. True, toward the end of middle adulthood some individuals may feel that their memories are slipping a bit or may begin to struggle with the sorts of unfamiliar problems that measure fluid intelligence, but most intellectual skills hold up well in middle age.

Personalities that took form during childhood and that solidified during adolescence and early adulthood tend to persist into later adulthood, although significant change is possible. According to Erikson, middle-aged adults successfully resolve the conflict of *generativity versus stagnation* if they can invest their energies in nurturing the younger generation or in producing something of lasting value, but they may experience a sense of stagnation if they feel they have failed their children or are preoccupied with their own needs. Midlife crisis is quite rare. Indeed, after the nest empties and middle-aged adults are freed of major parenting responsibilities, they often find their marriages more satisfying, take pride in their grown children and grandchildren, and become more androgynous, expressing both their masculine and feminine sides.

7. Older Adults (Age 65 and Up)

The poet Robert Browning expressed a very positive image of late adulthood when he wrote: "Grow old along with me! The best is yet to be, the last of life for which the first was made." By contrast, William Shakespeare, in *As You Like It* (Act II, Scene 7), characterized the seventh and final age of life as ". . . second childishness and mere oblivion; sans teeth, sans eyes, sans taste, sans every thing." The truth lies somewhere in between: Old age *does* bring with it some losses and declines in functioning, but it is also, for most, a period of continued growth and many satisfactions.

By the time adults are in their 60s and 70s, most of them have a physical impairment of some kind—a chronic disease, a disability, failing eyesight or hearing, or, at the least, slower reactions. As they enter their 80s and 90s, more and more adults take longer to learn things, experience periodic memory lapses, or have difficulty solving novel problems, although they usually retain well the knowledge that they have crystallized over a lifetime and the cognitive and linguistic skills that they practice every day. In short, there is no denying that physical and cognitive declines are part of the experience of aging for most adults.

Yet we should be equally impressed by how successfully most adults adapt to these changes. They typically continue to carry out daily activities effectively, and they enjoy just as much self-esteem and life satisfaction as younger adults do. They do not crumble in the face of life changes such as retirement or widowhood. They continue to lead active social lives, use their sophisticated social-cognitive skills to understand other people, and enjoy close ties with both family and friends. And in the end most are able to successfully resolve Erikson's conflict of *integrity versus despair,* finding meaning in their lives and coming to terms with the inevitability of death.

These, then, are the broad themes of later life. Yet what may be most striking of all about elderly adults is their immense diversity. Many people in their 60s to early 70s (the *young-old*) are healthy, active, and highly capable, whereas many adults in their 80s, 90s, and 100s (the *old-old* and the "very old") show clear signs of physical and cognitive decline. And, whether we look at the young-old or the old-old, we will find huge differences among individuals, for each adult carries into old age his or her own unique abilities, funds of knowledge, personality traits, and values and will cope with the challenges of aging and dying in his or her own way.

Table 18.1 summarizes much of this discussion of physical, cognitive, personal, and social development within each period of the life span. But, although this table can serve as a handy description of normal human development, we need to supplement it by turning to some of the processes and themes behind these changes.

TABLE 18.1 Summary of physical, cognitive, personal, and social development across the life span.

Period	*Physical Development*	*Cognitive Development*
Infant (0 to 2)	Rapid brain and body growth. Reflexes, then more voluntary motor control, walking at 1 year. Functioning senses at birth; early-emerging ability to make sense of sensory information.	Sensorimotor period: Through senses and actions, infants acquire symbolic capacity and object-permanence concept. Cooing, babbling, and then one-word and two-word sentences. Learning capacity and recognition memory from birth.
Preschool child (2 through 5)	Continued rapid brain development. Improved coordination and fine motor skills. Perceptual abilities are good; attention span is short.	Preoperational stage: Thought guided by perceptions rather than logic. Blossoming of symbolic capacity (language acquisition and pretend play). Some limits in information-processing capacity and reasoning; little deliberate use of memory strategies.
School-aged child (6 through 11)	Slow physical growth and improved motor skills. Increased ability to control attention and use senses intelligently.	Concrete operations stage: Logical actions in the head; mastery of conservation. Mastery of fine points of language; improved memory strategies and problem solving. IQs begin to stabilize.
Adolescent (12 through 19)	Dramatic growth spurt and attainment of sexual maturity. Improved physical functioning. Concern with body image.	Formal operations stage: Hypothetical and abstract thought. Continued improvement of information-processing skills.
Young adult (20 through 39)	Time of peak functioning, but gradual declines in physical and perceptual capacities begin.	Sophisticated cognitive skills, especially in areas of expertise. Possibility of growth beyond formal thought and gains in knowledge.
Middle-aged adult (40 through 64)	Physical declines become noticeable (e.g., some loss of endurance, need for reading glasses). Increased chronic illness. Menopause and male climacteric.	Mostly stable intellectual functioning and often peak expertise and creative achievement. Fluid intelligence may begin to decline, but crystallized knowledge is maintained well.
Older adult (65+)	Continued physical decline; more chronic disease, disability, and sensory impairment. Slower reaction time.	Declines in cognition are common, but not inevitable. Slower learning, memory problems, declines in IQ and problem solving, especially if skills are rarely exercised.

MAJOR THEMES IN HUMAN DEVELOPMENT

Another way in which to leave you with the big picture is by highlighting some major generalizations about human development. Many of these larger themes are incorporated in the life-span developmental perspective introduced in Chapter 1 (Baltes, 1987); some represent stands on the developmental issues laid out in Chapter 2; and most have been echoed throughout this book. We leave you with the following thoughts:

1. We Are Whole Persons throughout the Life Span

As our review of major developments in each life phase should make clear, it is the intermeshing of physical, cognitive, personal, and social development that gives each period of the life span—and each individual human—a distinctive and coherent quality. Thus the fact that 7-month-old infants become attached to their caregivers is not just a milestone in social development divorced from other aspects of development. The maturation of sensory and motor abilities permits infants to crawl after their parents to maintain the proximity they desire, and their cognitive growth makes them aware that caregivers continue to exist when they leave the room (and therefore can be retrieved). Moreover, the emergence of attachment bonds in turn affects development in other areas—for example, by providing toddlers with the security that allows them to explore the world around them and, in the process, develop their motor skills and cognitive capacities all the more. All the threads of development are interwoven in the whole developing person.

Personal Development	Social Development
Acquisition of sense of self, self-recognition, and awareness of gender identity. Temperament as basis of personality. Conflict of trust versus mistrust.	Social from birth. Attachment to caregiver at 7 months; separation and stranger anxiety follow. Increased social skills with parents and peers; capacity for simple pretend play. Family-centered lifestyle.
Concrete, physical self-concept. Rapid acquisition of gender role. Simple notions of morality. Conflicts of autonomy versus shame and initiative versus guilt.	Parent/child relationship still central in social world. Increased social-cognitive abilities, though egocentric in some ways. More cooperation with peers; social pretend play blossoms. Exposure to schooling.
Self-concept includes psychological traits. Personality "jells." Strong gender typing. Internalization of moral standards, but mainly preconventional morality. Much social comparison and conflict of industry versus inferiority.	Increased involvement with same-sex peers; formation of close chumships. Role-taking skills advance. Play centers on organized games with rules. School and television are important socialization agents.
More abstract and integrated self-concept. Adjustment to sexuality and gender role. Conventional moral reasoning. Conflict of identity versus role confusion.	Peak peer involvement and conformity. More emotionally intimate friendships; dating relationships begin. Parent/child relationship becomes more equal; autonomy increases. Involved in school and career exploration.
Continued work on identity. A minority of individuals shift to postconventional moral reasoning. Increased confidence. Divergence of roles in family according to sex. Personality fairly stable. Conflict of intimacy versus isolation.	Social networks continue to expand, and romantic relationships are formed. Most establish families and take on roles as spouses and parents. Careers are launched; much job switching. Period of much life change; high risk of divorce and psychological problems.
Continued personality stability, but possible midlife questioning and androgyny shift. Conflict of generativity versus stagnation.	Relations center within family. The nest empties and the grandparent role is often added to existing roles. High responsibility for younger and older generations. Career is more stable, and peak success is attained. Family and work roles dominate.
Most maintain characteristic personality traits, self-esteem, and life satisfaction. Growth for many as they resolve conflict of integrity versus despair.	Continued close ties to family and friends; loneliness is rare. Generally smooth adjustment to retirement, and maintenance of social activities. For women especially, adjustment to loss of spouse.

2. Development Proceeds in Multiple Directions

Heinz Werner (1957), a pioneering and influential developmental theorist, captured in what he called his **orthogenetic principle** much of what he had observed about the direction human development takes: "Wherever development occurs it proceeds from a state of relative globality and lack of differentiation to a state of increasing differentiation, articulation, and hierarchical integration" (p. 126). That is, developing humans increasingly master a range of more and more specific responses (differentiation) and combine these responses into more organized and coherent patterns (integration).

The orthogenetic principle is indeed a useful way of summarizing many developmental trends described in this book. The single, undifferentiated cell formed at conception becomes billions of highly specialized cells (neurons, blood cells, and so on), all organized into functioning systems (such as the brain). The young infant flails its whole body as a unit (global response); the older child moves specific parts of the body on command (differentiation) and coordinates separate movements to ride a bike (integration). Similarly, young children describe other people's personalities in only the most global terms ("He's nice" "She's mean"); school-aged children develop a more differentiated vocabulary of trait labels for characterizing companions; and adolescents become true personality theorists, integrating all they have learned about their companions—contradictions included—into coherent theories about what makes these people tick.

Werner's orthogenetic principle summarizes only *one* important direction of human development, however. Not all developmental change is a matter of acquiring more complex and organized behaviors or progressing toward some "mature" endpoint. As we have seen, human development involves gains *and* losses at every age, as well as systematic changes that make us neither better nor worse than we were before but simply different.

Thus children who are gaining many learning skills are also losing some of their intrinsic motivation to learn as they progress through school, and older adults are losing mental speed but at the same time gaining knowledge that helps them compensate for slower information processing. In fact, every gain may have its corresponding loss, and every loss its corresponding gain (Baltes, 1987). It is easy to see that spending all one's energies becoming an expert in this or that inevitably means losing touch with other possible areas of specialization. But consider too how Alice James, sister of pioneering psychologist William James and author Henry James, was able to see a positive side to her failing vision: "All loss is gain. Since I have become so near-sighted I see no dust or squalor, and therefore conceive of myself as living in splendor" (cited in Baltes, Smith, & Staudinger, 1992, p. 158).

We simply must abandon the old view that human development consists of growth or improvement up to adulthood; stability into middle age; and decline in old age. There are gains, losses, and just plain changes during *all* phases of the life span.

3. There Is Both Continuity and Discontinuity in Development

As we have seen throughout this book, developmentalists have long grappled with the issue of *continuity versus discontinuity* in human development. We can appreciate the wisdom of staking out a middle ground on the continuity/discontinuity issue by considering whether development is or is not stagelike and whether our early traits do or do not carry over into later life.

Do we progress through distinctly different stages of development or just gradually accumulate (or lose) knowledge and skills as we get older? Although some research supports Piaget's claim that children progress through qualitatively different stages of cognitive development, we now know that advances in cognitive development are achieved quite gradually and occur faster in familiar than in less familiar domains of cognitive functioning (Flavell, 1985). It seems that development often proceeds in a continuous, gradual manner that ultimately leads to stagelike discontinuities—qualitatively different performances that make us appreciate just how much growth has occurred.

Another variation on the continuity/discontinuity issue in development is this: Do our early traits predict our later traits, or is it quite possible for a shy and intelligent child to become an outgoing and not-so-intelligent adult? We have seen evidence that *some* traits, including general intelligence and extraversion/introversion, carry over from childhood and become even more stable and consistent during adulthood. However, this continuity or consistency is far from perfect, and there is ample room for change. A bright child may lose intellectual capacity if he or she is abused and neglected at home and attends inferior schools, and an introverted child may gain confidence and blossom into a more outgoing individual with the aid of supportive friends. Such discontinuity means that predicting the character of the adult from knowledge of the child remains a risky business, even in the face of much continuity in development.

4. There Is Much Plasticity in Human Development

Repeatedly we have seen that human beings of all ages are characterized by considerable *plasticity*—by a remarkable capacity to change in response to experience. Thus, infants whose intellectual development is stunted by early malnutrition can catch up if they are given adequate diets and enriching experiences, and aging adults not only learn new intellectual tricks but sprout new neural synapses in response to intellectual stimulation. Evidence of plasticity and change in later life is especially heartening to those of us who want to foster healthy development. Contrary to what Freud believed, early experiences rarely make or break us. Instead, there are opportunities throughout the life span—within limits, of course—to undo the damage done by early traumas, to teach new skills, and to redirect lives along more fruitful paths. If adverse early experiences are followed by adverse later experiences, we can expect poor outcomes. But, if potentially damaging early experiences are offset by favorable later experiences, we can expect developing humans to display considerable plasticity and resilience.

5. Nature and Nurture Truly Interact in Development

In a very important sense, the *nature/nurture issue* has been resolved. It is now clear that multiple causal forces, representing *both* nature and nurture and ranging from changes in cell chemistry to changes in the global economy, conspire to determine human development. Biological and environmental influences jointly explain both universal developmental trends and individual differences in development. Consider a universal accomplishment such as acquiring language. Biological maturation, guided by a species-wide genetic blueprint, clearly makes this achievement possible, for no amount of stimulation from adults can make a 1-month-old baby speak sentences. Yet, once an infant is maturationally ready, language skills will not be acquired without the input from the environment available in all societies—namely, opportunities to converse with speakers of the language. So it goes for many other developmental milestones: Nothing much happens unless the child is maturationally ready to learn *and* has the requisite learning experiences.

And why do individuals differ from one another in, for example, their command of language skills? We could argue that it is because different people inherit different intellectual potentials, but we would also have to acknowledge that a genetic potential for high intelligence would never be realized if a child is never exposed to language. We could stress the importance of linguistic stimulation, but we would have to acknowledge that children with the genes for high intelligence are more likely to actively seek out, elicit, and profit from such stimulation than children with limited genetic potential. In short, the experiences we have influence whether our genetic potentials are realized or not, and the genes we inherit influence what experiences we seek out and have and how we respond to them. Depending on which aspect of human development we study, we may find that either heredity or environment is more influential than the other, but we cannot escape the conclusion that there would be no development at all without the ongoing contributions of *both*.

As we have also seen, it is often the *goodness of fit* between person and environment that matters in human development (Lerner et al., 1989; Thomas & Chess, 1986). The child who is genetically predisposed to be irritable and difficult may become the rebellious, angry adolescent if parents are rigid, impatient, and punitive, but the same child may develop in more positive directions if the mesh between his or her temperament and the demands of the social environment is better. When there is goodness of fit between genetically influenced tendencies and environment, nature and nurture will work together in the person's favor.

6. We Are Individuals, Becoming Even More Diverse with Age

In any human development textbook, there is a tendency to emphasize developmental phenomena that are shared by all or most individuals — to highlight the regularities and commonalities. We do indeed share a good deal with our fellow developing humans. But let us not lose sight of the fact that each of us is truly one of a kind. Indeed, the diversity of developing humans is so impressive that it often seems impossible to generalize about them.

Individuality is apparent starting at birth if we look closely at each infant's temperament, daily rhythms, and rate of development. Yet young infants are not nearly the individuals that they will become, for early development is strongly channeled by a *specieswide* genetic blueprint and unfolds in remarkably predictable ways (McCall, 1981). After infancy our *individual* genetic endowments express themselves more fully, and we increasingly accumulate our own unique histories of life experiences. The result? We can tell a good deal about an individual just by knowing that he or she is 2 weeks or 2 years old, whereas we know very little indeed about a person simply from learning that he or she is 25 or 65. Indeed, because diversity increases with age, elderly adults are the most diverse group of human beings of all (Harris et al., 1992; Morse, 1993).

The fact that different individuals follow different developmental pathways over a lifetime is challenging to researchers who study adult development, for they rarely detect the universal age-related stages that students of infant and child development sometimes identify. Instead, it becomes necessary to look more closely at the major life events that individuals experience, regardless of how old they are at the time, and to trace the implications of these events for later functioning.

7. We Develop in a Cultural and Historical Context

Repeatedly we have seen that humans are embedded in a sociocultural context that affects their development. Human development takes different forms in different cultures, social classes, and racial and ethnic groups; human development in the 12th or 17th century was different from human development in the 20th century; and each person's development is influenced by social changes and historical events occurring during his or her lifetime. The implication? Our knowledge of human development is culture bound and time bound, for it is most often based on studies of children and adults in Western societies in the 20th century — and often white middle-class ones at that.

We know relatively little about human development in many non-Western societies. Our best guess is that people everywhere develop in some of the same directions but that they are also the products of a particular time and place.

The more developmentalists study cultural, subcultural, and historical variations in development, the more they appreciate the importance of contextual influences. We know that children reach puberty earlier and adults live longer now than they did a century ago. Today's cohorts of adults are also functioning better intellectually and maintaining their intellectual capacities longer than adults who were born early in this century and received less education and poorer health care (Schaie, 1989). Future cohorts of adults are likely to maintain their physical and mental abilities even longer. Changes in the family and in men's and women's roles, technological innovations such as genetic engineering, and significant social changes yet to take place may all make human development in the 21st century quite different from human development today.

8. We Are Active in Our Own Development

Early developmental theorists tended to view human beings as passively shaped by forces beyond their control. Sigmund Freud saw the developing child as driven by biological urges and molded by early experiences in the family; John Watson and other early learning theorists emphasized that human behavior is controlled by environmental stimuli. Jean Piaget did much to alter this image of developing humans by emphasizing how children *actively* explore the world around them and *actively* invent their own understandings, rather than merely absorbing lessons spoon-fed to them by adults. Piaget's insights about the developing child are now firmly embedded in our assumptions about human development at all ages. Certainly we are affected by those around us and are sometimes the passive recipients of environmental influence. But just as certainly we create our own environments, influence those around us, and, by doing so, contribute to our own development. It is this ongoing, dynamic transaction between an active person and a changing environment, each influencing the other in a reciprocal way, that steers development.

9. Development Is Best Viewed as a Lifelong Process

Developmentalists have never before been as aware of the importance of understanding linkages between earlier and later development as they are today. It is valuable, of course, to study infancy, adolescence, or any other developmental period in its own right. But it is more valuable still to view behavior during each phase of life from a life-span perspective. It helps to understand that the teenage girl who bickers with her parents in an effort to forge her own identity might not have the confidence to do so unless she had enjoyed a warm, secure attachment with them as an infant and child. It is important, too, to recognize that this adolescent's quest for a separate identity and increased independence will help her achieve a readiness for intimacy and interdependence with another person. Because development *is* a process, it helps to know where it started and where it is heading.

10. Development Is Best Viewed from Multiple Perspectives

As the content of this book testifies, many disciplines have something to contribute to a comprehensive understanding of human development. Geneticists, developmental neurologists, and other representatives of the biological sciences must help us understand the genes, hormones, and neural networks that guide human development and aging. Meanwhile, psychologists must help us understand the individual and his or her relationships, and anthropologists, sociologists, historians, and economists must tell us about the changing sociocultural context in which that individual develops.

Multiple theories must also be brought to bear on the task of understanding human development. As we noted in Chapter 2, many developmentalists are *eclectics*: they embrace several theories rather than feeling that they must select one and reject the rest. As we have seen throughout this book, psychoanalytic, social learning, cognitive-developmental, ethological, and contextual-dialectical theories *all* have something important to say about how and why we change and remain the same as we get older.

Some developmentalists believe that it is possible to integrate the best features of theories such as Freud's, Erikson's, and Piaget's, all of which propose universal stages of human development, with a contextual-dialectical perspective emphasizing variations in development (Lerner & Kauffman, 1985). Such an integrated theory would reflect our understanding that people all over the world develop along certain well-worn paths but that human development can also take quite different directions depending on the day-by-day transactions between the maturing individual and the particular social world in which he or she is developing.

Often it seems that, the more one learns about a topic, the more one realizes how much more there is to learn. This is certainly true of human development. As developmentalists increasingly incorporate contextual-dialectical assumptions into their thinking, they are asking new questions that might not have occurred to them in the past. How, for example, do children who are predisposed to be either sociable or shy influence the behavior of their parents, peers, and teachers over time? And how are changes in the ways in which others treat them linked to subsequent changes in their personalities? We know very little about how these sorts of transactions between changing persons and their changing environments actually play themselves out over the years.

For developmentalists, then, there are always more questions than answers. We find this to be both a humbling and an inspiring thought. And we hope that you, too, feel both humbled and inspired as you complete your introduction to life-span human development. For, much as you may have learned, there is much more to be discovered. We hope that you are intrigued enough to observe more closely your own development and that of those around you — or even to take further coursework. And we sincerely hope that you will use what you learn to steer your own and others' development in healthier directions.

KEY TERMS

orthogenetic principle

GLOSSARY

A, not B, error The tendency of 8- to 12-month-old infants to search for a hidden object in the place where they last found it (*A*) rather than in its new hiding place (*B*).

Ability tracking The practice in education of grouping students according to ability and then educating them in classes with students of comparable academic or intellectual standing.

Accommodation In Piaget's cognitive-developmental theory, the process of modifying existing schemata in order to incorporate or adapt to new experiences; contrast with *assimilation.*

Acquired immune deficiency syndrome (AIDS) The fatal disease in which a virus (HIV) destroys the immune system and makes victims susceptible to rare, "opportunistic" infections that eventually kill them; transmitted through sexual activity and drug needle sharing and from mother to child before or during birth.

Active euthanasia Deliberately causing a person's death; mercy killing. Contrast with *passive euthanasia.*

Activity/passivity issue Issue in developmental theory centering on whether humans are active contributors to their own development or are passively shaped by forces beyond their control.

Activity theory A perspective holding that aging adults will find satisfaction to the extent that they maintain an active lifestyle. Contrast with *disengagement theory.*

Adaptation In Piaget's cognitive-developmental theory, one's inborn tendency to adjust to the demands of the environment, consisting of the complementary processes of assimilation and accommodation.

Adolescent egocentrism A characteristic of adolescent thought that involves difficulty in differentiating between one's own thoughts and feelings and those of other people; evident in the *imaginary audience* and *personal fable* phenomena.

Adolescent growth spurt The rapid increase in physical growth that occurs during adolescence.

Age effects In developmental research, the effects of getting older or of developing. Contrast with *cohort effects* and *time of measurement effects.*

Age grades Socially defined age groups or strata, each with different statuses, roles, privileges, and responsibilities in society.

Age-irrelevant society A society in which age norms have loosened and many behaviors are acceptable at a wide range of ages.

Ageism Prejudice and discrimination directed at older people.

Age norm Expectations about what people should be doing or how they should behave at different points in the life span.

Age of viability A point (currently at about the 24th prenatal week) when a fetus may survive outside the uterus if excellent medical care is available.

Aging To the biologist, deterioration of the organism that leads inevitably to death; to most developmentalists, positive, negative, and neutral changes in the mature organism.

Alternative birth center A birthing room or facility that provides a homelike atmosphere but has medical technology available.

Alzheimer's disease A pathological condition of the nervous system that results in an irreversible loss of cognitive capacities; the leading cause of dementia.

Amniocentesis A method of extracting amniotic fluid from a pregnant woman so that fetal body cells within the fluid can be tested for chromosomal abnormalities and other genetic defects.

Amnion A watertight membrane that surrounds the developing embryo, serving to regulate its temperature and to cushion it against injuries.

Amoral Lacking any sense of morality; without standards of right and wrong.

Anal stage Freud's second stage of psychosexual development (from 1 to 3 years of age), in which anal activities such as defecation become the primary methods of gratifying the sex instinct.

Androgenized female Genetic female who was exposed to male sex hormones during the prenatal period and therefore developed malelike external genitalia and some masculine behaviors.

Androgens Male hormones that help trigger the adolescent growth spurt, as well as the development of the male sex organs, secondary sex characteristics, and sexual motivation.

Androgyny A gender-role orientation in which the person blends *both* positive masculine-stereotyped and positive feminine-stereotyped personality traits.

Androgyny shift A psychological change that begins in midlife, when parenting responsibilities are over, whereby both men and women retain their gender-typed qualities but add to them qualities traditionally associated with the other sex, thus becoming more androgynous.

Anorexia nervosa A life-threatening eating disorder characterized by failure to maintain a normal weight, a strong fear of weight gain, and a distorted body image; literally, "nervous lack of appetite."

Anoxia A lack of sufficient oxygen to the brain; may result in neurological damage or death.

Anticipatory grief Grieving prior to a death for what is happening and for what lies ahead.

Apgar test A test that is routinely used to assess a newborn's heart rate, respiration, color, muscle tone, and reflexes immediately after birth and then 5 minutes later; used to identify high-risk babies.

Aptitude-treatment interaction (ATI) A phenomenon in which characteristics of the student and of the school environment interact to affect student outcome, such that any given educational practice may be effective only with a particular kind of student.

Assimilation Piaget's term for the process by which children interpret new experiences in terms of their existing schemata. Contrast with *accommodation.*

Assisted suicide Making available to an individual who wishes to commit suicide the means by which he or she may do so, as when a physician provides a terminally ill patient who wants to die with enough medication to overdose.

Attachment A strong affectional tie that binds a person to an intimate companion; characterized by affection and a desire to maintain proximity.

Attention The focusing of perception and cognition on something in particular.

Attention-deficit hyperactivity disorder (ADHD) A disorder characterized by attentional difficulties, impulsive behavior, and overactive or fidgety behavior.

Attribution theory A theory of motivation emphasizing that explanations or causal attributions for outcomes influence future expectancies of success and motivation to succeed.

Authoritarian parenting A restrictive style of parenting in which adults impose many rules, expect strict obedience, and often rely on power tactics rather than explanations to elicit compliance.

Authoritative parenting A flexible style of parenting in which adults lay down clear rules but also grant a fair amount of autonomy to their children and explain the rationale for their restrictions.

Autism See *infantile autism.*

Autoimmune reactions Processes in which the immune system produces antibodies to attack and kill normal body cells; involved in rheumatoid arthritis and other diseases and possibly in aging and dying.

Automatization The process by which information processing becomes effortless and highly efficient as a result of continued practice or increased expertise.

Autonomous morality Piaget's second stage of moral development, in which children, starting at age 10 or 11, realize that rules are agreements between individuals that can be changed by consensus.

Autonomy The capacity to make decisions independently, serve as one's own source of emotional strength, and otherwise manage life tasks without being overdependent on other people; an important developmental task of adolescence.

Autonomy versus shame and doubt Psychosocial conflict in which toddlers attempt to demonstrate their independence from and control over other people; the second of Erikson's stages.

Avoidant attachment An insecure infant/caregiver bond or other intimate relationship characterized by little separation anxiety and a tendency to avoid or ignore the attachment object upon reunion.

Babbling An early form of vocalization that appears between 4 and 6 months of age and involves repeating consonant/vowel combinations such as "baba" or "dadada."

Baby biographies Carefully recorded observations of the growth and development of children by their parents over a period of time; the first scientific investigations of development.

Baby boom generation The huge generation of people born between 1945 (the close of World War II) and 1964.

Behavioral genetics The scientific study of the extent to which genetic and environmental differences among individuals are responsible for differences among them in traits such as intelligence and personality.

Behavioral inhibition A temperamental characteristic reflecting one's tendency to withdraw from unfamiliar people and situations.

Behaviorism A school of thought in psychology holding that conclusions about human development should be based on controlled observations of overt behavior rather than on speculation about unconscious motives or other unobservable phenomena; the philosophical underpinning for early theories of learning.

Bereavement A state of loss that provides the occasion for *grief* and *mourning.*

Blastula A hollow sphere of about 100 to 150 cells that the zygote forms by rapid cell division as it moves through the fallopian tube.

Brain growth spurt Period spanning the last three months of prenatal life and the first two years after birth in which the brain undergoes its most rapid development.

Breech presentation A delivery in which the fetus emerges feet first or buttocks first rather than head first.

Bulimia nervosa A life-threatening eating disorder characterized by recurrent eating binges followed by purging activities such as vomiting.

Canalization Ways in which genes work to limit or restrict development to a small number of possible outcomes, as when highly canalized traits such as babbling emerge in all normal children despite differences in their environments.

Career consolidation stage Psychosocial stage, added to Erikson's stage system by George Vaillant, in which adults in their 30s are concerned primarily with advancing in their careers and rarely question what they are doing.

Carrier In genetics, an individual who possesses a recessive gene associated with a disease and who, although he or she does not have the disease, can transmit the gene for it to offspring.

Case study A research method in which the investigator gathers extensive information about the life of a single individual and then tests hypotheses by analyzing this information.

Cataracts A pathologic condition of the eye involving opacification (clouding) of the lens; can impair vision or cause blindness.

Catch-up growth A phenomenon in which children who have experienced growth deficits will grow very rapidly to "catch up" to the growth trajectory that they are genetically programmed to follow.

Categorical self A person's classification of the self along socially significant dimensions such as age and sex.

Centenarian An individual who has lived to be 100 years of age.

Centration The tendency to focus on only one aspect of a problem when two or more aspects are relevant.

Cephalocaudal direction The principle that growth proceeds from the head (cephalic region) to the tail (caudal region).

Cerebral cortex The convoluted outer covering of the brain that is involved in voluntary body movements, perception, and higher intellectual functions such as learning, thinking, and speaking.

Cesarean section A surgical procedure in which a baby is removed from the mother through an incision made in her abdomen and uterus.

Child effects Instances in which children influence their parents rather than vice versa.

Chorion A membrane that surrounds the amnion and becomes attached to the uterine lining to gather nourishment for the embryo.

Chorionic villus biopsy An alternative to amniocentesis in which a catheter is inserted through the cervix to withdraw fetal cells from the chorion for prenatal testing to detect genetic defects.

Chromosome A threadlike structure made up of genes; in humans, there are 46 chromosomes in the nucleus of each cell.

Chromosome abnormalities Conditions in which a child has too few, too many, or incomplete chromosomes because of errors in the formation of sperm or ova.

Chumship A close friendship with a peer of the same sex that emerges at about age 9 to 12, according to Sullivan.

Classical conditioning A type of learning in which a stimulus that initially had no effect on the individual comes to elicit a response as a result of its association with a stimulus that already elicits the response.

Class inclusion The logical understanding that parts or subclasses are included in the whole class and that the whole is therefore greater than any of its parts.

Climacteric The loss of reproductive capacity in either sex in later life.

Clinical method An unstandardized interviewing procedure used by Jean Piaget in which a child's response to each successive question (or problem) determines what the investigator will ask next.

Clique A small friendship group that interacts frequently.

Codominance In genetics, an instance in which two different but equally powerful genes produce a phenotype in which both genes are equally expressed.

Coercive family environment A home in which family members are locked in power struggles, each trying to control the others through aggressive tactics such as threatening, yelling, and hitting.

Cognition The activity of knowing and the processes through which knowledge is acquired (e.g., attending, perceiving, remembering, thinking).

Cognitive development Changes in mental processes involved in perception, language use, learning, and thought.

Cognitive style An individual's characteristic ways of approaching problems and processing information, as illustrated by reflectivity/impulsivity.

Cohabitation The arrangement whereby two unmarried adults live together as a couple.

Cohort A group of people born at the same time; a particular generation of people.

Cohort effects In cross-sectional research, the effects on findings of the fact that the different age groups (cohorts) being compared were born at different times and had different formative experiences. Contrast with *age effects* and *time of measurement effects.*

Computer-assisted instruction Learning activities conducted with the aid of a computer, ranging from simple drills to elaborate problem-solving activities.

Conception The moment of fertilization, when a sperm penetrates an ovum, forming a zygote.

Concordance rate The percentage of cases in which a particular attribute is present for both members of a pair of people (e.g., twins) if it is present for one member.

Concrete operations stage Piaget's third stage of cognitive development, lasting from about age 7 to age 11, when children are acquiring logical operations and can reason effectively about real objects and experiences.

Conditioned response (CR) A learned response to a stimulus that was not originally capable of producing the response.

Conditioned stimulus (CS) An initially neutral stimulus that comes to elicit a particular response after being paired with an unconditioned stimulus that always elicits the response.

Confidant A spouse, relative, or friend to whom a person feels emotionally close and with whom he or she can share thoughts and feelings.

Conformity The tendency to go along with the opinions or wishes of someone else or to yield to group pressures.

Conservation The recognition that certain properties of an object or substance do not change when its appearance is altered in some superficial way.

Constraint-seeking questions In the Twenty Questions Task and similar hypothesis-testing tasks, questions that rule out more than one answer, thus narrowing the field of possible answers more quickly than would questions relating to only one hypothesis at a time.

Constructivism Piaget's position that children actively create their own understandings of the world from their experiences, as opposed to being born with innate ideas or being programmed by the environment.

Contact comfort The pleasurable tactile sensations provided by a parent or by a soft, terrycloth mother substitute; believed to foster attachments in infant monkeys and possibly humans.

Contextual-dialectical theories Theoretical perspectives holding that development arises from the ongoing interrelationships between a changing organism and a changing world.

Contextual model A world view that regards human development as an ongoing historical event or drama and emphasizes the ever-changing relationship between person and environment. Contrast with *mechanistic model* and *organismic model.*

Continuity/discontinuity issue The debate among theorists about whether human development is best characterized as gradual and continuous or abrupt and stagelike.

Continuous reinforcement A schedule of reinforcement in which every occurrence of an act is reinforced.

Contour The amount of light/dark transition or boundary area in a visual stimulus.

Contrived observation Observation of behavior conducted under special conditions created by the researcher so as to elicit the behavior of interest. Contrast with *naturalistic observation.*

Conventional morality Kohlberg's term for the third and fourth stages of moral reasoning, in which societal values are internalized and judgments are based on a desire to gain approval or uphold law and social order.

Convergent thinking Thinking that involves "converging" on the one best answer to a problem; what IQ tests measure. Contrast with *divergent thinking.*

Cooing An early form of vocalization that involves repeating vowel-like sounds.

Cooperative learning methods Procedures that involve assigning students, usually of different races or ability levels, to work teams that are reinforced for good group performance; meant to encourage cooperation among teammates.

Correlational method A research technique that involves determining whether two or more variables are related. It cannot indicate that one thing caused another, but it can *suggest* that a causal relationship exists or allow us to predict one characteristic from our knowledge of another.

Correlation coefficient A measure, ranging from $+1.00$ to -1.00, of the extent to which two variables or attributes are systematically related to each other in either a positive or a negative way.

Counterconditioning A treatment, based on classical-conditioning principles, in which the goal is to extinguish an undesirable response to a person, object, or situation and replace it with a new and more adaptive response.

Creativity The ability to produce novel responses or works.

Critical period A defined period in the development of an organism when it is particularly sensitive to certain environmental influences; outside this period, the same influences will have far less effect.

Crossing over A process in which genetic material is exchanged between pairs of chromosomes during meiosis.

Cross-linkage theory Theory of aging focusing on the increased interlinking or coupling of molecules of collagen or other substances in the body.

Cross-modal perception The ability to use one sensory modality to identify a stimulus or pattern of stimuli that is already familiar through another modality.

Cross-sectional design A developmental research design in which different age groups are studied and compared at the same point in time.

Crowd A network of heterosexual cliques that forms during adolescence and serves to arrange mixed-sex social activities.

Crystallized intelligence Those aspects of intellectual functioning that involve making use of knowledge acquired through experience. Contrast with *fluid intelligence.*

Cued recall memory Recollecting objects, events, or experiences in response to a hint or cue. Contrast with pure *recall memory* and *recognition memory.*

Cultural-familial retardation Mental retardation that appears to be due to some combination of low genetic potential and a poor family environment rather than to a specific biological cause. Contrast with *organic retardation.*

Cultural relativity The principle that a person's behavior can be understood only within the context of his or her cultural environment.

Culture A system of meanings shared by a population of people and transmitted from one generation to the next.

Culture bias The situation that arises in testing when one cultural or subcultural group is more familiar with test items than another group and therefore has an unfair advantage.

Cumulative-deficit hypothesis The notion that impoverished environments inhibit intellectual growth and that these inhibiting effects accumulate over time.

Cystic fibrosis A serious genetic disease, caused by a pair of recessive genes, that results when a child lacks an enzyme that prevents mucus from obstructing the lungs and digestive tract.

Daily hassles Everyday annoyances or chronic life strains that can mount up and cause psychological distress or physical illness.

Damage theories of aging Theories that emphasize a number of haphazard processes that cause cells and organ systems to deteriorate. Contrast with *programmed theories of aging.*

Dark adaptation The process by which the eyes become more sensitive to light over time as they remain in the dark.

Death anxiety A complex set of concerns about death and dying.

Decentration The ability to focus on two or more dimensions of a problem at one time.

Defense mechanisms Mechanisms used by the ego to defend itself against anxiety caused by conflict between the id's impulses and social demands.

Deferred imitation The imitation of models who are no longer present.

Delirium A clouding of consciousness characterized by alternating periods of disorientation and coherence.

Dementia A progressive loss of cognitive capacities (such as memory and judgment) that affects some aging individuals and that has a variety of causes.

Denial A defense mechanism in which anxiety-provoking thoughts are kept out of, or isolated from, conscious awareness.

Dependent variable The aspect of behavior that is measured in an experiment and that is assumed to be under the control of, or "dependent" on, the *independent variable.*

Depression See *major depression.*

Development Systematic changes in the individual occurring between conception and death; such changes can be positive, negative, or neutral.

Developmental norm The age at which half of a large group of infants or children master a skill or display a behavior; the average age for achieving a milestone in development.

Developmental psychopathology A field of study concerned with the origins and course of maladaptive or psychopathological behavior.

Developmental quotient (DQ) A numerical measure of an infant's performance on a developmental test relative to the performance of other infants of the same age.

Developmental stage A distinct phase within a larger sequence of development; a period characterized by a particular set of abilities, motives, behaviors, or emotions that occur together and form a coherent pattern.

Dialectical theory The view, set forth by Klaus Riegel, that development results from the continuous dialogues between a changing person and a changing world.

Dialectical thinking A form of post-formal-operational thought that involves uncovering and resolving contradictions between opposing ideas.

Diathesis/stress model The view that psychopathology results from the interaction of a person's predisposition to psychological problems and the experience of stressful events.

Differentiation theory A perspective holding that perception involves detecting distinctive features or cues that are contained in the sensory stimulation we receive. Contrast with *enrichment theory.*

Difficult temperament Characteristic mode of response in which the individual is irregular in his or her habits and adapts slowly—often with vigorous protest—to changes in routine or new experiences. Contrast with *easy temperament* and *slow-to-warm-up temperament.*

Diffusion status Identity status characterizing individuals who are not questioning who they are and have not committed themselves to an identity.

Disengagement theory A perspective holding that successful aging involves a mutually satisfying withdrawal of the aging individual and society from each other. Contrast with *activity theory.*

Disorganized/disoriented attachment An insecure infant/caregiver bond, common among abused children, that combines features of the resistant and avoidant attachment styles and is characterized by the infant's dazed response to reunion and confusion about whether to approach or avoid the caregiver.

Display rules Socially defined rules specifying what emotions should or should not be expressed under what circumstances.

Distinctive feature Any dimension on which two or more objects differ and can be discriminated.

Divergent thinking Thinking that requires coming up with a variety of ideas or solutions to a problem when there is no one right answer. Contrast with *convergent thinking.*

DNA repair theory Theory of aging that focuses on the deterioration of the genetic material DNA and the body's diminished ability to repair this damage.

Dominant gene A relatively powerful gene that is expressed phenotypically and masks the effect of a less powerful, *recessive gene.*

Double standard The view that sexual behavior appropriate for members of one gender is inappropriate for members of the other.

Down syndrome A chromosomal abnormality in which a child inherits an extra 21st chromosome and is, as a result, mentally retarded; also called trisomy 21.

Dying trajectory The perceived shape and duration of the path that the dying individual is following from life to death.

Dynamic assessment An approach to assessing intelligence that evaluates how well individuals learn new material when an examiner provides them with competent instruction.

Dyslexia Serious difficulties in learning to read by children who have normal intellectual ability and no sensory impairments or emotional difficulties that could account for their learning problems.

Easy temperament Characteristic mode of response in which the individual is even tempered, content, and quite open and adaptable to new experiences. Contrast with *difficult temperament* and *slow-to-warm-up temperament.*

Echolalia The repetition of sounds, as when an autistic child parrots back what someone else says.

Eclectic In the context of science, an individual who recognizes that no single theory can explain everything but that each theory has something to contribute to our understanding.

Ecological approach Bronfenbrenner's view emphasizing that the developing person is embedded in a series of environmental systems (*microsystem, mesosystem, exosystem,* and *macrosystem*).

Effectance motivation A motive to display competence, master challenges, and affect the world around one.

Ego Psychoanalytic term for the rational component of the personality.

Egocentrism The tendency to view the world from one's own perspective while failing to recognize that others may have different points of view.

Elaboration A memory strategy that involves adding something to or creating meaningful links between the bits of information one is trying to retain.

Electra complex Female version of the *Oedipus complex,* in which a 4- to 6-year-old girl is said to envy her father for possessing a penis and chooses him as a sex object in the hope of sharing this valuable organ that she lacks.

Emotion-focused coping An approach to dealing with stress that involves changing one's appraisal of and emotional response to a stressful situation rather than changing the situation itself (for example, distancing oneself from a problem, convincing oneself that it is not so bad). Contrast with *problem-focused coping.*

Empathy The vicarious experiencing of another person's feelings.

Empty nest Term used to describe the family after the last child departs the household.

Encoding The first step in learning and remembering something; the process of getting information into the information-processing system, learning it, and organizing it in a form suitable for storing.

Endocrine gland Type of gland that secretes chemicals called hormones directly into the bloodstream. Endocrine glands play critical roles in stimulating growth and regulating bodily functions.

Endocrine theory Theory of aging claiming that the genes program hormonal changes that bring about death.

Engrossment Parents' fascination with their neonate; a desire to touch, hold, caress, and talk to the newborn baby.

Enrichment theory A perspective on perception holding that we must "add to" sensory stimulation by drawing on stored knowledge in order to perceive a meaningful world. Contrast with *differentiation theory.*

Environment Events or conditions outside the person that are presumed to influence and be influenced by the individual.

Equity A balance of contributions and gains in a social relationship such that neither partner feels over- or underbenefited.

Estrogen The female hormone responsible for the development of the breasts, the female sex organs, and secondary sex characteristics, as well as the beginning of menstrual cycles.

Ethnic identity A sense of personal identification with one's ethnic group and its values and cultural traditions.

Ethology A discipline and theoretical perspective that focuses on the evolved behavior of different species in their natural environments.

Euthanasia Literally, "good death"; specifically, hastening, either actively or passively, the death of someone who is suffering from an incurable illness or injury.

Executive control processes Processes that direct and monitor the selection, organization, manipulation, and interpretation of information in the information-processing system.

Exosystem In Bronfenbrenner's ecological approach, settings that are not experienced directly by the individual but that still influence his or her development (e.g., effects on a child of events at a parent's workplace).

Expansion A conversational tactic used by adults in speaking to young children in which they respond to a child's utterance with a more grammatically complete expression of the same thought.

Experiment A research strategy in which the investigator manipulates or alters some aspect of a person's environment in order to measure what effect it has on the individual's behavior or development.

Experimental control In an experiment, holding all other factors besides the independent variable constant, so that any changes in the dependent variable can be said to be caused by the manipulation of the independent variable.

Explicit memory Memory that involves consciously recollecting the past. Contrast with *implicit memory.*

Expressive role A pattern of behavior, usually instilled in females, that stresses being kind, nurturant, cooperative, and sensitive to the needs of others.

Extended family household A family unit composed of parents and children living with other kin such as grandparents, aunts and uncles, and/or cousins. Compare to *nuclear family.*

Extinction The gradual weakening and disappearance of a learned response when it is no longer reinforced.

Extraversion/introversion A personality dimension indicating the extent to which a person is outgoing and socially oriented as opposed to shy, retiring, and uncomfortable around other people.

Factor analysis A technique that identifies clusters of tasks or test items (called factors) that are highly correlated with one another and unrelated to other items.

Failure to thrive A condition observed in infants who are emotionally deprived and characterized by stunted growth, weight loss, and delays in cognitive and socioemotional development.

Faith The ways in which we make or find meaning in our lives, within or outside the context of organized religion.

Family life cycle The sequence of changes in family composition, roles, and relationships that occurs from the time people marry until they die.

Fetal alcohol syndrome (FAS) A group of symptoms commonly observed in the offspring of mothers who use alcohol heavily during pregnancy, including a small head, widely spaced eyes, and mental retardation.

Filter model of mate selection Model proposed by Udry that views partner selection as a process of narrowing the field of all possible partners through considerations of propinquity, attractiveness, social background, and so on.

Fixation In psychoanalytic theory, a defense mechanism in which development is arrested and part of the libido remains tied to an early stage of development.

Fluid intelligence Those aspects of intelligence that involve actively thinking and reasoning to solve novel problems. Contrast with *crystallized intelligence.*

Foreclosure status Identity status characterizing individuals who appear to have committed themselves to a life direction but have adopted an identity prematurely, without much thought.

Formal operations stage Piaget's fourth and final stage of cognitive development (from age 11 or 12 and beyond), when the individual begins to think more rationally and systematically about abstract concepts and hypothetical ideas.

Fraternal twins Twins who are not identical; they result when a mother releases two ova at roughly the same time and each is fertilized by a different sperm.

Free radicals Molecules that have an extra or "free" electron, are chemically unstable, and react with other molecules in the body to produce substances that damage normal cells; highlighted in one damage theory of aging.

Functional grammar An analysis of the semantic relations (meanings) that children express in their earliest sentences.

Functional play Play that involves using objects appropriately to serve the functions they normally serve.

Gender consistency The stage of gender typing in which children realize that one's sex is stable across situations or despite changes in activities or appearance.

Gender identity One's awareness that one is either a male or a female.

Gender intensification A magnification of differences between males and females during adolescence; associated with increased pressure to conform to traditional gender roles.

Gender role A pattern of behaviors and traits that defines how a female or a male should act in a particular society.

Gender-role norms Society's expectations or standards concerning what males and females should be like and how they should behave.

Gender-role stereotypes Overgeneralized and largely inaccurate beliefs about what males and females are like.

Gender schemata Organized sets of beliefs and expectations about males and females that guide information processing.

Gender segregation The formation of separate boys' and girls' peer groups during childhood.

Gender stability The stage of gender typing in which children realize that sex remains stable over time.

Gender typing The process by which children become aware of their gender and acquire the motives, values, and behaviors considered appropriate for members of their biological sex.

Gene A functional unit of heredity made up of DNA and transmitted from generation to generation.

Gene/environment correlation A systematic interrelationship between an individual's genes and his or her environment; ways in which genes influence (1) the kind of home environment provided by parents (passive gene-environment correlation), (2) social reactions to the individual (evocative gene-environment correlations), and (3) the types of experiences the individual seeks out (active gene-environment correlation).

Gene/environment interaction The phenomenon whereby the effects of one's genes depend on the kind of environment one experiences and the effects of the environment depend on one's genetic endowment.

Generativity versus stagnation The psychosocial conflict in which middle-aged adults must gain the sense that they have produced something that will outlive them and genuinely care for younger generations in order to avoid self-preoccupation; the seventh of Erikson's stages.

Genetic counseling A service designed to inform people about genetic conditions they or their unborn children are at risk of inheriting.

Genital stage Freud's fifth and final stage of psychosexual development (from puberty onward), in which the underlying aim of the sex instinct is to establish an erotic relationship with another adult and to have children.

Genotype The genetic endowment that an individual inherits. Contrast with *phenotype.*

Germinal period First phase of prenatal development; lasts for about two weeks, from conception until the developing organism becomes attached to the wall of the uterus.

Gerontology The study of aging and old age.

Gestalt psychology A school of psychology emphasizing organization, patterning, and wholeness in human experience, especially innate principles for organizing visual stimuli into coherent patterns.

Giftedness The possession of unusually high general intellectual potential or of special abilities in such areas as creativity, mathematics, or the arts.

Goodness of fit The extent to which the child's temperament and the demands of the child's social environment are compatible or mesh; according to Thomas and Chess, development is likely to be optimized when the fit is good.

Grief The emotional response to loss.

Growth The physical changes that occur from conception to maturity.

Growth hormone Hormone produced by the pituitary gland that stimulates childhood physical growth and the adolescent growth spurt.

Habituation A simple form of learning that involves *not* responding to a stimulus that is repeated over and over; learning to be bored by the familiar.

Hayflick limit The estimate that human cells can double only 50 times, plus or minus 10, and then will die.

Heritability The amount of variability in a population on some trait dimension that is attributable to genetic differences among those individuals.

Heteronomous morality Piaget's first stage of moral development, in which children view the rules of authority figures as sacred and unalterable.

Holophrase A single-word utterance by an infant that represents an entire sentence's worth of meaning.

HOME inventory A widely used instrument that allows an observer to determine just how intellectually stimulating or impoverished a home environment is.

Hospice A program that supports dying persons and their families through a philosophy of "caring" rather than "curing," either in a facility or at home.

Hot flashes Sudden experiences of warmth and sweating, often followed by a cold shiver, that occur in menopausal women.

Huntington's disease A genetic disease caused by a single, dominant gene that strikes in middle age to produce a deterioration of physical and mental abilities and premature death.

Hyperactivity See *attention-deficit hyperactivity disorder (ADHD).*

Hypothesis A theoretical prediction about what will hold true if we observe a phenomenon.

Hypothetical-deductive reasoning A form of problem solving in which one starts with general or abstract ideas and deduces or traces their specific implications; "if–then" thinking.

Id Psychoanalytic term for the inborn component of the personality that is driven by the instincts or selfish urges.

Ideational fluency The most common measure of creativity; the sheer number of different, including novel, ideas that one can generate.

Identical twins Monozygotic twins who develop from a single zygote that later divides to form two genetically identical individuals.

Identification Freud's term for the individual's tendency to emulate, or adopt the attitudes and behaviors of, another person, particularly the same-sex parent.

Identity One's self-definition or sense of who one is, where one is going, and how one fits into society.

Identity achievement status Identity status characterizing individuals who have carefully thought through identity issues and made commitments or resolved their identity issues.

Identity versus role confusion The psychosocial conflict in which adolescents must form a coherent self-definition or else remain confused about their life directions; fifth of Erikson's stages.

Idiot savant A person who has an extraordinary talent but is otherwise mentally retarded.

Imaginary audience A form of adolescent egocentrism; involves confusing your own thoughts with those of a hypothesized audience for your behavior and concluding that others share your preoccupations.

Imaginary companions Pretend playmates invented by many preschool children during the peak of symbolic play.

Immanent justice In Piaget's heteronomous stage of moral development, the belief that rule violations will invariably be punished—that justice is ever present in the world.

Immune system theory Theory of aging focusing on (1) declines in the body's ability to defend itself successfully against potentially life-threatening foreign agents such as infection, and (2) autoimmune reactions that jeopardize normal body cells.

Implicit memory Memory that occurs unintentionally and without consciousness or awareness. Contrast with *explicit memory.*

Imprinting An innate form of learning in which the young of certain species will follow and become attached to moving objects (usually their mothers) during a critical period early in life.

Impulsivity A cognitive style characterized by quick responses to problems, often based on the first hypothesis or answer that comes to mind. Contrast with *reflectivity.*

Incomplete dominance Condition in which a stronger gene fails to mask all the effects of a weaker partner gene; a phenotype results that is similar but not identical to the effect of the stronger gene.

Independent variable The aspect of the environment that a researcher deliberately changes or manipulates in an experiment in order to see what effect it has on behavior; a causal variable. Contrast with *dependent variable.*

Indirect effects Instances in which the relationship between two individuals in a family is modified by the behavior or attitudes of a third family member.

Individuative-reflective faith In Fowler's theory of the development of faith, the stage that involves reflecting on the meaning of life and developing a belief system that is uniquely one's own.

Induction A form of discipline that involves explaining why a behavior is wrong and should be changed by emphasizing its effects on other people.

Industry versus inferiority Psychosocial conflict in which school-aged children must master important cognitive and social skills or else feel incompetent; the fourth of Erikson's stages.

Infantile amnesia A lack of memory for the early years of one's life.

Infantile autism A pervasive and severe developmental disorder that begins in infancy and is characterized by such problems as an aversion to social contact, deviant communication or mutism, and repetitive, stereotyped behavior.

Infant states The different levels of consciousness, such as sleep, alert inactivity, and crying, that young infants experience during a day.

Informal curriculum The non-academic instruction that children receive in school about how to fit into their culture (how to obey rules, cooperate, conform to important social values).

Information-processing approach An approach to cognition that emphasizes the fundamental mental processes involved in attention, perception, memory, and decision making.

Initiative versus guilt Psychosocial conflict in which preschool children must learn to initiate new activities and pursue bold plans or else become self-critical; the third of Erikson's stages.

Instinct An inborn biological force assumed to motivate a particular response or class of responses.

Instrumental role A pattern of behavior, usually instilled in males, that stresses being dominant, independent, assertive, and competitive.

Integrity versus despair Psychosocial conflict in which elderly adults attempt to find a sense of meaning in their lives and to accept the inevitability of death; the eighth of Erikson's stages.

Intelligence quotient (IQ) A numerical measure of a person's performance on an intelligence test relative to the performance of other examinees of the same age; typically a score of 100 is defined as average.

Internalization The process of adopting as one's own the attributes or standards of other people.

Internal working model Cognitive representations of self and others that children construct from their interactions with caregivers and that in turn shape their expectations about relationships.

Intimacy versus isolation Psychosocial conflict in which young adults must commit themselves to a shared identity with another person or else remain aloof and unconnected to others; the sixth of Erikson's stages.

Just-community approach A type of moral education advocated by Lawrence Kohlberg in which students and teachers jointly and democratically deal with the moral issues facing them.

Juvenile delinquency Lawbreaking behavior by a minor.

Karyotype A chromosomal portrait created by staining chromosomes, photographing them under a high power microscope, and arranging them into a predetermined pattern.

Klinefelter syndrome A sex chromosome abnormality in which males inherit two or more X chromosomes (XXY or XXXY); these males fail to develop secondary sex characteristics and often show deficiencies on tests of verbal abilities.

Knowledge base One's existing information about a content area; significant for its influence on how well one can learn and remember.

Lamaze method Prepared childbirth in which parents attend classes and learn mental exercises and relaxation techniques to ease delivery.

Language A symbolic system in which a limited number of signals can be combined according to rules to produce an infinite number of messages.

Language acquisition device (LAD) A set of linguistic processing skills that nativists believe to be innate; presumably the LAD enables a child to infer the rules governing others' speech and then to use these rules to produce language.

Latency period Freud's fourth stage of psychosexual development (age 6 to puberty), in which sexual desires are repressed and all the child's available libido is channeled into socially acceptable outlets such as schoolwork or rigorous play.

Lateralization The specialization of the two hemispheres of the cerebral cortex of the brain.

Learned helplessness A crippling inability to act based on the sense that one cannot control one's outcomes in life.

Learned helplessness orientation As contrasted with *mastery orientation,* a tendency to avoid challenges and to cease trying after failure experiences based on the belief that one can do little to improve.

Learning A relatively permanent change in behavior (or behavior potential) that results from one's experiences or practice.

Libido Freud's term for the biological energy of the sex instinct.

Life expectancy The average number of years a newborn baby today can be expected to live; 75 years at present in the United States.

Life review Process in which elderly adults reflect on unresolved conflicts of the past and evaluate their lives; may contribute to a sense of integrity and readiness for death.

Life-span perspective An emerging perspective that views development as a lifelong, multidirectional process that involves gain and loss, is characterized by considerable plasticity, is shaped by its historical/cultural context, has many causes, and is best viewed from a multidisciplinary perspective.

Life structure In Levinson's theory of adult development, an overall pattern of life that reflects the person's priorities and relationships.

Living Will A document in which a person states in advance an opposition to having extraordinary medical procedures applied if he or she becomes hopelessly ill.

Locus of control A personality dimension that differentiates between people who assume they are personally responsible for their life outcomes (internal locus) and people who believe that their outcomes depend on forces outside themselves (external locus).

Logical operation A type of cognitive schema in which an internal mental activity is performed on the objects of thought; an action such as mental addition or classification.

Longitudinal design A developmental research design in which one group of subjects is studied repeatedly over a period of months or years.

Long-term memory Memory store in which information that has been examined and interpreted is retained relatively permanently.

Looking-glass self The idea that a person's self-concept is largely a reflection of the ways in which other people respond to him or her.

Love withdrawal A form of discipline that involves withholding attention, affection, or approval after a child misbehaves.

Macrosystem In Bronfenbrenner's ecological approach, the larger cultural or subcultural context of development.

Mainstreaming The educational practice of integrating handicapped students into regular classrooms rather than placing them in segregated special education classes.

Major depression An affective or mood disorder characterized by at least one episode of feeling profoundly sad and hopeless and/or losing interest in almost all activities.

Masked depression Depression, particularly in a child, that seems to manifest itself more in problems such as aggression and anxiety than in overtly depressed behavior, and that is therefore "disguised" as problems other than depression.

Mastery orientation A tendency to enjoy challenges and to persist after failing, based on a belief that one has high ability and that continued effort will pay off. Contrast with *learned helplessness orientation.*

Maturation Developmental changes that are biologically programmed by genes rather than being caused by learning, injury, illness, or some other life experience.

Maximum life span A ceiling on the number of years that any member of a species will live; 110 to 120 for humans.

Mechanistic model A world view that regards human beings as machines shaped by outside forces and analyzable into their parts. Contrast with *contextual model* and *organismic model.*

Meiosis The process in which a germ cell divides, producing gametes (sperm or ova), each containing half of the parent cell's original complement of chromosomes; in humans, the products of meiosis normally contain 23 chromosomes.

Menarche A female's first menstrual period.

Menopause The ending of a woman's menstrual periods and reproductive capacity in midlife.

Mental age (MA) A measure of intellectual development that reflects the level of age-graded problems a child is able to solve; the age level at which a child functions intellectually.

Mental retardation Significant subaverage general intellectual functioning associated with impairments in adaptive behavior and manifested during the developmental period.

Mentor A guide or advisor who provides consultation and practical aid to a younger person.

Mesosystem In Bronfenbrenner's ecological approach, interrelationships between microsystems or immediate environments (e.g., ways in which events in the family affect a child's interactions at a day-care center).

Metacognition Knowledge of the human mind and of the whole range of cognitive processes, including thinking about one's own thought processes.

Metamemory One's knowledge about memory and memory processes.

Method of loci A mnemonic technique that involves establishing a mental map of a familiar route and then creating images linking each item to be learned to a landmark along the route.

Microsystem In Bronfenbrenner's ecological approach, the immediate settings in which the person functions (e.g., the family).

"Middle generation squeeze" Expression describing the phenomenon whereby middle-aged adults sometimes experience heavy responsibilities for both the younger and older generations in the family.

Middle school A school serving grades 6 to 8 and designed to make the transition from elementary school to high school easier for early adolescents.

Midlife crisis A period of major questioning, inner struggle, and reevaluation hypothesized to occur in an adult's early 40s.

Mitosis The process in which a cell duplicates its chromosomes and then divides into two genetically identical daughter cells.

Modified extended family Term used to describe an arrangement in which nuclear families that are related by kinship maintain separate households but frequently interact with one another rather than functioning in isolation.

Moral affect The emotional component of morality, including feelings of guilt, shame, and pride in ethical conduct.

Morality The ability to distinguish right from wrong and to act on this distinction; has affective, cognitive, and behavioral components.

Morality of care Gilligan's term for what she claims is the dominant moral orientation of females, in which the individual emphasizes concern and responsibility for the welfare of other people rather than abstract rights. Contrast with *morality of justice.*

Morality of justice Gilligan's term for what she claims is the dominant moral orientation of males, in which moral dilemmas are viewed as inevitable conflicts between the rights of two or more parties that must be settled by law. Contrast with *morality of care.*

Moral reasoning The cognitive component of morality; the thinking that occurs when people decide whether various acts are right or wrong.

Moral rules Standards of conduct that focus on the basic rights and privileges of individuals. Contrast with *social-conventional rules.*

Moratorium status Identity status characterizing individuals who are currently experiencing an identity crisis or period of questioning and have not yet resolved the issues they have raised.

Morpheme One of the smallest meaningful units of language; includes words and grammatical markers such as prefixes, suffixes, and verb tense modifiers (for example, *-ed, -ing*).

Motherese Baby talk, or the short, simple, high-pitched, and often repetitive sentences that adults use when talking with young children.

Mourning Culturally prescribed ways of displaying one's reactions to a loss.

Multi-infarct dementia A progressive loss of cognitive capacities caused by a series of minor strokes.

Mutation A change in the structure or arrangement of one or more genes that produces a new phenotype.

Myelin A waxy substance that insulates neural axons and thereby speeds the transmission of neural impulses.

Naturalistic observation A research method in which the scientist observes people as they engage in common everyday activities in their natural habitats. Contrast with *contrived observation.*

Natural selection The evolutionary principle that individuals who have characteristics advantageous for survival in a particular environment are the ones who are most likely to survive and reproduce. Over many generations, this process of "survival of the fittest" will lead to changes in a species and the development of new species.

Nature/nurture issue The debate within developmental psychology over the relative importance of biological predispositions (nature) and environmental influences (nurture) as determinants of human development.

Need for achievement (n Ach) A motive to compete and strive for success whenever one's behavior can be evaluated against a standard of excellence.

Negative identity A self-definition, built around socially devalued qualities, in which one attempts to become everything one is *not* supposed to become.

Negative reinforcement In operant conditioning, the process whereby a response is strengthened or made more probable when its consequence is the removal of an unpleasant stimulus from the situation.

Neonate A newborn infant from birth to approximately 1 month of age.

Neuron The basic unit of the nervous system; a nerve cell.

Neuroticism A personality dimension indicating the extent to which a person is psychologically stable or unstable (e.g., anxious, easily upset, depressed).

Nonnormative transition A life event that is idiosyncratic to the individual or that only a minority of people experience.

Nonshared environmental influences Experiences unique to the individual that are not shared by other members of the family and that tend to make members of the same family different from one another. Contrast with *shared environmental influences.*

Normal distribution A symmetrical (bell-shaped) curve that describes the variability of characteristics within populations; most people fall at or near the average score, with relatively few high or low scores.

Normative transition Life event or transition that is normal or typical in a society and that is experienced by most people.

Nuclear family A family unit consisting of husband/father, wife/mother, and at least one child. Compare to *extended family household.*

Object permanence The understanding that objects continue to exist when they are no longer visible or otherwise detectable to the senses; fully mastered by the end of infancy.

Observational learning Learning that results from observing the behavior of other people; emphasized in Bandura's social learning theory.

Oedipus complex Freud's term for the conflict that 4- to 6-year-old boys experience when they develop an incestuous desire for their mothers and, at the same time, a jealous and hostile rivalry with their fathers.

Old-old Older adults, most but not all of whom are 75 or older, who have chronic diseases and impairments, have suffered declines in their abilities, and often depend on others for care. Contrast with *young-old.*

Olfaction The sense of smell, made possible by sensory receptors in the nasal passage that react to chemical molecules in the air.

Operant conditioning A form of learning in which freely emitted acts (operants) become either more or less probable depending on the consequences they produce.

Oral stage Freud's first stage of psychosexual development (from birth to 1 year), in which children gratify the sex instinct by stimulating the mouth, lips, teeth, and gums.

Organic retardation Mental retardation due to some identifiable biological cause associated with hereditary factors, diseases, or injuries. Contrast with *cultural-familial retardation.*

Organismic model A world view that regards human beings as whole, living organisms who are active in their own development and who change in a stagelike manner. Contrast with *contextual model* and *mechanistic model.*

Organization In Piaget's cognitive-developmental theory, one's inborn tendency to combine and integrate available schemes into more coherent and complex systems or bodies of knowledge; as a memory strategy, a technique that involves grouping or classifying stimuli into meaningful clusters.

Orthogenetic principle Werner's principle that development proceeds from global and undifferentiated states toward more differentiated and integrated patterns of response.

Osteoporosis A disease in which bone tissue is lost, leaving bones fragile and easily fractured.

Overcontrolled disorders Childhood behavior problems that involve internalizing difficulties in ways that cause anxiety, depression, and other forms of inner distress. Contrast with *undercontrolled disorders.*

Overextension The young child's tendency to use a word to refer to a wider set of objects, actions, or events than is appropriate (for example, using the word *dog* to refer to all animals).

Overregularization The overgeneralization of observed grammatical rules to irregular cases to which the rules do not apply (for example, saying *mouses* rather than *mice*).

Parental imperative The notion that the demands of parenthood cause men and women to adopt distinct roles and psychological traits.

Partial reinforcement A schedule of reinforcement in which only some occurrences of a particular act are reinforced, often on an unpredictable schedule.

Passive euthanasia Allowing a terminally ill person to die, typically by withholding extraordinary life-saving treatments. Contrast with *active euthanasia.*

Peer A social equal; one who functions at one's own level of behavioral complexity; often someone of similar age.

Perception The interpretation of sensory input.

Perinatal environment The environment surrounding birth.

Period of the embryo Second phase of prenatal development, lasting from the third through the eighth prenatal week, during which the major organs and anatomical structures begin to develop.

Period of the fetus Third phase of prenatal development, lasting from the ninth prenatal week until birth;

during this period the major organ systems begin to function and the fetus grows rapidly.

Permissiveness/restrictiveness dimension A dimension of parenting that describes the amount of autonomy, or freedom from rules and demands, that parents allow their children.

Permissive parenting A lax style of parenting in which adults make few demands on their children and rarely attempt to control their behavior.

Personal fable A form of adolescent egocentrism that involves thinking that one's self, thoughts, and feelings are unique or special.

Personality The organized combination of attributes, motives, values, and behaviors that is unique to each individual.

Phallic stage Freud's third stage of psychosexual development (from 3 to 6 years of age), in which children gratify the sex instinct by fondling their genitals and developing an incestuous desire for the parent of the other sex.

Phenotype The way in which a person's *genotype* is actually expressed in observable or measurable characteristics.

Phenylketonuria (PKU) A genetic disease in which the child is unable to metabolize phenylalanine; if left untreated, it soon causes hyperactivity and mental retardation.

Phoneme One of the basic units of sound used in a particular spoken language.

Phonological awareness The understanding that spoken words can be decomposed into some number of basic sound units, or *phonemes*; an important skill in learning to read.

Phonology The sound system of a language and the rules for combining these sounds to produce meaningful units of speech.

Physical development Growth and aging of the body, including changes in the physiological functioning of the body's organs and in motor abilities.

Pincer grasp A grasp in which the thumb is used in opposition to the fingers, enabling an infant to become more dexterous at lifting and manipulating objects.

Pituitary gland The "master gland" located at the base of the brain that regulates the other endocrine glands and produces growth hormone.

Placenta An organ, formed from the chorion and the lining of the uterus, that provides for the nourishment of the unborn child and the elimination of its metabolic wastes.

Plasticity An openness of the brain cells (or of the organism as a whole) to positive and negative environmental influence; a capacity to change in response to experience.

Play Activity that is enjoyable, that is intrinsically motivated, and that has an unrealistic quality.

Polygenic trait A characteristic that is influenced by the action of many gene pairs rather than a single pair.

Population A well-defined group that a researcher studying a *sample* of individuals is ultimately interested in drawing conclusions about.

Positive reinforcement In operant conditioning, the strengthening of a response whose consequence is a pleasant event.

Postconventional morality Kohlberg's term for the fifth and sixth stages of moral reasoning, in which moral judgments are based on an abstract understanding of democratic social contracts or on universal principles of justice that have validity apart from the views of particular authority figures.

Postpartum depression An episode of severe, clinical depression lasting for months in a woman who has just given birth; to be contrasted with milder cases of the "maternity blues," in which a new mother is tearful and moody in the first days after birth.

Posttraumatic stress disorder A psychological disorder experienced by victims of extreme trauma, such as soldiers in combat and sexually abused children; involves flashbacks to traumatizing events, nightmares, and feelings of helplessness and anxiety in the face of danger.

Power assertion A form of discipline that involves the use of superior power to administer spankings, withhold privileges, and so on.

Pragmatics Rules specifying how language is to be used appropriately in different social contexts to achieve goals.

Preconventional morality Kohlberg's term for the first two stages of moral reasoning, in which society's rules are not yet internalized and judgments are based on the punishing or rewarding consequences of an act.

Premenstrual syndrome (PMS) A number of symptoms experienced shortly before each menstrual period; includes tenderness of the breasts, bloatedness, irritability, and moodiness.

Premoral period Piaget's term for the period, up to about age 6, in which children have little concern for or awareness of rules and are not yet really moral beings.

Prenatal environment The environment surrounding an organism between conception and birth.

Preoperational stage Piaget's second stage of cognitive development, lasting from about age 2 to age 7, when children think at a symbolic level but have not yet mastered logical operations.

Primary circular reaction A pleasurable action, centered on an infant's own body, that is discovered by chance and performed over and over.

Private speech Nonsocial speech, or speech for the self; commonly used by preschoolers to guide their activities and believed by Vygotsky to be the forerunner of inner speech, or silent thinking-in-words.

Problem-focused coping An approach to dealing with stress that involves attempting to change the stress-provoking situation or eliminate the problem (for example, confronting other people, actively planning ways to solve a problem, and seeking social support). Contrast with *emotion-focused coping.*

Problem solving The use of the information-processing system to achieve a goal or arrive at a decision.

Production deficiency A failure to spontaneously generate the mediators or strategies that would improve memory, even though one has the capacity to benefit from doing so.

Progeria A genetic disorder that results in premature aging and death in children.

Programmed theories of aging Theories that emphasize the systematic genetic control of aging processes. Contrast with *damage theories of aging.*

Prosocial behavior Positive actions toward other people, such as helping and cooperating.

Proximodistal direction In development, the principle that growth proceeds from the center of the body (or the proximal region) to the extremities (or distal regions).

Psychoanalytic theory The theoretical perspective associated with

Freud and his followers; emphasizes unconscious motivations for behavior, conflicts within the personality, and stages of psychosexual development.

Psychometric approach The research tradition that spawned standardized tests of intelligence and that views intelligence as a trait or set of traits that can be measured and that varies from person to person.

Psychosocial development Changes in personal and interpersonal qualities (such as motives and emotions, personality traits, interpersonal skills and relationships) and in roles played in the family and in the larger society.

Puberty The point at which a person reaches sexual maturity and is physically capable of conceiving a child.

Punisher Any consequence of an act that suppresses that act and/or decreases the probability that it will recur.

Punishment The process by which the consequence of an act suppresses the response and decreases the probability that it will recur.

Pygmalion effect The tendency of teacher expectancies to become self-fulfilling prophecies, causing students to perform better or worse depending on the teacher's estimation of their potential.

Random assignment A technique in which research participants are placed in experimental conditions in an unbiased or random way so that the resulting groups are not systematically different from one another.

Random sample A sample that is formed by identifying all members of the larger population of interest and then selecting a portion of them, in an unbiased or random way, to participate in the study; a technique to ensure that the sample studied is representative or typical of the larger population of interest.

Recall memory Recollecting or actively retrieving objects, events, and experiences when examples or cues are not provided. Contrast with *recognition memory.*

Recessive gene A less powerful gene that is not expressed phenotypically when paired with a *dominant gene.*

Reciprocal determinism In social learning theory, the notion that the flow of influence between people and their environments is a two-way street; the environment may affect the person, but the person's characteristics and behavior will also influence the environment.

Recognition memory Identifying an object or event as one that has been experienced before, as when one must select the correct answer from several options. Contrast with *recall memory.*

Reconstituted family A new family that forms after the remarriage of a single parent, sometimes involving the blending of two families into a new one.

Reflectivity A cognitive style characterized by relatively slow and deliberate responding based on a careful evaluation of alternative hypotheses. Contrast with *impulsivity.*

Reflex An unlearned and automatic response to a stimulus.

Regression A defense mechanism that involves retreating to an earlier, less traumatic stage of development.

Rehearsal A memory strategy that involves repeating the items one is trying to retain.

Reinforcer Any consequence of an act that increases the probability that the act will recur.

Relativistic thinking A form of postformal-operational thought in which it is understood that there are multiple ways of viewing a problem and that the solutions one arrives at will depend on one's starting assumptions and perspective.

Reliability The extent to which a research measure yields consistent information from occasion to occasion or yields agreement between different observers.

REM sleep A state of active, irregular sleep associated with dreaming; named for the rapid eye movements associated with it.

Repression A type of motivated forgetting in which anxiety-provoking thoughts and conflicts are forced out of conscious awareness.

Research ethics Standards of conduct that investigators are ethically bound to honor in order to protect their research participants from physical or psychological harm.

Reserve capacity The ability of many organ systems to respond to demands for extraordinary output, as when the heart and lungs work at maximal capacity.

Resilience The self-righting or recuperative capacity that allows many children to recover from early disadvantages and get back on a normal course of development.

Resistant attachment An insecure infant/caregiver bond or other intimate relationship characterized by strong separation anxiety and a tendency to show ambivalent reactions to the attachment object upon reunion, seeking and yet resisting contact.

Retrieval The process of getting information out of long-term memory when it is needed.

Reversibility The ability to reverse or negate an action by mentally performing the opposite action.

Rites of passage Rituals that signify the passage from one stage of life to another (for example, puberty rites).

Role conflict The sense of being pulled in different directions by the competing demands of different roles or activities.

Role overload The sense of having too much to do in carrying out one's major roles or life activities.

Role reversal A switching of child and parent roles late in life such that the parent becomes the dependent one and the child becomes the caregiver.

Role-taking skills The ability to assume another person's perspective and understand his or her thoughts, feelings, and behaviors.

Rubella A disease that has little effect on a pregnant woman but may cause a number of serious birth defects (such as blindness, deafness, and mental retardation) in fetuses exposed in the first three to four months of gestation; also called German measles.

Sample The group of individuals chosen to be the subjects of a study.

Scheme (or **schema**; plural, **schemes** or **schemata**) A cognitive structure or organized pattern of action or thought that is used to deal with experiences.

Schizophrenia A serious form of mental illness characterized by disturbances in logical thinking, emotional expression, and interpersonal behavior.

Scientific method An attitude or value about the pursuit of knowledge dictating that investigators must be objective and must allow their data to decide the merits of their theorizing.

Secondary circular reaction A pleasurable response, centered on an object in an infant's environment, that is discovered by chance and performed over and over.

Secular trend A trend in industrialized society toward earlier maturation and greater body size now than in the past.

Secure attachment An infant/caregiver bond or intimate relationship in which the individual welcomes close contact, uses the attachment object as a source of comfort, and dislikes but can manage separations.

Secure base A point of safety, represented by an infant's attachment figure, that permits exploration of the environment.

Selective breeding A method of studying genetic influence that involves determining whether a trait can be bred in animals through selective mating.

Selectivity hypothesis The notion that adults, as they age, narrow their social networks to those people who are most important to them and who are most likely to meet their emotional needs.

Self-concept One's perceptions of one's unique attributes or traits.

Self-esteem One's overall evaluation of one's worth as a person based on an assessment of the qualities that make up the self-concept.

Semantics The aspect of language centering on meanings.

Sensation The process by which information is detected by the sensory receptors and transmitted to the brain; starting point in *perception.*

Sensorimotor stage Piaget's first stage of cognitive development, spanning the first two years of life, in which infants rely on their senses and motor behaviors in adapting to the world around them.

Sensory register The first memory store in information processing, in which stimuli are noticed and are very briefly available for further processing.

Sensory threshold The point at which low levels of stimulation can be detected.

Separation anxiety A wary or fretful reaction that infants display when they are separated from their attachment objects.

Sequential design A developmental research design that combines the cross-sectional approach and the longitudinal approach in a single study to compensate for the weaknesses of each.

Seriation A logical operation that allows one to mentally order a set of stimuli along a quantifiable dimension such as height or weight.

Sex-linked characteristic An attribute determined by a gene that appears on one of the two types of sex chromosomes, usually the X chromosome.

Sexual orientation One's preference for sexual partners of the same or other sex, often characterized as primarily heterosexual, homosexual, or bisexual.

Shared environmental influences Experiences that individuals living in the same home environment share and that work to make them similar to one another. Contrast with *nonshared environmental influences.*

Short-term (or **working) memory** Memory store in which limited amounts of information are temporarily held and operated upon; called working memory when its active quality is being emphasized.

Sibling rivalry A spirit of competition, jealousy, or resentment that may arise between two or more brothers or sisters.

Sickle-cell disease A genetic blood disease in which red blood cells assume an unusual sickled shape and become inefficient at distributing oxygen throughout the body.

Single gene-pair inheritance Genetic mechanism through which a characteristic is influenced by only one pair of genes, one gene from the mother and its partner from the father.

Size constancy The tendency to perceive an object as the same size despite changes in its distance from the eyes.

Slow-to-warm-up temperament Characteristic mode of response in which the individual is relatively inactive and moody and displays mild resistance to new routines and experiences but gradually adapts. Contrast with *difficult temperament* and *easy temperament.*

Social clock A personal sense of when things should be done in one's life and when one is ahead of or behind the schedule dictated by age norms.

Social cognition Thinking about the thoughts, feelings, motives, and behavior of the self and other people.

Social comparison The process of defining and evaluating oneself in comparison to other people.

Social-conventional rules Standards of conduct determined by social consensus that indicate what is appropriate within a particular social setting. Contrast with *moral rules.*

Social convoy The changing cadre of significant people who serve as sources of social support to the individual during his or her life.

Socialization The process by which individuals acquire the beliefs, values, and behaviors judged important in their society.

Social learning theory Bandura's theory that children and adults can learn novel responses merely by observing the behavior of a model, making mental notes on what they have seen, and then using these mental representations to reproduce the model's behavior at some future time; more broadly, a learning perspective that emphasizes the cognitive processing of social experiences.

Social norm A socially defined expectation about how people should behave.

Social referencing The process, evident starting in infancy, of reading the emotional reactions of other people and using this information to guide one's own behavior in ambiguous situations.

Social support The several forms of assistance from other people that bolster individuals and protect them from stress.

Socioeconomic status (SES) The position people hold in society based on such factors as income, education, occupational status, and the prestige of their neighborhoods.

Sociometric techniques Methods for determining who is well liked and popular and who is disliked or neglected in a group.

Somatic symptoms Physical or bodily signs of distress such as loss of appetite or disruption of normal sleep patterns.

Species heredity The genetic endowment that members of a particular species have in common; responsible for universal species traits and patterns of maturation.

Stability of individual differences The extent to which individuals' rankings within a group on some trait dimension remain similar or change over time, as indicated by a correlation coefficient. Contrast with *stability of mean levels.*

Stability of mean levels The extent to which the average score in a group on some trait dimension remains constant or changes as people age. Contrast with *stability of individual differences.*

Storage In information processing, the holding of information in the long-term memory store.

Storm and stress G. Stanley Hall's term for the emotional ups and downs and rapid changes that he believed characterize adolescence.

Stranger anxiety A wary or fretful reaction that infants often display when approached by an unfamiliar person.

Strange Situation test A series of mildly stressful situations to which infants are exposed in order to determine the quality of their attachments.

Stress An aversive state brought about by events that seem to strain the person's coping capacities and threaten his or her well-being.

Structure-of-intellect model Guilford's factor-analytic model of intelligence; proposes that there are as many as 180 distinct mental abilities.

Substantive complexity The extent to which a job or activity provides opportunities for using one's mind and making independent judgments.

Superego Psychoanalytic term for the component of the personality that consists of one's internalized moral standards.

Symbolic capacity The capacity to use symbols such as words, images, or actions to represent or stand for objects and experiences; representational thought.

Symbolic play Pretend play; play in which one actor, object, or action represents another.

Synapse The point at which the axon or dendrite of one neuron makes a connection with another neuron.

Synchronized routines Harmonious, dancelike interactions between infant and caregiver in which each adjusts his or her behavior in response to that of the other.

Syntax Rules specifying how words can be combined to form meaningful sentences in a language.

Syphilis A common sexually transmitted disease that may cross the placental barrier in the middle and later stages of pregnancy, causing miscarriage or serious birth defects.

Systematic thinking A form of postformal-operational thought that involves thinking abstractly about entire systems of knowledge, as in comparing and contrasting theories or forming supertheories.

Tabula rasa The idea that the mind of an infant is a "blank slate" and that all knowledge, abilities, behaviors, and motives are acquired through experience.

Tay-Sachs disease A genetic disease, common among Jewish children, that is caused by a pair of recessive genes and that results in a degeneration of the nervous system and death.

Telegraphic speech Early sentences that consist primarily of content words, omitting the less meaningful parts of speech such as articles, prepositions, pronouns, and auxiliary verbs.

Temperament A pattern of tendencies to respond in predictable ways; building blocks of personality such as activity level, sociability, and emotionality.

Teratogen Any disease, drug, or other environmental agent that can harm a developing fetus.

Terminal drop A rapid decline in intellectual abilities that people who are within a few years of dying often experience.

Tertiary circular reaction An exploratory scheme in which an infant devises a new method of acting on objects to produce interesting results.

Test norms Standards of normal performance on psychometric instruments that are based on the average scores and range of scores obtained by a large, representative sample of test takers.

Testosterone The most important of the male hormones, or androgens; essential for normal sexual development during the prenatal period and at puberty.

Thalidomide A mild tranquilizer that, taken early in pregnancy, can produce a variety of malformations of the limbs, eyes, ears, and heart.

Theory A set of concepts and propositions designed to organize, describe, and explain a set of observations.

Theory of mind The understanding that people have mental states (feelings, desires, beliefs, and intentions) and that these states underlie and help to explain their behavior.

Time of measurement effects In developmental research, the effects on findings of historical events occurring at the time the data for a study are being collected (e.g., psychological changes brought about by an economic depression rather than by aging). Contrast with *age effects* and *cohort effects.*

Total brain death An irreversible loss of functioning in the entire brain, both the higher centers of the cerebral cortex that are involved in thought and the lower centers of the brain that control basic life processes such as breathing.

Transformational grammar Rules of syntax that allow one to transform declarative statements into questions, negatives, imperatives, and other kinds of sentences.

Transitivity The ability to recognize the necessary or logical relations among elements in a serial order (for example, that, if *A* is taller than *B,* and *B* is taller than *C,* then *A* must be taller than *C*).

Triarchic theory of intelligence An information-processing theory of intelligence that emphasizes three aspects of intelligent behavior: the context in which people display intelligence, the previous experience they have with cognitive tasks, and the information-processing components they use to go about solving problems.

Trust versus mistrust Psychosocial conflict of infancy, in which infants must learn to trust others to meet their needs in order to trust themselves; the first stage in Erikson's theory.

Turner syndrome A sex chromosome abnormality in which females inherit only one X chromosome (XO); they remain small in stature, fail to develop secondary sex characteristics, and may show some mental deficiencies.

Ultrasound Method of examining physical organs by scanning them with sound waves—for example, scanning the womb and thereby producing a visual outline of the fetus to detect gross abnormalities.

Umbilical cord A soft tube containing blood vessels that connects the embryo to the placenta and serves as a source of oxygen and nutrients and as a vehicle for the elimination of wastes.

Unconditioned response (UCR) The unlearned response elicited by an unconditioned stimulus.

Unconditioned stimulus (UCS) A stimulus that elicits a particular response without any prior learning.

Unconscious motivation Freud's term for feelings, experiences, and conflicts that influence a person's thinking and behavior, even though they cannot be recalled.

Undercontrolled disorders Childhood behavior problems that involve externalizing or acting out difficulties in ways that disturb other people. Contrast with *overcontrolled disorders.*

Underextension The young child's tendency to use general words to refer to a smaller set of objects, actions, or events than is appropriate (for example, using *candy* to refer only to mints).

Universality/particularity issue The debate over the extent to which developmental changes are common to everyone (*universal,* as in most stage theories) or different from person to person (*particularistic*).

Validity The extent to which a research instrument measures what it is intended to measure rather than something else.

Visual accommodation Changes in the shape of the eye's lens to bring objects at differing distances into focus.

Visual acuity The ability to perceive detail in a visual stimulus.

Visual cliff An elevated glass platform that creates an illusion of depth; used to test the depth perception of infants.

Warmth/hostility dimension A dimension of parenting that describes the amount of affection and approval parents display toward their children.

Wisdom Exceptional insight or judgment regarding life's problems.

X chromosome The longer of the two sex chromosomes; normal females have two X chromosomes, whereas normal males have only one.

Y chromosome The shorter of the two sex chromosomes; normal males have one Y chromosome, whereas females have none.

Young-old Older adults, often but not always between 55 and 75, who are relatively healthy, active, and socially involved. Contrast with *old-old.*

Zone of proximal development Vygotsky's term for the difference between what a learner can accomplish independently and what he or she can accomplish with the guidance and encouragement of a more skilled partner.

Zygote A single cell formed at conception from the union of a sperm and an ovum.

REFERENCES

Chapter 1: Understanding Life-Span Human Development

Abramovitch, R., Freedman, J. L., Thoden, K., & Nikolich, C. (1991). Children's capacity to consent to participation in psychological research: Empirical findings. *Child Development, 62,* 1100–1109.

American Psychological Association. (1982). *Ethical principles in the conduct of research with human participants.* Washington, DC: Author.

Ariès, P. (1962). *Centuries of childhood.* New York: Knopf.

Baltes, P. B. (1983). Life-span developmental psychology: Observations on history and theory revisited. In R. M. Lerner (Ed.), *Developmental psychology: Historical and philosophical perspectives.* Hillsdale, NJ: Erlbaum.

Baltes, P. B. (1987). Theoretical propositions of life-span developmental psychology: On the dynamics between growth and decline. *Developmental Psychology, 23,* 611–626.

Baltes, P. B., Reese, H. W., & Lipsitt, L. P. (1980). Life-span developmental psychology. *Annual Review of Psychology, 31,* 65–110.

Baltes, P. B., Smith, J., & Staudinger, U. M. (1992). Wisdom and successful aging. In T. B. Sonderegger (Ed.), *Nebraska Symposium on Motivation: Vol. 39. Psychology and aging.* Lincoln: University of Nebraska Press.

Bengtson, V. L., Cuellar, J. B., & Ragan, P. K. (1977). Stratum contrasts and similarities in attitudes toward death. *Journal of Gerontology, 32,* 76–88.

Biesele, M., & Howell, N. (1981). "The old people give you life": Aging among !Kung hunter-gatherers. In P. T. Amoss & S. Harrell (Eds.), *Other ways of growing old: Anthropological perspectives.* Stanford, CA: Stanford University Press.

Birren, J. E., & Zarit, J. M. (1985). Concepts of health, behavior, and aging. In J. E. Birren & J. Livington (Eds.), *Cognition, stress, and aging.* Englewood Cliffs, NJ: Prentice-Hall.

Borstelmann, L. J. (1983). Children before psychology: Ideas about children from antiquity to the late 1800s. In W. Kessen (Vol. Ed.; P. H. Mussen, General Ed.), *Handbook of child psychology: Vol. 1. History, theory, and methods* (4th ed.). New York: Wiley.

Bronfenbrenner, U. (1979). *The ecology of human development: Experiments by nature and design.* Cambridge, MA: Harvard University Press.

Charlesworth, W. R. (1992). Darwin and developmental psychology: Past and present. *Developmental Psychology, 28,* 5–16.

Clayton, V. P., & Birren, J. E. (1980). The development of wisdom across the life span: A reexamination of an ancient topic. In P. B. Baltes & O. G. Brim, Jr. (Eds.), *Life-span development and behavior* (Vol. 3). New York: Academic Press.

Coates, B., & Hartup, W. W. (1969). Age and verbalization in observational learning. *Developmental Psychology, 1,* 556–562.

Cole, T. R. (1992). *The journey of life: A cultural history of aging in America.* Cambridge, England: Cambridge University Press.

Darwin, C. A. (1877). A biographical sketch of an infant. *Mind, 2,* 285–294.

deMause, L. (1974). The evolution of childhood. In L. deMause (Ed.), *The history of childhood.* New York: Psychohistory Press.

Despert, J. L. (1965). *The emotionally disturbed child: Then and now.* New York: Brunner/Mazel.

Dublin, L. I., & Lotka, A. J. (1936). *Length of life: A study of the life table.* New York: Ronald Press.

Elder, G. H., Jr. (1974). *Children of the Great Depression.* Chicago: University of Chicago Press.

Elder, G. H., Jr. (1980). Adolescence in historical perspective. In J. Adelson (Ed.), *Handbook of adolescent psychology.* New York: Wiley.

Elder, G. H. Jr., & Caspi, A. (1988). Economic stress in lives: Developmental perspectives. *Journal of Social Issues, 44* (4), 25–45.

Elder, G. H., Jr., Liker, J. K., & Cross, C. E. (1984). Parent-child behavior in the Great Depression: Life course and intergenerational influences. In P. B. Baltes & O. G. Brim, Jr. (Eds.), *Life-span development and behavior* (Vol. 6). Orlando, FL: Academic Press.

Elkind, D. (1992, May/June). The future of childhood: Waaah!! Why kids have a lot to cry about. *Psychology Today,* pp. 38–41, 80–81.

Friedrich, L. K., & Stein, A. H. (1973). Aggressive and prosocial television programs and the natural behavior of preschool children. *Monographs of the Society for Research in Child Development, 38*(4, Serial No. 51).

Fry, C. L. (1985). Culture, behavior, and aging in the comparative perspective. In J. E. Birren & K. W. Schaie (Eds.), *Handbook of the psychology of aging* (2nd ed.). New York: Van Nostrand Reinhold.

Guemple, L. (1983). Growing old in Inuit society. In J. Sokolovsky (Ed.), *Growing old in different societies: Cross-cultural perspectives.* Belmont, CA: Wadsworth.

Haan, N. (1981). Common dimensions of personality development: Early adolescence to middle life. In D. H. Eichorn, J. A. Clausen, N. Haan, M. P. Honzik, & P. H. Mussen (Eds.), *Present and past in middle life.* New York: Academic Press.

Hall, G. S. (1891). The contents of children's minds on entering school. *Pedagogical Seminary, 1,* 139–173.

Hall, G. S. (1904). *Adolescence* (2 vols.). New York: Appleton.

Hall, G. S. (1922). *Senescence: The last half of life.* New York: Appleton.

Hareven, T. (1986). Life-course transitions and kin assistance in old age: A cohort comparison. In D. Van Tassel & P. N. Stearns (Eds.), *Old age in a bureaucratic society: The elderly, the experts, and the state of American history.* Westport, CT: Greenwood Press.

Hart, S. N. (1991). From property to person status: Historical perspective on children's rights. *American Psychologist, 46,* 53–59.

Hartmann, D. P. (1992). Design, measurement, and analysis: Technical issues in developmental research. In M. H. Bornstein & M. E. Lamb (Eds.), *Developmental psychology: An advanced textbook.* Hillsdale, NJ: Erlbaum.

Hartung, B., & Sweeney, K. (1991). Why adult children return home. *Social Science Journal, 28,* 467–480.

Haskett, M. E., & Kistner, J. A. (1991). Social interactions and peer perceptions of young physically abused children. *Child Development, 62,* 979–990.

Huston, A. C., Donnerstein, E., Fairchild, H., Feshbach, N. D., Katz, P. A., Murray, J. P., Rubinstein, E. A., Wilcox, B. L., & Zuckerman, D. (1992). *Big world, small screen.* Lincoln: University of Nebraska Press.

Kagan, J. (1986). Presuppositions in developmental inquiry. In L. Cirillo & S. Wapner (Eds.), *Value presuppositions in theories of human development.* Hillsdale, NJ: Erlbaum.

Kean, A. W. G. (1937). The history of the criminal liability of children. *Law Quarterly Review, 3,* 364–370.

Keith, J. (1985). Age in anthropological research. In R. H. Binstock & E. Shanas (Eds.), *Handbook of aging and the social sciences* (2nd ed.). New York: Van Nostrand Reinhold.

Keniston, K. (1970). Youth: A "new" stage of life. *American Scholar, 39,* 631–654.

Kett, J. F. (1977). *Rites of passage: Adolescence in America 1790 to the present.* New York: Basic Books.

McCall, R. B. (1977). Challenges to a science of developmental psychology. *Child Development, 48,* 333–344.

Miller, S. A. (1987). *Developmental research methods.* Englewood Cliffs, NJ: Prentice-Hall.

Minois, G. (1989). *History of old age. From antiquity to the Renaissance* (S. H. Tenison, Trans.). Cambridge, England: Polity Press. (Original work published 1987.)

Morse, C. K. (1993). Does variability increase with age? An archival study of cognitive measures. *Psychology and Aging, 8,* 156–164.

National Center for Health Statistics. (1992). *Vital statistics of the United States, 1989: Vol. 2, Sec. 6: Life tables.* (DHHS Publication No. PHS 93–1104). Washington, DC: Public Health Service.

Neugarten, B. L. (1975). The future and the young-old. *Gerontologist, 15* (P. 2), 4–9.

Neugarten, B. L., & Neugarten, D. A. (1986). Changing meanings of age in the aging society. In A. Pifer & L. Bronte (Eds.), *Our aging society: Paradox and promise.* New York: Norton.

Pifer, A., & Bronte, L. (1986). Introduction: Squaring the pyramid. In A. Pifer & L. Bronte (Eds.), *Our aging society: Paradox and promise.* New York: Norton.

Postman, N. (1982). *The disappearance of childhood.* New York: Delacorte.

Ratzan, R. M. (1986). Communication and informed consent in clinical geriatrics. *International Journal of Aging and Human Development, 23,* 17–26.

Reid, T. R. (1993, January 16). 2 million accept duty of being 20. *Washington Post,* pp. A14, A24.

Remley, A. (1988, October). The great parental value shift: From obedience to independence. *Psychology Today,* pp. 56–59.

Rosenmayr, L. (1985). Changing values and positions of aging in Western culture. In J. E. Birren & K. W. Schaie (Eds.), *Handbook of the psychology of aging* (2nd ed.). New York: Van Nostrand Reinhold.

Schaie, K. W. (1965). A general model for the study of developmental problems. *Psychological Bulletin, 64,* 91–107.

Schaie, K. W. (1986). Beyond calendar definitions of age, time, and cohort: The general developmental model revisited. *Developmental Review, 6,* 252–277.

Singer, J. L., & Singer, D. G. (1981). *Television, imagination, and aggression: A study of preschoolers.* Hillsdale, NJ: Erlbaum.

Society for Research in Child Development, Committee for Ethical Conduct in Child Development Research (1990, Winter). SRCD ethical standards for research with children. *SRCD Newsletter,* pp. 5–7.

Tangney, J. P. (1988). Aspects of the family and children's television viewing content preferences. *Child Development, 59,* 1070–1079.

Thompson, R. A. (1990). Vulnerability in research: A developmental perspective on research risk. *Child Development, 61,* 1–16.

U. S. Bureau of the Census. (1992). *Statistical abstract of the United States: 1992* (112th ed.). Washington, DC: U. S. Government Printing Office.

Vobejda, B. (1991, September 15). The future deferred: Longer road from adolescence to adulthood often leads back through parents' home. *Washington Post,* pp. A1, A29.

Willems, E. P., & Alexander, J. L. (1982). The naturalistic perspective in research. In B. B. Wolman (Ed.), *Handbook of developmental psychology.* Englewood Cliffs, NJ: Prentice-Hall.

Winn, M. (1983). *Children without childhood.* New York: Pantheon Books.

You didn't reveal your pain. (1992, March 30). *Newsweek,* p. 37.

Chapter 2: Theories of Human Development

Babikian, H. M., & Goldman, A. (1971). A study of teen-age pregnancy. *American Journal of Psychiatry, 128,* 755–760.

Balassone, M. L. (1991). A social learning model of adolescent contraceptive behavior. *Journal of Youth and Adolescence, 20,* 593–616.

Baltes, P. B. (1983). Life-span developmental psychology: Observations on history and theories revisited. In R. M. Lerner (Ed.), *Developmental psychology: Historical and philosophical perspectives.* Hillsdale, NJ: Erlbaum.

Bandura, A. (1977). *Social learning theory.* Englewood Cliffs, NJ: Prentice-Hall.

Bandura, A. (1986). *Social foundations of thought and action: A social cognitive theory.* Englewood Cliffs, NJ: Prentice-Hall.

Bandura, A. (1989). Social cognitive theory. In R. Vasta (Ed.), *Annals of child development: Vol. 6. Theories of child development: Revised formulations and current issues.* Greenwich, CT: JAI Press.

Beilin, H. (1992). Piaget's enduring contribution to developmental psychology. *Developmental Psychology, 28,* 191–204.

Bem, S. L. (1989). Genital knowledge and gender constancy in preschool children. *Child Development, 60,* 649–662.

Bijou, S. W., & Baer, D. M. (1961). *Child development: Vol. 1. A systematic and empirical theory.* New York: Appleton-Century-Crofts.

Brooks-Gunn, J., & Furstenberg, F. F., Jr. (1989). Long-term implications of fertility-related behavior and family formation on adolescent mothers and their children. In K. Kreppner & R. M. Lerner (Eds.), *Family systems and life-span development.* Hillsdale, NJ: Erlbaum.

Chilman, C. S. (1986). Some psychological aspects of adolescent sexual and contraceptive behaviors in a changing American society. In J. B. Lancaster & B. A. Hamburg (Eds.), *School-age pregnancy and parenthood: Biosocial dimensions.* New York: Aldine DeGruyter.

Cobliner, W. G. (1974). Pregnancy in the single adolescent girl: The role of cognitive functions. *Journal of Youth and Adolescence, 3,* 17–29.

Dixon, R. A., & Lerner, R. M. (1992). A history of systems in developmental psychology. In M. H. Bornstein & M. E. Lamb (Eds.), *Developmental psychology: An advanced textbook.* Hillsdale, NJ: Erlbaum.

Eisen, M., Zellman, G. L., & McAlister, A. L. (1990). Evaluating the impact of a theory-based sexuality and contraceptive education program. *Family Planning Perspectives, 22,* 261–271.

Emde, R. N. (1992). Individual meaning and increasing complexity: Contributions of Sigmund Freud and Rene Spitz to developmental psychology. *Developmental Psychology, 28,* 347–359.

Erikson, E. H. (1963). *Childhood and society* (2nd ed.). New York: Norton.

Erikson, E. H. (1968). *Identity: Youth and crisis.* New York: Norton.

Erikson, E. H. (1982). *The life cycle completed: A review.* New York: Norton.

Fabes, R. A., & Strouse, J. (1984). Youth's perceptions of models of sexuality: Implications for sex education. *Journal of Sex Education and Therapy, 10,* 33–37.

Finkel, M. L., & Finkel, D. J. (1978). Male adolescent contraceptive utilization. *Adolescence, 13,* 443–451.

Fisher, S., & Greenberg, R. P. (1977). *The scientific credibility of Freud's theories and therapy.* New York: Basic Books.

Freud, S. (1933). *New introductory lectures in psychoanalysis.* New York: Norton.

Freud, S. (1961). The dissolution of the Oedipus complex. In J. Strachey (Ed.), *The standard edition of the complete psychological works* of Sigmund Freud (Vol. 19). London: Hogarth Press. (Original work published 1924.)

Freud, S. (1964). An outline of psychoanalysis. In J. Strachey (Ed.), *The standard edition of the complete psychological works of Sigmund Freud* (Vol. 23). London: Hogarth Press. (Original work published 1940.)

Furstenberg, F. F., Jr., Brooks-Gunn, J., & Morgan, S. P. (1987). *Adolescent mothers in later life.* New York: Cambridge University Press.

Furstenberg, F. F., Jr., Lincoln, R., & Menken, J. (Eds.). (1981). *Teenage sexuality, pregnancy, and childbearing.* Philadelphia: University of Pennsylvania Press.

Gesell, A., & Ilg, F. L. (in collaboration with Ames, L. B., Learned, J., & Bullis, G. E.) (1949). *Child development: An introduction to the study of human growth. I. Infant and child in the culture of today. II. The child from five to ten.* New York: Harper & Brothers.

Gewirtz, J. L., & Pelaez-Nogueras, M. (1992). Skinner, B. F.: Legacy to human infant behavior and development. *American Psychologist, 47,* 1411–1422.

Grusec, J. E. (1992). Social learning theory and developmental psychology: The legacies of Robert Sears and Albert Bandura. *Developmental Psychology, 28,* 776–786.

Hall, C. S. (1954). *A primer of Freudian psychology.* New York: New American Library.

Hamburg, B. A. (1986). Subsets of adolescent mothers: Developmental, biomedical, and psychosocial issues. In J. B. Lancaster & B. A. Hamburg (Eds.), *School-age pregnancy and parenthood: Biosocial dimensions.* New York: Aldine DeGruyter.

Hatcher, S. L. M. (1973). The adolescent experience of pregnancy and abortion: A developmental analysis. *Journal of Youth and Adolescence, 2,* 53–102.

Henshaw, S. K., Koonin, L. M., & Smith, J. C. (1991). Characteristics of U.S. women having abortions, 1987. *Family Planning Perspectives, 23,* 75–81.

Hingson, R., & Strunin, L. (1992). Monitoring adolescents' response to the AIDS epidemic: Changes in knowledge, attitudes, beliefs, and behaviors. In R. J. DiClemente (Ed.), *Adolescents and AIDS. A generation in jeopardy.* Newbury Park, CA: Sage.

Horowitz, F. D. (1992). John B. Watson's legacy: Learning and environment. *Developmental Psychology, 28,* 360–367.

Inhelder, B., & Piaget, J. (1958). *The growth of logical thinking from childhood to adolescence: An essay on the construction of formal operational structures* (A. Parsons & S. Milgram, Trans.). New York: Basic Books.

Jung, C. G. (1933). *Modern man in search of a soul* (W. S. Dell & C. F. Baynes, Trans.). New York: Harcourt, Brace.

Kagan, J. (1980). Perspectives on continuity. In O. G. Brim, Jr., & J. Kagan (Eds.), *Constancy and change in human development.* Cambridge, MA: Harvard University Press.

Kagan, J. (1991). Continuity and discontinuity in development. In S. E. Brauth, W. S. Hall, & R. J. Dooling (Eds.), *Plasticity of development* (pp. 11–26). Cambridge, MA: Bradford Books, MIT Press.

Kaplan, B. (1983). A trio of trials. In R. M. Lerner (Ed.), *Developmental psychology: Historical and philosophical perspectives.* Hillsdale, NJ: Erlbaum.

Katcher, A. (1955). The discrimination of sex differences by young children. *Journal of Genetic Psychology, 87,* 131–143.

Kirby, D. (1985). The effects of selected sexuality education programs: Toward a more realistic view. *Journal of Sex Education and Therapy, 11,* 28–37.

Kirby, D., Waszak, C., & Ziegler, J. (1991). Six school-based clinics: Their reproductive health services and impact on sexual behavior. *Family Planning Perspectives, 23,* 6–16.

Lancaster, J. B., & Hamburg, B. A. (1986). The biosocial dimensions of school-age pregnancy and parenthood: An introduction. In J. B. Lancaster & B. A. Hamburg (Eds.), *School-age pregnancy and parenthood: Biosocial dimensions.* New York: Aldine DeGruyter.

Lerner, R. M. (1986). *Concepts and theories of human development* (2nd ed.). New York: Random House.

Lerner, R. M., & Kauffman, M. B. (1985). The concept of development in contextualism. *Developmental Review, 5,* 309–333.

McGillicuddy-DeLisi, A. V. (1985). The relationship between parental beliefs and children's cognitive level. In I. E. Sigel (Ed.), *Parental belief systems: The psychological consequences for children.* Hillsdale, NJ: Erlbaum.

Miller, S. A. (1988). Parents' beliefs about children's cognitive development. *Child Development, 59,* 259–285.

Morrison, D. M. (1985). Adolescent contraceptive behavior: A review. *Psychological Bulletin, 98,* 538–568.

Mosher, W. D., & McNally, J. W. (1991). Contraceptive use at first premarital intercourse: United States, 1965–1988. *Family Planning Perspectives, 23,* 108–116.

Overton, W. F. (1984). World views and their influence on psychological theory and research: Kuhn-Lakatos-Lauden. In H. W. Reese (Ed.), *Advances in child development and behavior* (Vol. 18). New York: Academic Press.

Pepper, S. C. (1942). *World hypotheses: A study in evidence.* Berkeley: University of California Press.

Phipps-Yonas, S. (1980). Teenage pregnancy and motherhood: A review of the literature. *American Journal of Orthopsychiatry, 50,* 403–431.

Piaget, J. (1950). *The psychology of intelligence.* New York: Harcourt Brace & World.

Piaget, J. (1952). *The origins of intelligence in children.* New York: International Universities Press.

Plomin, R. (1990). *Nature and nurture: An introduction to human behavioral genetics.* Pacific Grove, CA: Brooks/Cole.

Proctor, S. E. (1986). A developmental approach to pregnancy prevention with early adolescent females. *Journal of School Health, 56,* 313–316.

Reese, H. W., & Overton, W. F. (1970). Models of development and theories of development. In L. R. Goulet & P. B. Baltes (Eds.), *Life-span developmental psychology: Research and theory.* New York: Academic Press.

Riegel, K. F. (1976). The dialectics of human development. *American Psychologist, 31,* 689–700.

Riegel, K. F. (1979). *Foundations of dialectical psychology.* New York: Academic Press.

Sameroff, A. J. (1975). Transactional models in early social relations. *Human Development, 18,* 65–79.

Sameroff, A. J. (1983). Developmental systems: Contexts and evolution. In W. Kessen (Vol. Ed.; P. H. Mussen, General Ed.), *Handbook of child psychology: Vol. 1. History, theory, and methods* (4th ed.). New York: Wiley.

Schaffer, C., & Pine, F. (1972). Pregnancy, abortion, and the developmental tasks of adolescence. *Journal of the American Academy of Child Psychiatry, 11,* 511–536.

Schlinger, H. D. (1992). Theory of behavior analysis: An application to child development. *American Psychologist, 47,* 1396–1410.

Skinner, B. F. (1953). *Science and human behavior.* New York: Macmillan.

Thompson, L., & Spanier, G. B. (1978). Influence of parents, peers, and partners on the contraceptive use of college men and women. *Journal of Marriage and the Family, 40,* 481–492.

Tyson, P., & Tyson, R. L. (1990). *Psychoanalytic theories of development: An integration.* New Haven, CT: Yale University Press.

Watson, J. B. (1913). Psychology as the behaviorist views it. *Psychological Review, 20,* 158–177.

Watson, J. B. (1925). *Behaviorism.* New York: Norton.

Weisberg, P. (1963). Social and nonsocial conditioning of infant vocalization. *Child Development, 34,* 377–388.

Chapter 3: The Genetics of Life-Span Development

Ahern, F. M., Johnson, R. C., Wilson, J. R., McClearn, G. E., & Vandenberg, S. G. (1982). Family resemblances in personality. *Behavior Genetics, 12,* 261–280.

Anastasi, A. (1958). Heredity, environment, and the question "how?" *Psychological Review, 65,* 197–208.

Archer, J. (1992). *Ethology and human development.* Hertfordshire, England: Harvester Wheatsheaf.

Ayala, F. J., & Kiger, J. A. (1984). *Modern genetics.* Menlo Park, CA: Benjamin/Cummings.

Bailey, J. M., & Pillard, R. C. (1991). A genetic study of the male sexual orientation. *Archives of General Psychiatry, 48,* 1089–1096.

Baird, P. A., Anderson, T. W., Newcombe, H. B., & Lowry, R. B. (1988). Genetic disorders in children and young adults: A population study. *American Journal of Human Genetics, 42,* 677–693.

Baker, L. A., & Daniels, D. (1990). Nonshared environmental influences and personality differences in adult twins. *Journal of Personality and Social Psychology, 58,* 103–110.

Baker, L. A., Mack, W., Moffitt, T. E., & Mednick, S. (1989). Sex differences in property crime in a Danish adoption cohort. *Behavior Genetics, 19,* 355–370.

Bateson, P. (1985). Problems and possibilities in fusing developmental and evolutionary thought. In G. Butterworth, J. Rutkowska, & M. Scaife (Eds.), *Evolution and developmental psychology.* Brighton, England: Harvester.

Begley, S. (with M. Kasindorf) (1979, December 3). Twins: Nazi and Jew. *Newsweek,* p. 139.

Begley, S. (with A. Murr, K. Springen, J. Gordon, & J. Harrison) (1987, November 23). All about twins. *Newsweek,* pp. 58–69.

Belsky, J., Steinberg, L., & Draper, P. (1991). Childhood experience, interpersonal development, and reproductive strategy: An evolutionary theory of socialization. *Child Development, 62,* 647–670.

Bishop, J. A., & Cooke, L. M. (1975). Moths, melanism and clean air. *Scientific American, 232,* 90–99.

Bishop, J. E., & Waldholz, M. (1990). *Genome: The story of the most astonishing scientific adventure of our time—The attempt to map all the genes in the human body.* New York: Simon & Schuster.

Bouchard, T. J., Jr. (1984). Twins reared together and apart: What they tell us about human diversity. In S. W. Fox (Ed.), *Individuality and determinism: Chemical and biological bases.* New York: Plenum.

Bouchard, T. J., Jr., Lykken, D. T., McGue, M., Segal, N. L., & Tellegen, A. (1990). Sources of human psychological differences: The Minnesota study of twins reared apart. *Science, 250,* 223–228.

Bouchard, T. J., Jr., & McGue, M. (1981). Family studies of intelligence: A review. *Science, 212,* 1055–1059.

Braungart, J. M., Plomin, R., DeFries, J. C., & Fulker, D. W. (1992). Genetic influence on tester-rated infant temperament as assessed by Bayley's Infant Behavior Record: Nonadoptive and adoptive siblings and twins. *Developmental Psychology, 28,* 40–47.

Brown, W. T. (1985). Genetics of aging. In M. P. Janicki & H. M. Wisniewski (Eds.), *Aging and developmental disabilities: Issues and approaches.* Baltimore: Paul H. Brookes.

Burns, G. W., & Bottino, P. J. (1989). *The science of genetics* (6th ed.). New York: Macmillan.

Buss, A. H., & Plomin, R. (1984). *Temperament: Early developing personality traits.* Hillsdale, NJ: Erlbaum.

Carey, G. (1992). Twin imitation for antisocial behavior: Implications for genetic and family environment research. *Journal of Abnormal Psychology, 101,* 18–25.

Charlesworth, W. R. (1992). Darwin and developmental psychology: Past and present. *Developmental Psychology, 28,* 5–16.

Chipuer, H. M., Rovine, M. J., & Plomin, R. (1990). LISREL modeling: Genetic and environmental influences on IQ revisited. *Intelligence, 14,* 11–29.

Daniels, D. (1986). Differential experiences of siblings in the same family as predictors of adolescent sibling personality differences. *Journal of Personality and Social Psychology, 51,* 339–346.

Daniels, D., & Plomin, R. (1985). Differential experience of siblings in the same family. *Developmental Psychology, 21,* 747–760.

Darwin, C. (1859). *The origin of species.* New York: Modern Library.

DeBusk, F. L. (1972). The Hutchinson-Gilford progeria syndrome: Report of 4 cases and review of the literature. *Journal of Pediatrics, 80,* 697–724.

Denning, C. R., Kagan, B. M., Mueller, D. H., & Neu, H. C. (1991). The CF gene—One year later. *Cystic Fibrosis Currents, 6,* 1–19.

Downey, J., Elkin, E. J., Ehrhardt, A. A., Meyer-Bahlburg, H. F., Bell, J. J., & Morishima, A. (1991). Cognitive ability and everyday functioning in women with Turner syndrome. *Journal of Learning Disabilities, 24,* 32–39.

Dunn, J., & Plomin, R. (1990). *Separate lives: Why siblings are so different.* New York: Basic Books.

Dunn, J., & Stocker, C. (1989). The significance of differences in siblings' experiences within the family. In K. Kreppner & R. M. Lerner (Eds.), *Family systems and life-span development.* Hillsdale, NJ: Erlbaum.

Floderus-Myrhed, B., Pedersen, N., & Rasmuson, I. (1980). Assessment of heritability for personality, based on a short-form of the Eysenck Personality Inventory: A study of 12,898 twin pairs. *Behavior Genetics, 10,* 153–162.

Gandelman, R. (1992). *Psychobiology of behavioral development.* New York: Oxford University Press.

Gene therapy shown effective in combating cystic fibrosis. (1993, October 15). *Washington Post,* p. A12.

Goldsmith, H. H., & Campos, J. J. (1986). Fundamental issues in the study of early temperament: The Denver twin temperament study. In M. E. Lamb, A. L. Brown, & B. Rogoff (Eds.), *Advances in developmental psychology* (Vol. 4). Hillsdale, NJ: Erlbaum.

Gottesman, I. I., & Shields, J. (1982). *Schizophrenia: The epigenetic puzzle.* Cambridge, England: Cambridge University Press.

Gottlieb, G. (1991a). Experiential canalization of behavioral development: Results. *Developmental Psychology, 27,* 35–39.

Gottlieb, G. (1991b). Experiential canalization of behavioral development: Theory. *Developmental Psychology, 27,* 4–13.

Grilo, C. M., & Pogue-Geile, M. F. (1991). The nature of environmental influences on weight and obesity: A behavior genetic analysis. *Psychological Bulletin, 110,* 520–537.

Gusella, J. F., Wexler, N. S., Conneally, P. M., Naylor, S. L., Anderson, M. A., Tanzi, R. E., Watkins, P. C., Ottina, K., Wallace, M. R., Sakaguchi, A. Y., Young, A. B., Shoulson, I., Bonilla, E., & Martin, J. B. (1983). A polymorphic DNA marker genetically linked to Huntington disease. *Nature, 306,* 234–238.

Harris, J. R., Pedersen, N. L., McClearn, G. E., Plomin, R., & Nesselroade, J. R. (1992). Age differences in genetic and environmental influences for health from the Swedish Adoption/Twin Study of Aging. *Journal of Gerontology: Psychological Sciences, 47,* P213–P220.

Hebb, D. O. (1970). A return to Jensen and his social science critics. *American Psychologist, 25,* 568.

Heston, L. L. (1970). The genetics of schizophrenia and schizoid disease. *Science, 167,* 249–256.

Himelstein, S., Graham, S., & Weiner, B. (1991). An attributional analysis of maternal beliefs about the importance of child-rearing practices. *Child Development, 62,* 301–310.

Hinde, R. A. (1983). Ethology and child development. In M. M. Haith & J. J. Campos (Vol. Eds.; P. H. Mussen, General Ed.), *Handbook of child psychology: Vol. 2. Infancy and developmental psychobiology* (4th ed.). New York: Wiley.

Hoffman, L. W. (1991). The influence of the family environment on personality: Accounting for sibling differences. *Psychological Bulletin, 110,* 187–203.

Holtzman, N. A., Kronmal, R. A., Van Doorninck, W., Azen, C., & Koch, R. (1986). Effect of age at loss of dietary control on intellectual performance and behavior of children with phenylketonuria. *New England Journal of Medicine, 314,* 593–598.

Jarvik, L. F., & Bank, L. (1983). Aging twins: Longitudinal psychometric data. In K. W. Schaie (Ed.), *Longitudinal studies of adult psychological development.* New York: Guilford Press.

Kallmann, F. J., & Jarvik, L. F. (1959). Individual differences in constitution and genetic background. In J. E. Birren (Ed.), *Handbook of aging and the individual: Psychological and biological aspects.* Chicago: University of Chicago Press.

Kallmann, F. J., & Sander, G. (1949). Twin studies on senescence. *American Journal of Psychiatry, 106,* 29–36.

Kessler, S. (1975). Psychiatric genetics. In D. A. Hamburg & K. Brodie (Eds.), *American handbook of psychiatry: Vol. 6. New psychiatric frontiers.* New York: Basic Books.

Kettlewell, H. B. D. (1959). Darwin's missing evidence. *Scientific American, 200* (3), 48–53.

Lerner, R. M., & von Eye, A. (1992). Sociobiology and human development: Arguments and evidence. *Human Development, 35,* 12–33.

Lewontin, R. C., Rose, S., & Kamin, L. J. (1984). *Not in our genes: Biology, ideology, and human nature.* New York: Pantheon Books.

Little, P. (1992). Human Genome Project: Mapping the way ahead. *Nature, 359,* 367–368.

Loehlin, J. C. (1982). Are personality traits differentially heritable? *Behavior Genetics, 12,* 417–428.

Loehlin, J. C. (1985). Fitting heredity/environment models jointly to twin and adoption data from the California Psychological Inventory. *Behavior Genetics, 15,* 199–221.

Loehlin, J. C. (1992). *Genes and environment in personality development (Individual Differences and Development Series, Vol. 2).* Newbury Park, CA: Sage.

Loehlin, J. C., & Nichols, R. C. (1976). *Heredity, environment, and personality.* Austin: University of Texas Press.

Lykken, D. T., Tellegen, A., & Iacono, W. G. (1982). EEG spectra in twins: Evidence for a neglected mechanism of genetic determination. *Physiological Psychology, 10,* 60–65.

Lytton, H. (1977). Do parents create, or respond to, differences in twins? *Developmental Psychology, 13,* 456–459.

Magenis, R. E., Overton, K. M., Chamberlin, J., Brady, T., & Lorrien, E. (1977). Parental origin of the extra chromosome in Down's syndrome. *Human Genetics, 37,* 7–16.

Mandoki, M. W., Sumner, G. S., Hoffman, R. P., & Riconda, D. L. (1991). A review of Klinefelter's syndrome in children and adolescents. *Journal of the American Academy of Child and Adolescent Psychiatry, 30,* 167–172.

Martin, N. G., Oakeshott, J. G., Gibson, J. B., Starmer, G. A., Perl, J., & Wilkers, A. V. (1985). A twin study of psychomotor and physiological responses to an acute dose of alcohol. *Behavior Genetics, 15,* 305–347.

McCall, R. B. (1981). Nature-nurture and the two realms of development: A proposed integration with respect to mental development. *Child Development, 52,* 1–12.

McCartney, K., Harris, M. J., & Bernieri, F. (1990). Growing up and growing apart: A developmental meta-analysis of twin studies. *Psychological Bulletin, 107,* 226–237.

McClearn, G., & Foch, T. T. (1985). Behavioral genetics. In J. E. Birren & K. W. Schaie (Eds.), *Handbook of the psychology of aging* (2nd ed.). New York: Van Nostrand Reinhold.

McGue, M., & Lykken, D. T. (1992). Genetic influence on risk of divorce. *Psychological Science, 3,* 368–373.

McKusick, V. A. (1989). *Mendelian inheritance in man* (9th ed.). Baltimore: Johns Hopkins University Press.

Mills, R. G., & Weiss, A. S. (1990). Does progeria provide the best model of accelerated aging in humans? *Gerontology, 36,* 85–98.

Morrison, J. R., & Stewart, M. A. (1973). The psychiatric status of the legal families of adopted hyperactive children. *Archives of General Psychiatry, 28,* 888–891.

Neale, M. C., & Martin, N. G. (1989). The effects of age, sex, and genotype on self-report drunkenness following a challenge dose of alcohol. *Behavior Genetics, 19,* 63–78.

Nightingale, E. O., & Goodman, M. (1990). *Before birth: Prenatal testing for genetic disease.* Cambridge, MA: Harvard University Press.

O'Connor, M., Foch, T., Sherry, T., & Plomin, R. (1980). A twin study of specific behavioral problems of socialization as viewed by parents. *Journal of Abnormal Child Psychology, 8,* 189–199.

Omenn, G. S. (1983). Medical genetics, genetic counseling, and behavior genetics. In J. L. Fuller & E. C. Simmel (Eds.), *Behavior genetics: Principles and applications.* Hillsdale, NJ: Erlbaum.

Pedersen, N. L., McClearn, G. E., Plomin, R., & Friberg, L. (1985). Separated fraternal twins: Resemblance for cognitive abilities. *Behavior Genetics, 15,* 407–419.

Plomin, R. (1986). *Development, genetics, and psychology.* Hillsdale, NJ: Erlbaum.

Plomin, R. (1990). *Nature and nurture: An introduction to human behavioral genetics.* Pacific Grove, CA: Brooks/Cole.

Plomin, R., & Bergeman, C. S. (1991). The nature of nurture: Genetic influence on environmental measures. *Behavioral and Brain Sciences, 14,* 373–385.

Plomin, R., Corley, R., DeFries, J. C., & Fulker, D. W. (1990). Individual differences in television viewing in early childhood: Nature as well as nurture. *Psychological Science, 1,* 371–377.

Plomin, R., & DeFries, J. C. (1985). *Origins of individual differences in infancy: The Colorado adoption project.* Orlando, FL: Academic Press.

Plomin, R., DeFries, J. C., & Loehlin, J. C. (1977). Genotype-environment interaction and correlation in the analysis of human behavior. *Psychological Bulletin, 84,* 309–322.

Plomin, R., DeFries, J. C., & McClearn, G. E. (1990). *Behavioral genetics: A primer* (2nd ed.). San Francisco: W. H. Freeman.

Plomin, R., Lichtenstein, P., Pedersen, N. L., McClearn, G. E., & Nesselroade, J. R. (1990). Genetic influences on life events during the last half of the life span. *Psychology and Aging, 5,* 25–30.

Plomin, R., Pedersen, N. L., McClearn, G. E., Nesselroade, J. R., & Bergeman, C. S. (1988). EAS temperaments during the last half of the life span: Twins reared apart and twins reared together. *Psychology and Aging, 3,* 43–50.

Pueschel, S. M., & Goldstein, A. (1983). Genetic counseling. In J. L. Matson & J. A. Mulick (Eds.), *Handbook of mental retardation.* Oxford, England: Pergamon Press.

Reznikoff, M., Domino, G., Bridges, C., & Honeyman, M. (1973). Creative abilities in identical and fraternal twins. *Behavior Genetics, 3,* 365–377.

Riese, M. L. (1990). Neonatal temperament in monozygotic and dizygotic twin pairs. *Child Development, 61,* 1230–1237.

Rose, R. J., Koskenvuo, M., Kaprio, J., Sarna, S., & Langinvainio, H. (1988). Shared genes, shared experiences, and similarity of personality: Data from 14,288 adult Finnish co-twins. *Journal of Personality and Social Psychology, 54,* 161–171.

Rowe, D. C. (1983). Biometrical genetic models of self-reported delinquent behavior: A twin study. *Behavior Genetics, 13,* 473–489.

Rowe, D. C. (1993). *The limits of family influence: Genes, experience, and behavior.* New York: Guilford Press.

Rowe, D. C., & Plomin, R. (1981). The importance of nonshared (E1) environmental influences in behavioral development. *Developmental Psychology, 17,* 517–531.

Saudino, K. J., & Eaton, W. O. (1991). Infant temperament and genetics: An objective twin study of motor activity level. *Child Development, 62,* 1167–1174.

Scarr, S. (1991). Theoretical issues in investigating intellectual plasticity. In S. E. Brauth, W. S. Hall, & R. J. Dooling (Eds.), *Plasticity of development.* Cambridge, MA: Bradford/MIT Press.

Scarr, S., & Carter-Saltzman, L. (1983). Genetics and intelligence. In J. L. Fuller & E. C. Simmel (Eds.), *Behavior genetics: Principles and applications.* Hillsdale, NJ: Erlbaum.

Scarr, S., & Kidd, K. K. (1983). Developmental behavior genetics: In M. M. Haith & J. J. Campos (Vol. Eds.; P. H. Mussen, General Ed.), *Handbook of child psychology: Vol. 2. Infancy and developmental psychobiology* (4th ed.). New York: Wiley.

Scarr, S., & McCartney, K. (1983). How people make their own environments: A theory of genotype → environment effects. *Child Development, 54,* 424–435.

Scarr, S., & Weinberg, R. A. (1976). IQ test performance of black children adopted by white families. *American Psychologist, 31,* 1159–1166.

Scarr, S., & Weinberg, R. A. (1978). The influence of family background on intellectual attainment. *American Sociological Review, 43,* 674–692.

Scarr, S., & Weinberg, R. A. (1983). The Minnesota adoption studies: Genetic differences and malleability. *Child Development, 54,* 260–267.

Seligmann, J. (1990, October 1). Curing cystic fibrosis? Genes convert sick cells. *Newsweek,* p. 64.

Stevenson, J. (1992). Evidence for a genetic etiology in hyperactivity in children. *Behavior Genetics, 22,* 337–344.

Stevenson, J., Batten, N., & Cherner, M. (1992). Fears and fearfulness in children and adolescents: A genetic analysis of twin data. *Journal of Child Psychology and Psychiatry, 33,* 977–985.

Strayer, F. F. (1980). Social ecology of the preschool peer group. In W. A. Collins (Ed.), *Minnesota Symposia on Child Psychology: Vol. 13. Development of cognition, affect, and social relations.* Hillsdale, NJ: Erlbaum.

Strigini, P., Sansone, R., Carobbi, S., & Pierluigi, M. (1990). Radiation and Down's syndrome. *Nature, 347,* 717.

Swavely, S. M., & Falek, A. (1989). Huntington's disease: The prototype for late onset terminal genetic disorders. *Loss, Grief, & Care, 3,* 111–124.

Thompson, R. F. (1975). *Introduction to physiological psychology.* New York: Harper & Row.

Truett, K. R., Eaves, L. J., Meyer, J. M., Heath, A. C., & Martin, N. G. (1992). Religion and education as mediators of attitudes: A multivariate analysis. *Behavior Genetics, 22,* 43–62.

Tryon, R. C. (1940). Genetic differences in maze learning in rats. *Yearbook of the National Society for Studies in Education, 39,* 111–119.

Wachs, T. D. (1992). *The nature of nurture* (Individual Differences and Development Series, Vol. 3). Newbury Park, CA: Sage.

Waddington, C. H. (1966). *Principles of development and differentiation.* New York: Macmillan.

Weinberg, R. A., Scarr, S., & Waldman, I. D. (1992). The Minnesota Transracial Adoption Study: A follow-up of IQ test performance at adolescence. *Intelligence, 16,* 117–135.

Wiggins, S., Whyte, P., Huggins, M., Adam, S., Theilmann, J., Bloch, M., Sheps, S. B., Schechter, M. T., & Hayden, M. R. (1992). The psychological consequences of predictive testing for Huntington's disease. *New England Journal of Medicine, 327,* 1401–1405.

Wilson, R. S. (1978). Synchronies in mental development: An epigenetic perspective. *Science, 202,* 939–948.

Wilson, R. S. (1983). The Louisville twin study: Developmental synchronies in behavior. *Child Development, 54,* 298–316.

Wilson, R. S., & Matheny, A. P., Jr. (1986). Behavior-genetics research in infant temperament: The Louisville twin study. In R. Plomin & J. Dunn (Eds.), *The study of temperament: Changes, continuities, and challenges.* Hillsdale, NJ: Erlbaum.

Chapter 4: Environment and Life-Span Development

Abel, E. L. (1981). Behavioral teratology of alcohol. *Psychological Bulletin, 90,* 564–581.

Abel, E. L. (1989). *Behavioral teratogenesis and behavioral mutogenesis: A primer in abnormal development.* New York: Plenum

Abma, J. C., & Mott, F. L. (1991). Substance use and prenatal care during pregnancy among young women. *Family Planning Perspectives, 23,* 117–122, 128.

Achenbach, T. M., Phares, V., Howell, C. T., Rauh, V. A., & Nurcombe, B. (1990). Seven-year outcome of the Vermont Intervention Program for low-birthweight infants. *Child Development, 61,* 1672–1681.

Adler, J., & Carey, J. (1982, January 11). But is it a person? *Newsweek,* p. 44.

Ainsworth, M. D. S. (1967). *Infancy in Uganda: Infant care and the growth of love.* Baltimore: Johns Hopkins University Press.

Allen, M. C., & Capute, A. J. (1986). Assessment of early auditory and visual abilities of extremely premature infants. *Developmental Medicine and Child Neurology, 28,* 458–466.

Amoss, P. T. (1981). Coast Salish elders. In P. T. Amoss & S. Harrell (Eds.), *Other ways of growing old: Anthropological perspectives.* Stanford, CA: Stanford University Press.

Amoss, P. T., & Harrell, S. (1981). Introduction: An anthropological perspective. In P. T. Amoss & S. Harrell (Eds.), *Other ways of growing old: Anthropological perspectives.* Stanford, CA: Stanford University Press.

Anderson, R. L., & Golbus, M. S. (1989). Chemical teratogens. In M. I. Evans, J. C. Fletcher, A. O. Dixler, & J. D. Shulman (Eds.), *Fetal diagnosis and therapy: Science, ethics, and the law.* Philadelphia: Lippincott.

Apgar, V., & Beck, J. (1974). *Is my baby all right?* New York: Pocket Books.

Baird, P. A., Anderson, T. W., Newcombe, H. B., & Lowry, R. B. (1988). Genetic disorders in children and young adults: A population study. *American Journal of Human Genetics, 42,* 677–693.

Baker, R. L., & Mednick, B. R. (1984). *Influences on human development: A longitudinal perspective.* Boston: Kluwer Nijhoff.

Barker, J. C. (1990). Between humans and ghosts: The decrepit elderly in a Polynesian society. In J. Sokolovsky (Ed.), *The cultural context of aging: Worldwide perspectives.* New York: Bergin and Garvey.

Barnard, K. E., & Bee, H. L. (1983). The impact of temporally patterned stimulation on the development of preterm infants. *Child Development, 54,* 1156–1167.

Barr, H. M., & Streissguth, A. P. (1991). Caffeine use during pregnancy and child outcome: A 7-year prospective study. *Neurotoxicology and Teratology, 13,* 441–448.

Barr, H. M., Streissguth, A. P., Darby, B. L., & Sampson, P. D. (1990). Prenatal exposure to alcohol, caffeine, tobacco, and aspirin: Effects on fine and gross motor performance in 4-year-old children. *Developmental Psychology, 26,* 339–348.

Barry, H., Child, I. L., & Bacon, M. K. (1959). The relation of child training to subsistence economy. *American Anthropologist, 61,* 51–63.

Beckwith, L., & Parmelee, A. H., Jr. (1986). EEG patterns of preterm infants, home environment, and later IQ. *Child Development, 57,* 777–789.

Beidelman, T. O. (1971). *The Kagura: A matrilineal people of East Africa.* New York: Holt, Rinehart & Winston.

Bellinger, D., Leviton, A., Waternaux, C., Needleman, H., & Rabinowitz, M. (1987). Longitudinal analyses of prenatal and postnatal lead exposure and early cognitive development. *New England Journal of Medicine, 316,* 1037–1043.

Belsky, J. (1985). Experimenting with the family in the newborn period. *Child Development, 56,* 407–414.

Benedict, R. (1934). *Patterns of culture.* Boston: Houghton Mifflin.

Bengtson, V. L., Dowd, J. J., Smith, D. H., & Inkeles, A. (1975). Modernization, modernity, and perceptions of aging: A cross-cultural study. *Journal of Gerontology, 30,* 688–695.

Biesele, M., & Howell, N. (1981). "The old people give you life": Aging among !Kung hunter-gatherers. In P. T. Amoss & S. Harrell (Eds.), *Other ways of growing old: Anthropological perspectives.* Stanford, CA: Stanford University Press.

Bochner, S., & David, K. H. (1968). Delay of gratification, age, and intelligence in Aboriginal culture. *International Journal of Psychology, 3,* 167–174.

Brackbill, Y. (1979). Obstetrical medication and infant behavior. In J. D. Osofsky (Ed.), *Handbook of infant development.* New York: Wiley.

Brackbill, Y., McManus, K., & Woodward, L. (1985). *Medication in maternity: Infant exposure and maternal information.* Ann Arbor: University of Michigan Press.

Brazelton, T. B. (1979). Behavioral competence of the newborn infant. *Seminars in Perinatology, 3,* 35–44.

Brislin, R. (1993). *Understanding culture's influence on behavior.* Fort Worth, TX: Harcourt Brace Jovanovich.

Bronfenbrenner, U. (1979). *The ecology of human development: Experiments by nature and design.* Cambridge, MA: Harvard University Press.

Bronfenbrenner, U. (1989). Ecological systems theory. In R. Vasta (Ed.), *Annals of child development: Vol. 6. Theories of child development: Revised formulations and current issues.* Greenwich, CT: JAI Press.

Bronfenbrenner, U., & Crouter, A. C. (1983). The evolution of environmental models in developmental research. In W. Kessen (Vol. Ed.; P. H. Mussen, General Ed.), *Handbook of child psychology: Vol. 1. History, theory, and methods* (4th ed.). New York: Wiley.

Brooks-Gunn, J., Klebanov, P. K., Liaw, F., & Spiker, D. (1993). Enhancing the development of low birthweight, premature infants: Changes in cognition and behavior over the first three years. *Child Development, 64,* 736–753.

Brown, S. S. (Ed.). (1988). *Prenatal care: Reaching mothers, reaching infants.* Washington, DC: National Academy Press.

Burton, L. M. (1990). Teenage childbearing as an alternative life-course strategy in multigeneration black families. *Human Nature, 1,* 123–143.

Byrd, M., & Breuss, T. (1992). Perceptions of sociological and psychological age norms by young, middle-aged, and elderly New Zealanders. *International Journal of Aging and Human Development, 34,* 145–163.

Callahan, E. J., & McClusky, K. A. (Eds.). (1983). *Life-span developmental psychology: Nonnormative life events.* New York: Academic Press.

Campbell, S. B., Cohn, J. F., Flanagan, C., Popper, S., & Meyers, T. (1992). Course and correlates of postpartum depression during the transition to parenthood. *Development and Psychopathology, 4,* 29–47.

Christoffel, K. K., & Salafsky, I. (1975). Fetal alcohol syndrome in dizygotic twins. *Journal of Pediatrics, 87,* 963–967.

Cohen, S. E., Parmelee, A. H., Jr., Beckwith, L., & Sigman, M. (1986). Cognitive development in preterm infants: Birth to 8 years. *Developmental and Behavioral Pediatrics, 7,* 102–110.

Corah, N. L., Anthony, E. J., Painter, P., Stern, J. A., & Thurston, D. L. (1965). The effects of perinatal anoxia after seven years. *Psychological Monographs, 79*(Whole No. 596).

Cotterell, J. L. (1986). Work and community influences on the quality of child rearing. *Child Development, 57,* 362–374.

Curtiss, S. (1977). *Genie: A psycholinguistic study of a modern-day "wild child."* New York: Academic Press.

Datan, N., & Ginsberg, L. H. (Eds.). (1975). *Life-span developmental psychology: Normative life crises.* New York: Academic Press.

Dick-Read, G. (1972). *Childbirth without fear: The original approach to natural childbirth* (Rev. ed.). New York: Harper & Row. (Original work published 1933.)

Dowd, J. J., & Bengtson, V. L. (1978). Aging in minority populations: An examination of the double jeopardy hypothesis. *Journal of Gerontology, 33,* 427–436.

Draper, P., & Keith, J. (1992). Cultural contexts of care: Family caregiving for elderly in America and Africa. *Journal of Aging Studies, 6,* 113–134.

Edelman, C. L., & Mandle, C. L. (1990). *Health promotion throughout the lifespan.* St. Louis: Mosby.

Edwards, M., & Waldorf, M. (1984). *Reclaiming birth: History and heroines of American childbirth reform.* Trumansburg, NY: Crossing Press.

Ellis, G. J., & Petersen, L. R. (1992). Socialization values and parental control techniques: A cross-cultural analysis of child-rearing. *Journal of Comparative Family Studies, 23,* 39–54.

Estop, A. M., Cieply, K., VanKirk, V., Munne, S., & Garver, K. (1991). Cytogenetic studies in human sperm. *Human Genetics, 87,* 447–451.

Evans, M. I., Fletcher, J. C., Dixler, A. O., & Shulman, J. D. (1989). *Fetal diagnosis and therapy: Science, ethics, and the law.* Philadelphia: Lippincott.

Field, T., Sandberg, D., Garcia, R., Vega-Lahr, N., Goldstein, S., & Guy, L. (1985). Pregnancy problems, postpartum depression, and early mother-infant interactions. *Developmental Psychology, 21,* 1152–1156.

Finley, G. E. (1982). Modernization and aging. In T. M. Field, A. Huston, H. C. Quay, L. Troll, & G. E. Finley (Eds.), *Review of human development.* New York: Wiley-Interscience.

Finster, M., Pedersen, H., & Morishima, H. O. (1984). Principles of fetal exposure to drugs used in obstetric anesthesia. In B. Krauer, F. Krauer, F. E. Hytten, & E. del Pozo (Eds.), *Drugs and pregnancy: Maternal drug handling—fetal drug exposure.* Orlando, FL: Academic Press.

Fried, P. A. (1982). Marihuana use by pregnant women and effects on offspring: An update. *Neurobehavioral Toxicology and Teratology, 4,* 451–454.

Fried, P. A., O'Connell, C. M., & Watkinson, B. (1992). 60- and 72-month follow-up of children prenatally exposed to marijuana, cigarettes, and alcohol: Cognitive and language assessment. *Developmental and Behavioral Pediatrics, 13,* 383–391.

Fry, C. L. (1985). Culture, behavior, and aging in the comparative perspective. In J. E. Birren & K. W. Schaie (Eds.), *Handbook of the psychology of aging* (2nd ed.). New York: Van Nostrand Reinhold.

Fullerton, J. T., & Severino, R. (1992). In-hospital care for low-risk childbirth: Comparison with results from the National Birth Center Study. *Journal of Nurse Midwifery, 37,* 331–340.

Gabiano, C., Tovo, P. A., de Martino, M., Galli, L., Giaquinto, C., Loy, A., Schoeller, M. C., Giovannini, M., Ferranti, G., Rancilio, L., Caselli, D., Segni, G., Livadiotti, S., Conte, A., Rizzi, M., Viggiano, D., Mazza, A., Ferrazzin, A., Tozzi, A. E., & Cappello, N. (1992). Mother-to-child transmission of human immunodeficiency virus type 1: Risk of infection and correlates of transmission. *Pediatrics, 90,* 369–374.

Garbarino, J. (1992). The meaning of poverty in the world of children. *American Behavioral Scientist, 35,* 220–237.

Garmezy, N. (1987). Stress, competence, and development: Continuities in the study of schizophrenic adults, children vulnerable to psychopathology, and the search for stress-resistant children. *American Journal of Orthopsychiatry, 57,* 159–174.

Glascock, A. (1990). By any other name, it is still killing: A comparison of the treatment of the elderly in America and other societies. In J. Sokolovsky (Ed.), *The cultural context of aging: Worldwide perspectives.* New York: Bergin and Garvey.

Goldberg, S. (1983). Parent-infant bonding: Another look. *Child Development, 54,* 1355–1382.

Goodstein, A., & Goldstein, S. (1986). The challenge of an aging population: The case of the People's Republic of China. *Research on Aging, 8,* 179–200.

Gorman, K. S., & Pollitt, E. (1992). Relationship between weight and body proportionality at birth, growth during the first year of life, and cognitive development at 36, 48, and 60 months. *Infant Behavior and Development, 15,* 279–296.

Gotlib, I. H., Whiffen, V. E., Wallace, P. M., & Mount, J. (1991). Prospective investigation of postpartum depression: Factors involved in onset and recovery. *Journal of Abnormal Psychology, 100,* 122–132.

Gottlieb, S. E., & Barrett, D. E. (1986). Effects of unanticipated cesarian section on mothers, infants, and their interaction in the first month of life. *Developmental and Behavioral Pediatrics, 7,* 180–185.

Greenberg, M., & Morris, N. (1974). Engrossment: The newborn's impact upon the father. *American Journal of Orthopsychiatry, 44,* 520–531.

Greenberg, M. T., & Crnic, K. A. (1988). Longitudinal predictors of developmental status and social interaction in premature and full-term infants at age two. *Child Development, 59,* 554–570.

Guemple, L. (1983). Growing old in Inuit society. In J. Sokolovsky (Ed.), *Growing old in different societies: Cross-cultural perspectives.* Belmont, CA: Wadsworth.

Gunderson, V., & Sackett, G. P. (1982). Paternal effects on reproductive outcome and developmental risk. In M. E. Lamb & A. L. Brown (Eds.), *Advances in developmental psychology* (Vol. 2). Hillsdale, NJ: Erlbaum.

Half our pregnancies are unintentional. (1983, October 10). *Newsweek,* p. 37.

Hamm, A. C. (1981). *Questions and answers about DES exposure during pregnancy and birth.* NIH Pub. No. 81–1118. Washington, DC: National Institutes of Health, U.S. Department of Health and Human Services.

Hanshaw, J. B., Dudgeon, J. A., & Marshall, W. C. (1985). *Viral diseases of the fetus and newborn* (2nd ed.). Philadelphia: Saunders.

Harmon, T. M., Hynan, M. T., & Tyre, T. E. (1990). Improved obstetric outcomes using hypnotic analgesia and skill mastery combined with childbirth education. *Journal of Consulting and Clinical Psychology, 58,* 525–530.

Harrell, S. (1981). Growing old in rural Taiwan. In P. T. Amoss & S. Harrell (Eds.), *Other ways of growing old: Anthropological perspectives.* Stanford, CA: Stanford University Press.

Hawley, T. L., & Disney, E. R. (1992). Crack's children: The consequences of maternal cocaine abuse. *Social Policy Report, Society for Research in Child Development, 6,* 1–23.

Heinonen, O. P., Slone, D., & Shapiro, S. (1977). *Birth defects and drugs in pregnancy.* Littleton, MA: Publishing Sciences Group.

Helms, J. E. (1992). Why is there no study of cultural equivalence in standardized cognitive ability testing? *American Psychologist, 47,* 1083–1101.

Hodnett, E. D., & Osborn, R. W. (1989). A randomized trial of the effects of monitrice support during labor: Mothers' views two to four weeks postpartum. *Birth, 16,* 177–183.

Jacobson, J. L., Jacobson, S. W., Fein, G. G., Schwartz, P. M., & Dowler, J. K. (1984). Prenatal exposure to an environmental toxin. *Developmental Psychology, 20,* 523–532.

Jacobson, J. L., Jacobson, S. W., & Humphrey, H. E. (1990). Effects of in utero exposure to polychlorinated biphenyls and related contaminants on cognitive functioning in young children. *Journal of Pediatrics, 116,* 38–45.

Jacobson, J. L., Jacobson, S. W., Sokol, R. J., Martier, S. S., Ager, J. W., & Kaplan-Estrin, M. G. (1993). Teratogenic effects of alcohol on infant development. *Alcoholism: Clinical and Experimental Research, 17,* 174–183.

Jacobson, S. W., Fein, G. G., Jacobson, J. L., Schwartz, P. M., & Dowler, J. K. (1984). Neonatal correlates of exposure to smoking, caffeine, and alcohol. *Infant Behavior and Development, 7,* 253–265.

Johnson, D. L., Teigen, K., & Davila, R. (1983). Anxiety and social restriction: A study of children in Mexico, Norway, and the United States. *Journal of Cross-Cultural Psychology, 14,* 439–454.

Jones, D. S., Byers, R. H., Bush, T. J., Oxtoby, M. J., & Rogers, M. F. (1992). Epidemiology of transfusion-associated acquired immunodeficiency syndrome in children in the United States, 1981 through 1989. *Pediatrics, 89,* 123–127.

Jones, K. L., Smith, D. W., Ulleland, C. N., & Streissguth, A. P. (1973). Pattern of malformation in offspring of chronic alcoholic mothers. *Lancet, 1,* 1267–1271.

Kagan, J. (1986). Rates of change in psychological processes. *Journal of Applied Developmental Psychology, 7,* 125–130.

Kagan, S., & Masden, M. C. (1972). Rivalry in Anglo-American and Mexican children of two ages. *Journal of Personality and Social Psychology, 24,* 214–220.

Kaplan, B. J. (1986). A psychobiological review of depression during pregnancy. *Psychology of Women Quarterly, 10,* 35–48.

Keith, J. (1990). Age in social and cultural context: Anthropological perspectives. In R. H. Binstock & L. K. George (Eds.), *Handbook of aging and the social sciences* (3rd ed.). San Diego: Academic Press.

Kelley-Buchanan, C. (1988). *Peace of mind during pregnancy: An A–Z guide to the substances that could affect your unborn baby.* New York: Facts on File.

Kennell, J., Klaus, M., McGrath, S., Robertson, S., & Hinkley, C. (1991). Continuous emotional support during labor in a U.S. hospital: A randomized controlled trial. *Journal of the American Medical Association, 265,* 2197–2201.

Kennell, J. H., Voos, D. K., & Klaus, M. H. (1979). Parent-infant bonding. In J. D. Osofsky (Ed.), *Handbook of infant development.* New York: Wiley.

Kessner, D. M. (1973). *Infant death: An analysis by maternal risk and health care.* Washington, DC: National Academy of Sciences.

Kiefer, C. W. (1990). The elderly in modern Japan: Elite, victims, or plural players. In J. Sokolovsky (Ed.), *The cultural context of aging: Worldwide perspectives.* New York: Bergin and Garvey.

King, M. (1990). New lung power, *Atlanta Journal,* June 19, 1990; p. D5.

Klaus, M. H., & Kennell, J. H. (1976). *Maternal-infant bonding.* St. Louis: Mosby.

Klee, L. (1986). Home away from home: The alternative birth center. *Social Science and Medicine, 23,* 9–16.

Kochanevich-Wallace, P. M., McCluskey-Fawcett, K. A., Meck, N. E., & Simons, C. J. (1988). Method of delivery and parent-newborn interaction. *Journal of Pediatric Psychology, 13,* 213–221.

Kohlberg, L. (1966). Cognitive stages and preschool education. *Human Development, 9,* 5–17.

Kohn, M. L. (1969). *Class and conformity: A study of values.* Homewood, IL: Dorsey Press.

Konner, M. (1991). *Childhood.* Boston: Little, Brown.

Konner, M. J. (1976). Maternal care, infant behavior and development among the !Kung. In R. B. Lee & I. DeVore (Eds.), *Kalahari hunter-gatherers: Studies of the !Kung San and their neighbors.* Cambridge, MA: Harvard University Press.

Konner, M. J. (1981). Evolution of human behavior development. In R. H. Munroe, R. L. Munroe, & B. B. Whiting (Eds.), *Handbook of cross-cultural human development.* New York: Garland STPM Press.

Kopp, C. B., & Kahler, S. R. (1989). Risk in infancy. *American Psychologist, 44,* 224–230.

Kopp, C. B., & Krakow, J. B. (1983). The developmentalist and the study of biological risk: A view of the past with an eye toward the future. *Child Development, 54,* 1086–1108.

Kopp, C. B., & Parmelee, A. H. (1979). Prenatal and perinatal influences on infant behavior. In J. D. Osofsky (Ed.), *Handbook of infant development.* New York: Wiley.

Kraus, M. A., & Redman, E. S. (1986). Postpartum depression: An interactional view. *Journal of Marital and Family Therapy, 12,* 63–74.

Lamaze, F. (1958). *Painless childbirth: Psychoprophylactic method.* London: Burke.

Lefkowitz, M. M. (1981). Smoking during pregnancy: Long-term effects on offspring. *Developmental Psychology, 17,* 192–194.

Leroy, M. (1988). *Miscarriage.* London: Macdonald & Co.

Lester, B. M., Corwin, M. J., Sepkoski, C., Seifer, R., Peucker, M., McLaughlin, S., & Golub, H. L. (1991). Neurobehavioral syndromes in cocaine-exposed newborn infants. *Child Development, 62,* 694–705.

LeVine, R. A. (1974). Parental goals: A cross-cultural view. *Teachers College Record, 76,* 226–239.

LeVine, R. A. (1988). Human parental care: Universal goals, cultural strategies, individual behavior. In R. A. LeVine, P. M. Miller, & M. M. West (Eds.), *Parental behavior in diverse societies: New directions for child development* (No. 40). San Francisco: Jossey-Bass.

Lin, C. (1989). High risk situations: The very low birthweight fetus. In M. I. Evans et al. (Eds.), *Fetal Diagnosis and Therapy: Science, Ethics, and the Law.* Philadelphia: Lippincott.

Localio, A. R., Lawthers, A. G., Bengtson, J. M., Herbert, L. E., Weaver, S. L., Brennan, T. A., & Landis, R. (1993). Relationship between malpractice claims and Cesarean delivery. *Journal of the American Medical Association, 269,* 366–373.

Maccoby, E. E. (1980). *Social development: Psychological growth and the parent-child relationship.* San Diego: Harcourt Brace Jovanovich.

MacDonald, K. (1986). Early experience, relative plasticity, and cognitive development. *Journal of Applied Developmental Psychology, 7,* 101–124.

MacFarlane, A. (1977). *The psychology of childbirth.* Cambridge, MA: Harvard University Press.

Makonkawkeyoon, S., Limson-Pobre, R. N., Moreira, A. L., Schauf, V., & Kaplan, G. (1993). Thalidomide inhibits the replication of human immunodeficiency virus type 1. *Proceedings of the National Academy of Sciences, 90,* 5974–5978.

Markides, K. S., Boldt, J. S., & Ray, L. A. (1986). Sources of helping and intergenerational solidarity: A three-generations study of Mexican-Americans. *Journal of Gerontology, 41,* 506–511.

Markides, K. S., Liang, J., & Jackson, J. S. (1990). Race, ethnicity, and aging: Conceptual and methodological issues. In R. H. Binstock & L. K. George (Eds.), *Handbook of aging and the social sciences* (3rd ed.). San Diego: Academic Press.

McKinney, J. P. (1984). Becoming an adult in the 1980s. In R. P. Boger, G. E. Blom, & L. E. Lezotte (Eds.), *Child nurturance: Vol. 4. Child nurturing in the 1980s.* New York: Plenum.

McLanahan, S. S., & Sorensen, A. B. (1985). Life events and psychological well-being over the life course. In G. H. Elder, Jr. (Ed.), *Life course dynamics: Trajectories and transitions, 1968–1980.* Ithaca, NY: Cornell University Press.

McLoyd, V. C. (1990). The impact of economic hardship on black families and children: Psychological distress, parenting, and socioemotional development. *Child Development, 61,* 311–346.

Miller, S. S. (1976). *Symptoms: The complete home medical encyclopedia.* New York: Thomas Y. Crowell.

Mischel, W., & Metzner, R. (1962). Preference for delayed reward as a function of age, intelligence, and length of delay interval. *Journal of Abnormal and Social Psychology, 64,* 425–431.

Mitchell, J. L. (1989). Drug abuse and AIDS in women and their affected offspring. *Journal of the National Medical Association, 81,* 841–842.

Molfese, V. J. (1989). *Perinatal risk and infant development: Assessment and prediction.* New York: Guilford Press.

Moore, K. L. (1977). *The developing human.* Philadelphia: Saunders.

Morelli, G. A., Rogoff, B., Oppenheim, D., & Goldsmith, D. (1992). Cultural variation in infants' sleeping arrangements: Questions of independence. *Developmental Psychology, 28,* 604–613.

Murray, A. D., Dolby, R. M., Nation, R. L., & Thomas, D. B. (1981). Effects of epidural anesthesia on newborns and their mothers. *Child Development, 52,* 71–82.

Murray, L. (1992). The impact of postnatal depression on infant development. *Journal of Child Psychology and Psychiatry and Allied Disciplines, 33,* 543–561.

Myers, B. J. (1982). Early intervention using Brazelton training with middle-class mothers and fathers of newborns. *Child Development, 53,* 462–471.

Myers, R. E. (1980). Reply to Drs. Kron and Brackbill. *American Journal of Obstetrics and Gynecology, 136,* 819–820.

Myers, R. E., & Myers, S. E. (1979). Use of sedative, analgesic, and anesthetic drugs during labor and delivery: Bane or boon. *American Journal of Obstetrics and Gynecology, 133,* 83–104.

Nanson, J. L., & Hiscock, M. (1990). Attention deficits in children exposed to alcohol prenatally. *Alcoholism: Clinical and Experimental Research, 14,* 656–661.

Neugarten, B. L. (1968). Adult personality: Toward a psychology of the life cycle. In B. L. Neugarten (Ed.), *Middle age and aging: A reader in social psychology.* Chicago: University of Chicago Press.

Neugarten, B. L. (1975). The future and the young-old. *Gerontologist, 15*(Part II), 4–9.

Neugarten, B. L., Moore, J. W., & Lowe, J. C. (1965). Age norms, age constraints, and adult socialization. *American Journal of Sociology, 70,* 710–717.

Neugarten, B. L., & Neugarten, D. A. (1986). Changing meanings of age in the aging society. In A. Pifer & L. Bronte (Eds.), *Our aging society: Paradox and promise.* New York: Norton.

Neuspiel, D. R., & Hamel, S. C. (1991). Cocaine and infant behavior. *Developmental and Behavioral Pediatrics, 12,* 55–64.

Nsamenang, A. B. (1992). *Human development in cultural context—A third world perspective.* Newbury Park, CA: Sage.

Ogbu, J. U. (1981). Origins of human competence: A cultural-ethological perspective. *Child Development, 52,* 413–429.

O'Hara, M. W., Schlechte, J. A., Lewis, D. A., & Varner, M. W. (1991). Controlled prospective study of postpartum mood disorders: Psychological, environmental, and hormonal variables. *Journal of Abnormal Psychology, 100,* 63–73.

Osako, M. M., & Liu, W. T. (1986). Intergenerational relations and the aged among Japanese Americans. *Research on Aging, 8,* 128–155.

Paige, K. E., & Paige, J. M. (1981). *The politics of reproductive ritual.* Berkeley: University of California Press.

Palkovitz, R. (1985). Fathers' birth attendance, early contact, and extended contact with their newborns: A critical review. *Child Development, 56,* 392–406.

Peterson, G. H., Mehl, L. E., & Liederman, P. H. (1979). The role of some birth-related variables in father attachment. *American Journal of Orthopsychiatry, 49,* 330–338.

Pines, M. (1981, September). Update: The civilizing of Genie. *Psychology Today,* pp. 28–34.

Plath, D., & Ikeda, K. (1975). After coming of age: Adult awareness of age norms. In T. R. Williams (Ed.), *Socialization and communication in primary groups.* The Hague: Mouton.

Radke-Yarrow, M., Cummings, E. M., Kuczynski, L., & Chapman, M. (1985). Patterns of attachment in two- and three-year-olds in normal families and families with parental depression. *Child Development, 56,* 884–893.

Richman, A. L., LeVine, R. A., New, R. S., Howrigan, G. A., Welles-Nystrom, B., & LeVine, S. E. (1988). Maternal behavior to infants in five cultures. In R. A. LeVine, P. M. Miller, & M. M. West (Eds.), *Parental behavior in diverse societies: New directions for child development* (No. 40). San Francisco: Jossey-Bass.

Richman, A. L., Miller, P. M., & LeVine, R. A. (1992). Cultural and educational variations in maternal responsiveness. *Developmental Psychology, 28,* 614–621.

Roberts, C. J., & Lowe, C. R. (1975). Where have all the conceptions gone? *Lancet, 1,* 498–499.

Rode, S. S., Chang, P., Fisch, R. O., & Sroufe, L. A. (1981). Attachment patterns of infants separated at birth. *Developmental Psychology, 17,* 188–191.

Rohner, R. P. (1984). Toward a conception of culture for cross-cultural psychology. *Journal of Cross-Cultural Psychology, 15,* 111–138.

Roscoe, B., & Peterson, K. L. (1989). Age-appropriate behaviors: A comparison of three generations of females. *Adolescence, 24,* 167–178.

Rothberg, A. D., & Lits, B. (1991). Psychosocial support for maternal stress during pregnancy: Effect on birth weight. *American Journal of Obstetrics and Gynecology, 165,* 403–407.

Rubin, D. H., Krasilnikoff, P. A., Leventhal, J. M., Weile, B., & Berget, A. (1986). Effect of passive smoking on birth-weight. *Lancet, 2,* 415–417.

Rutter, M. (1980). Raised lead levels and impaired cognitive/behavioral functioning: A review of the evidence. *Developmental Medicine and Child Neurology, 22*(Suppl. 42), 1–26.

Rymer, R. (1993). *Genie: An abused child's first flight from silence.* New York: HarperCollins.

Sameroff, A. J. (1983). Developmental systems: Contexts and evolution. In W. Kessen (Vol. Ed.; P. H. Mussen, General Ed.), *Handbook of child psychology: Vol. 1. History, theory, and methods* (4th ed.). New York: Wiley.

Sameroff, A. J., & Chandler, M. J. (1975). Reproductive risk and the continuum of caretaking casualty. In F. D. Horowitz, M. Hetherington, S. Scarr-Salapatek, & G. Siegel (Eds.), *Review of child development research* (Vol. 4). Chicago: University of Chicago Press.

Scafidi, F. A., Field, T. M., Schanberg, S. M., Bauer, C. R., Vega-Lahr, N., Garcia, R., Poirier, J., Nystrom, G., & Kuhn, C. M. (1986). Effects of tactile/kinesthetic stimulation on the clinical course and sleep/wake behavior of preterm neonates. *Infant Behavior and Development, 9,* 91–105.

Scafidi, F. A., Field, T. M., Schanberg, S. M., Bauer, C. R., Vega-Lahr, N., Garcia, R., Poirier, J., Nystrom, G., & Kuhn, C. M. (1990). Massage stimulates growth in preterm infants: A replication. *Infant Behavior and Development, 13,* 167–188.

Schaefer, M., Hatcher, R. P., & Barglow, P. D. (1980). Prematurity and infant stimulation: A review of research. *Child Psychiatry and Human Development, 10,* 199–212.

Schardein, J. L. (1985). *Chemically induced birth defects.* New York: Dekker.

Schlegel, A., & Barry, H. III (1991). *Adolescence: An anthropological inquiry.* New York: Free Press.

Schnoll, S. H. (1986). Pharmacologic basis of perinatal addiction. In I. J. Chasnoff (Ed.), *Drug use in pregnancy: Mother and child.* Boston: MTP Press.

Singer, L., Farkas, K., & Kliegman, R. (1992). Childhood medical and behavioral consequences of maternal cocaine use. *Journal of Pediatric Psychology, 17,* 389–406.

Sokolovsky, J. (1990). Introduction. In J. Sokolovsky (Ed.), *The cultural context of aging: Worldwide perspectives.* New York: Bergin and Garvey.

Sontag, L. W. (1941). The significance of fetal environmental differences. *American Journal of Obstetrics and Gynecology, 42,* 996–1003.

Spiker, D., Ferguson, J., & Brooks-Gunn, J. (1993). Enhancing maternal interactive behavior and child social competence in low birthweight, premature infants. *Child Development, 64,* 754–768.

Spreen, O., Tupper, D., Risser, A., Tuokko, H., & Edgell, D. (1984). *Human developmental neuropsychology.* New York: Oxford University Press.

Stein, Z. A., & Susser, M. W. (1976). Prenatal nutrition and mental competence. In J. D. Lloyd-Still (Ed.), *Malnutrition and intellectual development.* Littleton, MA: Publishing Sciences Group.

Stein, Z. A., Susser, M. W., Saenger, G., & Marolla, F. (1975). *Famine and human development: The Dutch hunger winter of 1944–1945.* New York: Oxford University Press.

Stern, M., & Hildebrandt, K. A. (1986). Prematurity stereotyping: Effects on mother-infant interaction. *Child Development, 57,* 308–315.

Stone, R. (1992). Can a father's exposure lead to illness in his children? *Science, 258,* 31.

Stott, D. H., & Latchford, S. A. (1976). Prenatal antecedents of child health, development, and behavior: An epidemiological report of incidence and association. *Journal of the American Academy of Child Psychiatry, 15,* 161–190.

Streissguth, A. P., Barr, H. M., & Sampson, P. D. (1990). Moderate prenatal alcohol exposure: Effects on child IQ and learning problems at age 7½ years. *Alcoholism: Clinical and Experimental Research, 14,* 662–669.

Streissguth, A. P., Herman, C. S., & Smith, D. W. (1978). Stability of intelligence in the fetal alcohol syndrome: A preliminary report. *Alcoholism: Clinical and Experimental Research, 2,* 165–170.

Streissguth, A. P., Randels, S. P., & Smith, D. F. (1991). A test-retest study of intelligence in patients with fetal alcohol syndrome: Implications for care. *Journal of the American Academy of Child and Adolescent, 30,* 584–587.

Strigini, P., Sansone, R., Carobbi, S., & Pierluigi, M. (1990). Radiation and Down's syndrome. *Nature, 347,* 717.

Super, C. M., & Harkness, S. (1981). Figure, ground, and Gestalt: The cultural context of the active individual. In R. M. Lerner & N. A. Busch-Rossnagel (Eds.), *Individuals as producers of their development: A life-span perspective.* New York: Academic Press.

Super, C. M., Herrera, M. G., & Mora, J. O. (1990). Long-term effects of food supplementation and psychosocial intervention on the physical growth of Colombian infants at risk of malnutrition. *Child Development, 61,* 29–49.

Taffel, S. M., Placek, P. J., Moien, M., & Kosary, C. L. (1991). 1989 U.S. cesarean section rate steadies—VBAC rate rises to nearly one in five. *Birth, 18,* 73–77.

Tanner, J. M. (1990). *Foetus into man: Physical growth from conception to maturity* (rev. & enl. ed.). Cambridge, MA: Harvard University Press.

Task Force on Pediatric AIDS (1989). Pediatric AIDS and human immunodeficiency virus infection. *American Psychologist, 44,* 258–264.

Taylor, R. J., & Chatters, L. M. (1991). Extended family networks of older black adults. *Journal of Gerontology: Social Sciences, 46,* S210–S217.

Tronick, E. Z., Morelli, G. A., & Ivey, P. K. (1992). The Efe forager infant and toddler's pattern of social relationships: Multiple and simultaneous. *Developmental Psychology, 28,* 568–577.

U.S. Department of Health, Education and Welfare. (1979). *Smoking and health: A report to the Surgeon General.* DHEW Pub. No. PHS 79–50066. Washington, DC: U.S. Government Printing Office.

van Gennep, A. (1960). *The rites of passage* (M. B. Vizedom & G. L. Caffee, Trans.). Chicago: University of Chicago Press. (Original work published 1908.)

Vaughan, B. E., Bradley, C. F., Joffe, L. S., Seifer, R., & Barglow, P. (1987). Maternal characteristics measured prenatally are predictive of ratings of temperamental "difficulty" on the Carey Infant Temperament Questionnaire. *Developmental Psychology, 23,* 152–161.

Vaughn, V. C., McKay, J. R., & Behrman, R. E. (1984). *Nelson textbook of pediatrics* (12th ed.). Philadelphia: Saunders.

Vorhees, C. V., & Mollnow, E. (1987). Behavioral teratogenesis: Long-term influences on behavior from early exposure to environmental agents. In J. D. Osofsky (Ed.), *Handbook of infant development* (2nd ed.). New York: Wiley.

Weibel-Orlando, J. (1990). Grandparenting styles: Native American perspectives. In J. Sokolovsky (Ed.), *The cultural context of aging: Worldwide perspectives.* New York: Bergin and Garvey.

Werner, E. E. (1989). High-risk children in young adulthood: A longitudinal study from birth to 32 years. *American Journal of Orthopsychiatry, 59,* 72–81.

Werner, E. E., & Smith, R. S. (1982). *Vulnerable but invincible: A longitudinal study of resilient children and youth.* New York: McGraw-Hill.

Werner, E. E., & Smith, R. S. (1992). *Overcoming the odds: High-risk children from birth to adulthood.* Ithaca, NY: Cornell University Press.

Whiffen, V. E. (1992). Is postpartum depression a distinct diagnosis? *Clinical Psychology Review, 12,* 485–508.

Whiting, B. B., & Edwards, C. P. (1988). *Children of different worlds: The formation of social behavior.* Cambridge, MA: Harvard University Press.

Whiting, B. B., & Whiting, J. W. M. (1975). *Children of six cultures.* Cambridge, MA: Harvard University Press.

Wideman, M. V., & Singer, J. E. (1984). The role of psychological mechanisms in preparation for childbirth. *American Psychologist, 39,* 1357–1371.

Widmayer, S., & Field, T. (1980). Effects of Brazelton demonstrations on early interactions of preterm infants and their teenage mothers. *Infant Behavior and Development, 3,* 79–89.

Wilson, M. N. (1989). Child development in the context of the Black extended family. *American Psychologist, 44,* 380–385.

Wilson, R. S. (1985). Risk and resilience in early mental development. *Developmental Psychology, 21,* 795–805.

Winick, M. (1976). *Malnutrition and brain development.* New York: Oxford University Press.

Worobey, J., & Brazelton, T. B. (1986). Experimenting with the family in the newborn period: A commentary. *Child Development, 57,* 1298–1300.

Zepelin, H., Sills, R. A., & Heath, M. W. (1986–1987). Is age becoming irrelevant? An exploratory study of perceived age norms. *International Journal of Aging and Human Development, 24,* 241–256.

Zeskind, P. S., & Ramey, C. T. (1981). Preventing intellectual and interactional sequelae of fetal malnutrition: A longitudinal, transactional, and synergistic approach to development. *Child Development, 52,* 213–218.

Zuckerman, B., Frank, D. A., Hingson, R., Amaro, H., Levenson, S. M., Kayne, H., Parker, S., Vinci, R., Aboagye, K., Fried, L., Cabral, H., Timperi, R., & Bauchner, H. (1989). Effects of maternal marijuana and cocaine use on fetal growth. *New England Journal of Medicine, 320,* 762–768.

Chapter 5: The Physical Self

Adams, P., Davies, G. T., & Sweetnam, P. (1970). Osteoporosis and the effects of aging on bone mass in elderly men and women. *Quarterly Journal of Medicine, 39,* 601–615.

Ainscough, C. E. (1990). Premenstrual emotional changes: A prospective study of symptomatology in normal women. *Journal of Psychosomatic Research, 34,* 35–45.

Andres, R., & Tobin, J. D. (1977). Endocrine systems. In C. E. Finch & L. Hayflick (Eds.), *Handbook of the biology of aging.* New York: Van Nostrand Reinhold.

Archer, J. (1991). The influence of testosterone on human aggression. *British Journal of Psychology, 82,* 1–28.

Asso, D. (1983). *The real menstrual cycle.* Chichester, England: Wiley.

Ausman, L. M., & Russell, R. M. (1990). Nutrition and aging. In E. L. Schneider & J. W. Rowe (Eds.), *Handbook of the biology of aging* (3rd ed.). San Diego: Academic Press.

Bafitis, H., & Sargent, F. II. (1977). Human physiological adaptability through the life sequence. *Journal of Gerontology, 32,* 402–410.

Barry, D. (1990). *Dave Barry turns 40.* New York: Crown.

Benes, F. M. (1989). Myelination of cortical-hippocampal relays during late adolescence. *Schizophrenia Bulletin, 15,* 585–593.

Bennett, E. L., Diamond, M. C., Krech, D., & Rosenzweig, M. R. (1964). Chemical and anatomical plasticity of the brain. *Science, 146,* 610–619.

Berg, W. K., Adkinson, C. D., & Strock, B. D. (1973). Duration and frequency of periods of alertness in neonates. *Developmental Psychology, 9,* 434.

Berg, W. K., & Berg, K. M. (1979). Psychological development in infancy: State, sensory function, and attention. In J. D. Osofsky (Ed.), *Handbook of infant development.* New York: Wiley.

Berger, B., & Hecht, L. M. (1989). Exercise, aging, and psychological well-being: The mind-body question. In A. C. Ostrow (Ed.), *Aging and motor behavior.* Indianapolis: Benchmark Press.

Berscheid, E., Walster, E., & Bohrnstedt, G. (1973, June). The happy American body: A survey report. *Psychology Today,* pp. 119–131.

Birren, J. E., Butler, R. N., Greenhouse, S. W., Sokoloff, L., & Yarrow, M. R. (Eds.). (1963). *Human aging: A biological and behavioral study.* Washington, DC: U.S. Government Printing Office.

Birren, J. E., & Fisher, L. M. (1992). Aging and slowing of behavior: Consequences for cognition and survival. In T. B. Sonderegger (Ed.), *Nebraska Symposium on Motivation: Vol. 39. Psychology and aging.* Lincoln: University of Nebraska Press.

Black, J. E., Isaacs, K. R., & Greenough, W. T. (1991). Usual vs. successful aging: Some notes on experiential factors. *Neurobiology of Aging, 12,* 325–328.

Black, J. E., Sirevaag, A. M., Wallace, C. S., Savin, M. H., & Greenough, W. T. (1989). Effects of complex experience on somatic growth and organ development in rats. *Developmental Psychobiology, 22,* 727–752.

Boismier, J. D. (1977) Visual stimulation and the wake-sleep behavior in human neonates. *Developmental Psychobiology, 10,* 219–227.

Bondareff, W. (1985). The neural basis of aging. In J. E. Birren & K. W. Schaie (Eds.), *Handbook of the psychology of aging* (2nd ed.). New York: Van Nostrand Reinhold.

Bosman, E. A. (1993). Age-related differences in the motoric aspects of transcription typing skill. *Psychology and Aging, 8,* 87–102.

Bower, T. G. R. (1982). *Development in infancy* (2nd ed.). San Francisco: W. H. Freeman.

Brierley, J. (1976). *The growing brain.* London: NFER Publishing.

Brooks-Gunn, J., & Warren, M. P. (1988). The psychological significance of secondary sexual characteristics in nine- to eleven-year-old girls. *Child Development, 59,* 1061–1069.

Brown, J. L. (1964). States in newborn infants. *Merrill-Palmer Quarterly, 10,* 313–327.

Brown, M. A., & Woods, N. F. (1986). Sex role orientation, sex typing, occupational traditionalism, and perimenstrual symptoms. In V. L. Olesen & N. F. Woods (Eds.), *Culture, society, and menstruation.* Washington, DC: Hemisphere.

Buchanan, C. M., Eccles, J. S., & Becker, J. B. (1992). Are adolescents the victims of raging hormones: Evidence for activational effects of hormones on moods and behavior at adolescence. *Psychological Bulletin, 111,* 62–107.

Buell, S. J., & Coleman, P. D. (1979). Dendritic growth in the aged human brain and failure of growth in senile dementia. *Science, 206,* 854–856.

Campos, J. J., Bertenthal, B. I., & Kermoian, R. (1992). Early experience and emotional development: The emergence of wariness of heights. *Psychological Science, 3,* 61–64.

Case, R. (1992). The role of the frontal lobes in the regulation of cognitive development. *Brain and Cognition, 20,* 51–73.

Cherry, K. E., & Morton, M. R. (1989). Drug sensitivity in older adults: The role of physiologic and pharmacokinetic factors. *International Journal of Aging and Human Development, 28,* 159–174.

Christofalo, V. J. (1988). An overview of the theories of biological aging. In J. E. Birren & V. L. Bengtson (Eds.), *Emergent theories of aging.* New York: Springer.

Clark, D. O., & Maddox, G. L. (1992). Racial and social correlates of age-related changes in functioning. *Journal of Gerontology: Social Sciences, 47,* S222–S232.

Coleman, P. D., & Flood, D. G. (1987). Neuron numbers and dendritic extent in normal aging and Alzheimer's disease. *Neurobiology of Aging, 8,* 521–545.

Connor, J. R., Jr., Diamond, M. C., & Johnson, R. E. (1980). Aging and environmental influences on two types of dendritic spines in the rat occipital cortex. *Experimental Neurology, 70,* 371–379.

Corbin, C. (1973). *A textbook of motor development.* Dubuque, IA: William C. Brown.

Coren, S., Porac, C., & Duncan, P. (1981). Lateral preference behaviors in preschool children and young adults. *Child Development, 52,* 443–450.

Cowan, W. M. (1979). The development of the brain. *Scientific American, 241,* 112–133.

Cunningham, D. A., Rechnitzer, P. A., Pearce, M. E., & Donner, A. P. (1982). Determinants of self-selected walking pace across ages 19 to 66. *Journal of Gerontology, 37,* 560–564.

Davidson, J. M., Chen, J. J., Crapo, L., Gray, G. D., Greenleaf, W. J., & Catania, J. A. (1983). Hormonal changes and sexual function in aging men. *Journal of Clinical Endocrinology and Metabolism, 57,* 71–77.

Davis, M. A., Murphy, S. P., & Neuhaus, J. M. (1988). Living arrangements and eating behavior of older adults in the United States. *Journal of Gerontology: Social Sciences, 43,* S96–S98.

Dennis, W. (1960). Causes of retardation among institutional children: Iran. *Journal of Genetic Psychology, 96,* 47–59.

Dennis, W., & Dennis, M. G. (1940). The effect of cradling practices upon the onset of walking in Hopi children. *Journal of Genetic Psychology, 56,* 77–86.

Dubas, J. S., Graber, J. A., & Petersen, A. C. (1991). The effects of pubertal development on achievement during adolescence. *American Journal of Education, 99,* 444–460.

Duncan, P. D., Ritter, P. L., Dornbusch, S. M., Gross, R. T., & Carlsmith, J. M. (1985). The effects of pubertal timing on body image, school behavior, and deviance. *Journal of Youth and Adolescence, 14,* 227–235.

Dustman, R. E., Emmerson, R. Y., Steinhaus, L. A., Shearer, D. E., & Dustman, T. J. (1992). The effects of videogame playing on neuropsychological performance of elderly individuals. *Journal of Gerontology: Psychological Sciences, 47,* 168–171.

Dustman, R. E., Ruhling, R. O., Russell, E. M., Shearer, D. E., Bonekat, H. W., Shigeoka, J. W., Wood, J. S., & Bradford, D. C. (1989). Neurobiology of aging. In A. C. Ostrow (Ed.), *Aging and motor behavior.* Indianapolis: Benchmark Press.

Dyer, K. F. (1977). The trend of the male-female performance differential in athletics, swimming, and cycling, 1948–1976. *Journal of Biosocial Science, 9,* 325–338.

Eichorn, D. H. (1979). Physical development: Current foci of research. In J. D. Osofsky (Ed.), *Handbook of infant development.* New York: Wiley.

Englander-Golden, P., Sonleitner, F. J., Whitmore, M. R., & Corbley, G. J. M. (1986). Social and menstrual cycles: Methodological and substantive findings. In V. L. Olesen & N. F. Woods (Eds.), *Culture, society, and menstruation.* Washington, DC: Hemisphere.

Faust, M. S. (1960). Developmental maturity as a determinant of prestige in adolescent girls. *Child Development, 31,* 173–184.

Faust, M. S. (1977). Somatic development of adolescent girls. *Monographs of the Society for Research in Child Development, 42* (Whole No. 169).

Fentress, J. C., & McLeod, P. J. (1986). Motor patterns in development. In E. M. Blass (Ed.), *Handbook of behavioral neurobiology: Vol. 8. Developmental psychobiology and developmental neurobiology.* New York: Plenum.

Fischer, K. W., Kenny, S. L., & Pipp, S. L. (1990). How cognitive processes and environmental conditions organize discontinuities in the development of abstractions. In C. N. Alexander & E. J. Langer (Eds.), *Higher stages of human development: Perspectives on adult growth.* New York: Oxford University Press.

Flint, M. (1982). Male and female menopause: A cultural put-on. In A. M. Voda, M. Dinnerstein, & S. R. O'Donnell (Eds.), *Changing perspectives on menopause.* Austin: University of Texas Press.

Flood, D. G., Buell, S. J., Horwitz, G. J., & Coleman, P. D. (1987). Dendritic extent in human dentate gyrus granule cells in normal aging and senile dementia. *Brain Research, 402,* 205–216.

Flood, D. G., & Coleman, P. D. (1990). Hippocampal plasticity in normal aging and decreased plasticity in Alzheimer's disease. *Progress in Brain Research, 83,* 435–443.

Frankenburg, W. K., & Dodds, J. B. (1967). The Denver Development Screening Test. *Journal of Pediatrics, 71,* 181–191.

Fries, J. F., & Crapo, L. M. (1981). *Vitality and aging: Implications of the rectangular curve.* San Francisco: W. H. Freeman.

Frisch, R. E. (1983). Fatness, puberty, and fertility: The effects of nutrition and physical training on menarche and ovulation. In J. Brooks-Gunn & A. C. Petersen (Eds.), *Girls at puberty: Biological and psychosocial perspectives.* New York: Plenum.

Frisch, R. E., Wyshak, G., & Vincent, L. (1980). Delayed menarche and amenorrhea of ballet dancers. *New England Journal of Medicine, 303,* 17–19.

Gaddis, A., & Brooks-Gunn, J. (1985). The male experience of pubertal change. *Journal of Youth and Adolescence, 14,* 61–69.

Gandelman, R. (1992). *Psychobiology of behavioral development.* New York: Oxford University Press.

Goldberg, A. P., & Hagberg, J. M. (1990). Physical exercise in the elderly. In E. L. Schneider & J. W. Rowe (Eds.), *Handbook of the biology of aging* (3rd ed.). San Diego: Academic Press.

Goldfield, E. C. (1989). Transition from rocking to crawling: Postural constraints on infant movement. *Developmental Psychology, 25,* 913–919.

Greene, J. G. (1984). *The social and psychological origins of the climacteric syndrome.* Hants, England & Brookfield, VT: Gower.

Greenough, W. T. (1986). What's special about development? Thoughts on the bases of experience-sensitive synaptic plasticity. In W. T. Greenough & J. M. Juraska (Eds.), *Developmental neuropsychobiology.* Orlando, FL: Academic Press.

Greenough, W. T., Black, J. E., & Wallace, C. S. (1987). Experience and brain development. *Child Development, 58,* 539–559.

Greif, E. B., & Ulman, K. J. (1982). The psychological impact of menarche on early adolescent females: A review. *Child Development, 53,* 1413–1430.

Grilo, C. M., & Pogue-Geile, M. F. (1991). The nature of environmental influences on weight and obesity: A behavior genetic analysis. *Psychological Bulletin, 110,* 520–537.

Guigoz, Y., & Munro, H. N. (1985). Nutrition and aging. In C. E. Finch & E. L. Schneider (Eds.), *Handbook of the biology of aging* (2nd ed.). New York: Van Nostrand Reinhold.

Guralnik, J. M., & Kaplan, G. A. (1989). Predictors of healthy aging: Prospective evidence from the Alameda County Study. *American Journal of Public Health, 79,* 703–708.

Gustafson, G. E. (1984). Effects of the ability to locomote on infants' social and exploratory behaviors. *Developmental Psychology, 20,* 397–405.

Halverson, H. M. (1931). An experimental study of prehension in infants by means of systematic cinema records. *Genetic Psychology Monographs, 10,* 107–286.

Harman, S. M., & Talbert, G. B. (1985). Reproductive aging. In C. E. Finch & E. L. Schneider (Eds.), *Handbook of the biology of aging* (2nd ed.). New York: Van Nostrand Reinhold.

Harman, S. M., & Tsitouras, P. D. (1980). Reproductive hormones in aging men: I. Measurement of sex steroids, basal luteinizing hormone, and Leydig cell response to human chorionic gonadotropin. *Journal of Clinical Endocrinology and Metabolism, 51,* 35–40.

Harris, C. S. (1978). *Fact book on aging: A profile of America's older population.* Washington, DC: National Council on Aging.

Harris, J. R., Pedersen, N. L., McClearn, G. E., Plomin, R., & Nesselroade, J. R. (1992). Age differences in genetic and environmental influences for health from the Swedish Adoption/Twin Study of Aging. *Journal of Gerontology: Psychological Sciences, 47,* P213–P220.

Haywood, K. M. (1986). *Life span motor development.* Champaign, IL: Human Kinetics Publishers.

Heath, G. W., Hagberg, J. M., Ehsani, A. A., & Holloszy, J. O. (1981). A physiological comparison of young and older endurance athletes. *Journal of Applied Physiology, 51,* 634–640.

Herkowitz, J. (1978). Sex-role expectations and motor behavior of the young child. In M. V. Ridenour (Ed.), *Motor development: Issues and applications.* Princeton, NJ: Princeton Book Co.

Hill, J. P. (1988). Adapting to menarche: Familial control and conflict. In M. R. Gunnar & W. A. Collins (Eds.), *Development during the transition to adolescence: Vol. 21. Minnesota Symposia on Child Psychology.* Hillsdale, NJ: Erlbaum.

Hofsten, C. von. (1982). Eye-hand coordination in the newborn. *Developmental Psychology, 18,* 450–461.

Hofsten, C. von. (1984). Developmental changes in the organization of prereaching movements. *Developmental Psychology, 20,* 378–388.

Hofsten, C. von. (1991). Structuring of early reaching movements: A longitudinal study. *Journal of Motor Behavior, 23,* 280–292.

Hopkins, B. (1991). Facilitating early motor development: An intracultural study of West Indian mothers and their infants living in Britain. In J. K. Nugent, B. M. Lester, & T. B. Brazelton (Eds.), *The cultural context of infancy: Vol. 2. Multicultural and interdisciplinary approaches to parent-infant relations.* Norwood, NJ: Ablex.

Hopwood, N. J., Kelch, R. P., Hale, P. M., Mendes, T. M., Foster, C. M., & Beitins, I. Z. (1990). The onset of human puberty: Biological and environmental factors. In J. Bancroft & J. M. Reinisch (Eds.), *Adolescence and puberty.* New York: Oxford University Press.

Houx, P. J., Vreeling, F. W., & Jolles, J. (1991). Rigorous health screening reduces age effect on memory scanning task. *Brain and Cognition, 15,* 246–260.

Hutt, S. J., Lenard, H. G., & Prechtl, H. E. R. (1969). Psychophysiology of the newborn. In L. P. Lipsitt & H. W. Reese (Eds.), *Advances in child development and behavior.* New York: Academic Press.

Huttenlocher, P. R. (1979). Synaptic density in human frontal cortex—Developmental changes and effects of aging. *Brain Research, 163,* 195–205.

Janowsky, J. S., & Finlay, B. L. (1986). The outcome of perinatal brain damage: The role of normal neuron loss and axon retraction. *Developmental Medicine and Child Neurology, 28,* 375–389.

Johnson, W. R., & Buskirk, E. R. (1974). *Science and medicine of exercise and sport* (2nd ed.). New York: Harper & Row.

Johnston, C. C., Jr., Hui, S. L., Witt, R. M., Appledorn, R., Baker, R. S., & Longcope, C. (1985). Early menopausal changes in bone mass and sex steroids. *Journal of Clinical Endocrinology and Metabolism, 61,* 905–911.

Jones, M. C. (1965). Psychological correlates of somatic development. *Child Development, 36,* 899–911.

Jones, M. C., & Bayley, N. (1950). Physical maturing among boys as related to behavior. *Journal of Educational Psychology, 41,* 129–148.

Jones, M. C., & Mussen, P. H. (1958). Self-conceptions, motivations, and interpersonal attitudes of early- and late-maturing girls. *Child Development, 29,* 491–501.

Kail, R. (1991). Developmental change in speed of processing during childhood and adolescence. *Psychological Bulletin, 109,* 490–501.

Kail, R., & Park, Y. (1992). Global developmental change in processing time. *Merrill-Palmer Quarterly, 38,* 525–541.

Kendler, K. S., Silberg, J. L., Neale, M. C., Kessler, R. C., Heath, A. C., & Eaves, L. J. (1992). Genetic and environmental factors in the aetiology of menstrual, premenstrual and neurotic symptoms: A population-based twin study. *Psychological Medicine, 22,* 85–100.

Keough, J., & Sugden, D. (1985). *Movement skill development.* New York: Macmillan.

Kermoian, R., & Campos, J. J. (1988). Locomotor experience: A facilitator of spatial cognitive development. *Child Development, 59,* 908–917.

Kinsbourne, M. (1989). Mechanisms and development of hemisphere specialization in children. In C. R. Reynolds & E. Fletcher-Janzen (Eds.), *Handbook of clinical child neuropsychology.* New York: Plenum.

Kolb, B., & Fantie, B. (1989). Development of the child's brain and behavior. In C. R. Reynolds & E. Fletcher-Janzen (Eds.), *Handbook of clinical child neuropsychology.* New York: Plenum.

Kron, R. E. (1966). Instrumental conditioning of nutritive sucking behavior in the newborn. *Recent Advances in Biological Psychiatry, 9,* 295–300.

Lakatta, E. G. (1990). Heart and circulation. In E. L. Schneider & J. W. Rowe (Eds.), *Handbook of the biology of aging* (3rd ed.). San Diego: Academic Press.

Lamy, P. P. (1986). The elderly and drug interactions. *Journal of the American Geriatrics Society, 34,* 586–592.

Lenneberg, E. H. (1967). *Biological foundations of language.* New York: Wiley.

Lima, S. D., Hale, S., & Myerson, J. (1991). How general is general slowing: Evidence from the lexical domain. *Psychology and Aging, 6,* 416–425.

Lipsitt, L. P. (1990). Learning processes in the human newborn: Sensitization, habituation, and classical conditioning. *Annals of the New York Academy of Sciences, 608,* 113–127.

Livson, N., & Peskin, H. (1980). Perspectives on adolescence from longitudinal research. In J. Adelson (Ed.), *Handbook of adolescent psychology.* New York: Wiley.

Lock, M. (1986). Ambiguities of aging: Japanese experience and perceptions of menopause. *Culture, Medicine, and Psychiatry, 10,* 23–46.

Margolis, L. H., Sparrow, A. W., & Swanson, G. M. (1989). *Growing into healthy adults: Pediatric antecedents of adult disease* (Health Monograph Series No. 3). Lansing: Michigan Department of Public Health.

Marshall, W. A. (1977). *Human growth and its disorders.* New York: Academic Press.

Marshall, W. A., & Tanner, J. M. (1970). Variations in the pattern of pubertal changes in boys. *Archives of Disease in Childhood, 45,* 13–23.

Masoro, E. J. (1988). Minireview: Food restriction in rodents—An evaluation of its role in the study of aging. *Journal of Gerontology: Biological Sciences, 43,* B59–B64.

Masters, W. H., & Johnson, V. E. (1966). *Human sexual response.* Boston: Little, Brown.

Mathew, A., & Cook, M. L. (1990). The control of reaching movements by young infants. *Child Development, 61,* 1238–1257.

Matthews, K. A. (1992). Myths and realities of the menopause. *Psychosomatic Medicine, 54,* 1–9.

Matthews, K. A., Wing, R. R., Kuller, L. H., Meilahn, E. N., Kelsey, S. F., Costello, E. J., & Caggiula, A. W. (1990). Influences of natural menopause on psychological characteristics and symptoms of middle-aged healthy women. *Journal of Consulting and Clinical Psychology, 58,* 345–351.

McFarlane, J. A., & Williams, T. M. (1990). The enigma of premenstrual syndrome. *Canadian Psychology, 31,* 95–108.

McGandy, R. B., Barrows, C. H., Spanias, A., Meredith, A., Stone, J. L., & Norris, A. H. (1966). Nutrient intakes and energy expenditure in men of different ages. *Journal of Gerontology, 21,* 581–587.

McGanity, W. J. (1976). Problems of nutritional evaluation of the adolescent. In J. I. McKigney & H. N. Munro (Eds.), *Nutritional requirements in adolescence.* Cambridge, MA: MIT Press.

McKinlay, S. M., Brambilla, D. J., & Posner, J. G. (1992). The normal menopause transition. *Maturitas, 14,* 103–115.

Michel, G. F. (1981). Right-handedness: A consequence of infant supine head-orientation preference. *Science, 212,* 685–687.

Molfese, D. L. (1977). Infant cerebral asymmetry. In S. J. Segalowitz & F. A. Gruber (Eds.), *Language development and neurological theory.* Orlando, FL: Academic Press.

Montoye, H. J., & Lamphiear, D. E. (1977). Grip and arm strength in males and females, age 10 to 69. *Research Quarterly for Exercise and Sport, 48,* 108–120.

Morse, C. K. (1993). Does variability increase with age? An archival study of cognitive measures. *Psychology and Aging, 8,* 156–164.

Murray, M. P., Duthie, E. H., Jr., Gambert, S. R., Sepic, S. B., & Mollinger, L. A. (1985). Age-related differences in knee muscle strength in normal women. *Journal of Gerontology, 40,* 275–280.

Murray, M. P., Kory, R. C., & Clarkson, B. H. (1969). Walking patterns in healthy old men. *Journal of Gerontology, 24,* 169–178.

Must, A., Jacques, P. F., Dallal, G. E., Bajema, C. J., & Dietz, W. H. (1992). Long-term morbidity and mortality of overweight adolescents: A follow-up of the Harvard Growth Study of 1922 to 1935. *New England Journal of Medicine, 327,* 1350–1355.

National Center for Health Statistics. (1990). Americans assess their health: United States, 1987. *Vital and Health Statistics,* Series 10 (No. 174).

Neugarten, B. L., Wood, V., Kraines, R. J., & Loomis, B. (1963). Women's attitudes toward the menopause. *Vita Humana, 6,* 140–151.

Ochs, A. L., Newberry, J., Lenhardt, M. L., & Harkins, S. W. (1985). Neural and vestibular aging associated with falls. In J. E. Birren & K. W. Schaie (Eds.), *Handbook of the psychology of aging* (2nd ed.). New York: Van Nostrand Reinhold.

Oppenheim, R. W. (1980). Metamorphosis and adaptation in the behavior of developing organisms. *Developmental Psychology, 13,* 353–356.

Paikoff, R. L., & Brooks-Gunn, J. (1991). Do parent-child relationships change during puberty? *Psychological Bulletin, 110,* 47–66.

Peskin, H. (1973). Influence of the developmental schedule of puberty on learning and ego functioning. *Journal of Youth and Adolescence, 2,* 273–290.

Prechtl, H. F. R. (1981). The study of neural development as a perspective of clinical problems. In K. J. Connolly & H. F. R. Prechtl (Eds.), *Maturation and development.* Philadelphia: Lippincott.

Previc, F. H. (1991). A general theory concerning the prenatal origins of cerebral lateralization in humans. *Psychological Review, 98,* 299–334.

Rakic, P. (1991). Plasticity of cortical development. In S. E. Brauth, W. S. Hall, & R. J. Dooling (Eds.), *Plasticity of development.* Cambridge, MA: Bradford/MIT Press.

Richards, M. H., Boxer, A. W., Petersen, A. C., & Albrecht, R. (1990). Relation of weight to body image in pubertal girls and boys from two communities. *Developmental Psychology, 26,* 313–321.

Rierdan, J., & Koff, E. (1991). Depressive symptomatology among very early maturing girls. *Journal of Youth and Adolescence, 20,* 415–425.

Roffwarg, H. P., Muzio, J. W., & Dement, W. C. (1966). Ontogenetic development of the human sleep-dream cycle. *Science, 152,* 604–619.

Ruble, D. N., & Brooks-Gunn, J. (1982). The experience of menarche. *Child Development, 53,* 1557–1566.

Salthouse, T. A. (1984). Effects of age and skill in typing. *Journal of Experimental Psychology: General, 113,* 345–371.

Scherr, P. A., LaCroix, A. Z., Wallace, R. B., Berkman, L., Curb, J. D., Cornoni-Huntley, J., Evans, D. A., & Hennekens, C. H. (1992). Light to moderate alcohol consumption and mortality in the elderly. *Journal of the American Geriatrics Society, 40,* 651–657.

Schiavi, R. C., Schreiner-Engel, P., White, D., & Mandeli, J. (1991). The relationship between pituitary-gonadal function and sexual behavior in healthy aging men. *Psychosomatic Medicine, 53,* 363–374.

Segalowitz, S. J., Unsal, A., & Dywan, J. (1992). Cleverness and wisdom in 12-year-olds: Electrophysiological evidence for late maturation of the frontal lobe. *Developmental Neuropsychology, 8,* 279–298.

Selkoe, D. J. (1992). Aging brain, aging mind. *Scientific American, 267,* 135–142.

Shephard, R. J. (1978). *Physical activity and aging.* Chicago: Year Book Medical Publishers.

Shephard, R. J. (1990). The scientific basis of exercise prescribing for the very old. *Journal of the American Geriatrics Society, 38,* 62–70.

Shephard, R. J., & Montelpare, W. (1988). Geriatric benefits of exercise as an adult. *Journal of Gerontology: Medical Sciences, 43,* M86–M90.

Shirley, M. M. (1933). *The first two years: A study of 25 babies: Vol. 1. Postural and locomotor development.* Minneapolis: University of Minnesota Press.

Simmons, R. G., & Blyth, D. A. (1987). *Moving into adolescence: The impact of pubertal change and school context.* New York: Hawthorne, Aldine de Gruyter.

Smoll, F. L., & Schutz, R. W. (1990). Quantifying gender differences in physical performance: A developmental perspective. *Developmental Psychology, 26,* 360–369.

Soules, M. R., & Bremner, W. J. (1982). The menopause and climacteric: Endocrinologic basis and associated symptomatology. *Journal of the American Geriatrics Society, 30,* 547–561.

Spirduso, W. W., & MacRae, P. G. (1990). Motor performance and aging. In J. E. Birren & K. W. Schaie (Eds.), *Handbook of the psychology of aging* (3rd ed.). San Diego: Academic Press.

Stattin, H., & Magnusson, D. (1990). *Paths through life: Vol 2. Pubertal maturation in female development.* Hillsdale, NJ: Erlbaum.

Steinberg, L. D. (1981). Transformations in family relations at puberty. *Developmental Psychology, 17,* 833–840.

Steinberg, L. D. (1988). Reciprocal relation between parent-child distance and pubertal maturation. *Developmental Psychology, 24,* 122–128.

Stelmach, G. E., & Nahom, A. (1992). Cognitive-motor abilities of the elderly driver. *Human Factors, 34,* 53–65.

Stelmach, G. E., Phillips, J., DiFabio, R. P., & Teasdale, N. (1989). Age, functional postural reflexes, and voluntary sway. *Journal of Gerontology: Biological Sciences, 44,* B100–B106.

Stones, M. J., & Kozma, A. (1985). Physical performance. In N. Charness (Ed.), *Aging and human performance.* Chichester, England & New York: Wiley.

Stuss, D. T. (1992). Biological and psychological development of executive functions. *Brain and Cognition, 20,* 8–23.

Tanner, J. M. (1962). *Growth at adolescence* (2nd ed.). Oxford, England: Blackwell.

Tanner, J. M. (1981). Growth and maturation during adolescence. *Nutrition Review, 39,* 43–55.

Tanner, J. M. (1990). *Foetus into man: Physical growth from conception to maturity* (rev. & enl. ed.). Cambridge, MA: Harvard University Press.

Thatcher, R. W. (1992). Cyclic cortical reorganization during early childhood. *Brain and Cognition, 20,* 24–50.

Thelen, E. (1984). Learning to walk: Ecological demands and phylogenetic constraints. In L. P. Lipsitt & C. Rovee-Collier (Eds.), *Advances in infancy research* (Vol. 3). Norwood, NJ: Ablex.

Thoman, E. B., & Whitney, M. P. (1989). Sleep states of infants monitored in the home: Individual differences, developmental trends, and origins of diurnal cyclicity. *Infant Behavior and Development, 12,* 59–75.

Thomas, J. R., & French, K. E. (1985). Gender differences across age in motor performance: A meta-analysis. *Psychological Bulletin, 98,* 260–282.

Thomas, J. R., Gallagher, J. D., & Purvis, G. J. (1981). Reaction time and anticipation time: Effects of development. *Research Quarterly for Exercise and Sport, 52,* 359–367.

Treloar, A. E. (1982). Predicting the close of menstrual life. In A. M. Voda, M. Dinnerstein, & S. R. O'Donnell (Eds.), *Changing perspectives on menopause.* Austin: University of Texas Press.

Tsitouras, P. D., Martin, C. E., & Harman, S. M. (1982). Relationship of serum testosterone to sexual activity in healthy elderly. *Journal of Gerontology, 37,* 288–293.

Udry, J. R. (1990). Hormonal and social determinants of adolescent sexual initiation. In J. Bancroft & J. M. Reinisch (Eds.), *Adolescence and puberty.* New York: Oxford University Press.

Unger, R., & Crawford, M. (1992). *Women and gender: A feminist psychology.* Philadelphia: Temple University Press.

Wagner, E. H., LaCroix, A. Z., Buchner, D. M., & Larson, E. B. (1992). Effects of physical activity on health status in older adults: I. Observational studies. *Annual Review of Public Health, 13,* 451–468.

Walford, R. L. (1983). *Maximum life span.* New York: Norton.

Weg, R. B. (1983). Changing physiology of aging. In D. S. Woodruff & J. E. Birren (Eds.), *Aging: Scientific perspectives and social issues.* Pacific Grove, CA: Brooks/Cole.

Whipp, B. J., & Ward, S. A. (1992). Will women soon outrun men? *Nature, 355,* 25.

Whitall, J. (1991). The developmental effect of concurrent cognitive and locomotor skills: Time-sharing from a dynamic perspective. *Journal of Experimental Child Psychology, 51,* 245–266.

Whitbourne, S. K. (1985). *The aging body: Physiological changes and psychological consequences.* New York: Springer-Verlag.

Wilkinson, R. T., & Allison, S. (1989). Age and simple reaction time: Decade differences for 5,325 subjects. *Journal of Gerontology: Psychological Sciences, 44,* P29–P35.

Willemsen, E. (1979). *Understanding infancy.* San Francisco: W. H. Freeman.

Witelson, S. F. (1987). Neurobiological aspects of language in children. *Child Development, 58,* 653–688.

Wolff, P. H. (1966). The causes, controls, and organization of behavior in the neonate. *Psychological Issues, 5*(1, Whole No. 17).

Woods, N. F., Most, A., & Dery, G. K. (1982). Prevalence of perimenstrual symptoms. *American Journal of Public Health, 72,* 1257–1264.

Woollacott, M. H., Shumway-Cook, A., & Nashner, L. M. (1986). Aging and posture control: Changes in sensory organization and muscular coordination. *International Journal of Aging and Human Development, 23,* 97–114.

Wright, A. L. (1982). Variation in Navajo menopause: Toward an explanation. In A. M. Voda, M. Dinnerstein, & S. R. O'Donnell (Eds.), *Changing perspectives on menopause.* Austin: University of Texas Press.

Yamaura, H., Ito, M., Kubota, K., & Matsuzawa, T. (1980). Brain atrophy during aging: A quantitative study with computed tomography. *Journal of Gerontology, 35,* 492–498.

Zani, B. (1991). Male and female patterns in the discovery of sexuality during adolescence. *Journal of Adolescence, 14,* 163–178.

Zelazo, P. R., Zelazo, N. A., & Kolb, S. (1972). "Walking" in the newborn. *Science, 176,* 314–315.

Zeskind, P. S., & Ramey, C. T. (1981). Preventing intellectual and interactional sequelae of fetal malnutrition: A longitudinal, transactional, and synergistic approach to development. *Child Development, 52,* 213–218.

Chapter 6: Perception

Adams, M. J. (1990). *Beginning to read: Learning and thinking about print.* Cambridge, MA: MIT Press.

Anand, K. J., & Hickey, P. R. (1992). Halothane-morphine compared with high-dose sufentanil for anesthesia and postoperative analgesia in neonatal cardiac surgery. *New England Journal of Medicine, 326,* 1–9.

Anderson, D. R., Lorch, E. P., Field, D. E., Collins, P. A., & Nathan, J. G. (1986). Television viewing at home: Age trends in visual attention and time with TV. *Child Development, 57,* 1024–1033.

Arterberry, M., Yonas, A., & Bensen, A. S. (1989). Self-produced locomotion and the development of responsiveness to linear perspective and texture gradients. *Developmental Psychology, 25,* 976–982.

Aslin, R. N. (1987). Visual and auditory development in infancy. In J. D. Osofsky (Ed.), *Handbook of infant development* (2nd ed.). New York: Wiley.

Aslin, R. N., Pisoni, D. B., & Jusczyk, P. W. (1983). Auditory development and speech perception in infancy. In M. M. Haith & J. J. Campos (Eds.), *Handbook of child psychology: Vol. 2. Infancy and developmental psychobiology* (4th ed.). New York: Wiley.

Associated Press (1993, March 4). NIH panel urges testing of newborns for deafness. *Washington Post,* p. A13.

Baltes, P. B., Reese, H. W., & Nesselroade, J. R. (1977). *Life-span developmental psychology: Introduction to research methods.* Pacific Grove, CA: Brooks/Cole.

Banks, M. S., & Ginsburg, A. P. (1985). Infant visual preferences: A review and new theoretical treatment. In H. W. Reese (Ed.), *Advances in child development and behavior* (Vol. 19). Orlando, FL: Academic Press.

Banks, M. S., in collaboration with Salapatek, P. (1983). Infant visual perception. In M. M. Haith & J. J. Campos (Eds.; P. H. Mussen, Gen. Ed.), *Handbook of child psychology: Vol. 2. Infancy and developmental psychobiology* (4th ed.). New York: Wiley.

Barrera, M. E., & Maurer, D. (1981). Recognition of mother's photographed face by the three-month-old infant. *Child Development, 52,* 714–716.

Bartoshuk, L. M., & Weiffenbach, J. M. (1990). Chemical senses and aging. In E. L. Schneider & J. W. Rowe (Eds.), *Handbook of the biology of aging* (3rd ed.). San Diego: Academic Press.

Bergman, M. (1980). *Aging and the perception of speech.* Baltimore: University Park Press.

Bergman, M., Blumenfeld, V. G., Cascardo, D., Dash, B., Levitt, H., & Margulies, M. K. (1976). Age-related decrement in hearing for speech: Sampling and longitudinal studies. *Journal of Gerontology, 31,* 533–538.

Berry, J. W., Poortinga, Y. H., Segall, M., & Dasen, P. R. (1992). *Cross-cultural psychology: Research and applications.* Cambridge, England: Cambridge University Press.

Bertenthal, B. I. (1993, March). *Emerging trends in perceptual development.* Paper presented at the biennial meeting of the Society for Research in Child Development, New Orleans.

Bertenthal, B. I., & Campos, J. J. (1987). New directions in the study of early experience. *Child Development, 58,* 560–567.

Bess, F. H., & McConnell, F. E. (1981). *Audiology, education, and the hearing impaired child.* St Louis: Mosby.

Bornstein, M. H. (1992). Perception across the lifespan. In M. H. Bornstein & M. E. Lamb (Eds.), *Developmental psychology: An advanced textbook* (3rd ed.). Hillsdale, NJ: Erlbaum.

Bornstein, M. H., Ferdinandsen, K., & Gross, C. G. (1981). Perception of symmetry in infancy. *Developmental Psychology, 17,* 82–86.

Bornstein, M. H., Kessen, W., & Weiskopf, S. (1976). Color vision and hue categorization in young human infants. *Journal of Experimental Psychology: Human Perception and Performance, 2,* 115–129.

Botuck, S., & Turkewitz, G. (1990). Intersensory functioning: Auditory-visual pattern equivalence in younger and older children. *Developmental Psychology, 26,* 115–120.

Bower, T. G. R. (1982). *Development in infancy* (2nd ed.). San Francisco: W. H. Freeman.

Bower, T. G. R., Broughton, J. M., & Moore, M. K. (1970). The coordination of vision and tactile input in infancy. *Perception and Psychophysics, 8,* 51–53.

Bronson, G. W. (1991). Infant differences in rate of visual encoding. *Child Development, 62,* 44–54.

Bruck, M. (1990). Word recognition skills of adults with childhood diagnoses of dyslexia. *Developmental Psychology, 26,* 439–454.

Bruck, M. (1992). Persistence of dyslexics' phonological awareness deficits. *Developmental Psychology, 28,* 874–886.

Butler, R. N., & Lewis, M. I. (1977). *Aging and mental health* (2nd ed.). St. Louis: Mosby.

Butterfield, E. C., & Siperstein, G. N. (1972). Influence of contingent auditory stimulation upon non-nutritional suckle. In J. F. Bosma (Ed.), *Third symposium on oral sensation and perception: The mouth of the infant.* Springfield, IL: Charles C Thomas.

Cain, W. S., & Gent, J. F. (1991). Olfactory sensitivity: Reliability, generality, and association with aging. *Journal of Experimental Psychology: Human Perception and Performance, 17,* 382–391.

Campos, J. J., Bertenthal, B. I., & Kermoian, R. (1992). Early experience and emotional development: The emergence of wariness of heights. *Psychological Science, 3,* 61–64.

Campos, J. J., Hiatt, S., Ramsay, D., Henderson, C., & Svejda, M. (1978). The emergence of fear on the visual cliff. In M. Lewis & L. Rosenblum (Eds.), *The origins of affect.* New York: Plenum.

Campos, J. J., Langer, A., & Krowitz, A. (1970). Cardiac responses on the visual cliff in prelocomotor human infants. *Science, 170,* 196–197.

Catherwood, D., Crassini, B., & Freiberg, K. (1989). Infant response to stimuli of similar hue and dissimilar shape: Tracing the origins of the categorization of objects by hue. *Child Development, 60,* 752–762.

Cernoch, J. M., & Porter, R. H. (1985). Recognition of maternal axillary odors by infants. *Child Development, 56,* 1593–1598.

Chall, J. S. (1983). *Stages of reading development.* New York: McGraw-Hill.

Chang, H. W., & Trehub, S. E. (1977). Infants' perception of temporal grouping in auditory patterns. *Child Development, 48,* 1666–1670.

Clarkson, M. G., & Berg, W. K. (1983). Cardiac orienting and vowel discrimination in newborns: Crucial stimulation parameters. *Child Development, 54,* 162–171.

Colombo, J. (1986). Recent studies in early auditory development. In G. J. Whitehurst (Ed.), *Annals of child development: A research annual* (Vol. 3). Greenwich, CT: JAI Press.

Corso, J. F. (1963). Aging and auditory thresholds in men and women. *Archives of Environmental Health, 6,* 350–356.

Corso, J. F. (1981). *Aging sensory systems and perception.* New York: Praeger.

Crook, C. K. (1978). Taste perception in the newborn infant. *Infant Behavior and Development, 1,* 52–69.

Dannemiller, J. L., & Stephens, B. R. (1988). A critical test of infant pattern preference models. *Child Development, 59,* 210–216.

Davis, A. (1983). The epidemiology of hearing disorders. In R. Hinchcliffe (Ed.), *Hearing and balance in the elderly.* Edinburgh: Churchill Livingstone.

Day, R. H., & McKenzie, B. E. (1981). Infant perception of the invariant size of approaching and receding objects. *Developmental Psychology, 17,* 670–677.

DeCasper, A. J., & Fifer, W. P. (1980). Of human bonding: Newborns prefer their mothers' voices. *Science, 208,* 1174–1176.

DeCasper, A. J., & Spence, M. J. (1986). Prenatal maternal speech influences newborns' perception of speech sounds. *Infant Behavior and Development, 9,* 133–150.

DeCasper, A. J., & Spence, M. J. (1991). Auditorily mediated behavior during the perinatal period: A cognitive view. In M. J. S. Weiss & P. R. Zelazo, (Eds.), *Newborn attention: Biological constraints and the influence of experience.* Norwood, NJ: Ablex.

Descartes, R. (1965). La dioptrique. In R. J. Herrnstein & E. G. Boring (Eds.), *A source-book in the history of psychology.* Cambridge, MA: Harvard University Press. (Original work published 1638.)

Doty, R. L., Shaman, P., Applebaum, S. L., Giberson, R., Siksorski, L., & Rosenberg, L. (1984). Smell identification ability: Changes with age. *Science, 226,* 1441–1443.

Eimas, P. D. (1975a). Auditory and phonetic cues for speech: Discrimination of the (*r-l*) distinction by young infants. *Perception and Psychophysics, 18,* 341–347.

Eimas, P. D. (1975b). Speech perception in early infancy. In L. B. Cohen & P. Salapatek (Eds.), *Infant perception: From sensation to cognition.* New York: Academic Press.

Eimas, P. D. (1985). The perception of speech in early infancy. *Scientific American, 252,* 46–52.

Enns, J. T., & Akhtar, N. (1989). A developmental study of filtering in visual attention. *Child Development, 60,* 1188–1199.

Fantz, R. L. (1961). The origin of form perception. *Scientific American, 204,* 66–72.

Fantz, R. L. (1963). Pattern vision in newborn infants. *Science, 140,* 296–297.

Fantz, R. L., & Fagan, J. F. (1975). Visual attention to size and number of pattern details by term and preterm infants during the first six months. *Child Development, 46,* 3–18.

Farkas, M. S., & Hoyer, W. J. (1980). Processing consequences of perceptual grouping in selective attention. *Journal of Gerontology, 35,* 207–216.

Field, J., Muir, D., Pilon, R., Sinclair, M., & Dodwell, P. (1980). Infants' orientation to lateral sounds from birth to three months. *Child Development, 51,* 295–298.

Field, T. (1990). *Infancy.* Cambridge, MA: Harvard University Press.

Finitzo, T., Gunnarson, A. D., & Clark, J. L. (1990). Auditory deprivation and early conductive hearing loss from otitus media. *Topics in Language Disorders, 11,* 29–42.

Fletcher, A. B. (1987). Pain in the neonate. *New England Journal of Medicine, 317,* 1347–1348.

Fozard, J. L. (1990). Vision and hearing in aging. In J. E. Birren & K. W. Schaie (Eds.), *Handbook of the psychology of aging* (3rd ed.). San Diego: Academic Press.

Ganchrow, J. R., Steiner, J. E., & Daher, M. (1983). Neonatal facial expressions to different qualities and intensities of gustatory stimuli. *Infant Behavior and Development, 6,* 189–200.

Gandelman, R. (1992). *Psychobiology of behavioral development.* New York: Oxford University Press.

Gibson, E. J. (1969). *Principles of perceptual learning and development.* New York: Appleton-Century-Crofts.

Gibson, E. J. (1987). Introductory essay: What does infant perception tell us about theories of perception? *Journal of Experimental Psychology: Human Perception and Performance, 13,* 515–523.

Gibson, E. J. (1988). Exploratory behavior in the development of perceiving, acting, and the acquiring of knowledge. *Annual Review of Psychology, 39,* 1–41.

Gibson, E. J. (1991). *An odyssey in learning and perception.* Cambridge, MA: Bradford/MIT Press.

Gibson, E. J., Gibson, J. J., Pick, A. D., & Osser, H. A. (1962). A developmental study of the discrimination of letterlike forms. *Journal of Comparative and Physiological Psychology, 55,* 897–906.

Gibson, E. J., & Levin, H. (1975). *The psychology of reading.* Cambridge, MA: MIT Press.

Gibson, E. J., & Spelke, E. S. (1983). The development of perception. In J. H. Flavell & E. M. Markman (Eds.; P. H. Mussen, Gen. Ed.), *Handbook of child psychology: Vol. 3. Cognitive development* (4th ed.). New York: Wiley.

Gibson, E. J., & Walk, R. D. (1960). The "visual cliff." *Scientific American, 202,* 64–71.

Gibson, E. J., & Walker, A. S. (1984). Development of knowledge of visual-tactile affordances of substance. *Child Development, 55,* 453–460.

Goffinet, J. M. (1992). Hearing loss and hearing aid use by the elderly: A primer for the geriatric care professional. *Educational Gerontology, 18,* 257–264.

Greenberg, D. A., & Branch, L. G. (1982). A review of methodological issues concerning incidence and prevalence data of visual deterioration in elders. In R. Sekuler, D. Kline, & K. Dismukes (Eds.), *Aging and human visual function.* New York: Alan R. Liss.

Greenough, W. T., Black, J. E., & Wallace, C. S. (1987). Experience and brain development. *Child Development, 58,* 539–559.

Gross-Glenn, K., Duara, R., Barker, W. W., & Lowenstein, D. (1991). Positron emission tomographic studies during serial word-reading by normal and dyslexic adults. *Journal of Experimental Neuropsychology, 13,* 531–544.

Haith, M. M. (1980). Visual competence in early infancy. In R. Held, H. Liebowitz, & H. R. Teuber (Eds.), *Handbook of sensory physiology* (Vol. 8). Berlin: Springer-Verlag.

Harkins, S. W., Price, D. D., & Martelli, M. (1986). Effects of age on pain perception: Thermonociception. *Journal of Gerontology, 41,* 58–63.

Hartley, A. A. (1992). Attention. In F. I. M. Craik & T. A. Salthouse (Eds.), *Handbook of aging and cognition.* Hillsdale, NJ: Erlbaum.

Hasher, L., Stoltzfus, E. R., Zacks, R. T., & Rypma, B. (1991). Age and inhibition. *Journal of Experimental Psychology: Learning, Memory, and Cognition, 17,* 163–169.

Held, R., & Hein, A. (1963). Movement-produced stimulation in the development of visually guided behavior. *Journal of Comparative and Physiological Psychology, 56,* 872–876.

Hull, R. H. (1980). Hull's thirteen commandments for talking to the hearing-impaired older person. *ASHA, 22,* 427.

Hutchinson, K. M. (1989). Influence of sentence context on speech perception in young and older adults. *Journal of Gerontology: Psychological Sciences, 44,* P36–P44.

James, W. (1890). *Principles of psychology* (2 vols.). New York: Holt.

Kagan, J. (1971). *Change and continuity in infancy.* New York: Wiley.

Kahn, H. A., Leibowitz, H. M., Ganley, J. P., Kini, M. M., Colton, T., Nickerson, R. S., & Dawber, T. R. (1977). The Framingham eye study: I. Outline and major prevalence findings. *American Journal of Epidemiology, 106,* 17–32.

Kant, I. (1958). *Critique of pure reason.* New York: Modern Library. (Original work published 1781.)

Kellman, P. J., & Spelke, E. S. (1983). Perception of partly occluded objects in infancy. *Cognitive Psychology, 15,* 483–524.

Kenshalo, D. R. (1977). Age changes in touch, vibration, temperature, kinesthesis and pain sensitivity. In J. E. Birren & K. W. Schaie (Eds.), *Handbook of the psychology of aging.* New York: Van Nostrand Reinhold.

Kim, K., & Spelke, E. S. (1992). Infants' sensitivity to effects of gravity on visible object motion. *Journal of Experimental Psychology: Human Perception and Performance, 18,* 385–393.

Kisilevsky, B. S., & Muir, D. W. (1984). Neonatal habituation and dishabituation to tactile stimulation during sleep. *Developmental Psychology, 20,* 367–373.

Kline, D. W., Kline, T. J. B., Fozard, J. L., Kosnik, W., Schieber, F., & Sekuler, R. (1992). Vision, aging, and driving: The problems of older drivers. *Journal of Gerontology: Psychological Sciences, 47,* P27–P34.

Kline, D. W., & Schieber, F. (1985). Vision and aging. In J. E. Birren & K. W. Schaie (Eds.), *Handbook of the psychology of aging* (2nd ed.). New York: Van Nostrand Reinhold.

Kosnik, W., Winslow, L., Kline, D., Rasinski, K., & Sekuler, R. (1988). Visual changes in daily life throughout adulthood. *Journal of Gerontology: Psychological Sciences, 43,* P63–P70.

Kremenitzer, J. P., Vaughn, H. G., Jr., Kurtzberg, D., & Dowling K. (1979). Smooth-pursuit eye movements in the newborn infant. *Child Development, 50,* 442–448.

Krumhansl, C. L., & Jusczyk, P. W. (1990). Infants' perception of phrase structure in music. *Psychological Science, 1,* 70–73.

Kuhl, P. K. (1991). Perception, cognition, and the ontogenetic and phylogenetic emergence of human speech. In S. E. Brauth, W. S. Hall, & R. J. Dooling (Eds.), *Plasticity of development.* Cambridge, MA: Bradford/MIT Press.

Langlois, J. H., Roggman, L. A., Casey, R. J., Ritter, J. M., Reiser-Danner, L. A., & Jenkins, V. Y. (1987). Infant preferences for attractive faces: Rudiments of a stereotype? *Developmental Psychology, 23,* 363–369.

Lewkowicz, D. J. (1988). Sensory dominance in infants: 1. Six-month-old infants' response to auditory-visual compounds. *Developmental Psychology, 24,* 155–171.

Locke, J. (1939). An essay concerning human understanding. In E. A. Burtt (Ed.), *The English philosophers from Bacon to Mill.* New York: Modern Library. (Original work published 1690.)

Lynch, M. P., Eilers, R. E., Oller, D. K., & Urbano, R. C. (1990). Innateness, experience, and music perception. *Psychological Science, 1,* 272–276.

Maccoby, E. E. (1967). Selective auditory attention in children. In L. P. Lipsitt & C. C. Spiker (Eds.), *Advances in child development and behavior.* New York: Academic Press.

Marean, G. C., Werner, L. A., & Kuhl, P. K. (1992). Vowel categorization by very young infants. *Developmental Psychology, 28,* 396–405.

Maurer, D., & Salapatek, P. (1976). Developmental changes in the scanning of faces by young infants. *Child Development, 47,* 523–527.

Maxon, A. B., & Brackett, D. (1992). *The hearing-impaired child: Infancy through high school years.* Boston: Andover Medical Publishers.

Mayberry, R. I., & Eichen, E. B. (1991). The long-lasting advantage of learning sign language in childhood: Another look at the critical period for language acquisition. *Journal of Memory and Language, 30,* 486–512.

McDowd, J. M., & Birren, J. E. (1990). Aging and attentional processes. In J. E. Birren & K. W. Schaie (Eds.), *Handbook of the psychology of aging* (3rd ed.). San Diego: Academic Press.

McDowd, J. M., & Craik, F. I. M. (1988). Effects of aging and task difficulty on divided attention. *Journal of Experimental Psychology: Human Perception and Performance, 14,* 267–280.

Meadows-Orlans, K. P., & Orlans, H. (1990). Responses to loss of hearing in later life. In D. F. Moores & K. P. Meadows-Orlans (Eds.), *Educational and developmental aspects of deafness.* Washington, DC: Gallaudet University Press.

Meltzoff, A. N., & Borton, R. W. (1979). Intermodal matching by human neonates. *Nature, 282,* 403–404.

Miller, P. H., & Weiss, M. G. (1981). Children's attention allocation, understanding of attention, and performance on the incidental learning task. *Child Development, 52,* 1183–1190.

Mitchell, D. E. (1988). The recovery from early monocular visual deprivation in kittens. In A. Yonas (Ed.), *Minnesota Symposia on Child Psychology: Vol. 20. Perceptual development in infancy.* Hillsdale, NJ: Erlbaum.

Mitchell, D. E., Freeman, R. D., Millodot, M., & Haegerstrom, G. (1973). Meridional amblyopia: Evidence for modification of the human visual system by early visual experience. *Vision Research, 13,* 535–558.

Miyawaki, K., Strange, W., Verbrugge, R., Liberman, A. M., Jenkins, J. J., & Fujimura, D. (1975). An effect of linguistic experience: The discrimination of [r] and [*l*] by native speakers of Japanese and English. *Perception and Psychophysics, 18,* 331–340.

Morrison, F. J. (1984). Reading disability: A problem in rule learning and word decoding. *Developmental Review, 4,* 36–47.

Morrongiello, B. A., Fenwick, K. D., & Chance, G. (1990). Sound localization activity in very young infants: An observer-based testing procedure. *Developmental Psychology, 26,* 1003.

Moss, M. S., Lawton, M. P., & Glicksman, A. (1991). The role of pain in the last year of life of older persons. *Journal of Gerontology: Psychological Sciences, 46,* P51–P57.

Muir, D. W. (1985). The development of infants' auditory spatial sensitivity. In S. E. Trehub & B. Schneider (Eds.), *Advances in the study of communication and affect: Vol. 10. Auditory development in infancy.* New York: Plenum.

Murphy, C. (1985). Cognitive and chemosensory influences on age-related changes in the ability to identify blended foods. *Journal of Gerontology, 40,* 47–52.

Nanez, J. (1987). Perception of impending collision in 3- to 6-week-old infants. *Infant Behavior and Development, 11,* 447–463.

National Center for Health Statistics, G. S. Poc. (1983). Eye care visits and use of eyeglasses or contact lenses: United States, 1979 and 1980. *Vital and Health Statistics,* Series 10 (No. 145).

Nissen, M. J., & Corkin, S. (1985). Effectiveness of attentional cueing in older and younger adults. *Journal of Gerontology, 40,* 185–191.

Ochs, A. L., Newberry, J., Lenhardt, M. L., & Harkins, S. W. (1985). Neural and vestibular aging associated with falls. In J. E. Birren & K. W. Schaie (Eds.), *Handbook of the psychology of aging* (2nd ed.). New York: Van Nostrand Reinhold.

Olsho, L. W., Harkins, S. W., & Lenhardt, M. L. (1985). Aging and the auditory system. In J. E. Birren & K. W. Schaie (Eds.), *Handbook of the psychology of aging* (2nd ed.). New York: Van Nostrand Reinhold.

Owsley, C., Ball, K., Sloane, M. E., & Bruni, J. R. (1991). Visual/cognitive correlates of vehicle accidents in older drivers. *Psychology and Aging, 6,* 403–415.

Peeples, D. R., & Teller, D. Y. (1975). Color vision and brightness discrimination in two-month-old human infants. *Science, 189,* 1102–1103.

Piaget, J. (1954). *The construction of reality in the child.* New York: Basic Books.

Piaget, J. (1960). *Psychology of intelligence.* Paterson, NJ: Littlefield, Adams.

Pitts, D. G. (1982). The effects of aging on selected visual functions: Dark adaptation, visual acuity, stereopsis, and brightness contrast. In R. Sekuler, D. Kline, & K. Dismukes (Eds.), *Aging and human visual function.* New York: Alan R. Liss.

Plude, D. J., & Hoyer, W. J. (1981). Adult age differences in visual search as a function of stimulus mapping and processing load. *Journal of Gerontology, 36,* 598–604.

Plude, D. J., & Hoyer, W. J. (1985). Attention and performance: Identifying and localizing age deficits. In N. Charness (Ed.), *Aging and human performance.* Chichester, England: Wiley.

Porter, F. L., Miller, R. H., & Marshall, R. E. (1986). Neonatal pain cries: Effects of circumcision on acoustic features and perceived urgency. *Child Development, 57,* 790–802.

Porter, R. H., Makin, J. W., Davis, L. B., & Christensen, K. M. (1992). Breast-fed infants respond to olfactory clues from their own mother and unfamiliar lactating females. *Infant Behavior and Development, 15,* 85–93.

Pratt, K. C. (1954). The neonate. In L. Carmichael (Ed.), *Manual of child psychology* (2nd ed.). New York: Wiley.

Rango, N. (1985). The social epidemiology of accidental hypothermia among the aged. *Gerontologist, 25,* 424–430.

Reese, H. W. (1963). Perceptual set in young children. *Child Development, 34,* 151–159.

Riesen, A. H. (1965). Effects of visual deprivation on perceptual function and the neural substrate. In J. de Ajuriaguerra (Ed.), *Dessaferentation experimental et clinique.* Geneva: Georg.

Riesen, A. H., Chow, K. L., Semmes, J., & Nissen, H. W. (1951). Chimpanzee vision after four conditions of light deprivation. *American Psychologist, 6,* 282.

Rieser, J., Yonas, A., & Wilkner, K. (1976). Radial localization of odors by human newborns. *Child Development, 47,* 856–859.

Rose, S. A., Feldman, J. F., Wallace, I. F., & McCarton, C. (1991). Information processing at 1 year: Relation to birth status and developmental outcome during the first 5 years. *Developmental Psychology, 27,* 723–737.

Rose, S. A., Gottfried, A. W., & Bridger, W. H. (1981). Cross-modal transfer in 6-month-old infants. *Developmental Psychology, 17,* 661–669.

Rovee, C. K., Cohen, R. Y., & Shlapack, W. (1975). Life-span stability in olfactory sensitivity. *Developmental Psychology, 11,* 311–318.

Ruff, H. A., & Lawson, K. R. (1990). Development of sustained, focused attention in young children during free play. *Developmental Psychology, 26,* 85–93.

Ruff, H. A., Saltarelli, L. M., Coppozzoli, M., & Dubiner, K. (1992). The differentiation of activity in infants' exploration of objects. *Developmental Psychology, 27,* 851–861.

Russell, M. J., Cummings, B. J., Proffitt, B. F., Wysocki, C. J., Gilbert, A. N., & Cotman, C. W. (1993). Life span changes in verbal categorization of odors. *Journal of Gerontology: Psychological Sciences, 48,* P49–P53.

Salapatek, P. (1975). Pattern perception in early infancy. In L. B. Cohen & P. Salapatek (Eds.), *Infant perception: From sensation to cognition* (Vol. 1). New York: Academic Press.

Samuels, C. A., & Ewy, R. (1985). Aesthetic perception of faces during infancy. *British Journal of Developmental Psychology, 3,* 221–228.

Scarborough, H. S. (1990). Very early language deficits in dyslexic children. *Child Development, 61,* 1728–1743.

Schiff, A. R., & Knopf, I. J. (1985). The effect of task demands on attention allocation in children of different ages. *Child Development, 56,* 621–630.

Schiffman, S. (1977). Food recognition by the elderly. *Journal of Gerontology, 32,* 586–592.

Schiffman, S., & Pasternak, M. (1979). Decreased discrimination of food odors in the elderly. *Journal of Gerontology, 34,* 73–79.

Scialfa, C. T., Guzy, L. T., Liebowitz, H. W., & Garvey, P. M. (1991). Age differences in estimating vehicle velocity. *Psychology and Aging, 6,* 60–66.

Sivak, M., Olson, P. L., & Pastalan, L. A. (1981). Effect of driver's age on nighttime legibility of highway signs. *Human Factors, 23,* 59–64.

Slater, A., Mattock, A., Brown, E., & Bremner, J. G. (1991). Form perception at birth: Cohen and Younger (1984) revisited. *Journal* of *Experimental Child Psychology, 51,* 395–406.

Slater, A., Morison, V., Town, C., & Rose, D. (1985). Movement perception and identity constancy in the new-born baby. *British Journal of Developmental Psychology, 3,* 211–220.

Smith, F. (1977). Making sense of reading—and of reading instruction. *Harvard Educational Review, 47,* 386–395.

Spelke, E. S. (1990). Principles of object perception. *Cognitive Science, 14,* 29–56.

Spelke, E. S., Breinlinger, K., Macomber, J., & Jacobson, K. (1992). Origins of knowledge. *Psychological Review, 99,* 605–632.

Spelke, E. S., Hofsten, C. von, & Kestenbaum, R. (1989). Object perception in infancy: Interaction of spatial and kinetic information for object boundaries. *Developmental Psychology, 25,* 185–196.

Starkey, P., Spelke, E. S., & Gelman, R. (1990). Numerical abstraction by human infants. *Cognition, 36,* 97–127.

Steiner, J. E. (1979). Human facial expressions in response to taste and smell stimulation. In H. W. Reese & L. P. Lipsitt (Eds.), *Advances in child development and behavior* (Vol. 13). New York: Academic Press.

Stevens, J. C., & Cain, W. S. (1987). Old-age deficits in the sense of smell as gauged by thresholds, magnitude matching, and odor identification. *Psychology and Aging, 2,* 36–42.

Streri, A., & Pecheux, M. (1986a). Tactual habituation and discrimination of form in infancy: A comparison with vision. *Child Development, 57,* 100–104.

Streri, A., & Pecheux, M. (1986b). Vision-to-touch and touch-to-vision transfer of form in 5-month-old infants. *British Journal of Developmental Psychology, 4,* 161–167.

Strutt, G. F., Anderson, D. R., & Well, A. D. (1975). A developmental study of the effects of irrelevant information on speeded classification. *Journal of Experimental Child Psychology, 20,* 127–135.

Stryker, M. P., Sherk, H., Leventhal, A. G., & Hirsch, V. H. B. (1978). Physiological consequences for the cat's visual cortex of effectively restricting early visual experience with oriented contours. *Journal of Neurophysiology, 41,* 896–909.

Tanner, J. M. (1990). *Foetus into man: Physical growth from conception to maturity* (rev. & enl. ed.). Cambridge, MA: Harvard University Press.

Trehub, S. E. (1985). Auditory pattern perception in infancy. In S. E. Trehub & B. Schneider (Eds.), *Advances in the study of communication and affect: Vol. 10. Auditory development in infancy.* New York: Plenum.

Trehub, S. E., Schneider, B. A., Thorpe, L. A., & Judge, P. (1991). Observational measures of auditory sensitivity in early infancy. *Developmental Psychology, 27,* 40–49.

Treiber, F., & Wilcox, S. (1980). Perception of a "subjective contour" by infants. *Child Development, 51,* 915–917.

Tun, P. A., Wingfield, A., Stine, E. A. L., & Mecsas, C. (1992). Rapid speech processing and divided attention: Processing rate versus processing resources as an explanation of age effects. *Psychology and Aging, 7,* 546–550.

Van Giffen, K., & Haith, M. M. (1984). Infant visual response to Gestalt geometric forms. *Infant Behavior and Development, 7,* 335–346.

Vellutino, F. (1991). Introduction to three studies on reading acquisition: Convergent findings on theoretical foundations of code-oriented versus whole language approaches to reading instruction. *Journal of Educational Psychology, 83,* 437–443.

Verrillo, R. T., & Verrillo, V. (1985). Sensory and perceptual performance. In N. Charness (Ed.), *Aging and human performance.* Chichester, England: Wiley.

Vurpillot, E. (1968). The development of scanning strategies and their relation to visual differentiation. *Journal of Experimental Child Psychology, 6,* 632–650.

Walk, R. D. (1981). *Perceptual development.* Pacific Grove, CA: Brooks/Cole.

Weiffenbach, J. M., Cowart, B. J., & Baum, B. J. (1986). Taste intensity perception in aging. *Journal of Gerontology, 41,* 460–468.

Werker, J. F., Gilbert, J. H. V., Humphrey, K., & Tees, R. C. (1981). Developmental aspects of cross-language speech perception. *Child Development, 52,* 349–355.

Werker, J. F., & Tees, R. C. (1984). Cross-language speech perception: Evidence for perceptual reorganization during the first year. *Infant Behavior and Development, 7,* 49–63.

Werker, J. F., & Tees, R. C. (1992). The organization and reorganization of human speech perception. *Annual Review of Neuroscience, 15,* 377–402.

Wertheimer, M. (1923). Untersuchungen zur Lehre von der Gestalt. II. *Psychologische Forschung, 4,* 301–350.

Whitbourne, S. K. (1985). *The aging body: Physiological changes and psychological consequences.* New York: Springer-Verlag.

Williams, A. F., & Carsten, O. (1989). Driver age and crash involvement. *American Journal of Public Health, 79,* 326–327.

Wingfield, A., Poon, L. W., Lombardi, L., & Lowe, D. (1985). Speed of processing in normal aging: Effects of speech rate, linguistic structure, and processing time. *Journal of Gerontology, 40,* 579–595.

Witelson, S. F. (1977). Developmental dyslexia: Two right hemispheres and none left. *Science, 195,* 309–311.

Wynn, K. (1992). Addition and subtraction by human infants. *Nature, 358,* 749–750.

Yendovitskaya, T. V. (1971). Development of attention. In A. V. Zaporozhets & D. B. Elkonin (Eds.), *The psychology of preschool children.* Cambridge, MA: MIT Press.

Yonas, A. (1981). Infants' responses to optical information for collision. In R. N. Aslin, J. R. Alberts, & M. R. Petersen (Eds.), *Development of perception: Psychobiological perspectives. Vol. 2: The visual system.* New York: Academic Press.

Zaporozhets, A. V. (1965). The development of perception in the preschool child. *Monographs of the Society for Research in Child Development, 30*(2, Serial No. 100), 82–101.

Chapter 7: Cognition and Language

Acredolo, L., & Goodwyn, S. (1988). Symbolic gesturing in normal infants. *Child Development, 59,* 450–466.

Adey, P. S., & Shayer, M. (1992). Accelerating the development of formal thinking in middle and high school students: II. Postproject effects on science achievement. *Journal of Research in Science Teaching, 29,* 81–92.

Arnett, J. (1990). Contraceptive use, sensation seeking, and adolescent egocentrism. *Journal of Youth and Adolescence, 19,* 171–180.

Azmitia, M. (1992). Expertise, private speech, and the development of self-regulation. In R. M. Diaz & L. E. Berk (Eds.), *Private speech: From social interaction to self-regulation.* Hillsdale, NJ: Erlbaum.

Baillargeon, R., & DeVos, J. (1991). Object permanence in young infants: Further evidence. *Child Development, 62,* 1227–1246.

Baillargeon, R., & Graber, M. (1988). Evidence of location memory in 8-month-old infants in a nonsearch AB task. *Developmental Psychology, 24,* 502–511.

Bandura, A. (1971). An analysis of modeling processes. In A. Bandura (Ed.), *Psychological modeling.* New York: Lieber-Atherton.

Baron, N. S. (1992). *Growing up with language: How children learn to talk.* Reading, MA: Addison-Wesley.

Basseches, M. (1984). *Dialectical thinking and adult development.* Norwood, NJ: Ablex.

Bates, E., & MacWhinney, B. (1982). Functionalist approaches to grammar. In E. Wanner & L. Gleitman (Eds.), *Language acquisition: The state of the art.* Cambridge, England: Cambridge University Press.

Bates, E., O'Connell, B., & Shore, C. (1987). Language and communication in infancy. In J. D. Osofsky (Ed.), *Handbook of infant development* (2nd ed.). New York: Wiley.

Beal, C. R. (1987). Repairing the message: Children's monitoring and revision skills. *Child Development, 58,* 401–408.

Beal, C. R. (1990). The development of text evaluation and revision skills. *Child Development, 61,* 247–258.

Beal, C. R., & Belgrad, S. L. (1990). The development of message evaluation skills in young children. *Child Development, 61,* 705–712.

Behrend, D. A., Rosengren, K., & Perlmutter, M. (1989). A new look at children's private speech: The effects of age, task difficulty, and parent presence. *International Journal of Behavioral Development, 12,* 305–320.

Beilin, H. (1992). Piaget's enduring contribution to developmental psychology. *Developmental Psychology, 28,* 191–204.

Bellugi, U. (1988). The acquisition of a spatial language. In F. S. Kessel (Ed.), *The development of language and language researchers: Essays in honor of Roger Brown.* Hillsdale, NJ: Erlbaum.

Benedict, H. (1979). Early lexical development: Comprehension and production. *Journal of Child Language, 6,* 183–200.

Berg, C. A., & Sternberg, R. J. (1985). A triarchic theory of intellectual development during adulthood. *Developmental Review, 5,* 334–370.

Berk, L. E. (1992). Children's private speech: An overview of theory and the status of research. In R. M. Diaz & L. E. Berk (Eds.), *Private speech: From social interaction to self-regulation.* Hillsdale, NJ: Erlbaum.

Berk, L. E., & Landau, S. (1993). Private speech of learning disabled and normally achieving children in classroom academic and laboratory contexts. *Child Development, 64,* 556–571.

Bivens, J. A., & Berk, L. E. (1990). A longitudinal study of the development of elementary school children's private speech. *Merrill-Palmer Quarterly, 36,* 443–463.

Bjorklund, D. F. (1989). *Children's thinking: Developmental function and individual differences.* Pacific Grove, CA: Brooks/Cole.

Blackburn, J. (1984). The influence of personality, curriculum, and memory correlates on formal reasoning in young adults and elderly persons. *Journal of Gerontology, 39,* 207–209.

Blackburn, J. A., & Papalia, D. E. (1992). The study of adult cognition from a Piagetian perspective. In R. J. Sternberg & C. A. Berg (Eds.), *Intellectual development.* New York: Cambridge University Press.

Blake, J., & de Boysson-Bardies, B. (1992). Patterns in babbling: A cross-linguistic study. *Journal of Child Language, 19,* 51–74.

Bloom, L. (1970). *Language development: Form and function in emerging grammars.* Cambridge, MA: MIT Press.

Bohannon, J. N. III, MacWhinney, B., & Snow, C. (1990). No negative evidence revisited: Beyond learnability or who has to prove what to whom. *Developmental Psychology, 26,* 221–226.

Bohannon, J. N. III, & Stanowicz, L. (1988). The issue of negative evidence: Adult responses to children's language errors. *Developmental Psychology, 24,* 684–689.

Bohannon, J. N. III, & Warren-Leubecker, A. (1985). Theoretical approaches to language acquisition. In J. Berko Gleason (Ed.), *The development of language.* Columbus, OH: Merrill.

Bohannon, J. N. III, & Warren-Leubecker, A. (1989). Theoretical approaches to language acquisition. In J. B. Gleason (Ed.), *The development of language.* Columbus, OH: Merrill.

Boloh, Y., & Champaud, C. (1993). The past conditional verb form in French children: The role of semantics in late grammatical development. *Journal of Child Language, 20,* 169–189.

Bower, T. G. R. (1982). *Development in infancy.* San Francisco: W. H. Freeman.

Braine, M. D. S. (1963). The ontogeny of English phrase structure: The first phrase. *Language, 39,* 1–13.

Brainerd, C. J. (1978). The stage question in cognitive-developmental theory. *Behavioral and Brain Sciences, 2,* 173–213.

Bromley, D. B. (1991). Aspects of written language production over adult life. *Psychology and Aging, 6,* 296–308.

Brown, R. (1973). *A first language: The early stages.* Cambridge, MA: Harvard University Press.

Brown R., Cazden, C., & Bellugi, U. (1969). The child's grammar from I–III. In J. P. Hill (Ed.), *Minnesota Symposia on Child Psychology* (Vol. 2). Minneapolis: University of Minnesota Press.

Brown, R., & Hanlon, C. (1970). Derivational complexity and order of acquisition. In J. R. Hayes (Ed.), *Cognition and the development of language.* New York: Wiley.

Bruner, J. S. (1983). *Child's talk: Learning to use language.* New York: Norton.

Burke, D. M., MacKay, D. G., Worthley, J. S., & Wade, E. (1991). On the tip of the tongue: What causes word finding failures in young and older adults? *Journal of Memory and Language, 30,* 542–579.

Callanan, M. A., & Oakes, L. M. (1992). Preschoolers' questions and parents' explanations: Causal thinking in everyday activity. *Cognitive Development, 7,* 213–233.

Capelli, C. A., Nakagawa, N., & Madden, C. M. (1990). How children understand sarcasm: The role of context and intonation. *Child Development, 61,* 1824–1841.

Carey, S. (1977). The child as word learner. In M. Halle, J. Bresnan, & G. A. Miller (Eds.), *Linguistic theory and psychological reality.* Cambridge, MA: MIT Press.

Case, R. (1985). *Intellectual development: Birth to adulthood.* Orlando, FL: Academic Press.

Cavanaugh, J. C., Kramer, D. A., Sinnott, J. D., Camp, C. J., & Markley, R. P. (1985). On missing links and such: Interfaces between cognitive research and everyday problem-solving. *Human Development, 28,* 146–168.

Chandler, M. J., & Boutilier, R. G. (1992). The development of dynamic system reasoning. *Human Development, 35,* 121–137.

Chandler, M. J., Fritz, A. S., & Hala, S. (1989). Small-scale deceit: Deception as a marker of two-, three-, and four-year-olds' early theories of mind. *Child Development, 60,* 1263–1277.

Chapman, M., & Lindenberger, U. (1988). Functions, operations, and decalage in the development of transitivity. *Developmental Psychology, 24,* 542–551.

Chomsky, C. S. (1969). *The acquisition of syntax in children from 5 to 10.* Cambridge, MA: MIT Press.

Chomsky, N. (1968). *Language and mind.* New York: Harcourt Brace & World.

Chomsky, N. (1975). *Reflections on language.* New York: Pantheon Books.

Clark, E. V. (1983). Meanings and concepts. In J. H. Flavell and E. M. Markman (Eds.; P. H. Mussen, Series Ed.), *Handbook of child psychology. Vol. 3: Cognitive development.* New York: Wiley.

Clark, H. H., & Clark, E. V. (1977). *Psychology and language: An introduction to psycholinguistics.* New York: Harcourt Brace Jovanovich.

Commons, M. L., Richards, F. A., & Armon, C. (Eds.). (1984). *Beyond formal operations: Late adolescent and adult cognitive development.* New York: Praeger.

Commons, M. L., Richards, F. A., & Kuhn, D. (1982). Systematic and metasystematic reasoning: A case for levels of reasoning beyond Piaget's stage of formal operations. *Child Development, 53,* 1058–1069.

Cooper, R. P., & Aslin, R. N. (1990). Preference for infant-directed speech in the first month after birth. *Child Development, 61,* 1584–1595.

Cornelius, S. W., & Caspi, A. (1987). Everyday problem solving in adulthood and old age. *Psychology and Aging, 2,* 144–153.

Cowan, P. A. (1978). *Piaget: With feeling.* New York: Holt, Rinehart & Winston.

Dale, P. S. (1976). *Language development: Structure and function.* New York: Holt, Rinehart & Winston.

Davidson, P. M. (1992). Genevan contributions to characterizing the age 4 transition. *Human Development, 35,* 165–171.

de Boysson-Bardies, B., Sagart, L., & Durand, C. (1984). Discernible differences in the babbling of infants according to target language. *Journal of Child Language, 11,* 1–16.

De Lisi, R., & Staudt, J. (1980). Individual differences in college students' performance on formal operations tasks. *Journal of Applied Developmental Psychology, 1,* 163–174.

Denney, N. W. (1982). Aging and cognitive changes. In B. B. Wolman (Ed.), *Handbook of developmental psychology.* Englewood Cliffs, NJ: Prentice-Hall.

de Villiers, J. G., & de Villiers, P. A. (1973). A cross-sectional study of the acquisition of grammatical morphemes in child speech. *Journal of Psycholinguistic Research, 2,* 267–278.

de Villiers, P. A., & de Villiers, J. G. (1979). *Early language.* Cambridge, MA: Harvard University Press.

de Villiers, P. A., & de Villiers, J. G. (1992). Language development. In M. H. Bornstein & M. E. Lamb (Eds.), *Developmental psychology: An advanced textbook.* Hillsdale, NJ: Erlbaum.

Diamond, A. (1985). The development of the ability to use recall to guide action, as indicated by infants' performance on AB. *Child Development, 56,* 868–883.

Diaz, R. M. (1983). Thought and two languages: The impact of bilingualism on cognitive development. In W. W. Gordon (Ed.), *Review of research in education* (Vol. 10). Washington, DC: American Educational Research Association.

Diaz, R. M. (1985). Bilingual cognitive development: Addressing three gaps in recent research. *Child Development, 56,* 1376–1388.

Eimas, P. D. (1975). Speech perception in early infancy. In L. B. Cohen & P. Salapatek (Eds.), *Infant perception: From sensation to cognition* (Vol. 2). New York: Academic Press.

Elkind, D. (1967). Egocentrism in adolescence. *Child Development, 38,* 1025–1034.

Elkind, D., & Bowen, R. (1979). Imaginary audience behavior in children and adolescents. *Developmental Psychology, 15,* 38–44.

Enright, R., Lapsley, D., & Shukla, D. (1979). Adolescent egocentrism in early and late adolescence. *Adolescence, 14,* 687–695.

Farrar, M. J. (1992). Negative evidence and grammatical morpheme acquisition. *Developmental Psychology, 28,* 90–98.

Fernald, A. (1989). Intonation and communicative intent in mothers' speech to infants: Is the melody the message? *Child Development, 60,* 1497–1510.

Fernald, A., Taeschner, T., Dunn, J., Papousek, M., & Fukui, I. (1989). A cross-language study of prosodic modifications in mothers' and fathers' speech to preverbal infants. *Journal of Child Language, 16,* 477–501.

Field, D. (1981). Can preschool children really learn to conserve? *Child Development, 52,* 326–334.

Fischer, K. W. (1980). A theory of cognitive development: The control and construction of hierarchies of skills. *Psychological Review, 87,* 477–531.

Fischer, K. W., Kenny, S. L., & Pipp, S. L. (1990). How cognitive processes and environmental conditions organize discontinuities in the development of abstractions. In C. N. Alexander & E. J. Langer (Eds.), *Higher stages of human development: Perspectives on adult growth.* New York: Oxford University Press.

Flavell, J. H. (1963). *The developmental psychology of Jean Piaget.* New York: Van Nostrand Reinhold.

Flavell, J. H. (1985). *Cognitive development* (2nd ed.). Englewood Cliffs, NJ: Prentice-Hall.

Flavell, J. H., Everett, B. H., Croft, K., & Flavell, E. R. (1981). Young children's knowledge about visual perception: Further evidence for the level 1– level 2 distinction. *Developmental Psychology, 17,* 99–103.

Freedle, R., & Lewis, M. (1977). Prelinguistic conversation. In M. Lewis & L. Rosenblum (Eds.), *Interaction, conversation, and the development of language.* New York: Wiley.

Freund, L. S. (1990). Maternal regulation of children's problem-solving behavior and its impact on children's performance. *Child Development, 61,* 113–126.

Galambos, S. J., & Goldin-Meadow, S. (1990). The effects of learning two languages on levels of metalinguistic awareness. *Cognition, 34,* 1–56.

Gallagher, J. M., & Easley, J. A., Jr. (Eds.). (1978). *Knowledge and development. Vol. 2: Piaget and education.* New York: Plenum.

Gauvain, M., & Rogoff, B. (1989). Collaborative problem-solving and children's planning skills. *Developmental Psychology, 25,* 139–151.

Gelman, R. (1972). The nature and development of early number concepts. In H. W. Reese (Ed.), *Advances in child development and behavior* (Vol. 7). New York: Academic Press.

Gelman, R. (1978). Cognitive development. *Annual Review of Psychology, 29,* 297–332.

Gelman, R., & Shatz, M. (1977). Appropriate speech adjustments: The operation of conversational constraints on talk to two-year-olds. In M. Lewis & L. Rosenblum (Eds.), *Interaction, conversation, and the development of language.* New York: Wiley.

Glick, J. C. (1975). Cognitive development in cross-cultural perspective. In F. Horowitz (Ed.), *Review of child development research* (Vol. 1). Chicago: University of Chicago Press.

Gopnik, M., & Crago, M. B. (1991). Familial aggregation of a developmental language disorder. *Cognition, 39,* 1–50.

Gordon, P. (1990). Learnability and feedback. *Developmental Psychology, 26,* 217–220.

Gray, W. M., & Hudson, L. M. (1984). Formal operations and the imaginary audience. *Developmental Psychology, 20,* 619–627.

Greenfield, P. M., & Savage-Rumbaugh, E. S. (1993). Comparing communicative competence in child and chimp: The pragmatics of repetition. *Journal of Child Language, 20,* 1–26.

Greenfield, P. M., & Smith, J. H. (1976). *The structure of communication in early language development.* New York: Academic Press.

Hakuta, K. (1988). Why bilinguals? In F. S. Kessel (Ed.), *The development of language and language researchers: Essays in honor of Roger Brown.* Hillsdale, NJ: Erlbaum.

Hakuta, K., & Garcia, E. E. (1989). Bilingualism and education. *American Psychologist, 44,* 374–379.

Hala, S., Chandler, M., & Fritz, A. S. (1991). Fledgling theories of mind: Deception as a marker of three-year-olds' understanding of false belief. *Child Development, 61,* 653–663.

Harris, M. (1992). *Language experience and early language development: From input to uptake.* Hove, UK: Erlbaum.

Harter, S. (1982). Cognitive-developmental considerations in the conduct of play therapy. In C. E. Schaefer & K. J. O'Connor (Eds.), *Handbook of play therapy.* New York: Wiley.

Hooper, F. H., Hooper, J. O., & Colbert, K. K. (1985). Personality and memory correlates of intellectual functioning in adulthood: Piagetian and psychometric assessments. *Human Development, 28,* 101–107.

Hudak, M. A., & Anderson, D. E. (1990). Formal operations and learning style predict success in statistics and computer science courses. *Teaching of Psychology, 17,* 231–234.

Hunt, K. W. (1970). Syntactic maturity in schoolchildren and adults. *Monographs of the Society for Research in Child Development, 35*(1, Serial No. 134).

Huttenlocher, J., Haight, W., Bryk, A., Seltzer, M., & Lyons, T. (1991). Early vocabulary growth: Relation to language input and gender. *Developmental Psychology, 27,* 236–248.

Inhelder, B. (1966). Cognitive development and its contribution to the diagnosis of some phenomena of mental deficiency. *Merrill-Palmer Quarterly, 12, 299–319.*

Inhelder, B., & Piaget, J. (1964). *Early growth of logic in the child: Classification and seriation.* New York: Harper & Row.

Irwin, R. R. (1991). Reconceptualizing the nature of dialectical postformal operational thinking: The effects of affectively mediated social experiences. In J. D. Sinnott & J. C. Cavanaugh (Eds.), *Bridging paradigms: Positive development in adulthood and cognitive aging.* New York: Praeger.

Irwin, R. R., & Sheese, R. L. (1989). Problems in the proposal for a "stage" of dialectical thinking. In M. L. Commons, J. D. Sinnott, F. A. Richards, & C. Armon, (Eds.), *Adult development: Vol. 1. Comparisons and applications of developmental models.* New York: Praeger.

Jahnke, H. C., & Blanchard-Fields, F. (1993). A test of two models of adolescent egocentrism. *Journal of Youth and Adolescence, 22,* 313–326.

Johnson, J., & Newport, E. (1989). Critical period effects in second language learning: The influence of maturational state on the acquisition of English as a second language. *Cognitive Psychology, 21,* 60–99.

John-Steiner, V. (1992). Private speech among adults. In R. M. Diaz & L. E. Berk (Eds.), *Private speech: From social interaction to self-regulation.* Hillsdale, NJ: Erlbaum.

Keating, D. P. (1980). Thinking processes in adolescence. In J. Adelson (Ed.), *Handbook of adolescent psychology.* New York: Wiley.

Kemler Nelson, D. G., Hirsh-Pasek, K., Jusczyk, P. W., & Cassidy, K. W. (1989). How the prosodic cues in motherese might assist in language learning. *Journal of Child Language, 16,* 55–68.

Kemper, S. (1992). Language and aging. In F. I. M. Craik & T. A. Salthouse (Eds.), *Handbook of aging and cognition.* Hillsdale, NJ: Erlbaum.

Kenny, S. L. (1983). Developmental discontinuities in childhood and adolescence. In K. W. Fischer (Ed.), *Levels and transitions in children's development* (No. 21, New Directions for Child Development Series). San Francisco: Jossey-Bass.

Kitchener, K. S., & King, P. M. (1981). Reflective judgment: Concepts of justification and their relationship to age and education. *Journal of Applied Developmental Psychology, 2,* 89–116.

Kitchener, K. S., King, P. M., Wood, P. K., & Davison, M. L. (1989). Sequentiality and consistency in the development of reflective judgment: A six-year longitudinal study. *Journal of Applied Developmental Psychology, 10,* 73–95.

Kohlberg, L., Yaeger, J., & Hjertholm, E. (1968). Private speech: Four studies and a review of theories. *Child Development, 39,* 691–736.

Kramer, D. A. (1989). Development of an awareness of contradiction across the life span and the question of post-formal operations. In M. L. Commons, J. D. Sinnott, F. A. Richards, & C. Armon (Eds.), *Adult development: Vol. 1. Comparisons and applications of developmental models.* New York: Praeger.

Krauss, R. M., & Glucksberg, S. (1977). Social and nonsocial speech. *Scientific American, 236,* 100–105.

Kuhn, D. (1992). Cognitive development. In M. H. Bornstein & M. E. Lamb (Eds.),

Developmental psychology: An advanced textbook. Hillsdale, NJ: Erlbaum.

Labouvie-Vief, G. (1984). Logic and self-regulation from youth to maturity: A model. In M. L. Commons, F. A. Richards, & C. Armon (Eds.), *Beyond formal operations: Late adolescent and adult cognitive development.* New York: Praeger.

Labouvie-Vief, G. (1985). Intelligence and cognition. In J. E. Birren & K. W. Schaie (Eds.), *Handbook of the psychology of aging* (2nd ed.). New York: Van Nostrand Reinhold.

Labouvie-Vief, G. (1992). A neo-Piagetian perspective on adult cognitive development. In R. J. Sternberg & C. A. Berg (Eds.), *Intellectual development.* New York: Cambridge University Press.

Labouvie-Vief, G., Adams, C., Hakim-Larson, J., & Hayden, M. (1983, April). *Contexts of logic: The growth of interpretation from preadolescence to mature adulthood.* Paper presented at the biennial meeting of the Society for Research in Child Development, Detroit.

Lanza, E. (1992). Can bilingual 2-year-olds code-switch? *Journal of Child Language, 19,* 633–658.

Lapsley, D. K., Milstead, M., Quintana, S. M., Flannery, D., & Buss, R. R. (1986). Adolescent egocentrism and formal operations: Tests of a theoretical assumption. *Developmental Psychology, 22,* 800–807.

Lechner, C. R., & Rosenthal, D. A. (1984). Adolescent self-consciousness and the imaginary audience. *Genetic Psychology Monographs, 110,* 289–305.

Lenneberg, E. H. (1967). *Biological foundations of language.* New York: Wiley.

Leonard, L. B., Chapman, K., Rowan, L. E., & Weiss, A. L. (1983). Three hypotheses concerning young children's imitations of lexical items. *Developmental Psychology, 19,* 591–601.

Lewis, B. A., & Thompson, L. A. (1992). A study of developmental speech and language disorders in twins. *Journal of Speech and Hearing Research, 35,* 1086–1094.

Lewis, C., & Osborne, A. (1990). Three-year-olds' problems with false belief: Conceptual deficit or linguistic artifact? *Child Development, 61,* 1514–1519.

Light, L. L. (1990). Interactions between memory and language in old age. In J. E. Birren & K. W. Schaie (Eds.), *Handbook of the psychology of aging* (3rd ed.). San Diego: Academic Press.

Markman, E. M. (1989). *Categorization and naming in children.* Cambridge, MA: MIT Press.

Martorano, S. C. (1977). A developmental analysis of performance on Piaget's formal operations tasks. *Developmental Psychology, 13,* 666–672.

McGhee, P. E. (1979). *Humor: Its origin and development.* San Francisco: W. H. Freeman.

McGhee, P. E., & Chapman, A. J. (1980). *Children's humour.* London: Wiley.

McGhee-Bidlack, B. (1991). The development of noun definitions: A metalinguistic analysis. *Journal of Child Language, 18,* 417–434.

McNeill, D. (1970). *The acquisition of language.* New York: Harper & Row.

Mervis, C. B., & Johnson, K. E. (1991). Acquisition of the plural morpheme: A case study. *Developmental Psychology, 27,* 222–235.

Moerk, E. L. (1989). The LAD was a lady and the tasks were ill-defined. *Developmental Psychology, 9,* 21–57.

Neimark, E. D. (1975). Longitudinal development of formal operations thought. *Genetic Psychology Monographs, 91,* 171–225.

Neimark, E. D. (1979). Current status of formal operations research. *Human Development, 22,* 60–67.

Nelson, K. (1973). Structure and strategy in learning to talk. *Monographs of the Society for Research in Child Development, 38*(Serial No. 149).

Nelson, K., Hampson, J., & Shaw, L. K. (1993). Nouns in early lexicons: Evidence, explanations, and implications. *Journal of Child Language, 20,* 61–84.

Newport, E. L. (1991). Contrasting conceptions of the critical period for language. In S. Carey & R. Gelman (Eds.), *The epigenesis of mind: Essays on biology and cognition.* Hillsdale, NJ: Erlbaum.

Norman-Jackson, J. (1982). Family interactions, language development, and primary reading achievement of Black children in families of low income. *Child Development, 53,* 349–358.

Obler, L. K., & Albert, M. L. (1985). Language skills across adulthood. In J. E. Birren & K. W. Schaie (Eds.), *Handbook of the psychology of aging* (2nd ed.). New York: Van Nostrand Reinhold.

Ochs, E. (1982). Talking to children in western Samoa. *Language in Society, 11,* 77–104.

O'Connor, B. P., & Nikolic, J. (1990). Identity development and formal operations as sources of adolescent egocentrism. *Journal of Youth and Adolescence, 19,* 149–158.

Oller, D. K., & Eilers, R. E. (1988). The role of audition in infant babbling. *Child Development, 59,* 441–449.

Owens, R. E., Jr. (1984). *Language development: An introduction.* Columbus, OH: Merrill.

Pearce, K. A., & Denney, N. W. (1984). A life span study of classification preference. *Journal of Gerontology, 39,* 458–464.

Pegg, J. E., Werker, J. F., & McLeod, P. J. (1992). Preference for infant-directed over adult-directed speech: Evidence from 7-week-old infants. *Infant Behavior and Development, 15,* 325–345.

Penner, S. G. (1987). Parental responses to grammatical and ungrammatical child utterances. *Child Development, 58,* 376–384.

Perry, W. G., Jr. (1970). *Forms of intellectual and ethical development in the college years: A scheme.* New York: Holt, Rinehart & Winston.

Petitto, L. A., & Marentette, P. F. (1991). Babbling in the manual mode: Evidence for the ontogeny of language. *Science, 251,* 1493–1496.

Piaget, J. (1926). *Language and thought in the child.* London: Routledge & Kegan Paul.

Piaget, J. (1929). *The child's conception of the world.* New York: Harcourt, Brace & World.

Piaget, J. (1952). *The origins of intelligence in children.* New York: International Universities Press.

Piaget, J. (1954). *The construction of reality in the child.* New York: Basic Books.

Piaget, J. (1970). Piaget's theory. In P. H. Mussen (Ed.), *Carmichael's manual of child psychology* (Vol. 1). New York: Wiley.

Piaget, J. (1972). Intellectual evolution from adolescence to adulthood. *Human Development, 15,* 1–12.

Piaget, J. (1977). The role of action in the development of thinking. In W. F. Overton & J. M. Gallagher (Eds.), *Knowledge and development* (Vol. 1). New York: Plenum.

Piaget, J. (1985). *The equilibration of cognitive structures: The central problem of intellectual development.* (Trans. by T. Brown & K. J. Thampy). Chicago: University of Chicago Press.

Piaget, J., & Inhelder, B. (1956). *The child's conception of space.* New York: Norton.

Reich, P. A. (1986). *Language development.* Englewood Cliffs, NJ: Prentice-Hall.

Reznick, J. S., & Goldfield, B. A. (1992). Rapid change in lexical development in comprehension and production. *Developmental Psychology, 28,* 406–413.

Rice, M. L., & Woodsmall, L. (1988). Lessons from television: Children's word learning when viewing. *Child Development, 59,* 420–429.

Richards, F. A., & Commons, M. L. (1990). Postformal cognitive-developmental theory and research: A review of its current status. In C. N. Alexander & E. J. Langer (Eds.), *Higher stages of human development: Perspectives on adult growth.* New York: Oxford University Press.

Richman, A. L., Miller, P. M., & LeVine, R. A. (1992). Cultural and educational variations in maternal responsiveness. *Developmental Psychology, 28,* 614–621.

Riegel, K. F. (1973). Dialectic operations: The final period of cognitive development. *Human Development, 16,* 346–370.

Rosenthal, M. K. (1982). Vocal dialogues in the neonatal period. *Developmental Psychology, 18,* 17–21.

Ruffman, T. K., & Olson, D. R. (1989). Children's ascriptions of knowledge to others. *Developmental Psychology, 25,* 601–606.

Sachs, J. (1985). Prelinguistic development. In J. Berko Gleason (Ed.), *The development of language.* Columbus, OH: Merrill.

Sacks, O. (1989). *Seeing voices: A journey into the world of the deaf.* Berkeley: University of California Press.

Salthouse, T. A. (1990). Cognitive competence and expertise in aging. In J. E. Birren & K. W. Schaie (Eds.), *Handbook of the psychology of aging* (3rd ed.). San Diego: Academic Press.

Schaie, K. W. (1983). The Seattle longitudinal study: A 21-year exploration of psychometric intelligence in adulthood. In K. W. Schaie (Ed.), *Longitudinal studies of adult psychological development.* New York: Guilford Press.

Schieffelin, B. B. (1986). *How Kaluli children learn what to say, what to do, and how*

to feel. New York: Cambridge University Press.
Schieffelin, B. B., & Ochs, E. (1983). A cultural perspective on the transition from prelinguistic to linguistic communication. In R. M. Golinkoff (Ed.), *Transition from prelinguistic to linguistic communication.* Hillsdale, NJ: Erlbaum.
Scribner, S. (1984). Studying working intelligence. In B. Rogoff & J. Lave (Eds.), *Everyday cognition: Its development in social context.* Cambridge, MA: Harvard University Press.
Sinnott, J. D. (1989). Life span relativistic postformal thought: Methodology and data from everyday problem solving. In M. L. Commons, J. D. Sinnott, F. A. Richards, & C. Armon (Eds.), *Adult development: Vol. 1. Comparisons and applications of developmental models.* New York: Praeger.
Skinner, B. F. (1957). *Verbal behavior.* New York: Appleton-Century-Crofts.
Slobin, D. I. (1979). *Psycholinguistics.* Glenview, IL: Scott, Foresman.
Snow, C. E., Arlman-Rupp, A., Hassing, Y., Jobse, J., Joosken, J., & Vorster, J. (1976). Mother's speech in three social classes. *Journal of Psycholinguistic Research, 5,* 1–20.
Sudhalter, V., & Braine, M. D. S. (1985). How does comprehension of passives develop? A comparison of actional and experiential verbs. *Journal of Child Language, 12,* 455–470.
Taylor, M., & Gelman, S. A. (1988). Adjectives and nouns: Children's strategies for learning new words. *Child Development, 59,* 411–419.
Taylor, M., & Gelman, S. A. (1989). Incorporating new words into the lexicon: Preliminary evidence for language hierarchies in two-year-old children. *Child Development, 60,* 625–636.
Thomas, D., Campos, J. J., Shucard, D. W., Ramsay, D. S., & Shucard, J. (1981). Semantic comprehension in infancy: A signal detection approach. *Child Development, 52,* 798–803.
Thompson, J. R., & Chapman, R. S. (1977). Who is "Daddy" revisited? The status of two-year-olds' overextended words in use and comprehension. *Journal of Child Language, 4,* 359–375.
Tomlinson-Keasey, C., Eisert, D. C., Kahle, L. R., Hardy-Brown, K., & Keasey, B. (1979). The structure of concrete-operational thought. *Child Development, 50,* 1153–1163.
Trabasso, T. (1975). Representation, memory, and reasoning: How do we make transitive inferences? In A. D. Pick (Ed.), *Minnesota Symposia on Child Psychology* (Vol. 9). Minneapolis: University of Minnesota Press.
Tulkin, S. R., & Konner, M. J. (1973). Alternative conceptions of intellectual functioning. *Human Development, 16,* 33–52.
Valdez-Menchaca, M. C., & Whitehurst, G. J. (1992). Accelerating language development through picture book reading: A systematic extension to Mexican day care. *Developmental Psychology, 28,* 1106–1114.
Vygotsky, L. S. (1962). *Thought and language* (E. Hanfmann & G. Vakar, Eds. & Trans.). Cambridge, MA: MIT Press. (Original work published 1934.)
Vygotsky, L. S. (1978). *Mind in society: The development of higher mental processes* (M. Cole, V. John-Steiner, S. Scribner, & E. Souberman, Eds.). Cambridge, MA: Harvard University Press. (Original work published 1930, 1933, 1935.)
Ward, S. L., & Overton, W. F. (1990). Semantic familiarity, relevance, and the development of deductive reasoning. *Developmental Psychology, 26,* 488–493.
Waxman, S. R., & Hatch, T. (1992). Beyond the basics: Preschool children label objects flexibly at multiple hierarchical levels. *Journal of Child Language, 19,* 153–166.
Werker, J. F., Gilbert, J. H. V., Humphrey, K., & Tees, R. C. (1981). Developmental aspects of cross-language speech perception. *Child Development, 52,* 349–355.
Wertsch, J. V., & Tulviste, P. (1992). L. S. Vygotsky and contemporary developmental psychology. *Developmental Psychology, 28,* 548–557.
Whitehurst, G. J., Falco, F. L., Lonigan, C. J., Fischel, J. E., DeBaryshe, B. D., Valdez-Menchaca, M. C., & Caulfield, M. (1988). Accelerating language development through picture book reading. *Developmental Psychology, 24,* 552–559.
Whitehurst, G. J., & Valdez-Menchaca, M. C. (1988). What is the role of reinforcement in early language acquisition? *Child Development, 59,* 430–440.
Wishart, J. G., & Bower, T. G. (1985). A longitudinal study of the development of the object concept. *British Journal of Developmental Psychology, 3,* 243–258.
Wolff, P. H. (1969). The natural history of crying and other vocalizations in early infancy. In B. M. Foss (Ed.), *Determinants of infant behavior* (Vol. 4). London: Methuen.
Yalisove, D. (1978). The effect of riddle structure on children's comprehension of riddles. *Developmental Psychology, 14,* 173–180.

Chapter 8: Learning and Information Processing

Abravanel, E., & Gingold, H. (1985). Learning via observation during the 2nd year of life. *Developmental Psychology, 21,* 614–623.
Abravanel, E., & Sigafoos, A. D. (1984). Exploring the presence of imitation during early infancy. *Child Development, 55,* 381–392.
Adams, C. (1991). Qualitative age differences in memory for text: A life-span developmental perspective. *Psychology and Aging, 6,* 323–336.
Adams, C., Labouvie-Vief, G., Hobart, C. J., & Dorosz, M. (1990). Adult age group differences in story recall style. *Journal of Gerontology: Psychological Sciences, 45,* P17–P27.
Atkinson, R. C., & Shiffrin, R. M. (1968). Human memory: A proposed system and its control processes. In K. W. Spence & J. T. Spence (Eds.), *The psychology of learning and motivation: Advances in research and theory* (Vol. 2). New York: Academic Press.
Bahrick, H. P. (1984). Semantic memory content in permastore: Fifty years of memory for Spanish learned in high school. *Journal of Experimental Psychology: General, 113,* 1–29.
Bahrick, H. P., Bahrick, P. O., & Wittlinger, R. P. (1975). Fifty years of memory for names and faces: A cross-sectional approach. *Journal of Experimental Psychology: General, 104,* 54–75.
Bahrick, H. P., & Hall, L. K. (1991). Lifetime maintenance of high school mathematics content. *Journal of Experimental Psychology: General, 120,* 20–33.
Baker, L., & Brown, A. L. (1984). Metacognitive skills and reading. In P. D. Pearson (Ed.), *A handbook of reading research.* New York: Longman.
Baker-Ward, L., Ornstein, P. A., & Holden, D. J. (1984). The expression of memorization in early childhood. *Journal of Experimental Child Psychology, 37,* 555–575.
Baltes, M. M., & Wahl, H. W. (1992). The dependency-support script in institutions: Generalization to community settings. *Psychology and Aging, 7,* 409–418.
Baltes, P. B., & Kliegl, R. (1992). Further testing of limits of cognitive plasticity: Negative age differences in a mnemonic skill are robust. *Developmental Psychology, 28,* 121–125.
Baltes, P. B., Smith, J., & Staudinger, U. M. (1992). Wisdom and successful aging. In T. B. Sonderegger (Ed.), *Nebraska Symposium on Motivation: Vol. 39. Psychology and aging.* Lincoln: University of Nebraska Press.
Bandura, A. (1965). Influence of models' reinforcement contingencies on the acquisition of imitative responses. *Journal of Personality and Social Psychology, 1,* 589–595.
Bandura, A. (1977). *Social learning theory.* Englewood Cliffs, NJ: Prentice-Hall.
Bandura, A. (1986). *Social foundations of thought and action: A social cognitive theory.* Englewood Cliffs, NJ: Prentice-Hall.
Bandura, A. (1989). Social cognitive theory. In R. Vasta (Ed.), *Annals of child development. Vol. 6: Theories of child development: Revised formulations and current issues.* New York: Appleton-Century-Crofts.
Barrett, T. R., & Wright, M. (1981). Age-related facilitation in recall following semantic processing. *Journal of Gerontology, 36,* 194–199.
Bedard, J., & Chi, M. T. H. (1992). Expertise. *Current Directions in Psychological Science, 1,* 135–139.
Berg, C. A. (1989). Knowledge of strategies for dealing with everyday problems from childhood through adolescence. *Developmental Psychology, 25,* 607–618.
Best, D. L. (1993). Inducing children to generate mnemonic organizational strategies: An examination of long-term retention and materials. *Developmental Psychology, 29,* 324–336.
Biederman, I., Cooper, E. E., Fox, P. W., & Mahadevan, R. S. (1992). Unexceptional spatial memory in an exceptional memorist. *Journal of Experimental Psychology: Learning Memory and Cognition, 18,* 654–657.
Bjorklund, D. F. (1985). The role of conceptual knowledge in the development of

organization in children's memory. In C. J. Brainerd & M. Pressley (Eds.), *Basic processes in memory development: Progress in cognitive development research.* New York: Springer-Verlag.

Bjorklund, D. F. (1989). *Children's thinking: Developmental function and individual differences.* Pacific Grove, CA: Brooks/Cole.

Bjorklund, D. F., & Harnishfeger, K. K. (1990). The resources construct in cognitive development: Diverse sources of evidence and a theory of inefficient inhibition. *Developmental Review, 10,* 48–71.

Bjorklund, D. F., & Zeman, B. R. (1982). Children's organization and metamemory awareness in their recall of familiar information. *Child Development, 53,* 799–810.

Botwinick, J. (1984). *Aging and behavior: A comprehensive integration of research findings* (3rd ed.). New York: Springer.

Bray, N. W., Hersh, R. E., & Turner, L. A. (1985). Selective remembering during adolescence. *Developmental Psychology, 21,* 290–294.

Bray, N. W., Justice, E. M., & Zahm, D. N. (1983). Two developmental transitions in directed forgetting strategies. *Journal of Experimental Child Psychology, 36,* 43–55.

Brown, A. L. (1975). The development of memory: Knowing, knowing about knowing, and knowing how to know. In H. W. Reese (Ed.), *Advances in child development and behavior* (Vol. 10). New York: Academic Press.

Brown, A. L., Bransford, J. D., Ferrara, R. A., & Campione, J. C. (1983). Learning, remembering, and understanding. In J. H. Flavell & E. M. Markman (Eds.), *Handbook of child psychology: Vol. 3. Cognitive development* (4th ed.). New York: Wiley.

Brown, A. L., & Smiley, S. S. (1978). The development of strategies for studying text. *Child Development, 49,* 1076–1088.

Camp, C. J. (1989). World-knowledge systems. In L. W. Poon, D. C. Rubin, & B. A. Wilson (Eds.), *Everyday cognition in adulthood and late life.* Cambridge, England: Cambridge University Press.

Canestrari, R. E. (1963). Paced and self-paced learning in young and elderly adults. *Journal of Gerontology, 18,* 165–168.

Case, R. (1985). *Intellectual development: Birth to adulthood.* Orlando, FL: Academic Press.

Case, R. (1992). The role of the frontal lobes in the regulation of cognitive development. *Brain and Cognition, 20,* 51–73.

Cavanaugh, J. C. (1983). Comprehension and retention of television programs by 20- and 60-year-olds. *Journal of Gerontology, 38,* 190–196.

Cavanaugh, J. C., Grady, J. G., & Perlmutter, M. (1983). Forgetting and use of memory aids in 20 to 70 year olds' everyday life. *International Journal of Aging and Human Development, 17,* 113–122.

Cavanaugh, J. C., & Perlmutter, M. (1982). Metamemory: A critical examination. *Child Development, 53,* 11–28.

Cavanaugh, J. C., & Poon, L. W. (1989). Metamemorial predictors of memory performance in young and older adults. *Psychology and Aging, 4,* 365–368.

Cerella, J. (1990). Aging and information-processing rate. In J. E. Birren & K. W. Schaie (Eds.), *Handbook of the psychology of aging* (3rd ed.). San Diego: Academic Press.

Chi, M. T. H. (1978). Knowledge structures and memory development. In R. Siegler (Ed.), *Children's thinking: What develops?* Hillsdale, NJ: Erlbaum.

Chi, M. T. H., Glaser, R., & Rees, E. (1982). Expertise in problem solving. In R. J. Sternberg (Ed.), *Advances in the psychology of human intelligence* (Vol. 1). Hillsdale, NJ: Erlbaum.

Chi, M. T. H., Hutchinson, J. E. & Robin, A. F. (1989). How inferences about novel domain-related concepts can be constrained by structured knowledge. *Merrill-Palmer Quarterly, 35,* 27–62.

Coates, B., & Hartup, W. W. (1969). Age and verbalization in observational learning. *Developmental Psychology, 1,* 556–562.

Cornelius, S. W., & Caspi, A. (1987). Everyday problem solving in adulthood and old age. *Psychology and Aging, 2,* 144–153.

Cunningham, J. G., & Weaver, S. L. (1989). Young children's knowledge of their memory span: Effects of task and experience. *Journal of Experimental Child Psychology, 48,* 32–44.

Davis, J. M., & Rovee-Collier, C. K. (1983). Alleviated forgetting of a learned contingency in 8-week-old infants. *Developmental Psychology, 19,* 353–365.

DeLoache, J. S., Cassidy, D. J., & Brown, A. L. (1985). Precursors of mnemonic strategies in very young children's memory. *Child Development, 56,* 125–137.

Dempster, F. N. (1981). Memory span: Sources of individual and developmental differences. *Psychological Bulletin, 89,* 63–100.

Dempster, F. N. (1985). Short-term memory development in childhood and adolescence. In C. J. Brainerd & M. Pressley (Eds.), *Basic processes in memory development: Progress in cognitive development research.* New York: Springer-Verlag.

Dempster, F. N. (1992). The rise and fall of the inhibitory mechanism: Toward a unified theory of cognitive development and aging. *Developmental Review, 12,* 45–75.

Denney, N. W. (1980). Task demands and problem-solving strategies in middle-aged and older adults. *Journal of Gerontology, 35,* 559–564.

Denney, N. W. (1982). Aging and cognitive changes. In B. B. Wolman (Ed.), *Handbook of developmental psychology.* Englewood Cliffs, NJ: Prentice-Hall.

Denney, N. W. (1985). A review of life span research with the Twenty Questions Task: A study of problem-solving ability. *International Journal of Aging and Human Development, 21,* 161–173.

Denney, N. W. (1989). Everyday problem solving: Methodological issues, research findings, and a model. In L. W. Poon, D. C. Rubin, & B. A. Wilson (Eds.), *Everyday cognition in adulthood and late life.* Cambridge, England: Cambridge University Press.

Denney, N. W., & Pearce, K. A. (1989). A developmental study of practical problem solving in adults. *Psychology and Aging, 4,* 438–442.

Deptula, D., Singh, R., & Pomara, N. (1993). Aging, emotional states, and memory. *American Journal of Psychiatry, 150,* 429–434.

Dixon, R. A. (1992). Contextual approaches to adult intellectual development. In R. J. Sternberg & C. A. Berg (Eds.), *Intellectual development.* New York: Cambridge University Press.

Dixon, R. A., & Hultsch, D. F. (1983a). Metamemory and memory for text relationships in adulthood: A cross-validation study. *Journal of Gerontology, 38,* 689–694.

Dixon, R. A., & Hultsch, D. F. (1983b). Structure and development of metamemory in adulthood. *Journal of Gerontology, 38,* 682–688.

Domjan, M. J. (1993). *Principles of learning and behavior* (3rd ed.). Pacific Grove, CA: Brooks/Cole.

Ellis, N. R., Palmer, R. L., & Reeves, C. L. (1988). Developmental and intellectual differences in frequency processing. *Developmental Psychology, 24,* 38–45.

Ericsson, K. A., Chase, W. G., & Faloon, S. (1980). Acquisition of a memory skill. *Science, 208,* 1181–1182.

Fabricius, W. V., & Cavalier, L. (1989). The role of causal theories about memory in young children's memory strategy choice. *Child Development, 19,* 298–308.

Fagan, J. F., Jr. (1984). Infant memory: History, current trends, relations to cognitive psychology. In M. Moscovitch (Ed.), *Infant memory: Its relation to normal and pathological memory in humans and other animals.* New York: Plenum.

Field, T. M., Woodson, R., Greenberg, R., & Cohen, D. (1982). Discrimination and imitation of facial expressions by neonates. *Science, 218,* 179–181.

Fitzgerald, H. E., & Brackbill, Y. (1976). Classical conditioning in infancy: Development and constraints. *Psychological Bulletin, 83,* 353–376.

Fivush, R., Gray, J. T., & Fromhoff, F. A. (1987). Two-year-olds talk about the past. *Cognitive Development, 2,* 393–409.

Flavell, J. H. (1985). *Cognitive development* (2nd ed.). Englewood Cliffs, NJ: Prentice-Hall.

Flavell, J. H., Beach, D. R., & Chinsky, J. M. (1966). Spontaneous verbal rehearsal in a memory task as a function of age. *Child Development, 37,* 283–299.

Flavell, J. H., & Wellman, H. M. (1977). Metamemory. In R. V. Kail & J. W. Hagen (Eds.), *Perspectives on the development of memory and cognition.* Hillsdale, NJ: Erlbaum.

Friedman, S. B. (1972). Habituation and recovery of visual response in the alert human newborn. *Journal of Experimental Child Psychology, 13,* 339–349.

Gardner, H. (1985). *The mind's new science: A history of the cognitive revolution.* New York: Basic Books.

Graf, P. (1990). Life-span changes in implicit and explicit memory. *Bulletin of the Psychonomic Society, 28,* 353–358.

Guttentag, R. E. (1985). Memory and aging: Implications for theories of memory development during childhood. *Developmental Review, 5,* 56–77.

Hasher, L., & Zacks, R. T. (1979). Automatic and effortful processes in memory. *Journal of Experimental Psychology: General, 108,* 356–388.

Hasher, L., & Zacks, R. T. (1984). Automatic processing of fundamental information: The case of frequency of occurrence. *American Psychologist, 108,* 356–388.

Hasher, L., & Zacks, R. T. (1988). Working memory, comprehension, and aging: A review and a new view. In G. H. Bower (Ed.), *The psychology of learning and motivation* (Vol. 22). New York: Academic Press.

Hertzog, C., Hultsch, D. F., & Dixon, R. A. (1989). Evidence for the convergent validity of two self-report metamemory questionnaires. *Developmental Psychology, 25,* 687–700.

House, B. J. (1982). Learning processes: Developmental trends. In J. Worell (Ed.), *Psychological development in the elementary years.* New York: Academic Press.

Houx, P. J., Vreeling, F. W., & Jolles, J. (1991). Rigorous health screening reduces age effect on memory scanning task. *Brain and Cognition, 15,* 246–260.

Howe, M. L., & Courage, M. L. (1993). On resolving the enigma of infantile amnesia. *Psychological Bulletin, 113,* 305–326.

Hulicka, I. M. (1967). Age differences in retention as a function of interference. *Journal of Gerontology, 22,* 180–184.

Hultsch, D. F., & Dixon, R. A. (1984). Memory for text materials in adulthood. In P. B. Baltes & O. G. Brim, Jr. (Eds.), *Life-span development and behavior* (Vol. 6). New York: Academic Press.

Hultsch, D. F., & Dixon, R. A. (1990). Learning and memory in aging. In J. E. Birren & K. W. Schaie (Eds.), *Handbook of the psychology of aging* (3rd ed.). San Diego: Academic Press.

Hultsch, D. F., Hammer, M., & Small, B. J. (1993). Age differences in cognitive performance in later life: Relationships to self-reported health and activity life style. *Journal of Gerontology: Psychological Sciences, 48;* P1–P11.

Hultsch, D. F., Masson, M. E. J., & Small, B. J. (1991). Adult age differences in direct and indirect tests of memory. *Journal of Gerontology: Psychological Sciences, 46,* P22–P30.

Jensen, A. R. (1990). Speed of information processing in a calculating prodigy. *Intelligence, 14,* 259–274.

Jones, M. C. (1924). A laboratory study of fear: The case of Peter. *Pedagogical Seminary, 31,* 308–315.

Justice, E. M. (1985). Categorization as preferred memory strategy: Developmental changes during elementary school. *Developmental Psychology, 21,* 1105–1110.

Kail, R. (1990). *The development of memory in children* (3rd ed.). New York: W. H. Freeman.

Kail, R. (1991). Developmental change in speed of processing during childhood and adolescence. *Psychological Bulletin, 109,* 490–501.

Kail, R., & Bisanz, J. (1992). The information-processing perspective on cognitive development in childhood and adolescence. In R. J. Sternberg & C. A. Berg (Eds.), *Intellectual development.* New York: Cambridge University Press.

Kaitz, M., Meschulach-Sarfaty, O., Auerbach, J., & Eidelman, A. (1988). A reexamination of newborns' ability to imitate facial expressions. *Developmental Psychology, 24,* 3–7.

Kasworm, C. E., & Medina, R. A. (1990). Adult competence in everyday tasks: A cross-sectional secondary analysis. *Educational Gerontology, 16,* 27–48.

Kausler, D. H. (1990). Motivation, human aging, and cognitive performance. In J. E. Birren & K. W. Schaie (Eds.), *Handbook of the psychology of aging* (3rd ed.). San Diego: Academic Press.

Kee, D. W., & Bell, T. S. (1981). The development of organizational strategies in the storage and retrieval of categorical items in free-recall learning. *Child Development, 52,* 1163–1171.

Klahr, D., & Robinson, M. (1981). Formal assessment of problem-solving and planning processes in preschool children. *Cognitive Psychology, 13,* 113–148.

Klahr, D., & Wallace, J. C. (1976). *Cognitive development: An information-processing view.* Hillsdale, NJ: Erlbaum.

Kliegl, R., Smith, J., & Baltes, P. B. (1989). Testing-the-limits and the study of adult age differences in cognitive plasticity of a mnemonic skill. *Developmental Psychology, 25,* 247–256.

Kreutzer, M. A., Leonard, C., & Flavell, J. H. (1975). An interview study of children's knowledge about memory. *Monographs of the Society for Research in Child Development, 40*(1, Serial No. 159).

Kron, R. E. (1966). Instrumental conditioning of nutritive sucking behavior in the newborn. *Recent Advances in Biological Psychiatry, 9,* 295–300.

Kuhn, D. (1992). Cognitive development. In M. H. Bornstein & M. E. Lamb (Eds.), *Developmental psychology: An advanced textbook* (3rd ed.). Hillsdale, NJ: Erlbaum.

Lachman, M. E., & Leff, R. (1989). Perceived control and intellectual functioning in the elderly: A 5-year longitudinal study. *Developmental Psychology, 25,* 722–728.

Lange, G., & Pierce, S. H. (1992). Memory-strategy learning and maintenance in preschool children. *Developmental Psychology, 28,* 453–462.

Lesgold, A. M. (1984). Acquiring expertise. In J. R. Anderson & S. M. Kosslyn (Eds.), *Tutorials in learning and memory: Essays in honor of Gordon Bower.* San Francisco: W. H. Freeman.

Light, L. L. (1991). Memory and aging: Four hypotheses in search of data. *Annual Review of Psychology, 42,* 333–376.

Lipsitt, L. P. (1990). Learning and memory in infants. *Merrill-Palmer Quarterly, 36,* 53–66.

Lipsitt, L. P., & Kaye, H. (1964). Conditioned sucking in the human newborn. *Psychonomic Science, 1,* 29–30.

Loewen, E. R., Shaw, R. J., & Craik, F. I. (1990). Age differences in components of metamemory. *Experimental Aging Research, 16,* 43–48.

Mayer, R. E. (1985). Mathematical ability. In R. J. Sternberg (Ed.), *Human abilities: An information-processing approach.* New York: W. H. Freeman.

Meltzoff, A. N. (1988). Infant imitation and memory: Nine-month-olds in immediate and deferred tests. *Child Development, 59,* 217–225.

Meltzoff, A. N., & Moore, M. K. (1983). Newborn infants imitate adult facial gestures. *Child Development, 54,* 702–709.

Meltzoff, A. N., & Moore, M. K. (1989). Imitation in newborn infants: Exploring the range of gestures initiated and the underlying mechanisms. *Developmental Psychology, 25,* 954–962.

Miller, P. H., Seier, W. L., Probert, J. S., & Aloise, P. A. (1991). Age differences in the capacity demands of a strategy among spontaneously strategic children. *Journal of Experimental Child Psychology, 52,* 149–165.

Miller, P. H., & Weiss, M. G. (1981) Children's attention allocation, understanding of attention, and performance on the incidental learning task. *Child Development, 52,* 1183–1190.

Miller, P. H., Woody-Ramsey, J., & Aloise, P. A. (1991). The role of strategy effortfulness in strategy effectiveness. *Developmental Psychology, 27,* 738–745.

Mitchell, D. B. (1989). How many memory systems? Evidence from aging. *Journal of Experimental Psychology: Learning, Memory, and Cognition, 15,* 31–49.

Morrell, R. W., Park, D. C., & Poon, L. W. (1989). Quality of instructions on prescription drug labels: Effects on memory and comprehension in young and old adults. *Gerontologist, 29,* 345–354.

Morrow, D. G., Leirer, V. O., & Altieri, P. A. (1992). Aging, expertise, and narrative processing. *Psychology and Aging, 7,* 376–388.

Nelson, K. (1984). The transition from infant to child memory. In M. Moscovitch (Ed.), *Infant memory: Its relation to normal and pathological memory in humans and other animals.* New York: Plenum.

Nelson, K. (1992). Emergence of autobiographical memory at age 4. *Human Development, 35,* 172–177.

Newell, A., & Simon, H. A. (1961). Computer simulation of human thinking. *Science, 134,* 2011–2017.

Offenbach, S. I. (1974). A developmental study of hypothesis testing and cue selection strategies. *Developmental Psychology, 10,* 484–490.

Ornstein, P. A., Naus, M. J., & Liberty, C. (1975). Rehearsal and organizational processes in children's memory. *Child Development, 46,* 818–830.

Papoušek, H. (1967). Experimental studies of appetitional behavior in human newborns and infants. In H. W. Stevenson, E. H. Hess, & H. L. Rheingold (Eds.), *Early behavior: Comparative and developmental approaches.* New York: Wiley.

Park, D. C., Morrell, R. W., Frieske, D., & Kincaid, D. (1992). Medication adherence behaviors in older adults: Effects of external cognitive supports. *Psychology and Aging, 7,* 252–256.

Parke, R. D. (1977). Some effects of punishment on children's behavior—revisited. In E. M. Hetherington & R. D. Parke (Eds.), *Contemporary readings in child psychology.* New York: McGraw-Hill.

Parkin, A. J., & Streete, S. (1988). Implicit and explicit memory in young children and adults. *British Journal of Psychology, 79,* 361–369.

Pascual-Leone, J. (1970). A mathematical model for the transition rule in Piaget's developmental stages. *Acta Psychologica, 32,* 301–345.

Pascual-Leone, J. (1984). Attentional, dialectic, and mental effort: Toward an organismic theory of life stages. In M. L. Commons, F. A. Richards, & C. Armon (Eds.), *Beyond formal operations: Late adolescent and adult cognitive development.* New York: Praeger.

Perlmutter, M. (1986). A life-span view of memory. In P. B. Baltes, D. L. Featherman, & R. M. Lerner (Eds.), *Life-span development and behavior* (Vol. 7). Hillsdale, NJ: Erlbaum.

Perris, E. E, Myers, N. A., & Clifton, R. K. (1990). Long-term memory for a single infancy experience. *Child Development, 61,* 1796–1807.

Piaget, J., & Inhelder, B. (1969). *The psychology of the child* (H. Weaver, Trans.). New York: Basic Books. (Original work published 1966.)

Poon, L. W. (1985). Differences in human memory with aging: Nature, causes, and clinical implications. In J. E. Birren & K. W. Schaie (Eds.), *Handbook of the psychology of aging* (2nd ed.). New York: Van Nostrand Reinhold.

Poon, L. W., Fozard, J. L., Paulshock, D. R., & Thomas, J. C. (1979). A questionnaire assessment of age differences in retention of recent and remote events. *Experimental Aging Research, 5,* 401–411.

Pressley, M. (1982). Elaboration and memory development. *Child Development, 53,* 296–309.

Pressley, M. (1983). Making meaningful materials easier to learn: Lessons from cognitive strategy research. In M. Pressley & J. R. Levin (Eds.), *Cognitive strategy research: Educational applications.* New York: Springer-Verlag.

Pressley, M., Forrest-Pressley, D. L., Elliott-Faust, D., & Miller, G. (1985). Children's use of cognitive strategies, how to teach strategies, and what to do if they can't be taught. In M. Pressley & C. J. Brainerd (Eds.), *Cognitive learning and memory in children: Progress in cognitive development research.* New York: Springer-Verlag.

Pressley, M., & Levin, J. R. (1980). The development of mental imagery retrieval. *Child Development, 51,* 558–560.

Reder, L. M., Wible, C., & Martin, J. (1986). Differential memory changes with age: Exact retrieval versus plausible inference. *Journal of Experimental Psychology: Learning, Memory, and Cognition, 12,* 72–81.

Reese, H. W., & Rodeheaver, D. (1985). Problem solving and complex decision making. In J. E. Birren & K. W. Schaie (Eds.), *Handbook of the psychology of aging* (2nd ed.). New York: Van Nostrand Reinhold.

Roediger, H. L. (1990). Implicit memory: Retention without remembering. *American Psychologist, 45,* 1043–1056.

Rovee-Collier, C. K. (1984). The ontogeny of learning and memory in human infancy. In R. Kail & N. E. Spear (Eds.), *Comparative perspectives on the development of memory.* Hillsdale, NJ: Erlbaum.

Rovee-Collier, C. K. (1987). Learning and memory in infancy. In J. D. Osofsky (Ed.), *Handbook of infant development* (2nd ed.). New York: Wiley.

Rovee-Collier, C. K., Schechter, A., Shyi, G. C., & Shields, P. J. (1992). Perceptual identification of contextual attributes and infant memory retrieval. *Developmental Psychology, 28,* 307–318.

Salatas, H., & Flavell, J. H. (1976). Behavioral and metamnemonic indicators of strategic behaviors under remember instructions in first grade. *Child Development, 47,* 81–89.

Salthouse, T. A. (1990). Cognitive competence and expertise in aging. In J. E. Birren & K. W. Schaie (Eds.), *Handbook of the psychology of aging* (3rd ed.). San Diego: Academic Press.

Salthouse, T. A. (1992). Why do adult age differences increase with task complexity? *Developmental Psychology, 28,* 905–918.

Salthouse, T. A. (1993). Speed and knowledge as determinants of adult age differences in verbal tasks. *Journal of Gerontology: Psychological Sciences, 48,* P29–P36.

Schacter, D. L. (1992). Understanding implicit memory: A cognitive neuroscience approach. *American Psychologist, 47,* 559–569.

Schaie, K. W. (1977/1978). Toward a stage theory of adult cognitive development. *International Journal of Aging and Human Development, 8,* 129–138.

Schneider, W., Korkel, J., & Weinert, F. E. (1989). Domain-specific knowledge and memory performance: A comparison of high- and low-aptitude children. *Journal of Educational Psychology, 81,* 306–312.

Schneider, W., & Sodian, B. (1988). Metamemory-memory behavior relationships in young children: Evidence from a memory-for-location task. *Journal of Experimental Child Psychology, 45,* 209–233.

Scogin, F., & Bienias, J. L. (1988). A three-year follow-up of older adult participants in a memory-skills training progam. *Psychology and Aging, 3,* 334–337.

Sheingold, K., & Tenney, Y. J. (1982). Memory for a salient childhood event. In U. Neisser (Ed.), *Memory observed: Remembering in natural contexts.* San Francisco: W. H. Freeman.

Siegler, R. S. (1981). Developmental sequences within and between concepts. *Monographs of the Society for Research in Child Development, 46*(2, Serial No. 189).

Siegler, R. S., & Crowley, K. (1991). The microgenetic method: A direct means for studying cognitive development. *American Psychologist, 46,* 606–620.

Singer, J. M., & Fagen, J. W. (1992). Negative affect, emotional expression, and forgetting in young infants. *Developmental Psychology, 28,* 48–57.

Skinner, B. F. (1953). *Science and human behavior.* New York: Macmillan.

Skinner, B. F. (1983). Intellectual self-management in old age. *American Psychologist, 38,* 239–244.

Somerville, S. C., Wellman, H. M., & Cultice, J. C. (1983). Young children's deliberate reminding. *Journal of Genetic Psychology, 143,* 87–96.

Sophian, C. (1980). Habituation is not enough: Novelty preferences, search, and memory in infancy. *Merrill-Palmer Quarterly, 26,* 239–257.

Spilich, G. J., Vesonder, G. T., Chiesi, H. L., & Voss, J. F. (1979). Text processing of domain-related information for individuals with high and low domain knowledge. *Journal of Verbal Learning and Verbal Behavior, 18,* 275–290.

Storandt, M. (1992). Memory-skills training for older adults. In T. B. Sonderegger (Ed.), *Nebraska Symposium on Motivation: Vol. 39. Psychology and aging.* Lincoln: University of Nebraska Press.

Sunderland, A., Watts, K., Baddeley, A. D., & Harris, J. E. (1986). Subjective memory assessment and test performance in elderly adults. *Journal of Gerontology, 41,* 376–384.

Swain, I. U., Zelazo, P. R., & Clifton, R. K. (1993). Newborn infants' memory for speech sounds retained over 24 hours. *Developmental Psychology, 29,* 312–323.

Usher, J. A., & Neisser, U. (1993). Childhood amnesia and the beginnings of memory for four early life events. *Journal of Experimental Psychology: General, 122,* 155–165.

Verhaeghen, P., Marcoen, A., & Goossens, L. (1992). Improving memory performance in the aged through mnemonic training: A meta-analytic study. *Psychology and Aging, 7,* 242–251.

Verna, G. B. (1977). The effects of a four-hour delay of punishment under two conditions of verbal instruction. *Child Development, 48,* 621–624.

Vinter, A. (1986). The role of movement in eliciting early imitations. *Child Development, 57,* 66–71.

Waddell, K. J., & Rogoff, B. (1981). Effect of contextual organization on spatial memory of middle-aged and older women. *Developmental Psychology, 17,* 878–885.

Wagner, D. A. (1978). Memories of Morocco: The influence of age, schooling, and environment on memory. *Cognitive Psychology, 10,* 1–28.

Watson, J. B., & Raynor, R. (1920). Conditioned emotional reactions. *Journal of Experimental Psychology, 3,* 1–14.

Weiss, B., Dodge, K. A., Bates, J. E., & Pettit, G. S. (1992). Some consequences of early harsh discipline: Child aggression and a maladaptive social information processing style. *Child Development, 63,* 1321–1335.

Wellman, H. M. (1977). Preschoolers' understanding of memory relevant variables. *Child Development, 48,* 1720–1723.

West, R. L., Crook, T. H., & Barron, K. L. (1992). Everyday memory performance across the life span: Effects of age and noncognitive individual differences. *Psychology and Aging, 7,* 72–82.

White, S. H., & Pillemer, D. B. (1979). Childhood amnesia and the development of a socially accessible memory system. In J. F. Kihlstrom & F. J. Evans (Eds.), *Functional disorders of memory.* Hillsdale, NJ: Erlbaum.

Willemsen, E. (1979). *Understanding infancy.* San Francisco: W. H. Freeman.

Woodruff-Pak, D. S. (1990). Mammalian models of learning, memory, and aging. In J. E. Birren & K. W. Schaie (Eds.), *Handbook of the psychology of aging* (3rd ed.). San Diego: Academic Press.

Yussen, S. R., & Levy, V. M. (1975). Developmental changes in predicting one's own memory span of short-term memory. *Journal of Experimental Child Psychology, 19,* 502–508.

Zivian, M. T., & Darjes, R. W. (1983). Free recall by in-school and out-of-school adults: Performance and metamemory. *Developmental Psychology, 19,* 513–520.

Chapter 9: Mental Abilities

Alpaugh, P. K., & Birren, J. E. (1977). Variables affecting creative contributions across the adult life span. *Human Development, 20,* 240–248.

American Association on Mental Retardation (1992). *Mental retardation: Definition, classification, and systems of support* (9th ed.). Washington, DC: Author.

Anastasi, A. (1988). *Psychological testing* (6th ed.). New York: Macmillan.

Baltes, P. B., & Smith, J. (1990). Toward a psychology of wisdom and its ontogenesis. In R. J. Sternberg (Ed.), *Wisdom: Its nature, origins, and development.* Cambridge, England: Cambridge University Press.

Baltes, P. B., Sowarka, D., & Kliegl, R. (1989). Cognitive training research on fluid intelligence in old age: What can older adults achieve by themselves? *Psychology and Aging, 4,* 217–221.

Bayley, N. (1968). Behavioral correlates of mental growth: Birth to thirty-six years. *American Psychologist, 23,* 1–17.

Bayley, N. (1969). *Bayley Scales of Infant Development.* New York: Psychological Corp.

Bayley, N. (1993). *Bayley Scales of Infant Development* (2nd ed.). San Antonio, TX: Psychological Corp.

Berrueta-Clement, J. R., Schweinhart, L. J., Barnett, S. W., Epstein, A. S., & Weikart, D. P. (1984). *Changed lives: The effects of the Perry Preschool Program on youths through age 19.* Ypsilanti, MI: High/Scope Press.

Blagg, N. (1991). *Can we teach intelligence? A comprehensive evaluation of Feuerstein's instrumental enrichment program.* Hillsdale, NJ: Erlbaum.

Block, J., Gjerde, P. F., & Block, J. H. (1986). More misgivings about the Matching Familiar Figures Test as a measure of reflection-impulsivity: Absence of construct validity in preadolescence. *Developmental Psychology, 22,* 820–831.

Bornstein, M. H., & Sigman, M. D. (1986). Continuity in mental development from infancy. *Child Development, 57,* 251–274.

Bradley, R. H., & Caldwell, B. M. (1984). 174 children: A study of the relationship between home environment and cognitive development during the first 5 years. In A. W. Gottfried (Ed.), *Home environment and early cognitive development: Longitudinal research.* Orlando, FL: Academic Press.

Bradley, R. H., Caldwell, B. M., Rock, S. L., Ramey, C. T., Barnard, K. E., Gray, C., Hammond, M. A., Mitchell, S., Gottfried, A. W., Siegel, L., & Johnson, D. L. (1989). Home environment and cognitive development in the first 3 years of life: A collaborative study involving six sites and three ethnic groups in North America. *Developmental Psychology, 25,* 217–235.

Brody, E. B., & Brody, N. (1976). *Intelligence: Nature, determinants, and consequences.* New York: Academic Press.

Busse, E. W., & Maddox, G. L. (1985). *The Duke longitudinal studies of normal aging. 1955–1980: Overview of history, design, and findings.* New York: Springer.

Caldwell, B. M., & Bradley, R. H. (1984). *Manual for the Home Observation for Measurement of the Environment.* Little Rock: University of Arkansas.

Campbell, F. A., & Ramey, C. T. (1993, March). *Mid-adolescent outcomes for high risk students: An examination of the continuing effects of early intervention.* Paper presented at the biennial meeting of the Society for Research in Child Development, New Orleans.

Campione, J. C., Brown, A. L., Ferrara, R. A., & Bryant, N. R. (1984). The zone of proximal development: Implications for individual differences and learning. In B. Rogoff & J. V. Wertsch (Eds.), *Children's learning in the "zone of proximal development"* (New Directions for Child Development, No. 23). San Francisco: Jossey-Bass.

Carroll, J. B. (1992). Cognitive abilities: The state of the art. *Psychological Science, 3,* 266–270.

Cattell, R. B. (1963). Theory of fluid and crystallized intelligence: A critical experiment. *Journal of Educational Psychology, 54,* 1–22.

Clayton, V. P., & Birren, J. E. (1980). The development of wisdom across the life span: A reexamination of an ancient topic. In P. B. Baltes & O. G. Brim, Jr. (Eds.), *Life-span development and behavior* (Vol. 3). New York: Academic Press.

Coleman, L. J. (1985). *Schooling the gifted.* Menlo Park, CA: Addison-Wesley.

Coon, H., Fulker, D. W., DeFries, J. C., & Plomin, R. (1990). Home environment and cognitive ability of 7-year-old children in the Colorado Adoption Project: Genetic and environmental etiologies. *Developmental Psychology, 26,* 459–468.

Cornelius, S. W. (1984). Classic pattern of intellectual aging: Test familiarity, difficulty, and performance. *Journal of Gerontology, 39,* 201–206.

Cox, C. M. (1926). *Genetic studies of genius. Vol. 2: The early mental traits of three hundred geniuses.* Stanford, CA: Stanford University Press.

Cravens, H. (1992). A scientific project locked in time: The Terman Genetic Studies of Genius, 1920s–1950s. *American Psychologist, 47,* 183–189.

Crockenberg, S. (1983). Early mother and infant antecedents of Bayley Scale performance at 21 months. *Developmental Psychology, 19,* 727–730.

Cunningham, W. R., & Owens, W. A., Jr. (1983). The Iowa State study of the adult development of intellectual abilities. In K. W. Schaie (Ed.), *Longitudinal studies of adult psychological development.* New York: Guilford Press.

Darlington, R. B. (1991). The long-term effects of model preschool programs. In L. Okagaki & R. J. Sternberg (Eds.), *Directors of development: Influences on the development of children's thinking.* Hillsdale, NJ: Erlbaum.

Dennis, W. (1966). Creative productivity between the ages of 20 and 80 years. *Journal of Gerontology, 21,* 1–8.

Dixon, R. A., Kramer, D. A., & Baltes, P. B. (1985). Intelligence: A life-span developmental perspective. In B. B. Wolman (Ed.), *Handbook of intelligence: Theories, measurements, and applications.* New York: Wiley.

Eichorn, D. H., Hunt, J. V., & Honzik, M. P. (1981). Experience, personality, and IQ: Adolescence to middle age. In D. H. Eichorn, J. A. Clausen, N. Haan, M. P. Honzik, & P. H. Mussen (Eds.), *Present and past in middle life.* New York: Academic Press.

Erikson, E. H. (1982). *The life cycle completed: A review.* New York: Norton.

Escalona, S. (1968). *The roots of individuality: Normal patterns of individuality.* Chicago: Aldine.

Fagan, J. F. III, & McGrath, S. K. (1981). Infant recognition memory and later intelligence. *Intelligence, 5,* 121–130.

Feldman, D. H. (1980). *Beyond universals in cognitive development.* Norwood, NJ: Ablex.

Feldman, D. H. (1982). A developmental framework for research with gifted children. In D. H. Feldman (Ed.), *Developmental approaches to giftedness and creativity* (New Directions for Child Development, No. 17). San Francisco: Jossey-Bass.

Feldman, D. H. (1986). *Nature's gambit: Child prodigies and the development of human potential.* New York: Basic Books.

Feldman, R. D. (1982). *Whatever happened to the Quiz Kids? Perils and profits of growing up gifted.* Chicago: Chicago Review Press.

Feuerstein, R., Miller, R., Hoffman, M. B., Rand, Y., Mintzker, Y., & Jensen, M. R. (1981). Cognitive modifiability in adolescence: Cognitive structure and the effects of intervention. *Journal of Special Education, 15,* 269–287.

Feuerstein, R., Rand, Y., & Hoffman, M. B. (1979). *The dynamic assessment of retarded performers: The Learning Potential Assessment Device, theory, instruments, and techniques.* Baltimore: University Park Press.

Fincher, J. (1973). The Terman study is 50 years old: Happy anniversary and pass the ammunition. *Human Behavior, 2,* 8–15.

Fisher, M. A., & Zeaman, D. (1970). Growth and decline of retardate intelligence. In N. R. Ellis (Ed.), *International review of research in mental retardation* (Vol. 4). New York: Academic Press.

Flynn, J. R. (1987). Massive IQ gains in 14 nations: What IQ tests really measure. *Psychological Bulletin, 101,* 171–191.

Fraser, B. J., Walberg, H. J., Welch, W. W., & Hattie, J. A. (1987). Synthesis of educational productivity research. *International Journal of Educational Research, 11,* 145–252.

Frisby, C. L., & Braden, J. P. (1992). Feuerstein's dynamic assessment approach: A semantic, logical, and empirical critique. *Journal of Special Education, 26,* 281–301.

Gardner, H. (1983). *Frames of mind: The theory of multiple intelligences.* New York: Basic Books.

Gardner, H., Phelps, E., & Wolf, D. (1990). The roots of adult creativity in children's symbolic products. In C. N. Alexander & E. J. Langer (Eds.), *Higher stages of human development: Perspectives on adult growth.* New York: Oxford University Press.

Gardner, M. K., & Clark, E. (1992). The psychometric perspective on intellectual development in childhood and adolescence. In R. J. Sternberg & C. A. Berg (Eds.), *Intellectual development.* New York: Cambridge University Press.

Getzels, J. W., & Jackson, P. W. (1962). *Creativity and intelligence: Explorations with gifted children.* New York: Wiley.

Gottfredson, L. S. (1986). Societal consequences of the *g* factor in employment. *Journal of Vocational Behavior, 29,* 379–410.

Gottfried, A. W. (1984). Home environment and early cognitive development: Integration, meta-analyses, and conclusions. In A. W. Gottfried (Ed.), *Home environment and early cognitive development: Longitudinal research.* Orlando, FL: Academic Press.

Gottfried, A. W., & Gottfried, A. E. (1984). Home environment and cognitive development in young children of middle-socioeconomic–status families. In A. W. Gottfried (Ed.), *Home environment and early cognitive development: Longitudinal research.* Orlando, FL: Academic Press.

Gray, S. W., Ramsey, B. K., & Klaus, R. A. (1982). *From 3 to 20: The early training project.* Baltimore: University Park Press.

Gribbin, K., Schaie, K. W., & Parham, I. A. (1980). Complexity of life style and maintenance of intellectual abilities. *Journal of Social Issues, 36,* 47–61.

Grossman, H. J. (1983). *Classification in mental retardation.* Washington, DC: American Association on Mental Deficiency.

Gruber, H. E. (1982). On the hypothesized relation between giftedness and creativity. In D. H. Feldman (Ed.), *Developmental approaches to giftedness and creativity* (New Directions for Child Development, No. 17). San Francisco: Jossey-Bass.

Guilford, J. P. (1967). *The nature of human intelligence.* New York: McGraw-Hill.

Guilford, J. P. (1988). Some changes in the structure-of-the-intellect model. *Educational and Psychological Measurement, 40,* 1–4.

Harrell, T. W., & Harrell, M. S. (1945). Army General Classification Test scores for civilian occupations. *Educational and Psychological Measurement, 5,* 229–239.

Harrington, D. M., Block, J. H., & Block, J. (1983). Predicting creativity in preadolescence from divergent thinking in early childhood. *Journal of Personality and Social Psychology, 45,* 609–623.

Harrington, D. M., Block, J. H., & Block, J. (1987). Testing aspects of Carl Rogers's theory of creative environments: Child-rearing antecedents of creative potential in young adolescents. *Journal of Personality and Social Psychology, 52,* 851–856.

Hayslip, B., Jr. (1989). Alternative mechanisms for improvements in fluid ability performance among older adults. *Psychology and Aging, 4,* 122–124.

Helms, J. E. (1992). Why is there no study of cultural equivalence in standardized cognitive-ability testing? *American Psychologist, 47,* 1083–1101.

Hennessey, B. A., & Amabile, T. M. (1988). The conditions of creativity. In R. J. Sternberg (Ed.), *The nature of creativity: Contemporary psychological perspectives.* Cambridge, England: Cambridge University Press.

Hertzog, C. (1989). Influences of cognitive slowing on age differences in intelligence. *Developmental Psychology, 25,* 636–651.

Holliday, S. G., & Chandler, M. J. (1986). *Wisdom: Explorations in adult competence.* Basel, Switzerland: Karger.

Honzik, M. P. (1983). Measuring mental abilities in infancy: The value and limitations. In M. Lewis (Ed.), *Origins of intelligence: Infancy and early childhood* (2nd ed.). New York: Plenum.

Honzik, M. P., Macfarlane, J. W., & Allen, L. (1948). The stability of mental test performance between two and eighteen years. *Journal of Experimental Education, 17,* 309–324.

Horn, J. L., & Cattell, R. B. (1967). Age differences in fluid and crystallized intelligence. *Acta Psychologica, 26,* 107–129.

Horn, J. L., & Hofer, S. M. (1992). Major abilities and development in the adult period. In R. J. Sternberg & C. A. Berg (Eds.), *Intellectual development.* New York: Cambridge University Press.

Howieson, N. (1981). A longitudinal study of creativity: 1965–1975. *Journal of Creative Behavior, 15,* 117–134.

Hunt, J. M., & Paraskevopoulos, J. (1980). Children's psychological development as a function of the inaccuracy of their mothers' knowledge of their abilities. *Journal of Genetic Psychology, 136,* 285–298.

Hunter, J. E., & Hunter, R. F. (1984). Validity and utility of alternative predictors of job performance. *Psychological Bulletin, 96,* 72–98.

Jaquish, G. A., & Ripple, R. E. (1981). Cognitive creative abilities and self-esteem across the adult life-span. *Human Development, 24,* 110–119.

Jarvik, L. F., & Bank, L. (1983). Aging twins: Longitudinal psychometric data. In K. W. Schaie (Ed.), *Longitudinal studies of adult psychological development.* New York: Guilford Press.

Jayanthi, M., & Rogoff, B. (1985). A cultural perspective on the development of talent. In F. D. Horowitz & M. O'Brien (Eds.), *The gifted and talented: Developmental perspectives.* Washington, DC: American Psychological Association.

Jensen, A. R. (1969). How much can we boost IQ and scholastic achievement? *Harvard Educational Review, 39,* 1–123.

Jensen, A. R. (1977). Cumulative deficit in the IQ of blacks in the rural South. *Developmental Psychology, 13,* 184–191.

Jensen, A. R. (1980). *Bias in mental testing.* New York: Free Press.

Jensen, A. R. (1993). Why is reaction time correlated with psychometric *g*? *Current Directions in Psychological Science, 2,* 53–56.

Johansson, B., Zarit, S. H., & Berg, S. (1992). Changes in cognitive functioning of the oldest old. *Journal of Gerontology: Psychological Sciences, 47,* P75–P80.

Kagan, J., Rosman, B. L., Day, D., Albert, J., & Phillips, W. (1964). Information processing in the child: Significance of analytic and reflective attitudes. *Psychological Monographs, 78*(1, Whole No. 578).

Kerns, K. A., & Berenbaum, S. A. (1991). Sex differences in spatial ability in children. *Behavior Genetics, 21,* 383–396.

Kleemeier, R. W. (1962). Intellectual change in the senium. *Proceedings of the Social Statistics Section of the American Statistical Association,* 290–295.

Klineberg, O. (1963). Negro-white differences in intelligence test performance: A new look at an old problem. *American Psychologist, 18,* 198–203.

Kogan, N. (1983). Stylistic variation in childhood and adolescence: Creativity, metaphor, and cognitive styles. In J. H. Flavell & E. H. Markman (Eds.), *Handbook of child psychology: Vol. 3. Cognitive development* (4th ed.). New York: Wiley.

Labouvie-Vief, G. (1985). Intelligence and cognition. In J. E. Birren & K. W. Schaie (Eds.), *Handbook of the psychology of aging* (2nd ed.). New York: Van Nostrand Reinhold.

Lazar, I., & Darlington, R. (1982). Lasting effects of early education: A report from the Consortium for Longitudinal Studies. *Monographs of the Society for Research in Child Development, 47*(2–3, Serial No. 195).

Lee, V. E., Brooks-Gunn, J., & Schnur, E. (1988). Does Head Start work? A 1-year follow-up comparison of disadvantaged children attending Head Start, no preschool, and other preschool programs. *Developmental Psychology, 24,* 210–222.

Lee, V. E., Brooks-Gunn, J., Schnur, E., & Liaw, F. (1990). Are Head Start effects sustained? A longitudinal follow-up comparison of disadvantaged children attending Head

Start, no preschool, and other preschool programs. *Child Development, 61,* 495–507.

Lehman, H. C. (1953). *Age and achievement.* Princeton, NJ: Princeton University Press.

Lewontin, R. C. (1976). Race and intelligence. In N. J. Block & G. Dworkin (Eds.), *The IQ controversy.* New York: Pantheon Books.

Linn, M. C., & Petersen, A. C. (1985). Emergence and characterization of sex differences in spatial ability: A meta-analysis. *Child Development, 56,* 1479–1498.

Loehlin, J. C., Lindzey, G., & Spuhler, J. N. (1975). *Race differences in intelligence.* San Francisco: W. H. Freeman.

Longstreth, L., Davis, B., Carter, L., Flint, D., Owen, J., Rickert, M., & Taylor, E. (1981). Separation of home intellectual environment and maternal IQ as determinants of child IQ. *Developmental Psychology, 17,* 532–541.

Luster, T., & Dubow, E. (1992). Home environment and maternal intelligence as predictors of verbal intelligence: A comparison of preschool and school-age children. *Merrill-Palmer Quarterly, 38,* 151–175.

Maccoby, E. E., & Jacklin, C. N. (1974). *The psychology of sex differences.* Stanford, CA: Stanford University Press.

MacPhee, D., Ramey, C. T., & Yeates, K. O. (1984). Home environmental and early cognitive development: Implications for intervention. In A. W. Gottfried (Ed.), *Home environment and early cognitive development: Longitudinal research.* Orlando, FL: Academic Press.

McCall, R. B. (1981). Nature-nurture and the two realms of development: A proposed integration with respect to mental development. *Child Development, 55,* 1–12.

McCall, R. B. (1983). A conceptual approach to early mental development. In M. Lewis (Ed.), *Origins of intelligence: Infancy and early childhood* (2nd ed.). New York: Plenum.

McCall, R. B., Applebaum, M. I., & Hogarty, P. S. (1973). Developmental changes in mental test performance. *Monographs of the Society for Research in Child Development, 38*(3, Serial No. 150).

McCall, R. B., & Carriger, M. S. (1993). A meta-analysis of infant habituation and recognition memory performance as predictors of later IQ. *Child Development, 64,* 57–79.

McCall, R. B., Eichorn, D. H., & Hogarty, P. S. (1977). Transitions in early mental development. *Monographs of the Society for Research in Child Development, 42*(3, Serial No. 171).

McCrae, R. R., Arenberg, D., & Costa, P. T., Jr. (1987). Declines in divergent thinking with age: Cross-sectional, longitudinal, and cross-sequential analyses. *Psychology and Aging, 2,* 130–137.

McKenna, F. P. (1990). Learning implications of field dependence-independence: Cognitive style versus cognitive ability. *Applied Cognitive Psychology, 4,* 425–437.

Messer, S. B. (1976). Reflectivity-impulsivity: A review. *Psychological Bulletin, 83,* 1026–1052.

Miller, S. A. (1986). Parents' beliefs about their children's cognitive abilities. *Developmental Psychology, 22,* 276–284.

Minton, H. L., & Schneider, F. W. (1980). *Differential psychology.* Pacific Grove, CA: Brooks/Cole.

Monass, J. A., & Engelhard, J. A., Jr. (1990). Home environment and the competitiveness of accomplished individuals in four talent fields. *Developmental Psychology, 26,* 264–268.

Moore, E. G. J. (1986). Family socialization and the IQ test performance of traditionally and transracially adopted black children. *Developmental Psychology, 22,* 317–326.

Morse, C. K. (1993). Does variability increase with age? An archival study of cognitive measures. *Psychology and Aging, 8,* 156–164.

Mumford, M. D., & Gustafson, S. B. (1988). Creativity syndrome: Integration, application, and innovation. *Psychological Bulletin, 103,* 27–43.

Newcombe, N., & Bandura, M. M. (1983). Effect of age at puberty on spatial ability in girls: A question of mechanism. *Developmental Psychology, 19,* 215–224.

Newcombe, N., & Dubas, J. S. (1992). A longitudinal study of predictors of spatial ability in adolescent females. *Child Development, 63,* 37–46.

Newcombe, N., Dubas, J. S., & Baenninger, M. (1989). Associations of timing of puberty, spatial ability, and lateralization in adult women. *Child Development, 60,* 246–254.

Noble, K. D., Robinson, N. M., & Gunderson, S. A. (1993). All rivers lead to the sea: A follow-up study of gifted young adults. *Roeper Review, 15,* 124–130.

Oakland, T., & Parmelee, R. (1985). Mental measurement of minority-group children. In B. B. Wolman (Ed.), *Handbook of intelligence: Theories, measurements, and applications.* New York: Wiley.

Ochse, R. (1990). *Before the gates of excellence: The determinants of creative genius.* Cambridge, England: Cambridge University Press.

O'Connor, N., & Hermelin, B. (1991). Talents and preoccupations in idiot-savants. *Psychological Medicine, 21,* 959–964.

Okagaki, L., & Sternberg, R. J. (1993). Parental beliefs and children's school performance. *Child Development, 64,* 36–56.

Orwoll, L., & Perlmutter, M. (1990). The study of wise persons: Integrating a personality perspective. In R. J. Sternberg (Ed.), *Wisdom: Its nature, origins, and development.* Cambridge, England: Cambridge University Press.

Over, R. (1989). Age and scholarly impact. *Psychology and Aging, 4,* 222–225.

Owens, W. A., Jr. (1953). Age and mental abilities: A longitudinal study. *Genetic Psychology Monographs, 48,* 3–54.

Patterson, C. J., Kupersmidt, J. B., & Vaden, N. A. (1990). Income level, gender, ethnicity, and household composition as predictors of children's school-based competence. *Child Development, 61,* 485–494.

Piaget, J. (1950). *The psychology of intelligence.* New York: Harcourt Brace & World.

Plomin, R. (1990). *Nature and nurture: An introduction to behavior genetics.* Pacific Grove, CA: Brooks/Cole.

Ramey, C. T., & Ramey, S. L. (1992). Effective early intervention. *Mental Retardation, 30,* 337–345.

Reznikoff, M., Domino, G., Bridges, C., & Honeyman, M. (1973). Creative abilities in identical and fraternal twins. *Behavior Genetics, 3,* 365–377.

Richardson, T. M., & Benbow, C. P. (1990). Long-term effects of acceleration on the social-emotional adjustment of mathematically precocious youths. *Journal of Educational Psychology, 82,* 464–470.

Robinson, N. M., & Janos, P. M. (1986). Psychological adjustment in a college-level program of marked academic acceleration. *Journal of Youth and Adolescence, 15,* 51–60.

Robinson, N. M., & Robinson, H. B. (1982). The optimal match: Devising the best compromise for the highly gifted student. In D. H. Feldman (Ed.), *Developmental approaches to giftedness and creativity* (New Directions for Child Development, No. 17). San Francisco: Jossey-Bass.

Rose, S. A., Feldman, J. F., & Wallace, I. F. (1992). Infant information processing in relation to six-year cognitive outcomes. *Child Development, 63,* 1126–1141.

Rose, S. A., Feldman, J. F., Wallace, I. F., & McCarton, C. (1989). Infant visual attention: Relation to birth status and developmental outcome during the first 5 years. *Developmental Psychology, 25,* 560–576.

Ross, R. T., Begab, M. J., Dondis, E. H., Giampiccolo, J. S., Jr., & Meyers, C. E. (1985). *Lives of the mentally retarded: A forty-year follow-up study.* Stanford, CA: Stanford University Press.

Runco, M. A. (1992). Children's divergent thinking and creative ideation. *Developmental Review, 12,* 233–264.

Saccuzzo, D. P., Johnson, N. E., & Russell, G. (1992). Verbal versus performance IQs for gifted African-American, Caucasian, Filipino, and Hispanic children. *Psychological Assessment, 4,* 239–244.

Sacks, E. L. (1952). Intelligence scores as a function of experimentally established social relationships between child and examiner. *Journal of Abnormal and Social Psychology, 47,* 354–358.

Salkind, N. J., & Nelson, C. F. (1980). A note on the developmental nature of reflection-impulsivity. *Developmental Psychology, 16,* 237–238.

Salthouse, T. A. (1993). Speed and knowledge as determinants of adult age differences in verbal tasks. *Journal of Gerontology: Psychological Sciences, 48,* P29–P36.

Sameroff, A. J., Seifer, R., Baldwin, A., & Baldwin, C. (1993). Stability of intelligence from preschool to adolescence: The influence of social and family risk factors. *Child Development, 64,* 80–97.

Sanders, B., & Soares, M. P. (1986). Sexual maturation and spatial ability in college students. *Developmental Psychology, 22,* 199–203.

Scarr, S., & Weinberg, R. A. (1983). The Minnesota adoption studies: Genetic differences and malleability. *Child Development, 54,* 260–267.

Schaie, K. W. (1983). The Seattle longitudinal study: A 21-year exploration of psychometric intelligence in adulthood. In K. W. Schaie (Ed.), *Longitudinal studies of adult psychological development.* New York: Guilford Press.

Schaie, K. W. (1984). Midlife influences upon intellectual functioning in old age. *International Journal of Behavioral Development, 7,* 463–478.

Schaie, K. W. (1989a). The hazards of cognitive aging. *Gerontologist, 29,* 484–493.

Schaie, K. W. (1989b). Perceptual speed in adulthood: Cross-sectional and longitudinal studies. *Psychology and Aging, 4,* 443–453.

Schaie, K. W. (1990). Intellectual development in adulthood. In J. E. Birren & K. W. Schaie (Eds.), *Handbook of the psychology of aging* (3rd ed.). San Diego: Academic Press.

Schaie, K. W., & Hertzog, C. (1983). Fourteen-year cohort-sequential analyses of adult intellectual development. *Developmental Psychology, 19,* 531–543.

Schaie, K. W., & Hertzog, C. (1986). Toward a comprehensive model of adult intellectual development: Contributions of the Seattle longitudinal study. In R. J. Sternberg (Ed.), *Advances in the psychology of human intelligence* (Vol. 3). Hillsdale, NJ: Erlbaum.

Schaie, K. W., & Willis, S. L. (1986). Can decline in adult intellectual functioning be reversed? *Developmental Psychology, 22,* 223–232.

Schaie, K. W., & Willis, S. L. (1993). Age difference patterns of psychometric intelligence in adulthood: Generalizability within and across ability domains. *Psychology and Aging, 8,* 44–55.

Schalock, R. L., Holl, C., Elliott, B., & Ross, I. (1992). A longitudinal follow-up of graduates from a rural special education program. *Learning Disability Quarterly, 15,* 29–38.

Schuster, D. T. (1990). Fulfillment of potential, life satisfaction, and competence: Comparing four cohorts of gifted women at midlife. *Journal of Educational Psychology, 82,* 471–478.

Shepard, R. N., & Metzler, J. (1971). Mental rotation of three-dimensional objects. *Science, 171,* 701–703.

Shurkin, J. N. (1992). *Terman's kids: The groundbreaking study of how the gifted grow up.* Boston: Little, Brown.

Signorella, M. L., Jamison, W., & Krupa, M. H. (1989). Predicting spatial performance from gender stereotyping in activity preferences and in self-concept. *Developmental Psychology, 25,* 89–95.

Simonton, D. K. (1975). Age and literary creativity: A cross-cultural and trans-historical survey. *Journal of Cross-Cultural Psychology, 6,* 259–277.

Simonton, D. K. (1984). *Genius, creativity, and leadership: Historiometric inquiries.* Cambridge, MA: Harvard University Press.

Simonton, D. K. (1989). Age and creative productivity: Nonlinear estimation of an information-processing model. *International Journal of Aging and Human Development, 29,* 23–37.

Simonton, D. K. (1990). Creativity in the later years: Optimistic prospects for achievement. *Gerontologist, 30,* 626–631.

Simonton, D. K. (1991). Career landmarks in science: Individual differences and interdisciplinary contrasts. *Developmental Psychology, 27,* 119–130.

Smith, G., & Carlsson, I. (1985). Creativity in middle and late school years. *International Journal of Behavioral Development, 8,* 329–343.

Smith, J., & Baltes, P. B. (1990). Wisdom-related knowledge: Age/cohort differences in response to life-planning problems. *Developmental Psychology, 26,* 494–505.

Smith, J. D., & Caplan, J. (1988). Cultural differences in cognitive style development. *Developmental Psychology, 24,* 46–52.

Smith, J. D., & Kemler Nelson, D. G. (1988). Is the more impulsive child a more holistic processor? A reconsideration. *Child Development, 59,* 719–727.

Spearman, C. (1927). *The abilities of man.* New York: Macmillan.

Staudinger, U. M., Smith, J., & Baltes, P. B. (1992). Wisdom-related knowledge in a life review task: Age differences and the role of professional specialization. *Psychology and Aging, 7,* 271–281.

Sternberg, R. J. (1985). *Beyond IQ: A triarchic theory of human intelligence.* Cambridge, MA: Cambridge University Press.

Sternberg, R. J. (1988). *The triarchic mind: A new theory of human intelligence.* New York: Viking.

Sternberg, R. J. (Ed.) (1990). *Wisdom: Its nature, origins, and development.* Cambridge, England: Cambridge University Press.

Sternberg, R. J. (1991). Theory-based testing of intellectual abilities: Rationale for the triarchic abilities test. In H. A. H. Rowe (Ed.), *Intelligence: Reconceptualization and measurement.* Hillsdale, NJ: Erlbaum.

Sternberg, R. J. (1992). Ability tests, measurements, and markets. *Journal of Educational Psychology, 84,* 134–140.

Sternberg, R. J., & Berg, C. A. (1986). Quantitative integration: Definitions of intelligence: A comparison of the 1921 and 1986 symposia. In R. J. Sternberg & D. K. Detterman (Eds.), *What is intelligence? Contemporary viewpoints on its nature and definition.* Norwood, NJ: Ablex.

Subotnik, R. F., Karp, D. E., & Morgan, E. R. (1989). High IQ children at midlife: An investigation into the generalizability of Terman's genetic studies of genius. *Roeper Review, 11,* 139–144.

Taylor, R. E., & Richards, S. B. (1991). Patterns of intellectual differences of Black, Hispanic, and White children. *Psychology in the Schools, 28,* 5–9.

Terman, L. M. (1954). The discovery and encouragement of exceptional talent. *American Psychologist, 9,* 221–238.

Terman, L. M., & Oden, M. H. (1959). *The gifted group at mid-life.* Stanford, CA: Stanford University Press.

Thompson, L. A., Fagan, J. F., & Fulker, D. W. (1991). Longitudinal prediction of specific cognitive abilities from infant novelty preference. *Child Development, 62,* 530–538.

Thorndike, R. L., Hagen, E. P., & Sattler, J. M. (1986). *The Stanford-Binet Intelligence Scale* (4th ed.). Chicago: Riverside.

Thurstone, L. L. (1938). *Primary mental abilities.* Chicago: University of Chicago Press.

Thurstone, L. L., & Thurstone, T. G. (1941). Factorial studies of intelligence. *Psychometric Monographs,* No. 2.

Thurstone, L. L., & Thurstone, T. G. (1948). *SRA Primary Mental Abilities, Ages 11–17, Form AM.* Chicago: Science Research Associates.

Tomlinson-Keasey, C., & Little, T. D. (1990). Predicting educational attainment, occupational achievement, intellectual skill, and personal adjustment among gifted men and women. *Journal of Educational Psychology, 82,* 442–455.

Torrance, E. P. (1975). Creativity research in education: Still alive. In I. A. Taylor & J. W. Getzels (Eds.), *Perspectives in creativity.* Chicago: Aldine-Atherton.

Torrance, E. P. (1988). The nature of creativity as manifest in its testing. In R. J. Sternberg (Ed.), *The nature of creativity: Contemporary psychological perspectives.* Cambridge, England: Cambridge University Press.

Turkheimer, E. (1991). Individual and group differences in adoption studies of IQ. *Psychological Bulletin, 110,* 392–405.

Vincent, K. R. (1991). Black/White IQ differences: Does age make the difference? *Journal of Clinical Psychology, 47,* 266–270.

Waber, D. P. (1977). Sex differences in mental abilities, hemispheric lateralization, and rate of physical growth at adolescence. *Developmental Psychology, 13,* 29–38.

Wallace, A. (1986). *The prodigy: A biography of William Sidis.* New York: Dutton.

Wallach, M. A. (1971). *The intelligence-creativity distinction.* Morristown, NJ: General Learning Press.

Wallach, M. A. (1985). Creativity testing and giftedness. In F. D. Horowitz & M. O'Brien (Eds.), *The gifted and talented. Developmental perspectives.* Washington, DC: American Psychological Association.

Wallach, M. A., & Kogan, N. (1965). *Thinking in young children.* New York: Holt, Rinehart & Winston.

Wang, J. J., & Kaufman, A. S. (1993). Changes in fluid and crystallized intelligence across the 20-year to 90-year age range on the K-BIT. *Journal of Psychoeducational Assessment, 11,* 29–37.

Wechsler, D. (1981). *Wechsler Adult Intelligence Scale–Revised.* New York: Psychological Corp.

Wechsler, D. (1989). *WPPSI-R manual: Wechsler Preschool and Primary Scale of Intelligence–Revised.* San Antonio, TX: Psychological Corp.

Wechsler, D. (1991). *Manual, WISC-III: Wechsler Intelligence Scale for Children–Third Edition.* San Antonio, TX: Psychological Corp.

Weinberg, R. A. (1989). Intelligence and IQ: Landmark issues and great debates. *American Psychologist, 44,* 98–104.

Weinberg, R. A., Scarr, S., & Waldman, I. D. (1992). The Minnesota transracial adoption study: A follow-up of IQ test performance at adolescence. *Intelligence, 16,* 117–135.

Westling, D. L. (1986). *Introduction to mental retardation.* Englewood Cliffs, NJ: Prentice-Hall.

White, N., & Cunningham, W. R. (1988). Is terminal drop pervasive or specific? *Journal of Gerontology: Psychological Sciences, 43,* P141–144.

Yeates, K. O., MacPhee, D., Campbell, F. A., & Ramey, C. T. (1983). Maternal IQ and home environment as determinants of early childhood intellectual competence: A developmental analysis. *Developmental Psychology, 19,* 731–739.

Yerkes, R. M. (1921). Psychological examining in the U.S. Army. *Memoirs: National Academy of Science, 15,* 1–890.

Zelniker, T., & Jeffrey, W. E. (1976). Reflective and impulsive children: Strategies of information processes underlying differences in problem solving. *Monographs of the Society for Research in Child Development, 41*(5, Serial No. 168).

Zelniker, T., & Jeffrey, W. E. (1979). Attention and cognitive style in children. In G. A. Hale & M. Lewis (Eds.), *Attention and cognitive development.* New York: Plenum.

Zigler, E., Abelson, W. D., Trickett, P. K., & Seitz, V. (1982). Is an intervention program necessary to improve economically disadvantaged children's IQ scores? *Child Development, 53,* 340–348.

Zigler, E., & Hodapp, R. M. (1991). Behavioral functioning in individuals with mental retardation. *Annual Review of Psychology, 42,* 29–50.

Chapter 10: Self-Conceptions, Personality, and Emotional Expression

Archer, S. L. (1982). The lower age boundaries of identity development. *Child Development, 53,* 1551–1556.

Archer, S. L. (1992). A feminist's approach to identity research. In G. R. Adams, T. P. Gullotta, & R. Montemayor (Eds.), *Adolescent identity formation* (Advances in Adolescent Development, Vol. 4). Newbury Park, CA: Sage.

Asendorpf, J. B., & Van Aken, M. A. G. (1991). Correlates of the temporal consistency of personality patterns in childhood. *Journal of Personality, 59,* 689–703.

Bandura, A. (1986). *Social foundations of thought and action: A social cognitive theory.* Englewood Cliffs, NJ: Prentice-Hall.

Bengtson, V. L., Reedy, M. N., & Gordon, C. (1985). Aging and self-conceptions: Personality processes and social contexts. In J. E. Birren & K. W. Schaie (Eds.), *Handbook of the psychology of aging* (2nd ed.). New York: Van Nostrand Reinhold.

Bernstein, R. M. (1980). The development of the self-system during adolescence. *Journal of Genetic Psychology, 136,* 231–245.

Bertenthal, B. I., & Fischer, K. W. (1978). Development of self-recognition in the infant. *Developmental Psychology, 14,* 44–50.

Berzonsky, M. D. (1992). A process perspective on identity and stress management. In G. R. Adams, T. P. Gullotta, & R. Montemayor (Eds.), *Adolescent identity formation* (Advances in Adolescent Development, Vol. 4). Newbury Park, CA: Sage.

Bilsker, D., & Marcia, J. E. (1991). Adaptive regression and ego identity. *Journal of Adolescence, 14,* 75–84.

Bilsker, D., Schiedel, D., & Marcia, J. (1988). Sex differences in identity status. *Sex Roles, 18,* 231–236.

Blount, R. (1986, May 4). "I'm about five years ahead of my age." *Atlanta Journal and Constitution,* pp. C17–C20.

Bodily, C. L. (1991). "I have no opinions. I'm 73 years old": Rethinking ageism. *Journal of Aging Studies, 5,* 245–264.

Bornstein, R. F. (1992). The dependent personality: Developmental, social, and clinical perspectives. *Psychological Bulletin, 112,* 3–23.

Boyes, M. C., & Chandler, M. (1992). Cognitive development, epistemic doubt, and identity formation in adolescence. *Journal of Youth and Adolescence, 21,* 277–304.

Braungart, J. M., Plomin, R., DeFries, J. C., & Fulker, D. W. (1992). Genetic influence on tester-rated infant temperament as assessed by Bayley's Infant Behavior Record: Nonadoptive and adoptive siblings and twins. *Developmental Psychology, 28,* 40–47.

Bretherton, I., Fritz, J., Zahn-Waxler, C., & Ridgeway, D. (1986). Learning to talk about emotions: A functionalist perspective. *Child Development, 57,* 529–548.

Brooks-Gunn, J., & Lewis, M. (1981). Infant social perception: Responses to pictures of parents and strangers. *Developmental Psychology, 17,* 647–649.

Buss, A. H., & Plomin, R. (1984). *Temperament: Early developing personality traits.* Hillsdale, NJ: Erlbaum.

Butler, R. (1990). The effects of mastery and competitive conditions on self-assessment at different ages. *Child Development, 61,* 201–210.

Butler, R., & Ruzany, N. (1993). Age and socialization effects on the development of social comparison motives and normative ability assessment in kibbutz and urban children. *Child Development, 64,* 532–543.

Butler, R. N. (1963). The life review: An interpretation of reminiscence in the aged. *Psychiatry, 26,* 65–76.

Butler, R. N. (1975). *Why survive? Being old in America.* New York: Harper & Row.

Campbell, E., Adams, G. R., & Dobson, W. R. (1984). Familial correlates of identity formation in late adolescence: A study of the predictive utility of connectedness and individuality in family relations. *Journal of Youth and Adolescence, 13,* 509–525.

Caspi, A., Elder, G. H., Jr., & Bem, D. J. (1987). Moving against the world: Life-course patterns of explosive children. *Developmental Psychology, 23,* 308–313.

Caspi, A., Elder, G. H., Jr., & Bem, D. J. (1988). Moving away from the world: Life-course patterns of shy children. *Developmental Psychology, 24,* 824–831.

Chess, S., & Thomas, A. (1984). *Origins and evolution of behavior disorders: From infancy to early adult life.* New York: Brunner/Mazel.

Cole, P. M. (1985). Display rules and the socialization of affective displays. In G. Zivin (Ed.), *The development of expressive behavior: Biology-environment interactions.* Orlando, FL: Academic Press.

Cole, P. M. (1986). Children's spontaneous control of facial expression. *Child Development, 57,* 1309–1321.

Coles, R. (1970). *Erik H. Erikson: The growth of his work.* Boston: Little, Brown.

Connolly, J. J. (1991). Longitudinal studies of personality, psychopathology, and social behavior. In D. G. Gilbert & J. J. Connolly (Eds.), *Personality, social skills, and psychopathology: An individual differences approach.* New York: Plenum.

Cooley, C. H. (1902). *Human nature and the social order.* New York: Scribner's.

Coopersmith, S. (1967). *The antecedents of self-esteem.* San Francisco: W. H. Freeman.

Costa, P. T., Jr., & McCrae, R. R. (1988). Personality in adulthood: A six-year longitudinal study of self-reports and spouse ratings on the NEO Personality Inventory. *Journal of Personality and Social Psychology, 54,* 853–863.

Costa, P. T., Jr., & McCrae, R. R. (1992). Trait psychology comes of age. In T. B. Sonderegger (Ed.). *Nebraska Symposium on Motivation: Vol. 39. Psychology and aging.* Lincoln: University of Nebraska Press.

Costa, P. T., Jr., McCrae, R. R., & Arenberg, D. (1980). Enduring dispositions in adult males. *Journal of Personality and Social Psychology, 38,* 793–800.

Costa, P. T., Jr., McCrae, R. R., & Arenberg, D. (1983). Recent longitudinal research on personality and aging. In K. W. Schaie (Ed.), *Longitudinal studies of adult psychological development.* New York: Guilford Press.

Costa, P. T., Jr., McCrae, R. R., Zonderman, A. B., Barbano, H. E., Lebowitz, B., & Larson, D. M. (1986). Cross-sectional studies of personality in a national sample: 2. Stability in neuroticism, extraversion, and openness. *Psychology and Aging, 1,* 144–149.

Cote, J. E., & Levine, C. (1988). A critical examination of the ego identity status paradigm. *Developmental Review, 8,* 147–184.

Cousins, S. D. (1989). Culture and self-perception in Japan and the United States. *Journal of Personality and Social Psychology, 56,* 124–131.

Cross, S., & Markus, H. (1991). Possible selves across the life span. *Human Development, 34,* 230–255.

Damon, W., & Hart, D. (1982). The development of self-understanding from infancy through adolescence. *Child Development, 53,* 841–864.

Damon, W., & Hart, D. (1988). *Self-understanding in childhood and adolescence.* New York: Cambridge University Press.

Denham, S. A. (1989). Maternal affect and toddlers' social-emotional competence.

American Journal of Orthopsychiatry, 59, 368–376.

DeVries, M. W. (1984). Temperament and infant mortality among the Masai of East Africa. *American Journal of Psychiatry, 141,* 1189–1194.

Dixon, S., Tronick, E., Keefer, C., & Brazelton, T. B. (1981). Mother-infant interaction among the Gusii of Kenya. In T. M. Field, A. M. Sostek, P. Vietze, & P. H. Leiderman (Eds.), *Culture and early interactions.* Hillsdale, NJ: Erlbaum.

Doelling, J. L., & Johnson, J. H. (1990). Predicting success in foster placement: The contribution of parent-child temperament characteristics. *American Journal of Orthopsychiatry, 60,* 585–593.

Donahue, E. M., Robins, R. W., Roberts, B. W., & John, O. P. (1993). The divided self: Concurrent and longitudinal effects of psychological adjustment and social roles on self-concept differentiation. *Journal of Personality and Social Psychology, 64,* 834–846.

Douglas, K., & Arenberg, D. (1978). Age changes, cohort differences, and cultural change on the Guilford-Zimmerman Temperament Survey. *Journal of Gerontology, 33,* 737–747.

Dunn, J., Brown, J., & Beardsall, L. (1991). Family talk about feeling states and children's later understanding of children's emotions. *Developmental Psychology, 27,* 448–455.

Dusek, J., & Flaherty, J. (1981). The development of the self-concept during the adolescent years. *Monographs of the Society for Research in Child Development, 46*(4, Serial No. 191).

Dyk, P. H., & Adams, G. R. (1990). Identity and intimacy: An initial investigation of three theoretical models using cross-lag panel correlations. *Journal of Youth and Adolescence, 19,* 91–110.

Eccles, J., Wigfield, A., Harold, R. D., & Blumefeld, P. (1993). Age and gender differences in children's self- and task perceptions during elementary school. *Child Development, 64,* 830–847.

Eder, R. A. (1989). The emergent personologist: The structure and content of 3½, 5½, and 7 ½-year-olds' concepts of themselves and other persons. *Child Development, 60,* 1218–1228.

Eder, R. A. (1990). Uncovering young children's psychological selves: Individual and developmental differences. *Child Development, 61,* 849–863.

Erikson, E. H. (1963). *Childhood and society* (2nd ed.). New York: Norton.

Erikson, E. H. (1968). *Identity: Youth and crisis.* New York: Norton.

Erikson, E. H. (1982). *The life cycle completed: A review.* New York: Norton.

Erikson, E. H., Erikson, J. M., & Kivnick, H. Q. (1986). *Vital involvement in old age.* New York: Norton.

Feinman, S. (1992). *Social referencing and the social construction of reality in infancy.* New York: Plenum.

Feinman, S., & Lewis, M. (1983). Social referencing at 10 months: A second-order effect on infants' responses to strangers. *Child Development, 54,* 878–887.

Felson, R. B. (1990). Comparison processes in parents' and children's appraisals of academic performance. *Social Psychology Quarterly, 53,* 264–273.

Field, D., & Millsap, R. E. (1991). Personality in advanced old age: Continuity or change? *Journal of Gerontology: Psychological Sciences, 46,* P299–P308.

Finn, S. E. (1986). Stability of personality self-ratings over 30 years: Evidence for an age/cohort interaction. *Journal of Personality and Social Psychology, 50,* 813–818.

Fordham, S., & Ogbu, J. (1986). Black students' school success: Coping with the "burden of 'acting white.'" *Urban Review, 18,* 176–206.

Frey, K. S., & Ruble, D. N. (1985). What children say when the teacher is not around: Conflicting goals in social comparison and performance assessment in the classroom. *Journal of Personality and Social Psychology, 48,* 550–562.

Gallup, G. G., Jr. (1979). Self-recognition in chimpanzees and man: A developmental and comparative perspective. In M. Lewis & L. A. Rosenblum (Eds.), *Genesis of behavior: Vol. 2. The child and its family.* New York: Plenum.

Gambria, L. M. (1979–1980). Sex differences in daydreaming and related mental activity from the late teens to the early nineties. *International Journal of Aging and Human Development, 10,* 1–34.

Glick, M., & Zigler, E. (1985). Self-image: A cognitive-developmental approach. In R. L. Leahy (Ed.), *The development of the self.* Orlando, FL: Academic Press.

Gnepp, J., & Klayman, J. (1992). Recognition of uncertainty in emotional inferences: Reasoning about emotionally equivocal situations. *Developmental Psychology, 28,* 145–158.

Goldsmith, H. H., Buss, A. H., Plomin, R., Rothbart, M. K., Thomas, A., Chess, S., Hinde, R. A., & McCall, R. B. (1987). Roundtable: What is temperament? Four approaches. *Child Development, 58,* 505–529.

Gross, A. L., & Ballif, B. (1991). Children's understanding of emotion from facial expressions and situations: A review. *Developmental Review, 11,* 368–398.

Grotevant, H. D., & Cooper, C. R. (1986). Individuation in family relations: A perspective on individual differences in the development of identity and role-taking skills in adolescence. *Human Development, 29,* 82–100.

Haan, N. (1981). Common dimensions of personality development: Early adolescence to middle life. In D. H. Eichorn, J. A. Clausen, N. Haan, M. P. Honzik, & P. H. Mussen (Eds.), *Present and past in middle life.* New York: Academic Press.

Haight, B. K. (1988). The therapeutic role of a structured life review process in homebound elderly subjects. *Journal of Gerontology: Psychological Sciences, 43,* P40–P44.

Haight, B. K. (1992). Long-term effects of a structured life review process. *Journal of Gerontology: Psychological Sciences, 47,* P312–P315.

Halberstadt, A. G. (1991). Toward an ecology of expressiveness: Family socialization in particular and a model in general. In R. S. Feldman & B. Rime (Eds.), *Fundamentals of nonverbal behavior.* New York: Cambridge University Press.

Harris, P. L. (1989). *Children and emotion: The development of psychological understanding.* Oxford, England: Basil Blackwell.

Harris, P. L., Olthof, T., & Terwogt, M. M. (1981). Children's knowledge of emotion. *Journal of Child Psychology and Psychiatry, 22,* 247–261.

Harter, S. (1982). The perceived competence scale for children. *Child Development, 53,* 87–97.

Harter, S. (1983). Developmental perspectives on the self-system. In E. M. Hetherington (Vol. Ed; P. H. Mussen, General Ed.), *Handbook of child psychology: Vol. 4. Socialization, personality, and social development* (4th ed.). New York: Wiley.

Harter, S. (1986). Cognitive-developmental processes in the integration of concepts about emotions and the self. *Social Cognition, 4,* 119–151.

Harter, S. (1990a). Issues in the assessment of the self-concept of children and adolescents. In A. M. La Greca (Ed.), *Through the eyes of the child: Obtaining self-reports from children and adolescents.* Boston: Allyn & Bacon.

Harter, S. (1990b). Processes underlying adolescent self-concept formation. In R. Montemayor, G. R. Adams, & T. P. Gullotta (Eds.), *From childhood to adolescence: A transitional period?* Newbury Park, CA: Sage.

Harter, S., & Monsour, A. (1992). Development analysis of conflict caused by opposing attributes in the adolescent self-portrait. *Developmental Psychology, 28,* 251–260.

Harter, S., & Pike, R. (1984). The pictorial scale of perceived competence and social acceptance for young children. *Child Development, 55,* 1969–1982.

Heckhausen, J., & Krueger, J. (1993). Developmental expectations for the self and most other people: Age grading in three functions of social comparison. *Developmental Psychology, 29,* 539–548.

Helson, R., & Moane, G. (1987). Personality change in women from college to midlife. *Journal of Personality and Social Psychology, 53,* 176–186.

Helson, R., & Wink, P. (1992). Personality change in women from the early 40s to the early 50s. *Psychology and Aging, 7,* 46–55.

Hill, S. D., & Tomlin, C. (1981). Self-recognition in retarded children. *Child Development, 52,* 145–150.

Hodgson, J. W., & Fischer, J. L. (1979). Sex differences in identity and intimacy development in college youth. *Journal of Youth and Adolescence, 8,* 37–50.

Hoffner, C., & Badzinski, D. M. (1989). Children's integration of facial and situational cues to emotion. *Child Development, 60,* 411–422.

Isberg, R. S., Hauser, S. T., Jacobson, A. M., Powers, S. I., Noam, G., Weiss-Perry, B., & Follansbee, D. (1989). Parental contexts of adolescent self-esteem: A developmental perspective. *Journal of Youth and Adolescence, 18,* 1–23.

Izard, C. E. (1982). *Measuring emotions in infants and children.* New York: Cambridge University Press.

Izard, C. E. (1993). Four systems for emotion activation: Cognitive and noncognitive processes. *Psychological Review, 100,* 68–90.

Johnson, W., Emde, R. N., Pannabecker, B., Stenberg, C., & Davis, M. (1982). Maternal perception of infant emotion from birth through 18 months. *Infant Behavior and Development, 5,* 313–322.

Kagan, J. (1989). Temperamental contributions to social behavior. *American Psychologist, 44,* 668–674.

Kagan, J., & Moss, H. A. (1962). *Birth to maturity.* New York: Wiley.

Kagan, J., Reznick, J. S., Snidman, N., Gibbons, J., & Johnson, M. O. (1988). Childhood derivatives of inhibition and lack of inhibition to the unfamiliar. *Child Development, 59,* 1580–1589.

Kagan, J., Snidman, N., & Arcus, D. M. (1992). Initial reactions to unfamiliarity. *Current Directions in Psychological Science, 1,* 171–174.

Keller, A., Ford, L. H., Jr., & Meachum, J. A. (1978). Dimensions of self-concept in preschool children. *Developmental Psychology, 14,* 483–489.

Kerwin, C., Ponterotto, J. G., Jackson, B. L., & Harris, A. (1993). Racial identity in biracial children: A qualitative investigation. *Journal of Counseling Psychology, 40,* 221–231.

Klinnert, M. D., Emde, R. N., Butterfield, P., & Campos, J. J. (1986). Social referencing: The infant's use of emotional signals from a friendly adult with mother present. *Developmental Psychology, 22,* 427–432.

Knight, G. P., Bernal, M. E., Garza, C. A., Cota, M. K., & Ocampo, K. A. (1993). Family socialization and the ethnic identity of Mexican-American children. *Journal of Cross-Cultural Psychology, 24,* 99–114.

Kogan, N. (1990). Personality and aging. In J. E. Birren & K. W. Schaie (Eds.), *Handbook of the psychology of aging* (3rd ed.). San Diego: Academic Press.

Korn, S. J. (1984). Continuities and discontinuities in difficult/easy temperament: Infancy to young adulthood. *Merrill-Palmer Quarterly, 30,* 189–199.

Kowaz, A. M., & Marcia, J. E. (1991). Development and validation of a measure of Eriksonian industry. *Journal of Personality and Social Psychology, 60,* 390–397.

Kroger, J. (1988). A longitudinal study of ego identity status interview domains. *Journal of Adolescence, 11,* 49–64.

Lamborn, S. D., Mounts, N. S., Steinberg, L., & Dornbusch, S. M. (1991). Patterns of competence and adjustment among adolescents from authoritative, authoritarian, indulgent, and neglectful families. *Child Development, 62,* 1049–1065.

Lawton, M. P., Kleban, M. H., Rajagopal, D., & Dean, J. (1992). Dimensions of affective experience in three age groups. *Psychology and Aging, 7,* 171–184.

Leon, G. R., Gillum, B., Gillum, R., & Gouze, M. (1979). Personality stability and change over a 30-year period—middle age to old age. *Journal of Consulting and Clinical Psychology, 47,* 517–524.

Lerner, J. V., Nitz, K., Talwar, R., & Lerner, R. M. (1989). On the functional significance of temperamental individuality: A developmental contextual view of the concept of goodness of fit. In G. A. Kohnstamm, J. E. Bates, & M. K. Rothbart (Eds.), *Temperament in childhood.* Chichester, England: Wiley.

Levenson, R. W., Cartensen, L. L., Friesen, W. V., & Ekman, P. (1991). Emotion, physiology, and expression in old age. *Psychology and Aging, 6,* 28–35.

Lewis, M., Alessandri, S. M., & Sullivan, M. W. (1990). Violation of expectancy, loss of control, and anger expressions in young infants. *Developmental Psychology, 26,* 745–751.

Lewis, M., Alessandri, S. M., & Sullivan, M. W. (1992). Differences in shame and pride as a function of children's gender and task difficulty. *Child Development, 63,* 630–638.

Lewis, M., & Brooks-Gunn, J. (1979). *Social cognition and the acquisition of self.* New York: Plenum.

Lewis, M., & Michalson, L. (1983). *Children's emotions and moods: Developmental theory and measurement.* New York: Plenum.

Lewis, M., Stanger, C., & Sullivan, M. W. (1989). Deception in 3-year-olds. *Developmental Psychology, 25,* 439–443.

Lewis, M., Sullivan, M. W., Stanger, C., & Weiss, M. (1989). Self-development and self-conscious emotions. *Child Development, 60,* 146–156.

Livesley, W. J., & Bromley, D. B. (1973). *Person perception in childhood and adolescence.* London: Wiley.

Livson, F. B. (1976). Patterns of personality in middle-aged women: A longitudinal study. *International Journal of Aging and Human Development, 7,* 107–115.

Livson, F. B. (1981). Paths to psychological health in the middle years: Sex differences. In D. H. Eichorn, J. A. Clausen, N. Haan, M. P. Honzik, & P. H. Mussen (Eds.), *Present and past in middle life.* New York: Academic Press.

Loehlin, J. C. (1992). *Genes and environment in personality development.* Newbury Park, CA: Sage.

Mahler, M. S., Pine, F., & Bergman, A. (1975). *The psychological birth of the infant.* New York: Basic Books.

Malatesta, C. Z. (1981). Affective development over the lifespan: Involution or growth? *Merrill-Palmer Quarterly, 27,* 145–173.

Malatesta, C. Z., Culver, C., Tesman, J. R., & Shepard, B. (1989). The development of emotion expression during the first two years of life. *Monographs of the Society for Research in Child Development, 54*(1–2, Serial No. 219).

Malestesta, C. Z., Grigoryev, P., Lamb, C., Albin, M., & Culver, C. (1986). Emotional socialization and expressive development in preterm and full-term infants. *Child Development, 57,* 316–330.

Malatesta, C. Z., & Haviland, J. M. (1982). Learning display rules: The socialization of emotion expression in infancy. *Child Development, 53,* 991–1003.

Malatesta, C. Z., & Kalnok, M. (1984). Emotional experience in younger and older adults. *Journal of Gerontology, 39,* 301–308.

Marcia, J. E. (1966). Development and validation of ego identity status. *Journal of Personality and Social Psychology, 3,* 551–558.

Markstrom-Adams, C. (1992). A consideration of intervening factors in adolescent identity formation. In G. R. Adams, T. P. Gullotta, & R. Montemayor (Eds.), *Adolescent identity formation* (Advances in Adolescent Development, Vol. 4). Newbury Park, CA: Sage.

Markus, H. R., & Kitayama, S. (1991). Culture and the self: Implications for cognition, emotion, and motivation. *Psychological Review, 98,* 224–253.

Marsh, H. W. (1989). Age and sex effects in multiple dimensions of self-concept: Preadolescence to early adulthood. *Journal of Educational Psychology, 81,* 417–430.

Matula, K. E., Huston, T. L., Grotevant, H. D., & Zamutt, A. (1992). Identity and dating commitment among women and men in college. *Journal of Youth and Adolescence, 21,* 339–356.

Maziade, M., Caron, C., Côté, R., Merette, C., Bernier, H., Laplante, B., Boutin, P., & Thivierge, J. (1990). Psychiatric status of adolescents who had extreme temperaments at age 7. *American Journal of Psychiatry, 147,* 1531–1536.

McAdams, D. P., de St. Aubin, E., & Logan, R. L. (1993). Generativity among young, midlife, and older adults. *Psychology and Aging, 8,* 221–230.

McCrae, R. R., & Costa, P. T., Jr. (1990). *Personality in adulthood.* New York: Guilford Press.

McFarland, C., Ross, M., & Giltrow, M. (1992). Biased recollections in older adults: The role of implicit theories of aging. *Journal of Personality and Social Psychology, 62,* 837–850.

McGue, M., Bacon, S., & Lykken, D. T. (1993). Personality stability and change in early adulthood: A behavioral genetic analysis. *Developmental Psychology, 29,* 96–109.

McGue, M., Hirsch, B., & Lykken, D. T. (1993). Age and the self-perception of ability: A twin study analysis. *Psychology and Aging, 8,* 72–80.

McGuire, W. J., McGuire, C. V., Child, P., & Fujioka, T. (1978). Salience of ethnicity in the spontaneous self-concept as a function of one's ethnic distinctiveness in the social environment. *Journal of Personality and Social Psychology, 36,* 511–520.

Mead, G. H. (1934). *Mind, self, and society.* Chicago: University of Chicago Press.

Meilman, P. W. (1979). Cross-sectional age changes in ego identity status during adolescence. *Developmental Psychology, 15,* 230–231.

Michalson, L., & Lewis, M. (1985). What do children know about emotions and when do they know it? In M. Lewis & C. Saarni (Eds.), *The socialization of emotions.* New York: Plenum.

Mischel, W. (1973). Toward a cognitive social learning reconceptualization of personality. *Psychological Review, 80,* 252–283.

Molinari, V., & Reichlin, R. E. (1984–1985). Life review reminiscence in the elderly: A review of the literature. *International Journal of Aging and Human Development, 20,* 81–92.

Montemayor, R., & Eisen, M. (1977). The development of self-conceptions from childhood to adolescence. *Developmental Psychology, 13,* 314–319.

Mortimer, J. T., Finch, M. D., & Kumka, D. (1982). Persistence and change in development: The multidimensional self-concept. In P. B. Baltes & O. G. Brim, Jr. (Eds.), *Life-span development and behavior* (Vol. 4). New York: Academic Press.

Moss, H. A., & Susman, E. J. (1980). Longitudinal study of personality development. In O. G. Brim, Jr., & J. Kagan (Eds.), *Constancy and change in human development.* Cambridge, MA: Harvard University Press.

Mullis, A. K., Mullis, R. L., & Normandin, D. (1992). Cross-sectional and longitudinal comparisons of adolescent self-esteem. *Adolescence, 27,* 51–61.

Munro, G., & Adams, G. R. (1977). Ego-identity formation in college students and working youth. *Developmental Psychology, 13,* 523–524.

Neugarten, B. L. (1977). Personality and aging. In J. E. Birren & K. W. Schaie (Eds.), *Handbook of the psychology of aging.* New York: Van Nostrand Reinhold.

Ochse, R., & Plug, C. (1986). Cross-cultural investigation of the validity of Erikson's theory of personality development. *Journal of Personality and Social Psychology, 50,* 1240–1252.

Offer, D., Ostrov, E., & Howard, K. I. (1984). The self-image of normal adolescents. In D. Offer, E. Ostrov, & K. I. Howard (Eds.), *Patterns of adolescent self-image* (New Directions for Mental Health Services, No. 22). San Francisco: Jossey-Bass.

Ogbu, J. U. (1988). Black education: A cultural-ecological perspective. In H. P. McAdoo (Ed.), *Black families.* Beverly Hills, CA: Sage.

Orlovsky, J. L., Marcia, J. E., & Lesser, I. M. (1973). Ego identity status and the intimacy versus isolation crisis of young adulthood. *Journal of Personality and Social Psychology, 27,* 211–219.

Ozer, D. J., & Gjerde, P. F. (1989). Patterns of personality consistency and change from childhood through adolescence. *Journal of Personality, 57,* 483–507.

Patterson, S. J., Sochting, I., & Marcia, L. E. (1992). The inner space and beyond: Women and identity. In G. R. Adams, T. P. Gullotta, & R. Montemayor (Eds.), *Adolescent identity formation* (Advances in Adolescent Development, Vol. 4). Newbury Park, CA: Sage.

Phinney, J., & Chavira, V. (1992). Ethnic identity and self-esteem: An exploratory longitudinal study. *Journal of Adolescence, 15,* 271–281.

Phinney, J., & Nakayama, S. (1991, April). *Parental influence on ethnic identity formation in minority adolescents.* Paper presented at the biennial meeting of the Society for Research in Child Development, Seattle.

Phinney, J., & Rosenthal, D. A. (1992). Ethnic identity in adolescence: Process, context, and outcome. In G. R. Adams, T. P. Gullotta, & R. Montemayor (Eds.), *Adolescent identity formation* (Advances in Adolescent Development, Vol. 4). Newbury Park, CA: Sage.

Pipp, S., Easterbrooks, M. A., & Harmon, R. J. (1992). The relation between attachment and knowledge of self and mother in one-year-old infants to three-year-old infants. *Child Development, 63,* 738–750.

Plomin, R. (1986). *Development, genetics, and psychology.* Hillsdale, NJ: Erlbaum.

Plomin, R. (1990). *Nature and nurture: An introduction to behavior genetics.* Pacific Grove, CA: Brooks/Cole.

Raskin, P. M. (1986). The relationship between identity and intimacy in early adulthood. *Journal of Genetic Psychology, 147,* 167–181.

Reznick, J. S., Kagan, J., Snidman, N., Gersten, M., Baak, K., & Rosenberg, A. (1986). Inhibited and uninhibited children: A follow-up study. *Child Development, 57,* 660–680.

Robinson, J. L., Kagan, J., Reznick, J. S., & Corley, R. (1992). The heritability of inhibited and uninhibited behavior: A twin study. *Developmental Psychology, 28,* 1030–1037.

Rodin, J., & Langer, E. (1980). Aging labels: The decline of control and the fall of self-esteem. *Journal of Social Issues, 36*(2), 12–29.

Rosenholtz, S. J. (1977). *The multiple abilities curriculum: An intervention against the self-fulfilling prophecy.* Unpublished doctoral dissertation, Stanford University, Stanford, CA.

Rosenholtz, S. J. (1985). Modifying status expectations in the traditional classroom. In J. Berger & M. Zelditch, Jr. (Eds.), *Status, rewards, and influence.* San Francisco: Jossey-Bass.

Rosenthal, D. A., & Feldman, S. S. (1992). The relationship between parenting behaviour and ethnic identity in Chinese-American and Chinese-Australian adolescents. *International Journal of Psychology, 27,* 19–31.

Rovee-Collier, C. K. (1987). Learning and memory. In J. D. Osofsky (Ed.), *Handbook of infant development* (2nd ed.). New York: Wiley.

Ruble, D. N. (1983). The development of comparison processes and their role in achievement-related self-socialization. In E. T. Higgins, D. N. Ruble, & W. W. Hartup (Eds.), *Social cognition and social development: A sociocultural perspective.* New York: Cambridge University Press.

Ryff, C. D. (1991). Possible selves in adulthood and old age: A tale of shifting horizons. *Psychology and Aging, 6,* 286–295.

Saarni, C. (1984). An observational study of children's attempts to monitor their expressive behavior. *Child Development, 55,* 1504–1513.

Saarni, C. (1990). Emotional competence: How emotions and relationships become integrated. In R. A. Thompson (Ed.), *Nebraska Symposium on Motivation: Vol. 36. Socioemotional development.* Lincoln: University of Nebraska Press.

Samuels, C. (1986). Bases for the infant's development of self-awareness. *Human Development, 29,* 36–48.

Savin-Williams, R. C., & Demo, D. H. (1984). Developmental change and stability in adolescent self-concept. *Developmental Psychology, 20,* 1100–1110.

Scarr, S., & McCartney, K. (1983). How people make their own environments: A theory of genotype-environment effects. *Child Development, 54,* 424–435.

Schaie, K. W., & Parham, I. A. (1976). Stability of adult personality traits: Fact or fable? *Journal of Personality and Social Psychology, 34,* 146–158.

Schiedel, D. G., & Marcia, J. E. (1985). Ego identity, intimacy, sex role orientation, and gender. *Developmental Psychology, 21,* 149–160.

Scott, W. A., Scott, R., & McCabe, M. (1991). Family relationships and children's personality: A cross-cultural, cross-source comparison. *British Journal of Social Psychology, 30,* 1–20.

Secord, P. F., & Peevers, B. H. (1974). The development and attribution of person concepts. In T. Mischel (Ed.), *Understanding other persons.* Totowa, NJ: Rowman & Littlefield.

Selman, R. L. (1980). *The growth of interpersonal understanding.* New York: Academic Press.

Simmons, R. G., Burgeson, R., Carlton-Ford, S., & Blyth, D. A. (1987). The impact of cumulative change in early adolescence. *Child Development, 58,* 1220–1234.

Simmons, R. G., Rosenberg, F., & Rosenberg, M. (1973). Disturbance in self-image at adolescence. *American Sociological Review, 38,* 553–568.

Slugoski, B. R., Marcia, J. E., & Koopman, R. F. (1984). Cognitive and social interactional characteristics of ego identity statuses in college males. *Journal of Personality and Social Psychology, 47,* 646–661.

Spencer, M. B. (1988). Self-concept development. In D. T. Slaughter (Ed.), *Black children in poverty: Developmental perspectives.* San Francisco: Jossey-Bass.

Spencer, M. B., & Markstrom-Adams, C. (1990). Identity processes among racial and ethnic minority children in America. *Child Development, 61,* 290–310.

Stern, D. N. (1983). The early development of schemas of self, other, and "self with other." In J. D. Lictenberg & S. Kaplan (Eds.), *Reflections on self psychology.* Hillsdale, NJ: Erlbaum.

Stevens, D. P., & Truss, C. V. (1985). Stability and change in adult personality over 12 and

20 years. *Developmental Psychology, 21,* 568–584.

Stipek, D. (1983). A developmental analysis of pride and shame. *Human Development, 26,* 42–54.

Stipek, D., Gralinski, H., & Kopp, C. (1990). Self-concept development in the toddler years. *Developmental Psychology, 26,* 972–977.

Stipek, D., Recchia, S., & McClintic, S. (1992). Self-evaluation in young children. *Monographs of the Society for Research in Child Development, 57*(1, Serial No. 226).

Streitmatter, J. (1993). Gender differences in identity development: An examination of longitudinal data. *Adolescence, 28,* 55–66.

Taft, L. B., & Nehrke, M. F. (1990). Reminiscence, life review, and ego integrity in nursing home residents. *International Journal of Aging and Human Development, 30,* 189–196.

Thomas, A., & Chess, S. (1977). *Temperament and development.* New York: Brunner/Mazel.

Thomas, A., & Chess, S. (1986). The New York longitudinal study: From infancy to early adult life. In R. Plomin & J. Dunn (Eds.), *The study of temperament: Changes, continuities, and challenges.* Hillsdale, NJ: Erlbaum.

Thomas, A., Chess, S., & Birch, H. G. (1970). The origin of personality. *Scientific American, 223,* 102–109.

Tran, T. V., Wright, R., & Chatters, L. (1991). Health, stress, psychological resources, and subjective well-being among older Blacks. *Psychology and Aging, 6,* 100–108.

Vaillant, G. E. (1977). *Adaptation to life.* Boston: Little, Brown.

Vaillant, G. E. (1983). Childhood environment and maturity of defense mechanisms. In D. Magnusson & V. L. Allen (Eds.), *Human development: An interactional perspective.* New York: Academic Press.

Vaillant, G. E., & Milofsky, E. (1980). Natural history of male psychological health. IX: Empirical evidence for Erikson's model of the life cycle. *American Journal of Psychiatry, 137,* 1348–1359.

Veroff, J., Douvan, E., & Kulka, R. A. (1981). *The inner American. A self-portrait from 1957 to 1976.* New York: Basic Books.

Walden, T. A., & Ogan, T. A. (1988). The development of social referencing. *Child Development, 59,* 1230–1240.

Waterman, A. S. (1982). Identity development from adolescence to adulthood: An extension of theory and a review of research. *Developmental Psychology, 18,* 341–358.

Waterman, A. S. (1992). Identity as an aspect of optimal psychological functioning. In G. R. Adams, T. P. Gullotta, & R. Montemayor (Eds.), *Adolescent identity formation* (Advances in Adolescent Development, Vol. 4). Newbury Park, CA: Sage.

Waterman, A. S., & Archer, S. L. (1990). A life-span perspective on identity formation: Developments in form, function, and process. In P. B. Baltes, D. L. Featherman, & R. M. Lerner (Eds.), *Life-span development and behavior* (Vol. 10). Hillsdale, NJ: Erlbaum.

Webster, J. D. & Cappeliez, P. (1993). Reminiscence and autobiographical memory: Complementary contexts for cognitive aging research. *Developmental Review, 13,* 54–91.

Wells, L. E., & Stryker, S. (1988). Stability and change in the self over the life course. In P. B. Baltes, D. L. Featherman, & R. M. Lerner (Eds.), *Life-span development and behavior* (Vol. 8). Hillsdale, NJ: Erlbaum.

Whitbourne, S. K. (1986). *The me I know: A study of adult identity.* New York: Springer-Verlag.

Whitbourne, S. K., & Tesch, S. A. (1985). A comparison of identity and intimacy statuses in college students and alumni. *Developmental Psychology, 21,* 1039–1044.

Whitbourne, S. K., & Waterman, A. S. (1979). Psychosocial development during the adult years: Age and cohort comparisons. *Developmental Psychology, 15,* 373–378.

Whitbourne, S. K., Zuschlag, M. K., Elliot, L. B., & Waterman, A. S. (1992). Psychosocial development in adulthood: A 22-year sequential study. *Journal of Personality and Social Psychology, 63,* 260–271.

Wigfield, A., Eccles, J. S., Mac Iver, D., Reuman, D. A., & Midgley, C. (1991). Transitions during early adolescence: Changes in children's domain-specific self-perceptions and general self-esteem across the transition to junior high school. *Developmental Psychology, 27,* 552–565.

Wintre, M. G., Polivy, J., & Murray, M. A. (1990). Self-predictions of emotional response patterns: Age, sex, and situational determinants. *Child Development, 61,* 1124–1133.

Wong, P. T. P., & Watt, L. M. (1991). What types of reminiscence are associated with successful aging? *Psychology and Aging, 6,* 272–279.

Woodruff, D. S., & Birren, J. E. (1972). Age changes and cohort differences in personality. *Developmental Psychology, 6,* 252–259.

Wrightsman, L. S. (1988). *Personality development in adulthood.* Newbury Park, CA: Sage.

Chapter 11: Gender Roles and Sexuality

Abler, R. M., & Sedlacek, W. E. (1989). Freshman sexual attitudes and behaviors over a 15-year period. *Journal of College Student Development, 30,* 201–209.

Abrahams, B., Feldman, S. S., & Nash, S. C. (1978). Sex role self-concept and sex role attitudes: Enduring personality characteristics or adaptations to changing life situations? *Developmental Psychology, 14,* 393–400.

Allgood-Merten, B., & Stockard, J. (1991). Sex role identity and self esteem: A comparison of children and adolescents. *Sex Roles, 25,* 129–139.

Anderson, J. W., & Moore, M. (1993, February 14). Born oppressed: Women in the developing world face cradle-to-grave discrimination, poverty. *Washington Post,* pp. A1, A48–A49.

Arber, S., & Ginn, J. (1991). *Gender and later life: A sociological analysis of resources and constraints.* London, England: Sage.

Archer, J. (1991). The influence of testosterone on human aggression. *British Journal of Psychology, 82,* 1–28.

Atkinson, J., & Huston, T. L. (1984). Sex role orientation and division of labor early in marriage. *Journal of Personality and Social Psychology, 46,* 330–345.

Baier, J. L., Rosenzweig, M. G., & Whipple, E. G. (1991). Patterns of sexual behavior, coercion, and victimization of university students. *Journal of College Student Development, 32,* 310–322.

Bailey, J. M., & Pillard, R. C. (1991). A genetic study of male sexual orientation. *Archives of General Psychiatry, 48,* 1089–1096.

Bailey, J. M., Pillard, R. C., Neale, M. C., & Agyei, Y. (1993). Heritable factors influence sexual orientation in women. *Archives of General Psychiatry, 50,* 217–223.

Baker, D. P., & Jones, D. P. (1992). Opportunity and performance: A sociological explanation for gender differences in academic mathematics. In J. Wrigley (Ed.), *Education and gender equality.* London: Falmer Press.

Bakwin, H. (1973). Erotic feelings in infants and young children. *American Journal of Diseases of Children, 126,* 52–54.

Bandura, A. (1986). *Social foundations of thought and action: A social cognitive theory.* Englewood Cliffs, NJ: Prentice-Hall.

Barry, H. III, Bacon, M. K., & Child, I. L. (1957). A cross-cultural survey of some sex differences in socialization. *Journal of Abnormal and Social Psychology, 55,* 327–332.

Baruch, G. K., & Barnett, R. C. (1986). Father's participation in family work and children's sex-role attitudes. *Child Development, 57,* 1210–1223.

Beitchman, J. H., Zucker, K. J., Hood, J. E., daCosta, G. A., & Akman, D. (1991). A review of the short-term effects of child sexual abuse. *Child Abuse and Neglect, 15,* 537–556.

Bell, A. P., Weinberg, M. S., & Hammersmith, S. K. (1981). *Sexual preference: Its development in men and women.* Bloomington, IN: Indiana University Press.

Bem, S. L. (1974). The measurement of psychological androgyny. *Journal of Consulting and Clinical Psychology, 42,* 155–162.

Bem, S. L. (1975). Sex-role adaptability: One consequence of psychological androgyny. *Journal of Personality and Social Psychology, 31,* 634–643.

Bem, S. L. (1978). Beyond androgyny: Some presumptuous prescriptions for a liberated sexual identity. In J. A. Sherman & F. L. Denmark (Eds.), *The psychology of women: Future directions in research.* New York: Psychological Dimensions.

Bem, S. L. (1979). Theory and measurement of androgyny: A reply to the Podhazer-Tetenbaum and Locksley-Colten critiques. *Journal of Personality and Social Psychology, 37,* 1047–1054.

Bem, S. L. (1989). Genital knowledge and gender constancy in preschool children. *Child Development, 60,* 649–662.

Benbow, C. P., & Arjmand, O. (1990). Predictors of high academic achievement in mathematics and science by mathematically talented students: A longitudinal study. *Journal of Educational Psychology, 82,* 430–441.

Berenbaum, S. A., & Hines, M. (1992). Early androgens are related to childhood sex-typed toy preferences. *Psychological Science, 3,* 203–206.

Bergen, D. J., & Williams, J. E. (1991). Sex stereotypes in the United States revisited: 1972–1988. *Sex Roles, 24,* 413–424.

Bernstein, A. C., & Cowan, P. A. (1975). Children's concepts of how people get babies. *Child Development, 46,* 77–91.

Best, D. L., Williams, J. E., Cloud, J. M., Davis, S. W., Robertson, L. S., Edwards, J. R., Giles, H., & Fowles, J. (1977). Development of sex-trait stereotypes among young children in the United States, England, and Ireland. *Child Development, 48,* 1375–1384.

Bigler, R. S., & Liben, L. S. (1990). The role of attitudes and interventions in gender-schematic processing. *Child Development, 61,* 1440–1452.

Blakemore, J. E. O., LaRue, A. A., & Olejnik, A. B. (1979). Sex-appropriate toy preference and the ability to conceptualize toys as sex-role related. *Developmental Psychology, 15,* 339–340.

Block, J. H. (1976). Issues, problems, and pitfalls in assessing sex differences: A critical review of the psychology of sex differences. *Merrill-Palmer Quarterly, 22,* 283–308.

Boldizar, J. P. (1991). Assessing sex-typing and androgyny in children: The Children's Sex-role Inventory. *Developmental Psychology, 27,* 505–515.

Bradbard, M. R., Martin, C. L., Endsley, R. C., & Halverson, C. F. (1986). Influence of sex stereotypes on children's exploration and memory: A competence versus performance distinction. *Developmental Psychology, 22,* 481–486.

Brody, N. (1985). The validity of tests of intelligence. In B. B. Wolman (Ed.), *Handbook of intelligence.* New York: Wiley.

Brooks-Gunn, J., & Furstenberg, F. F., Jr. (1989). Long-term implications of fertility-related behavior and family formation on adolescent mothers and their children. In K. Kreppner & R. M. Lerner (Eds.), *Family systems and life-span development.* Hillsdale, NJ: Erlbaum.

Broverman, I. K., Vogel, S. R., Broverman, D. M., Clarkson, F. E., & Rosenkrantz, P. S. (1972). Sex-role stereotypes: A current appraisal. *Journal of Social Issues, 28,* 59–78.

Bukowski, W. M., Gauze, C., Hoza, B., & Newcombe, A. F. (1993). Differences and consistency between same-sex and other-sex peer relationships during early adolescence. *Developmental Psychology, 29,* 255–263.

Burnham, D. K., & Harris, M. B. (1992). Effects of real gender and labeled gender on adults' perceptions of infants. *Journal of Genetic Psychology, 153,* 165–183.

Bussey, K., & Bandura, A. (1992). Self-regulatory mechanisms governing gender development. *Child Development, 63,* 1236–1250.

Caldera, Y. M., Huston, A. C., & O'Brien, M. (1989). Social interactions and play patterns of parents and toddlers with feminine, masculine, and neutral toys. *Child Development, 60,* 70–76.

Caplan, P. J., MacPherson, G. M., & Tobin, P. (1985). Do sex-related differences in spatial abilities exist? *American Psychologist, 40,* 786–799.

Carter, D. B., & Levy, G. D. (1988). Cognitive aspects of early sex-role development: The influence of gender schemas on preschoolers' memories and preferences for sex-typed toys and activities. *Child Development, 59,* 782–792.

Carter, D. B., & McCloskey, L. A. (1983–1984). Peers and the maintenance of sex-typed behavior: The development of children's conceptions of cross-gender behavior in their peers. *Social Cognition, 2,* 294–314.

Carter, D. B., & Patterson, C. J. (1982). Sex roles as social conventions: The development of children's conceptions of sex-role stereotypes. *Developmental Psychology, 18,* 812–824.

Ceci, S. J., & Bruck, M. (1993). Suggestibility of the child witness: A historical review and synthesis. *Psychological Bulletin, 113,* 403–439.

Centers for Disease Control (1992). Sexual behavior among high school students—United States, 1990. *Morbidity and Mortality Weekly Reports, 40,* 885–888.

Coats, P. B., & Overman, S. J. (1992). Childhood play experiences of women in traditional and nontraditional professions. *Sex Roles, 26,* 261–271.

Cole, P. M., & Putnam, F. W. (1992). Effect of incest on self and social functioning: A developmental psychopathology perspective. *Journal of Consulting and Clinical Psychology, 60,* 174–184.

Coles, R., & Stokes, G. (1985). *Sex and the American teenager.* New York: Harper & Row.

Comfort, A. (1974). Sexuality in old age. *Journal of the American Geriatrics Society, 22,* 440–442.

Condry, J., & Condry, S. (1976). Sex differences: A study in the eye of the beholder. *Child Development, 47,* 812–819.

Cowan, C. P., Cowan, P. A., Heming, G., & Miller, N. B. (1991). Becoming a family: Marriage, parenting, and child development. In P. A. Cowan & M. Hetherington (Eds.), *Family transitions.* Hillsdale, NJ: Erlbaum.

Cowan, G., & Avants, S. K. (1988). Children's influence strategies: Structure, sex differences, and bilateral mother-child influences. *Child Development, 53,* 984–990.

Cunningham, J. D., & Antill, J. K. (1984). Changes in masculinity and femininity across the family life cycle: A reexamination. *Developmental Psychology, 20,* 1135–1141.

Dabbs, J. M., & Morris, R. (1990). Testosterone, social class, and antisocial behavior in a sample of 4,462 men. *Psychological Science, 1,* 209–211.

Damon, W. (1977). *The social world of the child.* San Francisco: Jossey-Bass.

Darling, C. A., Davidson, J. K., & Passarello, L. C. (1992). The mystique of first intercourse among college youth: The role of partners, contraceptive practices, and psychological reactions. *Journal of Youth and Adolescence, 21,* 97–117.

Darling, C. A., & Hicks, M. W. (1982). Parental influence on adolescent sexuality: Implications for parents and educators. *Journal of Youth and Adolescence, 11,* 231–245.

Darling, C. A., Kallen, D. J., & VanDusen, J. E. (1984). Sex in transition, 1900–1980. *Journal of Youth and Adolescence, 13,* 385–399.

Daubman, K., Heatherington, L., & Ahn, A. (1992). Gender and the self-presentation of academic achievement. *Sex Roles, 27,* 187–204.

Deaux, K., & Major, B. (1990). A social-psychological model of gender. In D. L. Rhode (Ed.), *Theoretical perspectives on sexual difference.* New Haven, CT: Yale University Press.

Diamond, M. (1982). Sexual identity, monozygotic twins reared in discordant sex roles, and a BBC follow up. *Archives of Sexual Behavior, 11,* 181–186.

Dittman, R. W., Kappes, M. E., & Kappes, M. H. (1992). Sexual behavior in adolescent and adult females with congenital adrenal hyperplasia. *Psychoneuroendocrinology, 17,* 153–170.

Dreyer, P. H. (1982). Sexuality during adolescence. In B. B. Wolman (Ed.), *Handbook of developmental psychology.* New York: Wiley.

Eagly, A. H. (1987). *Sex differences in social behavior: A social-role interpretation.* Hillsdale, NJ: Erlbaum.

Eagly, A. H., & Steffen, V. J. (1986). Gender and aggressive behavior: A meta-analytic review of the social psychological literature. *Psychological Bulletin, 100,* 309–330.

Eaton, W. O., & Enns, L. R. (1986). Sex differences in human motor activity level. *Psychological Bulletin, 100,* 19–28.

Eaton, W. O., & Yu, A. P. (1989). Are sex differences in child motor activity level a function of sex differences in maturational status? *Child Development, 60,* 1005–1011.

Eccles, J. S., Jacobs, J. E., & Harold, R. D. (1990). Gender role stereotypes, expectancy effects, and parents' socialization of gender differences. *Journal of Social Issues, 46,* 183–201.

Ehrhardt, A. A. (1985). The psychobiology of gender. In A. S. Rossi (Ed.), *Gender and the life course.* New York: Aldine.

Ehrhardt, A. A., & Baker, S. W. (1974). Fetal androgens, human central nervous system differentiation, and behavioral sex differences. In R. C. Friedman, R. M. Rickard, & R. L. Van de Wiele (Eds.), *Sex differences in behavior.* New York: Wiley.

Eisler, R. M., & Blalock, J. A. (1991). Masculine gender role stress: Implications for the assessment of men. *Clinical Psychology Review, 11,* 45–60.

Elias, J., & Gebhard, P. (1969). Sexuality and sexual learning in childhood. *Phi Delta Kappan, 50,* 401–405.

Ellis, L., Ames, M. A. Peckham, W., & Burke, D. M. (1988). Sexual orientation in human offspring may be altered by severe emotional distress during pregnancy. *Journal of Sex Research, 25,* 152–157.

Etaugh, C., Levine, D., & Mennella, A. (1984). Development of sex biases in children: 40 years later. *Sex Roles, 10,* 911–922.

Etaugh, C., & Liss, M. B. (1992). Home, school, and playroom: Training grounds for adult gender roles. *Sex Roles, 26,* 129–147.

Fabes, R. A., Eisenberg, N., & Miller, P. A. (1990). Maternal correlates of children's vicarious emotional responsiveness. *Developmental Psychology, 26,* 639–648.

Fagot, B. I. (1978). The influence of sex of child on parental reactions to toddler children. *Child Development, 49,* 459–465.

Fagot, B. I. (1985). Beyond the reinforcement principle: Another step toward understanding sex-role development. *Developmental Psychology, 21,* 1097–1104.

Fagot, B. I., & Leinbach, M. D. (1989). The young child's gender schema: Environmental input, internal organization. *Child Development, 60,* 663–672.

Fagot, B. I., & Leinbach, M. D. (1993). Gender-role development in young children: From discrimination to labeling. *Developmental Review, 13,* 205–224.

Fagot, B. I., Leinbach, M. D., & Hagan, R. (1986). Gender labeling and the adoption of sex-typed behaviors. *Developmental Psychology, 22,* 440–443.

Fagot, B. I., Leinbach, M. D., & O'Boyle, C. (1992). Gender labeling, gender stereotyping, and parenting behaviors. *Developmental Psychology, 28,* 225–230.

Feingold, A. (1988). Cognitive gender differences are disappearing. *American Psychologist, 43,* 95–103.

Feingold, A. (1992). Sex differences in variability in intellectual abilities: A new look at an old controversy. *Review of Educational Research, 62,* 61–84.

Feldman, S. S., Biringen, Z. C., & Nash, S. C. (1981). Fluctuations of sex-related self-attributions as a function of stage of family life cycle. *Developmental Psychology, 17,* 24–35.

Felstein, I. (1983). Dysfunction: Origins and therapeutic approaches. In R. B. Weg (Ed.), *Sexuality in the later years: Roles and behavior.* New York: Academic Press.

Finkelhor, D., Hotaling, G. T., Lewis, I. A., & Smith, C. (1989). Sexual abuse and its relationship to later sexual satisfaction, marital status, religion, and attitudes. *Journal of Interpersonal Violence, 4,* 379–399.

Ford, C. S., & Beach, F. A. (1951). *Patterns of sexual behavior.* New York: Harper & Row.

Forrest, J. D., & Singh, S. (1990). The sexual and reproductive behavior of American women, 1982–1988. *Family Planning Perspectives, 22,* 206–214.

Frable, D. E. S. (1989). Sex typing and gender ideology: Two facets of the individual's gender psychology that go together. *Journal of Personality and Social Psychology, 56,* 95–108.

Frey, K. S., & Ruble, D. N. (1992). Gender constancy and the cost of sex-typed behavior: A test of the conflict hypothesis. *Developmental Psychology, 28,* 714–721.

Friedman, K. S., & Pines, A. M. (1992). Increase in Arab women's perceived power in the second half of life. *Sex Roles, 26,* 1–9.

Fultz, N. H., & Herzog, A. R. (1991). Gender differences in affiliation and instrumentality across adulthood. *Psychology and Aging, 6,* 579–586.

Furstenberg, F. F., Jr., Brooks-Gunn, J., & Morgan, S. P. (1987). *Adolescent mothers in later life.* New York: Cambridge University Press.

Furstenberg, F. F., Jr., Lincoln, R., & Menken, J. (Eds.). (1981). *Teenage sexuality, pregnancy, and childbearing.* Philadelphia: University of Pennsylvania Press.

Galambos, N. L., Almeida, D. M., & Petersen, A. C. (1990). Masculinity, femininity, and sex role attitudes in early adolescence: Exploring gender intensification. *Child Development, 61,* 1905–1914.

Gandelman, R. (1992). *Psychobiology of behavioral development.* New York: Oxford University Press.

Garnets, L., & Kimmel, D. (1991). Lesbian and gay male dimensions of the psychological study of human diversity. In J. D. Goodchilds (Ed.), *Psychological perspectives on human diversity in America.* Washington, DC: American Psychological Association.

George, L. K., & Weiler, S. J. (1981). Sexuality in middle and late life: The effects of age, cohort, and gender. *Archives of General Psychiatry, 38,* 919–923.

Goldman, R., & Goldman, J. (1982). *Children's sexual thinking: A comparative study of children aged 5 to 15 years in Australia, North America, Britain, and Sweden.* London: Routledge & Kegan Paul.

Gordon, B. N., Schroeder, C. S., & Abrams, J. M. (1990). Children's knowledge of sexuality: A comparison of sexually abused and nonabused children. *American Journal of Orthopsychiatry, 60,* 250–257.

Green, R. (1987). *The "sissy boy syndrome" and the development of homosexuality.* New Haven, CT: Yale University Press.

Greenblat, C. S. (1983). The salience of sexuality in the early years of marriage. *Journal of Marriage and the Family, 45,* 289–299.

Gullotta, T. P., Adams, G. R., & Alexander, S. J. (1986). *Today's marriages and families: A wellness approach.* Pacific Grove, CA: Brooks/Cole.

Gutmann, D. (1975). Parenthood: Key to the comparative psychology of the life cycle? In N. Datan & L. H. Ginsberg (Eds.), *Life span developmental psychology: Normative life crises.* New York: Academic Press.

Gutmann, D. (1987). *Reclaimed powers: Toward a new psychology of men and women in later life.* New York: Basic Books.

Hall, J. A., & Halberstadt, A. G. (1980). Masculinity and femininity in children: Development of the Children's Personal Attributes Questionnaire. *Developmental Psychology, 16,* 270–280.

Hamilton, V. L., Blumenfeld, P. C., Akoh, H., & Miura, K. (1991). Group and gender in Japanese and American elementary classrooms. *Journal of Cross-Cultural Psychology, 22,* 317–346.

Hannah, J. S., & Kahn, S. E. (1989). The relationship of socioeconomic status and gender to the occupational choices of grade 12 students. *Journal of Vocational Behavior, 34,* 161–178.

Henker, B., & Whalen, C. K. (1989). Hyperactivity and attention deficits. *American Psychologist, 44,* 216–223.

Herdt, G. H., & Davidson, J. (1988). The Sambia "turnim-man": Sociocultural and clinical aspects of gender formation in male pseudohermaphrodites with 5-alpha-reductase deficiency in Papua New Guinea. *Archives of Sexual Behavior, 17,* 33–56.

Hetherington, E. M., & Frankie, G. (1967). Effect of parental dominance, warmth, and conflict on imitation in children. *Journal of Personality and Social Psychology, 6,* 119–125.

Hill, J. P., & Lynch, M. E. (1983). The intensification of gender-related role expectations during early adolescence. In J. Brooks-Gunn & A. C. Petersen (Eds.), *Girls at puberty: Biological and psychosocial perspectives.* New York: Plenum.

Huston, A. C. (1983). Sex-typing. In E. M. Hetherington (Vol. Ed.; P. H. Mussen, General Ed.), *Handbook of child psychology: Vol. 4. Socialization, personality, and social development.* New York: Wiley.

Huston, A. C. (1985). The development of sex typing: Themes from recent research. *Developmental Review, 5,* 1–17.

Hyde, J. S. (1981). How large are cognitive gender differences? A meta-analysis using ω^2 and *d. American Psychologist, 36,* 892–901.

Hyde, J. S. (1984). How large are sex differences in aggression? A developmental meta-analysis. *Developmental Psychology, 20,* 722–736.

Hyde, J. S., Fennema, E., & Lamon, S. J. (1990). Gender differences in mathematics performance: A meta-analysis. *Psychological Bulletin, 107,* 139–155.

Hyde, J. S., & Linn, M. C. (1988). Gender differences in verbal ability: A meta-analysis. *Psychological Bulletin, 104,* 53–69.

Hyde, J. S., Rosenberg, B. G., & Behrman, J. A. (1977). Tomboyism. *Psychology of Women Quarterly, 2,* 73–75.

Imperato-McGinley, J., Peterson, R. E., Gautier, T., & Sturla, E. (1979). Androgens and the evolution of male gender identity among male pseudohermaphrodites with 5a-reductase deficiency. *New England Journal of Medicine, 300,* 1233–1237.

Intons-Peterson, M. J., & Reddel, M. (1984). What do people ask about a neonate? *Developmental Psychology, 20,* 358–359.

Jacklin, C. N. (1989). Male and female: Issues of gender. *American Psychologist, 44,* 127–133.

Jacklin, C. N., & Maccoby, E. E. (1978). Social behavior at 33 months in same-sex and mixed-sex dyads. *Child Development, 49,* 557–569.

Jacobs, J. E., & Eccles, J. S. (1992). The impact of mothers' gender-role stereotypic beliefs on mothers' and children's ability perceptions. *Journal of Personality and Social Psychology, 63,* 932–944.

Jung, C. G. (1933). *Modern man in search of a soul* (W. S. Dell & C. F. Baynes, Trans.). New York: Harcourt, Brace.

Jussim, L., & Eccles, J. S. (1992). Teacher expectations II: Construction and reflection of student achievement. *Journal of Personality and Social Psychology, 63,* 947–961.

Katcher, A. (1955). The discrimination of sex differences by young children. *Journal of Genetic Psychology, 87,* 131–143.

Katz, P. A. (1979). The development of female identity. *Sex Roles, 5,* 155–178.

Katz, P. A. (1986). Modification of children's gender-stereotyped behavior: General issues and research considerations. *Sex Roles, 14,* 591–602.

Katz, P. A., & Walsh, P. V. (1991). Modification of children's gender-stereotyped behavior. *Child Development, 62,* 338–351.

Kendall-Tackett, K. A., Williams, L. M., & Finkelhor, D. (1993). Impact of sexual abuse on children: A review and synthesis of recent empirical studies. *Psychological Bulletin, 113,* 164–180.

Kerns, K. A., & Berenbaum, S. A. (1991). Sex differences in spatial ability in children. *Behavior Genetics, 21,* 383–396.

Kimura, D. (1992). Sex differences in the brain. *Scientific American, 267,* 119–125.

Kinsey, A. C., Pomeroy, W. B., & Martin, C. E. (1948). *Sexual behavior in the human male.* Philadelphia: Saunders.

Kinsey, A. C., Pomeroy, W. B., Martin, C. E., & Gebhard, P. H. (1953). *Sexual behavior in the human female.* Philadelphia: Saunders.

Kohlberg, L. (1966). A cognitive-developmental analysis of children's sex-role concepts and attitudes. In E. E. Maccoby (Ed.), *The development of sex differences.* Stanford, CA: Stanford University Press.

Kortenhaus, C. M., & Demarest, J. (1993). Gender role stereotyping in children's literature: An update. *Sex Roles, 28,* 219–232.

Kuhn, D., Nash, S. C., & Brucken, L. (1978). Sex-role concepts of two- and three-year-olds. *Child Development, 49,* 445–451.

Langlois, J. H., & Downs, A. C. (1980). Mothers, fathers, and peers as socialization agents of sex-typed play behaviors in young children. *Child Development, 51,* 1237–1247.

Lewin, M., & Tragos, L. M. (1987). Has the feminist movement influenced adolescent sex role attitudes? A reassessment after a quarter century. *Sex Roles, 16,* 125–135.

Lewis, M., & Brooks-Gunn, J. (1979). *Social cognition and the acquisition of self.* New York: Plenum.

Lewis, M., & Weinraub, M. (1979). Origins of early sex-role development. *Sex Roles, 5,* 135–153.

Liben, L. S., & Signorella, M. L. (1993). Gender-schematic processing in children: The role of initial interpretations of stimuli. *Developmental Psychology, 29,* 141–149.

Liebert, R. M., & Sprafkin, J. (1988). *The early window: Effects of television on children and youth* (3rd ed.). New York: Pergamon Press.

Linn, M. C., & Petersen, A. C. (1985). Emergence and characterization of sex differences in spatial ability: A meta-analysis. *Child Development, 56,* 1479–1498.

Lobel, T. E., & Menashri, J. (1993). Relations of conceptions of gender-role transgressions and gender constancy to gender-typed toy preferences. *Developmental Psychology, 29,* 150–155.

Lockheed, M. E. (1986). Reshaping the social order: The case of gender segregation. *Sex Roles, 14,* 617–628.

Loehlin, J. C. (1992). *Genes and environment in personality development* (Individual Differences and Development Series, Vol. 2). Newbury Park, CA: Sage.

Loewenstein, G., & Furstenburg, F. (1991). Is teenage sexual behavior rational? *Journal of Applied Social Psychology, 21,* 957–986.

Lorber, J. (1986). Dismantling Noah's ark. *Sex Roles, 14,* 567–580.

Lott, B. (1985). The potential enrichment of social/personality psychology through feminist research and vice versa. *American Psychologist, 40,* 155–164.

Lummis, M., & Stevenson, H. W. (1990). Gender differences in beliefs and achievement: A cross-cultural study. *Developmental Psychology, 26,* 254–263.

Lytton, H., & Romney, D. M. (1991). Parents' differential socialization of boys and girls: A meta-analysis. *Psychological Bulletin, 109,* 267–296.

Maccoby, E. E. (1980). *Social development.* New York: Harcourt Brace Jovanovich.

Maccoby, E. E. (1988). Gender as a social category. *Developmental Psychology, 24,* 755–765.

Maccoby, E. E. (1990). Gender and relationships: A developmental account. *American Psychologist, 45,* 513–520.

Maccoby, E. E., & Jacklin, C. N. (1974). *The psychology of sex differences.* Stanford, CA: Stanford University Press.

MacFarlane, A. (1977). *The psychology of childbirth.* Cambridge, MA: Harvard University Press.

Marcus, D. E., & Overton, W. F. (1978). The development of cognitive gender constancy and sex-role preferences. *Child Development, 49,* 434–444.

Marsiglio, W., & Donnelly, D. (1991). Sexual relations in later life: A national study of married persons. *Journal of Gerontology: Social Sciences, 46,* S338–S344.

Martin, C. L. (1989). Children's use of gender-related information in making social judgments. *Developmental Psychology, 25,* 80–88.

Martin, C. L. (1990). Attitudes and expectations about children with nontraditional gender roles. *Sex Roles, 22,* 151–165.

Martin, C. L., & Halverson, C. F., Jr. (1981). A schematic processing model of sex typing and stereotyping in children. *Child Development, 52,* 1119–1134.

Martin, C. L., & Halverson, C. F., Jr. (1983). The effects of sex-typing schemas on young children's memory. *Child Development, 54,* 563–574.

Martin, C. L., & Halverson, C. F., Jr. (1987). The roles of cognition in sex-roles and sex-typing. In D. B. Carter (Ed.), *Current conceptions of sex roles and sex-typing: Theory and research.* New York: Praeger.

Martin, C. L., & Little, J. K. (1990). The relation of gender understanding to children's sex-typed preferences and gender stereotypes. *Child Development, 61,* 1429–1439.

Massad, C. M. (1981). Sex-role identity and adjustment during adolescence. *Child Development, 52,* 1290–1298.

Masters, W. H., & Johnson, V. E. (1966). *Human sexual response.* Boston: Little, Brown.

Masters, W. H., & Johnson, V. E. (1970). *Human sexual inadequacy.* Boston: Little, Brown.

Masters, W. H., Johnson, V. E., & Kolodny, R. C. (1988). *Masters and Johnson on sex and human loving.* Glenview, IL: Scott Foresman.

Maticka-Tyndale, E. (1991). Modification of sexual activities in the era of AIDS: A trend analysis of adolescent sexual activities. *Youth and Society, 23,* 31–49.

McGhee, P. E., & Frueh, T. (1980). Television viewing and the learning of sex-role stereotypes. *Sex Roles, 6,* 179–188.

Mischel, W. (1970). Sex-typing and socialization. In P. H. Mussen (Ed.), *Carmichael's manual of child psychology* (Vol. 2). New York: Wiley.

Mitchell, J. E., Baker, L. A., & Jacklin, C. N. (1989). Masculinity and femininity in twin children: Genetic and environmental factors. *Child Development, 60,* 1475–1485.

Money, J. (1985). Pediatric sexology and hermaphroditism. *Journal of Sex and Marital Therapy, 11,* 139–156.

Money, J. (1988). *Gay, straight, and in-between: The sexology of erotic orientation.* New York: Oxford University Press.

Money, J., & Ehrhardt, A. (1972). *Man and woman, boy and girl.* Baltimore: Johns Hopkins University Press.

Money, J., & Tucker, P. (1975). *Sexual signatures: On being a man or a woman.* Boston: Little, Brown.

Morrison, D. M. (1985). Adolescent contraceptive behavior: A review. *Psychological Bulletin, 98,* 538–568.

Munroe, R. H., Shimmin, H. S., & Munroe, R. L. (1984). Gender understanding and sex-role preferences in four cultures. *Developmental Psychology, 20,* 673–682.

Mussen, P. H., & Rutherford, E. (1963). Parent-child relations and parental personality in relation to young children's sex-role preferences. *Child Development, 34,* 589–607.

O'Donohue, W. T., & Elliott, A. N. (1992). Treatment of the sexually abused child: A review. *Journal of Clinical Child Psychology, 21,* 218–228.

O'Heron, C. A., & Orlofsky, J. L. (1990). Stereotypic and nonstereotypic sex role trait and behavior orientations, gender identity, and psychological adjustment. *Journal of Personality and Social Psychology, 58,* 134–143.

Orlofsky, J. L., & O'Heron, C. A. (1987). Stereotypic and nonstereotypic sex role trait and behavior orientations: Implications for personal adjustment. *Journal of Personality and Social Psychology, 52,* 1034–1042.

Parsons, J. E., Adler, T. F., & Kaczala, C. M. (1982). Socialization of achievement attitudes and beliefs: Parental influences. *Child Development, 53,* 310–321.

Parsons, T. (1955). Family structure and the socialization of the child. In T. Parsons & R. F. Bales (Eds.), *Family socialization and interaction processes.* Glencoe, IL: Free Press.

Paul, J. P. (1993). Childhood cross-gender behavior and adult homosexuality: The resurgence of biological models of sexuality. *Journal of Homosexuality, 24,* 41–54.

Persson, G., & Svanborg, A. (1992). Marital coital activity in men at the age of 75: Relation to somatic, psychiatric, and social factors at the age of 70. *Journal of the American Geriatrics Society, 40,* 439–444.

Pfeiffer, E., Verwoerdt, A., & Davis, G. C. (1972). Sexual behavior in middle life. *American Journal of Psychiatry, 128,* 1262–1267.

Pleck, J. H. (1981). *The myth of masculinity.* Cambridge, MA: MIT Press.

Pleck, J. H. (1985). *Working wives/working husbands.* Beverly Hills, CA: Sage.

Pomerleau, A., Bolduc, D., Malcuit, G., & Cossette, L. (1990). Pink or blue: Environmental gender stereotypes in the first two years of life. *Sex Roles, 22,* 359–367.

Purifoy, F. E., Grodsky, A., & Giambra, L. M. (1992). The relationship of sexual daydreaming to sexual activity, sexual drive, and sexual attitudes for women across the life-span. *Archives of Sexual Behavior, 21,* 369–385.

Reinisch, J. M., Sanders, S. A., Hill, C. A., & Ziemba-Davis, M. (1992). High-risk sexual behavior among heterosexual undergraduates at a midwestern university. *Family Planning Perspectives, 24,* 116.

Resnick, S. M., Berenbaum, S. A., Gottesman, I. I., & Bouchard, T. J. (1986). Early hormonal influences on cognitive functioning in congenital adrenal hyperplasia. *Developmental Psychology, 22,* 191–198.

Rheingold, H. L., & Cook, K. V. (1975). The contents of boys' and girls' rooms as an index of parents' behavior. *Child Development, 46,* 459–463.

Richardson, J. G., & Simpson, C. H. (1982). Children, gender, and social structure: An analysis of the contents of letters to Santa Claus. *Child Development, 53,* 429–436.

Roberts, L. R., Sarigiani, P. A., Petersen, A. C., & Newman, J. L. (1990). Gender differences in the relationship between achievement and self image during early adolescence. *Journal of Early Adolescence, 10,* 159–175.

Robinson, C. C., & Morris, J. T. (1986). The gender-stereotyped nature of Christmas toys received by 36-, 48-, and 60-month-old children: A comparison between nonrequested vs. requested toys. *Sex Roles, 15,* 21–32.

Robinson, I., Ziss, K., Ganza, B., Katz, S., & Robinson, E. (1991). Twenty years of sexual revolution, 1965–1985: An update. *Journal of Marriage and the Family, 53,* 216–220.

Robinson, P. K. (1983). The sociological perspective. In R. B. Weg (Ed.), *Sexuality in the later years: Roles and behavior.* New York: Academic Press.

Rosen, R., & Hall, E. (1984). *Sexuality.* New York: Random House.

Rosenwasser, S. M., Lingenfelter, M., & Harrington, A. F. (1989). Nontraditional gender role portrayals on television and children's gender role perceptions. *Journal of Applied Developmental Psychology, 10,* 97–105.

Ross, C. A., Miler, S. D., Bjornson, L., Reagor, P., Fraser, G. A., & Anderson, G. (1991). Abuse histories in 102 cases of multiple personality disorder. *Canadian Journal of Psychiatry, 36,* 97–101.

Rubin, J. Z., Provenzano, F. J., & Luria, Z. (1974). The eye of the beholder: Parents' views on sex of newborns. *American Journal of Orthopsychiatry, 44,* 512–519.

Ruble, D. N. (1988). Sex-role development. In M. H. Bornstein & M. E. Lamb (Eds.), *Developmental psychology: An advanced textbook.* Hillsdale, NJ: Erlbaum.

Ruble, D. N., Balaban, T., & Cooper, J. (1981). Gender constancy and the effects of sex-typed televised toy commercials. *Child Development, 52,* 667–673.

Schiavi, R. C., Schreiner-Engel, P., White, D., & Mandeli, J. (1991). The relationship between pituitary-gonadal function and sexual behavior in healthy aging men. *Psychosomatic Medicine, 53,* 363–374.

Serbin, L. A., Powlishta, K. K., & Gulko, J. (1993). The development of sex typing in middle childhood. *Monographs of the Society for Research in Child Development, 58*(2, Serial No. 232).

Serbin, L. A., Tonick, I. J., & Sternglanz, S. H. (1977). Shaping cooperative cross-sex play. *Child Development, 48,* 924–929.

Shaffer, D. R., Pegalis, L. J., & Cornell, D. P. (1992). Gender and self-disclosure revisited: Personal and contextual variations in self-disclosure to same-sex acquaintances. *Journal of Social Psychology, 132,* 307–315.

Sigelman, C. K., Carr, M. B., & Begley, N. L. (1986). Developmental changes in the influence of sex-role stereotypes on person perception. *Child Study Journal, 16,* 191–205.

Signorielli, N., & Lears, M. (1992). Children, television, and conceptions about chores: Attitudes and behaviors. *Sex Roles, 27,* 157–170.

Slaby, R. G., & Frey, K. S. (1975). Development of gender constancy and selective attention to same-sex models. *Child Development, 46,* 849–856.

Smith, P. K., & Daglish, L. (1977). Sex differences in parent and infant behavior in the home. *Child Development, 48,* 1250–1254.

Smith, T. W. (1991). Adult sexual behavior in 1989: Number of partners, frequency of intercourse and risk of AIDS. *Family Planning Perspectives, 23,* 102–107.

Sonenstein, F. L., Pleck, J. H., & Ku, L. C. (1991). Levels of sexual activity among adolescent males in the United States. *Family Planning Perspectives, 23,* 162–167.

Spence, J. T. (1993). Gender-related traits and gender ideology: Evidence for a multifactorial theory. *Journal of Personality and Social Psychology, 64,* 624–635.

Spence, J. T., & Helmreich, R. L. (1978). *Masculinity and femininity: Their psychological dimensions, correlates, and antecedents.* Austin: University of Texas Press.

Sroufe, L. A., Bennett, C., Englund, M., Urban, J., & Shulman, S. (1993). The significance of gender boundaries in preadolescence: Contemporary correlates and antecedents of boundary violation and maintenance. *Child Development, 64,* 455–466.

Starr, B. D., & Weiner, M. B. (1981). *The Starr-Weiner report on sex and sexuality in the mature years.* New York: Stein & Day.

Stern, M., & Karraker, K. H. (1989). Sex stereotyping of infants: A review of gender labeling studies. *Sex Roles, 20,* 501–522.

Stevenson, M. R., & Black, K. N. (1988). Paternal absence and sex-role development: A meta-analysis. *Child Development, 59,* 793–814.

Stoddart, T., & Turiel, E. (1985). Children's concepts of cross-gender activities. *Child Development, 56,* 1241–1252.

Tharinger, D. (1990). Impact of child sexual abuse on developing sexuality. *Professional Psychology: Research and Practice, 21,* 331–337.

Thompson, S. K. (1975). Gender labels and early sex-role development. *Child Development, 46,* 339–347.

Thorne, B. (1993). *Gender play: Girls and boys in school.* New Brunswick, NJ: Rutgers University Press.

Todd, J., Friedman, A., & Kariuki, P. W. (1990). Women growing stronger with age: The effect of status in the United States and Kenya. *Psychology of Women Quarterly, 14,* 567–577.

Trickett, P. K., & Putnam, F. W. (1993). Impact of child sexual abuse on females: Toward a developmental, psychobiological integration. *Psychological Science, 4,* 81–87.

Unger, R., & Crawford, M. (1992). *Women and gender: A feminist psychology.* Philadelphia: Temple University Press.

Urberg, K. A. (1979). Sex-role conceptualization in adolescents and adults. *Developmental Psychology, 15,* 90–92.

Weizman, R., & Hart, J. (1987). Sexual behavior in healthy married elderly men. *Archives of Sexual Behavior, 16,* 39–44.

Whiting, B. B., & Edwards, C. P. (1988). *Children of different worlds: The formation of social behavior.* Cambridge, MA: Harvard University Press.

Whitley, B. E., Jr. (1983). Sex-role orientation and self-esteem: A critical meta-analytic review. *Journal of Personality and Social Psychology, 44,* 765–778.

Wielandt, H., & Boldsen, J. (1989). Age at first intercourse. *Journal of Biosocial Science, 21,* 169–177.

Wilkinson, L. C., & Marrett, C. B. (Eds.). (1985). *Gender influences in classroom interaction.* Orlando, FL: Academic Press.

Williams, J. E., & Best, D. L. (1990). *Measuring sex stereotypes: A multination study* (rev. ed.). Newbury Park, CA: Sage.

Wyatt, G. E., Guthrie, D., & Notgrass, C. M. (1992). Differential effects of women's child sexual abuse and subsequent sexual revictimization. *Journal of Consulting and Clinical Psychology, 60,* 167–173.

Young, W. C., Goy, R. W., & Phoenix, C. H. (1964). Hormones and sexual behavior. *Science, 143,* 212–218.

Zick, C. D., & McCullough, J. L. (1991). Trends in married couples' time use: Evidence from 1977–78 and 1987–88. *Sex Roles, 24,* 459–487.

Chapter 12: Choices: The Development of Morality and Motivation

Ainlay, S. C., & Smith, D. R. (1984). Aging and religious participation. *Journal of Gerontology, 39,* 357–363.

Anderson, K. E., Lytton, H., & Romney, D. M. (1986). Mothers' interactions with normal and conduct-disordered boys: Who affects whom? *Developmental Psychology, 22,* 604–609.

Arend, A., Gove, F. L., & Sroufe, L. A. (1979). Continuity of individual adaptation from infancy to kindergarten: A predictive study of ego-resiliency and curiosity in preschoolers. *Child Development, 50,* 950–959.

Atkinson, J. W. (1964). *An introduction to motivation.* Princeton, NJ: Van Nostrand.

Ayres, R., Cooley, E., & Dunn, C. (1990). Self-concept, attribution, and persistence in learning-disabled students. *Journal of School Psychology, 28,* 153–163.

Bandura, A. (1986). *Social foundations of thought and action: A social cognitive theory.* Englewood Cliffs, NJ: Prentice-Hall.

Bandura, A. (1991). Social cognitive theory of moral thought and action. In W. M. Kurtines & J. L. Gewirtz (Eds.), *Handbook of moral behavior and development: Vol. 1. Theory.* Hillsdale, NJ: Erlbaum.

Baruch, R. (1967). The achievement motive in women: Implications for career development. *Journal of Personality and Social Psychology, 5,* 260–267.

Battle, E. S. (1966). Motivational determinants of academic competence. *Journal of Personality and Social Psychology, 4,* 634–642.

Baumrind, D. (1973). The development of instrumental competence through socialization. In A. Pick (Ed.), *Minnesota Symposium on Child Psychology* (Vol. 7). Minneapolis: University of Minnesota Press.

Benenson, J. F., & Dweck, C. S. (1986). The development of trait explanations and self-evaluations in the academic and social domains. *Child Development, 57,* 1179–1187.

Berkowitz, M. W. (1985). The role of discussion in moral education. In M. W. Berkowitz & F. Oser (Eds.), *Moral education: Theory and application.* Hillsdale, NJ: Erlbaum.

Berkowitz, M. W., & Gibbs, J. C. (1983). Measuring the developmental features of moral discussion. *Merrill-Palmer Quarterly, 29,* 399–410.

Blasi, A. (1980). Bridging moral cognition and moral action: A critical review of the literature. *Psychological Bulletin, 88,* 1–45.

Blasi, A. (1984). Moral identity: Its role in moral functioning. In W. M. Kurtines & J. L. Gewirtz (Eds.), *Morality, moral behavior, and moral development.* New York: Wiley.

Blazer, D., & Palmore, E. (1976). Religion and aging in a longitudinal panel. *Gerontologist, 16,* 82–85.

Boggiano, A. K., & Katz, P. (1991). Maladaptive achievement patterns in students: The role of teachers' controlling strategies. *Journal of Social Issues, 47*(4), 35–51.

Boldizar, J. P., Perry, D. G., & Perry, L. C. (1989). Outcome values and aggression. *Child Development, 60,* 571–579.

Boldizar, J. P., Wilson, K. L., & Deemer, D. K. (1989). Gender, life experiences, and moral judgment development: A process-oriented approach. *Journal of Personality and Social Psychology, 57,* 229–238.

Brabeck, M. (1983). Moral judgment: Theory and research on differences between males and females. *Developmental Review, 3,* 274–291.

Brody, G. H., & Shaffer, D. R. (1982). Contributions of parents and peers to children's moral socialization. *Developmental Review, 2,* 31–75.

Bullock, M., & Lutkenhaus, P. (1988). The development of volitional behavior in the toddler years. *Child Development, 59,* 664–674.

Burton, R. V. (1963). The generality of honesty reconsidered. *Psychological Review, 70,* 481–499.

Burton, R. V. (1976). Honesty and dishonesty. In T. Lickona (Ed.), *Moral development and behavior.* New York: Holt, Rinehart & Winston.

Burton, R. V. (1984). A paradox in theories and research in moral development. In W. M. Kurtines & J. L. Gewirtz (Eds.), *Morality, moral behavior, and moral development.* New York: Wiley.

Bussey, K. (1992). Lying and truthfulness: Children's definitions, standards, and evaluative reactions. *Child Development, 63,* 129–137.

Butler, R. (1990). The effects of mastery and competitive conditions on self-assessment at different ages. *Child Development, 61,* 201–210.

Cairns, R. B., Cairns, B. D., Neckerman, H. J., Gest, S. D., & Gariepy, J. (1988). Social networks and aggressive behavior: Peer support or peer rejection? *Developmental Psychology, 24,* 815–823.

Cassidy, J. (1986). The ability to negotiate the environment: An aspect of infant competence as related to quality of attachment. *Child Development, 57,* 331–337.

Chap, J. B. (1985–1986). Moral judgment in middle and late adulthood: The effects of age-appropriate moral dilemmas and spontaneous role taking. *International Journal of Aging and Human Development, 22,* 161–171.

Coie, J. D., Dodge, K. A., Terry, R., & Wright, V. (1991). The role of aggression in peer relations: An analysis of aggression episodes in boys' play groups. *Child Development, 62,* 812–826.

Coke, M. M. (1992). Correlates of life satisfaction among elderly African Americans. *Journal of Gerontology: Psychological Sciences, 47,* P316–P320.

Colby, A., & Damon, W. (1992). *Pathways to commitment: Moral leaders in our time.* New York: Free Press.

Colby, A., & Kohlberg, L. (1987). *The measurement of moral judgment: Vol. 1. Theoretical foundations and research validation.* Cambridge, England: Cambridge University Press.

Colby, A., Kohlberg, L., Gibbs, J., & Lieberman, M. (1983). A longitudinal study of moral judgment. *Monographs of the Society for Research in Child Development, 48*(1–2, Serial No. 200).

Cole, P. M., Barrett, K. C., & Zahn-Waxler, C. (1992). Emotion displays in two-year-olds during mishaps. *Child Development, 63,* 314–324.

Coleman, J. S. (1961). *The adolescent society: The social life of the teenager and its impact on education.* Glencoe, IL: Free Press.

Costa, P. T., & McCrae, R. R. (1988). From catalog to classification: Murray's needs and the five-factor model. *Journal of Personality and Social Psychology, 55,* 258–265.

Crandall, V. C. (1967). Achievement behavior in young children. In *The young child: Reviews of research.* Washington, DC: National Association for the Education of Young Children.

Crandall, V. C. (1969). Sex differences in expectancy of intellectual and academic reinforcement. In C. P. Smith (Ed.), *Achievement-related motives in children.* New York: Russell Sage Foundation.

Crockenberg, S., & Litman, C. (1990). Autonomy as competence in 2-year-olds: Maternal correlates of child defiance, compliance, and self-assertion. *Developmental Psychology, 26,* 961–971.

Damon, W. (1977). *The social world of the child.* San Francisco: Jossey-Bass.

Damon, W., & Hart, D. (1992). Self-understanding and its role in social and moral development. In M. H. Bornstein & M. E. Lamb (Eds.), *Developmental psychology: An advanced textbook.* Hillsdale, NJ: Erlbaum.

de Vries, B., & Walker, L. J. (1986). Moral reasoning and attitudes toward capital punishment. *Developmental Psychology, 22,* 509–513.

Dishion, T. J., Patterson, G. R., Stoolmiller, M., & Skinner, M. L. (1991). Family, school, and behavioral antecedents to early adolescent involvement with antisocial peers. *Developmental Psychology, 27,* 172–180.

Dodge, K. A. (1980). Social cognition and children's aggressive behavior. *Child Development, 51,* 162–170.

Dodge, K. A. (1986). A social information processing model of social competence in children. In M. Perlmutter (Ed.), *Minnesota Symposia on Child Psychology* (Vol. 18). Hillsdale, NJ: Erlbaum.

Dodge, K. A. (1993). Social-cognitive mechanisms in the development of conduct disorder and depression. *Annual Review of Psychology, 44,* 559–584.

Dodge, K. A., & Frame, C. L. (1982). Social cognitive biases and deficits in aggressive boys. *Child Development, 53,* 620–635.

Dweck, C. S. (1975). The role of expectations and attributions in the alleviation of learned helplessness. *Journal of Personality and Social Psychology, 31,* 674–685.

Dweck, C. S. (1978). Achievement. In M. E. Lamb (Ed.), *Social and personality development.* New York: Holt, Rinehart & Winston.

Dweck, C. S., Davidson, W., Nelson, S., & Enna, B. (1978). Sex differences in learned helplessness: II. The contingencies of evaluative feedback in the classroom. III. An experimental analysis. *Developmental Psychology, 14,* 268–276.

Dweck, C. S., & Elliott, E. S. (1983). Achievement motivation. In E. M. Hetherington (Vol. Ed.; P. H. Mussen, General Ed.), *Handbook of child psychology: Vol. 4. Socialization, personality, and social development* (4th ed.). New York: Wiley.

Dweck, C. S., & Leggett, E. L. (1988). A social-cognitive approach to motivation and personality. *Psychological Review, 95,* 256–273.

Eccles, J. S., Jacobs, J. E., & Harold, R. D. (1990). Gender role stereotypes, expectancy effects, and parents' socialization of gender differences. *Journal of Social Issues, 46*(2), 183–201.

Eccles, J. S., Lord, S., & Midgley, C. (1991). What are we doing to early adolescents? The impact of educational contexts on early adolescents. *American Journal of Education, 99,* 521–542.

Eisenberg, N., Miller, P. A., Shell, R., McNalley, S., & Shea, C. (1991). Prosocial development in adolescence: A longitudinal study. *Developmental Psychology, 27,* 849–857.

Elliott, D. S., & Ageton, S. S. (1980). Reconciling race and class differences in self-reported and official estimates of delinquency. *American Sociological Review, 45,* 95–110.

Elliott, E. S., & Dweck, C. S. (1988). Goals: An approach to motivation and achievement. *Journal of Personality and Social Psychology, 54,* 5–12.

Emde, R. N., Biringen, Z., Clyman, R. B., & Oppenheim, D. (1991). The moral self of infancy: Affective core and procedural knowledge. *Developmental Review, 11,* 251–270.

Findley, M. J., & Cooper, H. M. (1983). Locus of control and academic achievement: A literature review. *Journal of Personality and Social Psychology, 44,* 419–427.

Fischer, K. W., & Lazerson, A. (1984). *Human development: From conception through adolescence.* New York: W. H. Freeman.

Fischer, W. F. (1963). Sharing in preschool children as a function of the amount and type of reinforcement. *Genetic Psychology Monographs, 68,* 215–245.

Ford, M. E., & Thompson, R. A. (1985). Perceptions of personal agency and infant attachment: Toward a life-span perspective on competence development. *International Journal of Behavioral Development, 8,* 377–406.

Ford, M. R., & Lowery, C. R. (1986). Gender differences in moral reasoning: A comparison of the use of justice and care orientations. *Journal of Personality and Social Psychology, 50,* 777–783.

Fordham, S., & Ogbu, J. U. (1986). Black students' school success: Coping with the "burden of 'acting white.'" *Urban Review, 18,* 176–206.

Fowler, J. W. (1981). *Stages of faith: The psychology of human development and the quest for meaning.* San Francisco: Harper & Row.

Fowler, J. W. (1991). The vocation of faith developmental theory. In J. W. Fowler, K. E. Nipkow, & F. Schweitzer (Eds.), *Stages of faith and religious development.* New York: Crossroad.

Frankel, K. A., & Bates, J. E. (1990). Mother-toddler problem-solving: Antecedents in attachment, home behavior, and temperament. *Child Development, 61,* 810–819.

Freud, S. (1960). *A general introduction to psychoanalysis.* New York: Washington Square Press. (Original work published 1935.)

Gibbs, J. C. (1979). Kohlberg's moral stage theory: A Piagetian revision. *Human Development, 22,* 89–112.

Gibbs, J. C., Basinger, K. S., & Fuller, D. (1992). *Moral maturity: Measuring the development of sociomoral reflection.* Hillsdale, NJ: Erlbaum.

Gibbs, J. C., & Schnell, S. V. (1985). Moral development "versus" socialization: A critique. *American Psychologist, 40,* 1071–1080.

Gilligan, C. (1977). In a different voice: Women's conceptions of self and morality. *Harvard Educational Review, 47,* 481–517.

Gilligan, C. (1982). *In a different voice: Psychological theory and women's development.* Cambridge, MA: Harvard University Press.

Gilligan, C. (1993). Adolescent development reconsidered. In A. Garrod (Ed.), *Approaches to moral development: New research and emerging themes.* New York: Teachers College Press.

Ginsburg, G. S., & Bronstein, P. (1993). Family factors related to children's intrinsic/extrinsic motivational orientation and academic performance. *Child Development, 64,* 1461–1474.

Graham, S., Hudley, C., & Williams, E. (1992). Attributional and emotional determinants of aggression among African-American and Latino young adolescents. *Developmental Psychology, 28,* 731–740.

Gralinski, J. H., & Kopp, C. B. (1993). Everyday rules for behavior: Mothers' requests to young children. *Developmental Psychology, 29,* 573–584.

Green, M. (1989). *Theories of human development: A comparative approach.* Englewood Cliffs, NJ: Prentice-Hall.

Grolnick, W. S., & Ryan, R. M. (1989). Parent styles associated with children's self-regulation and competence in school. *Journal of Educational Psychology,* 81, 143–154.

Grusec, J. E., Kuczynski, L., Rushton, J. P., & Simutis, Z. (1979). Learning resistance to temptation through observation. *Developmental Psychology, 15,* 233–240.

Guerra, N. G., & Slaby, R. G. (1990). Cognitive mediators of aggression in adolescent offenders: 2. Intervention. *Developmental Psychology, 26,* 269–277.

Haan, N., Aerts, E., & Cooper, B. A. B. (1985). *On moral grounds: The search for practical morality.* New York: New York University Press.

Haidt, J., Koller, S. H., & Dias, M. G. (1993). Affect, culture, and morality, or is it wrong to eat your dog? *Journal of Personality and Social Psychology, 65,* 613–628.

Harkness, S., Edwards, C. P., & Super, C. M. (1981). Social roles and moral reasoning: A case study in a rural African community. *Developmental Psychology, 17,* 595–603.

Hart, D., & Chmiel, S. (1992). Influence of defense mechanisms on moral judgment development: A longitudinal study. *Developmental Psychology, 28,* 722–730.

Harter, S. (1981). A new self-report scale of intrinsic versus extrinsic orientation in the classroom: Motivational and informational components. *Developmental Psychology, 17,* 300–312.

Hartshorne, H., & May, M. S. (1928–1930). *Studies in the nature of character: Vol. 1. Studies in deceit. Vol. 2. Studies in self-control. Vol. 3. Studies in the organization of character.* New York: Macmillan.

Hatch, L. R. (1991). Informal support patterns of older African-American and White women: Examining effects of family, paid work, and religious participation. *Research on Aging, 13,* 144–170.

Helmreich, R. L., Sawin, L. L., & Carsrud, A. L. (1986). The honeymoon effect in job performance: Temporal increases in the predictive power of achievement motivation. *Journal of Applied Psychology, 71,* 185–188.

Heyman, G. D., Dweck, C. S., & Cain, K. M. (1992). Young children's vulnerability to self-blame and helplessness: Relationship to beliefs about goodness. *Child Development, 63,* 401–415.

Hoffman, M. L. (1970). Moral development. In P. H. Mussen (Ed.), *Carmichael's manual of child psychology* (Vol. 2). New York: Wiley.

Hoffman, M. L. (1981). Is altruism part of human nature? *Journal of Personality and Social Psychology, 40,* 121–137.

Hoffman, M. L. (1983). Affective and cognitive processes in moral internalization. In E. T. Higgins, D. N. Ruble, & W. W. Hartup (Eds.), *Social cognition and social development: A sociocultural perspective.* Cambridge, England: Cambridge University Press.

Hoffman, M. L. (1988). Moral development. In M. H. Bornstein & M. E. Lamb (Eds.), *Developmental psychology: An advanced textbook* (2nd ed.). Hillsdale, NJ: Erlbaum.

Hoffman, M. L. (1993). Empathy, social cognition, and moral education. In A. Garrod (Ed.), *Approaches to moral development: New research and emerging themes.* New York: Teachers College Press.

Hooker, K., & Siegler, I. C. (1993). Life goals, satisfaction, and self-rated health: Preliminary findings. *Experimental Aging Research, 19,* 97–110.

Hudley, C., & Graham, S. (1993). An attributional intervention to reduce peer-directed aggression among African-American boys. *Child Development, 64,* 124–138.

Hyde, K. E. (1990). *Religion in childhood and adolescence: A comprehensive review of the research.* Birmingham, AL: Religious Education Press.

Ingrassia, M. (with P. Annin, N. A. Biddle, & S. Miller) (1993, July 19). "Life means nothing." *Newsweek,* pp. 16–17.

Jose, P. M. (1990). Just world reasoning in children's immanent justice judgments. *Child Development, 61,* 1024–1033.

Jussim, L., & Eccles, J. S. (1992). Teacher expectations: II. Construction and reflection of student achievement. *Journal of Personality and Social Psychology, 63,* 947–961.

Kagan, J. (1981). *The second year: The emergence of self-awareness.* Cambridge, MA: Harvard University Press.

Kagan, J., & Moss, H. A. (1962). *Birth to maturity.* New York: Wiley.

Kausler, D. H. (1990). Motivation, human aging, and cognitive performance. In J. E. Birren & K. W. Schaie (Eds.), *Handbook of the psychology of aging* (3rd ed.). San Diego: Academic Press.

Kochanska, G. (1993). Toward a synthesis of parental socialization and child temperament in early development of conscience. *Child Development, 64,* 325–347.

Kohlberg, L. (1963). The development of children's orientations toward a moral order: I. Sequence in the development of moral thought. *Vita Humana, 6,* 11–33.

Kohlberg, L. (1973). Continuities in childhood and adult moral development revisited. In P. B. Baltes & K. W. Schaie (Eds.), *Life-span developmental psychology: Personality and socialization.* New York: Academic Press.

Kohlberg, L. (1975, June). The cognitive-developmental approach to moral education. *Phi Delta Kappan,* pp. 670–677.

Kohlberg, L. (1981). *Essays on moral development: Vol. 1. The philosophy of moral development.* San Francisco: Harper & Row.

Kohlberg, L. (1984). *Essays on moral development: Vol. 2. The psychology of moral development.* San Francisco: Harper & Row.

Kohlberg, L. (1985). The just community approach to moral education in theory and practice. In M. W. Berkowitz & F. Oser (Eds.), *Moral education: Theory and application.* Hillsdale, NJ: Erlbaum.

Kohlberg, L., & Diessner, R. (1991). A cognitive-developmental approach to moral development. In J. L. Gewirtz & W. M. Kurtines (Eds.), *Intersections with attachment.* Hillsdale, NJ: Erlbaum.

Kreutz, D. (1991, May 1). Tucsonan who saved drowning man honored for act transcending heroism. *Arizona Daily Star,* pp. 1B–2B.

Krogh, K. M. (1985). Women's motives to achieve and to nurture in different life stages. *Sex Roles, 12,* 75–90.

Kruger, A. C. (1992). The effect of peer and adult-child transactive discussions on moral reasoning. *Merrill-Palmer Quarterly, 38,* 191–211.

Kruger, A. C., & Tomasello, M. (1986). Transactive discussions with peers and adults. *Developmental Psychology, 22,* 681–685.

Kurtines, W. M. (1986). Moral behavior as rule governed behavior: Person and situation effects on moral decision making. *Journal of Personality and Social Psychology, 50,* 784–791.

Lamborn, S. D., Mounts, N. S., Steinberg, L., & Dornbusch, S. M. (1991). Patterns of competence and adjustment among adolescents from authoritative, authoritarian, indulgent, and neglectful families. *Child Development, 62,* 1049–1065.

Lapsley, D. K., Harwell, M. R., Olson, L. M., Flannery, D., & Quintana, S. M. (1984). Moral judgment, personality, and attitude toward authority in early and late adolescence. *Journal of Youth and Adolescence, 13,* 527–542.

Lewis, M., Alessandri, S. M., & Sullivan, M. W. (1990). Violation of expectancy, loss of control, and anger expressions in young infants. *Developmental Psychology, 26,* 745–751.

Lin, C. C., & Fu, V. R. (1990). A comparison of child-rearing practices among Chinese, immigrant Chinese, and Caucasian-American parents. *Child Development, 61,* 429–433.

Linn, R. (1989). Hypothetical and actual moral reasoning of Israeli selective conscientious objectors during the war in Lebanon (1982–1985). *Journal of Applied Developmental Psychology, 10,* 19–36.

Lyons, N. P. (1983). Two perspectives: On self, relationships, and morality. *Harvard Educational Review, 53,* 125–145.

Lytton, H. (1990). Child and parent effects in boys' conduct disorder: A reinterpretation. *Developmental Psychology, 26,* 683–697.

Mac Iver, D. J., Stipek, D. J., & Daniels, D. H. (1991). Explaining within-semester changes in student effort in junior high school and senior high school courses. *Journal of Educational Psychology, 83,* 201–211.

MacTurk, R. H., McCarthy, M. E., Vietze, P. M., & Yarrow, L. J. (1987). Sequential analysis of mastery behavior in 6- and 12-month-old infants. *Developmental Psychology, 23,* 199–203.

Maehr, M. L., & Kleiber, D. A. (1981). The graying of achievement motivation. *American Psychologist, 36,* 787–793.

Malatesta, C. Z., & Culver, L. C. (1984). Thematic and affective content in the lives of adult women. In C. Z. Malatesta & C. E. Izard (Eds.), *Emotion in adult development.* Beverly Hills, CA: Sage.

Martin, G. B., & Clark, R. D. III. (1982). Distress crying in neonates: Species and peer specificity. *Developmental Psychology, 18,* 3–9.

Mayes, L. C., & Zigler, E. (1992). An observational study of the affective concomitants of mastery in infants. *Journal of Psychology and Psychiatry, 4,* 659–667.

McAdams, P. P., de St. Aubin, E., & Logan, R. L. (1993). Generativity among young, middle, and older adults. *Psychology and Aging, 8,* 221–230.

McClelland, D. C. (1985). How motives, skills, and values determine what people do. *American Psychologist, 40,* 812–825.

McClelland, D. C., Atkinson, J. W., Clark, R. A., & Lowell, E. L. (1953). *The achievement motive.* New York: Appleton-Century-Crofts.

Mellinger, J. C., & Erdwins, C. J. (1985). Personality correlates of age and life roles in adult women. *Psychology of Women Quarterly, 9,* 503–514.

Messer, D. J., McCarthy, M. E., McQuiston, S., MacTurk, R. H., Yarrow, L. J., & Vietze, P. M. (1986). Relation between mastery behavior in infancy and competence in early childhood. *Developmental Psychology, 22,* 366–372.

Milich, R., & Okazaki, M. (1991). An examination of learned helplessness among attention-deficit hyperactivity disordered boys. *Journal of Abnormal Child Psychology, 19,* 607–623.

Miller, A. (1985). A developmental study of the cognitive basis of performance impairment after failure. *Journal of Personality and Social Psychology, 49,* 529–538.

Mischel, W. (1974). Processes in the delay of gratification. In L. Berkowitz (Ed.), *Advances in experimental social psychology* (Vol. 7). New York: Academic Press.

Nelson, E. A., Grinder, R. E., & Biaggio, A. M. B. (1969). Relationships between behavioral, cognitive-developmental, and self-report measures of morality and personality. *Multivariate Behavioral Research, 4,* 483–500.

Nelson, E. A., Grinder, R. E., & Mutterer, M. L. (1969). Sources of variance in behavioral measures of honesty in temptation situations: Methodological analyses. *Developmental Psychology, 1,* 265–279.

Nelson, S. A. (1980). Factors influencing young children's use of motives and outcomes as moral criteria. *Child Development, 51,* 823–829.

Nelson-Le Gall, S. A. (1985). Motive-outcome matching and outcome foreseeability: Effects on attribution of intentionality and moral judgments. *Developmental Psychology, 21,* 332–337.

Nicholls, J. G. (1978). The development of the concepts of effort and ability, perception of academic attainment, and the understanding that difficult tasks require more ability. *Child Development, 49,* 800–814.

Nicholls, J. G., & Miller, A. T. (1984). Reasoning about the ability of self and others: A developmental study. *Child Development, 55,* 1990–1999.

Nucci, L. P., & Nucci, M. S. (1982). Children's responses to moral and social conventional transgressions in free-play settings. *Child Development, 53,* 1337–1342.

Olthof, T., Ferguson, T. J., & Luiten, A. (1989). Personal responsibility and antecedents of anger and blame reactions in children. *Child Development, 60,* 1326–1336.

Palmore, E. (1981). *Social patterns in normal aging: Findings from the Duke Longitudinal Study.* Durham, NC: Duke University Press.

Patterson, G. R. (1982). *Coercive family processes.* Eugene, OR: Castilia Press.

Patterson, G. R., DeBaryshe, B. D., & Ramsey, E. (1989). A developmental perspective on antisocial behavior. *American Psychologist, 44,* 329–335.

Perry, D. G., & Parke, R. D. (1975). Punishment and alternative response training as determinants of response inhibition in children. *Genetic Psychology Monographs, 91,* 257–279.

Phillips, D. (1984). The illusion of incompetence among academically competent children. *Child Development, 55,* 2000–2016.

Piaget, J. (1965). *The moral judgment of the child.* New York: Free Press. (Original work published 1932.)

Plomin, R. (1990). *Nature and nurture: An introduction to behavior genetics.* Pacific Grove, CA: Brooks/Cole.

Power, F. C., Higgins, A., & Kohlberg, L. (1989). *Lawrence Kohlberg's approach to moral education.* New York: Columbia University Press.

Pratt, M. W., Diessner, R., Hunsberger, B., Pancer, S. M., & Savoy, K. (1991). Four pathways in the analysis of adult development and aging: Comparing analyses of reasoning about personal-life dilemmas. *Psychology and Aging, 4,* 666–675.

Pratt, M. W., Golding, G., & Hunter, W. J. (1983). Aging as ripening: Character and consistency of moral judgment in young, mature, and older adults. *Human Development, 26,* 277–288.

Pratt, M. W., Golding, G., Hunter, W. J., & Norris, J. (1988). From inquiry to judgment: Age and sex differences in patterns of adult moral thinking and information-seeking. *International Journal of Aging and Human Development, 27,* 109–124.

Pratt, M. W., Golding, G., & Kerig, P. (1987). Lifespan differences in adult thinking about hypothetical and personal moral issues: Reflection or regression? *International Journal of Behavioral Development, 10,* 359–375.

Quiggle, N. L., Garber, J., Panak, W. F., & Dodge, K. A. (1992). Social information processing in aggressive and depressed children. *Child Development, 63,* 1305–1320.

Rapkin, B. D., & Fischer, K. (1992). Framing the construct of life satisfaction in terms of older adults' personal goals. *Psychology and Aging, 7,* 138–149.

Raynor, J. O. (1970). Relationships between achievement-related motives, future orientation, and academic performance. *Journal of Personality and Social Psychology, 15,* 28–33.

Raynor, J. O. (1982). A theory of personality functioning and change. In J. O. Raynor & E. E. Entin (Eds.), *Motivation, career striving, and aging.* Washington, DC: Hemisphere.

Reker, G. T., Peacock, E. J., & Wong, P. T. P. (1987). Meaning and purpose in life and well-being: A life-span perspective. *Journal of Gerontology, 42,* 44–49.

Rest, J. R. (1993). Research on moral judgment in college students. In A. Garrod (Ed.), *Approaches to moral development: New research and emerging themes.* New York: Teachers College Press.

Rest, J. R., & Thoma, S. J. (1985). Relation of moral judgment development to formal education. *Developmental Psychology, 21,* 709–714.

Rosen, B. C., & D'Andrade, R. (1959). The psychosocial origins of achievement motivation. *Sociometry, 22,* 185–218.

Rosenholtz, S. J., & Simpson, C. (1984). The formation of ability conceptions: Developmental trend or social construction? *Review of Educational Research, 54,* 31–63.

Rushton, J. P. (1980). *Altruism, socialization, and society.* Englewood Cliffs, NJ: Prentice-Hall.

Rushton, J. P., Fulker, D. W., Neale, M. C., Nias, K. K. B., & Eysenck, H. J. (1986). Altruism and aggression: The heritability of individual differences. *Journal of Personality and Social Psychology, 50,* 1192–1198.

Schlaefli, A., Rest, J. R., & Thoma, S. J. (1985). Does moral education improve moral judgment? A meta-analysis of intervention studies using the Defining Issues Test. *Review of Educational Research, 55,* 319–352.

Selman, R. L. (1980). *The growth of interpersonal understanding.* New York: Academic Press.

Shweder, R. A., Mahapatra, M., & Miller, J. G. (1990). Culture and moral development. In J. W. Stigler, R. A. Shweder, & G. Herdt (Eds.), *Cultural psychology: Essays on comparative human development.* Cambridge, England: Cambridge University Press.

Sigelman, C. K., & Waitzman, K. A. (1991). The development of distributive justice orientations: Contextual influences on children's resource allocations. *Child Development, 62,* 1367–1378.

Slaby, R. G., & Guerra, N. G. (1988). Cognitive mediators of aggression in adolescent offenders: 1. Assessment. *Developmental Psychology, 24,* 580–588.

Slaughter-Defoe, D. T., Nakagawa, K., Takanishi, R., & Johnson, D. J. (1990). Toward cultural/ecological perspectives on schooling and achievement in African- and Asian-American children. *Child Development, 61,* 363–383.

Smetana, J. G. (1981). Preschool children's conceptions of moral and social rules. *Child Development, 52,* 1333–1336.

Smetana, J. G. (1989). Toddlers' social interactions in the context of moral and conventional transgressions in the home. *Developmental Psychology, 25,* 499–508.

Smetana, J. G., Schlagman, N., & Adams, P. W. (1993). Preschool children's judgments about hypothetical and actual transgressions. *Child Development, 64,* 202–214.

Snarey, J. R. (1985). Cross-cultural universality of social-moral development: A critical review of Kohlbergian research. *Psychological Bulletin, 97,* 202–232.

Spence, J. T. (1985). Achievement American style: The rewards and costs of individualism. *American Psychologist, 40,* 1285–1295.

Steinberg, L., Dornbusch, S. M., & Brown, B. B. (1992). Ethnic differences in adolescent achievement: An ecological perspective. *American Psychologist, 47,* 723–729.

Steinberg, L., Elmen, J. D., & Mounts, N. S. (1989). Authoritative parenting, psychosocial maturity, and academic success among adolescents. *Child Development, 60,* 1424–1436.

Stevens, D. P., & Truss, C. V. (1985). Stability and change in adult personality over 12 and 20 years. *Developmental Psychology, 21,* 568–584.

Stewart, L., & Pascual-Leone, J. (1992). Mental capacity constraints and the development of moral reasoning. *Journal of Experimental Child Psychology, 54,* 251–287.

Stipek, D. J. (1984). The development of achievement motivation. In R. Ames & C. Ames (Eds.), *Research on motivation in education* (Vol. 1). Orlando, FL: Academic Press.

Stipek, D. J., & Gralinski, J. H. (1991). Gender differences in children's achievement-related beliefs and emotional responses to success and failure in mathematics. *Journal of Educational Psychology, 83,* 361–371.

Stipek, D. J., & Kowalski, P. S. (1989). Learned helplessness in task-orienting versus performance-orienting testing conditions. *Journal of Educational Psychology, 81,* 384–391.

Stipek, D. J., & Mac Iver, D. (1989). Developmental change in children's assessment of intellectual competence. *Child Development, 60,* 521–538.

Stipek, D. J., Recchia, A., & McClintic, S. (1992). Self-evaluation in young children. *Monographs of the Society for Research in Child Development, 57*(1, Serial No. 226).

Stipek, D. J., Roberts, T. A., & Sanborn, M. E. (1984). Preschool-age children's performance expectations for themselves and another child as a function of the incentive value of success and the salience of past performance. *Child Development, 55,* 1983–1989.

Surber, C. F. (1982). Separable effects of motives, consequences, and presentation order on children's moral judgments. *Developmental Psychology, 18,* 257–266.

Tharp, R. G. (1989). Psychocultural variables and constants: Effects on teaching and learning in schools. *American Psychologist, 44,* 349–359.

Thoma, S. J. (1986). Estimating gender differences in the comprehension and preference of moral issues. *Developmental Review, 6,* 165–180.

Thoma, S. J., Rest, J. R., & Davison, M. L. (1991). Describing and testing a moderator of the moral judgment and action relationship. *Journal of Personality and Social Psychology, 61,* 659–669.

Tietjen, A. M., & Walker, L. J. (1985). Moral reasoning and leadership among men in a Papua New Guinea society. *Developmental Psychology, 21,* 982–992.

Tisak, M. S. (1986). Children's conceptions of parental authority. *Child Development, 57,* 166–176.

Tisak, M. S., & Tisak, J. (1990). Children's conceptions of parental authority, friendship, and sibling relations. *Merrill-Palmer Quarterly, 36,* 347–368.

Tomlinson-Keasey, C., & Keasey, C. B. (1974). The mediating role of cognitive development in moral judgment. *Child Development, 45,* 291–298.

Toner, I. J., Parke, R. D., & Yussen, S. R. (1978). The effect of observation of model behavior on the establishment and stability of resistance to deviation in children. *Journal of Genetic Psychology, 132,* 283–290.

Toner, I. J., & Potts, R. (1981). Effect of modeled rationales on moral behavior, moral choice, and level of moral judgment in children. *Journal of Psychology, 107,* 153–162.

Trevethan, S. D., & Walker, L. J. (1989). Hypothetical versus real-life moral reasoning among psychopathic and delinquent youth.

Development and Psychopathology, 1, 91–103.

Turiel, E. (1978). The development of concepts of social structure: Social convention. In J. Glick & A. Clarke-Stewart (Eds.), *The development of social understanding.* New York: Gardner Press.

Turiel, E. (1983). *The development of social knowledge: Morality and convention.* Cambridge, England: Cambridge University Press.

Veroff, J., Atkinson, J. W., Feld, S. C., & Gurin, G. (1960). The use of thematic apperception to assess motivation in a nationwide interview study. *Psychological Monographs, 74*(12, Whole No. 499).

Veroff, J., Reuman, D., & Feld, S. (1984). Motives in American men and women across the adult life span. *Developmental Psychology, 20,* 1142–1158.

Walker, L. J. (1980). Cognitive and perspective-taking prerequisites of moral development. *Child Development, 51,* 131–139.

Walker, L. J. (1984). Sex differences in the development of moral reasoning: A critical review. *Child Development, 55,* 677–691.

Walker, L. J. (1989). A longitudinal study of moral reasoning. *Child Development, 60,* 157–166.

Walker, L. J., & Taylor, J. H. (1991). Family interactions and the development of moral reasoning. *Child Development, 62,* 264–283.

Watson, J. S., & Ramey, C. T. (1972). Reactions to response-contingent stimulation in early infancy. *Merrill-Palmer Quarterly, 18,* 219–228.

Weiner, B. (1974). *Achievement and attribution theory.* Morristown, NJ: General Learning Press.

Weiner, B. (1986). *An attributional theory of motivation and emotion.* New York: Springer-Verlag.

White, R. W. (1959). Motivation reconsidered: The concept of competence. *Psychological Review, 66,* 297–333.

Wigfield, A., & Eccles, J. S. (1992). The development of achievement task values: A theoretical analysis. *Developmental Review, 12,* 265–310.

Winterbottom, M. (1958). The relation of need for achievement to learning experiences in independence and mastery. In J. Atkinson (Ed.), *Motives in fantasy, action, and society.* Princeton, NJ: Van Nostrand.

Wolff, M., Rutten, P., & Bayer, A. F. III. (1992). *Where we stand: Can America make it in the race for health, wealth, and happiness?* New York: Bantam Books.

Yarrow, L. J., MacTurk, R. H., Vietze, P. M., McCarthy, M. E., Klein, R. P., & McQuiston, S. (1984). Developmental course of parental stimulation and its relationship to mastery motivation during infancy. *Developmental Psychology, 20,* 492–503.

Young, G., & Dowling, W. (1987). Dimensions of religiosity in old age: Accounting for variation in types of participation. *Journal of Gerontology, 42,* 376–380.

Zahn-Waxler, C., Radke-Yarrow, M., & King, R. A. (1979). Child rearing and children's prosocial initiations toward victims of distress. *Child Development, 50,* 319–330.

Zahn-Waxler, C., Radke-Yarrow, M., Wagner, E., & Chapman, M. (1992). Development of concern for others. *Developmental Psychology, 28,* 126–136.

Chapter 13: Participation in the Social World

Adams, R. G. (1985–1986). Emotional closeness and physical distance between friends: Implications for elderly women living in age-segregated and age-integrated settings. *International Journal of Aging and Human Development, 22,* 55–76.

Ainsworth, M. D. S. (1973). The development of infant-mother attachment. In B. M. Caldwell & H. N. Ricciuti (Eds.), *Review of child development research* (Vol. 3). Chicago: University of Chicago Press.

Ainsworth, M. D. S. (1979). Attachment as related to mother-infant interaction. In J. G. Rosenblatt, R. A. Hinde, C. Beer, & M. Busnel (Eds.), *Advances in the study of behavior* (Vol. 9). New York: Academic Press.

Ainsworth, M. D. S. (1989). Attachments beyond infancy. *American Psychologist, 44,* 709–716.

Ainsworth, M. D. S., Blehar, M., Waters, E., & Wall, S. (1978). *Patterns of attachment.* Hillsdale, NJ: Erlbaum.

Allan, G. (1986). Friendship and care for elderly people. *Aging and Society, 6,* 1–12.

Allen, J. P., Weissberg, R. P., & Hawkins, J. A. (1989). The relation between values and social competence in early adolescence. *Developmental Psychology, 25,* 458–464.

Alley, T. R. (1981). Head shape and the perception of cuteness. *Developmental Psychology, 17,* 650–654.

Antonucci, T. C. (1985). Personal characteristics, social support, and social behavior. In R. H. Binstock & E. Shanas (Eds.), *Handbook of aging and the social sciences* (2nd ed.). New York: Van Nostrand Reinhold.

Antonucci, T. C., & Akiyama, H. (1991). Social relationships and aging well. *Generations, 15,* 39–44.

Antonucci, T. C., Fuhrer, R., & Jackson, J. S. (1990). Social support and reciprocity: A cross-ethnic and cross-national perspective. *Journal of Social and Personal Relationships, 7,* 519–530.

Archer, J. (1992). Childhood gender roles: Social context and organization. In H. McGurk (Ed.), *Childhood social development: Contemporary perspectives.* Hove, UK: Erlbaum.

Arling, G. (1987). Strain, social support, and distress in old age. *Journal of Gerontology, 42,* 107–113.

Asher, S. R. (1986). An overview of intervention research with unpopular children. In S. R. Asher & J. Coie (Eds.), *Assessment of children's social status.* New York: Cambridge University Press.

Athey, I. (1984). Contributions of play to development. In T. D. Yawkey & A. D. Pelligrini (Eds.), *Child's play: Developmental and applied.* Hillsdale, NJ: Erlbaum.

Barenboim, C. (1981). The development of person perception in childhood and adolescence: From behavioral comparisons to psychological constructs to psychological comparisons. *Child Development, 52,* 129–144.

Barnas, M. V., Pollina, L., & Cummings, E. M. (1991). Life-span attachment: Relations between attachment and socioemotional functioning in adult women. *Genetic, Social, and General Psychology Monographs, 117,* 175–202.

Bartholomew, K., & Horowitz, L. M. (1991). Attachment styles among young adults: A test of a four-category model. *Journal of Personality and Social Psychology, 61,* 226–244.

Belsky, J. (1980). Child maltreatment: An ecological integration. *American Psychologist, 35,* 320–335.

Belsky, J., Rovine, M., & Taylor, D. G. (1984). The Pennsylvania infant and family development project. III: The origins of individual differences in infant-mother attachment: Maternal and infant contributions. *Child Development, 55,* 718–728.

Berman, W. H., & Sperling, M. B. (1991). Parental attachment and emotional distress in the transition to college. *Journal of Youth and Adolescence, 20,* 427–440.

Berndt, T. J. (1979). Developmental changes in conforming to peers and parents. *Developmental Psychology, 15,* 608–616.

Berndt, T. J. (1982). The features and effects of friendship in early adolescence. *Child Development, 53,* 1447–1460.

Berndt, T. J., & Hoyle, S. G. (1985). Stability and change in childhood and adolescent friendships. *Developmental Psychology, 21,* 1007–1015.

Berndt, T. J., & Perry, T. B. (1990). Distinctive features and effects of early adolescent friendships. In R. Montemayor, G. R. Adams, & T. P. Gullotta (Eds.), *From childhood to adolescence: A transitional period.* Newbury Park, CA: Sage.

Bierman, K. L., & Furman, W. (1984). The effects of social skills training and peer involvement on the social adjustment of preadolescents. *Child Development, 55,* 151–162.

Biller, H. B. (1993). *Fathers and families: Paternal factors in child development.* Westport, CT: Auburn House.

Biringen, A. (1990). Direct observation of maternal sensitivity and dyadic interactions in the home: Relations to maternal thinking. *Developmental Psychology, 26,* 278–284.

Bixenstine, V. C., DeCorte, M. S., & Bixenstine, B. A. (1976). Conformity to peer-sponsored misconduct at four grade levels. *Developmental Psychology, 12,* 226–236.

Blanchard-Fields, F. (1986a). Attributional processes in adult development. *Educational Gerontology, 12,* 291–300.

Blanchard-Fields, F. (1986b). Reasoning on social dilemmas varying in emotional saliency: An adult developmental perspective. *Psychology and Aging, 1,* 325–333.

Blieszner, R., & Adams, R. G. (1992). *Adult friendship.* Newbury Park, CA: Sage.

Bohlin, G., & Hagekull, B. (1993). Stranger wariness and sociability in the early years. *Infant Behavior and Development, 16,* 53–67.

Bossé, R., Aldwin, C. M., Levenson, M. R., Spiro, A. III, & Mroczek, D. K. (1993). Change in social support after retirement: Longitudinal findings from the Normative Aging Study. *Journal of Gerontology: Psychological Sciences, 48,* P210–P217.

Bowlby, J. (1969). *Attachment and loss: Vol. 1. Attachment.* New York: Basic Books.

Bowlby, J. (1973). *Attachment and loss: Vol. 2. Separation.* New York: Basic Books.

Bowlby, J. (1980). *Attachment and loss: Vol. 3. Loss, sadness, and depression.* New York: Basic Books.

Bowlby, J. (1988). *A secure base: Parent-child attachment and healthy human development.* New York: Basic Books.

Bretherton, I. (1990). Open communication and internal working models: Their role in the development of attachment relationships. In R. A. Thompson (Ed.), *Nebraska Symposium on Motivation: Vol. 36. Socioemotional development.* Lincoln: University of Nebraska Press.

Bretherton, I., Stolberg, U., & Kreye, M. (1981). Engaging strangers in proximal interaction: Infants' social initiative. *Developmental Psychology, 17,* 746–755.

Brook, J. S., Brook, D. W., Gordon, A. S., Whiteman, M., & Cohen, P. (1990). The psychosocial etiology of adolescent drug use: A family interactional approach. *Genetic, Social, and General Psychology Monographs, 116,* 111–267.

Brown, B. B., & Lohr, M. J. (1987). Peer-group affiliation and adolescent self-esteem: An integration of ego-identity and symbolic-interaction theories. *Journal of Personality and Social Psychology, 52,* 47–55.

Brown, B. B., Mounts, N., Lamborn, S. D., & Steinberg, L. (1993). Parenting practices and peer group affiliation in adolescence. *Child Development, 64,* 467–482.

Brownell, C. A. (1986). Convergent developments: Cognitive-developmental correlates of growth in infant/toddler peer skills. *Child Development, 57,* 275–286.

Brownell, C. A. (1990). Peer social skills in toddlers: Competencies and constraints illustrated by same-age and mixed-age interaction. *Child Development, 61,* 838–848.

Buhrmester, D., & Furman, W. (1986). The changing functions of friends in childhood: A neo-Sullivanian perspective. In V. J. Derlega & B. A. Winstead (Eds.), *Friendship and social interaction.* New York: Springer-Verlag.

Bukowski, W. M., Gauze, C., Hoza, B., & Newcomb, A. F. (1993). Differences and consistency between same-sex and other-sex peer relationships during early adolescence. *Developmental Psychology, 29,* 253–263.

Buss, D. M. (1985). Human mate selection. *American Scientist, 73,* 47–51.

Buss, D. M. (1989). Sex differences in human mate preferences: Evolutionary hypotheses tested in 37 cultures. *Behavioral and Brain Sciences, 12,* 1–49.

Caplan, M., Vespo, J., Pedersen, J., & Hay, D. F. (1991). Conflict and its resolution in small groups of one- and two-year-olds. *Child Development, 62,* 1513–1524.

Carlson, V., Cicchetti, D., Barnett, D., & Braunwald, K. (1989). Disorganized/disoriented attachment relationships in maltreated infants. *Developmental Psychology, 25,* 525–531.

Carstensen, L. L. (1992). Social and emotional patterns in adulthood: Support for socioemotional selectivity theory. *Psychology and Aging, 7,* 331–338.

Chatters, L. M., Taylor, R. J., & Jackson, J. S. (1986). Aged blacks' choices for an informal helper network. *Journal of Gerontology, 41,* 94–100.

Chen, X., Rubin, K. H., & Sun, Y. (1992). Social reputation in Chinese and Canadian children: A cross-cultural study. *Child Development, 63,* 1336–1343.

Christopher, J. S., Nangle, D. W., & Hansen, D. J. (1993). Social-skills interventions with adolescents: Current issues and procedures. *Behavior Modification, 17,* 314–338.

Cillessen, A. H., Van IJzendoorn, H. W., Van Lieshout, C. F., & Hartup, W. W. (1992). Heterogeneity among peer-rejected boys: Subtypes and stabilities. *Child Development, 63,* 893–905.

Coie, J. D., Dodge, K. A., & Coppotelli, H. (1982). Dimensions and types of social status: A cross-age perspective. *Developmental Psychology, 18,* 557–570.

Coie, J. D., Dodge, K. A., & Kupersmidt, J. B. (1990). Peer group behavior and social status. In S. R. Asher & J. D. Coie (Eds.), *Peer rejection in childhood.* Cambridge, England: Cambridge University Press.

Coie, J. D., & Kupersmidt, J. B. (1983). A behavioral analysis of emerging social status in boys' groups. *Child Development, 54,* 1400–1416.

Coie, J. D., Lochman, J. E., Terry, R., & Hyman, C. (1992). Predicting early adolescent disorder from childhood aggression and peer rejection. *Journal of Consulting and Clinical Psychology, 60,* 783–792.

Collins, N. L., & Read, S. J. (1990). Adult attachment, working models, and relationship quality in dating couples. *Journal of Personality and Social Psychology, 58,* 644–663.

Connidis, I. A., & Davies, L. (1992). Confidants and companions: Choices in later life. *Journal of Gerontology: Social Sciences, 47,* S115–S122.

Cox, M. J., Owen, M. T., Henderson, V. K., & Margand, N. A. (1992). Prediction of infant-father and infant-mother attachment. *Developmental Psychology, 28,* 474–483.

Cox, M. J., Owen, M. T., Lewis, J. M., & Henderson, V. K. (1989). Marriage, adult adjustment, and early parenting. *Child Development, 60,* 1015–1024.

Crockenberg, S. B. (1981). Infant irritability, mother responsiveness, and social support influences on the security of infant-mother attachment. *Child Development, 52,* 857–865.

Crowell, J. A., & Feldman, S. S. (1991). Mothers' working models of attachment relationships and mother and child behavior during separation and reunion. *Developmental Psychology, 27,* 597–605.

de Jong-Gierveld, J. (1986). Loneliness and the degree of intimacy in interpersonal relationships. In R. Gilmour & S. Duck (Eds.), *The emerging field of personal relationships.* Hillsdale, NJ: Erlbaum.

Denney, N. W. (1982). Aging and cognitive changes. In B. B. Wolman (Ed.), *Handbook of developmental psychology.* Englewood Cliffs, NJ: Prentice-Hall.

Dickens, W. J., & Perlman, D. (1981). Friendship over the life cycle. In S. Duck & R. Gilmour (Eds.), *Personal relationships: Vol. 2. Developing personal relationships.* London: Academic Press.

Dishion, T. J., Patterson, G. R., Stoolmiller, M., & Skinner, M. L. (1991). Family, school, and behavioral antecedents to early adolescent involvement with antisocial peers. *Developmental Psychology, 27,* 172–180.

Dodge, K. A., Coie, J. D., Pettit, G. S., & Price, J. M. (1990). Peer status and aggression in boys' groups: Developmental and contextual analysis. *Child Development, 61,* 1289–1309.

Dolen, L. S., & Bearison, D. J. (1982). Social interaction and social cognition in aging. *Human Development, 25,* 430–442.

Douvan, E., & Adelson, J. (1966). *The adolescent experience.* New York: Wiley.

Droege, K. L., & Stipek, D J. (1993). Children's use of dispositions to predict classmates' behavior. *Developmental Psychology, 29,* 646–654.

Dunn, J. (1993). *Young children's close relationships: Beyond attachment.* Newbury Park, CA: Sage.

Dunphy, D. C. (1963). The social structure of urban adolescent peer groups. *Sociometry, 26,* 230–246.

Eckerman, C. O., & Stein, M. R. (1990). How imitation begets imitation and toddlers' generation of games. *Developmental Psychology, 26,* 370–378.

Egeland, B., & Farber, E. A. (1984). Mother-infant attachment: Factors related to its development and changes over time. *Child Development, 55,* 753–771.

Elicker, J., Englund, M., & Sroufe, L. A. (1992). Predicting peer competence and peer relationships in childhood from early parent-child relationships. In R. D. Parke & G. W. Ladd (Eds.), *Family-peer relationships: Modes of linkage.* Hillsdale, NJ: Erlbaum.

Ellis, S., Rogoff, B., & Cromer, C. C. (1981). Age segregation in children's social interactions. *Developmental Psychology, 17,* 399–407.

Eyer, D. E. (1992). *Mother-infant bonding: A scientific fiction.* New Haven, CT: Yale University Press.

Feeney, J. A., & Noller, P. (1991). Attachment style and verbal descriptions of romantic partners. *Journal of Social and Personal Relationships, 8,* 187–215.

Feingold, A. (1992). Gender differences in mate selection preferences: A test of the parental investment model. *Psychological Bulletin, 112,* 125–139.

Feinman, S. (1992). *Social referencing and the social construction of reality in infancy.* New York: Plenum.

Felton, B. J., & Berry, C. A. (1992). Do the sources of the urban elderly's social support determine its psychological consequences? *Psychology and Aging, 7,* 89–97.

Field, D., & Minkler, M. (1988). Continuity and change in social support between young-old and old-old or very-old age. *Journal of Gerontology: Psychological Sciences, 43,* P100–P106.

Field, T. M. (1987). Affective and interactive disturbances in infants. In J. D. Osofsky (Ed.), *Handbook of infant development* (2nd ed.). New York: Wiley.

Fischer, C. S., & Phillips, S. L. (1982). Who is alone? Social characteristics of people with small networks. In L. A. Peplau & D. Perlman (Eds.), *Loneliness: A sourcebook of current theory, research and therapy.* New York: Wiley-Interscience.

Fischer, J. L., Sollie, D. L., Sorell, G. T., & Green, S. K. (1989). Marital status and career stage influences on social networks of young adults. *Journal of Marriage and the Family, 51,* 521–534.

Fitzgerald, J. M., & Martin-Louer, P. (1983–1984). Person perception in adulthood: A categories analysis. *International Journal of Aging and Human Development, 18,* 197–205.

Flavell, J. H. (1985). *Cognitive development* (2nd ed.). Englewood Cliffs, NJ: Prentice-Hall.

Fox, N. A., Kimmerly, N. L., & Schafer, W. D. (1991). Attachment to mother/attachment to father: A meta-analysis. *Child Development, 62,* 210–225.

Frankel, K. A., & Bates, J. E. (1990). Mother-toddler problem-solving: Antecedents in attachment, home behavior, and temperament. *Child Development, 61,* 810–819.

Fredrickson, B. L., & Carstensen, L. L. (1990). Choosing social partners: How old age and anticipated endings make people more selective. *Psychology and Aging, 5,* 335–347.

Freud, A., & Dann, S. (1951). An experiment in group upbringing. In R. Eisler, A. Freud, H. Hartmann, & E. Kris (Eds.), *The psychoanalytic study of the child* (Vol. 6). New York: International Universities Press.

Freud, S. (1930). *Three contributions to the theory of sex.* New York: Nervous and Mental Disease Pub. Co. (Original work published 1905.)

Fuligni, A. J., & Eccles, J. S. (1993). Perceived parent-child relationships and early adolescents' orientation toward peers. *Developmental Psychology, 29,* 622–632.

Furman, W., & Bierman, K. L. (1983). Developmental changes in young children's conceptions of friendship. *Child Development, 54,* 549–556.

Furman, W., & Buhrmester, D. (1992). Age and sex differences in perceptions of networks of personal relationships. *Child Development, 63,* 103–115.

Gauvain, M., & Rogoff, B. (1989). Collaborative problem solving and children's planning skills. *Developmental Psychology, 25,* 139–151.

Gavin, L. A., & Furman, W. (1989). Age differences in adolescents' perceptions of their peer groups. *Developmental Psychology, 25,* 827–834.

Giordano, P. C., Cernkovich, S. A., & DeMaris, A. (1993). The family and peer relations of black adolescents. *Journal of Marriage and the Family, 55,* 277–287.

Gnepp, J. (1989). Personalized inferences of emotions and appraisals: Component processes and correlates. *Developmental Psychology, 25,* 277–288.

Gnepp, J., & Chilamkurti, C. (1988). Children's use of personality attributions to predict other people's emotional and behavioral reactions. *Child Development, 59,* 743–754.

Goldberg, S. (1983). Parent-infant bonding: Another look. *Child Development, 54,* 1355–1382.

Goldberg, S., Perrotta, M., Minde, K., & Corter, C. (1986). Maternal behavior and attachment in low-birth-weight twins and singletons. *Child Development, 57,* 34–46.

Goldfarb, W. (1943). The effects of early institutional care on adolescent personality. *Journal of Experimental Education, 12,* 107–129.

Goldfarb, W. (1945). Effects of psychological deprivation in infancy and subsequent stimulation. *American Journal of Psychiatry, 102,* 18–33.

Goldfarb, W. (1947). Variations in adolescent adjustment in institutionally reared children. *Journal of Orthopsychiatry, 17,* 449–457.

Goldsmith, H. H., & Alansky, J. A. (1987). Maternal and infant temperamental predictors of attachment: A meta-analytic review. *Journal of Consulting and Clinical Psychology, 55,* 805–816.

Greene, J. G., Fox, N. A., & Lewis, M. (1983). The relationship between neonatal characteristics and three-month mother-infant interaction in high-risk infants. *Child Development, 54,* 1286–1296.

Grossmann, K., Grossmann, K. E., Spangler, S., Suess, G., & Unzner, L. (1985). Maternal sensitivity and newborn responses as related to quality of attachment in Northern Germany. In I. Bretherton & E. Waters, *Growing points of attachment theory. Monographs of the Society for Research in Child Development, 50*(1–2, Serial No. 209).

Grossmann, K. E., & Grossmann, K. (1991). Attachment quality as an organizer of emotional and behavioral responses in a longitudinal perspective. In C. M. Parker, J. Stevenson-Hinde, & P. Marris (Eds.), *Attachment across the life cycle.* London: Tavistock/Routledge.

Hanna, E., & Meltzoff, A. N. (1993). Peer imitation by toddlers in laboratory, home, and day-care contexts: Implications for social learning and memory. *Developmental Psychology, 29,* 701–710.

Harkness, S., & Super, C. M. (1985). The cultural context of gender segregation in children's peer groups. *Child Development, 56,* 219–224.

Harlow, H. F., & Harlow, M. K. (1977). The young monkeys. In *Readings in developmental psychology today* (3rd ed.). Del Mar, CA: CRM Books.

Harlow, H. F., & Zimmerman, R. R. (1959). Affectional responses in the infant monkey. *Science, 130,* 421–432.

Hartup, W. W. (1983). Peer relations. In M. Hetherington (Ed.; P. H. Mussen, General Ed.), *Handbook of child psychology: Vol. 4. Socialization, personality, and social development* (4th ed.). New York: Wiley.

Hartup, W. W. (1989). Social relationships and their developmental significance. *American Psychologist, 44,* 120–126.

Hartup, W. W. (1992). Friendships and their developmental significance. In H. McGurk (Ed.), *Childhood social development: Contemporary perspectives.* Hove, UK: Erlbaum.

Hay, D. F. (1985). Learning to form relationships in infancy: Parallel attainments with parents and peers. *Developmental Review, 5,* 122–161.

Hay, D. F., Nash, A., & Pedersen, J. (1983). Interaction between six-month-old peers. *Child Development, 54,* 557–562.

Hazan, C., & Shaver, P. R. (1987). Romantic love conceptualized as an attachment process. *Journal of Personality and Social Psychology, 52,* 511–524.

Hazan, C., & Shaver, P. R. (1990). Love and work: An attachment-theoretical perspective. *Journal of Personality and Social Psychology, 59,* 270–280.

Heller, K., Thompson, M. G., Trueba, P. E., Hogg, J. R., & Vlachos-Weber, I. (1991). Peer support telephone dyads for elderly women: Was this the wrong intervention? *American Journal of Community Psychology, 19,* 53–74.

Higley, J. D., Hopkins, W. D., Thompson, W. W., Byrne, E. A., Hirsh, R. M., & Suomi, S. J. (1992). Peers as primary attachment sources in yearling rhesus monkeys. *Development Psychology, 28,* 1163–1171.

Hodges, J., & Tizard, B. (1989). IQ and behavioural adjustment of ex-institutional adolescents. *Journal of Child Psychology and Psychiatry, 30,* 53–75.

Holahan, C. K., & Holahan, C. J. (1987). Self-efficacy, social support, and depression in aging: A longitudinal analysis. *Journal of Gerontology, 42,* 65–68.

Howes, C. (1983). Patterns of friendship. *Child Development, 54,* 1041–1053.

Howes, C., & Matheson, C. C. (1992). Sequences in the development of competent play with peers: Social and social pretend play. *Developmental Psychology, 28,* 961–974.

Howes, P., & Markman, H. J. (1989). Marital quality and child functioning: A longitudinal investigation. *Child Development, 60,* 1044–1051.

Hudson, L. M., Forman, E. R., & Brion-Meisels, S. (1982). Role-taking as a predictor of prosocial behavior in cross-age tutors. *Child Development, 53,* 1320–1329.

Isabella, R. A. (1993). Origins of attachment: Maternal interactive behavior across the first year. *Child Development, 64,* 605–621.

Isabella, R. A., & Belsky, J. (1991). Interactional synchrony and the origins of infant-mother attachment: A replication study. *Child Development, 62,* 373–384.

Izard, C. E., Haynes, O. M., Chisholm, G., & Baak, K. (1991). Emotional determinants of infant-mother attachment. *Child Development, 62,* 906–917.

Jones, W. H., Hobbs, S. A., & Hockenbury, D. (1982). Loneliness and social skill deficits. *Journal of Personality and Social Psychology, 42,* 682–689.

Kagan, J. (1972). Do infants think? *Scientific American, 226,* 74–82.

Kagan, J. (1976). Emergent themes in human development. *American Scientist, 64,* 186–196.

Kahn, R. L., & Antonucci, T. C. (1980). Convoys over the life course: Attachment, roles, and social support. In P. B. Baltes & O. G. Brim, Jr. (Eds.), *Life-span development and behavior* (Vol. 3). New York: Academic Press.

Keller, H., & Scholmerich, A. (1987). Infant vocalizations and parental reactions during the first four months of life. *Developmental Psychology, 23,* 62–67.

Kendig, H. L., Coles, R., Pittelkow, Y., & Wilson, S. (1988). Confidants and family structure in old age. *Journal of Gerontology: Social Sciences, 43,* S31–S40.

Kenny, M. E. (1987). The extent and function of parental attachment among first-year college students. *Journal of Youth and Adolescence, 16,* 17–29.

Kenny, M. E., & Donaldson, G. A. (1991). Contributions of parental attachment and family structure to the social and psychological functioning of first-year college students. *Journal of Counseling Psychology, 38,* 479–486.

Kessen, W. (1975). *Childhood in China.* New Haven, CT: Yale University Press.

Kinney, D. A. (1993). From nerds to normals: The recovery of identity among adolescents from middle school to high school. *Sociology of Education, 66,* 21–40.

Klaus, H. M., & Kennell, J. H. (1976). *Maternal-infant bonding.* St. Louis: Mosby.

Kobak, R. R., Cole, H. E., Ferenz-Gilles, R., Fleming, W. S., & Gamble, W. (1993). Attachment and emotional regulation during mother-teen problem solving: A control theory analysis. *Child Development, 64,* 231–245.

Kobak, R. R., & Hazan, C. (1991). Attachment in marriage: Effects of security and accuracy of working models. *Journal of Personality and Social Psychology, 60,* 861–869.

Kobak, R. R., & Sceery, A. (1988). Attachment in late adolescence: Working models, affect regulation, and representations of self and others. *Child Development, 59,* 135–146.

Kohlberg, L. (1969). Stage and sequence: The cognitive-developmental approach to socialization. In D. A. Goslin (Ed.), *Handbook of socialization theory and research.* Chicago: Rand McNally.

Krause, N., Liang, J., & Yatomi, N. (1989). Satisfaction with social support and depressive symptoms: A panel analysis. *Psychology and Aging, 4,* 88–97.

Kupersmidt, J. B., & Coie, J. D. (1990). Preadolescent peer status, aggression, and school adjustment as predictors of externalizing problems in adolescence. *Child Development, 61,* 1350–1362.

Kurdek, L. A., & Krile, D. (1982). A developmental analysis of the relation between peer acceptance and both interpersonal understanding and perceived social self-competence. *Child Development, 53,* 1485–1491.

Ladd, G. W. (1990). Having friends, keeping friends, making friends, and being liked by peers in the classroom: Predictors of children's early school adjustment. *Child Development, 61,* 1081–1100.

Ladd, G. W., Price, J. M., & Hart, C. H. (1990). Preschoolers' behavioral orientations and patterns of peer contact: Predictive of peer status? In S. R. Asher & J. D. Coie (Eds.), *Peer rejection in childhood.* New York: Cambridge University Press.

Lamb, M. E. (1987). Predictive implications of individual differences in attachment. *Journal of Consulting and Clinical Psychology, 55,* 817–824.

Langlois, J. H. (1986). From the eye of the beholder to behavioral reality: Development of social behaviors and social relations as a function of physical attractiveness. In C. P. Herman, M. P. Zanna, & E. T. Higgins (Eds.), *Physical appearance, stigma, and social behavior: The Ontario Symposium, Volume 3.* Hillsdale, NJ: Erlbaum.

Lapsley, D. K., Rice, K. G., & FitzGerald, D. P. (1990). Adolescent attachment, identity, and adjustment to college: Implications for the continuity of adaptation hypothesis. *Journal of Counseling and Development, 68,* 561–565.

Larson, R., Zuzanek, J., & Mannell, R. (1985). Being alone versus being with people: Disengagement in the daily experience of older adults. *Journal of Gerontology, 40,* 375–381.

LeMare, L. J., & Rubin, K. H. (1987). Perspective taking and peer interaction: Structural and developmental analyses. *Child Development, 58,* 306–315.

Lempers, J. D., & Clark-Lempers, D. S. (1992). Young, middle, and late adolescents' comparisons of the functional importance of five significant relationships. *Journal of Youth and Adolescence, 21,* 53–96.

Lester, B. M., Corwin, M. J., Sepkoski, C., Seifer, R., Peucker, M., McLaughlin, S., & Golub, H. L. (1991). Neurobehavioral syndromes in cocaine-exposed newborn infants. *Child Development, 62,* 694–705.

Lester, B. M., Kotelchuck, M., Spelke, E., Sellers, M. J., & Klein, R. E. (1974). Separation protest in Guatemalan infants: Cross-cultural and cognitive findings. *Developmental Psychology, 10,* 79–85.

Levesque, R. J. R. (1993). The romantic experience of adolescents in satisfying love relationships. *Journal of Youth and Adolescence, 22,* 219–251.

Levitt, M. J. (1991). Attachment and close relationships: A life-span perspective. In J. L. Gewirtz & W. M. Kurtines (Eds.), *Intersections with attachment.* Hillsdale, NJ: Erlbaum.

Levy, M. B., & Davis, K. E. (1988). Lovestyles and attachment styles compared: Their relations to each other and to various relationship characteristics. *Journal of Social and Personal Relationships, 5,* 439–471.

Levy-Shiff, R., Goldshmidt, I., & Har-Even, D. (1991). Transition to parenthood in adoptive families. *Developmental Psychology, 27,* 131–140.

Lewis, M., & Rosenblum, M. A. (1975). *Friendship and peer relations.* New York: Wiley.

Lieberman, A. F., Weston, D. R., & Pawl, J. H. (1991). Preventive intervention and outcome with anxiously attached dyads. *Child Development, 62,* 199–209.

Livesley, W. J., & Bromley, D. B. (1973). *Person perception in childhood and adolescence.* London: Wiley.

Lorenz, K. Z. (1937). The companion in the bird's world. *Auk, 54,* 245–273.

Louis Harris and Associates (1981). *Aging in the eighties: America in transition.* Washington, DC: National Council on Aging.

Lyons-Ruth, K., Alpern, L., & Repacholi, B. (1993). Disorganized infant attachment classification and maternal psychosocial problems as predictors of hostile-aggressive behavior in the preschool classroom. *Child Development, 64,* 572–585.

Lyons-Ruth, K., Connell, D. B., Grunebaum, H. U., & Botein, S. (1990). Infants at social risk: Maternal depression and family support services as mediators of infant development and security of attachment. *Child Development, 61,* 85–98.

Maccoby, E. E. (1990). Gender and relationships: A developmental account. *American Psychologist, 45,* 513–520.

Main, M., & Cassidy, J. (1988). Categories of response to reunion with the parent at age 6: Predictable from infant attachment classifications and stable over a 1–month period. *Developmental Psychology, 24,* 415–426.

Main, M., & Goldwyn, R. (in press). Interview-based adult attachment classifications: Related to infant-mother and infant-father attachment. *Developmental Psychology.*

Main, M., & Solomon, J. (1990). Procedures for identifying infants as disorganized/disoriented during the Ainsworth Strange Situation. In M. T. Greenberg, D. Cicchetti, & E. M. Cummings (Eds.), *Attachment in the preschool years: Theory, research, and intervention.* Chicago: University of Chicago Press.

Main, M., & Weston, D. R. (1981). The quality of the toddler's relationship to mother and to father: Related to conflict and the readiness to establish new relationships. *Child Development, 52,* 932–940.

Mangelsdorf, S. C. (1992). Developmental changes in infant-stranger interaction. *Infant Behavior and Development, 15,* 191–208.

Mangelsdorf, S. C., Gunnar, M., Kestenbaum, R., Lang, S., & Andreas, D. (1990). Infant proneness-to-distress temperament, maternal personality, and mother-infant attachment:

Associations and goodness of fit. *Child Development, 61,* 820–831.

Matthews, S. H. (1986). *Friendships through the life course: Oral biographies in old age* (Vol. 161, Sage Library of Social Research). Beverly Hills, CA: Sage.

McDavid, J. W., & Harari, H. (1966). Stereotyping of names and popularity in grade school children. *Child Development, 37,* 453–459.

McGuire, K. D., & Weisz, J. R. (1982). Social cognition and behavior correlates of preadolescent chumship. *Child Development, 53,* 1478–1484.

Miller, B. C., McCoy, J. K., & Olson, T. D. (1986). Dating age and stage as correlates of adolescent sexual attitudes and behavior. *Journal of Adolescent Research, 1,* 361–371.

Miller, P. H., & Aloise, P. A. (1989). Young children's understanding of the psychological causes of behavior: A review. *Child Development, 60,* 257–285.

Morgan, G. A., & Ricciuti, H. N. (1969). Infants' responses to strangers during the first year. In B. M. Foss (Ed.), *Determinants of infant behavior* (Vol. 4). London: Methuen.

Morison, P., & Masten, A. S. (1991). Peer reputation in middle childhood as a predictor of adaptation in adolescence: A seven-year follow-up. *Child Development, 62,* 991–1007.

Mueller, E., & Lucas, T. (1975). A developmental analysis of peer interactions among toddlers. In M. Lewis & L. Rosenblum (Eds.), *Friendship and peer relations.* New York: Wiley.

Mueller, E., & Vandell, D. (1979). Infant-infant interaction. In J. Osofsky (Ed.), *Handbook of infant development.* New York: Wiley.

Murstein, B. I. (1980). Mate selection in the 1970s. *Journal of Marriage and the Family, 42,* 777–792.

Oden, S., & Asher, S. R. (1977). Coaching children in social skills for friendship making. *Child Development, 48,* 495–506.

Okonjo, K. (1992). Aspects of continuity and change in mate-selection among the Igbo west of the River Niger. *Journal of Comparative Family Studies, 23,* 339–360.

O'Mahony, J. F. (1986). Development of person description over adolescence. *Journal of Youth and Adolescence, 15,* 389–403.

Oppenheim, D., Sagi, A., & Lamb, M. E. (1988). Infant-adult attachments on the kibbutz and their relation to socioemotional development 4 years later. *Developmental Psychology, 24,* 427–433.

Parker, J. G., & Asher, S. R. (1993). Friendship and friendship quality in middle childhood: Links with peer group acceptance and feelings of loneliness and social dissatisfaction. *Developmental Psychology, 29,* 611–621.

Parkhurst, J. T., & Asher, S. R. (1992). Peer rejection in middle school: Subgroup differences in behavior, loneliness, and interpersonal concerns. *Developmental Psychology, 28,* 231–241.

Parlee, M. B., & the Editors of Psychology Today (1979, October). The friendship bond. *Psychology Today,* pp. 42–54, 113.

Passman, R. H. (1977). Providing attachment objects to facilitate learning and reduce distress: Effects of mothers and security blankets. *Developmental Psychology, 13,* 25–28.

Peevers, B. H., & Secord, P. F. (1973). Developmental changes in attribution of descriptive concepts to persons. *Journal of Personality and Social Psychology, 27,* 120–128.

Piaget, J. (1965). *The moral judgment of the child.* New York: Free Press. (Original work published 1932.)

Pilisuk, M., & Minkler, M. (1980). Supportive networks: Life ties for the elderly. *Journal of Social Issues, 36*(2), 95–116.

Pipp, S., Easterbrooks, M. A., & Harmon, R. J. (1992). The relation between attachment and knowledge of self and mother in one- to three-year-old infants. *Child Development, 63,* 738–750.

Pratt, M. W., Diessner, R., Hunsberger, B., Pancer, S. M., & Savoy, K. (1991). Four pathways in the analysis of adult development and aging: Comparing analyses of reasoning about personal-life dilemmas. *Psychology and Aging, 6,* 666–675.

Provence, S., & Lipton, R. C. (1962). *Infants in institutions.* New York: International Universities Press.

Putallaz, M., & Wasserman, A. (1989). Children's naturalistic entry behavior and sociometric status: A developmental perspective. *Developmental Psychology, 25,* 297–305.

Rabiner, D. L., Keane, S. P., & MacKinnon-Lewis, C. (1993). Children's beliefs about familiar and unfamiliar peers in relation to their sociometric status. *Developmental Psychology, 29,* 236–243.

Radke-Yarrow, M., Cummings, E. M., Kuczynski, L., & Chapman, M. (1985). Patterns of attachment in two- and three-year-olds in normal families and families with parental depression. *Child Development, 56,* 884–893.

Reis, H. T., Lin, Y., Bennett, M. E., & Nezlek, J. B. (1993). Change and consistency in social participation during early adulthood. *Developmental Psychology, 29,* 633–645.

Rholes, W. S., Newman, L. S., & Ruble, D. N. (1990). Understanding self and other: Developmental and motivational aspects of perceiving persons in terms of invariant dispositions. In E. T. Higgins & R. M. Sorrentino (Eds.), *Handbook of motivation and cognition: Vol. 2. Foundations of social behavior.* New York: Guilford Press.

Rholes, W. S., & Ruble, D. N. (1984). Children's understanding of dispositional characteristics of others. *Child Development, 55,* 550–560.

Rice, K. G. (1990). Attachment in adolescence: A narrative and meta-analytic review. *Journal of Youth and Adolescence, 19,* 511–538.

Roberto, K. A., & Kimboko, P. J. (1989). Friendships in later life: Definitions and maintenance patterns. *International Journal of Aging and Human Development, 28,* 9–19.

Roberto, K. A., & Scott, J. P. (1986). Equity considerations in the friendships of older adults. *Journal of Gerontology, 41,* 241–247.

Rode, S. S., Chang, P., Fisch, R. O., & Sroufe, L. A. (1981). Attachment patterns of infants separated at birth. *Developmental Psychology, 17,* 188–191.

Rook, K. S. (1984). Promoting social bonding: Strategies for helping the lonely and socially isolated. *American Psychologist, 39,* 1389–1407.

Rook, K. S. (1991). Facilitating friendship formation in late life: Puzzles and challenges. *American Journal of Community Psychology, 19,* 103–110.

Rose, S., & Frieze, I. H. (1993). Young singles' contemporary dating scripts. *Sex Roles, 28,* 499–509.

Rosen, K. S., & Rothbaum, F. (1993). Quality of parental caregiving and security of attachment. *Developmental Psychology, 29,* 358–367.

Schaffer, H. R., & Emerson, P. E. (1964). The development of social attachments in infancy. *Monographs of the Society for Research in Child Development, 29*(3, Serial No. 94).

Schneider, B. H. (1992). Didactic methods for enhancing children's peer relations: A quantitative review. *Clinical Psychology Review, 12,* 363–382.

Sebald, H. (1986). Adolescents' shifting orientation toward parents and peers: A curvilinear trend over recent decades. *Journal of Marriage and the Family, 48,* 5–13.

Selman, R. L. (1976). Social-cognitive understanding: A guide to educational and clinical experience. In T. Lickona (Ed.), *Moral development and behavior: Theory, research and social issues.* New York: Holt, Rinehart & Winston.

Selman, R. L. (1980). *The growth of interpersonal understanding.* New York: Academic Press.

Selman, R. L., Beardslee, W., Schultz, L. H., Krupa, M., & Podorefsky, D. (1986). Assessing adolescent interpersonal negotiation strategies: Toward the integration of structural and functional models. *Developmental Psychology, 22,* 450–459.

Senchak, M., & Leonard, K. E. (1992). Attachment styles and marital adjustment among newlywed couples. *Journal of Social and Personal Relationships, 9,* 51–64.

Shantz, C. U. (1987). Conflicts between children. *Child Development, 58,* 283–305.

Sharabany, R., Gershoni, R., & Hofman, J. E. (1981). Girlfriend, boyfriend: Age and sex differences in intimate friendship. *Developmental Psychology, 17,* 800–808.

Shea, L., Thompson, L., & Blieszner, R. (1988). Resources in older adults' old and new friendships. *Journal of Social and Personal Relationships, 5,* 83–96.

Silverstein, M., & Waite, L. J. (1993). Are blacks more likely than whites to receive and provide social support in middle and old age?—Yes, no, and maybe so. *Journal of Gerontology: Social Sciences, 48,* S212–S222.

Skolnick, A. (1986). Early attachment and personal relationships across the life course. In P. B. Baltes, D. L. Featherman, & R. M. Lerner (Eds.), *Life-span development and behavior* (Vol. 7). Hillsdale, NJ: Erlbaum.

Sroufe, L. A. (1977). Wariness of strangers and the study of infant development. *Child Development, 48,* 1184–1199.

Sroufe, L. A. (1985). Attachment classification from the perspective of infant-caregiver relationships and infant temperament. *Child Development, 56,* 1–14.

Sroufe, L. A., Bennett, C., Englund, M., Urban, J., & Shulman, S. (1993). The significance of gender boundaries in preadolescence: Contemporary correlates and antecedents of boundary violation and maintenance. *Child Development, 64,* 455–466.

Sroufe, L. A., Fox, N. E., & Pancake, V. R. (1983). Attachment and dependency in developmental perspective. *Child Development, 54,* 1615–1627.

Sroufe, L. A., Waters, E., & Matas, L. (1974). Contextual determinants of infant affectional response. In M. Lewis & L. A. Rosenblum (Eds.), *The origins of fear.* New York: Wiley.

Steele, B. F., & Pollack, C. B. (1974). A psychiatric study of parents who abuse infants and small children. In R. E. Helfer & C. H. Kempe (Eds.), *The battered child.* Chicago: University of Chicago Press.

Steinberg, L., & Silverberg, S. B. (1986). The vicissitudes of autonomy in early adolescence. *Child Development, 57,* 841–851.

Stern, D. (1977). *The first relationship: Infant and mother.* Cambridge, MA: Harvard University Press.

Stevenson, M. B., VerHoeve, J. N., Roach, M. A., & Leavitt, L. A. (1986). The beginning of conversation: Early patterns of mother-infant vocal responsiveness. *Infant Behavior and Development, 9,* 423–440.

Sullivan, H. S. (1953). *The interpersonal theory of psychiatry.* New York: Norton.

Suomi, S. J., & Harlow, H. F. (1972). Social rehabilitation of isolate reared monkeys. *Developmental Psychology, 6,* 487–496.

Takahashi, K. (1990). Are the key assumptions of the "Strange Situation" procedure universal? A view from Japanese research. *Human Development, 33,* 23–30.

Terry, R., & Coie, J. D. (1991). A comparison of methods for defining sociometric status among children. *Developmental Psychology, 27,* 867–880.

Teti, D. M., Nakagawa, M., Das, R., & Wirth, O. (1991). Security of attachment between preschoolers and their mothers: Relations among social interaction, parenting stress, and mothers' sorts of the Attachment Q-Set. *Developmental Psychology, 27,* 440–447.

Thompson, R. A., & Lamb, M. E. (1984). Continuity and change in socioemotional development during the second year. In R. N. Emde & R. J. Harmon (Eds.), *Continuities and discontinuities in development.* New York: Plenum.

Thorne, B. (1993). *Gender play: Girls and boys in school.* New Brunswick, NJ: Rutgers University Press.

Tizard, B. (1977). *Adoption: A second chance.* London: Open Books.

Tronick, E. Z. (1989). Emotions and emotional communication in infants. *American Psychologist, 44,* 112–119.

Tronick, E. Z., Morelli, G. A., & Ivey, P. K. (1992). The Efe forager infant and toddler's pattern of social relationships: Multiple and simultaneous. *Developmental Psychology, 28,* 568–577.

Tudge, J. R. H. (1992). Processes and consequences of peer collaboration: A Vygotskian analysis. *Child Development, 63,* 1364–1379.

Udry, J. R. (1971). *The social context of marriage* (2nd ed.). Philadelphia: Lippincott.

Vandell, D. L., & Wilson, K. S. (1987). Infants' interactions with mother, sibling, and peer: Contrasts and relations between interaction systems. *Child Development, 58,* 176–186.

Vandell, D. L., Wilson, K. S., & Buchanan, N. R. (1980). Peer interaction in the first year of life: An examination of its structure, content, and sensitivity to toys. *Child Development, 51,* 481–488.

van IJzendoorn, M. H. (1992). Intergenerational transmission of parenting: A review of studies in nonclinical populations. *Developmental Review, 12,* 76–99.

van IJzendoorn, M. H., Goldberg, S., Kroonenberg, P. M., & Frenkel, O. J. (1992). The relative effects of maternal and child problems on the quality of attachment: A meta-analysis of attachment in clinical samples. *Child Development, 63,* 840–858.

van IJzendoorn, M. H., & Kroonenberg, P. M. (1988). Cross-cultural patterns of attachment: A meta-analysis of the Strange Situation. *Child Development, 59,* 147–156.

Vaughn, B. E., Egeland, B. R., Sroufe, L. A., & Waters, E. (1979). Individual differences in infant-mother attachment at twelve and eighteen months: Stability and change in families under stress. *Child Development, 50,* 971–975.

Vaughn, B. E., Lefever, G. B., Seifer, R., & Barglow, P. (1989). Attachment behavior, attachment security, and temperament during infancy. *Child Development, 60,* 728–737.

Vaughn, B. E., Stevenson-Hinde, J., Waters, E., Kotsaftis, A., Lefever, G. B., Shouldice, A., Trudel, M., & Belsky, J. (1992). Attachment security and temperament in infancy and early childhood: Some conceptual clarifications. *Developmental Psychology, 28,* 463–473.

Vormbrock, J. K. (1993). Attachment theory as applied to wartime and job-related marital separation. *Psychological Bulletin, 114,* 122–144.

Walster, E., Walster, G. W., & Berscheid, E. (1978). *Equity: Theory and research.* Boston: Allyn & Bacon.

Ward, R. A., Sherman, S. R., & LaGory, M. (1984). Subjective network assessments and subjective well-being. *Journal of Gerontology, 39,* 93–101.

Waters, E., Vaughn, B. E., & Egeland, B. R. (1980). Individual differences in mother-infant attachment relationships at age one: Antecedents in neonatal behavior in an urban, economically disadvantaged sample. *Child Development, 51,* 208–216.

Waters, E., Wippman, J., & Sroufe, L. A. (1979). Attachment, positive affect, and competence in the peer group: Two studies in construct validation. *Child Development, 50,* 821–829.

Weinraub, M., & Lewis, M. (1977). The determinants of children's responses to separation. *Monographs of the Society for Research in Child Development* (4, Serial No. 172).

Weiss, R. S. (1991). The attachment bond in childhood and adulthood. In C. M. Parker, J. Stevenson-Hinde, & P. Marris (Eds.), *Attachment across the life cycle.* London: Tavistock/Routledge.

Wellman, H. M. (1990). *The child's theory of mind.* Cambridge, MA: MIT Press.

Whiting, B. B., & Edwards, C. P. (1988). *Children of different worlds: The formation of social behavior.* Cambridge, MA: Harvard University Press.

Wilks, J. (1986). The relative importance of parents and friends in adolescent decision making. *Journal of Youth and Adolescence, 15,* 323–334.

Winstead, B. A. (1986). Sex differences in same-sex friendships. In V. J. Derlega & B. A. Winstead (Eds.), *Friendship and social interaction.* New York: Springer-Verlag.

Wolff, P. H. (1963). Observations on the early development of smiling. In B. M. Foss (Ed.), *Determinants of infant behavior* (Vol. 2). London: Methuen.

Wright, P. H. (1982). Men's friendships, women's friendships and the alleged inferiority of the latter. *Sex Roles, 8,* 1–20.

Wright, P. H., & Scanlon, M. B. (1991). Gender role orientations and friendship: Some attenuation, but gender differences abound. *Sex Roles, 24,* 551–566.

Yeates, K. O., & Selman, R. L. (1989). Social competence in the schools: Toward an integrative developmental model for intervention. *Developmental Review, 9,* 64–100.

Youniss, J. (1980). *Parents and peers in social development: A Sullivan-Piaget perspective.* Chicago: University of Chicago Press.

Youniss, J., & Smollar, J. (1985). *Adolescent relations with mothers, fathers, and friends.* Chicago: University of Chicago Press.

Yuill, N. (1992). Children's conception of personality traits. *Human Development, 35,* 265–279.

Zaslow, M. (1980). Relationships among peers in kibbutz toddler groups. *Child Psychiatry and Human Development, 10,* 178–189.

Chapter 14: The Family

Abramovitch, R., Corter, C., & Pepler, D. J. (1980). Observations of mixed-sex sibling dyads. *Child Development, 51,* 1268–1271.

Abramovitch, R., Corter, C., Pepler, D. J., & Stanhope, L. (1986). Sibling and peer interaction: A final follow-up and a comparison. *Child Development, 57,* 217–229.

Agnew, R., & Huguley, S. (1989). Adolescent violence toward parents. *Journal of Marriage and the Family, 51,* 699–711.

Aizenberg, R., & Treas, J. (1985). The family in later life: Psychosocial and demographic considerations. In J. E. Birren & K. W. Schaie (Eds.), *Handbook of the psychology of aging* (2nd ed.). New York: Van Nostrand Reinhold.

Al Awad, A. M., & Sonuga-Barke, E. J. (1992). Childhood problems in a Sudanese city: A comparison of extended and nuclear families. *Child Development, 63,* 906–914.

Allison, P. D., & Furstenberg, F. F., Jr. (1989). How marital dissolution affects children: Variations by age and sex. *Developmental Psychology, 25,* 540–549.

Amato, P. R. (1989). Family processes and the competence of adolescents and primary school children. *Journal of Youth and Adolescence, 18,* 39–53.

Amato, P. R. (1993). Children's adjustment to divorce: Theories, hypotheses, and empirical support. *Journal of Marriage and the Family, 55,* 23–38.

Amato, P. R., & Keith, B. (1991a). Parental divorce and adult well-being: A meta-analysis. *Journal of Marriage and the Family, 53,* 43–58.

Amato, P. R., & Keith, B. (1991b). Parental divorce and the well-being of children: A meta-analysis. *Psychological Bulletin, 110,* 26–46.

Ambert, A. (1992). *The effect of children on parents.* New York: Haworth.

Anderson, K. E., Lytton, H., & Romney, D. M. (1986). Mothers' interactions with normal and conduct-disordered boys: Who affects whom? *Developmental Psychology, 22,* 604–609.

Aquilino, W. S. (1991). Predicting parents' experiences with coresident adult children. *Journal of Family Issues, 12,* 323–342.

Atkinson, M. P., Kivett, V. R., & Campbell, R. T. (1986). Intergenerational solidarity: An examination of a theoretical model. *Journal of Gerontology, 41,* 408–416.

Axinn, W. G., & Thornton, A. (1993). Mothers, children, and cohabitation: The intergenerational effects of attitudes and behavior. *American Sociological Review, 58,* 233–246.

Azmitia, M., & Hesser, J. (1993). Why siblings are important agents of cognitive development: A comparison of siblings and peers. *Child Development, 64,* 430–444.

Barber, B. L., & Eccles, J. S. (1992). Long-term influence of divorce and single parenting on adolescent family- and work-related values, behaviors, and aspirations. *Psychological Bulletin, 111,* 108–126.

Barnett, R. C., & Baruch, G. K. (1987). Determinants of father's participation in family work. *Journal of Marriage and the Family, 49,* 29–40.

Baskett, L. M., & Johnson, S. M. (1982). The young child's interaction with parents versus siblings: A behavioral analysis. *Child Development, 53,* 643–650.

Baumrind, D. (1967). Child care practices anteceding three patterns of preschool behavior. *Genetic Psychology Monographs, 75,* 43–88.

Baumrind, D. (1977, March). *Socialization determinants of personal agency.* Paper presented at the biennial meeting of the Society for Research in Child Development, New Orleans.

Baumrind, D. (1991). Effective parenting during the early adolescent transition. In P. A. Cowan & M. Hetherington (Eds.), *Family transitions.* Hillsdale, NJ: Erlbaum.

Bell, A. P., & Weinberg, M. S. (1978). *Homosexualities: A study of diversity among men and women.* New York: Simon & Schuster.

Belsky, J. (1980). Child mistreatment: An ecological integration. *American Psychologist, 35,* 320–335.

Belsky, J. (1981). Early human experience: A family perspective. *Developmental Psychology, 17,* 3–23.

Belsky, J., Gilstrap, B., & Rovine, M. (1984). The Pennsylvania infant and family development project. I: Stability and change in mother-infant and father-infant interaction in a family setting at one, three, and nine months. *Child Development, 55,* 692–705.

Belsky, J., & Isabella, R. A. (1985). Marital and parent-child relationships in family of origin and marital change following the birth of a baby: A retrospective analysis. *Child Development, 56,* 342–349.

Belsky, J., Lang, M. E., & Rovine, M. (1985). Stability and change in marriage across the transition to parenthood: A second study. *Journal of Marriage and the Family, 47,* 855–865.

Bengtson, V., Rosenthal, C., & Burton, L. (1990). Families and aging: Diversity and heterogeneity. In R. H. Binstock & L. K. George (Eds.), *Handbook of aging and the social sciences* (3rd ed.). San Diego: Academic Press.

Biller, H. B. (1993). *Fathers and families: Paternal factors in child development.* Westport, CT: Auburn House.

Block, J. H., Block, J., & Gjerde, P. F. (1986). The personality of children prior to divorce: A prospective study. *Child Development, 57,* 827–840.

Blumstein, P., & Schwartz, P. (1983). *American couples: Money, work, sex.* New York: Morrow.

Booth, A., & Amato, P. (1991). Divorce and psychological stress. *Journal of Health and Social Behavior, 32,* 396–407.

Booth, A., & Edwards, J. N. (1992). Starting over: Why remarriages are more unstable. *Journal of Family Issues, 13,* 179–194.

Booth, A., & Johnson, D. (1988). Premarital cohabitation and marital success. *Journal of Family Issues, 9,* 255–272.

Brody, E. M. (1985). Parent care as a normative family stress. *Gerontologist, 25,* 19–29.

Brody, E. M. (1990). *Women in the middle: Their parent-care years.* New York: Springer.

Brody, E. M., Johnsen, P. T., & Fulcomer, M. C. (1984). What should adult children do for elderly parents? Opinions and preferences of three generations of women. *Journal of Gerontology, 39,* 736–746.

Brody, E. M., Litvin, S. J., Hoffman, C., & Kleban, M. H. (1992). Differential effects of daughters' marital status on their parent care experiences. *Gerontologist, 32,* 58–67.

Brody, G. H., Neubaum, E., & Forehand, R. (1988). Serial marriage: A heuristic analysis of an emerging family form. *Psychological Bulletin, 103,* 211–222.

Bronfenbrenner, U. (1979). Contexts of child rearing: Problems and prospects. *American Psychologist, 34,* 844–850.

Bronfenbrenner, U. (1989). Ecological systems theory. In R. Vasta (Ed.), *Annals of child development: Vol. 6. Theories of child development: Revised formulations and current issues.* Greenwich, CT: JAI Press.

Brown, B. B., Mounts, N., Lamborn, S. D., & Steinberg, L. (1993). Parenting practices and peer group affiliation in adolescence. *Child Development, 64,* 467–482.

Buehler, C. A., Hogan, M. J., Robinson, B. E., & Levy, R. J. (1985–1986). The parental divorce transition: Divorce-related stressors and well-being. *Journal of Divorce, 9,* 61–81.

Bugental, D. B., Blue, J., & Cruzcosa, M. (1989). Perceived control over caregiving outcomes: Implications for child abuse. *Developmental Psychology, 25,* 532–539.

Buhrmester, D., & Furman, W. (1990). Perceptions of sibling relationships during middle childhood and adolescence. *Child Development, 61,* 1387–1398.

Bumpass, L. L. (1990). What's happening to the family? Interactions between demographic and institutional change. *Demography, 27,* 483–498.

Bursik, K. (1991). Adaptation to divorce and ego development in adult women. *Journal of Personality and Social Psychology, 60,* 300–306.

Burton, L. M. (1990). Teenage childrearing as an alternative life-course strategy in multigenerational black families. *Human Nature, 1,* 123–143.

Burton, L. M., & Dilworth-Anderson, P. (1991). The intergenerational family roles of aged Black Americans. *Marriage and Family Review, 16,* 311–330.

Camara, K. A., & Resnick, G. (1988). Interparental conflict and cooperation: Factors moderating children's postdivorce adjustment. In E. M. Hetherington & J. D. Arasteh (Eds.), *Impact of divorce, single-parenting, and stepparenting on children.* Hillsdale, NJ: Erlbaum.

Carstensen, L. L. (1992). Social and emotional patterns in adulthood: Support for socioemotional selectivity theory. *Psychology and Aging, 7,* 331–338.

Caspi, A., Herbener, E. S., & Ozer, D. J. (1992). Shared experiences and the similarity of personalities: A longitudinal study of married couples. *Journal of Personality and Social Psychology, 62,* 281–291.

Castro Martin, T., & Bumpass, L. L. (1989). Recent trends in marital disruption. *Demography, 26,* 37–51.

Chadwick, B. A., & Heaton, T. B. (1992). *Statistical handbook on the American family.* Phoenix: Onyx Press.

Cherlin, A. J., & Furstenberg, F. F., Jr. (1986). *The new American grandparent: A place in the family, a life apart.* New York: Basic Books.

Cherlin, A. J., Furstenberg, F. F., Jr., Chase-Lansdale, P. L., Kiernan, K. E., Robins, P. K., Morrison, D. R., & Teitler, J. O. (1991). Longitudinal studies of effects of divorce on children in Great Britain and the United States. *Science, 252,* 1386–1389.

Cicchetti, D., & Barnett, D. (1991). Attachment organization in maltreated preschoolers. *Development and Psychopathology, 3,* 397–411.

Cicirelli, V. G. (1982). Sibling influence throughout the life span. In M. E. Lamb & B. Sutton-Smith (Eds.), *Sibling relationships: Their nature and significance across the lifespan.* Hillsdale, NJ: Erlbaum.

Cicirelli, V. G. (1989). Feelings of attachment to siblings and well-being in later life. *Psychology and Aging, 4,* 211–216.

Cicirelli, V. G. (1991). Sibling relationships in adulthood. *Marriage and Family Review, 16,* 291–310.

Cicirelli, V. G. (1993). Attachment and obligation as daughters' motives for caregiving behavior and subsequent effect on subjective burden. *Psychology and Aging, 8,* 144–155.

Clingempeel, W. G., Colyar, J. J., Brand, E., & Hetherington, E. M. (1992). Children's relationships with maternal grandparents: A longitudinal study of family structure and pubertal status effects. *Child Development, 63,* 1404–1422.

Clingempeel, W. G., Ievoli, R., & Brand, E. (1984). Structural complexity and the quality of stepparent-stepchild relationships. *Family Processes, 23,* 547–560.

Clingempeel, W. G., & Segal, S. (1986). Stepparent-stepchild relationships and the psychological adjustment of children in stepmother and stepfather families. *Child Development, 57,* 474–484.

Collins, W. A., & Russell, G. (1991). Mother-child and father-child relationships in middle childhood and adolescence: A developmental analysis. *Developmental Review, 11,* 99–136.

Conger, R. D., Conger, K. J., Elder, G. H., Jr., Lorenz, F. O., Simons, R. L., & Whitbeck, L. B. (1992). A family process model of economic hardship and adjustment of early adolescent boys. *Child Development, 63,* 526–541.

Conger, R. D., Conger, K. J., Elder, G. H., Jr., Lorenz, F. O., Simons, R. L., & Whitbeck, L. B. (1993). Family economic stress and adjustment of early adolescent girls. *Developmental Psychology, 29,* 206–219.

Cowan, C. P., Cowan, P. A., Heming, G., & Miller, N. B. (1991). Becoming a family: Marriage, parenting, and child development. In P. A. Cowan & M. Hetherington (Eds.), *Family transitions.* Hillsdale, NJ: Erlbaum.

Cox, M. J., Owen, M. T., Henderson, V. K., & Margand, N. A. (1992). Prediction of infant-father and infant-mother attachment. *Developmental Psychology, 28,* 474–483.

Cox, M. J., Owen, M. T., Lewis, J. M., & Henderson, V. K. (1989). Marriage, adult adjustment, and early parenting. *Child Development, 60,* 1015–1024.

Crnic, K. A., & Booth, C. (1991). Mothers' and fathers' perceptions of daily hassles of parenting across early childhood. *Journal of Marriage and the Family, 53,* 1042–1050.

Crnic, K. A., Greenberg, M. T., Ragozin, A. S., Robinson, N. M., & Basham, R. B. (1983). Effects of stress and social support on mothers and premature and full-term infants. *Child Development, 54,* 209–217.

Crockenberg, S., & Litman, C. (1990). Autonomy as competence in 2-year-olds: Maternal correlates of child defiance, compliance, and self-assertion. *Developmental Psychology, 26,* 961–971.

Crouter, A. C., & McHale, S. M. (1993). The long arm of the job: Influences of parental work on childrearing. In T. Luster & L. Okagaki (Eds.), *Parenting: An ecological perspective.* Hillsdale, NJ: Erlbaum.

Culp, R. E., Little, V., Letts, D., & Lawrence, H. (1991). Maltreated children's self-concept: Effects of a comprehensive treatment program. *American Journal of Orthopsychiatry, 61,* 114–121.

Deimling, G. T., & Bass, D. M. (1986). Symptoms of mental impairment among elderly adults and their effects on family caregivers. *Journal of Gerontology, 41,* 778–784.

DeMaris, A., & MacDonald, W. (1993). Premarital cohabitation and marital instability: A test of the unconventionality hypothesis. *Journal of Marriage and the Family, 55,* 399–407.

DeMaris, A., & Rao, K. V. (1992). Premarital cohabitation and subsequent marital stability in the United States: A reassessment. *Journal of Marriage and the Family, 54,* 178–190.

Demo, D. H. (1992). Parent-child relations: Assessing recent changes. *Journal of Marriage and the Family, 54,* 104–117.

Dishion, T. J., Patterson, G. R., Stoolmiller, M., & Skinner, M. L. (1991). Family, school, and behavioral antecedents to early adolescent involvement with antisocial peers. *Developmental Psychology, 27,* 172–180.

Dornbusch, S. M., Carlsmith, J. M., Bushwall, S. J., Ritter, P. L., Leiderman, H., Hastorf, A. H., & Gross, R. T. (1985). Single parents, extended households, and the control of adolescents. *Child Development, 56,* 326–341.

Draper, P., & Buchanan, A. (1992). If you have a child you have a life: Demographic and cultural perspectives on fathering in old age in !Kung society. In B. S. Hewlett (Ed.), *Father-child relations: Cultural and biosocial contexts.* New York: Aldine de Gruyter.

Dunn, J. (1993). *Young children's close relationships: Beyond attachment.* Newbury Park, CA: Sage.

Dunn, J., & Kendrick, C. (1981). Interaction between young siblings: Association with the interaction between mother and firstborn child. *Developmental Psychology, 17,* 336–343.

Dunn, J., & Kendrick, C. (1982). *Siblings: Love, envy, and understanding.* Cambridge, MA: Harvard University Press.

Duvall, E. M. (1977). *Marriage and family development* (5th ed.). Philadelphia: Lippincott.

Dwyer, J. W., & Coward, R. T. (1991). A multivariate comparison of the involvement of adult sons versus daughters in the care of impaired parents. *Journal of Gerontology: Social Sciences, 46,* S259–S269.

East, P. L., & Rook, K. S. (1992). Compensatory patterns of support among children's peer relationships: A test using school friends, nonschool friends, and siblings. *Developmental Psychology, 28,* 163–172.

Easterbrooks, M. A., & Goldberg, W. A. (1984). Toddler development in the family: Impact of father involvement and parenting characteristics. *Child Development, 55,* 740–752.

Eccles, J. S., Midgley, C., Wigfield, A., Buchanan, C. M., Reuman, D., Flanagan, C., & Mac Iver, D. (1993). Development during adolescence: The impact of stage-environment fit on young adolescents' experiences in schools and in families. *American Psychologist, 48,* 90–101.

Eckenrode, J., Laird, M., & Doris, J. (1993). School performance and disciplinary problems among abused and neglected children. *Developmental Psychology, 29,* 53–62.

Egeland, B. (1979). Preliminary results of a prospective study of the antecedents of child abuse. *International Journal of Child Abuse and Neglect, 3,* 269–278.

Egeland, B., Jacobvitz, D., & Sroufe, L. A. (1988). Breaking the cycle of abuse. *Child Development, 59,* 1080–1088.

Egeland, B., & Sroufe, L. A. (1981). Attachment and early maltreatment. *Child Development, 52,* 44–52.

Egeland, B., Sroufe, L. A., & Erickson, M. (1983). The developmental consequences of different patterns of maltreatment. *International Journal of Child Abuse and Neglect, 7,* 459–469.

Egerton, J. (1983). *Generations: An American family.* Lexington: University Press of Kentucky.

Eggebeen, D. J., & Lichter, D. T. (1991). Race, family structure, and changing poverty among American children. *American Sociological Review, 56,* 801–817.

Emery, R. E. (1989). Family violence. *American Psychologist, 44,* 321–328.

Emery, R. E., & Tuer, M. (1993). Parenting and the marital relationship. In T. Luster & L. Okagaki (Eds.), *Parenting: An ecological perspective.* Hillsdale, NJ: Erlbaum.

Fagot, B. I., & Kavanaugh, K. (1993). Parenting during the second year: Effects of children's age, sex, and attachment classification. *Child Development, 64,* 258–271.

Falbo, T. (1991). The impact of grandparents on children's outcomes in China. *Marriage and Family Review, 16,* 369–376.

Falbo, T., & Polit, D. F. (1986). Quantitative review of the only child literature: Research evidence and theory development. *Psychological Bulletin, 100,* 176–189.

Falbo, T., & Poston, D. L., Jr. (1993). The academic, personality, and physical outcomes of only children in China. *Child Development, 64,* 18–35.

Fantuzzo, J. W. (1990). Behavioral treatment of the victims of child abuse and neglect. *Behavior Modification, 14,* 316–339.

Fantuzzo, J. W., DePaola, L. M., Lambert, L., Martino, T., Anderson, G., & Sutton, S. (1991). Effects of interparental violence on the psychological adjustment and competencies of young children. *Journal of Consulting and Clinical Psychology, 59,* 258–265.

Field, D., Minkler, M., Falk, R. F., & Leino, E. V. (1993). The influence of health on family contacts and family feelings in advanced old age: A longitudinal study. *Journal of Gerontology: Psychological Sciences, 48,* P18–P28.

Fine, M. A., & Schwebel, A. I. (1991). Stepparent stress: A cognitive perspective. *Journal of Divorce and Remarriage, 17,* 1–15.

Fitzgerald, L. F., & Shullman, S. L. (1993). Sexual harrassment: A research analysis and agenda for the 1990s. *Journal of Vocational Behavior, 42,* 5–27.

Frodi, A. M., & Lamb, M. E. (1980). Child abusers' responses to infant smiles and cries. *Child Development, 51,* 238–241.

Furman, W., & Buhrmester, D. (1985a). Children's perceptions of the personal relationships in their social networks. *Developmental Psychology, 21,* 1016–1024.

Furman, W., & Buhrmester, D. (1985b). Children's perceptions of the qualities of sibling relationships. *Child Development, 56,* 448–461.

Furman, W., & Buhrmester, D. (1992). Age and sex differences in perceptions of networks of personal relationships. *Child Development, 63,* 103–115.

Galambos, N. L. (1992). Parent-adolescent relations. *Current Directions in Psychological Science, 1,* 146–149.

Garbarino, J. (1992). *Children and families in the social environment* (2nd ed.). New York: Aldine de Gruyter.

Garbarino, J., & Sherman, D. (1980). High-risk neighborhoods and high-risk families: The human ecology of child maltreatment. *Child Development, 51,* 188–198.

Gelles, R. J. (1992). Poverty and violence toward children. *American Behavioral Scientist, 35,* 258–274.

Gigy, L., & Kelly, J. B. (1992). Reasons for divorce: Perspectives of divorcing men and women. *Journal of Divorce and Remarriage, 18,* 169–187.

Gil, D. G. (1970). *Violence against children.* Cambridge, MA: Harvard University Press.

Glenn, N. D. (1975). Psychological well-being in the postparental stage: Some evidence from national surveys. *Journal of Marriage and the Family, 37,* 105–110.

Glenn, N. D., & McLanahan, S. (1981). The effects of offspring on the psychological well-being of older adults. *Journal of Marriage and the Family, 43,* 409–421.

Glenn, N. D., & McLanahan, S. (1982). Children and marital happiness: A further specification of the relationship. *Journal of Marriage and the Family, 44,* 63–72.

Glenn, N. D., & Weaver, C. N. (1988). The changing relationship of marital status to reported happiness. *Journal of Marriage and the Family, 50,* 317–324.

Glick, P. C. (1989). Remarried families, stepfamilies, and stepchildren: A brief demographic profile. *Family Relations, 38,* 24–47.

Glick, P. C., & Lin, S. (1987). Remarriage after divorce: Recent changes and demographic variations. *Sociological Perspectives, 30,* 162–179.

Goetting, A. (1986). The developmental tasks of siblingship over the life cycle. *Journal of Marriage and the Family, 48,* 703–714.

Gottman, J., & Levenson, R. (1992). Marital processes predictive of later dissolution: Behavior, physiology, and health. *Journal of Personality and Social Psychology, 63,* 221–233.

Gray, J. D., & Silver, R. C. (1990). Opposite sides of the same coin: Former spouses' divergent perspectives in coping with their divorce. *Journal of Personality and Social Psychology, 59,* 1180–1191.

Greene, A. L., & Boxer, A. M. (1986). Daughters and sons as young adults: Restructuring the ties that bind. In N. Datan, A. L. Greene, & H. W. Reese (Eds.), *Life-span developmental psychology: Intergenerational relations.* Hillsdale, NJ: Erlbaum.

Greene, J. G., Fox, N. A., & Lewis, M. (1983). The relationship between neonatal characteristics and three-month mother-infant interactions in high-risk infants. *Child Development, 54,* 1286–1296.

Grolnick, W. S., & Ryan, R. M. (1989). Parent styles associated with children's self-regulation and competence in school. *Journal of Educational Psychology, 81,* 143–154.

Grossman, F. K., Eichler, L. S., Winickoff, S. A., & Associates (1980). *Pregnancy, birth, and parenthood: Adaptations of mothers, fathers, and infants.* San Francisco: Jossey-Bass.

Grotevant, H. D., & Cooper, C. R. (1986). Individuation in family relations: A perspective on individual differences in the development of identity and role-taking skills in adolescence. *Human Development, 29,* 82–100.

Grych, J. H., & Fincham, F. D. (1992). Interventions for children of divorce: Toward greater integration of research and action. *Psychological Bulletin, 111,* 434–454.

Gwartney-Gibbs, P. A. (1986). The institutionalization of premarital cohabitation: Estimates from marriage license applications, 1970–1980. *Journal of Marriage and the Family, 48,* 423–434.

Hackel, L. S., & Ruble, D. N. (1992). Changes in the marital relationship after the first baby is born: Predicting the impact of expectancy disconfirmation. *Journal of Personality and Social Psychology, 62,* 944–957.

Hagestad, G. O. (1985). Continuity and connectedness. In V. L. Bengtson & J. F. Robertson (Eds.), *Grandparenthood.* Beverly Hills, CA: Sage.

Hagestad, G. O., & Burton, L. M. (1986). Grandparenthood, life context, and family development. *American Behavioral Scientist, 29,* 471–484.

Haggstrom, G. W., Kanouse, D. E., & Morrison, P. A. (1986). Accounting for the educational shortfalls of mothers. *Journal of Marriage and the Family, 48,* 175–186.

Harkins, E. B. (1978). Effects of empty nest transition on self-report of psychological and physical well-being. *Journal of Marriage and the Family, 40,* 549–556.

Hart, S. N., & Brassard, M. R. (1987). A major threat to children's mental health: Psychological maltreatment. *American Psychologist, 42,* 160–165.

Haskett, M. E., & Kistner, J. A. (1991). Social interactions and peer perceptions of young physically abused children. *Child Development, 62,* 979–990.

Hetherington, E. M. (1981). Children and divorce. In R. W. Henderson (Ed.), *Parent-child interaction: Theory, research and prospects.* New York: Academic Press.

Hetherington, E. M. (1989). Coping with family transitions: Winners, losers, and survivors. *Child Development, 60,* 1–14.

Hetherington, E. M., & Camara, K. A. (1984). Families in transition: The processes of dissolution and reconstitution. In R. D. Parke (Ed.), *Review of child development research: Vol. 7. The family.* Chicago: University of Chicago Press.

Hetherington, E. M., Clingempeel, W. G., & Associates. (1992). Coping with marital transitions. *Monographs of the Society for Research in Child Development, 57*(2–3, Serial No. 227).

Hetherington, E. M., Cox, M., & Cox, R. (1982). Effects of divorce on parents and children. In M. E. Lamb (Ed.), *Nontraditional families.* Hillsdale, NJ: Erlbaum.

Hewlett, B. S. (1992). Introduction. In B. S. Hewlett (Ed.), *Father-child relations: Cultural and biosocial contexts.* New York: Aldine de Gruyter.

Hill, R. (1986). Life cycle stages for types of single parent families: Of family development theory. *Family Relations, 35,* 19–29.

Himes, C. L. (1992). Future caregivers: Projected family structures of older persons. *Journal of Gerontology: Social Science, 47,* S17–S26.

Hoffman, L. W., & Manis, J. D. (1979). The value of children in the United States: A new approach to the study of fertility. *Journal of Marriage and the Family, 41,* 583–596.

Holden, G. W., & Ritchie, K. L. (1991). Linking extreme marital discord, child rearing, and child behavior problems: Evidence from battered women. *Child Development, 62,* 311–327.

Holmbeck, G. N., & Hill, J. P. (1991). Conflictive engagement, positive affect, and menarche in families with seventh-grade girls. *Child Development, 62,* 1030–1048.

Howe, N., & Ross, H. S. (1990). Socialization, perspective-taking, and the sibling relationship. *Developmental Psychology, 26,* 160–165.

Howes, P., & Markman, H. J. (1989). Marital quality and child functioning: A longitudinal investigation. *Child Development, 60,* 1044–1051.

Hudson, M. F. (1986). Elder mistreatment: Current research. In K. A. Pillemer & R. S. Wolf (Eds.), *Elder abuse: Conflict in the family.* Dover, MA: Auburn House.

Huston, T. L., McHale, S. M., & Crouter, A. C. (1986). When the honeymoon's over: Changes in the marriage relationship over the first year. In R. Gilmour & S. Duck (Eds.), *The emerging field of personal relationships.* Hillsdale, NJ: Erlbaum.

Huston, T. L., & Vangelisti, A. L. (1991). Socioemotional behavior and satisfaction in marital relationships: A longitudinal study. *Journal of Personality and Social Psychology, 6,* 721–733.

Jacobson, C. K., & Heaton, T. B. (1991). Voluntary childlessness among American men and women in the late 1980s. *Social Biology, 38,* 79–93.

Johnson, C. L., & Troll, L. (1992). Family functioning in late late life. *Journal of Gerontology: Social Sciences, 47,* S566–S572.

Johnson, D. R., Amoloza, T. O., & Booth, A. (1992). Stability and developmental change in marital quality: A three-wave panel analysis. *Journal of Marriage and the Family, 54,* 582–594.

Julian, T. W., McKenry, P. C., & McKelvey, M. W. (1991). Mediators of relationship stress between middle-aged fathers and their adolescent children. *Journal of Genetic Psychology, 152,* 381–386.

Kalmuss, D., Davidson, A., & Cushman, L. (1992). Parenting expectancies, experiences, and adjustment to parenthood: A test of the violated expectations framework. *Journal of Marriage and the Family, 54,* 516–526.

Kaufman, J., & Zigler, E. (1989). The intergenerational transmission of child abuse. In D. Cicchetti & V. Carlson (Eds.), *Child maltreatment: Theory and research on the causes and consequences of child abuse and neglect.* New York: Cambridge University Press.

Keith, J. (1992). Care-taking in cultural context: Anthropological queries. In H. L. Kendig, A. Hashimoto, & L. C. Coppard (Eds.), *Family support for the elderly: The international experience.* Oxford, England: Oxford University Press.

Keller, B. B., & Bell, R. Q. (1979). Child effects on adult's method of eliciting altruistic behavior. *Child Development, 50,* 1004–1009.

Kelley, M. L., Power, T. G., & Wimbush, D. D. (1992). Determinants of disciplinary practices in low-income Black mothers. *Child Development, 63,* 573–582.

Kempe, R. S., & Kempe, C. H. (1978). *Child abuse.* Cambridge, MA: Harvard University Press.

Kiernan, K. E. (1989). Who remains childless? *Journal of Biosocial Science, 21,* 387–398.

Kinard, E. M., & Reinherz, H. (1986). Effects of marital disruption on children's school aptitude and achievement. *Journal of Marriage and the Family, 48,* 285–293.

Kitson, G. C., Babri, K. B., & Roach, M. J. (1985). Who divorces and why: A review. *Journal of Family Issues, 6,* 255–293.

Kitson, G. C., & Morgan, L. A. (1990). The multiple consequences of divorce: A decade review. *Journal of Marriage and the Family, 52,* 913–924.

Klein, M., & Stern, L. (1971). Low birth weight and the battered child syndrome. *American Journal of Diseases of Childhood, 122,* 15–18.

Klimes-Dougan, B., & Kistner, J. (1990). Physically abused preschoolers' responses to peers' distress. *Developmental Psychology, 26,* 599–602.

Kline, M., Tschann, J. M., Johnston, J. R., & Wallerstein, J. S. (1989). Children's adjustment in joint and sole physical custody families. *Developmental Psychology, 25,* 430–438.

Klineberg, S. L. (1984). Social change, world views, and cohort succession: The United States in the 1980s. In K. A. McCluskey & H. W. Reese (Eds.), *Lifespan developmental psychology: Historical and generational effects.* Orlando, FL: Academic Press.

Knight, B. G., Lutzky, S. M., & Macofsky-Urban, F. (1993). A meta-analytic review of interventions for caregiver distress: Recommendations for future research. *Gerontologist, 33,* 240–248.

Kobak, R. R., Cole, H.E., Ferenz-Gilles, R., Fleming, W. S., & Gamble, W. (1993). Attachment and emotional regulation during mother-teen problem solving: A control theory analysis. *Child Development, 64,* 231–245.

Koestner, R., Zuroff, D. C., & Powers, T. A. (1991). Family origins of adolescent self-criticism and its continuity into adulthood. *Journal of Abnormal Psychology, 100,* 191–197.

Kohn, M. L. (1969). *Class and conformity: A study of values.* Homewood, IL: Dorsey Press.

Kreppner, K., Paulsen, S., & Schuetze, Y. (1982). Infant and family development: From triads to tetrads. *Human Development, 25,* 373–391.

Kurdek, L. A. (1991a). Correlates of relationship satisfaction in cohabiting gay and lesbian couples: Integration of contextual investment, and problem-solving models. *Journal of Personality and Social Psychology, 61,* 910–922.

Kurdek, L. A. (1991b). The relations between reported well-being and divorce history, availability of a proximate adult, and gender. *Journal of Marriage and the Family, 53,* 71–78.

Kurdek, L. A., & Schmitt, J. P. (1986). Early development of relationship quality in heterosexual married, heterosexual cohabiting, gay, and lesbian couples. *Developmental Psychology, 22,* 305–309.

Lamb, M. E. (1981). *The role of the father in child development.* New York: Wiley.

Lamb, M. E., & Elster, A. B. (1985). Adolescent mother-infant-father relationships. *Developmental Psychology, 21,* 768–773.

Lamborn, S. D., Mounts, N. S., Steinberg, L., & Dornbusch, S. M. (1991). Patterns of competence and adjustment among adolescents from authoritative, authoritarian, indulgent, and neglectful families. *Child Development, 62,* 1049–1065.

Lamborn, S. D., & Steinberg, L. (1993). Emotional autonomy redux: Revisiting Ryan and Lynch. *Child Development, 64,* 483–499.

Lauer, R. H., & Lauer, J. C. (1986). Factors in long-term marriages. *Journal of Family Issues, 7,* 382–390.

Lee, G. R. (1988). Marital satisfaction in later life: The effects of nonmarital roles. *Journal of Marriage and the Family, 50,* 775–783.

Lempers, J. D., & Clark-Lempers, D. S. (1992). Young, middle and late adolescents' comparisons of the functional importance of five significant relationships. *Journal of Youth and Adolescence, 21,* 53–96.

Lerner, J. V. (1993). The influence of child temperamental characteristics on parent behaviors. In T. Luster & L. Okagaki (Eds.), *Parenting: An ecological perspective.* Hillsdale, NJ: Erlbaum.

Lerner, M. J., Somers, D. G., Reid, D., Chiriboga, D., & Tierney, M. (1991). Adult children as caregivers: Egocentric biases in judgments of sibling contributions. *Gerontologist, 31,* 746–755.

Levenson, R. W., Carstensen, L. L., & Gottman, J. M. (1993). Long-term marriage: Age, gender, and satisfaction. *Psychology and Aging, 8,* 310–313.

Levinson, D. (1989). *Family violence in cross-cultural perspective.* Newbury Park, CA: Sage.

Lewis, R. A., Freneau, P. J., & Roberts, C. L. (1979). Fathers and the postparental transition. *Family Coordinator, 28,* 514–520.

Litwak, E. (1960). Geographic mobility and extended family cohesion. *American Sociological Review, 25,* 385–394.

Lustig, J. L., Wolchik, S. A., & Braver, S. L. (1992). Social support in chumships and adjustment in children of divorce. *American Journal of Community Psychology, 20,* 393–399.

Lytton, H. (1990). Child and parent effects in boys' conduct disorder: A reinterpretation. *Developmental Psychology, 26,* 683–697.

Lytton, H., & Romney, D. M. (1991). Parents' differential socialization of boys and girls: A meta-analysis. *Psychological Bulletin, 109,* 267–296.

Maccoby, E. E. (1980). *Social development.* San Diego: Harcourt Brace Jovanovich.

Maccoby, E. E. (1984). Middle childhood in the context of the family. In W. A. Collins (Ed.), *Development during middle childhood: The years from six to twelve.* Washington, DC: National Academy Press.

Maccoby, E. E., & Martin, J. A. (1983). Socialization in the context of the family: Parent-child interaction. In E. M. Hetherington (Ed.; P. H. Mussen, General Ed.), *Handbook of child psychology: Vol. 4. Socialization, personality, and social development* (4th ed.). New York: Wiley.

MacDonald, K. (1992). Warmth as a developmental construct: An evolutionary analysis. *Child Development, 63,* 753–773.

MacKinnon, C. E. (1989). An observational investigation of sibling interactions in married and divorced families. *Developmental Psychology, 25,* 36–44.

Main, M., & George, C. (1985). Responses of abused and disadvantaged toddlers to distress in agemates: A study in the day-care setting. *Developmental Psychology, 21,* 407–412.

Main, M., & Weston, D. R. (1981). The quality of the toddler's relationship to mother and to father: Related to conflict and the readiness to establish new relationships. *Child Development, 52,* 932–940.

Malinosky-Rummell, R., & Hansen, D. J. (1993). Long-term consequences of childhood physical abuse. *Psychological Bulletin, 114,* 68–79.

Markides, K. S., Boldt, J. S., & Ray, L. A. (1986). Sources of helping and intergenerational solidarity: A three-generations study of Mexican Americans. *Journal of Gerontology, 41,* 506–511.

Markides, K. S., Liang, J., & Jackson, J. S. (1990). Race, ethnicity, and aging: Conceptual and methodological issues. In R. H. Binstock & L. K. George (Eds.), *Handbook of aging and the social sciences* (3rd ed.). San Diego: Academic Press.

Matthews, S. H., & Sprey, J. (1985). Adolescents' relationships with grandparents: An empirical contribution to conceptual clarification. *Journal of Gerontology, 40,* 621–626.

McHale, S. M., & Gamble, W. C. (1989). Sibling relationships of children with disabled and nondisabled brothers and sisters. *Developmental Psychology, 25,* 421–429.

McLanahan, S. S., & Sorenson, A. B. (1985). Life events and psychological well-being over the life course. In G. H. Elder, Jr. (Ed.), *Life course dynamics: Trajectories and transitions, 1968–1980.* Ithaca, NY: Cornell University Press.

McLoyd, V. C. (1989). Socialization and development in a changing economy: The effects of paternal job and income loss on children. *American Psychologist, 44,* 293–302.

McLoyd, V. C. (1990). The impact of economic hardship on Black families and children: Psychological distress, parenting, and socioemotional development. *Child Development, 61,* 311–346.

Menaghan, E. G. (1983). Marital stress and family transitions: A panel analysis. *Journal of Marriage and the Family, 45,* 371–386.

Menaghan, E. G., & Lieberman, M. A. (1986). Changes in depression following divorce: A panel study. *Journal of Marriage and the Family, 48,* 319–328.

Meyer, D. R., & Garasky, S. (1993). Custodial fathers: Myths, realities, and child support policy. *Journal of Marriage and the Family, 55,* 73–89.

Montemayor, R. (1982). The relationship between parent-adolescent conflict and the amount of time adolescents spend alone and with parents and peers. *Child Development, 53,* 1512–1519.

Myers-Walls, J. A. (1984). Balancing multiple roles responsibilities during the transition to parenthood. *Family Relations, 33,* 267–271.

Newcomb, P. R. (1979). Cohabitation in America: An assessment of consequences. *Journal of Marriage and the Family, 41,* 597–603.

Nock, S. L. (1987). *Sociology of the family.* Englewood Cliffs, NJ: Prentice-Hall.

Norman-Jackson, J. (1982). Family interactions, language development, and primary reading achievement of Black children in families of low income. *Child Development, 53,* 349–358.

Norton, A. J., & Moorman, J. E. (1987). Current trends in marriage and divorce among American women. *Journal of Marriage and the Family, 49,* 3–14.

Nydegger, C. N. (1986). Asymmetrical kin and the problematic son-in-law. In N. Datan, A. L. Greene, & H. W. Reese (Eds.), *Life-span developmental psychology: Intergenerational relations.* Hillsdale, NJ: Erlbaum.

Oates, K. (1986). *Child abuse and neglect: What happens eventually?* New York: Brunner/Mazel.

Offer, D., Ostrov, E., & Howard, K. I. (1981). *The adolescent: A psychological self-portrait.* New York: Basic Books.

Ogbu, J. U. (1981). Origins of human competence: A cultural-ethological perspective. *Child Development, 52,* 413–429.

Okraku, I. O. (1987). Age and attitudes toward multigenerational residence, 1973 to 1983. *Journal of Gerontology, 42,* 280–287.

Oyserman, D., Radin, N., & Benn, R. (1993). Dynamics in a three-generational family: Teens, grandparents, and babies. *Developmental Psychology, 29,* 564–572.

Paikoff, R. L., & Brooks-Gunn, J. (1991). Do parent-child relationships change during puberty? *Psychological Bulletin, 110,* 47–66.

Palkovitz, R. (1984). Parental attitudes and fathers' interactions with their 5-month-old infants. *Developmental Psychology, 20,* 1054–1060.

Parke, R. D. (1979). Perspectives on father-infant interaction. In J. Osofsky (Ed.), *Handbook of infant development.* New York: Wiley.

Parke, R. D., & Lewis, N. G. (1981). The family in context: A multilevel interactional analysis of child abuse. In R. W. Henderson (Ed.), *Parent-child interaction: Theory, research, and prospects.* New York: Academic Press.

Parke, R. D., & Sawin, D. B. (1976). The father's role in infancy: A reevaluation. *Family Coordinator, 25,* 365–371.

Patterson, G. R., & Stouthamer-Loeber, M. (1984). The correlation of family management practices and delinquency. *Child Development, 55,* 1299–1307.

Paulhus, D., & Shaffer, D. R. (1981). Sex differences in the impact of number of older and number of younger siblings on scholastic aptitude. *Social Psychology Quarterly, 44,* 363–368.

Paveza, G. J., Cohen, D., Eisdorfer, C., Freels, S., Semla, T., Ashford, J. W., Gorelick, P., Hirschman, R., Luchins, D., & Levy, P. (1992). Severe family violence and Alzheimer's disease: Prevalence and risk factors. *Gerontologist, 32,* 493–497.

Pearson, J. L., Hunter, A. G., Ensminger, M. E., & Kellam, S. G. (1990). Black grandmothers in multigenerational households: Diversity in family structure and parenting involvement in the Woodlawn community. *Child Development, 61,* 434–442.

Pedro-Carroll, J. L., & Cowen, E. L. (1985). The children of divorce intervention program: An investigation of the efficacy of a school-based prevention program. *Journal of Consulting and Clinical Psychology, 53,* 603–611.

Peterson, J. W. (1990). Age of wisdom: Elderly black women in family and church. In J. Sokolovsky (Ed.), *The cultural context of aging: Worldwide perspectives.* New York: Bergin and Garvey.

Pinto, A., Folkers, E., & Sines, J. O. (1991). Dimensions of behavior and home environment in school-age children: India and the United States. *Journal of Cross-Cultural Psychology, 22,* 491–508.

Rempel, J. (1985). Childless elderly: What are they missing? *Journal of Marriage and the Family, 47,* 343–348.

Richards, L. N., Bengtson, V. L., & Miller, R. B. (1989). The "generation in the middle": Perceptions of changes in adults' intergenerational relationships. In K. Kreppner & R. M. Lerner (Eds.), *Family systems and life-span development.* Hillsdale, NJ: Erlbaum.

Roberto, K. A., & Stroes, J. (1992). Grandchildren and grandparents: Roles, influences, and relationships. *International Journal of Aging and Human Development, 34,* 227–239.

Rollins, B. C., & Feldman, H. (1970). Marital satisfaction over the family life cycle. *Journal of Marriage and the Family, 32,* 20–28.

Ross, H. G., & Milgram, J. I. (1982). Important variables in adult sibling relationships: A qualitative study. In M. E. Lamb & B. Sutton-Smith (Eds.), *Sibling relationships: Their nature and significance across the lifespan.* Hillsdale, NJ: Erlbaum.

Rossi, A. S., & Rossi, P. H. (1990). *Of human bonding: Parent-child relations across the life course.* New York: Aldine de Gruyter.

Rowland, D. T. (1991). Family diversity and the life cycle. *Journal of Comparative Family Studies, 22,* 1–14.

Rubinstein, R. L., Alexander, R. B., Goodman, M., & Luborsky, M. (1991). Key relationships of never married, childless older women: A cultural analysis. *Journal of Gerontology: Social Sciences, 46,* S270–S277.

Russell, R. J., & Wells, P. A. (1991). Personality similarity and quality of marriage. *Personality and Individual Differences, 12,* 407–412.

Ryan, R. M., & Lynch, J. H. (1989). Emotional autonomy versus detachment: Revisiting the vicissitudes of adolescence and young adulthood. *Child Development, 60,* 340–356.

Salzinger, S., Feldman, R. S., Hammer, M., & Rosario, M. (1993). The effects of physical abuse on children's social relationships. *Child Development, 64,* 169–187.

Schaefer, E. S. (1959). A circumplex model for maternal behavior. *Journal of Abnormal and Social Psychology, 59,* 226–235.

Schinke, S. P., Schilling, R. F. II, Barth, R. P., Gilchrist, L. D., & Maxwell, J. S. (1986). Stress-management intervention to prevent family violence. *Journal of Family Violence, 1,* 13–26.

Schumm, W. R., & Bugaighis, M. A. (1986). Marital quality over the marital career: Alternative explanations. *Journal of Marriage and the Family, 48,* 165–168.

Scott, W. A., Scott, R., & McCabe, M. (1991). Family relationships and children's personality: A cross-cultural, cross-source comparison. *British Journal of Social Psychology, 30,* 1–20.

Seltzer, J. A., & Bianchi, S. M. (1988). Children's contact with absent parents. *Journal of Marriage and the Family, 50,* 663–677.

Shanas, E. (1980). Older people and their families: The new pioneers. *Journal of Marriage and the Family, 42,* 9–15.

Sherrod, K. B., O'Connor, S., Vietze, P. M., & Altemeier, W. A. III. (1984). Child health and maltreatment. *Child Development, 55,* 1174–1183.

Sigelman, C. K., Berry, C. J., & Wiles, K. A. (1984). Violence in college students' dating relationships. *Journal of Applied Social Psychology, 14,* 530–548.

Silverberg, S. B., & Steinberg, L. (1987). Adolescent autonomy, parent-adolescent conflict, and parental well-being. *Journal of Youth and Adolescence, 16,* 293–312.

Silverberg, S. B., & Steinberg, L. (1990). Psychological well-being of parents with early adolescent children. *Developmental Psychology, 26,* 658–666.

Simons, R. L., & Beaman, J., Conger, R. D., & Chao, W. (1993). Stress, support, and antisocial behavior trait as determinants of emotional well-being and parenting practices among single mothers. *Journal of Marriage and the Family, 55,* 385–398.

Simons, R. L., Robertson, J. F., & Downs, W. R. (1989). The nature of the association between parental rejection and delinquent behavior. *Journal of Youth and Adolescence, 18,* 297–310.

Simons, R. L., Whitbeck, L. B., Conger, R. D., & Wu, C. (1991). Intergenerational transmission of harsh parenting. *Developmental Psychology, 27,* 159–171.

Sirignano, S. W., & Lachman, M. E. (1985). Personality change during the transition to parenthood: The role of perceived infant temperament. *Developmental Psychology, 21,* 558–567.

Skolnick, A. (1981). Married lives: Longitudinal perspectives on marriage. In D. H. Eichorn, J. A. Clausen, N. Haan, M. P. Honzik, & P. H. Mussen (Eds.), *Present and past in middle life.* New York: Academic Press.

Smith, T. W. (1990). Academic achievement and teaching younger siblings. *Social Psychology Quarterly, 53,* 352–363.

Smock, P. J. (1993). The economic costs of marital disruption for young women over the past two decades. *Demography, 30,* 353–371.

Snow, M. E., Jacklin, C. N., & Maccoby, E. E. (1983). Sex-of-child differences in father-child interaction at one year of age. *Child Development, 54,* 227–232.

Spanier, G. B. (1983). Married and unmarried cohabitation in the United States: 1980. *Journal of Marriage and the Family, 45,* 277–288.

Steinberg, L. (1981). Transformations in family relations at puberty. *Developmental Psychology, 17,* 833–840.

Steinberg, L., Mounts, N. S., Lamborn, S. D., & Dornbusch, S. M. (1991). Authoritative parenting and adolescent adjustment across varied ecological niches. *Journal of Research on Adolescence, 1,* 19–36.

Stemp, P. S., Turner, J., & Noh, S. (1986). Psychological distress in the postpartum period: The significance of social support. *Journal of Marriage and the Family, 48,* 271–277.

Stets, J. E. (1992). Interactive processes in dating aggression: A national study. *Journal of Marriage and the Family, 54,* 165–177.

Stevenson, M. R., & Black, K. N. (1988). Paternal absence and sex-role development: A meta-analysis. *Child Development, 59,* 793–814.

Stewart, R. B., & Marvin, R. S. (1984). Sibling relations: The role of conceptual perspective-taking in the ontogeny of sibling caregiving. *Child Development, 55,* 1322–1332.

Stewart, R. B., Mobley, L. A., Van Tuyl, S. S., & Salvador, M. A. (1987). The firstborn's adjustment to the birth of a sibling: A longitudinal assessment. *Child Development, 58,* 341–355.

Stocker, C., Dunn, J., & Plomin, R. (1989). Sibling relationships: Links with child temperament, maternal behavior, and family structure. *Child Development, 60,* 715–727.

Straus, M. A. (1980). A sociological perspective on the causes of family violence. In M. R. Green (Ed.), *Violence and the family* (AAAS Selected Symposium No. 47). Boulder, CO: Westview.

Straus, M. A., & Gelles, R. J. (1986). Societal change and change in family violence from 1975 to 1985 as revealed by two national surveys. *Journal of Marriage and the Family, 48,* 465–479.

Straus, M. A., & Gelles, R. J. (Edited with C. Smith). (1990). *Physical violence in American families: Risk factors and adaptations to violence in 8,145 families.* New Brunswick, NJ: Transaction.

Stroebe, W., & Stroebe, M. S. (1986). Beyond marriage: The impact of partner loss on health. In R. Gilmour & S. Duck (Eds.), *The emerging field of personal relationships.* Hillsdale, NJ: Erlbaum.

Stull, D. E., & Scarisbrick-Hauser, A. (1989). Never-married elderly: A reassessment with implications for long-term care policy. *Research on Aging, 11,* 124–139.

Suitor, J. J. (1991). Marital quality and satisfaction with the division of household labor across the family life cycle. *Journal of Marriage and the Family, 53,* 221–230.

Sweet, J. A., & Bumpass, L. L. (1987). *American families and households.* New York: Russell Sage Foundation.

Taeuber, C. (1990). Diversity: The dramatic reality. In S. A. Bass, E. A. Kutza, & F. M. Torres-Gil (Eds.), *Diversity in aging.* Glenview, IL: Scott, Foresman.

Tanfer, K. (1987). Patterns of premarital cohabitation among never-married women in the United States. *Journal of Marriage and the Family, 49,* 483–497.

Thomson, E., & Colella, U. (1992). Cohabitation and marital stability: Quality or commitment. *Journal of Marriage and the Family, 54,* 259–267.

Tietjen, A. M., & Bradley, C. F. (1985). Social support and maternal psychosocial adjustment during the transition to parenthood. *Canadian Journal of Behavioral Science, 17,* 109–121.

Trickett, P. K., Aber, J. L., Carlson, V., & Cicchetti, D. (1991). Relationship of socioeconomic status to the etiology and developmental sequelae of physical child abuse. *Developmental Psychology, 27,* 148–158.

Trickett, P. K., & Susman, E. J. (1988). Parental perceptions of child-rearing practices in physically abusive and nonabusive families. *Developmental Psychology, 24,* 270–276.

Umberson, D. (1992). Relationships between adult children and their parents: Psychological consequences for both generations. *Journal of Marriage and the Family, 54,* 664–674.

U.S. Bureau of the Census (1993). *Statistical abstract of the United States: 1993* (113th ed.). Washington, DC: U.S. Government Printing Office.

van IJzendoorn, M. H. (1992). Intergenerational transmission of parenting: A review of studies in nonclinical populations. *Developmental Review, 12,* 76–99.

Veroff, J., Douvan, E., & Kulka, R. A. (1981). *The inner American: A self-portrait from 1957 to 1976.* New York: Basic Books.

Volling, B. L., & Belsky, J. (1992). The contribution of mother-child and father-child relationships to the quality of sibling interaction: A longitudinal study. *Child Development, 63,* 1209–1222.

Vondra, J., & Belsky, J. (1993). Developmental origins of parenting: Personality and relationship factors. In T. Luster & L. Okagaki (Eds.), *Parenting: An ecological perspective.* Hillsdale, NJ: Erlbaum.

Wallerstein, J. S. (1984). Children of divorce: Preliminary report of a ten-year follow-up of young children. *American Journal of Orthopsychiatry, 54,* 444–458.

Wallerstein, J. S. (1987). Children of divorce: Report of a ten-year follow-up of early latency-age children. *American Journal of Orthopsychiatry, 57,* 199–211.

Wallerstein, J. S. (1991). The long-term effects of divorce on children: A review. *Journal of the American Academy of Child and Adolescent Psychiatry, 30,* 349–360.

Wallerstein, J. S., & Blakeslee, S. (1989). *Second chances: Men, women, and children a decade after divorce.* New York: Ticknor & Fields.

Ward, R., Logan, J., & Spitze, G. (1992). The influence of parent and child needs on coresidence in middle and later life. *Journal of Marriage and the Family, 54,* 209–221.

Ward, R., & Spitze, G. (1992). Consequences of parent-adult child coresidence. *Journal of Family Issues, 13,* 533–572.

Waters, E., Wippman, J., & Sroufe, L. A. (1979). Attachment, positive affect, and competence in the peer group: Two studies in construct validation. *Child Development, 50,* 821–829.

Weibel-Orlando, J. (1990). Grandparenting styles: Native American perspectives. In J. Sokolovsky (Ed.), *The cultural context of aging: Worldwide perspectives.* New York: Bergin and Garvey.

Weisner, T. S., & Gallimore, R. (1977). My brother's keeper: Child and sibling caretaking. *Current Anthropology, 18,* 169–190.

Whitbourne, S. K. (1986). *The me I know: A study of adult identity.* New York: Springer-Verlag.

White, K., Speisman, J. C., & Costos, D. (1983). Young adults and their parents: Individuation to mutuality. In H. D. Grotevant & C. R. Cooper (Eds.), *Adolescent development in the family* (New Directions for Child Development, No. 22). San Francisco: Jossey-Bass.

White, L., & Edwards, J. N. (1990). Emptying the nest and parental well-being: An analysis of national panel data. *American Sociological Review, 55,* 235–242.

Widmayer, S., & Field, T. (1980). Effects of Brazelton demonstrations on early interactions of preterm infants and their teen-age mothers. *Infant Behavior and Development, 3,* 79–89.

Wiehe, V. R. (1990). *Sibling abuse: Hidden physical, emotional, and sexual trauma.* Lexington, MA: Lexington Books.

Wilkie, C. F., & Ames, E. W. (1986). The relationship of infant crying to parental stress in the transition to parenthood. *Journal of Marriage and the Family, 48,* 545–550.

Wilson, M. N. (1986). The black extended family: An analytical consideration. *Developmental Psychology, 22,* 246–258.

Wilson, M. N. (1989). Child development in the context of the Black extended family. *American Psychologist, 44,* 380–385.

Wolf, R. S., & Pillemer, K. A. (1989). *Helping elderly victims: The reality of elder abuse.* New York: Columbia University Press.

Wolfe, D. A., Edwards, B., Manion, I., & Koverola, C. (1988). Early intervention for parents at risk of child abuse and neglect: A preliminary investigation. *Journal of Consulting and Clinical Psychology, 56,* 40–47.

Wolfner, G. D., & Gelles, R. J. (1993). A profile of violence toward children: A national study. *Child Abuse and Neglect, 17,* 197–212.

Wolfson, C., Handfield-Jones, R., Glass, K. C., McClaran, J., & Keyserlingk, E. (1993). Adult children's perceptions of their responsibility to provide care for dependent elderly parents. *Gerontologist, 33,* 315–323.

Youniss, J., & Smollar, J. (1985). *Adolescent relations with mothers, fathers, and friends.* Chicago: University of Chicago Press.

Zaslow, M. J. (1989). Sex differences in children's response to parental divorce: 2. Samples, variables, ages, and sources. *American Journal of Orthopsychiatry, 59,* 118–141.

Zigler, E., & Finn Stevenson, M. F. (1993). *Children in a changing world: Developmental and social issues.* Pacific Grove, CA: Brooks/Cole.

Chapter 15: Lifestyles: Play, School, and Work

Alexander, K. L., & Entwisle, D. R. (1988). Achievement in the first two years of school: Patterns and processes. *Monographs of the Society for Research in Child Development, 53*(2, Serial No. 218).

Anderson, D. R., & Collins, P. A. (1988). *The impact on children's education: Television's influence on cognitive development.* Washington, DC: U.S. Department of Education.

Aneshensel, C. S., & Rosen, B. C. (1980). Domestic roles and sex differences in occupational expectations. *Journal of Marriage and the Family, 42,* 121–131.

Anson, A. R., Cook, T. D., Habib, F., Grady, M. K., Haynes, N., & Comer, J. P. (1991). The Comer school development program: A theoretical analysis. *Urban Education, 26,* 56–82.

Arber, S., & Ginn, J. (1991). *Gender and later life: A sociological analysis of resources and constraints.* London: Sage.

Aronson, E., Blaney, N., Stephan, C., Sikes, J., & Snapp, M. (1978). *The jigsaw classroom.* Beverly Hills, CA: Sage.

Atchley, R. C. (1976). *The sociology of retirement.* Cambridge, MA: Schenkman.

Athey, I. (1984). Contributions of play to development. In T. D. Yawkey & A. D. Pelligrini (Eds.), *Child's play: Developmental and applied.* Hillsdale, NJ: Erlbaum.

Avioli, P., & Kaplan, E. (1992). A panel study of married women's work patterns. *Sex Roles, 26,* 227–242.

Bachman, J. G., & Schulenberg, J. (1993). How part-time work intensity relates to drug use, problem behavior, time use, and satisfaction among high school seniors: Are these consequences or merely correlates? *Developmental Psychology, 29,* 220–235.

Banks, J. A. (1993). Multicultural education: Historical development, dimensions, and practice. *Review of Educational Research, 19,* 3–49.

Baran, S. J., Chase, L. J., & Courtright, J. A. (1979). Television drama as a facilitator of prosocial behavior: "The Waltons." *Journal of Broadcasting, 23,* 277–284.

Barglow, P., Vaughn, B. E., & Molitor, N. (1987). Effect of maternal absence due to employment on the quality of infant-mother attachment in a low-risk sample. *Child Development, 58,* 945–954.

Barnes, K. E. (1971). Preschool play norms: A replication. *Developmental Psychology, 5,* 99–103.

Baruch, G. K., & Barnett, R. (1986). Role quality, multiple role involvement, and psychological well-being in midlife women. *Journal of Personality and Social Psychology, 51,* 578–585.

Baruch, G. K., Biener, L., & Barnett, R. C. (1987). Women and gender in research on work and family stress. *American Psychologist, 42,* 130–136.

Baydar, N., & Brooks-Gunn, J. (1991). Effects of maternal employment and child-care arrangements on preschoolers' cognitive and behavioral outcomes: Evidence from the children of the National Longitudinal Survey of Youth. *Developmental Psychology, 27,* 932–945.

Belsky, J., & Most, R. (1981). From exploration to play: A cross-sectional study of infant free-play behavior. *Developmental Psychology, 17,* 630–639.

Belsky, J., & Rovine, M. J. (1988). Nonmaternal care in the first year of life and the security of infant-parent attachment. *Child Development, 59,* 157–167.

Bizot, E. B., & Goldman, S. H. (1993). Prediction of satisfactoriness and satisfaction: An 8-year follow-up. *Journal of Vocational Behavior, 43,* 19–29.

Bogatz, G. A., & Ball, S. (1972). *The second year of Sesame Street: A continuing evaluation.* Princeton, NJ: Educational Testing Service.

Bossé, R., Aldwin, C. M., Levenson, M. R., Spiro, A. III, & Mroczek, D. K. (1993). Change in social support after retirement: Longitudinal findings from the Normative Aging Study. *Journal of Gerontology: Psychological Sciences, 48,* P210–P217.

Bradbard, M. R., & Endsley, R. C. (1979). What do licensers say to parents who ask their help with selecting quality day care? *Child Care Quarterly, 8,* 307–312.

Braddock, J. H. II, & McPartland, J. M. (1993). Education of early adolescents. *Review of Educational Research, 19,* 135–170.

Bray, D. W., & Howard, A. (1983). The AT&T longitudinal studies of managers. In K. W. Schaie (Ed.), *Longitudinal studies of adult psychological development.* New York: Guilford Press.

Brookover, W., Beady, C., Flood, P., Schweitzer, J., & Wisenbaker, J. (1979). *School social systems and student achievement: Schools can make a difference.* New York: Praeger.

Brooks, L. (1991). Recent developments in theory-building. In D. Brown, L. Brooks, & Associates (Eds.), *Career choice and development: Applying contemporary theories to practice* (2nd ed.). San Francisco: Jossey-Bass.

Brophy, J. (1979). Teacher behavior and its effects. *Journal of Educational Psychology, 71,* 733–750.

Brown, B. B., Mounts, N., Lamborn, S. D., & Steinberg, L. (1993). Parenting practices and peer group affiliation in adolescence. *Child Development, 64,* 467–482.

Brownell, C. A. (1988). Combinatorial skills: Converging developments over the second year. *Child Development, 59,* 675–685.

Brownell, C. A., & Carriger, M. S. (1990). Changes in cooperation and self-other differentiation during the second year. *Child Development, 61,* 1164–1174.

Buysse, V., & Bailey, D. B. (1993). Behavioral and developmental outcomes in young children with disabilities in integrated and segregated settings: A review of comparative studies. *Journal of Special Education, 26,* 434–461.

Ceci, S. J. (1991). How much does schooling influence general intelligence and its cognitive components? A reassessment of the evidence. *Developmental Psychology, 27,* 703–722.

Chadwick, B. A., & Heaton, T. B. (1992). *Statistical handbook on the American family.* Phoenix: Onyx Press.

Chambré, S. M. (1993). Volunteerism by elders: Past trends and future prospects. *Gerontologist, 33,* 221–228.

Chen, C., & Stevenson, H. W. (1989). Homework: A cross-cultural examination. *Child Development, 60,* 551–561.

Clark, D. O., & Maddox, G. L. (1992). Racial and social correlates of age-related changes in functioning. *Journal of Gerontology: Social Sciences, 47,* S222–S223.

Clarke-Stewart, A. (1993). *Daycare* (rev. ed.). Cambridge, MA: Harvard University Press.

Clausen, J. A., & Gilens, M. (1990). Personality and labor force participation across the life course: A longitudinal study of women's careers. *Sociological Forum, 5,* 595–618.

Clements, D. H. (1990). Metacomponential development in a Logo programming environment. *Journal of Educational Psychology, 82,* 141–149.

Clements, D. H. (1991). Enhancement of creativity in computer environments. *American Educational Research Journal, 28,* 173–187.

Coleman, J. (1961). *The adolescent society.* New York: Free Press.

Collins, W. A., Sobol, B. L., & Westby, S. (1981). Effects of adult commentary on children's comprehension and inferences about a televised aggressive portrayal. *Child Development, 52,* 158–163.

Comer, J. P. (1988, November). Educating poor minority children. *Scientific American, 259*(5), 42–48.

Comer, J. P. (1991). The black child in school. In M. Lewis (Ed.), *Child and adolescent psychiatry: A comprehensive textbook.* Baltimore: Williams & Wilkins.

Comstock, G. (with H. Paik). (1991). *Television and the American child.* New York: Academic Press.

Connolly, J. A., & Doyle, A. B. (1984). Relation of social fantasy play to social competence in preschoolers. *Developmental Psychology, 20,* 797–806.

Corrigan, R. (1987). A developmental sequence of actor-object pretend play in young children. *Merrill-Palmer Quarterly, 33,* 87–106.

Costa, P. T., Jr., McCrae, R. R., & Arenberg, D. (1983). Recent longitudinal research on personality and aging. In K. W. Schaie (Ed.), *Longitudinal studies of adult psychological development.* New York: Guilford Press.

Costa, P. T., Jr., McCrae, R. R., Zonderman, A. B., Barbano, H. E., Lebowitz, B., & Larson, D. M. (1986). Cross-sectional studies of personality in a national sample: 2. Stability in neuroticism, extraversion, and openness. *Psychology and Aging, 1,* 144–149.

Cox, T. H., & Harquail, C. V. (1991). Career paths and career success in the early career stages of male and female MBAs. *Journal of Vocational Behavior, 39,* 54–75.

Crockenberg, S., & Litman, C. (1991). Effects of maternal employment on maternal and two-year-old child behavior. *Child Development, 61,* 930–953.

Cronbach, L. J., & Snow, R. E. (1977). *Aptitudes and instructional methods: A handbook for research on interactions.* New York: Irvington.

Crook, C. (1992). Cultural artefacts in social development: The case of computers. In H. McGurk (Ed.), *Childhood social development: Contemporary perspectives.* Hove, UK: Erlbaum.

Crosby, F. J. (1991). *Juggling: The unexpected advantages of balancing career and home for women and their families.* New York: Free Press.

Crouter, A. C., MacDermid, S. M., McHale, S. M., & Perry-Jenkins, M. (1990). Parental monitoring and perceptions of children's school performance and conduct in dual- and single-career families. *Developmental Psychology, 26,* 649–657.

Crouter, A. C., & McHale, S. M. (1993). The long arm of the job: Influences of parental work on childrearing. In T. Luster & L. Okagaki (Eds.), *Parenting: An ecological perspective.* Hillsdale, NJ: Erlbaum.

Crystal, S., Shea, D., & Krishnaswami, S. (1992). Educational attainment, occupational history, and stratification: Determinants of later-life economic outcomes. *Journal of Gerontology: Social Sciences, 47,* S213–S221.

Csikszentmihalyi, M., & Larson, R. (1984). *Being adolescent: Conflict and growth in the teenage years.* New York: Basic Books.

Cumming, E., & Henry, W. E. (1961). *Growing old: The process of disengagement.* New York: Basic Books.

Curry, N. E., & Arnaud, S. H. (1984). Play in developmental preschool settings. In T. D. Yawkey & A. D. Pelligrini (Eds.), *Child's play: Developmental and applied.* Hillsdale, NJ: Erlbaum.

Dancer, L. S., & Gilbert, L. A. (1993). Spouses' family work participation and its relation to wives' occupational level. *Sex Roles, 28,* 127–145.

Drabman, R. S., & Thomas, M. H. (1974). Does media violence increase children's tolerance of real-life aggression? *Developmental Psychology, 10,* 418–421.

Drebing, C. E., & Gooden, W. E. (1991). The impact of the dream on mental health functioning in the male midlife transition. *International Journal of Aging and Human Development, 32,* 277–287.

Eccles, J. S., Lord, S., & Midgley, C. (1991). What are we doing to early adolescents? The impact of educational contexts on early adolescents. *American Journal of Education, 99,* 521–542.

Eccles, J. S., Midgley, C., Wigfield, A., Buchanan, C. M., Reuman, D., Flanagan, C., & Mac Iver, D. (1993). Development during adolescence: The impact of stage-environment fit on young adolescents' experiences in schools and in families. *American Psychologist, 48,* 90–101.

Ekerdt, D. J., Bossé, R., & Levkoff, S. (1985). Empirical test for phases of retirement: Findings from the Normative Aging Study. *Journal of Gerontology, 40,* 95–101.

Ekerdt, D. J., & DeViney, S. (1993). Evidence for a preretirement process among older male workers. *Journal of Gerontology: Social Sciences, 48,* S35–S43.

Ekerdt, D. J., & Vinick, B. H. (1991). Marital complaints in husband-working and husband-retired couples. *Research on Aging, 13,* 364–382.

Elkind, D. (1981). *The hurried child: Growing up too fast too soon.* Reading, MA: Addison-Wesley.

Ensminger, M. E., & Slusarcick, A. L. (1992). Paths to high school graduation or dropout: A longitudinal study of a first-grade cohort. *Sociology of Education, 65,* 95–113.

Entwisle, D. R., & Alexander, K. L. (1992). Summer setback: Race, poverty, school composition, and mathematics achievement in the first two years of school. *American Sociological Review, 57,* 72–84.

Eron, L. D. (1982). Parent-child interaction, television violence, and aggression of children. *American Psychologist, 37,* 197–211.

Etaugh, C., & Liss, M. B. (1992). Home, school, and playroom: Training grounds for adult gender roles. *Sex Roles, 26,* 129–147.

Evans, L., Ekerdt, D. J., & Bossé, R. (1985). Proximity to retirement and anticipatory involvement: Findings from the Normative Aging Study. *Journal of Gerontology, 40,* 368–374.

Farrell, M. P., & Rosenberg, S. D. (1981). *Men at midlife.* Dover, MA: Auburn House.

Featherman, D. L. (1980). Schooling and occupational careers: Constancy and change in worldly success. In O. G. Brim, Jr., & J. Kagan (Eds.), *Constancy and change in human development.* Cambridge, MA: Harvard University Press.

Fein, G. G. (1981). Pretend play: An integrative review. *Child Development, 52,* 1095–1118.

Fein, G. G. (1986). The affective psychology of play. In A. W. Gottfried & C. C. Brown (Eds.), *Play interactions: The contributions of play material and parental involvement to children's development.* Lexington, MA: Lexington Books.

Fiorentine, R. (1988). Increasing similarity in the values and life plans of male and female college students? Evidence and implications. *Sex Roles, 18,* 143–158.

Fisher, E. P. (1992). The impact of play on development: A meta-analysis. *Play and Culture, 5,* 159–181.

Fitzgerald, L. F., & Shullman, S. L. (1993). Sexual harassment: A research analysis and agenda for the 1990s. *Journal of Vocational Behavior, 42,* 5–27.

Folk, K. F., & Beller, A. H. (1993). Part-time work and child care choices for mothers of preschool children. *Journal of Marriage and the Family, 55,* 146–157.

Fraser, B. J., Walberg, H. J., Welch, W. W., & Hattie, J. A. (1987). Synthesis of educational productivity research. *International Journal of Educational Research, 11,* 145–252.

Frueh, T., & McGhee, P. H. (1975). Traditional sex-role development and the amount of time spent watching television. *Developmental Psychology, 11,* 109.

Fry, P. S. (1992). Major social theories of aging and their implications for counseling concepts and practice: A critical review. *Counseling Psychologist, 20,* 246–329.

Gandelman, R. (1992). *Psychobiology of behavioral development.* New York: Oxford University Press.

Garcia, E. E. (1993). Language, culture, and education. *Review of Educational Research, 19,* 51–98.

Gaskill, L. R. (1991). Same-sex and cross-sex mentoring of female proteges: A comparative analysis. *Career Development Quarterly, 40,* 48–63.

Gerbner, G., Gross, L., Signorielli, N., & Morgan, M. (1986). *Television's mean world: Violence profile No. 14–15.* Philadelphia: Annenberg School of Communications, University of Pennsylvania.

Giffin, H. (1984). The coordination of meaning in the creation of a shared make-believe reality. In I. Bretherton (Ed.), *Symbolic play: The*

development of social understanding. Orlando, FL: Academic Press.
Ginzberg, E. (1972). Toward a theory of occupational choice: A restatement. *Vocational Guidance Quarterly, 20,* 169–176.
Ginzberg, E. (1984). Career development. In D. Brown, L. Brooks, & Associates (Eds.), *Career choice and development.* San Francisco: Jossey-Bass.
Gordon, D. E. (1993). The inhibition of pretend play and its implications for development. *Human Development, 36,* 215–234.
Gottfredson, L. S. (1981). Circumscription and compromise: A developmental theory of occupational aspirations. *Journal of Counseling Psychology, 28,* 545–579.
Greenberger, E., & Steinberg, L. (1986). *When teenagers work: The psychological and social costs of adolescent employment.* New York: Basic Books.
Grotevant, H. D., & Cooper, C. R. (1988). The role of family experience in career exploration: A life-span perspective. In P. B. Baltes, D. L. Featherman, & R. M. Lerner (Eds.), *Life-span development and behavior* (Vol. 8). Hillsdale, NJ: Erlbaum.
Grotevant, H. D., Cooper, C. R., & Kramer, K. (1986). Exploration as a predictor of congruence in adolescents' career choices. *Journal of Vocational Behavior, 29,* 201–215.
Grotevant, H. D., & Durrett, M. E. (1980). Occupational knowledge and career development in adolescence. *Journal of Vocational Behavior, 17,* 171–182.
Guralnick, M. J., & Groom, J. M. (1988). Friendships of preschool children in mainstreamed playgroups. *Developmental Psychology, 24,* 595–604.
Gutek, B. A. (1985). *Sex and the workplace.* San Francisco: Jossey-Bass.
Gutek, B. A., & Koss, M. P. (1993). Changed women and changed organizations: Consequences of and coping with sexual harassment. *Journal of Vocational Behavior, 42,* 28–48.
Gutek, B. A., Searle, S., & Klepa, L. (1991). Rational versus gender role explanations for work-family conflict. *Journal of Applied Psychology, 76,* 560–568.
Hannah, J. S., & Kahn, S. E. (1989). The relationship of socioeconomic status and gender to the occupational choices of grade 12 students. *Journal of Vocational Behavior, 34,* 161–178.
Harris, M. J., & Rosenthal, R. (1986). Four factors in the mediation of teacher expectancy effects. In R. S. Feldman (Ed.), *The social psychology of education: Current research and theory.* Cambridge, England: Cambridge University Press.
Harris, P. L., & Kavanaugh, R. D. (1993). Young children's understanding of pretense. *Monographs of the Society for Research in Child Development, 58*(1, Serial No. 181).
Havighurst, R. J. (1982). The world of work. In B. B. Wolman (Ed.), *Handbook of developmental psychology.* Englewood Cliffs, NJ: Prentice-Hall.
Havighurst, R. J., Neugarten, B. L., & Tobin, S. S. (1968). Disengagement and patterns of aging. In B. L. Neugarten (Ed.), *Middle age and aging.* Chicago: University of Chicago Press.
Hedlund, B., & Ebersole, P. (1983). A test of Levinson's mid-life reevaluation. *Journal of Genetic Psychology, 143,* 189–192.
Helson, R., & Wink, P. (1992). Personality change in women from the early 40s to the early 50s. *Psychology and Aging, 7,* 46–55.
Henderson, S., Hesketh, B., & Tuffin, K. (1988). A test of Gottfredson's theory of circumscription. *Journal of Vocational Behavior, 32,* 37–48.
Herring, C., & Wilson-Sadberry, K. R. (1993). Preference or necessity? Changing work roles of black and white women, 1973–1990. *Journal of Marriage and the Family, 55,* 314–325.
Herzog, A. R., House, J. S., & Morgan, J. N. (1991). Relation of work and retirement to health and well-being in older age. *Psychology and Aging, 6,* 202–211.
Herzog, A. R., Kahn, R. L., Morgan, J. N., Jackson, J. S., & Antonucci, T. C. (1989). Age differences in productive activities. *Journal of Gerontology: Social Sciences, 44,* S129–S138.
Hetherington, E. M., Cox, M., & Cox, R. (1979). Play and social interaction in children following divorce. *Journal of Social Issues, 35,* 26–49.
Hoffman, L. W. (1989). Effects of maternal employment in the two-parent family. *American Psychologist, 44,* 283–292.
Holland, J. L. (1973). *Making vocational choices: A theory of careers.* Englewood Cliffs, NJ: Prentice-Hall.
Holland, J. L. (1985). *Making vocational choices: A theory of vocational personalities and work environments* (2nd ed.). Englewood Cliffs, NJ: Prentice-Hall.
Howard, A., & Bray, D. W. (1988). *Managerial lives in transition: Advancing age and changing times.* New York: Guilford Press.
Howes, C. (1988). Relations between early child care and schooling. *Developmental Psychology, 24,* 53–57.
Howes, C. (1990). Can the age of entry into child care and the quality of child care predict adjustment in kindergarten? *Developmental Psychology, 26,* 292–303.
Howes, C., & Matheson, C. C. (1992). Sequences in the development of competent play with peers: Social and social pretend play. *Developmental Psychology, 28,* 961–974.
Howes, C., Phillips, D. A., & Whitebook, M. (1992). Thresholds of quality: Implications for the social development of children in center-based child care. *Child Development, 63,* 449–460.
Huesmann, L. R. (1986). Psychological processes promoting the relation between exposure to media violence and aggressive behavior by the viewer. *Journal of Social Issues, 42*(3), 125–139.
Huesmann, L. R., Eron, L. D., Lefkowitz, M. M., & Walder, L. O. (1984). Stability of aggression over time and generations. *Developmental Psychology, 20,* 1120–1134.
Huston, A. C., Donnerstein, E., Fairchild, H., Feshbach, N. D., Katz, P. A., Murray, J. P., Rubinstein, E. A., Wilcox, B. L., & Zuckerman, D. (1992). *Big world, small screen.* Lincoln: University of Nebraska Press.
Huston, A. C., Wright, J. C., Rice, M. L., Kerkman, D., & St. Peters, M. (1990). Development of television viewing patterns in early childhood: A longitudinal investigation. *Developmental Psychology, 26,* 409–420.
Hyson, M. C., Hirsch-Pasek, K., & Rescorla, L. (1989). *Academic environments in early childhood: Challenge or pressure?* Summary report to the Spencer Foundation.
Jenkins, S. R. (1989). Longitudinal prediction of women's careers: Psychological, behavioral, and social-structural influences. *Journal of Vocational Behavior, 34,* 204–235.
Johnsen, E. P. (1991). Searching for the social and cognitive outcomes of children's play: A selective second look. *Play and Culture, 4,* 201–213.
Johnson, D. W., Johnson, R. T., & Maruyama, G. (1983). Interdependence and interpersonal attraction among heterogeneous and homogeneous individuals: A theoretical formulation and a meta-analysis of the research. *Review of Educational Research, 53,* 5–54.
Jussim, L., & Eccles, J. S. (1992). Teacher expectations. II: Construction and reflection of student achievement. *Journal of Personality and Social Psychology, 63,* 947–961.
Kagan, J., Kearsley, R. B., & Zelazo, P. R. (1978). *Infancy: Its place in human development.* Cambridge, MA: Harvard University Press.
Keating, N., & Jeffrey, B. (1983). Work careers of ever married and never married retired women. *Gerontologist, 23,* 416–421.
Kee, D. W. (1986). Computer play. In A. W. Gottfried & C. C. Brown (Eds.), *Play interactions. The contribution of play materials and parental involvement to children's development.* Lexington, MA: Lexington Books.
Kelso, G. I. (1977). The relation of school grade to ages and stages in vocational development. *Journal of Vocational Behavior, 10,* 287–301.
Kleiber, D., Larson, R., & Csikszentmihalyi, M. (1986). The experience of leisure in adolescence. *Journal of Leisure Research, 18,* 169–176.
Kohn, M. L., & Schooler, C. (1982). Job conditions and personality: A longitudinal assessment of their reciprocal effects. *American Journal of Sociology, 87,* 1257–1286.
Kohn, M. L., & Schooler, C. (in collaboration with J. Miller, K. A. Miller, C. Schoenbach, & R. Schoenberg). (1983). *Work and personality: An inquiry into the impact of social stratification.* Norwood, NJ: Ablex.
Kulik, J. A., & Kulik, C. C. (1992). Meta-analytic findings on grouping programs. *Gifted Child Quarterly, 36,* 73–77.
Kunkel, D., & Roberts, D. (1991). Young minds and marketplace values: Issues in children's advertising. *Journal of Social Issues, 47*(1), 57–72.
Lamb, M. E., Hwang, C., Bookstein, F. L., Broberg, A., Hult, G., & Frodi, M. (1988). Determinants of social competence in Swedish

preschoolers. *Developmental Psychology, 24,* 58–70.

Lamb, M. E., Sternberg, K. J., & Prodromidis, M. (1992). Nonmaternal care and the security of infant-mother attachment: A reanalysis of the data. *Infant Behavior and Development, 15,* 71–83.

Larwood, L., & Gutek, B. A. (1987). Working toward a theory of women's career development. In B. A. Gutek & L. Larwood (Eds.), *Women's career development.* Newbury Park, CA: Sage.

Lauver, P. J., & Jones, R. M. (1991). Factors associated with perceived career options in American Indian, White, and Hispanic rural high school students. *Journal of Counseling Psychology, 38,* 159–166.

Lee, V. E., Brooks-Gunn, J., Schnur, E., & Liaw, F. (1990). Are Head Start effects sustained? A longitudinal follow-up comparison of disadvantaged children attending Head Start, no preschool, and other preschool programs. *Child Development, 61,* 495–507.

Lepper, M. R. (1985). Microcomputers in education: Motivational and social issues. *American Psychologist, 40,* 1–18.

Lepper, M. R., & Gurtner, J. (1989). Children and computers: Approaching the twenty-first century. *American Psychologist, 44,* 170–178.

Lerner, J. V., Nitz, K., Talwar, R., & Lerner, R. M. (1989). On the functional significance of temperamental individuality: A developmental contextual view of the concept of goodness of fit. In G. A. Kohnstamm, J. E. Bates, & M. K. Rothbart (Eds.), *Temperament in childhood.* Chichester, England: Wiley.

Levinson, D. J. (1986). A conception of adult development. *American Psychologist, 41,* 3–13.

Levinson, D. J. (1990). A theory of life structure development in adulthood. In C. N. Alexander & E. J. Langer (Eds.), *Higher stages of human development: Perspectives on adult growth.* New York: Oxford University Press.

Levinson, D. J., with Darrow, C. N., Klein, E. B., Levinson, M. H., & McKee, B. (1978). *The seasons of a man's life.* New York: Ballantine Books.

Liebert, R. M., & Sprafkin, J. (1988). *The early window: Effects of television on children and youth* (3rd ed.). New York: Pergamon Press.

Lillard, A. S. (1993). Pretend play skills and the child's theory of mind. *Child Development, 64,* 348–371.

Linney, J. A., & Seidman, E. (1989). The future of schooling. *American Psychologist, 44,* 336–340.

Lloyd, D. N. (1978). Prediction of school failure from third-grade data. *Educational and Psychological Measurement, 38,* 1193–1200.

Lonner, W. J., Thorndike, R. M., Forbes, N. E., & Ashworth, C. (1985). The influence of television on measured cognitive abilities: A study with native Alaskan children. *Journal of Cross-Cultural Psychology, 16,* 355–380.

Mac Iver, D., & Reuman, D. A. (1988, April). *Decision-making in the classroom and early adolescents' valuing of mathematics.* Paper presented at the annual meeting of the American Educational Research Association, New Orleans.

Madden, N. A., & Slavin, R. E. (1983). Mainstreaming students with mild handicaps: Academic and social outcomes. *Review of Educational Research, 53,* 519–569.

McCaul, E. J., Donaldson, G. A., Coladarci, T., & Davis, W. E. (1992). Consequences of dropping out of school: Findings from high school and beyond. *Journal of Educational Research, 85,* 198–207.

McCune-Nicolich, L., & Fenson, L. (1984). Methodological issues in studying early pretend play. In T. D. Yawkey & A. D. Pellegrini (Eds.), *Child's play: Developmental and applied.* Hillsdale, NJ: Erlbaum.

McEvoy, G. M., & Cascio, W. F. (1989). Cumulative evidence of the relationship between employee age and job performance. *Journal of Applied Psychology, 74,* 11–17.

Menaghan, E. G., & Parcel, T. L. (1991). Transitions in work and family arrangements: Mothers' employment conditions, children's experiences, and child outcomes. In K. Pillemer & K. McCartney (Eds.), *Parent-child relations throughout life.* Hillsdale, NJ: Erlbaum.

Mercer, R. T., Nichols, E. G., & Doyle, G. C. (1989). *Transitions in a woman's life: Major life events in developmental context.* New York: Springer.

Midgley, C., Feldlaufer, H., & Eccles, J. S. (1989). Student/teacher relations and attitudes toward mathematics before and after the transition to junior high school. *Child Development, 60,* 981–992.

Minuchin, P. P., & Shapiro, E. K. (1983). The school as a context for social development. In E. M. Hetherington (Ed; P. H. Mussen, General Ed.), *Handbook of child psychology. Vol 4: Socialization, personality, and social development.* New York: Wiley.

Moen, P. (1985). Continuities and discontinuities in women's labor force activity. In G. H. Elder, J. (Ed.), *Life course dynamics. Trajectories and transitions, 1968–1980.* Ithaca, NY: Cornell University Press.

Moen, P. (1992). *Women's two roles: A contemporary dilemma.* New York: Auburn House.

Moorehouse, M. J. (1991). Linking maternal employment patterns to mother-child activities and children's school competence. *Developmental Psychology, 27,* 295–303.

National Education Goals Panel (1992). *The National Education Goals Report, 1992.* Washington, DC: U.S. Department of Education.

Nicolich, L. M. (1977). Beyond sensorimotor intelligence: Assessment of symbolic maturity through analysis of pretend play. *Merrill-Palmer Quarterly, 23,* 89–99.

Nock, S. L., & Kingston, P. W. (1988). Time with children: The impact of couples' work-time commitment. *Social Forces, 67,* 59–85.

O'Connell, B., & Bretherton, I. (1984). Toddler's play, alone and with mother: The role of maternal guidance. In I. Bretherton (Ed.), *Symbolic play: The development of social understanding.* Orlando, FL: Academic Press.

Odden, A. (1990). Class size and student achievement: Research-based policy alternatives. *Educational Evaluation and Policy Analysis, 12,* 213–227.

Ogbu, J. U. (1990). Cultural model, identity, and literacy. In J. W. Stigler, R. A. Shweder, & G. Herdt (Eds.), *Cultural psychology: Essays on comparative human development.* Cambridge, England: Cambridge University Press.

Ogletree, S. M., & Williams, S. W. (1990). Sex and sex-typing effects on computer attitudes and aptitude. *Sex Roles, 23,* 703–712.

O'Reilly, A. W., & Bornstein, M. H. (1993). Caregiver-child interaction in play. In M. H. Bornstein & A. W. O'Reilly (Eds.), *The role of play in the development of thought* (New Directions for Child Development, No. 59). San Francisco: Jossey-Bass.

Ornstein, S., & Isabella, L. A. (1990). Age vs. stage models of career attitudes of women: A partial replication and extension. *Journal of Vocational Behavior, 36,* 1–19.

Palmore, E. B., Burchett, B. M., Fillenbaum, G. G., George, L. K., & Wallman, L. M. (1985). *Retirement: Causes and consequences.* New York: Springer.

Parnes, H. S., & Less, L. (1985). Variation in selected forms of leisure activity among elderly males. In Z. S. Blau (Ed.), *Current perspectives on aging and the life cycle: Vol. 1. Work, retirement and social policy.* Greenwich, CT: JAI Press.

Parten, M. B. (1932). Social participation among preschool children. *Journal of Abnormal and Social Psychology, 27,* 243–269.

Pence, A. R. (1986). Infant schools in North America, 1825–1840. In S. Kilmer (Ed.), *Advances in early education and day care: A research annual* (Vol. 4). Greenwich, CT: JAI Press.

Peterson, P. L. (1977). Interactive effects of student anxiety, achievement orientation, and teacher behavior on student achievement and attitude. *Journal of Educational Psychology, 69,* 779–792.

Phillips, S. D. (1982). Career exploration in adulthood. *Journal of Vocational Behavior, 20,* 129–140.

Piaget, J. (1962). *Play, dreams and imitation in childhood.* New York: Norton. (Original work published 1951.)

Piaget, J. (1965). *The moral judgment of the child.* New York: Free Press. (Original work published 1932.)

Pines, M. (1978, September). Invisible playmates. *Psychology Today,* pp. 38–42, 106.

Pleck, J. H. (1985). *Working wives/working husbands.* Beverly Hills, CA: Sage.

Price, R. H. (1992). Psychosocial impact of job loss on individuals and families. *Current Directions in Psychological Science, 1,* 9–11.

Ragins, B. R., & McFarlin, D. B. (1990). Perceptions of mentor roles in cross-gender mentoring relationships. *Journal of Vocational Behavior, 37,* 321–339.

Ramey, C. T., & Ramey, S. L. (1992). Effective early intervention. *Mental Retardation, 30,* 337–345.

Rapkin, B. D., & Fischer, K. (1992). Personal goals of older adults: Issues in assessment and prediction. *Psychology and Aging, 7,* 127–137.

Reid, P. T., & Stephens, D. S. (1985). The roots of future occupations in childhood: A review of the literature on girls and careers. *Youth and Society, 16,* 267–288.

Rexroat, C. (1992). Changes in the employment continuity of succeeding cohorts of young women. *Work and Occupations, 19,* 18–34.

Reynolds, D. (1992). School effectiveness and school improvement: An updated review of the British literature. In D. Reynolds & P. Cuttance (Eds.), *School effectiveness: Research, policy, and practice.* London: Cassell.

Rhodes, S. R. (1983). Age-related differences in work attitudes and behavior: A review and conceptual analysis. *Psychological Bulletin, 93,* 328–367.

Rice, M. L., Huston, A. C., Truglio, R., & Wright, J. (1990). Words from 'Sesame Street': Learning vocabulary while viewing. *Developmental Psychology, 26,* 421–428.

Rist, R. C. (1970). Student social class and teacher expectations: The self-fulfilling prophecy in ghetto education. *Harvard Educational Review, 40,* 411–451.

Roberts, P., & Newton, P. M. (1987). Levinsonian studies of women's adult development. *Psychology and Aging, 2,* 154–163.

Rogoff, B. (1990). *Apprenticeship in thinking: Cognitive development in social context.* New York: Oxford University Press.

Rogoff, B., Mistry, J., Goncu, A., & Mosier, C. (1991). Cultural variation in the role relations of toddlers and their families. In M. H. Bornstein (Ed.), *Cultural approaches to parenting.* Hillsdale, NJ: Erlbaum.

Rosenthal, R., & Jacobson, L. (1968). *Pygmalion in the classroom.* New York: Holt, Rinehart & Winston.

Rosenwasser, S. M., Lingenfelter, M., & Harrington, A. F. (1989). Nontraditional gender role portrayals and children's gender role perceptions. *Journal of Applied Developmental Psychology, 10,* 97–105.

Rubin, K. H. (1982). Nonsocial play in preschoolers: Necessarily evil? *Child Development, 53,* 651–657.

Rubin, K. H., Fein, G., & Vandenberg, B. (1983). Play. In E. M. Hetherington (Ed.; P. H. Mussen, General Ed.), *Handbook of child psychology: Vol. 4. Socialization, personality, and social development.* New York: Wiley.

Ruff, H. A., & Saltarelli, L. M. (1993). Exploratory play with objects: Basic cognitive processes and individual differences. In M. H. Bornstein & A. W. O'Reilly (Eds.), *The role of play in the development of thought* (New Directions for Child Development, No. 59). San Francisco: Jossey-Bass.

Rutter, M. (1983). School effects on pupil progress: Research findings and policy implications. *Child Development, 54,* 1–29.

Rutter, M., Maughan, B., Mortimore, P., Ouston, J., & Smith, A. (1979). *Fifteen thousand hours: Secondary schools and their effects on children.* Cambridge, MA: Harvard University Press.

Scarr, S. (1984). *Mother care/other care.* New York: Basic Books.

Scarr, S., & Eisenberg, M. (1993). Child care research: Issues, perspectives, and results. *Annual Review of Psychology, 44,* 613–644.

Schor, J. B. (1991). *The overworked American: The unexpected decline of leisure.* New York: Basic Books.

Schramm, W., Lyle, J., & Parker, E. B. (1961). *Television in the lives of our children.* Stanford, CA: Stanford University Press.

Seleen, D. R. (1982). The congruence between actual and desired use of time by older adults: A predictor of life satisfaction. *Gerontologist, 22,* 95–99.

Shelton, B. A. (1992). *Women, men, and time: Gender differences in paid work, housework, and leisure.* Westport, CT: Greenwood Press.

Shore, C. (1986). Combinatorial play, conceptual development, and early multiword speech. *Developmental Psychology, 22,* 184–190.

Sigman, M., & Sena, R. (1993). Pretend play in high-risk and developmentally delayed children. In M. H. Bornstein & A. W. O'Reilly (Eds.), *The role of play in the development of thought.* (New Directions for Child Development, No. 59). San Francisco: Jossey-Bass.

Signorielli, N. (1991). *A sourcebook on children and television.* Westport, CT: Greenwood Press.

Simmons, R. G., & Blyth, D. A. (1987). *Moving into adolescence: The impact of pubertal change in school context.* New York: Aldine de Gruyter.

Singer, D. G., & Singer, J. L. (1990). *The house of make-believe: Children's play and the developing imagination.* Cambridge, MA: Harvard University Press.

Slade, A. (1987). Quality of attachment and early symbolic play. *Developmental Psychology, 23,* 78–85.

Slaughter-Defoe, D. T., Nakagawa, K., Takanishi, R., & Johnson, D. J. (1990). Toward cultural/ecological perspectives on schooling and achievement in African- and Asian-American children. *Child Development, 61,* 363–383.

Slavin, R. E. (1986). Cooperative learning: Engineering social psychology in the classroom. In R. S. Feldman (Ed.), *The social psychology of education: Current research and theory.* Cambridge, England: Cambridge University Press.

Slavin, R. E. (1989). Class size and student achievement: Small effects of small classes. *Educational Psychologist, 24,* 99–110.

Slavin, R. E. (1991). Cooperative learning and group contingencies. *Journal of Behavioral Education, 1,* 105–115.

Smith, P. K. (1978). A longitudinal study of social participation in preschool children: Solitary and parallel play reexamined. *Developmental Psychology, 14,* 517–523.

Sorensen, A. (1983). Women's employment patterns after marriage. *Journal of Marriage and the Family, 45,* 311–321.

Sorensen, A. B., & Hallinan, M. T. (1986). Effects of ability grouping on growth in academic achievement. *American Educational Research Journal, 23,* 519–542.

Sorensen, E. (1991). *Exploring the reasons behind the narrowing gender gap in earnings* (Urban Institute Report 1991–1992). Washington, DC: Urban Institute Press.

Spade, J. Z., & Reese, C. A. (1991). We've come a long way, maybe: College students' plans for work and family. *Sex Roles, 24,* 309–321.

Spitze, G. (1988). Women's employment and family relations: A review. *Journal of Marriage and the Family, 50,* 595–618.

Steinberg, L. (1984). The varieties and effects of work during adolescence. In M. E. Lamb, A. L. Brown, & B. Rogoff (Eds.), *Advances in developmental psychology* (Vol. 3). Hillsdale, NJ: Erlbaum.

Steinberg, L., & Dornbusch, S. M. (1991). Negative correlates of part-time employment during adolescence: Replication and elaboration. *Developmental Psychology, 27,* 304–313.

Steinberg, L., Dornbusch, S. M., & Brown, B. B. (1992). Ethnic differences in adolescent achievement: An ecological perspective. *American Psychologist, 47,* 723–729.

Steinberg, L., Fegley, S., & Dornbusch, S. M. (1993). Negative impact of part-time work on adolescent adjustment: Evidence from a longitudinal study. *Developmental Psychology, 29,* 171–180.

Stephan, W. G. (1978). School desegregation: An evaluation of the predictions made in Brown vs. Board of Education. *Psychological Bulletin, 85,* 217–238.

Stevenson, H. W., Chen, C., & Lee, S. Y. (1993). Mathematics achievement of Chinese, Japanese, and American children: Ten years later. *Science, 259,* 53–58.

Stevenson, H. W., Chen, C., & Uttal, D. H. (1990). Beliefs and achievement: A study of Black, White, and Hispanic children. *Child Development, 61,* 508–523.

Stevenson, H. W., & Lee, S. Y. (1990). Contexts of achievement: A study of American, Chinese, and Japanese children. *Monographs of the Society for Research in Child Development, 55*(1–2, Serial No. 221).

Stevenson, H. W., Lee, S. Y., & Stigler, J. W. (1986). Mathematics achievement of Chinese, Japanese, and American children. *Science, 231,* 693–699.

Stevenson, H. W., Stigler, J. W., Lee, S. Y., Lucker, G. W., Litamura, S., & Hsu, C. (1985). Cognitive performance and academic achievement of Japanese, Chinese, and American children. *Child Development, 56,* 718–734.

Stigler, J. W., Lee, S. Y., & Stevenson, H. W. (1987). Mathematics classrooms in Japan, Taiwan, and the United States. *Child Development, 58,* 1272–1285.

St. John, N. H. (1975). *School desegregation: Outcomes for children.* New York: Wiley.

Stroud, J. G. (1981). Women's careers: Work, family, and personality. In D. H. Eichorn, J. A. Clausen, N. Haan, M. P. Honzik, & P. H. Mussen (Eds.), *Present and past in middle life.* New York: Academic Press.

Sue, S., & Okazaki, S. (1990). Asian-American educational achievements: A phenomenon in search of explanation. *American Psychologist, 45,* 913–920.

Super, D. E. (1957). *The psychology of careers.* New York: Harper & Row.

Super, D. E. (1980). A life-span life-space approach to career development. *Journal of Vocational Behavior, 13,* 282–298.

Super, D. E. (1985). Coming of age in Middletown: Careers in the making. *American Psychologist, 40,* 405–414.

Super, D. E. (1991). A life-span life-space approach to career development: In D. Brown, L. Brooks, & Associates (Eds.), *Career choice and development: Applying contemporary theories to practice* (2nd ed.). San Francisco: Jossey-Bass.

Taylor, A. R., Asher, S. R., & Williams, G. A. (1987). The social adaptation of mainstreamed mildly retarded children. *Child Development, 58,* 1321–1334.

Taylor, M., Cartwright, B. S., & Carlson, S. M. (1993). A developmental investigation of children's imaginary companions. *Developmental Psychology, 29,* 276–285.

Thomas, M. H., Horton, R. W., Lippincott, E. C., & Drabman, R. S. (1977). Desensitization to portrayals of real-life aggression as a function of exposure to television violence. *Journal of Personality and Social Psychology, 35,* 450–458.

Trice, A. D., & McClellan, N. (1993). Do children's career aspirations predict adult occupations? An answer from a secondary analysis of a longitudinal study. *Psychological Reports, 72,* 368–370.

Unger, R., & Crawford, M. (1992). *Women and gender: A feminist psychology.* Philadelphia: Temple University Press.

Vaillant, G. E. (1977). *Adaptation to life.* Boston: Little, Brown.

Vandenberg, B. R. (1986). Beyond the ethology of play. In A. W. Gottfried & C. C. Brown (Eds.), *Play interactions. The contributions of play materials and parental involvement to children's development.* Lexington, MA: Lexington Books.

Vannoy, D., & Philliber, W. W. (1992). Wife's employment and quality of marriage. *Journal of Marriage and the Family, 54,* 387–398.

Van Velsor, E., & O'Rand, A. M. (1984). Family life cycle, work career patterns, and women's wages at midlife. *Journal of Marriage and the Family, 46,* 365–373.

Vondracek, F. W., Lerner, R. M., & Schulenberg, J. E. (1986). *Career development: A life-span developmental approach.* Hillsdale, NJ: Erlbaum.

Waite, L. J., Haggstrom, G., & Kanouse, D. E. (1986). The effects of parenthood on the career orientation and job characteristics of young adults. *Social Forces, 65,* 43–73.

Waldman, D. A., & Avolio, B. J. (1986). A meta-analysis of age differences in job performance. *Journal of Applied Psychology, 71,* 33–38.

Waldman, E. (1985). Today's girls in tomorrow's labor force: Projecting their participation and occupations. *Youth and Society, 16,* 375–392.

Warr, P. (1992). Age and occupational well-being. *Psychology and Aging, 7,* 37–45.

Weinstein, C. S. (1991). The classroom as a social context for learning. *Annual Review of Psychology, 42,* 493–525.

Weisner, T. S. (1984). Ecocultural niches of middle childhood: A cross-cultural perspective. In W. A. Collins (Ed.), *Development during middle childhood: The years from six to twelve.* Washington, DC: National Academy Press.

Williamson, R. C., Rinehart, A. D., & Blank, T. O. (1992). *Early retirement: Promises and pitfalls.* New York: Plenum.

Zaslow, M. J. (1991). Variation in child care quality and its implications for children. *Journal of Social Issues, 47*(2), 125–138.

Zigler, E. F. (1987). Formal schooling for four-year-olds? No. *American Psychologist, 42,* 254–260.

Zigler, E. F., & Finn Stevenson, M. F. (1993). *Children in a changing world: Developmental and social issues.* Pacific Grove, CA: Brooks/Cole.

Chapter 16: Psychological Disorders throughout the Life Span

Achenbach, T. M. (1982). *Developmental psychopathology* (2nd ed.). New York: Wiley.

Achenbach, T. M., & Edelbrock, C. S. (1978). The classification of child psychopathology: A review and analysis of empirical efforts. *Psychological Bulletin, 85,* 1275–1301.

Achenbach, T. M., Verhulst, F. C., Edelbrock, C. S., Baron, G. D., & Akkerhuis, G. W. (1987). Epidemiological comparisons of American and Dutch children: II. Behavioral/emotional problems reported by teachers for ages 6 to 11. *Journal of the American Academy of Child Psychiatry, 26,* 326–332.

Allen, A., & Blazer, D. G. (1991). Mood disorders. In J. Sadavoy, L. W. Lazarus, & L. F. Jarvik (Eds.), *Comprehensive review of geriatric psychiatry.* Washington, DC: American Psychiatric Press.

American Psychiatric Association. (1987). *Diagnostic and statistical manual of mental disorders (3rd ed., rev.) DSM-III-R.* Washington, DC: Author.

Anderson, K. E., Lytton, H., & Romney, D. M. (1986). Mothers' interactions with normal and conduct-disordered boys: Who affects whom? *Developmental Psychology, 22,* 604–609.

Angold, A., & Rutter, M. (1992). Effects of age and pubertal status on depression in a large clinical sample. *Development and Psychopathology, 4,* 5–28.

Arling, G., Harkins, E. B., & Capitman, J. A. (1986). Institutionalization and personal control: A panel study of impaired older people. *Research on Aging, 8,* 38–56.

Associated Press (1993, September 10). Alzheimer's treatment wins approval by FDA. *Washington Post,* p. A26.

Atlas, J. A., & Lapidus, L. (1987). Patterns of symbolic expression in subgroups of the childhood psychoses. *Journal of Clinical Psychology, 43,* 177–188.

Attie, I., & Brooks-Gunn, J. (1989). Development of eating problems in adolescent girls: A longitudinal study. *Developmental Psychology, 25,* 70–79.

Barkley, R. A., Fischer, M., Edelbrock, C., & Smallish, L. (1991). The adolescent outcome of hyperactive children diagnosed by research criteria: Mother-child interactions, family conflicts and maternal psychopathology. *Journal of Child Psychology and Psychiatry and Allied Disciplines, 32,* 233–255.

Baron-Cohen, S., Leslie, A. M., & Frith, U. (1985). Does the autistic child have a "theory of mind"? *Cognition, 21,* 37–46.

Baumrind, D. (1985). Familial antecedents of adolescent drug use: A developmental perspective. In C. L. Jones & R. J. Battjes, *Etiology of drug abuse: Implications for prevention* (NIDA Research Monograph No. 56, DHHS Pub. No. (ADM) 85–1335). Washington, DC: U.S. Government Printing Office.

Beardslee, W. R., Keller, M. B., Lavori, P. W., Staley, J., & Sacks, N. (1993). The impact of parental affective disorder on depression in offspring: A longitudinal follow-up in a nonreferred sample. *Journal of the American Academy of Child and Adolescent Psychiatry, 32,* 723–730.

Bemporad, J. R. (1979). Adult recollections of a formerly autistic child. *Journal of Autism and Developmental Disorders, 9,* 179–197.

Bemporad, J. R., & Wilson, A. (1978). A developmental approach to depression in childhood and adolescence. *Journal of the American Academy of Psychoanalysis, 6,* 325–352.

Berman, A. L., & Jobes, D. A. (1991). *Adolescent suicide: Assessment and intervention.* Washington, DC: American Psychological Association.

Blazer, D. G., Burchett, B., Service, C., & George, L. K. (1991). The association of age and depression among the elderly: An epidemiologic exploration. *Journal of Gerontology: Medical Sciences, 46,* M210–M215.

Bolla-Wilson, K., & Bleecker, M. L. (1989). Absence of depression in elderly adults. *Journal of Gerontology: Psychological Sciences, 44,* P53–P55.

Brandtstädter, J., & Renner, G. (1990). Tenacious goal pursuit and flexible goal adjustment: Explication and age-related analysis of assimilative and accommodative strategies of coping. *Psychology and Aging, 5,* 58–67.

Brinich, E., Drotar, D., & Brinich, P. (1989). Security of attachment and outcome of preschoolers with histories of nonorganic failure to thrive. *Journal of Clinical Child Psychology, 18,* 142–152.

Brook, J. S., Brook, D. W., Gordon, A. S., Whiteman, M., & Cohen, P. (1990). The psychosocial etiology of adolescent drug use: A family interactional approach. *Genetic, Social, and General Psychology Monographs, 116,* 111–267.

Brooks-Gunn, J., & Warren, M. P. (1989). Biological and social contributions to negative affect in young adolescent girls. *Child Development, 60,* 40–55.

Brown, G. W., & Harris, T. O. (1978). *Social origins of depression.* New York: Free Press.

Buhrmester, D., Camparo, L., Christensen, A., Gonzales, L. S., & Hinshaw, S. P. (1992). Mothers and fathers interacting in dyads and triads with normal and hyperactive sons. *Developmental Psychology, 28,* 500–509.

Cantwell, D. P., & Baker, L. (1992). Attention deficit disorder with and without hyperactivity: A review and comparison of matched groups. *Journal of the American Academy of Child and Adolescent Psychiatry, 31,* 432–438.

Chiverton, P., & Caine, E. D. (1989). Education to assist spouses in coping with Alzheimer's disease. *Journal of the American Geriatrics Society, 37,* 593–598.

Cicchetti, D., Beeghly, M., Carlson, V., Coster, W., Gersten, M., Rieder, C., & Toth, S. (1991). Development and psychopathology: Lessons from the study of maltreated children. In D. P. Keating & H. Rosen (Eds.), *Constructivist perspectives on developmental psychopathology and atypical development.* Hillsdale, NJ: Erlbaum.

Conn, D. K. (1991). Delirium and other organic mental disorders. In J. Sadavoy, L. W. Lazarus, & L. F. Jarvik (Eds.), *Comprehensive review of geriatric psychiatry.* Washington, DC: American Psychiatric Press.

Costa, P. T., Jr., Zonderman, A. B., & McCrae, R. R. (1991). Personality, defense, coping, and adaptation in older adulthood. In E. M. Cummings, A. L. Greene, & K. H. Karraker (Eds.), *Life-span developmental psychology: Perspectives on stress and coping.* Hillsdale, NJ: Erlbaum.

Coyne, J. C., & Downey, G. (1991). Social factors and psychopathology: Stress, social support, and coping processes. *Annual Review of Psychology, 42,* 401–425.

Crook, W. G. (1980). Can what a child eats make him dull, stupid, or hyperactive? *Journal of Learning Disabilities, 13,* 53–58.

Cunningham, C. E., & Barkley, R. A. (1979). The interactions of normal and hyperactive children with their mothers in free play and structured tasks. *Child Development, 50,* 217–224.

Deutsch, C. K., & Kinsbourne, M. (1990). Genetics and biochemistry in attention deficit disorder. In M. Lewis & S. M. Miller (Eds.), *Handbook of developmental psychopathology.* New York: Plenum.

DiBattista, D., & Shepherd, M. (1993). Primary school teachers' beliefs and advice to parents concerning sugar consumption and activity in children. *Psychological Reports, 72,* 47–55.

Dishion, T. J., Patterson, G. R., Stoolmiller, M., & Skinner, M. L. (1991). Family, school, and behavioral antecedents to early adolescent involvement with antisocial peers. *Developmental Psychology, 21,* 172–180.

Donenberg, G., & Baker, B. L. (1993). The impact of young children with externalizing behaviors on their families. *Journal of Abnormal Child Psychology, 21,* 179–198.

Dubow, E. F., Kausch, D. F., Blum, M. C., Reed, J., & Bush, E. (1989). Correlates of suicidal ideation and attempts in a community sample of junior high and high school students. *Journal of Clinical Child Psychology, 18,* 158–166.

DuPaul, G. J., & Barkley, R. A. (1993). Behavioral contributions to pharmacotherapy: The utility of behavioral methodology in medication treatment of children with Attention Deficit Hyperactivity Disorder. *Behavior Therapy, 24,* 47–65.

DuPaul, G. J., Barkley, R. A., & McMurray, M. B. (1991). Therapeutic effects of medication on ADHD: Implications for school psychologists. *School Psychology Review, 20,* 203–219.

Ellickson, P. L., & Hays, R. D. (1992). On becoming involved with drugs: Modeling adolescent drug use over time. *Health Psychology, 11,* 377–385.

Eron, L. D. (1987). The development of aggressive behavior from the perspective of a developing behaviorism. *American Psychologist, 42,* 435–442.

Esser, S. R., & Vitaliano, P. P. (1988). Depression, dementia, and social supports. *International Journal of Aging and Human Development, 26,* 289–301.

Farrell, A. D., Danish, S. J., & Howard, C. W. (1992). Relationship between drug use and other problem behaviors in urban adolescents. *Journal of Consulting and Clinical Psychology, 60,* 705–712.

Feingold, B. F. (1975). *Why your child is hyperactive.* New York: Random House.

Feinson, M. C., & Thoits, P. A. (1986). The distribution of distress among elders. *Journal of Gerontology, 41,* 225–233.

Felton, B. J., & Revenson, T. A. (1987). Age differences in coping with chronic illness. *Psychology and Aging, 2,* 164–170.

Felts, W. M., Chenier, T., & Barnes, R. (1992). Drug use and suicide ideation and behavior among North Carolina public school students. *American Journal of Public Health, 82,* 870–872.

Field, T. (1992). Infants of depressed mothers. *Development and Psychopathology, 4,* 49–66.

Fischer, M., Barkley, R. A., Edelbrock, C. S., & Smallish, L. (1990). The adolescent outcome of hyperactive children diagnosed by research criteria: II. Academic, attentional, and neuropsychological status. *Journal of Consulting and Clinical Psychology, 58,* 580–588.

Fischer, M., Barkley, R. A., Fletcher, K. E., & Smallish, L. (1993). The adolescent outcome of hyperactive children: Predictors of psychiatric, academic, social, and emotional adjustment. *Journal of the American Academy of Child and Adolescent Psychiatry, 32,* 324–332.

Fischer, M., Rolf, J. E., Hasazi, J. E., & Cummings, L. (1984). Follow-up of a preschool epidemiological sample: Cross-age continuities and predictions of later adjustment with internalizing and externalizing dimensions of behavior. *Child Development, 55,* 137–150.

Folkman, S., Lazarus, R. S., Pimley, S., & Novacek, J. (1987). Age differences in stress and coping processes. *Psychology and Aging, 2,* 171–184.

Folstein, S., & Rutter, M. (1977). Infantile autism: A genetic study of 21 twin pairs. *Journal of Child Psychology and Psychiatry, 18,* 297–321.

Frith, U. (1989). Autism and "theory of mind." In C. Gillberg (Ed.), *Diagnosis and treatment of autism.* New York: Plenum.

Garber, J. (1984). The developmental progression of depression in female children. In D. Cicchetti & K. Schneider-Rosen (Eds.), *Childhood depression* (New Directions for Child Development, No. 26). San Francisco: Jossey-Bass.

Garber, J., Weiss, B., & Shanley, N. (1993). Cognitions, depressive symptoms, and development in adolescents. *Journal of Abnormal Psychology, 102,* 47–57.

Gardner, L. J. (1972). Deprivation dwarfism. *Scientific American, 227,* 76–82.

Gardner, R. A. (1993). *Psychotherapy with children.* Northvale, NJ: Jason Aronson.

Garland, A., & Zigler, E. (1993). Adolescent suicide prevention: Current research and social policy implications. *American Psychologist, 48,* 169–182.

Garmezy, N. (1991). Resilience and vulnerability to adverse developmental outcomes associated with poverty. *American Behavioral Scientist, 34,* 416–430.

Gatz, M., & Hurwicz, M. L. (1990). Are old people more depressed? Cross-sectional data on Center for Epidemiological Studies depression scale factors. *Psychology and Aging, 5,* 284–290.

Gatz, M., & Pearson, C. G. (1988). Ageism revised and the provision of psychological services. *American Psychologist, 43,* 184–188.

Gatz, M., Popkin, S. J., Pino, C. D., & VandenBos, G. R. (1985). Psychological interventions in older adults. In J. E. Birren & K. W. Schaie (Eds.), *Handbook of the psychology of aging* (2nd ed.). New York: Van Nostrand Reinhold.

Gatz, M., & Smyer, M. (1992). The mental health system and older adults in the 1990s. *American Psychologist, 47,* 741–751.

Gelfand, D. M., & Peterson, L. (1985). *Child development and psychopathology.* Beverly Hills, CA: Sage.

Gillberg, C. (1991). Outcome in autism and autistic-like conditions. *Journal of the American Academy of Child and Adolescent Psychiatry, 30,* 375–382.

Gillberg, C., & Steffenburg, S. (1987). Outcome and prognostic factors in infantile autism and similar conditions: A population-based study of 46 cases followed through puberty. *Journal of Autism and Developmental Disorders, 17,* 273–287.

Girard, C. (1993). Age, gender, and suicide: A cross-national analysis. *American Sociological Review, 58,* 553–574.

Gold, M., & Petronio, R. J. (1980). Delinquent behavior in adolescence. In J. Adelson (Ed.), *Handbook of adolescent psychology.* New York: Wiley-Interscience.

Goodman, S. H., Brogan, D., Lynch, M. E., & Fielding, B. (1993). Social and emotional competence in children of depressed mothers. *Child Development, 64,* 516–531.

Goodyear, P., & Hynd, G. W. (1992). Attention-deficit disorder with (ADD/H) and without (ADD/WO) hyperactivity: Behavioral and neuropsychological differentiation. *Journal of Clinical Child Psychology, 21,* 273–305.

Gordon, R. A. (1990). *Anorexia and bulimia: Anatomy of a social epidemic.* Cambridge, MA: Basil Blackwell.

Gorman, J., Leifer, M., & Grossman, G. (1993). Nonorganic failure to thrive: Maternal history and current maternal functioning. *Journal of Clinical Child Psychology, 22,* 327–336.

Gotlib, I. H., & Hammen, C. L. (1992). *Psychological aspects of depression: Toward a cognitive-interpersonal integration.* Chichester, England: Wiley.

Green, W. H. (1986). Psychosocial dwarfism: Psychological and etiological considerations. In B. B. Lahey & A. E. Kazdin (Eds.), *Advances in clinical child psychology* (Vol. 9). New York: Plenum.

Gross, M. D., Tofanelli, R. A., Butzirus, S. M., & Snodgrass, E. W. (1987). The effect of diets rich in and free from additives on the behavior of children with hyperkinetic and learning disorders. *Journal of the American Academy of Child and Adolescent Psychiatry, 26,* 53–55.

Gurland, B. (1991). Epidemiology of psychiatric disorders. In J. Sadavoy, L. W. Lazarus, & L. F. Jarvik (Eds.), *Comprehensive review of geriatric psychiatry.* Washington, DC: American Psychiatric Press.

Hall, G. S. (1904). *Adolescence* (2 vols). New York: Appleton.

Harley, J. P., Ray, R. S., Tomasi, L., Eichman, P. L., Matthews, C. G., & Chun, R. (1978). Hyperkinesis and food additives: Testing the Feingold hypothesis. *Pediatrics, 61,* 818–828.

Harris, S. L., Handleman, J. S., Gordon, R., Kristoff, B., & Fuentes, F. (1991). Changes in cognitive and language functioning of preschool children with autism. *Journal of Autism and Developmental Disorders, 21,* 281–290.

Hawkins, J. D., Catalano, R. F., & Miller, J. Y. (1992). Risk and protective factors for alcohol and other drug problems in adolescence and early adulthood: Implications for substance abuse prevention. *Psychological Bulletin, 112,* 64–105.

Hechtman, L., Weiss, G., & Perlman, T. (1984). Young adult outcomes of hyperactive children who received long-term stimulant treatment. *Journal of the American Academy of Child Psychiatry, 23,* 261–269.

Henggeler, S. W. (1989). *Delinquency in adolescence.* (Developmental Clinical Psychology and Psychiatry, Vol. 18). Newbury Park, CA: Sage.

Heston, L. L., & White, J. A. (1991). *The vanishing mind: A practical guide to Alzheimer's disease and other dementias.* New York: W. H. Freeman.

Hill, P. (1993). Recent advances in selected aspects of adolescent development. *Journal of Child Psychology and Psychiatry and Allied Disciplines, 34,* 69–99.

Hinshaw, S. P. (1991). Stimulant medication and the treatment of aggression in children with attention deficits. *Journal of Clinical Child Psychology, 20,* 301–312.

Hinz, L. D., & Williamson, D. A. (1987). Bulimia and depression: A review of the affective variant hypothesis. *Psychological Bulletin, 102,* 150–158.

Holahan, C. J., & Moos, R. H. (1986). Personality, coping, and family resources in stress resistance: A longitudinal analysis. *Journal of Personality and Social Psychology, 51,* 389–395.

Holahan, C. J., & Moos, R. H. (1987). Personal and contextual determinants of coping strategies. *Journal of Personality and Social Psychology, 52,* 946–955.

Holroyd, S., & Baron-Cohen, S. (1993). How far can people with autism go in developing a theory of mind? *Journal of Autism and Developmental Disorders, 23,* 379–385.

Horwitz, A. V., & White, H. R. (1987). Gender role orientations and styles of pathology among adolescents. *Journal of Health and Social Behavior, 28,* 158–170.

Howard-Pitney, B., LaFramboise, T. D., Basil, M., September, B., & Johnson, M. (1992). Psychological and social indicators of suicide ideation and suicide attempts in Zuni adolescents. *Journal of Consulting and Clinical Psychology, 60,* 473–476.

Hsu, L. K. G. (1990). *Eating disorders.* New York: Guilford Press.

Hughes, C., & Russell, J. (1993). Autistic children's difficulty with mental disengagement with an object: Its implications for theories of autism. *Developmental Psychology, 29,* 498–510.

Irion, J. C., & Blanchard-Fields, F. (1987). A cross-sectional comparison of adaptive coping in adulthood. *Journal of Gerontology, 42,* 502–504.

Jacobvitz, D., & Sroufe, L. A. (1987). The early caregiver-child relationship and attention-deficit disorder with hyperactivity in kindergarten: A prospective study. *Child Development, 58,* 1496–1504.

Jessor, R. (1987). Problem-behavior theory, psychosocial development, and adolescent problem drinking. *British Journal of Addiction, 82,* 331–342.

Jessor, R., Donovan, J. E., & Costa, F. M. (1991). *Beyond adolescence: Problem behavior and young adult development.* Cambridge, England: Cambridge University Press.

Joffe, R. T., & Offord, D. R. (1990). Epidemiology. In G. MacLean (Ed.), *Suicide in children and adolescents.* Toronto: Hogrefe and Huber.

Johnson, C. L., Stuckey, M. K., Lewis, L. D., & Schwartz, D. M. (1982). Bulimia: A descriptive survey of 316 cases. *International Journal of Eating Disorders, 2,* 3–16.

Johnson, J. H., Rasbury, W. C., & Siegel, L. J. (1986). *Approaches to child treatment: Introduction to theory, research, and practice.* New York: Pergamon Press.

Johnston, L. D., O'Malley, P. M., & Bachman, J. G. (1985). *Use of licit and illicit drugs by America's high school students 1975–1984* (DHHS Publication No. ADM 85–1394). Rockville, MD: National Institute on Drug Abuse.

Jones, D. J., Fox, M. M., Babigian, H. M., & Hutton, H. E. (1980). Epidemiology of anorexia nervosa in Monroe County, New York: 1960–1976. *Psychosomatic Medicine, 42,* 551–558.

Jorm, A. F. (1987). Sex and age differences in depression: A quantitative synthesis of published research. *Australian and New Zealand Journal of Psychiatry, 21,* 46–53.

Kandel, D. B., & Davies, M. (1991). Decline in use of illicit drugs by high school students in New York State: A comparison with national data. *American Journal of Public Health, 81,* 1064–1067.

Kanner, A. D., Coyne, J. C., Schaefer, C., & Lazarus, R. S. (1981). Comparison of two modes of stress measurement: Daily hassles and uplifts versus major life events. *Journal of Behavioral Medicine, 4,* 1–39.

Kanner, L. (1943). Autistic disturbances of affective contact. *Nervous Child, 2,* 217–250.

Kashani, J. H., & Carlson, G. A. (1985). Major depressive disorder in a preschooler. *Journal of the American Academy of Child Psychiatry, 24,* 490–494.

Kashani, J. H., Orvaschel, H., Rosenberg, T. K., & Reid, J. C. (1989). Psychopathology in a community sample of children and adolescents: A developmental perspective. *Journal of the American Academy of Child and Adolescent Psychiatry, 28,* 701–706.

Kaszniak, A. W. (1990). Psychological assessment of the aging individual. In J. E. Birren & K. W. Schaie (Eds.), *Handbook of the psychology of aging* (3rd ed.). San Diego: Academic Press.

Kendall, P. C., Lerner, R. M., & Craighead, W. E. (1984). Human development and intervention in childhood psychopathology. *Child Development, 55,* 71–82.

Kendler, K. S., Kessler, R. C., Neale, M. C., Heath, A. C., & Eaves, L. J. (1993). The prediction of major depression in women: Toward an integrated etiologic model. *American Journal of Psychiatry, 150,* 1139–1148.

Kendler, K. S., MacLean, C., Neale, M. C., Kessler, R. C., Heath, A. C., & Eaves, L. J. (1991). The genetic epidemiology of bulimia nervosa. *American Journal of Psychiatry, 148,* 1627–1637.

Kendler, K. S., Neale, M. C., Kessler, R. C., Heath, A. C., & Eaves, L. J. (1992). A population-based twin study of major depression in women: The impact of varying definitions of illness. *Archives of General Psychiatry, 49,* 257–266.

Kessler, R. C., Foster, C., Webster, P. S., & House, J. S. (1992). The relationship between age and depressive symptoms in two national surveys. *Psychology and Aging, 7,* 119–126.

King, N. J., Ollendick, T. H., & Gullone, E. (1991). Negative affectivity in children and adolescents: Relations between anxiety and depression. *Clinical Psychology Review, 11,* 441–459.

Klerman, G. L. (1983). Problems in the definition and diagnosis of depression in the elderly. In L. D. Breslau & M. R. Haug (Eds.), *Depression and aging: Causes, care, and consequences.* New York: Springer.

Kosky, R. (1983). Childhood suicidal behavior. *Journal of Child Psychology and Psychiatry, 24,* 457–468.

Kovacs, M., Feinberg, T. L., Crouse-Novak, M., Paulauskas, S. L., Pollock, M., & Finkelstein, R. (1984). Depressive disorders in childhood: II. A longitudinal study of the risk for a subsequent major depression. *Archives of General Psychiatry, 41,* 643–649.

Kovacs, M., & Goldston, D. (1991). Cognitive and social cognitive development of depressed children and adolescents. *Journal of the American Academy of Child and Adolescent Psychiatry, 30,* 388–392.

Lachenmeyer, J. R., & Davidovicz, H. (1987). Failure to thrive: A critical review. In B. B. Lahey & A. E. Kazdin (Eds.), *Advances in clinical child psychology* (Vol. 10). New York and London: Plenum.

Lambert, M. C., Weisz, J. R., & Knight, F. (1989). Over- and undercontrolled clinic referral problems of Jamaican and American children and adolescents: The culture general and the culture specific. *Journal of Consulting and Clinical Psychology, 57,* 467–472.

Lambert, M. C., Weisz, J. R., Knight, F., Desrosiers, M., Overly, K., & Thesiger, C. (1992). Jamaican and American adult perspectives on child psychopathology: Further exploration of the threshold model. *Journal of Consulting and Clinical Psychology, 60,* 146–149.

Langer, E. J., & Rodin, J. (1976). The effects of choice and enhanced personal responsibility for the aged: A field experiment in an institutional setting. *Journal of Personality and Social Psychology, 34,* 191–198.

Larson, R., & Ham, M. (1993). Stress and "storm and stress" in early adolescence: The relationship of negative events with dysphoric affect. *Developmental Psychology, 29,* 130–140.

Larson, R., & Lampman-Petraitis, C. (1989). Daily emotional states as reported by children and adolescents. *Child Development, 60,* 1250–1260.

La Rue, A., Dessonville, C., & Jarvik, L. F. (1985). Aging and mental disorders. In J. E. Birren & K. W. Schaie (Eds.), *Handbook of the psychology of aging* (2nd ed.). New York: Van Nostrand Reinhold.

Lasoski, M. C., & Thelen, M. H. (1987). Attitudes of older and middle-aged persons toward mental health intervention. *Gerontologist, 27,* 288–292.

Lazarus, L. W., Sadavoy, J., & Langsley, P. R. (1991). Individual psychotherapy. In J. Sadavoy, L. W. Lazarus, & L. F. Jarvik (Eds.), *Comprehensive review of geriatric psychiatry.* Washington, DC: American Psychiatric Press.

Lazarus, R. S. (1993). From psychological stress to the emotions: A history of changing outlooks. *Annual Review of Psychology, 44,* 1–21.

Lazarus, R. S., & DeLongis, A. (1983). Psychological stress and coping in aging. *American Psychologist, 38,* 245–254.

Lazarus, R. S., & Folkman, S. (1984). *Stress, appraisal, and coping.* New York: Springer.

Leslie, A. M. (1992). Pretense, autism, and theory-of-mind module. *Current Directions in Psychological Science, 1,* 18–21.

Lieberman, M. A. (1983). Social contexts of depression. In L. D. Breslau & M. R. Haug (Eds.), *Depression and aging: Causes, care, and consequences.* New York: Springer.

Loeber, R. (1982). The stability of antisocial and delinquent child behavior: A review. *Child Development, 53,* 1431–1446.

Lord, C., Mulloy, C., Wendelboe, M., & Schopler, E. (1991). Pre- and perinatal factors in high-functioning females and males with autism. *Journal of Autism and Developmental Disorders, 21,* 197–209.

Lovaas, O. I. (1987). Behavioral treatment and normal educational and intellectual functioning in young autistic children. *Journal of Consulting and Clinical Psychology, 55,* 3–9.

Lovaas, O. I., Smith, T., & McEachin, J. J. (1989). Clarifying comments on the young autism study: Reply to Schopler, Short, and Mesibov. *Journal of Consulting and Clinical Psychology, 57,* 165–167.

Lozoff, B. (1989). Nutrition and behavior. *American Psychologist, 44,* 231–236.

Lynam, D., Moffitt, T., & Stouthamer-Loeber, M. (1993). Explaining the relation between IQ and delinquency: Class, race, test motivation, school failure, or self-control. *Journal of Abnormal Psychology, 102,* 187–196.

Mannuzza, S., Klein, R. G., Bessler, A., Malloy, P., & LaPadula, M. (1993). Adult outcome of hyperactive boys: Educational achievement, occupational rank, and psychiatric status. *Archives of General Psychiatry, 50,* 565–576.

Manuelidis, E. E., De Figueiredo, J. M., Kim, J. H., Fritch, W. W., & Manuelidis, L. (1988). Transmission studies from blood of Alzheimer disease patients and healthy relatives. *Proceedings of the National Academy of Sciences, 85,* 4898–4901.

McCall, P. L. (1991). Adolescent and elderly white male suicide trends: Evidence of changing well-being? *Journal of Gerontology: Social Sciences, 46,* S43–S51.

McConville, B. J., Boag, L. C., & Purohit, A. P. (1973). Three types of childhood depression. *Canadian Psychiatric Association Journal, 18,* 133–138.

McCrae, R. R. (1982). Age differences in the use of coping mechanisms. *Journal of Gerontology, 37,* 454–460.

McCrae, R. R., & Costa, P. T., Jr. (1986). Personality, coping, and coping effectiveness in an adult sample. *Journal of Personality, 54,* 385–405.

McLanahan, S. S., & Sorensen, A. B. (1985). Life events and psychological well-being over the life course. In G. H. Elder, Jr. (Ed.), *Life course dynamics: Trajectories and transitions, 1968–1980.* Ithaca, NY: Cornell University Press.

Milich, R., & Loney, J. (1979). The role of hyperactive and aggressive symptomology in predicting adolescent outcome among hyperactive children. *Journal of Pediatric Psychology, 4,* 93–112.

Milich, R., & Pelham, W. E. (1986). Effects of sugar ingestion on the classroom and playgroup behavior of attention deficit disordered boys. *Journal of Consulting and Clinical Psychology, 54,* 714–718.

Milich, R., Wolraich, M., & Lindgren, S. (1986). Sugar and hyperactivity: A critical review of empirical findings. *Clinical Psychology Review, 6,* 493–513.

Minuchin, S., Rosman, B. L., & Baker, L. (1978). *Psychosomatic families: Anorexia nervosa in context.* Cambridge, MA: Harvard University Press.

Moldin, S. O., Reich, T., & Rice, J. P. (1991). Current perspectives on the genetics of unipolar depression. *Behavior Genetics, 21,* 211–242.

Monroe, S. M., & Simons, A. D. (1991). Diathesis-stress theories in the context of life stress research: Implications for the depressive disorders. *Psychological Bulletin, 110,* 406–425.

Mulvey, E. P., Arthur, M. W., & Reppucci, N. D. (1993). The prevention and treatment of juvenile delinquency: A review of the research. *Clinical Psychology Review, 13,* 133–167.

Myers, J. K., Weissman, M. M., Tischler, G. L., Holzer, C. E. III, Leaf, P. J., & Orvaschel, H. (1984). Six-month prevalence of psychiatric disorders in three communities. *Archives of General Psychiatry, 41,* 959–967.

Newmann, J. P. (1989). Aging and depression. *Psychology and Aging, 4,* 150–165.

Nolen-Hoeksema, S. (1990). *Sex differences in depression.* Stanford, CA: Stanford University Press.

Nolen-Hoeksema, S., Girgus, J. S., & Seligman, M. E. P. (1986). Learned helplessness in children: A longitudinal study of depression, achievement, and explanatory style. *Journal of Personality and Social Psychology, 51,* 435–442.

Nolen-Hoeksema, S., Girgus, J. S., & Seligman, M. E. P. (1992). Predictors and consequences of childhood depressive symptoms: A 5-year longitudinal study. *Journal of Abnormal Psychology, 101,* 405–422.

Nolen-Hoeksema, S., Morrow, J., & Fredrickson, B. L. (1993). Response styles and the duration of episodes of depressed mood. *Journal of Abnormal Psychology, 102,* 20–28.

Offer, D., & Schonert-Reichl, K. A. (1992). Debunking the myths of adolescence: Findings from recent research. *Journal of the American Academy of Child and Adolescent Psychiatry, 31,* 1003–1013.

Ostrov, E., Offer, D., & Howard, K. I. (1989). Gender differences in adolescent symptomatology: A normative study. *Journal of the American Academy of Child and Adolescent Psychiatry, 28,* 394–398.

Pagel, M., & Becker, J. (1987). Depressive thinking and depression: Relations with personality and social resources. *Journal of Personality and Social Psychology, 52,* 1043–1052.

Pastalan, L. A. (1983). Environmental displacement: A literature reflecting old-person-environment transactions. In G. D. Rowles & R. J. Ohta (Eds.), *Aging and milieu: Environmental perspectives on growing old.* New York: Academic Press.

Pataki, C. S., & Carlson, G. A. (1990). Major depression in childhood. In M. Hersen and C. G. Last (Eds.), *Handbook of child and adult psychopathology: A longitudinal perspective.* New York: Pergamon Press.

Pearlin, L. I. (1980). Life strains and psychological distress among adults. In N. J. Smelser &

E. H. Erikson (Eds.), *Themes of work and love in adulthood.* Cambridge, MA: Harvard University Press.

Pelham, W. E., Jr., Carlson, C., Sams, S. E., Vallano, G., Dixon, M. J., & Hoza, B. (1993). Separate and combined effects of methylphenidate and behavior modification on boys with attention deficit-hyperactivity disorder in the classroom. *Journal of Consulting and Clinical Psychology, 61,* 506–515.

Petersen, A. C., Compas, B. E., Brooks-Gunn, J., Stemmler, M., Ey, S., & Grant, K. E. (1993). Depression in adolescence. *American Psychologist, 48,* 155–168.

Petersen, A. C., & Hamburg, B. A. (1986). Adolescence: A developmental approach to problems and psychopathology. *Behavior Therapy, 17,* 480–499.

Petersen, A. C., Sarigiani, P. A., & Kennedy, R. E. (1991). Adolescent depression: Why more girls? *Journal of Youth and Adolescence, 20,* 247–271.

Peterson, C., & Seligman, M. E. P. (1984). Causal explanations as a risk factor for depression: Theory and evidence. *Psychological Review, 91,* 347–374.

Pfeffer, C. R. (1986). *The suicidal child.* New York: Guilford Press.

Pfeffer, C. R., Klerman, G. L., Hurt, S. W., Lesser, M., Peskin, J. R., & Siefker, C. A. (1991). Sucidal children grow up: Demographic and clinical risk factors for adolescent suicide attempts. *Journal of the American Academy of Child and Adolescent Psychiatry, 30,* 609–616.

Pfeiffer, E. (1977). Psychopathology and social pathology. In J. E. Birren & K. W. Schaie (Eds.), *Handbook of the psychology of aging.* New York: Van Nostrand Reinhold.

Phares, V., & Compas, B. (1992). The role of fathers in child and adolescent psychopathology: Make room for daddy. *Psychological Bulletin, 111,* 387–412.

Polivy, J., & Herman, C. P. (1985). Dieting and binging: A causal analysis. *American Psychologist, 40,* 193–201.

Quay, H. C., Routh, D. K., & Shapiro, S. K. (1987). Psychopathology of childhood: From description to validation. *Annual Review of Psychology, 38,* 491–532.

Regier, D. A., Boyd, J. H., Burke, J. D., Rae, D. F., Myers, J. K., Kramer, M., Robins, L. N., George, L. K., Karno, M., & Locke, B. Z. (1988). One-month prevalence of mental disorders in the United States. *Archives of General Psychiatry, 45,* 977–986.

Reich, J. W., & Zautra, A. J. (1989). A perceived control intervention for at-risk older adults. *Psychology and Aging, 4,* 415–424.

Reich, J. W., & Zautra, A. J. (1990). Dispositional control beliefs and the consequences of a control-enhancing intervention. *Journals of Gerontology: Psychological Sciences, 45,* P46–P51.

Renner, L. (1985, March 2). Hyperactivity difficult to diagnose, control. *Lexington Herald-Leader,* p. B6.

Robins, L. N. (1966). *Deviant children grow up: A sociological and psychiatric study of sociopathic personality.* Baltimore: Williams & Wilkins.

Robins, L. N. (1979). Follow-up studies. In H. C. Quay & J. S. Werry (Eds.), *Psychopathological disorders of childhood* (2nd ed.). New York: Wiley.

Robins, L. N., & Regier, D. A. (Eds.). (1991). *Psychiatric disorders in America: The Epidemiologic Catchment Area Study.* New York: Free Press.

Rodin, J. (1986). Aging and health: Effects of the sense of control. *Science, 233,* 1271–1276.

Rodin, J., & Langer, E. J. (1977). Long-term effects of a control-relevant intervention with the institutionalized aged. *Journal of Personality and Social Psychology, 35,* 897–902.

Rodin, J., Striegel-Moore, R. H., & Silberstein, L. R. (1990). Vulnerability and resilience in the age of eating disorders: Risk and protective factors for bulimia nervosa. In J. Rolf, A. S. Masten, D. Cicchetti, K. H. Nuechterlein, & S. Weintraub (Eds.), *Risk and protective factors in the development of psychopathology.* Cambridge, England: Cambridge University Press.

Rook, K., Dooley, D., & Catalano, R. (1991). Age differences in workers' efforts to cope with economic distress. In J. Eckenrode (Ed.), *The social context of coping.* New York: Plenum.

Rosenthal, P. A., & Rosenthal, S. (1984). Suicidal behavior by preschool children. *American Journal of Psychiatry, 141,* 520–525.

Rowe, D. C., Rodgers, J. L., Meseck-Bushey, S., & St. John, C. (1989). Sexual behavior and nonsexual deviance: A sibling study of their relationship. *Developmental Psychology, 25,* 61–69.

Rubenstein, J. L., Heeren, T., Housman, D., Rubin, C., & Stechler, G. (1989). Suicidal behavior in "normal" adolescents: Risk and protective factors. *American Journal of Orthopsychiatry, 59,* 59–71.

Russell, G. F. M., Szmukler, G. I., Dare, C., & Eisler, I. (1987). An evaluation of family therapy in anorexia nervosa and bulimia nervosa. *Archives of General Psychiatry, 44,* 1047–1056.

Rutter, M. (1979). Protective factors in children's responses to stress and disadvantage. In M. W. Kent & J. E. Rolf (Eds.), *Primary prevention of psychopathology: Vol. 3. Social competence in children.* Hanover, NH: University Press of New England.

Rutter, M. (1987). Psychosocial resilience and protective mechanisms. *American Journal of Orthopsychiatry, 57,* 316–331.

Rutter, M. (1989). Pathways from childhood to adult life. *Journal of Child Psychology and Psychiatry, 30,* 23–51.

Rutter, M., & Schopler, E. (1987). Autism and pervasive developmental disorders: Concepts and diagnostic issues. *Journal of Autism and Developmental Disorders, 17,* 159–186.

Ryan, N. D., Puig-Antich, J., Ambrosini, P., Rabinovich, H., Robinson, D., & Nelson, B. (1987). The clinical picture of major depression in children and adolescents. *Archives of General Psychiatry, 44,* 854–861.

Sadowski, C., & Kelley, M. L. (1993). Social problem-solving in suicidal adolescents. *Journal of Consulting and Clinical Psychology, 61,* 121–127.

Sampson, R. J., & Laub, J. H. (1993). *Crime in the making: Pathways and turning points through life.* Cambridge, MA: Harvard University Press.

Scalf-McIver, L., & Thompson, J. K. (1989). Family correlates of bulimic characteristics in college females. *Journal of Clinical Psychology, 45,* 467–472.

Schopler, E., Short, A., & Mesibov, G. (1989). Relation of behavioral treatment to "normal functioning": Comment on Lovaas. *Journal of Consulting and Clinical Psychology, 57,* 162–164.

Scott, D. W. (1986). Anorexia nervosa: A review of possible genetic factors. *International Journal of Eating Disorders, 5,* 1–20.

Shavit, Y., & Rattner, A. (1988). Age, crime, and the early life course. *American Journal of Sociology, 93,* 1457–1470.

Shedler, J., & Block, J. (1990). Adolescent drug use and psychological health. *American Psychologist, 45,* 612–630.

Silver, L. B. (1992). *Attention-deficit hyperactivity disorder: A clinical guide to diagnosis and treatment.* Washington, DC: American Psychiatric Press.

Simons, R. F., Robertson, J. F., & Downs, W. R. (1989). The nature of the association between parental rejection and delinquent behavior. *Journal of Youth and Adolescence, 18,* 297–309.

Sines, J. O. (1987). Influence of the home and family environment on childhood dysfunction. In B. B. Lahey & A. E. Kazdin (Eds.), *Advances in clinical child psychology* (Vol. 10). New York and London: Plenum.

Smith, K., & Crawford, S. (1986). Suicidal behavior among "normal" high school students. *Suicide and Life-Threatening Behavior, 16,* 313–325.

Smolak, L., & Levine, M. P. (1993). Separation-individuation difficulties and the distinction between bulimia nervosa and anorexia nervosa in college women. *International Journal of Eating Disorders, 14,* 33–41.

Smoller, J. W. (1986). The etiology and treatment of childhood. In G. C. Ellenbogen (Ed.), *Oral sadism and the vegetarian personality: Readings from the Journal of Polymorphous Perversity.* New York: Brunner/Mazel. (Originally published by Wry-Bred Press.)

Spitz, R. A. (1946). Anaclitic depression: An inquiry into the genesis of psychiatric conditions in early childhood, II. *Psychoanalytic Study of the Child, 2,* 313–342.

Spitzer, R. L., Yanovski, S., Wadden, T., Wing, R., Marcus, M. D., Stunkard, A., Devlin, M., Mitchell, J., Hasin, D., & Horne, R. L. (1993). Binge eating disorder: Its further validation in a multisite study. *International Journal of Eating Disorders, 13,* 137–153.

Sroufe, L. A., & Rutter, M. (1984). The domain of developmental psychopathology. *Child Development, 55,* 17–29.

Stapley, J. C., & Haviland, J. M. (1989). Beyond depression: Gender differences in normal adolescents' emotional experiences. *Sex Roles, 20,* 295–308.

Steffenburg, S., Gillberg, C., Hellgren, L., Andersson, L., Gillberg, I. C., Jakobsson, G., & Bohman, M. (1989). A twin study of autism in Denmark, Finland, Iceland, Norway, and Sweden. *Journal of Child Psychology and Psychiatry, 30,* 405–416.

Steffensmeier, D., & Streifel, C. (1991). Age, gender, and crime across three historical periods—1935, 1960, and 1985. *Social Forces, 69,* 869–894.

Stevenson, J. (1992). Evidence for a genetic etiology in hyperactivity in children. *Behavior Genetics, 22,* 337–344.

Stewart, M. A., Pitts, F. N., Craig, A. G., & Dieruf, W. (1966). The hyperactive child syndrome. *American Journal of Orthopsychiatry, 36,* 861–867.

St. George-Hyslop, P. H., Tanzi, R. E., Polinsky, R. J., Haines, J. L., Nee, L., & Watkins, P.C. (1987). The genetic defect causing familial Alzheimer's disease maps on chromosome 21. *Science, 235,* 885–889.

Strober, M. (1986). Psychopathology in adolescence revisited. *Clinical Psychology Review, 6,* 199–209.

Strober, M., & Humphrey, L. L. (1987). Familial contributions to the etiology and course of anorexia nervosa and bulimia. *Journal of Consulting and Clinical Psychology, 55,* 654–659.

Susman, E. J., Dorn, L. D., & Chrousos, G. P. (1991). Negative affect and hormone levels in young adolescents: Concurrent and predictive perspectives. *Journal of Youth and Adolescence, 20,* 167–190.

Tanner, J. M. (1990). *Foetus into man: Physical growth from conception to maturity* (2nd ed.). Cambridge, MA: Harvard University Press.

Tannock, R., Schachar, R. J., & Logan, G. D. (1993). Does methylphenidate induce overfocusing in hyperactive children? *Journal of Clinical Child Psychology, 22,* 28–41.

Teri, L., & Wagner, A. (1992). Alzheimer's disease and depression. *Journal of Consulting and Clinical Psychology, 60,* 379–391.

Theander, S. (1985). Outcome and prognosis in anorexia nervosa and bulimia: Some results of previous investigations compared with those of a Swedish long-term study. *Journal of Psychiatric Research, 19,* 493–508.

Thelen, M. H., Powell, A. L., Lawrence, C., & Kuhnert, M. E. (1992). Eating and body image concerns among children. *Journal of Clinical Child Psychology, 21,* 41–46.

Trad, P. V. (1986). *Infant depression: Paradigms and paradoxes.* New York: Springer.

U.S. Bureau of the Census (1992). *Statistical abstract of the United States: 1992* (112th ed.). Washington, DC: U.S. Government Printing Office.

U.S. Bureau of the Census (1993). *Statistical abstract of the United States: 1993* (113th ed.). Washington, DC: U.S. Government Printing Office.

Vaillant, G. E. (1977). *Adaptation to life.* Boston: Little, Brown.

Volkmar, F. R., & Cohen, D. J. (1988). Neurobiologic aspects of autism. *New England Journal of Medicine, 318,* 1390–1392.

von Knorring, A., Andersson, O., & Magnusson, D. (1987). Psychiatric care and course of psychiatric disorders from childhood to early adulthood in a representative sample. *Journal of Child Psychology and Psychiatry, 28,* 329–341.

Wallander, J. L., & Hubert, N. C. (1985). Long-term prognosis for children with attention deficit disorder with hyperactivity (ADD/H). In B. B. Lahey & A. E. Kazdin (Eds.), *Advances in clinical child psychology* (Vol. 8). New York: Plenum.

Weisman, M. M., Bruce, M. L., Leaf, P. J., Florio, L. P., & Holzer, C. III (1991). Affective disorders. In L. N. Robins & D. A. Regier (Eds.), *Psychiatric disorders in America: The Epidemiologic Catchment Area Study.* New York: Free Press.

Weiss, B., Weisz, J. R., Politano, M., Carey, M., Nelson, W. M., & Finch, A. J. (1992). Relations among self-reported depressive symptoms in clinic-referred children versus adolescents. *Journal of Abnormal Psychology, 101,* 391–397.

Weisz, J. R., Sigman, M., Weiss, B., & Mosk, J. (1993). Parent reports of behavioral and emotional problems among children in Kenya, Thailand, and the United States. *Child Development, 64,* 98–109.

Weisz, J. R., Suwanlert, S., Chaiyasit, W., Weiss, B., Achenbach, T. M., & Eastman, K. L. (1993). Behavioral and emotional problems among Thai and American adolescents: Parent reports for ages 12–16. *Journal of Abnormal Psychology, 102,* 395–403.

Weisz, J. R., & Weiss, B. (1993). *Effects of psychotherapy with children and adolescents* (Vol. 27, Developmental Clinical Psychology and Psychiatry Series). Newbury Park, CA: Sage.

Weisz, J. R., Weiss, B., Alicke, M. D., & Klotz, M. L. (1987). Effectiveness of psychotherapy with children and adolescents: A meta-analysis for clinicians. *Journal of Consulting and Clinical Psychology, 55,* 542–549.

Whalen, C. K., & Henker, B. (1991). Therapies for hyperactive children: Comparisons, combinations, and compromises. *Journal of Consulting and Clinical Psychology, 59,* 126–137.

Whalen, C. K., Henker, B., Buhrmester, D., Hinshaw, S. P., Huber, A., & Laski, K. (1989). Does stimulant medication improve the peer status of hyperactive children? *Journal of Consulting and Clinical Psychology, 57,* 545–549.

Whitbeck, L. B., Hoyt, D. R., Simons, R. L., Conger, R. D., Elder, G. H., Jr., Lorenz, F. O., & Huck, S. (1992). Intergenerational continuity of parental rejection and depressed affect. *Journal of Personality and Social Psychology, 63,* 1036–1045.

Wilens, T. E., & Biederman, J. (1992). The stimulants. *Psychiatric Clinics of North America, 15,* 191–222.

Williams, G. J., Power, K. G., Millar, H. R., Freeman, C. P., Yellowlees, A., Dowds, T., Walker, M., Campsie, L., MacPherson, F., & Jackson, M. A. (1993). Comparison of eating disorders and other dietary/weight groups on measures of perceived control, assertiveness, self-esteem, and self-directed hostility. *International Journal of Eating Disorders, 14,* 27–32.

Williamson, D. A., Cubic, B. A., & Gleaves, D. H. (1993). Equivalence of body image disturbances in anorexia and bulimia nervosa. *Journal of Abnormal Psychology, 102,* 177–180.

Williamson, D. A., Davis, C. J., Goreczny, A. J., & Blouin, D. C. (1989). Body-image disturbances in bulimia nervosa: Influences of actual body size. *Journal of Abnormal Psychology, 98,* 97–99.

Wrightsman, L. S., Sigelman, C. K., & Sanford, F. H. (1979). *Psychology: A scientific study of human behavior.* Pacific Grove, CA: Brooks/Cole.

Yamaguchi, K., & Kandel, D. B. (1984). Patterns of drug use from adolescence to young adulthood: II. Sequences of progression. *American Journal of Public Health, 74,* 668–672.

Yirmiya, N., & Sigman, M. (1991). High functioning individuals with autism—Diagnosis, empirical findings, and theoretical issues. *Clinical Psychology Review, 11,* 669–683.

Zahn-Waxler, C., Cummings, E. M., Iannotti, R. J., & Radke-Yarrow, M. (1984). Young offspring of depressed parents: A population at risk for affective problems. In D. Cicchetti & K. Schneider-Rosen (Eds.), *Childhood depression* (New Directions for Child Development, No. 26). San Francisco: Jossey-Bass.

Zarit, S. H., Eiler, J., & Hassinger, M. (1985). Clinical assessment. In J. E. Birren & K. W. Schaie (Eds.), *Handbook of the psychology of aging* (2nd ed.). New York: Van Nostrand Reinhold.

Zarit, S. H., Orr, N. K., & Zarit, J. M. (1985). *The hidden victims of Alzheimer's disease: Families under stress.* New York: New York University Press.

Zerbe, K. J. (1993). *The body betrayed: Women, eating disorders, and treatment.* Washington, DC: American Psychiatric Press.

Zigler, E., Taussig, C., & Black, K. (1992). Early childhood intervention: A promising preventative for juvenile delinquency. *American Psychologist, 47,* 997–1006.

Chapter 17: The Final Challenge: Death and Dying

Adams, D. W., & Deveau, E. J. (1986). Helping dying adolescents: Needs and responses. In C. A. Corr & J. N. McNeil (Eds.), *Adolescence and death.* New York: Springer.

Adams, D. W., & Deveau, E. J. (1987). When a brother or sister is dying of cancer: The vulnerability of the adolescent sibling. *Death Studies, 11,* 279–295.

Applebaum, D. R., & Burns, G. L. (1991). Unexpected childhood death: Posttraumatic stress disorder in surviving siblings and parents. *Journal of Clinical Child Psychology, 20,* 114–120.

Ariès, P. (1981). *The hour of our death* (H. Weaver, Trans.). New York: Knopf. (Original work published 1977.)

Baker, S. R. (1991). Utilizing art and imagery in death and dying counseling. In D. Papadatou

& C. Papadatos (Eds.), *Children and death.* New York: Hemisphere.

Bankoff, E. A. (1983). Aged parents and their widowed daughters: A support relationship. *Journal of Gerontology, 38,* 226–230.

Bennett, N. G., & Garson, L. K. (1986). Extraordinary longevity in the Soviet Union: Fact or artifact. *Gerontologist, 26,* 358–361.

Berger, A. S. (1993). *Dying and death in law and medicine: A forensic primer for health and legal professionals.* Westport, CT: Praeger.

Bertman, S. L. (1991). Children and death: Insights, hindsights, and illuminations. In D. Papadatou & C. Papadatos (Eds.), *Children and death.* New York: Hemisphere.

Bifulco, A., Harris, T., & Brown, G. W. (1992). Mourning or early inadequate care? Reexamining the relationship of maternal loss in childhood with adult depression and anxiety. *Development and Psychopathology, 4,* 433–449.

Black, D. (1991). Family intervention with families bereaved or about to be bereaved. In D. Papadatou & C. Papadatos (Eds.), *Children and death.* New York: Hemisphere.

Bluebond-Langner, M. (1977). Meanings of death to children. In H. Feifel (Ed.), *New meanings of death.* New York: McGraw-Hill.

Bohannon, J. R. (1990–1991). Grief responses of spouses following the death of a child: A longitudinal study. *Omega, 22,* 109–121.

Bohannon, J. R. (1991). Religiosity related to grief levels of bereaved mothers and fathers. *Omega, 23,* 153–159.

Bowlby, J. (1980). *Attachment and loss: Vol. 3. Loss, sadness and depression.* New York: Basic Books.

Brent, S. B., & Speece, M. W. (1993). "Adult" conceptualization of irreversibility: Implications for the development of the concept of death. *Death Studies, 17,* 203–224.

Brent, S. B., Speece, M. W., Gates, M. F., Mood, D., & Kaul, M. (1991). The contribution of death-related experiences to health care providers' attitudes toward dying patients. I. Graduate and undergraduate nursing students. *Omega, 23,* 249–278.

Bunch, J. (1972). Recent bereavement in relation to suicide. *Journal of Psychosomatic Research, 16,* 361–366.

Butterfield-Picard, H., & Magno, J. B. (1982). Hospice the adjective, not the noun: The future of a national priority. *American Psychologist, 37,* 1254–1259.

Cesario, T. C., & Hollander, D. (1991). Life span extension by means other than control of disease. In F. C. Ludwig (Ed.), *Life span extension: Consequences and open questions.* New York: Springer.

Cook, A. S., & Dworkin, D. S. (1992). *Helping the bereaved: Therapeutic interventions for children, adolescents, and adults.* New York: Basic Books.

Corr, C. A. (1991). Understanding adolescents and death. In D. Papadatou & C. Papadatos (Eds.), *Children and death.* New York: Hemisphere.

Corr, C. A. (1993). Coping with dying: Lessons that we should and should not learn from the work of Elisabeth Kübler-Ross. *Death Studies, 17,* 69–83.

Corr, C. A., & Corr, D. M. (1992). Children's hospice care. *Death Studies, 16,* 431–449.

Cotton, C. R., & Range, L. M. (1990). Children's death concepts: Relationship to cognitive functioning, age, experience with death, fear of death, and hopelessness. *Journal of Clinical Child Psychology, 19,* 123–127.

Davies, B. (1991). Responses of children to the death of a sibling. In D. Papadatou & C. Papadatos (Eds.), *Children and death.* New York: Hemisphere.

DeFrain, J. D., Jakub, D. K., & Mendoza, B. L. (1991–1992). The psychological effects of sudden infant death on grandmothers and grandfathers. *Omega, 24,* 165–182.

DeFrain, J. D., Taylor, J., & Ernst, L. (1982). *Coping with sudden infant death.* Lexington, MA: Lexington Books.

Dickinson, G. E. (1992). First childhood death experiences. *Omega, 25,* 169–182.

Diggory, J. C., & Rothman, D. Z. (1961). Values destroyed by death. *Journal of Abnormal and Social Psychology, 63,* 205–210.

Durlak, J. A., & Riesenberg, L. A. (1991). The impact of death education. *Death Studies, 15,* 39–58.

Elizur, E., & Kaffman, M. (1983). Factors influencing the severity of childhood bereavement reactions. *American Journal of Orthopsychiatry, 53,* 668–676.

Finch, C. E. (1976). The regulation of physiological changes during mammalian aging. *Quarterly Review of Biology, 51,* 49–83.

Florian, V., & Kravetz, S. (1985). Children's concepts of death: A cross-cultural comparison among Muslims, Druze, Christians, and Jews in Israel. *Journal of Cross-Cultural Psychology, 16,* 174–189.

Furman, E. (1984). Children's patterns in mourning the death of a loved one. In H. Wass & C. A. Corr (Eds.), *Childhood and death.* Washington, DC: Hemisphere.

Futterman, A., Gallagher, D., Thompson, L. W., Lovett, S., & Gilewski, M. (1990). Retrospective assessment of marital adjustment and depression during the first 2 years of spousal bereavement. *Psychology and Aging, 5,* 277–283.

Gesser, G., Wong, P. T. P., & Reker, G. T. (1987–1988). Death attitudes across the life-span: The development and validation of the Death Attitude Profile (DAP). *Omega, 18,* 113–128.

Gilewski, M. J., Farberow, N. L., Gallagher, D. E., & Thompson, L. W. (1991). Interaction of depression and bereavement on mental health in the elderly. *Psychology and Aging, 6,* 67–75.

Glaser, B. G., & Strauss, A. L. (1968). *Time for dying.* Chicago: Aldine.

Graham-Pole, J., Wass, H., Eyberg, S., Chu, L., & Olejnik, S. (1989). Communicating with dying children and their siblings: A retrospective analysis. *Death Studies, 13,* 463–483.

Haas-Hawkings, G., Sangster, S., Ziegler, M., & Reid, D. (1985). A study of relatively immediate adjustment to widowhood in later life. *International Journal of Women's Studies, 8,* 158–166.

Harlow, S. D., Goldberg, E. L., & Comstock, G. W. (1991). A longitudinal study of the prevalence of depressive symptomatology in elderly widowed and married women. *Archives of General Psychiatry, 48,* 1065–1068.

Harman, D. (1981). The aging process. *Proceedings of the National Academy of Sciences of the USA, 78,* 7124–7128.

Harris, E. S. (1991). Adolescent bereavement following the death of a parent: An exploratory study. *Child Psychiatry and Human Development, 21,* 267–281.

Harris, T., & Bifulco, A. (1991). Loss of parent in childhood, attachment style, and depression in adulthood. In C. M. Parkes, J. Stevenson-Hinde, & P. Marris (Eds.), *Attachment across the life cycle.* London: Tavistock/Routledge.

Hart, R. W., & Setlow, R. B. (1974). Correlation between deoxyribonucleic acid excision-repair and life-span in a number of mammalian species. *Proceedings of the National Academy of Sciences of the USA, 71,* 2169–2173.

Hart, R. W., & Turturro, A. (1983). Theories of aging. In M. Rothstein (Ed.), *Review of biological research in aging* (Vol. 1). New York: Alan R. Liss.

Hayflick, L. (1976). The cell biology of human aging. *New England Journal of Medicine, 295,* 1302–1308.

Helsing, K. J., Szklo, M., & Comstock, G. W. (1981). Factors associated with mortality after widowhood. *American Journal of Public Health, 71,* 802–809.

Hickson, J., Housley, W. F., & Boyle, C. (1988). The relationship of locus of control, age, and sex to life satisfaction and death anxiety in older persons. *International Journal of Aging and Human Development, 26,* 191–199.

Hinton, J. (1975). The influence of previous personality on reactions to having terminal cancer. *Omega, 6,* 95–111.

Hoffman, S. I., & Strauss, S. (1985). The development of children's concepts of death. *Death Studies, 9,* 469–482.

Hutti, M. H. (1992). Parents' perceptions of the miscarriage experience. *Death Studies, 16,* 401–415.

Jacobs, S. C. (1993). *Pathological grief: Maladaptation to loss.* Washington, DC: American Psychiatric Press.

Jacobs, S. C., Kosten, T. R., Kasl, S. V., Ostfeld, A. M., Berkman, L., & Charpentier, P. (1987–1988). Attachment theory and multiple dimensions of grief. *Omega, 18,* 41–52.

Kalish, R. A. (1981). *Death, grief, and caring relationships.* Pacific Grove, CA: Brooks/Cole.

Kalish, R. A., & Reynolds, D. K. (1976). *Death and ethnicity: A psychocultural study.* Los Angeles: Ethel Percy Andrus Gerontology Center, University of Southern California.

Kalish, R. A., & Reynolds, D. K. (1977). The role of age in death attitudes. *Death Education, 1,* 205–230.

Kaminer, H., & Lavie, P. (1993). Sleep and dreams in well-adjusted and less adjusted Holocaust survivors. In M. S. Stroebe, W. Stroebe, & R. O. Hansson (Eds.), *Handbook of bereavement: Theory, research, and intervention.* Cambridge, England: Cambridge University Press.

Kaprio, J., Koskenvuo, M., & Rita, H. (1987). Mortality after bereavement: A prospective study of 95,647 widowed persons. *American Journal of Public Health, 77,* 283–287.

Kastenbaum, R. J. (1985). Dying and death: A life-span approach. In J. E. Birren & K. W. Schaie (Eds.), *Handbook of the psychology of aging* (2nd ed.). New York: Van Nostrand Reinhold.

Kastenbaum, R. J. (1986). *Death, society, and human experience* (3rd ed.). Columbus, OH: Merrill.

Kastenbaum, R. J. (1991). *Death, society, and human experience* (4th ed.). New York: Macmillan.

Kinsella, K., & Taeuber, C. M. (1993). *An aging world II* (International Population Reports, P25, 92–3). Washington, DC: U.S. Bureau of the Census.

Klass, D. (1993). Solace and immortality: Bereaved parents' continuing bond with their children. *Death Studies, 17,* 343–368.

Klenow, D. J., & Youngs, G. A., Jr. (1987). Changes in doctor/patient communication of a terminal prognosis: A selective review and critique. *Death Studies, 11,* 263–277.

Knapp, R. J. (1986). *Beyond endurance: When a child dies.* New York: Schocken.

Koocher, G. P. (1973). Childhood, death, and cognitive development. *Developmental Psychology, 9,* 369–375.

Koocher, G. P. (1974). Talking with children about death. *American Journal of Orthopsychiatry, 44,* 404–411.

Kristal, B. S., & Yu, B. P. (1992). An emerging hypothesis: Synergistic induction of aging by free radicals and maillard reactions. *Journal of Gerontology: Biological Sciences, 47,* B107–B114.

Kübler-Ross, E. (1969). *On death and dying.* New York: Macmillan.

Kübler-Ross, E. (1974). *Questions and answers on death and dying.* New York: Macmillan.

Lamberti, J. W., & Detmer, C. M. (1993). Model of family grief assessment and treatment. *Death Studies, 17,* 55–67.

Lang, A., & Gottlieb, L. (1993). Parental grief reactions and marital intimacy following infant death. *Death Studies, 17,* 233–255.

Leahy, J. M. (1992–1993). A comparison of depression in women bereaved of a spouse, child, or a parent. *Omega, 26,* 207–217.

Lehman, D. R., Davis, C. G., DeLongis, A., Wortman, C. B., Bluck, S., Mandel, D. R., & Ellard, J. H. (1993). Positive and negative life changes following bereavement and their relations to adjustment. *Journal of Social and Clinical Psychology, 12,* 90–112.

Lehman, D. R., Ellard, J. H., & Wortman, C. B. (1986). Social support for the bereaved: Recipients' and providers' perspectives on what is helpful. *Journal of Consulting and Clinical Psychology, 54,* 438–446.

Lehman, D. R., Wortman, C. B., & Williams, A. F. (1987). Long-term effects of losing a spouse or child in a motor vehicle crash. *Journal of Personality and Social Psychology, 52,* 218–231.

Lehr, U. M. (1982). Social-psychological correlates of longevity. In C. Eisdorfer (Ed.), *Annual review of gerontology and geriatrics* (Vol. 3). New York: Springer.

Lesher, E. L., & Bergey, K. J. (1988). Bereaved elderly mothers: Changes in health, functional activities, family cohesion, and psychological well-being. *International Journal of Aging and Human Development, 26,* 81–90.

Lester, D., & Templer, D. (1992–1993). Death anxiety scales: A dialogue. *Omega, 26,* 239–253.

Leviton, D., & Forman, E. C. (1974). Death education for children and youth. *Journal of Clinical Child Psychology, 3,* 8–10.

Lieberman, M. A. (1993). Bereavement self-help groups: A review of conceptual and methodological issues. In M. S. Stroebe, W. Stroebe, & R. O. Hansson (Eds.), *Handbook of bereavement: Theory, research, and intervention.* Cambridge, England: Cambridge University Press.

Lieberman, M. A., & Videka-Sherman, L. (1986). The impact of self-help groups on the mental health of widows and widowers. *American Journal of Orthopsychiatry, 56,* 435–449.

Littlefield, C. H., & Rushton, J. P. (1986). When a child dies: The sociobiology of bereavement. *Journal of Personality and Social Psychology, 51,* 797–802.

Lockshin, R. A., & Zakeri, Z. F. (1990). Programmed cell death: New thoughts and relevance to aging. *Journal of Gerontology: Biological Sciences, 45,* B135–B140.

Lohr, J. B. (1991). Oxygen radicals and neuropsychiatric illness: Some speculations. *Archives of General Psychiatry, 48,* 1097–1106.

Lonetto, R., & Templer, D. I. (1986). *Death anxiety.* Washington, DC: Hemisphere.

Lopata, H. Z. (1979). Widowhood and husband sanctification. In L. A. Bugen (Ed.), *Death and dying: Theory, research, practice.* Dubuque, IA: William C. Brown.

Lund, D. A., & Caserta, M. S. (1992). Older bereaved spouses' participation in self-help groups. *Omega, 25,* 47–61.

Lund, D. A., Dimond, M. F., Caserta, M. S., Johnson, R. J., Poulton, J. L., & Connelly, J. R. (1985–1986). Identifying elderly with coping difficulties after two years of bereavement. *Omega, 16,* 213–224.

Masoro, E. J. (1988). Minireview: Food restriction in rodents—An evaluation of its role in the study of aging. *Journal of Gerontology: Biological Sciences, 43,* B59–B64.

Maurer, A. (1961). The child's knowledge of non-existence. *Journal of Existential Psychiatry, 2,* 193–212.

Mazess, R. B., & Forman, S. H. (1979). Longevity and age exaggeration in Vilcabamba, Ecuador. *Journal of Gerontology, 34,* 94–98.

McClearn, G., & Foch, T. T. (1985). Behavioral genetics. In J. E. Birren & K. W. Schaie (Eds.), *Handbook of the psychology of aging* (2nd ed.). New York: Van Nostrand Reinhold.

McGoldrick, M., Almeida, R., Hines, P. M., Garcia-Preto, N., Rosen, E., & Lee, E. (1991). Mourning in different cultures. In F. Walsh & M. McGoldrick (Eds.), *Living beyond loss: Death in the family.* New York: Norton.

McIntyre, M. S., Angle, C. R., & Struempler, L. J. (1972). The concept of death in midwestern children and youth. *American Journal of Diseases of Children, 123,* 527–532.

McWhirter, L., Young, V., & Majury, J. (1983). Belfast children's awareness of violent death. *British Journal of Social Psychology, 22,* 81–92.

Medvedev, Z. A. (1991). The structural basis of aging. In F. C. Ludwig (Ed.), *Life span extension: Consequences and open questions.* New York: Springer.

Meshot, C. M., & Leitner, L. M. (1992–1993). Adolescent mourning and parental death. *Omega, 26,* 287–299.

Metcalf, P., & Huntington, R. (1991). *Celebrations of death: The anthropology of mortuary ritual* (2nd ed.). Cambridge, England: Cambridge University Press.

Mikulincer, M., Florian, V., & Tolmacz, R. (1990). Attachment styles and fear of personal death: A case study of affect regulation. *Journal of Personality and Social Psychology, 58,* 273–280.

Moss, M. S., Moss, S. Z., Rubinstein, R., & Resch, N. (1993). Impact of elderly mother's death on middle age daughters. *International Journal of Aging and Human Development, 37,* 1–22.

Murrell, S. A., & Himmelfarb, S. (1989). Effects of attachment bereavement and pre-event conditions on subsequent depressive symptoms in older adults. *Psychology and Aging, 4,* 166–172.

Nagy, M. (1948). The child's theories concerning death. *Journal of Genetic Psychology, 73,* 3–27.

National Center for Health Statistics. (1992). *Vital statistics of the United States, 1989: Vol. 2, Sec. 6: Life tables.* (DHHS Publ. No. PHS 93–1104). Washington, DC: Public Health Service.

Norris, F. H., & Murrell, S. A. (1990). Social support, life events, and stress as modifiers of adjustment to bereavement by older adults. *Psychology and Aging, 5,* 429–436.

Oken, D. (1961). What to tell cancer patients. *Journal of the American Medical Association, 175,* 1120–1128.

Orbach, I., Gross, Y., Glaubman, H., & Berman, D. (1986). Children's perception of various determinants of the death concept as a function of intelligence, age, and anxiety. *Journal of Clinical Child Psychology, 15,* 120–126.

Osterweis, M., Solomon, F., & Green, M. (Eds.). (1984). *Bereavement: Reactions, consequences, and care.* Washington, DC: National Academy Press.

Parkes, C. M. (1986). *Bereavement: Studies of grief in adult life* (2nd ed.). London: Tavistock.

Parkes, C. M. (1991). Attachment, bonding, and psychiatric problems after bereavement in adult life. In C. M. Parkes, J. Stevenson-Hinde, & P. Marris (Eds.), *Attachment across the life cycle.* London: Tavistock/Routledge.

Parkes, C. M., & Weiss, R. S. (1983). *Recovery from bereavement.* New York: Basic Books.

Pennebaker, J. W., & O'Heeron, R. C. (1984). Confiding in others and illness rate among spouses of suicide and accidental-death victims. *Journal of Abnormal Psychology, 93,* 473–476.

Peppers, L. G. (1987–1988). Grief and elective abortion: Breaking the emotional bond? *Omega, 18,* 1–12.

Perry, H. L. (1993). Mourning and funeral customs of African Americans. In D. P. Irish, K. F. Lundquist, & V. J. Nelson (Eds.), *Ethnic variations in dying, death, and grief: Diversity in universality.* Washington, DC: Taylor and Francis.

Piper, W. E., McCallum, M., & Azim, H. F. A. (1992). *Adaptation to loss through short-term group psychotherapy.* New York: Guilford Press.

Ponzetti, J. J. (1992). Bereaved families: A comparison of parents' and grandparents' reactions to the death of a child. *Omega, 25,* 63–71.

Quill, T. E. (1993). *Death and dignity: Making choices and taking charge.* New York: Norton.

Rando, T. A. (1986). A comprehensive analysis of anticipatory grief: Perspectives, processes, promises, and problems. In T. A. Rando (Ed.), *Loss and anticipatory grief.* Lexington, MA: Lexington Books.

Rando, T. A. (1991). Parental adjustment to the loss of a child. In D. Papadatou & C. Papadatos (Eds.), *Children and death.* New York: Hemisphere.

Raphael, B. (1983). *The anatomy of bereavement.* New York: Basic Books.

Rappaport, H., Fossler, R. J., Bross, L. S., & Gilden, D. (1993). Future time, death anxiety, and life purpose among older adults. *Death Studies, 17,* 369–379.

Rosen, H. (1986). *Unspoken grief: Coping with childhood sibling loss.* Lexington, MA: Lexington Books.

Rosenblatt, P. C. (1993). Cross-cultural variation in the experience, expression, and understanding of grief. In D. P. Irish, K. F. Lundquist, & V. J. Nelson (Eds.), *Ethnic variations in dying, death, and grief: Diversity in universality.* Washington, DC: Taylor and Francis.

Rosenfeld, A. (1985). *Prolongevity II.* New York: Knopf.

Rubin, S. S. (1993). The death of a child is forever: The life course impact of child loss. In M. S. Stroebe, W. Stroebe, & R. O. Hansson (Eds.), *Handbook of bereavement: Theory, research, and intervention.* Cambridge, England: Cambridge University Press.

Sable, P. (1989). Attachment, anxiety, and loss of a husband. *American Journal of Orthopsychiatry, 59,* 550–556.

Sanders, C. M. (1979–1980). A comparison of adult bereavement in the death of a spouse, child and parent. *Omega, 10,* 303–322.

Sanders, C. M. (1982–1983). Effects of sudden vs. chronic illness death on bereavement outcome. *Omega, 13,* 227–241.

Sanders, C. M. (1993). Risk factors in bereavement outcome. In M. S. Stroebe, W. Stroebe, & R. O. Hansson (Eds.), *Handbook of bereavement: Theory, research, and intervention.* Cambridge, England: Cambridge University Press.

Sandler, I. N., West, S. G., Baca, L., Pillow, D. R., Gersten, J. C., Rogosch, F., Virdin, L., Beals, J., Reynolds, K. D., Kallgren, C., Tein, J., Kriege, G., Cole, E., & Ramirez, R. (1992). Linking empirically based theory and evaluation: The family bereavement program. *American Journal of Community Psychology, 20,* 491–521.

Saunders, C. (1977). Dying they live: St. Christopher's Hospice. In H. Feifel (Ed.), *New meanings of death.* New York: McGraw-Hill.

Schachter, S. (1991–1992). Adolescent experiences with the death of a peer. *Omega, 24,* 1–11.

Scharlach, A. E., & Fredriksen, K. I. (1993). Reactions to the death of a parent during midlife. *Omega, 27,* 307–319.

Schonfeld, D. J., & Kappelman, M. (1990). The impact of school-based education on the young child's understanding of death. *Developmental and Behavioral Pediatrics, 11,* 247–252.

Schulz, R., & Aderman, D. (1974). Clinical research and the stages of dying. *Omega, 5,* 137–143.

Schulz, R., & Schlarb, J. (1987–1988). Two decades of research on dying: What do we know about the patient? *Omega, 18,* 299–317.

Schwab, R. (1992). Effects of a child's death on the marital relationship: A preliminary study. *Death Studies, 16,* 141–154.

Seale, C. F. (1989). What happens in hospices: A review of research evidence. *Social Science and Medicine, 28,* 551–559.

Seale, C. F. (1991). A comparison of hospice and conventional care. *Social Science and Medicine, 32,* 147–152.

Selkoe, D. J. (1992). Aging brain, aging mind. *Scientific American, 267,* 135–142.

Shneidman, E. S. (1973). *Deaths of man.* New York: Quadrangle.

Shneidman, E. S. (1980). *Voices of death.* New York: Harper & Row.

Shuchter, S. R., & Zisook, S. (1993). The course of normal grief. In M. S. Stroebe, W. Stroebe, & R. O. Hansson (Eds.), *Handbook of bereavement: Theory, research, and intervention.* Cambridge, England: Cambridge University Press.

Siebold, C. (1992). *The hospice movement: Easing death's pains.* New York: Twayne.

Silverman, P. R. (1969). The widow-to-widow program: An experiment in preventive intervention. *Mental Hygiene, 53,* 333–337.

Silverman, P. R. (1981). *Helping women cope with grief* (Sage Human Services Guide No. 25). Beverly Hills, CA: Sage.

Silverman, P. R., & Worden, J. W. (1993). Children's reactions to the death of a parent. In M. S. Stroebe, W. Stroebe, & R. O. Hansson (Eds.), *Handbook of bereavement: Theory, research, and intervention.* Cambridge, England: Cambridge University Press.

Smith, G. S., & Walford, R. L. (1977). Influence of the main histocompatibility complex on aging in mice. *Nature, 270,* 727–729.

Speece, M. W., & Brent, S. B. (1984). Children's understanding of death: A review of three components of a death concept. *Child Development, 55,* 1671–1686.

Speece, M. W., & Brent, S. B. (1992). The acquisition of a mature understanding of three components of the concept of death. *Death Studies, 16,* 211–229.

Spinetta, J. J. (1974). The dying child's awareness of death: A review. *Psychological Bulletin, 81,* 256–260.

Stambrook, M., & Parker, K. C. H. (1987). The development of the concept of death in childhood: A review of the literature. *Merrill-Palmer Quarterly, 33,* 133–157.

Stein, S., Linn, M. W., & Stein, E. M. (1989). Psychological correlates of survival in nursing home cancer patients. *Gerontologist, 29,* 224–228.

Stroebe, M. S., Gergen, M. M., Gergen, K. J., & Stroebe, W. (1992). Broken hearts or broken bonds. *American Psychologist, 47,* 1205–1212.

Stroebe, M. S., & Stroebe, W. (1993). The mortality of bereavement: A review. In M. S. Stroebe, W. Stroebe, & R. O. Hansson (Eds.), *Handbook of bereavement: Theory, research, and intervention.* Cambridge, England: Cambridge University Press.

Stroebe, W., & Stroebe, M. S. (1993). Determinants of adjustment to bereavement in younger widows and widowers. In M. S. Stroebe, W. Stroebe, & R. O. Hansson (Eds.), *Handbook of bereavement: Theory, research, and intervention.* Cambridge, England: Cambridge University Press.

Thomas, L. E., DiGiulio, R. C., & Sheehan, N. W. (1988). Identity loss and psychological crisis in widowhood: A re-evaluation. *International Journal of Aging and Human Development, 26,* 225–239.

Thompson, L. W., Gallagher-Thompson, D., Futterman, A., Gilewski, M. J., & Peterson, J. (1991). The effects of late-life spousal bereavement over a 30-month interval. *Psychology and Aging, 6,* 434–441.

Umberson, D., Wortman, C. B., & Kessler, R. C. (1992). Widowhood and depression: Explaining long-term gender differences in vulnerability. *Journal of Health and Social Behavior, 33,* 10–24.

Urofsky, M. I. (1993). *Letting go: Death, dying, and the law.* New York: Scribner's.

U.S. Bureau of the Census. (1993). *Statistical abstract of the United States: 1993* (113th ed.). Washington, DC: U.S. Government Printing Office.

van der Wal, J. (1989–1990). The aftermath of suicide: A review of empirical evidence. *Omega, 20,* 149–171.

Van Dongen, C. J. (1993). Social context of postsuicide bereavement. *Death Studies, 17,* 125–141.

Van Eerdewegh, M. M., Clayton, P. J., & Van Eerdewegh, P. (1985). The bereaved children: Variables influencing early psychopathology. *British Journal of Psychiatry, 147,* 188–194.

Waechter, E. H. (1984). Dying children: Patterns of coping. In H. Wass & C. A. Corr (Eds.), *Childhood and death.* Washington, DC: Hemisphere.

Walford, R. L. (1983). *Maximum life span.* New York: Norton.

Wass, H. (1991). Helping children cope with death. In D. Papadatou & C. Papadatos (Eds.), *Children and death.* New York: Hemisphere.

Wenestam, C., & Wass, H. (1987). Swedish and U.S. children's thinking about death: A qualitative study and cross-cultural comparison. *Death Studies, 11,* 99–121.

Wikan, U. (1988). Bereavement and loss in two Muslim communities: Egypt and Bali compared. *Social Science and Medicine, 27,* 451–460.

Wikan, U. (1991). *Managing turbulent hearts.* Chicago: University of Chicago Press.

Worchel, F. F., Copeland, D. R., & Barker, D. G. (1987). Control-related coping strategies in pediatric oncology patients. *Journal of Pediatric Psychology, 12,* 25–38.

Worden, J. W. (1991). *Grief counseling and grief therapy: A handbook for the mental health practitioner* (2nd ed.). New York: Springer.

Worden, J. W., & Silverman, P. S. (1993). Grief and depression in newly widowed parents with school-age children. *Omega, 27,* 251–261.

Wortman, C. B., & Silver, R. C. (1989). The myths of coping with loss. *Journal of Consulting and Clinical Psychology, 57,* 349–357.

Zisook, S., & Shuchter, S. R. (1991). Depression through the first year after the death of a spouse. *American Journal of Psychiatry, 148,* 1346–1352.

Chapter 18: Epilogue: Fitting the Pieces Together

Baltes, P. B. (1987). Theoretical propositions of life-span developmental psychology: On the dynamics between growth and decline. *Developmental Psychology, 23,* 611–626.

Baltes, P. B., Smith, J., & Staudinger, U. M. (1992). Wisdom and successful aging. In T. B. Sonderegger (Ed.), *Nebraska Symposium on Motivation: Vol. 39. Psychology and aging.* Lincoln: University of Nebraska Press.

Flavell, J. H. (1985). *Cognitive development* (2nd ed.). Englewood Cliffs, NJ: Prentice-Hall.

Harris, J. R., Pedersen, N. L., McClearn, G. E., Plomin, R., & Nesselroade, J. R. (1992). Age differences in genetic and environmental influences for health from the Swedish Adoption/Twin Study of Aging. *Journal of Gerontology: Psychological Sciences, 47,* P213–P220.

Lerner, J. V., Nitz, K., Talwar, R., & Lerner, R. M. (1989). On the functional significance of temperamental individuality: A developmental contextual view of the concept of goodness of fit. In G. A. Kohnstamm, J. E. Bates, & M. K. Rothbart (Eds.), *Temperament in childhood.* Chichester, England: Wiley.

Lerner, R. M., & Kauffman, M. B. (1985). The concept of development in contextualism. *Developmental Review, 5,* 309–333.

McCall, R. B. (1981). Nature-nurture and the two realms of development: A proposed integration with respect to mental development. *Child Development, 52,* 1–12.

Morse, C. K. (1993). Does variability increase with age? An archival study of cognitive measures. *Psychology and Aging, 8,* 156–164.

Schaie, K. W. (1989). The hazards of cognitive aging. *Gerontologist, 29,* 484–493.

Thomas, A., & Chess, S. (1986). The New York longitudinal study: From infancy to early adult life. In R. Plomin & J. Dunn (Eds.), *The study of temperament: Changes, continuities, and challenges.* Hillsdale, NJ: Erlbaum.

Werner, H. (1957). The concept of development from a comparative and organismic point of view. In D. B. Harris (Ed.), *The concept of development: An issue in the study of human behavior.* Minneapolis: University of Minnesota Press.

NAME INDEX

SUBJECT INDEX

Page numbers followed by "b" designate boxes; page numbers followed by "f" designate figures or photos; page numbers followed by "t" designate tables; page numbers followed by "n" designate footnotes.

CREDITS

PHOTOGRAPHS

CHAPTER 1

2: W. H. Owens/Black Star. **4:** Gale Zucker. **6:** Henry Lillie Pierce Fund, Courtesy, Museum of Fine Arts, Boston. **8:** Reuters/Bettmann. **10:** The Bettmann Archive. **14:** Gail Meese/Meese Photo Research. **17:** Wide World Photos. **22:** Barbara Rios/Photo Researchers, Inc.

CHAPTER 2

28: Gale Zucker. **32:** UPI/Bettmann. **38:** The Bettmann Archive. **39:** B. F. Skinner. **40:** (top), Chuck Painter, News and Publications Service, Stanford University. **40:** (bottom), Marianne Gontarz. **43:** Yves de Braine/Black Star. **44:** Erika Stone/Photo Researchers, Inc. **46:** Bob Kalmbach, News & Information Services, University of Michigan. **47:** Steve Kagan/Photo Researchers, Inc.

CHAPTER 3

56: Thomas S. England/Photo Researchers, Inc. **61:** Biophoto Association/Photo Researchers, Inc. **63:** Nigel Calder/Photo Researchers, Inc. **65:** Gale Zucker. **75:** Wide World Photos. **76:** Frank L. DeBusk/University of Florida. **81:** E. Novitski.

CHAPTER 4

87: Tomas Friedmann/Photo Researchers, Inc. **89:** Omikron/Photo Researchers, Inc. **90:** Omikron/Photo Researchers, Inc. **94:** Stern Hamburg/Black Star. **95:** Streissguth, Ann. P., Ph.D; Aase, Jon M., M.D.; Clarren, Sterling K., MD; Randels, Sandra P., RN; LaDue, Robin A., PhD; and Smith, David F., MD (1991). Fetal Alcohol Syndrome in Adolescents and Adults. *The Journal of the American Medical Association. 265*(15), 1961–1967. **97:** Junebug Clark/Photo Researchers, Inc. **104:** P. Amranand/SuperStock, Inc. **106:** David Grossman/Photo Researchers, Inc. **107:** Jean Claude Bouvier/Photo Researchers, Inc. **110:** B. Wickley/SuperStock, Inc. **112:** Ed Lettau/Photo Researchers, Inc.

CHAPTER 5

119: (left), Ellis Herwig/Stock, Boston. **119:** (right), Allen Zak/Meese Photo Research. **125:** T. Rosenthal/SuperStock, Inc. **126:** Wide World Photos. **127:** R. Llewellen/SuperStock, Inc. **131:** David Young Wolff/Tony Stone Images, Inc. **133:** Jacques M. Chenet/Woodfin Camp. **137:** Mimi Forsyth/Monkmeyer Press Photo Service. **138:** Susan Wagner/Photo Researchers, Inc. **141:** Christopher Morris/Black Star. **142:** Suzanne Murphy/Tony Stone Images, Inc.

CHAPTER 6

149: Suzanne Szasz/Photo Researchers, Inc. **151:** William Vandivert. **154:** Schuster/SuperStock, Inc.. **156:** Cathy Watterson/Meese Photo Research. **157:** Suzanne Szasz/Photo Researchers, Inc. **159:** Katrina Thomas/Photo Researchers, Inc. **163:** Richard Hutchings/Photo Researchers, Inc. **165:** Gail Meese/Meese Photo Research. **169:** Telex Communications, Inc.

CHAPTER 7

175: Gale Zucker/Meese Photo Research. **176:** Rivera Collection/SuperStock, Inc. **186:** R. Heinzen/SuperStock, Inc. **187:** Arthur Tress/Photo Researchers, Inc. **189:** Gale Zucker. **191:** Terry Wild Studio. **193:** Peter Buckley/Photo Researchers, Inc. **201:** Gale Zucker. **204:** Gail Meese/Meese Photo Research.

CHAPTER 8

213: David Strickler/Meese Photo Research. **215:** From "Imitation of Film-Mediated Aggressive Models" by A. Bandura, D. Ross, S. A. Ross. 1963, *Journal of Abnormal and Social Psychology,* pp. 3–11. Copyright 1963 by the American Psychological Association. **218:** From Field, T. M., Woodson, R., Greenberg, R., & Cohen, D. (1982) Discrimination and imitation of facial expressions by neonates. *Science, 218,* 179–181; Figure 1, p. 180. Copyright 1982 by the AAAS. Courtesy Tiffany Field, University of Miami Medical School. **219:** Carolyn K. Rovee-Collier/Rutgers University. **224:** Marianne Gontarz. **227:** Tim Davis/Photo Researchers, Inc. **230:** Marianne Gontarz. **232:** Leslie Holzer/Photo Researchers, Inc.

CHAPTER 9

240: Gail Meese/Meese Photo Research. **242:** Mimi Forsyth/Monkmeyer Press Photo Service. **255:** Carol Bernson/Black Star. **256:** Wide World Photos. **262:** Audrey Topping/Photo Researchers, Inc.

CHAPTER 10

268: Harvard University Archives. **271:** Paul Damien/Tony Stone Images, Inc. **274:** Marvin Wax. **282:** Lawrence Migdale/Tony Stone Images, Inc. **283:** Ulrike Welsch. **288:** Photo Researchers, Inc. **289:** SuperStock, Inc. **290:** Larry Busacca/Retna, Ltd. **293:** C. Izard/University of Delaware. **294:** (top), Crampon/Jerrican/Photo Researchers, Inc. **294:** (bottom), Gale Zucker.

CHAPTER 11

300: John Running/Black Star. **302:** Paul Conklin/Meese Photo Research. **311:** Wide World Photos. **315:** Gail Meese/Meese Photo Research. **320:** Gail Meese/Meese Photo Research. **323:** Marleen Ferguson/Tony Stone Images, Inc. **325:** Marianne Gontarz.

CHAPTER 12

331: Gale Zucker. **336:** David Shaffer. **339:** Bruce Kliewe/Jeroboam. **343:** Andrew Lichtenstein/Impact Visuals. **345:** Jim Pickerell/Tony Stone Images,

Inc. **347:** David Austen/Tony Stone Images, Inc. **348:** Pam Hasegawa/Impact Visuals. **350:** Sue Ann Miller/Tony Stone Images, Inc. **351:** David Shaffer. **354:** Alexander Lowry/Photo Researchers, Inc. **355:** George Robinson/Tony Stone Images, Inc.

CHAPTER 13

361: Gale Zucker. **363:** Ursula Markus/Photo Researchers, Inc. **365:** Chester Higgins, Jr./Photo Researchers, Inc. **366:** Nina Leen/Life Magazine. **368:** Harlow Primate Lab. **370:** Jeremy Horner/Tony Stone Images, Inc. **372:** Gail Meese/Meese Photo Research. **375:** Terry Wild Studio. **377:** Terry Wild Studio. **380:** Shirley Zeiberg/Photo Researchers, Inc. **385:** Marianne Gontarz. **386:** Billy E. Barnes/Tony Stone Images, Inc.

CHAPTER 14

390: David S. Strickler/Meese Photo Research. **394:** T. Rosenthal/SuperStock, Inc. **399:** Pennie Tweedie/Tony Stone Images, Inc. **403:** Spencer Grant/Photo Researchers, Inc. **404:** Jim Pickerell/Tony Stone Images, Inc. **405:** Marianne Gontarz. **409:** Jerry Mesmer/Tony Stone Images, Inc. **414:** Wide World Photos.

CHAPTER 15

420: Robert Frerck/Tony Stone Images, Inc. **422:** Lawrence Migdale/Photo Researchers, Inc. **425:** Myrleen Ferguson/Tony Stone Images, Inc. **427:** Gail Meese/Meese Photo Research. **431:** Arthur Tress/Magnum. **433:** J. Meyers/SuperStock, Inc. **437:** Gail Meese/Meese Photo Research. **441:** Andy Sacks/Tony Stone Images, Inc. **446:** Marianne Gontarz.

CHAPTER 16

453: Meri Houtchens-Kitchen/The Picture Cube. **461:** T. Rosenthal/SuperStock, Inc. **463:** William Thompson/The Picture Cube. **466:** Jon Riley/Tony Stone Images, Inc. **472:** David Butow/Black Star. **475:** Gale Zucker. **477:** Gale Zucker.

CHAPTER 17

481: Terry Wild Studio. **484:** Bernard Wolff/Photo Researchers, Inc. **487:** Wide World Photos. **490:** Spencer Grant/Photo Researchers, Inc. **491:** Gale Zucker. **496:** Marvin Wax. **500:** Sarah Putnam/The Picture Cube. **502:** Bernard Wolff/Photo Researchers, Inc. **505:** Spencer Grant/The Picture Cube.

CHAPTER 18

510: Library of Congress Archives. **512:** Bettie Lou Sjoberg. **514:** Larry Hamill. **519:** Wide World Photos.

TABLES AND FIGURES

CHAPTER 1

13: Figure 1.2 from "Stratum Contrasts and Similarities in Attitudes toward Death," by V. L. Bengtson, J. B. Cuellar, and P. K. Ragan, 1977, *Journal of Gerontology, 32.* Reprinted by permission.

CHAPTER 3

70: Figure 3.7 data from "The Louisville Twin Study: Developmental Synchronies in Behavior," by R. S. Wilson, 1983, *Child Development, 54,* pp. 298–316. © 1983 by The Society for Research in Child Development, Inc. Reprinted by permission. **74:** Figure 3.9 adapted from "Sources of Human Psychological Differences: The Minnesota Study of Twins Reared Apart," by T. J. Bouchard, Jr., D. T. Lykken, M. McGue, N. L. Segal, and A. Tellegen, 1990, *Science, 250,* pp. 223–228.

CHAPTER 4

88: Figure 4.1 adapted from *The Child: Development in a Social Context,* by Claire B. Kopp and Joanne B. Krakow, p. 648. Copyright © 1982, Addison-Wesley Publishing Co., Inc. Reprinted by permission of the publisher. **92:** Figure 4.5 adapted from a figure in *The Developing Human,* by K. L. Moore, 1988 (4th ed.). Philadelphia, W. B. Saunders. Reprinted by permission.

CHAPTER 5

117: Figure 5.1 from *Growth at Adolescence* (2nd ed.), by J. M. Tanner, 1962, Blackwell Scientific Publications Ltd., London; redrawn from "The Measurement of the Body in Childhood," by R. E. Scammon. In J. A. Harris, C. M. Jackson, D. G. Paterson, and R. E. Scammon (Eds.), *The Measurement of Man,* 1930, University of Minnesota Press. Reprinted by permission. **124:** Table 5.4 adapted from "The Denver Development Screening Test," by W. K. Frankenburg and J. B. Dodds, 1967, *Journal of Pediatrics, 71,* pp. 181–191. Reprinted by permission. **129:** Figure 5.4 from "Variations in the Pattern of Pubertal Changes in Boys," by W. A. Marshall, and J. M. Tanner, 1970, *Archives of Disease in Childhood, 45,* pp. 13–23. Reprinted by permission of the BMJ Publishing Group, London. **132:** Figure 5.5 from *Science and Medicine of Exercise and Sport* (2nd ed.), edited by Warren K. Johnson and Elsworth R. Buskirk. Reprinted by permission of Harper and Row, Publishers, Inc. **134:** Figure 5.7 data from "Human Physiological Adaptability through the Life Sequence," by H. Bafitis and F. Sargent II, 1977, *Journal of Gerontology, 32.* Reprinted by permission. **135:** Table 5.5 data from "Prevalence of Perimenstrual Symptoms," by N. F. Woods, A. Most, and G. K. Dery, 1982, *American Journal of Public Health, 72,* pp. 1257–1264. © 1982 American Journal of Public Health. Reprinted by permission. **140:** Figure in Box 5.3 from "Effects of Age and Skill in Typing," by T. A. Salthouse, 1984, *Journal of Experimental Psychology: General, 113,* pp. 345–371. Copyright 1984 by the American Psychological Association. Reprinted by permission. **143:** Figure 5.9 adapted from "Predictors of Healthy Aging; Prospective Evidence from the Alameda County Study," by J. M. Guralnik, and G. A. Kaplan, 1989, *American Journal of Public Health, 79,* pp. 703–708.

CHAPTER 6

147: Figure 6.1 adapted from "Perceptual Set in Young Children," by H. W. Reese, 1963, *Child Development, 34.* © 1963 by The Society for Research in Child Development, Inc. Reprinted by permission. **149:** Figure 6.2 from "Infant Visual Perception," by M. S. Banks, in collaboration with P. Salapatek. In M. M. Haith and J. J. Campos (Eds.; P. H. Mussen, Gen. Ed.), *Handbook of Child Psychology: Vol. 2. Infancy and Developmental Psychobiology* (4th ed.), 1983. Copyright © 1983 by John Wiley and Sons, Inc. Reprinted by permission. **150:** Figure 6.3 adapted from "Pattern Perception in Infancy," by P. Salapatek. In L. B. Cohen and P. Salapatek (Eds.), *Infant Perception: From Sensation to Cognition,* Volume 1, 1975. Copyright 1975 by Academic Press, Inc. Reprinted by permission. **153:** Figure in Box 6.1 reprinted with permission from *Nature, 358,* "Addition and Subtraction by Human Infants," by K. Wynn, 1992, pp. 749–750. Copyright 1992 Macmillan Magazines Limited. **161:** Figure 6.7 adapted from "A Developmental Study of the Discrimination of Letter-Like Forms," by E. J. Gibson, J. J. Gibson, A. D. Pick, and H. A. Osser, 1962, *Journal of Comparative and Physiological Psychology, 55,* pp. 897–906. Copyright © 1962 by the American Psychological Association. Reprinted by permission. **166:** Figure 6.9 from "Age-Related Decrement in Hearing for Speech: Sampling and Longitudinal Studies," by M. Bergman, V. G. Blumenfeld, D. Cascardo, B. Dash, H. Levitt, and M. K. Margulies, 1976, *Journal of Gerontology, 31.* Reprinted by permission. **167:** Table 6.1 from "Food Recognition by the Elderly," by S. Schiffman, 1977, *Journal of Gerontology, 32.* Reprinted by permission.

CHAPTER 7

179: Figure in Box 7.1 adapted from "Evidence of Location Memory in 8-Month-Old Infants in a Nonsearch AB Task," by R. Baillargeon and M. Graber, 1988, *Developmental Psychology, 24,* pp. 502–511. Copyright 1988 by the American Psychological Association. Reprinted by permission. **188:** Figure 7.5 data from "Individual Differences in College Students' Performance on Formal Operations Tasks," by R. DeLisi and J. Staudt, 1980, *Journal of Applied Developmental Psychology, 1,* pp. 163–174. **197:** Table 7.2 from *Psycholinguistics,* 2nd Edition, by Dan I. Slobin. Copyright © 1979, 1974 by Scott, Foresman and Company. Reprinted by permission of HarperCollins College Publishers. **199:** Table 7.4 adapted from "Order of Acquisition of English Grammatical Morphemes," from *Psychology and Language: An Introduction to Psycholinguistics,* by Herbert H. Clark and Eve V. Clark, p. 345. Copyright © 1977 by Harcourt Brace & Company. Reprinted by permission of the publisher. **200:** Table 7.5 adapted from "Social and Non-Social Speech," by R. M. Krauss and S. Glucksberg, February 1977, *Scientific American, 236,* pp. 100–105. Copyright © 1977 by Scientific American, Inc. All rights reserved. **203:** Figure in Box 7.3 from "Critical Period Effects in Second Language Learning: The Influence of Maturational State on the Acquisition of English as a Second Language," by J. S. Johnson, and E. L. Newport, 1989, *Cognitive Psychology, 21,* pp. 60–99. Copyright 1989 by Academic Press. Reprinted by permission.

CHAPTER 8

214: Figure 8.3 adapted from "Influence of Models' Reinforcement Contingencies on the Acquisition of Imitative Responses," by A. Bandura, 1965, *Journal of Personality and Social Psychology, 1,* pp. 589–595. Copyright 1965 by the American Psychological Association. Reprinted by permission. **216:** Figure 8.4 adapted from "Human Memory: A Proposed System and Its Control Processes," by R. C. Atkinson and R. M. Shiffrin. In K. W. Spence and J. T. Spence (Eds.), *The Psychology of Learning and Motivation: Advances in Research and Theory* (Vol. 2), 1968, Academic Press. Reprinted by permission. **220:** Graph in Box 8.2 from "Childhood Amnesia and the Beginnings of Memory for Four Early Life Events," by J. A. Usher and U. Neisser, 1993, *Journal of Experimental Psychology: General, 122,* pp. 155–165. Copyright 1993 by the American Psychological Association. Reprinted by permission. **221:** Figure 8.7 from *Intellectual Development: Birth to Adulthood,* by R. Case, 1985. Orlando, FL: Academic Press. **224:** Figure 8.9 adapted from "Knowledge Structures and Memory Development," by M. T. H. Chi. In R. Siegler (Ed.), *Children's Thinking: What Develops?* 1978. Copyright 1978 by Lawrence Erlbaum Associates, Inc. Reprinted by permission. **225:** Table 8.1 adapted from "Developmental Sequences within and between Concepts," by R. S. Siegler, 1981. *Monographs of the Society for Research in Child Development, 46* (Serial No. 189). © 1981 by The Society for Research in Child Development, Inc. Reprinted by permission. **229:** Figure 8.12 adapted from "Differential Memory Changes with Age: Exact Retrieval Versus Plausible Inference, by L. M. Reder, C. Wible, and J. Martin, 1986, *Journal of Experimental Psychology: Learning, Memory, and Cognition, 12,* p. 76. Copyright 1986 by the American Psychological Association. Adapted by permission. **233:** Figure 8.13 from "Effect of Contextual Organization on Spatial Memory of Middle-Aged and Older Women," by K. J. Waddell, and B. Rogoff, 1981, *Developmental Psychology, 17,* pp. 878–885. Copyright 1981 by the American Psychological Association. Reprinted by permission. **235:** Figure 8.15 adapted from "Further Testing of Limits of Cognitive Plasticity: Negative Age Differences in a Mnemonic Skill Are Robust," by P. B. Baltes, and R. Kliegl, 1992 *Developmental Psychology, 28,* pp. 121–125. Copyright 1992 by the American Psychological Association. Reprinted by permission.

CHAPTER 9

241: Figure 9.1 adapted from *The Nature of Human Intelligence,* by J. P. Guilford, 1967. New York: McGraw-Hill. Reprinted with permission of McGraw-Hill. **246:** Table 9.1 from "The Stability of Mental Test Performance between Two and Eighteen Years," by . P. Honzik, J. W. Macfarlane, and L. Allen, 1948, *Journal of Experimental Education, 17,* pp. 309–324. **247:** Figure in Box 9.1 from "Information Processing in the Child: Significance of Analytic and Reflective Attitudes," by J. Kagan, B. L. Rosman, D. Day, J. Albert, and W. Phillips, 1964, *Psychological Monographs, 78,* pp. 1–37. Copyright © 1964 by the American Psychological Association. Reprinted by permission. **248:** Figure 9.3 from "Mental Rotation of Three-Dimensional Objects," by R. N. Shepard, and J. Metzler, 1971, *Science, 171,* pp. 701–703. Copyright 1971 by the American Association for the Advancement of Science. **249:** Table 9.2 from "Army General Classification Test Scores for Civilian Populations," by T. W. Harrell and M. S. Harrell, 1945, *Educational and Psychological Measurement, 5,* pp. 299–239. Reprinted by permission. **251:** Table 9.3 modified from "The Seattle Longitudinal Study: A 21-Year Exploration of Psychometric Intelligence in Adulthood," by K. W. Schaie, 1983, in K. W. Schaie (Ed.), *Longitudinal Studies of Adult Psychological Development.* New York: Guilford Press. Reprinted by permission. **253:** Table 9.5 adapted from B. M. Caldwell and R. H. Bradley, *Manual for the HOME Observation for Measurement of the Environment,* 1984. Little Rock: University of Arkansas Press. Adapted by permission of the authors. **259:** Figure 9.4 abridged from *Modes of Thinking in Young Children,* by Michael A. Wallach and Nathan Kogan, copyright © 1965 by Holt, Rinehart and Winston, Inc. **261:** Figure 9.5 data from "Creative Productivity between the Ages of 20 and 80 Years," by W. Dennis, 1966, *Journal of Gerontology, 21,* p. 2. Reprinted by permission. **265:** Figure 9.6 from "Can Decline in Adult Intellectual Functioning Be Reversed?" by K. W. Schaie and S. L. Willis, 1986, *Developmental Psychology, 22,* p. 228. Copyright 1986 by the American Psychological Association. Reprinted by permission.

CHAPTER 10

276: Figure 10.1 adapted from *Birth to Maturity,* by K. Kagan and H. A. Moss, 1962. Copyright © 1962 by John Wiley and Sons, Inc. Reprinted by permission of the author. **279:** Figure 10.2 from "Developmental Analysis of Conflict Caused by Opposing Attributes in the Adolescent Self-Portrait," by S. Harter and A. Monsour, 1992, *Developmental Psychology, 28,* pp. 251–260. Copyright 1992 by the American Psychological Association. Reprinted by permission. **281:** Figure 10.3 adapted from "Cross-Sectional Age Changes in Ego Identity Status during Adolescence," by P. W. Meilman, 1979, *Developmental Psychology, 15,* pp. 230–231. Copyright 1979 by the American Psychological Association. Reprinted by permission. **284:** Figure 10.4 adapted from "Possible Selves in Adulthood and Old Age: A Tale of Shifting Horizons," by C. D. Ryff, 1991, *Psychology and Aging, 6,* pp. 286–295. Copyright 1991 by the American Psychological Association. Reprinted by permission. **286:** Table 10.3 data partially from "Trait Psychology Comes of Age," by P. T. Costa, Jr., and R. R. McCrae, 1992. In T. B. Sonderegger (Ed.), *Nebraska Symposium on Motivation: Vol. 39. Psychology and Aging.* Lincoln, NB: University of Nebraska Press.

CHAPTER 11

303: Figure 11.1 adapted from "Gender Differences in Mathematics Performance: A Meta-Analysis," by J. S. Hyde, E. Fennema, and S. J. Lamon, 1990, *Psychological Bulletin, 107,* pp. 139–155. Copyright 1990 by the American Psychological Association. Reprinted by permission. **306:** Figure 11.2 based on "Social Behavior at 33 Months in Same-Sex and Mixed-Sex Dyads," by C. N. Jacklin and E. E. Maccoby, 1978, *Child Development, 49,* pp. 557–569. © 1978 by The Society for Research in Child Development, Inc. Reprinted by permission. **307:** Table 11.1 based on "Children, Gender, and Social Structure: An Analysis of the Contents of Letters to Santa Claus," by J. G. Richardson and C. H. Simpson, 1982, *Child Development, 53,* pp. 429–436. © 1982 by The Society for Research in Child Development, Inc. Reprinted by permission. **308:** Figure 11.3 from *Man and Woman, Boy and Girls,* by J. Money and A. Ehrhardt, 1972, Johns Hopkins University Press. Reprinted by permission. **313:** Figure 11.4 adapted from "The Roles of Cognition in Sex Roles and Sex Typing," by C. L. Martin and C. F. Halverson, J., 1987, in D. B. Carter (Ed.), *Current Conceptions of Sex Roles and Sex Typing: Theory and Research.* Copyright 1987 by Praeger Publishing. Reprinted by permission of Greenwood Publishing Group, Inc., Westport, CT. **317:** Figure 11.5 adapted from "Children's Concepts of Cross-Gender Activities," by T. Stoddart and E. Turiel, 1985, *Child Development, 56,* pp. 1241–1252. © 1985 by The Society for Research in Child Development, Inc. Reprinted by permission.

CHAPTER 12

338: Figures 12.1 and 12.2 adapted from "Factors Influencing Young Children's Use of Motives and Outcomes as Moral Criteria," by S. A. Nelson, 1980, *Child Development, 51,* pp. 823–829. © 1980 by The Society for Research in Child Development, Inc. Reprinted by permission. **340:** Table 12.2 adapted from "Contributions of Parents and Peers to Children's Moral Socialization," by G. H. Brody and D. R. Shaffer, 1982, *Developmental Review, 2,* pp. 31–75. Reprinted by permission of Academic Press, Inc. **341:** Figure 12.3 from "A Longitudinal Study of Moral Judgment," by A. Colby, L. Kohlberg, J. Gibbs, and M. Lieberman, 1983, *Monographs of the Society for Research in Child Development, 48* (Nos. 1–2, Serial No. 200). © 1983 by The Society for Research in Child Development, Inc. Reprinted by permission. **348:** Graph in Box 12.3 from "Culture and Moral Development," by R. A. Shweder, M. Mahapatra, and J. G. Miller, 1990, in J. W. Stigler, R. A. Shweder, and G. Herdt (Eds.), *Cultural Psychology Essays on Comparative Human Development.* Copyright 1990 by Cambridge University Press. Reprinted with the permission of Cambridge University Press.

CHAPTER 13

374: Figure 13.2 from "Age Segregation in Children's Social Interactions," by S. Ellis, B. Rogoff, and C. C. Cromer, 1981, *Developmental Psychology, 17,* pp. 399–407. Copyright 1981 by the American Psychological Association. Reprinted by permission. **378:** Figure 13.3 from "Girlfriend, Boyfriend: Age and Sex Differences in Intimate Friendship," by R. Sharabany, R. Gershoni, and J. E. Hofman, 1981, *Developmental Psychology 17,* pp. 800–808. Copyright 1981 by the American Psychological Association. Reprinted by permission. **379:** Figure 13.4 from "The Social Structure of Urban Adolescent Peer Groups," by D. C. Dunphy, 1963, *Sociometry, 26,* pp. 230–246. Reprinted by permission. **381:** Figure 13.5 adapted from "Reasoning on Social Dilemmas Varying in Emotional Saliency: An Adult Developmental Perspective," by F. Blanchard-Fields, 1986, *Psychology and Aging, 1,* pp. 325–333. Copyright

1986 by the American Psychological Association. Reprinted by permission. **383:** Figure 13.6 from *The Social Context of Marriage,* by J. Richard Udry (2nd ed.), 1971. Copyright © 1971 by J. B. Lippincott Company. Reprinted by permission. **384:** Box 13.3 adapted from "Love and Work: An Attachment-Theoretical Perspective," by C. Hazan and P. R. Shaver, 1990, *Journal of Personality and Social Psychology, 59*(2), pp. 270–280. Copyright 1990 by the American Psychological Association. Reprinted by permission.

CHAPTER 14

391: Figure 14.1 from "Early Human Experience: A Family Perspective," by J. Belsky, 1981, *Developmental Psychology, 17,* pp. 3–23. Copyright 1981 by the American Psychological Association. Reprinted by permission. **392:** Table 14.1 from E. M. Duvall, *Marriage and Family Development,* 1978. Copyright © 1978 by J. B. Lippincott Company. Reprinted by permission of Harper and Row, Publishers, Inc. **397:** Figure 14.3 from "A Family Process Model of Economic Hardship and Adjustment of Early Adolescent Boys," by R. D. Conger, K. J. Conger, G. H. Elder, Jr., F. O. Lorenz, R. L. Simons, and L. B. Whitbeck, 1992, *Child Development, 63,* pp. 526–541. Copyright © 1992 by The Society for Research in Child Development, Inc. Adapted by permission. **400:** Table 14.2 adapted from *The Adolescent: A Psychological Self-Portrait,* by Daniel Offer, Eric Ostrov, and Kenneth I. Howard. Copyright © 1981 by Basic Books, Inc. Reprinted by permission of Basic Books, Publishers, New York. **407:** Figure 14.4 from "Marital Satisfaction over the Family Life Cycle," by B. C. Rollins and H. Feldman, 1970, *Journal of Marriage and the Family, 32,* pp. 20–28. Copyrighted 1970 by the National Council on Family Relations, 3989 Central Avenue, N.E., Suite #550, Minneapolis, MN 55421.Reprinted by permission. **411:** Table 14.3 adapted from "Reasons for Divorce: Perspectives of Divorcing Men and Women," by L. Gigy and J. B. Kelly, 1992, *Journal of Divorce and Remarriage, 18,* pp. 169–187. Adapted by permission of Haworth Press, Inc. **417:** Figure 14.5 adapted from "Responses of Abused and Disadvantaged Toddlers to Distress in Agemates: A Study in the Day-Care Setting," by M. Main and C. George, 1985, *Developmental Psychology, 21,* pp. 407–412. Copyright 1985 by the American Psychological Association. Reprinted by permission.

CHAPTER 15

424: Figure 15.1 adapted from "Preschool Play Norms: A Replication," by K. E. Barnes, 1971, *Developmental Psychology, 5,* pp. 99–103. Copyright 1971 by the American Psychological Association. Reprinted by permission. **430:** Figure 15.2 from *The Early Window: Effects of Television on Children and Youth,* by Robert M. Liebert and Joyce Sprakfin (3rd ed.). Copyright © 1988 by Allyn & Bacon. Reprinted by permission. **434:** Figure 15.3 from *Being Adolescent,* by M. Csikszentmihalyi and R. Larson. Copyright © 1984 by Basic Books, Inc. Reprinted by permission of Basic Books, Inc., Publishers, New York. **439:** Figure 15.4 from "The AT&R Longitudinal Studies of Managers," by D. W. Bray and A. Howard. In K. W. Schaie (Ed.), *Longitudinal Studies of Adult Psychological Development,* 1983. Reprinted by permission of The Guilford Press.

CHAPTER 16

462: Table 16.2 adapted from "Follow-Up of a Preschool Epidemiological Sample: Cross-Age Continuities and Predictions of Later Adjustment with Internalizing and Externalizing Dimensions of Behavior," by M. Fischer, J. E. Rolf, J. E. Hasazi, and L. Cummings, 1984, *Child Development, 55,* pp. 137–150. © 1984 by The Society for Research in Child Development, Inc. Reprinted by permission. **467:** Figure 16.2 data from National Center for Health Statistics, reported in: U.S. Bureau of the Census (1992); Statistical Abstract of the United States, 1992 (112th ed.). Washington, D.C.: U.S. Government Printing Office; p. 90 (1989 data). **470:** Figure 16.3 adapted from "Six-Month Prevalence of Psychiatric Disorders in Three Communities," by J. K. Myers, M. M Weissman, G. L. Tischler, C. E. Holzer, II, P. J. Leaf, and H. Orvaschel, 1984, *Archives of General Psychiatry, 41,* pp. 959–567. **474:** Figure 16.4 from *The Vanishing Mind* by L. L. Heston and J. A. White. Copyright © 1991 by W. H. Freeman and Company. Reprinted by permission.

CHAPTER 17

492: Figure 17.3 reprinted from *Omega, 18,* by S. C. Jacobs, T. R. Kosten, S. V. Kasl, A. M. Ostfeld, L. Berkman, and P. Charpentier, "Attachment Theory and Multiple Dimensions of Grief," pp. 41–52, Copyright 1987–1988, with the kind permission of Elsevier Science Ltd., The Boulevard, Langford Lane, Kidlington OX5 1GB, UK. **494** & **497:** Figures 17.4 and 17.6 from *Death Studies, 1987, Vol. 11,* pp. 109 and 111, Wenestam & Wass, New York: Hemisphere Publishing Corporation. Reproduced with permission. **495:** Figure 17.5 from *Children and Death,* p. 165, D. Papadatou and C. Papadatou, (Eds.), New York: Hemisphere Publishing Corporation, 1991. Reproduced with permission. **498:** Table 17.2 from "The Role of Age in Death Attitudes," by R. A. Kalish and D. K. Reynolds, *Death Education, 1,*(2), p. 225. Copyright 1977 by Hemisphere Publishing Corp. Reprinted by permission. **499:** Table 17.3 adapted from C. M. Parkes, *Bereavement: Studies of Grief in Adult Life* (2nd ed.), 1986, Tavistock Publications. Reprinted by permission.

TO THE OWNER OF THIS BOOK:

We hope that you have found *Life-Span Human Development* (Second Edition) useful. So that this book can be improved in a future edition, would you take the time to complete this sheet and return it? We'd really like to hear what you think.

School and address: ____

Department: ____

Name of course: ______________________ Instructor's name: ____________________

1. What I like most about this book is: ____

____

____

2. What I like least about this book is: ____

____

____

3. This book could be improved by: ____

____

____

4. Were all of the chapters of the book assigned for you to read? Yes No

If not, which ones weren't? ____

____

5. In the space below, or on a separate sheet of paper, please write specific suggestions for improving this book and anything else you'd care to share about your experience in using the book.

Optional:

Your name: ______________________________ Date: ______________________________

May Brooks/Cole quote you, either in promotion for *Life-Span Human Development* (Second Edition) or in future publishing ventures?

Yes: __________ No: __________

Thanks for your help,

Carol K. Sigelman
David R. Shaffer

FOLD HERE

NO POSTAGE NECESSARY IF MAILED IN THE UNITED STATES

BUSINESS REPLY MAIL

FIRST CLASS PERMIT NO. 358 PACIFIC GROVE, CA

POSTAGE WILL BE PAID BY ADDRESSEE

ATT: *Carol K. Sigelman & David R. Shaffer*

Brooks/Cole Publishing Company
511 Forest Lodge Road
Pacific Grove, California 93950-9968

FOLD HERE